Tour of Website for
INFORMATION TECHNOLOGY FOR MANAGEMENT 5th Edition
wiley.com/college/turban

The website accompanying this book offers students a range of interactive study resources:

➡ Student Practice Quizzes

➡ Lecture Slides in PowerPoint

➡ Additional Chapter Material that provides in-depth information on key topics in each chapter. Throughout the book, these icons will direct you to the website for more information.

➡ Virtual Company Website

About the Virtual Company Case and Website

Students solve realistic IT problems when they are "hired" as interns at The Wireless Café, a simulated high-tech restaurant in Shanghai.

At the end of each chapter, look for the Virtual Company box to find summaries of the assignments. To find the assignments, go to The Wireless Café's website.

Students can then use the information in the chapter and website to develop creative solutions to IT problems such as:

➡ Wireless: Advertising and/or taking orders through mobile devices

➡ Data Management: Helping the Wireless Café manage its inventory by tracking its food and beverages on spreadsheets.

➡ E-commerce: Making epayments to suppliers

To Access The Wireless Café's Website:

1. Go to wiley.com/college/turban

2. Select Student Resources site

3. Click on Virtual Company

5TH EDITION

Information Technology for Management

TRANSFORMING ORGANIZATIONS IN THE DIGITAL ECONOMY

EFRAIM TURBAN, *University of Hawaii at Manoa*

DOROTHY LEIDNER, *Baylor University*

EPHRAIM MCLEAN, *Georgia State University*

JAMES WETHERBE, *Texas Tech University*

with contributions by:

CHRISTY CHEUNG, *City University of Hong Kong*

DANIEL TSE, *City University of Hong Kong*

MAGGIE LEW, *TSE Computer Ltd., Hong Kong*

WILEY   JOHN WILEY & SONS, INC.

EXECUTIVE EDITOR	Beth Lang Golub
ASSOCIATE EDITOR	Lorraina Raccuia
DEVELOPMENT EDITOR	Ann Torbert
MARKETING MANAGER	Jillian Rice
MEDIA EDITOR	Allison Morris
EDITORIAL ASSISTANT	Ame Esterline
SENIOR DESIGNER	Maddy Lesure
TEXT DESIGNER	Kenny Beck
SENIOR ILLUSTRATION EDITOR	Anna Melhorn
SENIOR PRODUCTION EDITOR	Patricia McFadden
SENIOR PHOTO EDITOR	Lisa Gee
PRODUCTION MANAGEMENT	Ingrao Associates
COVER PHOTO	Michael Freeman/Digital Vision

This book was set in 10/12 Meridien Roman by TechBooks and printed and bound by Von Hoffmann, Inc. The cover was printed by Von Hoffmann Press.

This book is printed on acid free paper. ∞

ISBN 0-471-70522-5

Printed in the United States of America

10 9 8 7 6 5 4 3 2 1

Preface

THE WEB REVOLUTION

In the last decade, we have been witnessing one of the most important technological revolutions in the modern era—the Web revolution. The Web is not only changing the way that we work, study, play, and conduct our lives, but it is doing so much more quickly than any other revolution (such as the Industrial Revolution), with impacts that are more far-reaching. For example, two years ago, when we last revised this book, blogging was a novelty. Today more than two million bloggers are active on the Web. In another developing technology, Apple sold over 100 million songs on iTunes during the first year of operation (July 2003 to July 2004.) Furthermore, we have seen only the tip of the iceberg. The Web revolution is facilitated by ever-changing information technologies.

Information Technology for Management, 5th Edition, addresses the basic principles of MIS in light of these new developments. For example, one of the major changes occurring in IT is the ability to deliver systems over the Internet. This option, which is delivered by application server providers, is a strategic option for prudent managers of the digital economy. It is the beginning of the move toward utility, or "on-demand," computing which may change the need for software and hardware. But does utility computing fit all organizations? Such issues resulting from the Web revolution are discussed in this textbook. Its major objective is to prepare managers and staff in the modern enterprise to understand the role of information technology in the digital economy.

TRANSFORMING ORGANIZATIONS TO THE DIGITAL ECONOMY

This book is based on the fundamental premise that the major role of information technology is to provide organizations with *strategic advantage by facilitat-*ing problem solving, increasing productivity and quality, increasing speed, improving customer service, enhancing communication and collaboration, and *enabling business process restructuring*. By taking a practical, managerial-oriented approach, the book demonstrates that IT can be provided not only by information systems departments but also by end users and vendors as well. Managing information resources, new technologies, and communications networks is becoming a—or even *the*—critical success factor in the operations of many organizations, private and public, and will be essential to the survival of organizations in the digital economy.

While recognizing the importance of the technology, system development, and functional transaction processing systems, we emphasize the *innovative* uses of information technology throughout the enterprise. The rapidly increased use of the Web, the Internet, intranets, extranets, e-business and e-commerce, and mobile computing changes the manner in which business is done in almost all organizations. This fact is reflected in our book: Every chapter and major topic point to the role of the Web in facilitating competitiveness, effectiveness, and profitability. Of special importance is the emergence of the second-generation e-commerce applications such as m-commerce, c-commerce, e-learning, and e-government. Also, the integration of ERP, CRM, and knowledge management with e-commerce is of great importance.

FEATURES OF THIS TEXT

In developing the 5th Edition of *Information Technology for Management*, we have tried to craft a book that will serve the needs of tomorrow's managers. This book reflects our vision of where information systems are going and the direction of IS education in business and e-business programs. This vision is represented by the following features that we have integrated throughout the book.

• *Global Perspective and New Chapter on Global Information Systems.* The importance of global competition, partnerships, and trading is rapidly increasing; we've added a new chapter that focuses on global information systems (Chapter 8). International examples are highlighted with a special globe icon, a Global Index appears at the back of the book, and the book's Web site includes several international cases.

• *Focus on Security.* Computer and IT security issues are becoming more important, at the personal, organizational, and global levels. For example, spyware software is becoming more common, and the world's first mobile phone virus has been found. We show how IT is used to counter cyberterrorism on the personal and organizational levels, in addition to showing how governments use IT to strengthen homeland security.

• *Digital Economy Focus.* This book recognizes that organizations desire to transform themselves successfully to the digital economy. To do so companies need not only to use Web-based systems, but also to have an appropriate e-strategy and ability to implement click-and-mortar systems as well as new business models. Furthermore, they need to plan the transformation process, which is dependent on information technology and enabled by it.

• *Managerial Orientation.* Most IS textbooks identify themselves as either technology or sociobehavioral oriented. While we recognize the importance of both, our emphasis is on *managerial* orientation. To implement this orientation, we assembled all of the major technological topics in six Technology Guides, located on the book's Web site. Furthermore, we attempted not to duplicate detailed presentations of behavioral sciences topics, such as dealing with resistance to change or motivating employees. Instead, we concentrate on managerial decision making, cost-benefit justification, supply chain management, organizational restructuring, and CRM as they relate to information technology.

• *Functional Relevance.* Frequently, non–IS major students wonder why they must learn technical details. In this text the relevance of information technology to the major functional areas is an important theme. We show, through the use of icons, the relevance of topics to accounting, finance, marketing, production/operations management, human resources management, and government. Finally, our examples also cover small service industries as well as the international setting.

• *E-Business, E-Commerce, and the Use of the Web.* We strongly believe that e-business, e-commerce, and the use of the Internet, intranets, and extranets are changing the world of business. Not only is an entire chapter (Chapter 4) dedicated to e-business, but we also demonstrate the significance of e-business in every chapter and major topic. In this edition, we also have expanded coverage of m-commerce and commercial mobile computing applications.

• *Real-World Orientation.* Extensive, vivid examples from large corporations, small businesses, government, and not-for-profit agencies make concepts come alive by showing students the capabilities of information technology, its cost and justification, and some of the innovative ways real corporations are using IT in their operations.

• *Failures and Lessons Learned.* We acknowledge the fact that many systems do fail. Many chapters include discussion or examples of failures, and the lessons learned from them. For example, Chapter 7 cites some ERP failures, and Chapter 13 discusses economic aspects of failures and runaway projects.

• *Solid Theoretical Backing.* Throughout the book we present the theoretical foundation necessary for understanding information technology, ranging from Moore's Law to Porter's competitiveness models, including his latest e-strategy adaptation.

• *Up-to-Date Information.* The book presents the most current topics of information technology, as evidenced by the many new cases and examples throughout the book and by 2003 and 2004 citations. Every topic in the book has been researched to find the most up-to-date information and features.

• *Economic Justification.* Information technology is mature enough to stand the difficult test of economic justification. It is our position that investment in information technology must be scrutinized like any other investment, despite the difficulties of measuring technology benefits. In addition to discussion throughout the text, we devote a complete chapter (Chapter 13, "IT Economics") to this subject. We emphasize enterprisewide interorganizational and global systems. We also present technologies that support this integration, including Web Services and XML.

• *Ethics.* The importance of ethics is growing rapidly in the digital economy. Topics relating to ethics are introduced in every chapter, and are highlighted by icons in the margin. We introduce the essentials of ethics as an online file to Chapter 1 (Online File W1.4). Also, a primer on ethics is also provided in

Online File W1.4; this resource poses 14 ethics scenarios and asks students to think about responses to these situations.

WHAT'S NEW IN THIS EDITION?

In preparing the new, 5th Edition we made the following large-scale changes:

- Online Interactive Learning Sessions: The book's Student Web site contains engaging activities including interactive drag-and-drop exercises and simulations, as well as animations that help students to visualize IT processes.
- Revised coverage of supply chain management, including added materials on enterprisewide systems and CRM. (Chapter 7).
- New chapter on Interorganizational and Global Information Systems (Chapter 8).
- New materials on strategic IS with IT Strategy and Planning (Chapter 12).
- Focused Chapter 14 (on IT acquisition) on management issues and business process redesign; all technology issues surrounding systems analysis and design have moved to online Technology Guide 6.
- Increased emphasis on trends toward utility computing, grid computing, and outsourcing.
- Increased coverage of information security and homeland security, especially in Chapters 10, 11, and 15.
- Revised Chapter 16, "Impacts of IT on Organizations, Individuals, and Society," to include more current issues.
- Completely revised most of the chapters, to introduce new research, current examples and case studies, and updated reference materials.
- Streamlined and smoothed the logical flow throughout the text, eliminating duplications.

ORGANIZATION OF THE BOOK

The book is divided into five major parts, composed of 16 regular chapters supplemented by six Technology Guides. Parts and chapters break down as follows.

- *Part I: IT in the Organization.* Part I gives an overview of IT in the organization. Chapter 1 introduces the drivers of the use of information technology in the digital economy and gives an overview of information systems and IT trends. Chapter 2 presents the foundations of information systems and their strategic use. Special attention is given to the role information systems play in facilitating Web-based business models.

- *Part II: The Web Revolution.* The three chapters in Part II introduce the Web-based technologies and applications, starting with telecommunications networks and the role of the Internet, intranets, and extranets in contributing to communication, collaboration, and information discovery (Chapter 3). The topic of e-business and e-commerce is presented in a comprehensive way (Chapter 4), followed by mobile and wireless computing in Chapter 5.

- *Part III: Organizational Applications.* Part III begins with the basics: IT applications in transaction processing, functional applications, and integration of functional systems (Chapter 6). We then cover supply chain management, Web-based enterprise systems, and customer relationship management (CRM) (Chapter 7). Chapter 8 focuses on interorganizational and global systems.

- *Part IV: Managerial and Decision Support Systems.* Part IV discusses the many ways information systems can be used to support the day-to-day operations of a company, with a strong emphasis on the use of IT in managerial decision making. The three chapters in this part address some of the ways businesses are using information technology to solve specific problems and to build strategic, innovative systems that enhance quality and productivity. Special attention is given to innovative applications of knowledge management (Chapter 9), data analysis and data management (Chapter 10), and decision support and intelligent support systems (Chapter 11).

- *Part V: Implementing and Managing IT.* Part V explores several topics related to the implementation, evaluation, construction, and maintenance of information systems. First we cover use of IT for strategic advantage, including the topic of IT planning (Chapter 12). Then we consider several issues ranging from the economics of information technology (Chapter 13), to acquiring (building or outsourcing) information systems (Chapter 14), to the management of IT resources and IT security (Chapter 15). Finally, Chapter 16 assesses the impact of IT on individuals, organizations, and society.

The six **Technology Guides,** which are available online at the book's Web site, cover hardware, software, databases, telecommunications, and the essentials of the Internet, and an introduction to systems analysis and design. They contain condensed, up-to-date presentations of all the material necessary for the understanding of these technologies. They can be used as a self-study refresher or as a basis for a class presentation. The Technology Guides are supplemented online by a glossary for the terms in the Tech Guides, questions for review and discussion, and case studies, all of which are available on our Web site (www.wiley.com/college/turban).

PEDAGOGICAL FEATURES

We developed a number of pedagogical features to aid student learning and tie together the themes of the book.

• **Chapter Outline.** The chapter outline provides a quick indication of the major topics covered in the chapter.

• **Learning Objectives.** Learning objectives listed at the beginning of each chapter help students focus their efforts and alert them to the important concepts that will be discussed.

• **Opening Cases.** Each chapter opens with a *real-world* example that illustrates the use of information technology in modern organizations. These cases have been carefully chosen to demonstrate the relevance, for business students, of the topics introduced in the chapter. They are presented in a standard format (problem or opportunity, IT solution, and results) that helps model a way to think about business problems. The opening case is followed by a brief section called "Lessons Learned from This Case" that ties the key points of the opening case to the topic of the chapter.

• **"IT at Work" Boxes.** The IT at Work boxes spotlight some real-world innovations and new technologies that companies are using to solve organizational dilemmas or create new business opportunities. Each box concludes with "for further exploration" questions and issues. Some of these boxes are online.

• **"A Closer Look" Boxes.** These boxes contain detailed, in-depth discussions of specific concepts or procedures, often using real-world examples. Some boxes enhance the in-text discussion by offering an alternative approach to information technology. Some of these boxes are included in the online materials.

• **Highlighted Icons.** Icons appear throughout the text to relate the topics covered within each chapter to some major themes of the book. The icons alert students to the related functional areas, to IT failures, and to global and ethical issues. Icons also indicate where related enrichment resources can be found on the book's companion Web site. The following list summarizes these icons. (They also are summarized for students in a marginal annotation on page 6 in Chapter 1.)

 Ethics-related topic

 Global organizations and issues

 Lessons to be learned from IT failures

 Accounting example

 Finance example

 Government example

 Human resources management example

 Marketing example

 Production/operations management example

 Service-company example (for example, health services, educational services, and other non-manufacturing examples)

 Material at the book's Web site: *www.wiley/com/college.turban*

• ***Online Chapter Resources.*** Each chapter is supported by many online files (up to 30 per chapter). These files are cited in the text, as they include in-depth discussions, technically oriented materials, examples, cases, and illustrations. The Online Chapter Resources can be accessed by going to the Student Website at *www.wiley.com/college/turban*, then clicking on Online Chapter Resources.

• ***Managerial Issues.*** The final text section of every chapter explores some of the special concerns managers face as they adapt to an increasingly technological environment. The issues highlighted in this section can serve as a springboard for class discussion and challenge business students to consider some of the actions they might take if placed in similar circumstances.

• ***Key Terms.*** The key terms and concepts are typeset in boldface blue when first introduced in a chapter, and are listed at the end of the chapter. All key terms are defined in the end-of-book glossary.

• ***Chapter Highlights.*** All the important concepts covered in the chapter are listed at the end of the chapter and are linked by number to the learning objectives introduced at the beginning of each chapter, to reinforce the important ideas discussed.

• ***Virtual Company Assignment.*** The Virtual Company Assignment centers around the ongoing situation at a simulated company, The Wireless Café. Students are "hired" by the restaurant as consultants and in each chapter are given assignments that require them to use the information presented in the chapter to develop solutions and produce deliverables to present to the owners of The Wireless Café. These assignments get the student into active, hands-on learning to complement the conceptual coverage of the text. The assignments are found on the Student Resources site at *www.wiley.com/college/turban.*

• ***End-of-Chapter Questions and Exercises.*** Different types of questions measure student comprehension and students' ability to apply knowledge. Questions for Review ask students to summarize the concepts introduced. Discussion Questions are intended to promote class discussion and develop critical thinking skills. Exercises are more challenging assignments that require students to apply what they have learned.

• ***Group Assignments.*** Comprehensive group assignments, including Internet research, oral presentations to the class, and debates are available in each chapter.

• ***Internet Exercises.*** Close to 200 hands-on exercises send the students to interesting Web sites to explore those sites, find resources, investigate an application, compare, analyze, and summarize information, or learn about the state of the art of a topic.

• ***Minicases.*** Two real-world cases at the end of each chapter highlight some of the problems encountered by corporations as they develop and implement information systems. Discussion questions and assignments are included. A number of additional minicases are available online at the book's Web site.

SUPPLEMENTARY MATERIALS

An extensive package of instructional materials is available to support this 5th edition.

• ***Instructor's Manual.*** The Instructor's Manual presents objectives from the text with additional information to make them more appropriate and useful for the instructor. The manual also includes practical applications of concepts, case study elaboration, answers to end-of-chapter questions, questions for review, questions for discussion, and Internet exercises.

• ***Test Bank.*** The test bank contains over 1,000 questions and problems (about 70 per chapter) consisting of multiple-choice, short answer, fill-ins, and critical thinking/essay questions.

• ***Computerized Test Bank.*** This electronic version of the test bank allows instructors to customize tests and quizzes for their students.

• ***PowerPoint Presentation.*** A series of slides designed around the content of the text incorporates key points from the text and illustrations where appropriate.

• ***Video Series.*** A collection of video clips provides students and instructors with dynamic international business examples directly related to the concepts introduced in the text. The video clips illustrate the ways in which computer information systems are utilized in various companies and industries.

• ***Business Extra Select.*** (*www.wiley.com/college/bxs*) Business Extra Select enables you to add copyright-cleared articles, cases, and readings from such leading business resources as *INSEAD, Ivey* and *Harvard Business School Cases, Fortune, The Economist, The Wall Street Journal,* and more. You can create your own custom CoursePack, combining these resources along with content from Wiley's Business Textbooks, your own content such as lecture notes, and any other third-party content. Or you can use a ready-made CoursePack for Turban's *IT for Management*, 5th Edition.

• **The Turban Web Site.** (*www.wiley.com/college/turban*). The book's Web site greatly extends the content and themes of the text to provide extensive support for instructors and students. Organized by chapter, it includes Chapter Resources: tables, figures, cases, questions, exercises, and downloadable PowerPoint slides, self-testing material for students, working students' experiences with using IT, links to resources on the Web, and links to many of the companies discussed in the text and to the Virtual Company Web site.

ACKNOWLEDGMENTS

Several individuals helped us with the creation of the 5th Edition: Christy Cheung helped in revising most of the chapters. Daniel Tse and Maggie Lew helped to update Technology Guides 1 through 6 and helped to revise Chapter 15. Joyce Chan, Mei-Ting Cheung, and Felix Leung, all of City University of Hong Kong, helped review several chapters. Thanks to all for their contributions.

Faculty feedback was essential to the development of the book. Many individuals participated in focus groups and/or acted as reviewers. Several others created portions of chapters or cases, especially international cases, some of which are in the text and others on the Web site:

Thanks, first, to Carolyn Jacobson, Marymount University, who read through the 4th Edition and offered valuable insights.

Thanks, too, to the following reviewers: Lawrence Andrew, Western Illinois University; Bay Arinze, Drexel University; Benli Asilani, University of Tennessee Chattanooga; Mary Astone, Troy State University; Cynthia Barnes, Lamar University; Andy Borchers, Kettering University; Sonny Butler, Georgia Southern University; Jason Chen, Gonzaga University; Roland Eichelberger, Baylor University; Jerry Flatto, University of Indianapolis; Marvin Golland, Polytechnic University of Brooklyn; Vipul Gupta, St. Joseph's University; Jeet Gupta, University of Alabama, Hunstville; David Harmann, University of Central Oklahoma; Shohreh, University of Houston, Downtown; Richard Herschel, Saint Joseph's University; Phil Houle, Drake University; Jonatan Jelan, Mercy College; Tim Jenkins, ITT Institute of Technology, San Bernadino; Gerald Karush, Southern New Hampshire University; Joseph Kasten, Dowling College; Stephen Klein, Ramapo College; Kapil Ladha, Drexel University; Albert Lederer, University of Kentucky; Chang-Yang Lin, Eastern Kentucky University; Liping Liu, The University of Akron; Steve Loy, Eastern Kentucky University; Dana Kristin McCann, Central Michigan University; Roberto Mejias, Purdue University; Luvai Motiwalla, University of Massachusetts, Lowell; Sean Neely, City University Bellevue; Luis Rabelo, University of Central Florida; W. Raghupathi, Fordham University; Mahesh Raisinghani, University of Dallas; Tom Schambach, Illinois State University; Werner Schenk, University of Rochester; Sheryl Schoenacher, SUNY Farmingdale; Richard Segall, Arkansas State University; Victor Smolensky, San Diego State University; Bruce White, Quinnipiac University; Geoffrey Willis, University of Central Oklahoma; Marie Wright, Western Connecticut State University.

Please see *wiley.com/college/turban* for a list of acknowledgements for past editions of this book.

Many individuals helped us with the administrative work. Of special mention is Christy Cheung of City University of Hong Kong who devoted considerable time to typing and editing. Christy also contributed cases, conducted research, and assisted in many other aspects of the book. Several other individuals helped with typing, figure drawing, and more. Among those are Eric Leung and Daphne Turban. Hugh Watson of the University of Georgia, the Information Systems Advisor to Wiley, guided us through various stages of the project.

Finally, we would like to thank the dedicated staff of John Wiley & Sons: Lorraina Raccuia, Jeanine Furino, and Trish McFadden. A special thank you to Beth Lang Golub, Ann Torbert, Suzanne Ingrao of Ingrao Associates, and Shelley Flannery, whose considerable energy, time, expertise, and devotion have contributed significantly to the success of this project. Most of all the dedication of Ann Torbert, development editor, was extremely critical to the success of this edition.

Finally, we recognize the various organizations and corporations that provided us with material and permissions to use it.

Efraim Turban
Dorothy Leidner
Ephraim McLean
James Wetherbe

About the Authors

DR. EFRAIM TURBAN

Dr. Efraim Turban obtained his M.B.A. and Ph.D. degrees from the University of California, Berkeley. His industry experience includes eight years as an industrial engineer, three of which were spent at General Electric Transformers Plant in Oakland, California. He also has extensive consulting experience to small and large corporations as well as to governments. In his over thirty years of teaching, Professor Turban has served as Chaired Professor at Eastern Illinois University, and as Visiting Professor at City University of Hong Kong, Nanyang Technological University in Singapore, and University of Science and Technology in Hong Kong. He has also taught at UCLA; USC; Simon Fraser University; Lehigh University; California State University, Long Beach; and Florida International University.

Dr. Turban was a co-recipient of the 1984/85 National Management Science Award (Artificial Intelligence in Management). In 1997 he received the Distinguished Faculty Scholarly and Creative Achievement Award at California State University, Long Beach.

Dr. Turban has published over 110 articles in leading journals, including the following: *Management Science, MIS Quarterly, Operations Research, Journal of*
MIS, Communications of the ACM, International Journal of Electronic Commerce, Information Systems Frontiers, Decision Support Systems, International Journal of Information Management, Heuristics, Expert Systems with Applications, International Journal of Applied Expert Systems, Journal of Investing, Accounting, Management and Information Systems, Computers and Operations Research, Computers and Industrial Engineering, IEEE Transactions on Engineering Management, Omega, International Journal of Electronic Commerce, Organizational Computing and Electronic Commerce, and *Electronic Markets.* He has also published 22 books, including best sellers such as *Neural Networks: Applications in Investment and Financial Services* (2nd edition) (co-editor with R. Trippi), Richard D. Irwin, 1996; *Decision Support Systems and Intelligent Systems* (Prentice Hall, 7th edition, 2005); *Expert Systems and Applied Artificial Intelligence,* (MacMillan Publishing Co., 1992), *Electronic Commerce: A Managerial Approach, 4th edition,* (Prentice Hall, 2006), *Introduction to Information Technology 3rd edition* (Wiley, 2005), and *Introduction to Electronic Commerce* (Prentice Hall, 2003).

Professor Turban is a Visiting Scholar with the Pacific Institute for Information Systems Management College of Business University of Hawaii at Manoa. His major research interests include electronic commerce, strategy, and implementation.

DR. DOROTHY LEIDNER

Dr. Dorothy E. Leidner is the Randall W. and Sandra Ferguson Professor of Information Systems and Director of the Center for Knowledge Management at Baylor University. Prior to rejoining the Baylor faculty, she was associate professor at INSEAD and at Texas Christian University. She has also been visiting professor at Instituto Tecnologico y des Estudios Superiores de Monterrey, Mexico, at the Institut d'Administration Des Entreprises at the Universite de Caen, France, and at Southern Methodist University. Dr. Leidner received her Ph.D. in Information Systems from the University of Texas at Austin, where she also obtained her M.B.A. and
her B.A. in Plan II. Dr Leidner's research has been published in a variety of journals, such as *MIS Quarterly, Information Systems, Decision Sciences, Decision Support Systems,* and *Organization Science.* She has received best-paper awards in 1993 from the Hawaii International Conference on Systems Sciences, in 1995 from *MIS Quarterly,* and in 1999 from the Academy of Management. She is currently serving as co-editor of the journal *Data Base for Advances in Information Systems.* She is also an associate editor for *MIS Quarterly* and a senior editor for the *Journal of Strategic Information Systems,* and is on the editorial board of *MISQ Executive.*

DR. EPHRAIM R. McLEAN

Dr. Ephraim McLean earned his Bachelor of Mechanical Engineering degree from Cornell University in 1958. After brief service in the U.S. Army Ordinance Corps, he worked for the Procter & Gamble Co. for seven years, first in manufacturing management and later as a computer systems analyst. In 1965, he left P&G and entered the Sloan School of Management at the Massachusetts Institute of Technology, obtaining his master's degree in 1967 and his doctorate in 1970.

While at M.I.T., he began an interest in the application of computer technology to medicine, working on his dissertation at the Lahey Clinic in Boston. While there, he was instrumental in developing the Lahey Clinic Automated Medical History System. During the same period, he served as an instructor at M.I.T. and also assisted in the preparation of the books *The Impact of Computers on Management* (MIT Press, 1967), *The Impact of Computers on Collective Bargaining* (MIT Press, 1969), and *Computers in Knowledge-Based Fields* (MIT Press, 1970). While at M.I.T., he was elected to Sigma XI, the scientific research society.

Dr. McLean left M.I.T. and joined the faculty of the Anderson Graduate School of Management at The University of California, Los Angeles (UCLA) in winter 1970. He was the founding Director of the Information Systems Research Program and the first Chairman of the Information Systems area, both within the Anderson Graduate School of Management. In fall 1987, he was named to the George E. Smith Eminent Scholar's Chair in the Robinson College of Business at Georgia State University in Atlanta; in 2002, was appointed Regent's Professor in the University System of Georgia.

Dr. McLean has published over 125 articles in such publications as the *Harvard Business Review, Sloan Management Review, California Management Review, Communications of the ACM, MIS Quarterly, Information Systems Research, Management Science, Journal of MIS, Information & Management, DATABASE, InformationWEEK, DATAMATION, ComputerWorld,* and the *Proceedings of ICIS. HICSS,* and *AMCIS.* He is the co-author (with John Soden of Mckinsey & Co.) of *Strategic Planning for MIS* (Wiley Interscience, 1977), co-editor of a book of programs entitled *APL Applications in Management* (UCLA, 1981), and co-editor of *The Management of Information Systems* (Dryden Press, 2nd ed., 1994). He was a founding associate editor for Research of the *MIS Quarterly,* and for seven years the senior co-editor of *The DATA BASE for Advances in Information Systems.*

He has served four times on the national Executive Council of the Society for Information Management (SIM). In 1980, he co-chaired the organizing committee for the International Conference on Information Systems (ICIS) and was Conference Co-chairman in 1981 in Cambridge, MA; Conference Chairman in 1986 in San Diego, CA; and Conference Co-chairman in 1997 in Atlanta, CA. He is currently the Executive Director of the ICIS and of the Association for Information Systems (AIS) of which he was one of the founding members. In 1999, he was named a fellow of the AIS, one of the first in the world so honored. In 2003, he was named IS Educator of the Year by the Special Interest Group on Education of the Association for Information Technology Professionals (AITP).

DR. JAMES C. WETHERBE

Dr. James C. Wetherbe is Stevenson Chair of Information Technology at Texas Tech University as well as Professor of MIS at the University of Minnesota where he directed the MIS Research Center for 20 years. He is internationally known as a dynamic and entertaining speaker, author, and leading authority on the use of computers and information systems to improve organizational performance and competitiveness. He is particularly appreciated for his ability to explain complex technology in straightforward, practical terms that can be strategically applied by both executives and general management.

Dr. Wetherbe is the author of 18 highly regarded books and is quoted often in leading business and information systems journals. He has also authored over 200 articles, was ranked by *InformationWEEK* as one of the top dozen information technology consultants, and is the first recipient of the MIS Quarterly Distinguished Scholar Award. He has also served on the faculties of the University of Memphis, where he was Fed Ex Professor and Director of the Center for Cycle Time Research, and the University of Houston.

Dr. Wetherbe received his Ph.D. from Texas Tech University.

Brief Contents

PART I
IT in the Organization

1   Strategic Use of Information Technology in the Digital Economy **1**
2   Information Technologies: Concepts and Management **48**

PART II
The Web Revolution

3   Network Computing: Discovery, Communication, and Collaboration **89**
4   E-Business and E-Commerce **137**
5   Mobile, Wireless, and Pervasive Computing **185**

PART III
Organizational Applications

6   Transaction Processing, Functional Applications, and Integration **244**
7   Enterprise Systems: From Supply Chains to ERP to CRM **293**
8   Interorganizational and Global Information Systems **331**

PART IV
Managerial and Decision Support Systems

9   Knowledge Management **365**
10 Data Management: Warehousing, Analyzing, Mining, and Visualization **406**
11 Management Decision Support and Intelligent Systems **456**

PART V
Implementing and Managing IT

12 Using Information Technology for Strategic Advantage **505**
13 Information Technology Economics **553**
14 Acquiring IT Applications and Infrastructure **594**
15 Managing Information Resources and Security **632**
16 The Impacts of Information Technology on Organizations, Individuals, and Society **688**

Glossary

Technology Guides
Online at
www.wiley.com/
college/turban

T1 Hardware
T2 Software
T3 Data and Databases
T4 Telecommunications
T5 The Internet and the Web
T6 A Technical View of Systems Analysis and Design

Contents

PART I
IT In The Organization

1 Strategic Use of Information Technology in the Digital Economy 1
   Siemans AG **2**
1.1 Doing Business in the Digital Economy **3**
1.2 Business Pressures, Organizational Responses, and IT Support **12**
1.3 Information Systems: Definitions and Examples **20**
1.4 Information Technology Developments and Trends **26**
1.5 Why Should You Learn About Information Technology? **34**
1.6 Plan of the Book **35**
   Minicases: (1) Dartmouth College /
    (2) Wal-Mart **40**

Appendix 1A Porter's Models **44**

2 Information Technologies: Concepts and Management **48**
   Building an E-Business at FedEx Corporation **49**
2.1 Information Systems: Concepts and Definitions **51**
2.2 Classification and Evolution of Information Systems **53**
2.3 Transaction Processing versus Functional Information Systems **58**
2.4 How IT Supports Organizational Activities **60**
2.5 How IT Supports Supply Chain, CRM, PRM Operations **63**
2.6 Information Systems Infrastructure and Architecture **66**
2.7 Web-based Systems **71**
2.8 New Computing Environments **74**
2.9 Managing Information Resources **77**
   Minicases: (1) Maybelline / (2) J. P. Morgan **83**

Appendix 2A Build-to-Order Production **87**

PART II
The Web Revolution

3 Network Computing: Discovery, Communication, and Collaboration **89**
   Safeway Collaborates in Designing Stores **90**
3.1 Network Computing—An Overview **91**
3.2 Discovery **95**
3.3 Communication **104**
3.4 Collaboration **108**
3.5 Collaboration-Enabling Tools: From Workflow to Groupware **116**
3.6 E-Learning and Virtual Work **120**
3.7 Some Ethical and Integration Issues **124**
   Minicases: (1) General Motors / (2) Cisco **131**

4 E-Business and E-Commerce **137**
   Buy Chocolate Online? try godiva.com **138**
4.1 Overview of E-Business and E-Commerce **139**
4.2 Major EC Mechanisms **143**
4.3 Business-to-Consumer Applications **146**
4.4 Online Advertising **153**
4.5 B2B Applications **157**
4.6 Intrabusiness and Business-to-Employees EC **161**
4.7 E-Government and Consumer-to-Consumer EC **161**
4.8 E-Commerce Support Services **164**
4.9 Ethical and Legal Issues in E-Business **170**
4.10 Failures and Strategies for Success **174**
   Minicases: (1) FreeMarkets.com / (2) Hi-Life Corporation **181**

5 Mobile, Wireless, and Pervasive Computing **185**
   Nextbus **186**
5.1 Mobile Computing and Commerce: Overview, Benefits, and Drivers **187**
5.2 Mobile Computing Infrastructure **193**
5.3 Mobile Applications in Financial Services **202**
5.4 Mobile Shopping, Advertising, and Content-Providing **204**

5.5 Mobile Intrabusiness and Enterprise Applications **208**

5.6 Mobile B2B and Supply Chain Applications **214**

5.7 Mobile Consumer and Personal Service Applications **214**

5.8 Location-Based Commerce **218**

5.9 Pervasive Computing **222**

5.10 Inhibitors and Barriers of Mobile Computing **232**
Minicases: (1) Hertz / (2) Washington Township (OH) **239**

PART III
Organizational Applications

6 Transaction Processing, Functional Applications, and Integration **244**
Dartmouth-Hitchcock Medical Center **245**

6.1 Functional Information Systems **247**

6.2 Transaction Processing Information Systems **249**

6.3 Managing Production/Operations and Logistics **255**

6.4 Managing Marketing and Sales Systems **260**

6.5 Managing the Accounting and Finance Systems **269**

6.6 Managing Human Resources Systems **276**

6.7 Integrating Functional Information Systems **282**
Minicases: (1) Dollar General / (2) 99 Cents Only Stores **289**

7 Enterprise Systems: From Supply Chains to ERP to CRM **293**
ChevronTexaco **294**

7.1 Essentials of Enterprise Systems and Supply Chains **295**

7.2 Supply Chain Problems and Solutions **299**

7.3 Computerized Enterprise Systems: MRP, MRP II, SCM and Software Integration **309**

7.4 Enterprise Resource Planning and Supply Chain Management **311**

7.5 CRM and Its support by IT **318**
Minicases: (1) Northern Digital / (2) QVC **327**

8 Interorganizational and Global Information Systems **331**
Dell **332**

8.1 Interorganizational Systems **334**

8.2 Global Information Systems **336**

8.3 B2B Exchanges, Hubs, and Directories **341**

8.4 Virtual Corporations and IT Support **344**

8.5 Electronic Data Interchange (EDI) **345**

8.6 Extranets, XML, and Web Services **349**

8.7 IOS Implementation Issues **354**
Minicases: (1) Volkswagen / (2) Six Flags **361**

PART IV
Managerial and Decision Support Systems

9 Knowledge Management **365**
KM Portal at Frito-Lay Assists Dispersed Sales Teams **366**

9.1 Introduction to Knowledge Management **367**

9.2 Knowledge Management Initiatives **372**

9.3 Approaches to Knowledge Management **374**

9.4 Information Technology in Knowledge Management **376**

9.5 Knowledge Management Systems Implementation **380**

9.6 Roles of People in Knowledge Management **388**

9.7 Ensuring Success of KM Efforts **391**
Minicases: (1) DaimlerChrysler / (2) Buckman Labs **400**

10 Data Management: Warehousing, Analyzing, Mining, and Visualization **406**
Harrah's Entertainment **407**

10.1 Data Management: A Critical Success Factor **409**

10.2 Data Warehousing **417**

10.3 Information and Knowledge Discovery with Business Intelligence **422**

10.4 Data Mining Concepts and Applications **428**

10.5 Data Visualization Technologies **432**

10.6 Marketing Databases in Action **440**

10.7 Web-Based Data Management Systems **443**
Minicases: (1) Homeland Security / (2) Sears **451**

11 Management Decision Support and Intelligent Systems **456**
New Balance **457**

11.1 Managers and Decision Making **459**

11.2 Decision Support Systems **465**

11.3 Group Decision Support Systems **471**

11.4 Enterprise and Executive Decision Support Systems **471**

11.5 Intelligent Support Systems: The Basics **476**

11.6 Expert Systems **480**

11.7 Other Intelligent Systems **484**

11.8 Web-Based Management Support Systems **492**

11.9 Advanced and Special Decision Support Topics **492**

Minicases: (1) Netherlands Railway / (2) Singapore and Malaysia Airlines **500**

PART V
Implementing and Managing IT

12 Using Information Technology for Strategic Advantage **505**
Dell's Direct Path to Success **506**

12.1 Strategic Advantage and Information Technology **508**

12.2 Porter's Value Chain Model **513**

12.3 Strategic Resources and Capabilities **515**

12.4 IT Planning—A Critical Issue for Organizations **519**

12.5 Strategic IT Planning (Stage 1) **521**

12.6 Information Requirements Analysis, Resource Allocation, and Project Planning (Stages 2–4) **528**

12.7 Planning IT Architectures **531**

12.8 Some Issues in IT Planning **536**
Minicase (1) Cisco Systems / (2) National City Bank **547**

13 Information Technology Economics **552**
State of Iowa **553**

13.1 Financial and Economic Trends and the Productivity Paradox **554**

13.2 Evaluating IT Investment: Benefits, Costs, and Issues **560**

13.3 Methods for Evaluating and Justifying IT Investment **566**

13.4 IT Economics Strategies: Chargeback and Outsourcing **574**

13.5 Economics of Web-Based Systems and E-Commerce **580**

13.6 Other Economic Aspects of Information Technology **582**
Minicases: (1) Intranets / (2) Kone Inc. **589**

14 Acquiring IT Applications and Infrastructure **594**
How Sterngold Acquired an e-Commerce System **595**

14.1 The Landscape and Framework of IT Application Acquisition **597**

14.2 Identifying, Justifying, and Planning Information System Applications (Step 1) **600**

14.3 Acquiring IT Applications: Available Options (Step 3) **602**

14.4 Outsourcing and Application Service Providers **608**

14.5 Vendor and Software Selection and Other Implementation Issues **611**

14.6 Connecting to Databases and Business Partners: Integration (Step 4) **614**

14.7 Business Process Redesign **615**

14.8 The Role of IT in Business Process Redesign **617**

14.9 Restructuring Processes and Organizations **621**
Minicase (1) Pioneer Inc. / (2) McDonald's **628**

15 Managing Information Resources and Security **632**
Cybercrime in the New Millennium **633**

15.1 The IS Department and End Users **634**

15.2 The CIO in Managing the IS Department **639**

15.3 IS Vulnerability and Computer Crimes **641**

15.4 Protecting Information Resources: From National to Organizational Efforts **652**

15.5 Securing the Web, Intranets, and Wireless Networks **660**

15.6 Business Continuity and Disaster Recovery Planning **667**

15.7 Implementing Security: Auditing and Risk Management **670**

15.8 Information Technology in Counterterrorism **676**
Minicases: (1) Home Depot / (2) Zions Bancorporation **683**

16 The Impacts of Information Technology on Individuals, Organizations, and Society **688**
Movie Piracy **689**

16.1 Introduction **691**

16.2 IT Is Eliminating the Barriers of Time, Space, and Distance **692**

16.3 Information Is Changing from a Scarce Resource to an Abundant Resource **696**

16.4 Machines Are Performing Functions Previously Performed by Humans **703**

16.5 Information Technology Urges People to Reexamine Their Value Systems **711**

16.6 Conclusion **716**
 Minicases: (1) ChoicePoint: / (2) Australian Fishing Community **720**

Technology Guides (Online)

T1 Hardware
T1.1 What Is a Computer System?
T1.2 The Evolution of Computer Hardware
T1.3 Types of Computers
T1.4 The Microprocessor and Primary Storage
T1.5 Input/Output Devices

T2 Software
T2.1 Types of Software
T2.2 Application Software
T2.3 Systems Software
T2.4 Programming Languages
T2.5 Software Development and CASE Tools
T2.6 Software Issues and Trends

T3 Data and Databases
T3.1 File Management
T3.2 Databases and Database Management Systems
T3.3 Logical Data Organization
T3.4 Creating Databases
T3.5 Emerging Database Models
T3.6 Data Warehouses

T3.7 Physical Database Organization
T3.8 Database Management
T3.9 An Emerging Technology: IP-based Storage

T4 Telecommunications
T4.1 Telecommunications Concepts
T4.2 Communications Media (Channels)
T4.3 Network Systems: Protocols, Standards, Interfaces, and Topologies
T4.4 Network Architecture: Open Systems and Enterprise Networking
T4.5 Telecommunications Applications

T5 The Internet and the Web
T5.1 What Is the Internet?
T5.2 Basic Characteristics and Capabilities of the Internet
T5.3 Browsing and the World Wide Web

T6 A Technical View of Systems Analysis and Design
T6.1 Developing an IT Architecture
T6.2 Overview of the SDLC
T6.3 Alternative Methods and Tools for Systems Development
T6.4 Component-Based Development and Web Services

Glossary G-1
Photo Credits P-1
Name Index NI-1
Subject Index SI-1

PART I
IT in the Organization

▶ 1. **Strategic Use of Information Technology in the Digital Economy**
2. **Information Technologies: Concepts and Management**

CHAPTER
1

Strategic Use of Information Technology in the Digital Economy

1.1 Doing Business in the Digital Economy

1.2 Business Pressures, Organizational Responses, and IT Support

1.3 Information Systems: Definitions and Examples

1.4 Information Technology Developments and Trends

1.5 Why Should You Learn About Information Technology?

1.6 Plan of the Book

Minicases:
1. Dartmouth College
2. Wal-Mart

Appendix 1A: Porter's Models

LEARNING OBJECTIVES

After studying this chapter, you will be able to:

❶ Describe the characteristics of the digital economy and e-business.

❷ Recognize the relationships between business pressures, organizational responses, and information systems.

❸ Identify the major pressures in the business environment and describe the major organizational responses to them.

❹ Define computer-based information systems and information technology.

❺ Describe the role of information technology in supporting the functional areas, public services, and specific industries.

❻ List the new technology developments in the areas of generic and networked computing and Web-based systems.

❼ Understand the importance of learning about information technology.

SIEMENS AG IS TRANSFORMING ITSELF INTO AN E-BUSINESS

 THE PROBLEM

Siemens AG (*siemens.com*) is a German-based 150-year-old diversified and global manufacturer. With 484,000 employees, Siemens does business in 190 countries and has 600 manufacturing and R & D (research and development) facilities in over 50 countries. Its product lines and services are extremely varied, including communication and information, automation and controls, power, transportation, medical equipment, and lighting. Besides its own 13 operating divisions, Siemens AG has interests in other companies like Bosch (household appliances), Framatome (in France's nuclear power industry), and Fujitsu computers.

Facing hundreds of competitors, most of which are in foreign countries, the company had difficulties expanding its business in a fast-changing business environment and was unable to enjoy the profit margin of some of its competitors. A major problem area was the coordination of the internal units of the company. Another one was the collaboration with so many suppliers and customers. In particular, its *supply chain*—the flow of materials from suppliers through manufacturing, distribution, and sales—is very complex. Finally, it was necessary to find ways to contain costs and to increase customer service.

 THE SOLUTION

By the late 1990s the company decided to transform itself into a 100 percent "e-business"—a company that performs various business functions electronically. It would do so by introducing Web-based systems and electronic commerce applications in all of its operations. The reason for such an ambitious goal was the need to solve the problems caused by multiple supply chain operations. Embarking on a four-year plan, the company started the transformation in 1999.

Siemens had decided on a dual approach: It would use its own in-house information systems capabilities where it made sense to do so, but it would also go out-of-house to purchase some systems from major vendors. Siemens strategic goals were to:

- Improve its readiness for extended electronic commerce by standardizing hundreds of business processes across multiple divisions. (For example, the company went from over 300 different process applications to 29.)
- Redesign the information technology infrastructure to enable integration of "best-of-breed" software (software components that best fit the company's needs, each from a different vendor), integrated into an enterprisewide platform.

Besides being able to handle electronic transactions, Siemens also wanted to create an easily accessible central corporate *knowledge base*—a companywide storehouse of proven methodologies (known as "best practices"; see Chapter 9).

Using SAP R/3 systems (see Chapter 7), along with software from i2 Technology and IBM, the company built functional systems that link the enterprise, ensure support functions, and connect with the company's supply chain partners. Functions such as taking customer orders, online procuring of materials and components that go into the manufacturing process, collaborating with business partners in developing products, and transporting finished products were integrated across the company, using the Internet as much as possible. Also, the system was designed to provide better customer service to Siemens's business customers.

 THE RESULTS

In its 2000 fiscal year, the company saw its online sales and its electronic procurement transactions reach 10 percent of its total sales and purchases, respectively. In 2002, online sales increased by 25 percent, and e-procurement grew 60 percent over its 2000 level.

As of January 2004, most employees are networked throughout the company. They have direct access to the Internet, and a portal through which employees can access corporate information is in use. This portal offers various workplace aids, including search engines, forms, travel booking, and electronic expense account reporting.

The transformation to an e-business cost Siemens around 1 billion euros. President and CEO Heinrich von Pierer says, "This will make us faster and help us further cut costs. . . . All of this is aimed at meeting today's e-economy goals directly, with the promise of operational economies in return."

Sources: Compiled from Schultz (2002), *aberdeen.com* (accessed September 2002), and *siemens.com* (accessed May 2004).

 LESSONS LEARNED FROM THIS CASE

This brief "Lessons Learned" section ties the key points of the opening case to the topics that will be covered in the chapter.

This case illustrates that fierce global competition drives even large corporations to find ways to reduce costs, increase productivity, and improve customer service, which increase competitive advantage. These efforts are best achieved by using Web-based systems, which are the major enablers in the transformation to an *e-business* or *e-company* in the digital economy.

In this chapter we present characteristics and concepts of the digital economy and how it is changing business processes. We also describe the extremely competitive business environment in which companies operate today, the business pressures to which they are subject, and what companies are doing to counter these pressures, especially in strategic management. Futhermore, you will learn what makes information technology a necessity in supporting organizations, and why any manager in the twenty-first century should know about it.

Many new terms and concepts are introduced in Chapter 1 and discussed in more detail in later chapters. You will benefit most from Chapter 1 by reading it as an overview—aim to get the "big picture" in this chapter and plan to fill in the details later.

1.1 DOING BUSINESS IN THE DIGITAL ECONOMY

Conducting business in the digital economy means using Web-based systems on the Internet and other electronic networks to do some form of electronic commerce. First we will consider the concepts of electronic commerce and networked computing and then look at the impact they have made on how companies do business.

Electronic Commerce and Networked Computing

As described in the opening case, Siemens AG was an established "old-economy" company that has seen the need to transform itself into an *e-business,* a company that performs most of its business functions electronically, in order to enhance its operations and competitiveness (Chapter 12). Its use of Web-based systems to support buying, selling, and customer service exemplifies *electronic commerce* (*EC* or *e-commerce*). In e-commerce (Chapter 4), business transactions are done electronically over the Internet and other computing networks. EC is becoming a very significant global economic element in the twenty-first century (see Evans and Wurster, 2000 and Drucker, 2002).

The infrastructure for EC is **networked computing** (also known as *distributed computing*), which connects computers and other electronic devices via telecommunication networks. Such connections allow users to access information stored in many places and to communicate and collaborate with others, all from their desktop (or even mobile) computers. While some people still use a standalone computer exclusively, or a network confined to one location, the vast majority of people use multiple-location networked computers. These may be connected to the *global networked environment,* known as the *Internet,* or to its counterpart within organizations, called an *intranet.* In addition, some companies link their intranets to those of their business partners over networks called *extranets.* The connection typically is done via wireline systems, but since 2000 more and more communication and collaboration is done via wireless systems.

Networked computing is helping some companies excel and is helping others simply to survive. Broadly, the collection of computing systems used by an organization is termed **information technology (IT),** which is the focus of this book. In the developed countries, almost all medium and large organizations, and many small ones, private or public, in manufacturing, agriculture, or services, use information technologies, including electronic commerce, to support their operations.

Why is this so? The reason is simple: IT has become the major facilitator of business activities in the world today. (See, for instance, Dickson and DeSanctis, 2001; Huber, 2004; and Tapscott et al., 2000.) Note that here and throughout the book, in using the term "business" we refer not only to for-profit organizations, but also to not-for-profit public organizations and government agencies, which need to be run like a business. IT is also a catalyst of fundamental changes in the strategic structure, operations, and management of organizations (see Carr, 2001), due to the capabilities shown in Table 1.1. These capabilities, according to Wreden (1997), support the following five business objectives: (1) improving productivity (in 51% of corporations), (2) reducing costs (39%), (3) improving decision making (36%), (4) enhancing customer relationships (33%), and (5) developing new strategic applications (33%). Indeed, IT is creating a transformation in the way business is conducted, facilitating a transition to a digital economy.

What Is the Digital Economy?

The **digital economy** refers to an economy that is based on digital technologies, including digital communication networks (the Internet, intranets, and private *value-added networks* or VANs), computers, software, and other related information technologies. The digital economy is also sometimes called the *Internet economy,* the *new economy,* or the *Web economy* (see Brynolfsson et al., 2003 and Liebowitz, 2002).

TABLE 1.1 Major Capabilities of Information Systems
● Perform high-speed, high-volume, numerical computations.
● Provide fast, accurate, and inexpensive communication within and between organizations.
● Store huge amounts of information in an easy-to-access, yet small space.
● Allow quick and inexpensive access to vast amounts of information worldwide.
● Enable communication and collaboration anywhere, any time.
● Increase the effectiveness and efficiency of people working in groups in one place or in several locations.
● Vividly present information that challenges the human mind.
● Facilitate work in hazardous environments.
● Automate both semiautomatic business processes and manually done tasks.
● Facilitate interpretation of vast amounts of data.
● Facilitate global trade.
● Can be wireless, thus supporting unique applications anywhere.
● Accomplish all of the above much less expensively than when done manually.

In this new economy, digital networking and communication infrastructures provide a global platform over which people and organizations devise strategies, interact, communicate, collaborate, and search for information. This platform includes, for example, the following, according to Choi and Whinston (2000):

● A vast array of digitizable products—databases, news and information, books, magazines, TV and radio programming, movies, electronic games, musical CDs, and software—which are delivered over the digital infrastructure any time, anywhere in the world

● Consumers and firms conducting financial transactions digitally—through digital currencies or financial tokens carried via networked computers and mobile devices

● Physical goods such as home appliances and automobiles, which are equipped with microprocessors and networking capabilities

The following icon is used throughout the book to indicate that additional related resources are available at the book's Web site, *www.wiley.com/college/turban.*

The term *digital economy* also refers to the convergence of computing and communication technologies on the Internet and other networks, and the resulting flow of information and technology that is stimulating e-commerce and vast organizational change. This convergence enables all types of information (data, audio, video, etc.) to be stored, processed, and transmitted over networks to many destinations worldwide. The digital economy has helped create an economic revolution, which was evidenced by unprecedented economic performance and the longest period of uninterrupted economic expansion in history, from 1991 until 2000. (See Online File W1.1 for some statistics related to the "digital revolution.")

OPPORTUNITIES FOR ENTREPRENEURS. The new digital economy is providing unparalleled opportunities for thousands of entrepreneurs, some of them in their teens, to apply EC business models to many business areas. As we will see throughout the book, many of these initiatives were started by one or two individuals. Others were started by large corporations. These startup companies not only sold products, but many also provided support services ranging from computer infrastructure to electronic payments. Known as *dot-coms*, these companies saw an opportunity to do global business electronically. An interesting example is entrepreneur Don Kogen and his Thaigem.com business, described in *IT at Work 1.1*.

"IT at Work" boxes spotlight innovations and technologies used by real organizations to solve business problems.

"Integrating IT" icons highlight examples of IT applications in major functional areas of business, in government, and in public services. The codes used in these turquoise-colored icons are:

ACC—accounting

POM—production/operations management
MKT—marketing
HRM—human resources management
FIN—finance
GOV—government
SVC—other public services and service industries

IT at Work 1.1
DIAMONDS FOREVER—ONLINE

The gems market is a global one with thousands of traders buying and selling about $40 billion worth of gems each year. This age-old business is very inefficient in terms of pricing: Several layers of intermediaries can jack up the price of a gem 1,000 percent between wholesale and final retail prices.

Chanthaburi, Thailand, is one of the world's leading centers for processing gems, and that is where Don Kogen landed, at the age of 15, to search for his fortune. And indeed, he found it there. After failing to become a gem cutter, Kogen moved into gem sorting, and soon he learned to speak Thai. After three years of observing how gem traders haggle over stones, he decided to try the business himself. Having only a small amount of "seed" money, Kogen started by purchasing low-grade gems from sellers who arrived early in the morning and selling them for a small profit to dealers from India and Pakistan who usually arrived late in the day. Using advertising, he reached the U.S. gem market and soon had 800 potential overseas customers. Using faxes, he shortened the order time, which resulted in decreasing the entire time from order to delivery. These various business methods enabled him to grow his mail-order business to $250,000 per year by 1997.

In 1998, Kogen decided to use the Internet. Within a month, he established a Web site, *thaigem.com*, and sold his first gem online. By 2001, the revenue reached $4.3 million, growing to $9.8 million in 2002. Online sales account for 85 percent of the company's revenue. The buyers are mostly jewelry dealers or retailers such as Wal-Mart or QVC. Kogen buys raw or refined gems from all over the world, some online, trying to cater to the demands of his customers.

Thaigem's competitive edge is low prices. The proximity to gem-processing factories and the low labor cost enable Kogen to offer prices significantly lower than his online competitors (such as Tiffany's at *tiffany.com*). Kogen makes only 20 to 25 percent profit, much less than other dealers make. To make the business even more competitive, Kogen caters even to small buyers. Payments are made safely, securely, and conveniently using either PayPal or Escrow.com. Delivery to any place is made via Federal Express, at $15 per shipment.

Dissatisfied customers can return merchandise within 30 days, no questions asked. No jewel is guaranteed, but Kogen's name is trusted by over 68,000 potential customers worldwide. Kogen enjoys a solid reputation on the Web. For example, he uses eBay to auction gems as an additional selling channel. Customers' comments on eBay are 99 percent positive versus 1 percent negative.

Thaigem.com is further expanding its customer-service program. The company has implemented a 24-hour "Live Support" chat service, Monday through Friday, further augmenting this service with the addition of a 1-800 (toll-free) number for U.S. customers. This "Live Support" chat software allows Thaigem.com to track the movement of customers and know exactly what products or content pages customers are viewing.

Sources: Compiled from *thaigem.com* (April 2004) and from Mevedoth (2002).

For Further Exploration: Go to *blackstartrading.com* and compare it to *thaigem.com*; which site do you think is better? What kinds of business and revenue models were used? Were they effective? How is competitive advantage gained in this case?

The New vs. the Old: Illustrative Examples

The changes brought by the digital economy are indeed significant. Computer-based information systems of all kinds have been enhancing business competitiveness and creating strategic advantage on their own or in conjunction with e-commerce applications (see Carr, 2001; Basu and Muylle, 2003; and Li et al., 2003). In a study conducted by Lederer et al. (1998), companies ranked the number-one benefit of Web-based systems as "enhancing competitiveness or creating strategic advantage."

Let's look at a few examples that illustrate differences between doing business in the new economy and the old one.

EXAMPLE #1: PAYING FOR GOODS: THE CHECKOUT EXPERIENCE. It sometimes takes more time to check out than to shop, which can be a really frustrating experience.

Old Economy. In the "old-old" economy, when you visited stores that sold any type of retail product (e.g., groceries, office supplies), you placed your items in a shopping cart and proceeded to checkout. At the checkout counter, you stood in line while a clerk punched in the price of each item on a manual adding machine. After the clerk added up all your items, you paid for them in cash. Note that in this situation no information was gathered about the item itself, other than the price.

Using the next generation of checkout technology, you take your items to a clerk, who swipes (sometimes twice or more) the barcode of each item over a "reader." The reader captures data on the price and description of each item and automatically enters that data into the organization's database. You receive an itemized account of your purchases and the total price.

New Economy. In the new economy, you take your items to a self-service kiosk, where you swipe the barcode of each item over a reader. After you have swiped all of your items, the kiosk gives you directions about how to pay (cash, credit card, or debit card). You still may have to wait if there are lines to get to the self-service kiosk; often, other shoppers need help to learn the technology. But, your checkout time is much faster.

In the coming generation of checkout technology, all items will have wireless radio frequency identification (RFID) tags (see Chapters 2 and 5) either attached to or embedded in them. After you have finished shopping, you will simply walk your cart with all its items through a device similar to an airport security scanner. This device will "read" the wireless signals from each item, generate an itemized account of all your purchases, total up the price, and debit your debit card or credit card (after recognizing your face or fingerprint), all in a few seconds. You will not wait in line at all.

An ethical issue here is what happens to the RFID tags. If they are not removed after you pay, it is theoretically possible for someone to track your whereabouts, which many consider an invasion of privacy. But removing these tags costs money and takes time, an added burden to retailers. Pending legislation in Massachusetts is attempting to force retailers to remove the tags. Pending legislation in California tries to limit the information placed on RFIDs, to ensure privacy.

EXAMPLE #2: CROSSING INTERNATIONAL BORDERS. Assume you are traveling to another country, say Australia. Your plane lands after a long flight, but before you can make your way to your lodgings, you must first go through immigration.

Old Economy. You wait in line to be processed by the immigration officers. The inspectors are slow, and some are new and need help from time to time. Processing certain people takes several minutes. You are tired, upset, and stressed. You may wait 10 minutes, 20 minutes, or even close to an hour.

New Economy. You submit your passport and it is scanned. At the same time, a photo of your face is taken. A computer compares that picture with the picture in the passport and with one in a database. In 10 seconds you are through immigration and on your way out of the airport. The world's first system of this kind was initiated in Australia in 2003. In some countries (e.g., Israel), an image of your fingerprints is taken and compared to a stored image. Again, in seconds you are on your way. These systems use a technology called *biometrics* (see Chapter 15) that not only expedites processing but also increases security by eliminating the entry of people with false passports.

EXAMPLE #3: SUPPLYING COMMERCIAL PHOTOS. Thousands of companies around the globe provide photos of their products to retailers who advertise products in newspapers, in paper catalogs, or online. The new economy has changed the process by which these photos are supplied.

Old Economy. In the old economy, the retailer sends the manufacturer a request for a picture of the item to be advertised, say a Sony TV set. Sony then sends to a designated ad agency, by courier, alternative pictures that the agency can use. The agency selects a picture, designs the ad, gets an approval from the retailer, and sends the picture by courier to the printer. There it is rephotographed and entered into production for the catalog. (An improvement introduced several years ago allows the ad agency to send the picture to a scanning house. There, a digital image is made, and that image is moved to the printer.) Both the retailer and the ad agency may be involved in a quality check at various times, slowing the process. The cycle time per picture can be four to six weeks. The total processing cost per picture is about $80.

New Economy. Orbis Inc., a very small Australian company, changed the above old-economy linear supply chain to a hub-like supply chain, as shown in Figure 1.1. In the new process, the manufacturer (e.g., Sony) sends many

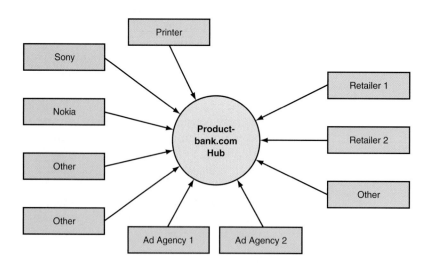

FIGURE 1.1 Changing a linear supply chain to a hub.

digitized pictures to Orbis (at *productbank.com.au*), and Orbis organizes the pictures in a database. When a retailer needs a picture, it enters the database and selects a picture, or several alternatives. The ID number of the chosen picture is e-mailed to the ad agency. The agency enters the database, views the digitized pictures, and works on them. Then, after the client's approval, either the final digitized pictures are e-mailed to the printer, or the printer is told to pick them up from the database. The entire process takes less than a week at a cost of about $50 per picture.

EXAMPLE #4: PAYING FOR TRANSPORTATION IN NEW YORK CITY. Millions of people all over the world take public transportation. Metal tokens were the preferred solution in some major cities for generations.

Old Economy. For over 50 years, New Yorkers have used tokens to pay for transportation on buses and subways. The tokens save time and are liked by travelers. However, it costs $6 million a year to manufacture replacement tokens and to collect the tokens out of turnstiles and fare boxes ("NYC Transit Tokens. . . ," 2003). New York City needs this money badly for other services.

New Economy. The new-economy solution has been to switch to Metro-Cards. By 2002, only 9 percent of all commuters were still using tokens. Despite the fact that they have to occasionally swipe the MetroCard through the card reader several times, travelers generally like the new cards. (A new generation of contactless cards does not have this problem.) MetroCards are offered at discounts, which riders like.

Other cities have made the transition to electronic cards as well. Chicago's transit moved to cards in 1999, replacing the century-old tokens. Washington, D.C., Paris, and London also use transit cards. In Hong Kong, millions use a contactless card not only for transportation but also to pay for telephone, Internet access, food in vending machines, and much more.

EXAMPLE #5: IMPROVING THE LAUNDRY EXPERIENCE FOR COLLEGE STUDENTS. Millions of college students use dorm laundry facilities worldwide. What is their experience?

Old Economy. You run to the laundry room only to find out that all machines are taken. You wait for a machine, and when you finally get one, you realize that you are short on coins. You manage to find someone who will make change for you, and now you are set to start. But you do not remember how your mother instructed you to wash the dirty shirts, and now there is no one around to ask. You put everything into the washer, start it, and hope for the best. Rather than hang around the laundry room, you go away to study, and when you come back you find that someone took out your clean stuff and placed it on the dirty counter. You transfer the laundry to the dryer, and go back to study some more. This time you come back before the dryer is finished, so you must wait, wasting more time.

New Economy. Dryers and washers in your college are hooked to the Web. You punch a code into your cell phone or sign in at *esuds.net,* and you can check for availability of laundry machines. Furthermore, you can pay with your student ID or with a credit card, and you will receive e-mail alerts when your wash and dry cycles are complete. Once in the laundry room, you activate this system by swiping your student ID card (or key in a PIN number). The system automatically injects premeasured amounts of detergent and fabric softener, at the right cycle time.

The machine owners benefit too: They can monitor machine performance, arrange for some maintenance, eliminate vandalism (no cash in the machines), and enjoy higher utilization (more students use the campus machines). Sound great? If you do not have it on your campus yet, it will come soon.

EXAMPLE #6: THE POWER OF E-COMMERCE. The power of e-commerce is demonstrated in the following three examples:

Every year, Warren Buffett, the most famous U.S. stock investor and investment guru, invites eight people to lunch with him. The eight pay big money for the pleasure. The money is donated to San Francisco's needy people. In the past, Buffett charged $30,000 per person. In 2003, Buffett placed the invitation in an online auction. Bidders pushed the price from $30,000 to over $200,000.

Initial public offerings (IPOs) of equity securities (stocks) can make their buyers rich, since on the first day of trading prices can go up considerably, frequently over 100 percent. Initial stock allocations typically have been offered for sale to stockbrokers and to some interest groups (e.g., mutual funds and pension funds). In August 2004, Google.com went public with its IPO by conducting a Dutch auction on the Internet (see Chapter 4). Using this method for its stock offering, the company collected much more money and the shares were distributed in a fair manner.

Chris Moneymaker won $2.5 million in May 2003 in the World Series of Poker. Chris, a 27-year-old, had never before sat down at a poker tournament table. Yet, he cleaned out many skilled professionals. How did he do it? Although Chris had never sat in a room with players, he had played extensively online, where the game is much faster, but the money is just as real. (Interested? See Wayner, 2003 and *playwinningpoker.com*.)

In each of the examples above, we can see the advantage of the new way of doing business over the old one in terms of at least one of the following: cost, quality, speed, strategic competitive advantage, and customer service. What is amazing is the *magnitude* of this advantage. In the past, business improvements were in the magnitude of 10 to 25 percent. Today, improvements can be hundreds or even thousands of times faster or cheaper. For example, it is about 250 times faster to get through immigration now, and there are fewer mistakes (Walker, 2003). The new economy brings not only digitization but also the opportunity to use new business models, such as Don Kogen uses at Thaigem.com—selling from the Internet.

Business Models in the Digital Economy

The Internet is challenging the economic, societal, and technological foundations of the old economy. In essence, a *revolution* has been underway. And like all successful revolutions, when it ends, the landscape will look significantly different. Entrepreneurs are developing new models for business, the economy, and government.

A **business model** is a method of doing business by which a company can generate revenue to sustain itself. The model spells out how the company creates (or adds) value that consumers are willing to pay for, in terms of the goods and/or services the company produces in the course of its operations. Some models are very simple. For example, Nokia makes and sells cell phones and generates profit from these sales. On the other hand, a TV station provides free broadcasting. Its survival depends on a complex model involving factors such as advertisers and content providers. Internet portals, such as Yahoo, also use a similar complex business model.

Some examples of new business models brought about by the digital revolution are listed in *A Closer Look 1.1*. Further discussion of these models will be found throughout the book (especially in Chapter 4), and also in Afuah and Tucci (2003), Brynolfsson et al. (2003), Weill and Vitale (2001), and Turban et al. (2006), and at *digitalenterprise.org*. In part, these new business models have sprung up in response or reaction to business pressures, which is the topic we turn to next.

"A Closer Look" boxes contain detailed, in-depth discussion of specific concepts, procedures, or approaches.

A CLOSER LOOK

1.1 FIVE REPRESENTATIVE BUSINESS MODELS OF THE DIGITAL AGE

NAME-YOUR-OWN-PRICE. Pioneered by Priceline.com, this model allows the buyer to state a price he or she is willing to pay for a specific product or service. Using information in its database, Priceline will try to match the buyer's request with a supplier willing to sell on these terms. Customers may have to submit several bids before they find a price match for the product they want. Priceline's major area of operation is travel (airline tickets, hotels).

TENDERING VIA REVERSE AUCTIONS. If you are a big buyer, private or public, you are probably using a *tendering* (bidding) system to make your major purchases. In what is called a *request for quote* (RFQ), the buyer indicates a desire to receive bids on a particular item, and would-be sellers bid on the job. The lowest bid wins (if price is the only consideration), hence the name *reverse auction*. Now tendering can be done online, saving time and money (see Chapter 4). Pioneered by General Electric Corp. (*gxs.com*), tendering systems are gaining popularity. Indeed, several government entities are mandating electronic tendering as the only way to sell to them. Electronic reverse auctions are fast, they reduce administrative costs by as much as 85 percent, and products' prices can be 5 to 20 percent lower.

AFFILIATE MARKETING. *Affiliate marketing* is an arrangement in which marketing partners place a banner ad for a company, such as Amazon.com, on their Web site. Every time a customer clicks on the banner, moves to the advertiser's Web site, and makes a purchase there, the advertiser pays a 3 to 15 percent commission to the host site. In this way, businesses can turn other businesses into their *virtual commissioned sales force*. Pioneered by CDNow (see Hoffman and Novak, 2000), the concept is now employed by thousands of retailers or direct sellers. For details see Chapter 4 and Helmstetter and Metiviers (2000).

GROUP PURCHASING. It is customary to pay less per unit when buying more units. Discounts are usually available for such quantity purchases. Using e-commerce and the concept of *group purchasing,* in which purchase orders of many buyers are aggregated, a small business or even an individual can participate and get a discount. EC brings in the concept of *electronic aggregation* for group purchasing, in which a third party finds the individuals or *SMEs* (small/medium enterprises) that want to buy the same product, aggregates their small orders, and then negotiates (or conducts a tender) for the best deal. The more that join the group, the larger the aggregated quantity, and the lower the price paid. Some leading aggregators are *buyerzone.com* and *allbusiness.com*.

E-MARKETPLACES AND EXCHANGES. Electronic marketplaces have existed in isolated applications for decades. An example is the stock exchanges, some of which have been fully computerized since the 1980s. But, since 1999, thousands of electronic marketplaces of different varieties have sprung up. E-marketplaces introduce operating efficiencies to trading, and if well organized and managed, they can provide benefits to both buyers and sellers. Of special interest are *vertical marketplaces,* which concentrate on one industry (e.g., *chemconnect.com* in the chemical industry). (Chapter 4 will explore e-marketplaces and exchanges in more detail.)

1.2 BUSINESS PRESSURES, ORGANIZATIONAL RESPONSES, AND IT SUPPORT

Environmental, organizational, and technological factors are creating a highly competitive business environment in which customers are the focal point. Furthermore, these factors can change quickly, sometimes unpredictably (see Tapscott et al., 2000). A Gartner Group survey, Gartner G2 (2004), revealed that the most important business issues of 2004 were retaining loyal customers, improving productivity, cutting costs, increasing market share, and providing timely organizational response. As we will see throughout the book, IT is a major enabler for dealing with these issues.

Companies need to react frequently and quickly to both the *problems* and the *opportunities* resulting from this new business environment (see Arens and Rosenbloom, 2003 and Drucker, 2001). Because the pace of change and the degree of uncertainty in tomorrow's competitive environment are expected to accelerate, organizations are going to operate under increasing pressures to produce more, using fewer resources.

Boyett and Boyett (1995) emphasize this dramatic change and describe it with a set of what they call **business pressures,** or *drivers*. These business pressures are forces in the organization's environment that create pressures on (that is, that "drive") the organization's operations.

Boyett and Boyett maintain that in order to succeed (or even merely to survive) in this dynamic world, companies must not only take traditional actions such as lowering costs, but also undertake innovative activities (such as changing structure or processes) or devise a competitive strategy (Chapter 12). We refer to these reactions, some of which are interrelated, as **critical response activities.** These activities can be performed in some or all of the processes of the organization, from the daily routines of preparing payroll and order entry, to strategic activities such as the acquisition of a company. A response can be a reaction to a pressure already in existence, an initiative intended to defend an organization against future pressures, or an activity that exploits an opportunity created by changing conditions. Most response activities can be greatly facilitated by information technology. In some cases IT is the only solution to these business pressures (see Simpson, 2003 and Arens and Rosenbloom, 2003).

The relationships among business pressures, organizational responses, and IT are shown in Figure 1.2. This figure illustrates a model of the new world of

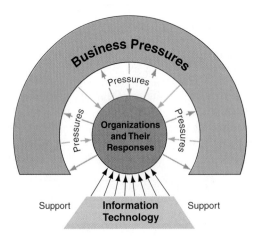

FIGURE 1.2 IT support for organizational responses.

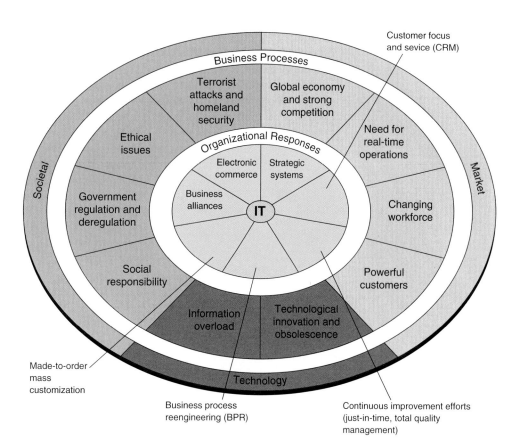

FIGURE 1.3 Business pressures, organizational responses, and IT support.

business. The business environment contains pressures on organizations, and organizations respond with activities supported by IT (hence the bidirectional nature of the arrows in the figure).

In the remainder of this section, we will examine two components of the model—business pressures and organizational responses—in more detail.

Business Pressures   The business environment consists of a variety of factors—social, technological, legal, economic, physical, and political (see Huber, 2004). Significant changes in any of these factors are likely to create business pressures on organizations. In this book, we will focus on the following business pressures: market pressures, technology pressures, and societal pressures. Figure 1.3 presents a schematic view of these major pressures, which may interrelate and affect each other. These pressures are described next.

MARKET PRESSURES.   The market pressures that organizations feel come from a global economy and strong competition, the changing nature of the workforce, and powerful customers. (These are shown in a tan color in Figure 1.3.)

Global Economy and Strong Competition.   Within the last 20 or so years, the foundation necessary for a global economy has taken shape. This move to globalization has been facilitated by advanced telecommunication networks and especially by the Internet. Regional agreements such as the North American Free Trade Agreement (United States, Canada, and Mexico) and the creation of a unified European market with a single currency, the euro, have contributed to increased world trade. Further, reduction of trade barriers has allowed products and services to flow more freely around the globe.

One particular pressure that exists for businesses in a global market is the cost of labor. Labor costs differ widely from one country to another. While the hourly industrial wage rate (excluding benefits) is over $25 in some developed countries, it can be less than $1 in many developing countries, including those in Asia, South America, Eastern Europe, and Africa. Therefore, many companies in labor-intensive industries have found it necessary to move their manufacturing facilities to countries with low labor costs. Such a global strategy requires extensive communication and collaboration, frequently in several languages and under several cultural, ethical, and legal conditions. This can be greatly facilitated with IT (Chapter 8).

Using IT in a multicountry/multicultural environment may create ethical issues, such as invasion of privacy of individuals whose private data are taken across borders. *Global competition* is especially intensified when governments become involved through the use of subsidies, tax policies, import/export regulations, and other incentives. Rapid and inexpensive communication and transportation modes increase the magnitude of international trade even further. Competition is now becoming truly global.

Need for Real-Time Operations. The world is moving faster and faster. Decisions need to be made very quickly, and speed is needed to remain competitive (Gates, 1999; Davis, 2001; and Huber, 2004). Led by Cisco Systems, some companies are even attempting to close their accounting books in a day— a process that used to take as many as 10 days (McCleanahen, 2002).

Changing Nature of the Workforce. The workforce, particularly in developed countries, is changing rapidly. It is becoming more diversified as increasing numbers of women, single parents, minorities, and persons with disabilities work in all types of positions. In addition, more employees than ever prefer to defer retirement. Finally, more and more workers are becoming knowledge workers (Drucker, 2002). Information technology is easing the integration of this wide variety of employees into the traditional workforce, and it enables homebound people to work from home (telecommute). (For more, see the discussions of telecommuting in Chapter 16.)

Powerful Customers. Consumer sophistication and expectations increase as customers become more knowledgeable about the availability and quality of products and services. On the Web, consumers can now easily find detailed information about products and services, compare prices, and buy at electronic auctions. As we mentioned earlier, in some cases buyers can even name the price they are willing to pay. Therefore, consumers have considerable power (Pitt et al., 2002). Companies need to be able to deliver information quickly to satisfy these customers.

Customers today also want *customized products and services,* with high quality and low prices. Vendors must respond, or lose business. For example, a large department store in Japan offers refrigerators in 24 different colors with a delivery time of just a few days. Dell Computer will take an order over the Internet for a computer, made to specifications of your choice, and will deliver that computer to your home within 3 to 7 days. And Nike will let you design your own sneakers online and will make and ship them to arrive at your home in two weeks (*nike.com*). Finally, automakers are selling build-to-order cars whose configuration is done on the Internet (see *jaguar.com*). The old saying, "The customer is king," has never before been so true.

The importance of customers has created "competition over customers." This competition forces organizations to increase efforts to acquire and retain customers. An enterprisewide effort to do just that is called *customer relationship management (CRM)* (see Greenberg, 2002). This topic will be addressed in detail in Chapter 6.

TECHNOLOGY PRESSURES. The second category of business pressures consists of those related to technology (shown in red in Figure 1.3). Two major pressures in this category are technological innovation and information overload.

Technological Innovation and Obsolescence. Technology is playing an increased role in both manufacturing and services. New and improved technologies create or support substitutes for products, alternative service options, and superb quality. In addition, some of today's state-of-the-art products may be obsolete tomorrow. Thus, technology accelerates the competitive forces. Many technologies affect business in areas ranging from genetic engineering to food processing. However, probably the technology with the greatest impact is Web-based information technology (see Evans and Wurster, 2000; Carr, 2001; and Motiwalla and Hashimi, 2003).

An example of technological obsolesence is illustrated in Minicase 1 (Maybelline) at the end of Chapter 2. The technology of interactive voice response (IVR), which is still new for many companies, is being replaced by mobile devices, which are being replaced by wireless devices and by voice portals.

Information Overload. The Internet and other telecommunication networks increase the amount of information available to organizations and individuals. Furthermore, the amount of information available on the Internet more than doubles every year, and most of it is free! The information and knowledge generated and stored inside organizations is also increasing exponentially. The world is facing a flood of information. Thus, the accessibility, navigation, and management of data, information, and knowledge, which are necessary for managerial decision making, become critical. The only effective solutions are provided by information technology (e.g., search engines, intelligent databases).

SOCIETAL PRESSURES. The third category of business pressures consists of those related to society (in blue in Figure 1.3). The "next society," as Drucker (2001, 2002) calls it, will be a knowledge society, and also a society of aging populations. Both of these have important societal implications related to education and health care (e.g., see the case of Elite-Care in Chapter 5), and handling of such issues likely will involve various information technologies (see Sipior et al., 2004). Other important societal issues include social responsibility, government regulation/deregulation, spending for social programs, and ethics.

Social Responsibility. The interfaces between organizations and society are both increasing and changing rapidly. Social issues that affect business range from the state of the physical environment to companies' contributions to education (e.g., by allowing interns to work in the companies). Corporations are becoming more aware of these and other social issues, and some are willing to spend time and/or money on solving various social problems. Such activity is known as organizational *social responsibility*. Online File W1.2 at the book's Web site lists some major areas of social responsibility related to business.

Government Regulations and Deregulation. Several social responsibility issues are related to government regulations regarding health, safety, environmental control, and equal opportunity. For example, U.S. companies that spray products with paint must use paper to absorb the overspray. The paper must then be disposed of by a licensed company, usually at a high cost.

A recent example is the Sarbanes-Oxley Act that requires extensive controls and reporting (see Online File W1.3). Government regulations cost money and make it more difficult to compete with countries that lack such regulations. In general, deregulation intensifies competition.

Terrorist Attacks and Protection. Since September 11, 2001, organizations have been under increased pressure to protect themselves against terrorist attacks. In addition, employees in the military reserves may be called up for active duty, creating personnel problems. Information technology and especially intelligent systems may make a valuable contribution in the area of protection, by providing security systems and possibly identifying patterns of behavior that will help to prevent terrorist attacks and cyberattacks against organizations.

Homeland Security. The National Strategy for Homeland Security of the United States includes a "National Vision" for the sharing of information related to the detection of terrorist activities. Its goals are to build a national environment that enables the sharing of essential homeland security information. It will be a system of systems that can integrate knowledge that resides across many disparate data sources, while ensuring that privacy and civil liberties are adequately safeguarded. Information will be shared across each level of government and among federal, state, and local governments, private industry, and citizens. With the proper use of people, processes, and technology, U.S. homeland security officials can have common awareness of threats and vulnerabilities as well as knowledge of the personnel and resources available to address these threats. Officials will receive the information they need so they can anticipate threats and respond rapidly and effectively.

These goals can be accomplished only if there is a means to facilitate the sharing of information among numerous agencies that currently maintain independent data silos. Border security alone engages 11 agencies. Ultimately a data warehouse of homeland security information will lead to increased security for the United States. It will be a model for how all countries can interact to protect their borders and ensure the safety of their citizenry. To accomplish the project, a data warehouse (Chapter 10) will be constructed. In Chapters 10 and 11 we will discuss the implementation of this project. Related to this project are some ethical issues about protecting the privacy of citizens. For further information, consult *whitehouse.gov/homeland/book/index.html*.

Use of this icon highlights IT-related ethics discussions.

Ethical Issues. **Ethics** relates to standards of right and wrong, and *information ethics* relates to standards of right and wrong in information processing practices. Organizations must deal with ethical issues relating to their employees, customers, and suppliers. Ethical issues are very important since they have the power to damage the image of an organization and to destroy the morale of the employees. Ethics is a difficult area because ethical issues are not cut-and-dried. What is considered ethical by one person may seem unethical to another. Likewise, what is considered ethical in one country may be seen as unethical in another.

The use of information technology raises many ethical issues. These range from the monitoring of electronic mail to the potential invasion of privacy of millions of customers whose data are stored in private and public databases. At this chapter's Web site, in Online File W1.4, you will find resources that will help you develop and strengthen your understanding of ethical issues related to business, and to IT management in particular. The online file consists of two parts: (1) a general framework of ethics in business and society, and (2) an Ethics Primer that poses various ethical situations and asks you to think about responses to these situations. In addition to the materials in Online File W1.4, specific ethical issues are discussed in all chapters of the book (and are highlighted by an icon in the margin).

The environments that surrounded organizations are becoming more complex and turbulent. Advances in communications, transportation, and technology create many changes. Other changes are the result of political or economic activities. Thus, the pressures on organizations are mounting, and organizations must be ready to take responsive actions if they are to succeed. In addition, organizations may see opportunities in these pressures. (For a framework for change analysis, see Online File W1.5 at the book's Web site.) Organizational responses to the increasing business pressures are described next.

Organizational Responses

Traditional organizational responses may not be effective with new types of pressures. Therefore many old solutions need to be modified, supplemented, or eliminated. Organizations can also take *proactive* measures, to create a change in the marketplace. Such activities also include exploiting opportunities created by the external pressures.

Organizations' major responses are divided here into seven categories: strategic management and systems, customer focus, continuous improvement, restructuring, make-to-order and mass customization, business alliances, and e-business. These responses can be interrelated, so the categories sometimes overlap.

Strategic Management and Systems. An important response activity is to develop a corporate strategy of how to handle the business pressures. Once such strategy is developed (including the supporting role of IT), the company can develop its tactical and operational plans as well as specific strategic IT-supported systems. For discussion of a well-known framework for analyzing competitive forces and developing strategic responses, see Appendix 1A at the end of this chapter.

Strategic systems provide organizations with strategic advantages that enable them to increase their market share and/or profit, to better negotiate with suppliers, or to prevent competitors from entering their territory (Callon, 1996). There are a variety of IT-supported strategic systems, as we will show throughout the book. According to Moss-Kanter (2001), the Internet is transforming companies and their strategies, changing the competitive landscape and requiring commitment to change. In particular these days, Web-based systems are providing considerable strategic advantage to companies (Lederer et al., 2001; Li et al., 2003; and Basu and Muylle, 2003).

A prime example of strategic systems is Federal Express's overnight delivery system, which can track the status of every individual package, anywhere in the delivery chain. The Federal Express (FedEx) system is heavily supported by IT. A major challenge with this kind of strategic system is the difficulty of sustaining competitive advantage. Most of FedEx's competitors duplicated the system. So FedEx moved the system to the Internet. However, the competitors quickly followed, and FedEx is now continuously introducing new innovations to keep or expand market share. For example, in an application called "My Account,"

FedEx provides you with comprehensive account management, including an on-line address checker (for shipping destinations) and an online wireless portal. An increasing number of mobile-computing-based strategic systems are appearing (e.g., see the Expedia case in Chapter 12). Strategic systems relate to appropriate decision-making practices and tools, as advocated by Huber (2004).

CUSTOMER FOCUS.   Organizational attempts to provide superb customer service sometimes make the difference between attracting and keeping customers, or losing them to other organizations. With a slew of IT tools, sophisticated mechanisms and innovations are designed to make customers happy (see Chapter 7).

CONTINUOUS IMPROVEMENTS.   Many companies continuously conduct programs that attempt to improve their productivity and quality (see Brue, 2002), and they frequently do so with the facilitation of IT. Examples of such programs include total quality management (TQM) and Six Sigma, knowledge management, productivity and creativity improvements, just-in-time (JIT) processing, improvements in decision-making processes, change management, and customer service improvements. The underlying purpose of IT support in continuous improvement is (1) to monitor and analyze performance and productivity and (2) to gather, share, and better use organizational knowledge. (See Online File W1.6 for more details.) We will provide examples throughout the book of how IT is contributing to continuous improvement.

RESTRUCTURING BUSINESS PROCESSES.   Organizations may discover that continuous improvement efforts have limited effectiveness in an environment full of strong business pressures. Therefore, a relatively new approach may be needed. This approach, initially called *business process reengineering (BPR)*, refers to a situation in which an organization fundamentally and radically redesigns its business processes to achieve dramatic improvements (Hammer and Champy, 2001). Such redesign effects a major innovation in an organization's structure and the way it conducts its business. If done on a smaller scale than corporatewide, the redesign process may be referred to as a *restructuring* (see El-Sawy, 2001). Technological, human, and organizational dimensions of a firm may all be changed in restructuring and BPR (see Chapter 14). The major areas in which IT supports restructuring are described in Chapter 14.

MAKE-TO-ORDER AND MASS CUSTOMIZATION.   A major response area is the trend to produce customized products and services. This strategy is referred to as *build-to-order.* As today's customers demand customized products and services, the business problem is how to provide customization and do it efficiently. This can be done, in part, by changing manufacturing processes from mass production to mass customization (Anderson, 2002; Smith and Rupp, 2002; and Zhu and Kraemer, 2002; see also Appendix 2A in this book). In mass production, a company produces a large quantity of identical items. In *mass customization,* items are produced in a large quantity but are customized to fit the desires of each customer. IT and EC are ideal facilitators of mass customization, for example, by enabling interactive communication between buyers and designers so that customers can quickly and correctly configure the products they want. Also, electronic ordering reaches the production facility in minutes.

BUSINESS ALLIANCES.   Many companies realize that alliances with other companies, even competitors, can be very beneficial. For example, General Motors and Ford created a joint venture to explore electronic-commerce applications, and the major airlines in Southeast Asia created a joint portal in 2003 that promotes travel to the region. There are several types of alliances: sharing resources, doing procurement jointly, establishing a permanent supplier-company relationship, and creating joint research efforts. Any of these might be undertaken in response to business pressures and usually is supported by IT.

One of the most interesting types of business alliance is the *virtual corporation,* which operates through telecommunications networks, usually without a permanent headquarters. (The term is used by some to describe a purely online business that does not have physical stores.) Virtual corporations may be temporary or permanent. A *temporary* virtual corporation is typically a joint venture in which companies form a special company for a specific, limited-time mission. A *permanent* virtual corporation is designed to create or assemble productive resources rapidly or frequently, on an ongoing basis. The virtual corporation form of organization could become common in the future. More details of virtual corporations are provided in Chapter 8.

All types of business alliances can be heavily supported by information technologies ranging from collaborative portals to electronic transmission of drawings.

ELECTRONIC BUSINESS AND E-COMMERCE.   As seen in the opening case, companies are transforming themselves into e-businesses. Doing business electronically is the newest and perhaps most promising strategy that many companies can pursue (see Turban et al., 2006). Several of the business models introduced earlier (in *A Closer Look 1.1,* page 11) are in fact e-commerce. Chapter 4 will focus extensively on this topic, and e-commerce applications are introduced throughout the book.

To illustrate the importance of e-commerce, let's look at what a management guru, Peter Drucker, has to say about EC.

> The truly revolutionary impact of the Internet Revolution is just beginning to be felt. But it is not "information" that fuels this impact. It is not "artificial intelligence." It is not the effect of computers and data processing on decision-making, policy-making, or strategy. It is something that practically no one foresaw or, indeed even talked about ten or fifteen years ago: e-commerce—that is, the explosive emergence of the Internet as a major, perhaps eventually *the* major, worldwide distribution channel for goods, for services, and, surprisingly, for managerial and professional jobs. This is profoundly changing economics, markets and industry structure, products and services and their flow, consumer segmentation, consumer values and consumer behavior, jobs and labor markets. But the impact may be even greater on societies and politics, and above all, on the way we see the world and ourselves in it. (Drucker, 2002, pp. 3–4)

E-business not only is revolutionizing business but, according to Earl and Khan (2001), is changing the face of IT by pushing companies to redefine technology's role in new business models. For example, many EC systems need to be built quickly and inexpensively since they are used only for a short time, due to rapid technological and market changes. Some companies are introducing dozens of EC projects that enable them to compete globally. For example, see Online Minicase W1.1 about Qantas Airlines at the book's Web site.

While some critical response activities can be executed manually, the vast majority require the support of information systems. Before we provide more examples on the role of information systems and IT, let us briefly explore the terms themselves.

1.3 INFORMATION SYSTEMS: DEFINITIONS AND EXAMPLES

What Is an Information System?

An **information system (IS)** collects, processes, stores, analyzes, and disseminates information for a specific purpose. Like any other system, an information system includes *inputs* (data, instructions) and *outputs* (reports, calculations). It *processes* the inputs by using technology such as PCs and produces outputs that are sent to users or to other systems via electronic networks. A *feedback* mechanism that controls the operation may be included (see Figure 1.4). Like any other system, an information system also includes people, procedures, and physical facilities, and it operates within an *environment*. An information system is not necessarily computerized, although most of them are. (For a more general discussion of *systems,* see Online File W1.7 at the book's Web site.)

FORMAL AND INFORMAL INFORMATION SYSTEMS. An information system can be formal or informal. *Formal* systems include agreed-upon procedures, standard inputs and outputs, and fixed definitions. A company's accounting system, for example, would be a formal information system that processes financial transactions. *Informal* systems take many shapes, ranging from an office gossip network to a group of friends exchanging letters electronically. Both types of information systems must be studied.

WHAT IS A COMPUTER-BASED INFORMATION SYSTEM? A **computer-based information system (CBIS)** is an information system that uses computer technology to perform some or all of its intended tasks. Such a system can include as little as a personal computer and software. Or it may include several thousand computers of various sizes with hundreds of printers, plotters, and other devices, as well as communication networks (wireline and wireless) and databases. In most cases an information system also includes people. The basic

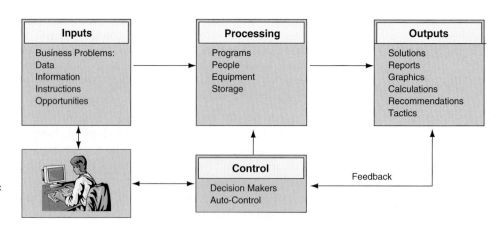

FIGURE 1.4 A schematic view of an information system.

components of information systems are listed below. Note that not every system includes all these components.

- *Hardware* is a set of devices such as processor, monitor, keyboard, and printer. Together, they accept data and information, process them, and display them.
- *Software* is a set of programs that instruct the hardware to process data.
- A *database* is a collection of related files, tables, relations, and so on, that stores data and the associations among them.
- A *network* is a connecting system that permits the sharing of resources by different computers. It can be wireless.
- *Procedures* are the set of instructions about how to combine the above components in order to process information and generate the desired output.
- *People* are those individuals who work with the system, interface with it, or use its output.

In addition, all information systems have a *purpose* and a *social context*. A typical purpose is to provide a solution to a business problem. In the Siemens case, for example, the purpose of the system was to coordinate internal units, to collaborate with the many suppliers and customers, and to improve costs and customer service. The social context of the system consists of the values and beliefs that determine what is admissible and possible within the culture of the people and groups involved.

THE DIFFERENCE BETWEEN COMPUTERS AND INFORMATION SYSTEMS. Computers provide effective and efficient ways of processing data, and they are a necessary part of an information system. An IS, however, involves much more than just computers. The successful application of an IS requires an understanding of the business and its environment that is supported by the IS. For example, to build an IS that supports transactions executed on the New York Stock Exchange, it is necessary to understand the procedures related to buying and selling stocks, bonds, options, and so on, including irregular demands made on the system, as well as all related government regulations.

In learning about information systems, it is therefore not sufficient just to learn about computers. Computers are only one part of a complex system that must be designed, operated, and maintained. A public transportation system in a city provides an analogy. Buses are a necessary ingredient of the system, but more is needed. Designing the bus routes, bus stops, different schedules, and so on requires considerable understanding of customer demand, traffic patterns, city regulations, safety requirements, and the like. Computers, like buses, are only one component in a complex system.

WHAT IS INFORMATION TECHNOLOGY? Earlier in the chapter we broadly defined *information technology* as the collection of computer systems used by an organization. Information technology, in its narrow definition, refers to the technological side of an information system. It includes the hardware, software, databases, networks, and other electronic devices. It can be viewed as a subsystem of an information system. Sometimes, though, the term information technology is also used interchangeably with *information system*. In this book, we use the term *IT* in its broadest sense—to describe an organization's collection of information systems, their users, and the management that oversees them. The purpose of this book is to acquaint you with all aspects of information systems/information technology.

Now that the basic terms have been defined, we present some examples of IS applications worldwide.

Examples of Information Systems

Millions of different information systems are in use throughout the world. The following examples are intended to show the diversity of applications and the benefits provided. At the end of each example, we list the *critical response activities* supported by the system.

As the examples in this section show, information systems are being used successfully in all functional areas of business. We provide here five examples, one for each of the major functional areas: accounting, production/operations management, marketing, human resource management, and finance.

Beginning here, and continuing throughout the book, icons positioned in the margins will call out the functional areas to which our real-world examples apply. In addition we will point to IT applications in government and in other public services such as health care and education by using icons. Finally, you've already seen that other icons will identify global examples—IT used by non-U.S.-based companies or by any company with significant business outside the United States. For a key that identifies the icons, see the note on page 6 or in the preface.

Managing Accounting Information Across Asia.   Le Saunda Holding Company (Hong Kong) manages 32 subsidiaries in four Asian countries, mostly in the manufacture, import, and sale of shoes (*lesaunda.com.hk*). Managing the financing and cash flow is a complex process. All accounting information flows to headquarters electronically. Also, sales data are electronically collected at point-of-sale (POS) terminals. The sales data, together with inventory data (which are updated automatically when a sale occurs), are transferred to headquarters. Other relevant data, such as advertising and sales promotions, merchants, and cash flow, are also transmitted electronically and collected in a centralized database for storage and processing.

To cope with the rapid growth of the company, a sophisticated accounting software package was installed. The result was radical improvements in accounting procedures. For example, it now takes less than 10 minutes, rather than a day, to produce an ad-hoc complex report. The company's accountants can generate reports as they are needed, helping functional managers make quicker and better decisions. The system is also much more reliable, and internal and external auditing is easier. Headquarters knows what is going on almost as soon as it occurs. All these improvements have led to a substantial growth in revenue and profits for the firm. (*Source: lesaunda.com.hk*, press releases.)

Critical response activities supported: decision making, managing large amounts of information, improved quality, reduced cycle time, enhanced strategic competitiveness.

The Dallas Mavericks: Using IT for Successful Play and Business.   Mark Cuban, the owner of the Dallas Mavericks of the National Basketball Association (NBA), expects the franchise to play well and also to perform as a business. He wants to fill every seat at every game and to maximize sales from concessions and souvenir sales.

Cuban's strategy to reach his business goals is to give fans the best possible experience, with a high-quality team on the court and excellent service at arena bars, barbecue stands, and souvenir shops. In the 2002 season, the "Mavs" filled the 19,200-seat American Airlines Center to 103.7 percent capacity, bringing in folding chairs to handle the overflow demand for tickets. Dallas was named in 2003 the best NBA city by *The Sporting News*.

Filling seats is critical. To track attendance, the Mavs became the first NBA team to put barcodes on tickets and then scan them, in part to find out if group sales and community-organization giveaways were putting bodies in seats or just wasting tickets. The team's business managers have found other uses for the attendance information as well. By enabling improved attendance forecasting for particular games, for example, the system has helped reduce beverage inventories by 50 percent.

Each of the 144 luxury suites in the Center is equipped with PCs that handle orders for merchandise, food, and beverages. Wireless access from all seats in the arena is available so that fans can place orders directly from their seats. All 840 cash registers at concessions stands, restaurants, stores, and bars use a sophisticated point-of-sale system. In the big retail store on the ground floor, salespeople using hand-held computing devices ring up credit-card purchases when lines get too long. The system allows the Mavs to process credit-card transactions in only 3 seconds, because there is an always-on Internet connection to the processing facility. During a game, managers can see which concession stands are busy and which ones can be closed early to cut labor costs.

Technology also supports the Mavs on the court. The team has 10 assistant coaches, and each has a laptop computer and a hand-held computing device. Game film is streamed over the Web for coaches to view on the road or at home. A digital content management system developed in-house matches game footage with the precise, to-the-minute statistics provided for every play of every game by the NBA. The searchable database allows coaches to analyze the effectiveness of particular plays and combinations of players in different game situations.

In 2002, the Mavs started using hand-held computers to track the performance of each referee in every one of their games. The coaches can look at trends—for example, to see which referee favors a given team or which one calls more 3-second violations—and they can tell the team's players. Another program logs different offensive and defensive schemes used against the Mavs. This system will let coaches make real-time adjustments using statistics from previous games. (*Source:* Cone, 2003.)

Critical response activities supported: Decision making, increased sales, improved customer service, improved inventory management, better utilization of capacity.

 The Success Story of Campusfood.com. Campusfood.com's recipe for success was a simple one: Provide interactive menus to college students, using the power of the Internet to enhance traditional telephone ordering of meals. Launched at the University of Pennsylvania, the company has taken thousands of orders for local restaurants, bringing pizza, hoagies, and wings to the Penn community.

Founder Michael Saunders began developing the site in 1997, while he was a junior at Penn, and with the help of some classmates, launched the site in 1998. After graduation, Saunders began building the company's customer base.

This involved registering other schools, attracting students, and generating a list of local restaurants from which students could order food to be delivered. Currently, this activity is outsourced to a marketing firm, and schools nationwide are being added to the list. By 2003 there were more than 200 participating schools and more than 1,000 participating restaurants.

Financed through private investors, friends, and family members, the site was built on an investment of less than $1 million. (For comparison, another company, with services also reaching the college-student market, has investment of $100 million.) Campusfood.com's revenue is generated through transaction fees; the site takes a 5 percent commission on each order.

When you visit *Campusfood.com,* you can do the following: Search a list of local restaurants, their hours of operation, addresses, phone numbers, and other information. Browse an interactive menu, which shows each participating restaurant's standard print menus, including the latest prices and a listing of every topping, every special, and every drink offered. Bypass busy-signals and place an order without being placed on hold, and avoid miscommunications on orders. Get access to more specials, including discounts and meal deals available online exclusively to Campusfood.com customers. Have access to electronic payment capabilities and your own account record ("My Account"). (*Source:* Prince, 2002 and *campusfood.com.*)

Critical response activities supported: customer service, improved cycle time, and innovative marketing method.

State-of-the-Art Human Resources Management in China. International Information Products Company LTD (IIPC) produces IBM personal computers (PCs) in Shenzhen, China. The company is one of China's top-10 exporters and one of the world's most efficient manufacturers of IBM PCs. The company's success is attributed, in part, to its world-class Human Resources Information System (powered by PeopleSoft's HRMS). In operation since October 2001, the system includes these basic elements: employee record management, recruitment, variable pay analysis, performance appraisal, payroll, and management of fringe benefits and absence records. In addition, employees can self-manage their personal data and report leaves and absences on the intranet. Using e-kiosks placed in several locations within the plant (e.g., the cafeteria), employees who do not have Internet access at work or home can use the system as well.

China's employee tax and benefits systems (e.g., health care and social insurance) are very complex, requiring many computations. Using HRMS and its Global Payroll component, IIPC was able to reduce the payroll cycle from 11 days to 4 days, and to reduce the computation run time from 6 hours to 2 hours, while eliminating errors. The system automates labor-intensive HR processes such as workforce administration, enabling HR staff to concentrate on staffing, training, career planning, rewards and promotions, and other nonclerical HR services. Furthermore, the data collected in the system are used by top management for supporting strategic decisions. (*Source:* Smith, 2002.)

Critical response activities supported: improved cycle time, improved dissemination of information, automated clerical tasks, use by employees for self-service.

Mobile Banking at Handelsbanken of Sweden. Handelsbanken of Sweden is the largest bank in Scandinavia, where more than 80 percent of the population over 15 years old carry mobile phones. Operating in a very competitive banking environment, the bank is trying to meet customers' expectations of using their mobile phones to organize their personal and working lives while on the move. Mobile banking services, including stock trading, was an opportunity for the bank to gain a competitive edge, and so the bank become the world's first to have mobile banking applications.

An interactive service allows customers to access up-to-the-minute banking information, including the latest stock market and interest rate data, whenever and wherever they like. Handelsbanken's e-banking has become so popular that it is used by tens of thousands of customers. It opens up critical business and personal information to safe and easy access from mobile devices. Both the bank's financial advisors and its customers can access general and personalized stock market and account information, transfer money, request loans, buy and sell stocks and bonds, and pay bills. This move into mobile banking is a key first step in a strategy to exploit the potential of e-business, while also extending the bank's brand reach. (*Sources:* Compiled from IBM's case study: Handelsbanken at *www-3.ibm.com/e-business/doc/ content/casestudy/35433.html,* accessed March 2003, and from press releases at *handelsbanken.com.*)

Critical response activities supported: improved customer service, innovative strategic marketing methods, competitive advantage.

In addition to functional areas, we can classify applications by the industry in which they are used. For example, retailing, financial services, education, health care, social services, and government are heavy users. An example of a government service is provided in Online Minicase W1.2.

Information Systems Failures

Use of the icon on the right indicates a description of an IT failure, and discussion of the lessons that can be learned from it.

So far we have introduced you to many success stories. You may wonder, though, is IT always successful? The answer is, "Absolutely not." There are many failures. We will show you some of these (marked with a "lessons from failures" icon) in this book, and in some cases we present them on our Web site. (See, for example, the 2000 U.S. Presidential Election Case in Online File W1.8 at the Web site.) We can learn from failures as much as we can learn from successes, as illustrated in *IT at Work 1.2* (page 26).

One area of IT failure is that of the dot-coms. As will be seen in Chapter 4, hundreds of dot-coms folded in 2000 and 2001. It was a shakeout that resulted from a rush to capitalize on e-commerce (see Kaplan, 2002). In addition there were many failures of Internet projects in established companies. (For example, the Go.com project of Walt Disney Company was supposed to manage all the Web sites owned by Disney and generate money from advertisers at the sites. Unfortunately, the income generated from advertising was not sufficient to keep the site going.) Like the gold rush and the rush to create companies when the automobile was invented, only a relatively few made it. The rest failed. According to Barva et al. (2001), the reason for EC failures is that many of the models used were too narrow. In place of these models, they offer an e-business value model, which we describe in Chapter 4.

Another reason for failure is that it is hard to predict the future. It is especially hard to predict the future in the field of information technology, which is evolving and continuously changing, as shown in Section 1.4.

IT at Work 1.2
HOW NIKE'S $400 MILLION SUPPLY CHAIN MANAGEMENT SOFTWARE SYSTEM FAILED

In certain retail stores, fans of Nike's Air Terra Humara 2 running shoe hit the jackpot. Once selling for over $100 US, they were selling for less than $50 in fall 2001. The cheaper shoes were the aftermath of the breakdown in Nike's supply chain, a breakdown attributed to a software problem.

Nike had installed a $400 million supply chain system in early 2001. The system was supposed to forecast sales demand and plan supplies of raw materials and finished products accordingly. However, the newly deployed demand and supply planning application apparently overestimated the demand for certain shoes in some locations and underestimated demand in others. As a result, some raw materials were overpurchased, while inventory levels of other materials were insufficient. Some shoes were over-manufactured, while the most-demanded ones were undermanufactured. To speed the right shoes to market, Nike had to spend around $5 a pair in air freight cost, compared to the usual cost of 75 cents by ocean shipping. In all, Nike attributed some $100 million in lost sales in the third quarter of 2001 alone to this problem.

What went wrong? The system was developed with software from i2, a major software producer. However, Nike insisted on modifying the i2 standard software, customizing it to its needs. Specifically, Nike wanted a forecast by style, by color, and by size (several thousand combinations). This resulted in a need to make thousands of forecasts, very rapidly, to quickly respond to changing market conditions and consumer preferences. To meet Nike's need it was necessary to customize the standard software, and to do so quickly because Nike wanted the system fast. The reprogramming was apparently done *too* fast. The software had bugs in it when it was deployed. Almost any new software contains bugs that need to be fixed; appropriate testing is critical, and it is a time-consuming task (see Murphy, 2003). Nike and i2 failed to recognize what was achievable.

Customizing standard software requires a step-by-step systematic process (see Technology Guide 6). It should be done only when it is absolutely necessary, and it must be planned for properly. Furthermore, Nike could have discovered the problem early enough if they had used appropriate deployment procedures (see Chapter 14).

To avoid disasters such as the one Nike experienced, companies must fully understand what they are trying to achieve and why. They must use performance-level indicators to properly measure the system during testing. Incidentally, Nike fixed the problem after spending an undisclosed amount of time and money in 2002.

Sources: Compiled from Sterlicchi and Wales (2001) and from *nike.com* press releases, 2002, 2003.

For Further Exploration: Why did Nike need the detailed forecasting? How can a company determine if it really needs to customize software? Whose responsibility is it to test and deploy the software: the software vendor's or the user's?

1.4 INFORMATION TECHNOLOGY DEVELOPMENTS AND TRENDS

In the previous sections, we described the role of IT in supporting business activities. We also pointed out (in Table 1.1, page 5) some of the capabilities that enable IT to play a support role. Next we will describe some of IT's developments and trends, and especially the move toward Web-based computing, wireless applications, and intelligent systems.

First imagine this scenario: It's a Monday morning in the year 2008. Executive Joanne Smith gets into her car, and her voice activates a wireless telecommunications-access workstation. She requests that all open and pending voice and mail messages, as well as her schedule for the day, be transmitted to her car. The office workstation consolidates these items from home and office databases. The message-ordering "knowbot" (knowledge robot), which is an enhanced e-mail messaging system, delivers the accumulated messages (in the order she prefers) to the voice and data wireless device in Joanne's car. By the time

Joanne gets to the office, she has heard the necessary messages, sent some replies, revised her day's schedule, and completed a to-do list for the week, all of which have been filed in her virtual database by her personal organizer knowbot. She has also accessed the Internet by voice and checked the traffic conditions, stock prices, and top news stories.

The virtual organizer and the company intranet have made Joanne's use of IT much easier. No longer does she have to be concerned about the physical location of data. She is working on a large proposal for the Acme Corporation today; and although segments of the Acme file physically exist on several data-bases, she can access the data from her *wireless workstation* wherever she happens to be. To help manage this information resource, Joanne uses an *information visualizer* that enables her to create and manage dynamic relationships among data collections. This information visualizer has extended the graphical user interface to a three-dimensional graphic structure.

Joanne could do even more work if her car were able to drive itself and if it were able to find an empty parking space on its own. Although this kind of car is still in an experimental stage, it will probably be in commercial use before 2015 due to developments in pervasive computing (see Chapter 5).

It may be possible for parts of this year-2008 scenario to become a reality even sooner, owing to important trends in information technology. For example, voice access to the Internet is already becoming popular (e.g., see *tellme.com* and *bevocal.com*). These trends, which are listed in Table 1.2 (page 28), fall into two categories: general and networked computing. Here we describe only *selected* items from Table 1.2. The rest are described in Chapter 2 and in the Technology Guides on the book's Web site.

Six Technology Guides at the book's Web site provide up-to-date presentations on hardware, software, databases, telecommunications, the Internet, and a technical view of systems analysis.

General Technological Trends

General trends are relevant to any computing system. Two representative examples are discussed below. Additional trends are presented in Chapter 2 and in the online Technology Guides.

COST-PERFORMANCE RATIO OF CHIPS: IMPROVEMENT BY A FACTOR OF AT LEAST 100. In about 10 years, a computer will cost the same as it costs today but will be about 50 times more powerful (in terms of processing speed, memory, and so on). At the same time labor costs could double, so the cost-performance ratio of computers versus manual work will improve by a factor of 100. This means that computers will have increasingly greater *comparative advantage* over people in performing certain types of work. This phenomenon is based on a prediction made in 1965 by Gordon Moore, the co-founder of Intel. Popularly called **Moore's Law,** this prediction was that the processing power of silicon chips would double every 18 months. And so it has, resulting in enormous increases in computer processing capacity and a sharp decline in cost (see Chapter 13).

Moore's Law applies to electronic chips. An extension of Moore's Law, according to McGarvey (2000) and *tenornetworks.com,* states that the performance of optical communication networks (see Technology Guide 4) is growing by a factor of 10 every three years. For example, according to Donofrio (2001), IBM is working on a supercomputer that will run at a petaflop (10^{15}) operations per second—which is 500 times faster than the fastest supercomputer of 2002. Such a computer will tackle brain-related diseases (such as Alzheimer's and stroke). It is expected to reach a speed of 20 to 30 petaflops in 2010.

TABLE 1.2 Major Technological Developments and Trends

General Developments and Trends
- The cost-performance advantage of computers over manual labor will increase.
- Graphical and other user-friendly interfaces will dominate PCs.
- Storage capacity will increase dramatically.
- Data warehouses will store ever-increasing amounts of information.
- Multimedia use, including virtual reality, will increase significantly.
- Intelligent systems, especially artificial neural computing and expert systems, will increase in importance and be embedded in other systems.
- The use of intelligent agents will make computers "smarter."
- There is a push for open architecture (e.g., the use of Web Services and Linux).
- Object-oriented programming and document management will be widely accepted.
- Artificial intelligence systems are moving to learning-management systems.
- Computers will be increasingly compact and more portable.
- There is proliferation of embedded technologies (especially intelligent ones).
- The use of plug-and-play software will increase.

Networked Computing Developments and Trends
- Optical computing will increase network capacity and speed, facilitating the use of the Internet.
- Storage networks will become popular.
- Mobile and wireless applications will become a major component of IT.
- Home computing will be integrated with the telephone, television, and other electronic services to create smart appliances.
- The use of the Internet will grow, and it will change the way we live, work, and learn.
- Corporate portals will connect companies with their employees, business partners, and the public.
- Intranets will be the dominating network systems in most organizations.
- E-commerce over the Internet will grow rapidly, changing the manner in which business is conducted.
- Intelligent software agents will roam through databases and networks, conducting time-consuming tasks for their masters.
- Interpersonal transmission will grow (one-to-one, one-to-many, many-to-many).
- More transactions among organizations will be conducted electronically, in what is called business-to-business (B2B) commerce.
- Networks and intelligent systems will be major contributors toward improved national security and counter-terrorism efforts.
- RFID (radio frequency identification) will change supply chains and retailing.

STORAGE. Whereas Moore's Law expresses computing speed, improvements in storage contribute to the cost-performance ratio in a similar way. Large storage capabilities are essential for advanced applications. There are several new devices and methods to increase storage (see Technology Guide 3). Of special interest are memory sticks that in 2004 were capable of storing 150 gigabytes in a device the size of a credit card.

OBJECT-ORIENTED ENVIRONMENT, COMPONENTS, AND WEB SERVICES. An *object-oriented environment* is an innovative way of programming and using computers that significantly reduces the costs of building and maintaining information systems. **Object technology** enables the development of self-contained units of software that can be shared, purchased, and/or reused. This technology enables developers to assemble information systems rather than building them from scratch. This is a faster and cheaper process. This environment includes object-oriented programming, databases, and operating systems (Elrad et al., 2001). Object technology applications include component-based development and Web Services, both of which are based in part on object-oriented technology (described in Chapter 14 and Technology Guide 6).

SELF-HEALING COMPUTERS. IBM Corp. is developing computers, called *self-healing computers,* that can take care of themselves. The first such computer (named eLiza), a supercomputer at the National Center for Atmosphere Research, was installed at Blue Sky. With 2 trillion calculations per second, this computer (which, incidentally, is the world's most powerful) has the ability to repair itself and keep running without human intervention. For details see Van (2003).

QUANTUM COMPUTING. Researchers are looking into using the basic quantum states of matter as a fundamental unit of computing. If successful, quantum computers will be hundreds of times faster than today's fastest supercomputers.

NANOTECHNOLOGY. Sometime in the future there will be superfast molecular computers. Built on a crystalline structure, these still-experimental computers will be very tiny so they could be woven into our clothing. They will require very little power, yet they will have huge storage capacities and be immune to computer viruses, crashes, and other glitches.

Networked and Distributed Computing

The technology of networked and distributed computing enables users to reach other users and to access databases anywhere in the organization and in any other place, using intranets and the Internet. The networks' power stems from what is called **Metcalfe's Law.** Robert Metcalfe, a pioneer of computer networks, claimed that the value of a network grows roughly in line with the square of the number of its users (or nodes). Thus, if you increase the number of users, say from 2 to 10, the network's value will change from 2^2 (4) to 10^2 (100), or 25 times more. With 350 million Internet users, the value is (350 million)^2, an astronomical number.

Kelly (1999), in what is called *Kelly's Extension* of Metcalfe's Law, claims that the value of the Internet is actually much larger. The reason is that Metcalfe's Law of n^2 is based on the idea of the telephone network, where the connections are point-to-point. On the Internet we can make multiple simultaneous connections between groups of people. So, claims Kelly, the potential value of the Internet is n^n, which is obviously a much larger number.

Network-based technologies are some of the most exciting IT developments, which we will discuss throughout the text. Here we provide an overview of some representative network-based technologies.

THE INTERNET AND THE WEB. From about 50 million Internet users in 1997, there could be as many as 1.46 billion by 2007 (*Computer Industry Almanac*, 2004). The wireless devices that access the Internet and the integration of television and computers will allow the Internet to reach every home, business, school, and other organization. Then the **information superhighway** will be complete. This is a national fiber-optic-based network and wireless infrastructure that will connect all Internet users in a country, and will change the manner in which we live, learn, and work. Singapore is likely to be the first country to have such a national information superhighway completely installed. Maui, Hawaii, is the first community in the United States to have a wireless Internet all over the island.

INTRANETS AND EXTRANETS.   Just as use of the Internet is becoming common, so too is the use of *intranets* ("internal networks") that connect the computing devices within individual organizations. As the intranet concept spreads and the supporting hardware and software are standardized, it is logical to assume that most organizations will use an intranet for internal communication. In addition, combining an intranet with the Internet, in what is called an *extranet,* creates powerful interorganizational systems (Chapter 8) for communication and collaboration.

MOBILE COMPUTING AND M-COMMERCE.   *M-commerce (mobile commerce)* refers to the conduct of e-commerce via wireless devices. It is the commercial application of *mobile computing,* which is computing using mobile devices and done primarily by wireless networks (see Chapter 5). There is a strong interest in the topic of mobile commerce because according to industry research firms, the number of mobile commerce users will grow from about 95 million in 2003 to about 1.7 billion by 2008. In addition, revenues from mobile commerce are expected to grow globally from nearly $7 billion in 2003 to over $554 billion in 2008 (*cellular.co.za,* 2004). Furthermore, these devices can be connected to the Internet, enabling transactions to be made from anywhere and enabling many applications (see Sadeh, 2002 and *A Closer Look 1.2*). For example, m-commerce can offer customers the location information of anything they want to purchase. This is a useful feature for customers, but it is even more important for merchants because it enables customers to act instantly on any shopping impulse. This wireless application is referred to as *location-based commerce,* or *l-commerce.* (For details, see Chapter 5.)

PERVASIVE COMPUTING.   Strongly associated with m-commerce and wireless networks is *pervasive computing,* in which computation becomes part of the environment. The computer devices (personal computer, personal digital assistant, game player) through which we now relate to computation will occupy only a small niche in this new computational world. Our relationship to pervasive computing will differ radically from our current relationship with computers. In pervasive computing, computation will be embodied in many things, not in what we now know as computers. RFID is an example.

RFID.   *Radio frequency identification* uses tiny tags that contain a processor and an antenna and can communicate with a detecting unit. (See Chapter 5 for details.) With their declining cost, RFIDs will have many applications, one of which is supply chain improvement and inventory control (see Minicase 2 at the end of this chapter).

We can already put computation almost anywhere. Embedded computation controls braking and acceleration in our cars, defines the capability of medical instruments, and runs virtually all machinery. Hand-held devices (especially cell phones and pagers) are commonplace; useful computational wristwatches and other wearables are becoming practical; computational furniture, clothes, and rooms are in the demonstration stage. Soon, *smart appliances,* which are home appliances that are connected to the Internet and among themselves for increased capabilities, will be integrated and managed in one unit. (See Chapter 5 for further discussion.)

At present, most large-scale applications of pervasive computing, such as intelligent cities, hospitals, or factories, are still under development. However,

A CLOSER LOOK
1.2 MOBILE AND WIRELESS APPLICATIONS: A SAMPLER

Mobile computing supports existing and entirely new kinds of applications. For example, each of the following can be done from any place, at any time.

- *Mobile personal communications capabilities,* such as personal digital assistants (PDAs) and cell phones for networked communications and applications.
- *Online transaction processing.* For example, a salesperson in a retail environment can enter an order for goods and also charge a customer's credit card to complete the transaction.
- *Remote database queries.* For example, a salesperson can use a mobile network connection to check an item's availability or the status of an order, directly from the customer's site or on the road.
- *Dispatching,* like air traffic control, rental car pickup and return, delivery vehicles, trains, taxis, cars, and trucks.
- *Front-line IT applications.* Instead of the same data being entered multiple times as they go through the value chain (the series of business activities that add value to a company's product or service), they are entered only once at any time and place and transmitted electronically thereafter.
- *M-commerce.* Users of wireless devices can access the Internet, conduct information searches, collaborate with others and make decisions jointly, and buy and sell from anywhere.

Wireless communications support both mobile computing applications and low-cost substitutions for communication cables. For example:

- Temporary offices can be set up quickly and inexpensively by using wireless network connections.
- Wireless connections to permanent office locations are often practical in difficult or hazardous wiring environments.
- Installing a wireless connection can replace leased lines that are used to connect local area networks (LANs), thus eliminating the costs of monthly line leases.

There are mobile and wireless application opportunities in many industries, such as:

- *Retail.* Retail applications have been very successful to date, particularly in department stores where there are frequent changes of layout. Also, retail sales personnel can conduct inventory inquiries or even sales transactions on the retail floor with wireless access from PCs or cell phones. Radio-frequency devices are helping retailers in inventory and security management.
- *Wholesale/distribution.* Wireless networking is used for inventory picking in warehouses with PCs mounted on forklifts, and for delivery and order status updates with mobile PCs inside distribution trucks.
- *Field service/sales.* Mobile computing can be used for dispatching, online diagnostic support from customer sites, and parts-ordering/inventory queries in all types of service and sales functions.
- *Factories/manufacturing.* Environments and applications include mobile shop-floor quality control systems or wireless applications that give added flexibility for temporary setups.
- *Health care/hospitals.* Health care personnel can access and send data to patient records, or consult comparative diagnosis databases, wherever the patient or the health care worker may be located.
- *Education.* Pilot applications equip students with PCs in lecture halls, linked by a wireless network, for interactive quizzes, additional data and graphics lecture support, and online handout materials. (See Minicase 1 at the end of the chapter and Chapter 5.)
- *Finance.* Mobile transactional capabilities can assist in purchasing, selling, inquiry, brokerage, and other dealings, using wireless devices.
- *Banking.* Mobile personal, programmable communications devices (e.g., hand-held computers such as PDAs) are effective for authorizing and managing payment and banking transactions.
- *Entertainment.* New technologies accelerate the quality of the end-user experience of mobile entertainment services. With the improvement of ringtone quality (from monophonic to polyphonic) and the development of streaming audio, mobile music creates immense revenues for operators and content providers. Through third-generation networks and improved multimedia, mobile video offers a widely touted capability that will enrich the mobile entertainment experience immeasurably.

smaller-scale applications, such as the "intelligent restaurant" described in *IT at Work 1.3*, are already in place.

CORPORATE PORTALS. A *corporate portal* refers to a company's Web site that is used as a *gateway* to the corporate data, information, and knowledge. Corporate portals may be used both by employees and by outsiders, such as customers or suppliers. (Employees have a password that allows them to access data through the portal that are not available to the public.) A variety of corporate portals provide a wide range of functionalities (see Chapter 3 for details).

THE NETWORKED ENTERPRISE. The various components and technologies just described can be integrated together into an *enterprisewide network* that is a seamless system, extending the corporate contacts to all entities a company does business with. The networked enterprise provides two primary benefits: First, by creating new types of services, businesses can engage customers in a direct interactive relationship that results in customers getting precisely what they want when they want it, resulting in stronger customer relationships and better relationships with suppliers and other business partners. Second, by taking the entire product design process online—drawing partners and customers into the process and removing the traditional communication barriers that prevent rapid product design and creation—companies can bring products and services to market far more quickly.

The networked enterprise is shown schematically in Online File W1.9 at the book's Web site. As a result of the technology pressures discussed earlier, companies that implement standards-based intranets can quickly create or join extranets, as we discuss in Chapters 4 and 8.

THE NETWORK COMPUTER. In 1997, the *network computer* was introduced. This computer does not have a hard drive. Instead, it is served by a central computing station. At a "dumb" (passive) terminal, it temporarily receives and can use applications and data stored elsewhere on the network. Also called "thin clients," network computers are designed to provide the benefits of desktop computing without the high cost of PCs. Prices of network computers are getting close to $200. A variation of the thin client is the *Simputer* or "simple computer" (see *simputer.org*).

OPTICAL NETWORKS. A major revolution in network technology is *optical networks*. These are high-capacity telecommunication networks that convert signals in the network to colors of light and transmit these over fiber-optic filaments. Optical networks are useful in Internet, video, multimedia interaction, and advanced digital services. (For more, see Technology Guide 4.)

STORAGE NETWORKS. **Network storage devices** are attached to the corporate network (usually intranets) and can be accessed from network applications throughout the enterprise. Their benefits are optimal data sharing, simplicity, scalability (ability to adapt to increased demands), and manageability. Online storage is also available from independent vendors.

Rather than handling their own server computers, many corporations are relying on outside outfits to manage their technology at remote data centers, which pipe data to their premises via the Web. Ferelli (2004) discusses the issue of

IT at Work 1.3
PERVASIVE COMPUTING AT ROYAL MILE PUB

All of us are familiar with the service at restaurants, and most of us have encountered inconvenient scenarios such as long waits, cold food, or even service of a wrong order. These inconveniences are the result of a conventional process that works like this: A server takes your drink order and then walks to the bar to place the order. She or he knows that after approximately five minutes your drink will be ready, so in the meantime the server takes an order from someone else and then heads back to the bar. If your order is not ready, the server comes to your table, apologizes for the delay, and takes your food order. That order is written on a piece of paper, which the server carries to the kitchen and places on a revolving wheel, which the chef rotates into view when he or she is ready to begin preparing the next order. At that point, the server may find that the kitchen is out of this selection, so he or she comes to your table and asks you to reorder. Sometimes, the server makes a mistake in writing your order, or the chef reads the handwritten order incorrectly. In such a case, after a long wait, the customer is frustrated at getting the wrong food.

The situation is different at Royal Mile Pub (Silver Springs, Maryland), thanks to pervasive computing. The Royal Mile is a medium-size restaurant (about 20 tables), with a bar that specializes in a wide selection of beverages. But what is really different about the Royal Mile is that the servers' green order pads have been replaced with iPaq PDAs connected to the kitchen using wireless networking.

The new system works as follows: The server uses a special PDA to take the orders. Most menu items are visible on the PDA, which also has handwriting capabilities for writing in special instructions. To take drink or food orders requires only one or two keystrokes. The server glances at the screen to verify that the correct item has appeared. Experienced servers can be trained in about 15 minutes on how to use the devices.

The Wi-Fi (wireless fidelity) system, which is a local area network, transmits the orders within the range of the restaurant (described further in Chapter 5). The orders appear immediately on screens in the kitchen and bar. After transmitting an order, the server can move to the next table rather than hurrying off to hand the orders to the cooks or bartenders.

The system is liked by all. Servers can spend more time with each customer and handle more tables because they make half as many trips out of the serving area. The PDA interface tells servers which menu items are unavailable; getting that information immediately to the customers reduces servers' trips to the kitchen, thus eliminating another source of customer and server dissatisfaction. Because the kitchen becomes aware of orders immediately, the food arrives more quickly. The system also totals each bill, eliminating arithmetic errors.

The owner is very positive about the system's effects on his business. The order system costs about $30,000 to install. Its benefits include fewer errors, better inventory control, and smaller payrolls. As orders transmit,

PPT 8800 from Symbol Technologies, another type of personal digital assistant, used for the same purpose as an iPaq PDA.

they are processed against the inventory database, allowing kitchen managers to track raw material purchases against the food orders and identify waste or other delivery and processing problems. Integration with the enterprise database and inventory control systems is fundamental to realizing cost reductions, improved workflow, and inventory and personnel management. The pervasive order system has reduced the error rate from several wrong meals per night to about one every two nights. Improvements occur not only in wasted (and replacement) meals, but also in customer satisfaction. In addition, now only three food servers are needed, meaning lasting cost reductions and lower overhead. Also, three data-entry stations on the serving floor for processing credit card charges were reduced to one, freeing up space on the serving floor.

Sources: Compiled from Stanford (2003), and *royalmilepub.com* (accessed March 2003).

For Further Exploration: Why would customers appreciate this pervasive computing system? What strategic advantage is generated? If such a system is beneficial to all, why have not all restaurants adopted it? Why it is classified as pervasive computing?

security in storage networks, as well as major benefits and implementation issues. Data centers are operated by a third party, such as application service providers (ASPs) (see Chapters 13 and 14). Major software vendors, including IBM and SAP, are in this business. For details on storage networks, see Technology Guide 3.

WEB SERVICES.   By using universal prefabricated business process software, called *Web Services,* computer users will soon be able to integrate applications, business processes, databases, and more into all kinds of applications, and do so rapidly and inexpensively. By using agreed-upon protocols and standards for the Web Services, developers can create a truly open computing environment independent of any vendor or product. Web Services will impact e-business application development, application integration, and application access. See Chapters 2, 3, 4, and Technology Guide 6 for details. Also see Clark et al. (2002).

All of these developments and prospects will increase the importance of IT both at home and at work. Therefore, it is obvious that to function effectively in the digital era, it makes sense to learn about IT.

1.5 WHY SHOULD YOU LEARN ABOUT INFORMATION TECHNOLOGY?

The field of IT is growing rapidly, especially with the introduction of the Internet and e-commerce, so the organizational impacts keep increasing. We are becoming more and more dependent on information systems. For example, on March 1, 2003, a computer glitch disturbed hundreds of flights in Japan.

In this part of the chapter we describe some specific benefits you can derive from studying IT.

Benefits from Studying IT

A major role of IT is being a *facilitator* of organizational activities and processes. That role will become more important as time passes. Therefore, it is necessary that every manager and professional staff member learn about IT not only in his or her specialized field, but also in the entire organization and in interorganizational settings as well.

Obviously, you will be more effective in your chosen career if you understand how successful information systems are built, used, and managed. You also will be more effective if you know how to recognize and avoid unsuccessful systems and failures. Also, in many ways, having a comfort level with information technology will enable you, off the job and in your private life, to take advantage of new IT products and systems as they are developed. (Wouldn't you rather be the one explaining to friends how some new product works, than the one asking about it? For help in that role, by the way, see *howthingswork.com*.) Finally, you should learn about IT because being knowledgeable about information technology can also increase employment opportunities. Even though computerization eliminates some jobs, it also creates many more.

The demand for traditional information technology staff—such as programmers, systems analysts, and designers—is substantial. In addition, many well-paid opportunities are appearing in emerging areas such as the Internet and e-commerce, m-commerce, network security, object-oriented programming, telecommunications, multimedia design, and document management. (See Online File W1.10 at the book's Web site for a listing of jobs in e-commerce.)

According to a study by the U.S. Bureau of Labor Statistics, each of the top seven fastest-growing occupations projected through 2010 fall within an IT- or computer-related field. These top seven occupations are (Pollock, 2003):

1. Computer software applications engineers
2. Computer support specialists
3. Computer software systems engineers
4. Network and computer systems administrators
5. Network systems and data communications analysts
6. Desktop publishers
7. Database administrators

At about $60,000 per year, workers in the software and information services industries were the highest-paid U.S. wage earners in 2000, about twice that of the average worker in the private sector. Furthermore, earnings of IT employees were growing twice as fast as those in the entire private sector. Thus, salaries for IT employees are generally high.

To exploit the high-paying opportunities in IT, a college degree in any of the following fields, or combination of them, is advisable: computer science, computer information systems (CIS), management information systems (MIS), electronic commerce, and e-business. Within the last few years, many universities have started e-commerce or e-business degrees (e.g., see *is.cityu.edu.hk* and *cgu.edu*). Many schools offer graduate degrees with specialization in information technology.

Majoring in an IT-related field can be very rewarding. For example, students graduating with baccalaureate degrees in MIS usually earn the highest starting salaries of all undergraduate business majors (more than $45,000 per year). MBAs with experience in Web technologies and e-commerce are getting starting salaries of over $100,000/year, plus bonuses. Many students prefer a double major, one of which is MIS. Similarly, MBAs with an undergraduate degree in computer science have little difficulty getting well-paying jobs, even during recessionary times. Many MBA students select IS as a major, a second major, or an area of specialization. In addition, nondegree programs are also available on hundreds of topics. For details about careers in IT, see *techjourney.com* and also "Career resources" and "Technology careers" at *wageweb.com*.

Finally, another benefit from studying IT is that it may contribute to future organizational leadership. In the past, most CEOs came from the areas of finance and marketing. Lately, however, we see a trend to appoint CEOs who have strong IT knowledge and who have emerged from the technology area.

1.6 PLAN OF THE BOOK

A major objective of this book is to demonstrate how IT in general and Web systems in particular support different organizational activities. In addition, we will illustrate the role that networked computing plays in our society today and will play tomorrow. Furthermore, we describe how information systems should be developed, maintained, and managed.

The book is divided into six parts. Figure 1.5 (page 36) shows how the chapters are positioned in each part and how the parts are connected. Notice that in the center of the figure are the six Technology Guides. These guides can be found on the book's Web site (*wiley.com/college/turban*).

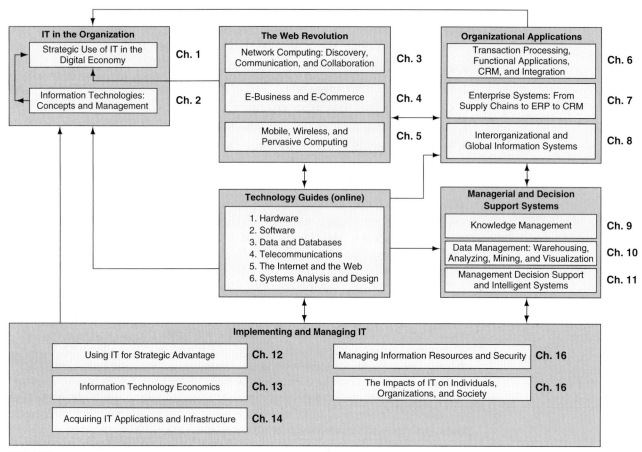

FIGURE 1.5 Plan of the book.

MANAGERIAL ISSUES

At the end of every chapter, you will find a list of some of the special concerns managers face as they adapt technology to their organization's needs.

1. *Recognizing opportunities for using IT and Web-based systems for strategic advantage.* These opportunities are highlighted and discussed in most chapters of the book, but especially in Chapters 3, 4, 5, 6, 7, and 13.

2. *Who will build, operate, and maintain the information systems?* This is a critical issue because management wants to minimize the cost of IT while maximizing its benefits. Some alternatives are to outsource portions, or even all, of the IT activities, and to divide the remaining work between the IS department and the end users. Details are provided in Chapters 13 through 15 and in Technology Guide 6.

3. *How much IT?* This is a critical issue related to IT planning. IT does not come free, but *not* having it may be much costlier. Chapters 12 and 13 deal with this issue.

4. *How important is IT?* In some cases, IT is the only approach that can help organizations. As time passes, the *comparative advantage* of IT increases.

5. *Is the situation going to change?* Yes, the pressures will be stronger as time passes. Therefore, the IT role will be even more important.

6. ***Globalization.*** Global competition will have an impact on many companies. However, globalization opens many opportunities, ranging from selling and buying products and services online in foreign markets, to conducting joint ventures or investing in them. IT supports communications, collaboration, and discovery of information regarding all the above (Chapter 8).

7. ***Ethics and social issues.*** The implementation of IT involves many ethical and social issues that are constantly changing due to new developments in technologies and environments. These topics should be examined any time an IT project is undertaken. Online File W1.4 at the book's Web site presents an introduction to ethics. Ethical issues are highlighted in most chapters throughout the book.

8. ***Transforming the organization to the digital economy.*** The transformation can be done on several fronts, as Siemens AG did. Management should study the opportunities, consider alternatives, and prioritize them. A prime area to start with is e-procurement (Chapters 4 and 7).

KEY TERMS

Business model *10*

Business pressures *12*

Computer-based information system (CBIS) *20*

Critical response activities *12*

Digital economy *4*

Ethics *16*

Information superhighway *29*

Information system (IS) *20*

Information technology (IT) *4*

Metcalfe's Law *29*

Moore's Law *27*

Network storage device *32*

Networked computing *4*

Object technology *28*

CHAPTER HIGHLIGHTS (Numbers Refer to Learning Objectives)

① The world is moving to a digital economy, which can be viewed as a major economic, societal, and organizational revolution. This revolution automates business processes by using the Internet, intranets, VANs, and extranets to connect organizations and people.

① The digital economy is characterized by extensive use of information technology in general and the Internet in particular. These drive new business models that dramatically reduce cost and increase quality, customer service, and speed.

① Companies are trying to transform themselves to e-businesses by converting their information systems to Web-based and by automating as many business processes as possible.

② Many market, technology, and societal pressures surround the modern organization, which is responding with critical response activities supported by information technology.

③ An accelerated rate of technological change, complexity, and turbulence and a move toward a global economy today characterize the business environment. In addition, the competition faced by businesses is ever increasing.

③ Organizational responses include strategic information systems, continuous improvements, business process restructuring, electronic commerce, and business alliances. IT plays a major role in all of these.

③ Organizations are adopting a customer-focused approach in order to succeed.

③ Organizations are changing their mode of operation by using IT-supported innovative approaches such as e-commerce, mass customization, CRM, and business alliances.

④ An information system collects, processes, stores, and disseminates information for a specific purpose. A computer-based information system uses computers to perform some or all of these activities.

④ Information technology refers to the network of all information systems in an organization.

⑤ Information technology is a major agent of change, supporting critical response activities in all functional areas, in all industries, and in both the private and the public sectors.

⑥ The major generic technological developments in IT are: increasing cost/performance, proliferation of object technology, and introduction of component-based development.

⑥ The major networked-computing developments are: increasing use of the Internet and intranets, mobile commerce, portals, optical networks, storage networks, and Web Services.

⑦ Learning about IT is essential because the role of IT is rapidly increasing in the support of organizations. We are getting more dependent on IT as time passes. Also, more IT-related jobs with high salaries are available.

VIRTUAL COMPANY ASSIGNMENT

Instructions for accessing The Wireless Café on the Student Web Site

1. Go to
   wiley.com/college/turban
2. Select Turban/Leidner/
   McLean/Wetherbe's
   Information Technology for Management, Fifth Edition.
3. Click on Student
   Resources site, in the tool-bar on the left.
4. Click on the link for
   Virtual Company Web site
5. Click on Wireless Café.

Starting Your Internship at The Wireless Café
Go to The Wireless Café's link on the Student Web Site. There you will find a description of your internship at this restaurant, as well some assignments that will help you learn more about how IT solutions could help the restaurant improve its business.

More Resources
More resources and study tools are located on the Student Web Site. You'll find additional chapter materials and useful Web links. In addition, self-quizzes that provide individualized feedback are available for each chapter.

QUESTIONS FOR REVIEW

1. Define an information system and list its major components.
2. Define digital economy and list its major characteristics.
3. Define a business model by giving an example of one.
4. What are the major pressures in the business environment?
5. List the major critical response activities used by organizations.
6. Define information technology.
7. What is a virtual corporation?
8. Define mobile computing and m-commerce.
9. Define corporate portals.
10. Describe mass customization.
11. What are Moore's Law and Metcalfe's Law?
12. What is cycle-time reduction? Why is it important?
13. Define Web Services.
14. List the major capabilities of IT.
15. Define optical networks and network storage.
16. Describe a Simputer (simple computer).
17. Define the Internet, an intranet, and an extranet.
18. Define networked computing and networked organizations.
19. Describe pervasive computing.

QUESTIONS FOR DISCUSSION

1. Discuss the motivation for becoming an e-business.
2. Review the examples of the new versus the old economy cases. In what way did IT make the difference?
3. Explain why IT is a business pressure and also an enabler of response activities that counter business pressures.
4. Why is m-commerce perceived as being able to increase EC applications?
5. Explain why the cost-performance ratio of IT will improve by a factor of 100, while performance is expected to improve only by a factor of 50.
6. Is IT a strategic weapon or a survival tool? Discuss.
7. It is said that networked computing changes the way we live, work, and study. Why?
8. Relate cycle-time reduction to improved financial and business performance.
9. Distinguish between network computers and networked computing.
10. Why is the Internet said to be the creator of new business models?
11. Explain why mass customization is desirable.
12. Discuss why some information systems fail.
13. Discuss the potential impact of utility computing.
14. Discuss the ethics related to use of RFID tags.

EXERCISES

1. Review the examples of IT applications in Section 1.3, and identify the business pressures in each example.
2. The market for optical copiers is shrinking rapidly. It is expected that by 2005 as much as 85 percent of all duplicated documents will be done on computer printers. Can a company such as Xerox Corporation survive?
   a. Read about the problems and solution of Xerox in 2000–2003 at *fortune.com, findarticles.com,* and *google.com.*
   b. Identify all the business pressures on Xerox.
   c. Find some of Xerox's response strategies (see *xerox.com, fortune.com,* and *forbes.com*).
   d. Identify the role of IT as a contributor to the business technology pressures.
   e. Identify the role of IT as a facilitator of the critical response activities.
3. Reread the Siemens case at the start of the chapter and prepare a presentation to the CEO of a competing company. Stress both the benefits and the cost and limitations of such a transformation.

GROUP ASSIGNMENTS

1. Review the *Wall Street Journal, Fortune, Business Week,* and local newspapers of the last three months to find stories about the use of Web-based technologies in organizations. Each group will prepare a report describing five applications. The reports should emphasize the role of the Web and its benefit to the organizations. Cover issues discussed in this chapter, such as productivity, quality, cycle time, and globalization. One of the groups should concentrate on m-commerce and another on electronic marketplaces. Present and discuss your work.
2. Identify Web-related new business models in the areas of the group's interests. Identify radical changes in the operation of the functional areas (accounting, finance, marketing, etc.), and tell the others about them.
3. Enter *digitalenterprise.org;* go to Net-centrism and read the latest "hungry minds" items there. Prepare a report regarding the latest in the digital age.

INTERNET EXERCISES

1. Enter the Web site of UPS (*ups.com*).
   a. Find out what information is available to customers before they send a package.
   b. Find out about the "package tracking" system; be specific.
   c. Compute the cost of delivering a $10'' \times 20'' \times 15''$ box, weighing 40 pounds, from your hometown to Long Beach, California. Compare the fastest delivery against the least cost.

2. Surf the Internet (use *google.com, brint.com,* or a similar engine) to find information about:
   a. International virtual corporations (at least two examples).
   b. Virtual corporations in general.

3. Enter *digitalenterprise.org*. Prepare a report regarding the latest EC developments in the digital age.

4. Visit some Web sites that offer employment opportunities in IT (such as *execunet.com* and *monster.com*). Compare the IT salaries to salaries offered to accountants. For other information on IT salaries, check *Computerworld's* annual salary survey and *techjourney.com*.

5. Prepare a short report on the role of information technology in government. Start with *whitehouse.gov/omb/egov/2003egov-strat.pdf, ctg.albany.edu, e-government.govt.nz,* and *worldbank.org/publicsector/egov*. Find e-government plans in Hong Kong and in Singapore (*cca.gov.sg;* check action plan).

6. Enter *x-home.com* and find information about the easy life of the future.

7. Enter *tellme.com* and *bevocal.com*. Observe the demos. Write a report on the benefits of such technologies.

8. Experience customization by designing your own shoes at *nike.com*, your car at *jaguar.com*, your CD at *saregama.com*, and your business card at *iprint.com*. Summarize your experiences.

9. Enter *dell.com* and configure the computer of your dreams. (You do not have to buy it.) What are the advantages of such configuration?

Minicase 1
Dartmouth College Goes Wireless

Dartmouth College, one of the oldest in the United States (founded in 1769), was one of the first to embrace the wireless revolution. Operating and maintaining a campuswide information system with wires is very difficult, since there are 161 buildings with more than 1,000 rooms on campus. In 2000, the college introduced a campuswide wireless network that includes more than 500 Wi-Fi (wireless fidelity; see Chapter 5) systems. By the end of 2002, the entire campus became a fully wireless, always-connected community—a microcosm that provides a peek at what neighborhood and organizational life may look like for the general population in just a few years.

To transform a wired campus to a wireless one requires lots of money. A computer science professor who initiated the idea at Dartmouth in 1999 decided to solicit the help of alumni working at Cisco Systems. These alumni arranged for a donation of the initial system, and Cisco then provided more equipment at a discount. (Cisco and other companies now make similar donations to many colleges and universities, writing off the difference between the retail and the discount prices for an income tax benefit.)

As a pioneer in campuswide wireless, Dartmouth has made many innovative usages of the system, some of which are the following:

● Students are developing new applications for the Wi-Fi. For example, one student has applied for a patent on a personal-security device that pinpoints the location of campus emergency services to one's mobile device.

● Students no longer have to remember campus phone numbers, as their mobile devices have all the numbers and can be accessed anywhere on campus.

● Students primarily use laptop computers on the network. However, an increasing number of Internet-enabled PDAs and cell phones are used as well. The use of regular cell phones is on the decline on campus.

● An extensive messaging system is used by the students, who send SMSs (Short Message Services) to each other. Messages reach the recipients in a split second, any time, anywhere, as long as they are sent and received within the network's coverage area.

● Usage of the Wi-Fi system is not confined just to messages. Students can submit their classwork by using the network, as well as by watching streaming video and listening to Internet radio.

● An analysis of wireless traffic on campus showed how the new network is changing and shaping campus behavior patterns. For example, students log on in short bursts, about 16 minutes at a time, probably checking their messages. They tend to plant themselves in a few favorite spots (dorms, TV room, student center, and on a shaded bench on the green) where they use their computers, and they rarely connect beyond those places.

- Some students invented special complex wireless games that they play online.
- One student has written a code that calculates how far away a networked PDA user is from his or her next appointment, and then automatically adjusts the PDA's reminder alarm schedule accordingly.
- Professors are using wireless-based teaching methods. For example, students armed with Handspring Visor PDAs, equipped with Internet access cards, can evaluate material presented in class and can vote on a multiple-choice questionnaire relating to the presented material. Tabulated results are shown in seconds, promoting discussions. According to faculty, the system "makes students want to give answers," thus significantly increasing participation.

- Faculty and students developed a special voice-over-IP application for PDAs and iPAQs that uses live two-way voice-over-IP chat.

Sources: Compiled from McHugh (2002), Hafner (2003), and *dartmouth.edu* (March 2003).

Questions for Minicase 1

1. In what ways is the Wi-Fi technology changing the life of Dartmouth students?
2. Some say that the wireless system will become part of the background of everybody's life—that the mobile devices are just an afterthought. Explain.
3. Is the system contributing to improved learning, or just adding entertainment that may reduce the time available for studying? Debate your point of view with students who hold a different opinion.
4. What are the major benefits of the wireless system over the previous wireline one? Do you think wireline systems will disappear from campuses one day? (Do some research on the topic.)

Minicase 2
Wal-Mart Leads RFID Adoption

In the first week of April 2004, Wal-Mart Stores Inc. (*walmart.com*) launched its first live test of RFID-tracing technology. One distribution center, seven stores, and 21 products from participating vendors were in the pilot test.

In the supply chain pilot application, passive RFID chips with small antennae are attached to cases and pallets. When passed near an RFID "reader," the chip activates, and its unique product identifier code is transmitted back to an inventory control system. Cases and pallets containing the 21 products featuring RFID tags are delivered to the distribution center in Sanger, Texas, where RFID readers installed at the dock doors notify both shippers and Wal-Mart what products enter the Wal-Mart distribution center and where the products are stored. RFID readers are also installed in other places, such as conveyor belts, so that each marked case can be tracked. Readers used by Wal-Mart have an average range of 15 feet. (For more detail, see discussion in Chapters 5 and 7 of how RFID works.)

Wal-Mart has set a January 2005 target for its top 100 suppliers to be placing RFID tags on cases and pallets destined for Wal-Mart stores, and believes that the implementation of this pilot scheme will pave the way for achieving this goal. The system is expected to improve flows along the supply chain, reduce theft, increase sales and reduce inventory costs (by eliminating both overstocking and understocking), and gain visibility and accuracy throughout Wal-Mart's supply chain.

While some of Wal-Mart's suppliers are late in implementing the system, it is clear that if the pilot is successful (and so far it is), RFID will become an industry standard. After all, nearly $70 billion is lost in the retail sector in the United States every year, due to products lost in the supply chain or being stored in wrong places.

The next step in Wal-Mart's pilot is to mark each individual item with a tag. This plan raises a possible privacy issue: What if the tags are not removed from the products? People fear that they will be tracked after leaving the store.

Wal-Mart also can use RFIDs for many other applications. For example, it could attach tags to shoppers' children, so if they are lost in the megastore, they could be tracked in seconds.

Retailers such as Wal-Mart believe that the widespread implementation of RFID technology marks a revolutionary change in supply chain management, much as the introduction of barcodes was seen as revolutionary two decades ago.

Sources: Condensed from Landoline (2003), *BusinessWeek Online* (2004), and *FoodProductionDaily.com* (2004).

Questions for Minicase 2

1. Assuming the cost of RFID is low (less than $0.05 per tagged item), what advantages can you see for tagging individual items in each store? Is it necessary to do it?
2. Find some information regarding the advantages of RFIDs over regular barcodes.
3. Is this an e-business application? Why, or why not? If yes, can you identify the business model used?
4. What are some of the business pressures that drive use of RFID in retailing?

REFERENCES

Aberdeen.com, "Siemens' Private Marketplace Turns Procurement into Profit Center," Aberdeen Group Report, *aberdeen.com/2001/research/04012501.asp.* Boston, April 2001 (accessed September 18, 2002).

Afuah, A., and C. L. Tucci, *Internet Business Models and Strategies,* 2nd ed. New York: McGraw Hill, 2003.

Anderson, D., *Build-to-Order and Mass Customization.* Los Angeles, CA: CIM Press, 2002.

Arens, Y., and P. S. Rosenbloom, "Responding to the Unexpected," *Association for Computing Machinery: Communications of the ACM,* September 2003.

Barva A., et al., "Driving Business Excellence," *MIT Sloan Management Review,* Fall 2001.

Basu, A., and S. Muylle, "Online Support for Commerce Processes by Web Retailers," *Decision Support Systems,* 34(4), 2003.

Boyett, J. H., and J. T. Boyett, *Beyond Workplace 2000: Essential Strategies for the New American Corporation.* New York: Dutton, 1995.

Brue, G., *Six Sigma for Managers.* New York: McGraw-Hill, 2002.

Brynolfsson, E., et al., "Consumer Surplus in the Digital Economy: Estimating the Value of Increased Product Variety at Online Booksellers," *Management Science,* 49(11), 2003.

BusinessWeek Online, news item, March 18, 2004.

Callon, J. D., *Competitive Advantage Through Information Technology.* New York: McGraw-Hill, 1996.

Campusfood.com (accessed January 2003).

Carr, N. G. (ed.), *The Digital Enterprise.* Boston: Harvard Business School Press, 2001.

Cellular.co.za/news_2004/april/040104-Mobile_commerce_has_taken_off.htm (accessed April 2004).

Choi, S. Y., and A. B. Whinston, *The Internet Economy: Technology and Practice.* Austin, TX: Smartecon.com pub, 2000.

Clark, M., et al., *Web Services: Business Strategies and Architectures.* South Bend, IN: Expert Press, 2002.

Computer Industry Almanac, 2004, p. 28.

Cone, E., "Dallas Mavericks," *Baseline Magazine,* October 1, 2003.

Dartmouth.edu (accessed March 2003).

Davis, B., *Speed Is Life.* New York: Doubleday, 2001.

Dickson, G. W., and G. DeSanctis, *Information Technology and the Future Enterprise: New Models for Managers.* Upper Saddle River, NJ: Prentice-Hall, 2001.

Donofrio, N., "Technology Innovation for a New Era," *Computing & Control Engineering Journal,* June 2001.

Drucker, P. F., "The Next Society," *The Economist,* November 3, 2001.

Drucker, P. F., *Managing in the Next Society.* New York: Truman Talley Books, 2002.

Earl M., and B. Khan, "E-Commerce Is Changing the Face of IT," *MIT Sloan Management Review,* Fall, 2001.

El-Sawy, O., *Redesigning Enterprise Processes for E-Business.* New York: McGraw-Hill, 2001.

Elrad, T., et al., "Aspect-Oriented Programming," *Association for Computing Machinery: Communications of the ACM,* October 2001.

Evans, P. B., and T. S. Wurster, *Blown to Bits: How the New Economics of Information Transforms Strategy.* Boston: Harvard Business School Press, 2000.

Ferelli, M., "SANs More Menaced from Within than Without: Security Is a People Thing," *Computer Technology Review,* February 1, 2004.

FoodProductionDaily.com, Breaking News, March 5, 2004.

Gartner G2, "2004 Key Business Issues, A Gartner/Forbes.com Survey of CEOs," Report #220092990, February 2004.

Gates, H. B., *Business @ the Speed of Thought.* New York: Penguin Books, 1999.

Greenberg, P., *CRM at the Speed of Light: Capturing and Keeping Customers in Internet Real Time,* 2nd ed. New York: McGraw-Hill, 2002.

Hafner, K., "A New Kind of Revolution in the Dorms of Dartmouth," *New York Times,* September 23, 2003.

Hammer, M., and J. Champy, *Reengineering the Corporation Revised Edition: Manifesto for Business Revolution.* New York: Harper Business, 2001.

Hammer, M., and J. Champy, *Reengineering the Corporation.* Revised Edition. New York: Harper Business, 2001.

"Handelsbanken," IBM Case Study, *www-3.ibm.com/e-business/doc/content/casestudy/35433.html.* Accessed March 10, 2002.

Handelsbanken.com (accessed March 2003).

Helmstetter, G., and P. Metivier, *Affiliate Selling: Building Revenue on the Web.* New York: Wiley, 2000.

Hoffman, D. L., and T. P. Novak, "How to Acquire Customers on the Web," *Harvard Business Review,* May–June 2000.

Huber, G., *The Necessary Nature of Future Firms: Attributes of Survivors in a Changing World.* San Francisco: Sage Publications, 2004.

Kaplan, P. J., *F'D Companies: Spectacular Dot.com Flameouts*. New York: Simon & Schuster, 2002.

Kelly, K., *New Rules for the New Economy*. New York: Penguin USA, 1999.

Landoline, K., "Untangling the RFID Labyrinth," *IT Agenda*, July 23, 2003 (*rfgonline.com*).

Lederer, A. D., et al., "The Search for Strategic Advantage from the World Wide Web," *International Journal of Electronic Commerce*, 5(4), Summer 2001.

Lederer, A. L., et al., "Using Web-based Information Systems to Enhance Competitiveness," *Communications of the ACM*, July 1998.

LeSaunda.com (accessed January 2003).

Li, Y. N., et al., "Factor Analysis of Service Quality Dimension Shifts in the Information Age," *Managerial Auditing Journal*, 18(4), 2003.

Liebowitz, S., *Rethinking the Network Economy: The True Forces that Drive the Digital Marketplace*. New York: AMACOM, 2002.

McCleanahen, J., "The Book on the One-Day Close," *industryweek.com*, April 2002, pp. 31–33.

McGarvey, J., "Net Gear Breaks Moore's Law," *Interactive Week*, April 17, 2000.

McHugh, J., "Unplugged U.," *Wired*, October 2002.

Mevedoth, R., "From Rocks to Riches," *Forbes Global*, September 2, 2002.

Moss-Kanter, R., "You Are Here," *INC.*, February 2001.

Motiwalla, L., and A. Hashimi, "Web-Enabling for Competitive Advantage: A Case Study of Himalayan Adventures," *Annals of Cases on Information Technology*, 2003.

Murphy, V., "The Exterminator," *Forbes Global*, May 26, 2003.

"New York City Transit Tokens May Take a Hike," *Associated Press*, January 27, 2003.

Nike.com (accessed January 2003).

Papazoglou, M. P., and D. Georgakopoulos, "Special Section: Service-Oriented Computing," *Communications of the ACM*, October 2003.

Pitt, L. F., et al., "The Internet and the Birth of Real Consumer Power," *Business Horizons*, July–August, 2002.

PlayWinningPoker.com.

Pollock, J., "The 7 Fastest Growing Occupations," *http://encarta.msn.com/encnet/departments/elearning/?article=7fastestgrowing* (accessed December 20, 2003).

Prince, M., "Easy Doesn't Do It," *Wall Street Journal*, July 17, 2002.

RoyalMilePub.com (accessed March 2003).

Sadeh, N., *Mobile Commerce: New Technologies, Services and Business Models*. New York: Wiley, April 2002.

Schultz, G., "Siemens: 100% E-Business," *APICS*, April 2002. pp. 25–32.

Siemens.com (accessed May 2004).

Simpson, R. L., "Today's Challenges Shape Tomorrow's Technology, Part 2," *Nursing Management*, December 2003.

Sipior, J. C., et al., "A Community Initiative that Diminished the Digital Divide," *Communications of the Association for Information Systems*, 13, 2004.

Smith, A. D., and W. T., Rupp, "Information Management Leveraging in the Case of E-Folios: Mass Customization Approaches in an E-Commerce Environment," *Services Marketing Quarterly*, 2003.

Smith K., "IIPC: Vision to See, Faith to Believe, Courage to Do," *People Talk*, September–December, 2002.

Stanford V., "Pervasive Computing Puts Food on the Table," *Pervasive Computing*, January 2003.

Sterlicchi, J., and E. Wales, "Custom Chaos: How Nike Just Did It Wrong," *Business Online* (BolWeb.com), June 2001.

Tapscott, D., et al., *Digital Capital*. Boston: Harvard Business School Press, 2000.

Thaigem.com (accessed April 2004).

Tellme.com (accessed May 2004).

Turban, E., et al., *Electronic Commerce 2006*. Upper Saddle River, NJ: Prentice Hall, 2006.

Van, J., "Self-Healing Computers Seen as Better Fix," *Chicago Tribune*, March 24, 2003.

Walker, C., "World-First Technology Launched at Sydney International Airport," Western Australia E-Commerce Centre, February 4, 2003.

Wayner, P., "Learn When to Hold 'Em (Online)," *International Herald Tribune*, July 11, 2003.

Weill, P., and M. R. Vitale, *Place to Space: Migrating to eBusiness Models*. Boston: Harvard Business School Press, 2001.

Wreden, N., "Business-Boosting Technologies," *Beyond Computing*, November–December 1997.

Zhu, K., and K. L., Kraemer, "E-Commerce Metrics for Net-Enhanced Organizations: Assessing the Value of E-Commerce to Firm Performance in the Manufacturing Sector," *Information Systems Research*, 13(3), 2002.

APPENDIX 1A

PORTER'S MODELS

Researcher Michael Porter has proposed two models that have become classic ways to study and explain basic business activities—the *competitive forces model* and the *value chain model*. We present an overview of these two models in this appendix, and will refer to these models throughout the book.

Porter's Competitive Forces Model and Strategies

The most well-known framework for analyzing competitiveness is Porter's **competitive forces model** (Porter, 1985). It has been used to develop strategies for companies to increase their competitive edge. It also demonstrates how IT can enhance the competitiveness of corporations.

The model recognizes five major forces that could endanger a company's position *in a given industry.* (Other forces, such as those cited in Chapter 1, including the impact of government, affect all companies in the industry and therefore may have less impact on the relative success of a company within its industry.) Although the details of the model differ from one industry to another, its general structure is universal.

The five major forces in an industry can be generalized as follows:

1. The threat of entry of new competitors
2. The bargaining power of suppliers
3. The bargaining power of customers (buyers)
4. The threat of substitute products or services
5. The rivalry among existing firms in the industry

The strength of each force is determined by factors related to the industry's structure, as shown in Figure 1A.1 on the next page. Companies need to protect themselves against the forces, or they can use the forces to improve their position or to challenge the leaders in the industry.

Some have suggested semiradical changes in Porter's model. For example, Harmon et al. (2001) proposed adding a sixth force—bargaining power of employees—to the original five. Another major force is the Internet, which has changed the nature of doing business as well as the nature of competition in many industries.

Porter's model identifies the forces that influence competitive advantage in the marketplace. Of greater interest to most managers is the development of a *strategy* aimed at performing activities differently from a competitor. Porter (1985) proposed three such strategies—cost leadership, differentiation, and niche strategies. Other strategic-management authors have proposed additional strategies (e.g., see Neumann, 1994; Wiseman, 1988; and Frenzel, 1996).

In Table 1A.1 we cite 12 general strategies for competitive advantage. Each of these strategies (and some others) can be enhanced by IT, as will be shown throughout the book and especially in Chapter 12. Forthcoming chapters will show: (1) how different information technologies impact the five forces, and (2) how IT facilitates the 12 strategies.

Porter's Value Chain Model

According to Porter's **value chain model** (Porter, 1985), the activities conducted in any manufacturing organization can be divided into two parts: *primary activities and support activities.*

The **primary activities** are those business activities through which a company produces goods, thus creating value for which customers are willing to pay. Primary activities involve the purchase of materials, the processing of materials into products, and delivery of products to customers. Typically, there are five primary activities:

1. Inbound logistics (inputs)
2. Operations (manufacturing and testing)
3. Outbound logistics (storage and distribution)
4. Marketing and sales
5. Services

The primary activities usually take place in a sequence from 1 to 5. As work progresses according to the sequence, value is added to the product in each activity. To be more specific, the incoming materials (1) are processed (in receiving, storage, etc.) in activities called *inbound logistics*. Next, the materials are used in *operations* (2), where significant value is added by the process of turning raw materials into products. The products need to be prepared for delivery (packaging, storing, and shipping) in the

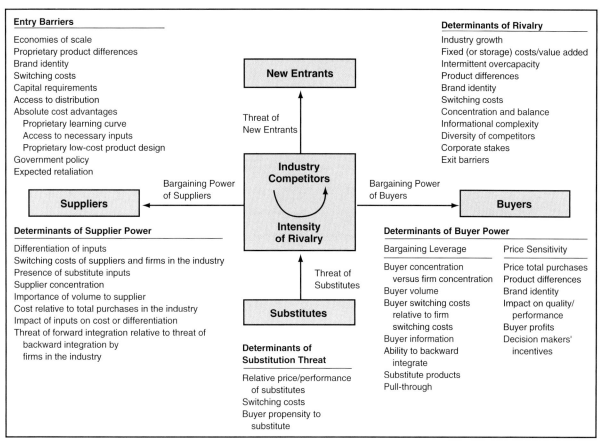

FIGURE 1A.1 Porter's five forces model, including the major determinant of each force. (*Source:* Adapted with permission of the Free Press, a division of Simon & Schuster, Inc., from Michael Porter, *Competitive Advantage: Creating and Sustaining Superior Performance*, p. 6. © 1985, 1998 by Michael Porter.)

TABLE 1A.1 Twelve Strategies for Competitive Advantage

Strategy	Description
Cost leadership	Produce product/service at the lowest cost in the industry.
Differentiation	Offer different products, services, or product features.
Niche	Select a narrow-scope segment (*market niche*) and be the best in quality, speed, or cost in that segment.
Growth	Increase market share, acquire more customers, or sell more types of products.
Alliance	Work with business partners in partnerships, alliances, joint ventures, or virtual companies.
Innovation	Introduce new products/services; put new features in existing products/services; develop new ways to produce products/services.
Operational effectiveness	Improve the manner in which internal business processes are executed so that the firm performs similar activities better than rivals.
Customer orientation	Concentrate on customer satisfaction.
Time	Treat time as a resource, then manage it and use it to the firm's advantage.
Entry barriers	Create barriers to entry. By introducing innovative products or using IT to provide exceptional service, companies can create entry barriers to discourage new entrants.
Lock in customers or suppliers	Encourage customers or suppliers to stay with you rather than going to competitors. Locking in customers has the effect of reducing their bargaining power.
Increase switching costs	Discourage customers or suppliers from going to competitors for economic reasons.

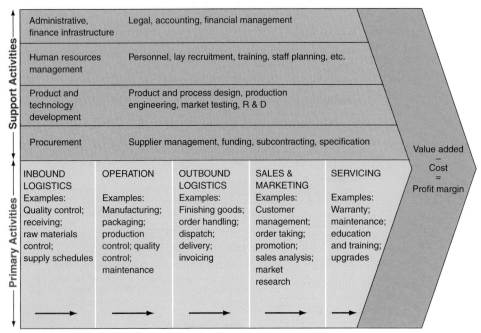

FIGURE 1A.2 The firm's value chain. The arrows illustrate the flow of goods and services (the internal part of the supply chain). (*Source:* Drawn by E. Turban.)

outbound logistics activities (3). Then *marketing and sales* (4) attempt to sell the products to customers, increasing product value by creating demand for the company's products. (The value of a sold item is much larger than that of an unsold one.) Finally, *after-sales service* (5) such as warranty service or upgrade notification is performed for the customer, further adding value. The goal of these value-adding, primary activities is to make a profit for the company.

Primary activities are sustained and furthered by the following **support activities:**

1. The firm's infrastructure (accounting, finance, management)
2. Human resources management
3. Technology development (R&D)
4. Procurement

Each support activity can be applied to any or all of the primary activities, and the support activities may also support each other (see Figure 1A.2). For an

example of Porter's value chain model applied to the airline industry, see Online File W1.11.

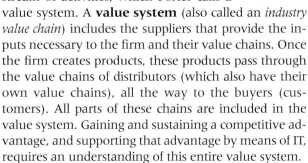

A firm's value chain is part of a larger stream of activities, which Porter calls a value system. A **value system** (also called an *industry value chain*) includes the suppliers that provide the inputs necessary to the firm and their value chains. Once the firm creates products, these products pass through the value chains of distributors (which also have their own value chains), all the way to the buyers (customers). All parts of these chains are included in the value system. Gaining and sustaining a competitive advantage, and supporting that advantage by means of IT, requires an understanding of this entire value system.

In forthcoming chapters, we will show how different functional departments relate to Porter's value chain model and how IT impacts the addition of value (and hopefully profit) in companies. For in-depth discussion, see Chapter 12.

KEY TERMS FOR APPENDIX 1A

Competitive forces model *44*
Primary activities *44*
Support activities *46*

Value chain model *44*
Value system *46*

References for Appendix 1A

Frenzel, C. W., *Management of Information Technology,* 2nd ed. Cambridge, MA: Course Technology, 1996.

Harmon, P., et al., *Developing E-Business Systems and Architectures: A Manager's Guide.* San Francisco: Morgan Kaufmann Publishers, 2001.

Neumann, S., *Strategic Information Systems—Competition Through Information Technologies.* New York: Macmillan, 1994.

Porter, M. E., *Competitive Advantage: Creating and Sustaining Superior Performance.* New York: Free Press, 1985.

Wiseman, C., *Strategic Information Systems.* Burr Ridge, IL: Richard D. Irwin, 1988.

PART I
IT in the Organization

1. Strategic Use of Information Technology in the Digital Economy
▶ 2. Information Technologies: Concepts and Management

CHAPTER 2

Information Technologies: Concepts and Management

2.1 Information Systems: Concepts and Definitions

2.2 Classification and Evolution of Information Systems

2.3 Transaction Processing versus Functional IS

2.4 How IT Supports Organizational Activities

2.5 How IT Supports Supply Chains, CRM, and PRM Operations

2.6 IS Infrastructure and Architecture

2.7 Web-Based Systems

2.8 New Computing Environments

2.9 Managing Information Resources

Minicases:
1. Maybelline
2. J.P. Morgan

Appendix 2A: Build-to-Order Production

LEARNING OBJECTIVES

After studying this chapter, you will be able to:

❶ Describe various information systems and their evolution, and categorize specific systems you observe.

❷ Describe and contrast transaction processing and functional information systems.

❸ Identify the major internal support systems and relate them to managerial functions.

❹ Describe the support IT provides along the supply chain, including CRM.

❺ Discuss information infrastructure and architecture.

❻ Compare client/server architecture, mainframe-based legacy systems, and P2P architecture, and comment on their differences.

❼ Describe the major types of Web-based information systems and understand their functionalities.

❽ Describe new computing environments.

❾ Describe how information resources are managed and what are the roles of the ISD and end users.

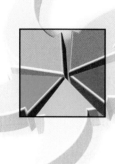

BUILDING AN E-BUSINESS AT FEDEX CORPORATION

FedEx Corporation was founded in 1973 by entrepreneur Fred Smith. Today, with a fully integrated physical and virtual infrastructure, FedEx's business model supports 24–48-hour delivery to anywhere in the world. FedEx operates one of the world's busiest data-processing centers, handling over 100 million information requests per day from more than 3,000 databases and more than 500,000 archive files. It operates one of the largest real-time, online client/server networks in the world. The core competencies of FedEx are now in express transportation and in e-solutions.

THE PROBLEM/OPPORTUNITY

Initially, FedEx grew out of pressures from mounting inflation and global competition. These pressures gave rise to greater demands on businesses to expedite deliveries at a low cost and to improve customer services. FedEx didn't have a business problem per se but, rather, has endeavored to stay ahead of the competition by looking ahead at every stage for opportunities to meet customers' needs for fast, reliable, and affordable overnight deliveries. Lately, the Internet has provided an inexpensive and accessible platform upon which FedEx has seen further opportunities to expand its business scope, both geographically and in terms of service offerings. FedEx is attempting to fulfill two of its major goals simultaneously: 100 percent customer service and 0 percent downtime.

THE IT SOLUTION/PROJECT

A prime software application used by FedEx is e-Shipping Tools, a Web-based shipping application that allows customers to check the status of shipments through the company's Web page. FedEx is also providing integrated solutions to address the entire selling and supply chain needs of its customers. Its e-Commerce Solutions provides a full suite of services that allow businesses to integrate FedEx's transportation and information systems seamlessly into their own operations. These solutions have taken FedEx well beyond a shipping company.

FedEx markets several e-commerce hardware/software solutions: FedEx PowerShipMC (a multicarrier hardware/software system), FedEx Ship Manager Server (a hardware/software system providing high-speed transactions and superior reliability, allowing an average of eight transactions per second), FedEx ShipAPI™ (an Internet-based application that allows customization, eliminating redundant programming), and FedEx Net-Return® (a Web-based item-return management system). This infrastructure is now known as FedEx Direct Link. It enables business-to-business electronic commerce through combinations of global virtual private network (VPN) connectivity, Internet connectivity, leased-line connectivity, and VAN (value-added network) connectivity.

Figure 2.1 (page 50) provides an example of one of FedEx's e-commerce solutions. It shows how FedEx customers can tap into a network of systems through the Internet. When a customer places an online order, it is sent to a FedEx Web server. Information about the order and the customer is then sent to the merchant's PC, and a message is sent to the customer to confirm receipt of the order. After the order is received and acknowledged, the FedEx Web server sends

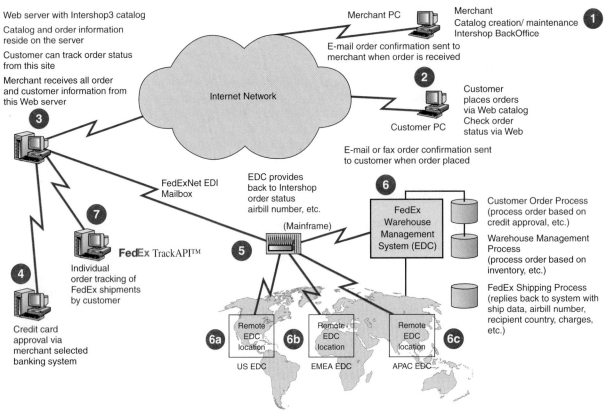

FIGURE 2.1 An example of a FedEx e-commerce solution. *Source:* Based on a SIM 2000 award-winning paper written by William L. Conley, Ali F. Farhoomand, and Pauline S.P. Ng, at *simnet.org/ library/doc/2ndplace.doc,* accessed 2003. Courtesy of William Conley.

a message to the merchant's bank to obtain credit approval. At the same time, the order is sent via electronic data interchange (EDI) to a FedEx mainframe that activates the *warehouse management system.* The order is processed (goods are picked and packed), the warehouse inventory system is updated, and the shipping process is activated. Information regarding the processing of the order is accessible at the three remote electronic data centers (EDCs) located in the United States, the Europe/Mediterranean (EMEA) region, and the Asia Pacific (APAC) region. During the entire process the customer, the merchant, and FedEx employees may track at any time the status of the order and its fulfillment via the Web.

 THE RESULTS

The new e-commerce-based FedEx business model creates value for customers in a number of ways: It facilitates better communication and collaboration between the various parties along the selling and supply chains. It promotes efficiency gains by reducing costs and speeding up the order cycle. It encourages customers not only to use FedEx as a shipper but also to outsource to FedEx all their logistics activities. It also provides FedEx a competitive edge and increased revenue and profits. Thus, FedEx has changed from an old-economy shipping company to an e-business logistics enterprise.

Sources: Based on a SIM 2000 award-winning paper written by William L. Conley, Ali F. Farhoomand, and Pauline S.P. Ng, *simnet.org/library/doc/2ndplace.doc* (accessed February 2003). Courtesy of William Conley. Updated with information from *fedex.com* (accessed February 2003).

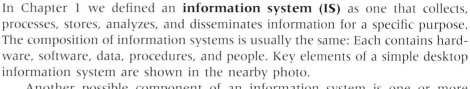 **LESSONS LEARNED FROM THIS CASE**

In the digital economy, how well companies transform themselves from traditional modes of operation to e-business will depend on how well they can adapt their structure and processes to take advantage of emerging technologies and what architecture and infrastructure they use. FedEx has transformed itself into an e-business by integrating physical and virtual infrastructures across information systems, business processes, and organizational bounds. FedEx's experience in building an e-business shows how a company can successfully apply its information technology expertise in order to pioneer "customercentric" innovations with sweeping structural and strategic impacts. It also shows the role of outsourcing, which frees companies to concentrate on their core business. In this chapter we describe how information systems of different kinds are structured, organized, and managed so that they can support businesses in the twenty-first century.

2.1 INFORMATION SYSTEMS: CONCEPTS AND DEFINITIONS

In Chapter 1 we defined an **information system (IS)** as one that collects, processes, stores, analyzes, and disseminates information for a specific purpose. The composition of information systems is usually the same: Each contains hardware, software, data, procedures, and people. Key elements of a simple desktop information system are shown in the nearby photo.

Another possible component of an information system is one or more smaller information systems. Information systems that contain smaller systems are typical of large companies. For example, FedEx's corporate information system contains hundreds of smaller information systems, which are referred to as "applications." An **application program** is a computer program designed to support a specific task or a business process (such as execute the payroll) or, in some cases, another application program.

There are dozens of applications in each functional area. For instance, in managing human resources, it is possible to find one application for screening job applicants and another for monitoring employee turnover. Some of the applications might be completely independent of each other, whereas others are interrelated. The collection of application programs in a single department is usually considered a *departmental information system*, even though it is made up of many applications. For example, the collection of application programs in the human resources area is called the *human resources information system (HRIS)*.

Information systems are usually connected by means of *electronic networks*. The connecting networks can be *wireline* and/or *wireless*. Information systems can connect an entire organization, or even multiple organizations. If the entire company is networked and people can communicate with each other and access information throughout the organization, then the arrangement is known as an *enterprisewide information system*. An *interorganizational information system*, such as FedExNet, involves information flow among two or more organizations, and is used primarily in e-business applications.

The organization and management of information systems is emerging as a theoretical discipline, rather than simply as an applied field of study (O'Donovan and Roode, 2002). Before we focus on the details of IT and its management, it is necessary to describe the major concepts of information systems and organize the systems in some logical manner. That is the major purpose of this chapter.

Data, Information, and Knowledge

Information systems are built to attain several goals. One of the primary goals is to economically process data into information or knowledge. Let us define these concepts:

Data items refer to an elementary description of things, events, activities, and transactions that are recorded, classified, and stored, but not organized to convey any specific meeting. Data items can be numeric, alphanumeric, figures, sounds, or images. A student grade in a class is a data item, and so is the number of hours an employee worked in a certain week. A **database** consists of stored data items organized for retrieval.

Information is data that have been organized so that they have meaning and value to the recipient. For example, a student's grade point average is information. The recipient interprets the meaning and draws conclusions and implications from the data. Data items typically are processed into information by means of an application. Such processing represents a more specific use and a higher added value than simple retrieval and summarization from a database. The application might be a Web-based inventory management system, a university online registration system, or an Internet-based buying and selling system.

Finally, **knowledge** consists of data and/or information that have been organized and processed to convey understanding, experience, accumulated learning, and expertise as they apply to a current problem or activity. Data that are processed to extract critical implications and to reflect past experiences and expertise provide the recipient with *organizational knowledge,* which has a very high potential value. Currently, *knowledge management* is one of the hottest topics in the IT field (see Chapter 9).

Data, information, and knowledge can be *inputs* to an information system, and they can also be *outputs.* For example, data about employees, their wages, and time worked are processed as inputs in order to produce an organization's payroll information (output). The payroll information itself can later be used as an input to another system that prepares a budget or advises management on salary scales.

Information Systems Configurations

Information systems are made out of components that can be assembled in many different configurations, resulting in a variety of information systems and applications, much as construction materials can be assembled to build different homes. The size and cost of a home depend on the purpose of the building, the availability of money, and constraints such as ecological and environmental legal requirements. Just as there are many different types of houses, so there are many different types of information systems. We classify houses as single-family homes, apartments (or flats), townhouses, and cottages. Similarly, it is useful to classify information systems into groups that share similar characteristics. Such a classification may help in identifying systems, analyzing them, planning new systems, planning integration of systems, and making decisions such as the possible outsourcing of systems. This classification can be done in several alternative ways, as shown next.

2.2 CLASSIFICATION AND EVOLUTION OF INFORMATION SYSTEMS

Information systems are classified in this section by organizational levels and by the type of support provided. The section also looks at the evolution of support systems.

Classification by Organizational Levels

Organizations are made up of components such as divisions, departments, and work units, organized in hierarchical levels. For example, most organizations have functional departments, such as production and accounting, which report to plant management, which in turn reports to a division head. The divisions report to the corporate headquarters. Although some organizations have restructured themselves in innovative ways, such as those based on cross-functional teams, today the vast majority of organizations still have a traditional hierarchical structure. Thus, we can find information systems built for headquarters, for divisions, for the functional departments, for operating units, and even for individual employees. Such systems can stand alone, but usually they are interconnected.

Typical information systems that follow the organizational structure are *functional (departmental), enterprisewide,* and *interorganizational.* These systems are organized in a hierarchy in which each higher-level system consists of several (even many) systems from the level below it, as shown in Figure 2.2. As can be seen in the figure, a departmental system supports the functional areas in each company. At a higher level, the enterprisewide system supports the entire company, and interorganizational systems connect different companies.

FUNCTIONAL (DEPARTMENTAL) INFORMATION SYSTEMS. The major functional information systems are organized around the traditional departments—

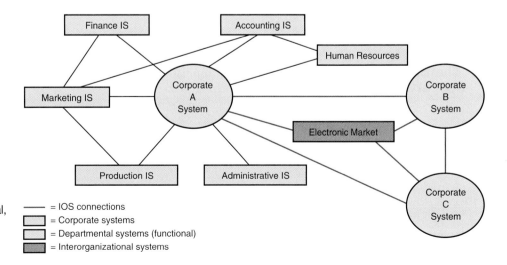

FIGURE 2.2 Departmental, corporate, and interorganizational information systems.

——— = IOS connections
▢ = Corporate systems
▢ = Departmental systems (functional)
▮ = Interorganizational systems

functions—in a company: manufacturing (operations/production), accounting, finance, marketing, and human resources. Functional systems are described in Chapter 6.

A special system that crosses several departments is the *transaction processing system (TPS)*. The TPS automates routine and repetitive tasks that are critical to the operation of the organization, such as preparing a payroll or billing customers. Transaction processing systems are described in Section 2.3 and in Chapter 6.

ENTERPRISE INFORMATION SYSTEMS. While a departmental information system is usually related to a functional area, other information systems serve several departments or the entire enterprise. These information systems together with the departmental applications comprise the *enterprisewide information system (EIS)*. One of the most popular enterprise applications is *enterprise resources planning (ERP)*, which enables companies to plan and manage the resources of an entire enterprise. ERP systems present a relatively new model of enterprisewide computing (see Chapter 7).

INTERORGANIZATIONAL SYSTEMS. Some information systems connect two or more organizations. They are referred to as *interorganizational information systems (IOSs)*. For example, the worldwide airline reservation system is composed of several systems belonging to different airlines. Of these, American Airlines' SABRE system is the largest; thousands of travel agents and hundreds of airlines are connected to it. Such systems are common among business partners. Those that support international or global operations may be especially complex (see Mol and Koppius, 2002). Interorganizational information systems play a major role in e-commerce, as well as in supply chain management support. (See Chapter 8.)

Classification by the Type of Support Provided

Another way to classify information systems is according to the type of support they provide, regardless of the functional area. For example, an information system can support office workers in almost any functional area. Likewise, managers working from various geographical locations can be supported by a computerized decision-making system. The main types of support systems are listed and described in Table 2.1 (page 55) together with the types of employees they support. The evolution of these systems and a brief description of each follow. For more detail, see Online File W2.1.

The Evolution of Support Systems

The first business applications of computers did repetitive, large-volume, transactions-computing tasks. The computers "crunched numbers," summarizing and organizing transactions and data in the accounting, finance, and human resources areas. Such systems are called, generally, *transaction processing systems*.

As the per-transaction cost of computing decreased and computers' capabilities increased, a new breed of information system, called *management information systems (MISs)*, started to develop. These systems accessed, organized, summarized, and displayed information for supporting routine decision making in the functional areas. In addition, *office automation systems (OASs)* such as word processing systems and airline reservation systems were developed to support office workers. Computers also were introduced in the manufacturing

TABLE 2.1 Main Types of IT Support Systems

System	Employees Supported	Description	Detailed Description In:
Transaction processing system (TPS)	All employees	Processes an organization's basic business transactions (e.g., purchasing, billing, payroll).	Chapter 6
Management information system (MIS)	All employees	Provides routine information for planning, organizing, and controlling operations in functional areas.	Chapter 6
Office automation system (OAS)	Office workers	Increases productivity of office workers; includes word processing.	Chapters 3, 6
Word processing system	Office workers	Helps create, edit, format, distribute, and print documents.	Chapter 3
CAD/CAM	Engineers, draftspeople	Allows engineers to design and test prototypes; transfers specifications to manufacturing facilities.	Chapter 6
Communication and collaboration systems (e.g., e-mail, voice mail, call centers, others)	All employees	Enable employees and customers to interact and work together more efficiently.	Chapter 3
Desktop publishing system	Office workers	Combines text, photos, graphics to produce professional-quality documents.	Chapter 3
Document management system (DMS)	Office workers	Automates flow of electronic documents.	Chapter 10
Decision support system (DSS)	Decision makers, managers	Combines models and data to solve semistructured problems with extensive user involvement.	Chapter 11
Executive support system (ESS)	Executives, senior managers	Supports decisions of top managers.	Chapter 11
Group support system (GSS)	People working in groups	Supports working processes of groups of people (including those in different locations).	Chapter 11
Expert system (ES)	Knowledge workers, nonexperts	Provides stored knowledge of experts to nonexperts and decision recommendations based on built-in expertise.	Chapters 9, 10
Knowledge work system (KWS)	Managers, knowledge workers	Supports the gathering, organizing, and use of an organization's knowledge.	Chapters 9, 10, 11
Neural networks, case-based reasoning	Knowledge workers, professionals	Learn from historical cases, even with vague or incomplete information.	Chapters 9, 10
Data warehouse	Managers, knowledge workers	Stores huge amounts of data that can be easily accessed and manipulated for decision support.	Chapters 10, 11
Business intelligence	Decision makers, managers	Gathers and uses large amounts of data for analysis by DSS, ESS, and intelligent systems.	Chapter 10
Mobile computing systems	Mobile employees	Support employees who work with customers or business partners outside the physical boundaries of the organization.	Chapter 5

environment, with applications ranging from robotics to computer-aided design and manufacturing (CAD/CAM).

Further, additional increasing computing capabilities and reduced costs justified computerized support for a growing number of nonroutine applications, and *decision support systems* were developed to provide computerized support for complex, nonroutine decisions. The microcomputer revolution, which started around 1980, began the era of **end-user computing,** in which analysts, managers, and many other professionals are building and using systems on their own desktop computers. Decision support expanded in two directions: first, toward executives and to other managers (*executive support systems* and *enterprisewide information systems*), and second, to people working in groups (*group support systems*).

Eventually, interest in programming computers to perform intelligent problem solving led to commercial applications known as *intelligent support systems (ISSs)*. These include *expert systems,* which provide the stored knowledge of experts needed to help nonexperts, and a new breed of intelligent systems with *machine-learning* capabilities (such as artificial neural networks; Chapter 11) that can learn from historical cases.

As our economy has become more focused on knowledge work, *knowledge work systems* have been developed specifically to support the creating, gathering, organizing, integrating, and disseminating of an organization's knowledge. Included in this category are software products for word processing, document management, and desktop publishing.

A major innovation in the evolution of support systems has been the development of *data warehousing*. A data warehouse is a database designed to support DSS, ESS, and other analytical and end-user activities. The use of data warehouses is a part of *business intelligence,* the gathering and use of large amounts of data for query or analysis by DSS, ESS, and intelligent systems.

The latest support system in organizations is *mobile computing*. Mobile computing supports mobile employees, those who are working with customers or business partners, outside the physical boundaries of their companies. The mobile employees carry portable devices, ranging from PDAs to cell phones, digital cameras, and notebook computers, that can access the Internet. These devices enable communication with organizations and other individuals via wireline or wireless networks.

The information systems described so far were designed mostly to support the activities inside organizations. However, companies discovered that their *external* activities also can be improved with IT. The first type of IT system, developed in the 1980s, to improve communications with business partners was *electronic data interchange (EDI),* which involved computer-to-computer direct communication of standard business documents (such as orders and order confirmations) between business partners. These systems became the basis for *electronic markets,* which later developed into *electronic commerce*. These expanded later to improved *collaboration* of planning and other business activities among business partners, and some of the enterprisewide systems expanded to include more formalized business partner relationships. Later on came a wave of systems intended to support customers; these were grouped under the umbrella term *customer relationship management (CRM),* and they include services such as *call centers* (Chapter 7). Some of these external support systems are described further in Section 2.5.

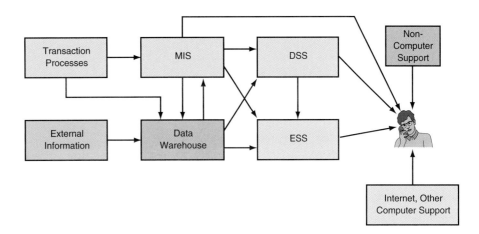

FIGURE 2.3 Interrelated support systems. The TPS collects information that is used to build the DSS and ESS. The information in the data warehouse and DSS can be used as an input to the ESS.

Major advances in external support are attributed to Web-based and mobile systems. *Web-based systems* started to be developed in the mid-1990s and picked up momentum in 2000. As their name implies, these systems deliver business applications via the Internet. As shown in the Siemens case in Chapter 1 and the FedEx case here, organizations are using Web-based systems to transform themselves into e-businesses. As will be shown *throughout the text,* today many—and probably most—of the innovative and strategic systems in medium and large organizations are Web-based. Using their browsers, people in these organizations communicate, collaborate, access vast amounts of information, and run most of the organization's tasks and processes by means of Web-based systems. (For more, see Section 2.7.)

In summary, the relationship among the different types of support systems can be described as follows: Each support system has sufficiently unique characteristics that it can be classified as a special entity. Moreover, there is information flow among these entities and systems. For example, an MIS extracts information from a TPS, and an ESS receives information from data warehouses and MIS (see Figure 2.3). In many cases, two or more support systems can be integrated to form a hybrid system, as is the case in business intelligence or CRM. Finally, as the technologies change, the interrelationships and coordination among the different types of systems continue to evolve. Ten years from now, the relationships shown in Figure 2.3 will probably look different from the way they look today.

INTEGRATED SUPPORT SYSTEMS. From the time of their inception, support systems were used both as standalone systems and as integrated systems composed of two or more of the support systems. Notable were systems that include some intelligent components (e.g., a DSS-ES combination). Such integration provides extended functionalities, making these systems more useful. As will be discussed in Chapter 6, there is an increasing trend to integrate the various support systems as well as to integrate support systems with other systems. Integrated support systems can provide solutions to complex problems, as shown in *A Closer Look 2.1.*

Now that we have completed an overview of the different types of support systems and their evolution, we will look at some of the key systems in more detail.

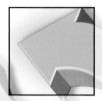

A CLOSER LOOK
2.1 INTELLIGENT PRICE SETTING
IN RETAILING

Pricing several thousands of items at Longs Drug Stores (a U.S. chain of about 400 drug stores, *longs.com*) is decentralized. Each store is empowered to price each of the items it carries in the store, in order to better compete locally. Pricing traditionally was done manually by modifying the manufacturer's suggested retail price. Similar practices existed in most other retail chains, including supermarkets. Furthermore, when a price war occurred, or when a seasonal sales time arrived, prices were slashed across the board, without paying attention to demand forecast, profitability, pricing strategy, or price consistency across stores.

Now price setting is undergoing a radical change, largely as a result of improved IT support systems. Following what airlines and car leasing companies were doing for years, the retail industry, including Longs Drug Stores and about half of all other U.S. retailers, is introducing *price-optimization* programs. How do these programs work? Price-optimization programs (offered by Demand-Tech Inc., and others) combine support systems such as DSS, intelligent systems, data warehouses, and more to form a system that recommends a price for each item in each store. The input data used are seasonal sales figures, actual sales at each store (in real time), each

product's price-demand curve, competitors' prices, profitability metrics, and more. The process is illustrated in Online File W2.2 at the book's Web site. Using the program, retailers can identify the most price-sensitive products, and they can test within seconds what impact a price change would have on profit margin (or other desired goal, such as sales volume). Using each store's priorities, strategies can be developed and tested.

The models used are similar to *yield-management* models pioneered by the airline industry in the 1980s and since adopted by the car-leasing, financial services, consumer electronics, transportation, and other industries. Even casinos are introducing similar programs to determine the optimal payout for slot machines.

Initial results at Longs Drugs and at other retail stores that have used similar programs show volume, revenue, and profit increases of between 2 and 10 percent. The software is still fairly expensive, so only large retailers can use it now. As more competitors produce similar software, it will become cheaper in the future, and consumers will be the ultimate beneficiaries.

Source: Condensed from Cortese (2002).

2.3 TRANSACTION PROCESSING VERSUS FUNCTIONAL INFORMATION SYSTEMS

Any organization that performs periodic financial, accounting, and other routine business activities faces repetitive information processing tasks. For example, employees are paid at regular intervals, customers place purchase orders and are billed, and expenses are monitored and compared to the budget. Table 2.2 (page 59) presents a list of representative routine, repetitive business transactions in a manufacturing organization. The information system that supports such processes is called the *transaction processing system.*

Transaction Processing Systems

A **transaction processing system (TPS)** supports the monitoring, collection, storage, processing, and dissemination of the organization's basic business transactions. It also provides the input data for many applications involving support systems such as DSS. Sometimes several TPSs exist in one company. The transaction processing systems are considered critical to the success of any organization since they support core operations, such as purchasing of materials, billing customers, preparing a payroll, and shipping goods to customers.

TABLE 2.2 Routine Business Transactions
in a Manufacturing Company

Payroll and personnel	*Sales*
Employee time cards	Sales records
Employee pay and deductions	Invoices and billings
	Accounts receivable
Payroll checks	Sales returns
Fringe benefits	Shipping
Purchasing	*Production*
Purchase orders	Production reports
Deliveries	Quality-control reports
Payments (accounts payable)	*Inventory management*
	Material usage
Finance and accounting	Inventory levels
Financial statements	
Tax records	
Expense accounts	

The TPS collects data continuously, frequently on a daily basis, or even in *real time* (i.e., as soon as they are generated). Most of these data are stored in the corporate databases or data warehouse and are available for processing.

EXAMPLES OF TPS. In retail stores, data flow from POS (point-of-sale) terminals to a database where they are aggregated. Sales reduce the level of inventory on hand, and the collected revenue from sales increases the company's cash position. TPS data may be analyzed by data-mining tools to find emerging patterns in what people buy. Such transactions occur all the time.

In banking, TPSs cover the area of deposits and withdrawals (which are similar to inventory levels). They also cover money transfers between accounts in the bank and among banks. Generating monthly statements for customers and setting fees charged for bank services are also typical transaction-processing activities for a bank.

Payroll is another area covered by TPSs for a business. Further details on TPSs are provided in Chapter 6.

Functional Management Information Systems

The transaction-processing system covers the core activities of an organization. The *functional areas,* however, perform many other activities; some of these are repetitive, while others are only occasional. For example, the human resources department hires, advises, and trains people. Each of these tasks can be divided into subtasks. Training may involve selecting topics to teach, selecting people to participate in the training, scheduling classes, finding teachers, and preparing class materials. These tasks and subtasks are frequently supported by information systems specifically designed to support functional activities. Such systems are referred to as **functional management information systems,** or just **MIS.***

Functional management information systems are put in place to ensure that business strategies come to fruition in an efficient manner. Typically, a

*The term MIS here refers to a specific *application in* a functional area. The term MIS is also used in another context to describe the area of *management of* information systems.

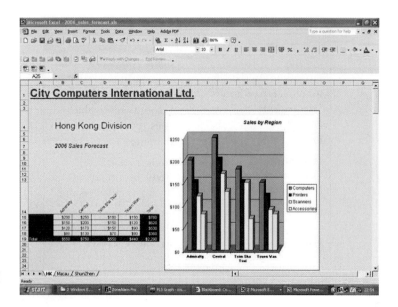

FIGURE 2.4 Sales forecast by region, generated by marketing MIS.

functional MIS provides periodic information about such topics as operational efficiency, effectiveness, and productivity by extracting information from databases and processing it according to the needs of the user.

Management information systems are also used for planning, monitoring, and control. For example, a sales forecast by region is shown in Figure 2.4. Such a report can help the marketing manager make better decisions regarding advertising and pricing of products. Another example is that of a human resources information system (HRIS), which provides a manager with a daily report of the percentage of people who were on vacation or called in sick, as compared to forecasted figures.

So far we described what the support systems are. Now let's see *how* they support employees in organizations.

2.4 HOW IT SUPPORTS ORGANIZATIONAL ACTIVITIES

Another important way to classify information systems is by the nature of activities they support. Such support can be for operational, managerial, or strategic activities, as well as for knowledge workers in an organization.

Operational Activities

Operational activities deal with the day-to-day operations of an organization, such as assigning employees to tasks and recording the number of hours they work, or placing a purchase order. Operational activities are short-term in nature. The information systems that support them are mainly TPSs, MISs, and mobile systems. Operational systems are used by supervisors (first-line managers), operators, and clerical employees.

Managerial Activities

Managerial activities, also called tactical activities or decisions, deal in general with middle-management activities such as short-term planning, organizing, and control. Computerized managerial systems are frequently *equated with MISs,* because MISs are designed to summarize data and prepare reports. Middle managers also can get quick answers to queries from such systems as the need for answers arises.

TABLE 2.3 Support Provided by MISs for Managerial Activities	
Task	**MIS Support**
Statistical summaries	Summaries of new data (e.g., daily production by item, monthly electricity usage).
Exception reports	Comparison of actual performances to standards (or target). Highlight only deviations from a threshold (e.g., above or below 5%).
Periodic reports	Generated at predetermined intervals.
Ad-hoc reports	Generated as needed, on demand. These can be routine reports or special ones.
Comparative analysis and early detection of problems	Comparison of performance to metrics or standards. Includes analysis such as trends and early detection of changes.
Projections, forecasting	Projection of future sales, cash flows, market share, etc.
Automation of routine decisions	Standard modeling techniques applied to routine decisions such as when and how much to order or how to schedule work.
Connection and collaboration	Internal and external Web-based messaging systems, e-mail, voice mail, and groupware (see Chapter 3).

Managerial information systems are broader in scope than operational information systems, but like operational systems, they use mainly internal sources of data. They provide the major, representative types of support shown in Table 2.3.

Strategic Activities   *Strategic activities* are activities or decisions that deal with situations that may significantly change the manner in which business is done. Traditionally, strategic activities involved only long-range planning. Introducing a new product line, expanding the business by acquiring supporting businesses, and moving operations to a foreign country, are prime examples of long-range activities. A long-range planning document traditionally outlines strategies and plans for the next five or even 10 years. From this plan, companies derive their shorter-range planning, budgeting, and resource allocation. In the digital economy, the planning period has been dramatically reduced to one to two years, or even months. Strategic activities help organizations in two other ways.

First, *strategic response* activities can react quickly to a major competitor's action or to any other significant change in the enterprise's environment. Although they can sometimes be planned for as a set of contingencies, strategic responses are frequently not included in the long-range plan because the situations they respond to are unpredictable. IT is often used to support the response or to provide the response itself. For instance, when Kodak Corporation learned that a Japanese company was developing a disposable camera, Kodak decided to develop one too. However, Kodak faced a time problem because the Japanese were already in the middle of the development process. By using computer-aided design and other information technologies, Kodak was able to cut its design time by half and beat the Japanese in the race to be the first to have the cameras in retail outlets.

Second, instead of waiting for a competitor to introduce a major change or innovation, an organization can be the *initiator of change*. Such innovative strategic activities are frequently supported by IT, as shown by FedEx in the opening case and by many startup companies that exploit opportunities by using IT (e.g., see the Thaigem story in Chapter 1 and the Amazon.com story in Chapter 4).

E-BUSINESS STRATEGIC SYSTEMS. As we saw in Chapter 1, e-commerce and e-business have become a new way of conducting business in the last decade or so. In this new approach, business transactions take place via telecommunications networks, primarily the Internet. E-business refers not only to buying and selling electronically, but also involves e-collaboration and e-learning. It aims at increasing productivity, reaching new customers, and sharing knowledge across institutions for competitive advantage. EC-supported strategic systems are changing how business is done. We will provide e-business strategic examples throughout the book.

Who Performs What Activities in Organizations? So far in this section, we have looked at operational, managerial, and strategic activities, and at how IT supports them. Here, we take a different look at these activities by looking at the people who typically perform them in an organization. For example, line managers and operators usually make operational decisions, and middle managers make most of the managerial decisions. Strategic decisions are made almost entirely by an organization's top managers. The relationships between the people supported and the decision type are shown in Figure 2.5. The

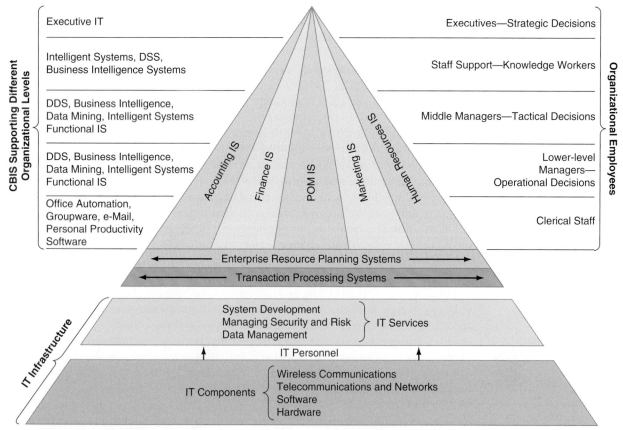

FIGURE 2.5 The information systems support of people in organizations.

triangular shape of the figure also illustrates the quantity of employees involved in the various types of activities and the decisions relating to those activities. Top managers are few, and they sit at the top of the triangle.

KNOWLEDGE WORKERS, CLERICAL STAFF, AND DATA WORKERS. As you can see in Figure 2.5, an additional level of *staff support* is introduced between top and middle management. These are professional people, such as financial and marketing analysts. They act as advisors and assistants to both top and middle management. Many of these professional workers are classified as **knowledge workers,** people who create information and knowledge as part of their work and integrate it into the business. Knowledge workers are engineers, financial and marketing analysts, production planners, lawyers, and accountants, to mention just a few. They are responsible for finding or developing new knowledge for the organization and integrating it with existing knowledge. Therefore they must keep abreast of all developments and events related to their profession. They also act as change agents by introducing new procedures, technologies, or processes. In many developed countries, 60 to 80 percent of all workers are knowledge workers.

Information systems that support knowledge workers range from Internet search engines (which help knowledge workers find information) and expert systems (which support information interpretation), to Web-based computer-aided design (which shape and speed the design process) and sophisticated data management systems (which help increase productivity and quality of work). Knowledge workers are the major users of the Internet for business purposes.

Another large class of employees is *clerical workers,* who support managers at all levels. Among clerical workers, those who use, manipulate, or disseminate information are referred to as **data workers.** These include bookkeepers, secretaries who work with word processors, electronic file clerks, and insurance claim processors. Data workers are supported by office automation and communication systems including document management, workflow, e-mail, and coordination software.

INFRASTRUCTURE FOR THE SUPPORT SYSTEMS. All of the systems in the support triangle are built on *information infrastructure.* Consequently, all of the employees who are supported work with infrastructure technologies such as the Internet, intranets, corporate portals, and corporate databases. Therefore, the information infrastructure is shown as the *foundation* of the triangle in Figure 2.5; it is described in more detail in Section 2.6.

2.5 HOW IT SUPPORTS SUPPLY CHAINS, CRM, AND PRM OPERATIONS

As indicated in Chapter 1, organizations work with business partners in several areas, frequently along the supply chain.

The Basics of Supply Chains and Their Management

A **supply chain** is a concept describing the flow of materials, information, money, and services from raw material suppliers through factories and warehouses to the end customers. A supply chain also includes the *organizations* and *processes* that create and deliver these products, information, and services to the end customers. The term *supply chain* comes from a picture of how the partnering organizations are linked together. As shown in Figure 2.6 (page 64), a simple linear supply chain links a company that processes milk (middle of the chain) with its suppliers (on the bottom) and its distributors and customers (on the top). The supply chain

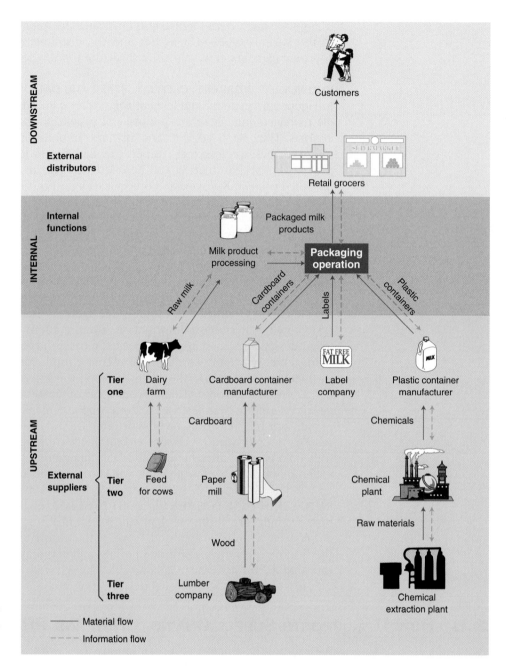

FIGURE 2.6 A simple supply chain for a manufacturer. Note: Only representative processes are shown. (*Source:* Modified from Reid and Sanders, 2002).

shown in Figure 2.6 is fairly simple. As will be shown in Chapter 7, supply chains can be much more complex. Note that the supply chain shows both physical flows and the flow of information. Not shown is the flow of money, which goes in the direction opposite to the flow of the physical materials.

SUPPLY CHAIN PARTS.   A supply chain can be broken into three major parts: upstream, internal, and downstream as shown in Figure 2.6.

- *The upstream supply chain.* The *upstream* part of the supply chain includes the activities of a company (a milk producer, in our case), with its first-tier suppliers and their connection to their suppliers (referred to as second-tier suppliers). The supplier relationship can be extended several tiers, all the way to the origin of the material (e.g., mining ores, growing crops). In the upstream supply chain, the major activity is *procurement*.

- **The internal supply chain.** The *internal* part of the supply chain includes all of the *in-house* processes used in transforming the inputs received from the suppliers into the organization's outputs. It extends from the time the inputs enter an organization to the time that the products go to distribution outside of the organization. The internal supply chain is mainly concerned with production management, manufacturing, and inventory control (e.g., processing and packaging in Figure 2.6).
- **The downstream supply chain.** The *downstream* part of the supply chain includes all the activities involved in delivering the products to the final customers. The downstream supply chain is directed at distribution, warehousing, transportation, and after-sale services (e.g., retail grocers in Figure 2.6).

A company's supply chain involves an array of business processes that not only effectively transform raw items to finished goods or services but that also make those goods or services attractive to customers. The activities that add value to the company's goods or services are part of what is called the *value chain*, which we discuss in Chapter 12.

**IT Support of
Supply Chains**

Managing supply chains can be complex and difficult to manage due to the need to coordinate several business partners, several internal corporate departments, numerous business processes, and possibly many customers. Managing medium to large supply chains manually is almost impossible. IT support of supply chains can be divided according to the three segments of the supply chain.

SUPPORT OF THE INTERNAL SUPPLY CHAIN. The IT support of the internal supply chain was described in the previous two sections. It involves the TPS and other corporatewide information systems, and it includes all of the functional information systems. (These will be described in detail in Chapter 6.) It also supports the various types of activities and participants described in Section 2.4.

SUPPORT OF THE UPSTREAM SUPPLY CHAIN. The major IT support of the upstream supply chain is to improve procurement activities and relationships with suppliers. As will be seen in Chapters 4 and 6, using e-procurement is becoming very popular, resulting in major savings and improvements in buyer-seller relationships. E-procurement is done in private and public exchanges (Chapter 4 and Turban et al., 2006). Relationships with suppliers can be improved by using a supplier portal (Chapter 3) and other supplier-relationship IT tools.

SUPPORT OF THE DOWNSTREAM SUPPLY CHAIN. IT support of the downstream segment of the supply chain is done in two areas. First, IT supports customer relationship management activities such as providing a customer call center. Second, IT supports order taking and shipments to customers (Chapters 4 and 7).

Many companies provide IT support to both the upstream and downstream segments of the supply chain, as described in the story about Best Buy in Online File W2.3.

MANAGING SUPPLY CHAINS. IT provides two major types of software solutions for managing—planning, organizing, coordinating, and controlling—supply chain activities. First is *enterprise resource planning (ERP)* software, which helps in managing both the internal and the external relationships with the business partners. Second is *supply chain management (SCM)* software, which helps in decision making related both to internal segments and to their relationships with external segments. Both types of software are described in Chapter 7.

Finally, the concepts of build-to-order production and of e-commerce have put a new spin on supply chain management; for elaboration, see Appendix 2A at the end of this chapter.

2.6 INFORMATION SYSTEMS INFRASTRUCTURE AND ARCHITECTURE

Infrastructure

An **information infrastructure** consists of the physical facilities, services, and management that support all shared computing resources in an organization. There are five major components of the infrastructure: (1) computer hardware, (2) software, (3) networks and communication facilities (including the Internet and intranets), (4) databases, and (5) information management personnel. Infrastructures include these resources as well as their integration, operation, documentation, maintenance, and management. If you go back and examine Figure 2.1 (which describes the architecture of the FedExNet), and introduce specific names instead of general ones (e.g., instead of "Merchant PC," say "Dell server"), you will get a picture of the system's infrastructure. Infrastructures are further discussed in Chapters 13 and 14, and in Broadbent and Weill (1997), Weill and Vitale (2001), HP Company (2004), and Seven Spaces (2004). IT infrastructure is derived from the IT architecture.

The IT Architecture

Technology Guides are located at the book's Web site.

Information technology architecture is a high-level map or plan of the information assets in an organization including the physical design of the building that holds the hardware.* On the Web, IT architecture includes the content and organization of the site and the interface to support browsing and search capabilities. The IT architecture of an e-business (a travel agency) is shown in Technology Guide 6. IT architecture is a guide for current operations and a blueprint for future directions. It assures managers that the organization's IT structure will meet its strategic business needs. (See the *Journal of Information Architecture* for examples, tutorials, news, products, etc.)

Creating the IT architecture is a cyclical process, which is driven by the business architecture. This process is described in Technology Guide 6. It is based on **business architecture,** which describes organizational plans, visions, objectives and problems, and the information required to support them. The potential users of IT must play a critical role in the creation of business architecture, in order to ensure that business architectures are properly linked and meet the organization's long-term needs.

Once the business architecture is finished, the system developer can start a five-step process of building the IT architecture. The details and definitions of those steps are provided by Koontz (2000) and are shown in Technology Guide 6. Translating the business objectives into IT architecture can be a very complex undertaking. For a translation guide in the e-business environment, see Whipple (2001).

Let's look now at various basic elements of IT architecture.

Information technology architecture needs to be distinguished from *computer architecture* (see Technology Guide 1). For example, the architecture for a computer may involve several processors, or it may have special features to increase speed such as *reduced instruction set computing* (RISC). Our interest here is in information architecture only.

Information Architecture According to Computing Paradigms (Environments)

A common way to classify information architecture is by computing paradigms, which are the core of the architecture. The major computing paradigms discussed here are: the mainframe environment, the PC environment, distributed computing, client/server architecture, and legacy systems. (For further details, see Technology Guide 1.)

MAINFRAME ENVIRONMENT. In the mainframe environment, processing is done by one or more mainframe computers. The users work with passive (or "dumb") terminals, which are used to enter or change data and access information from the mainframe and are controlled by it. This was the dominant architecture until the mid-1980s. Very few organizations use this type of architecture exclusively today due to its inflexibility and poor price-to-performance ratio (Ahmad, 2000).

An extension of this paradigm is an architecture that combines a mainframe with a number of PCs that are used as smart terminals. A **smart terminal** (also called *intelligent terminal*) contains a keyboard and screen (as does a "dumb terminal"), but it also comes with a disk drive that enables it to perform limited processing tasks when not communicating directly with the central computer. Yet the core of the system is the mainframe with its powerful storage and computational capabilities. The network computers (NCs) that were introduced in 1997 (see the discussion of client/server architecture, next page) redefined the role of the centralized mainframe computing environment (for details see Amato-McCoy, 2002, and Ahmad, 2000).

PC ENVIRONMENT. In the PC configuration, *only* PCs (no mainframes) provide the computing power in the information system. Initially there was only one PC in each information system. Later it became possible to network several PCs together.

PC-LANs. When PCs are connected via local area networks (LANs), a more flexible PC system is created. New functionalities can be added, including e-mail, Internet access, and the sharing of devices such as printers. This paradigm offers scalability (the ability to handle an increased load) and effectiveness, but it generally lacks the high security and integrity of a mainframe system, as well as efficient device coordination capability.

Wireless LANs. A wireless LAN (WLAN) is a flexible data communications system implemented as an extension to, or alternative for, a wired LAN within a building, plant, or campus. Using electromagnetic waves, WLANs transmit and receive data through the air, minimizing the need for wired connections. See Chapter 5 and Technology Guide 4 for details.

DISTRIBUTED PROCESSING. **Distributed processing** (*distributed computing*) divides the processing work between two or more computers, using a network for connection. The participating computers can be all mainframes, all PCs, or as in most cases, a combination of the two types. They can be in one location or in several. **Cooperative processing** is a type of distributed processing in which two or more geographically dispersed computers are teamed together to execute a specific task.

Thanks to communication networks and especially the Internet and intranets, distributed computing has become the dominant architecture of most organizations. This architecture permits intra- and interorganizational cooperation in computing; accessibility to vast amounts of data, information, and knowledge; and high efficiency in the use of computing resources. The concept of distributed computing drives today's new architectures, including those that are Web-based. An example is provided in *IT at Work 2.1* (page 69).

The Impact of Distributed Computing on IT. Traditional applications such as word processing were modeled as standalone applications: They offered users the capabilities to perform tasks using data stored on the system. Most new software programs, in contrast, are based on the *distributed computing* model, where applications collaborate to provide services and expose functionality to each other. As a result, the primary role of many new software programs is to support information exchange (through Web servers and browsers), collaboration (e.g., through e-mail and instant messaging), and individual expression (through Weblogs and e-zines).

The most important configuration of distributed processing is the *client/server architecture*, where several computers share resources and are able to communicate with many other computers via networks. The Internet, intranets, and extranets are based on the client/server model of distributed computing.

Client/Server Architecture. **Client/server architecture** divides distributed computing units into two major categories, *clients* and *servers*, all of which are connected by a network of some sort. A **client** is a computer such as a PC attached to a network, which is used to access shared network resources. A **server** is a machine that is attached to this same network and provides clients with some services. Examples of servers are a *database server* that provides a large storage capacity, or a *communication server* that provides connection to another network, to commercial databases, or to a powerful processor. In some client/server systems there are additional computing units, referred to as *middleware* (see Technology Guide 2).

There are several models of client/server architecture. In the most traditional model, the mainframe acts as a database server, providing data for analysis done by the PC clients using spreadsheets, database management systems, and application software. For other models and more details see Technology Guide 2.

The Benefits of Client/Server Architecture. The purpose of client/server architecture is to maximize the use of computer resources. Client/server architecture provides a way for different computing devices to work together, each doing the job for which it is best suited. For example, large storage and heavy computation power is more cost-effective on a mainframe than on a PC. Common office computing, such as word processing, is more conveniently handled by a PC. The role of each machine need not be fixed. A PC, for example, can be a client in one task and a server in another. Another important element is *sharing*. The clients, which are usually inexpensive PCs, share more expensive devices, the servers.

Client/server architecture gives a company as many access points to data as there are PCs on the network. It also lets a company use more tools to process data and information. Client/server architecture has changed the way people work in organizations. For example, people are empowered to access databases at will.

Enterprisewide Computing. Client/server computing can be implemented in a small work area or in one department, where its main benefit would be the sharing of resources within that department. However, many users frequently

IT at Work 2.1
FLEXIBLE IT ARCHITECTURE AT CHASE MANHATTAN BANK

Chase Manhattan Bank and Chemical Bank merged in 1996, creating the then-largest bank in the United States. (It has since merged with J.P. Morgan, and now is J.P. Morgan Chase Company, *jpmorganchase.com.*) The unified Chase Manhattan Bank had to process 16 million checks daily across 700 locations in 58 countries. It also had to serve 25 million retail customers and thousands more institutional customers, with the customer base expected to grow by 6 to 10 percent a year. The problem was how to merge the different information systems of the two banks and create an IT architecture that would support the new bank's activities, including its future growth and additional planned acquisitions.

Previous mergers and acquisitions involving both Chase and Chemical had resulted in many problems in developing the IT architecture. "We needed to blueprint an architectural platform that provided operational excellence and customer privacy," says Dennis O'Leary, CEO and executive vice president of the new bank. "The platform also had to be functional and have the ability to integrate business at the retail, national, and global enterprise levels." One problem was the worldwide connectivity among more than 60,000 desktop computers, 14 large mainframes, 300 minicomputers, 1,100 T1 telecommunication lines, and more than 1,500 core applications.

The new architecture was constructed incorporating the Internet and intranets. (Specifically, the new architecture was based on the TCP/IP model, as described in Technology Guide 5.) An innovative three-layer system was designed. First was a global infrastructure; second were distribution networks that routed traffic among business units; and third were numerous access networks. This flexible structure allowed the addition of networks whenever needed. The global infrastructure was a network built on wide area networks (WANs), satellites, and related technologies. The architectural plan included several security devices, including *firewalls,* mainly in the distribution network layer. The access networks were the internal networks of the different business units, now reformulated as intranets. The system also had many client/server applications as well as mainframes. All the desktops were managed on Windows NT. The bank also uses data and voice communications services to streamline business operations.

In order to reduce costs associated with information technology, J.P. Morgan Chase is outsourcing part of its IT infrastructure to its outsourcing partners. For example, it signed a 5-year agreement with Aurum Technology in October 2002 to provide the bank with check-imaging services. It has also outsourced its data center to IBM Global Services (IGS) since February 2003. Under terms of the JPM Chase deal, 4,000 IT employees will join IGS, where they will continue to run the bank's data-center operations. IGS will assume ownership of the bank's systems, but the bank's IT management will still control the infrastructure deployed. This arrangement allows the bank to reduce its annual spending in IT, yet guarantees that the transition does not affect its daily operations.

In 1998/99 Chase Manhattan embarked on a major e-banking initiative, based on improved architecture. By 2003 the bank offered a wide range of online services such as Chase Online Plus for managing multiple accounts, extensive online shopping, online deep-discount investment services, an online service for small businesses, and a special online payroll system (called PowerPay). In addition, the bank offered services to large businesses and partners. Mobile banking was introduced in 2004. All of these initiatives are easily scalable, so accommodating more acquisitions and mergers, like the one with J.P. Morgan, creates no problems.

All of this massive networking has one goal: giving customers extensive real-time access to accounts and a view of their assets.

As a nice bonus, J.P. Morgan Chase Company won the Computerworld Honors Medal of Achievement 2004, presented annually for visionary use of information technology, for a financial-derivatives modeling system that enables the bank to increase competitiveness and market response.

Sources: Condensed from Girishankar (1997), Schwartz (2003), and Bills (2002); from miscellaneous Chase Manhattan and J.P. Morgan Chase press releases in 2002 and 2003; and from *https://secure.cwheroes.org* (2004).

For Further Exploration: What competitive advantage is provided by networks? What are the advantages of moving to e-business? What types of support systems discussed in this chapter may be appropriate here?

need access to data, applications, services, electronic mail, and real-time flows of data from different departments or in different databases. The solution is to deploy **enterprisewide computing,** a client/server architecture that connects data within an entire organization. This combination of client/servers and broad access to data forms a cohesive, flexible, and powerful computing environment. An example of such an architecture is provided in the FedExNet opening case. This architecture is the core of Web-based systems.

An enterprisewide client/server architecture provides total integration of departmental and corporate IS resources. It thereby allows for an additional class of applications that span the enterprise and benefit both corporate central management (providing controls) and end-user systems (providing empowerment). It also provides better control and security over data in a distributed environment. By implementing client/server computing as the architecture for enterprisewide information systems, organizations can maximize the value of information by increasing its availability.

Many new IT developments are based on the client/server concept. These include enterprise group support technologies such as Lotus Notes/Domino, Microsoft Exchange, and Microsoft Outlook (see Chapter 3) as well as Web-based systems and the Internet, intranets, and extranets. Client/server architecture is quickly becoming a part of, or is being replaced by, Web-based systems.

We need to discuss a couple more topics related to information architecture—legacy systems and peer-to-peer architecture—before we close this section and move to Web-based systems.

LEGACY SYSTEMS. **Legacy systems** are older, usually mature, information systems. Although legacy systems are normally less desirable than and less compatible with modern equivalents, they are still, in some cases, part of the backbone of the overall IT infrastructure within an organization. They are usually part of a pure mainframe system or a distributed system in which the mainframe plays the major role. Newer legacy systems may include one or more LANs and even early client/server implementations.

Legacy systems were developed from the late 1950s through the 1980s for general-purpose business use in medium- to large-size companies. They were the primary mechanism for high-volume processing applications. Legacy systems typically are housed in a secured and costly computer center, operated by IS professional staff rather than by end users. Much of their work is repetitive, mainly in transaction processing. Some legacy systems are very large, including hundreds or even thousands of remote terminals networked to the mainframe processor.

Because companies invested lots of money and expertise in building legacy systems, many companies try to reengineer these systems rather than to replace them (see Martin, 2002). Erlikh (2002) provides some guidelines on how to leverage legacy systems with Web-based architecture. An emerging way to integrate legacy systems with Web-based systems is by using Web Services.

PEER-TO-PEER ARCHITECTURE. In a client/server architecture some computers or devices serve others. Peer-to-peer architecture is a special client/server architecture that provides some additional new and useful functionalities.

Peer-to-peer (P2P) architecture is a type of network in which each client computer shares files or computer resources (like processing power) *directly* with others *but not through a central server*. This is in contrast with the traditional client/sever architecture in which some computers serve other computers via a central server. P2P sharing typically had been done over private networks, but recently it moved to the Internet. P2P architecture is really two different things—the direct sharing of digital files, and the sharing of different computers' processing power.

The main benefit of P2P is that it can expand enormously the universe of information accessible from a personal computer or a mobile device. Additionally, some proponents claim that a well-designed P2P architecture, especially when done on the Web, can offer better security, reliability, and availability of content than the client/server model, on which the Web is currently based (e.g., see Agre, 2003 and Kini, 2002). Other advantages over client/server are that there is no need for a network administrator, the network is fast and inexpensive to set up and maintain, and each PC can make a backup copy of its data to other PCs for improved security. The technology is more productive than client/server because it enables direct connections between computers, so there is no need to incur the cost of setting up and maintaining servers.

P2P architecture is the basis of *file sharing* over the Web and the basis on which companies such as Napster, Kazaa, and Gnutella operate (see Chapter 16). A scalable P2P architecture is also suitable for supporting networked virtual environments, such as multiplayer online role-playing games with hundreds or thousands of participants (Kawahara et al., 2004).

2.7 WEB-BASED SYSTEMS

The concept of client/server architecture has dominated IT architecture for several decades. But even the specially structured client/server applications that were considered revolutionary in the mid-1990s may soon become obsolete due to the rapid development of Web-based systems, as well as the introduction of new concepts such as utility computing and Web Services (presented in Section 2.8). Although most of these new technologies are based on the client/server concept, their implementation is considerably less expensive than that of many specially structured client/server systems. Furthermore, the conversion of existing systems to Web-based ones can be easy and fast, and the functionalities of the Web-based can be larger than those available in non-Web-based client/server systems. Therefore, as is shown throughout the book and especially in Chapters 3 and 4, the Internet, intranets, and sometimes extranets are becoming an indispensable part of most IT architectures. New Web-based architectures may replace old architectures, or may integrate legacy systems into their structure (see Erlikh, 2002).

Technically, the term **Web-based systems** refers to those applications or services that are resident on a server that is accessible using a Web browser and is therefore accessible from anywhere in the world via the Web. The only client-side software needed to access and execute Web-based applications is a Web browser environment, and of course the applications must conform to the Internet protocols. An example of such an application would be an online store. Additionally, two other very important features of Web-based functionalities are (1) that the generated content/data are updated in real time, and (2) that Web-based systems are universally accessible via the Web to users (dependent on defined user-access rights). The major communication networks of the Web environments are the Internet, intranets, and extranets.

The Internet

Sometimes called simply "the Net," the **Internet** is a worldwide system of computer networks—a network of networks, in which users at any one computer can get information from any other computer (and sometimes talk directly to users at other computers). Today, the Internet is a public, cooperative, and self-sustaining facility accessible to hundreds of millions of people worldwide.

Physically, the Internet uses a portion of the total resources of the currently existing public telecommunication networks. Technically, what distinguishes the Internet is its use of a set of protocols called TCP/IP (for Transmission Control Protocol/Internet Protocol). The Internet applications and technology are discussed in more detail in Technology Guide 5. Two adaptations of Internet technology, intranets and extranets, also make use of the TCP/IP protocol.

Intranets

The concept of an intranet is a natural progression in the marriage of the enterprise and the Internet. An **intranet** is the use of Web technologies to create a private network, usually within one enterprise. Although an intranet may be a single local area network (LAN) segment that uses the TCP/IP protocol, it is typically a complete LAN, or several intraconnected LANs. A security gateway such as a firewall is used to segregate the intranet from the Internet and to selectively allow access from outside the intranet. (See Online Minicase W2.1 for an example in academia.)

Intranets have a variety of uses, as we show throughout the book and especially in Chapters 3 and 4. They allow for the secure online distribution of many forms of internal company information. Intranets are used for workgroup activities and the distributed sharing of projects within the enterprise. Other uses include controlled access to company financial documents, use of knowledge management, research materials, online training, and other information that requires distribution within the enterprise. Intranets are usually combined with and accessed via a corporate portal.

CORPORATE PORTALS. *Corporate portals* are Web sites that provide the gateway to corporate information from a single point of access. They aggregate information from many files and present it to the user. The function of corporate portals is often described as "corecasting," since they support decisions central to particular goals of the enterprise. Corporate portals also help to personalize information for individual customers and for employees. For further discussion of corporate portals, see Chapter 3.

Extranets

Extranets connect several intranets via the Internet, by adding to the Internet a security mechanism (VPN; see Technology Guide 4) and possibly some functionalities. They form a larger virtual network that allows remote users (such as business partners or mobile employees) to securely connect over the Internet to the enterprise's main intranet. Typically, remote access software is used to authenticate and encrypt the data that pass between the remote user and the intranet. Extranets allow two or more enterprises to share information in a controlled fashion, and therefore they play a major role in the development of business-to-business electronic commerce (see Chapter 8 for details).

Web-Based E-Commerce Systems

Most e-commerce applications run on the Internet, intranet and extranets, using Web-based features. Therefore, Web-based systems are the engines of e-commerce. They enable business transactions to be conducted seamlessly 24 hours a day, seven days a week. A central property of the Web and e-commerce is that you can instantly reach millions of people, anywhere, any time. The major components of Web-based EC are electronic storefronts and malls (Chapter 5), electronic markets, mobile commerce, and the Enterprise Web.

ELECTRONIC MARKETS. Web-accessed electronic markets are rapidly emerging as a vehicle for conducting e-commerce. An **electronic market** is a network of interactions and relationships over which information, products, services, and payments are exchanged. When the marketplace is electronic, the business center is not a physical building but a Web-based location where business interactions occur. In electronic markets, the principal participants—transaction handlers, buyers, brokers, and sellers—not only are at different locations but seldom even know one another. The means of interconnection vary among parties and can change from event to event, even between the same parties. Electronic markets can reside in one company, where there is either one seller and many buyers, or one buyer and many sellers. These are referred to as *private marketplaces*. (See Online Minicase W2.2 for an example of a Web-based private marketplace.) Alternatively, electronic markets can have many buyers and many sellers. Then they are known as *public marketplaces* or *exchanges*.

Electronic Exchanges. A form of electronic markets is **electronic exchanges,** which are Web-based public marketplaces where many business buyers and many sellers interact dynamically. They were originally set as trading places for commodities. Since then a variety of exchanges have emerged for all kinds of products and services (see Chapter 4).

MOBILE COMPUTING AND MOBILE COMMERCE. **Mobile computing** is a computing paradigm designed for mobile employees and others who wish to have a real-time connection between a mobile device and other computing environment. **Mobile commerce** or **m-commerce** (see Chapter 5) is commerce (buying and selling of goods and services) in a *wireless environment,* such as through wireless devices like cellular telephones and PDAs. Also called "next-generation e-commerce," m-commerce enables users to access the Internet without needing to find a place to plug in. So-called *smart phones* offer Internet access, fax, e-mail, and phone capabilities all in one, paving the way for m-commerce to be accepted by an increasingly mobile workforce as well as millions of consumers. As *wireless computing*—content delivery over wireless devices—becomes faster, more secure, and scalable, there is wide speculation that m-commerce will surpass wireline e-commerce as the method of choice for digital commerce transactions (see *IT at Work 2.2,* page 74).

ENTERPRISE WEB. The **Enterprise Web** is an open environment for managing and delivering Web applications. It is the sum of a company's systems, information, and services that are available on the Web, working together as one entity. The Enterprise Web combines services from different vendors in a technology layer that spans rival platforms and business systems, creating a foundation for building applications at lower cost. This foundation consists of the services most commonly used by Web applications, including business integration,

IT at Work 2.2
WIRELESS PEPSI INCREASES PRODUCTIVITY

Pepsi Bottling Group (PBG), the largest manufacturer, seller, and distributor of Pepsi-Cola, has a mountainous job stocking and maintaining their Pepsi vending machines—including a huge amount of paperwork and frustrating searches for parts and equipment necessary to fix the machines. Any time a machine is out of stock or not functioning, the company loses revenue and profits. There are tens of thousands of machines to serve.

In 2002, the company began to equip its service technicians with hand-held devices, hooked into a wireless wide area network (WWAN). A mobile database application allows wireless communications around the country in real time. The database includes the repair parts inventory that is available on each service truck, so dispatchers know where and who to send for maintenance at any given moment. It also has a back-office system that maintains the overall inventory. In the near future the company will also be able to locate the whereabouts of each truck in real

time, using global positioning systems (GPSs). The aim is to make scheduling and dispatching more effective.

In the summer of 2002 only about 700 technicians used the wireless system, but already the company was saving $7 million per year. Each technician has been able to handle one more service call each day than previously. PBG provided the wireless capability to about 300 more technicians in 20 more locations in late 2002, and many more technicians will be similarly equipped later on.

Sources: Compiled from Rhey (2002) and from *pepsi.com* (accessed March 2003).

For Further Exploration: What are the capabilities of the hand-held devices? Relate the hand-held devices to the mobile database. The case deals with the maintenance issue. In what ways, if any, can wireless help with stocking issues? How is Pepsi's competitive advantage increased?

---

collaboration, content management, identity management, and search, which work together via integrating technologies such as middleware (see Technology Guide 2), component-based development (Technology Guide 6), and Web Services (Technology Guide 6).

The result is an environment that spans the entire enterprise, is open to all platforms for which adapters are available (or completely open with Web Services), and is available to all audiences. Enterprise Web environments are available from all major software vendors (e.g., Microsoft, IBM, SAP, Oracle, BEA Software, PeopleSoft, and more). For more on the Enterprise Web, see Online File W2.4 at the book's Web site.

2.8 NEW COMPUTING ENVIRONMENTS

During the last decade several new computing environments have emerged, some of which are based on Web technology. These systems are in the early stages of usage, and some are still under development, but they may reshape the IT field. In this section we provide several examples of these new initiatives. For a discussion of the issues that new networked computing systems need to address, see Online File W2.5. The following are representative initiatives of emerging computing environments.

Utility Computing   According to Bill Gates, **utility computing** is computing that is as available, reliable, and secure as electricity, water services, and telephony (Gates, public speech, January 2003). The vision behind utility computing is to have computing resources flow like electricity on demand from virtual utilities around the globe—always on and highly available, secure, efficiently metered, priced on a pay-as-you-use basis, dynamically scaled, self-healing, and easy to manage. In this setting, enterprises would plug in, turn on the computer, and (it is hoped) save lots of money. IBM (*On-Demand* project), HP, Microsoft, Oracle, Sun Microsystems, SAP, and other major software companies are backing the idea (see Cone, 2001).

If (or when) it becomes successful, utility computing will change the way software is sold, delivered, and used in the world. Some experts believe that all software will become a service and be sold as a utility one day (Cone, 2001). Preparing for this day, IBM is moving aggressively into the application services provider (ASP) area. The ASPs will operate the supply channels of utility computing (see Chapters 13 and 14).

An example of using utility computing is the case of the Mobil Travel Guide, which rates over 25,000 restaurants and hotels in the United States and publishes travel guides for various regions. To accommodate the ever-increasing traffic of Web servers that are looking for the ratings, the company is using IBM's *on-demand* hosting services. With this service, the company not only solved all capacity problems but also increased security—all at a 30 percent cost reduction compared to having its own servers (Greenmeier, 2003).

Despite the bright promises and the efforts of the major vendors, progress is slow. According to Margulius (2002), key pieces of the technology are still missing. For example, utility computing is hard to do in heterogeneous data centers. Also, the utility concept works better for some applications than for others. Furthermore, utility computing needs extra security when traveling online. Finally, distribution of software differs from distribution of utilities (see Wainewright, 2002).

In addition, other fundamental issues, such as granular accounting reporting, project cost allocation, and operational processes, are not yet in place (Kumar, 2003). According to a recent survey, 55.6 percent of the 310 respondents cited security and privacy as the number-one concern for failure to adopt utility computing (Dubie and Bernarz, 2004). Other concerns included vendor dependency and lock-in (50.8%), performance and reliability (45.9%), business data too critical to trust to outsiders (41.6%), and loss of control over key resources (38.3%).

These drawbacks need to be overcome by vendors in order to offer utility computing in a way that appeals to customers. However, it looks like utility computing will start inside companies, where the IT department can offer utility-style services to business units for internal use, and from there may eventually spread to the computing public (see Margulius, 2002).

SUBSCRIPTION COMPUTING. **Subscription (service) computing,** a variety of utility computing, puts the pieces of a computing platform together as services, rather than as a collection of separately purchased components (Bantz et al., 2002). Users can get programs, information, or storage over the Internet (usually protected by virtual private networks; see Technology Guide 4). The services provided by subscription computing and their value to users are summarized in Online File W2.6.

An interesting alternative to utility computing is grid computing.

Grid Computing   Conventional networks, including the Internet, are designed to provide communication among devices. The same networks can be used to support the concept of **grid computing,** in which the unused processing cycles of all computers in a given network can be harnessed to create powerful computing capabilities.

Grid computing coordinates the use of a large number of servers and storage, acting as one computer. (See Online File W2.7.) Thus problems of spikes in demand are solved without the cost of maintaining reserve capacity (see *oracle.com/grid*).

Grid computing is already in limited use, and many of the current grid applications are in areas that formerly would have required supercomputers. Mason (2004) urged that companies doing multi-hour-long processing jobs, making complex scientific and mathematical calculations, and processing large data sets for business intelligence would be good candidates for taking advantage of the faster processing speed of grid computing.

A well-known grid-computing project is the SETI (Search for Extraterrestrial Intelligence) @Home project. In this project, PC users worldwide donate unused processor cycle times to help the search for signs of extraterrestrial life by analyzing signals coming from outer space. The project relies on individual volunteers to allow the project to harness the unused processing power of the users' computers. This method saves the project both money and resources.

A major commercial application of grid computing in the consumer market is Sony's attempt to link online thousands of Sony video-game consoles. For details see Lohr (2003). An example of real-world use is provided in Minicase 2.

Pervasive Computing

As discussed in Chapter 1, with **pervasive computing** we envision a future in which computation becomes part of the environment. Computation will be embedded in *things,* not in computers. The use of pervasive computing does not just improve efficiency in work and living tasks but also enriches the quality of life through art, design, and entertainment (Benford et al., 2004). Relentless progress in semiconductor technology, low-power design, and wireless technology will make embedded computation less and less obtrusive. Pervasive computing is closely related with IT support systems, especially intelligent systems and DSS.

Web Services

Web Services are self-contained, self-describing business and consumer modular applications, delivered over the Internet, that users can select and combine through almost any device, ranging from personal computers to mobile phones. By using a set of shared protocols and standards, these applications permit disparate systems to "talk" with one another—that is, to share data and services—without requiring human beings to translate the conversation. The result promises to be on-the-fly and in-real-time links among the online processes of different systems and companies. These links could shrink corporate IT departments, foster new interactions among businesses, and create a more user-friendly Web for consumers. Web Services provide for inexpensive and rapid solutions for application integration, access to information, and application development. In September 2003, Microsoft and IBM demonstrated how Web Services technology can allow their software to interact, and they pledged to cooperate in establishing standards. Such cooperation is expected to help speed up the adoption of Web Services (*The Economist,* 2004). For more, see Technology Guide 6 and also the special section on Web Services in *Communications of the ACM* (October 2003).

SERVICE-ORIENTED ARCHITECTURE. A by-product of Web Services is *service-oriented architecture,* which defines how two computing entities interact in such a way as to enable one entity to perform a unit of work (service) on behalf of another entity. See Technology Guide 6 for details.

Commercial Efforts in New Computing Environments

Three software companies currently are developing major products in the emerging computer environments. All will incorporate utility computing, pervasive computing, and Web Services sometime in the future. Microsoft is launching a major research effort, known as *Microsoft.Net* (*www.microsoft.com/net/default.asp*). IBM is developing its WebSphere platform (*ibm.com/software/websphere*). And Sun Microsystems is building a new system architecture in its N1 Project. For more about these commercial ventures, see Online File W2.8.

Whether an organization uses mainframe-based legacy systems or cutting-edge Web-based ones, its information resources are extremely important organizational assets that need to be protected and managed. This topic is presented in Section 2.9.

2.9 MANAGING INFORMATION RESOURCES

A modern organization possesses many information resources. In addition to the infrastructures, numerous applications exist, and new ones are continuously being developed. Applications have enormous strategic value. Firms rely on them so heavily that, in some cases, when they are not working even for a short time, an organization cannot function. Furthermore, the acquisition, operation, security, and maintenance of these systems may cost a considerable amount of money. Therefore, it is essential to manage these information systems properly.

There are many types of information systems resources, and their components may be from multiple vendors and of different brands. The major categories are *hardware* (all types of computers, servers, and other devices), *software* (development tools, languages, and applications), *databases, networks* (local, wide, Internet, intranets and extranets, and supporting devices), *procedures, security facilities,* and *physical buildings*. The resources are scattered throughout the organization, and some of them change frequently. Therefore, it may be rather difficult to manage IS resources.

Which IT Resources Are Managed by Whom?

The responsibility for the management of information resources is divided between two organizational entities: the *information systems department (ISD),* which is a corporate entity, and the *end users,* who are scattered throughout the organization. This division of responsibility raises important questions such as: Which resources are managed by whom? What is the role of the ISD, its structure, and its place in the organization? What are the relationships between the ISD and the end users? Brief answers to these questions are provided in this section.

There is no standard menu for the division of responsibility for the development and maintenance of IS resources between the ISD and end users. In some organizations, the ISD manages most of these resources, regardless of where they are located and how they are used. In others, the ISD manages only a few. The division depends on many things: the size and nature of the organization, the amount and type of IT resources, the organization's attitudes toward computing, the attitudes of top management toward computing, the maturity level of the technology, the amount and nature of outsourced IT work, and even the country in which the company operates.

Generally speaking, the ISD is responsible for corporate-level and *shared resources,* while the end users are responsible for departmental resources. Sometimes the division between the ISD and the end users is based on other approaches. For example, the ISD may acquire or build systems and the end users operate and maintain them.

Because of interdependencies of information resources, it is important that the ISD and the end users work closely together and cooperate regardless of who is doing what. We discuss this below and also in Chapter 15.

The Role of the IS Department

As Table 2.4 shows, the role of the ISD is changing from purely technical to more managerial and strategic. As a result of this changing role, the position of the ISD within the organization is tending to be elevated from a unit reporting to a functional department (such as accounting) to a unit reporting to a senior vice president of administration or even to the CEO. In this new role, the ISD must be able to work closely with external organizations such as vendors, business partners, consultants, research institutions, and universities. In addition, the ISD and the end-user units must be close partners. The mechanisms that build the required cooperation are described in Chapter 15.

The role of the director of the ISD is also changing, from a technical manager to a senior executive, sometimes referred to as the **chief information officer (CIO),** or the *chief technology officer (CTO)*. Details are provided in Ball (2002), in *cio.com/summaries/roledescription,* and in Chapter 15.

IT ISSUES. In late 2004, the major issues in IT management were how to get guidance from top managers, how to reduce IT costs, how to align the IT architecture, how to move an organization's IT systems to fit the digital age, how to integrate applications, how to secure information systems, how much to outsource, how to measure the return on IT investment and justify it, and how to deal with emerging technologies such as Web Services. All of these issues are covered in many places throughout this book.

THE FUTURE OF THE ISD. The growing strategic importance of IT and the new architecture will change the role of the ISD. According to Popp et al. (2004), we are in a transition toward such a change. (For more, see Chapter 15, Figure 15.1.)

TABLE 2.4 The Changing Role of the Information Systems Department

Traditional Major IS Functions
Managing systems development and systems project management
Managing computer operations, including the computer center
Staffing, training, and developing IS skills
Providing technical services

Managing Security
Educating the non-IS managers about IT
Educating the IS staff about the business
Supporting end-user computing

New (Additional) Major IS Functions
Initiating and designing specific strategic information systems
Infrastructure planning, development, and control
Incorporating the Internet and electronic commerce into the business
Managing system integration including the Internet, intranets, and extranets
Partnering with the executive level that runs the business
Managing outsourcing
Proactively using business and technical knowledge to "seed" innovative ideas about IT
Creating business alliances with vendors and IS departments in other organizations
Providing new computing environments (e.g., wireless)

➡ **MANAGERIAL ISSUES**

1. ***The transition to e-business.*** Converting an organization to a networked-computing-based e-business may be a complicated process. The e-business requires a client/server architecture, an intranet, an Internet connection, and e-commerce policy and strategy, all in the face of many unknowns and risks. However, in many organizations this potentially painful conversion may be the only way to succeed or even to survive. When to do it, how to do it, what will be the role of the enabling information technologies, and what will be the impacts of such a conversion are major issues for organizations to consider.

2. ***From legacy systems to client/server to intranets, corporate portals, and Web-based systems.*** Related major issues are whether and when and how to move from the legacy systems to a Web-based client/server enterprisewide architecture. While the general trend is toward Web-based client/server, there have been several unsuccessful transformations and many unresolved issues regarding the implementation of these systems. The introduction of intranets seems to be much easier than that of other client/server applications. Yet, moving to any new architecture requires new infrastructure and a decision about what to do with the legacy systems, which may have a considerable impact on people, quality of work, and budget (see Minicase 2). A major aspect is the introduction of wireless infrastructure. These important issues are discussed in detail in Chapters 8 and 14 and in Technology Guide 6.

   It should be noted that many companies need high-speed computing of high-volume data. Here the client/server concept may not be effective. In such cases, management should consider transformation of the legacy systems to new types of mainframes that use innovations that make the systems smaller and cheaper. Other options such as grid computing are available.

3. ***How to deal with the outsourcing and utility computing trends.*** As opportunities for outsourcing (e.g., ASPs) are becoming cheaper, available, and viable, the concept becomes more attractive. In the not-so-distant future, we will see outsourcing in the form of utility computing. How much to outsource is a major managerial issue (see Chapters 13 and 14). Another issue is the offshore outsourcing to countries such as India and China.

4. ***How much infrastructure?*** Justifying information system applications is not an easy job due to the intangible benefits and the rapid changes in technologies that often make systems obsolete. Justifying infrastructure is even more difficult since many users and applications share the infrastructure that will be used for several years in the future. This makes it almost impossible to quantify the benefits. Basic architecture is a necessity, but there are some options. Various justification methodologies are presented in Chapter 13.

5. ***The roles of the ISD and end users.*** The role of the ISD can be extremely important, yet top management frequently mistreats it. By constraining the ISD to technical duties, top management may jeopardize an organization's entire future. However, it is not economically feasible for the ISD to develop and manage all IT applications in an organization. End users play an important role in IT development and management. The end users know best what their information needs are and to what degree they are fulfilled. Properly managed end-user computing is essential for the betterment of all organizations (see Chapter 14).

6. *Ethical issues.* Systems developed by the ISD and maintained by end users may introduce some ethical issues. The ISD's major objective should be to build efficient and effective systems. But, such systems may invade the privacy of the users or create advantages for certain individuals at the expense of others. See Ethics in IT Management, including the Ethics Primer (Online File W1.4), and Chapter 16 for details.

KEY TERMS

Application program *51*

Business architecture *66*

Chief information officer (CIO) *78*

Client *68*

Client/server architecture *68*

Cooperative processing *67*

Data item *52*

Data workers *63*

Database *52*

Distributed processing (computing) *67*

Electronic exchanges *73*

Electronic markets *73*

End-user computing *56*

Enterprise Web *73*

Enterprisewide computing *70*

Extranets *72*

Functional MIS *59*

Grid computing *75*

Information *52*

Information infrastructure *66*

Information system (IS) *51*

Information technology architecture *66*

Internet *72*

Intranet *72*

Knowledge *52*

Knowledge workers *63*

Legacy system *70*

Mobile commerce (m-commerce) *73*

Mobile computing *73*

Peer-to-peer (P2P) architecture *70*

Pervasive computing *76*

Server *68*

Smart terminal *67*

Subscription computing *75*

Supply chain *63*

Transaction processing system (TPS) *58*

Utility computing *74*

Web-based systems *71*

Web Services *76*

CHAPTER HIGHLIGHTS (Numbers Refer to Learning Objectives)

① Information systems can be organized according to organizational hierarchy (e.g., departmental, enterprisewide, and interorganizational) or by the nature of supported task (e.g., operational, managerial, and strategic).

① Interorganizational information systems (IOSs) connect two or more organizations and play a major role in e-business.

② The transaction processing system (TPS) covers the core repetitive organizational transactions such as purchasing, billing, or payroll.

② The data collected in a TPS are used to build other support systems.

② The major functional information systems in an organization are accounting, finance, manufacturing (operations), human resources, and marketing.

②, ③ The term *management information system (MIS)* refers to the department that manages information systems in organizations. The acronym MIS is also used more generally to describe the field of IT.

③ The main IT support systems are TPS, MIS, office automation systems, decision support systems, executive support systems, group support systems, knowledge management systems, enterprise information systems, expert systems, and artificial neural networks. (See Online File W2.1.)

③ Managerial activities and decisions can be classified as operational, managerial (tactical), and strategic.

④ Two of the major IT-supported managerial activities are (1) improving supply chain operations and (2) the introduction of a variety of customer relationship management (CRM) activities. IT is a major enabler of both.

⑤ Information architecture provides the conceptual foundation for building the information infrastructure and specific applications. It maps the information requirements as they relate to information resources.

5 There are three major configurations of information architecture: the mainframe environment, the PC environment, and the distributed (networked) environment. An emerging architecture is peer-to-peer.

5 The information infrastructure refers to the shared information resources (such as corporate networks, databases) and their linkages, operation, maintenance, and management. These support an array of applications.

6 In client/server architecture, several PCs (the clients) are networked among themselves and are connected to databases, telecommunications, and other devices (the servers) that provide services to the client computers.

6 An enterprisewide information system is a system that provides computing capabilities to all of the organization's employees. It also provides accessibility to any data or information needed by any employee at any location.

6 Legacy systems are typically older systems in which the mainframe is at the core of the system.

7 Web-based systems refer to those applications or services that reside on a server that is accessible using a Web browser and work with Internet protocols. Examples are e-procurement, corporate portals, electronic markets and exchanges, and mobile commerce.

8 There is a trend for renting application software as needed rather buying it. This way, there is no need to build systems or own software. This approach, called *utility computing,* is similar to buying water or electricity when needed.

8 Wireless computing is becoming a major computing environment.

9 Information resources are extremely important, and they must be managed properly by both the ISD and end users. In general, the ISD manages shared enterprise information resources such as networks, while end users are responsible for departmental information resources, such as PCs and functional applications.

9 The role of the ISD is becoming more managerial, and its importance is rapidly increasing.

VIRTUAL COMPANY ASSIGNMENT

Information Architecture at The Wireless Café
Go to The Wireless Café's link on the Student Web Site. There you will be asked to study the restaurant's existing information technologies and document its information architecture.

More Resources
More resources and study tools are located on the Student Web Site. You'll find additional chapter materials and useful Web links. In addition, self-quizzes that provide individualized feedback are available for each chapter.

Instructions for accessing The Wireless Café on the Student Web Site

1. Go to
   wiley.com/college/turban
2. Select Turban/Leidner/ McLean/Wetherbe's *Information Technology for Management,* Fifth Edition.
3. Click on Student Resources site, in the toolbar on the left.
4. Click on the link for Virtual Company Web Site
4. Click on Wireless Café.

QUESTIONS FOR REVIEW

1. Define data, information, and knowledge.
2. Describe a TPS.
3. What is an MIS?
4. Explain the role of the DSS.
5. How does a KMS work?
6. Describe operational, managerial, and strategic activities.
7. What information systems support the work of groups?
8. What is an enterprisewide system?
9. What is information architecture?
10. Define information infrastructure.
11. Describe the evolution of support systems over time.
12. What is a Web-based system?
13. Define the Internet, intranet, and extranet.
14. What is mobile commerce?
15. List the information resources that are usually managed by end users.
16. Distinguish between a mainframe and a distributed environment.
17. Define a legacy system.
18. What is a client/server system?
19. Define utility computing.
20. What/who are knowledge workers?
21. Define peer-to-peer architecture.
22. Define grid computing.
23. Define Web Services.

QUESTIONS FOR DISCUSSION

1. Discuss the logic of building information systems in accordance with the organizational hierarchical structure.
2. Distinguish between interorganizational information systems (IOS) and electronic markets.
3. Describe how business architecture, IT architecture, and information infrastructure are interrelated.
4. Explain how operational, managerial, and strategic activities are related to various IT support systems.
5. Relate the following concepts: client/server, distributed processing, and enterprisewide computing.
6. Discuss the capabilities of P2P architecture.
7. Web-based applications such as e-commerce and e-government exemplify the platform shift from client/server computing to Web-based computing.
   Discuss the advantages of a Web-based computing environment.
8. Is the Internet an infrastructure, architecture, or application program? Why? If none of the above, then what is it?
9. There is wide speculation that m-commerce will surpass wireline e-commerce (e-commerce that takes place over wired networks) as the method of choice for digital commerce transactions. What industries or application areas will be most affected by m-commerce?
10. Some speculate that utility computing will be the dominating option of the future. Do you agree? Discuss why or why not.
11. Compare and contrast grid computing and utility computing.

EXERCISES

1. Classify each of the following systems as one (or more) of the IT support systems:
   a. A student registration system in a university.
   b. A system that advises farmers about which fertilizers to use.
   c. A hospital patient-admission system.
   d. A system that provides a marketing manager with demand reports regarding the sales volume of specific products.
   e. A robotic system that paints cars in a factory.
2. Select two companies you are familiar with and find their mission statement and current goals (plans). Explain how these goals are related to operational, managerial, and strategic activities on a one-to-one basis. Then explain how information systems (by type) can support the activities (be specific).
3. Review the list of key IT management issues (see the subsection titled, "The Role of the IS Department," page 78).
   a. Present these issues to IT managers in a company you can access. (You may want to develop a questionnaire.)
   b. Have the managers vote on the importance of these items. Also ask them to add any items that are important to them but don't appear on the list. Report the results.
4. Review the following systems in this chapter and identify the support provided by IT:
   ● Chase Manhattan Bank (page 69)
   ● Maybelline (Minicase 1)
   ● J.P. Morgan (Minicase 2)
   ● Bomb detection by the FAA (see Online File W2.1)
   ● Best Buy online (see Online File W2.3)

GROUP ASSIGNMENTS

1. Observe a checkout counter in a supermarket that uses a scanner. Find some material that describes how the scanned code is translated into the price that the customers pay.

   a. Identify the following components of the system: inputs, processes, and outputs.

   b. What kind of a system is the scanner (TPS, DSS, ESS, ES, etc.)? Why did you classify it as you did?

   c. Having the information electronically in the system may provide opportunities for additional managerial uses of that information. Identify such uses.

   d. Checkout systems are now being replaced by self-service checkout kiosks and scanners. Compare the two.

2. Divide the class into teams. Each team will select a small business to start (a restaurant, dry cleaning business, small travel agency, etc.). Assume the business wants to become an e-business. Each team will plan the architecture for the business's information systems, possibly in consultation with Microsoft or another vendor. Make a class presentation.

INTERNET EXERCISES

1. Enter the site of Federal Express (*fedex.com*) and find the current information systems used by the company or offered to FedEx's customers. Explain how the systems' innovations contribute to the success of FedEx.

2. Surf the Internet for information about airport security regarding bomb- and weapon-detecting devices. Examine the available products, and comment on the IT techniques used.

3. Enter the Web site of Hershey Foods (*hersheys.com*). Examine the information about the company and its products and markets. Explain how an intranet can help such a company compete in the global market.

4. Investigate the status of utility computing by visiting *infoworld.com/forums/utility, aspnews.com* (discussion forum), *google.com, ibm.com, oracle.com,* and *cio.com.* Prepare a report that will highlight the progress today and the current inhibitors.

5. Enter *argus-acia.com* and learn about new developments in the field of information architecture. Also, view the tutorials at *hotwired.com/webmonkey* on this topic. Summarize major new trends.

6. Investigate the status of pervasive computing by looking at *ibm.com/software/pervasive, computer.org/pervasive,* and *percom.org.* Prepare a report.

7. Enter *cio.com* and find recent information on the changing role of the CIO and the ISD. Prepare a report.

8. Enter *oracle.com* and *mysap.com* and identify material related to supply chain and enterprisewide systems. Prepare a report.

9. Enter *oracle.com* and read about grid computing. View the demo. Write a summary on business applications of grid computing.

Minicase 1
E-Commerce Supports Field Employees at Maybelline

The Business Problem

Maybelline is a leader in color cosmetics products (eye shadow, mascara, etc.), selling them in more than 70 countries worldwide (*maybelline.com*). The company uses hundreds of salespeople (field merchandising representatives, or "reps"), who visit drugstores, discount stores, supermarkets, and cosmetics specialty stores, in an attempt to close deals. This method of selling has proved to be fairly effective, and it is used by hundreds of other manufacturers such as Kodak, Nabisco, and Procter & Gamble. Sales managers from any company need to know, as quickly as

possible, when a deal is closed or if there is any problem with the customer.

Information technology has been used extensively to support sales reps and their managers. Until 2000, Maybelline, as well as many other large consumer product manufacturers, equipped reps with an interactive voice response (IVR) system, by means of which they were to enter, every evening, information about their daily activities. This solution required that the reps collect data with paper-based surveys completed for every store they visited each day. For example, the reps noted how each product was displayed, how much stock was available, how items were promoted, etc. In addition to the company's products the reps surveyed the competitors' products as well. In the evening, the reps translated the data collected into answers to the voice response system, which asked them routine questions. The reps answered by pressing the appropriate telephone keys.

The IVR system was not the perfect way to transmit sales data. For one thing, the IVR system consolidated information, delivering it to top management as a hard copy. Also, unfortunately, these reports sometimes reached top management days or weeks too late, missing important changes in trends and the opportunities to act on them in time. Frequently, the reps themselves were late in reporting, thus further delaying the needed information.

Even if the reps did report on time, information was inflexible, since all reports were menu-driven. With the voice system the reps answered only the specific questions that applied to a situation. To do so, they had to wade through over 50 questions, skipping the irrelevant ones. This was a waste of time. In addition, some of the material that needed to be reported had no matching menu questions. Considered a success in the 1990s, the system was unable to meet the needs of the twenty-first century. It was cumbersome to set up and operate and was also prone to input errors.

The E-Business Solution

Maybelline replaced the IVR system by equipping its reps with a mobile system, called Merchandising Sales Portfolio (MSP), from Thinque Corp. (*thinque.com*, now part of *meicpg.com*). It runs on hand-held, pen-based PDAs (personal digital assistants), which have hand-writing recognition capability (from NEC), powered by Microsoft's CE operating system. The system enables reps to enter their information by hand-writing their reports directly at the clients' sites. From the hand-held device, data can be uploaded to a Microsoft SQL Server database at headquarters every evening. A secured Internet connection links the PDA to the corporate intranet (a synchronization process). The new system also enables district managers to electronically send daily schedules and other important information to each rep.

The system also replaced some of the functions of the EDI (electronic data interchange) system, the pride of the 1990s. For example, the reps' reports include inventory-scanned data from retail stores. These are processed quickly by an *order management system*, and passed whenever needed to the shipping department for inventory replenishment.

In addition to routine information, the new system is used for decision support. It is not enough to speed information along the supply chain; managers need to know

the *reasons why* certain products are selling well, or not so well, in every location. They need to know what the conditions are at retail stores affecting the sales of each product, and they need to know it in a timely manner. The new system offers those capabilities.

The Results

The system provided managers at Maybelline headquarters with an interactive link with the mobile field force. Corporate planners and decision makers can now respond much more quickly to situations that need attention. The solution is helping the company forge stronger ties with its retailers, and it considerably reduces the amount of after-hours time that the reps spend on data transfer to headquarters (from 30–50 minutes per day to seconds).

The new system also performs market analysis that enables managers to optimize merchandising and customer service efforts. It also enables Maybelline to use a more sophisticated interactive voice response unit—to capture data for special situations. Moreover, it provides browser-based reporting tools that enable managers, regardless of where they are, to view retail information within hours of its capture. Using the error-checking and validation feature in the MSP system, reps make significantly fewer data entry errors.

Finally, the quality of life of Maybelline reps has been greatly improved. Not only do they save 30 to 40 minutes per day, but also their stress level has been significantly reduced. As a result, employee turnover has declined appreciably, saving money for the company.

Source: Compiled from "Industry Solutions—Maybelline," at *thinque.com* (accessed May 15, 2002).

Questions for Minicase 1

1. IVR systems are still popular. What advantages do they have over even older systems in which the reps mailed or faxed reports?

2. Summarize the advantages of the new system over the IVR one.

3. Explain why Maybelline's new reporting system is an e-commerce application.

4. The existing technology enables transmission of data any time an employee can access the Internet with a wireline. Technically, the system can be enhanced so that the data can be sent *wirelessly* from any location as soon as they are entered. Would you recommend a wireless system to Maybelline? Why or why not?

5. According to In-Stat Group (*instat.com*), voice portals compete directly with IVRs. Examine the capabilities of such portals (see *tellme.com* and *bevocal.com*), and discuss their possible application at Maybelline.

Minicase 2
Grid Computing at J.P. Morgan

J.P. Morgan Chase Investment Bank (*jpmorgan.com*) provides investment banking and commercial banking products and services. It also advises on corporate strategy and structure, risk management, and raising of capital. J.P. Morgan Chase, the largest financial institution in the United States, employs 11,000 IT professionals.

The company faced a problem of ever-increasing demand for computing resources. There were 2,000 PCs that run on 50 midsize servers. Some were overutilized, whereas others were underutilized, creating staffing inefficiencies and poor service to the company's securities traders. The PCs were designed to help traders assess and manage financial exposures, such as interest rates, equities, foreign exchange, and credit derivatives.

In 2003, the company began use of grid computing, at a cost of $4.5 million. The system saved $1 million in computing costs in 2003 and $5 million in 2004. The savings come from lower costs for hardware, reduced development and operation costs, and a more effective system management. For example, when an isolated server fails, the system can still provide the real-time information required by the traders.

The system also provides scalability: New applications are now being built in 10 weeks instead of 20. Also, any increase in new business volume is handled quickly and efficiently. The system was considered the world's largest-known grid computing commercial application in 2004.

The introduction of grid computing was an impressive project because of the huge mindshift away from the old system. It was necessary to make an organizational shift, overcoming skepticism from internal users who for years had run applications on their own dedicated servers. It was necessary to take away the perceived flexibility that the business units thought they had, and there was lots of resistance to the change (see Chapter 16). A major success factor was the emphasis on problem-solving rather than on pushing a new technology.

Sources: Compiled from Hamblen (2004) and *jpmorgan.com* (accessed May 8, 2004).

Questions for Minicase 2

1. List the business problems, and explain how they were solved by grid computing.

2. Which of the support systems described in this chapter may support the work of the internal securities traders?

3. Would you advise the company to use utility computing instead of grid computing? Why, or why not?

4. Classify the information systems for the professional traders according to the chapter's classification.

5. In your opinion, is this system related to the Internet, to an extranet, to an intranet? (Tip: The system is for internal users only).

REFERENCES

Agre, P. E., "P2P and the Promise of Internet Equality," *Communications of the ACM*, 46(2), February 2003.

Ahmad, I., "Network Computers: The Changing Face of Computing," *IEEE Concurrency*, 8(4), October–December 2000.

Amato-McCoy, D. M., "Thin-Client Technology Trims IT Maintenance Costs, Adds Flexibility and Growth," *Stores*, November 2002.

Ball, L. D., "CIO on Center Stage: 9/11 Changes Everything," *Journal of Information Systems Management*, Spring 2002.

Bantz, D. F., et al., "The Emerging Model of Subscription Computing," *IT Pro*, 4(4), July–August 2002.

Benford, S., et al., "Guest Editors' Introduction: Art, Design, and Entertainment in Pervasive Environments," *Pervasive Computing, IEEE*, 3(1), January–March 2004, pp. 12–13.

Best Buy, "Making the Best Buying Decisions," e-business case study, *http://www-3.ibm.com/e-business/doc/content/casestudy/43886.html* (accessed March 18, 2003).

Bills, S., "In Brief: Aurum to Do Imaging for JPM Chase Unit," *American Banker*, 167(210), October 22, 2002.

Broadbent, M., and P. Weill, "Management by Maxim: How Business IT Managers Can Create IT Infrastructures," *Sloan Management Review*, Spring 1997.

"Business: The Next Big Thing?: The Future of Computing," *The Economist*, 370(8358) January 17, 2004, p. 57.

Coffee, P., "Grid Computing in the Enterprise," *eWeek*, February 9, 2004.

Conley, W. L. et al., "Building an E-Business at FedEx Corporation," *Society for Information Management Annual Awards Paper Competition*, 2000, *simnet.org/library/doc/2ndplace.doc*.

Cone, E., "New World Order: Software Giants Vie to Control the Supernet," *Interactive Week*, June 25, 2001.

Cortese, A., "The Power of Optimal Pricing," *Business 2.0*, September 2002.

Dubie, D., and A. Bednarz, "Utility Computing Services Catching On," *Network World,* 21(15), April 12, 2004, p. 10.

Erlikh, L., "Leveraging Legacy Systems in Modern Architecture," *Journal of Information Technology Cases and Applications,* July–September 2002.

FedEx.com (accessed February 2003).

Gens, F., "IDC Predictions 2004: New IT Growth Wave, New Game Plan," IDC.com, *www.idc.com/getdoc.jsp?containerId=30499_S-004&element* (Accessed December 2003).

Girishankar, S., "Modular Net Eases Merger," *techweb.com/se/directlink.cgi, CWK19970421S0005,* April 1997.

Greenemeier, L., "IBM Expands On-Demand Services," *InformationWeek,* September 30, 2003.

Hamblen, M., "J.P. Morgan Harnesses Power with Grid Computing System," *ComputerWorld,* March 15, 2004.

Hewlett-Packard Company, "IT Consolidation: Journey to an Adaptive Enterprise—An Overview," *hp.com,* February 1, 2004.

https://secure.cwheroes.org/briefingroom_2004/detail.asp?id=20044909 (accessed April 2004).

"Industry Solutions—Maybelline," *Thinque.com,* May 15, 2002.

Kawahara, Y., et al., "A Peer-to-Peer Message Exchange Scheme for Large-Scale Networked Virtual," *Telecommunications Systems,* 25(3–4), March–April 2004, p. 353.

Kini, R. B., "Peer-to-Peer Technology: A Technology Reborn," *Information Systems Management,* Summer 2002.

Koontz, C., "Develop a Solid Architecture," *e-Business Advisor,* January 2000.

Kumar, R., "Do Not Expect Utility Computing to Deliver Until 2006; Beware Utility Promises," *Computer Weekly,* October 28, 2003.

Lohr, S., "Sony to Supercharge Online Gaming," *International Herald Tribune,* February 28, 2003.

Margulius, D., "The Realities of Utility Computing," *Infoworld.com,* April 15, 2002.

Marson, B., "Grid Computing: More Questions than Answers," CIO.com, *www2.cio.com/analyst/report2153.html* (accessed April 2004).

Martin, C. F., "Legacy Value Engineering," *Information Technology: The Executive's Journal,* 2002.

Mol, M. J., and Koppius O. R., "Information Technology and the Internationalization of the Firm," *Journal of Global Information Management,* October–December 2002.

O'Donovan, B., and D. Roode, "A Framework for Understanding the Emerging Discipline of Information Systems," *Information Technology and People,* 15(1), 2002.

Pepsi.com (accessed March 2003).

Popp, R., et al., "Countering Terrorism through Information Technology," *Communications of the ACM,* March 2004.

Reid, D., and N. Sanders, *Operations Management.* New York: John Wiley & Sons, 2002.

Rhey, E., "Pepsi Refreshes, Wirelessly," *PC,* September 17, 2002, pp. 4–5.

Santosus, M., "Wire Education," *CIO Web Bulletin,* October 1998.

Scannell, E., and T. Sullivan, "Utility Computing on Tap for 2004," *Info World,* 26(1) January 5, 2004, p. 16.

Schwartz, J., "Banking on Outsourcing: Jumbo Deals with Outsourcers Are Enabling Major Banks to Save on Costs," *VARbusiness,* February 24, 2003.

Turban, E. et al., *Electronic Commerce 2006.* Upper Saddle River, NJ: Prentice Hall, 2006.

Wainewright, P., "The Power of Utility Computing," *ASPnews.com,* September 30, 2002.

Weill, P., and M. R. Vitale, *Place to Space: Migrating to eBusiness Models.* Boston: Harvard Business Press, 2001.

Whipple, L. C., "Master the Art of Translation," *e-Business Advisor,* March 2001.

Zhang, W., et al., "Multisite Task Scheduling on Distributed Computing Grid," *Grid and Cooperative Computing: Second International Workshop,* GCC 2003, Shanghai, China, December 7–10, 2003. Revised Papers, Part II, *Lecture Notes in Computer Science,* 3033, Springer-Verlag: Heidelberg, 2004, pp. 57–64.

APPENDIX 2A

BUILD-TO-ORDER PRODUCTION

The concept of build-to-order means that you start to make a product (service) only *after* an order for it is placed. This concept is as old as commerce itself, and was the only method of production until the Industrial Revolution began. According to this concept, if you need a pair of shoes, you go to a shoemaker who takes the measurement. You negotiate quality, design, and price, and you make a down payment. The shoemaker buys the materials and makes a customized product for you. Customized products were expensive, and it took a long time to finish them. This changed with the coming of the Industrial Revolution.

The Industrial Revolution started with the concept of dividing work into small parts. Such *division of labor* makes the work simpler, requiring less training for employees. It also allows for *specialization*. Different employees become experts in executing certain tasks. Because the work segments are simpler, it is easier to *automate* them. All this reduces the prices to consumers, and demand increases. So the concept of *build-to-market* developed. To build to market, it was necessary to design standard products, produce them, store them, and then sell them. The creation of standard products by automation drove prices down still further and demand accelerated. To meet the ever-increasing demand, the solution of mass production was created.

According to the concept of *mass production,* a manufacturer produces large amounts of standard products at a very low cost, and then "pushes" (markets) them to consumers. With increased competition and the desire to sell in remote markets, it was necessary to create special marketing organizations to do the sales. This new model also required the creation of large factories, and finance, accounting, personnel, and other departments to keep track of the many new and specialized business activities. In mass production, the workers do not know who the customers are, and frequently do not care about customers' needs or product quality. But the products are inexpensive, and their price fueled demand, so the concept became a dominant one. Mass production also required inventory systems at various places in the supply chain, which were based on forecasted demand. If the forecasted demand was wrong, the inventories were incorrect: Either the inventories were insufficient to meet demand, or there was too much inventory at hand.

As society became more affluent, the demand for customized products, especially cars, increased. To make sales, manufacturers had to meet this kind of demand. As long as the demand for customized product was small, there was no problem of meeting it. In purchasing a new car, for example, customers were asked to pay a premium and wait for a long time, and they were willing to do so. Slowly, the demand for customized products and services increased. In the 1970s, Burger King introduced the concept of "having it your way," and manufacturers began looking for solutions for providing customized products in large quantities. This idea is the essence of *mass customization.* Such solutions were usually enhanced by some kind of information technologies (Pine and Gilmore, 1999). Later, Dell Computer introduced the idea of customized PCs. This customization strategy was so successful that many other industries also wanted to try mass customization. However, they found that it is not so easy to do so (Zipkin, 2001 and Agrawal et al., 2001).

Using e-commerce can facilitate the use of customization and even the use of mass customization (Holweg and Pil, 2001). To understand this strategy, let's look first at a comparison of mass production, also known as a *push system,* with mass customization, also known as a *pull system,* as shown in Figure 2A.1.

One important area in the supply chain is ordering. Using EC a customer can self-configure the desired product online. The order is received in seconds, and once it is verified and payment arranged, the order is sent electronically to the production floor. This saves processing time and money. For complex products, customers may collaborate in real time with the manufacturer's designers, as is done at Cisco Systems. Again, time and money are saved, and errors are reduced due to better communication and collaboration.

Other contributions of EC to mass customization are the following: The customers' needs are

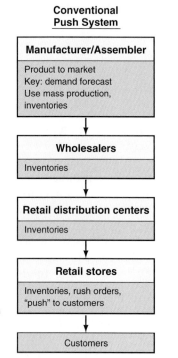
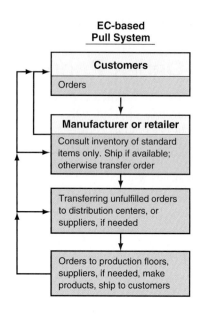

FIGURE 2A.1 Comparison of a push-based supply chain and a pull-based supply chain.

visible to all partners in the order-fulfillment chain (fewer delays, faster response time); inventories are reduced due to rapid communication; and digitizable products and services can be delivered electronically, at almost no additional cost.

Another key area in mass customization is understanding what the customers want, and EC is also very helpful here (see Chapter 4 and Holweg and Pil, 2001). E-commerce can help in expediting the production changeover from one item to another. Also, since most mass production is based on assembly of standard components, EC can help make the production configuration in minutes, including the identification of the needed components and their

location. Furthermore, a production schedule can be automatically generated, detailing deployment of all needed resources, including money. This is why many industries, and particularly the auto manufacturers, are planning to move to build-to-order using EC. As a result of this change in production methods, they are expecting huge cost reductions, shorter order-to-delivery time, and lower inventory costs. (See Exhibit 1 in Agrawal et al., 2001, and Holweg and Pil, 2001.)

Mass customization on a large scale is not easy to attain (Zipkin, 2001 and Agrawal et al., 2001), but if properly performed, it may become the dominant model in many industries.

References for Appendix 2A

Agrawal, M. T. V. et al., "The False Promise of Mass Customization," *McKinsey Quarterly,* No. 3, 2001.

Holweg, M., and F. Pil, "Successful Build-to-Order Strategies Start with the Customer," *MIT Sloan Management Journal,* 43(1), Fall 2001, pp. 74–83.

Pine, B. J., and J. Gilmore, "The Four Faces of Mass Customization," *Harvard Business Review,* January–February 1997.

Zipkin, P., "The Limits of Mass Customization," *MIT Sloan Management Review,* Spring 2001.

PART II
The Web Revolution

▶ 3. Network Computing: Discovery, Communication, and Collaboration
4. E-Business and E-Commerce
5. Mobile, Wireless, and Pervasive Computing

CHAPTER

3

Network Computing: Discovery, Communication, and Collaboration

3.1 Network Computing—An Overview

3.2 Discovery

3.3 Communication

3.4 Collaboration

3.5 Collaboration-Enabling Tools: From Workflow to Groupware

3.6 E-Learning and Virtual Work

3.7 Some Ethical and Integration Issues

Minicases:
1. General Motors
2. Cisco

LEARNING OBJECTIVES

After studying this chapter, you will be able to:

❶ Understand the concepts of the Internet and the Web, their importance, and their capabilities.

❷ Understand the role of intranets, extranets, and corporate portals for organizations.

❸ Identify the various ways in which communication is executed over the Internet.

❹ Demonstrate how people collaborate over the Internet, intranets, and extranets using various supporting tools, including voice technology and teleconferencing.

❺ Describe groupware capabilities.

❻ Describe and analyze the role of e-learning and distance learning.

❼ Analyze telecommuting (teleworking) as a technosocial phenomenon.

❽ Consider ethical and integration issues related to the use of network computing.

SAFEWAY COLLABORATES IN DESIGNING STORES

➡ THE PROBLEM

Safeway PLC, a large food retailer in the UK (now a subsidiary of Morrison Supermarkets), builds about 10 new stores every year and renovates over 100. Being in stiff competition with other supermarkets, the company must manage this construction carefully so it meets the budget and time plans. This is not an easy job, given that hundreds of the company's employees must collaborate with hundreds of vendors throughout the life-cycle of a building, including design, construction, and ongoing facility management.

In addition to stores, Safeway frequently builds public structures, such as a school or bridge, which it donates to a community in exchange for a parcel of land for a store. The diversity of structures (there are four types of stores plus community structures) adds to the difficulties in managing the construction projects. Previously, communications were handled primarily through the postal system and e-mail, an often slow and inefficient process, especially with stores scattered throughout England, Scotland, Wales, and Northern Ireland.

➡ THE SOLUTION

By using an online project collaboration service, called Buzzsaw (from Autodesk.com), Safeway can store and share project information in a secure location that can be accessed any time and anywhere (using a Web-based extranet). This online collaboration enhances communication between internal departments and outside partners (such as developers, planning consultants, architects, structural and mechanical engineers, builders, repair staff, and building enforcement authorities). Key users can view drawings online, mock up drawings, make changes, and post revisions for other staff to view, all in real time (e.g., using screen-sharing capability). Buzzsaw also automatically tracks and logs what's been changed. Even banks with ATMs located in the stores can use Buzzsaw, since their input is needed for designers.

➡ THE RESULTS

The communication lag time plummeted from 2 to 3 weeks to 5 to 10 minutes. Another benefit is the reduction in travel time and costs of architects and structural and mechanical engineers, who can stay in their offices collaborating electronically (10–15% reduction). Printing costs of architectural drawings have been reduced by 30 percent. Also, project turnaround time is shorter. Store modifications have been reduced from 6 months to as little as 3 months. Design changes are now transmitted in 5 to 10 minutes instead of 1 to 2 days. Also, because the design process is rapid, designs now include cutting-edge features; all supermarkets want the latest design. Buzzsaw is helping Safeway to be *first to market* with innovative new formats such as a design for Internet cafés and for certain store departments.

Collaboration is taken to a better, more integrated level. Users can monitor crucial information and the software, letting them know when decisions are required. Finally, Buzzsaw provides enhanced e-mail that helps users to prioritize the large number of messages.

Source: Compiled from Parks (2004).

 LESSONS LEARNED FROM THIS CASE

The Safeway opening case demonstrates the use of online communication and collaboration, via network computing, within a company and with its business partners. The system provides many capabilities, including the discovery of information and data. It has also resulted in significant improvements to the company and its business partners.

In this chapter we learn about the major capabilities of network computing to support discovery of information, communication, and collaboration activities in organizations. We also learn how organizations are exploiting network computing for e-learning and telecommuting.

3.1 NETWORK COMPUTING—AN OVERVIEW

An Overview of the Internet and the Web

Technology Guides are located at the book's Web site.

Many aspects of the way we work and live in the twenty-first century will be determined by the vast web of electronic networks, which was referred to generally as the information superhighway but now is usually called the Internet. As you know from previous chapters, the Internet is a *global network of computer networks*. It links the computing resources of businesses, government, and educational institutions using a common computer communication protocol, TCP/IP (described in Technology Guide 5). Because of its capabilities, the Internet (frequently referred to as "the Net") is rapidly becoming one of the most important information technologies today. It is clearly the most widely discussed IT topic of the new century.

Future versions of the Internet will allow even larger volume and a more rapid flow of information. Eventually we may see several information superhighways. It is probable that the original concept of a scientific-educational system will be separated from the commercial one. For example, in order to support advanced network applications and technologies, over 260 U.S. universities, working in partnership with industry and government, are working on a project named **Internet2** (*internet2.edu*). On Internet2, advanced next-generation applications such as remote diagnosis, digital libraries, distance education, online simulation, and virtual laboratories will enable people to collaborate and access information in ways not possible using today's Internet (Choi and Whinston, 2000). Another vision is that there will be several types of interrelated Internets, one for e-commerce, one for education, and so forth.

THE WORLD WIDE WEB. The **World Wide Web—the Web**—is the most widely used application on the Internet. Are the Internet and the World Wide

Web the same thing? Many people believe that the Web is synonymous with the Internet, but that is not the case. The Internet functions as the *transport mechanism,* and the Web (WWW, or W3) is an *application* that *uses* those transport functions. Other applications also run on the Internet, with e-mail being the most widely used.

The Web is a system with universally accepted standards for storing, retrieving, formatting, and displaying information via client/server architecture. The Web handles all types of digital information, including text, hypermedia, graphics, and sound. It uses graphical user interfaces, so it is very easy to use. See Technology Guide 5 for details.

THE EVOLUTION OF COMMERCIAL APPLICATIONS ON THE INTERNET. With the commercialization of the Internet in the early 1990s, we have seen an explosion of commercial applications. These applications evolve through four major phases: *presence, e-commerce, collaboration,* and *integration.* The major characteristics of each phase as they evolved over time are illustrated in Figure 3.1. Specific applications in each phase are demonstrated throughout this book.

Another way to look at the applications of the Internet is via the generic categories that they support, as presented next.

INTERNET APPLICATION CATEGORIES. The Internet supports applications in the following major categories:

- *Discovery.* Discovery involves browsing and information retrieval. As shown in the opening case, it provides customers the ability to view information in databases, download it, and/or process it. Discovery is automated by software agents since the amount of information on the Internet and

TIME →

	Presence	E-commerce	Collaboration and Interaction	Integration and Services
Emphasis	Eyeballs (human review)	Revue, expansion	profit	Capabilities, services
Type of transaction	No transaction	B2C, C2C, C2B, G2C, e-CRM	B2B, B2E, supply chain, c-commerce, G2B	Portals, e-learning, m-commerce, L-commerce
Nature	Publish information	Process transaction	Collaborate	Integrate, provide services
Target	Pages	Process transaction	Digital systems	Digital environments
Concentrate on	Web sites	Web-enabled existing systems, dot-coms	Business transformation and consolidation	Internal and external integration
	1993–1994	**1995–1999**	**2000–2001**	**2001–2005**

FIGURE 3.1 The evolution of the Internet over time.

intranets is growing rapidly. Discovery methods and issues are described in Section 3.2.

- *Communication.* The Internet provides fast and inexpensive communication channels that range from messages posted on online bulletin boards to complex information exchanges among many organizations. It also includes information transfer (among computers and via wireline and wireless) and information processing. E-mail, chat groups, and newsgroups (Internet chat groups focused on specific categories of interest) are examples of major communication media presented in Section 3.3 and in Technology Guide 5.

- *Collaboration.* Due to improved communication, electronic collaboration between individuals and/or groups and collaboration between organizations are increasing rapidly. Several tools can be used, ranging from screen sharing and teleconferencing to group support systems, as we will illustrate in Section 3.5. Collaboration also includes resource-sharing services, which provide access to printers and specialized servers. Several collaboration software products, called groupware and workflow, can be used on the Internet and on other networks.

The Net is also used for education, entertainment, and work. People can access the content of newspapers, magazines, and books. They can download documents, and they can do research. They can correspond with friends and family, play games, listen to music, view movies and other cultural events, and even visit many major museums and galleries worldwide.

The Network Computing Infrastructure: Intranets and Extranets

In addition to the Internet and the Web there are a few other major infrastructures of network computing: value-added networks (VANs) (see Technology Guide 4), intranets, and extranets.

INTRANETS. As discussed in Chapter 2, an *intranet* is a network designed to serve the internal informational needs of a company, using Internet concepts and tools. It is a network confined to an organization for its internal use. It provides easy and inexpensive browsing and search capabilities.

Intranets also support communication and collaboration. They are frequently connected to the Internet, enabling a company to conduct e-commerce activities. (Such activities are facilitated by *extranets,* as described later in this chapter and in Chapter 8.) Using screen sharing and other groupware tools, intranets can be used to facilitate the work of groups. Companies also publish newsletters and deliver news to their employers via their intranets. For extensive information about intranets, see *intranetjournal.com.*

Intranets have the power to change organizational structures and cultures as well as procedures, and to help restructure corporations. Intranets can be implemented using different types of local area network (LAN) technologies including wireless LANs (see Technology Guide 4 and Chapter 5). *IT at Work 3.1* (page 94) illustrates how a wireless LAN contributes to competitive advantage.

Intranets are used in all types of organizations, from manufacturers to health care providers to government agencies to educational institutions. Examples of several intranet applications are available in Online File W3.1 at the book's Web site.

IT at Work 3.1
WIRELESS LANs SPEED STOCK REFILL

EMKE Groups, a retail giant in the Middle East, is using a wireless retail solution in its retail outlets in the United Arab Emirates (UAE). The solution allows EMKE staff to make online requisition of goods from the retail outlets to a central warehouse, thus ensuring faster and correct replenishment of goods.

The group was using hand-held devices in a "batch process" to scan goods and upload the information to the back-office systems, entailing delays of several hours to update the system. Now it updates the system on wireless local area networks (WLANs) for its new stores; the new technology enables real-time updates. Real-time updates through the new system will give the retail group a strong advantage in a very competitive market, since stocks and merchandising can change quite regularly.

While implementing the new solution, the company shifted from traditional DOS-based mobile computers to the latest Pocket PC mobile computers, which enables staff to use multiple applications using the same hardware.

Performance of the new system turns out to be satisfactory. The group is going to implement the next generation of solutions in its upcoming new stores and its existing store in the UAE. It also intends to implement similar WLAN solutions in outlets in Kuwait and Oman.

Source: Compiled from Haugseth (2004).

For Further Exploration: What are possible disadvantages of using a wireless LAN?

EXTRANETS. An intranet's infrastructure is confined to an organization's boundaries, but not necessarily geographical ones; intranets can also be used to connect offices of the same company in different locations. As described in Chapter 2, another type of infrastructure that connects the intranets of *different organizations* is an *extranet.* An extranet is an infrastructure that allows *secure communications* among *business partners* over the Internet (using VPN; see Technology Guide 4). It offers secured accessibility to the intranets of the participating companies, as well as the necessary interorganizational communications, using Internet tools.

The use of extranets is rapidly increasing due to the large savings in communication costs (replacing expensive VANs) that can materialize. Extranets enable innovative applications of business-to-business (B2B) e-commerce (see Chapter 4). The National Semiconductor Corporation case study in Online Minicase W3.1 illustrates how NSC's customers could save time and effort in design by using design assistance offered through extranets. Finally, extranets are closely related to improved communications along the supply chain (for details see Technology Guide 4 and Chow, 2004).

The Internet, intranets, and extranets can be used in various ways in a corporate environment in order to gain competitive advantage. Examples are provided throughout the book and in Online File W3.2. An example of how a hypothetical company, Toys Inc., might use all network computing infrastructures is shown in Figure 3.2 (page 95). In addition, VANs are used by banks.

The *discovery, communication,* and *collaboration* capabilities available at low cost on the Internet, intranets, and extranets provide for a large number of useful applications. In the next four sections of this chapter, we discuss these capabilities. Many other applications are presented in Chapter 4 and throughout the book.

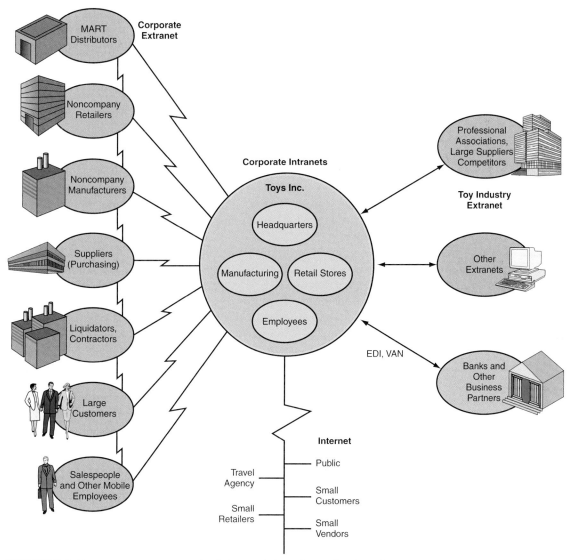

FIGURE 3.2 How a company uses the Internet, intranets, and extranets.

3.2 DISCOVERY

The Internet permits users to access information located in databases all over the world. Although only a small portion of organizational data may be accessible to Internet users, even that limited amount is enormous. Many fascinating resources are accessible. The discovery capability can facilitate education, government services, entertainment, and commerce. Discovery is done by *browsing* and *searching* data sources on the Web. Information can be either *static,* meaning staying basically unchanged, or *dynamic*. Dynamic information, such as stock prices or news, is changing constantly. The major problem of discovery is the huge amount of information available. The solution is to use different types of search and other software agents.

The Role of Internet Software Agents

A large number of Internet software agents can be used to automate and expedite discovery. **Software agents** are computer programs that carry out a set of routine computer tasks on behalf of the user and in so doing employ some sort of knowledge of the user's goals. We examine some of these agents in this section.

SEARCH ENGINES, DIRECTORIES, SOFTWARE, AND INTELLIGENT AGENTS. The amount of information on the Web is (at least) doubling every year. This makes navigating through the Web and gaining access to necessary information more and more difficult. *Search engines* and *directories* are two fundamentally different types of search facilities available on the Web.

A **search engine** (e.g., Altavista, Google) maintains an index of hundreds of millions of Web pages and uses that index to find pages that match a set of user-specified keywords. Such indexes are created and updated by software robots called **softbots.**

A **directory** (e.g., Yahoo, About.com), on the other hand, is a hierarchically organized collection of links to Web pages. Directories are compiled manually. Somewhat similar to directorles, indexes are generated by computers.

Search engines and directories often present users with links to thousands or even millions of pages. It is quite difficult to find information of interest from such a large number of links. Therefore we can use additional tools to refine the search. For example, *meta searchers* search several engines at once (e.g., Metacrawler.com). Most of these helpers use software agents, some of which exhibit intelligent behavior and learning and are called **intelligent agents** (D'Invetno and Luck, 2004; Wooldridge, 2002). The topic of intelligent agents is discussed more fully in Chapter 11. Here we present only a few examples of Internet-based software agents, which appear under names such as *wizards, softbots,* and *knowbots.* Three major types of agents available for help in browsing and searching are Web-browsing-assisting agents, FAQ agents, and indexing agents.

Web-Browsing-Assisting Agents. Some agents can facilitate browsing by offering the user a tour of the Internet. Known as *tour guides,* they work while the user browses. For example, WebWatcher is a personal agent, developed at Carnegie Mellon University, that helps find pages related to the current page, adding hyperlinks to meet the user's search goal and giving advice on the basis of the user's preference.

NetCaptor (*netcaptor.com*) is a custom browser application with a simple-to-navigate Windows interface that makes browsing (only with Internet Explorer) more pleasurable and productive. NetCaptor opens a separate tabbed space for each Web site visited by the user. Users can easily switch between different tabbed spaces. The CaptorGroup feature creates a group of links that are stored together so the user can get single-click access to multiple Web sites. The PopupCaptor feature automatically closes pop-up windows ("ad blocking," see Chapter 4) that are displayed during browsing. NetCaptor also includes a utility, called Flyswat, to turn certain words and phrases into hyperlinks. Clicking on these links opens a window with links to Web sites with relevant information. (Take the tour.)

For more details on Web-browsing assistants see Tan and Kumar (2002), *botspot.com,* and Lieberman et al. (2001).

Frequently Asked Questions (FAQ) Agents. *FAQ agents* guide people to the answers to frequently asked questions. When searching for information, people tend to ask the same or similar questions. In response, newsgroups, support staffs, vendors, and others have developed files of those FAQs and an appropriate answer to each. But there is a problem: People use natural language, asking the same questions in several different ways. The FAQ agent (such as FAQFinder developed at the University of Chicago) addresses this problem by indexing a large number of FAQ files. Using the text of a question submitted in natural language, the software agent can locate the appropriate answer. GTE Laboratories developed an FAQ agent that accepts natural-language questions from users of Usenet News Groups and answers them by matching question-answer pairs. A solution to natural language may be provided by a semantic Web. (See Chapter 11, Berners-Lee et al., 2001, and Van Den Heuvel and Maamar, 2003.)

AskJeeves (*askjeeves.com*), another popular FAQ assistant, makes it easy to find answers on the Internet to questions asked in plain English. The system responds with one or more closely related questions to which the answers are available. Parts of such questions may contain drop-down menus for selecting from different options. After the user selects the question that is closest to the original question, the system presents a reply page containing different sources that can provide answers. Due to the limited number of FAQs and the semistructured nature of the questions, the reliability of FAQ agents is very high.

Search and Indexing Agents. Another type of discovery agent on the Internet traverses the Web and performs tasks such as information retrieval and discovery, validating links, and generating statistics. Such search agents are called *Web robots, spiders,* and *wanderers.*

Indexing agents can carry out a massive autonomous search of the Web on behalf of a user or, more commonly, of a search engine like Google, HotBot, or Altavista. First, they scan millions of documents and store an index of words found in document titles, key words, and texts. The user can then query the search engine to find documents containing certain key words.

Special indexing agents are being developed for knowledge sharing and knowledge acquisition in large databases and documents. **Metasearch engines** integrate the findings of the various search engines to answer queries posted by the users. (Examples include *Infospace, QueryServer, seek2.com, surfwax, Metacrawler, Profusion, Infofetcher, Search, ixquick, All-in-One, Dogpile, Copernic,* and *Mamma*. See *suite101.com* for details.)

Visual interface search tools display search results in a way that assists users' search for better-targeted information. Vivisimo and WiseNet group the text-based search results into categories relevant to the search terms. KartOO and Mooter provide a visual representation of the search term that attempts to cluster together similar sites or results via a visual mapping metaphor. WebBrain combines the two ways of search-result display.

IT at Work 3.2 (page 98) provides an insight into a specific application of search and indexing technology in health care. An example in education is provided in Online File W3.3.

Internet-Based Web Mining

The term *data mining* refers to sophisticated analysis techniques for sifting through large amounts of information. Data mining permits new patterns and relationships to be discovered through the use of software that can do much of the mining

IT at Work 3.2
KAISER PERMANENTE USES GOOGLE TO BUILD A PORTAL

Kaiser Permanente (*kaiserpermanente.org*), America's largest not-for-profit health maintenance organization (HMO), has almost 9 million members. The amount of available medical knowledge doubles about every 7 years, so keeping up with new knowledge is an important aspect of good caregiving by HMOs.

When Kaiser Permanent developed a clinical-knowledge corporate portal for its 50,000 doctors, nurses, and other caregivers, search was a part of the plan. The Permanente Knowledge Connection, available from anywhere in the Kaiser wide area network, gives medical staff access to diagnostic information, best practices, publications, educational material, and other clinical resources. The portal's resources are distributed across the entire United States. Putting the right information quickly and easily into caregivers' hands is essential to the clinical portal's success.

Kaiser turned to the Google Search Appliance, which enabled the HMO to index 150,000 documents across the Kaiser network. Clinicians now search the site in situations that range from leisurely research to urgent care, from the exam room to the emergency room. Doctors and nurses use the search engine to help them reach diagnoses and specify treatments, check the side-effects of new medications, and consult clinical research studies and other medical publications. Google's spell checking capability is especially useful in the medical profession: Doctors' handwriting can be problematic, and pharmaceutical product names are difficult.

Source: Compiled from *services.google.com/marketing/links/banner_gsa03_eweek/casestudies* (accessed May 2004).

For Further Exploration: Why did Kaiser Permanente need Google's Search Appliance? What benefits did Kaiser gain from implementing Google's Search Appliance?

---

process (see Chapter 10). Software agents are key tools in discovering previously unknown relationships, especially in complex data structures. *Query-and-reporting tools,* on the other hand, demand a predefined database structure and are most valuable when asking specific questions to confirm hypotheses. For more on Web mining and its varieties, see Chapter 10.

Other Discovery Aids

Hundreds of other search engines and discovery aids are available (e.g., see McLaughlin, 2004, for over 100 sites; also see Carroll, 2003 and Sullivan, 2004). Here are some useful ones:

- *Webopedia.com.* This is a directory of technology-related terms, which are arranged alphabetically. If you know the term for which you want a definition, you can go to it directly. In addition to a definition you will find relevant Internet resources with links. If you do not know the exact term you are looking for, you can use some key word to find it.
- *What Is?* (*whatis.techtarget.com*). This knowledge exploration tool provides information about IT, especially about the Internet and computers. It contains over 4,000 individual encyclopedic definitions/topics and a number of "Fast Reference" pages. The topics contain about 12,000 hyperlinked cross-references between definitions/topics and to other sites for further information.
- *eBizSearch* (*gunther.smeal.psu.edu*). This engine searches the Web as well as academic and commercial articles for various aspects of e-business.
- *High Beam* (*highbeam.com*). This site searches for books, articles, maps, pictures, and so on that you can have for a seven-day free trial. After that, you must pay for the files. Abstracts are free.

- *Howstuffworks.com.* You can learn about thousands of products, things, concepts, etc. at this educational and entertaining site. It combines a search engine and a menu system.
- *Findarticles.com.* This search engine specializes in finding articles, usually from trade magazines, on topics of your choice. Like library search engines, it is limited to certain magazines.

Toolbars

To get the most out of search engines, you may use add-on toolbars and special software. Some are attached to the popular search engines, others are independent. Most are free. Examples are: Google Toolbar (*toolbar.google.com*), Copernic Agent Basic (*copernic.com*), KartOO (*kartoo.com*), Yahoo Companion (*companion.yahoo.com*), and Grokker (*groxis.com*).

Discovery of Material in Foreign Languages

There is a huge amount of information on the Internet in languages that you may not know. Some of this is vendors' information intended for global reach. Alternatively, you may need to create a foreign-language Web site for your company. Asking human translators for help is expensive and slow. A more useful tool is *automatic translation* of Web pages. Such translation is available to and from all major languages, and its quality is improving with time. We distinguish between real-time translation, which is offered by browsers, and delayed translation, which is offered by many others. For details and examples of both types, see *A Closer Look 3.1.*

Information and Corporate Portals

With the growing use of intranets and the Internet, many organizations encounter information overload at a number of different levels. Information is scattered across numerous documents, e-mail messages, and databases at

---

A CLOSER LOOK

3.1 AUTOMATIC TRANSLATION OF WEB PAGES

Automatic translation of Web pages is an application offered by many vendors. Not all automatic translations are equally good, so some evaluation of these products is needed. According to Sullivan (2001), the best way to assess machine translation is to use the following three criteria: (1) intelligibility—how well a reader can get the gist of a translated document, (2) accuracy—how many errors occur during a translation, and (3) speed—how many words per second are translated. Because the quality of automatic translation has not always been as good as human translation, many experts advocate use of the computer as a productivity booster, with human translation as a double-check. However, as time passes, automatic translation is becoming better (see Sullivan, 2001).

There are three Web page translation methods: (1) dictionary-based translation, (2) machine translation, and (3) methods using a linguistic jargon called parallel corpora. Direct dictionary-based translation is the simplest method. However, it suffers from some problems, among which are: (1) the problem of inflection (a translation problem due to differences between written and spoken words), (2) translation ambiguity, (3) how to handle compound words and phrases, and (4) how to translate proper names and other untranslatable words (Hedlund et al., 2004).

Some major translation products are: WorldPoint Passport (*worldpoint.com*), Babel Fish Translation (*world. altavista. com*), *AutoTranslate* (offered in Netscape browser), "BETA" (*google.com/languagetools*), *Freetranslation.com,* and products and services available at *tranexp.com* and *translationzone.com.* For details on these and other automatic translators, see Online File W3.4 at the book's Web site.

different locations and systems. Accessing relevant and accurate information is often time-consuming and may require access to multiple systems.

As a consequence, organizations lose a lot of productive employee time. One solution to this problem is to use portals. A **portal** is a Web-based personalized gateway to information and knowledge in network computing. It attempts to address information overload through an intranet-based environment to search and access relevant information from disparate IT systems and the Internet, using advanced search and indexing techniques. A portal is the one screen from which we do all our relevant work on the Web. In general, portals are referred to as information portals.

INFORMATION PORTALS.   An **information portal** is a single point of access through a Web browser to critical business information located inside and outside of an organization, and it can be personalized for each user. One way to distinguish among portals is to look at their content, which can vary from narrow to broad, and their community or audience, which can also vary. (For a classification, see *PortalsCommunity.com/library/fundamentals.cfm.*) We distinguish seven types of portals, described below.

1. *Commercial (public) portals* offer content for diverse communities and are the most popular portals on the Internet. Although they offer customization of the user interface, they are still intended for broad audiences and offer fairly routine content, some in real time (e.g., a stock ticker and news on a few preselected items). Examples are *yahoo.com, lycos.com,* and *msn.com.*

2. *Publishing portals* are intended for communities with specific interests. These portals involve relatively little customization of content, but they provide extensive online search in a specific area and some interactive capabilities. Examples are *techweb.com* and *zdnet.com.*

3. *Personal portals* target specific filtered information for individuals. They offer relatively narrow content but are typically much more personalized, effectively having an audience of one.

4. *Affinity portals* support communities such as hobby groups or a political party (Tedeschi, 2000). They offer a single point of entry to an entire community of affiliated interests (e.g., *espn.com*).

5. *Mobile portals* are portals accessible from mobile devices. Although most of the other portals mentioned here are PC-based, increasing numbers of portals are accessible via mobile devices. One example is i-mode from DoCoMo in Japan.

6. *Voice portals* (also called *vortals*) are Web portals with audio interfaces, which enables them to be accessed by a standard or cell phone. In a voice portal, input from the user is made via spoken command, which the system can accept thanks to *advanced speech recognition (ASR)* techniques. Output from the system back to the user is performed by *text-to-speech (TTS)* (Boothroyd, 2003). AOLbyPhone is an example of a service that allows you to retrieve e-mail, news, and other content by voice. (See Figure 3.3.) Companies such as *tellme.com* and *bevocal.com* offer the software for such services. Voice portals use both speech recognition and text-to-speech technologies. The 511 system described in Online Minicase W1.2 is an example of an e-government voice portal.

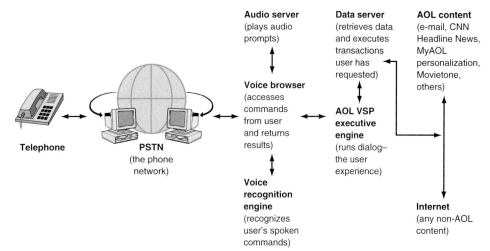

FIGURE 3.3 AOLbyphone. (*Source:* DeYoung, 2001, p. 10.)

7. *Corporate portals* coordinate rich content within relatively narrow corporate and partners' communities. Kounadis (2000) defines a corporate portal as a personalized, single point of access through a Web browser to critical business information located inside and outside of an organization. They are also known as *enterprise portals* or *enterprise information portals*.

CORPORATE PORTALS. In contrast with publishing and commercial portals such as Yahoo, which are gateways to general information on the Internet, **corporate portals** provide single-point access to *specific* enterprise information and applications available on the Internet, intranets, and extranets.

Corporate portals offer employees, business partners, and customers an organized focal point for their interactions with the firm any time and from anywhere. Through the portal, these people can have structured and personalized access to information across large, multiple, and disparate enterprise information systems, as well as the Internet. Many large organizations have already implemented corporate portals to cut costs, free up time for busy executives and managers, and improve profitability. (See ROI white papers and reports at *plumtree.com*.) In addition, corporate portals enable efficient knowledge management (Benbya et al., 2004) and offer customers and employees self-service opportunities (see CRM in Chapter 7), which reduces a company's cost. (See discussion and examples at *Peoplesoft.com*.) *A Closer Look 3.2* (page 102) describes several types of corporate portals. (For more, see Sullivan, 2003 and Jafair et al., 2003).

Figure 3.4 (page 103) depicts a corporate portal framework based on Aneja et al. (2000) and Kounadis (2000). This framework illustrates the features and capabilities required to support various organizational activities using internal and external information sources. Online File W3.5 takes a look at the corporate portals of some well-known companies. Also, look at Online Minicase W3.2, which tells about a business intelligence portal at Amway.

APPLICATIONS OF CORPORATE PORTALS. According to a survey by the Delphi Group, over 55 percent of its 800 respondents had begun corporate portal projects, with about 42 percent of them conducting the projects at the enterprisewide

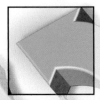

A CLOSER LOOK
3.2 TYPES OF CORPORATE PORTALS

The following types of portals can be found in organizations.

A PORTAL FOR SUPPLIERS. Using corporate portals, suppliers can manage their own inventories online. They can view what they sold to the portal owner and at what price. They can see the inventory levels of products at the portal owner's organization, and they can send material and supplies when they see that a reorder level is reached. Suppliers can also collaborate with corporate buyers and other staff via the portal.

A PORTAL FOR CUSTOMERS. Customers can use a *customer-facing portal* for viewing products and services and placing orders, which they can later self-track. They can view their own accounts and see what is going on there in almost real time. Thus, customers personalize their views of the corporate portal. They can configure products (services), place orders, and pay for and arrange delivery and warranty. They can see their order status and outstanding invoices as well.

For example, Halliburton (*halliburton.com*) created a portal, called myHalliburton, to provide its customers access to technical tools, best practices, SAP account data, and private forums for project management. The company's 5,000 customers worldwide can also gather product information, track invoices, tap a knowledge base of technical expertise, and collaborate securely with Halliburton teams through the portal.

A PORTAL FOR EMPLOYEES. Such portals are used for training, dissemination of news and information, and workplace discussion groups. They also are used for self-service activities, mainly in the human resources area (e.g., change your address, fill in an expense report, register for classes, get reimbursed for tuition). Employees' portals are sometimes bundled with supervisors' portals (see next item).

For example, in the myHalliburton portal described earlier, corporate geologists, geophysicists, and production engineers, located at customer sites, can use 3-D simulators, unit conversion calculators, custom-tool builders, and other interactive tools integrated into the portal, allowing them to isolate problems and make decisions more quickly.

SUPERVISORS' PORTALS. These portals, sometimes called *workforce portals,* enable managers and supervisors to control the entire workforce management process—from budgeting to scheduling workforce.

For example, Mazda North America Operations provides its field managers, who supervise 700-some dealerships, with a Dealer Analysis portal. The portal integrates application information and resources from diverse repositories into a "dashboard." Using the dashboard on the portal, regional managers can analyze consolidated data on both sales and customer support performance, 24 hours a day, and can track near-real-time sales figures for all dealerships nationwide.

OTHER TYPES. Several other types of corporate portals also exist: *business intelligence portals* (Imhoff, 2001; Ferguson, 2001), *intranet portals* (Ferguson, 2001), and *knowledge portals* (Kesner, 2003).

level (cited in Stackpole, 1999). The number of corporate portals can only have increased since that study was conducted. The top portal applications cited in the study, in decreasing order of importance, were: knowledge bases and learning tools; business process support; customer-facing sales, marketing, and service; collaboration and project support; access to data from disparate corporate systems; internal company information, policies, and procedures; best practices and lessons learned; human resources and benefits; directories and bulletin boards; identification of subject matter experts; and news and Internet access.

The Delphi Group also found that poor organization of information and lack of navigation and retrieval tools contributed to over 50 percent of the problems for corporate portal users. For this reason it is advisable for organizations to develop a corporate portal strategy, as discussed in Online File W3.6.

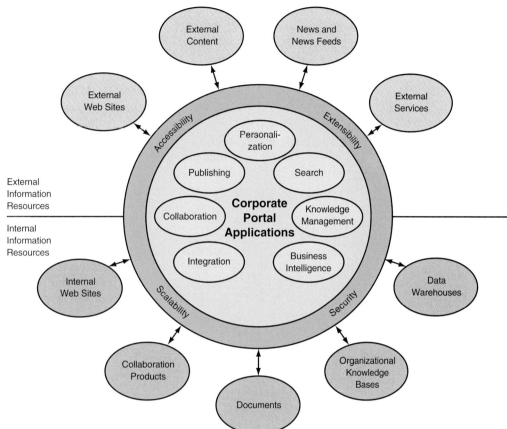

FIGURE 3.4 A corporate portal framework. (*Sources:* Compiled from A. Aneja et al., "Corporate Portal Framework for Transforming Content Chaos on Intranets," *Intel Technology Journal,* Q1, 2000, and from T. Kounadis, "How to Pick the Best Portal," *e-Business Advisor,* August 2000.)

INTEGRATION OF PORTALS.   Many organizations are creating several corporate portals. While in some cases these portals are completely independent of each other, in other cases they are interrelated. For example, they may share content, and they may draw from the same applications and databases.

Tool-building software, such as WebSphere Portal (from IBM), allows companies to create multiple portals as one unit. It enables three different portals to be used by a single company—a portal for business partners (B2B), a portal for employees (B2E), and a portal for customers (B2C). If portals are built one at a time over a long period, and possibly with different tools, it is wise to keep in mind that it may be beneficial to integrate them (Ojala, 2002).

INDUSTRYWIDE COMMUNICATION NETWORKS (PORTALS).   In addition to single-company portals, there are also portals for entire industries. Thanks to the Internet, entire industries can now create communication networks (industry portals). For example, *chaindrugstore.net* links retailers and product manufacturers, and provides product and industry news and recall and promotional information. The site was created in 2001 by the National Association of Chain Drug Stores. The objective is to facilitate the rapid exchange of needed information. The site has an offshoot for independent pharmacies (called CommunityDrugStore.net). The service, according to Brookman (2003), reaches more than 130 retailers representing 32,000 stores. The service is free to the retailers; suppliers pay annual fees in exchange for being able to use the portal to communicate information to retailers (e.g., to advertise special deals, to notify retailers about price changes). The portal also provides industry news, and it can be personalized for individual retailers. Retailers also use it as a productivity tool. For example, the site has "Call Me" and "Send Me" buttons, so retailers can click and receive product information in seconds. Although some people fear that the site will reduce the effectiveness of face-to-face meetings, the participants are more than happy with the communication and collaboration support. The membership renewal rate has been 100 percent, and additional members have joined. For details see Brookman (2003).

3.3 COMMUNICATION

Communication is an interpersonal process of sending and receiving symbols with messages attached to them. Through communication, people exchange and share information as well as understand and influence each other. Most managers spend as much as 90 percent of their time communicating. Managers serve as "nerve centers" in the information-processing networks called organizations, where they collect, distribute, and process information continuously. Since poor communication can mean poor management, managers must communicate effectively among themselves and with others, both inside and outside of organizations. Information technologies have come to play a major role in providing communication support for organizations.

On the Web we distinguish three communication modes:

1. *People-to-people.* This was the earliest mode of network communication, when people used e-mail and newsgroups. They also discovered information on bulletin boards and communicated there.

2. *People-to-machine.* This was the next step, when people conducted discovery on the Web, searching and finding information.

3. *People and machine-to-machine.* This mode occurs when applications need to "talk" to applications, either in complete automation or in automation but including people.

Factors Determining the Uses of Information Technologies for Communication

Several factors determine the IT technologies that could be used to provide communication support to a specific organization or group of users. The major ones are the following:

- *Participants.* The number of people sending and receiving information can range from two to many thousands.

- *Nature of sources and destinations.* Sources and destinations of information can include people, databases, sensors, and so on.

- *Media.* Communication can involve one or several IT-supported media, such as text, voice, graphics, video, pictures, and animation. Using different media for communicating can increase the effectiveness of a message, expedite learning, and enhance problem solving. Working with multiple media may, however, reduce the efficiency and effectiveness of the system (its speed, capacity, quality) and may significantly increase its cost.

		PLACE	
		Same	**Different**
TIME	**Same**	A decision room GDSS (see Chapter 10) Whiteboard Other real-time collaboration (RTC) tools	Videoconferencing Instant messenger Screen sharing Whiteboard Chat room Internet telephony Other RTC tools
	Different	Multishift control center E-mail Workflow	E-mail Bulletin board Web-based call center Workflow GDSS Autoresponder (Chapter 7)

FIGURE 3.5 A framework for IT communication support.

- *Place (location).* The sender(s) and receiver(s) can be in the same room (face-to-face) or at different locations.
- *Time.* Messages can be sent at a certain time and received almost simultaneously. Such **synchronous (real-time) communication** is provided by telephones, instant messaging online, teleconferencing, and face-to-face meetings. **Asynchronous communication,** on the other hand, refers to communication in which the receiver gets an answer sometime after a request was sent. E-mail and electronic bulletin boards are examples.

A TIME/PLACE FRAMEWORK. The last two factors in the preceding list—place and time—were used by DeSanctis and Gallupe (1987) to create a framework for classifying IT communication and collaboration support technologies. According to this framework, IT communication can be divided into four cells, as shown in Figure 3.5, with representative technologies in each cell. The time/place cells are as follows:

1. *Same-time/same-place.* In this setting, participants meet face-to-face in one place and at the same time. An example is communication in a meeting room, which can be electronically supported by group support system software (see *groupsystems.com* and Chapter 11).
2. *Same-time/different-place.* This setting refers to a meeting whose participants are in different places but communicate at the same time. A telephone conference call, desktop videoconferencing, chat rooms, and instant messaging are examples of such situations.
3. *Different-time/same-place.* This setting can materialize when people work in shifts. The first shift leaves electronic or voice messages for the second shift.
4. *Different-time/different-place.* In this setting, participants are in different places, and sending and/or receiving messages at different times (e.g., e-mail). This setting is known as *virtual meetings.*

Businesses require that messages be transmitted as fast as they are needed, that the intended receiver properly and timely interprets them, and that the cost of doing this be reasonable. Communication systems that meet these conditions have several characteristics. They allow two-way communication:

Messages flow in different directions, sometimes almost simultaneously, and messages reach people regardless of where they are located. Efficient systems also allow people to access various sources of information (such as databases). IT helps to meet these requirements through the electronic transfer of information using tools such as e-mail.

The Internet has become a major supporter of interactive communications. People are using a variety of Internet technologies—Internet phones, smart cell phones, Internet videoconferencing, Internet radio, whiteboards, chat rooms, and more—for communication. In Section 3.5 we will discuss some of the IT tools cited in connection with Figure 3.5. E-mail, including instant and universal messaging services, is discussed in Online File W3.7 at the book's Web site. Other Internet-based communication tools and technologies are described in Technology Guide 4.

Web-Based Call Centers

Effective personalized customer contact is becoming an important aspect of customer support through the Web. Such service is provided through *Web-based call centers* (also known as *customer care centers, contact centers,* or *customer interaction centers*). Enabling Web collaboration and simultaneous voice/Web contact can differentiate a company from its competitors. There are at least four categories of capabilities employed by Web-based call centers—e-mail, interactive text chat, callbacks, and simultaneous voice and Web sessions. (For discussion of how companies might decide among the possible choices for Web-based call centers, see Sharp, 2003.) WebsiteAlive (*websitealive.com*), a Web-based call center support product, delivers live customer-service capabilities for any online company. Further details and examples are provided in Chapter 7.

Electronic Chat Rooms

Electronic chat refers to an arrangement whereby participants exchange messages in real time. The software industry estimates that millions of chat rooms exist on the Internet. A **chat room** is a virtual meeting place where groups of regulars come to gab. Chat programs allow you to send messages to people who are connected to the same channel of communication *at the same time*. It is like a global conference call system. Anyone can join in the online conversation. Messages are displayed on your screen as they arrive, even if you are in the middle of typing a message.

The chat rooms can be used to build a community, to promote a commercial, political, or environmental cause, to support people with medical problems, or to let hobbyists share their interest. And since many customer-supplier relationships have to be sustained without face-to-face meetings, online communities are increasingly being used to serve business interests, including advertising (see *Parachat.com* and Technology Guide 5). Chat capabilities can be added to a business site by letting software chat vendors host your session on their site. You simply put a chat link on your site and the chat vendor does the rest, including the advertising that pays for the session.

Two major types of chat programs exist: (1) Web-based chat programs, which allow you to send messages to Net users using a Web browser and visiting a Webchat site (e.g., *chat.yahoo.com*), and (2) an e-mail-based (text only) program called **Internet relay chat (IRC).** A business can use IRC to interact with customers, provide online experts' answers to questions, and so on.

Today, there are several hundred IRC networks in operation in the world. They run various implementations of IRC servers, and are administered by various groups of IRC operators. The largest IRC networks have traditionally been grouped as the "Big Four": EFNet, IrcNet, QuakeNet, and UnderNet. The most popular IRC client at the moment is called mIRC (*mirc.com*).

The biggest difference between IRC and *instant messaging (IM)* applications (such as ICQ and MSN Messenger, which allow users to exchange real time messages) is the fact that all the users on IRC channels normally see everything other users say—in other words, it is real-time *public* conversation. In addition to this, IRC also supports IM-style private messaging between users as well. Many long-time IRC users see IM applications as just a sidekick of the IRC phenomenon. (For further information about IRC, refer to *irchelp.org* and *mirc.com/links.html*.)

Voice Communication

The most natural mode of communication is voice. When people need to communicate with each other from a distance, they use the telephone more frequently than any other communication device. Voice communication enables workers, from forklift drivers to disabled employees to military pilots, to have portable, safe, and effective access to computer technology from their work areas. In addition, voice communication is faster than typing (about two and half times faster), and fewer errors in voice data entry are made compared to keyboard data entry. Voice communication can now be done on the Internet using a microphone and a sound card (see *protocols.com/pbook/VOIP*). You can even talk long distance on the Internet without paying the normal long distance telephone charges. This is known as **Internet telephony (voice-over IP),** and it is described in Technology Guide 5.

You can get freeware (free software) for Internet telephony from *pc-telephone. com*. Also, some browsers provide you with Internet telephony capability. To connect from computers to regular telephones try, for example, *dialpad.com,* which offers low-cost long-distance calls through the Internet to regular telephones in U.S. cities from anywhere in the world. For more information see *tmcnet.com/it*.

Voice and data can work together to create useful applications. *Voice mail,* a well-known computerized system for storing, forwarding, and routing telephone messages, is one such application. For some other applications of voice technologies, see Online File W3.8 at the book's Web site. More advanced applications of voice technology such as natural language speech recognition and voice synthesis are described in Chapter 11.

Weblogging (Blogging)

The Internet offers an opportunity for individuals to do personal publishing using a technology known as **Weblogging,** or **blogging.** A **blog** is a personal Web site, open to the public, in which the owner expresses his or her feelings or opinions. People can write stories, tell news, and provide links to other articles and Web sites. At some blogs you can find fascinating items that you might otherwise have overlooked. At others, you can rapidly get up to speed on an issue of special interest. Blogs are growing rapidly, estimated by BBC News (February 2003) to be close to 500,000.

Blogs became very popular after the terrorist attacks of September 11, 2001, and during the 2003 Iraqi war. People were looking for as many sources of information as possible and for personal connections. Blogs are comforting for people in times of stress. They are a place at which people feel their ideas get noticed, and they can result in two-way communication and collaboration and group discussion.

Building blogs is becoming easier and easier. Programs downloadable from *blogger.com, pitas.com,* and others are very user friendly. "Bloggers" (the people who create and maintain blogs) are handed a fresh space on their Web site to write in each day. They can easily edit, add entries, and broadcast whatever they want by simply clicking on the send key. Other services are provided by *zblogger.com* and *moveabletype.org*.

As indicated by MacDonald (2004), one of the greatest limitations of blogs is their temporal nature. Postings are always arranged in date order, irrespective of their other dimensions (e.g., importance, substance, and popularity). This limitation leads to problems in the documentation, management, and search of information in the blogs.

Blogs are also criticized for their tendency to coalesce into self-referential cliques. Bloggers are blamed for their mutual backslapping, endlessly praising and linking to one another's sites. However, bloggers are creating their own communities and have developed a rich terminology. (For a bloggers' dictionary, see *marketingterms.com/dictionary/blog* and *samizdata.net/blog/glossary*.) Blogs have just begun to be used for commercial purposes. For example, Weidlich (2003) reports that some company executives use blogs for informal talk to customers. Also see Lewin (2003). For further discussion on blogs, see Stauffer (2002) and Stone (2002).

3.4 COLLABORATION

One of the abiding features of a modern organization is that people collaborate to perform work or attain a goal. **Collaboration** refers to mutual efforts by two or more individuals who perform activities in order to accomplish certain tasks. The individuals may represent themselves or organizations, or they may be members of a team or a group. Group members work together on tasks ranging from designing products and documents, to teaching each other, to executing complementary subtasks. Also, people work with customers, suppliers, and other business partners in an effort to improve productivity and competitiveness. Finally, group members participate in decision making. In all of the above cases they need to collaborate. Collaboration can be supported electronically by several technologies as described later in this chapter.

The Nature of Group Work

Group work is increasing in importance. Indeed, it is a cornerstone in some business process restructuring (BPR) projects and in e-commerce. Also, group work is needed in virtual corporations as well as in multinational organizations. The use of group work is also increasing due to the support provided by IT, especially the support provided to groups whose members are in different locations.

The term *workgroup* refers to two or more individuals who act together to perform some task. The group can be permanent or temporary. It can be in one location (face-to-face meetings) or in several. If group members are in different locations we say we have a **virtual group (team),** and they conduct **virtual meetings** (they are in different locations, so "meet" electronically). Members can meet concurrently or at different times. The group can be a committee, a review panel, a task force, an executive board, a team, or a department. Groups conduct their work by using different approaches or processes.

CONVENTIONAL APPROACH TO GROUP WORK. For years, people have recognized the benefits of collaborative work. Typical benefits that relate to decision making in groups are listed in Table 3.1. But despite the many benefits of group interaction, groups are not always successful. The reason is that the process of collaborative work is frequently plagued by dysfunctions, as listed in Table 3.2.

TABLE 3.1 Benefits of Working in a Group
● Groups are better than individuals at understanding problems.
● People are accountable for decisions in which they participate.
● Groups are better than individuals at catching errors.
● A group has more information (knowledge) than any one member and, as a result, more alternatives are generated for problem solving.
● Synergy can be produced, so the effectiveness and/or quality of group work can be greater than the sum of what is produced by independent individuals.
● Working in a group may stimulate the participants and the process.
● Group members have their egos embedded in the decision they make, so they will be committed to its implementation.

TABLE 3.2 Dysfunctions of Group Process
● Social pressures to conform ("groupthink") may eliminate superior ideas.
● Group process can be time-consuming, slow, and costly.
● Work done in a group may lack appropriate coordination.
● Some members may dominate the agenda.
● Some group members ("free riders") may rely on others to do most of their work.
● The group may compromise on solutions of poor quality.
● The group may be unable to complete a task.
● Unproductive time is spent socializing, getting ready, waiting for people, or repeating what has already been said.
● Members may be afraid to speak up.

To reconcile these differences, researchers have worked for many years to improve the process used by people working in groups. If the causes of group dysfunctions could be lessened or eliminated, the benefits of group work would be greatly enhanced. Several approaches have been developed to attempt to solve the problems inherent in group work. Two representative manual methods are the *nominal group technique* and the *Delphi method* (see Online File W3.9 for explanations of those two methods).

The limited success of the above approaches to group work and the availability of IT tools and the Internet has created an opportunity for supporting groups electronically, which is part of virtual collaboration. We describe the general support in this section. The support that is intended to facilitate decision making is described in Chapter 11.

VIRTUAL TEAMS. Much of the work in transnational corporations, and increasingly even in domestic firms, is performed by virtual teams—teams whose members are spread across countries and continents. Virtual teams help employers recruit qualified employees from a larger talent pool dispersed across multiple geographic locations and allow companies to minimize travel and relocation expenses. Furthermore, locating staff in different time zones simplifies the challenge of around-the-clock operations that many firms face. Another benefit of virtual teams stems from the fact that the teams work in a digital environment, where most communications are digitally encoded and can be stored in a central repository. Thus, virtual teams reduce information loss and facilitate knowledge transfer throughout the organization (Alexander, 2000).

Virtual teams transform the work environment, changing organizational cultures, job content, and job requirements, as well as the nature of supervision and evaluation. Virtual teams tend to promote a more formal organizational culture in which interactions among employees take place mainly through reports and e-mails as opposed to informal conversations in the hallways of traditional organizations (Alexander, 2000). They change job content by placing a greater emphasis on regular, accurate, and precise communications among team members via telephone, video conferencing, e-mail, instant messaging, and other communication and collaboration systems.

Skills and qualities required to succeed in virtual teams are quite different from the demands of traditional workgroups. Virtual team members must be self-starters to set their individual goals and must proactively work toward the goals without direct supervision from the boss located hundreds or thousands of miles away. Supervision and employee evaluations also need to be adapted to the virtual team environment. Managers are more likely to evaluate what virtual team members actually accomplish as opposed to relying on observations of whether they appear to be working, which are commonly used in traditional workplaces. *IT at Work 3.3* illustrates the use of virtual teams at Sabre, Inc.

While virtual teams represent a compelling work arrangement for many organizations, they can be challenging to implement and manage. Members of virtual teams face such issues as rapidly learning to work with individuals whom they do not know and with whom they may not share a common background. Conflict in virtual teams can occur as a result of relationship difficulties, task difficulties, or process difficulties (Hinds and Bailey, 2003). These difficulties are exacerbated in situations where the teams engage in little, if any, face-to-face communication. High-performing virtual teams exhibit marked differences in their patterns of communication compared with lower-performing virtual teams. High-performance teams have been shown to engage in regular, predictable, content-focused communication, whereas low-performance teams often exhibit irregular patterns of communication such that team members fail to keep current by reading each other's messages (Jarvenpaa and Leidner, 1999).

Managers of virtual teams also face unique challenges, in that they are not aware of the day-to-day activities of those whom they are responsible for supervising. Effective leaders must ensure that all team members share an understanding of the team's task and of the individual members' roles (Kayworth and Leidner, 2002). Effective leaders must learn to display both assertiveness and empathy using predominantly computer-based communication (Kayworth and Leidner, 2002). For many managers, this is difficult to accomplish and the performance of the team suffers as a result.

Virtual Collaboration

Virtual collaboration (or *e-collaboration*) refers to the use of digital technologies that enable organizations or individuals to collaboratively plan, design, develop, manage, and research products, services, and innovative IT and EC applications. Although e-collaboration can involve noncommerce applications, the term frequently refers to **collaborative commerce**—collaboration among business partners. An example would be a company that is collaborating electronically with a vendor that designs a product or a part for the company (see Minicase 1, about General Motors). Collaborative commerce implies communication, information sharing, and collaborative planning done electronically through tools such as groupware and specially designed EC collaboration tools. For details see Turban et al. (2006) and Poirier (2001).

Numerous studies (e.g., *line56.com*, 2002) suggest that collaboration is a set of relationships that can bring significant improvements in organizations' performance. Major benefits cited are cost reduction, increased revenue, and improved customer retention. These benefits are the results of fewer stockouts, less exception-processing (doing things as an exception to the standard way, usually more expensive than the standard way), reduced inventory throughout the supply chain, lower material costs, increased sales volume, and increased competitive advantage. According to a survey conducted by Deloitte Consulting

IT at Work 3.3
VIRTUAL TEAMS AT SABRE, INC.

Sabre, Inc. is one of the leading firms providing travel reservation services worldwide. The company's roots go back to 1960, when American Airlines developed a proprietary computerized travel reservation system. This unique system made American Airlines the originator of electronic commerce in the travel industry. In March 2000, AMR (the parent company of American Airlines) spun off Sabre as a separate company headquartered in Texas. Today, Sabre, Inc. employs over 6,000 people in 45 countries and generates over $2 billion in annual revenues. Sixty thousand travel agents in 114 countries rely on Sabre to make travel arrangements for their clients. The total volume of reservations processed by the system each year exceeds 400 million, which represents 40 percent of all travel reservations worldwide. Consumers may be familiar with Travelocity.com, which is Sabre's business-to-consumer travel site; corporate travel agents would recognize GetThere—the world's leading supplier of business-to-business online travel reservation systems operated by Sabre.

With employees working both in headquarters and field offices scattered around the globe, Sabre made a decision to use *virtual teams,* whose overall purpose was to improve customer focus, enhance productivity, and grow market share and profitability. The company discovered that cross-functional teams were better suited for the marketplace demands than the single-function teams it had used in the past. Now, a typical virtual team at Sabre includes representatives from several areas of the company: Account executives sell reservation systems, technicians install and service the systems, trainers teach travel agents how to use the systems, account management specialists handle billing and collections, and customer service representatives respond to miscellaneous inquiries.

Following the introduction of virtual teams, Sabre encountered several challenges related to managing and working in the teams. One of the primary challenges was building trust among team members. Managers and employees soon recognized that building trust requires a high level of responsiveness to electronic communications from other team members, dependable performance, and a proactive approach to completing team tasks. The second challenge involved generating synergy in virtual teams—making the team greater than the sum of its parts. To resolve this challenge, Sabre offered team-building activities, as well as extensive classroom and computer-based training that preceded the launch of new virtual teams.

A third challenge was that team members had to cope with the feeling of isolation and detachment that characterizes virtual teamwork. The company discovered that certain employees preferred independent work and operated well without much social interaction. Thus, Sabre conducted interviews with potential team members to determine their suitability for virtual teamwork. Furthermore, the company's teams are only partially virtual—the relationships may occasionally involve face-to-face interactions during certain meetings and teambuilding exercises. In addition, employees have the option to work either from home or from an office where they can interact with other employees, who may or may not be their teammates.

The fourth challenge involved balancing technical and interpersonal skills among team members. Sabre was surprised to find that despite the infrequent face-to-face communications, interpersonal abilities were extremely valuable and important to virtual teams. As a result, the company made a change in its hiring and team-member selection practices, to shift the emphasis from technical to interpersonal skills.

A fifth major challenge was related to employee evaluation and performance measurement. Over time, the company implemented a system of team-level and individual metrics that were intended to measure objective, quantifiable contributions of each team member and the performance of the virtual team as a whole. Nevertheless, the company admits that striking the right balance between the measures of individual contributions and group performance continues to be difficult.

The results of creating virtual teams at Sabre have been quite positive. Most managers and emplyees of the company agree that the shift from functional face-to-face teams to cross-functional virtual teams improved customer service. Customers themselves support these assertions: Sabre's customer satisfaction ratings have increased from 68 percent in 1997 to 85 percent in 2000. Besides, the company increased its market share in North America from 43 percent in 1997 to 50 percent in 2000. While virtual teams are not the only factor contributing to these positive changes, they seem to indicate that the use of virtual teams may be a rewarding choice for a global organization.

Sources: Compiled from Kirkman et al. (2002) and *sabre-holdings.com* (2004).

For Further Exploration: Are the challenges faced by virtual teams at Sabre unique to this company? What additional challenges with virtual teams might Sabre encounter in the future? If you were an employee at Sabre, would you prefer to work in a physical face-to-face environment or in a virtual team?

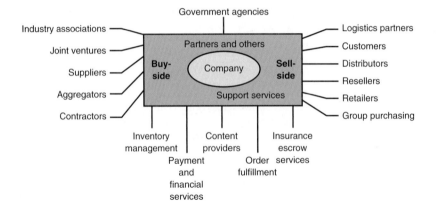

FIGURE 3.6
E-collaboration for
commerce.

and reported in *Manageradvisor.com* (2002), 70 percent of the companies conducting collaborative commerce are showing higher profitability than those that do not. Of those companies surveyed, 75 percent consider online collaboration (especially linking business processes) to be a top executive priority. These figures, gathered in 2002, are more than 20 percent higher than responses from a 2000 survey. Finally, 85 percent of all companies plan to have advanced collaborative commerce initiatives by 2005. Some of the major strategic benefits reported are an increase in process flexibility, faster delivery speed, and improved customer service (see Powell et al., 2004).

C-commerce activities are usually conducted between and among supply chain partners. For example, see the opening case in this chapter, which shows how one company becomes a *nucleus firm,* or a hub, for collaboration. Such an arrangement can be expanded to include all business partners, as shown in Figure 3.6. This concept is the basis for many-to-many e-marketplaces (see Chapter 4), in which a third-party company is the nucleus firm, creating a place not only for collaboration but also for trade.

There are several other varieties of virtual collaboration, ranging from joint design efforts to forecasting. Collaboration can be done both between and within organizations. The following are some types and examples of virtual collaboration.

COLLABORATIVE NETWORKS. Traditionally, collaboration has taken place among supply chain members, frequently those that were close to each other (e.g., a manufacturer and its distributor, or a distributor and a retailer). Even if more partners were involved, the focus has been on the optimization of information and product flow between existing nodes in the traditional supply chain.

The traditional collaboration resulted in a vertically integrated supply chain. However, as discussed in earlier chapters, IT and Web technologies can *fundamentally change* the shape of the supply chain, as well as the number of players within it and their individual roles and collaboration patterns. The new supply chain can be a hub or even a network. A comparison between the traditional supply chain collaboration and the collaborative network is shown in Figure 3.7. Notice that the traditional chain (part a, for the food industry) is basically linear. The collaborative network (part b) shows that partners at any point in the network can interact with each other, bypassing traditional partners. Interaction may occur among several manufacturers and/or distributors, as well as with new

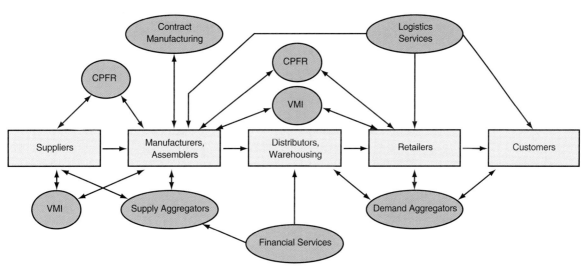

Part (a) Traditional collaboration, including CPFR. Collaboration agents and services are shown as ovals. (VMI and CPFR are defined later in this section.)

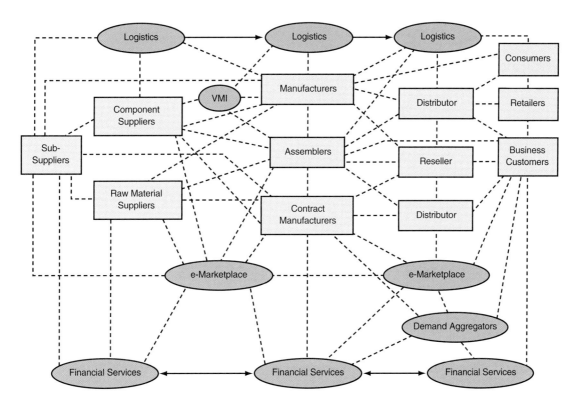

Part (b) Supply chains are evolving into collaborative networks. Ovals designate agents and services.

FIGURE 3.7 Comparing traditional supply chain collaboration and collaborative networks. Collaborative places and efforts are shown as ovals. (*Sources:* Part a based on Walton and Princi, 2000, p. 193, Fig. 1.8. Part b based on Poirier, 2001, p. 9-8, Fig. 1.)

players such as software agents that act as aggregators, B2B e-marketplaces, or logistics providers.

The collaborative network can take different shapes depending on the industry, the product (or service), the volume of flow, and more. Examples of collaborative networks are provided by Poirier (2001) and by Szekely (2003).

As the mobile technologies mature, mobile collaborative networks will gradually develop. These networks have the ability to share valuable business information in mobile scenarios with people who are co-located or remote, and not necessarily from the same company. Mobile workers will be able to communicate and share information any time, anywhere (Bartram and Blackstock, 2003 and Divitini et al., 2004). The latest and most ambitious attempt at collaborative networks is *grid computing* (see Chapter 2, *ibm.com/grid, oracle.com/grid*, and Vallés et al., 2004.)

REPRESENTATIVE EXAMPLES OF VIRTUAL COLLABORATION.   Leading businesses are moving quickly to realize the benefits of e-collaboration. For example, the real estate franchiser RE/MAX uses an e-collaboration platform to improve communications and collaboration among its nationwide network of independently owned real estate franchises, sales associates, and suppliers. Similarly, Marriott International, the world's largest hospitality company, started with an online brochure and then developed a c-commerce system that links corporations, franchisees, partners, and suppliers, as well as customers, around the world. In addition, as described in Online File W3.10, Nygard of Canada has developed a collaborative system along its entire supply chain.

There are many examples of e-collaboration. Here we present some additional representative ones. For more see Frank (2004), and Davison and de Vreede (2001).

Information Sharing Between Retailers and Their Suppliers: P&G and Wal-Mart.   One of the most publicized examples of information sharing is between Procter & Gamble (P&G) and Wal-Mart. Wal-Mart provides P&G access to sales information on every item Wal-Mart buys from P&G. The information is collected by P&G on a daily basis from every Wal-Mart store, and P&G uses the information to manage the inventory replenishment for Wal-Mart. This is known as *VMI, vendor-managed inventories* (see Chapter 8). By monitoring the inventory level of each P&G item in every Wal-Mart store, P&G knows when the inventories fall below the threshold that triggers a shipment. All this is done electronically. The benefit for P&G is that they can sell to a good customer, and the benefit to Wal-Mart is adequate inventory on its shelves. P&G has similar agreements with other major retailers.

Retailer–Supplier Collaboration: Asda Corporation.   Supermarket chain Asda (*asda.com*) has begun rolling out Web-based electronic data interchange (EDI) technology to 650 suppliers. Web-EDI technology is based on the AS2 standard, an internationally accepted HTTP-based protocol used to send real-time data in multiple formats securely over the Internet. It promises to improve the efficiency and speed of traditional EDI communications, which route data over third-party value-added networks (VANs). Asda believes that Web-EDI will bring a number of benefits. Parent-company Wal-Mart has been using the technology in the United States since 2003. The technology will speed up the stock replenishment cycle, give flexibility to increase data volume at no extra cost, and improve tracking of inbound and outbound data (*http://articles,* . . . Jan. 27, 2004).

Lower Transportation and Inventory Costs and Reduced Stockouts: Unilever.
Unilever's 30 contract carriers deliver 250,000 truckloads of shipments annu-ally. Unilever's Web-based database, the Transportation Business Center (TBC), provides these carriers with site specification requirements when they pick up a shipment at a manufacturing or distribution center or when they deliver goods to retailers. TBC gives carriers all the vital information they need: contact names and phone numbers, operating hours, the number of dock doors at a location, the height of the dock doors, how to make an appointment to deliver or pick up shipments, pallet configuration, and other special requirements. All mission-critical information that Unilever's carriers need to make pickups, shipments, and deliveries is now available electronically 24/7. TBC also helps Unilever organize and automate its carrier selection processes based on contract provisions and commitments. When a primary carrier is unable to accept a shipment, TBC automatically recommends alternative carriers (*http://articles* . . . Aug. 4, 2004).

Reduction of Product Development Time: Caterpillar, Inc.   Caterpillar, Inc. (*caterpillar.com*) is a multinational heavy-machinery manufacturer. In the tradi-tional mode of operation, cycle time along the supply chain was long because the process involved paper-document transfers among managers, salespeople, and technical staff. To solve the problem, Caterpillar connected its engineering and manufacturing divisions with its active suppliers, distributors, overseas fac-tories, and customers, through an extranet-based global collaboration system. By means of the collaboration system, a request for a customized tractor com-ponent, for example, can be transmitted from a customer to a Caterpillar dealer and on to designers and suppliers, all in a very short time. Customers also can use the extranet to retrieve and modify detailed order information while the vehicle is still on the assembly line. Remote collaboration capabilities between the customer and product developers have decreased cycle time delays caused by rework time. Suppliers are also connected to the system, so they can deliver materials or parts directly to Caterpillar's repair shops or directly to the customer if appropriate. The system also is used for expediting maintenance and repairs.

For comprehensive coverage of collaborative virtual design environments, see Ragusa and Bochenek (2001) and Manninen (2004). See also Minicase 1 at the end of this chapter.

Barriers to E-Collaboration and C-Commerce

Despite the many potential benefits, e-collaboration and c-commerce are moving ahead fairly slowly. Reasons cited in various studies include technical reasons involving integration, standards, and networks; security and privacy concerns over who has access to and control of information stored in a partner's database; internal resistance to information sharing and to new approaches; and lack of internal skills to conduct collaborative commerce (Murphy, 2003). A big stum-bling block to the adoption of c-commerce is the lack of defined and universally agreed-on standards. New approaches such as the use of XML and its variants and the use of Web Services could lessen significantly the problem of standards. (See Bradley, 2002, and *cpfr.com* for discussion of the *CPFR*—collaboration, plan-ning, forecasting, and replenishing—*initiative*.)

Sometimes collaboration is an organizational culture shock—people simply resist sharing. One reason is the lack of trust, especially in ad-hoc relationships. According to Gibson-Paul (2003), companies such as Boeing and Spalding are grappling with the trust factor. Some techniques she suggested include starting small (e.g., synchronizing one type of sales data), picking up projects that are likely to provide a quick return on investment for both sides, meeting face-to-face at the beginning of a collaboration; and showing the benefits to all parties. Despite initial lack of trust, if potential collaborators judge the benefits of collaboration to be sufficient, and about equal among collaborators, they will be more eager to join in.

Finally, global collaboration (Chapter 8) involves all of these potential barriers, and more. For further discussion, see Davison and de Vreede (2001) and Carmel (1999).

3.5 COLLABORATION-ENABLING TOOLS: FROM WORKFLOW TO GROUPWARE

As mentioned earlier, corporate portals facilitate e-collaboration. Also available for this purpose are a large number of tools and methodologies, whose types and features are listed in Online File W3.11. In this section we present workflow technologies, groupware, and other collaboration-enabling tools. For an e-collaboration technologies framework, see Brown and Sappenfield (2003).

Workflow Technologies

Workflow is the movement of information as it flows through the sequence of steps that make up an organization's work procedures. **Workflow management** is the automation of workflows, so that documents, information, or tasks are passed from one participant to another in a way that is governed by the organization's rules or procedures. Workflow management involves all of the steps in a business process from start to finish, including all exception conditions.

The key to workflow management is the tracking of process-related information and the status of each activity of the business process, which is done by workflow systems (see van der Aalst, 2002). **Workflow systems** are business process automation tools that place system controls in the hands of user departments. They employ a set of software programs that automate almost any information-processing task. The major workflow activities to be managed are job routing and monitoring, document imaging, document management, supply chain optimization, and control of work. These activities are done by workflow applications. See Online File W3.12 and Online Minicase W3.3.

There are multiple benefits of workflow management systems. For example, they improve control of business processes, with far less management intervention and far less chance for delays or misplaced work than other systems. They also improve the quality of services, by quicker response, with the best person available. They lower costs, both of staff training (since the work can be guided through complex procedures) and of management in general, because managers can have a far wider span of control while also being able to concentrate on nurturing the employees and handling special cases rather than routine reporting and distribution issues. Finally, workflow management systems also improve user satisfaction. Users typically have greater confidence that they are doing the best they can and the satisfaction of completing that work with fewer conflicting requirements. For more information on workflow management, see Fischer, 2002, and Basu and Kumar, 2002. Also, visit *wfmc.org, aim.org,* and *waria.com.*

Since workflow management systems usually support more than one individual, they are considered by some to be a subset of groupware, our next topic.

Groupware

Groupware refers to software products that support groups of people who share a common task or goal and who collaborate on its accomplishment. These products provide a way for groups to share resources and opinions. Groupware implies the use of networks to connect people electronically, even if the people are in the same room. Many groupware products are available on the Internet or an intranet, enhancing the collaboration of a large number of people worldwide. There are many different approaches and technologies for the support of groups on the Internet.

Groupware products come either as a standalone product supporting one task (such as e-mail), or as an integrated kit that includes several tools. In general, groupware technology products are fairly inexpensive and can be easily incorporated into existing information systems. The Internet, intranets, extranets, and private communication lines provide the infrastructure needed for the hardware and software of groupware. The software products are mostly Web-based, which is the trend today. In this section we will describe some of the most common groupware products.

ELECTRONIC MEETING SYSTEMS.   An important area of virtual collaboration is electronic meetings. For decades, people have attempted to improve face-to-face meetings. Initially, people attempted to better organize group meetings in one room by using a facilitator and established procedures (known as *group dynamics*). More recently, there have been numerous attempts to improve meetings by using information technologies. The advancement of Web-based systems opens the door for electronically supported *virtual meetings,* those whose members are in different locations, frequently in different countries.

The events of September 11, 2001 and the economic slowdown of 2001–2003 made virtual meetings more popular, as corporate travel waned. It is also hard for companies to ignore reported cost savings, such as the $4 million a month that IBM reported it saved just from cutting travel expenses to meetings (Callaghan, 2002). In addition, improvements in supporting technology, reductions in the price of technology, and the acceptance of virtual meetings as a respected way of doing business are fueling their growth (see Vinas, 2002).

Virtual meetings can be supported by a variety of tools, as will be shown in the remainder of this section. The direct support provided to decision making is presented in Chapter 11.

ELECTRONIC TELECONFERENCING.   **Teleconferencing** is the use of electronic communication that allows two or more people at different locations to have a simultaneous conference. There are several types of teleconferencing. The oldest and simplest is a telephone conference call, where several people talk to each other from three or more locations. The biggest disadvantage is that it does not allow for face-to-face communication. Also, participants in one location cannot see graphs, charts, and pictures at other locations. One solution is *video teleconferencing,* in which participants can see each other as well as the documents.

Video Teleconferencing.   In a **video teleconference** (or *videoconference*), participants in one location can see participants at other locations. Dynamic pictures of the participants can appear on a large screen or on a desktop computer. Originally, video teleconferencing was the transmission of live, compressed TV sessions between two or more points. Video teleconferencing today, however, is a digital technology capable of linking various types of computers across networks. Once conferences are digitized and transmitted over networks, they become a computer application.

With videoconferencing, participants can share data, voice, pictures, graphics, and animation. Data can also be sent along with voice and video. Such **data**

conferencing makes it possible to work on documents together and to exchange computer files during videoconferences. This allows several geographically dispersed groups to work on the same project and to communicate by video simultaneously.

Video teleconferencing offers various benefits. We've already mentioned three of them—providing the opportunity for face-to-face communication for individuals in different locations, supporting several types of media during conferencing, and lower travel time and costs. Other benefits of video teleconferencing are shown in Online File W3.13 at the book's Web site.

Web Conferencing. **Web conferencing** is conducted on the Internet for as few as two and as many as thousands of people. Web conferencing is done *solely* on the Web. (Videoconferencing is usually done on regular telephone lines, although it may also be done on the Web.) Like video teleconferencing, Web conferencing allows users to simultaneously view something, such as a sales presentation in Microsoft PowerPoint or a product drawing, on their computer screens; interaction takes place via messaging or a simultaneous phone teleconference. (Without such interaction, it is simply Webcasting.) Web conferencing is much cheaper than videoconferencing because it runs on the Internet.

The latest technological innovations permit both business-to-business and business-to-consumer applications of Web conferencing. For example, banks in Alaska use *video kiosks* in sparsely populated areas instead of building branches that will be underutilized. The video kiosks operate on the banks' intranet and provide videoconferencing equipment for eye-to-eye interactions. Some examples of other uses are: to educate staff members about a new product line or technology; to amplify a meeting with investors; or to walk a prospective client though an introductory presentation.

Web conferencing is becoming very popular. Some Web conferencing products provide whiteboarding (see discussion below) and polling features, and allow you to give presentations and demos and to share applications. Popular Web conferencing products are: Centra EMeeting (*centra.com*), Genesys Meeting Center (*genesys.com*), PlaceWare (*placeware.com*; see the demos), and WebEx Meeting Center.

RTC TOOLS. The Internet, intranets, and extranets offer tremendous potential for real-time and synchronous interaction of people working in groups. *Real-time collaboration (RTC)* tools (see same time–different location in Figure 3.5, page 105) help companies bridge time and space to make decisions and to collaborate on projects. RTC tools support synchronous communication of graphical and text-based information. These tools are being used in distance training, product demonstrations, customer support, and sales applications. RTC tools can be either purchased as standalone tools or used on a subscription basis. Some examples follow.

Interactive Whiteboards. Computer-based **whiteboards** work like the "physical world" whiteboards with markers and erasers, except with one big difference: Instead of one person standing in front of a meeting room drawing on the whiteboard, all participants can join in. Throughout a meeting, each user can view and draw on a single document "pasted" onto the electronic whiteboard on a computer screen. Digital whiteboarding sessions can also be saved for later reference or other uses. Some whiteboarding products let users insert graphics files that can be annotated by the group.

Take, for example, an advertisement that needs to be cleared by a senior manager. The proposed ad would be scanned into a PC, and both parties would see it on their screens. If the senior manager does not like something, he or she can highlight what needs to be changed, using a stylus pen. The two parties can also share applications. For example, if party A works with Excel, party B does not have to have Excel in order to work with it in the whiteboarding tool.

Besides being used for supporting people working on the same task, whiteboards are also used for training and learning. See Online File W3.14 for a description of two whiteboarding products that can be used for training and learning.

Screen Sharing. In collaborative work, members are frequently in different locations. Using **screen sharing** software, group members can work on the same document, which is shown on the PC screen of each participant. For example, two authors can work on a single manuscript. One may suggest a correction and execute it so the other author can see the change. Collaborators can work simultaneously on the same spreadsheet or on the resulting graphics. Changes can be done by using the keyboard or by touching the screen. This capability can expedite the design of products, the preparation of reports and bids, and the resolution of conflicts. A special screen sharing capability is offered by Groove Inc. (*groove.net*). Its product synchronizes people, computers, and information to enable the joint creation and/or editing of documents on your PC.

Instant Video. With the spread of instant messaging and Internet telephony has come the idea to link people via both voice and audio. Called *instant video,* the idea is for a kind of video chat room. It allows you to chat in real time, seeing the person you are communicating with. A simple way to do it is to add video cameras to the participants' computers. A more sophisticated approach that produces pictures of better quality is to integrate existing online videoconferencing service with instant messaging software, creating a service that offers the online equivalent of a videophone.

INTEGRATION AND GROUPWARE SUITES. Because groupware technologies are computer-based, it makes sense to integrate them with other computer-based or computer-controlled technologies. A *software suite* is created when several products are integrated into one system. Integrating several technologies can save time and money for users. For example, PictureTel Corporation (see *polycom.com*), in an alliance with software developer Lotus, developed an integrated desktop video teleconferencing product that uses Lotus Notes. Using this integrated system, publisher Reader's Digest has built several applications combined with videoconferencing capabilities. A seamless integration is provided in *groupware suites*. Lotus Notes/Domino suite (from IBM) is one example of popular groupware suites. For discussion of others, see Online File W3.15.

Lotus Notes/Domino. The **Lotus Notes/Domino** suite provides online collaboration capabilities, workgroup e-mail, distributed databases, bulletin whiteboards, text editing, (electronic) document management, workflow capabilities, instant virtual meetings, application sharing, instant messaging, consensus building, voting, ranking, and various application development tools. All these capabilities are integrated into one environment with a graphic menu-based user interface.

Group members using Lotus Notes/Domino might store all their official memos, formal reports, and informal conversations related to particular projects in a shared, online database. Then, as individual members need to check on the contents, they can access the shared database to find the information they need. For an interesting Notes/Domino application, see Online Minicase W3.4.

By the end of 2002, there were over 60 million Notes users worldwide (*ibm.com/software/lotus*, 2002). For even more capabilities of Lotus Notes/Domino, see Internet Exercise 3 at the end of the chapter.

SOCIAL SOFTWARE. **Social software** can be defined as any software that supports actual human interactions. According to Udell (2004), the category includes groupware and knowledge management tools, as well as other computer-mediated communication, Weblogs ("blogs") and *wikis* (a collaborative site on which many authors post their collective work), and large numbers of other products. (See the sampler listing social software at Online File W3.16.) These tools can help workers build relationships based on what they know and who they know. For how social networks provide competitive advantage, see Tynan (2004).

Implementation Issues of Virtual Collaboration

Throughout this chapter we have described a variety of online collaboration methods. Here we mention a few implementation issues that must be addressed when planning online collaboration. First, to connect you and your business partners, you need an effective collaborative environment. Such an environment is provided by groupware suites such as Lotus Notes/Domino. Another issue is the need to connect collaborative tools with file management products on the intranet. Two such products are e/pop servers and clients (*wiredred.com*) and eRoom's server (from *documentum.com*).

In addition, throughout the book, we have documented the general trend toward moving e-commerce applications onto the Web. To change the read-only Web to a truly collaborative environment, one needs *protocols,* rules that determine how two computers communicate with one another over a network. The protocols make possible the integration of different applications and standardize communication. One such protocol, which is relatively new, is WebDAV (Web Distributed Authoring and Versioning protocol). For details see *webdav.org*.

Finally, we should point out that online collaboration is not a panacea for all occasions or in all situations. Many times, a face-to-face meeting is a must. Human workers do sometimes need the facial cues and the physical closeness that no computer system can currently provide. (*Pervasive computing* attempts to remove some of these limitations, e.g., by interpreting facial cues. For more, see Chapter 5.) For implementation guidelines, see Buy IT Best Practice Network (2004).

3.6 E-LEARNING AND VIRTUAL WORK

Web-based systems enable many applications related to discovery, communication, and collaboration. Three additional, important applications are presented in this section—e-learning, distance learning, and telecommuting.

E-Learning versus Distance Learning

There can be some confusion between e-learning and distance learning since they overlap each other. Therefore we begin with brief definitions.

E-learning refers to learning supported by the Web. It can be done inside classrooms, as was demonstrated in the Dartmouth College Minicase in Chapter 1. It can be done as a support to conventional teaching, such as when students work on the Web at home or in the classroom. It also can be done in *virtual classrooms,* in which the entire coursework is done online and classes do not meet face-to-face, and in that case it is a part of distance learning.

Distance learning (DL) refers to situations where teachers and students do not meet face-to-face. It can be done in different ways. The oldest mode was correspondence, where all communication was done by "snail mail." As early as the 1920s the radio was added to support DL. Then came voice cassettes, videotapes, and TV for delivering lectures. Students communicated with professors by "snail mail," telephone, and faxes. A breakthrough occurred when the CD-ROM was introduced, since CD-ROMs are media-rich and enabled self-testing and feedback. Finally the Web provided a multimedia interactive environment for self-study. (For an overview of DL see Shin and Chan, 2004 and Keart et al., 2004.)

E-learning is only one channel of distance learning. At the same time, some types of e-learning are done in the face-to-face mode, and not from a distance. What is common to the two is some of the delivery tools as well as some pedagogical issues. In both cases, Web-enabled systems make knowledge accessible to those who need it, when they need it, any time, anywhere. E-learning and DL can be useful both as an environment for facilitating learning at schools and as an environment for efficient and effective corporate training.

Liaw and Huang (2002) describe how Web technologies can facilitate learning. For an overview and research issues related to e-learning, see Piccoli et al. (2001); this resource also provides a comparison of e-learning with traditional classroom teaching. Our discussion here concentrates on e-learning, which in its broader scope is known as *e-education* (see Albalooshi, 2003).

The Benefits of E-Learning

In theory, there are many benefits to e-learning: Self-paced and self-initiated learning has been shown to increase content retention (Urdan and Weggen, 2002). Online materials offer the opportunity to deliver very current content, of high quality (created by content experts), and consistent (presented the same way every time). Students in e-learning situations have the flexibility of learning from any place, at any time, and at their own pace. Finally, some learners in both educational and corporate settings appreciate what they perceive as the risk-free environment offered by e-learning, in which they feel more free to express themselves than in a face-to-face learning setting. In corporate e-training centers, learning time generally is shorter, and more people can be trained due to the faster training time. As a result, training costs can be reduced by 50 to 70 percent (Urdan and Weggen, 2002), and savings can be made on facility space as well.

E-learning provides a new set of tools that can add value to traditional learning modes. It does not usually replace the classroom setting, but enhances it, taking advantage of new content and delivery technologies. The better the match of content and delivery vehicle to an individual's learning style, the greater the content retention, and the better the learning results. Advanced e-learning support environments, such as Blackboard and WebCT, add value to traditional learning in higher education. See *A Closer Look 3.3* (page 122) for descriptions of these e-learning tools, with which you may already be familiar from personal experience. Several other e-learning courseware tools are discussed in Online File W3.17.

Some drawbacks do exist that offset the benefits of e-learning. Issues cited as possible drawbacks of e-learning are discussed in Online File W3.18 at the book's Web site. Suggestions on how to overcome such drawbacks and prevent e-learning failures are provided by Weaver (2002) and by Hricko (2003).

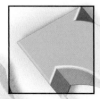

A CLOSER LOOK
3.3 BLACKBOARD AND WEBCT

There is a good chance that you will use the Blackboard Inc. or WebCT frameworks when taking a college class. These competing products provide the Internet infrastructure software for e-learning in schools, serving one of the fastest-growing industry segments in the world. Eduventures.com, a leading independent e-learning industry analyst, projected that the higher-education e-learning market will grow from $4 billion in 2001 to $11 billion by 2005 (*eduventures.com*, 2001).

The publisher places a book's content, teaching notes, quizzes, etc. on Blackboard or WebCT in a standardized format. Instructors can access modules and transfer them into their own specific Blackboard or WebCT sites, which can be accessed by their students.

Blackboard Inc. offers a complete suite of enterprise software products and services that power a total "e-education infrastructure" for schools, colleges, universities, and other education providers. Through this system, instructors can electronically manage the collection and organization of assignments. The built-in assessment management function allows simple assessment of workflow and provides flexibility in deploying tests and surveys. Of special interest are the discussion rooms that can be for everyone or for a restricted group. Last but not least, Blackboard also enables customization, extension, and integration of the sections of each course, providing flexibility in curriculum management.

WebCT provides a similar set of tools, but with a different vision and strategy. It uses advanced pedagogical tools to help institutions of higher education make distance-learning courses possible. Such courses enable schools to expand campus boundaries, attract and retain students and faculty, and continually improve course and degree program quality.

Textbook publishers are embracing these tools by making their major textbooks Blackboard and/or WebCT enabled. Thus, your professor can easily incorporate this book's content into the software that is used by thousands of universities worldwide. (For comparison between the two systems, refer to Siekmann, 2001 and CMS Task Force, 2002.)

Sources: Compiled from *webct.com* and *blackboard.com* (spring 2004).

Virtual Universities

The concept of **virtual universities**—online universities from which students take classes from home or an off-site location, via the Internet—is expanding rapidly. Hundreds of thousands of students in dozens of countries, from Great Britain to Israel to Thailand, are studying via such institutions. A large number of existing universities, including Stanford University and other top-tier institutions, offer online education of some form. Some universities, such as University of Phoenix (*phoenix.edu*), California Virtual Campus (*cvc.edu*), and the University of Maryland (*umuc.edu/distance*), offer thousands of courses and dozens of degrees to students worldwide, all online. Other universities offer limited online courses and degrees and also use innovative teaching methods and multimedia support in the traditional classroom.

The virtual university concept allows universities to offer classes worldwide. Moreover, we may soon see integrated degrees, where students can customize a degree that will best fit their needs by taking courses at different universities. Several all-virtual schools include *eschool-world.com*, *walden.com*, and *trainingzone.co.uk*.

For information about specific e-learning programs, see *Petersons.com*, *ECollege.com*, *icdl.open.ac.uk*, and *usdla.org*. For experiences in moving courses to e-learning environments, see Gale (2003). Hofmann (2002) describes the role of the Internet in distance learning in higher education, surveying implementation issues in terms of technology, course content, and pedagogy.

Online Corporate Training

Like educational institutions, a large number of business organizations are using e-learning in at least some courses (e.g., see Kapp, 2002). Web-based learning technologies allow organizations to keep their employees up-to-date, and training via the Web can run 24 hours per day, every day ("24/7"). Online corporate training also offers striking cost advantages: Conventional classroom training costs (in 2000) were about $75 an hour, with full-week programs costing $3,000 to $5,000 (*ENTmag.com,* 2000). Computer-based training costs about half that amount, without travel costs or class-size restrictions. IBM estimates a savings of $500,000 for every 1,000 hours of training not done in the traditional corporate-training classroom (Reeder, 2002). E-learning can provide 30 percent more training content in 40 percent less time and at 33 percent of the cost of more traditional techniques (Beckett, 2004).

Corporate training is often done via the intranet and corporate portals. However, in large corporations with multiple sites, and for studies from home, the Internet is used to access the online material. Some companies, like Barclays Bank, COX Industries, and Qantas Airways, offer online training in learning centers that they call "universities." For discussion of strategies for implementing corporate e-learning, see Delahoussaye and Zemke (2001). Vendors of online training and educational materials can be found at *digitalthink.com, click2learn.com, deitel.com,* and *smartplanet.com.*

E-learning is radically changing education and corporate training, and the socioeconomic and technological changes should be examined as the learning behaviors and expectations of learners change. There is a sharply growing demand for flexible and adaptive learning environments that are independent of time and geography (Meso and Liegle, 2000). For an overview of and guidelines for e-learning, see Piskurich (2003), Hartley (2002), and Cone and Robinson (2001).

Virtual Work and Telecommuting

Virtual (distributed) work environments refer to geographically distributed work teams, global project teams, interorganizational teams, and nontraditional work environments such as virtual organizations, satellite work centers, and telecommuting. The use of such distributed work environments in organizations is increasing rapidly. Many of the participants in such environments are mobile workers. The popularity of these environments is growing in direct relationship to the IT support for them. Wireless and wearable devices are one example, and the groupware tools described earlier are another.

Due to the large number of people participating in virtual work, organizations are faced with problems of how to implement virtual work environments and how to use the IT support (see Belanger et al., 2002). In Chapter 11 we will deal with one aspect of virtual work, the support to group decision making. The topic of supporting mobile employees is covered throughout the book. Here we deal with one such virtual work environment—telecommuting.

TELECOMMUTING. **Telecommuting,** or **teleworking,** refers to an arrangement whereby employees can work at home, at the customer's premises, in special work places, or while traveling, usually using a computer linked to their place of employment. Regular and overnight mail, special messengers, and fax typically have been used to support telecommuting, but they are relatively slow and expensive, and the Internet is gradually replacing them. Almost all groupware technologies can be used to support telecommuting. With laptops, broadband, and IP phones, maintaining a home office can be less expensive, and more productive, than setting up workers in larger facilities (Willis, 2004). For more on telecommuting, see Chapter 16.

3.7 SOME ETHICAL AND INTEGRATION ISSUES

Of the many issues involved in implementing network computing environments, ethics and integration issues are discussed here.

Ethics on the Net

Several ethical, legal, and security issues have been raised as a result of the use of electronic networks in general and the Internet in particular. For example:

- Does an employer have the right to look at your e-mail without your permission? (Yes, it is legal. But is it ethical?)
- Is someone's desire to download pornographic images from a newsgroup protected by freedom of speech and privacy laws?
- Should someone post critical or negative comments about a product, service, or person to a newsgroup?
- Should an Internet access provider be held liable for the content of the traffic on its network?

Whenever there are no specific answers to such questions and their legal dimensions are vague, ethics become an important factor. Here we discuss some representative ethical issues.

PRIVACY AND ETHICS IN E-MAIL. The increased use of e-mail raises the question of privacy. While letters are sealed, e-mail material is open (unless encrypted). Many organizations are monitoring e-mail, which they have the *legal* right to do in most states; this raises questions of invasion of privacy. (For more on privacy, see Chapter 16.) Other issues include the use of e-mail at work for personal purposes and for sending and receiving material that is not related to work. (For privacy protection tips surrounding e-mail, see *PC World,* February 1997.)

RIGHT TO FREE SPEECH. The dissemination of information such as pornographic and racist material via e-mail, newsgroups, electronic bulletin boards, and public networks may offend some people. But dissemination of such information in the United States is believed to be a right protected by the U.S. Constitution. At the time of this writing, the degree of freedom in the online world, and who should be liable for transmissions that are illegal, is still very much in debate. Legislation has been proposed that would require Internet access providers to create filters allowing adults to keep children from accessing inappropriate material. In fact, the commercial online providers have largely done so. The Internet, however, remains entirely accessible for anyone with a direct connection.

COPYRIGHT. The material you access on the Internet may be marked as being in the public domain; in that case it can be used by anyone for any purpose. Some material is marked as "copyrighted," which indicates that you need permission for anything other than a "fair use." *Fair use* refers to use for educational and not-for-profit activities. If you make a profit from use of copyrighted material, you should pay the copyright owner some fee or royalties.

Much of the material on the Internet is not marked as either in the public domain or copyrighted. Therefore, at least from an ethical point of view, it should be considered copyrighted. This includes software: You cannot legally copy any licensed software. However, *freeware* on the Internet can be downloaded and distributed. *Shareware* can be downloaded for review, but you are expected to pay for it if you decide you want to use it.

THE PRIVACY OF PATIENTS' INFORMATION. In the United States, several specialized online healthcare networks exist, such as Telemed, a network that tracks tuberculosis patients in order to prescribe the most suitable drugs. These systems could be abused. How do patients know they are getting qualified advice? What if personal medical records fall into the wrong hands? The growth of computerized networks makes medical confidentiality harder to preserve. The problem is how to strike a balance between the benefits of health information systems and their potential ethical problems.

INTERNET MANNERS. Two well-known behaviors on the Internet are spamming and flaming. **Spamming** refers to indiscriminate distribution of messages, without consideration for their appropriateness. Spamming is a major online problem since it is widely used by advertisers (see Chapters 4 and 16). Spamming is frequently answered by **flaming,** which refers to sending angry messages. The Internet can become a war zone between spammers and flamers. Both sides may be equally guilty of ruining newsgroups. Flamers are known for their attacks on inexperienced visitors to newsgroups as well as on those who make spelling errors. A *spam shield* can stop spamming (for examples see *spamcop.com* and *mailwatch.com/stopspam.cfm*). For more discussion of spamming and legislation to control it, see Chapter 16.

There are certain general "rules," called *netiquette* (network etiquette), governing Internet manners. One of these "rules," for example, is to think carefully before sending a public message; keep in mind that you are making your reputation internationally through the messages you send out. Another useful rule of Internet manners is to apply the Golden Rule: Do unto others in cyberspace as you would do unto them face to face, which is, of course, as you would want them to do unto you. A list of various "netiquette" rules is shown in Online File W3.19 at the book's Web site.

Likewise, it is far easier to take offense online because online interaction excludes the nuances of body language, rhythm, mood, and context. E-mail users developed an expressive language that can be used to overcome this problem. A sample is shown in Online File W3.20.

UNSOLICITED ADVERTISING. An extension of spamming is the use of junk mail which may clog providers' systems and which frequently annoys people. Similarly, the use of pop-ups (see Chapter 4) irritates many people.

MONITORING EMPLOYEES' USE OF THE INTERNET. Some companies use special software that monitors time spent on the Internet by each employee (and by site address). The objective is to eliminate abuse of access during working hours and the accessing of "indecent" sites. Other companies simply disconnect sites they do not want their employees to visit. Some people believe that such monitoring is either unethical or an infringement of their freedom of speech. Is freedom of speech an absolute right, or does it also involve associated responsibilities?

MONITORING STUDENTS' USE OF THE INTERNET. In recent years, the issue of using a university's network for nonstudy use (e.g., for P2P file sharing) has cropped up. At many universities, this usage has resulted in insufficient bandwidth and so has compromised use of the network for academic purposes. Some universities monitor students' activities on the Internet. Some students question whether it is ethical for universities to do so.

Integration Issues   When people discover, communicate, and collaborate by using just the Internet or other open systems, there are no problems of doing so. But in many cases, network computing involves other types of networks, such as value-added networks (VANs), as well as legacy and other specialized systems, such as computer-aided-design (CAD) or wireless systems. In such a case, users may encounter problems in connecting applications to such systems, a problem known as *integration*. The problem of integration was ranked by a group of chief information officers (CIOs) surveyed in 2001, 2002, and 2003 as their number-one or number-two technology problem.

The integration issue can be complicated since information systems involve not only networks, applications, and people, but also hardware, software, and support services of multiple organizations. We discussed the integration problem briefly in Chapter 2 and here. Many possible solutions to the integration problem have been developed over the years. They will be discussed in Chapters 4, 6, 7, and 14. One of the newest and most promising approaches to this problem is Web Services, as discussed in Chapter 2 and in Technology Guide 6. An example of how Expedia is using Web Services is provided in Chapter 12.

➡ MANAGERIAL ISSUES

1. *Security of communication.* Communication via networks raises the issue of the integrity, confidentiality, and security of the data being transferred. The protection of data in networks across the globe is not simple (see Chapter 15).

2. *Installing digital dashboards.* Many companies are installing "digital dashboards," which are a sort of one-way portal display that is continuously updated with online displays. The dashboard is available to employees and visitors in visible places around the company and is also accessible from PCs, PDAs, etc. Large companies, such as General Electric, believe that the cost of the dashboards can be justified by the better discovery and communication they promote within the company.

3. *Control of employee time and activities.* To control the time that employees might waste "surfing the Net" during working hours, some companies limit the information that employees have access to or they use special monitoring software. Providing guidelines for employee use of the Internet is a simple but fairly effective approach.

4. **How many portals?** A major issue for some companies is how many portals to have. Should there be separate portals for customers, suppliers, employees, for example? Regardless of the answer, it is a good idea to integrate the separate portals. If you build a separate portal, make sure it can be easily connected to the others (see the tips at "Experts offer key tips. . . ," 2002).

5. **Organizational impacts.** Technology-supported communication may have major organizational impacts. For example, intranets and groupware force people to cooperate and share information. Therefore, their use can lead to significant changes in both organizational culture and the execution of business process restructuring. Further impacts may be felt in corporate structure and the redistribution of organizational power.

6. **Telecommuting.** Telecommuting is a compelling venture, but management needs to be careful. Not all jobs are suitable for telecommuting, and allowing only some employees to telecommute may create jealousy. Likewise, not all employees are suitable telecommuters; some need the energy and social contact found in an office setting.

7. **Cost-benefit justification.** The technologies described in this chapter do not come free, and many of the benefits are intangible. However, the price of many networking technologies is decreasing.

8. **Controlling access to and managing the content of the material on an intranet.** This is becoming a major problem due to the ease of placing material on an intranet and the huge volume of information. Flohr (1997) suggests tools and procedures to manage the situation.

KEY TERMS

Asynchronous
  communication *105*
Blog *107*
Blogging (Weblogging) *107*
Chat room *106*
Collaboration *108*
Collaborative commerce *110*
Corporate portals *101*
Data conferencing *117*
Directories *96*
Distance learning (DL) *121*
E-learning *120*
Flaming *123*
Groupware *116*
Information portal *100*

Intelligent agents *96*
Internet relay chat (IRC) *106*
Internet2 *91*
Internet telephony (voice-over IP) *107*
Lotus Notes/Domino *119*
Metasearch engines *97*
Portal *100*
Screen sharing *119*
Search engine *96*
Social software *120*
Softbot *96*
Software agents *96*
Spamming *125*
Synchronous (real-time)
  communication *105*

Telecommuting (teleworking) *123*
Teleconferencing *117*
Video teleconference *117*
Virtual collaboration *110*
Virtual group (team) *108*
Virtual meetings *108*
Virtual universities *122*
Virtual work
  (distributed work) *123*
Web conferencing *118*
Whiteboard (electronic) *118*
World Wide Web (the Web) *91*
Workflow *116*
Workflow management *116*
Workflow systems *116*

CHAPTER HIGHLIGHTS (Numbers Refer to Learning Objectives)

❶ The Internet is a network of many networks.

❶ The Internet and the Web will enable us to integrate voice, text, and other interactive media and bring them into every home, school, and business.

❷ Intranets are an implementation and deployment of Web-based network services within a company.

❷ Intranets and extranets have the potential to change organizational structures and procedures.

❸ There are four configurations of supporting communication in meetings: same-time/same-place, same-time/different-place, different-time/same-place, and different-time/different-place.

❸ Electronic mail allows quick communication across the globe at minimal cost.

❹ Electronic meeting systems, computer-supported co-operative work, groupware, and other names designate various types of computer support to groups.

❹ Video teleconferencing utilizes several technologies that allow people to communicate and view each other as well as view and transfer documents.

❹ Voice technologies can be used to increase productivity and usability of communication.

❺ Lotus Notes/Domino is a major integrated software suite that supports the work of dispersed individuals and groups.

❻ Software agents help to carry out mundane tasks on the Internet such as searching, browsing, and sorting e-mail.

❼ Distance learning and telecommuting are supported by network computing.

❽ Ethical behavior on the Internet is critical in order to conduct business in a professional way. You need to know what is right and wrong.

VIRTUAL COMPANY ASSIGNMENT

Network Computing at The Wireless Café
Go to The Wireless Café's link on the Student Web Site. There you will find a description of some communications problems the restaurant is having as a result of its 24/7 operations. You will be asked to identify ways network computing can facilitate better staff communications.

More Resources
More resources and study tools are located on the Student Web Site. You'll find additional chapter materials and useful Web links. In addition, self-quizzes that provide individualized feedback are available for each chapter.

Instructions for accessing The Wireless Café on the Student Web Site

1. Go to
   wiley.com/college/turban
2. Select Turban/Leidner/ McLean/Wetherbe's *Information Technology for Management, Fifth Edition.*
3. Click on Student Resources site, in the tool-bar on the left.
4. Click on the link for Virtual Company Web site.
5. Click on Wireless Café.

QUESTIONS FOR REVIEW

1. List the major advantages of the Internet.
2. Define an intranet.
3. Define discovery, communication, and collaboration.
4. Describe corporate portals and their benefits.
5. Distinguish corporate portals from information (Internet) portals.
6. What are some major benefits and limitations of working in groups?

7. Describe the time/place framework.

8. Define software agents applications and list their Internet applications.

9. Describe differences and relationships between intranets and extranets.

10. Define groupware.

11. Describe the major capabilities of real-time collaboration tools.

12. List the major capabilities of teleconferencing.

13. Define workflow systems.

14. Describe software agents.

15. List the major Internet-based agents.

16. Define Internet and Internet2.

17. Define voice technology and list its major business uses.

18. Describe and distinguish between DL and e-learning.

19. Define telecommuting and describe its benefits.

20. Define flaming and contrast it with spamming.

21. Define netiquette.

QUESTIONS FOR DISCUSSION

1. Identify some commercial tools that allow users to conduct browsing, communication, and collaboration simultaneously.

2. Describe how software agents can help people find specific information quickly.

3. Explain the advantages of electronic mail over regular mail.

4. Discuss the role of Web-based call centers and their contribution to competitive advantage.

5. Explain why the topic of group work and its support is getting increased attention.

6. It is said that collaboration tools can change organizational culture. Explain how.

7. How can computers support a team whose members work at different times?

8. Based on what you know about Lotus Notes, can it support different-time/different-place work situations?

9. Relate telecommuting to networks.

10. Distinguish between flaming and spamming. How are they related? How is flaming related to netiquette?

EXERCISES

1. From your own experience or from vendors' information, list the major capabilities of Lotus Notes/Domino. Do the same for Microsoft Exchange. Compare and contrast the products. Explain how the products can be used to support knowledge workers and managers.

2. Visit *polycom.com* and sites of other companies that manufacture conferencing products for the Internet. Prepare a report. Why are conferencing products considered part of video commerce?

3. Marketel is a fast-growing (hypothetical) telemarketing company whose headquarters are in Colorado, but the majority of its business is in California. The company has eight divisions, including one in Chicago. (The company has just started penetrating the Midwest market.) Recently the company was approached by two large telephone companies, one in Los Angeles and one in Denver, for discussions regarding a potential merger.

   Nancy Miranda, the corporate CEO who was involved in the preliminary discussions, notified all division managers on the progress of the discussions. Both she and John Miner, the chief financial officer, felt that an immediate merger would be extremely beneficial. However, the vice presidents for marketing and operations thought the company should continue to be independent for at least two to three years. "We can get a much better deal if we first increase our market share," commented Sharon Gonzales, the vice president for marketing.

   Nancy called each of the division managers and found that five of them were in favor of the merger proposal and three objected to it. She also found that the division managers from the West Coast strongly opposed discussions with the Colorado company, and the other managers were strongly against discussions with the Los Angeles company. Memos, telephone calls, and meetings of two or three people at a time resulted in frustration. It became apparent that a meeting of all concerned individuals was needed. Nancy wanted to have the meeting as soon as possible in spite of the busy travel schedules of most division managers. She also wanted the meeting to be as short as possible. Nancy called Bob Kraut, the chief information officer, and asked for suggestions about how to conduct a conference electronically. The options he outlined are as follows.

   (1) Use the corporate intranet. Collect opinions from all division managers and vice presidents, then disseminate them to all parties, get feedback, and repeat the process until a solution is achieved.

   (2) Fly all division managers to corporate headquarters and have face-to-face meetings there until a solution is achieved.

(3) Use the Web for a meeting.

(4) Fly all division managers to corporate headquarters. Rent a decision room (a facility designed for electronic meetings) and a facilitator from the local university for $2,000 per day, and conduct the meetings there.

(5) Conduct a videoconference. Unfortunately, appropriate facilities exist only at the headquarters and in two divisions. The other division managers can be flown to the nearest division that has equipment. Alternatively, videoconferencing facilities can be rented in all cities.

(6) Use a telephone conference call.

Answer the following questions:

a. Which of these options would you recommend to management and why?

b. Is there a technology not listed that might do a better job?

c. Is it possible to use more than one alternative in this case? If yes, which technologies would you combine, and how would you use them?

GROUP ASSIGNMENTS

1. You are a member of a team working for a multinational finance corporation. Your team's project is to prepare a complex financing proposal for a client within one week. Two of the team members are in Singapore, one is in Seoul, South Korea, one is in London, and one is in Los Angeles. You cannot get the team members together in one place. Your team does not have all the required expertise, but other corporate employees may have it. There are 8,000 employees worldwide; many of them travel. You do not know exactly who are the experts in your company.

Your company has never prepared such a proposal, but you know that certain parts of the proposal can be adapted from previous proposals. These proposals are filed electronically in various corporate databases, but you are not sure exactly where. (The company has over 80 databases, worldwide.) Finally, you will need a lot of external information, and you will need to communicate with your client in China, with investment groups in Japan and New York, and with your corporate headquarters in London.

If the client accepts your proposal, your company will make more than $5 million in profit. If the contract goes to a competitor, you may lose your job.

Your company has all the latest information and communication technologies.

a. Prepare a list of tasks and activities that your team will need to go through in order to accomplish the mission.

b. Describe what information technologies you would use to support the above tasks. Be specific, explaining how each technology can facilitate the execution of each task.

2. The world of the Internet is growing very fast, and it keeps changing. The task for the group is to report on the latest developments on the Internet's uses. Members of the group will prepare a report to include the following:

a. New business applications on the Internet.

b. New books about the Internet.

c. Information about new software products related to the Internet.

d. New managerial and technological issues related to the Internet.

e. Also, send an e-mail message about a topic of concern to you to the White House and include the reply in your report.

3. Assign each group member to an integrated group support tool kit (Lotus Notes, Exceloncorp.com, GroupWise, etc.). Have each member visit the Web site of the commercial developer and obtain information about this product. As a group, prepare a comparative table of the major similarities and differences among the kits.

4. Assign each team to a college collaborative tool such as Blackboard, WebCT, etc. Establish common evaluative criteria. Have each team evaluate the capabilities and limitations of its tool, and convince each team that its product is superior.

5. Have each team download a free copy of Groove from *groove.net*. Install the software on the members' PCs and arrange collaborative sessions. What can the free software do for you? What are its limitations?

INTERNET EXERCISES

1. Your friend wishes to pursue graduate studies in accounting in the United States. She is especially interested in two universities: the University of Illinois and the University of Southern California. Use the Internet to find information that will help her choose between the two universities. Such information should include, *but not be limited to,* the following:

a. The types of degree programs in accounting offered by the two universities.

b. The admission procedures and school calendar.

c. Coursework and dissertation requirements of the programs under consideration.

d. The costs of tuition and other expenses associated with the programs.

2. You plan to take a three-week vacation in Hawaii this December, visiting the big island of Hawaii. Using the Internet, find information that will help you plan the trip. Such information includes, *but is not limited to,* the following:

a. Geographical location and weather conditions in December.

b. Major tourist attractions and recreational facilities.

c. Travel arrangements (airlines, approximate fares).

d. Car rental; local tours.

e. Alternatives for accommodation (within a moderate budget) and food.

f. Estimated cost of the vacation (travel, lodging, food, recreation, shopping, etc.).

g. State regulations regarding the entrance of your dog that you plan to take with you.

h. Shopping (try to find an electronic mall).

3. Enter *lotus.com* and identify the various tools it provides for collaboration. Mark the capabilities that are not cited in this chapter.

4. Visit *cdt.org*. Find what technologies are available to track users' activities on the Internet.

5. You are assigned the task of buying desktop teleconferencing equipment for your company. Using the Internet:

a. Identify three major vendors.

b. Visit their Web sites and find information about their products and capabilities.

c. Compare the least expensive products of two vendors.

d. Find a newsgroup that has an interest in video teleconferencing. Post new questions regarding the products selected. (For example, what are the users' experiences with the products?)

e. Prepare a report of your findings.

6. Both Microsoft Explorer and Netscape Navigator have the capability for Internet telephony; all you need is a sound card, microphone, and speakers on your PC. (If you do not have these browsers, access the VocalTec Web site at *vocaltec.com/*, and download and install its fully functional Internet long-distance telephone software.) Get a friend in another city to do the same. Contact each other via the Internet using your computer as a telephone. What are the advantages and disadvantages of using the Internet for telephone service? Compare your experience to that of making a standard telephone call.

7. Visit *albion.com/netiquette/netiquiz.html* and take the online quiz about netiquette.

8. Visit *tibco.com* and examine its Smartsockets product. Read the Southwest Airlines case at that site and prepare a list of the advantages of the system.

9. Visit *microsoft.com* and *slipstick.com* and find information about their digital dashboards. Examine their capabilities and compare them to information portals.

10. Enter *intranets.com*. Is this site a portal or an advertising company? Why are the services provided of interest to real estate companies?

11. Enter *hpe-learning.com*. Find what programs they have and how they conduct training. Write a report.

12. Enter *setiathome.ssl.Berkeley.edu* and download the free software. Join the efforts to analyze radiotelescope data. Comment about this collaborative effort. Explain why it uses P2P technology.

13. Enter *PCSVision.com*. Describe its services.

 ## *Minicase 1*
How General Motors Is Collaborating Online

The Problem

Designing a car is a complex and lengthy task. Take, for example, General Motors (GM). Each model created needs to go through a frontal crash test. So the company builds prototypes that cost about one million dollars for each car and tests how they react to a frontal crash. GM crashes these cars, makes improvements, then makes new prototypes and crashes them again. There are other tests and more crashes. Even as late as the 1990s, GM crashed as many as 70 cars for each new model.

The information regarding a new design and its various tests, collected in these crashes and other tests, has to be shared among close to 20,000 designers and engineers in hundreds of divisions and departments at 14 GM design labs, some of which are located in different countries. In addition, communication and collaboration is needed with design engineers of the more than 1,000 key suppliers. All of these necessary communications slowed the design process and increased its cost. It took over four years to get a new model to the market.

The Solution

GM, like its competitors, has been transforming itself into an e-business. This gradual transformation has been going on since the mid-1990s, when Internet bandwidth increased sufficiently to allow Web collaboration. The first task was to examine over 7,000 existing legacy IT systems, reducing them to about 3,000, and making them Web-enabled. The EC system is centered on a computer-aided design (CAD) program from EDS (a large IT company, subsidiary of GM). This system, known as Unigraphics, allows 3-D design documents to be *shared online* by both the internal and external designers and engineers, all of whom are hooked up with the EDS software. In addition, collaborative and Web-conferencing software tools, including Microsoft's NetMeeting and EDS's eVis, were added to enhance teamwork. These tools have radically changed the vehicle-review process.

An even more recent innovation is GM's Advanced Design Studio. Here, three 20-foot "power walls" wrap around one section of the room, displaying larger-than-life, three-dimensional projections of vehicles in progress, for everyone to examine and dissect. Engineers, designers, digital sculptors, and software programmers sit side by side, collaborating on various aspects of each vehicle appearing on the screens. The vehicle model manager addresses the Smart Board, a 50-inch flat-panel computer display synchronized with the power wall. He maneuvers around the screen 3-D sketches of upcoming GM vehicles.

GM also has a Virtual Reality Lab, equipped with a wraparound, floor-to-ceiling display wall. Wearing special 3-D glasses, managers can occupy the virtual space of the driver's seat and get a sense of the interior. They can also "drive" the prospective vehicle through simulations of downtown Las Vegas or along a twisting highway. The lab is digitally linked to all 14 GM engineering centers overseas via a corporate intranet, allowing executives and designers to collaborate on product reviews with colleagues around the world and around the clock.

To see how GM now collaborates with a supplier, take as an example a needed cost reduction of a new seat frame made by Johnson Control. GM electronically sends its specifications for the seat to the vendor's product data system. Johnson Control's collaboration systems (eMatrix) is integrated with EDS's Unigraphics. This integration allows joint searching, designing, tooling, and testing of the seat frame in real time, expediting the process and cutting costs by more than 10 percent.

Another area of collaboration is that of crashing cars. Here designers need close collaboration with the test engineers. Using simulation, mathematical modeling, and a Web-based review process, GM is able now to electronically "crash" cars rather than to do it physically.

The Results

Now it takes less than 18 months to bring a new car to market, compared to 4 or more years before, and at a much lower design cost. For example, 60 cars are now "crashed" electronically, and only 10 are crashed physically. The shorter cycle time enables more new car models, providing GM with a competitive edge. All this has translated into profit. Despite the economic slowdown, GM's revenues increased more than 6 percent in 2002, while its earnings in the second quarter of 2002 doubled that of 2001.

Sources: Compiled from Sullivan (2002), press releases at *gm.com,* and from *amrresearch.com* as reported by Sullivan (October 2002).

Questions for Minicase 1

1. Why did it take GM over four years to design a new car?
2. Who collaborated with whom to reduce the time-to-market?
3. How has IT helped to cut the time-to-market?

Minicase 2
Cisco Systems Pioneers E-Learning

The Problem

Cisco Systems is one of the fastest-growing high-tech companies in the world, selling devices that connect computers and networks to the Internet and other networks. Cisco's products are continuously being upgraded or replaced; so extensive training of employees and customers is needed. Cisco has recognized that its employees, business partners, and independent students seeking professional certification all require training on a continuous basis. Traditional classroom training was flawed by its inability to scale rapidly enough. Cisco offered in-house classes for each course, 6 to 10 times a year, in many locations, but the rapid growth in the number of students, coupled with the fast pace of technological change, made the training both expensive and ineffective.

The Solution

Cisco believes that *e-learning* is a revolutionary way to empower its workforce and partners with the skills and knowledge needed to turn technological change to an advantage. Therefore, Cisco implemented e-learning programs that allow students to learn new software, hardware, and procedures. Cisco believes that once people experience e-learning, they will recognize that it is the fastest, easiest way to get the information they need to be successful. The company created the Delta Force—made up of the CEO, the IT unit, and the Internet Learning Solution Group—to implement e-learning. The first project was to build two learning portals, one for 40 partner companies that sell Cisco products, and one for 4,000 systems engineers who implement the products after the sale.

To encourage its employees to use e-learning, Cisco:

- Makes e-learning "nonthreatening" by using an anonymous testing and scoring process that focuses on helping people improve rather than penalizing those who fail
- Gives those who fail the tests precision learning targets (remedial work, modules, exercises, or written materials) to help them pass and remove the fear associated with testing
- Enables managers to track, manage, and ensure employee development, competency change, and, ultimately, performance change
- Offers additional incentives and rewards such as stock grants, promotions, and bonuses to employees who pursue specialization and certification through e-learning
- Adds e-learning as a strategic top-down metric for Cisco executives, who are measured on their deployment of IT in their departments
- Makes e-learning a mandatory part of employees' jobs
- Offers easy access to e-learning tools via the Web

Cisco also wants to serve as a model of e-learning for its customers, hoping to convince them to use e-learning programs.

Cisco operates E-Learning Centers for Excellence that offer training at Cisco's centers as well as at customers' sites via intranets and the Internet. Some of the training requires the use of partnering vendors. Cisco offers a variety of training programs supported by e-learning. For example, in 2001, Cisco converted a popular 4 1/2-day, instructor-led training (ILT) course on Cisco's signature IOS (interorganizational information system) technologies into an e-learning program that blends both live and self-paced components. The goal was to teach seasoned systems engineers how to sell, install, configure, and maintain those key IOS technologies, and to do so in a way that would train more people than the 25 employees the ILT course could hold.

The Results

On the IOS course alone, Cisco calculated its return on investment as follows:

- It cost $12,400 in labor to develop the blended course.
- The course saved each system engineer one productivity day and 20 percent of the travel and lodging cost of a one-week training course in San Jose. Estimating $750 for travel and lodging and $450 for the productivity day, the savings totaled $1,200 per engineer.
- Seventeen system engineers attended the course the first time it was offered, for a total savings of $20,400. Cisco therefore recovered the development costs in the first offering—and saved $8,000 over and above the development costs. Since March 2001, the IOS Learning Services team has presented two classes of 40 engineers per month. At that rate, Cisco saves $1,152,000 net for just this one course every 12 months.

In 2003, there were over 10,000 corporate salespeople, 150,000 employees of business partners, and 200,000 independent students, all taking courses at Cisco learning centers, many using the e-learning courses. By 2003, Cisco had developed over 100 e-learning courses and was planning to develop many more soon. According to Galagan (2002), e-learning became a major force in Cisco's economic recovery, which started in 2002.

Sources: Compiled from miscellaneous news items at *Cisco.com* (2001–2003), Galagan (2002), and Delahoussaye and Zemke (2001).

Questions for Minicase 2

1. What were the drivers of e-learning at Cisco?
2. How can e-learning empower employees and partners?
3. What, in your opinion, made this project a success?
4. Can a small company use such e-training? Why or why not?

REFERENCES

Albalooshi, F., *Virtual Education: Cases in Learning and Teaching Technologies.* Hershey, PA: The Idea Group, 2003.

Alexander, S., "Virtual Teams Going Global," *InfoWorld,* 22(46), November 13, 2000.

Aneja, A. et al., "Corporate Portal Framework for Transforming Content Chaos on Intranets," *Intel Technology Journal,* Q1, 2000.

Bartram, L., and M. Blackstock, "Designing Portable Collaborative Networks," *Queue,* 1(3), May 2003, pp. 40–49.

Basu, A., and A. Kumar, "Research Commentary: Workflow Management Issues in e-Business," *Information System Research,* March 2002.

BBC, "Blogging Goes Mobile," *BBC News,* February 23, 2003, *news.bbc.co.uk/1/hi/technology/2783951.stm.* (Accessed May 13, 2003.)

Beckett, H., "Blend Skills for a Better Class of E-Learning," *Computer Weekly,* January 20, 2004.

Belanger, F. et al., "Technology Requirements and Work Group Communication for Telecommuters," *Information Systems Research,* June 2001.

Benbya, H., et al., "Corporate Portal: A Tool for Knowledge Management Synchronization," *International Journal of Information Management,* 24(3), June 2004, pp. 201–220.

Berners-Lee, T. J. et al., "The Semantic Web," *Scientific American,* May 2001, *scientificamerican.com/article.cfm?articleID=00048144-10D2-1C70-84A9809EC588EF21&catID=2.* (Accessed May 2003.)

blackboard.com. (Accessed spring 2004.)

Boothroyd, D., "Opening Up the Internet through Voice Portals," *HLTCentral,* January 27, 2003, *hltcentral.org/page=883.0.shtml.* (Accessed May 2004.)

Bradley, P., "CPFR Gaining Converts," *Logistics,* April 2002.

Brookman, F., "ChainDrugStore.Net Facilitates Rapid Exchange of Needed Information," *Stores,* January 2003.

Brown, M., and D. Sappenfield, "Collaborative Commerce: Not Dead Yet," *Intelligent Enterprise,* March 1, 2003.

BuyIT Best Practice Network, *e-Collaboration: A BuyIT e-Business Guideline,* January 2004, *buyitnet.org/Best_Practice_Guidelines/e-Business/docs/e-Collaboration%20Full.pdf.* (Accessed May 8, 2004.)

Cadinfo.NET, "Collaborative Workflow Streamlines Engineering Process Change," *cadinfo.net/editorial/dct.htm.* (Accessed January 3, 2003.)

Callaghan, D., "IBM: E-Meetings Save $4 Million a Month," *eWeek,* June 26, 2002.

Carmel, E., *Global Software Teams: Collaboration Across Borders and Time Zones.* Upper Saddle River, NJ: Prentice Hall, 1999.

Carroll, S., "How to Find Anything Online," *PC Magazine,* May 27, 2003, *pcmag.com/article2/0,4149,1047718,00.asp.* (Accessed May 30, 2003.)

Choi, S. Y., and A. B. Whinston, *The Internet Economy: Technology and Practice.* Austin: TX: SmartEcon Publishing, 2000.

Cone, J. W., and D. G. Robinson, "The Power of E-Performance," *Training and Development,* August 2001.

Chow, W. S., "An Exploratory Study of the Success Factors for Extranet Adoption in E-supply Chain," *Journal of Global Information Management,* 12(1), January–March 2004, pp. 60–67.

CMS Task Force, *WebCT vs. Blackboard: Report of the Course Management Task Force,* Course Management System Task Force, Office of the CIO, Western Carolina University, 5 December 2002, *wcu.edu/it/cio/planning/cmsfinalreport.pdf.* (Accessed May 8, 2004.)

Davison, R., and G. de Vreede, "The Global Application of Collaborative Technologies," *Communications of the ACM,* 44(12), 2001.

Delahoussaye, M., and R. Zemke, "About Learning Online," *Training,* September 2001.

DeSanctis, G., and B. Gallupe, "A Foundation for the Study of Group Decision Support Systems," *Management Science,* 33(5), 1987.

DeYoung, J., "Through the Voice Portal," *PC Magazine,* August 2001, p. 10.

D'Inverno, M., and M. Luck, *Understanding Agent Systems,* 2nd Ed., Springer Series on Agent Technology. Berlin: Springer Verlag, January 2004.

Divitini, M., et al., "Mobile Computing and Applications (MCA): UbiCollab: Collaboration Support for Mobile Users," *Proceedings of the 2004 ACM Symposium on Applied Computing,* Nicosia, Cyprus, March 14–17, 2004, pp. 1191–1195.

Eduventures.com, "Eduventures Releases Study of Higher Education E-Learning Market, a Subset of E-Education; Forecasts E-Education Market Growth from $4.5 Billion in 2001 to $11 Billion in 2005," *Eduventures.com,* December 18, 2001, *eduventures.com/about/press_room/12_18_01.cfm.* (Accessed May 2003.)

ENTmag.com, "Lessons in Technical Training," ENTmag.com, June 2000, *entmag.com/archives/article.asp?EditorialsID=5273.* (Accessed May 2003.)

"Experts Offer Key Tips on Building, Integrating Portal Marts," *I/S Analyzer,* September 2002.

Ferguson, M., "Corporate and E-Business Portals," *myITAdvisor,* April 2001.

Fischer, L., *Workflow Handbook 2002.* Lighthouse Point, FL: Future Strategies, 2002.

Fisher, K., and M. D. Fisher, *The Distance Manager.* New York, McGraw-Hill, 2000.

Flohr, U., "Intelligent Intranets: Intranets Can Be Anarchy Until You Manage Who Can Do What, Where," *Byte,* August 1997.

Frank, M., "Industry Showcase: LANSA Delivers e-Collaboration On Demand," *LANSA,* February 2004, *lansa.com/casestudies/ecoll-aboration.htm.* (Accessed May 7, 2004.)

Galagan, P. A., "Delta Force at Cisco," *Training and Development,* July 2002.

Gale, S. F., "Making E-Learning More than 'Pixie Dust'," *Workforce,* March 2003.

Gibson-Paul, L., "Suspicious Minds," *CIO Magazine,* January 15, 2003.

Hartley, D. E., "All Aboard the E-Learning Train," *Productivity Digest,* December 2002.

Haugseth, C., "Retail Giant, EMKE Group, Adopts Wireless Technology," *Middle East Company News,* April 10, 2004, *ameinfo.com/news/Detailed/37509.html.* (Accessed May 7, 2004.)

Hedlund, T., et al., "Dictionary-Based Cross-Language Information Retrieval: Learning Experiences from CLEF 2000–2002," *Information Retrieval,* 7(1–2), January–April 2004, pp. 99–119.

Hinds, P. J., and D. E. Bailey, "Out of Sight, Out of Sync: Understanding Conflict in Distributed Teams," *Organization Science,* 14(6), 2003, pp. 615–632.

http://articles.findarticles.com/p/articles/mi_m0COW/is_2004_Jan_27/ai_112588979.

http://articles.findarticles.com/p/articles/mi_m0DIS/is_8_4/ai_107180498.

Hofmann, D. W., "Internet-Based Learning in Higher Education," *Techdirections,* August 2002, *computerworld.com/managementtopics/management/helpdesk/story/0,10801,61019,00.html.* (Accessed April 28, 2002.)

Hricko, M. F., *Design and Implementation of Web-Enabled Teaching Tools*. Hershey PA: The Idea Group, 2003.

Imhoff, C., "Power Up Your Enterprise Portal," *e-Business Advisor,* May 2001.

Interactive Week, January 12, 1998.

"Intranet Corner: How Big 5 Consulting Firms Use Intranets to Manage Their Employees', and Industry Experts' Knowledge and What They Can Teach Us," *Intranet Journal,* July 2000, *intranetjournal.com/articles/200007/ic_07_26_00e.html.* (Accessed May 2003.)

Jafair, A., et al., *Designing Portals: Opportunities & Challenges.* IRM Press, September 2003.

Jarvenpaa, S., and D. Leidner, "Communication and Trust in Global Virtual Teams," *Organization Science,* Winter 1999, pp. 791–815.

Kapp, K., "Anytime E-Learning Takes Off in Manufacturing," *APICS,* June 2002.

Kayworth, T., and D. Leinder, "The Leadership of Global Virtual Teams," *Journal of Management Information Systems,* Winter 2002, pp. 7–40.

Keart, K., et al., "Using Information and Communication Technology in a Modular Distance Learning Course," *European Journal of Engineering Education,* 29(1), March 2004, pp. 17–25.

Kesner, R. M., "Building a Knowledge Portal: A Case Study in Web-Enabled Collaboration," *Information Strategy: The Executive Journal,* 2003.

Khalifa, M., and R. Davison, "Exploring the Telecommuting Paradox," *Communications of the ACM,* 43(3), March 2000.

Kirkman, B., et al., "Five Challenges to Virtual Team Success: Lessons from Sabre, Inc.," *Academy of Management Executive,* 16(3), August 2002.

Kounadis, T., "How to Pick the Best Portal," *e-Business Advisor,* August 2000.

Lewin, J., "Learning from Blogs," *ecommerce_in_action@itw.itworld.com.* (Accessed December 2003.)

Liaw, S., and H. Huang, "How Web Technology Can Facilitate Learning," *Information Systems Management,* Winter 2002.

Lieberman, H., et al., "Exploring the Web with Reconnaissance Agents," *Communications of the ACM,* 44(8), August 2001, pp. 69–75.

line56.com, "Transportation and Warehousing: Improving the Value of Your Supply Chain through Integrated Logistics," May 1, 2002, *elibrary.line56.com/data/detail?id=1043954015_280&type=RES&x=1033897490.* (Accessed August 17, 2002.)

Lotus.com, "Integration of TRADOS Software to Increase Functionality of Lotus Notes, September 25, 2002, *lotus.com, lotus.com/products/dmlt.nsf/0/90ff6c4f8a851a1485256966007084e6?OpenDocument.* (Accessed May 2003.)

Lotus Solutions, Winter 1998, pp. 10–11.

MacDonald, N., "The Future of Weblogging," *The Register,* April 18, 2004, *theregister.co.uk/2004/04/18/blogging_future.* (Accessed May 7, 2004.)

Manageradvisor.com, "Collaborative Commerce, the Way to Go?," *Manageradvisor.com, manageradvisor.com/doc/11546* (2002). (Accessed May 12, 2003.)

Manninen, M., *Rich Interaction Model for Game and Virtual Environment Design,* Academic Dissertation, 2004, *herkules.oulu.fi/isbn9514272544/isbn9514272544.pdf.* (Accessed May 8, 2004.)

McLaughlin, L., "Beyond Google," *PCWorld.com,* April 2004.

Meso, P. N., and J. O. Liegle, "The Future of Web-Based Instruction Systems," *Proceedings of the Americas Conference of the Association for Information Systems,* Milwaukee, WI, August 2000.

Murphy, J. V., "Forget the 'E'! C-Commerce Is the Next Big Thing," *Global Logistics & Supply Chain Strategies,* February 22, 2003,

transmontaigne.com/articles/TransMontaigneReprint.pdf. (Accessed May 8, 2003.)

Ojala, M., "Drowning in a Sea of Information," *Econtent Magazine,* June 2002, *econtentmag.com/Articles/ArticleReader.aspx?ArticleID= 977.* (Accessed May 12, 2003.)

Parks, L., "Buzzsaw Keeps Safeway Store Design on the Cutting Edge," *Stores,* February 2004.

PC World, February 1997.

Piccoli, G. et al., "Web-Based Virtual Learning Environments," *MIS Quarterly,* December 2001.

Piskurich, G. M., *Preparing Learners for E-Learning.* New York: Wiley, 2003.

Poirier, C. C., "Collaborative Commerce: Wave Two of the Cyber Revolutions," *Computer Science Corporation Perspectives,* 2001.

Powell, A., et al., "Virtual Teams: A Review of Current Literature and Directions for Future Research," *The DATA BASE for Advances in Information Systems,* 35(1), Winter 2004, pp. 6–36.

Ragusa, J. M., and G. M. Bochenek, "Collaborative Virtual Design Environments," *Communications of the ACM,* 44(12), 2001.

Reeder, J., "E-Learning: Not Your Father's Correspondence Course," *Sireview.com,* 2002, *sireview.com/articles/elearning.html.* (Accessed May 2003.)

Sabre, Inc., *http://www.sabre-holdings.com.* (Accessed May 2004.)

Sharp, D., *Call Center Operation: Design, Operation, and Maintenance.* Digital Press, 2003.

Shin, N., and J. K. Y. Chan, "Direct and Indirect Effects of Online Learning on Distance Education," *British Journal of Educational Technology,* 35(3), June 2004, pp. 275–288.

Siekmann, S., "Which Web Course Management System Is Right for Me? A Comparison of WebCT 3.1 and Blackboard 5.0," *CALICO Software Report,* June 2001, *calico.org/CALICO_Review/review/webct-bb00.htm.* (Accessed May 8, 2004.)

Stackpole, B., "Rent an App and Relax," *Datamation,* July 1999.

Stauffer, T., *Blog On: Building Online Communities with Web Logs.* McGraw-Hill Osborne, October 2002.

Stone, B., *Blogging: Genius Strategies for Instant Web Content.* New Riders, September 2002.

Suitt, H., "A Blogger in Their Midst," *Harvard Business Review,* September 2003.

Sullivan, D., "Machine Translation: It Can't Match the Human Touch," *E-Business Advisor,* June 2001.

Sullivan, D., "Major Search Engines and Directories," *SearchEngineWatch.com,* April 28, 2004, *searchenginewatch.com/links/article.php/2156221.* (Accessed May 7, 2004.)

Sullivan, D., *Proven Portals: Best Practices for Planning, Designing, and Developing Enterprise Portals.* Addison Wesley, September 2003.

Sullivan, M., "GM Moves into the Passing Lane," *Forbes* (*Best of the Web* supplement), October 7, 2002.

Szekely, B., "Build a Life Sciences Collaboration Network with LSID," *IBM DeveloperWorks,* August 15, 2003, *www-106.ibm.com/developerworks/webservices/library/os-lsid2.* (Accessed May 8, 2004.)

Tedeschi, B., "A Fresh Spin on 'Affinity Portals' to the Internet," *New York Times,* April 17, 2000.

Trados.com, *Integration of TRADOS Software to Increase Functionality of Lotus Notes,* Press Release, September 25, 2002, *trados.com/press_release.asp?page=796.* (Accessed May 2003.)

Turban, E. et al., *Electronic Commerce,* 4th ed. Upper Saddle River, NJ: Prentice Hall, 2006.

Tynan, D., "Tech Advantage," *Sales and Marketing Management,* April 2004.

Udell, J., "The New Social Enterprise," *Infoworld.com*, March 29, 2004.

Urdan, T., and C. Weggen, "Corporate E-Learning: Exploring a New Frontier," W.R. Hambrecht & Co., March 2002, *http://www. e-learning.nl/publicaties/marktonderzoek/New_Frontier.pdf.* (Accessed May 13, 2003.)

Vallés, J., et al., "The Grid for e-Collaboration and Virtual Organisations," *Proceedings of the Second European Across Grids Conference,* Nicosia, Cyprus, January 28–30, 2004.

Van Den Heuvel, W. J., and Z. Maamar, "Intelligent Web Services Moving toward a Framework to Compose," *Communications of the ACM*, 46(10), October 2003, pp. 103–109.

van der Aalst, W. M. P., *Workflow Management: Models, Methods and Systems.* Boston: MIT Press, 2002.

Vinas, T., "Meeting Makeover," *Industryweek,* February 2002.

Walton B., and M. Princi, "From Supply Chain to Collaborative Network," white paper, Gordon Andersen Consulting, 2000 (see *Walton.ASCET.com*).

Weaver, P., "Preventing E-Learning Failure," *Training and Development,* 56(8), August 2002.

webct.com. (Accessed Spring 2004.)

Weidlich, T., "The Corporate Blog Is Catching On," *New York Times,* June 22, 2003.

Willis, D., "Let My People Go," *Network Computing*, 15(4), March 4, 2004.

Wooldridge, M., *An Introduction to MultiAgent Systems.* New York: Wiley, March 2002.

PART II
The Web Revolution

3. Network Computing: Discovery, Communication, and Collaboration
▶ 4. E-Business and E-Commerce
5. Mobile, Wireless, and Pervasive Computing

CHAPTER

4

E-Business and E-Commerce

4.1 Overview of E-Business and E-Commerce

4.2 Major EC Mechanisms

4.3 Business-to-Consumer Applications

4.4 Online Advertising

4.5 B2B Applications

4.6 Intrabusiness and Business-to-Employees EC

4.7 E-Government and Consumer-to-Consumer EC

4.8 E-Commerce Support Services

4.9 Ethical and Legal Issues in E-Business

4.10 Failures and Strategies for Success

Minicases:
1. FreeMarkets.com
2. Hi-Life Corporation

LEARNING OBJECTIVES

After studying this chapter, you will be able to:

❶ Describe electronic commerce, its scope, benefits, limitations, and types.

❷ Understand the basics of how online auctions and bartering work.

❸ Describe the major applications of business-to-consumer commerce, including service industries, and the major issues faced by e-tailers.

❹ Discuss the importance and activities of online advertising.

❺ Describe business-to-business applications.

❻ Describe intrabusiness and B2E e-commerce.

❼ Describe e-government activities and consumer-to-consumer e-commerce.

❽ Describe the e-commerce support services, specifically payments and logistics.

❾ Discuss some ethical and legal issues relating to e-commerce.

❿ Describe EC failures and strategies for success.

BUY CHOCOLATE ONLINE? TRY GODIVA.COM

THE BUSINESS OPPORTUNITY

The demand for high-quality chocolate has been increasing rapidly since the early 1990s. Several local and global companies are competing in this market. Godiva Chocolatier is a well-known international company (based in New York) whose stores can be found in hundreds of malls worldwide. The problem for the company was to discover new ways to increase its sales. After rejecting the use of a CD-ROM catalog, Godiva had the courage to try to sell online as early as 1994. The company was a pioneering "click-and-mortar" e-business that exploited an opportunity years before its competitors.

THE PROJECT

Teaming with Fry Multimedia (an e-commerce pioneer), Godiva.com was created as a division of Godiva Chocolatier. The objective of the project was to sell online both to individuals and to businesses. Since 1994 the Godiva.com story parallels the dynamic growth of e-commerce (see Reda, 2004). It went through difficult times—testing e-commerce technologies as they appeared, failing at times—while remaining continuously committed to online selling, and finally becoming the fastest-growing division of Godiva, outpacing projections. This is truly a success story. Here we present some of the milestones encountered.

The major driving factors in 1994 were Internet *user groups* of chocolate lovers, who were talking about Godiva, to whom the company hoped to sell its product online. Like other pioneers, Godiva had to build its Web site from scratch, without EC-building tools. A partnership was made with *Chocolatier Magazine,* allowing Godiva.com to showcase articles and recipes from the magazine on its site in exchange for providing an online magazine subscription form to e-shoppers. The recognition of the importance of relevant content was correct, as was the perceived need for fresh content. The delivery of games and puzzles, which was considered necessary to attract people to EC sites, was found to be a failure. People were coming to learn about chocolate and Godiva and to buy—not to play games. Another concept that failed was the attempt to build the Web site to look like the physical store. It was found that different marketing channels should look different.

If you visit Godiva.com, you will find a user-friendly place to shop. Included in its major features are: electronic catalogs, some of which are constructed for special occasions (e.g., Mother's and Father's Days); a store locator (how to find the nearest physical store); a shopping cart, for easy collection of items to buy; a gift selector and gift finder; custom photography of the products for the Web site; a search engine, by products, by price, and so on; instructions of how to shop online (take the tour); a chocolate guide that shows you exactly what is inside each box; a place to click for live assistance or for a paper catalog, if you wish; the ability to create an address list for shipping gifts to your friends or employees; "My Godiva," a personalized place for your order history, account, order status, and so on; general content about chocolate (e.g., recipes); and shipment and payment arrangements.

Sales are both to individuals and to corporations. For corporations, incentive programs are offered, including address lists of employees or customers to whom the chocolate is to be sent directly. (This sales model is called *business-to-business-to-customers*, or B2B2C; see Turban et al., 2006).

Godiva continues to add features to stay ahead of the competition. Lately, it embarked on use of wireless technologies. For example, the store locator is available to wireless phone users and to Palm Pilot users who also can download mailing lists for gift sending.

 THE RESULTS

Godiva.com's online sales have been growing at a double-digit rate every year, outpacing the company's "old economy" divisions as well as the online stores of competitors.

Sources: Compiled from Reda (2004) and from *godiva.com* (accessed June 2004).

 LESSONS LEARNED FROM THIS CASE

Selling online can be a success if properly done. Trial and error enabled Godiva to be a leader in e-commerce (EC). Also, good alliances helped. Building an e-store requires special consideration for e-shoppers, especially user friendliness and fast services. Powerful multimedia eliminates the need to go to a physical store. This case demonstrated online business-to-customer (B2C) retailing, one of the topics of this chapter. Other online channels (B2B, C2C, G2C, etc.) are also described in this chapter as well as EC support services, strategies for success, and implementation issues.

4.1 OVERVIEW OF E-BUSINESS AND E-COMMERCE

Definitions and Concepts

Electronic commerce (EC or e-commerce) describes the process of buying, selling, transferring, or exchanging products, services, or information via computer networks, including the Internet. Some people view the term *commerce* as describing only *transactions* conducted between business partners. When this definition is used, some people find the term *electronic commerce* to be fairly narrow. Thus, many use the term *e-business* instead. **E-business** refers to a broader definition of EC, not just the buying and selling of goods and services, but also servicing customers, collaborating with business partners, conducting e-learning, and conducting electronic transactions within an organization. Others view e-business as the "other than buying and selling" activities on the Internet, such as collaboration and intrabusiness activities.

In this book we use the broadest meaning of electronic commerce, which is basically equivalent to e-business. The two terms *will be used interchangeably* throughout the chapter and the remainder of the text.

PURE VERSUS PARTIAL EC. Electronic commerce can take several forms depending on the *degree of digitization*—the transformation from physical to digital—involved. The degree of digitization can relate to: (1) the product (service) sold, (2) the process, or (3) the delivery agent (or intermediary).

Choi et al. (1997) created a framework that explains the possible configurations of these three dimensions. A product can be physical or digital, the process can be physical or digital, and the delivery agent can be physical or digital. In traditional commerce all three dimensions are physical. Purely physical organizations are referred to as **brick-and-mortar organizations.** In *pure EC* all dimensions are digital. All other combinations that include a mix of digital and physical dimensions are considered EC (but not pure EC).

If there is at least one digital dimension, we consider the situation *partial EC*. For example, buying a shirt at Wal-Mart Online or a book from Amazon.com is partial EC, because the merchandise is physically delivered by a shipper. However, buying an e-book from Amazon.com or a software product from Buy.com is *pure EC*, because the product, its delivery, payment, and transfer agent are all done online. In this book we use the term EC to denote either pure or partial EC.

EC ORGANIZATIONS.   Companies that are engaged only in EC are considered **virtual** (or pure-play) **organizations. Click-and-mortar** (or click-and-brick) **organizations** are those that conduct some e-commerce activities, yet their primary business is done in the physical world. Gradually, many brick-and-mortar companies are changing to click-and-mortar ones (e.g., Wal-Mart Online). Indeed, in many ways e-commerce is now simply a part of traditional commerce, and like the introduction of innovations such as barcodes a generation ago, many people expect companies to offer some form of e-commerce.

Types of E-Commerce Transactions

E-commerce transactions can be done between various parties. The common types of e-commerce transactions are described below.

- **Business-to-business (B2B):** In B2B transactions, both the sellers and the buyers are business organizations. The vast majority of EC volume is of this type.

- **Collaborative commerce (c-commerce):** In c-commerce, business partners collaborate (rather than buy or sell) electronically. Such collaboration frequently occurs between and among business partners along the supply chain (see Chapter 7).

- **Business-to-consumers (B2C):** In B2C, the sellers are organizations, and the buyers are individuals. B2C is also known as *e-tailing*.

- **Consumer-to-consumer (C2C):** In C2C, an individual sells products or services to other individuals. You also will see the term C2C used as "customer-to-customer." The terms are interchangeable, and both will be used in this book to describe individuals selling products and services to each other.

- **Business-to-business-to-consumers (B2B2C):** In this case a business sells to a business but delivers the product or service to an individual consumer, such as in Godiva's case.

- **Consumers-to-businesses (C2B):** In C2B, consumers make known a particular need for a product or service, and suppliers compete to provide the product or service to consumers. An example is Priceline.com, where the customer names a product and the desired price, and Priceline tries to find a supplier to fulfill the stated need.

- **Intrabusiness (intraorganizational) commerce:** In this case an organization uses EC internally to improve its operations. A special case of this is known as **B2E (business-to-its-employees) EC,** in which an organization delivers products or services to its employees.

- **Government-to-citizens (G2C) and to others:** In this case a government entity (unit) provides services to its citizens via EC technologies. Government units can do business with other government units **(G2G)** or with businesses **(G2B)**.
- **Mobile commerce (m-commerce):** When e-commerce is done in a wireless environment, such as using cell phones to access the Internet and shop there, we call it m-commerce.

EC Business Models

Each of the above types of EC is executed in one or more *business models,* the method by which a company generates revenue to sustain itself. For example, in B2B one can sell from catalogs or in auctions. The major business models of EC are summarized in Table 4.1. For finding the right business model for EC, see Sawhney (2002).

TABLE 4.1 E-Commerce Business Models

EC Model	Description
Online direct marketing	Manufacturers or retailers sell directly online to customers. Very efficient for digital products and services. Can allow for product or service customization.
Electronic tendering system	Businesses conduct online tendering, requesting quotes from suppliers. Uses B2B with a *reverse auction* mechanism (see Section 4.2).
Online auctions	Companies or individuals run auctions of various types on the Internet. Fast and inexpensive way to sell or liquidate items.
Name-your-own-price	Customers decide how much they are willing to pay. An intermediary (e.g., Priceline.com) tries to match a provider.
Find-the-best-price	Customers specify a need; an intermediary (e.g., Hotwire.com) compares providers and shows the lowest price. Customers must accept the offer in a short time or may lose the deal.
Affiliate marketing	Vendors ask partners to place logos (or banners) on partner's site. If customers click on logo, go to vendor's site, and buy, then vendor pays commissions to partners. (See *performics.com.*)
Viral marketing	Receivers send information about your product to their friends. (Be on the watch for viruses.)
Group purchasing (e-co-ops)	Small buyers aggregate demand to get a large volume; then the group conducts tendering or negotiates a low price.
Product customization	Customers use the Internet to self-configure products or services. Sellers then price them and fulfill them quickly (*build-to-order*).
Electronic marketplaces and exchanges	Transactions are conducted efficiently (more information to buyers and sellers, less transaction cost) in virtual marketplaces (private or public).
Value-chain integrators	Integrators aggregate information and package it for customers, vendors, or others in the supply chain.
Value-chain service providers	Service provider offers specialized services in supply chain operations such as providing logistics or payment services.
Information brokers	Brokers provide services related to EC information such as trust, content, matching buyers and sellers, evaluating vendors and products.
Bartering online	Intermediary administers online exchange of surplus products and/or company receives "points" for its contribution, and the points can be used to purchase other needed items.
Deep discounters	Company (e.g., Half.com) offers deep price discounts. Appeals to customers who consider only price in their purchasing decisions.
Membership	Only members can use the services provided, including access to certain information, conducting trades, etc. (e.g., Egreetings.com).
Supply-chain improvers	Organizations restructure supply chains to hubs or other configurations. Increases collaboration, reduces delays, and smoothes supply chain flows.

**Brief History and
Scope of EC**

E-commerce applications began in the early 1970s with such innovations as electronic transfer of funds. However, the applications were limited to large corporations and a few daring small businesses. Then came electronic data interchange (EDI), which automated routine transaction processing and extended EC to all industries. (See Chapter 8 for details about EDI.)

In the early 1990s, EC applications expanded rapidly, following the commercialization of the Internet and the introduction of the Web. A major shakeout in EC activities began in 2000 and lasted about three years; hundreds of dot-com companies went out of business. Since 2003, EC has continued to show steady progress. Today, most medium and large organizations and many small ones are practicing some EC.

THE SCOPE OF EC. Figure 4.1 describes the broad field of e-commerce. As can be seen in the figure, there are many EC applications (top of the figure); many

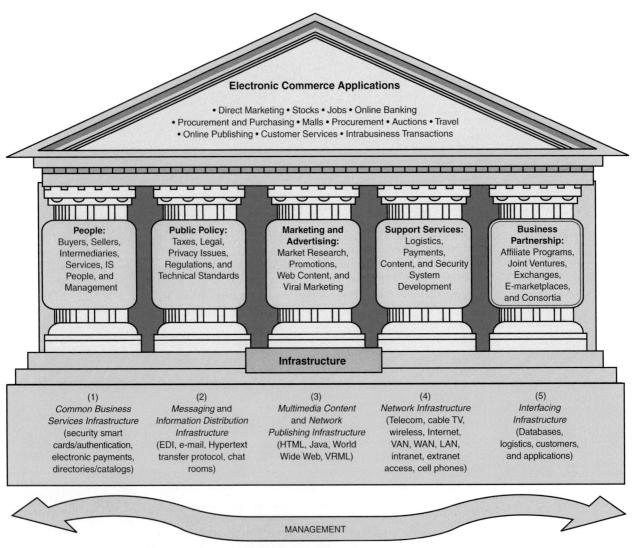

FIGURE 4.1 A framework for e-commerce. (*Source:* Drawn by E. Turban.)

of these are shown throughout the book. To execute these applications, companies need the right information, infrastructure, and support services. Figure 4.1 shows that the EC applications are supported by an infrastructure which includes hardware, software, and networks, ranging from browsers to multimedia, and also by the following five support areas:

1. *People.* They are the sellers, buyers, intermediaries, information systems specialists and other employees, and any other participants.
2. *Public policy.* There are legal and other policy and regulating issues, such as privacy protection and taxation, that are determined by the government.
3. *Marketing and advertising.* EC usually requires the support of marketing and advertising, like any other business. This is especially important in B2C online transactions where the buyers and sellers usually do not know each other.
4. *Support services.* Many services, ranging from payments to order delivery and content creation, are needed to support EC.
5. *Business partnerships.* Joint ventures, e-marketplaces, and business partnerships are common in EC. These occur frequently throughout the supply chain (i.e., the interactions between a company and its suppliers, customers, and other partners).

All of these EC components require good *management practices*. This means that companies need to plan, organize, motivate, devise strategy, and restructure processes as needed.

Benefits and Limitations/Failures of E-Commerce

Few innovations in human history encompass as many benefits to organizations, individuals, and society as does e-commerce. These benefits have just begun to materialize, but they will increase significantly as EC expands. The major benefits are listed in Table 4.2 (page 144).

Counterbalancing its many benefits, EC has some limitations, both technological and nontechnological, which have slowed its growth and acceptance. The major limitations are listed in Table 4.3 (page 144). As time passes, the limitations, especially the technological ones, will lessen or be overcome. In addition, appropriate planning can minimize the negative impact of some of them.

Despite its limitations, e-commerce has made very rapid progress. Also, various B2B activities, e-auctions, e-government, e-learning, and some B2C activities are ballooning. As experience accumulates and technology improves, the ratio of EC benefits to cost will increase, resulting in an even greater rate of EC adoption.

4.2 MAJOR EC MECHANISMS

The major mechanisms for buying and selling on the Internet are electronic catalogs, electronic auctions, and online bartering. (Other mechanisms—e-storefronts, e-malls, and e-marketplaces—are described later; see Sections 4.3 and 4.5.)

Electronic Catalogs

Catalogs have been printed on paper for generations. Recently, electronic catalogs on CD-ROM and the Internet have gained popularity. Electronic catalogs consist of a product database, directory and search capabilities, and a presentation

TABLE 4.2 Benefits of E-Commerce

To Organizations

- Expands a company's marketplace to national and international markets. With minimal capital outlay, a company can quickly locate more customers, the best suppliers, and the most suitable business partners worldwide.
- Enables companies to procure material and services from other countries, rapidly and at less cost.
- Shortens or even eliminates marketing distribution channels, making products cheaper and vendors' profits higher.
- Decreases (by as much as 90 percent) the cost of creating, processing, distributing, storing, and retrieving digitizable products and services (e.g., music, software).
- Allows lower inventories by facilitating "pull"-type supply chain management (see Appendix 2A). This allows product customization and reduces inventory costs.
- Lowers telecommunications costs because the Internet is much cheaper than value-added networks (VANs).
- Helps some small businesses compete against large companies.
- Enables a very specialized niche market (e.g., *cattoys.com*).

To Customers

- Frequently provides less expensive products and services by allowing consumers to conduct quick online searches and comparisons.
- Gives consumers more choices in selecting products and vendors.
- Enables customers to shop or make other transactions 24 hours a day, from almost any location.
- Retrieves relevant and detailed information in seconds.
- Enables consumers to get customized products, from PCs to cars, at competitive prices.
- Makes it possible for people to work and study at home.
- Makes possible electronic auctions that benefit buyers and sellers (see Section 4.2).
- Allows consumers to interact in electronic communities and to exchange ideas and compare experiences.

To Society

- Enables individuals to work at home and to do less traveling, resulting in less road traffic and less air pollution.
- Allows some merchandise to be sold at lower prices, thereby increasing people's standard of living.
- Enables people in developing countries and rural areas to enjoy products and services that otherwise are not available. This includes opportunities to learn professions and earn college degrees, or to receive better medical care.
- Facilitates delivery of public services, such as government entitlements, reducing the cost of distribution and chance of fraud, and increasing the quality of social services, police work, health care, and education.

TABLE 4.3 Limitations of E-Commerce

Technological Limitations	Nontechnological Limitations
- Lack of universally accepted standards for quality, security, and reliability.	- Unresolved legal issues (see Section 4.9).
- Insufficient telecommunications bandwidth.	- Lack of national and international government regulations and industry standards.
- Still-evolving software development tools.	- Lack of mature methodologies for measuring benefits of and justifying EC.
- Difficulties in integrating the Internet and EC applications and software with some existing (especially legacy) applications and databases.	- Many sellers and buyers waiting for EC to stabilize before they take part.
- Need for special Web servers in addition to the network servers.	- Customer resistance to changing from a real to a virtual store. Many people do not yet sufficiently trust paperless, faceless transactions.
- Expensive and/or inconvenient Internet accessibility for many would-be users.	- Perception that EC is expensive and unsecured.
	- An insufficient number (critical mass) of sellers and buyers exists for many profitable EC products and services.

function. They are the backbone of most e-commerce sites. For merchants, the objective of electronic catalogs is to advertise and promote products and services. For the customer, the purpose of such catalogs is to provide a source of information on products and services.

Electronic catalogs can be classified according to three dimensions:

1. ***The dynamics of the information presentation.*** Catalogs can be static or dynamic. *Static catalogs* present information in text and static pictures. *Dynamic catalogs* present information in motion pictures or animation, possibly with supplemental sound.

2. ***The degree of customization.*** Catalogs can be standard or customized. In *standard catalogs,* merchants offer the same catalog to any customer. *Customized catalogs* tailor content, pricing, and displays to the characteristics of specific customers.

3. ***The degree of integration with other business processes or features.*** Catalogs can be classified according to the degree of integration with the following business processes or features: order taking and fulfillment; electronic payment systems; intranet workflow software and systems; inventory and accounting systems; and suppliers' or customers' extranets. For example, when you place an order with Amazon.com, your order will be automatically transferred to a computerized inventory check.

For a comparison of paper and online catalogs, see Online File W4.1.

Electronic Auctions (E-Auctions)

An **auction** is a competitive process in which either a seller solicits consecutive bids from buyers or a buyer solicits bids from sellers. The primary characteristic of auctions, whether offline or online, is that prices are determined dynamically by competitive bidding. Auctions have been an established method of commerce for generations, and they are well-suited to deal with products and services for which conventional marketing channels are ineffective or inefficient. Electronic auctions generally increase revenues for sellers by broadening the customer base and shortening the cycle time of the auction. Buyers generally benefit from e-auctions by the opportunity to bargain for lower prices and the convenience of not having to travel to an auction site to "attend" the auction. Additional benefits of electronic auctions are shown in Online File W4.2.

The Internet provides an efficient infrastructure for executing auctions at lower administrative cost and with many more involved sellers and buyers (see Kambil and van Heck, 2002). Individual consumers and corporations alike can participate in this rapidly growing form of e-commerce. There are several types of electronic auctions, each with its motives and procedures. Auctions are divided here into two major types: *forward* auctions and *reverse* auctions.

FORWARD AUCTIONS. **Forward auctions** are auctions that *sellers* use as a selling channel to many potential buyers. Usually, items are placed at a special site for auction, and buyers will bid continuously for the items. The highest bidder wins the items. Sellers and buyers can be individuals or businesses. The popular auction site eBay.com conducts mostly forward auctions.

According to Gallaugher (2002) there are two types of forward e-auctions. One is to *liquidate* existing inventory, the other one is to *increase marketing efficiency.* Customers in the first type seek the lowest price on widely available goods or services; customers in the second type seek access to unique products or services. Online File W4.3 graphically demonstrates these two types of forward auctions.

REVERSE AUCTIONS. In **reverse auctions,** there is one buyer, usually an organization, that wants to buy a product or a service. Suppliers are invited to submit bids. Online bidding is much faster than conventional bidding, and it usually attracts many more bidders. The reverse auction is the most common auction model for large purchases (in terms of either quantities or price). Everything else being equal, the lowest-price bidder wins the auction. Governments and large corporations frequently mandate this approach, which may provide considerable savings.

Auctions are used in B2C, B2B, C2B, e-government, and C2C commerce, and they are becoming popular in many countries (see Minicase 1). The Internet opens many opportunities for e-auctions. Auctions can be conducted from the seller's site, the buyer's site, or from a third party's site. For example, as described in *IT at Work 4.1,* eBay, the best-known third-party site, offers hundreds of thousands of different items in several types of auctions. Over 300 other major companies, including Amazon.com and Dellauction.com, offer online auctions as well.

Bartering

Related to auctions is **electronic bartering,** the electronically supported exchange of goods or services *without a monetary transaction.* Electronic bartering is done through means of individual-to-individual bartering ads that appear in some newsgroups, bulletin boards, and chat rooms. There also are several intermediaries that arrange for corporate e-bartering (e.g., *barterbrokers.com*). These intermediaries try to match online partners to a barter transaction.

4.3 BUSINESS-TO-CONSUMER APPLICATIONS

B2C E-commerce began when companies like Amazon.com and Godiva.com started selling directly to consumers using the Internet. Here we will look at some of the major categories of B2C applications, which are expected to reach $1 trillion by 2005.

Electronic Retailing Mechanisms: Storefronts and Malls

For generations home shopping from catalogs has flourished, and television shopping channels have been attracting millions of shoppers for more than two decades. Shopping online offers an alternative to catalog and television shopping. **Electronic retailing (e-tailing)** is the direct sale of products and services through electronic storefronts or electronic malls, usually designed around an electronic catalog format and/or auctions. For the difference between retailing and e-tailing, see Online File W4.4 and also Lee and Brandberry (2003).

Like any mail-order shopping experience, e-commerce enables you to buy from home, and to do so 24 hours a day, 7 days a week. However, EC offers a wider variety of products and services, including the most unique items, often at lower prices. Furthermore, within seconds, shoppers can get very detailed supplementary information on products and can easily search for and compare competitors' products and prices. Finally, using the Internet, buyers can find hundreds of thousands of sellers.

IT at Work 4.1
E-BAY—THE WORLD'S LARGEST AUCTION SITE

EBay (*ebay.com*) is the world's largest auction site, and one of the most profitable e-businesses. The successful online auction house has its roots in a 50-year-old novelty item—Pez candy dispensers. Pamela Kerr, an avid collector of Pez dispensers, came up with the idea of trading them over the Internet. When she shared this idea with her boyfriend (now her husband), Pierre Omidyar, he was instantly struck with the soon-to-be-famous e-business auction concept.

In 1995, the Omidyars started the company, later renamed eBay, that has since become the premier online auction house. The business model of eBay was to provide an electronic infrastructure for conducting mostly C2C auctions, although it caters to small businesses as well. Technology replaces the traditional auctioneer as the intermediary between buyers and sellers.

On eBay, people can buy and sell just about anything. It has millions of unique auctions in progress and over 500,000 new items are added each day. The company collects a submission fee upfront, plus a commission as a percentage of the sale amount. The submission fee is based on the amount of exposure you want your item to receive. For example, a higher fee is required if you would like to be among the "featured auctions" in your specific product category, and an even higher fee if you want your item to be listed on the eBay home page under Featured Items.

The seller must specify a minimum opening bid. Sellers might set the opening bid lower than the *reserve price*, a minimum acceptable bid price, in order to generate bidding activity. If a successful bid is made, the seller and the buyer negotiate the payment method, shipping details, warranty, and other particulars. eBay serves as a liaison between the parties; it is the interface through which sellers and buyers can conduct business.

After a few years of successful operations and tens of millions of loyal users, eBay started to do B2C (e-tailing), mostly in fixed prices. By 2003, eBay operated several specialty sites, such as eBay Motors. eBay also operates a *business exchange* in which small- and medium-sized enterprises can buy and sell new and used merchandise, in B2B or B2C modes. In addition, *half.com*, the famous discount e-tailer, is now part of eBay and so is PayPal.com, the person-to-person payment company. eBay has become so popular that it has led to academic recognition with the creation of a new course at the University of Birmingham (UK). The course, "Buying and Selling on eBay.co.uk," offers a step-by-step guide to trading online (Lyons, 2004).

eBay operates *globally*, permitting international trades to take place. Country-specific sites are located in over 25 countries. Buyers from more than 160 other countries also participate. Finally, eBay operates locally: It has over 60 local sites in the United States that enable users to easily find items located near them, to browse through items of local interest, and to meet face-to-face to conclude transactions. As of spring 2004, eBay had over 95 million registered users. According to company financial statements, eBay reported $24 billion in sales in 2003, and it expects net revenue of $3 billion in 2004.

Sources: Compiled from press releases at *eBay.com* (2002–2004) and from Deitel et al. (2001).

For Further Exploration: Does eBay's 2003 change of business model, from pure auctions to adding e-tailing, make sense? Why are wireless auctions promoted?

Both goods and services are sold online. Goods that are bought most often online are computers and computer-related items, office supplies, books and magazines, CDs, cassettes, movies and videos, clothing and shoes, and toys. Services that are bought most often online include entertainment, travel services, stocks and bonds trading, electronic banking, insurance, and job matching. (Services will be presented as a separate topic later in this section.) Directories and hyperlinks from other Web sites and intelligent search agents help buyers find the best stores and products to match their needs.

Two popular shopping mechanisms online are electronic storefronts and electronic malls.

ELECTRONIC STOREFRONTS. Hundreds of thousands of solo storefronts can be found on the Internet, each with its own Internet address (URL), at which orders can be placed. Called **electronic storefronts,** they may be an *extension* of physical stores such as Home Depot, The Sharper Image, Godiva.com, or Wal-Mart. Or they may be new businesses started by entrepreneurs who saw a niche on the Web, such as CDNow.com, Uvine.com, Restaurant.com, and Alloy.com. Besides being used by retailers (e.g., Officedepot.com), storefronts also are used by manufacturers (e.g., Dell.com). Retailers' and manufacturers' storefronts may sell to individuals (B2C) and/or to organizations (B2B).

There are two types of storefronts, general and specialized. The *specialized* store sells one or a few products (e.g., chocolates, flowers, wines, or dog toys). The *general* storefronts sell many products (e.g., Amazon.com).

ELECTRONIC MALLS. An **electronic mall,** also known as a cybermall or e-mall, is a collection of individual shops under one Internet address. The basic idea of an electronic mall is the same as that of a regular shopping mall—to provide a one-stop shopping place that offers many products and services. Each cybermall may include thousands of vendors. For example, *shopping.yahoo.com* and *eshop.msn.com* include tens of thousands of products from thousands of vendors. A special mall that provides discounts and cash back is *cashbackstores.net.*

Two types of malls exist. First, there are *referral malls* (e.g., *hawaii.com*). You cannot buy in such a mall, but instead you are transferred from the mall to a participating storefront. In the second type of mall (e.g., *shopping.yahoo.com*), you can actually make a purchase. At this type of mall, you might shop from several stores but you make only one purchase transaction at the end; an *electronic shopping cart* enables you to gather items from various vendors and pay for them all together in one transaction. (The mall organizer, such as Yahoo, takes a commission from the sellers for this service.)

As is true for vendors that locate in a physical shopping mall, a vendor that locates in an e-mall gives up a certain amount of independence. Its success depends on the popularity of the mall, as well as on its own marketing efforts. On the other hand, malls generate streams of prospective customers who otherwise might never have stopped by the store. For interesting malls, see *shopping-headquarters.com* and *smartmall.biz.*

E-Tailing: The Essentials

The concept of retailing implies sales of goods and/or services to individual customers. One of the most interesting properties of e-tailing as a type of retailing is the ability to offer *customized* products and services to individual customers at a reasonable price and fairly fast (as done by Dell Computer). Many sites (e.g., *nike.com* and *lego.com*) offer product self-configuration from their B2C portals. The most well known B2C site is *Amazon.com,* whose story is presented in *IT at Work 4.2.*

Online Service Industries

Selling books, toys, computers, and most other products on the Internet may reduce vendors' selling costs by 20 to 40 percent. Further reduction is difficult to achieve because the products must be delivered physically. Only a few products (such as software or music) can be digitized to be delivered online for additional savings. On the other hand, delivery of *services,* such as buying an airline ticket or buying stocks or insurance online, can be done 100 percent electronically, with considerable cost reduction potential. Therefore, online delivery of services is growing very rapidly, with millions of new customers being added annually.

IT at Work 4.2
AMAZON.COM: THE KING OF E-TAILING

Entrepreneur and e-tailing pioneer Jeff Bezos, envisioning the huge potential for retail sales over the Internet, selected books as the most logical product for e-tailing. In July 1995, Bezos started Amazon.com, offering books via an electronic catalog from its Web site. Key features offered by the Amazon.com "superstore" were broad selection, low prices, easy searching and ordering, useful product information and personalization, secure payment systems, and efficient order fulfillment. Early on, recognizing the importance of order fulfillment, Amazon.com invested hundreds of millions of dollars in building physical warehouses designed for shipping small packages to hundreds of thousands of customers.

Over the years since its founding, Amazon.com has continually enhanced its business model by improving the customer's experience. For example, customers can personalize their Amazon accounts and manage orders online with the patented "One-Click" order feature. This personalized service includes an *electronic wallet*, which enables shoppers to place an order in a secure manner without the need to enter their address, credit card number, and so forth, each time they shop. One-Click also allows customers to view their order status and make changes on orders that have not yet entered the shipping process.

In addition, Amazon has been adding services and alliances to attract customers to make more purchases. For example, the company now offers specialty stores, such as its professional and technical store. It also is expanding its offerings beyond books. For example, in June 2002 it became an authorized dealer of Sony Corp. for selling Sony products online. Today you can find almost any product that sells well on the Internet, ranging from beauty aids to sporting goods to cars.

Amazon has more than 500,000 affiliate partners that refer customers to Amazon.com. Amazon pays a 3 to 5 percent commission on any resulting sale. In yet another extension of its services, in September 2001 Amazon signed an agreement with Borders Group Inc., providing Amazon's users with the option of picking up books, CDs, and so on at Borders' physical bookstores. Amazon.com also is becoming a Web-fulfillment contractor for national chains such as Target and Circuit City.

In January 2002, Amazon.com declared its first-ever profit—for the 2001 fourth quarter—and followed that by a profitable first quarter of 2002. 2003 was the first year with profit in each quarter.

Sources: Compiled from C. Bayers (2002), and from Daisey (2002).

For Further Exploration: What are the critical success factors for Amazon.com? What advantages does it have over other e-tailers (e.g., Wal-Mart Online or *barnesandnoble.com*)? What is the purpose of the alliances Amazon.com has made?

We will take a quick look here at the leading online service industries: banking, trading of securities (stocks, bonds), job matching, travel services, and real estate.

CYBERBANKING. Electronic banking, also known as **cyberbanking,** includes various banking activities conducted from home, a business, or on the road instead of at a physical bank location. Electronic banking has capabilities ranging from paying bills to applying for a loan. It saves time and is convenient for customers. For banks, it offers an inexpensive alternative to branch banking (for example, about 2 cents' cost per transaction versus $1.07 at a physical branch) and a chance to enlist remote customers. Many banks now offer online banking, and some use EC as a major competitive strategy. In addition to regular banks with added online services, we are seeing the emergence of *virtual banks,* dedicated solely to Internet transactions, such as *netbank.com.*

International and Multiple-Currency Banking. International banking and the ability to handle trading in multiple currencies are critical for international trade. Transfers of electronic funds and electronic letters of credit are important services in international banking. An example of support for EC global trade is provided by TradeCard (*tradecard.com*) in conjunction with MasterCard. Banks and companies such as Oanda also provide currency conversion of over 160 currencies. Although some international retail purchasing can be done by giving a credit card number, other transactions may require cross-border banking support. For example, Hong Kong and Shanghai Bank (*hsbc.com.hk*) has developed a special system (called Hexagon) to provide electronic banking in 60 countries. Using this system, the bank has leveraged its reputation and infrastructure in the developing economies of Asia, to rapidly become a major international bank without developing an extensive new branch network.

ONLINE SECURITIES TRADING. Emarketer.com (2003) has estimated that by the year 2004 about 35 million people in the United States would be using computers to trade stocks, bonds, and other financial instruments. In Korea, more than half of stock traders are already using the Internet for that purpose. Why? Because it makes a lot of dollars and "sense": An online trade typically costs the trader between $5 and $15, compared to an average fee of $100 from a full-service broker and $25 from a discount broker. Orders can be placed from anywhere, any time, even from your cell phone, and there is no waiting on busy telephone lines. Furthermore, the chance of making mistakes is small because online trading does away with oral communication of orders. Investors can find on the Web a considerable amount of information regarding specific companies or mutual funds in which to invest (e.g., *money.cnn.com*, *bloomberg.com*).

Example: Let's say, for example, that you have an account with Charles Schwab. You access Schwab's Web site (*schwab.com*) from your PC or your Internet-enabled mobile device, enter your account number and password to access your personalized Web page, and then click on "stock trading." Using a menu, you enter the details of your order (buy or sell, margin or cash, price limit, market order, etc.). The computer tells you the current "ask" and "bid" prices, much as a broker would do on the telephone, and you can approve or reject the transaction. Some well-known companies that offer only online trading are E*Trade, Ameritrade, and Suretrade.

However, both online banking and securities trading require tight security. Otherwise, your money could be at risk. (See Online File W4.5 for an example.) Most online banks and stock traders use only ID numbers and passwords. Yet even this may not be secure enough. See Section 4.8 on how to improve online security.

THE ONLINE JOB MARKET. The Internet offers a promising new environment for job seekers and for companies searching for hard-to-find employees. Thousands of companies and government agencies advertise available positions of all types of jobs, accept résumés, and take applications via the Internet. The online job market is especially effective for technology-oriented jobs.

The online job market is used by job seekers to reply online to employment ads, to place résumés on various sites, and to use recruiting firms (e.g., *monster.com*, *jobdirect.com*, *jobcenter.com*). Companies who have jobs to offer advertise openings on their Web sites or search the bulletin boards of recruiting firms. In many countries governments must advertise job openings on the Internet. In addition, hundreds of job-placement brokers and related services are active on the Web. (You can get help from *jobweb.com* or *brassring.com* to write your résumé.)

TRAVEL SERVICES.   The Internet is an ideal place to plan, explore, and economically arrange almost any trip. Online travel services allow you to purchase airline tickets, reserve hotel rooms, and rent cars. Most sites also offer a fare-tracker feature that sends you e-mail messages about low-cost flights to your favorite destinations or from your home city. Examples of comprehensive online travel services are Expedia.com, Travelocity.com, and Orbitz.com. Services are also provided online by all major airline vacation services, large conventional travel agencies, car rental agencies, hotels (e.g., *hotels.com*), and tour companies. Priceline.com allows you to set a price you are willing to pay for an airline ticket or hotel accommodations and then attempts to find a vendor that will match your price. A similar service offered by Hotwire.com tries to find the lowest available price for you.

REAL ESTATE.   Real estate transactions are an ideal area for e-commerce. You can view many properties on the screen, and can sort and organize properties according to your preferences and decision criteria. In some locations brokers allow the use of real estate databases only from their offices, but considerable information is now available on the Internet. For example, Realtor.com allows you to search a database of over 1.2 million homes across the United States. The database is composed of local "multiple listings" of all available properties, in hundreds of locations. Those who are looking for an apartment can try Apartments.com.

Customer Service

Whether an organization is selling to organizations or to individuals, in many cases a competitive edge is gained by providing superb customer service, which is part of CRM (Chapter 7). In e-commerce, customer service becomes even more critical, since customers and merchants do not meet face-to-face.

PHASES IN THE CUSTOMER SERVICE LIFE CYCLE.   Customer service should be approached as a business life cycle process, with the following four phases:

> *Phase 1: Requirements.* Assist the customer to determine needs by providing photographs of a product, video presentations, textual descriptions, articles or reviews, sound bites on a CD, or downloadable demonstration files. Also use intelligent agents to make requirements suggestions.
>
> *Phase 2: Acquisition.* Help the customer to acquire a product or service (online order entry, negotiations, closing of sale, and delivery).
>
> *Phase 3: Ownership.* Support the customer on an ongoing basis (interactive online user groups, online technical support, FAQs [frequently asked questions] and answers, resource libraries, newsletters, and online renewal of subscriptions).
>
> *Phase 4: Retirement.* Help the client to dispose of a service or product (online resale, classified ads).

Many activities can be conducted in each of these phases. For example, when an airline offers information such as flight schedules and fare quotes on its Web site, it is supporting phases 1 and 2. Similarly, when computer vendors provide electronic help desks for their customers, they are supporting phase 3. Dell will help you to auction your obsolete computer, and Amazon.com will help you to sell used books, activities that support phase 4.

Example: Fidelity Investments provides investors with "the right tools to make their own best investment decisions." The site (*fidelity.com*) has several sections, which include daily updates of financial news, information about Fidelity's mutual funds, material for interactive investment and retirement planning, and brokerage services. This is an example of support given to phase 1 in the online selling of services. The site also helps customers buy Fidelity's products (phase 2), handle their accounts (phase 3), and sell the securities (phase 4).

FACILITATING CUSTOMER SERVICE. Various tools are available for facilitating online customer service: Companies can use e-mail to send confirmations, product information, and instructions to customers and also to take orders, complaints, and other inquiries. Customers can track the status of their orders, services (such as FedEx shipments, banking or stock-trading activities), or job applications online at the company Web site. They can build individualized pages at the vendor's site, at which customized information can be provided. In company-sponsored chat rooms, customers can interact with each other and with the vendor's personnel, who monitor the chat room. And at Web-based call centers a company can handle customers' inquiries in any form they come (fax, telephone, e-mail, letters) and answer them quickly and automatically, whenever possible. Customers can also interact with the vendor and get quick problem resolution through these communication centers. (See Chapter 3 for details and more tools.) An example of a Web-based call center is included in Online File W4.6 about Canadian Tire's integrated call center.

Issues in E-Tailing   Despite e-tailing's ongoing growth, many e-tailers continue to face some major issues related to e-tailing. If not solved, they can slow the growth of an organization's e-tailing efforts. These issues are described below.

1. *Resolving channel conflict.* If a seller is a click-and-mortar company, such as Levi's or GM, it may face a conflict with its regular distributors when it sells directly online. Known as **channel conflict,** this situation can alienate the regular distributors. Channel conflict has forced some companies (e.g., Lego.com, see Chapter 8) to limit their B2C efforts; others (e.g., some automotive companies) have decided not to sell direct online. An alternative approach is to try to collaborate in some way with the existing distributors whose services may be restructured. For example, an auto company could allow customers to configure a car online, but require that the car be picked up from a dealer, where customers could arrange financing, warranties, and service.

2. *Resolving conflicts within click-and-mortar organizations.* When an established company decides to sell direct online on a large scale, it may create a conflict within its offline operations. Conflicts may arise in areas such as pricing of products and services, allocation of resources (e.g., advertising budget), and logistics services provided by the offline activities to the online activities (e.g., handling of returns of items bought online). As a result of these conflicts, some companies have completely separated the "clicks" (the online portion of the organization) from the "mortar" or "bricks" (the traditional brick-and-mortar part of the organization). Such separation may increase expenses and reduce the synergy between the two organizational parts.

3. *Organizing order fulfillment and logistics.* E-tailers face a difficult problem of how to ship very small quantities to a large number of buyers. This can be a difficult undertaking, especially when returned items need to be handled.

4. ***Determining viable and risk of online e-tailers.*** Many purely online e-tailers folded in 2000–2002 (see Kaplan, 2002), the result of problems with cash flow, customer acquisition, order fulfillment, and demand forecasting. Online competition, especially in commodity-type products such as CDs, toys, books, or groceries, became very fierce due to the ease of entry to the marketplace. So a problem most young e-tailers face is to determine how long to operate while you are still losing money and how to finance the losses.

5. ***Identifying appropriate revenue models.*** One early dot-com model was to generate enough revenue from advertising to keep the business afloat until the customer base reached critical mass. This model did not work. Too many dot-coms were competing for too few advertising dollars, which went mainly to a small number of well-known sites such as AOL, MSN, Google, and Yahoo. Advertising is the primary source of income of such portals (Luo and Najdaw, 2004). In addition, there was a "chicken-and-egg" problem: Sites could not get advertisers to come if they did not have enough visitors. To succeed in EC, it is necessary to identify appropriate revenue models. (For further discussion of EC revenue models, see Turban et al., 2006.)

To successfully implement e-tailing and solve the five issues just discussed, it is frequently necessary to conduct market research. Market research is needed for product design, marketing, and advertising decisions and strategy. For a discussion of market research in e-commerce, see Online File W4.7.

4.4 ONLINE ADVERTISING

Advertising is an attempt to disseminate information in order to influence a buyer–seller transaction. Traditional advertising on TV or in newspapers is impersonal, one-way mass communication. Direct-response marketing (telemarketing) contacts individuals by direct mail or telephone and requires them to respond in order to make a purchase. The direct-response approach personalizes advertising and marketing, but it can be expensive, slow, and ineffective (and from the consumer's point of view, annoying).

Internet advertising redefines the advertising process, making it media-rich, dynamic, and interactive. It improves on traditional forms of advertising in a number of ways: Internet ads can be updated any time at minimal cost and therefore can be always timely. Internet ads can reach very large numbers of potential buyers all over the world, and they are sometimes cheaper in comparison to print (newspaper and magazine), radio, or television ads. Internet ads can be interactive and targeted to specific interest groups and/or to individuals. Finally, it makes sense to move advertising to the Internet, where the number of viewers is rapidly growing.

Nevertheless, the Internet as an advertising medium does have some shortcomings, most of which relate to the difficulty in measuring the effectiveness and cost-justification of the ads. For example, it is difficult to measure the actual results of placing a banner ad or sending a marketing e-mail.

Advertising Methods The most common online advertising methods are banners, pop-ups, and e-mails. The essentials of these and some other methods are presented next.

BANNERS. **Banners** are simply electronic billboards. Typically, a banner contains a short text or graphical message to promote a product or a vendor. It may even contain video clips and sound. When customers *click* on a banner, they are *transferred* to the advertiser's home page. Banner advertising is the most commonly used form of advertising on the Internet. Advertisers go to great lengths to design banners that catch consumers' attention. (See Amiri and Menton, 2003.)

There are two types of banners: **Key-word banners** appear when a predetermined word is queried from a search engine. This is effective for companies who want to narrow their target to consumers interested in particular topics. **Random banners** appear randomly; they might be used to introduce new products to the widest possible audience or to promote brand recognition.

A major advantage of banners is that they can be customized to the target audience (a market segment or even an individual user). If the computer system knows who you are or what your profile is, you may be sent a banner that is supposed to match your interests. However, one of the major drawbacks of banners is that limited information is allowed due to their small size. Hence advertisers need to think of creative but short messages to attract viewers. Another drawback is that banners are ignored by many viewers today. A new generation of banner-like ads are the pop-ups.

POP-UP, POP-UNDER, AND SIMILAR ADS. Pop-up, pop-under, and similar ads are contained in a new browser window that is automatically launched when one enters or exits a Web site or by other triggers such as a delay during Internet surfing. A **pop-up ad** appears in front of the current browser window. A **pop-under ad** appears underneath the active window; when users close the active window, they see the ad. Pop-ups and pop-unders are sometime difficult to close. These methods are controversial: Many users strongly object to these ads, which they consider intrusive.

For many years, pop-up ads generated a steady source of income for online publishers, but this is no longer the case. Pop-up ad blockers such as Pop-up Stopper, STOPzilla, and Pop-up Eraser have become increasingly popular. Also, toolbars with built-in functions that stop pop-up ads are provided by Google, Yahoo, MSN, and AOL. The new version of the Internet Explorer browser (June 2004) includes a built-in blocker.

E-MAIL ADVERTISING. E-mail is emerging as an Internet advertising and marketing channel. It is generally cost-effective to implement and provides a better and quicker response rate than other advertising channels (such as print ads). Marketers develop or purchase a list of e-mail addresses, place them in a customer database, and then send advertisements via e-mail. A list of e-mail addresses can be a very powerful tool because the marketer can target a group of people or even individuals. For example, Restaurants.com (see Online Mini-case W4.1) uses e-mail to send restaurant coupons to millions of customers. However, as with pop-ups, there is a potential for misuse of e-mail advertising, and some consumers are receiving a flood of unsolicited mail. (We address the topic of unsolicited advertising on the next page.)

ELECTRONIC CATALOGS AND BROCHURES. As described earlier, the merchant's objective in using online catalogs is to advertise and promote products and services. Sometimes merchants find it useful to provide a *customized electronic* *catalog* to some individual customers. Each catalog is assembled specifically for the particular buyer, usually a company but sometimes even an individual consumer who buys frequently or in large quantities.

SPYWARE BANNERS. **Spyware** is Internet jargon for advertising-supported software (adware). It is a way for shareware authors to make money from a product, other than by selling it to users. Several large media companies offer to place banner ads in their products in exchange for a portion of the revenue from banner sales. If end users find the banners annoying, there is usually an option to remove them. These days, spyware can even be found accompanying hardware you buy and install in your system. The software that end users install with hardware purchased from certain manufacturers may include spyware agents.

Spyware threats come in different flavors. A spyware agent can be any of the following: A *hijacker* redirects your browser to Web sites. A *dialer* dials a service, most likely porn sites, for which you are billed. A *Trojan horse* is attached to a program and performs undesirable tasks on your computer. *Collectware* collects information about you and your surfing habits, and those who gathered that information may try to sell it to advertisers. (See Online File W4.8 for additional discussion of the categories of spyware.)

OTHER FORMS OF INTERNET ADVERTISING. Online advertising can be done in several other forms, including posting advertising in chat rooms (newsgroups) and in classified ads (see *infospace.com/info.cls2K/*). Advertising on Internet radio is just beginning, and soon advertising on Internet television will commence. Of special interest is advertising to members of Internet communities. Community sites (such as *geocities.com*) are gathering places for people of similar interests and are therefore a logical place to promote products related to those interests. Another interesting method is wireless ads, which we describe in Chapter 5.

Some Advertising Issues and Approaches

There are many issues related to the implementation of Internet advertising: how to design ads for the Internet, where and when to advertise, and how to integrate online and offline ads. Most such decisions require the input of marketing and advertising experts. Here, we present some illustrative issues in online advertising.

UNSOLICITED ADVERTISING. As discussed in Chapter 3, spamming is the indiscriminate distribution of electronic messages without permission of the receiver. E-mail spamming, also known as *unsolicited commercial e-mail (UCE)*, has been part of the Internet for years. Another form of spamming is the pop-up ad. Unfortunately, spamming seems to be getting worse over time. The drivers of spamming and some potential solutions are described in Online File W4.9 and Chapter 16.

On October 22, 2003, the U.S. Senate passed an antispam bill requiring spammers to clearly identify themselves and the products they are selling. Since the bill became law, several companies were fined in court.

Permission marketing is one answer to e-mail and pop-up spamming.

PERMISSION MARKETING. **Permission marketing** asks consumers to give their permission to voluntarily accept online advertising and e-mail. Typically, consumers are asked to complete an electronic form that asks what they are interested in and requests permission to send related marketing information. Sometimes consumers are offered incentives to receive advertising; at the least, marketers try to send information in an entertaining, educational, or other interesting manner.

Permission marketing is the basis of many Internet marketing strategies. For example, millions of users receive e-mails periodically from airlines such as American and Southwest. Users of this marketing service can ask for notification of low fares from their hometown or to their favorite destinations. Users can easily unsubscribe at any time. Permission marketing is also extremely important for market research (e.g., see Media Metrix at *comscore.com*).

In one particularly interesting form of permission marketing, companies such as Clickdough.com, Getpaid4.com, and CashSurfers.com have built customer lists of millions of people who are happy to receive advertising messages whenever they are on the Web. These customers are paid $0.25 to $0.50 an hour to view messages while they do their normal surfing. They may also be paid $0.10 an hour for the surfing time of any friends they refer to the site.

VIRAL MARKETING. **Viral marketing** refers to online "word-of-mouth" marketing. The main idea in viral marketing is to have people forward messages to friends, suggesting that they "check this out." A marketer can distribute a small game program, for example, embedded with a sponsor's e-mail, that is easy to forward. By releasing a few thousand copies, vendors hope to reach many more thousands.

Word-of-mouth marketing has been used for generations, but its speed and reach are multiplied manyfold by the Internet. Viral marketing is one of the new models being used to build brand awareness at a minimal cost. It has long been a favorite strategy of online advertisers pushing youth-oriented products.

Unfortunately, though, several e-mail hoaxes have spread via viral marketing. Also, a more serious danger of viral marketing is that a destructive computer virus can be added to an innocent advertisement, game, or message. However, when used properly, viral marketing can be both effective and efficient.

INTERACTIVE ADVERTISING AND MARKETING. All advertisers, whether online or not, attempt to target their ads to the desired market and, if possible, even to individuals. A good salesperson is trained to interact with sales prospects, asking questions about the features they are looking for and handling possible objections as they come up. Online advertising comes closer to supporting this one-to-one selling process than more traditional advertising media possibly can.

Ideally, in interactive marketing, advertisers present customized, one-on-one ads. The term *interactive* points to the ability to address an individual, to gather and remember that person's responses, and to serve that customer based on his or her previous, unique responses. When the Internet is combined with databases, interactive marketing becomes a very effective and affordable competitive strategy.

ONLINE PROMOTIONS: ATTRACTING VISITORS TO A SITE. A Web site without visitors has little value. The following are three representative ways to attract visitors to a Web site.

Making the Top of the List of a Search Engine. Web sites submit their URLs to search engines. The search engine's intelligent program (called a *spider*) crawls through the submitted site, indexing all related content and links. Some lists generated by search engines include hundreds or thousands of items. Users that view the results submitted by a search engine typically start by clicking on the first 10 or so items, and soon get tired. So, for best exposure, advertisers like to be in the top 10 on the list.

How does one make the top 10? If a company understands how a search engine's program ranks its findings, it can get to the top of a search engine's list merely by adding, removing, or changing a few sentences on its Web pages. However, this is not easy, as everyone wants to do it, so there are sometimes several thousand entries competing to be in the top 10. It may be easier to pay the search engine to put a banner at the top of the lists (e.g., usually on the right-hand side or the top of the screen at *google.com*'s results).

Online Events, Promotions, and Attractions. People generally like the idea of something funny or something free, or both. Contests, quizzes, coupons, and free samples are therefore an integral part of e-marketing. Running promotions on the Internet is similar to running offline promotions. These mechanisms are designed to attract visitors and to keep their attention. For innovative ideas for promotions and attractions used by companies online, see Strauss et al. (2003).

Online Coupons. Just as in offline advertising, online shoppers can get discounts via coupons. You can gather any discount coupons you want by accessing sites like *hotcoupons.com* or *coupons.com*, selecting the store where you plan to redeem the coupons, and printing them. In the future, transfer of coupons directly to a virtual supermarket (such as Peapod.com or Netgrocer.com) will be available so that you can receive discounts on the items you buy there. Coupons also can be distributed via wireless devices, based on your location. As you approach a restaurant, for example, you may be offered a 15 percent discount electronic coupon to show to the proprietors when you arrive.

4.5 B2B APPLICATIONS

In *business-to-business (B2B) applications*, the buyers, sellers, and transactions involve only organizations. Business-to-business comprises about 85 percent of EC volume. It covers a broad spectrum of applications that enable an enterprise to form electronic relationships with its distributors, resellers, suppliers, customers, and other partners. By using B2B, organizations can restructure their supply chains and partner relationships.

There are several business models for B2B applications. The major ones are sell-side marketplaces, buy-side marketplaces, and electronic exchanges. Other B2B systems are described in Chapter 8.

Sell-Side Marketplaces

In the **sell-side marketplace** model, organizations attempt to sell their products or services to other organizations electronically from their own private e-marketplace and/or from a third-party site. This model is similar to the B2C model in which the buyer is expected to come to the seller's site, view catalogs, and place an order. In the B2B sell-side marketplace, however, the buyer is an organization.

The key mechanisms in the sell-side model are: (1) electronic catalogs that can be customized for each large buyer and (2) forward auctions. Sellers such as Dell Computer (*dellauction.com*) use auctions extensively. In addition to auctions from their own Web sites, organizations can use third-party auction sites, such as eBay, to liquidate items. Companies such as FreeMarkets.com (see *ariba.com*) are helping organizations to auction obsolete and old assets and inventories (see Minicase 1).

The sell-side model is used by hundreds of thousands of companies and is especially powerful for companies with superb reputations. The seller can be either a manufacturer (e.g., Dell, IBM), a distributor (e.g., *avnet.com*), or a retailer (e.g., *bigboxx.com*). The seller uses EC to increase sales, reduce selling and advertising expenditures, increase delivery speed, and reduce administrative costs. The sell-side model is especially suitable to customization. For example, organizational customers can configure their orders online at *cisco.com*, *dell.com*, and others. Self-configuration of orders results in fewer misunderstandings about what customers want and in much faster order fulfillment.

Buy-Side Marketplaces

The **buy-side marketplace** is a model in which organizations attempt to buy needed products or services from other organizations electronically. A major method of buying goods and services in the buy-side model is a *reverse auction*. Here, a company that wants to buy items places a *request for quotation (RFQ)* on its Web site or in a third-party bidding marketplace. Once RFQs are posted, sellers (usually preapproved suppliers) submit bids electronically. Such auctions attract large pools of willing sellers, who can be either manufacturers, distributors, or retailers. The bids are routed via the buyer's intranet to the engineering and finance departments for evaluation. Clarifications are made via e-mail, and the winner is notified electronically.

The buy-side model uses EC technology to streamline the purchasing process in order to reduce the cost of items purchased, the administrative cost of procurement, and the purchasing cycle time. Procurements using a third-party buy-side marketplace model are especially popular for medium and small organizations.

E-PROCUREMENT. Purchasing by using electronic support is referred to as **e-procurement.** E-procurement uses *reverse auctions* (as discussed above) as well as two other popular mechanisms: group purchasing and desktop purchasing.

Group Purchasing. In **group purchasing,** the orders of many buyers are aggregated so that they total to a large volume, in order to merit more seller attention. The aggregated order can then be placed on a reverse auction, and a volume discount can be negotiated. Typically, the orders of small buyers are aggregated by a third-party vendor, such as United Sourcing Alliance *(usa-llc.com)*. Group purchasing is especially popular in the health care industry (see *all-health.com*) and education (*tepo.org*).

Desktop Purchasing. In a special case of e-procurement known as **desktop purchasing,** suppliers' catalogs are aggregated into an internal master catalog on the buyer's server, so that the company's purchasing agents (or even end users) can shop more conveniently. Desktop purchasing is most suitable for *indirect maintenance, replacement, and operations (MRO) items*, such as office supplies. (The term *indirect* refers to the fact that these items are not inputs to manufacturing.) In the desktop purchasing model, a company has many suppliers, but the quantities purchased from each are relatively small. This model is most appropriate for government entities and for large companies, such as Schlumberger, as described in *IT at Work 4.3.*

IT at Work 4.3
E-PROCUREMENT AT SCHLUMBERGER

Schlumberger is an $8.5 billion company with 60,000 employees in 100 countries. That makes it the world's largest oil-service company. In 2000 the company installed a Web-based automated procurement system in Oilfield Services, its largest division. With this system, employees can buy office supplies and small equipment as well as computers direct from their desktops. The single desktop system streamlined and sped up the purchasing operation, reducing both costs and the number of people involved in the process. The system also enables the company to consolidate purchases for volume discounts from vendors.

The system has two parts: The internal portion uses CommerceOne's BuySite procurement software and runs on the company's intranet. Once the employee selects the item, the system generates the requisition, routes it electronically to the proper people for approval, and turns it into a purchase order. The second part of the system, CommerceOne's MarketSite, transmits the purchase orders to the suppliers. This B2B Internet marketplace connects Schlumberger with hundreds of suppliers with a single, low-cost, many-to-many system.

Negotiation of prices is accomplished with individual vendors. For example, Office Depot's entire catalog is posted on the MarketSite, but the Schlumberger employees see only the subset of previously negotiated products and prices. (In the future, the company plans to negotiate prices in *real time* through auctions and other bidding systems.)

The benefits of the system are evident in both cost and processes. The cost of goods has been reduced, as have the transaction costs. Employees spend much less time in the ordering process, giving them more time for their true work. The system is also much more cost efficient for the suppliers, who can then pass along savings to customers. Procurement effectiveness can be increased because tracing the overall procurement activity is now possible.

Getting the system up and running was implemented in stages and ran at the same time as existing systems. There were no implementation issues for employees (once the system was in place, the old system was disabled), and there were no complaints in regard to the old system being shut down (no one was using the old system anymore).

Sources: Compiled from Ovans (2000) and CommerceOne.com, "Schlumberger Oilfield Services Selects Commerce One Solution to Fully Automate Its Worldwide Procurement Process" (February 1, 1999), *commerceone.com/news/releases/schlumberger.html* (accessed July 2003); CommerceOne.com, "Customer Snapshot: Schlumberger" (2003), *commerceone.com/customers/profiles/schlumberger.pdf* (accessed May 2004); and *Schlumberger.com* (2003).

For Further Exploration: What are the benefits of the e-procurement system to Schlumberger? How does it empower the buyers? Why would real-time price negotiations be beneficial?

Public Exchanges E-marketplaces in which there are many sellers and many buyers, and entry is open to all, are called **public exchanges** (in short, **exchanges**). They frequently are owned and operated by a third party. According to Kaplan and Sawhney (2000), there are four basic types of exchanges:

1. ***Vertical distributors for direct materials.*** These are B2B marketplaces where *direct materials* (materials that are inputs to manufacturing) are traded, usually in large quantities in an environment of long-term relationship known as *systematic sourcing*. Examples are Plasticsnet.com and Papersite.com. Both fixed and negotiated prices are common in this type of exchange.

2. ***Vertical exchanges for indirect materials.*** Here indirect materials in *one industry* are purchased usually on an as-needed basis (called *spot sourcing*). Buyers and sellers may not even know each other. ChemConnect.com and Isteelasia.com are examples. In such vertical exchanges, prices are continually changing, based on the matching of supply and demand. Auctions are typically used in this kind of B2B marketplace, sometimes done in private trading rooms, which are available in exchanges like ChemConnect.com (see *IT at Work 4.4* on page 160).

IT at Work 4.4
CHEMICAL COMPANIES "BOND" AT CHEMCONNECT

Buyers and sellers of chemicals and plastics today can meet electronically in a large vertical exchange called ChemConnect (*chemconnect.com*). Using this exchange, *global* chemical-industry leaders such as British Petroleum, Dow Chemical, BASF, Hyundai, and Sumitomo can reduce trading cycle time and cost and can find new markets and trading partners around the globe.

ChemConnect provides a public trading marketplace and an information portal to more than 9,000 members in 150 countries. In 2003, over 60,000 products were traded in this public, third-party-managed e-marketplace. Chemconnect provides three marketplaces (as of October 11, 2003): a commodity markets platform, a marketplace for sellers, and a marketplace for buyers, as described below.

At the *commodity markets platform*, prequalified producers, customers, and distributors come together in real time to sell and buy chemical-related commodities like natural-gas liquids, oxygenates, olefins, and polymers. They can even simultaneously execute multiple deals. Transactions are done through regional trading hubs.

The *marketplace for sellers* has many tools ranging from electronic catalogs to forward auctions. It enables companies to find buyers all over the world. ChemConnect provides all the necessary tools to expedite selling and achieving the best prices. It also allows for negotiations.

The *marketplace for buyers* is a place where thousands of buyers shop for chemical-related indirect materials (and a few direct materials). The market provides for automated request for proposal (RFP) tools as well as a complete on-line reverse auction. The sellers' market is connected to the buyers' market, so that sellers can connect to the RFPs posted on the marketplace for buyers. (Note that RFP and RFQ are interchangeable terms; RFP is used more in government bidding.)

In the three marketplaces, ChemConnect provides logistics and payment options. In all of its trading mechanisms, up-to-the-minute market information is available and can be translated to 30 different languages. Members pay transaction fees only for successfully completed transactions. Business partners provide several support services, such as financial services for the market members. The marketplaces work with certain rules and guidelines that ensure an unbiased approach to the trades. There is full disclosure of all legal requirements, payments, trading rules, and so on. (Click on "Legal info and privacy issues" at the ChemConnect Web site.) ChemConnect is growing rapidly, adding members and trading volume.

Source: Compiled from *chemconnect.com* (accessed October 11, 2003).

For Further Exploration: What are the advantages of the ChemConnect exchange? Why are there three trading places? Why does the exchange provide information portal services?

3. **Horizontal distributors.** These are many-to-many e-marketplaces for indirect (MRO) materials, such as office supplies, used by *any industry*. Prices are fixed or negotiated in this systematic sourcing-type exchange. Examples are EcEurope.com, Globalsources.com, and Alibaba.com.

4. **Functional exchanges.** Here, needed services such as temporary help or extra space are traded on an as-needed basis (spot sourcing). For example, Employease.com can find temporary labor using employers in its Employease Network. Prices are dynamic, and they vary depending on supply and demand.

All four types of exchanges offer diversified support services, ranging from payments to logistics. Vertical exchanges are frequently owned and managed by a group of big players in an industry (referred to as a *consortium*). For example, Marriott and Hyatt own a procurement consortium for the hotel industry, and ChevronTexaco owns an energy e-marketplace. The vertical e-marketplaces offer services particularly suited to the community they serve.

Since B2B activities involve many companies, specialized network infrastructure is needed. Such infrastructure works either as an Internet/EDI or as extranets (see Chapter 8). A related EC activity, usually done between and among organizations, is collaborative commerce (see Chapters 3 and 8).

4.6 INTRABUSINESS AND BUSINESS-TO-EMPLOYEES EC

E-commerce can be done not only between business partners but also *within* organizations. Such activity is referred to as *intrabusiness* EC or in short, **intrabusiness.** Intrabusiness can be done between a business and its employees (B2E), among units within the business (usually done as collaborative commerce), and among employees in the same business.

Business-to-Its-Employees (B2E) Commerce

Companies are finding many ways to do business electronically with their own employees. They disseminate information to employees over the company intranet, for example. (See Minicase 2.) They also allow employees to manage their fringe benefits and take training classes electronically. In addition, employees can buy on the corporate intranet discounted insurance, travel packages, and tickets to events, and they can electronically order supplies and material needed for their work. Also, many companies have electronic corporate stores that sell the company's products to its employees, usually at a discount.

E-Commerce between and among Units within the Business

Large corporations frequently consist of independent units, or *strategic business units (SBUs)*, which "sell" or "buy" materials, products, and services from each other. Transactions of this type can be easily automated and performed over the intranet. An SBU can be considered as either a seller or a buyer. An example would be company-owned dealerships, which buy goods from the main company. This type of EC helps improve the internal supply chain operations.

The major benefits of such c-commerce are smoothing the supply chain, reducing inventories along the supply chain, reducing operating costs, increasing customer satisfaction, and increasing a company's competitive edge. The challenges faced by the collaborators are software integration issues, technology selection, trust and security, and resistance to change and collaboration.

E-Commerce between and among Corporate Employees

Many large organizations allow employees to post classified ads on the company intranet, through which employees can buy and sell products and services from each other. This service is especially popular in universities, where it has been conducted since even before the commercialization of the Internet. The Internet is used for other collaborations as well, such as scheduling of employee athletic and social events.

4.7 E-GOVERNMENT AND CONSUMER-TO-CONSUMER EC

E-Government

As e-commerce matures and its tools and applications improve, greater attention is being given to its use to improve the business of public institutions and governments (country, state, county, city, etc). **E-government** is the use of Internet technology in general and e-commerce in particular to deliver information and public services to citizens, business partners and suppliers of

IT at Work 4.5
E-GOVERNMENT IN WESTERN AUSTRALIA

The focus of the Western Australian (WA) government agency Contract and Management Services (CAMS) is to develop online contract management solutions for the public sector. CAMS Online allows government agencies to search existing contracts to discover how to access the contracts that are in common use by different government agencies (for example, lightbulbs or paper towels bought by various government units). It also enables suppliers wanting to sell to the government to view the current tenders (bids) on the Western Australia Government Contracting Information Bulletin Board and to download tender documents from that site.

CAMS Online also provides government departments and agencies with unbiased expert advice on e-commerce, Internet, and communication services, and how-to's on building a bridge between the technological needs of the public sector and the expertise of the private sector.

WA's e-commerce activities include electronic markets for government buying. The *WA Government Electronic Market* provides online supplier catalogs, electronic purchase orders, and electronic invoicing, EFT, and check and credit card payments (*doir.wa.gov.au/aboutus/ecc.asp*, September 2002).

Government-to-government e-commerce functions include *DataLink*, which enables the transfer of data using a secure and controlled environment. *DataLink* is an ideal solution for government agencies needing to exchange large volumes of operational information. An intragovernment EC application is a videoconferencing service that offers two-way video and audio links, enabling government employees to meet together electronically from up to eight sites at any one time.

In addition to G2B functions, the G2C Web site also offers online training to citizens. A service called *Westlink* delivers adult training and educational programs to remote areas and schools, including rural and regional communities.

Source: Compiled from *business.wa.gov.au* (February 2001) and *doir.wa.gov.au/aboutus/ecc.asp* (June–November 2002).

For Further Exploration: How is contract management of the Western Australian government agency facilitated by e-commerce tools? Why would government want to take on a role in promoting e-learning?

government entities, and those working in the public sector. It is also an efficient way of conducting business transactions with citizens and businesses and within the governments themselves.

E-government offers a number of potential benefits: It improves the efficiency and effectiveness of the functions of government, including the delivery of public services. It enables governments to be more transparent to citizens and businesses by giving access to more of the information generated by government. E-government also offers greater opportunities for citizens to provide feedback to government agencies and to participate in democratic institutions and processes. As a result, e-government may facilitate fundamental changes in the relationships between citizens and governments.

E-government applications can be divided into three major categories: *government-to-citizens (G2C), government-to-business (G2B)*, and *government-to-government (G2G)*. In the G2C category, government agencies increasingly are using the Internet to provide services to citizens. An example is *electronic benefits transfer (EBT)*, in which governments (usually state or national) transfer benefits, such as Social Security and pension payments, directly to recipients' bank accounts or to smart cards. In G2B, governments use the Internet to sell to or buy from businesses. For example, electronic tendering systems using reverse auctions are becoming mandatory, to ensure the best price for government procurement of goods and services. G2G includes intragovernment EC (transactions between different governments) as well as services among different governmental agencies. For an example of an e-government initiative in Australia, see *IT at Work 4.5*. For an overview, see *egov.gov*.

IMPLEMENTING E-GOVERNMENT. Like any other organization, government entities want to move into the digital era, becoming click-and-mortar organizations. However, the transformation from traditional delivery of government services to full implementation of online government services may be a lengthy process.

The business consulting firm Deloitte & Touche conducted a study (Wong, 2000) that identified six stages in the transformation to e-government: *stage 1:* information publishing/dissemination; *stage 2:* "official" two-way transactions, with one department at a time; *stage 3:* multipurpose portals; *stage 4:* portal personalization; *stage 5:* clustering of common services; *stage 6:* full integration and enterprise transformation.

The speed at which a government moves from stage 1 to stage 6 varies, but usually the transformation is very slow. Deloitte & Touche found that in 2000, most governments were still in stage 1 (Wong, 2000).

The implementation issues that are involved in the transformation to e-government depend on which of the six stages of development a government is in, on the plan for moving to higher stages, and on the available funding. In addition, governments are concerned about maintaining the security and privacy of citizens' data, so time and effort must be spent to ensure that security.

In general, implementation of G2B is easier than implementation of G2C. In some countries, such as Hong Kong, G2B implementation is outsourced to a private company that pays all of the startup expenses in exchange for collecting future transaction fees. As G2B services have the potential for rapid cost savings, they can be a good way to begin an e-government EC initiative.

Consumer-to-Consumer E-Commerce

Consumer-to-consumer (C2C) e-commerce refers to e-commerce in which both the buyer and the seller are individuals (not businesses). C2C is conducted in several ways on the Internet, where the best-known C2C activities are auctions.

C2C AUCTIONS. In dozens of countries, C2C selling and buying on auction sites is exploding. Most auctions are conducted by intermediaries, like eBay.com. Consumers can select general sites such as *800webmall.com* or *auctionanything.com*; they also can use specialized sites such as *buyit.com* or *bid2bid.com*. In addition, many individuals are conducting their own auctions. For example, *greatshop.com* provides software to create online C2C reverse auction communities.

CLASSIFIED ADS. People sell to other people every day through classified ads in newspapers and magazines. Internet-based classified ads have one big advantage over these more traditional types of classified ads: They offer a national, rather than a local, audience (e.g., see *traderonline.com*). This wider audience greatly increases the supply of goods and services available and the number of potential buyers. Internet-based classifieds often can be edited or changed easily, and in many cases they display photos of the product offered for sale.

The major categories of online classified ads are similar to those found in the newspaper: vehicles, real estate, employment, pets, tickets, and travel. Classified ads are available through most Internet service providers (AOL, MSN, etc.), at some portals (Yahoo, etc.), and from Internet directories, online newspapers, and more. To help narrow the search for a particular item on several sites, shoppers can use search engines. Once users find an ad and get the details, they can e-mail or call the other party for additional information or to make a purchase. Classified sites generate revenue from affiliate sites.

PERSONAL SERVICES. Numerous personal services (lawyers, handy helpers, tax preparers, investment advisors, dating services) are available on the Internet. Some are in the classified ads, but others are listed in specialized Web sites and directories. Some are for free, some for a fee. *Be very careful before you purchase any personal services online.* Fraud or crime could be involved. For example, an online lawyer may not be an expert in the area he or she professes, or may not deliver the service at all.

SUPPORT SERVICES TO C2C. When individuals buy products or services from individuals, they usually buy from strangers. The issues of ensuring quality, receiving payments, and preventing fraud are critical to the success of C2C. One service that helps C2C is payments by companies such as PayPal.com (see Section 4.8). Another one is *escrow services,* intermediaries that take the buyer's money and the purchased goods, and only after making sure that the seller delivers what was agreed upon, deliver the goods to the buyer and the money to the seller (for a fee).

4.8 E-COMMERCE SUPPORT SERVICES

The implementation of EC may require several support services. B2B and B2C applications require payments and order fulfillment; portals require content. Figure 4.2 portrays the collection of the major EC services. They include: e-infrastructure (mostly technology consultants, system developers and integrators, hosting, security, wireless, and networks), e-process (mainly payments and logistics), e-markets (mostly marketing and advertising), e-communities (different audiences and business partners), e-services (CRM, PRM, and directory services), and e-content (supplied by content providers). All of these services support the EC applications in the center of the figure, and all of the services need to be managed.

Here we will focus on two of the above topics—payments and order fulfillment. For details on the other services, see Turban et al. (2006).

Electronic Payments

Payments are an integral part of doing business, whether in the traditional way or online. Unfortunately, in most cases traditional payment systems are not effective for EC, especially for B2B. Cash cannot be used because there is no face-to-face contact. Not everyone accepts credit cards or checks, and some buyers do not have credit cards or checking accounts. Finally, contrary to what many people believe, it may be less secure for the buyer to use the telephone or mail to arrange or send payment, especially from another country, than to complete a secured transaction on a computer. For all of these reasons, a better way is needed to pay for goods and services in cyberspace. This better way is *electronic payment systems.*

ELECTRONIC PAYMENT SYSTEMS. As in the traditional marketplace, so too in cyberspace, diversity of payment methods allows customers to choose how they wish to pay. Here we will look at some of the most popular electronic payment mechanisms.

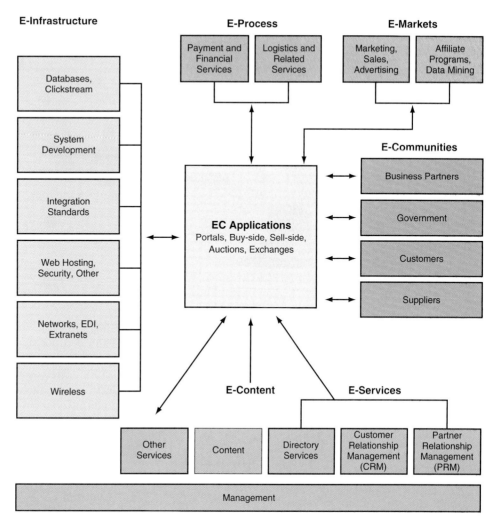

FIGURE 4.2 E-commerce support services.
(*Source:* Drawn by E. Turban. Based on S. Y. Choi et al. 1997, p. 18.)

Electronic Checks. *Electronic checks (e-checks)* are similar to regular paper checks. They are used mostly in B2B (Reda, 2002). First, the customer establishes a checking account with a bank. When the customer contacts a seller and buys a product or a service, he or she e-mails an encrypted electronic check to the seller. The seller deposits the check in a bank account, and funds are transferred from the buyer's account and into the seller's account.

Like regular checks, e-checks carry a signature (in digital form) that can be verified (see *echeck.net*). Properly signed and endorsed e-checks are exchanged between financial institutions through electronic clearinghouses (see *eccho.org* and Echecksecure from *etroqgroup.com* for details).

Electronic Credit Cards. *Electronic credit cards* make it possible to charge online payments to one's credit card account. For security, only encrypted credit cards should be used. Credit card details can be encrypted by using the SSL protocol in the buyer's computer (available in standard browsers). (Payment protocols are described in Online File W4.10.)

Here is how electronic credit cards work: When you buy a book from Amazon, your credit card information and purchase amount are encrypted in your

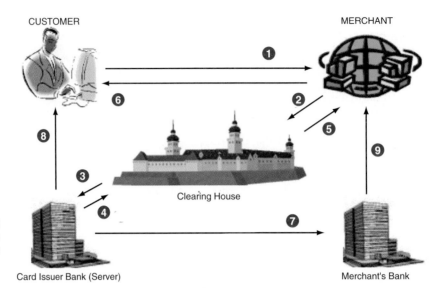

FIGURE 4.3 How e-credit cards work. (The numbers 1–9 indicate the sequence of activities.) (*Source:* Drawn by E. Turban.)

browser, so the information is safe while "traveling" on the Internet. Furthermore, when this information arrives at Amazon, it is not opened but is transferred automatically (in encrypted form) to a clearinghouse, where the information is decrypted for verification and authorization. The complete process of how e-credit cards work is shown in Figure 4.3. Electronic credit cards are used mainly in B2C and in shopping by SMEs (small-to-medium enterprises).

Purchasing Cards. The B2B equivalent of electronic credit cards is *purchasing cards*. In some countries, companies pay other companies primarily by means of purchasing cards, rather than by paper checks. Unlike credit cards, where credit is provided for 30 to 60 days (for free) before payment is made to the merchant, payments made with purchasing cards are settled within a week.

Purchasing cards typically are used for unplanned B2B purchases, and corporations generally limit the amount per purchase (usually $1,000 to $2,000). Purchasing cards can be used on the Internet much like regular credit cards. They expedite the process of unplanned purchases, usually as part of *desktop purchasing* (described earlier).

Electronic Cash. Cash is the most prevalent consumer payment instrument in offline transactions. Some buyers pay with cash because they do not have checks or credit cards, or because they want to preserve their anonymity. Traditional brick-and-mortar merchants prefer cash since they do not have to pay commissions to credit card companies, and they can put the money to use as soon as it is received. It is logical, therefore, that EC sellers and some buyers may prefer electronic cash. *Electronic cash (e-cash)* appears in three major forms: stored-value money cards, smart cards, and person-to-person payments.

Stored-Value Money Cards. Although they look like credit cards, **stored-value money cards** actually are a form of e-cash. The cards that you use to pay for photocopies in your library, for transportation, or for telephone calls are stored-value money cards. They allow a fixed amount of prepaid money to be stored. Each time you use the card, the amount is reduced. Millions of travelers, around the world, pay for transportation with such cards. Some of these cards are reloadable, and some are discarded when the money is depleted.

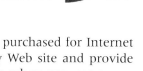

A stored-value money card from the Chicago Transit Authority (CTA).

Cards with stored-value money can be also purchased for Internet use. To use such cards, you enter a third-party Web site and provide an ID number and a password, much as you do when you use a prepaid phone card. The money can be used only in participating stores online.

Smart Cards. Although some people refer to stored-value money cards as smart cards, they are not really the same. True **smart cards** contain a microprocessor (chip) that enables them to store a considerable amount of information (more than 100 times that of a stored-value money card) and to conduct processing. Such cards are frequently *multipurpose;* they can be used as a credit card, debit card, or stored-value money card. In addition, when used in department store chains (as a *loyalty card*), they may contain the purchasing information of shoppers.

Advanced smart cards have the ability to support funds transfer, bill payments, and purchasing from vending machines, or to pay for services such as those offered on television or PCs (Shelter and Procaccino, 2002). Money values can be loaded onto advanced smart cards at ATMs, kiosks, or from your PC. For example, the VISA Cash Card allows you to buy goods or services at participating gas stations, fast-food outlets, pay phones, discount stores, post offices, convenience stores, coffee shops, and even movie theaters. Like stored-value money cards, smart cards are ideal for *micropayments* (small payments of a few dollars or less), but smart cards have additional functions as well. In Hong Kong, the transportation card called Octopus is a stored-value money card that can be used for trains and buses; however, as its capabilities have expanded so that it can be used in stores and vending machines, it is moving to a smart card.

Smart cards can also be used to transfer benefits from companies to their employees (as when retirees get their pension payments) and from governments that pay citizens various entitlements. The money is transferred electronically to a smart card at an ATM, kiosk, or PC.

Person-to-Person Payments. **Person-to-person payments** are a form of e-cash that enable the transfer of funds between two individuals, or between an individual and a business, without the use of a credit card. They are one of the newest and fastest-growing payment mechanisms. They can be used for a variety of purposes, like repaying money borrowed from a friend, sending money to students at college, paying for an item purchased at an online auction, or sending a gift to a family member.

One of the first companies to offer this service was PayPal. PayPal (now an eBay company) claimed to have had about 40 million customer accounts in 2004, handling more than 35 percent of all transactions of eBay and funneling $12.2 billion in payments through its servers annually (*paypal.com,* accessed May 2004). Other companies offer similar services: AOL QuickCash, Bank One's eMoneyMail, Yahoo PayDirect, and WebCertificate (*webcertificate.com*) are all PayPal competitors.

Virtually all of these person-to-person payment services work in a similar way. First, you select a service and open up an account. Basically, this entails creating a user name, selecting a password, and providing the service with a credit card or bank account number. Next, you add funds from your credit card or bank account to your new account. Now you're ready to send money to someone over the Internet. You access PayPal (for example) with your user name and password, and you specify the e-mail address of the person to receive the money, along with the dollar amount that you want to send. An e-mail is sent to the payee's e-mail address. The e-mail will contain a link back to the service's Web site. When the recipient clicks on the link, he or she will be taken to the service. The recipient will be asked to set up an account to which the money that was sent will be credited. The recipient can then credit the money from this account to either his or her credit card or bank account. The payer pays a small amount (around $1) per transaction.

Electronic Bill Presentment and Payments (EBPP). An increasing number of people prefer to pay their recurring monthly bills (such as telephone, utilities, credit cards, mortgage, rent, and cable TV) online. The recipients of such payments are even more enthusiastic about such service than the payers, since online payments enable them to reduce processing costs significantly and they receive the funds sooner.

Paying Bills at ATMs. In some countries (e.g., Hong Kong, Singapore) customers can pay bills at regular ATMs. The bills are sent by regular mail or can be viewed online. When you receive the bills, you go to an ATM, slide in your bank card, enter a password, and go to "bill payments" on the menu. All you need to do is insert the account number of the biller and the amount you want to pay; that amount will be charged to your bank card and sent to the biller. You get a printed receipt on the spot. Many merchants give a discount to those who use the service.

SECURITY IN ELECTRONIC PAYMENTS. Two main issues need to be considered under the topic of payment security: what is required in order to make EC payments safe, and the methods that can be used to do so.

Security Requirements. Security requirements for conducting EC are the following:

- *Authentication.* The buyer, the seller, and the paying institutions must be assured of the identity of the parties with whom they are dealing.
- *Integrity.* It is necessary to ensure that data and information transmitted in EC, such as orders, replies to queries, and payment authorizations, are not accidentally or maliciously altered or destroyed during transmission.
- *Nonrepudiation.* Merchants need protection against the customer's unjustified denial of placing an order. On the other hand, customers need protection against merchants' unjustified denial of payments made. (Such denials, of both types, are called *repudiation*.)
- *Privacy.* Many customers want their identity to be secured. They want to make sure others do not know what they buy. Some prefer complete anonymity, as is possible with cash payments.
- *Safety.* Customers want to be sure that it is safe to provide a credit card number on the Internet. They also want protection against fraud by sellers or by criminals posing as sellers.

Security Protection. Several methods and mechanisms can be used to fulfill the above requirements. One of the primary mechanisms is *encryption* (making messages indecipherable by using a key), which is often part of the most useful security schemes. For more detailed explanation of encryption, see Online File W4.11. Other representative methods are discussed below.

E-Wallets. **E-wallets** (or **digital wallets**) are software mechanisms that provide security measures, combined with convenience, to EC purchasing. The wallet stores the financial information of the buyer, such as credit card number, shipping information, and more. Thus, sensitive information does not need to be reentered for each purchase. If the wallet is stored at the vendor's site, it does not have to travel on the Net for each purchase, making the information more secure.

The problem is that you need an e-wallet with each merchant. One solution is to have a wallet installed on your computer (e.g., MasterCard Wallet or AOL Wallet). In that case, though, you cannot use the e-wallet to make a purchase from another computer, nor is it a totally secured system. Another solution is a *universal* e-wallet such as Microsoft's Passport (Rosenbaum, 2002) and the Liberty Alliance (Costa, 2002). Universal systems are becoming popular because they provide a *digital identity* as well.

Virtual Credit Cards. A **virtual credit card** allows you to shop with an ID number and a password instead of with a credit card number. Such cards are used primarily by people who do not trust browser encryption sufficiently to use their credit card numbers on the Internet. The virtual credit card gives an extra layer of security. The bank that supports your traditional credit card, for example, can provide you with a transaction number valid for online use for a short period. For example, if you want to make a $200 purchase, you would contact your credit card company to charge that amount to your regular credit card account. You would be given a transaction number that is good for charges up to $200. This transaction number is encrypted for security, but even in the worst possible case (that some unauthorized entity obtained the transaction number), your loss would be limited, in this case to $200.

Payment Using Fingerprints. An increasing number of supermarkets allow their regular customers to pay by merely using their fingerprint for identification. A computer template of your fingerprint is kept in the store's computer system. Each time you shop, your fingerprint is matched with the template at the payment counter. You approve the amount, which is then charged either to your credit card or bank account.

Order Fulfillment

We now turn our attention to another important EC support service—*order fulfillment*. Any time a company sells direct to customers it is involved in various order-fulfillment activities. It must perform the following activities: Quickly find the products to be shipped; pack them; arrange for the packages to be delivered speedily to the customer's door; collect the money from every customer, either in advance, by COD, or by individual bill; and handle the return of unwanted or defective products.

It is very difficult to accomplish these activities both effectively and efficiently in B2C, since a company may need to ship small packages to many customers, and do it quickly. For this reason, both online companies and click-and-mortar companies often have difficulties in their B2C supply chain. Here, we provide a brief overview of order fulfillment. For a more detailed discussion, see Bayles (2001), Croxton (2003), and Turban et al. (2006).

Order fulfillment includes not only providing customers with what they ordered and doing it on time, but also providing all related customer service.

For example, the customer must receive assembly and operation instructions to a new appliance. (A nice example is available at *livemanuals.com*.) In addition, if the customer is not happy with a product, an exchange or return must be arranged. (See *fedex.com* for how returns are handled via FedEx.) Order fulfillment is basically a part of what are called a company's *back-office operations* (activities such as inventory control, shipment, and billing).

In the late 1990s, e-tailers faced continuous problems in order fulfillment, especially during the holiday season. The problems resulted in inability to deliver on time, delivery of wrong items, high delivery costs, and the need to heavily compensate unhappy customers. Several factors can be responsible for delays in deliveries. They range from inability to forecast demand accurately to ineffective supply chains. Some such problems exist also in offline businesses. One factor that is typical of EC, though, is that it is based on the concept of "pull" operations, which begin with an order, frequently a customized one (see Appendix 2A on build-to-order). In the pull case it is more difficult to forecast demand, due to unique demands of customized orders and lack of sufficient years of experience.

For many e-tailers, taking orders over the Internet could well be the easy part of B2C e-commerce. Fulfillment to customers' doors is the sticky part. Fulfillment can be less complicated in B2B where several effective methods are in use (see Bayles, 2001).

4.9 ETHICAL AND LEGAL ISSUES IN E-BUSINESS

Ethical standards and their incorporation into law frequently trail technological innovation. E-commerce is taking new forms and enabling new business practices that may bring numerous risks—particularly for individual consumers—along with their advantages. We begin by considering ethical issues relating to e-business.

Ethical Issues

Many of the ethical and global issues related to IT in general apply also to e-business. These are discussed in the Ethics Primer at our Web site (Online File W1.4). In this section we touch on issues particularly related to e-commerce.

PRIVACY. Most electronic payment systems know who the buyers are; therefore, it may be necessary to protect the buyers' identities. A privacy issue related to employees also involves tracking: Many companies monitor employees' e-mail and have installed software that performs in-house monitoring of Web activities in order to discover employees who extensively use company time for non-business-related activities, including harassing other employees. Yet many employees don't want to feel like they are under the watchful eye of "Big Brother," even while at work.

WEB TRACKING. Log files are the principal resources from which e-businesses draw information about how visitors use a site. Applying analytics to log files means either turning log data over to an application service provider (ASP) or installing software that can pluck relevant information from files in-house. By using tracking software, companies can track individuals' movements on the Internet. Programs such as cookies raise a batch of privacy concerns. The tracking history is stored on your PC's hard drive, and any time you revisit a certain Web site, the computer knows it (see NetTracker at *sane.com*). In response, some users install programs such as Cookie Cutter, CookieCrusher, and Spam Butcher, which are designed to allow users to have some control over cookies.

However, the battle between computer end users and Web trackers has just begun. There are more and more "pesticides" for killing these "parasites." For example, Privacy Guardian, MyPrivacy, and Tracks Eraser Pro are examples of software that can protect users' online privacy by erasing a browser's cache, surfing histories, and cookies. Programs like Ad-Aware are specially designed to detect and remove spyware and data miners such as SahAgent, an application that collects and combines users' Internet browsing behavior and sends it to ShopAtHomeSelect servers. (For more information about anti-spy software, see *coast-info.org*.)

LOSS OF JOBS. The use of EC may result in the elimination of some of a company's employees as well as brokers and agents. The manner in which these unneeded workers, especially employees, are treated may raise ethical issues, such as how to handle the displacement and whether to offer retraining programs.

DISINTERMEDIATION AND REINTERMEDIATION. One of the most interesting EC issues relating to loss of jobs is that of *intermediation*. Intermediaries provide two types of services: (1) matching and providing information and (2) value-added services such as consulting. The first type of services (matching and providing information) can be fully automated, and therefore these services are likely to be assumed by e-marketplaces and portals that provide free services. The second type of services (value-added services) requires expertise, and these can be only partially automated. Intermediaries who provide only (or mainly) the first type of service may be eliminated, a phenomenon called **disintermediation** (elimination of the intermediaries). On the other hand, brokers who provide the second type of service or who manage electronic intermediation, also known as *infomediation*, are not only surviving, but may actually prosper. This phenomenon is called **reintermediation.**

Disintermediation may cause channel conflicts. Intermediaries therefore fight back against manufacturers in fear that the traditional sales channel will be negatively affected by disintermediation (Lee et al., 2003). For instance, Wal-Mart and Home Depot warned Black & Decker that they would take its products off their shelves if Black & Decker began to sell its products through the Internet. In another example, just one month after it started selling guitars online at a 10 percent discount, Gibson Musical Instruments backed away from its disintermediation efforts due to strong resistance from intermediaries. Also, confronted with dealer complaints, Ford executives recently agreed to discontinue plans for future direct online car sales.

The Web offers new opportunities for reintermediation by providing services (manual or computerized) required to support or complement EC. First, services are especially valuable when the number of participants is enormous, as with job finding, or when complex information products are exchanged. Second, many brokering services require extensive information processing; electronic versions of these services can offer more sophisticated features at a lower cost than is possible with human labor. Finally, for delicate negotiations, a computer mediator may be more predictable, and hence more trustworthy, than a human. For example, suppose a mediator's role is to inform a buyer and a seller whether a deal can be made, without revealing either side's initial price to the other. An independent auditor can verify that a software-based mediator will reveal only the information it is supposed to; a human mediator's fairness is less easily verified. For reintermediation in the travel industry, see Gilden (2004).

Legal Issues Specific to E-Commerce

Many legal issues are related to e-commerce. When buyers and sellers do not know each other and cannot even see each other (they may even be in different countries), there is a chance that dishonest people will commit fraud and other crimes over the Internet. During the first few years of EC, the public witnessed many of these, ranging from the creation of a virtual bank that disappeared along with the investors' deposits, to manipulation of stock prices on the Internet. Unfortunately, fraudulent activities on the Internet are increasing. Representative examples of legal issues specific to e-commerce are discussed below.

FRAUD ON THE INTERNET. Internet fraud and its sophistication have grown as much as, and even faster than, the Internet itself. For example, stock promoters falsely spread positive rumors about the prospects of the companies they touted, to boost the stock price. In other cases the information provided might have been true, but the promoters did not disclose that they were paid to talk up the companies. Stock promoters specifically target small investors who are lured by the promise of fast profits.

Stocks are only one of many areas where swindlers are active. Auctions are especially conducive to fraud, by both sellers and buyers. Other areas of potential fraud include selling bogus investments and phantom business opportunities. Financial criminals now have access to many more people, mainly due to the availability of electronic mail and pop-up ads. The U.S. Federal Trade Commission (*ftc.gov*) regularly publishes examples of scams most likely to arrive via e-mail or be found on the Web. Some ways in which consumers and sellers can protect themselves from online fraud are discussed later in this section.

DOMAIN NAMES. Another legal issue involves competition over domain names. Internet addresses are known as **domain names**. Domain names appear in levels. A top-level name is *wiley.com* or *stanford.edu*. A second-level name will be *wiley.com/turban* or *ibm.com.hk* (for IBM in Hong Kong). Top-level domain names are assigned by central nonprofit organizations that check for conflicts and possible infringement of trademarks (e.g., see *networksolutions.com*). Obviously, companies that sell goods and services over the Internet want customers to be able to find them easily, so it is best when the domain name matches the company's name.

Problems arise when several companies that have similar names compete over a domain name. For example, if you want to book reservations at Holiday Inn hotels on a cross-country trip you are planning and you go to *holidayinn.com*, you get the Web site for a hotel at Niagara Falls, New York; to get to the *hotel chain's* Web site, you have to go to *holiday-inn.com*. Several cases of disputed names are already in court. An international arbitration organization is available as an alternative to the courts. The problem of domain names was alleviated somewhat in 2001 after several upper-level names were added to "com" (such as "info" and "coop").

Cybersquatting. **Cybersquatting** refers to the practice of registering domain names in the hope of selling them later at a higher price. For example, the original owner of *tom.com* received about $8 million for the name. The case of *tom.com* was ethical and legal. But in other cases, cybersquatting can be illegal or at least unethical (see Stead and Gilbert, 2001). Companies such as Christian Dior, Nike, Deutsche Bank, and even Microsoft have had to fight or pay to get the domain name that corresponds to their company's name. The Anticybersquatting Consumer Protection Act (1999) lets trademark owners in the United States sue for statutory damages.

TAXES AND OTHER FEES. In offline sales, most states and localities tax business done within their jurisdiction, through sales taxes and other taxes. Federal, state, and local authorities have been scrambling to figure out how to get a piece of the revenue created by e-business. The problem is particularly complex for interstate and international commerce. For example, some claim that even the state in which a *server* is located deserves to receive some sales tax from an e-commerce transaction. Others say that the state in which the *seller* is located deserves the entire sales tax (or in some countries, value-added tax, VAT).

In addition to sales tax, there is a question about where (and in some cases, whether) electronic sellers should pay business license tax, franchise fees, gross-receipts tax, excise tax, privilege tax, and utility tax. Also, there is the issue of taxing Internet access. Currently there is no tax on fees you pay to AOL or to DSL or Internet service providers. Furthermore, how should tax collection be controlled? Legislative efforts to impose taxes on e-commerce are opposed by an organization named the Internet Freedom Fighters. Their efforts have been successful so far: At the time this edition was written (June 2004), there was a sales tax ban on business done on the Internet in the United States and many other countries, which could remain valid until fall 2006. At that time also, buyers were exempt from tax on Internet access (subject to renewal in 2004).

COPYRIGHT. Intellectual property, in its various forms, is protected by copyright laws and cannot be used freely. In EC it is very difficult to protect intellectual property. For example, some people mistakenly believe that if they have bought a piece of software, they have the right to share it with others. What they have bought is the right to *use* the software, not the right to distribute it—that right remains with the copyright holder. Similarly, it violates copyright laws to copy material from Web sites without permission. For further discussion of issues relating to intellectual property protection, see Chapter 16.

Protection of EC Buyers and Sellers

There are several ways buyers can be protected against fraud in e-commerce. Representative methods are described next.

BUYER PROTECTION. Some tips for safe electronic shopping are shown in Table 4.4 (page 174). In short, do not forget that you have shopper's rights. Consult your local or state consumer protection agency for general information on your consumer rights.

TABLE 4.4 Tips for Safe Electronic Shopping
● Look for reliable brand names at sites like Wal-Mart Online, Disney Online, and Amazon.com. Before purchasing, make sure that the site is authentic by entering the site directly and not from an unverified link.
● Search any unfamiliar selling site for the company's address and phone and fax numbers. Call up and quiz the employees about the seller.
● Check out the vendor with the local Chamber of Commerce or Better Business Bureau (*bbbonline.org*). Look for seals of authenticity such as TRUSTe.
● Investigate how secure the seller's site is by examining the security procedures and by reading the posted privacy policy.
● Examine the money-back guarantees, warranties, and service agreements.
● Compare prices to those in regular stores. Too-low prices could prove too good to be true, and some "catch" is probably involved.
● Ask friends what they know. Find testimonials and endorsements in community sites and well-known bulletin boards.
● Find out what your rights are in case of a dispute. Consult consumer protection agencies and the National Fraud Information Center (*fraud.org*).
● Check *consumerworld.org* for a listing of useful resources.
● Check *cfenet.com*, *isaca.org*, and *agacgfm.gov*.

SELLER PROTECTION.   Online sellers, too, may need protection. They must be protected against consumers who refuse to pay or who pay with bad checks and from buyers' claims that the merchandise did not arrive. They also have the right to protect against the use of their name by others as well as to protect the use of their unique words and phrases, slogans, and Web address (trademark protection). Security features such as authentication, nonrepudiation, and escrow services provide some needed protections. Another seller protection applies particularly to electronic media: Sellers have legal recourse against customers who download without permission copyrighted software and/or knowledge and use it or sell it to others.

4.10 FAILURES AND STRATEGIES FOR SUCCESS

E-Commerce Failures

In this concluding section we consider some EC failures and successes. A well known pre-Internet failure involving a U.S. Food and Drug Administration system is presented in Online File W4.12.

Failures of EC initiatives are fairly common. Furthermore, during 2000–2002, large numbers of dot-com companies failed. In this section we will look at some examples of failures and their causes. We will also look into some success factors that can be used to prevent failure.

INTERNET-RELATED EC FAILURES.   Pioneering organizations saw the potential for e-commerce, but expertise and EC business models were just developing. Failures of EC projects started as early as 1996. However, the major wave of Internet-based EC failures started in 2000, as second-round funding (funding subsequent to a firm's original funding but before it goes to the stock market with a stock offering) began to dry up. Here are some examples. (In the list we have highlighted, in italics, key reasons for the failure.)

● Dr. Koop, a medical portal, was unable to raise the needed advertising money, so the company folded. The diagnosis: death due to *incorrect business model*.

● An Internet mall operated by Open Market was closed in 1996 due to *an insufficient number of buyers*.

● Garden.com closed its doors in December 2000 due to *lack of cash*. Suppliers of venture capital were unwilling to give the company any more money to "burn."

● Several toy companies—Red Rocket, eParties.com, and BabyBucks.com—failed due to *too much competition*. This competition led vendors to lower their prices, which resulted in insufficient profits.

● Living.com, the online furniture store, closed in 2000. The *customer acquisition cost* was too high.

● PaperX.com, an online paper exchange in the UK, folded due to *lack of second-round funding*.

● Webvan, an online grocery and same-day delivery company, made a huge *investment* (over $1 billion) *in infrastructure of warehouses and logistics*. But its income was insufficient to convince investors to fund it further. It collapsed in 2002.

● In late 2000 Chemdex.com, the "granddaddy" of the third-party exchanges, closed down. Ventro.com, its parent company, said that the *revenue growth* was too slow and that a *new business model was needed*. Chemdex was not alone: During 2001–2003 large numbers of exchanges folded or changed their business models.

According to Useem (2000), the major reasons for EC failure are: incorrect revenue model, lack of strategy and contingency planning, inability to attract enough customers, lack of funding, channel conflict with distributors, too much online competition in standard (commodity) products (e.g., CDs, toys), poor order-fulfillment infrastructure, and lack of qualified management. To learn more about EC failures, visit *whytheyfailed.com* and *techdirt.com*.

FAILED EC INITIATIVES WITHIN ORGANIZATIONS. Whereas failed companies, especially publicly listed ones, are well advertised, failed EC initiatives within companies, especially within private companies, are less known. However, news about some failed EC initiatives has been publicized. For example, Levi Strauss stopped online direct sales of its apparel (jeans and its popular Levi's and Dockers brands) on its Web site (*levistrauss.com*) after its major distributors and retailers put pressure on the company not to compete with their brick-and-mortar outlets (channel conflict). Another EC initiative that failed was a joint venture between Intel and SAP, two world-class companies, which was designed to develop low-cost solutions for SMEs. It collapsed in August 2000 due to low demand and too few customers. Large companies such as Citicorp, Disney, and Merrill Lynch also closed EC initiatives after losing millions of dollars in them.

Success Stories and Lessons Learned

Offsetting the failures are hundreds of EC success stories, primarily in specialty and niche markets (see Athitakis, 2003). Here are some of the reasons for EC success and some suggestions from EC experts on how to succeed:

- Thousands of brick-and-mortar companies are slowly adding online channels with great success. Examples are Godiva.com, Uniglobe.com, Staples.com, Homedepot.com, Clearcommerce.com, 1-800-FLOWERS (*800flowers.com*), and Southwest Airlines (*iflyswa.com*).
- As of late 2000, more companies were pursuing mergers and acquisitions (e.g., Ivillage.com with Women.com, though each maintains its separate Web site). Mergers seem to be a growing trend.
- Peter Drucker, the management guru, provides the following advice: "Analyze the opportunities, go out to look, keep it focused, start small (one thing at a time), and aim at market leadership."
- A group of Asian CEOs recommends the following factors that are critical for success: Select robust business models, foster e-innovation, co-brand, carefully evaluate a spinoff strategy, employ ex-dot-com staffers, and focus on the e-generation (young adults) as your market (e.g., *alloy.com* and *bolt.com*).
- Consultant PricewaterhouseCoopers (*pwcglobal.com*) suggests taking extra care to avert technology malfunctions (e.g., inability to handle a surge of orders quickly enough), which erode consumer trust.
- Many experts (e.g., The National Institute for Standards and Technology, NIST) recommend contingency planning and preparing for disasters.
- Huff et al. (1999) suggest the following critical success factors for e-commerce: Add value, focus on a niche and then extend that niche, maintain flexibility, get the technology right, manage critical perceptions, provide excellent customer service, create effective connectedness, and understand Internet culture.

Conclusion

Analyzing successful companies, researchers have suggested that if they do careful planning to reach profitability quickly, many click-and-mortar companies are likely to succeed. Joint ventures and partnerships are very valuable, and planning for satisfactory infrastructure and logistics to meet high demand is needed. In short, do not forget that e-business has a "business" side!

Finally, let's not forget that history repeats itself. When the automobile was invented, there were 240 startup companies between 1904 and 1908. In 1910 there was a shakeout, and today there are only three U.S. automakers. However, the auto industry has grown by a hundredfold. The same is happening in EC: Despite the 2000–2003 failures, the total volume of EC activities continued to grow exponentially. For example, *emarketer.com* reported on May 19, 2003, that B2C revenues in 2002 reached $76 billion; a 48 percent increase over 2001. The figure for 2003 was over $96 billion—close to a 30 percent increase over 2002.

→ MANAGERIAL ISSUES

1. *Managing resistance to change.* Electronic commerce can result in a fundamental change in how business is done, and resistance to change from employees, vendors, and customers may develop. Education, training, and publicity over an extended time period offer possible solutions to the problem.

2. *Integration of e-commerce into the business environment.* E-commerce needs to be integrated with the rest of the business. Integration issues involve planning, competition for corporate resources with other projects, and interfacing EC with databases, existing IT applications, and infrastructure.

3. *Lack of qualified personnel and outsourcing.* Very few people have expertise in e-commerce. There are many implementation issues that require expertise, such as when to offer special promotions on the Internet, how to integrate an e-market with the information systems of buyers and sellers, and what kind of customer incentives are appropriate under what circumstances. For this reason, it may be worthwhile to outsource some e-commerce activities. Yet, as shown in Chapter 13, outsourcing decisions are not simple.

4. *Alliances.* It is not a bad idea to join an alliance or consortium of companies to explore e-commerce. Alliances can be created at any time. Some EC companies (e.g., Amazon.com) have thousands of alliances. The problem is which alliance to join, or what kind of alliance to form and with whom.

5. *Implementation plan.* Because of the complexity and multifaceted nature of EC, it makes sense to prepare an implementation plan. Such a plan should include goals, budgets, timetables, and contingency plans. It should address the many legal, financial, technological, organizational, and ethical issues that can surface during implementation.

6. *Choosing the company's strategy toward e-commerce.* Generally speaking there are three major options: (1) *Lead:* Conduct large-scale innovative e-commerce activities. (2) *Watch and wait:* Do nothing, but carefully watch what is going on in the field in order to determine when EC is mature enough to enter it. (3) *Experiment:* Start some e-commerce experimental projects (learn by doing). Each of these options has its advantages and risks.

7. *Privacy.* In electronic payment systems, it may be necessary to protect the identity of buyers. Other privacy issues may involve tracking of Internet user activities by intelligent agents and cookies, and in-house monitoring of employees' Web activities.

8. *Justifying e-commerce by conducting a cost-benefit analysis is very difficult.* Many intangible benefits and lack of experience may produce grossly inaccurate estimates of costs and benefits. Nevertheless, a feasibility study must be done, and estimates of costs and benefits must be made. For example, see the proposal for assessing EDI investment presented by Hoogewelgen and Wagenaar (1996).

9. *Order fulfillment.* Taking orders in EC may be easier than fulfilling them. To learn about the problems and solutions related to order fulfillment, see Chapter 7.

10. *Managing the impacts.* The impacts of e-commerce on organizational structure, people, marketing procedures, and profitability may be dramatic. Therefore, establishing a committee or organizational unit to develop strategy and to manage e-commerce is necessary.

KEY TERMS

Auction *145*

B2E (business-to-its-employees) EC *140*

Banners *154*

Brick-and-mortar organizations *140*

Business-to-business (B2B) *140*

Business-to-business-to-consumers (B2B2C) *140*

Business-to-consumers (B2C) *140*

Buy-side marketplace *158*
Channel conflict *152*
Click-and-mortar organizations *140*
Collaborative commerce
  (c-commerce) *140*
Consumer-to-consumer (C2C) *140*
Consumers-to-businesses (C2B) *140*
Cyberbanking *149*
Cybersquatting *173*
Desktop purchasing *158*
Disintermediation *171*
Domain name *172*
E-business *139*
E-government *161*
E-procurement *158*
E-wallets (digital wallets) *169*

Electronic bartering *146*
Electronic commerce
  (e-commerce, EC) *139*
Electronic mall *148*
Electronic retailing (e-tailing) *146*
Electronic storefront *148*
Forward auction *145*
Government-to-business (G2B) *141*
Government-to-citizens (G2C) *141*
Government-to-government
  (G2G) *141*
Group purchasing *158*
Intrabusiness *161*
Intrabusiness (intraorganizational)
  commerce *140*
Key-word banner *154*

Mobile commerce (m-commerce) *141*
Permission marketing *155*
Person-to-person payment *167*
Pop-under ad *154*
Pop-up ad *154*
Public exchanges (exchanges) *159*
Random banner *154*
Reintermediation *171*
Reverse auction *146*
Sell-side marketplace *157*
Smart card *000*
Spyware *155*
Stored-value money card *166*
Viral marketing *155*
Virtual credit card *169*
Virtual organizations *140*

CHAPTER HIGHLIGHTS (Numbers Refer to Learning Objectives)

1 E-commerce can be conducted on the Web and on other networks. It is divided into the following major types: business-to-business, collaborative commerce, business-to-consumers, consumer-to-consumer, business-to-business-to consumer, consumers-to-business, intrabusiness, e-government, and mobile commerce. In each type you can find several business models.

1 E-commerce offers many benefits to organizations, consumers, and society, but it also has limitations (technological and nontechnological). The current technological limitations are expected to lessen with time.

2 A major mechanism in EC is auctions. The Internet provides an infrastructure for executing auctions at lower cost, and with many more involved sellers and buyers, including both individual consumers and corporations. Two major types of auctions exist: forward auctions and reverse auctions. Forward auctions are used in the traditional process of *selling* to the highest bidder. Reverse auctions are used for *buying,* using a tendering system to buy at the lowest bid.

2 A minor mechanism is online bartering, in which companies or individuals arrange for *exchange* of physical items and/or services.

3 B2C e-tailing can be pure (such as Amazon.com), or part of a click-and-mortar organization. Direct marketing is done via solo storefronts or in malls. It can be done via electronic catalogs or by using electronic auctions. The leading online B2C service industries are banking, securities trading, job markets, travel, and real estate.

3 The major issues faced by e-tailers are channel conflict, conflict within click-and-mortar organizations, order fulfillment, determining viability and risk, and identifying appropriate revenue models.

4 Like any type of commerce, e-commerce requires advertising support. In EC, though, much of the advertising can be done online by methods such as banner ads, pop-ups, e-mail, electronic catalogs, and customized ads. Permission marketing, interactive and viral marketing, making it to the top of search-engine listings, and online promotions offer additional ways for vendors to reach more customers.

5 The major B2B applications are selling from catalogs and by forward auctions (the sell-side marketplace), buying in reverse auctions and in group and desktop purchasing (the buy-side marketplace), and trading in electronic exchanges.

6 EC activities can be conducted inside organizations. Three types are recognized: between a business and its employees, between units of the business, and among employees of the same organizations.

7 E-government commerce can take place between government and citizens, between businesses and governments, or among government units. It makes government operations more effective and efficient.

7 EC also can be done between consumers (C2C), but should be undertaken with caution. Auctions are the most popular C2C mechanism. C2C also can be done by use of online classified ads.

⑧ New electronic payment systems are needed to complete transactions on the Internet. Electronic payments can be made by e-checks, e-credit cards, purchasing cards, e-cash, stored-value money cards, smart cards, person-to-person payments via services like PayPal, electronic bill presentment and payment, and e-wallets.

⑧ Order fulfillment is especially difficult and expensive in B2C, because of the need to ship relatively small orders to many customers.

⑨ There is increasing fraud and unethical behavior on the Internet, including invasion of privacy by sellers and misuse of domain names.

⑨ The value of domain names, taxation of online business, and how to handle legal issues in a multicountry environment are major legal concerns.

⑨ Protection of customers, sellers, and intellectual property is also important.

⑩ Periods of innovation produce both successes and failures. There have been many of both in e-commerce. Major reasons for failure are insufficient cash flow, too much competition, conflicts with existing systems, wrong revenue models, and lack of planning. Despite the failures, overall EC volume is growing exponentially.

⑩ Five key strategies for EC success are: an appropriate revenue model, sufficient funding for the initial period, selection of the right products to sell online, entry into an area with not too many competitors, and proper planning.

VIRTUAL COMPANY ASSIGNMENT

E-Commerce at The Wireless Café
Go to The Wireless Café's link on the Student Web Site. There you will find a description of the e-commerce activities that have been taking place at the restaurant. You will be asked to identify ways to use both B2C and B2B e-commerce at The Wireless Café.

More Resources
More resources and study tools are located on the Student Web Site. You'll find additional chapter materials and useful Web links. In addition, self-quizzes that provide individualized feedback are available for each chapter.

Instructions for accessing The Wireless Café on the Student Web Site

1. Go to
   wiley.com/college/turban
2. Select Turban/Leidner/
   McLean/Wetherbe's
   Information Technology for Management, Fifth Edition.
3. Click on Student
   Resources site, in the toolbar on the left.
4. Click on the link for
   Virtual Company Web site.
5. Click on Wireless Café.

QUESTIONS FOR REVIEW

1. Define e-commerce and distinguish it from e-business.
2. List the major types of EC (by transaction).
3. Distinguish between business-to-consumer, business-to-business, and intrabusiness EC.
4. Describe forward and reverse auctions.
5. How are forward auctions used as a selling channel?
6. Describe the process of using reverse auctions for purchasing.
7. Define electronic bartering.
8. Describe electronic storefronts and malls.
9. What are some general features (critical success factors) that make the delivery of online services (e.g.,

cyberbanking, securities trading, job hunting, travel services) successful for both sellers and buyers?

10. Describe how customer service is provided online and list its four phases.

11. List the major issues relating to e-tailing.

12. Describe online advertising, its methods, and benefits.

13. Discuss spamming and permission marketing.

14. What is viral marketing?

15. List popular online promotion methods.

16. Briefly differentiate between the sell-side marketplace and the buy-side marketplace.

17. Describe how forward and reverse auctions are used in B2B commerce.

18. Describe the various methods of e-procurement.

19. Describe the role of exchanges in B2B.

20. Describe intrabusiness EC and list its major types.

21. Define B2E.

22. Define e-government and list its various types.

23. Describe typical G2B activities.

24. Describe the six phases of e-government implementation.

25. Define C2C EC and list some types of C2C activities.

26. List the various electronic payment mechanisms. Which of these are most often used for B2B payments?

27. List the security requirements for EC.

28. Describe the issues in EC order fulfillment.

29. List some ethical issues in EC.

30. List the major legal issues of EC.

31. Describe buyer protection in EC.

32. Describe seller protection in EC.

33. List five reasons for EC failures.

34. List five suggestions for EC success.

QUESTIONS FOR DISCUSSION

1. Discuss the major limitations of e-commerce. Which of them are likely to disappear? Why?

2. Discuss the reasons for having multiple EC business models.

3. Distinguish between business-to-business forward auctions and buyers' bids for RFQs.

4. Discuss the benefits to sellers and buyers of a B2B exchange.

5. What are the major benefits of e-government?

6. Discuss the various ways to pay online in B2C. Which one(s) would you prefer and why?

7. Why is order fulfillment in B2C considered difficult?

8. Discuss the reasons for EC failures.

EXERCISES

1. Assume you're interested in buying a car. You can find information about cars at *autos.msn.com*. Go to *autoweb.com* or *autobytel.com* for information about financing and insurance. Decide what car you want to buy. Configure your car by going to the car manufacturer's Web site. Finally, try to find the car from *autobytel.com*. What information is most supportive of your decision-making process? Write a report about your experience.

2. Consider Minicase 2 about Hi-Life.
   a. How was the corporate decision making improved?
   b. Summarize the benefits to the customers, suppliers, store management, and employees.
   c. The data collected at Activesys can be uploaded to a PC and transmitted to the corporate intranet via the Internet. It is suggested that transmission be done using a wireless system. Comment on the proposal.

3. Compare the various electronic payment methods. Specifically, collect information from the vendors cited in the chapter and find more with *google.com*. Pay attention to security level, speed, cost, and convenience.

4. Prepare a study on how to stop pop-ups. Look at *find.pcworld.com/27401 and 28221, 27424, 27426*. Consider *adsubstract.com, guidescope.com, symantac.com* (Norton). Investigate what AOL and Yahoo offer. What is new in legislation regarding spamming in your country?

GROUP ASSIGNMENTS

1. Have each team study a major bank with extensive EC strategy. For example, Wells Fargo Bank is well on its way to being a cyberbank. Hundreds of brick-and-mortar branch offices are being closed. In Spring 2003 the bank served more than a 1.2 million cyberaccounts (see *wellsfargo.com*). Other banks to look at are Citicorp, Netbank, and HSBC (Hong Kong). Each team should attempt to convince the class that its e-bank activities are the best.

2. Assign each team to one industry. Each team will find five real-world applications of the major business-to-business models listed in the chapter. (Try success stories of vendors and EC-related magazines.) Examine the problems they solve or the opportunities they exploit.

3. Have teams investigate how B2B payments are made in global trade. Consider instruments such as electronic letters of credit and e-checks. Visit *tradecard.com* and examine their services to SMEs. Also, investigate what Visa and MasterCard are offering. Finally, check Citicorp and some German and Japanese banks.

INTERNET EXERCISES

1. Access *etrade.com* and register for the Internet stock simulation game. You will be bankrolled with $100,000 in a trading account every month. Play the game and relate your experiences to IT.

2. Use the Internet to plan a trip to Paris. Visit *lonelyplanet.com, yahoo.com,* and *expedia.com.*
   a. Find the lowest airfare.
   b. Examine a few hotels by class.
   c. Get suggestions of what to see.
   d. Find out about local currency, and convert $1,000 to that currency with an online currency converter.
   e. Compile travel tips.
   f. Prepare a report.

3. Access *realtor.com.* Prepare a list of services available on this site. Then prepare a list of advantages derived by the users and advantages to realtors. Are there any disadvantages? To whom?

4. Enter *alibaba.com.* Identify the site's capabilities. Look at the site's private trading room. Write a report. How can such a site help a person who is making a purchase?

5. Enter *campusfood.com.* Explore the site. Why is the site so successful? Could you start a competing one? Why or why not?

6. Enter *dell.com,* go to "desktops" and configure a system. Register to "my cart" (no obligation). What calculators are used there? What are the advantages of this process as compared to buying a computer in a physical store? What are the disadvantages?

7. Enter *checkfree.com* and find their services. Prepare a report.

8. Enter *resumix.yahoo.com* and summarize the services they provide.

9. Enter *techjourney.com* and go to "Compensation." Find how much money you can earn.

Minicase 1
FreeMarkets.com

FreeMarkets (*freemarkets.com*) is a leader in creating B2B online auctions for buyers of industrial parts, raw materials, commodities, and services around the globe. The company has created auctions for goods and services in hundreds of industrial product categories. FreeMarkets auctions more than $5 billion worth of purchase orders a year and saves buyers an estimated 2 to 25 percent of total expenses (administrative and items).

FreeMarkets operates two types of marketplaces. First, the company helps customers purchase goods and services through its B2B global marketplace where reverse auctions usually take place. Second, FreeMarkets helps companies improve their asset-recovery results by getting timely market prices for surplus assets through the FreeMarkets Asset Exchange, employing a *forward auction* process, as well as other selling models.

FreeMarkets Onsite Auctions include (1) asset disposal recovery and (2) sourcing (e-procurement) functions. These functions provide the following:

- **Asset disposal analysis.** Market makers work with sellers to determine the best strategy to meet asset-recovery goals.
- **Detailed sales offering.** The company collects and consolidates asset information into a printed or online sales offering for buyers.
- **Targeted market outreach.** FreeMarkets conducts targeted advertising to a global database of 500,000 buyers and suppliers.
- **Event coordination.** The company prepares the site, provides qualified personnel, and enforces auction rules.
- **Sales implementation.** FreeMarkets summarizes auction results and assists in closing sales.

Asset-Recovery Success Stories

FreeMarkets helped the following companies make asset recoveries:

New Line Cinema (*newline.com*) had unique memorabilia that they had stored for years. In 2001 they decided to auction these via FreeMarkets' auction marketplace (Asset Exchange). The release of a movie sequel titled *Austin Powers: The Spy Who Shagged Me* provided an opportunity for New Line to experiment with the asset-recovery auction. Items from the original production were put up for auction; these items included a 1965 Corvette driven by Felicity Shagwell (sold in the auction for $121,000) and one of Austin's suits (sold for $7,500). In addition to freeing storage space and generating income, the auction provided publicity for the sequel through the newspaper and television coverage it received. An additional benefit was that the auction was linked to the company's online store. If you were unable to afford the 1965 Corvette, you instead could have purchased a new T-shirt or a poster of the new movie. Finally, the auction created a dedicated community of users. The auction was a great success, and since then New Line Cinema has conducted similar auctions on a regular basis.

Another success story for FreeMarkets' auctions was American Power Conversion Corp. (*apcc.com*), which needed a channel for end-of-life (old models) and refurbished power-protection products. These were difficult to sell in the regular distribution channels. Before using auctions, the company used special liquidation sales, which were not very successful. FreeMarkets deployed the auction site (using its standard technology, but customizing the applications). It also helped the company determine the auction strategies (such as starting-bid price and auction running length), which were facilitated by DSS modeling. The site became an immediate success. The company is considering selling regular products there, but only merchandise for which there would be no conflict with the company's regular distributors.

E-Procurement (Sourcing) Success Story

Besides providing companies with successful efforts in asset recovery, FreeMarkets has also helped companies conduct reverse auctions either from their own sites (with necessary expertise provided by FreeMarkets) or from FreeMarkets' site. Singapore Technologies Engineering (STE), a large integrated global engineering group specializing in the fields of aerospace, electronics, land systems, and marine had the following goals when it decided to use e-procurement (sourcing) with the help of FreeMarkets: to minimize the cost of products they need to buy, such as board parts; to identify a new global supply base for their multisourcing strategy; to ensure maximized efficiency in the procurement process; to find new, quality suppliers for reliability and support; and to consolidate existing suppliers. These are typical goals of business purchasers.

FreeMarkets started by training STE's corporate buyers and other staff. Then it designed an improved process that replicated the traditional negotiations with suppliers. Finally, it took a test item and prepared an RFQ, placing it for bid in the FreeMarkets Web site. FreeMarkets uses a five-step tendering process that starts with the RFQ and ends with supplier management (which includes suppliers' verification and training). STE saved 35 percent on the cost of printed circuit board assemblies.

In 2004 FreeMarkets took over the auction activities of the auto-industry exchange *covisint.com*. In 2004 Freemarkets merged with Ariba.com.

Sources: Compiled from *freemarkets.com;* see success stories (accessed December 15, 2002 and March 28, 2003); and from *ariba.com* (accessed September 3, 2004).

Questions for Minicase 1

1. What makes FreeMarkets different from eBay?
2. Why do you think FreeMarkets concentrates on asset recovery and on e-procurement?
3. Why is the RFQ mechanism popular?
4. In 2003 the company shifted attention to global supply management. What does the company mean by that?

Minicase 2
E-Commerce Improves Inventory Control at Hi-Life Corporation

The Business Problem

Hi-Life Corporation owns and operates 720 convenience retail stores in Taiwan, where the company sells over 3,000 different products. A major problem is keeping a proper level of inventory of each product in each store. Over-

stocking is expensive due to storage costs and tying up space and money to buy and maintain the inventory. Understocking reduces potential sales and could result in unhappy customers who may go to a competitor.

To calculate the appropriate level of inventory, it is necessary to know exactly how many units of each product are in stock at specific times. This is done by what is known as *stock count*. Periodic stock count is needed since the actual amount in stock frequently differs from the computed one (inventory = previous inventory − sales + new arrivals). The difference is due to "shrinkage" (e.g., theft, misplaced items, spoilage, etc.). Until 2002, stock counts at Hi-Life were done manually. Employees counted the quantity of each product and recorded it on data collection sheets on which the products' names were preprinted. Then, the data were painstakingly keyed into each store's PC. The process took over 21 person-hours, in each store, each time a count was needed, sometimes once a week. This process was expensive and frequently was delayed, causing problems along the entire supply chain due to delays in count and mismatches of computed and actual inventories.

The IT Solution

The first phase of improvement was introduced in spring 2002. Management introduced a Pocket PC (a hand-held device) from Hewlett-Packard. The Pocket PC (called Jornada) enables employees to enter the inventory tallies directly into electronic forms using Chinese characters for additional notes. Once the Pocket PC is placed in its synchronized cradle (see Chapter 5), inventory information can be relayed instantly to Hi-Life's headquarters.

In the second phase of improvement, in summer 2003, a compact barcode scanner was added on in the Pocket PC's expansion slot. Employees can now scan the products' barcodes and then enter the quantity found on the shelf. This new feature expedites data entry and minimizes errors in product identification. The up-to-the second information enables headquarters to compute appropriate inventory levels in minutes, to better schedule shipments, and to plan purchasing strategies using decision-support system formulas. The stores use the Internet (with a secured feature known as VPN; see Technology Guide 4) to upload data to the intranet at headquarters.

The Results

The results have been astonishing. Inventory taking has been reduced from 21 to less than 4 hours per store, per count. Errors are down by more than 90 percent, order placing is simple and quick, and administrative paperwork has been eliminated. Furthermore, quicker and more precise inventory counts have resulted in lower inventory levels and in quicker response times for changes in demand. The entire product-management process has become more efficient, including stocking, price checks, and reticketing.

For the employees, the new system is very user friendly, both to learn and to operate. Hi-Life's employees now have more time to plan, manage, and chat with customers. More important, faster and better inventory and purchasing decisions are enabled at headquarters, contributing to greater competitiveness and profitability for Hi-Life.

Sources: Compiled from *hp.com/jornada* (accessed May 2003) and from *microsoft.com/asia/mobile* (accessed May 2003).

Questions for Minicase 2

1. Explain why this is B2E.
2. How is corporate decision making improved?
3. Summarize the benefits to customers, employees, and the company.

REFERENCES

Amiri, A., and S. Menon, "Efficient Scheduling of Internet Banner Advertisements," *ACM Transactions on Internet Technology*, 3(4), November 2003, pp. 334–346.

Athitakis, M., "How to Make Money on the Net," *Business 2.0*, May 2003.

Bayers, C., "The Last Laugh (of Amazon's CEO)," *Business 2.0*, September 2002.

Bayles, D. L., *E-Commerce Logistics and Fulfillment*. Upper Saddle River, NJ: Prentice Hall, 2001.

Choi, S. Y., et al., *The Economics of Electronic Commerce*. Indianapolis, IN: Macmillan Technical Publications, 1997.

Croxton, K. L., "The Order Fulfillment Process," *International Journal of Logistics Management*, 14(1), 2003, pp. 19–32.

Daisey, M., *21 Dog Years: Doing Time @ amazon.com*. New York: Free Press, 2002.

Deitel, H. M., et al., *e-Business and e-Commerce for Managers*. Upper Saddle River, NJ: Prentice Hall, 2001.

Gallaugher, J. M., "E-Commerce and the Undulating Distribution Channel," *Communications of the ACM*, July 2002.

Gilden, J., "Popularity of Web Forces Travel Agents to Adjust," *Chicago Tribune*, March 14, 2004.

Huff, S. L., et al., "Critical Success Factors for Electronic Commerce," in *Cases in Electronic Commerce*. New York: Irwin/McGraw-Hill, 1999.

Kambil, A., and E. van Heck, *Making Markets*. Boston: Harvard Business School Press, 2002.

Kaplan, S., and M. Sawhney, "E-Hubs: The New B2B Marketplaces," *Harvard Business Review*, May 1, 2000.

Lee, S. C., and A. A. Brandberry, "The E-Tailer's Dilemma," *Data Base*, Spring 2003.

Lee, Y., et al., "Coping with Internet Channel Conflict," *Communications of the ACM*, 46(7), 2003, pp. 137–142.

Luo, W., and M. Najdawi, "Trust-Building Measures: A Review of Consumer Health Portals," *Communications of the ACM*, 47(1), 2004, pp. 108–113.

Lyons, R., "eBay Course for Beginners at University," *Birmingham Post*, Birmingham, UK, April 23, 2004, p. 4.

Mann, R. J., "Regulating Internet Payment Intermediaries," *Proceedings of the 5th International Conference on Electronic Commerce*, Pittsburgh, September 30–October 3, 2003, pp. 376–386.

Mulrean, J., "Protect Yourself: The Safest Ways to Pay Online," *http://moneycentral.msn.com/content/Savinganddebt/Finddealsonline/P36487.asp* (accessed July 2004).

Ovans, A., "E-Procurement at Schlumberger," *Harvard Business Review,* May–June 2000.

Reda, S., "Godiva.com's Story Parallels Dynamic Growth of E-Commerce," *Stores*, February 2004.

Reda, S., "Online Check Service Expands Internet Payment Options," *Stores*, February 2002.

Roy, S., "OK, You Are Now an Approved Supplier—But You Still Do Not Get Orders: Understanding the Case of the P-Card," *Industrial Marketing Management*, 32(7), October 2003, pp. 605–613.

Sawhney, M., "Fields of Online Dreams," *CIO Magazine*, October 15, 2002.

Shelter, K. M., and J. D. Procaccino, "Smart Card Evaluation," *Communications of the ACM,* July 2002.

Stead, B. A., and J. Gilbert, "Ethical Issues in Electronic Commerce," *Journal of Business Ethics*, No. 34, 2001.

Strauss, J., et al., *E-Marketing*, 3rd ed. Upper Saddle River, NJ: Prentice Hall, 2003.

Turban, E., et al., *Electronic Commerce 2006*. Upper Saddle River, NJ: Prentice Hall, 2006.

Useem, J., "Dot-Coms: What Have We Learned?" *Fortune*, October 2000.

Wong, W. Y., *At the Dawn of E-Government*. New York: Deloitte Research, Deloitte & Touche, 2000.

PART II
The Web Revolution

3. Network Computing: Discovery, Communication, and Collaboration
4. E-Business and E-Commerce
▶ 5. Mobile, Wireless, and Pervasive Computing

CHAPTER
5

Mobile, Wireless, and Pervasive Computing

5.1 Mobile Computing and Commerce: Overview, Benefits, and Drivers

5.2 Mobile Computing Infrastructure

5.3 Mobile Applications in Financial Services

5.4 Mobile Shopping, Advertising, and Content-Providing

5.5 Mobile Intrabusiness and Enterprise Applications

5.6 Mobile B2B and Supply Chain Applications

5.7 Mobile Consumer and Personal Service Applications

5.8 Location-Based Commerce

5.9 Pervasive Computing

5.10 Inhibitors and Barriers of Mobile Computing

Minicases:
1. Hertz
2. Washington Township (OH)

LEARNING OBJECTIVES

After studying this chapter, you will be able to:

❶ Discuss the characteristics and attributes of mobile computing and m-commerce.

❷ Describe the drivers of mobile computing.

❸ Understand the technologies that support mobile computing.

❹ Describe wireless standards and transmission networks.

❺ Discuss m-commerce applications in financial and other services, advertising, and providing of content.

❻ Describe the applications of m-commerce within organizations.

❼ Understand B2B and supply chain applications of m-commerce.

❽ Describe consumer and personal applications of m-commerce.

❾ Describe some non-Internet m-commerce applications.

❿ Describe location-based commerce (l-commerce).

⓫ Discuss the key characteristics and current uses of pervasive computing.

⓬ Describe the major inhibitors and barriers of mobile computing and m-commerce.

NEXTBUS: A SUPERB CUSTOMER SERVICE

➡ **THE PROBLEM**

Buses in certain parts of San Francisco have difficulty keeping up with the posted schedule, especially in rush hours. Generally, buses are scheduled to arrive every 20 minutes, but at times, passengers may have to wait 30 to 40 minutes. The schedules become meaningless, and passengers are unhappy because they waste time.

➡ **THE SOLUTION**

San Francisco bus riders carrying an Internet-enabled wireless device, such as a cell phone or PDA, can quickly find out when a bus is likely to arrive at a particular bus stop. The system tracks public transportation buses in *real time*. Knowing where each bus is and factoring in traffic patterns and weather reports, NextBus (*nextbus.com*) dynamically calculates the estimated arrival time of the bus to each bus stop on the route. The arrival times are also displayed on the Internet and on a public screen at each bus stop.

The NextBus system has been used successfully in several other cities around the United States, in Finland, and in several other countries. Figure 5.1 shows how the NextBus system works. The core of the NextBus system is a GPS satellite that can tell the NextBus information center where a bus is at any given time. Based on

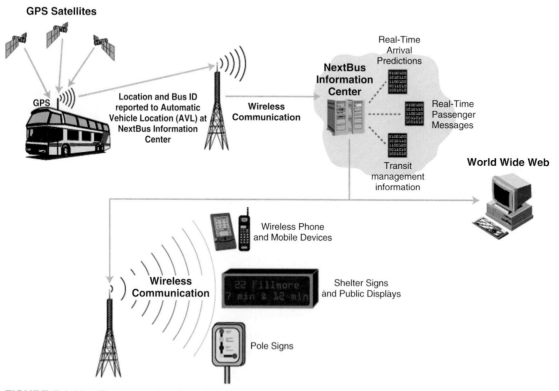

FIGURE 5.1 NextBus operational model. (*Source: NextBus.com/corporate/works/index.htm, 2002.* Used with permission of NextBus Information Systems.)

a bus's location, the scheduled arrival time at each stop can be calculated in real time. Users can access the information from their cell phones or PCs, any time, anywhere. NextBus schedules are also posted in real time on passenger's shelters at bus stops and public displays.

Currently, NextBus is an ad-free customer service, but in the near future advertising may be added. As the system knows exactly where you are when you request information and how much time you have until your next bus, it could send you to the nearest Starbucks for a cup of coffee, giving you an electronic discount coupon for a cup of coffee as you wait.

 THE RESULTS

Passengers in San Francisco are happy with the NextBus system; worries about missing the bus are diminished. A similar system is used in rural areas in Finland, where buses are infrequent and winters are very cold; passengers can stay in a warm coffeehouse not far from the bus stop rather than waiting in the cold for a bus that may be an hour late. Also, using the system, a bus company can do better scheduling, arrange more quickly for extra buses when needed, and improve its operations.

Sources: Compiled from ITS America 2001; Murphy (1999); and *nextbus.com* (accessed June 2004).

 LESSONS LEARNED FROM THIS CASE

This opening vignette is an example of location-based e-commerce, which is an application of *mobile commerce,* in which EC services are provided to customers located at specific places at the time they need services. This capability, which is not available in regular EC, may change many things in our lives. The vignette also exemplifies *pervasive computing,* in which services are seamlessly blended into the environment without the user being aware of the technology behind the scenes. This application is also a part of *mobile computing,* a computing paradigm designed for workers who travel outside the boundaries of their organizations or for people on the move.

Mobile computing and commerce are spreading rapidly, replacing or supplementing wired computing. Mobile computing involves mostly wireless infrastructure. Mobile computing may reshape the entire IT field (see Deans, 2004; Sadeh, 2002; and Mennecke and Strader, 2003). The technologies, applications, and limitations of mobile computing and mobile commerce are the main focus of this chapter. Later in the chapter, we will look briefly at futuristic applications of *pervasive computing.*

5.1 MOBILE COMPUTING AND COMMERCE: OVERVIEW, BENEFITS, AND DRIVERS

The Mobile Computing Landscape

In the traditional computing environment it was necessary to come to the computer to do some work on it. All computers were connected to each other, to networks, servers, etc. via *wires.* This situation limited the use of computers and created hardship for people and workers on the move. In particular, salespeople, repair people, service employees, law enforcement agents, and utility workers can be more effective if they can use information technology while at their jobs in the field or in transit. There are also mobile vacationers, people on holiday who wish to be connected with the Internet from any place, at any time.

The first solution was to make computers small enough so they can be easily carried around. First, the laptop computer was invented, and later on smaller and smaller computers, such as the PDAs and other hand-helds, appeared. These carriable computers are called *mobile devices*. They have become lighter with time and more powerful as far as processing speed and storage. At the end of the day, mobile workers could download (or upload) information from (or to) a regular desktop computer in a process known as *synchronization*. To speed up the "sync," special connecting cradles (docking stations) were created (see Minicase 2 at the end of this chapter and the Maybelline Minicase in Chapter 2).

These devices provided the first application of *mobile computing,* a computing paradigm designed for workers who travel outside the boundaries of their organizations or for anyone on the move. Salespeople were able to make proposals at customers' offices; a traveler could read and answer all of the day's e-mails while on the road. One could work with the mobile device as long as the battery was working.

For example, Millstone Coffee equipped its 300 drivers with hand-held devices and mobile applications for use while they are with clients selling roasted coffee beans to 13,000 stores in the United States. Using the devices, the drivers can track inventory, generate invoices, and capture detailed sales and marketing data at each store. The system does not use wireless; instead, the drivers synchronize ("sync") their hand-helds with the company's main system at the end of the day, a process that takes only 2 minutes. This strategy has proven to be cheaper for Millstone than going wireless, at least with the 2002 technology (see Cohen, 2002).

The second solution to the need for mobile computing was to replace wires with *wireless communication media.* Wireless systems have been in use in radio, TV, and telephones for a long time, so it was natural to adapt them to the computing environment (for more, see *Wired,* 2003).

The third solution was a combination of the first two, namely to use mobile devices in a wireless environment. Referred to as **wireless mobile computing,** this combination enables a real-time connection between a mobile device and other computing environments, such as the Internet or an intranet. This innovation is creating a revolution in the manner in which people use computers. It is spreading at work and at home. It is also used in education, health care, entertainment, security, and much more. The new computing model is basically leading to *ubiquity*—meaning that computing is available anywhere, at any time. (Note: Since many mobile applications now go wireless, the term *mobile computing* today is often used generally to describe wireless mobile computing.)

Due to some current technical limitations, we cannot (yet) do with mobile computing all the things that we do with regular computing. However, as time passes we can do more and more. On the other hand, we can do things in mobile computing that we cannot do in the regular computing environment. A major boost to mobile computing was provided in 2003 by Intel with its Centrino chip. This chip, which will be a standard feature in most laptops by 2005 (Estrada, 2002), includes three important capabilities: (1) a connection device to a wireless local area network, (2) low usage of electricity, enabling users to do more work on a single battery charge, and (3) a high level of security. The Centrino is expected to make mobile computing the common computing environment.

A second driving development of mobile computing is the introduction of the third- and fourth-generation wireless environments known as 3G and 4G. We will describe these later on.

Mobile Commerce

While the impact of mobile computing on our lives will be very significant, a similar impact is already occurring in the way we conduct business. This impact is described as *mobile commerce* (also known as *m-commerce* and *m-business*), which is basically any e-commerce or e-business done in a wireless environment, especially via the Internet. Like regular EC applications, m-commerce can be done via the Internet, private communication lines, smart cards, or other infrastructures (e.g., see Sadeh, 2002; Mennecke and Strader, 2003; Shi, 2004; and Kalakota and Robinson, 2001).

M-commerce is not merely a variation on existing Internet services; it is a natural extension of e-business. Mobile devices create an opportunity to deliver new services to existing customers and to attract new ones. Varshney and Vetter (2000) classified the applications of m-commerce into 12 categories, as shown in Table 5.1. (A classification by industry is provided at *mobile.commerce.net*. Also see *mobiforum.org*.)

Many of these applications, as well as some additional ones, will be discussed in this chapter. According to Sarshar (2003), as much as $1.8 trillion in consumer transactions could be made from mobile devices by the year 2005. The Yankee Group forecasted that mobile transactions will exceed $15 billion in the U.S. alone (TechLive, 2001).

Mobile Computing Basic Terminology

Let's build a foundation for further discussion by defining some common mobile computing terms:

- *Global positioning system (GPS).* A satellite-based tracking system that enables the determination of a GPS device's location. (See Section 5.8 for more on GPS.)

TABLE 5.1 Classes of M-Commerce Applications

Class of Applications	Examples
1. Mobile financial applications (B2C, B2B)	Banking, brokerage, and payments by mobile users
2. Mobile advertising (B2C)	Sending user-specific and location-sensitive advertising to users
3. Mobile inventory management (B2C, B2B)	Location tracking of goods, boxes, troops, and people
4. Proactive service management (B2C, B2B)	Transmitting to vendors information related to distributing components
5. Product locating and shopping (B2C, B2B)	Locating/ordering certain items from a mobile device
6. Wireless reengineering (B2C, B2B)	Improvement of business services
7. Mobile auction or reverse auction (B2C)	Services for customers to buy or sell certain items
8. Mobile entertainment services (B2C)	Video-on-demand and other services to a mobile user
9. Mobile office (B2C)	Working from traffic jams, airports, and conferences
10. Mobile distance education (B2C)	Taking a class using streaming audio and video
11. Wireless data center (B2C, B2B)	Downloading information by mobile users/vendors
12. Mobile music/music-on-demand (B2C)	Downloading and playing music using a mobile device

Source: Varshney and Vetter (2000), pp. 107–109.

- **Personal digital assistant (PDA).** A small portable computer, such as the family of Palm hand-helds and the Pocket PC devices from companies like HP.
- **Short Messaging Service (SMS).** A technology, in existence since 1991, that allows for the sending of short text messages (up to 160 characters in 2005) on certain cell phones. Data are borne by the radio resources reserved in cellular networks for locating mobile devices and connecting calls. SMS messages can be sent or received concurrently, even during a voice or data call. Used by hundreds of millions of users, SMS is known as "the e-mail of m-commerce."
- **Enhanced Messaging Service (EMS).** An extension of SMS that is capable of simple animation, tiny pictures, and short melodies.
- **Multimedia Messaging Service (MMS).** The next generation of wireless messaging, this technology will be able to deliver rich media.
- **Bluetooth.** A chip technology wireless standard designed for temporary, short-range connection (data and voice) among mobile devices and/or other devices (see *bluetooth.org*).
- **Wireless Application Protocol (WAP).** A technology that offers Internet browsing from wireless devices (see Section 5.2).
- **Smartphones.** Internet-enabled cell phones that can support mobile applications. These "phones with a brain" are becoming standard devices. They include WAP microprocessors for Internet access and the capabilities of PDAs as well.
- **Wi-Fi** *(short for* **Wireless Fidelity***).* Refers to a standard 802.11b on which most of the wireless local area networks (WLANs) run.
- **WLAN (Wireless Local Area Network).** A broad term for all 802.11 standards. Basically, it is a wireless version of the Ethernet networking standard. (For discussion of the Ethernet standard, see Technology Guide 4.)

Technology Guides are located at the book's Web site.

With these terms in mind, we can now look more deeply at the attributes and drivers of mobile computing.

Attributes and Drivers of Mobile Computing

Generally speaking, many of the EC applications described in Chapter 4 can be done in m-commerce. For example, e-shopping, e-banking, and e-stock trading are gaining popularity in wireless B2C. Auctioning is just beginning to take place on cell phones, and wireless collaborative commerce in B2B is emerging. However, there are several *new* applications that are possible only in the mobile environment. To understand why this is so, let's examine the major attributes of mobile computing and m-commerce.

SPECIFIC ATTRIBUTES OF MOBILE COMPUTING AND M-COMMERCE. Mobile computing has two major characteristics that differentiate it from other forms of computing: *mobility* and *broad reach.*

1. *Mobility.* Mobile computing and m-commerce are based on the fact that users carry a mobile device everywhere they go. Mobility implies portability. Therefore, users can initiate a *real-time* contact with other systems from wherever they happen to be if they can connect to a wireless network.
2. *Broad reach.* In mobile computing, people can be reached at any time. Of course, users can block certain hours or certain messages, but when users carry an open mobile device, they can be reached instantly.

These two characteristics break the barriers of geography and time. They create the following five value-added attributes that drive the development of m-commerce: ubiquity, convenience, instant connectivity, personalization, and localization of products and services.

Ubiquity. *Ubiquity* refers to the attribute of being available at *any location* at *any given time*. A mobile terminal in the form of a smartphone or a PDA offers ubiquity—that is, it can fulfill the need both for real-time information and for communication, independent of the user's location.

Convenience. It is very convenient for users to operate in the wireless environment. All they need is an Internet-enabled mobile device such as a smartphone. By using *GPRS* (General Packet Radio Service, a cell phone standard), it is easier and faster to access the Web without booting up a PC or placing a call via a modem. Also, more and more places are equipped with Wi-Fi, enabling users to get online from portable laptops any time (as was shown in the Dartmouth College case in Chapter 1). You can even watch an entire movie on a PDA (see *pocketpcfilms.com*).

Instant Connectivity. Mobile devices enable users to connect easily and quickly to the Internet, intranets, other mobile devices, and databases. Thus, wireless devices could become the preferred way to access information.

Personalization. *Personalization* refers to the preparation of customized information for individual consumers. For example, a user who is identified as someone who likes to travel might be sent travel-related information and advertising. Product personalization is still limited on mobile devices. However, the emerging need for conducting transactions electronically, combined with availability of personalized information and transaction feasibility via mobile portals, will move personalization to new levels, leading ultimately to the mobile device becoming a major EC tool. The process of personalization is illustrated in Online File W5.1 and is described by Dogac and Turner (2002).

Localization of Products and Services. Knowing where the user is physically located at any particular moment is key to offering relevant products and services. E-commerce applications based on localization of products and services are known as **location-based e-commerce** or **l-commerce.** Precise location information is known when a GPS is attached to a user's wireless device. For example, you might use your mobile device to find the nearest ATM or FedEx drop box. In addition, the GPS can tell others where you are. Localization can be general, such as to anyone in a certain location (e.g., all shoppers at a shopping mall). Or, even better, it can be targeted so that users get messages that depend both on where they are and what their preferences are, thus combining localization and personalization. For instance, if it is known that you like Italian food and you are strolling in a mall that has an Italian restaurant, you might receive an SMS that tells you that restaurant's "special of the day" and gives you a 10 percent discount. GPS may be a standard feature in many mobile devices by 2007.

DRIVERS OF MOBILE COMPUTING AND M-COMMERCE. In addition to the value-added attributes just discussed, the development of mobile computing and m-commerce is driven by the following factors.

Widespread Availability of Mobile Devices. The number of cell phones throughout the world exceeds 1.3 billion (*cellular.co.za/stats/stats-main.htm*). It is estimated that within a few years, about 70 percent of cell phones will have Internet access. Thus, a potential mass market is available for conducting discovery, communication, collaboration, and m-commerce. Cell phones are spreading quickly even in developing countries. In 2004, for example, the number of cell phones in China exceeded 310 million, exceeding the number of fixed line phones in that country (CellularOnline, 2004). This growth enables developing countries to leap-frog to m-commerce.

No Need for a PC. Because the Internet can be accessed via smartphone or other Internet-enabled wireless device, there is no need for a PC to access the Internet. Even though the cost of a PC that is used primarily for Internet access, such as the Simputer (a "simple computer"), can be as low as $300 (or even less), that amount is still a major expense for the vast majority of people in the world. Furthermore, one needs to learn how to operate a PC, service it, and replace it every few years to keep it up-to-date. Smartphones and other wireless devices obviate the need for a PC.

The Handset Culture. Another driver of m-commerce is the widespread use of cell phones, which is becoming a social phenomenon, especially among the 15-to-25-year-old age group. These users will constitute a major force of online buyers once they begin to make and spend larger amounts of money. The use of SMS has been spreading like wildfire in several European and Asian countries. In the Philippines, for example, SMS is a national phenomenon in the youth market. As another example, Japanese send many more messages through mobile phones than do Americans, who prefer the desktop for e-mail.

Vendors' Push. Vendors also are pushing m-commerce. Both mobile communication network operators and manufacturers of mobile devices are advertising the many potential applications of mobile computing and m-commerce so that they can sell new technologies, products, and services to buyers.

Declining Prices and Increased Functionalities. With the passage of time, the price of wireless devices is declining, and the per-minute pricing of mobile services is expected to decline by 50 to 80 percent before 2006. At the same time, functionalities are increasing. For ROI studies, see Chapter 13.

Improvement of Bandwidth. To properly conduct m-commerce, it is necessary to have sufficient bandwidth for transmitting text; however, bandwidth is also required for voice, video, and multimedia. The 3G (third-generation) technology (described in Section 5.2) provides the necessary bandwidth, at a data rate of up to 2 Mbps. This enables information to move 35 times faster than when 56K modems are used. Wi-Fi moves information even faster, at 11 Mbps. New Wi-Fi standards move information at 54 Mbps.

M-Commerce Value Chain and Revenue Models

Like EC, m-commerce is a complex process involving a number of operations and a number of players (customers, merchants, mobile operators, and the like). The key elements in the m-commerce value chain (for delivering m-commerce content and applications to end users) are summarized in Online File W5.2. Several types of vendors provide value-added services to m-commerce. These include: mobile portals, advertisers, software vendors, content providers, mobile portal, mobile network operators, and more. (See Sadeh, 2002, p. 34.)

The revenue models of m-commerce are the following: access fees, subscription fees, pay-per-use, advertising, transaction fees, hosting, payment clearing, and point-of-traffic (Coursaris and Hassanein, 2002).

The capabilities and attributes of mobile computing presented earlier provide for many applications, as shown in Figure 5.2. These attributes are supported by infrastructure.

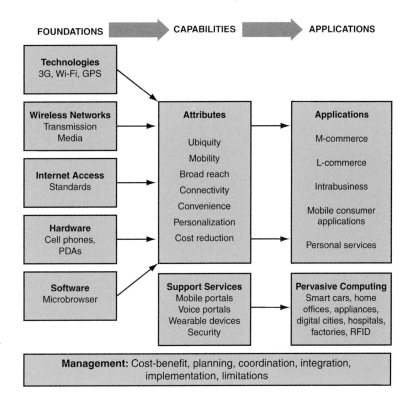

FIGURE 5.2 The landscape of mobile computing and commerce. (*Source:* Drawn by E. Turban.)

5.2 MOBILE COMPUTING INFRASTRUCTURE

Mobile computing requires hardware, software, and networks. The major infrastructure components of mobile computing are described in this section.

Mobile Computing Hardware

Several mobile computing devices are used in m-commerce. The major ones are:

- *Cellular (mobile) phones.* All major cell phone manufacturers are making Internet-enabled phones, also known as *smartphones.* These cell phones are improving with time, adding more features, larger screens, keyboards, camera, and more. Over 40 percent of the new cell phones have color screens (Fusco, 2003), for example. An example of an Internet-enabled cell phone is the Nokia 3510i, which includes Internet access, multimedia messaging (MMS), support for small Java applications (like games), a calculator, scheduler, address book, and more. Note that even phones without screen displays (regular or cellular phones) can be used to retrieve voice information from the Web (see *tellme.com* and the discussion of voice portals later in this section).

- *Attachable keyboard.* Transactions can be executed with the regular handset entry keys, but it is fairly time-consuming to do so. An alternative is to use a larger cell phone such as the Nokia 9500 that contains a small-scale keyboard. Yet another solution is to plug an attachable keyboard into the cell phone. (Attachable keyboards are also available for other wireless devices, such as PDAs.)

- *PDAs.* Personal digital assistants (PDAs) with Internet access are now available from several vendors, and their capabilities are increasing. Using special software, users can connect these PDAs to the Internet via a wireless modem. PDAs for *corporate users* include additional capabilities, such as e-mail synchronization and exchange of data and backup files with corporate servers. (Examples of PDAs for corporate users are Jornada, iPAQ from HP, CLIE from Sony, and MobilePro from NEC.)

- *Interactive pagers.* Some two-way pagers can be used to conduct limited mobile computing and m-commerce activities on the Internet (mainly sending and receiving text messages, such as stock market orders).

- *Screenphones.* A telephone equipped with a color screen, possibly a keyboard, e-mail, and Internet capabilities, is referred to as a **screenphone.** As of 2000, wireless screenphones became available.

- *E-mail hand-helds.* To enhance wireless e-mail capabilities, one can use devices such as the BlackBerry Hand-held (*blackberry.net*). This device, which includes a keypad, is an integrated package, so there is no need to dial into an Internet provider for access. A variety of services for data communication enable users to receive and send messages from anywhere. For example, the law firm of Paul, Hastins, Janofsky, & Walker (with offices in major U.S. cities) has deployed BlackBerry hand-helds to its 900 lawyers, who can now receive their e-mail in real time and can enter billing information while on the road. Furthermore, they can be alerted whenever they have a voice mail or fax waiting. A third of the company's lawyers have returned their laptops, and the company has saved $260,000 each year. New applications are coming with each new version of the hand-helds (for details, see Cohen, 2002). A product demo is available at *blackberry.net.*

- *Other devices.* Many other wireless support devices are on the market. For example, the Seiko SmartPad (*siibusinessproducts.com*) allows you to handwrite from a notepad instantly to a cell phone or PDA screen, overcoming the small screen size of these devices. Some new cell phones have built-in cameras; you can take a picture and e-mail it immediately from your mobile location. Finally there is a wireless mouse, which works up to 15 feet, so it can be used for presentations. For an overview of devices see Kridel (2003).

There is a significant trend toward the *convergence* of PDAs and cell phones. On the one hand, the PDA manufacturers are providing PDAs with cellular or wireless capabilities. On the other hand, the cellular phone manufacturers and systems providers are offering phones with PDA capabilities.

In addition to the hardware described above, mobile computing and m-commerce also require the following infrastructure hardware, most of which the user does not see or know about, but which is essential for wireless connectivity.

- A suitably configured wireline or wireless *WAN modem, wireless LAN adapter,* or *wireless MAN* (metro-area network) adapter.

- A *Web server* with wireless support, a WAP gateway, a communications server, and/or a mobile communications server switch (MCSS). Such a Web server provides communications functionality that enables the hand-held device to communicate with the Internet or intranet infrastructure (see *mobileinfo.com*).

- An *application* or *database server* with application logic and a business application database.

TABLE 5.2 Software for Mobile Computing

Software	Description
Microbrowser	A browser with limited bandwidth and memory requirements. Provides wireless access to the Internet.
Operating system (OS) for mobile client	An OS for mobile devices. Examples: Palmos, Windows 2001NT, Win CE. Specialized OSs: BlackBerry and Web browser.
Bluetooth (named for a Viking king)	Chip technology for short-range (30 meters in 2003) communication among wireless devices. Uses digital two-way radio frequency (RF). It is an almost universal standard for wireless Personal Area Network (WPAN) for data and voice. See *bluetooth.com.*
User interface	Application logic for hand-held devices. It is often controlled by the microbrowser.
Legacy application software	Residing on the mainframe, it is a major source of data to wireless systems.
Application middleware	Provides connection among applications, databases, and Web-based servers.
Wireless middleware	Links wireless networks to application servers.
Wireless Application Protocol (WAP)	A set of communication protocols that enables wireless devices to "talk" to a server on a mobile network, so users can access the Internet. Specially designed for small screen. A competing standard is the J2ME platform that offers better security and graphics (see *wapforum.org*).
Wireless Markup Language (WML)	An XML-based scripting language for creating content for wireless systems.
Voice XML	An extension of XML designed to accommodate voice.

- A large *enterprise application server.*
- A *GPS locator* that is used to determine the location of the person carrying the mobile computing device. This is the basis for location-based applications, as described in Section 5.8.

Mobile Computing Software

Developing software for wireless devices is challenging because, as of June 2004, there is no widely accepted standard for wireless applications. Therefore, software applications need to be customized for each type of device with which the application may communicate. The major software products required for mobile computing are presented in Table 5.2.

Wireless Wide Area Networks (WWANs)

At the core of most mobile computing applications are *mobile networks.* These are of two general types: the *wide area* and the *local area.* The wide area networks for mobile computing are known as **wireless wide area networks (WWANs).** The breadth of coverage of WWANs directly affects the availability of services (see Intel, 2002). Breadth of coverage depends on the transmission media and the generation of wireless.

The global communications and cellular phone companies operate most of the wireless wide area networks. A very simple mobile system is shown in Figure 5.3. At the edge of the system are the mobile handsets. A **mobile handset** consists of two parts—terminal equipment that hosts the applications (e.g., a PDA) and a mobile terminal (e.g., a cell phone) that connects to the mobile network.

TRANSMISSION MEDIA. Several transmission media can be used for wireless transmission. These media differ in both capabilities and cost. The major ones are shown in Technology Guide 4.

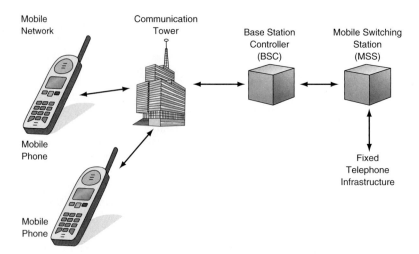

FIGURE 5.3 Mobile system architecture.

COMMUNICATION GENERATIONS OF WIRELESS WIDE AREA NETWORKS. The success of mobile computing depends on the capabilities of the WWAN communication systems. Four generations of communications technology are distinguished:

- **1G.** The first generation of wireless technology. It was an analog-based technology, in effect from 1979 to 1992.
- **2G.** The second generation of digital wireless technology. In existence today, 2G is based on digital radio technology and mainly accommodates text.
- **2.5G.** An interim technology based on GPRS (General Packet Radio Services) and EDGE (Enhanced Data Rates for Global Evaluation) that can accommodate limited graphics.
- **3G.** The third generation of digital wireless technology, which supports rich media such as video clips. It started in 2001 in Japan, and reached Europe in 2002 and the United States in 2003. As of 2004, the number of 3G cell phones in operation was around 180 million (a small percentage of the total number of cell phones in use today) (Dunne, 2001, and *mobiforum.org*).
- **4G.** The expected next generation after 3G. The arrival of 4G, which will provide faster display of multimedia, is expected between 2006 and 2010. Experimental 4Gs were used in Japan as early as 2003.

For details on transmission media, see Sadeh (2002) and Mennecke and Strader (2003).

COMMUNICATION PROTOCOLS IN WWAN. One of the major problems facing the mobile communication system providers is how to service extremely large numbers of users given limited communication bandwidth. This can be done through multiplexing protocols (see Technology Guide 4). In today's mobile world (2004), there are three main protocols:

1. **Frequency Division Multiple Access (FDMA).** Used by 1G systems, this protocol gives each user a different frequency to communicate on.
2. **Time Division Multiple Access (TDMA).** Used with some of the more popular 2G systems, this protocol assigns different users different time slots on a given communications channel (e.g., every 1/8 time slot).

3. **Code Division Multiple Access (CDMA).** Used with most 2.5G and 3G systems, this protocol separates different users by assigning different codes to the segments of each user's communications.

In today's mobile world most of the networks rely on either TDMA or CDMA. The relationships between these two multiplexing methods and the major network standards are detailed in Online File W5.3 along with the evolution of these standards from today's 2G world to tomorrow's 3G and 4G world.

Wireless Local Area Networks and Wi-Fi

For the past few years, wireless local area networks have been making their way to the wireless forefront. As the name implies, a *wireless LAN (WLAN)* is like a wired LAN but without the cables. WLANs transmit and receive data over the airwaves but only from a short distance.

In a typical configuration, a transmitter with an antenna, called a **wireless access point,** connects to a wired LAN from a fixed location or to satellite dishes that provide an Internet connection. A wireless access point provides service to a number of users within a small geographical perimeter (up to a couple hundred feet), known as a "hotspot zone," or **hotspot.** Several wireless access points are needed to support larger numbers of users across a larger geographical area. End users can access a WLAN with their laptops, desktops, or PDAs by adding a wireless network card. As of 2004 most PC and laptop manufacturers incorporate these cards directly in their PCs (as an option). For how to connect your PC quickly and securely with no wires, see Stafford and Brandt (2002). Figure 5.4 (page 198) shows how Wi-Fi works. Null et al. (2004) provide a step-by-step guide for building Wi-Fi at home or in small-business settings.

WLANs provide fast and easy Internet or intranet broadband access from public hotspots like airports, hotels, Internet cafes, and conference centers. WLANs are also being used in universities (recall the Dartmouth case in Chapter 1), offices, and homes in place of the traditional wired LANs. In this way users are free to roam across the campus, office, or throughout their homes (see *weca.net*).

Most of today's WLANs run on a standard known as **802.11b** that was developed by the IEEE (Institute of Electrical and Electronics Engineers). That standard is also called *Wi-Fi (wireless fidelity).* WLANs employing this standard have communication speeds of 11 Mbps. While most wired networks run at 100 Mbps, 11 Mbps is actually sufficient for many applications. Two other new standards, 802.11a and 802.11g, support data transmissions at 54 Mbps. The 802.11g standard is beginning to show up in commercial products because it is compatible with the 802.11b standard. While PCs can take advantage of 54 Mbps, today's (2004) PDAs cannot, because their expansion (network) cards are limited to the 11 Mbps speed. As of 2004 there is even hardware and software that supports voice over Wi-Fi (*telephony*).

The major benefits of Wi-Fi are its lower cost and its ability to provide simple Internet access. As a matter of fact it is the greatest facilitator of the *wireless Internet* (see Anderson, 2003).

WIRELESS PERSONAL AREA NETWORKS (WPANs). A *wireless personal area network (WPAN)* is a kind of WLAN that people have at their home or small offices. With such a network, one can connect PCs, PDAs, mobile phones, and digital music players that detect each other and can interact. Also, one can add a digital payment

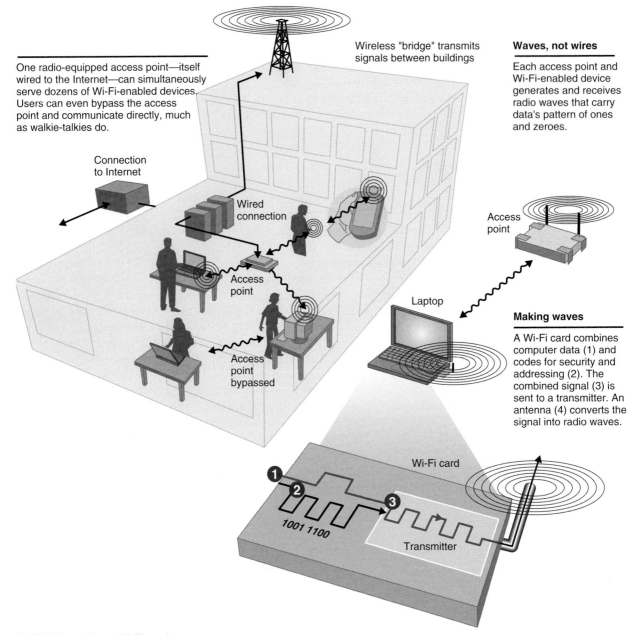

FIGURE 5.4 How Wi-Fi works. (*Source:* Perry, 2003, p. 81).

system and personal security technologies. The network maintains constant connectivity among devices, which is useful for users in office settings, including those who use wearable devices.

ILLUSTRATIVE APPLICATIONS OF WI-FI. The year 2004 was a breakthrough year for wireless networking in offices, airports, hotels, and campuses around the United States. Each month brings new examples of businesses that have added Wi-Fi services for their employees or customers. Several examples are presented below. Many more examples of Wi-Fi are included in this chapter and throughout the book.

- Like a number of airports in the United States, the Minneapolis–St. Paul International airport is served by Wi-Fi. The Northstar Crossing concession area, the Northwest Airlines' World Club lounge (started in Japan), the United Airlines' Red Carpet Club, and many of the main terminal concourses provide wireless Internet access to anyone with a laptop or hand-held device and a Wi-Fi network card. iPass is hosting the Internet service. The fee is $7.95 for unlimited daily access. Northwest had 570 hotspots in the United States (*JiWire.com* and *wifinefnews.com*, accessed May 2004).

- Lufthansa offers in-flight Wi-Fi service on its long-haul fleet. The hotspots on the aircrafts are connected to the Internet via satellites. While a news channel is free, there is a charge of $25 for use of other channels during the flight (Bloomberg News, 2003).

- Since 2002, T-Mobile has installed Wi-Fi networks in several thousand Starbucks stores in the United States. Starbucks has plans to add Wi-Fi to 70 percent of its 6,000 locations worldwide over the next few years. T-Mobile is also installing Wi-Fi in hundreds of Borders Books & Music stores. T-Mobile is charging $30 a month for unlimited access, with walk-in customers paying $2.99 for the first 15 minutes and 25 cents a minute thereafter.

- McDonald's piloted a program in April 2003 in which it initially offered Wi-Fi wireless access in 10 restaurants in New York City (*mcdwireless.com*). The company has an access point (hotspot) in each of these restaurants. If you buy a "value meal" you get one hour of free access. Alternatively, you can pay $3 an hour (which is significantly cheaper than the $12 an hour charged by Kinko's and many others for using regular desktop computers). McDonald's will eventually offer the program in thousands of its restaurants (watch for the window sign on the restaurants, that will combine McDonald's arches with a Wi-Fi symbol). With tens of thousands of McDonald's restaurants worldwide, this service can greatly help travelers accessing the Internet. Furthermore, if you have an Internet access via AOL or other ISPs, you will get the services free, even without buying the value meal.

- Similarly, Panera Bread Company has added hotspots in many of its restaurants in St. Louis, Missouri, where Panera is headquartered. The addition of hotspots is a marketing tactic aimed at attracting customers.

- Using a wireless ticketing system, Universal Studios in Hollywood is shortening the waiting lines for tickets at its front gate. The ticket sellers, armed with Wi-Fi–enabled devices and belt-mounted printers, not only sell tickets but also provide information. For details, see Scanlon (2003).

- CVS Corp., the largest retail pharmacy in the United States, uses Wi-Fi–based devices throughout its 4,100 stores. The hand-held computers support a variety of in-store applications, including direct store delivery, price management, inventory control, and receiving. Benefits include faster transfer rates, increasing productivity and performance, reduced cost, and improved customer service. For details see *symbol.com* (1998, 2003).

BARRIERS TO COMMERCIAL WI-FI GROWTH. Two factors are standing in the way of Wi-Fi market growth: cost and security. First, some analysts question why

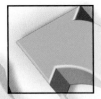

A CLOSER LOOK
5.1 WAR CHALKING AND WAR DRIVING

Free Wi-Fi Internet hubs are marked in some places by symbols on sidewalks and walls to indicate nearby wireless access. This practice is called *war chalking*. It was inspired by the practice of hobos during the Great Depression who used chalkmarks to indicate which homes were friendly.

A number of people have also made a hobby or sport out of war driving. *War driving* is the act of locating wireless local area networks while driving around a city or elsewhere (see *wardriving.com*). To war drive, you need a vehicle, a computer or PDA, a wireless card, and some kind of an antenna that can be mounted on top of or positioned inside the car. Because a WLAN may have a range that extends beyond the building in which it is located, an outside user may be able to intrude into the network, obtain a free Internet connection, and possibly gain access to important data and other resources. The term war driving was coined by computer security consultant Peter Shipley. (It derives from the term *war dialing*, a technique in which a hacker programs his or her system to call hundreds of phone numbers in search of poorly protected computer dial-ups. The term war dialing in turn came from the movie *WarGames*, which features Matthew Broderick performing the technique.)

Source: Compiled from Kellner (2003).

anyone would pay $30 a month, $7.95 a day, or any other fee for Wi-Fi access when it is readily available in many locations for free. Because it's relatively inexpensive to set up a wireless access point that is connected to the Internet, a number of businesses (e.g., Panera Bread Co.) offer their customers Wi-Fi access without charging them for the service. In fact, there is an organization, Freenetworks.org, aimed at supporting the creation of free community wireless network projects around the globe. In areas like San Francisco, where there is a solid core of high-tech professionals, many "gear heads" have set up their own wireless hotspots that give passersby free Internet connections. This is a part of a new culture known as *war chalking* and *war driving* (see *A Closer Look 5.1*).

One of the primary aims of people engaged in war driving is to highlight the lax security of Wi-Fi hotspots. This is the second barrier to widespread acceptance of Wi-Fi. Using radio waves, Wi-Fi can be interrupted by walls (resulting in poor quality at times), and it is difficult to protect. Wi-Fi does have a built-in security system, known as **Wireless Encryption Protocol (WEP),** which encrypts the communications between a client machine (laptop or PDA) and a wireless access point. However, WEP provides weak encryption, meaning that it is secured against casual hacking as long as the person setting up the network remembers to turn on the encryption. Unfortunately, many small business owners and homeowners with wireless LANs fail to do just that. For more on WEP, see Online File W5.4. For more on Wi-Fi security, see Judge (2004).

Mobile Computing and M-Commerce Security Issues

In 2001 a hacker sent an e-mail message to 13 million users of the i-mode wireless data service in Japan. The message had the potential to take over the recipient's phone, causing it to dial Japan's emergency hotline (1-1-0). NTT Docomo, which provides the i-mode service, rapidly fixed the problem so no damage was done. At the beginning of 2002, researchers in Holland discovered a bug in the operating system used by many Nokia phones that would enable a hacker to exploit the system by sending a malformed SMS message capable of crashing the system. Again, no real damage was done.

Today, most of the Internet-enabled cell phones in operation are incapable of storing applications and, in turn, incapable of propagating a virus, worm, or other rogue program from one phone to another. Most of these cell phones also have their operating systems and other functionalities "burned" right into the hardware. This makes it difficult for a rogue program to permanently alter the operation of a cell phone. However, as the capabilities of cellular phones increase and the functionality of PDAs and cell phones converge, the threat of attack from malicious code will certainly increase.

Beginning in 2004, there were several attacks made on mobile phones. These included the first known mobile virus, called Cabir. The virus was developed in Europe by a global group that creates viruses to demonstrate that no technology is wholly reliable and safe from viruses (see *forbes.com,* June 6, 2004).

Just because a mobile device is less susceptible to attack by malicious code does not mean that m-commerce is more secure than e-commerce in the wired world. By their very nature mobile devices and mobile transactions produce some unique security challenges. See Raina and Harsh (2002), and Online File W5.5.

Because m-commerce transactions eventually end up on a wired Internet, many of the processes, procedures, and technologies used to secure e-commerce transactions can also be applied in mobile environments. Of particular importance is the *public key infrastructure* (see Chapter 4, Online File W4.11). The security approaches that apply directly to mobile devices and networks are presented in Online File W5.6.

Voice Systems for M-Commerce

The most natural mode of human communication is voice. When people need to communicate with each other from a distance, they use the telephone more frequently than any other communication device. Voice communication can now also be done on the computer using a microphone and a sound card. As computers are getting better at recognizing and understanding the human voice, voice systems are improving, and the number and types of voice technology applications are growing. (For further discussion of voice recognition, see Kumagai, 2002, and Chapter 11 of this book.)

Voice technologies have various advantages: The most obvious one is portability; users do not have to go to a stationary computer. The hands- and eyes-free operations of voice technologies increase the productivity, safety, and effectiveness of mobile computer users, ranging from forklift drivers to military pilots. Also, for those users in dirty or moving environments, voice terminals operate better than keyboards because they are more rugged. Voice technologies also enable disabled people to tell a computer to perform various tasks. Another advantage is speed; people can communicate about two-and-a-half times faster talking than typing. In most circumstances, speaking also results in fewer data entry errors than does keyboard data entry, assuming a reliable voice recognition system is used.

Voice and data can work together to create useful applications. For example, operators of PBXs (private branch exchanges, which are basically the command center of intracompany phone systems) are letting callers give simple computer commands using interactive voice response (e.g., spelling the last name of the person one is calling).

VOICE PORTALS. A **voice portal** is a Web site with an audio interface. Voice portals are not really Web sites in the normal sense because they are accessed through a standard phone or a cell telephone. A certain phone number connects you to a participating Web site where you can request information by speaking. The system finds the information, translates it into a computer-generated voice reply, and tells you what you want to know. Several of these new sites are in operation. An example of this application is the voice-activated 511 traveler information line developed by Tellme.com (see Online Minicase W1.2). *Tellme.com* and *bevocal.com* allow callers to request information about weather, local restaurants, current traffic, and other handy information (see Kumagai, 2002).

In addition to retrieving information, some sites provide true interaction. *iPing.com* is a reminder and notification service that allows users to enter information via the Web and receive reminder calls. In addition, iPing.com can call a group of people to notify them of a meeting or conference call.

The real value for Internet marketers is that these voice portals can help businesses find new customers. Several of these sites are supported by ads; thus, the customer profile data they have available can deliver targeted advertising very precisely. For instance, a department-store chain with an existing brand image can use short audio commercials on these sites to deliver a message related to the topic of the call.

With the development of technical standards and continuing growth of wireless technologies, the number of m-commerce applications is growing rapidly. Applications are derived from providing wireless access to existing B2C, intrabusiness, and CRM applications and from creating new location-based and SMS-based applications. In Sections 5.3 through 5.8 of this chapter, we will study m-commerce applications in a number of diverse categories.

5.3 MOBILE APPLICATIONS IN FINANCIAL SERVICES

Mobile financial applications include banking, wireless payments and micropayments, wireless wallets, bill payment services, brokerage services, and money transfers. While many of these services are simply a subset of their wire-line counterparts, they have the potential to turn a mobile device into a business tool, replacing banks, ATMs, and credit cards by letting a user conduct financial transactions with a mobile device, any time and from anywhere. In this section we will look at some of the most popular mobile applications in financial services.

Mobile Banking Throughout Europe, the United States, and Asia, an increasing percentage of banks offer mobile access to financial and account information. For instance, Merita Bank in Sweden pioneered many services (Sadeh, 2002), and Citibank in the U.S. has a diversified mobile banking service. Consumers in such banks can use their mobile handsets to access account balances, pay bills, and transfer funds using SMS. The Royal Bank of Scotland, for example, uses a mobile payment service (Lipset, 2002), and Banamex, one of Mexico's largest banks, is a strong provider of wireless services to customers. Many banks in Japan allow for all banking transactions to be done via cell phone. A study of banks in Germany, Switzerland, and Austria found that over 60 percent offered some form of mobile financial services (Hornberger and Kehlenbeck, 2002).

To date, though, the uptake of mobile banking has been minimal. Yet surveys indicate there is strong latent demand for these offerings; customers seem to be waiting for the technology and transmission speeds to improve. The same picture holds true for other mobile financial applications like mobile brokering, insurance, and stock market trades.

Wireless Electronic Payment Systems

Wireless payment systems transform mobile phones into secure, self-contained purchasing tools capable of instantly authorizing payments over the cellular network. In Italy, for example, DPS-Promatic has designed and installed the first parking meter payable by mobile telephone (DPS-Promatic, 2002). In the United States, Cellbucks offers a mobile payment service to participating sports stadiums that enables fan to purchase food, beverages, and merchandise by cell phone and have it delivered to their seats. Any fan who is a member of the Cellbucks Network can dial a toll-free number provided on a menu of choices, enter his or her pass code and seat location, then select numbered items that correspond to desired menu selections. Once authorized, the purchase is passed on to stadium personnel and is in turn delivered to the fan's seat. An e-mail detailing the transaction is sent to the fan as further confirmation of the order. In Europe and Japan, wireless purchase of tickets to movies and other events is popular (Sadeh, 2002).

Micropayments

If you were in Frankfurt, Germany, and took a taxi ride, you could pay the taxi driver using your cell phone. As discussed in Chapter 4, electronic payments for small-purchase amounts (generally a few dollars or less) are called *micropayments*. The demand for wireless micropayments systems is fairly high. An A.T. Kearney study (*clickz.com/stats*, 2002) found that more than 40 percent of mobile phone users surveyed would like to use their mobile phone for small cash transactions such as transit fares or vending machines. The desire for such service was highest in Japan (50 percent) and lowest in the United States (38 percent). The percentage of mobile phone users who had actually used their phones for this purpose was only 2 percent, reflecting the fact that very few vendors participate in micropayments systems.

An Israeli firm, TeleVend, Inc. (*televend.com*), has pioneered a secure platform that allows subscribers to make payments using mobile phones of any type on any cellular infrastructure. A customer places a mobile phone call to a number stipulated by the merchant, to authorize a vending device to dispense the service. Connecting to a TeleVend server, the user selects the appropriate transaction option to authorize payment. Billing can be made to the customer's bank or credit card account or to the mobile phone bill.

Micropayment technology has wide-ranging applications, such as making payments to parking garages, restaurants, grocery stores, and public transportation. The success of micropayment applications, however, ultimately depends on the costs of the transactions. Transaction costs will be small only if there is a large volume of transactions.

Mobile (Wireless) Wallets

An *e-wallet* (see Chapter 4) is a piece of software that stores an online shopper's credit card numbers and other personal information so that the shopper does not have to reenter that information for every online purchase. In the recent past, companies like SNAZ offered **m-wallet** (*mobile wallet*, also known as *wireless wallet*) technologies that enabled cardholders to make purchases with a single click from their mobile devices. While most of these companies are now

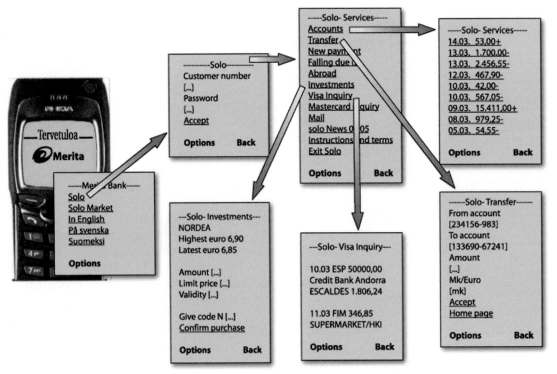

FIGURE 5.5 Nordea's WAP Solo banking portal. (*Source:* Sadeh, 2002, Fig. 1.4.)

defunct, some cell phone providers have incorporated m-wallets in their offerings. A good example is the Nokia wallet. This application provides users with a secure storage space in their phones for information (such as credit card numbers) to be used in mobile payments. The information can also be used to authenticate transactions by signing them digitally. Microsoft is offering its e-wallet, Passport, in a wireless environment.

Wireless Bill Payments

In addition to paying bills through wireline banking or from ATMs, a number of companies are now providing their customers with the option of paying their bills directly from a cell phone (Lipset, 2003). HDFC Bank of India (*hdfcbank.com*), for example, allows customers to pay their utility bills using SMS. An example of how bill payments can be made using a mobile device is shown in Figure 5.5. This service is offered by Nordea, a pioneering provider of wireless banking services in Scandinavia. According to Poropudas (2003), more and more ATMs and vending machines can communicate with mobile phones, giving consumers the opportunity to gain access to virtual cash, to buy goods or services, or to pay bills.

5.4 MOBILE SHOPPING, ADVERTISING, AND CONTENT-PROVIDING

Like EC, m-commerce B2C applications are concentrated in three major areas—retail shopping (for products and services), advertising, and providing content for a fee (see Rupp and Smith, 2002).

Shopping from Wireless Devices

An increasing number of online vendors allow customers to shop from wireless devices. For example, customers who use Internet-ready cell phones can shop at certain sites such as *mobile.yahoo.com* or *amazon.com*. Shopping from wireless devices enables customers to perform quick searches, compare prices, use a shopping cart, order, and view the status of their order using their cell phones or wireless PDAs. Wireless shoppers are supported by services similar to those available for wireline shoppers.

An example of restaurant food shopping from wireless devices is that of a joint venture between Motorola and Food.com. The companies offer restaurant chains an infrastructure that enables consumers to place an order for pickup or delivery virtually any time, anywhere. Donatos Pizzeria was the first chain to implement the system in 2002.

Cell phone users can also participate in online auctions. For example, eBay offers "anywhere wireless" services. Account holders at eBay can access their accounts, browse, search, bid, and rebid on items from any Internet-enabled phone or PDA. The same is true for participants in Amazon.com Auctions.

An example of purchasing movie tickets by wireless device is illustrated in Figure 5.6. Notice that the reservation is made directly with the merchant. Then money is transferred from the customer's account to the merchant's account.

Targeted Advertising

Knowing the current location of mobile users (using GPS) and their preferences or surfing habits, marketers can send user-specific advertising messages to wireless devices. Advertising can also be location-sensitive, informing a user about shops, malls, and restaurants close to where a potential buyer is. SMS messages and short paging messages can be used to deliver this type of advertising to cell

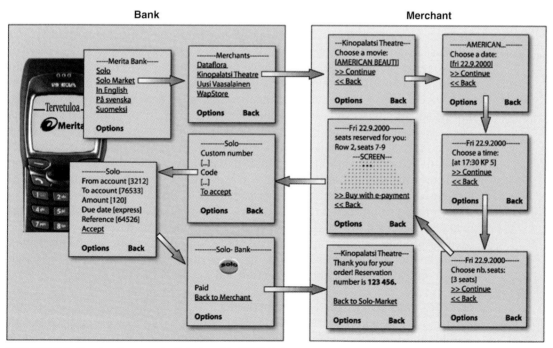

FIGURE 5.6 Purchasing movie tickets with WAP Solo. (*Source:* Sadeh, 2002, Fig. 1.5.)

A CLOSER LOOK
5.2 WIRELESS ADVERTISING IN ACTION

The following are a few examples of wireless advertising in action.

Vindigo.com (*vindigo.com*) has a large database of customers (over a million in May 2004) willing to accept promotional materials on their wireless devices. This is known as *permission marketing.* The users download special software on their PDAs that allows Vindigo.com to deliver timely, accurate information about places to go and things to do in their area. Along with every listing, the company can deliver a customized message to the users at a time and place where it is of most interest to them and they are most likely to act on it.

The company targets ads by city (New York, San Francisco, Los Angeles, etc.) and channel (Eat, Shop, or Play). Vindigo.com tracks which ads a user sees and selects, and even allows a user to request information from an advertiser via e-mail. Vindigo.com determines a user's location through GPS or by asking which neighborhoods they want to be matched with. For example, if you own an Italian restaurant chain, you can use Vindigo.com to send a message to anyone looking for Italian food within a few blocks of one of your locations. You can give them directions to that restaurant and even offer them the list of specials on the menu and discounts (see *vindigostudies.com*).

MyAvantGo.Com (*avantgo.com*) has several thousand content channels and over 8 million registered users (AvantGo, 2004). The content is delivered to PDAs and handsets running Palm or PocketPC operating systems. MyAvantgo offers an m-business channel and direct promotions to deliver advertising from some of the world's top brands including American Airlines, Chevy Trucks, the Golf Channel, CNN, the *New York Times,* and Yahoo. For details see Stanford (2002).

Hoping to become the king of location-based Web domains, Go2Online (*go2online.com*) helps mobile travelers find everything from lodging (choose *go2hotels*) to Jiffy Lube stations. Partnering with Sprint, NexTel, Verizon, and BellSouth, Go2 makes its services available on every Web-enabled phone, Palm i705, and BlackBerry RIM pager in America. Entering "JiffyLube" or any of hundreds of other brand names into the Go2 system will bring up the nearest location where one can find that product or service.

Sources: Compiled from the Web sites of Vindigo.com, AvantGo.com, and GO2Online.com.

---

phones and pagers, respectively. Many companies are capitalizing on targeted advertising, as shown in *A Closer Look 5.2*.

As more wireless bandwidth becomes available, content-rich advertising involving audio, pictures, and video clips will be generated for individual users with specific needs, interests, and inclinations. Also, depending on the interests and personality types of individual mobile users, the network provider may consider using "push" or "pull" methods of mobile advertising on a per-user basis or to a class of users (market segmentation). The number of ads pushed to an individual customer should be limited, to avoid overwhelming a user with too much information and also to avoid the possibility of congestion over the wireless networks. Wireless network managers may consider ad traffic to be of a lower priority compared with ordering or customer interaction. Finally, since ad pushers need to know a user's current location, a third-party vendor may be used to provide location services. This will require a sharing of revenues with a location service provider. A futuristic area of advertisement, which is based on GPS tracking, is described in Section 5.8.

GETTING PAID TO LISTEN TO ADVERTISING. Would you be willing to listen to a 10-second ad when you dial your cell phone if you were paid 2 minutes of free long-distance time? As in the wireline world, some consumers are willing to be paid for exposure to advertising. It depends on which country you are in.

In most places where it was offered in the United States, this service was a flop and was discontinued.

In Singapore, though, getting paid to listen to advertising works very well. Within a few months of offering the ads, more than 100,000 people subscribed to the free minutes in exchange for listening to the ads offered by SingTel Mobile (Eklund, 2001). Subscribers to SingTel's service fill out a personal questionnaire when they sign up. This information is fed into the Spotcast database (*spotcast-network.com*) and encrypted to shield subscribers' identities—Spotcast cannot match phone numbers to names, for example. To collect their free minutes—one minute per call, up to 100 minutes a month—subscribers dial a four-digit code, then the phone number of the person they want to talk to. The code prompts SingTel to forward the call to Spotcast and, in an instant, Spotcast's software finds the best ad to send to the subscriber based on the subscriber's profile.

THE FUTURE OF WIRELESS ADVERTISING. In 2002, the Yankee Group concluded that the U.S. wireless advertising market would be worth only $10 million by 2004, substantially below earlier estimates that pegged the market at $130 million by that year (Yankee Group, 2002). By 2003 almost all wireless advertising initiatives have been merely trials. As the Yankee Group noted, the most promising avenues of success for wireless advertising will incorporate it with other advertising media (e.g., hardcopy advertising that directs consumers to wireless or mobile ads offering incentives) or wireless ads directing users to Web sites or physical locations. According to the Yankee Group, many wireless advertising firms are betting their futures on the wide-scale acceptance of SMS, even in the United States where its usage currently is small.

Mobile Portals

A **mobile portal** is a customer channel, optimized for mobility, that aggregates and provides content and services for mobile users (see Bughin et al., 2001; Sadeh, 2002; and Chapter 3 for additional discussion of portals). Examples of best "pure" mobile portals (those whose only business is to be a mobile portal) are Room 33 (*room33.com*) in Europe and *zed.com* from Sonera in Finland. Nordea's Solo banking portal was illustrated in Figure 5.5. The world's best-known mobile portal, with over 40 million members, mostly in Japan, is i-mode from DoCoMo.

The services provided by mobile portals include news, sports, e-mail, entertainment and travel information; restaurants and event information; leisure-related services (e.g., games, TV and movie listings); community services; and stock trading. A sizeable percentage of the portals also provide downloads and messaging, music-related services, and health, dating, and job information. Mobile portals frequently charge for their services. For example, you may be asked to pay 50 cents to get a weather report over your mobile phone. Alternatively, you may pay a monthly fee for the portal service and get the report free any time you want it. In Japan, for example, i-mode generates revenue mainly from subscription fees.

Increasingly, the field of mobile portals is being dominated by a few big companies (Global Mobile Suppliers Association, 2002). The big players in Europe, for instance, are companies like Vodafone, Orange, O2, and T-Mobile; in the United States the big players are Cingular, Verizon, and Sprint PCS. Also, mobile-device manufactures offer their own portals (e.g., Club Nokia portal, My Palm portal). And, finally, the traditional portals (such as Yahoo, AOL, and MSN) have mobile portals as well.

5.5 MOBILE INTRABUSINESS AND ENTERPRISE APPLICATIONS

Although B2C m-commerce is getting considerable publicity, most of today's applications are used within organizations. According to Estrada (2002), employees connected to Wi-Fi increase their productivity by up to 22 percent due to better and faster connectivity. This section looks at how mobile devices and technologies can be used *within* organizations.

Support of Mobile Workers

Mobile workers are those working outside the corporate premises. Examples of mobile workers are salespeople in the field, traveling executives, telecommuters, people working in corporate yards and warehouses, and repair or installation employees who work at customers' sites or on utility lines. These mobile workers need the same corporate data available to employees working inside the company's offices. Yet, using wireline-based devices, even portable ones, may be inconvenient or impossible when employees are away from their offices.

The solution is myriad smaller, simple wireless devices—the smartphones and hand-held companions carried by mobile workers and the in-vehicle information systems installed in cars. Many of these wireless devices are wearable.

WEARABLE DEVICES. Employees who work on buildings, electrical poles, or other difficult-to-climb places may be equipped with a special form of mobile wireless computing devices called **wearable devices.** People wear these devices on their bodies (e.g., arms, clothes, or helmets). Examples of wearable devices include:

- *Screen.* A computer screen is mounted on a safety hat, in front of the wearer's eyes, displaying information to the worker.
- *Camera.* A camera is mounted on a safety hat. Workers can take digital photos and videos and transmit them instantly to a portable computer nearby. (Photo transmission is made possible via Bluetooth technology.)
- *Touch-panel display.* In addition to the wrist-mounted keyboard, mobile employees can use a flat-panel screen, attached to the hand, which responds to the tap of a finger or stylus.
- *Keyboard.* A wrist-mounted keyboard enables typing by the other hand. (Wearable keyboards are an alternative to voice recognition systems, which are also wireless.)
- *Speech translator.* For those mobile employees who do not have their hands free to use a keyboard, a wearable speech translator is handy (see Smailagic et al., 2001).

For an example of wearable devices used to support mobile employees, see *IT at Work 5.1, xybernaut.com, essworld.net,* and *media.mit.edu/wearable.*

JOB DISPATCH. Mobile devices are becoming an increasingly integral part of groupware and workflow applications. For example, nonvoice mobile services can be used to assist in dispatch functions—to assign jobs to mobile employees, along with detailed information about the task. The target areas for mobile delivery and dispatch services include the following: transportation (delivery of food, oil, newspapers, cargo, courier services, tow trucks, and taxis); utilities (gas, electricity, phone, water); field service (computer, office equipment, home repair);

IT at Work 5.1
WEARABLE DEVICES FOR BELL CANADA WORKERS

For years mobile employees, especially those who had to climb trees, electric poles, or tall buildings, were unable to enjoy the new technologies designed to make employees work or feel better. Thus, their productivity and comfort were inferior, especially where computers were involved. That is all beginning to change.

On a cold, damp November day in Toronto, Chris Holm-Laursen, a field technician with Bell Canada (*bell.ca*), is  out and about as usual, but this time with a difference: A small but powerful computer sits in a pocket of his vest, a keyboard is attached to the vest's upper-left side, and a flat-panel display screen hangs by his waist. A video camera attached to his safety hat enables him to take pictures without using his hands and send them immediately to the office. A cell phone is attached as well, connected to the computer. A battery pack to keep everything going sits against his back. (See nearby photo.)

Holm-Laursen and 18 other technicians on this pilot project were equipped like this for 10 weeks during fall 2000. By summer 2003 an increasing number of Bell Canada's employees have been equipped with similar devices. The wearable devices enabled the workers to access work orders and repair manuals wherever they were. These workers are not typical of the group usually most wired up, that is, white-collar workers. The hands-free aspect and the ability to communicate any time, from anywhere, represent major steps forward for these utility workers. A wide variety of employees—technicians, medical practitioners, aircraft mechanics, and contractors—are using or testing such devices.

So far, only a few companies make and sell wearables for mobile workers. Bell Canada's system was developed by Xybernaut, a U.S. company that in 2002 had more than a thousand of its units in use around the world, some in operation and others in pilot programs (see *xybernaut.com*, 2003). Minneapolis-based ViA is another supplier, most of whose systems are belt-worn (*bell.ca*). Meanwhile, Bell Canada was impressed with the initial results, and is equipping most of its technicians with wearable devices.

Of course, a practical problem of wearable devices in many countries is the weather: What happens when the temperature is minus 50 degrees or the humidity is 99 percent? Other potential problems also exist: If you are wearing thick gloves, how can you use a keyboard? If it is pouring rain, will the battery short circuit? Various solutions are being developed, such as voice input, tapping on a screen instead of typing, and rainproof electrical systems.

Sources: Compiled from XyberFlash (2000), and *xybernaut.com* (2003).

For Further Exploration: What are some other industrial applications of similar wearable devices? How do you think wearable devices could be used in entertainment?

---

health care (visiting nurses, doctors, social services); and security (patrols, alarm installation).

A dispatching application for wireless devices allows improved response with reduced resources, real-time tracking of work orders, increased dispatcher efficiency, and a reduction in administrative work. AirIQ (*edispatch.com*), for example, offers an interesting solution. AirIQ's OnLine system combines Internet, wireless, GPS, digital mapping, and intelligent information technologies. The system tracks vital information about a vehicle's direction, speed, and location which is provided by a device housed in each of the vehicles being tracked. Managers can view and access information about the fleet on digital maps, monitor vehicles on the Internet, and maintain top operating condition

IT at Work 5.2

U.S. FLEET SERVICES AND WIRELESS NETWORKING

Started in 1997, U.S. Fleet Services URL (*usfleet.com*) has grown to be the leading provider of mobile, onsite fueling in the United States with customers such as FedEx, Home Depot, Coca-Cola, Nabisco, and Office Max. Using trucks that resemble home fuel-delivery vehicles, U.S. Fleet travels to its customers, refueling the customers' vehicles onsite, usually during off-hours. In 1999 U.S. Fleet considered building a wireless network for its drivers, but decided against it. Managers considered the project too hard and too expensive given the expected return on investment. However, toward the end of 2001, they changed their minds.

While a mobile wireless solution was the end goal, the first step in the project actually involved the implementation of an ERP system. This was followed by a Web-based application built on top of the ERP that provided customers with information about their fuel consumption and local gas taxes, enabling them to do better fleet management. Finally, U.S. Fleet equipped its drivers with hand-held devices that could communicate with the company's intranet using Wi-Fi.

The hand-held device U.S. Fleet selected was the Intermec 710 (*intermec.com*). Besides having a built-in barcode scanner, this device also runs Microsoft's Pocket PC operating system, supports Visual Basic programs, handles CompactFlash cards, and has an integrated wireless radio for short-range Wi-Fi communications. The device is fairly lightweight with a drop-resistant case that is sealed to protect against harsh weather conditions.

The way the system works is this: Branch managers enter a delivery route and schedule for each driver into a centralized database via the company's intranet. Each driver starts his or her shift by downloading the route and

schedule over the company's Wi-Fi network into a hand-held. When the driver reaches a customer stop, the hand-held is used to scan a barcode attached to the customer's truck. This provides the driver with the type of fuel required by the truck. After the truck is fueled, a meter on the delivery truck sends a wireless signal to the hand-held. The hand-held then syncs with the meter, capturing the type and quantity of fuel delivered. The data are stored on the hand-held's CompactFlash memory card. When the driver returns to the home base, the data are unloaded over the Wi-Fi network to the central database. At this point, the data are available for U.S. Fleet and its customers to analyze using business intelligence tools.

Before the hand-helds were deployed, drivers would record the data manually. The data were then faxed from the branch offices to headquarters and entered by hand into the system. Not only were there delays but the data were also subject to entry errors at both ends of the line. Now, the company and its customers have accurate data in a timely fashion, which provides the company with faster invoicing and cash flow. On average, the new system has also enabled drivers to service six to seven more stops per shift.

Sources: Compiled from Ludorf (2002), *intermec.com* (2001), and *usfleet.com* (2003).

For Further Exploration: What systems did U.S. Fleet put in place before implementing its wireless solution? Why did U.S. Fleet select the device? How does the Intermec 710 hand-held device communicate with the company's intranet? What are the major benefits that U.S. Fleet has realized by combining hand-held devices with Wi-Fi?

---

of their fleet. AirIQ promises savings of about 30 percent in communication costs and increases in workforce efficiency of about 25 percent (*edispatch.com*).

IT at Work 5.2 provides a detailed description of a job-dispatching system being used by U.S. Fleet to benefit both itself and its customers.

SUPPORTING OTHER TYPES OF WORK. Wireless devices may support a wide variety of mobile workers. The applications will surely grow as the technology matures and as workers think up new ways to apply the functions of wireless devices to their jobs. Here are four examples.

1. Tractors equipped with sensors, onboard computers, and a GPS help farmers save time, effort, and money. GPS determines the precise location of

the tractor and can direct its automatic steering. Because the rows of planting resulting from GPS-guiding are more exact, the farmers save both on seeds and on fertilizers, due to minimized overlapping and spillage. Farmers can also work longer hours with the satellite-controlled steering, taking advantage of good weather, for example. Another saving is due to instant notification to the service department of any machine that breaks down. For details see Scanlon (2003).

2. Taco Bell provided its "mystery shoppers" (shoppers who visit restaurants to conduct a survey unknown to the owners) with hand-held computers so that they can communicate more quickly with the company's headquarters. The visitors must answer 35 questions, ranging from the speed of service to food quality. Before the devices, information was provided by filling out paper forms that were mailed overnight. This information was scanned into computers for processing. The information flow using the hand-helds is both faster and more accurate.

3. Like e-mail, SMS can be used to bolster collaboration; because of its reach it has special applications. According to Kontzer (2003), the following are 10 applications of SMS for mobile workers: (1) alerting mobile technicians to system errors, (2) alerting mobile execs to urgent voice messages, (3) confirming with mobile sales personnel that a faxed order was received, (4) informing travelers of delays and changes, (5) enabling contract workers to receive and accept project offers, (6) keeping stock traders up to date on urgent stock activity, (7) reminding data services subscribers about daily updates, (8) alerting doctors to urgent patient situations, (9) enabling mobile sales teams to input daily sales figures into corporate database, and (10) sending mobile sales reps reminders of appointments and other schedule details.

4. To increase national security and safeguard national borders, countries are using facial-recognition and iris-scanning biometrics (Chapter 15), both of which are supported by wireless systems (see Jones, 2003).

Customer Support and CRM

Mobile access extends the reach of CRM—both inside and outside the company—to both employees and business partners on a 24/7 basis, to any place where recipients are located. According to Eklund (2002), 12 percent of companies in the United States provided (in 2002) corporate users with mobile access to their CRM systems.

In the large software suites like Siebel's CRM, the two CRM functions that have attracted the most interest are *sales force automation* and *field service*. For instance, a sales person might be on a sales call and need to know recent billing history for a particular customer. Or, a field service representative on a service call might need to know current availability of various parts in order to fix a piece of machinery. It is these sorts of situations where mobile access to customer and partner data is invaluable. Two of the more recent offerings in this arena are Salesforce.com's Airforce Wireless Edition and Upshot's Alerts (*upshot.com*) (see Hill, 2002). See *A Closer Look 5.3* (page 212) for descriptions of the use of mobile applications for customer support.

Voice portal technology can also be used to provide enhanced customer service or to improve access to data for employees. For example, customers who are away from the office could use a vendor's voice portal to check on the status of deliveries to a job site. Salespeople could check on inventory status during

A CLOSER LOOK
5.3 MOBILE WORKPLACE APPLICATIONS FOR CUSTOMER SUPPORT

The following are two scenarios of wireless applications for mobile employees.

SALES SUPPORT. Linda is a member of the field sales team at Theru Tools (a fictitious company). Each day she drives out to her customers in a van stocked with products. For each sale, she has to note the customer name, the number and type of products sold, and any special discounts made. This record-keeping used to be done manually, and many errors were made, leading to customer complaints and lost sales.

Theru implemented a system using low-cost but powerful hand-held wireless devices. Using Mobile Sales (an application for hand-helds), accessed via the *mysap.com* Mobile Workplace, Linda and her coworkers in the field now have information at their fingertips, including updates on new products and special promotions. Linda can place orders without delay and get immediate feedback on product availability and delivery times. What's more, the system can prompt Linda as she enters orders, and it also can make plausibility checks on the orders, eliminating many of the errors associated with the manual process. It also checks to see if she is giving the right discounts to the right customer, and immediately triggers the invoicing process or prints out a receipt on the spot.

CUSTOMER SERVICE SUPPORT. Michael works for Euroblast, Inc. (another fictitious company) as a service engineer. It is his job to provide time-critical maintenance and support for the company's customers' electromechanical control systems. To do so, he needs to know immediately when a customer's system is faltering, what is malfunctioning, and what type of service contract is in effect.

Michael does not need to carry all of this information in his head, but instead has it in the palm of his hand. With only a few taps of a stylus, Michael accesses the *mysap.com* Mobile Workplace for all the data he requires, including the name and address of the next customer he should visit, equipment specifications, parts inventory data, and so forth.

Once he has completed the job, he can report back on the time and materials he used, and these data can be employed for timely billing and service quality analysis. In addition, his company is able to keep track of his progress and monitor any major fluctuations in activities. As a result, both Michael and his supervisors are better informed and better able to serve their customers.

Source: Compiled from SAP AG Corp. (2000) (advertisement).

---

a meeting to help close a sale. There are a wide variety of CRM applications for voice portal technology. The challenge is in learning how to create the navigation and other aspects of interaction that makes customers feel comfortable with voice-access technology.

Wireless Intrabusiness Applications

Wireless applications in the non-Internet environment have been around since the early 1990s. Examples include such applications as: wireless networking, used to pick items out of storage in warehouses via PCs mounted on forklifts; delivery-status updates, entered on PCs inside distribution trucks; and collection of data such as competitors' inventories in stores and customer orders, using a hand-held (but not networked) device, from which data were transferred to company headquarters each evening. (See the Maybelline minicase in Chapter 2, and the Hi-Life minicase in Chapter 4.)

Since then, a large number of Internet-based wireless applications have been implemented inside enterprises. Three examples of such intrabusiness applications are described below. For other examples, see Online File W5.7 at the book's Web site.

1. Employees at companies such as Telecom Italia Mobile (Republica IT, 2001) get their monthly pay slips as SMS messages sent to their mobile phone. The money itself is transferred electronically to a designated bank account. The

method is much cheaper for the company and results in less paperwork than the old method of mailing monthly pay slips.

2. Kemper Insurance Company has piloted an application that lets property adjusters report from the scene of an accident. Kemper attached a wireless digital imaging system to a camera that lets property adjusters take pictures in the field and transmit them to a processing center (Henning, 2002; Nelson, 2000). The cameras are linked to Motorola's StarTac data-enabled cellular phone service, which sends the information to a database. These applications eliminate delays in obtaining information and in film processing that exist with conventional methods.

3. A medical care organization developed a mobile enterprise application that allows sales representatives to check orders and inventories during their visits with physicians and instantly report on what they can deliver to the physician's office and when (Ellison, 2004).

As these three examples indicate, a variety of intrabusiness workflow applications are possible. Table 5.3 shows typical intrabusiness workflow applications before and after the introduction of wireless services. Some of these can be delivered on a wireless intranet; some are offered on the Internet. (For details on intrabusiness applications, see *mdsi-advantex.com* and *symbol.com*. The advantages offered by intrabusiness wireless solutions can be seen through an examination of workflow applications at *mdsi-advantex.com*.) Finally, RFID is gaining popularity in both intrabusiness and interbusiness applications (see the Wal-Mart minicase in Chapter 1).

Mobile intrabusiness applications are very popular and are typically easier to implement than interbusiness applications, such as B2B and supply chain, discussed next.

TABLE 5.3 Intrabusiness Workflow Applications	
Before Wireless	**With Wireless**
Work orders are manually assigned by multiple supervisors and dispatchers.	Work orders are automatically assigned and routed within minutes for maximum efficiency.
Field service technicians commute to dispatch center to pick up paper work orders.	Home-based field service technicians receive first work order of the day via mobile terminal and proceed directly to first assignment.
Manual record keeping of time, work completed, and billing information.	Automated productivity tracking, record keeping, and billing updates.
Field service technicians call in for new assignments and often wait because of radio traffic or unavailable dispatcher.	Electronic transmittal of additional work orders with no waiting time.
Complete work orders dropped off at dispatch center at the end of the day for manual entry into the billing or tracking system. Uncompleted orders are manually distributed to available technicians. Overtime charges often result.	Technicians close completed work orders from the mobile terminals as they are completed. At the end of the shift, the technicians sign off and go home.

Source: From the publicly distributed brochure "RALI Mobile" from Smith Advanced Technology, Inc. (2001).

5.6 MOBILE B2B AND SUPPLY CHAIN APPLICATIONS

Mobile computing solutions are also being applied to B2B and supply chain relationships. Such solutions enable organizations to respond faster to supply chain disruptions by proactively adjusting plans or by shifting resources related to critical supply chain events as they occur. With the increased interest in collaborative commerce comes the opportunity to use wireless communication to collaborate along the supply chain. For this to take place, integration is needed.

An integrated messaging system is at the center of B2B communications. By integrating the mobile terminal into the supply chain, it is possible to make mobile reservations of goods, check availability of a particular item in the warehouse, order a particular product from the manufacturing department, or provide security access to obtain confidential financial data from a management information system.

One example of an integrated messaging system is wireless *telemetry*, which combines wireless communications, vehicle monitoring systems, and vehicle location devices. (Telemetry is described further in Section 5.8.) This technology makes possible large-scale automation of data capture, improved billing timeliness and accuracy, less overhead than with the manual alternative, and increased customer satisfaction through service responsiveness. For example, vending machines can be kept replenished and in reliable operation by wirelessly polling inventory and service status continually to avert costly machine downtime.

Mobile devices can also facilitate collaboration among members of the supply chain. There is no longer any need to call a partner company and ask someone to find certain employees who work with your company. Instead, you can contact these employees directly, on their mobile devices.

By enabling sales force employees to type orders straight into the ERP while at a client's site, companies can reduce clerical mistakes and improve supply chain operations. By allowing them to check production schedules and inventory levels, and to access product configuration and *available-to-promise/capacity-to-promise* (ATP/CTP) functionality to obtain real-time delivery quotes, they empower their sales force to make more competitive and realistic offers to customers. Today's ERP systems tie into broader supply chain management solutions that extend visibility across multiple tiers in the supply chain. Mobile supply chain management (mSCM) empowers the workforce to leverage these broader systems through inventory management and ATP/CTP functionality that extend across multiple supply chain partners and take into account logistics considerations. Finally, RFIDs will automate many activities of supply chain management (e.g., see Caton, 2004).

5.7 MOBILE CONSUMER AND PERSONAL SERVICE APPLICATIONS

A large number of applications exist that support consumers and provide personal services (see Coursaris and Hassanein, 2002, and Sadeh, 2002). As an example, consider the situation of a person going to an international airport. Tasks such as finding the right check-in desk, checking for delayed flights, waiting for lost luggage, and even finding a place to eat or the nearest washroom can be assisted by mobile devices. Online File W5.8 at the book's Web site lists 12 problem areas at airports that can be solved using mobile devices. The capabilities shown in the table in Online File W5.8 are now possible in some places and are expected to be more widely available by 2006.

Other consumer and personal service areas in which wireless devices can be used are described in the following sections. (See also *attws.com.*)

Mobile Games

In the hand-held segment of the gaming market, Nintendo has been the long-time leader. In contrast, Nintendo has shown minimal interest in online or mobile games. Here, Sega has capitalized on the popularity of games such as Sonic the Hedgehog to garner 2.5 million Japanese subscribers for its mobile games and entertainment services (Becker, 2002). In Japan, where millions of commuters kill time during long train rides, cell phone games have become a cultural phenomenon.

With more than 1.3 billion cell phones in use by 2003 (CellularOnline, 2003), the potential audience for mobile games is substantially larger than the market for other platforms, Playstation and Gameboy included. Because of the market potential, Nokia has decided to enter the mobile gaming world, producing not only the phone/console but also the games that will be delivered on memory cards. It seeks to develop and market near-distance multiplayer gaming (over Bluetooth) and wide area gaming (using cellular networks) (Nokia, 2002).

In July 2001, Ericsson, Motorola, Nokia, and Siemens established the Mobile Games Interoperability Forum (MGIF) (*openmobilealliance.org*) to define a range of technical standards that will make it possible to deploy mobile games across multi-game servers, wireless networks, and over different mobile devices. Microsoft is moving into this field as well.

A topic related to games is *mobile entertainment,* discussed in Online File W5.9. Mobile gambling, another related topic, is extremely popular in some countries (e.g., horse racing in Hong Kong and racing and other events in Australia). (For more on mobile gambling, see *sportodds.com.*)

Hotel Services Go Wireless

A number of hotels now offer their guests in-room, high-speed Internet connection. Some of these same hotels are beginning to offer Wi-Fi Internet access in public areas and meeting rooms. One of these is Marriott, which manages 2,500 hotels worldwide. After a seven-month test, Marriott has partnered with STSN (*stsn.com*), an Internet service provider specializing in hotels, to provide Wi-Fi services in the 400 Marriott hotels that already have in-room broadband Internet access (Reuters, 2002). In the same vein, AT&T has partnered with Wayport Inc. to offer Wi-Fi in 475 hotels throughout the United States. In India the Taj Group is offering Wi-Fi access in its hotels (Taj Hotel, 2002), and Megabeam (a wireless provider in England) is starting to offer the same service in select Holiday Inn and Crowne Plaza hotels in London.

While Wi-Fi provides guests with Internet access, to date it has had minimal impact on other sorts of hotel services (e.g., check-in). However, a small number of hotels are testing use of the Bluetooth technology. Guests are provided with Bluetooth-enabled phones that can communicate with access points located throughout the hotel. This technology can be used for check-in and check-out, for making purchases from hotel vending machines and stores, for tracking loyalty points (see *tesalocks.com*), and for opening room doors in place of keys

(Mayor, 2001). In 2001, Classwave signed a deal with Starwood Hotels & Resorts worldwide to enable Bluetooth solutions within Starwood's hotels (Houck, 2001).

For a comparison of traditional and m-commerce hotel services, see Online File W5.10. These capabilities are now available in only some locations, but are expected to be widely available by 2006.

Wireless Telemedicine

Today there are two different kinds of technology used for *telemedicine* applications: (1) storage of data and transferring of digital images from one location to another, and (2) videoconferencing used for "real-time" consultation between a patient in one location and a medical specialist in another. In most of the real-time consultations, the patient is in a rural area and the specialist is in an urban location.

There are a number of impediments to telemedicine. Some states do not allow physicians to provide medical advice across state lines. The threat of malpractice suits is another issue since there is no "hands-on" interaction between the physician and patient. In addition, from a technical standpoint, many telemedicine projects are hindered by poor telecommunications support. However, those who are looking ahead to the needs of the aging population are seeing opportunities to meet some of those needs in emerging technologies. The new wireless and mobile technologies, especially the forthcoming generation, not only offer the possibility of overcoming the hurdles imposed by remote locations but also open a number of new and novel application opportunities. Examples include the following.

- Typically, physicians write a prescription and you take it to the pharmacy where you wait 15–30 minutes for it to be filled. Instead, some new mobile systems allow physicians to enter the patient prescription onto a palm-size device. That information goes by cellular modem (or Wi-Fi) to Med-i-nets (*med-i-nets.com*) (or similar companies). There, the information is checked for insurance eligibility and conformity to insurance company and government regulations. If all checks out, the prescription is transferred electronically to the appropriate pharmacy. In addition, for patients who need refills, the system tracks and notifies physicians when it is time to reorder, and the doctor can reissue a prescription with a few clicks.

- At the first warning signs of a heart attack, people are advised to contact emergency facilities as soon as possible. Manufacturers are working on wearable heart monitors linked to cell phones that can automatically contact doctors or family members at the first sign of trouble.

- The Swiss Federal Institute of Technology is designing portable devices that transmit the vital signs of avalanche victims up to 80 meters away (Baard, 2002). Not only does the device provide location information but it also provides information about body orientation that helps reduce injuries as rescuers dig for the victims.

- In-flight medical emergencies occur more frequently than one might think. Alaska Airlines, for example, deals with about 10 medical emergencies per day (Conrad, 2002). Mobile communications are already being used to attend to medical emergencies occurring on planes. MedLink (*medlink.com*), a service of MedAire in Phoenix, provides around-the-clock access to board-certified emergency physicians. These mobile services can also remotely control medical equipment, like defibrillators, located on board the plane.

● The military is involved in developing mobile telesurgery applications that enable surgeons in one location to remotely control robotic arms for surgery in another location. The technology was proven to be particularly useful in battlefield situations during the 2003 Iraq War.

Other Mobile-Computing Services for Consumers

Many other mobile computer services exist for consumers, in a variety of service categories. Examples include services providing news, weather, and sports reports; online language translations; information about tourist attractions (hours, prices); and emergency services. CVC Pharmacy stores allow you to print photos directly from your mobile phone at kiosks in the stores. For more examples, see the case studies at *mobileinfo.com*.

Non-Internet Mobile-Computing Applications for Consumers

Non-Internet mobile applications for consumers, mainly those using smart cards, have existed since the early 1990s. Active use of the cards is reported in transportation, where millions of "contactless" cards (also called *proximity cards*) are used to pay bus and subway fares and road tolls. Amplified remote-sensing cards that have an RF (radio frequency) of up to 30 meters are used in several countries for toll collection. *IT at Work 5.3* describes one use of proximity cards for toll collection.

IT at Work 5.3
THE HIGHWAY 91 PROJECT

Route 91 is a major eight-lane, east-west highway near Los Angeles. Traffic is especially heavy during rush hours. California Private Transportation Company (CPT) built six express toll lanes along a 10-mile stretch in the median of the existing Highway 91. The express lane system has only one entrance and one exit, and it is totally operated with EC technologies. The system works as follows.

Only prepaid subscribers can drive on the road. Subscribers receive an automatic vehicle identification (AVI) device that is placed on the rearview mirror of the car. The device, about the size of a thick credit card, includes a microchip, an antenna, and a battery. A large sign over the tollway tells drivers the current fee for cruising the express lanes. In a recent year it varied from $0.50 in slow traffic hours to $3.25 during rush hours.

Sensors in the pavement let the tollway computer know that a car has entered; the car does not need to slow or stop. The AVI makes radio contact with a transceiver installed above the lane. The transceiver relays the car's identity through fiber-optic lines to the control center, where a computer calculates the fee for that day's trip. The system accesses the driver's account and the fare is auto-

matically deducted from the driver's prepaid account. A monthly statement is sent to the subscriber's home.

Surveillance cameras record the license numbers of cars without AVIs. These cars can be stopped by police at the exit or fined by mail. Video cameras along the tollway also enable managers to keep tabs on traffic, for example, sending a tow truck to help a stranded car. Also, through knowledge of the traffic volume, pricing decisions can be made. Raising the price as traffic increases ensures that the tollway will not be jammed.

The system saves commuters between 40 and 90 minutes each day, so it is in high demand. An interesting extension of the system is the use of the same AVIs for other purposes. For example, they can be used in paid parking lots. Someday you may be even recognized when you enter the drive-through lane of McDonald's and a voice asks you, "Mr. Smart, do you want your usual meal today?"

Source: 91expresslanes.com (2002).

For Further Exploration: What is the role of the wireless component of this system? What are the advantages of the system to commuters? (Take the virtual "test drive.")

5.8 LOCATION-BASED COMMERCE

As discussed in Section 5.1, *location-based commerce (l-commerce)* refers to the localization of products and services. Location-based services are attractive to both consumers and businesses alike. From a consumer's or business user's viewpoint, l-commerce offers safety (you can connect to an emergency service with a mobile device and have the service pinpoint your exact location), convenience (you can locate what is near you without having to consult a directory, pay phone, or map), and productivity (you can optimize your travel and time by determining points of interest within close proximity). From a business supplier's point of view, l-commerce offers an opportunity to provide services that meet customers' needs.

The basic l-commerce services revolve around five key areas:

1. *Location:* determining the basic position of a person or a thing (e.g., car or boat)
2. *Navigation:* plotting a route from one location to another
3. *Tracking:* monitoring the movement of a person or a thing (e.g., a vehicle or package)
4. *Mapping:* creating maps of specific geographical locations
5. *Timing:* determining the precise time at a specific location

L-Commerce Technologies

Providing location-based services requires the following location-based and network technologies:

- *Position Determining Equipment (PDE).* This equipment identifies the location of the mobile device (either through GPS or by locating the nearest base station). The position information is sent to the mobile positioning center.
- *Mobile Positioning Center (MPC).* The MPC is a server that manages the location information sent from the PDE.
- *Location-based technology.* This technology consists of groups of servers that combine the position information with geographic- and location-specific content to provide an l-commerce service. For instance, location-based technology could present a list of addresses of nearby restaurants based on the position of the caller, local street maps, and a directory of businesses.
- *Geographic content.* Geographic content consists of streets, road maps, addresses, routes, landmarks, land usage, Zip codes, and the like. This information must be delivered in compressed form for fast distribution over wireless networks.
- *Location-specific content.* Location-specific content is used in conjunction with the geographic content to provide the location of particular services. Yellow-pages directories showing the location of specific business and services exemplify this type of content.

Figure 5.7 shows how these technologies are used in conjunction with one another to deliver location-based services. Underlying these technologies are global positioning and geographical information systems.

GLOBAL POSITIONING SYSTEM (GPS). As indicated at the start of the chapter, a **global positioning system (GPS)** is a wireless system that uses satellites to enable users to determine their position anywhere on the earth. GPS equipment

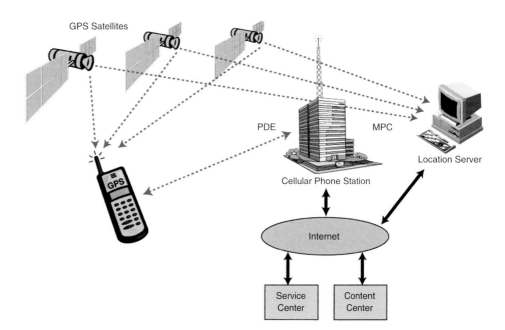

FIGURE 5.7 A smart-phone with GPS system in I-commerce.

has been used extensively for navigation by commercial airlines and ships and for locating trucks and buses (as in the opening case study).

GPS is supported by 24 U.S. government satellites that are shared worldwide. Each satellite orbits the earth once every 12 hours on a precise path, at an altitude of 10,900 miles. At any point in time, the exact position of each satellite is known, because the satellite broadcasts its position and a time signal from its onboard atomic clock, which is accurate to one-billionth of a second. Receivers also have accurate clocks that are synchronized with those of the satellites.

GPS handsets can be standalone units or can be plugged into or embedded in a mobile device. They calculate the position (location) of the handsets (or send the information to be calculated centrally). Knowing the speed of the satellite signals (186,272 miles per second), engineers can find the location of any receiving station (latitude and longitude) to within 50 feet by *triangulation,* using the distance from a GPS to *three* satellites to make the computation. GPS software then computes the latitude and longitude of the receiver. For an online tutorial on GPS, see *trimble.com/gps.*

GEOGRAPHICAL INFORMATION SYSTEM (GIS). The location provided by GPS is expressed in terms of latitude and longitude. To make that information useful to businesses and consumers it is necessary in many cases to relate those measures to a certain place or address. This is done by inserting the latitude and longitude onto an electronic map, which is known as a **geographical information system (GIS).** The GIS data visualization technology integrates GSP data onto digitized map displays. (See the description in Chapter 10 and also Steede-Terry, 2000, for more explanation.) Companies such as *mapinfo.com* provide the GIS core spatial technology, maps, and other data content needed in order to power location-based GIS/GPS services (see Figure 5.8, page 220).

An interesting application of GPS/GIS is now available from several car manufacturers (e.g., Toyota, Cadillac) and car rental companies (e.g., Hertz,

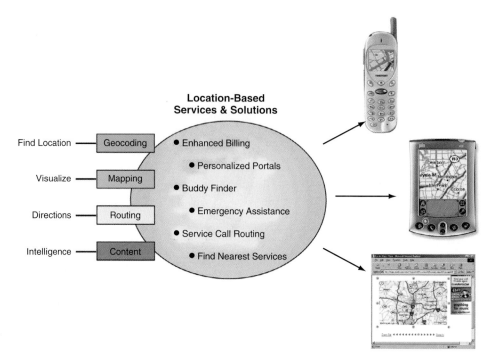

FIGURE 5.8 Location-based services involving maps. (*Source: Mapinfo.com,* 2001.)

Avis). Some cars have a navigation system that indicates how far away the driver is from gas stations, restaurants, and other locations of interest. The GPS knows where the car is at any time, so the application can map the route for the driver to a particular destination. Any GPS application can be classified as *telemetry,* a topic discussed further later on.

LOCATION-BASED ADVERTISING. Imagine that you are walking near a Starbucks store, but you do not even know that one is there. Suddenly your cell phone beeps with a message: "Come inside for a latte." The location of your wireless device was detected, and similar to the pop-up ads on your PC, advertising was directed your way (Needleman, 2002). You could use permission marketing to shield yourself from location-based advertising; if the system knows that you do not drink coffee, for example, you would not be sent a message from Starbucks.

Another (futuristic) use of wireless devices for advertising is described by Raskin (2003). In this case, a dynamic billboard ad could be personalized specifically for you when your car approaches a certain billboard and the system knows what your likes and preferences are. Your car will be tracked by a GPS, every 20 seconds. A computer scans the areas in which billboards are visible, and by cross-referencing information about your location and your likes, a *personalized ad* could be placed on the billboard so you would see it as you pass.

Yet another method of location-based advertising involves putting ads on the top of taxicabs. The ad will be changed based on the taxi location. For example, a taxi cruising in the theater district in New York City might show an ad for a play or a restaurant in that area; when the cab goes to another neighborhood, the ad might be for a restaurant or a business in the other area of the city.

E-911 Emergency Cell Phone Calls

If someone dials 911 from a regular wired phone, it is easy for the emergency 911 service to pinpoint the location of the phone. But, what happens if someone places a 911 call from a mobile phone? How can the emergency service locate the caller? A few years ago, the U.S. Federal Communication Commission (FCC) issued a directive to wireless carriers, requiring that they establish services to handle **wireless 911 (e-911)** calls. To give you an idea of the magnitude of this requirement, more than 156,000 wireless 911 calls are made every day, representing more than half the 911 calls made daily in the United States (Sarkar, 2003).

The e-911 directive is to take effect in two phases, although the specifics of the phases vary from one wireless carrier (e.g., T-Mobile, Cingular, Sprint, etc.) to another. Phase I requires carriers, upon appropriate request by a local *Public Safety Answering Point (PSAP),* to report the telephone number of a wireless 911 caller and the location of the cellular antenna that received the call. Phase II, which is being rolled out over a four-year period from October 2002 to December 2005, requires wireless carriers to provide information that will enable the PSAP to locate a caller within 50 meters 67 percent of the time and within 150 meters 95 percent of the time. By the end of Phase II, 100 percent of the new cell phones and 95 percent of all cell phones will have these location capabilities. It is expected that many other countries will follow the example of the United States in providing e-911 service.

Some expect that in the future cars will have a device for **automatic crash notification (ACN).** This still-experimental device will automatically notify the police of an accident involving an ACN-equipped car and its location. Also, following a school bus hijacking in Pennsylvania, the state legislature is considering a bill to mandate satellite tracking in all school buses.

Telematics and Telemetry Applications

Telematics refers to the integration of computers and wireless communications in order to improve information flow (see Chatterjee et al., 2002, and Zhao, 2002). It uses the principles of *telemetry,* the science that measures physical remoteness by means of wireless transmission from a remote source (such as a vehicle) to a receiving station. MobileAria (*mobilearia.com*) is a proposed standards-based telematics platform designed to bring multimedia services and m-commerce to automobiles.

Using *mobile telemetry,* technicians can diagnose from a distance maintenance problems in equipment. Car manufacturers use the technology for remote vehicle diagnosis and preventive maintenance. Finally, doctors can monitor patients and control medical equipment from a distance.

General Motors Corporation popularized automotive telematics with its OnStar system. Nokia has set up a business unit, called Smart Traffic Products, that is focusing solely on telematics. Nokia believes that every vehicle will be equipped with at least one Internet Protocol (IP) address by the year 2010. Smart cars and traffic products are discussed in more detail in Section 5.9.

Barriers to L-Commerce

What is holding back the widespread use of location-based commerce? Several factors come into play:

● *Accuracy.* Some of the location technologies are not as accurate as people expect them to be. However, a good GPS provides a location that is accurate up to 15 meters. Less expensive, but less accurate, technologies can be used instead to find an approximate location (within about 500 meters).

- *The cost-benefit justification.* For many potential users, the benefits of l-commerce do not justify the cost of the hardware or the inconvenience and time required to utilize the service (e.g., Hamblen, 2001). After all, they seem to feel, they can just as easily obtain information the old-fashioned way.

- *The bandwidth of GSM networks.* GSM bandwidth is currently limited; it will be improved as 3G technology spreads. As bandwidth improves, applications will improve, which will attract more customers.

- *Invasion of privacy.* When "always-on" cell phones are a reality, many people will be hesitant to have their whereabouts and movements tracked throughout the day, even if they have nothing to hide. This issue will be heightened when our cars, homes, appliances, and all sorts of other consumer goods are connected to the Internet, as discussed in the next section.

5.9 PERVASIVE COMPUTING

Steven Spielberg's sci-fi thriller *Minority Report* depicts the world of 2054. Based on a 1956 short story by Philip K. Dick, the film immerses the viewer in the consumer-driven world of pervasive computing 50 years from now. Spielberg put together a three-day think tank, headed by Peter Schwartz, president of Global Business Network (*gbn.com*), to produce a realistic view of the future (Mathieson, 2002). The think tank projected out from today's marketing and media technologies—Web cookies, GPS, Bluetooth, personal video recorders, barcode scanners, and the like—to create a society where billboards beckon you by name, newspapers are delivered instantly over broadband wireless networks, holographic hosts greet you at retail stores, and cereal boxes broadcast live commercials. While the technologies in the film were beyond the leading edge, none was beyond the realm of the plausible.

A world in which virtually every object has processing power with wireless or wired connections to a global network is the world of **pervasive computing.** (The term *pervasive computing* also goes by the names *ubiquitous computing, embedded computing,* or *augmented computing.*) The idea of pervasive computing has been around for years. However, the current version was articulated by Mark Weiser in 1988 at the computer science lab of Xerox PARC. From Weiser's perspective, pervasive computing was the opposite of virtual reality. In virtual reality, the user is immersed in a computer-generated environment. In contrast, pervasive computing is invisible "everywhere computing" that is embedded in the objects around us—the floor, the lights, our cars, the washing machine, our cell phones, our clothes, and so on (Weiser, 1991, 2002).

Invisible Computing Everywhere

By "invisible," Weiser did not mean to imply that pervasive computing devices would not be seen. He meant, rather, that unlike a desktop computer, these embedded computers would not intrude on our consciousness. Think of a pair of eyeglasses. The wearer does not have to think about using them. He or she simply puts them on and they augment the wearer's ability to see. This is Weiser's vision for pervasive computing. The user does not have to think about how to use the processing power in the object; rather, the processing power automatically helps the user perform a task.

Invisible is how you would describe some of the new embedded technology already in use at Prada's "epicenter" stores in New York, San Francisco, and

Los Angeles (Duan, 2002). Prada is a high-end fashion retailer. In the company's epicenters, the items for sale have an **RFID (radio frequency identification)** tag attached. The tag contains a processor and an antenna. If a customer wants to know about a particular item, she or he can move with the item toward one of the many displays around the store. The display automatically detects the item and provides sketches, video clips of models wearing the item, and information about the item (color, cut, fabric, materials, and availability). If a customer takes a garment into one of the dressing rooms, the tags are automatically scanned and detected via an antenna embedded in the dressing room. Information about the item will be automatically displayed on an interactive touch screen in the dressing room. The dressing rooms also have a video-based "Magic Mirror." When the customer tries on the garment and turns around in front of the mirror, the images will be captured and played back in slow motion. (See Section 5.10 for a related privacy issue.)

Invisible is also a term that characterizes a device manufactured and sold by Fitsense Technology (*fitsense.com*), a Massachusetts developer of Internet sports and fitness monitors. With this one-ounce device that is clipped to a shoelace, runners are able to capture their speed and the distance they have run. The device transmits the data via a radio signal to a wrist device that can capture and transmit the data wirelessly to a desktop computer for analysis. Along the same lines, Champion Chip (*championchip.com*), headquartered in the Netherlands, has developed a system that keeps track of the tens of thousands of participants in very popular long-distance races. The tracking system includes miniature transponders attached to the runners' shoelaces or ankle bracelets and antenna mats at the finish line that use radio frequencies to capture start times, splits, and finish times as the runners cross them.

Active badges can be worn as ID cards by employees who wish to stay in touch at all times while moving around the corporate premises. The clip-on badge contains a microprocessor that transmits its (and its wearer's) location to the building's sensors, which send it to a computer. When someone wants to contact the badge wearer, the phone closest to the person is identified automatically. When badge wearers enter their offices, their badge identifies them and logs them on to their personal computers.

Similarly, *memory buttons* are nickel-sized devices that store a small database relating to whatever it is attached to. These devices are analogous to a bar code, but with far greater informational content and a content that is subject to change. For example, the U.S. Postal Service is placing memory buttons in some mailboxes to track and improve collection and delivery schedules.

For a short list of the technical foundation of pervasive computing, see Online File W5.11 at the book's Web site.

Contextual Computing and Context Awareness

Location can be a significant differentiator when it comes to advertising services. However, knowing that the user is at the corner of the street will not tell you what he or she is looking for. For this, we might need to know the time of day, or access our user's calendar or other relevant *contextual attributes.* **Context awareness** refers to capturing a broad range of contextual attributes to better understand what the consumer needs, and what products or services he or she might possibly be interested in.

Context awareness is part of **contextual computing,** which refers to the enhancement of a user's interactions by understanding the user, the context, and the applications and information being used, typically across a wide set of user goals (see Pitkow et al., 2002 for details). Contextual computing is about actively adapting the computational environment for each user, at each point of computing.

Contextual computing and context awareness are viewed by many as the Holy Grail of m-commerce. They feel that contextual computing ultimately offers the prospect of applications that could anticipate our every wish and provide us with the exact information and services we are looking for—and also help us filter all those annoying promotional messages that we really do not care for. Such applications are futuristic at the present time, but as shown in *IT at Work 5.4* they already exist in a research university.

Applications of Pervasive Computing

According to Estrin et al. (2000), 98 percent of all processors on the planet are not in traditional desktop computer systems, nor even in laptops. They are in household appliances, vehicles, and machines. Such existing and future applications of pervasive computing are illustrated in Figure 5.9 (page 226). Notice that all 14 devices can be connected to the Internet. Several of these applications are described in the remainder of this section. We will look at four applications in particular: smart homes, smart appliances, smart cars, and smart things.

Smart Homes

In a *smart home*, your home computer, television, lighting and heating controls, home security system, and many appliances within the home can "talk" to each other via the Internet or a home intranet. These linked systems can be controlled through various devices.

In the United States, tens of thousands of homes are already equipped with home-automation devices, and there are signs that Europe—which has much lower home Internet penetration levels—is also warming to the idea. For instance, a 2001 study by the UK's Consumers' Association found that almost half those surveyed were interested in having the functions a "smart home" could offer, if they were affordable (Edgington, 2001).

Some of the tasks supported today by home automation systems are:

- *Lighting.* You can program your lights to go on, off, or dim to match your moods and needs for comfort and security.
- *Energy management.* A home's HVAC (heat, ventilation, and air conditioning) system can be programmed for maximum energy efficiency, controlled with a touch panel, and can be accessed via your telephone or PDA.
- *Water control.* Watercop (*watercop.com*) is a device that relies on a series of strategically placed moisture-detection sensors. When the moisture level rises in one of these sensors, it sends a wireless signal to the Watercop control unit, which turns off the main water supply.
- *Home security and communications.* The window blinds, garage doors, front door, smoke detectors, and home security systems can all be automated from a network control panel. These can all be programmed to respond to scheduled events (e.g., when you go on vacation).
- *Home theater.* You can create a multisource audio and video center around your house that you can control with a touch pad or remote. For example, if you have a DVD player in your bedroom but want to see the same movie in your child's room, you can just click a remote to switch rooms.

Analysts generally agree that the market opportunities for smart homes will take shape over the next 3 to 5 years. These opportunities are being driven by

IT at Work 5.4
CONTEXT-AWARE ENVIRONMENT
AT CARNEGIE MELLON UNIVERSITY

Carnegie Mellon University (CMU) is known for its advanced science projects including robotics and artificial intelligence. Students participate in a context-awareness experiment in the following manner: Each participating student is equipped with a PDA from which he or she can access Internet services via the campus Wi-Fi network. The students operate in a context-aware environment whose architecture is shown in the attached figure.

messages, and determine what to show to the students, and when. For example, while attending classes the student may block all messages. That is, certain messages will be shown only if the student is in a certain place and/or time; others will not be shown at all.

A user's context information can be accessed by a collection of *personal agents,* each in charge of assisting with different tasks, while locating and invoking relevant Internet services identified through services registries (see the figure).

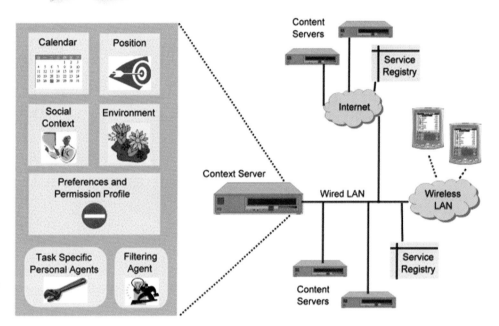

Carnegie Mellon's context-awareness system
(*Source:* Sadeh, 2002.)

A user's context (left of figure) includes his or her:

- Calendar information
- Current location (position), which is regularly updated using location-tracking technology
- Weather information, indicating whether it is sunny, raining, or snowing, and the current outside temperature (environment)
- Social context information, including the student's friends and his or her teachers, classmates, and so forth

The preferences of each student are solicited and entered into system, to create a personal profile, shown as "Preferences and Permissions" in the figure. All of the above information helps the system to filter incoming

An example of a simple agent is a *restaurant concierge* that gives suggestions to students about places to have lunch, depending on their food preferences, the time they have available before their next class, their location on campus, and the weather. For example, when it is raining, the agent attempts to find a place that does not require going outside of the building where the student is located. The recommendation (usually several choices) appears on the PDA, with an overall rating and a "click for details" possibility.

Source: Compiled from Sadeh (2002).

For Further Exploration: Does the usefulness of such a service justify the need to disclose private preferences? Can such a system be developed for consumers who are not members of a defined community such as a university?

FIGURE 5.9 Embedded computing devices everywhere. (*Source:* Estrin et al., 2000, pp. 38–39.)

1. Smart building materials:
   - Sense vibrations, temperature, moisture
   - Monitor premises for intruders
   - Cancel street noise
2. Bridge deck erected with smart building materials:
   - Senses and reports traffic, wind loads
   - Monitors structural integrity
3. Autonomous robo-sweeper
4. Wireless communication, including links to GPS satellites, Net access
5. Smart sensor pills:
   - Programmable delivery vehicles for pharmaceuticals
   - Internal sensing applications
6. Embedded automobile devices (such as antilock brakes, air bags):
   - Evaluate performance
   - Provide Net access
7. Fire hydrant measures water flow, senses heat, offers security mechanisms.
8. Autonomous robo-mailbot performing nominally manual labor.

9. Street light senses foot and motor traffic, polices area.
10. Banking/business:
   - Uses ATM machines, cash registers, bar-code readers, credit card devices
   - Security devices offer personal IDs, but also sense vibrations and (body) heat and motion and monitors premises for intruders.
11. Home networks:
   - Most electrical appliances, including dishwashers, toasters, cable TV set-top boxes, toys, phones, thermostats, PCs
12. Smart building materials:
   - Smart paint
   - Smart concrete
   - Smart gels
13. Smart cement detects earthquake activity.
14. Collar on dog for wireless location via GPS link. Clothes on man (personal cybernetics) offer similar abilities as well as networking and heat sensors.

the increasing adoption of broadband (cable or DSL) services and the proliferation of wireless local area networks (Wi-Fi) within the home and by the trend to integrate currently independent devices. Online File W5.12 shows a wireless connected house.

Smart Appliances

One of the key elements of a smart home is the *smart appliance,* an Internet-ready appliance that can be controlled by a small hand-held device or desktop computer via a home intranet (wireline or wireless) or the public Internet.

One organization that is focused on smart appliances is the Internet Home Alliance (*internethomealliance.com*). The alliance is made up of a number of appliance manufacturers (e.g., Whirlpool and Sunbeam), computer hardware companies (e.g., IBM and Cisco), retailers (e.g., Best Buy), and vendors specializing in home automation (e.g., Lutron Electronics). The mission of the alliance is to accelerate the process of researching, developing, and testing new home products and services that require a broadband or persistent connection to the Internet. Online File W5.13 exemplifies some the types of smart appliances being developed by members of the alliance; in this case, however, the appliances are being used for commercial purposes, not in the home.

The appliance manufacturers are interested not only in the sale of appliances but also in service. In most cases, when an appliance is purchased and taken home, the manufacturer loses touch with the appliance unless the customer registers the product for warranty purposes. Potentially, a networked appliance could provide a manufacturer, as well as the owner of the appliance, with information that could be used to capture or report on the operation, performance, and usage of a device. In addition, the networked appliance could provide information for diagnostic purposes—for monitoring, troubleshooting, repairing, or maintaining the device (Pinto, 2002).

To date, however, consumers have shown little interest in smart appliances. As a result, the manufacturers of these appliances are focusing on improving people's lives by eliminating repetitive, nonquality tasks. One example is Sunbeam's corded HLT (Home Linking Technology) products that communicate with one another using an embedded technology called PLC (Power Line Communication). For instance, an HTL alarm clock can coordinate an entire morning's routine: The heating system, the coffee maker, and the lights in the kids' rooms go on, and the electric blanket goes off.

Whether offerings of this sort will prove successful is an open question. In the near term, one of the biggest technical barriers to widespread adoption of smart appliances will continue to be the fact that most homes lack broadband connection to the Internet. However, this situation is rapidly changing.

Smart Cars

Every car today has at least one computer on board to operate the engine, regulate fuel consumption, and control exhaust emissions. The average automobile on the road today has 20 or more microprocessors, which are truly invisible. They are under the hood, behind the dash, in the door panels, and on the undercarriage. Microprocessors control the radio, decide when your transmission should shift gears, remember your seat position, and adjust the temperature in the passenger cabin. They can make the suspension work better, help you see in the dark, and warn when a tire is low. In the shop, the onboard microprocessors are used to diagnose problems. Car computers often operate independently, but some swap data among themselves—a growing trend. The microprocessors in a car require little maintenance, continuing to operate through extreme temperature, vibration, and humidity.

In 1998, the U.S. Department of Transportation (DOT) identified eight areas where microprocessors and intelligent systems could improve or impact auto safety (*www.its.dot.gov/ivi/ivi.htm*). The list included four kinds of collision avoidance (see Jones, 2001), computer "vision" for cars, vehicle stability, and two kinds of driver monitoring. The automotive industry is in the process of testing a variety of experimental systems addressing the areas identified by the DOT. For example, GM in partnership with Delphi Automotive Systems has developed an Automotive Collision Avoidance System that employs radar, video cameras, special sensors, and GPS to monitor traffic and driver actions in an effort to reduce collisions with other vehicles and pedestrians (Sharke, 2003).

There is also a growing trend to connect car microprocessors to mobile networks and to the Internet (see Moore, 2000). Emergency assistance, driving directions, and e-mail are some of the services these connections can support. To increase safety, drivers can use voice-activated controls, even to access the Web (Bretz, 2001) GM's OnStar system (*onstar.com*) already supports many of these services (see Online File W5.14).

OnStar is the forerunner of smart cars of the future. The next generation of smart cars is likely to provide even more automated services, especially in emergency situations. For instance, although OnStar will automatically signal the service center when the air bags are deployed and will immediately contact emergency services if the driver and passengers are incapacitated, what OnStar cannot provide is detailed information about a crash. Newer systems are under development that will automatically determine the speed upon impact, whether the car has rolled over, and whether the driver and passengers were wearing seat belts. Information of this sort might be used by emergency personnel to determine the severity of the accident and what types of services will be needed.

Ideally smart cars eventually will be able to drive themselves. Known as *autonomous land vechicles* (ALVs), these cars follow GIS maps and use sensors in a wireless environment to identify obstacles. These vehicles are already on the roads in California, Pennsylvania, and Germany (on an experimental basis, of course).

Smart "Things"

Several other devices and instruments can be made to be "smart." Some examples are discussed below.

BARCODES. A typical barcode, known as the *Universal Product Code (UPC),* is made up of 12 digits, in various groups. The first two show the country where it was issued, the next four represent the manufacturer, and the remaining six are the product code assigned by the manufacturer. On a package the code is represented by a series of bars and spaces of varying widths.

Barcodes are used at various points in the supply chain to track inventory and shipments and to identify items at the point of sale. A barcode scanner is required to support these tasks. It consists of a scanning device for reading the code and translating it into an electrical output, a decoder for converting the electrical output to data that a computer or terminal can recognize, and a cable that connects the decoder to a computer or terminal.

Barcodes have worked pretty well over the past 25 years. But, they have their limitations. First, they require line-of-sight of the scanning device. This is fine in a store but can pose substantial problems in a manufacturing plant, a warehouse, or on a shipping/receiving dock. Second, they are printed on paper, meaning that they can be ripped, soiled, or lost. Third, the barcode identifies the manufacturer and product, not the item. For example, every carton of milk of a given producer has the same barcode, regardless of when it was produced. This makes a barcode useless in determining things like the expiration date. There is an alternative identification method, called Auto-ID, that overcomes the limitations of barcodes.

AUTO-ID. This method has been promoted over the past couple of years by the **Auto Identification (Auto-ID) Center** (*autoidcenter.org*), a joint partnership among more than 87 global companies and three of the world's leading research universities—MIT in the United States, the University of Cambridge in the UK, and the University of Adelaide in Australia. The companies include manufacturers (e.g., Coca-Cola, Gillette, and Canon), retailers (e.g., Wal-Mart, Tesco in the UK), shippers (e.g., UPS and the U.S. Postal Service), standards bodies (e.g., Uniform Code Council), and government agencies (e.g., the U.S. Department of Defense).

The mission of the Auto-ID Center goes well beyond replacing one code with another. Its stated aim is to create an **Internet of things,** a network that connects computers to objects—boxes of laundry detergent, pairs of jeans, airplane engines. This Internet of things will provide the ability to track individual items as they move from factories to store shelves to recycling facilities. This will make possible near-perfect supply chain visibility.

The key technical elements of the Auto-ID system and the explanation of how it will work are provided in Online File W5.15. The earliest Auto-ID device is the RFID.

RFID: Capabilities and Cost

RFID has been around awhile. During World War II, RFIDs were used to identify friendly aircraft. Today, they are used in wireless tollbooth systems, such as E-Z Pass. In Singapore they are used in a system called Electronic Road Pricing, which charges different prices to drive on different roads at different times, encouraging drivers to stay off busy roads at busy times. Every car has an RFID tag that communicates with card readers on the major roads (similar to the story of Highway 91 in *IT at Work 5.3*, page 217).

Until now the problem with RFID has been the expense. Tags have cost at least 50 cents, which makes them unusable for low-priced items. A California company called Alien Technology (*alientechnology.com*) has invented a way to mass-produce RFID tags for less than 10 cents apiece for large production runs. In January 2003, Gillette placed an order with Alien Technology for 500 million RFID tags (*RFID Journal,* 2002). Gillette is using the tags in a number of trial programs. In one of the early trials, Gillette attached the tags to the Mach 3 razors they ship to Wal-Mart, whose store shelves are equipped with special RFID readers. The overall success of RFID tags in the marketplace will depend on the outcome of trials such as this.

IMPLEMENTING RFID. The major expected benefit of RFID is its potential for revolutionizing supply chain management, as explained in Chapter 1 and as demonstrated in Chapter 7. For example, NATO is using RFID to manage the flow of military supplies from Europe to Afghanistan, and it soon will be used in all 19 NATO countries in defense-related transactions. But RFID could have many other applications, ranging from payment collection on tollways, to finding lost kids in amusement parks to preventing cell phones from being stolen (a use that Nokia is working on).

Several factors will determine the speed with which RFID will take off. The first of these is how many companies will mandate that business partners use RFID. So far, only Wal-Mart and the U.S. Department of Defense have required such use. The second factor is the success of attempted legislation to limit the amount of information on the tag (pending in the state of California) or to force removal of the tags when customers pay for the items (state of Massachusetts). More legislation will be attempted to protect the privacy of consumers. In the interim, some companies maintain a wait-and-see attitude. Finally, the cost of the tags and the needed information systems support is still high and is likely to remain so (Spivey-Overby, 2004). However, Ryan (2004) suggests that in order to be winners, manufacturers must embrace the technology. For an overview of the implementation issues and attempted solutions, see Kharif (2004).

Large-Scale Pervasive Systems

Smart appliances, cars, and barcodes can certainly make our lives more comfortable, but pervasive computing can make an even larger contribution when large numbers of computing devices are put together, creating massive intelligent systems. These systems include factories, airports, schools, and even entire cities. At the moment most of them are experimental and on a relatively small scale. Let's look at some examples.

SMART SCHOOLS. The University of California at Los Angeles is experimenting with a smart kindergarten (Chen et al., 2002). Exploring communication between students, teachers, and the environment, the project aims to create a smart learning environment.

INTELLIGENT ELDER CARE. The increased age of the population in many countries brings a problem of caring for more elderly for longer times. Long-term care facilities, where different patients require different levels of care, bring the problem of how to provide such care efficiently and effectively. The experimental project titled Elite Care has demonstrated the benefits of using pervasive computing in such settings, as described in *IT at Work 5.5*.

SMART OFFICES. The original work of Weiser (1991) centered around an intelligent office. And indeed several projects are experimenting with such an environment which can interact with users through voice, gesture, or movements and can anticipate their activities. By monitoring office employees, the SmartOffice (Le Gal et al., 2001) even anticipates user intentions and augments the environment to communicate useful information.

DIGITAL CITIES. According to Ishida (2002a) the concept of *digital cities* is to build an area in which people in regional communities can interact and share knowledge, experiences, and mutual interests. Digital cities integrate urban information (both real time and stored) and create public spaces for people living in or visiting the cities. Digital cities are being developed all over the world (see Ishida, 2002a, 2002b). In Europe alone there are over 100 projects (e.g., Amsterdam, Helsinki).

In the city of Kyoto, Japan, for example, the digital city complements and corresponds to the physical city (Ishida, 2002a). Three layers are constructed: The first is an information layer, where Web archives and real-time sensory data

IT at Work 5.5
USING PERVASIVE COMPUTING TO DELIVER ELDER CARE

Delivering health services to the elderly is becoming a major societal problem in many countries, especially in countries where there are relatively fewer and fewer young people to take care of more and more elderly. The problem is already acute in Japan, and it is expected to be very serious in 10 to 15 years in several European countries and in China. Managing and delivering health care involves large numbers of diversified decisions, ranging from allocation of resources to determining what treatment to provide to each patient at each given time.

Elderly residents in assisted-living facilities require differing levels of care. Some residents need minimal assistance, others have short-term memory problems, and yet others have more severe problems like Alzheimer's disease so they require more supervision and help. At Elite Care's Estates Cluster Residential Care Facility in Milwaukie, Oregon, pervasive computing is being used to increase the autonomy and care level of all of its residents, regardless of their individual needs.

Elite Care, a family-owned business (*elite-care.com*), has been built from the ground up to provide "high-tech, high-touch" programs. Its advisory committee, which includes, among others, representatives from the Mayo Clinic, Harvard University, the University of Michigan, the University of Wisconsin, and Sandia National Laboratory, has contributed a number of ideas that have been put into practice.

The entire facility is designed with a 30-mile network (wireline and wireless) of unobtrusive sensors and other devices including: biosensors (e.g., weight sensors) attached to each resident's bed; movement sensors embedded in badges worn by the residents and staff; panic buttons used to call for help; Internet access via touch screens in each room; video conferencing using Webcams; and climate control, lights, and other regulated appliances.

These devices and others allow the staff to monitor various patient activity. For example, staff can determine the location of any patient, to tell whether he or she is in an expected area of the facility. Devices that monitor length of absence from bed might alert personnel that the patient has fallen or is incapacitated in other ways. Medical personnel can watch for weight loss (possibly indicating conditions like impending congestive heart failure), restlessness at night (indicating conditions like insufficient pain medication), and frequency of trips to the bathroom (indicating medical problems like infection). Also, close monitoring of conditions enables staff to give medicine and/or other treatments as needed, rather than at predetermined periods. All of these capabilities enable true one-to-one care, which is both more effective and less expensive.

One of the initial concerns with these monitors is that the privacy of the residents would be unnecessarily invaded. To alleviate these concerns, residents and their families are given the choice of participating or not. Most choose to participate because the families believe that these monitors provide better tracking and care. The monitors also increase the autonomy of all the patients because their use reduces the need for staff to constantly monitor residents in person, especially those with more acute care needs.

All of these sensors and systems are connected through a high-speed Ethernet (see Technology Guide 4). The data produced by the sensors and systems are stored in a database and can be used to alert the staff in real time if necessary. These data are used for analytical purposes and for developing individualized care programs. The same database is also used for administrative purposes such as monitoring staff performance in timely delivery.

A similar concept is used in Swan Village of Care in Bentley, Australia. At the present time such projects are experimental and expensive, but some day they will be affordable to many.

Sources: Compiled from Stanford (2002), *elite-care.com,* and *ECC. online.wa.gov.au/news* (January 14, 2003).

For Further Exploration: What types of data do these devices provide? How can pervasive computing increase the quality of elder care? What about the privacy issue?

---

are integrated to provide information anywhere, any time. The second layer is 2-D and 3-D interfaces, which provide views of cars, buses, and pictures that illustrate city services (for attractive and natural presentation). Finally, there is an interactive layer. Extensive use of GIS supports the project. One area of emphasis is a digital tour guide for visitors. Also, the system uses avatars (animated computer characters) that appear on a hand-held device and "walk" with visitors around the city in real time.

Another digital-city experiment is the city of Lancaster (UK), where wireless devices are being used to improve services to both visitors and residents (Davies et al., 2002). The experimental Lancaster City Guide is based on a network of Wi-Fi context-sensitive and location-aware applications. One area that was developed first is services to tourists. By knowing where the tourist is (using a GPS) and his or her preferences, the system can recommend tourist sites in the same general area. (This application is similar to the Carnegie Mellon application described in *IT at Work 5.4*, page 225.)

For other digital-city experiments, see Raskin (2003), Mankins (2002), and Fleck et al. (2002). For information on other large-scale pervasive computing projects, see Weise (2002), and Stanford (2002).

5.10 INHIBITORS AND BARRIERS OF MOBILE COMPUTING

Several limitations are either slowing down the spread of mobile computing or are leaving many m-commerce customers disappointed or dissatisfied (e.g., see Islam and Fayad, 2003). Representative inhibitors and barriers of mobile computing are covered in the following discussion.

The Usability Problem

When mobile Internet users visit mobile Internet sites, the *usability* of the site is critical to attract attention and retain "user stickiness" (the degree to which users stay at a site). There are three dimensions to usability, namely *effectiveness, efficiency,* and *satisfaction.* However, users often find current mobile devices to be ineffective, particularly with respect to restricted keyboards and pocket-size screens, limiting their usability. In addition, because of the limited storage capacity and information access speed of most smartphones and PDAs, it is often difficult or impossible to download large files to these devices.

Mobile visitors to a Web site are typically paying premium fees for connections and are focused on a specific goal (e.g., conducting a stock trade). Therefore, if customers want to find exactly what they are looking for, easily and quickly, they need more than text-only devices with small screens. In 2003, many WAP applications were still text-based, and had only simple black-and-white graphics. This made tasks such as mobile shopping difficult. Because all the transactions were essentially text-based, mobile users could not "browse" an online picture-based catalog. However, more and faster multimedia are becoming available as 3G spreads.

The major technical and other limitations that have slowed the spread of m-commerce are summarized in Table 5.4.

Ethical and Legal Issues

Several ethical and legal issues are unique to mobile computing. For example, fashion retailer Benetton Group SpA was considering attaching RFID "smart tags" to its Sisley line of clothing to help track shipping, inventory, and sales in the company's 5,000 stores worldwide. (Also, the tags could help prevent shoplifting.) The idea was to integrate the RFID tag into the clothing labels. Using the tags, the store would know where each piece of clothing is, at any given time. However, privacy groups expressed concern that the tags could also be used to track buyers, and some groups even urged that the company's clothing be boycotted. As a result, Benetton backed away from the plan, at least until an impact study is done (Rosencrance, 2003).

TABLE 5.4 Technical and Other Limitations of Mobile Computing	
Limitation	Description
Insufficient bandwidth	Sufficient bandwidth is necessary for widespread use and it must be inexpensive. It will take a few years until 3G is in many places. Wi-Fi solves some of the problem.
Security standards	Universal standards were not available in 2003. It may take 3 or more years to have them.
Power consumption	Batteries with long life are needed for mobile computing. Color screens and Wi-Fi consume more electricity, but new chips are solving some of the power-consumption problems.
Transmission interferences	Weather and terrain problems as well as distance-limited connection exist with some technologies. Reception in tunnels and some buildings is poor.
GPS accuracy	GPS may be inaccurate in a city with tall buildings.
WAP limitations	According to *mofileinfo.com*, in 2002 there were only about 50,000 WAP sites (compared to millions of Web sites). WAP still is a cumbersome process to work with.
Potential health hazards	Potential health damage from cellular radio frequency emission is not known yet. However, more car accidents are related to drivers who were talking (some places bar the use of cell phones while you drive). Also, cell phones may interfere with sensitive medical devices.
Legal issues	Potential legal issues against manufacturers of cell phones and against service providers exist, due to the potential health problems.
Human interface with device	Screens and keyboards are too small and uncomfortable and tedious for many people to use.
Complexity	Too many optional add-ons are available (e.g., battery chargers, external keyboards, headset, microphones, cradles). Storing and using the optional add-ons is a problem to some.

According to Hunter (2002), privacy is in great danger in the world of ubiquitous computing because of the proliferation of networked devices used by individual, businesses, and government. The Elite Care project described in *IT at Work 5.5* (page 231), for example, raised the issue of protecting information collected by sensors. Also, privacy is difficult to control in other types of context-aware systems (e.g., see Jiang and Landay, 2002). As indicated earlier, security is especially difficult in Wi-Fi systems.

Challenges in Deploying Ubiquitous Systems

For pervasive (ubiquitous) systems to be widely deployed, it is necessary to overcome both the technical and ethical/legal barriers associated with wireless computing, plus overcoming other barriers unique to pervasive computing. Davies and Gellersen (2002) provide a comprehensive list of technical challenges, social and legal issues, and economic concerns (including finding appropriate business models) in deploying ubiquitous systems. They also cite research challenges such as component interaction, adaptation and contextual sensitivity, user interface interaction, and appropriate management mechanisms.

Failures in Mobile Computing and M-Commerce

As with any other technology, especially a new one, there have been many failures of applications as well as entire companies in mobile computing and m-commerce. It is important to anticipate and plan for possible failures as well as to learn from them.

The case of Northeast Utilities provides some important insights. According to Hamblen (2001), Northeast Utilities (located in Berlin, Connecticut), which supplies energy products and services to 1.2 million customers from Maine to Maryland, embarked on a wireless project in 1995 in which its field inspectors used wireless devices to track spills of hazardous material and report them to headquarters in real time. After spending a year and a half and $1 million, the project failed. Some of the lessons learned were:

● Do not start without appropriate infrastructure.
● Do not start a full-scale implementation; use a small pilot for experimentation.
● Pick up an appropriate architecture. Some users don't need to be persistently connected, for example.
● Talk with a range of users, some experienced and some not, about usability issues.
● Users must be involved; hold biweekly meetings if possible.
● Employ wireless experts if you are not one.
● Wireless is a different medium from other forms of communication. Remember that people are not used to the wireless paradigm.

Having learned from the failure, Northeast made its next wireless endeavor a success. Today, 15 field inspectors carry rugged wireless laptops that are connected to the enterprise intranet and databases. The wireless laptops are used to conduct measurements related to electricity transformers, for example. Then the laptops transmit the results, in real time, to chemists and people who prepare government reports about hazardous materials spills. In addition, time is saved, because all the information is entered directly into proper fields of electronic forms without having to be transcribed. The new system is so successful that it has given IT workers the confidence to launch other applications such as sending power-outage reports to managers via smart phones and wireless information to crews repairing street lights.

MANAGERIAL ISSUES

1. *Comparing wireless to synchronized mobile devices.* In many cases, transmitting data in the evening, using a docking device, is sufficient. In others, real-time communication is needed, justifying a wireless system.

2. *Timetable.* Although there has been much hype about m-commerce in the last few years, only a small number of large-scale mobile computing applications have been deployed to date. The most numerous applications are in e-banking, stock trading, emergency services, and some B2B tasks. Companies still have time to carefully craft an m-commerce strategy. This will reduce the number of failed initiatives and bankrupted companies. For calculating the total cost of wireless computing ownership and how to justify it, see Intel (2002).

3. *Setting applications priorities.* Finding and prioritizing applications is a part of an organization's e-strategy. Although location-based advertising is logically attractive, its effectiveness may not be known for several years. Therefore, companies should be very careful in committing resources to m-commerce. For the near term, applications that enhance the efficiency and effectiveness of mobile workers are likely to have the highest payoff.

4. *Just a buzzword?* In the short run, mobile computing, m-commerce, and especially l-commerce, may be just buzzwords due to the many limitations they now face. However, in the long run, the concepts will be increasingly popular. Management should monitor the technological developments and make plans accordingly.

5. *Choosing a system.* The multiplicity of standards, devices, and supporting hardware and software can confuse a company planning to implement mobile computing. An unbiased consultant can be of great help. Checking the vendors and products carefully, as well as who is using them, is also critical. This issue is related to the issue of whether or not to use an application service provider (ASP) for m-commerce.

KEY TERMS

1G *196*
2G *196*
2.5G *196*
3G *196*
4G *196*
802.11b *197*
Auto Identification (Auto-ID) Center *229*
Automatic crash notification (ACN) *221*
Bluetooth *190*
Code Division Multiple Access (CDMA) *197*
Context awareness *223*
Contextual computing *223*
Enhanced Messaging Service (EMS) *190*
Frequency Division Multiple Access (FDMA) *196*

Geographical information system (GIS) *219*
Global positioning system (GPS) *218*
Hotspot *197*
Internet of things *229*
Location-based commerce (l-commerce) *191*
M-wallet (mobile wallet) *203*
Mobile handset *195*
Mobile portals *207*
Multimedia Messaging Service (MMS) *190*
Personal digital assistant (PDA) *190*
Pervasive computing *222*
Radio frequency identification (RFID) *223*
Screenphones (wireless) *194*

Short Messaging Service (SMS) *190*
Smartphone *190*
Telematics *221*
Time Division Multiple Access (TDMA) *196*
Voice portal *202*
Wearable devices *208*
Wireless access point (for Wi-Fi) *197*
Wireless Application Protocol (WAP) *190*
Wireless Encryption Protocol (WEP) *200*
Wireless fidelity (Wi-Fi) *190*
Wireless local area network (WLAN) *190*
Wireless 911 (e-911) *221*
Wireless mobile computing *188*
Wireless wide area networks (WWAN) *195*

CHAPTER HIGHLIGHTS (Numbers Refer to Learning Objectives)

❶ Mobile computing is based on mobility and reach. These characteristics provide ubiquity, convenience, instant connectivity, personalization, and product and service localization.

❷ The major drivers of mobile computing are: large numbers of users of mobile devices, especially cell phones; no need for a PC; a developing "cell phone culture" in some areas; vendor marketing; declining prices; increasing bandwidth; and the explosion of EC in general.

❸ Mobile computing and m-commerce require mobile devices (e.g., PDAs, cell phones) and other hardware, software, and wireless technologies. Commercial services and applications are still emerging. These technologies allow users to access the Internet any time, anywhere.

❸ For l-commerce, a GPS receiver is also needed.

❹ Standards are being developed by several organizations in different countries, resulting in competing systems. It is expected that with time some of these will converge.

❺ Many EC applications in the service industries (e.g., banking, travel, and stocks) can be conducted with wireless devices. Also, shopping can be done from mobile devices.

❺ Location-based advertising and advertising via SMSs on a very large scale is expected.

❺ Mobile portals provide content (e.g., news) to millions.

❻ Large numbers of intrabusiness applications, including inventory management, sales force automation, wireless voice, job dispatching, wireless office, and more are already evident inside organizations.

7 Emerging mobile B2B applications are being integrated with the supply chain and are facilitating cooperation between business partners.

8 M-commerce is being used to provide applications in travel, gaming, entertainment, and delivery of medical services. Many other applications for individual consumers are planned for, especially targeted advertising.

9 Most non-Internet applications involve various types of smart cards. They are used mainly in transportation, security, and shopping from vending machines and gas pumps.

10 Location-based commerce, or l-commerce, is emerging in applications such as calculating arrival time of buses (using GPS) and emergency services (wireless 911). In the future, it will be used to target advertising to individuals based on their location. Other innovative applications also are expected.

11 In the world of invisible computing virtually every object has an embedded microprocessor that is connected in a wired and/or wireless fashion to the Internet. This Internet of things—homes, appliances, cars, and any manufactured items—will provide a number of life-enhancing, consumer-centric, and B2B applications.

11 In context-aware computing, the computer captures the contextual variables of the user and the environment and then provides, in real time, various services to users.

12 The major limitations of mobile computing are: small screens on mobile devices, limited bandwidth, high cost, lack of (or small) keyboards, transmission interferences, unproven security, and possible health hazards. Many of these limitations are expected to diminish over time. The primary legal/ethical limitations of m-commerce relate to privacy issues.

VIRTUAL COMPANY ASSIGNMENT

Instructions for accessing The Wireless Café on the Student Web site:

1. Go to

   wiley.com/college/turban

2. Select Turban/Leidner/McLean/Wetherbe's *Information Technology for Management, Fifth Edition.*

3. Click on Student Resources site, in the toolbar on the left.

4. Click on the link for Virtual Company Web site.

5. Click on Wireless Café.

Mobile Computing at The Wireless Café

Go to The Wireless Café's link on the Student Web Site. You will be asked to consider mobile and wireless applications that can be implemented at the restaurant.

More Resources

More resources and study tools are located on the Student Web Site. You'll find additional chapter materials and useful Web links. In addition, self-quizzes that provide individualized feedback are available for each chapter.

QUESTIONS FOR REVIEW

1. Define mobile computing and m-commerce.

2. Define the following terms: PDA, WAP, SMS, GPS, Wi-Fi, and smartphone.

3. List the value-added attributes of mobile computing.

4. List at least five major drivers of mobile computing.

5. Describe the major hardware devices used for mobile computing.

6. List the major software items used for mobile computing.

7. Describe the major components of a mobile network.

8. Define the terms FDMA, TDMA, and CDMA.

9. List the major standards used by mobile phone systems (e.g., GSM).

10. Describe the major components of a WLAN.

11. Define 1G, 2G, 2.5G, 3G, and 4G.

12. List some of the key security issues in an m-commerce transaction.

13. List some of the uses of voice portals.

14. Discuss mobile micropayments.

15. Describe the m-wallet and wireless bill payments.

16. Describe how mobile devices can be used to shop.

17. Explain targeted advertising in the wireless environment and in pervasive computing.

18. Describe mobile portals and what kind of information they provide.

19. Describe wireless job dispatch.

20. Discuss how wireless applications can be used to provide customer support.

21. List some of the major intrabusiness wireless applications.

22. Describe wireless support along the supply chain.

23. How can telemetry improve supply chain operations?

24. Describe the application of wireless and mobile technologies to games and entertainment.

25. Discuss some of the potential applications of Wi-Fi and Bluetooth technologies in hotels.

26. Describe some potential uses of mobile and wireless technologies in providing medical care.

27. Describe some of the potential uses of l-commerce.

28. Discuss the technologies used in providing l-commerce services.

29. Describe GPS and GIS.

30. Discuss telematics.

31. List some of the barriers to l-commerce.

32. Define pervasive computing.

33. List some of the major properties of pervasive computing.

34. Discuss some of the ways that pervasive computing can be used in the home.

35. Describe a smart car.

36. Describe some of the ways that microprocessors are being used to enhance the intelligence of appliances.

37. What is contextual computing?

38. Discuss the role that usability plays in the adoption of m-commerce.

39. List the technical limitations of m-commerce.

QUESTIONS FOR DISCUSSION

1. Discuss how mobile computing can solve some of the problems of the *digital divide* (the gap within a country or between countries with respect to people's ability to access the Internet). (See International Communications Union 1999 and Chapter 16).

2. Discuss how m-commerce can expand the reach of e-business.

3. Explain the role of protocols in mobile computing.

4. Discuss the impact of wireless computing on emergency medical services.

5. How do smartphones and screenphones differ? What characteristics do they share?

6. How are GIS and GPS related?

7. List three to four major advantages of wireless commerce to consumers, presented in this chapter, and explain what benefits they provide to consumers.

8. You can use location-based tools to help you find your car or the closest gas station. However, some people see location-based tools as an invasion of privacy. Discuss the pros and cons of location-based tools.

9. Discuss how wireless devices can help people with disabilities.

10. Discuss the benefits of telemetry-based systems.

11. Discuss the ways in which Wi-Fi is being used to support mobile computing and m-commerce. Describe the ways in which Wi-Fi is affecting the use of cellular phones for m-commerce.

12. Which of the applications of pervasive computing—smart cars, homes, appliances, and things—do you think are likely to gain the greatest market acceptance of the next few years? Why?

13. Which of the current mobile computing and m-commerce limitations do you think will be minimized within 5 years? Which ones will not?

14. Describe some m-commerce B2B applications along the supply chain.

15. It is said that Wi-Fi is winning a battle against 3G. In what sense is this true? In what sense is this false?

EXERCISES

1. Investigate the status of commercial applications of voice portals. Visit at least five vendors (e.g., *tellme.com*, *bevocal.com*, etc.). View the demos and lists of products at the sites.
   a. Prepare a list of capabilities offered by the different vendors.
   b. Prepare a list of actual applications.
   c. Comment on the value of such applications to users. How can the benefits be assessed?

2. Conduct a study on wearable computers. Find five vendors. Start with *nexttag.com*, *mobileinfo.com*, *xybernaut.com*, and *eg3.com*, and look for others as well.

   a. Identify 5 to 10 consumer-oriented wearable devices. What are the capabilities of these products? What advantages do they offer users?
   b. Identify 5 to 10 industry-oriented wearable devices. What are the capabilities of these products? What advantages do they offer users?
   c. See if you can find "What's cooking" in the research labs. For example, visit MIT's wearable computing lab.

3. Investigate commercial uses of GPS. Start with *gpshome.ssc.nasa.gov*; then go to *gpsstore.com*. Can some of the consumer-oriented products be used in industry? Prepare a report on your finding.

GROUP ASSIGNMENTS

1. Each team should examine a major vendor of mobile devices (Nokia, Kyocera, Motorola, Palm, BlackBerry, etc.). Each team will research the capabilities and prices of the devices offered by each company and then make a class presentation, the objective of which is to convince the rest of the class why one should buy that company's products.

2. Each team should explore the commercial applications of m-commerce in one of the following areas: financial services, including banking, stocks, and insurance; marketing and advertising; manufacturing; travel and transportation; human resources management; public services; and health care. Each team will present a report to the class based on their findings. (Start at *mobiforum.org*.)

3. Each team will investigate a global organization involved in m-commerce, such as *openmobilealliance.com*. The teams will investigate the membership and the current projects the organization is working on and then present a report to the class based on their findings.

4. Each team will investigate a standards-setting organization and report on its procedures and progress in developing wireless standards. Start with the following: *atis.org*, *etsi.org*, and *tiaonline.org*.

5. Each team should take one of the following areas—homes, cars, appliances, or other consumer goods like clothing—and investigate how embedded microprocessors are currently being used and will be used in the future to support consumer-centric services. Each team will present a report to the class based on their findings.

INTERNET EXERCISES

1. Learn about PDAs by visiting vendors' sites such as Palm, SONY, Hewlett-Packard, IBM, Phillips, NEC, Hitachi, Casio, Brother, Texas Instruments, and others. List some m-commerce devices manufactured by these companies.

2. Access *progressive.com*, an insurance company, from your cell phone (use the "Go to..." feature). If you have a Sprint PCS wireless phone, do it via the Finance menu. If you have a Palm i705 (or newer), you can download the Web-clipping application from Progressive. Report on these capabilities.

3. Research the status of 3G and the future of 4G by visiting *itu.int*, *4g.newstrove.com*, and *3gnewsroom.com*. Prepare a report on the status of 3G and 4G based on your findings.

4. Explore *nokia.com*. Prepare a summary of the types of mobile services and applications Nokia currently supports and plans to support in the future.

5. Enter *kyocera-wireless.com*. Take the smart tour and view the demos. What is a smartphone? What are its capabilities? How does it differ from a regular cell phone?

6. Enter *mobile.commerce.net* and find information about car navigation systems. Write a report.

7. Enter *ibm.com*. Search for *wireless e-business*. Research the resulting stories to determine the types of wireless capabilities and applications IBM's software and hardware supports. Describe some of the ways these applications have helped specific businesses and industries.

8. Using a search engine, try to determine whether there are any commercial Wi-Fi hotspots in your area. Enter *wardriving.com*. Based on information provided at this site, what sorts of equipment and procedures could you use to locate hotspots in your area?

9. Enter *mapinfo.com* and look for the location-based services demos. Try all the demos. Find all of the wireless services. Summarize your findings.

10. Visit *ordersup.com, astrology.com,* and similar sites that capitalize on l-commerce. What features do these sites share?

11. Enter *packetvideo.com* and *microsoft.com/mobile/pocketpc*. Examine their demos and products and list their capabilities.

12. Enter *internethomealliance.com* and review their white-papers. Based on these papers, what are the major appliances that are currently in most U.S. homes? Which of these appliances would most homeowners be likely to connect to a centrally controlled network?

13. Enter *onstar.com*. What types of *fleet* services does OnStar provide? Are these any different from the services OnStar provides to individual car owners?

14. Enter *autoidcenter.org*. Read about the Internet of Things. What is it? What types of technologies are needed to support it? Why is it important?

15. Enter *mdsi-advantex.com* and review the wireless products for the enterprise. Summarize the advantages of the different products.

16. Enter *attwireless.com/mlife* and prepare a list of the services available there.

17. Enter *wirelesscar.com*. Examine all the services provided and relate them to telemetry.

18. Enter the site of a wireless e-mail provider (BlackBerry, T-mobile, Handspring); collect information about the capabilities of the products and compare them.

19. Enter *zilog.com/about/partners/011600.html* and find information about smart appliances.

20. Enter *media.mit.edu/wearables* and prepare a report about new developments (most recent 12 months).

21. Enter *med-i-nets.com* and find information about Pharm-i-net. Trace the supply chain and the support of wireless. Make a diagram of the supply chain.

Minicase 1
Hertz Goes Wireless

The car rental industry is very competitive, and Hertz (*hertz.com*), the world's largest car rental company, competes against hundreds of companies in thousands of locations. The competition focuses on customer acquisition and loyalty. In the last few years, competition has intensified, and profits in the industry have been drifting downward. Hertz has been a "first mover" to information technologies since the 1970s, so it has naturally looked for new technologies to improve its competitive position. In addition to data warehousing and mining, a superb executive information system, and e-commerce, Hertz has pioneered some mobile commerce applications:

● *Quick rentals.* Upon arrival at the airport, Hertz's curbside attendant greets you and transmits your name wirelessly to the renting booth. The renting-booth employee advises the curbside attendant about the location of your car. All you need to do is go to the slot where the car is parked and drive away. This system, which once operated over a WLAN, is now part of a national wireless network that can check credit cards, examine your rental history, determine which airline to credit your loyalty mileage to, and more.

● *Instant returns.* Pioneered by Hertz in 1987, a hand-held device connected to a database via a wireless system expedites the car return transaction. Right in the parking lot, the lot attendant uses a hand-held device to calculate the cost of the rental and print a receipt for the renter. You check out in less than a minute, and you do not have to enter the renting booth at all.

● *In-car cellular phones.* Starting in 1988, Hertz began renting cell phones with its cars. Today, of course, this is not as big a deal as it was in 1988, when it was a major innovation.

● *NeverLost Onboard.* Some cars come equipped with an onboard GPS system, which provides route guidance in the form of turn-by-turn directions to many destinations. The information is displayed on a screen with computer-generated voice prompts. An electronic mapping system (GIS) is combined with the GPS, enabling you to see on the map where you are and where you are going. Also, consumer information about the locations of the nearest hospitals, gas stations, restaurants, and tourist areas is provided.

- *Additional customer services.* Hertz's customers can download city guides, Hertz's location guide, emergency telephone numbers, city maps, shopping guides, and even reviews of restaurants, hotels, and entertainment into their PDAs and other wireless devices. Of course, driving directions are provided.
- *Car locations.* Hertz is experimenting with a GPS-based car-locating system. This will enable the company to know where a rental car is at any given time, and even how fast it is being driven. Although the company promises to provide discounts based on your usage pattern, this capability is seen by many as an invasion of privacy. On the other hand, some may feel safer knowing that Hertz knows where they are at all times.

Hertz has been the top car rental company and still maintains that position. It is also a very profitable company that is expanding and growing continuously. Its success is attributed to being customer-centric, as facilitated by its use of wireless technologies and EC.

Source: hertz.com (2003) and Martin (2003).

Questions for Minicase 1

1. Which of these applications are intrabusiness in nature?
2. Identify any finance- and marketing-oriented applications.
3. What are the benefits to Hertz of knowing exactly where each of its cars is? As a renter, how do you feel about this capability?

Minicase 2
Washington Township Fire Department Goes Wireless

The Washington Township Fire Department (WTFD) is located just north of Columbus, Ohio. WTFD responds to more than 4,500 emergency medical services (EMS) calls every year. Time is critical when WTFD is responding to emergencies, which range from heart attacks to fire injuries to highway accidents. The service is run by emergency medical technicians (EMTs).

Rushing victims to the hospital is only one part of the service offered by these dedicated technicians. Providing first aid at the accidents' scene and while transporting the injured in the ambulances is the other part. When a patient is transferred to the hospital, the EMTs must also provide information on what treatments and medications were administered, and what health-related signs they observed in the patient. Such patient care reports are critical to the continuance of the treatment in the hospital, and they become a permanent part of the medical record. The information is also used to keep EMS records for planning, budgeting, training, and reporting to the state of Ohio.

In the past, the department had problems using 8" × 14," multipart, multicopy paper forms. According to Jack McCoy, using paper forms caused several problems. First, not everyone's handwriting is legible, so it was often difficult for hospital personnel as well as the WTFD office people to decipher the information. Second, on many occasions, the information was incomplete, or even inaccurate. To restore the information took considerable valuable time. Office employees at WTFD had to

spend close to 1,800 hours a year processing information after the completion of the patient care report. In fact, 85 percent of one full-time office employee's time was required just to re-enter data that were already entered on the paper reports. But the major problem was the time spent by EMTs filling out forms, since this prevented them from returning quickly to the station, to respond to other emergency calls.

A solution to the paperwork problems was a mobile data collection device (MobilEMS of Clayton I.D.S. Corp. powered by SQL Anywhere Studio from Sybase Corp.). The device allows EMTs to collect patient information quickly, easily, and accurately at the scene and to deliver that information to the hospital in a print-out. This is done by using a series of data entry screens with drop-down menus containing vital information such as diagnoses, treatment rendered, drug administered, and even street names. It also includes a signature-capture feature that allows EMTs to document a patient's refusal of treatment as well as transfer of care to the hospital.

Once the incident data are entered into the system's embedded SQL database, printing reports is simple. The technician beams the information from MobilEMS to the hospital printer's infrared port and a clear document is produced. Back at the station, the EMTs synchronize the data in their hand-helds with the department computer systems by placing MobilEMS in a docking station.

According to McCoy, it takes about 15 seconds to move the data into the system. This is a significant improvement

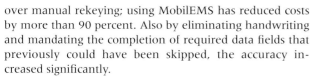

over manual rekeying; using MobilEMS has reduced costs by more than 90 percent. Also by eliminating handwriting and mandating the completion of required data fields that previously could have been skipped, the accuracy increased significantly.

Finally, the system is customizable. Fields can be added and additional information can be stored. Thus, additional applications are leading to a completely paperless environment.

Source: Compiled from Sybase.com (2003).

Question for Minicase 2

1. The system uses a mobile device with a docking station for data synchronization, but no wireless is used. Would you recommend adding wireless? What for? Why or why not?

2. What are the potential legal issues in this case?

3. The system is based on electronic forms with checkmarks. Why not use a similar set of paper forms?

4. What are the benefits of the mobile system to the patient, to the hospital, and to the employees?

5. What are the benefits to WTFD?

REFERENCES

91expresslanes.com (accessed May 2002).

Anderson, C., "Wi-Fi Revolution," special Wired report, May 2004, *wired.com/wired/archive/11.05/unwired/wifirevolution.html* (accessed June 2003).

AvantGo, "My AvantGo Hits 7 Million Registered Users." *Press Release*, November 12, 2002, *avantgo.com/news/press/press_archive/2002/release11_12_02.html* (accessed May 2004).

Baard, M., "After the Fall: Help for Climbers," *Wired News.* December 24, 2002, *wired.com/news/technology/0,1282,56146,00.html* (accessed May 2004).

Becker, D., "Sega Forms Mobile Games Division," *CNET News.com,* April 2002, *news.zdnet.co.uk/story/0,t269-s2108679,00.html* (accessed May 2004).

Bloomberg News, "Lufthansa to Launch In-Flight Wi-Fi Service," May 28, 2003, *seattletimes.nwsource.com/html/boeingaerospace/134830929_ boeingnet28.html* (accessed June 2003).

Bretz, E., "The Car, Just a Web Browser with Tires," *IEEE Spectrum,* 38(1), January 2001, pp. 92–94.

Bughin, J., et al., "Mobile Portals Mobilize for Scale," *The McKinsey Quarterly*, April–June, 2001.

Caton, M., "RFID Reshapes Supply Chain Management,"*e-Week,* April 19, 2004.

CellularOnline, "China Mobile Subscribers Outstrip Landlines," March 22, 2004, *cellular.co.za/news_2004/march/032204-china-mobile-subs.htm* (accessed May 2004).

CellularOnline, "China Now Has More Than 200 Million Mobile Phone Users," November 2003, *cellular.co.za/news_2003/011003-china_now_has_more_than_200_mill.htm,* (accessed May 2004).

CellularOnline, "Latest Mobile, GSM, Global, Handset, Base Station, & Regional Cellular Statistics," *cellular.co.za/stats/stats-main.htm* (accessed May 2004).

Chatterjee, A., et al., "A Road Map for Telematics," *McKinsey Quarterly*, April–June, 2002.

Chen, A., et al., "A Support Infrastructure for Smart Kindergarten," *Pervasive Computing,* 1(2) April–June, 2002, pp. 49–57.

Cohen, A., "Off-Site, Online," *PC Magazine,* Sept, 17, 2002, *pcmag.com/article2/0,4149,481823,00.asp* (accessed May 2004).

Conrad, D., "Medlink to the Rescue," March 11, 2002, *alaskasworld.com/news/2002/03/11_MedLink.asp* (accessed June 2003).

Coursaris, C., and H., Hassanein, "Understanding M-Commerce: A Consumer-Centric Model," *Quarterly Journal of Electronic Commerce,* 3(3), July–September 2002, pp. 247–271.

Davies, N., and H. W., Gellersen, "Beyond Prototyping: Challenges in Deploying Ubiquitous Systems," *Pervasive Computing,* January–March 2002 available at *ee.oulu.fi/~skidi/teaching/mobile_and_ubiquitous_multimedia_2002/beyond_prototypes_challenges.pdf* (accessed May 2004).

Davies, N., et al., "Future Wireless Applications for a Networked City," *IEEE Wireless Communications,* February 2002.

Deans, P. C., *E-Commerce and M-Commerce Technologies*. Hershey, PA: IRM Press, 2004.

Dogac, A., and A. Tumer, "Issues in Mobile Electronic Commerce," *Journal of Database Management*, January–February 2002.

DPS-Promatic, "Innovative Pay-by-GSM Meter." 2002, *dpspro.com/tcs_news_park.html,* (accessed May 2004).

Duan, M. "Enhancing the Shopping Experience, One $2,000 Suit at a Time," *Mpulse Magazine,* November 2002, *cooltown.hp.com/mpulse/1102-prada.asp* (accessed June 2003).

Dunne, D., "What Is 3G Technology?" *Darwin Magazine,* October 18, 2001, *darwinmag.com/learn/curve/column.html?ArticleID=182* (accessed May 2004).

Edgington, C., "How Internet Gateways and Smart Appliances Will Transform Our Homes," *TNTY Futures,* 1(6), 2001, *tnty.com/newsletter/futures/technology.html* (accessed May 2004).

Eklund, B., "Wireless Advertising's Home of the Free," *RedHerring.com,* March 6, 2001, *redherring.com/Article.aspx?a=1294* (accessed May 2004).

Eklund, R., "Mobile CRM Comes of Age," *CRM Magazine.* July 15, 2002, *destinationcrm.com/articles/default.asp?ArticleID=2352* (accessed May 2004).

elite-care.com (accessed May 2004).

Ellison, C., "Palm Sees Uptick in Development of Mobile Enterprise Applications," *e-Week*, May 18, 2004.

Estrada, M., "Bridging the Wireless Gap," *Knowledgestorm: The Upshot,* October 2002, *knowledgestorm.com/info/user_newsletter/092402/wireless.jsp* (accessed May 2004).

Estrin, D., et al., "Embedding the Internet," *Communications of the ACM*, 43(5), May 2000, pp. 38–42.

Fleck, M., et al., "From Informing to Remembering: Ubiquitous Systems in Interactive Museums," *Pervasive Computing,* April–June 2002, *computer.org/pervasive/pc2002/b2013abs.htm* (accessed June 2003).

Fusco, P., "Get the Picture?," December 17, 2003, *internetnews.com/bus-news/article.php/3289711* (accessed May 2004).

Global Mobile Suppliers Association (GSA), "Survey of Mobile Portal Services," Quarter 4, 2002, *gsacom.com/downloads/MPSQ4_2002.pdf* (accessed May 2004).

Hamblen, M., "Get Payback on Wireless," *Computer World*, January 1, 2001, *computerworld.com/mobiletopics/mobile/story/0,10801,54798,00.html* (accessed May 2004).

hertz.com (accessed May 2003).

Henning, T., "Wireless Imaging," *The Future Image Report*. 2002.

Hill, K., "Mobile CRM Software: The Race Is On," *CRM Daily*, December 3, 2002, *wireless.newsfactor.com/story.xhtml?story_id=20135* (accessed May 2004).

Hornberger, M., and C. Kehlenbeck, "Mobile Financial Services On The Rise In Europe," September 19, 2002, *banktech.com/story/wireless/BNK20020919S0005* (accessed May 2004).

Houck, J., "For Hotel Check-in, Press 1 Now," *Wireless News Factor*, February 15, 2001.

Hunter, R., *World without Secrets: Business, Crime, and Privacy in the Age of Ubiquitous Computing*. New York: Wiley, 2002.

Intel, "Building the Foundation for Anytime Anywhere Computing," White Paper 25 1290–002 Intel Corporation, June 13, 2002, *intel.com/eBusiness/it/management/pp022402_sum.htm* (accessed June 2003).

Intermec.com, "U.S. Fleet Services Refuels America's Commercial Fleets Using Intermec 710 Mobile Computer," December 18, 2001, *home.intermec.com/eprise/main/Intermec/Content/About/NewsPages/pressRelease?section=about&pressID=339* (accessed May 2004).

International Telecommunications Union, "Challenges to the Network: Internet for Development," October 1999, *itu.int/ITU-D/ict/publications/inet/1999/chal_exsum.pdf* (accessed June 2003).

Ishida, T., "Digital City Kyoto," *Communications of the ACM*, 45(7), July 2002a, pp. 76–81.

Ishida, T. (ed.), *Understanding Digital Cities: Cross Cultural Perspective*. Cambridge MA: MIT Press, 2002b.

Islam, N., and M. Fayad, "Toward Ubiquitous Acceptance of Ubiquitous Computing," *Communications of the ACM*, February 2003.

ITS America, "NextBus Expands Real-Time Transit Information in the Bay Area with AC Transit," August 9, 2001, *itsa.org/ITSNEWS.NSF/0/34c13fd8352c4c3f85256aa400497aad?OpenDocument* (accessed May 2004).

Jiang, X., and J. A. Landay, "Modeling Privacy Control in Context-Aware Systems," *Pervasive Computing*, July–Sept. 2002.

Jones, J., "A Moving Target," *FCW.com*, May 21, 2004.

Jones, W. D., "Keeping Cars from Crashing," *IEEE Spectrum*, 38(9), September 2001, pp. 40–45.

Judge, P., "Wi-Fi Switch Security Nothing but a White Elephant," *security.itworld.com*, May 14, 2004.

Kalakota, R., and M. Robinson, *E-Businesses: Roadmap for Success*. Reading, MA: Addison Wesley, 2001.

Kellner, M., "Is This the Year for Wireless Gear?" *GCN*, January 27, 2003, *gcn.com/22_2/buyers_guide/20950–1.html* (accessed June 2003).

Kharif, O., "Like It or Not, RFID Is Coming," *Business Week Online*, March 18, 2004.

Kontzer, T., "Top Ten Uses for SMS," *Information Week*, June 11, 2003, *informationweek.com/techcenters/networking/wireless* (accessed June 2003).

Kridel, T., "30 Mobile Miracles for Today and Tomorrow," *Laptop*, April 24, 2003, available at *bluetooth.com/news/news.asp?A=2&PID=689* (accessed June 2003).

Kumagai, J., "Talk to the Machine," *IEEE Spectrum*, 39(9), September 2002, pp. 60–64, *ieeexplore.ieee.org/xpl/abs_free.jsp?orNumber=1030970ddl.co.uk/newsevents/press/articles/200209(talktothemachine).pdf* (accessed May 2004).

Le Gal, C., et al., "Smart Office: Design of an Intelligent Environment," *IEEE Intelligent Systems*, 16(4), July–August, 2001, pp. 60–66.

Lipset, V., "Bluefish and Zaryba Enable Mobile Bill Payment," *MCommerce Times*, January 21, 2003, *mcommercetimes.com/Solutions/309* (accessed June 2003).

Lipset, V., "Magex Launches Mobile Payments Using SMS," *MCommerce Times*, December 3, 2002, *mcommercetimes.com/Solutions/299* (accessed June 2003).

Ludorf, C., "U.S. Fleet Services and Wireless Networking," *Transportation and Technology Today*, August 2002.

Mankins, M., "The Digital Sign in the Wired City," *IEEE Wireless Communication*, February 2002.

Martin, J. A., "Mobile Computing: Hertz In-Car GPS," *PC World*, March 13, 2003, *pcworld.com/howto/article/0,aid,109560,00.asp* (accessed June 2003).

Mathieson, R., "The Future According to Spielberg: Minority Report and the World of Ubiquitous Computing," *MPulse*. August, 2002, *cooltown.com/mpulse/0802-minorityreport.asp* (accessed May 2004).

Mayor, M., "Bluetooth App Slams Door on Hotel Room Keys," *Wireless NewsFactor*, April 4, 2001, *wirelessnewsfactor.com/perl/story/8704.html* (accessed May 2004).

Mennecke, B. E., and T. J. Strader, *Mobile Commerce: Technology, Theory and Applications*, Hershey, PA.: Idea Group Publishing, 2003.

Moore, J. F., "The Race to Put the Web into Cars," *Business 2.0*, Dec. 6, 2000, *business2.com/b2/web/articles/0,17863,530182,00.html* (accessed May 2004).

Mobileinfo.com, 2002. "Wireless Application Protocol–WAP: Future Outlook for WAP," *mobileinfo.com/WAP/future_outlook.htm*, 2001 (accessed June 2003).

Murphy, P., "Running Late? Take the NextBus," *Environmental News Network*, September 7, 1999, *enn.com/enn-features-archive/1999/09/090799/nextbus_4692.asp* (accessed May 2004).

Needleman, R., "Targeted Wi-Fi," *Business 2.0*, December 2002, *business2.com/b2/web/articles/0,17863,532732,00.html* (accessed May 2004).

Nelson, M., "Wireless Photos Speed Damage Claims: Kemper Insurance Uses Wireless Digital Imaging to Lower Costs, Streamline Process," *InformationWeek*, September 25, 2000, *informationweek.com/805/photo.htm* (accessed May 2004). *nextbus.com* (accessed May 2004).

Nokia, "Nokia Brings Mobility to the Games Industry by Making Rich Games Mobile.," November 4, 2002 *nokia-asia.com/apc/about_nokia/press/0,5854,36_2_71,00.html* (accessed May 2004).

Null, C., et al., "Building the Unwired Workplace," *Mobile PC*, June 2004.

Perry, R., "Wireless Fidelity," *Technology Review*, September 2003.

Pinto, J., "The Pervasive Internet & Its Effect on Industrial Automation," *AutomationTechies.com*, November 2002, *jimpinto.com/writings/pervasive.html* (accessed May 2004).

Pitkow, J., et al., "Personalized Search," *Communications of the ACM*, 45(9), September 2002, pp. 50–55.

Poropudas, T., "ATM Connection to Boost Mobile Payments," *Mobile CommerceNet*, February 15, 2003.

Raina, K., and A. Harsh, *MCommerce Security*. New York: Osborne, 2002.

Raskin, A.,"Your Ad Could Be Here! (And Now We Can Tell You Who Will See It)," *Business 2.0*, May 2003, *business2.com/b2b/web/articles/0,17863,515629,00.html* (accessed May 2004).

Republica IT, "Busta Paga in Pensione Lo Stipendio Arriva Via Sms," March 20, 2001, *repubblica.it/online/tecnologie_internet/tim/tim/tim.html* (accessed May 2004).

Reuters, "Marriott Hotels to Offer Wi-Fi Access," News.com, December 18, 2002, *news.com.com/2100-1033-978411.html* (accessed May 2004).

RFID Journal, "Gillette to Buy 500 Million EPC Tags," November 15, 2002, *216.121.131.129/article/articleprint/115/-1/1/* (accessed May 2004).

Rosencrance, L., "Update: Benetton Backs away from 'Smart Tags' in Clothing Line," *Computer World*, April 4, 2003, *computerworld.com/industrytopics/retail/story/0,10801,80061,00.html* (accessed May 2004).

Rupp, W. T., and A. D. Smith, "Mobile Commerce: New Revenue Machine, or a Black Hole?" *Business Horizons*, July–August, 2002.

Ryan, T., "RFID in the Consumer Industries," Research Report, Aberdeen Group, March 2004.

Sadeh, N., *M-Commerce*. New York: Wiley, 2002.

Sanford, V., "Wearable Computing Goes Live in Industry," *IEEE Pervasive Computing*, October–December 2004.

SAP AG Corp., "CRM and the mySAP.com Mobile Workplace," (a publicly available brochure), 2000.

Sarkar, D., "Lawmakers Form 911 Caucus," *Federal Computer Week*, February 25, 2003, *fcw.com/fcw/articles/2003/0224/web-caucus-02-25-03.asp* (accessed May 2004).

Sarshar, A., "How Do 'Dot-Net,' Mobile Computing and PDAs Contribute to Your Bottom Line?" *Knowledgestorm: The Upshot*, February 2003, *knowledgestorm.com/info/user_newsletter/022003/geneva.jsp* (accessed May 2004).

Scanlon, J., "The Way We Work," special Wired Report, *Wired*, May, 2003, *wired.com/wired/archive/11.05/unwired* (accessed May 2004).

Sharke, P., "Smart Cars," Mechanical Engineering, May 2003, *memagazine.org/contents/current/features/smartcar/smartcar.html* (accessed May 2004).

Shi, N., *Wireless Communications and Mobile Commerce*. Hershey, PA: Idea Group Publishing, 2004.

Spivey-Overby, "RFID at What Cost? What Wal-Mart Compliance Really Means," ForrTel (Webcast plus telephone), Forrester Research, May 25, 2004, 11 A.M.

Stafford, A., and A. Brandt, "The No-Hassle Networking Guide," *PC World* (accessed May 2002).

Stanford, V., "Using Technology to Empower Assisted Living Patients," *Healthcare Review*, July 2, 2000.

Stanford, V., "Pervasive Computing Goes to Work: Interfacing to the Enterprise," *Pervasive Computing*, 1(3), July–September 2002, pp. 6–12, *ee.oulu.fi/~skidi/teaching/mobile_and_ubiquitous_ multimedia_2002/pervasive_computing_goes_to_work.pdf* (accessed May 2004).

Steede-Terry, K., *Integrating GIS and the Global Positioning System*. Redlands, CA: Environmental Systems Research Institute, 2000.

Sybase.com, "Clayton I.D.S and Washington/Norwich Township Fire Departments," Sybase Inc., *sybase.com/detail/1,6904,1023367,00.html* (accessed June 2003).

Symbol.com, "CVS Selects Symbol's Wireless Network System, Hand-Held Computers, June 3, 1998, *symbol.com/news/pressreleases/cvs.html* (accessed June 2003).

Taj Hotel, "Taj Hotels Introduce WiFi Facilities," *The Hindu*. July 31, 2002, *thehindu.com/2002/07/31/stories/2002073102321600.htm* (accessed June 2003).

Tech Live Staff, "Future of Mobile Commerce Murky," techtv.com, November 2, 2001, *techtv.com/news/internet/story/0,24195,3357949,00.html* (accessed May 2004).

Varshney, U., and R. Vetter, "Recent Advances in Wireless Networking," *IEEE Computer*, 33(6), June 2000, pp. 107–109.

Weise, E., "Laundry Spins on the High Tech Cycle," *USA Today*, September 3, 2002, *usatoday.com/tech/techreviews/products/2002-09-02-wired-washers_x.htm* (accessed June 2003).

Weiser, M., "The Computer for the Twenty-First Century," *Scientific American*, September 1991. Reprinted in *Pervasive Computing*, January–March, 2002, available at *ubiq.com/hypertext/weiser/SciAmDraft3.html* (accessed May 2004).

Wired, "Get Wireless," Special Wired Report. Supplement to *Wired*, May 2003 (11 articles), *wired.com/wired/current.html* (accessed May 2004).

XyberFlash, "Wearable Computers for the Working Class," *New York Times*, December 14, 2000.

Xybernaut.com, "Xybernaut Mobile Assistant: Productivity Gains in the Telecommunication Field," *xybernaut.com/case_studies/PDFs/Telecommunication_CS.pdf* (accessed June 2003).

Yankee Group, "Wireless Advertising: Still Waiting for Takeoff." October 30, 2002. *yankeegroup.com/public/products/research_note.jsp?ID=8907* (accessed June 2003).

Zhao, Y., "Telematics: Safe and Fun Driving," *IEEE Intelligent Systems*, 17(1), January/February 2002, pp. 10–14. *ce.unipr.it/people/broggi/publications/si-its-01-2002.pdf* (accessed May 2004).

PART III
Organizational Applications

▶ 6. Transaction Processing, Functional Applications, and Integration
7. Enterprise Systems: From Supply Chains to ERP to CRM
8. Interorganizational and Global Information Systems

CHAPTER

6

Transaction Processing, Functional Applications, and Integration

6.1 Functional Information Systems

6.2 Transaction Processing Information Systems

6.3 Managing Production/Operations and Logistics

6.4 Managing Marketing and Sales Systems

6.5 Managing the Accounting and Finance Systems

6.6 Managing Human Resources Systems

6.7 Integrating Functional Information Systems

Minicases:
1. Dollar General
2. 99 Cents Only Stores

LEARNING OBJECTIVES

After studying this chapter, you will be able to:

❶ Relate functional areas and business processes to the value chain model.

❷ Identify functional management information systems.

❸ Describe the transaction processing system and demonstrate how it is supported by IT.

❹ Describe the support provided by IT and the Web to production/operations management, including logistics.

❺ Describe the support provided by IT and the Web to marketing and sales.

❻ Describe the support provided by IT and the Web to accounting and finance.

❼ Describe the support provided by IT and the Web to human resources management.

❽ Describe the benefits and issues of integrating functional information systems.

WIRELESS INVENTORY MANAGEMENT SYSTEM AT DARTMOUTH-HITCHCOCK MEDICAL CENTER

➡ THE PROBLEM

Dartmouth-Hitchcock Medical Center (DHMC) is a large medical complex in New Hampshire with hospitals, a medical school, and over 600 practicing physicians in its many clinics. DHMC is growing rapidly and is encountering a major problem in the distribution of medical supplies. These supplies used to be ordered by nurses. But nurses are usually in short supply, so having nurses spending valuable time ordering supplies left them less time for their core competency—nursing. Furthermore, having nurses handling supply orders led to inventory management problems: Busy nurses tended to overorder in an effort to spend less time managing inventory. On the other hand, they frequently waited until the last minute to order supplies, which led to costly rush orders.

One solution would have been to transfer the task of inventory ordering and management to other staff, but doing so would have required hiring additional personnel and the DHMC was short on budget. Also, the coordination with the nurses to find what was needed and when, as well as maintaining the stock, would have been cumbersome.

What the medical center needed was a solution that would reduce the burden on the nurses, but also reduce the inventory levels and the last-minute, expensive ordering. Given the size of the medical center, and the fact that there are over 27,000 different inventory items, this was not a simple task.

➡ THE SOLUTION

DHMC realized that their problem was related to the supply chain, and so it looked to IT for solutions. The idea the DHMC chose was to connect wireless hand-held devices with a purchasing and inventory management information system. Here is how the new system works (as of the summer of 2002): The medical center has a wireless LAN (Wi-Fi) into which hand-helds are connected. Information about supplies then can be uploaded and downloaded from the devices to the network from anywhere within the range of the Wi-Fi. In remote clinics without Wi-Fi, the hand-helds are docked into wire-line network PCs.

For each item in stock a "par level" (the level at which supplies must be reordered) was established, based on actual usage reports and in collaboration between the nurses and the materials management staff. Nurses simply scan an item when it is consumed, and the software automatically adjusts the recorded inventory level. When a par level is reached for any inventory item, an order to the supplier is generated automatically. Similarly, when the inventory level at each nursing station dips below the station's par level, a shipment is arranged from the central supply room to that nursing station. The system also allows for nurses to make restocking requests, which can be triggered by scanning an item. The system works for the supplies of all non-nursing departments as well (e.g., human resources or accounting). Overall, the Wi-Fi system includes over 27,000 line items.

The system is integrated with other applications from the same vendor (PeopleSoft Inc.). One such application is Express PO, which enables purchasing managers to review standing purchase orders, e-procurement, and contract management.

THE RESULTS

Inventory levels were reduced by 50 percent, paying for the system in just a few months. Materials purchasing and management now are consistent across the enterprise, the time spent by nurses on tracking materials has been drastically reduced, and access to current information has been improved. All of this contributed to reduced costs and improved patient care.

Sources: Compiled from Grimes (2003), and *peoplesoft.com* (accessed March 31, 2003).

LESSONS LEARNED FROM THIS CASE

The DHMC case provides some interesting observations about implementing IT: First, IT can support the routine processes of inventory management, enabling greater efficiency, more focus on core competencies, and greater satisfaction for employees and management. The new system also helped to modernize and re-design some of the center's business processes (e.g., distribution, procurement), and was able to support several business processes (e.g., operations, finance, and accounting), not just one. Although the system's major application is in inventory management, the same software vendor provided ready-made modules, which were *integrated* with the inventory module and with each other (for example, with purchasing and contract management). The integration also included connection to suppliers, using the Internet. This IT solution has proven useful for an organization whose business processes cross the traditional functional departmental lines. (In this case nursing is considered operations/production; inventory control, purchasing, and contract management are in the finance/accounting area.)

To offer service in the digital economy, companies must continuously upgrade their functional information systems by using state-of-the-art technology. Furthermore, the functional processes must be improved as needed. Finally, as we will show in Chapter 7, supply chain software is needed in some segments of the supply chain. These segments may include functional information systems.

Functional information systems get much of their data from the systems that process routine transactions (*transaction processing systems, TPSs*). Also, many applications in business intelligence, e-commerce, CRM, and other areas use data and information from two or more functional information systems. Therefore, there is a need to integrate the functional systems applications among themselves, with the TPS, and with other applications. These relationships are shown in Figure 6.1 (page 247), which provides a pictorial view of the topics discussed in this chapter. (Not shown in the figure are applications discussed in other chapters, such as e-commerce and knowledge management.)

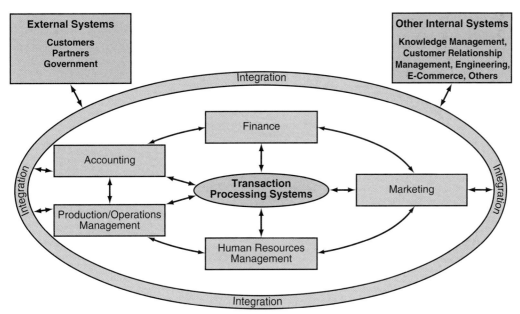

FIGURE 6.1 The functional areas, TPS, and integration connection. Note the flow of information from the TPS to the functional systems. Flow of information between and among functional systems is done via the integration component. (Not shown in the figure are applications discussed in other chapters, such as CRM, e-commerce, and knowledge management.)

6.1 FUNCTIONAL INFORMATION SYSTEMS

The major functional areas in many companies are the production/operations, marketing, human resources, accounting and finance departments. (See the value chain model in Chapter 12 for their role.) Traditionally, information systems were designed within each functional area, to support the area by increasing its internal effectiveness and efficiency. However, as we will discuss in Chapter 7, the traditional functional hierarchical structure may not be the best structure for some organizations, because certain business processes involve activities that are performed in several functional areas. Suppose a customer wants to buy a particular product. When the customer's order arrives at the marketing department, the customer's credit needs to be approved by Finance. Someone (usually in the production/operations area) checks to find if the product is in the warehouse. If it is there, then someone needs to pack the product and forward it to Shipping, which arranges for delivery. Accounting prepares a bill for the customer, and Finance may arrange for shipping insurance. The flow of work and information between the different departments may not work well, creating delays or poor customer service.

One possible solution is to restructure the organization. For example, the company can create cross-functional teams, each responsible for performing a complete business process. Then, it is necessary to create appropriate information systems applications for the restructured processes. As we will discuss in Chapter 14, this arrangement can be a difficult-to-implement solution. In other cases, the company can use IT to create minor changes in the business

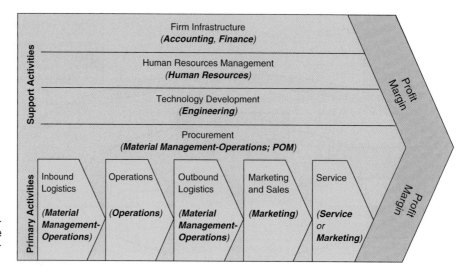

FIGURE 6.2 Typical functional areas mapped on the value chain of a manufacturing company.

processes and organizational structure, but this solution may not solve problems such as lack of coordination or an ineffective supply chain. One other remedy may be an *integrated approach* that keeps the functional departments as they are, but creates an integrated supportive information system to help communication, coordination, and control. The integrated approach is discussed in Section 6.7.

Before we demonstrate how IT facilitates the work of the functional areas, and makes possible their integration, we need to see how they are organized and how they relate to the corporate value chain and the supply chain.

Porter's Value Chain Model and the Supply Chain

The *value chain* model, introduced in Appendix 1A, views activities in organizations as either primary (reflecting the flow of goods and services) or secondary (supporting the primary activities). The organizational structure of firms is intended to support both of these types of activities. Figure 6.2 maps the major *functional departments* onto the value chain structure (both as primary and support activities).

As described in Chapter 2, the *supply chain* is a business process that links all the procurement from suppliers, the transformation activities inside a firm, and the distribution of goods or services to customers via wholesalers and retailers. In this chapter we present innovative applications that increase mainly internal functional efficiency, and we provide examples of improved communication and collaboration with customers and business partners as a result of these applications. First, let us examine the characteristics of functional information systems.

Major Characteristics of Functional Information Systems

Functional information systems share the following characteristics:

- *Composed of smaller systems.* A functional information system consists of several smaller information systems that support specific activities performed in the functional area.
- *Integrated or independent.* The specific IS applications in any functional area can be integrated to form a coherent departmental functional system, or they

can be completely independent. Alternatively, some of the applications within each area can be integrated across departmental lines to match a business process.

- **Interfacing.** Functional information systems may interface with each other to form the organization-wide information system. Some functional information systems interface with the environment outside the organization. For example, a human resources information system can collect data about the labor market.

- **Supportive of different levels.** Information systems applications support the three levels of an organization's activities: *operational, managerial,* and *strategic* (see Chapter 2).

A model of the IS applications in the production/operations area is provided in Online File W6.1. Other functional information systems have a similar basic structure.

In this chapter we describe IT applications in some of the key primary and support areas of the value chain. However, since information systems applications receive much of the data that they process from the corporate *transaction processing system,* we deal with this system first.

6.2 TRANSACTION PROCESSING INFORMATION SYSTEMS

The core operations of organizations are enabled by transaction processing systems.

Computerization of Routine Transaction Processes

In every organization there are business transactions that provide its mission-critical activities. Such transactions occur when a company produces a product or provides a service. For example, to produce toys, a manufacturer needs to buy materials and parts, pay for labor and electricity, build the toys, ship them to customers, bill customers, and collect money. A bank that maintains the toy company's checking account must keep the account balance up-to-date, disperse funds to back up the checks written, accept deposits, and mail a monthly statement.

Every transaction may generate additional transactions. For example, purchasing materials will change the inventory level, and paying an employee reduces the corporate cash on hand. Because the computations involved in most transactions are simple and the transaction volume is large and repetitive, such transactions are fairly easy to computerize.

The *transaction processing system* (TPS) monitors, collects, stores, processes, and disseminates information for all routine core business transactions. These data are input to functional information systems applications, as well as to decision support systems (DSSs), customer relationship management (CRM), and knowledge management (KM). The TPS also provides critical data to e-commerce, especially data on customers and their purchasing history.

Transaction processing occurs in all functional areas. Some TPSs occur within one area, others cross several areas (such as payroll). Online File W6.2 provides a list of TPS activities by the major functional areas. The information systems that automate transaction processing can be part of the departmental systems, and/or part of the enterprisewide information systems. For a

---

TABLE 6.1 The Major Characteristics of a TPS

- Typically, *large amounts of data* are processed.
- The *sources of data are mostly internal,* and the output is intended mainly for an *internal audience.* This characteristic is changing somewhat, since trading partners may contribute data and may be permitted to use TPS output directly.
- The TPS processes information on a *regular basis:* daily, weekly, biweekly, and so on.
- *Large storage (database) capacity* is required.
- *High processing speed* is needed due to the high volume.
- The TPS basically *monitors and collects past data.*
- Input and output *data are structured.* Since the processed data are fairly stable, they are formatted in a standard fashion.
- A *high level of detail* (raw data, not summarized) is usually observable, especially in input data but often in output as well.
- *Low computation complexity* (simple mathematical and statistical operations) is usually evident in a TPS.
- A high level of *accuracy, data integrity, and security* is needed. Sensitive issues such as privacy of personal data are strongly related to TPSs.
- *High reliability* is required. The TPS can be viewed as the lifeblood of the organization. Interruptions in the flow of TPS data can be fatal to the organization.
- *Inquiry processing* is a must. The TPS enables users to query files and databases (even online and in real time).

---

comprehensive coverage of TPSs, see Subrahmanyam (2002) and Bernstein and Newcomer (1997).

Objectives of TPS

The primary goal of a TPS is to provide all the information needed by law and/or by organizational policies to keep the business running properly and efficiently. Specifically, a TPS has to efficiently handle high volume, avoid errors due to concurrent operations, be able to handle large variations in volume (e.g., during peak times), avoid downtime, never lose results, and maintain privacy and security (see Bernstein and Newcomer, 1997). To meet these goals, a TPS is usually automated and is constructed with the major characteristics listed in Table 6.1

Specific objectives of a TPS may include one or more of the following: to allow for efficient and effective operation of the organization, to provide timely documents and reports, to increase the competitive advantage of the corporation, to provide the necessary data for tactical and strategic systems such as Web-based applications, to ensure accuracy and integrity of data and information, and to safeguard assets and security of information. It also is important to remember that TPSs must closely interface with many IT initiatives, especially with e-payment, e-procurement, and e-marketing.

Activities and Methods of TPS

Regardless of the specific data processed by a TPS, a fairly standard process occurs, whether in a manufacturer, in a service firm, or in a government organization. First, data are collected by people or sensors and entered into the computer via any input device. Generally speaking, organizations try to automate the TPS data entry as much as possible because of the large volume involved.

Next, the system processes data in one of two basic ways: *batch* or *online processing.* In **batch processing,** the firm collects data from transactions as they occur, storing them in groups or batches. The system then prepares and processes the batches periodically (say, every night). Batch processing is particularly useful

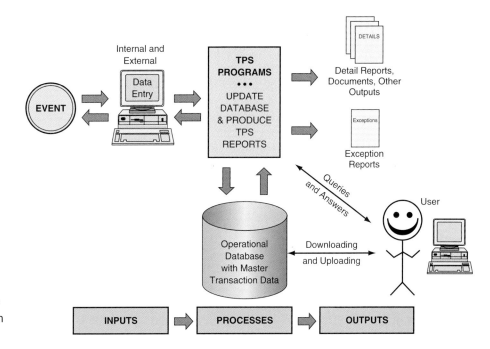

FIGURE 6.3 The flow of information in transaction processing.

for operations that require processing for an extended period of time. Once a batch job begins, it continues until it is completed or until an error occurs. In **online processing,** data are processed as soon as a transaction occurs, possibly even in real time (instantly).

To implement online transaction processing, *master files* containing key information about important business entities are placed on hard drives, where they are directly accessible. The *transaction files* containing information about activities concerning these business entities, such as orders placed by customers, are also held in online files until they are no longer needed for everyday transaction processing activity. This ensures that the transaction data are available to all applications, and that all data are kept up-to-the-minute. These data can also be processed and stored in a data warehouse (Chapter 10). The entire process is managed by a *transaction manager* (see Subrahmanyam, 2002, for details).

The flow of information in a typical TPS is shown in Figure 6.3. An event, such as a customer purchase, is recorded by the TPS program. The processed information can be either a report or an activity in the database. In addition to a scheduled report, users can query the TPS for nonscheduled information (such as, "What was the impact of our price cut on sales during the first five days, by day?"). The system will provide the appropriate answer by accessing a database containing transaction data.

Web-Based and Online Transaction Processing Systems

Transaction processing systems may be fairly complex, involving customers, vendors, telecommunications, and different types of hardware and software. Traditional TPSs are centralized and run on a mainframe. However, innovations such as online transaction processing require a client/server architecture. In **online transaction processing (OLTP),** transactions are processed as soon as they occur. For example, when you pay for an item at a POS at a store, the system records the effects of the sale by reducing the inventory on hand by a unit, increasing the store's cash position by the amount you paid, and increasing sales figures for the item by one unit. A relatively new form of Web-based transaction processing is *object-oriented transaction processing,* which is described in Online File W6.3.

With OLTP and Web technologies such as an extranet, suppliers can look at the firm's inventory level or production schedule in *real time*. The suppliers themselves, in partnership with their customers, can then assume responsibility for inventory management and ordering. Such Web-based systems would be especially useful in processing orders involving several medium-to-large business partners. Customers too can enter data into the TPS to track orders and even query it directly, as described in *IT at Work 6.1*.

WEB-BASED INTERACTIVE TRANSACTION PROCESSING. Rather than isolated exchanges of simple text and data over private networks, such as traditional EDI and EFT, transactions are increasingly conducted over the Internet and intranets

---

IT at Work 6.1
MODERNIZING THE TPS CUTS DELIVERY TIME AND SAVES MONEY

Here are some examples of how modernizing transaction processing systems has saved time and/or money:

KINKO'S. Each time you make a copy at Kinko's, a copying transaction and a payment transaction occur. In the past you received a device (a card, the size of a credit card) and inserted it into a control device attached to the copy machine, and it recorded the number of copies that you made. Then you stood in line to pay: The cashier placed the device in a reader to see how many copies were made. Your bill was computed, with tax added. Kinko's cost was high in this system, and some customers were unhappy about standing in line to pay for only a few copies. Today, using Kinko's new system, you insert your credit card (or a stored-value card purchased from a machine) into a control device, make the copies, print a receipt, and go home. You no longer need to see a Kinko's employee to complete your purchase.

CARNIVAL LINE. Carnival Line, the operator of cruise ships, needs to rapidly process sometimes over 2,500 people leaving the ship at the ports of call, and later returning to the ship. The company used to use printed name lists with room for checkmarks. Today, passengers place a smart card into a reader. This way the company knows who left the ship and when, and who returns. Each smart-card reader can process over 1,000 people in 30 minutes. In the past it was necessary to use 10–15 employees to process the people leaving and

returning to the ship, and it took almost an hour. Today, one person supervises two card readers for less than 30 minutes.

CALIFORNIA DEPARTMENT OF MOTOR VEHICLES. The California DMV processes 14 million vehicle registration fees each year. To smooth the process, the DMV is using a rule-based expert system that calculates the fees (see *blazesoft.com* for details).

UPS STORE. Seconds after you enter an address and a Zip code into a terminal at UPS delivery outlets at a UPS Store, a shipping label and a receipt are generated. Your shipping record stays in the database, so if you send another package to the same person, you do not need to repeat the address again.

SPRINT INC. Using an object-oriented approach, Sprint Inc. has improved its order processing for new telephones. In the past it took a few days for a customer to get a new telephone line; with its new system, Sprint can process an order in only a few hours. The order application itself takes less than 10 minutes, experiences fewer errors, and can be executed on electronic forms on a salesperson's desktop or laptop computer.

For Further Exploration: Could Kinko's operate without employees at their outlets? What effect does Carnival's smart-card reader have on security? Whose time is being saved at UPS and Sprint?

in a more complex manner. As a result, OLTP has broadened to become *interactive Internet TPS*. Internet transaction processing software and servers allow multimedia data transfer, fast response time, and storage of large amount of graphics and video—all in real time and at low cost. The interactivity feature allows for easy and fast response to queries. OLTP also offers flexibility to accommodate unpredictable growth in processing demand (scalability) and timely search and analysis of large databases. Companies that accept and process large number of orders, such as Dell Computer, tend to have a sophisticated Web-based ordering system.

Typical Tasks in Transaction Processing

Transaction processing exists in all functional areas. In later sections (6.3 through 6.6) we will describe the key TPS activities in major functional areas. Here we describe in some detail one application that crosses several functional areas—order processing.

ORDER PROCESSING. Orders for goods and/or services may flow from customers to a company by phone, on paper, or electronically. Fast and effective order processing is recognized as a key to customer satisfaction. Orders can also be internal—from one department to another. Once orders arrive, an order processing system needs to receive, document, route, summarize, and store the orders. A computerized system can also track sales by product, by zone, or by salesperson, providing sales or marketing information that may be useful to the organization. As described in Chapters 4 and 5, more and more companies are providing systems for their salespeople that enable them to enter orders from a business customer's site using wireless notebook computers, PDAs, or Web-enabled cell phones. Some companies spend millions of dollars reengineering their order processing as part of their transformation to e-business (e.g., see Siemens case, Chapter 1). IBM, for example, restructured its procurement system so its own purchasing orders are generated quickly and inexpensively in its e-procurement system.

Orders can be for services as well as for products. Otis Elevator Company, for example, tracks orders for elevator repair. The processing of repair orders is done via wireless devices that allow effective communication between repair crews and Otis physical facilities. Orders also can be processed by using innovative IT technologies such as global positioning systems; see *IT at Work 6.2* (page 254).

OTHER TPS ACTIVITIES. Other typical TPS activities are summarized in Table 6.2 (page 255). Most of these routine tasks are computerized.

Transaction Processing Software

There are dozens of commercial TPS software products on the market. Many are designed to support Internet transactions. (See a sampler of TPS software products and vendors in Online File W6.4.)

The problem, then, is how to evaluate so many software packages. In Chapter 14, there is a discussion on software selection that applies to TPS as well. But the selection of a TPS software product has some unique features. Therefore, one organization, the Transaction Processing Performance Council (*tpc.org*), has been trying to assist in this task. This organization is conducting *benchmarking* for TPS. It checks hardware vendors, database vendors, middleware vendors, and so forth. Recently it started to evaluate e-commerce transactions (*tpc.org/tpcw;* there, see "transactional Web e-commerce benchmark"). Also, the organization has several decision support benchmarks (e.g., TPC-H, and TPC-R).

IT at Work 6.2

AUTOMATIC VEHICLE LOCATION AND DISPATCH SYSTEM IN SINGAPORE

Taxis in Singapore are tracked by a *global positioning system (GPS)*, which is based on the 24 satellites originally set up by the U.S. government. The GPS allows its users to get an instant fix on the geographical position of each taxi (see figure below).

Here's how the system works: Customer orders are usually received via cell phone, regular telephone, fax, or e-mail. Customers can also dispatch taxis from special kiosks (called CabLink) located in shopping centers and hotels. Other booking options include portable taxi-order terminals placed in exhibition halls. Frequent users enter orders from their offices or homes by keying in a PIN number over the telephone. That number identifies the user automatically, together with his or her pickup point. Infrequent customers use an operator-assisted system.

The computerized ordering system is connected to the GPS. Once an order has been received, the GPS finds a vacant cab nearest the caller, and a display panel in the taxi alerts the driver to the pickup address. The driver has 10 seconds to push a button to accept the order. If he does not, the system automatically searches out the next-nearest taxi for the job.

The system completely reengineered taxi order processing. First, the transaction time for processing an order for a frequent user is much shorter, even during peak demand, since they are immediately identified. Second, taxi drivers are not able to pick and choose which trips they want to take, since the system will not provide the commuter's destination. This reduces the customer's average waiting time significantly, while minimizing the travel distance of empty taxis. The system increases the capacity for taking incoming calls by 1,000 percent, providing a competitive edge to those cab companies that use the system. It also reduces misunderstanding between drivers and dispatchers, and driver productivity increased since they utilize their time more efficiently. Finally, customers who use terminals do not have to wait a long time just to get a telephone operator (a situation that exists during rush hours, rain, or any other time of high demand for taxis). Three major taxi companies with about 50,000 taxis are connected to the system.

Source: Compiled from Liao (2003) and author's experience.

For Further Exploration: What tasks do computers execute in this order processing system? What kinds of priorities can be offered to frequent taxi customers?

Location tracking of taxicabs in Singapore

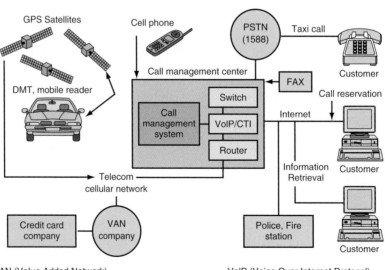

VAN (Value Added Network)
PSTN (Public Switched Telecommunication)

VoIP (Voice Over Internet Protocol)
CTI (Computer Telephone Integration)

TABLE 6.2 Typical TPS Activities	
Activities	Description
The ledger	The entire group of an organization's financial accounts. Contains all of the assets, liabilities, and owner's (stockholders') equity accounts.
Accounts payable and receivable	Records of all accounts to be paid and those owed by customers. Automated system can send reminder notes about overdue accounts.
Receiving and shipping records	Transaction records of all items sent or received, including returns.
Inventory-on-hand records	Records of inventory levels as required for inventory control and taxation. Use of barcodes improves ability to count inventory periodically.
Fixed-assets management	Records of the value of an organization's fixed assets (e.g., buildings, cars, machines), including depreciation rate and major improvements made in assets, for taxation purposes.
Payroll	All raw and summary payroll records.
Personnel files and skills inventory	Files of employees' history, evaluations, and record of training and performance.
Reports to government	Reports on compliance with government regulations, taxes, etc.
Other periodic reports and statements	Financial, tax, production, sales, and other routine reports.

6.3 MANAGING PRODUCTION/OPERATIONS AND LOGISTICS

The *production and operations management (POM)* function in an organization is responsible for the processes that transform inputs into useful outputs (see Figure 6.4). In comparison to the other functional areas, the POM area is very diversified and so are its supporting information systems. It also differs considerably among organizations. For example, manufacturing companies use completely different processes than do service organizations, and a hospital operates

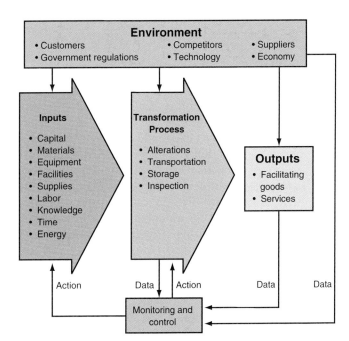

FIGURE 6.4 The production/operations management functions transform inputs into useful outputs. (*Source:* J. R. Meredith and S. M. Shafer, *Operations Management.* New York: Wiley, 2002. Reprinted by permission of John Wiley & Sons, Inc.)

much differently from a university. (Look again at Online File W6.1 for an example of the complexity of the POM field. Note that the internal interfaces are on the left and the external ones on the right.)

Because of the breadth and variety of POM functions, here we present four IT-supported POM topics: in-house logistics and materials management, planning production/operations, computer-integrated manufacturing (CIM), and product lifecycle management (PLM). A fifth topic, automating design work and manufacturing, is presented in Online File W6.5.

In-House Logistics and Materials Management

Logistics management deals with ordering, purchasing, inbound logistics (receiving), and outbound logistics (shipping) activities. In-house logistics activities are a good example of processes that cross several primary and support activities in the value chain. Both conventional purchasing and e-procurement result in incoming materials and parts. The materials received are inspected for quality and then stored. While the materials are in storage, they need to be maintained until distributed to those who need them. Some materials are disposed of when they become obsolete or their quality becomes unacceptable.

All of these activities can be supported by information systems (Robb, 2003). For example, many companies today are moving to some type of e-procurement (Chapter 4). Scanners and voice technologies, including wireless ones, can support inspection, and robots can perform distribution and materials handling. Large warehouses use robots to bring materials and parts from storage, whenever needed. The parts are stored in bins, and the bins are stacked one above the other (similar to the way safe deposit boxes are organized in banks). Whenever a part is needed, the storekeeper keys in the part number. The mobile robot travels to the part's "address," takes the bin out of its location (e.g., using magnetic force), and brings the bin to the storekeeper. Once a part is taken out of the bin, the robot is instructed to return the bin to its permanent location. In intelligent buildings in Japan, robots bring files to employees and return them for storage. In some hospitals, robots even dispense medicines.

INVENTORY MANAGEMENT. *Inventory management* determines how much inventory to keep. Overstocking can be expensive; so is keeping insufficient inventory. Three types of costs play important roles in inventory decisions: the cost of maintaining inventories, the cost of ordering (a fixed cost per order), and the cost of not having inventory when needed (the shortage or opportunity cost). The objective is to minimize the total of these costs.

Two basic decisions are made by operations: when to order, and how much to order. Inventory models, such as the economic order quantity (EOQ) model, support these decisions. Dozens of models exist, because inventory scenarios can be diverse and complex. A large number of commercial inventory software packages to automate the application of these models are available at low cost. For example, using DSS models in a Web-based system, more and more companies are improving their inventory management and replenishment, better meeting customers' demand (Amato-McCoy, 2002c).

Once management has made decisions about how much to order and when, an information system can track the level of inventory for each item that management wants to control. (Not every item needs such control. For example, items whose consumption is basically fixed, such as toilet paper or pencils, may not be closely controlled.) When the inventory falls to a certain level, called the *reorder point,* the computer automatically generates a purchase order. The order is transferred electronically either to a vendor or, if the item is manufactured in-house, to the manufacturing department.

Many large companies (such as Wal-Mart) allow their suppliers to monitor the inventory level and ship when needed, eliminating the need for sending purchasing orders. Such a strategy, in which the supplier monitors inventory levels and replenishes when needed, is called **vendor-managed inventory (VMI).** The monitoring can be done by using mobile agents over the Internet. It also can be done by using Web services, as Dell Computer is doing. In the near future this will be done with RFIDs (Chapter 7).

In Chapter 7 we demonstrate how IT and EC help in reducing inventories.

QUALITY CONTROL. Manufacturing quality-control systems can be standalone systems or can be part of an enterprisewide total quality management (TQM) effort. They provide information about the quality of incoming materials and parts, as well as the quality of in-process semifinished and finished products. Such systems record the results of all inspections. They also compare actual results to metrics.

Quality-control data may be collected by Web-based sensors and interpreted in real time, or they can be stored in a database for future analysis. Also, RFIDs can be used to collect data. Periodic reports are generated (such as percentage of defects, percentage of rework needed), and management can compare performance among departments on a regular basis or as needed.

Web-based quality control information systems are available from several vendors (e.g., HP and IBM) for executing standard computations such as preparing quality control charts. First, manufacturing data are collected for quality-control purposes by sensors and other instruments. After the data have been recorded, it is possible to use Web-based expert systems to make interpretations and recommend actions (e.g., to replace equipment).

Planning Production/ Operations

The POM planning in many firms is supported by IT. Some major areas of planning and their computerized support are described here.

MATERIAL REQUIREMENTS PLANNING (MRP). Inventory systems that use an EOQ approach are designed for those individual items for which demand is completely independent (for example, the number of chairs a furniture manufacturer will sell). However, in manufacturing systems, the demand for some items can be interdependent. For example, a company may make three types of chairs that all use the same legs, screws, and bolts. Thus, the demand for legs, screws, and bolts depends on the total demand for all three types of chairs and their shipment schedule.

The software that facilitates the plan for acquiring (or producing) parts, subassemblies, or materials in the case of interdependent items is called **material requirements planning (MRP).** MRP is computerized because of the complex interrelationship among many products and their components, and the need to change the plan each time that a delivery date or the order quantity is changed. Several MRP packages are commercially available.

MRP deals only with production scheduling and inventories. A more complex process will also involve allocation of related resources. In such a case, more complex, integrated software is available—MRP II.

MANUFACTURING RESOURCE PLANNING (MRP II). A POM system called **manufacturing resource planning (MRP II)** adds functionalities to a regular MRP. For example, in addition to the output similar to that of MRP, MRP II determines the costs of parts and the cash flow needed to pay for parts. It also estimates costs of labor, tools, equipment repair, and energy. Finally, it provides a detailed, computerized budget for the parts involved. Several MRP II software packages are commercially available. MRP II evolved to ERP, which is described in Chapter 7.

JUST-IN-TIME SYSTEMS. In mass customization and build-to-order production, the just-in-time concept is frequently used. **Just-in-time (JIT)** is an approach that attempts to minimize waste of all kinds (of space, labor, materials, energy, and so on) and to continuously improve processes and systems. For example, if materials and parts arrive at a workstation *exactly when needed,* there is no need for inventory, there are no delays in production, and there are no idle production facilities or underutilized workers. Many JIT systems are supported by software from vendors such as HP, IBM, CA, and Cincom Systems.

JIT systems have resulted in significant benefits. At Toyota, for example, benefits included reducing production cycle time from 15 days to 1 day, reducing cost by 30 to 50 percent, and achieving these cost savings while increasing quality. JIT is especially useful in supporting Web-based mass customization, as in the case of Dell Computer's model of assembling computers only after orders are received. To ship computers quickly, components and parts are provided just in time. As of 2001, car manufacturers were rapidly adopting a make-to-order process. To deliver customized cars quickly and with cost efficiency, manufacturers need a JIT system. Oracle, PeopleSoft, and other vendors offer a demand-driven *lean manufacturing*, which is a derivative of JIT.

PROJECT MANAGEMENT. A *project* is usually a one-time effort composed of many interrelated activities, costing a substantial amount of money, and lasting for weeks or years. The management of a project is complicated by the following characteristics.

- Most projects are unique undertakings, and participants have little prior experience in the area.
- Uncertainty exists due to the generally long completion times.
- There can be significant participation of outsiders, which is difficult to control.
- Extensive interaction may occur among participants.
- The many interrelated activities make changes in planning and scheduling difficult.
- Projects often carry high risk but also high profit potential.

The management of projects is enhanced by computerized project management tools such as the *program evaluation and review technique (PERT)* and the *critical path method (CPM)*. For example, developing Web applications is a major project, and several IT tools are available to support and help manage these activities (see *citadon.com*). Merrill-Lynch uses such computerized tools to plan and manage its main projects (Bielski, 2002), significantly improving resource allocation and decision making. For project cost estimation using special software, see Vijayakumar (2002). Project management can be streamlined through online solutions, as demonstrated by Perkins-Munn and Chen (2004).

TROUBLESHOOTING. Finding what's wrong in the factory's internal operations can be a lengthy and expensive process. Intelligent systems can come to the rescue. Bizworks (*bizworks.co.nz*) is an example of a successful software product that tackles thorny POM problems, such as interpretation of data gathered by factory sensors. The product is useful for quality control, maintenance management, and more. Similar products cut diagnosis time from hours to seconds. Many detecting systems are Web-based (see *gensym.com*).

OTHER AREAS. Many other areas of planning production and operations are improved by IT. For example, Lee and Chen (2002) developed a Web-based production planning optimization tool. Factory layout planning and design also have been greatly improved due to IT tools (Benjaafar et al., 2002).

Korolishin (2003) describes a Web-based system at Office Depot that matches employee scheduling with store traffic patterns to increase customer satisfaction and reduce costs. Parks (2004) describes how Schurman Fine Papers (a retailer and manufacturer of greeting cards and specialty products) uses special *warehouse management software* to improve forecasting and inventory processes. Its two warehouses distribute products to over 30,000 retail stores.

Computer-Integrated Manufacturing

Computer-integrated manufacturing (CIM) is a concept or philosophy that promotes the integration of various computerized factory systems. CIM has three basic goals: (1) the *simplification* of all manufacturing technologies and techniques, (2) *automation* of as many of the manufacturing processes as possible, and (3) *integration and coordination* of all aspects of design, manufacturing, and related functions via computer hardware and software. Typical technologies to be integrated are flexible-manufacturing systems (FMSs), JIT, MRP, CAD, CAE, and group technology (GT). For details see Online File W6.6.

The major advantages of CIM are its comprehensiveness and flexibility. These are especially important in business processes that are being completely restructured or eliminated. Without CIM, it may be necessary to invest large amounts of money to change existing information systems to fit the new processes. For an example of how a furniture company uses CIM, see *kimball.com* (click on Electronic Manufacturing Services). For more on a unified framework for integrated manufacturing see Zaremba and Morel (2003).

Product Lifecycle Management (PLM)

Product lifecycle management (PLM) is a business strategy that enables manufacturers to control and share product-related data as part of product design and development efforts and in support of supply chain operations (see Day, 2002). In PLM, Web-based and other new technologies are applied to *product development* to automate its *collaborative aspects,* which even within a given organization can prove tedious and time-consuming. By overlapping formerly disparate functions, such as a manufacturing process and the logistics that support it, a dynamic collaboration takes place among the functions, essentially forming a single large product team from the product's inception.

An example of a Web-based PLM product (from PTC Corp.) for designing popular ATV bikes is provided in Figure 6.5 (page 260). The collaboration is achieved via "ProjectLink" (at the center of the figure). Using this PLM, bike-maker Cannondale Corp. was able to design its 2003 model significantly faster.

PLM can have a significant beneficial impact in engineering change, cycle time, design reuse, and engineering productivity. Studies have shown that

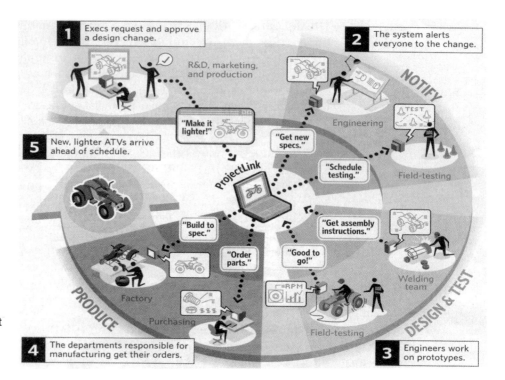

FIGURE 6.5 How product life cycle management works. (*Source:* Raskin, 2002, p. 50.)

electronic-based collaboration can reduce product cost and travel expenses, as well as significantly reduce costs associated with product-change management. Moreover, an explosion of new products that have short life cycles, as well as increasing complexity in supply chain management, are driving the need for PLM.

PLM is a big step for an organization, requiring it to integrate a number of different processes and systems. Ultimately, its overall goal from the organization's point of view is to move information through an organization as quickly as possible in order to reduce the time it takes to get a product to market and to increase profitability. PLM tools are offered by SAP (MYSAP PLM), Matrix One, EDS, PTC, Dassault Systems, and IBM (IBM PLM).

6.4 MANAGING MARKETING AND SALES SYSTEMS

In Chapters 1 through 5 we emphasized the increasing importance of a customer-focused approach and the trend toward customization and consumer-based organizations. How can IT help? First we need to understand how products reach customers, which takes place through a series of marketing entities known as *channels*.

Channel systems (in marketing) are all the systems involved in the process of getting a product or service to customers and dealing with all customers' needs. The complexity of channel systems can be observed in Figure 6.6 (page 261), where six major marketing systems are interrelated.

Channel systems can link and transform marketing, sales, procurement, logistics and delivery, and other activities. Added market power comes from the integration of channel systems with the corporate functional areas. The problem is that a change in any of the channels may affect the other channels. Therefore, the supporting information systems must be coordinated or even integrated.

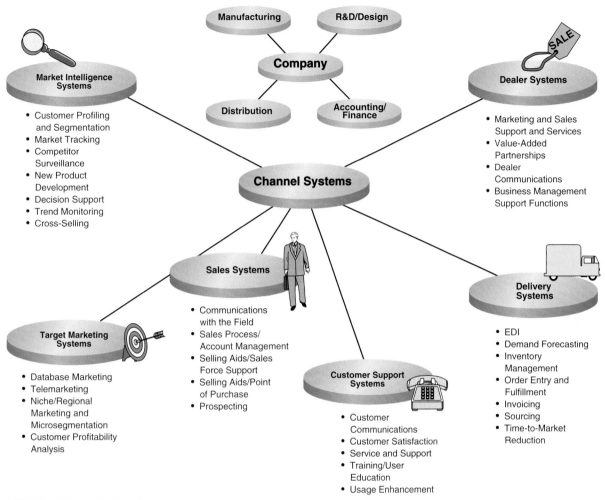

FIGURE 6.6 Marketing channel systems.

We describe only a few of the many channel-system activities here, organizing them into three groups: customer relations, distribution channels and in-store innovations, and marketing management. A fourth topic, telemarketing and online shopping, is presented in Online File W6.7.

"The Customer Is King/Queen"

It is essential for companies today to know who their customers are and to treat them like royalty. New and innovative products and services, successful promotions, customization, and world-class customer service are becoming a necessity for many organizations. In this section we will briefly describe a few activities related to *customer-centric* organizations. More are described in Chapter 7, where customer relationship management (CRM) is presented.

CUSTOMER PROFILES AND PREFERENCE ANALYSIS. Information about existing and potential customers is critical for success. Sophisticated information systems have been developed to collect data on customers, their demographics (age, gender, income level), and preferences. For example, shoppers' in-store activities can be monitored and then analyzed to better arrange the layouts and employees' scheduling.

Consumer behavior online can be tracked by cookies (small data files placed on a user's hard drive by a Web server). Then the consumer's online behavior can be analyzed and used for marketing purposes. By checking the demographics of its millions of customers and their locations, America Online (AOL), for example, can match appropriate ads of advertisers with specific customers. The effectiveness of such ads is very high. Even more powerful is the combination of offline and online data (e.g., see *doubleclick.com*). For approaches to targeted marketing and/or advertising, see Chapter 4 and Strauss et al. (2003).

PROSPECTIVE CUSTOMER LISTS AND MARKETING DATABASES. All firms need to know who their customers are, and IT can help create customer databases of both existing and potential customers. It is possible today to purchase computerized lists from several sources and then merge them electronically. These prospective-customer lists then can be analyzed and sorted by any desired classification for direct mailing, e-mailing, or telemarketing. Customer data can be stored in a corporate database or in special marketing databases for future analysis and use. For how Sears uses a marketing database, see Amato-McCoy (2002b). (We discuss database marketing further in Chapter 10.)

MASS CUSTOMIZATION. Increasingly, today's customers want customized products. Some manufacturers offer different product configurations, and in some products dozens of options are available. The result is *mass customization*, as practiced successfully by Dell Computer and many other companies (see Appendix 2A). Customization is possible both in manufactured goods and in services.

Wind (2001) analyzed the impact of customization on marketing and the resultant changes (see Table 6.3). As shown throughout this book, these changes are being supported by IT. For example, the Web can be used to expedite the ordering and fulfillment of customized products, as demonstrated in *IT at Work 6.3* (page 264), about building a Jaguar.

Mass customization is not for everyone, and it does have several limitations (Zipkin, 2001). The major limitations are that it requires a highly flexible production technology, an elaborate system for eliciting customers' wants and needs, and strong direct-to-customer logistics system. Another limitation is cost: some people are unable or unwilling to pay even the slightly higher prices that customization often entails. Holweg and Pil (2001) provide some guidelines for how to overcome these limitations.

PERSONALIZATION. Using cameras, retailers can find what people are doing while they visit physical stores. Similarly, tracking software can find what people are doing in a virtual store. This technology provides information for real-time marketing and is also used in m-commerce (see Chapter 5 and also Sadeh, 2002). Personalized product offers then are made, based on where the customer spent the most time and on what what he or she purchased. A similar approach is used in Web-based *cross-selling* (or *up-selling*) efforts, in which advertising of related products is provided. For example, if you are buying a car, car insurance is automatically offered (see Strauss et al., 2003).

ADVERTISING AND PROMOTIONS. The Internet opens the door to a new advertising medium. As was shown in Chapter 4, online advertising, mainly via

TABLE 6.3 The Changing Face of Marketing	Old Model	New Model
	Mass and Segmented Marketing	Customization
Relationships with customers	Customer is a passive participant in the exchange	Customer is an active co-producer
Customer needs	Articulated	Articulated and unarticulated
Segmentation	Mass market and target segments	Segments looking for customized solutions and "segments one" (a segment of only one person)
Product and service offerings	Line extensions and modification	Customized products, services, and marketing
New-product development	Marketing and R&D drive new-product development	R&D focuses on developing the platforms that allow consumers to customize
Pricing	Fixed prices and discounting	Customer-determined pricing (e.g., Priceline.com; auctions); value-based pricing models
Communication	Advertising and public relations	Integrated, interactive, and customized marketing communication, education, and entertainment
Distribution	Traditional retailing and direct marketing	Direct (online) distribution and rise of third-party logistics services
Branding	Traditional branding and co-branding	Use of the customer's name as the brand (e.g., My brand or Brand 4 ME)
Basis of competitive advantage	Marketing power	Marketing finesse and "capturing" the customer as "partner" while integrating marketing, operations, R&D, and information

Source: Wind (2001), p. 41.

e-mail and banners, is growing rapidly. Innovative methods such as viral marketing (Reda, 2002) are possible only on the Internet. Wireless and pervasive computing applications also are changing the face of advertising (Chapter 5). For example, in order to measure attention to advertising, a mobile-computing device from Arbitron (see Portable People Meter at *arbitron.com*) is carried by customers. Whoever is wearing the device automatically logs advertising seen or heard any time, anywhere in their daily movements.

Distribution Channels and In-Store Innovations

Organizations can distribute their products and services through several delivery channels. For instance, a company may use its own outlets or distributors. Digitizable products can be distributed online, or can be delivered on CD-ROMs. Other products can be delivered by trucks or trains, with the movement of goods monitored by IT applications. The Web is revolutionizing distribution channels (Chaudhury et al., 2001). Here we look at some representative topics relating to distribution channels.

NEW IT-SUPPORTED DISTRIBUTION CHANNELS. In addition to the Internet, IT enables other (new or improved) channels through which to distribute goods or services. For example, by connecting mapping technology with databases of local employers, retailers and fast-food marketers are providing goods and

IT at Work 6.3
BUILD YOUR JAGUAR ONLINE

Prospective Jaguar car buyers can build, see, and price the car of their dreams online. As of October 2000, you can configure the car at *jaguar.com* in real time. Cars have been configured online since 1997, but Jaguar was the industry's first to offer comprehensive services, delivered in many languages.

Using a virtual car, users can view more than 1,250 possible exterior combinations, rotating the car through 360 degrees, by moving directional arrows. As you select the model, color, trim, wheels, and accessories, both image and price information automatically update. The design choices are limited to current models. Up to 10 personalized car selections per customer can be stored in a "virtual garage." Customers can "test" virtual cars and conduct comparisons of different models. Once the buyer makes a decision, the order is forwarded to a dealer of his or her choice.

Like most other car manufacturers, Jaguar will not let you consummate the purchase online. To negotiate price, customers can go to a Jaguar dealer or use Auto By Tel (*autobytel.com*), which connects nearby dealers to the customer. However, Jaguar's system helps get customers to the point of purchase. It helps them *research* the purchase and explore, price, and visualize options. Customers thus

familiarize themselves with the Jaguar before even visiting a showroom. The ability to see a 3-D photo of the car is an extremely important customer service. Finally, the order for the customer-configured car can be transmitted electronically to the production floor, reducing the time-to-delivery cycle.

The IT support for this innovation includes a powerful configuration database integrated with Jaguar's production system (developed by Ford Motor Company and Trilogy Corp.) and the "virtual car" (developed by Global Beach Corp.).

As of mid-2000, most car manufacturers had introduced Web-based make-to-order systems. In order to avoid channel conflicts, these systems typically involve the dealers in the actual purchase. All major car manufacturers are attempting to move some part of car ordering to the Web.

Sources: Compiled from *jaguar.com* press releases (October–November 2000); *ford.com* (2000) (go to Services); and *autobytel.com* (2002).

For Further Exploration: Why would manufacturers be interested in the Web if the actual purchase is done at the dealers' site?

---

services to employees during their lunch breaks. Using the Internet, retailers offer special incentives (e.g., coupons) to lunchtime shoppers. According to Seidman (2002), fast food, paint, and tires top the list of items sold in this new channel. A leading vendor in this area is SBS Technologies (*sbs.com*); it works with Mapinfo.com, which provides electronic maps showing a marketer who is working where, so they can design promotions accordingly.

Another new distribution channel is self-service convenience kiosks, which are popular at railway stations, highway rest areas, airports, and gasoline stations. While some of these have a sales employee or two, most are without employees. They are used by manufacturers (e.g., Mattel) as well as by retailers to offer their products to the public. What is new about this distribution channel is that payment can be made by inserting a credit card into a card reader or by using a smart card, even for a small purchase amount.

IMPROVING SHOPPING AND CHECKOUT AT RETAIL STORES. The modern shopper is often pressed for time, and most are unhappy about waiting in long lines. Using information technology, it is possible to reengineer the shopping and the checkout process. For example:

- Several companies use hand-held wireless devices that scan the barcode UPC of the product you want to buy, giving you all product information, including options such as maintenance agreements. The desired purchase is matched with your smart card (or credit card), and an order to send the product(s) to the cashier is issued. By the time you arrive at the cashier, the bill and the merchandise are ready.

- An alternative to the hand-held computer is the information kiosk. The kiosks enable customers to view catalogs in stores, conduct product searches, and even compare prices with those of competitors. Kiosks at some stores (e.g., 7-Eleven stores in some countries) can be used to place orders on the Internet. (For details about use of in-store kiosks, see Online File W6.8 and Sweeney, 2001.)

- Video-based systems count the number of shoppers and track where they go in physical stores. These are not security systems per se; rather, their purpose is to gather information about shopping patterns. The collected data are analyzed and used for computer-based decisions regarding displays, store design, and in-store marketing messages and promotions. The information is also used to determine when shopping traffic is heaviest, in order to schedule employees (see Kroll, 2002, for details).

- Some stores that have many customers who pay by check (e.g., large grocery stores, Costco, Wal-Mart stores) have installed check-writers. All you have to do is submit the blank check to the cashier, who runs it through a machine attached to the cash register. The machine prints the name of the store as the payee and the amount, you sign the check, and in seconds the check is validated, your bank account is debited, and you are out of the store with your merchandise.

- Computerization of various activities in retail stores can save time and money and provide better customer service. Cash Register Express offers many products, such as Video Express and portable data collectors. For details about computerized cash register services, see *pcamerica.com*.

- The ExxonMobile Speedpass allows customers to fill their tanks by waving a token, embedded with an RFID device, at a gas-pump sensor. Then the RFID starts an authorization process, and the purchase is charged to your credit card. Customers no longer need to carry their Mobile credit cards (See *mobil.com/speedpass*.)

U-Scan kiosk

- An increasing number of retailers are installing self-checkout machines. For example, Home Depot in 2003 added self-checkouts in their stores. Not only does the retailer save the cost of employees' salaries, but customers are happier for saving time. (And some enjoy "playing cashier" briefly.) A major device is U-Scan, which is used in many supermarkets (see photo). Soon, RFIDs will improve the process even further.

DISTRIBUTION CHANNELS MANAGEMENT. Once products are in the distribution channels, firms need to monitor and track them, since only fast and accurate delivery times guarantee high customer satisfaction and repeat business. FedEx, UPS, HDL, and other large shipping companies provide customers with sophisticated tracking systems. These shippers track the location of their trucks and airplanes using GPSs; they also scan the packages so they know their whereabouts. Shipping companies also offer customers the ability to self-track packages using Web-based systems, thus reducing the need for customer service employees. Tracking will be significantly improved with RFIDs.

Marketing Management

Many marketing management decision applications are supported by computerized information systems. (Online File W6.9 shows the marketing management decision framework.) Here are some representative examples of how marketing management is being done.

PRICING OF PRODUCTS OR SERVICES. Sales volumes are largely determined by the prices of products or services. Price is also a major determinant of profit. Pricing is a difficult decision, and prices may need to be changed frequently. For example, in response to price changes made by competitors, a company may need to adjust its prices or take other actions. Checking competitors' prices is commonly done by retailers. But instead of carrying paper and pen, one can use wireless price checkers (e.g., PriceMaster Plus, from SoftwarePlus). These devices make data collection easy.

Pricing decisions are supported by a number of computerized systems. Three pricing models for retailers with thousands of items to price were developed by Sung and Lee (2000). Many companies are using online analytical processing (OLAP) to support pricing and other marketing decisions (see Chapters 10 and 11). In Chapter 2 we discussed the optimization models used to support prices at Longs Drug Stores and others (see *A Closer Look 2.1*). Web-based comparison engines enable customers to select a vendor at the price they want, and they also enable vendors to see how their prices compare with others. For an overview on pricing and the Internet, including quick price testing, see Baker et al. (2001).

SALESPERSON PRODUCTIVITY. Salespeople differ from each other; some excel in selling certain products, while others excel in selling to a certain type of customer or in a certain geographical zone. This information, which is usually collected in the sales and marketing TPS, can be analyzed, using a comparative performance system, in which sales data by salesperson, product, region, and even the time of day are evaluated. Actual current sales can be compared to historical data and to standards. Multidimensional spreadsheet software facilitates this type of analysis. Assignment of salespeople to regions and/or products and the calculation of bonuses can also be supported by this system.

In addition, sales productivity can be boosted by Web-based systems. For example, in a Web-based call center, when a customer calls a sales rep, the rep can look at the customer's history of purchases, demographics, services available where the customer lives, and more. This information enables reps to work faster, while providing better customer service. Customers' information can be provided by marketing customer information file technology (MCIF) (see Totty, 2000).

Sales Force Automation. The productivity of salespeople in the field also can be greatly increased by what is known as **sales force automation**—providing salespeople with mobile devices, access to databases, and so on. It empowers the field sales force to close deals at the customer's office and to configure marketing strategies at home. (Recall the Maybelline case, Chapter 2; for additional examples, see Brewin, 2004, and O'Donnell, 2004.) For other uses of the Web by the sales force, see Varney (1996) and the case of PAVECA in Online File W6.10.

Sales force automation can be boosted in many ways by using Web-based tools. For example, Netgain (from *netgainservices.com*) lets a multimedia company's design and sales teams collaborate over the Web, passing off sales leads, bringing in new sales reps to clinch different parts of a deal, and tracking reports on sales progress.

Productivity Software. **Sales automation software** is especially helpful to small businesses, enabling them to rapidly increase sales and growth. Such Web-based software (e.g., from *salesforce.com*) can manage the flow of messages and assist in writing contracts, scheduling, and making appointments. Of course it provides word processing and e-mail, and it helps with mailings and follow-up letters. Electronic stamps (e.g., *stamps.com*) can assist with mass mailings.

PROFITABILITY ANALYSIS. In deciding on advertising and other marketing efforts, managers often need to know the profit contribution of certain products and services. Profitability information for products and services can be derived from the cost-accounting system. For example, profit performance analysis software available from IBM, Siebel Systems, and Microstrategy, Inc. is designed to help managers assess and improve the profit performance of their line of business, products, distribution channels, sales regions, and other dimensions critical to managing the enterprise. Northwest Airlines, for example, uses expert systems and DSS to set prices based on profitability. They also use a similar system to audit tickets and for calculating commissions to travel agents.

In addition, identification of profitable customers and the frequency with which they interact with the organization can be derived from special promotional programs, such as hotels' frequent-stayer programs. This information can be used for loyalty and other programs.

SALES ANALYSIS AND TRENDS. The marketing TPS collects sales figures that can be segregated along several dimensions for early detection of problems and opportunities, by searching for trends and relationships. For example, if sales of a certain product show a continuous decline in certain regions but not in other regions, management can investigate the declining region. Similarly, an increasing sales volume of a new product calls attention to an opportunity if it is found to be statistically significant. This application demonstrates the reliance of decision making on the TPS. Also, data mining can be used to find relationships and patterns in large databases (see Chapter 10).

NEW PRODUCTS, SERVICES, AND MARKET PLANNING. The introduction of new or improved products and services can be expensive and risky. An important question to ask about a new product or service is, "Will it sell?" An appropriate answer calls for careful analysis, planning, and forecasting. These can best be executed with the aid of IT because of the large number of determining factors and the uncertainties that may be involved. Market research also can be conducted on the Internet, as described in Online File W4.7. A related issue is the speed with which products are brought to market. An example of how Procter & Gamble expedites the time-to-market by using the Internet is provided in *IT at Work 6.4* (page 268).

WEB-BASED SYSTEMS IN MARKETING. The use of Web-based systems in support of marketing and sales has grown rapidly, as demonstrated by the P&G case. A summary of some Web-based impacts is provided in Figure 6.7 (page 268).

OTHER APPLICATIONS. Many other applications exist. For example, Howarth (2004a) describes the use of IT to reduce theft in stores.

Marketing activities conclude the *primary* activities of the value chain. Next we look at the functional systems that are *secondary* (support) activities in the value chain: accounting/finance and human resources management.

IT at Work 6.4

INTERNET MARKET RESEARCH EXPEDITES
TIME-TO-MARKET AT PROCTER & GAMBLE

For decades, Procter & Gamble (P&G) and Colgate-Palmolive have been competitors in the market for personal care products. Developing a major new product, from concept to market launch, used to take over 5 years. First, a concept test was done; the companies sent product photos and descriptions to potential customers, asking whether they might buy it. If the feedback was negative, they tried to improve the product concept and then repeated the concept testing. Once positive response was achieved, sample products were mailed out, and customers were asked to fill out detailed questionnaires. When customers' responses met the companies' internal hurdles, the company would start with mass advertising on television and in magazines.

However, thanks to the Internet, it took P&G only three-and-a-half years to get Whitestrips, the teeth-brightening product, onto the market and to a sales level of $200 million a year—considerably quicker than other oral care products. In September 2000, P&G threw out the old marketing test model and instead introduced Whitestrips on the Internet, offering the product for sale on P&G's Web site. The company spent several months studying who was coming to the site and buying the product; it collected responses to online questionnaires, which was much faster than the old mail-outs.

The online research, which was facilitated by data mining conducted on P&G's huge historical data (stored in a data warehouse) and the new Internet data, revealed the most enthusiastic groups. These included teenage girls, brides-to-be, and young Hispanic Americans. Immediately, the company started to target these segments with appropriate advertising. The Internet created a product awareness of 35 percent, even before any shipments were made to stores. This "buzz" created a huge demand for the product by the time it hit the shelves.

From this experience, P&G learned important lessons about flexible and creative ways to approach product innovation and marketing. The whole process of studying the product concept, segmenting the market, and expediting product development has been revolutionized.

Sources: Compiled from Buckley (2002), and from *pg.com* (February–December 2002).

For Further Exploration: How did the Internet decrease time-to-market in this situation? What is the role of data mining? Why is so much testing needed?

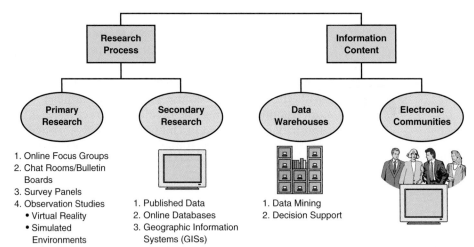

FIGURE 6.7 The impact of the Web on marketing information services. Channel-driven advantages are (1) transaction speed (real-time response) because of the interactive nature of the process, (2) global reach, (3) reduced costs, (4) multimedia content, and (5) reliability. (*Source:* P. K. Kannan et al., "Marketing Information on the I-Way," *Communications of the ACM*, 1999, p. 36. (Association for Computing Machinery, Inc. Reprinted by permission.)

6.5 MANAGING THE ACCOUNTING AND FINANCE SYSTEMS

A primary mission of the accounting/finance functional area is to manage money flows into, within, and out of organizations. This is a very broad mission since money is involved in all functions of an organization. Some repetitive accounting/financing activities such as payroll, billing, and cash management were computerized as early as the 1950s. Today, accounting/finance information systems are very diverse and comprehensive.

The general structure of an accounting/finance system is presented in Figure 6.8. It is divided into three levels: strategic, tactical, and operational. Information technology can support almost all the activities listed, as well as the communication and collaboration of accounting/finance with internal and external environments. We describe some selected activities in the rest of this section. For others, see Reed et al. (2001).

Financial Planning and Budgeting

Appropriate management of financial assets is a major task in financial planning and budgeting. Managers must plan for both the acquisition of financial

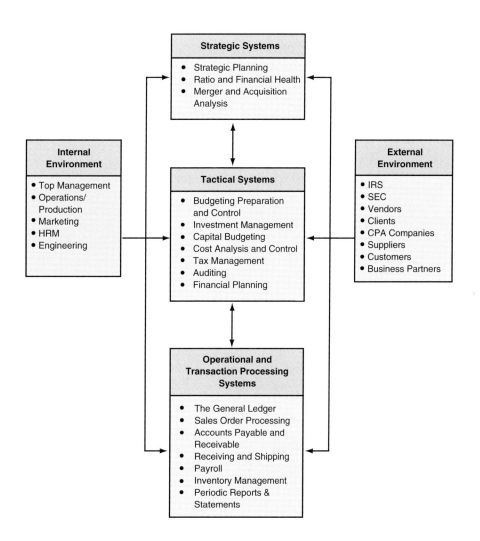

FIGURE 6.8 Major activities of the accounting/finance system.

resources and their use. Financial planning, like any other functional planning, is tied to the overall organizational planning and to other functional areas. It is divided into short-, medium-, and long-term horizons, much like activities planning. Financial analysts use Web resources and computerized spreadsheets to accomplish the organization's financial planning and budgeting activities.

FINANCIAL AND ECONOMIC FORECASTING. Knowledge about the availability and cost of money is a key ingredient for successful financial planning. Especially important is the projection of cash flow, which tells organizations what funds they need and when, and how they will acquire them. This function is important for all firms, but is especially so for small companies, which tend to have little financial cushion. Inaccurate cash flow projection is the number one reason why many small businesses go bankrupt. Availability and cost of money depend on corporate financial health and the willingness of lenders and investors to infuse money into the company (see Banks, 2001).

Financial and economic analysis is facilitated by intelligent systems such as neural computing (Chapter 11). Many software packages are available for conducting economic and financial forecasting, which are frequently available for a fee, over the Internet.

BUDGETING. The best-known part of financial planning is the annual budget, which allocates the financial resources of an organization among participants and activities. The budget is the financial expression of the organization's plans. It allows management to allocate resources in the way that best supports the organization's mission and goals. IT enables the introduction of financial intelligence into the budgeting process.

Software Support. Several software packages, many of which are Web-based, are available to support budget preparation and control (e.g., Budget 2000 from PROPHIX Software, and budgeting modules from PeopleSoft and Capterra.com) and to facilitate communication among all participants in the budget preparation.

Since budget preparation may involve both top-down and bottom-up processes, modeling capabilities in some packages allow the budget coordinator to take the top-down numbers, compare them with the bottom-up data from the users, and reconcile the two.

Software also makes it easier to build complex budgets that involve multiple sites, including foreign countries. Budgeting software also allows various internal and external comparisons. One of the latest trends is industry-specific packages such as for hospitals, banks, or retailers. Budgeting software is frequently bundled with financial analysis and reporting functions.

The major benefits of using budgeting software are that it can: reduce the time and effort involved in the budget process, explore and analyze the implications of organizational and environmental changes, facilitate the integration of the corporate strategic objectives with operational plans, make planning an ongoing, continuous process, and automatically monitor exceptions for patterns and trends.

CAPITAL BUDGETING. *Capital budgeting* is the financing of asset acquisitions, including the disposal of major organizational assets. It usually includes a comparison of options, such as keep the asset, replace it with an identical new asset, replace it with a different one, or discard it. The capital budgeting process also evaluates buy-versus-lease options.

Capital budgeting analysis uses standard financial models, such as net present value (NPV), internal rate of return (IRR), and payback period, to evaluate alternative investment decisions. Most spreadsheet packages include built-in functions of these models.

Managing Financial Transactions

An accounting/finance information system is also responsible for gathering the raw data necessary for the accounting/finance TPS, transforming the data into information, and making the information available to users, whether aggregate information about payroll, the organization's internal managers, or external reports to stockholders or government agencies.

Many packages exist to execute routine accounting transaction processing activities. Several are available free on the Internet (try *tucows.com*). Many software packages are integrated. In these integrated systems, the accounting/finance activities are combined with other TPSs such as those of marketing and production and operations management. The data collected and managed for the accounting/finance transaction processing system are also inputs for the various functional information systems.

One such integrated system is MAS 90 and MAS 200 (from *bestsoftware.com*). It is a collection of standard accounting modules, as shown in Figure 6.9 (the "wheel" in the diagram). Communication and inquiry modules (right side) support the accounting modules. The user can integrate as many of the modules as needed for the business. On the left side is a list of other business processes and functional applications that can interface with accounting applications. Note that the software includes an e-commerce module, which provides dynamic

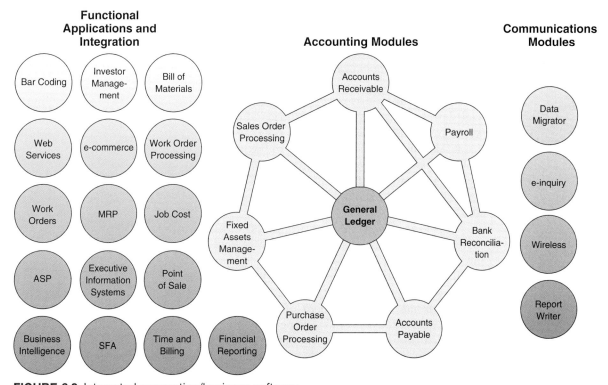

FIGURE 6.9 Integrated accounting/business software.

Web access to MAS 90. This module includes account and order inquiry capabilities as well as a shopping cart for order entry. The 2004 version of MAS 90 includes modules for business intelligence, e-commerce, CRM, sales force automation (SFA), and financial reporting.

Another integrated accounting software package is *peachtree.com* (from Best Software), which offers a sales ledger, purchase ledger, cash book, sales order processing, invoicing, stock control, job casting, fixed-assets register, and more. Other software vendors are Great Plains and Solomon (see Business Solutions at Microsoft.com); see their demos. Other accounting packages can be found at *2020software.com* and *findaccountingsoftware.com*.

The accounting/finance TPS also provides a complete, reliable audit trail of all transactions transmitted through the network. This feature is vital to accountants and auditors. (For more, see the "Control and Auditing" section below.)

E-COMMERCE APPLICATIONS OF FINANCIAL TRANSACTIONS. Companies doing e-commerce need to access financial data of customers (e.g., credit line), inventory levels, and manufacturing databases (to see available capacity, to place orders, etc.). Great Plains (*bestsoftware.com*) offers 50 modules to choose from, to meet the most common financial, project, distribution, manufacturing, and e-business needs.

Diversified financial transactions also lend themselves to e-commerce applications, especially Web-based ones. In Chapter 4, we described e-banking, online securities trading, and more. Many of these can be done in a wireless environment (Chapter 5, and the Handlesbanken case in Chapter 1, page 24). Here we provide a few other examples.

Global Stock Exchanges. According to Maxemchuk and Shur (2001), financial markets are moving toward global, 24-hour, distributed electronic stock exchanges that will use the Internet for both the transactions and multicasting of real-time stock prices.

Handling Multiple Currencies. Global trade involves financial transactions in different currencies. Conversion ratios of many of them change every minute. Zakaria (2002) reports on a Web-based system (from SAP AG) that takes financial data from seven Asian countries and converts the currencies to dollars in seconds. Reports based on these data, which used to take weeks to generate, now take minutes. The system handles the multiplicity of languages as well.

E-Bonds. The World Bank is now using e-bonds, a system for marketing, distributing, and trading bonds over the Internet. The system expanded in 2003 to include electronic applications to currency and derivatives trading. For details see *gs.com* (2001).

Factoring Online. *Factors* are financial institutions that buy accounts receivable, usually at a discount. Factoring of receivables gives the selling company an immediate cash inflow. The factor takes on the risks and expenses of collecting the debts. Factoring on the Web is becoming very popular. For details see Salodof-MacNeil (2002).

Electronic Re-presentment of Checks. Companies face a problem of bad checks (insufficient funds). Paper checks that do not clear are usually re-presented (manually or electronically). Electronic re-presentment can be organized as part of cash management information systems. Such systems consolidate checks from different banks and conduct a return analysis (analysis of why checks are not honored, who is likely to pass bad checks, etc.).

Electronic Bill Presentment and Payments. One of the most successful areas of e-commerce is that of electronic presentment and payments. In its simplest form it is an electronic payment of bills. However, third-party companies provide a service in which they calculate, print, and electronically present the bills to customers (see Chapter 4 and Boucher-Ferguson, 2002).

VIRTUAL CLOSE. Companies close their books (accounting records) quarterly, mainly to meet regulatory requirements. Some companies want to be able to close their books any time, on short notice. Called a **virtual close,** the ability to close the books quickly may give almost real-time information on the financial health of a company (see McClenahen, 2002). With an advanced IT program developed by Cisco (see Online File W6.11) it will soon be possible, even for a large multinational corporation, to close the books in a matter of hours.

INTEGRATION OF FINANCIAL TRANSACTIONS WITH E-COMMERCE APPLICATIONS. ACCPAC International (*accpaconline.com*) integrated its financial accounting software with e-business solutions (software, system building, consulting, and integration) to help global traders. The e-commerce module (eTransact) is tightly integrated with ACCPAC for Windows, offering a single, unifying financial and business management system.

EXPENSE MANAGEMENT AUTOMATION. **Expense management automation (EMA)** refers to systems that automate data entry and processing of travel and entertainment expenses. These expenses can account for 20 percent of the operating expenses of large corporations (Degnan, 2003). EMA systems (by companies such as Captura, Concur, Extensity, and Necho) are Web-based applications that replace the paper forms and rudimentary spreadsheet. These systems let companies quickly and consistently collect expense information, enforce company policies and contracts, and reduce unplanned purchases of airline and hotel services. The software forces travelers to be organized before a trip starts. In addition to benefits to the companies, employees also benefit from quick reimbursement (since expense approvals are not held up by sloppy or incomplete documentation). (For details, see "What EMA systems now offer…," 2002.)

Investment Management

Effective investment management is a difficult task, both for individuals and for corporations. For one thing, there are thousands of investment alternatives. On the New York Stock Exchange alone, there are more than 2,000 stocks, and millions of possible combinations for creating portfolios. Investment decisions are based on economic and financial forecasts and on various multiple and conflicting objectives (such as high yield, safety, and liquidity). The investment environment also includes opportunities in other countries. Another factor that contributes to the complexity of investment management is that investments made by many organizations are subject to complex regulations and tax laws. Finally, investment decisions need to be made quickly and frequently. Decision makers can be in different locations, and they need to cooperate and collaborate. Therefore, computerization is especially popular in financial institutions that are involved in investments, as illustrated in *IT at Work 6.5* (page 274). Many other banks and financial institutions have similar systems, especially for portfolio management. An example is Opti-Money, which is successfully used in Israel (see Avriel et al., 2004).

IT at Work 6.5
MATLAB MANAGES EQUITY PORTFOLIOS AT DAIWA SECURITIES

Daiwa Securities of Japan (*daiwa.co.jp*) is one of the world's largest and most profitable multinational securities firms. Many of the company's traders are engineers and mathematicians who use computers to constantly buy and sell securities for the company's own portfolio. Daiwa believes that identifying mispricings in the stock markets holds great profit potential. Toward this end the company uses leading-edge computerized quantitative analysis methods to look for securities that are underpriced by the market. The software compares stock price performance of individual companies to that of other companies in the same market sector. In an attempt to minimize risk, the model then suggests a buy, sell, or sell-short solution for each investigated security.

The company is using an *arbitrage* approach, which looks for the opportunity to make profits with very little risk. It may keep undervalued stocks, but it sells short overvalued stocks and futures. The buy-sell recommendations are generated by a system (coded in MATLAB, from Mathworks.com) that is based on modern portfolio theory. The system uses two models: one for the short term (3 to 10 days) and one for the longer term (3 to 6 weeks). It follows over 1,200 stocks and includes many variables, some of which are very volatile. Changes in the MATLAB model can be made quickly on the Excel spreadsheet it uses. Complex statistical tools are used for the computations. The system attempts to minimize the risk of the portfolio yet maximize its profit. Since these two goals usually contradict each other, trade-offs must be considered.

The system is based on neural networks and fuzzy logic. The advantage of neural networks is that they can closely approximate the underlying processes that may be moving the financial markets in a particular direction.

To motivate the traders to use the system, as well as to quickly build modifications using Excel, the company pays generous bonuses for successful trades. As a matter of fact, some young MBA and PhD traders have commanded bonuses of hundreds of thousands of dollars each year.

Sources: Compiled from Pittaras (1996), and *daiwa.co.jp* (press releases 2000).

For Further Exploration: What is the logic of the arbitrage strategy? Why would bonuses be used to motivate employees to use the system?

In addition, data-mining tools and neural networks (Chapter 11) are used by many institutional investment managers to analyze historical databases, so they can make better predictions. For a data-mining tool, see *wizsoft.com*. Some typical financial applications of neural computing are provided in Online File W6.12.

The following are the major areas of support that IT can provide to investment management.

ACCESS TO FINANCIAL AND ECONOMIC REPORTS. Investment decisions require managers to evaluate financial and economic reports and news provided by federal and state agencies, universities, research institutions, financial services, and corporations. There are hundreds of Web sources, many of which are free; a sampling is listed in Online File W6.13. Most of these services are useful both for professional investment managers and for individual investors.

FINANCIAL ANALYSIS. Financial analysis can be executed with a spreadsheet program, or with commercially available ready-made decision support software (e.g., see *tradeportal.com/tradematrix.asp*). Or it can be more sophisticated, involving intelligent systems. Other information technologies can be used as well. For example, Morgan Stanley and Company uses virtual reality on its intranet to display the results of risk analysis in three dimensions. Seeing data in 3-D makes it easier to make comparisons and intuitive connections than would seeing a two-dimensional chart or spreadsheet data.

One area of analysis that is becoming popular is referred to as **financial value chain management (FVCM).** According to this approach, financial analysis is combined with operations analysis. All financial functions are analyzed (including international trades). Combining financial and operations analysis provides better financial control. For example, if the organization runs its operations at a lower-than-planned level, it is likely to need less money; if it exceeds the operational plan, it may well be all right to exceed the budgeted amounts for that plan. For details see Aberdeen.com (2002).

Control and Auditing

A major reason organizations go out of business is their inability to forecast and/or secure sufficient *cash flow.* Underestimated expenses, overspending, financial mismanagement, and fraud can lead to disaster. Good planning is necessary, but not sufficient, and must be supplemented by skillful control. Control activities in organizations take many forms, including control and auditing of the information systems themselves (see Chapter 15). Information systems play an extremely important role in supporting organizational control, as we show throughout the text. Specific forms of financial control are presented next.

RISK ANALYSIS. Companies need to analyze the risk of doing business with partners or in other countries. Giving credit to customers can be risky, so one can use products such as FICO (from *fairisaac.com*) for calculating risk.

BUDGETARY CONTROL. Once the annual budget has been decided upon, it is divided into monthly allocations. Managers at various levels then monitor departmental expenditures and compare them against the budget and operational progress of the corporate plans. Simple reporting systems summarize the expenditures and provide *exception reports* by flagging any expenditure that exceeds the budget by a certain percent or that falls significantly below the budget. More sophisticated software attempts to tie expenditures to program accomplishment. Numerous software programs can be used to support budgetary control; most of them are combined with budget preparation packages from vendors such as *outlooksoft.com, clarifysystems.com,* and *capterra.com.*

AUDITING. The major purpose of auditing is to ensure the accuracy and condition of the financial health of an organization. Internal auditing is done by the organization's accounting/finance personnel, who also prepare for external auditing by CPA companies.

IT can facilitate auditing. For example, intelligent systems can uncover fraud by finding financial transactions that significantly deviate from previous payment profiles. Also, IT provides real-time data whenever needed (see *peoplesoft.com/go/ pt_financials*).

FINANCIAL RATIO ANALYSIS. A major task of the accounting/finance department is to watch the financial health of the company by monitoring and assessing a set of financial ratios. These ratios are mostly the same as those used by external parties when they are deciding whether to invest in an organization, loan money to it, or buy it. But internal parties have access to much more detailed data for use in calculating financial ratios.

The collection of data for ratio analysis is done by the transaction processing system, and computation of the ratios is done by financial analysis models. The *interpretation* of the ratios, and especially the prediction of their future behavior, requires expertise and is sometimes supported by expert systems.

PROFITABILITY ANALYSIS AND COST CONTROL. Many companies are concerned with the profitability of individual products or services as well as with the financial health of the entire organization. Profitability analysis DSS software (see Chapter 11) allows accurate computation of profitability. It also allows allocation of overheads. One way to control cost is by properly estimating it. This is done by special software; see Vijayakumar (2002).

BUSINESS PERFORMANCE MANAGEMENT (BPM). Business performance management unifies budgeting with planning forecasting, reporting, analysis, and scoreboarding. (See *outlooksoft.com* for a product demo, and *frango.com*.) BPM is revisited in Chapter 11.

PRODUCT PRICING. The pricing of products is an important corporate decision since it determines competitiveness and profitability. The marketing department may wish to reduce prices in order to increase market share, but the accounting/finance system must check the relevant cost in order to provide guidelines for such price reductions. Decision support models can facilitate product pricing. Accounting, finance, and marketing, supported by integrated software and intranets, can team up to jointly set appropriate product prices.

Several more applications in the financial/accounting area are described in Online File W6.14. Many more can be found at Reed et al. (2001).

6.6 Managing Human Resources Systems

Developments in Web-based systems increased the popularity of human resources information systems (HRISs) as of the late 1990s. Initial HRIS applications were mainly related to transaction processing systems. (For examples, see Thomas and Ray, 2000; and Bussler and Davis, 2001–2002.) In recent years, as systems generally have been moved to intranets and the Web, so have HRIS applications, many of which can be delivered via an HR portal (see Online File W6.15). Many organizations use their Web portals to advertise job openings and conduct online hiring and training. Ensher et al. (2002) describe the impact of the Internet on acquiring, rewarding, developing, protecting, and retaining human resources. Their findings are summarized in Table 6.4. Perhaps the biggest benefit to companies of human relations IT services is the release of HR staff from intermediary roles (e.g., by self-services, such as self-entry of an address change), so they can focus on strategic planning and human resources organization and development. In the following sections we describe in more detail how IT facilitates the management of human resources (HRM).

Recruitment *Recruitment* is finding employees, testing them, and deciding which ones to hire. Some companies are flooded with viable applicants, while others have difficulty finding the right people. Information systems can be helpful in both cases. Here we present some examples.

TABLE 6.4 Comparison of Traditional Human Resources to E-Human Resources

Key HR Process	Traditional HR	E-HR
Acquiring Human Resources Recruitment and selection	• Paper résumés and paper postings • Positions filled in months • Limited by geographical barriers	• Electronic résumés and Internet postings • Positions filled in weeks or days • Unlimited access to global applicants
Selection	• Costs directed at attracting candidates • Manual review of resumes • Face-to-face (FTF) interviewing process	• Costs directed at selecting candidates • Electronic review of resumes (scanning) • Some distance interviewing (mostly still FTF)
Rewarding Human Resources Performance evaluation	• Supervisor evaluation • Face-to-face evaluation	• 360-degree evaluation • Appraisal software (online and hard copy)
Compensation and benefits	• Time spent on paperwork (benefits changes) • Emphasis on salary and bonuses • Naïve employees • Emphasis on internal equity • Changes made by HR	• Time spent on assessing market salaries • Emphasis on ownership and quality of work-life • Knowledgeable employees • Emphasis on external equity • Changes made by employees online
Developing Human Resources Training and development	• Standardized classroom training • Development process is HR-driven	• Flexible online training • Development process is employee-driven
Career management	• HR lays out career paths for employees • Reactive decisions • Personal networking (local area only)	• Employees manage their careers in concert with HR • Proactive planning with technology • Electronic and personal networking
Protecting Human Resources Health and safety	• Building and equipment safety • Physical fatigue • Mostly reactive programs • Limited to job-related stressors • Focus on employee–management relations	• Ergonomic considerations • Mental fatigue and wellness • Proactive programs to reduce stress • Personal and job-related stressors • Focus on employee–employee relations
Employee relations/legal	• Stronger union presence • Sexual harassment/discrimination • Task performance monitoring	• Weaker union presence • Equal employment opportunity • Use of technology monitoring/big brother • Intellectual property/data security • Inappropriate uses of technology
Retaining Human Resources Retention strategies	• Not a major focal point	• Currently the critical HR activity • Online employee opinion surveys • Cultivating an effective company culture • Mundane tasks done by technology, freeing time for more interesting work
Work–family balance	• Not a major focal point	• Development and monitoring of programs • Providing childcare and eldercare • Erosion of work–home boundaries

Source: Ensher et al. (2002), p. 240, Table 1.

USING THE WEB FOR RECRUITMENT. With millions of resumes available online, it is not surprising that companies are trying to find appropriate candidates on the Web, usually with the help of specialized search engines. Also, hundreds of thousands of jobs are advertised on the Web (see Thomas and Ray, 2000, and Jandt and Nemnich, 1999). Many matching services exist (see Internet Exercise 3). Online recruiting is able to "cast a wide net" to reach more candidates, which may bring in better applicants. In addition, the costs of online recruitment are lower. Other benefits of online recruitment for employers, plus some disadvantages, are shown in Online File W6.16.

Recruitment online is beneficial for candidates as well. They are exposed to a larger number of job offerings, can get details of the positions quickly, and can begin to evaluate the prospective employer. To check the competitiveness of salary offerings, or to see how much one can make elsewhere in several countries, job candidates can go to *monster.com.*

Online recruitment may be facilitated by intelligent systems such as Resumix, described in *IT at Work 6.6.*

For a complete analysis of and guidelines for e-recruitment, see Thomas and Ray (2000) and Borck (2000).

POSITION INVENTORY. Large organizations frequently need to fill vacant positions. To do so, they maintain a file that lists all open positions by job title, geographical area, task content, and skills required. Like any other inventory, this position inventory is updated each time a position is added, modified, and so on. The government of the Philippines, for example, provides a list of available positions in that country, and that list is accessible via the Internet. For those people without Internet access, the government provides access via computers in kiosks in public places and government facilities.

IT at Work 6.6
RESUMIX

From the time a position becomes available or a résumé is received, Resumix (*resumix.com,* now a subsidiary of Yahoo Enterprise Solutions) gives the recruiter the control while dispersing the work of processing job applications. Hiring managers can view job applications; operators can scan résumés; and a recruiter can search for a candidate or identify existing employees for training programs, redeployment opportunities, or new initiatives.

The core of this powerful system is Resumix's Knowledge Base. As a computerized intelligent system, it goes beyond simply matching words. The Knowledge Base interprets a candidate's resume, determining skills based on context and matching those skills to the position criteria. For example,

you might be looking for a product manager. Being a member of the AMA (American Marketing Association) might be one of the desirable properties for the job. However, with a basic keyword search, you might get candidates who have listed with AMA, but are really members of the American Medical Association or American Meatpackers Association. Those are not relevant to your search. Resumix Knowledge Base would select only the candidates with relevant skills.

Source: resumix.yahoo.com (accessed June 2004).

For Further Exploration: Can Resumix eliminate human résumé evaluators? Is a machine probing into your résumé an invasion of privacy?

An advanced intranet-based position inventory system keeps the position inventory list current, matches openings with available personnel, and allows data to be viewed by an employee over the corporate portal from any location at any time. Outsiders can view openings from the Internet. In addition, it is possible to match openings to available personnel.

By analyzing the position inventory and its changes over time, human resources personnel can find other useful information, such as those jobs with high turnover. Such information can support decisions about promotions, salary administration, and training plans.

HRM PORTALS AND SALARY SURVEYS. One advantage of the Web is the large amount of information related to job matching. There are also many private and public HR-related portals. The portal is a search engine, an index of jobs, posted on corporate-member sites. For example, several large companies (e.g., IBM, Xerox, GE) created jointly with 120 companies a career portal called DirectEmployers.com. Commercial, public online recruiters, such as Monster.com, help corporate recruiters find candidates for difficult-to-fill positions. For details see Harrington (2002).

Another area for HR portals is salary surveys. Salary surveys help companies determine how much to pay their employees. Companies used to pay consultants up to $10,000 for a one-time survey (Bussler and Davis, 2001–2002). Now they can conduct such surveys themselves by utilizing free data from vendors such as Salary.com (check "What you are worth").

EMPLOYEE SELECTION. The human resources department is responsible for screening job applicants, evaluating, testing, and selecting them in compliance with state and federal regulations. The process of employee selection can be very complex since it may involve many external and internal candidates and multiple criteria. To expedite the testing and evaluation process and ensure consistency in selection, companies use information technologies such as Web-based expert systems. Figure 6.10 shows the multiple criteria involved in employee

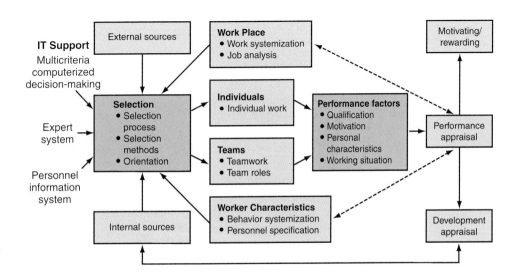

FIGURE 6.10 Intelligent personnel selection model. (*Source:* Jareb and Rajkoric, 2001.)

selection and illustrates the role of an expert system in this process and in related tasks such as performance appraisal.

Human Resources Maintenance and Development

Once recruited, employees become part of the corporate human resources pool, which needs to be maintained and developed. Some activities supported by IT are the following.

PERFORMANCE EVALUATION. Most employees are periodically evaluated by their immediate supervisors. Peers or subordinates may also evaluate others. Evaluations are usually recorded on paper or electronic forms. Using such information manually is a tedious and error-prone job. Once digitized, evaluations can be used to support many decisions, ranging from rewards to transfers to layoffs. For example, many universities evaluate professors online. The evaluation form appears on the screen, and the students fill it in. Results can be tabulated in minutes. Corporate managers can analyze employees' performances with the help of expert systems, which provide systematic interpretation of performance over time.

Wage review is related to performance evaluation. For example, Hewlett-Packard's Atlanta-based U.S. Field Services Operations (USFO) Group has developed a paperless wage review (PWR) system. The Web-based system uses intelligent agents to deal with quarterly reviews of HP's 15,000 employees. (A similar system is used by most other groups, covering a total of 150,000 employees.) The agent software lets USFO managers and personnel access employee data from both the personnel and functional databases. The PWR system tracks employee review dates and automatically initiates the wage review process. It sends wage review forms to first-level managers by e-mail every quarter.

TRAINING AND HUMAN RESOURCES DEVELOPMENT. Employee training and retraining is an important activity of the human resources department. Major issues are planning of classes and tailoring specific training programs to meet the needs of the organization and employees. Sophisticated human resources departments build a career development plan for each employee. IT can support the planning, monitoring, and control of these activities by using workflow applications.

IT also plays an important role in training (see discussion on e-learning, Chapter 3). Some of the most innovative developments are in the areas of *intelligent computer-aided instruction (ICAI)* and application of multimedia support for instructional activities. Instruction is provided online at 38 percent of all Fortune 1,000 corporations, according to OmniTech Consulting ("Web Breathes Life," 1988). Training salespeople is an expensive and lengthy proposition. To save money on training costs, companies are providing sales-skills training over the Internet or intranet. Online File W6.17 provides examples of the variety of employee training available on the Internet and intranets. Interesting implementations of computer-based training at Shoney's are reported by McKinley (2003) and at Sheetz convenience stores by Korolishin (2004b).

Training can be improved using Web-based video clips. For example, using a digital video-editing system, Dairy Queen's in-house video production department produced a higher-quality training video at 50 percent lower cost than by outsourcing it. The affordability of the videos encourages more Dairy Queen franchisees to participate in the training program. This improves customer service as well as employee skill.

Finally, training can be enhanced by virtual reality. Intel, Motorola, Samsung Electronic, and IBM are using virtual reality (Chapter 10) to simulate different scenarios and configurations. The training is especially effective in complex environments where mistakes can be very costly (see Boisvert, 2000).

Human Resources Planning and Management

Managing human resources in large organizations requires extensive planning and detailed strategy (Bussler and Davis, 2001–2002). In some industries, labor negotiation is a particularly important aspect of human resources planning. For most companies, administering employee benefits is also a significant part of the human resources function. Here are some examples of how IT can help.

PERSONNEL PLANNING AND HR STRATEGIES. The human resources department forecasts requirements for people and skills. In some geographical areas and for overseas assignments it may be difficult to find particular types of employees. In such cases the HR department plans how to find (or develop from within) sufficient human resources.

Large companies develop qualitative and quantitative workforce planning models. Such models can be enhanced if IT is used to collect, update, and process the information. Radio Shack uses special software to develop HR strategies (see Reda, 2004, for details).

LABOR–MANAGEMENT NEGOTIATIONS. Labor–management negotiations can take several months, during which time employees may present management with a large number of demands. Both sides need to make concessions and trade-offs. Large companies (like USX, formerly U.S. Steel, in Pittsburgh, Pennsylvania) have developed computerized DSS models that support such negotiations. The models can simulate financial and other impacts of fulfilling any demand made by employees, and they can provide answers to queries of the negotiators in a matter of seconds.

Another information technology that has been successfully used in labor–management negotiations is group decision support systems (see Chapter 11), which have helped improve the negotiation climate and considerably reduced the time needed to reach an agreement.

PAYROLL AND EMPLOYEES' RECORDS. The HR department is responsible for payroll preparation, which can be executed in-house or may be outsourced. It is usually done with the help of computers that print the payroll checks or transfer the money electronically to the employees' bank accounts (Bussler and Davis, 2001–2002). The HR department is also responsible for all personnel record keeping and its privacy and security. In most companies this is done electronically.

BENEFITS ADMINISTRATION. Employees' contributions to their organizations are rewarded by salary/wage, bonuses, and other benefits. Benefits include those for health and dental care as well as contributions for pensions. Managing the benefits system can be a complex task, due to its many components and the tendency of organizations to allow employees to choose and trade off benefits ("cafeteria style"). In large companies, using computers for benefits selection can save a tremendous amount of labor and time for HR staff.

Providing flexibility in selecting benefits is viewed as a competitive advantage in large organizations. It can be successfully implemented when supported by computers. Some companies have automated benefits enrollments. Employees can self-register for specific benefits using the corporate portal or voice technology. Employees self-select desired benefits from a menu. Payroll pay cards are now in use in numerous companies, such as Payless Shoes, which has 30,000 employees in 5,000 stores (see Korolishin, 2004a). The system specifies the value of each benefit and the available benefits balance of each employee. Some companies use intelligent agents to assist the employees and monitor their actions. Expert systems can answer employees' questions and offer advice online. Simpler systems allow for self-updating of personal information such as changes in address, family status, etc. Self-entry saves money for the company and is usually more accurate.

For a comprehensive resource of HRM on the Web, see *shrm.org/hrlinks.*

EMPLOYEE RELATIONSHIP MANAGEMENT.   In their effort to better manage employees, companies are developing *human capital management (HCM),* facilitated by the Web, to streamline the HR process. These Web applications are more commonly referred to as **employee relationship management (ERM).** For example, self-services such as tracking personal information and online training are very popular in ERM. Improved relationships with employees results in better retention and higher productivity. For an example of how ERM is done in a global grocery chain, see Buss (2002). ERM technologies and applications are very similar to those of customer relationship management (CRM), which we discuss in Chapter 7.

6.7 INTEGRATING FUNCTIONAL INFORMATION SYSTEMS

Functional information systems can be built in-house, they can be purchased from large vendors (such as Computer Associates, Best Software Inc., Microsoft, Oracle, IBM, or PeopleSoft), or they can be leased from application service providers (ASPs). In any of these cases, there is a need for their integration with other information systems, including databases.

Reasons for Integration   For many years most IT applications were developed in the functional areas, independent of each other. Many companies developed their own customized systems that dealt with standard procedures to execute transaction processing/operational activities. These procedures are fairly similar, regardless of what company is performing them. Therefore, the trend today is to buy commercial, off-the-shelf functional applications or to lease them from ASPs. The smaller the organization, the more attractive such options are. Indeed, several hundred commercial products are available to support each of the major functional areas.

Development tools are also available to build custom-made applications in a specific functional area. For example, there are software packages for building financial applications, a hospital pharmacy management system, and a university student registration system. Some software vendors specialize in one or a few areas. For example, Lawson Software concentrates on retailing (see Minicase1), and PeopleSoft's strength is in HRM.

However, to build information systems along business processes (which cross functional lines) requires a different approach. Matching business processes with a combination of several functional off-the-shelf packages may be a solution in some areas. For example, it may be possible to integrate manufacturing, sales, and accounting software if they all come from the same software vendor (as shown in the opening case). However, combining existing packages from several vendors may not be practical or effective. To build applications that will easily cross functional lines and reach separate databases often requires new approaches such as Web Services and integrated suites, such as Oracle 9i (McCullough, 2002).

Information systems integration tears down barriers between and among departments and corporate headquarters and reduces duplication of effort. For example, Palaniswamy and Frank (2000) studied five ERP systems and found in all cases that better cross-functional integration was a critical success factor. A framework for an integrated information system was developed by Yakhou and Rahali (1992) and is shown in Online File W6.18. In their integrated framework, there is data sharing as well as joint execution of business processes across functional areas, allowing individuals in one area to quickly and easily provide input to another area. Various functional managers are linked together in an enterprisewide system.

Technology Guides are located at the book's Web site.

One of the key factors for integration, especially with business partners, is agreement on appropriate standards (see *openapplications.org*). Integration can be done by middleware (Technology Guide 2) and by Web Services (Technology Guide 6).

Integrated information systems can be built easily in a small company. In large organizations, and even in multinational corporations, integration may require more effort, as shown in *IT at Work 6.7* (page 284).

Another approach to integration of information systems is to use ERP software (Chapter 7). However, ERP requires a company to fit its business processes to the software. As an alternative to ERP, companies can choose the *best-of-breed systems* on the market, or use some of their own home-grown systems and integrate them. The latter approach may not be simple, but it may be more effective.

By whatever method it is accomplished, integrating information systems helps to reduce cost, increase employees' productivity, and facilitate information sharing and collaboration, which are necessary for improving customer service.

Integration of Front-Office with Back-Office Operations

In Chapters 2 and 4 we discussed the need to integrate front-office with back-office operations. This is a difficult task. It is easier to integrate the front-office operations among themselves and the back-office operations among themselves (which is basically what systems such as MAS 90 are doing).

Software from various vendors offers some front-office and back-office integration solutions. Oracle Corp., for example, is continuously expanding its front-office software, which offers a capability of connecting back-office operations with it. To do so, the software uses new integration approaches, such as process-centric integration. **Process-centric integration** refers to integration solutions designed, developed, and managed from a business-process perspective, instead of from a technical or middleware perspective. The Oracle 9i product, for example, offers not only internal integration of the back office and front office, but also integration with business partners (see McCullough, 2002). Among its capabilities are:

- *Field sales online:* a Web-based customer management application.
- *Service contracts:* contract management and service options.
- *Mobile sales and marketing:* wireless groupware for connecting different management groups.
- *Call center and telephony suite:* a Web-based call center.

IT at Work 6.7
WEB-BASED INTEGRATED EMPLOYEES
AND CUSTOMER PORTALS AT EUROPCAR

Europcar International (*europcar.com*), the largest European-based car rental agency, changed the structure of its entire organization, in addition to changing everyday work processes and methods. To support these changes, the company combined 55 different mainframe and minicomputer systems into a single client/server center known as Greenway. Located at corporate headquarters near Paris, the $400 million system initially combined data from nine different countries within Europe, and today it has expanded to a global system (118 countries in 2004).

The 55 original independent systems used various data types, many of which were incompatible and needed to be integrated. Europcar was interested in integrating the business processes, customer preferences, and related data into a single system. To complicate matters, the company had to simultaneously develop a uniform set of business practices (corporate standards) to support the new single business entity. Furthermore, Europcar had to consider the variety of languages spoken in the nine countries involved, as well as different cultures and currencies (before the euro was adopted).

Key business processes—including reservations, billing, fleet management, cost control, and corporate finance—were all integrated into Greenway. The system serves employees via an employee portal and customers via a customer portal. As Europcar has expanded to 100 countries worldwide (as of 2003), its information system has expanded considerably as well. Reservations can be made on the corporate portal, and a smart card is available to enable customers to check in and out rapidly. Other customer-related benefits include: (1) fast service to calling customers since clerks no longer have to manually verify credit cards or calculate bills, (2) reservation desks linked to airline reservation systems like SABRE or Amadeus, (3) online reservations accessed via the customers' portal, and (4) corporate customers managed from one location.

Europcar originally grew through the acquisition of geographically and culturally disparate entities. Through reengineering, IT helps support these business alliances to present more of a multicountry team-based organization. By 2004, several thousand Europcar employees at about 1,000 offices worldwide were using Greenway.

Sources: Based on *europcar.com* (press releases 2000–2004).

For Further Exploration: What are some of the difficulties of integrating 55 systems from nine countries speaking different languages? What functional areas can you identify in the integrated system? What is the role of the different portals?

- ***Internet commerce:*** an order-taking and payment unit interconnected with ERP back-office applications. It is also tightly connected to the call center for order taking.
- ***Business intelligence:*** identification of most-valuable customers, analysis of why customers leave, and evaluation of sales forecast accuracy.

Another integration software product is IBM's WebSphere architecture, which includes front office (WebSphere Portal), back office, and supportive infrastructure. Special software for integrating front- and back-office applications is provided by Best Software.

Many other vendors offer complete enterprise packages. For example, Synco Software (*syncosoft.com*) offers ERP services, which include accounting, finance, marketing, production, and executive information system modules. SAP-AG, in its ERP R/3 product, offers more than 70 integrated modules, as will be shown in Chapter 7.

 ## MANAGERIAL ISSUES

1. ***Integration of functional information systems.*** Integration of existing stand-alone functional information systems is a major problem for many organizations. Although client/server architecture is more amenable to integration than

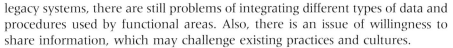

legacy systems, there are still problems of integrating different types of data and procedures used by functional areas. Also, there is an issue of willingness to share information, which may challenge existing practices and cultures.

2. ***Priority of transaction processing.*** Transaction processing may not be an exotic application, but it deals with the core processes of organizations. It must receive top priority in resource allocation, balanced against innovative applications needed to sustain competitive advantage and profitability, because the TPS collects the information needed for most other applications.

3. ***Finding innovative applications.*** Tools such as Lotus Notes, corporate portals, and Web-based business intelligence enable the construction of many applications that can increase productivity and quality. Finding opportunities for such applications can best be accomplished cooperatively by end users and the IS department.

4. ***Using the Web.*** Web-based systems should be considered in all functional areas. They are effective, cost relatively little, and are user friendly. In addition to new applications, companies should consider conversion of existing applications to Web-based ones.

5. ***Systems integration.*** Although functional systems are necessary, they may not be sufficient if they work independently. It is difficult to integrate functional information systems, but there are several approaches to doing so. In the future, Web Services could solve many integration problems, including connecting to a legacy system.

6. ***Ethical issues.*** Many ethical issues are associated with the various topics of this chapter. Professional organizations, relating to the functional areas (e.g., marketing associations), have their own codes of ethics. These codes should be taken into account in developing functional systems. Likewise, organizations must consider privacy policies. Several organizations provide comparisons of privacy policies and other ethics-related topics. For an example, see *socap.org*.

HRM applications are especially prone to ethical and legal considerations. For example, training activities that are part of HRM may involve ethical issues in recruiting and selecting employees and in evaluating performance. Likewise, TPS data processing and storage deal with private information about people, their performance, etc. Care should be taken to protect this information and the privacy of employees and customers.

For more on business ethics as it applies to topics in this chapter, see *ethics.ubc.ca/resources/business*.

KEY TERMS

Batch processing *250*

Channel systems *260*

Computer-integrated manufacturing (CIM) *259*

Employee relationship management (ERM) *282*

Expense management automation (EMA) *273*

Financial value chain management (FVCM) *275*

Just-in-time (JIT) *258*

Manufacturing resource planning (MRP II) *258*

Material requirements planning (MRP) *257*

Online processing *251*

Online transaction processing (OLTP) *251*

Process-centric integration *283*

Product lifecycle management (PLM) *259*

Sales automation software *267*

Sales force automation *266*

Vendor-managed inventory (VMI) *257*

Virtual close *273*

CHAPTER HIGHLIGHTS (Numbers Refer to Learning Objectives)

❶ Information systems applications can support many functional activities. Considerable software is readily available on the market for much of this support (for lease or to buy).

❷ The major business functional areas are production/operations management, marketing, accounting/finance, and human resources management.

❸ The backbone of most information systems applications is the transaction processing system (TPS), which keeps track of the routine, mission-central operations of the organization.

❹ The major area of IT support to production/operations management is in logistics and inventory management: MRP, MRP II, JIT, mass customization, PLM, and CIM.

❺ Marketing and sales information systems deal with all activities related to customer orders, sales, advertising and promotion, market research, customer service, and product and service pricing. Using IT can increase sales, customers' satisfaction, and profitability.

❻ Financial information systems deal with topics such as investment management, financing operations, raising capital, risk analysis, and credit approval.

❻ Accounting information systems also cover many non-TPS applications in areas such as cost control, taxation, and auditing.

❼ Most tasks related to human resources development can be supported by human resources information systems. These tasks include employee recruitment and selection, hiring, performance evaluation, salary and benefits administration, training and development, labor negotiations, and work planning.

❼ Web-based HR systems are extremely useful for recruiting and training.

❽ Integrated functional information systems are necessary to ensure effective and efficient execution of activities that cross functional lines or that require functional cooperation.

❽ Integrating applications is difficult; it can be done in different ways, such as buying off-the-shelf applications from one vendor or using special connecting software known as middleware. A promising new approach is that of Web Services.

VIRTUAL COMPANY ASSIGNMENT

Instructions for accessing The Wireless Café on the Student Web Site

1. Go to
   wiley.com/college/turban
2. Select Turban/Leidner/McLean/Wetherbe's *Information Technology for Management, Fifth Edition.*
3. Click on Student Resources site, in the toolbar on the left.
4. Click on the link for Virtual Company Web site.
5. Click on Wireless Café.

Transaction Processing at The Wireless Café
Go to The Wireless Café's link on the Student Web Site. There you will be asked to think about the business activities and transactions, other than cooking, that the restaurant engages in. You will be asked to consider types of transaction processing applications that could be implemented at The Wireless Café.

More Resources
More resources and study tools are located on the Student Web Site. You'll find additional chapter materials and useful Web links. In addition, self-quizzes that provide individualized feedback are available for each chapter.

QUESTIONS FOR REVIEW

1. What is a functional information system?
2. List the major characteristics of a functional information system.
3. What are the objectives of a TPS?
4. List the major characteristics of a TPS.
5. Distinguish between batch and online TPS.
6. Explain how the Web enables mass customization.
7. Describe MRP.
8. Describe MRP II.
9. Describe VMI.
10. Define CIM, and list its major benefits.
11. Describe PLM, and list its benefits.
12. Define channel systems.
13. Define JIT, and list some of its benefits.
14. Define sales force automation.
15. What is product/customer profitability?
16. Describe some tactical and strategic accounting/finance applications.
17. List some budgeting-related activities.
18. List some EC activities in finance.
19. List IT-supported recruitment activities.
20. How can training go online?
21. Explain human resources information systems.
22. Describe the need for application integration.

QUESTIONS FOR DISCUSSION

1. Why is it logical to organize IT applications by functional areas?
2. Describe the role of a TPS in a service organization.
3. Why are transaction processing systems a major target for restructuring?
4. Which functional areas are related to payroll, and how does the relevant information flow?
5. Discuss the benefits of Web-based TPS.
6. It is said that in order to be used successfully, MRP must be computerized. Why?
7. The Japanese implemented JIT for many years without computers. Discuss some elements of JIT, and comment on the potential benefits of computerization.
8. Describe the role of computers in CIM.
9. Explain how Web applications can make the customer king/queen.
10. Why are information systems critical to sales-order processing?
11. Describe how IT can enhance mass customization.
12. Marketing databases play a major role in channel systems. Why?
13. Geographical information systems are playing an important role in supporting marketing and sales. Provide some examples not discussed in the text.
14. What is the role of software in PLM? Can PLM be done manually?
15. Discuss how IT facilitates the budgeting process.
16. Why is risk management important, and how can it be enhanced by IT?
17. Compare bill presentment to check re-presentment. How are they facilitated by IT?
18. How can the Internet support investment decisions?
19. Describe the benefits of an accounting integrated software such as MAS 90; compare it to MAS 200.
20. Discuss the role IT plays in support of auditing.
21. Investigate the role of the Web in human resources management.
22. Geographical information systems are playing an important role in supporting marketing and sales. Provide some examples not discussed in the text. (See Chapter 10.)
23. Discuss the need for application integration and the difficulty of doing it.
24. Discuss the approaches and reasons for integrating front-office with back-office operations.

EXERCISES

1. Review the Dartmouth-Hitchcock Medical center case. Assume that RFID tags cost 5 cents each. How might use of RFID tags change the supply chain management? Would the new system at the medical center still be needed? Write a report on your conclusions.
2. The chart shown in Figure 6.4 portrays the flow of routine activities in a typical manufacturing organization. Explain in what areas IT can be most valuable.
3. Argot International (a fictitious name) is a medium-sized company in Peoria, Illinois, with about 2,000

employees. The company manufactures special machines for farms and food-processing plants, buying materials and components from about 150 vendors in six different countries. It also buys special machines and tools from Japan. Products are sold either to wholesalers (about 70) or directly to clients (from a mailing list of about 2,000). The business is very competitive.

The company has the following information systems in place: financial/accounting, marketing (primarily information about sales), engineering, research and development, and inventory management. These systems are independent of each other although they are all connected to the corporate intranet.

Argot is having profitability problems. Cash is in high demand and short supply, due to strong business competition from Germany and Japan. The company wants to investigate the possibility of using information technology to improve the situation. However, the vice president of finance objects to the idea, claiming that most of the tangible benefits of information technology are already being realized.

You are hired as a consultant to the president. Respond to the following:

a. Prepare a list of 10 potential applications of information technologies that you think could help the company.

b. From the description of the case, would you recommend any portals? Be very specific. Remember, the company is in financial trouble.

c. How can Web Services help Argot?

4. Enter *resumix.yahoo.com*. Take the demo. Prepare a list of all the product's capabilities.

GROUP ASSIGNMENTS

1. Each group should visit (or investigate) a large company in a different industry and identify its channel systems. Prepare a diagram that shows the six components shown in Figure 6.7. Then find how IT supports each of those components. Finally, suggest improvements in the existing channel system that can be supported by IT technologies and that are not in use by the company today. Each group presents its findings.

2. The class is divided into groups of four. Each group member represents a major functional area: production/operations management, sales/marketing, accounting/ finance, and human resources. Find and describe several examples of processes that require the integration of functional information systems in a company of your choice. Each group will also show the interfaces to the other functional areas.

3. Each group investigates an HRM software vendor (Oracle, Peoplesoft, SAP, Lawson Software). The group prepares a list of all HRM functionalities supported by the software. Then the groups make a presentation to convince the class that its vendor is the best.

INTERNET EXERCISES

1. Surf the Net and find free accounting software (try *shareware.cnet.com, clarisys.ca/free, rkom.com, tucows.com, passtheshareware.com,* and *freeware-guide.com*). Download the software and try it. Write a report on your findings.

2. Enter the site of Federal Express (*fedex.com*) and learn how to ship a package, track the status of a package, and calculate its cost. Comment on your experience.

3. Finding a job on the Internet is challenging; there are almost too many places to look. Visit the following sites: *headhunter.net, careermag.com, hotjobs.com, jobcenter.com,* and *monster.com*. What do these sites provide you as a job seeker?

4. Enter the Web sites *tps.com* and some of those listed in Online File W6.4, and find information about software products available from those sites. Identify the software that allows Internet transaction processing. Prepare a report about the benefits of the products identified.

5. Enter the Web site *peoplesoft.com* and identify products and services in the area of integrated software. E-mail PeopleSoft to find out whether its product can fit the organization where you work or one with which you are familiar.

6. Examine the capabilities of the following financial software packages: TekPortal (from *teknowledge.com*), Financial Analyzer (from Oracle), and CFO Vision (from SAS Institute). Prepare a report comparing the capabilities of the software packages.

7. Surf the Internet and find information from three vendors on sales force automation (try *sybase.com* first). Prepare a report on the state of the art.

8. Enter *teknowledge.com* and review the products that help with online training (training systems). What are the most attractive features of these products?

9. Enter *microsoft.com/businessSolutions/Solomon/default.mspx*. View three of the demos in different functional areas of your choice. Prepare a report on the capabilities.

10. Enter *sage.com/solutions/solutions.htm*. Identify functional software, CRM software, and e-business software products. Are these standalone or integrated? Explain.

Minicase 1
Dollar General Uses Integrated Software

Dollar General (*dollargeneral.com*) operates more than 6,000 general stores in the United States, fiercely competing with Wal-Mart, Target, and thousands of other stores in the sale of food, apparel, home-cleaning products, health and beauty aids, and more. The chain doubled in size between 1996 and 2002 and has had some problems in addition to the stiff competition, due to its rapid expansion. For example, moving into new states means different sales taxes, and these need to be closely monitored for changes. Personnel management also became more difficult with the organization's growth. An increased number of purchasing orders exacerbated problems in the accounts payable department, which was using manual matching of purchasing orders, invoices, and what was actually received in the "receiving" department before bills were paid.

The IT department was flooded with requests to generate long reports on topics ranging from asset management to general ledgers. It became clear that a better information system was needed. Dollar General started by evaluating information requirements that would be able to solve the above and other problems that cut into the company's profit.

A major factor in deciding which software to buy was the integration requirement among the existing information systems of the various functional areas, especially the financial applications. This led to the selection of the Financials suite (from Lawson Software). The company started to implement applications one at a time. Before 1998, the company installed the suite's asset management, payroll, and some HR applications which allow the tens of thousands of employees to monitor and self-update their benefits, 401k contributions, and personal data (resulting in big savings to the HR department). After 1998, the accounts payable and general ledger modules of Lawson Software were activated. The accounting modules allow employees to route, extract, and analyze data in the accounting/finance area with little reliance on IT personnel. During 2001–2003, Dollar General moved into the sales and procurement areas, thus adding the marketing and operation activities to the integrated system.

Here are a few examples of how various parts of the new system work: All sales data from the point-of-sale scanners of some 6,000 stores are pulled each night, together with financial data, discounts, etc., into the business intelligence application for financial and marketing analysis. Employee payroll data, from each store, are pulled once a week. This provides synergy with the sales audit system (from STS Software). All sales data are processed nightly by the STS System, broken into hourly journal entries, processed and summarized, and then entered into the Lawson's general ledger module.

The original infrastructure was mainframe based (IBM AS 400). By 2002, the 800 largest suppliers of Dollar General were submitting their bills on the EDI. This allowed instantaneous processing in the accounts payable module. By 2003, service providers, such as utilities, were added to the system. To do all this the system was migrated in 2001 from the old legacy system to the Unix operating system, and then to a Web-based infrastructure, mainly in order to add Web-based functionalities and tools.

A development tool embedded in Lawson's Financials allowed users to customize applications without touching the computer programming code. This included applications that are not contained in the Lawson system. For example, an employee-bonus application was not available at Lawson, but was added to Financial's payroll module to accommodate Dollar General's bonus system. A customized application that allowed additions and changes in dozens of geographical areas also solved the organization's state sales-tax collection and reporting problem.

The system is very scalable, so there is no problem in adding stores, vendors, applications, or functionalities. In 2003, the system was completely converted to Web-based, enabling authorized vendors, for example, to log on the Internet and view the status of their invoices by themselves. Also, the Internet/EDI enables small vendors to use the system. (An EDI is too expensive for small vendors, but the EDI/Internet is affordable.) Also, the employees can update personal data from any Web-enabled desktop in the store or at home. Future plans call for adding an e-purchasing (procurement) module using a desktop purchasing model (see Chapter 4).

Sources: Compiled from Amato-McCoy (2002a) and *lawson.com* (accessed May 2004).

Questions for Minicase 1

1. Explain why the old, nonintegrated functional system created problems for the company. Be specific.
2. The new system cost several million dollars. Why, in your opinion, was it necessary to install it?
3. Lawson Software Smart Notification Software (*lawson.com*) is being considered by Dollar General. Find information about the software and write an opinion for adoption or rejection.
4. Another new product of Lawson is Services Automation. Would you recommend it to Dollar General? Why or why not?

Minicase 2
99 Cents Only Stores Use IT to Improve Operations

Finding items in a 750,000-square-foot distribution center is not a simple job. Dozens of "pickers" work at 99 Cents Only (*www.99only.com*) Stores' two distribution centers, fulfilling orders from 189 stores. Until 2003, the workers spent lots of time looking for items and trying to avoid crashing into one another. The pickers use electric carts to move items on pallets, which are then loaded on trucks to be delivered to individual stores.

A new system was installed in 2003, using proven information technologies. Here's how the system works: New products arrive and are stored. The computer-generated voice system analyzes each store's order and then instructs pickers how to fulfill the order in real time. Directed by computer-generated voice, pickers pick needed items from a certain section, row, and bin and deliver them to the truck. The computerized system also calculates the most efficient route for the pickers to drive their carts. The process is illustrated in Online File W6.19.

The voice system enables the pickers to confirm finding the items, or to notify of shortages. Other computer systems support the cash registers in each store, provide Wi-Fi service for internal communication in each store and in the warehouses, provide Internet access, and run all the back-office operations.

Being relatively small, the company integrates only proven technologies into its overall IT system. The results of the computer-generated voice system alone show an increase in picking accuracy (to 99% from about 90%) and productivity improvement of about 15 percent.

Source: Compiled from Rae-Dupree (2004).

Questions for Minicase 2

1. Identify the improvements made by IT and relate them to the functional departments. (Try to match with the specific topics discussed in each functional area.)
2. Relate this case to the topic of systems integration.
3. Envision how RFID may improve on the new system in the future.
4. In your opinion, is the system connected to the TPS? (Consider also the in-store applications.)
5. Enter High Jump Software Inc. (*highjumpsoftware.com*), the vendor of the warehouse-management package, and identify the capabilities of the system.

REFERENCES

Aberdeen.com, "Best Practices in Streamlining the Financial Value Chain: Top Seven FVCM Implementations," *Aberdeen Group*, 2002, *aberdeen.com/ab_company/hottopics/fvcm2002/default.htm* (accessed June 2003).

Amato-McCoy, D. M., "Dollar General Rings Up Back-Office Efficiencies with Financial Suite," *Stores,* October 2002a.

Amato-McCoy, D. M., "Sears Combines Retail Reporting and Customer Databases on a Single Platform," *Stores,* November 2002b.

Amato-McCoy, D. M., "Linens 'n Things Protects Inventory Investment with Supply Planning Suite," *Stores,* November 2002c.

Asian Wall Street Journal, February 2000.

autobytel.com, 2002.

Avriel, M., et al., "Opti-Money at Bank Hapoalim," *Interfaces*, January–February 2004.

Baker, W. et al., "Price Smarter on the Net," *Harvard Business Review*, February 2001.

Banks, E., *E-Finance: The Electronic Revolution*. London: John Wiley and Sons, Ltd., 2001.

Benjaafar, S. et al., "Next Generation Factory Layouts," *Interfaces*, November–December 2002.

Bernstein, P. A., and E. Newcomer, *The Principles of Transaction Processing*. San Francisco: Morgan Kaufmann, 1997.

Bielski, L., "Cutting Cost, Retaining Project Detail," *ABA Banking Journal*, May 2002.

Boisvert, L., "Web-based Learning," *Information Systems Management*, Winter 2000.

Bolton, M., "Customer Centric Business Processing," *International Journal of Productivity and Performance Management*, 53(12), 2004.

Borck, J. R., "Recruiting Systems Control Resume Chaos," *Infoworld*, July 24, 2000.

Boucher-Ferguson, R., "A New Shipping Rout (Web-EDI)," *eWeek*, September 23, 2002.

Brewin, B., "Verizon Plans Faster Wireless Data Network," *Computerworld*, January 12, 2004.

Buckley, N., "E-Route to Whiter Smile," *Financial Times*, August 26, 2002.

Buss, D., "Extended POS Initiative Aims to Connect Store and Consumer to the Entire Enterprise," *Store*, October 2002.

Bussler, L., and Davis, "Information Systems: The Quiet Revolution in Human Resource Management," *Journal of Computer Information Systems*, Winter 2001–2002.

Chaudhury, A. et al., "Web Channels in E-Commerce," *Communications of the ACM*, January 2001.

cscresearchservices.com, "The Long-Standing Gulf between Objects and Transactions Is Being Bridged," 1997, *cscresearchservices.com/foundation/library/104/RP19.asp* (accessed July 2003).

Copeland, J., "Making HR Your Business," *CA Magazine*, April 2004.

daiwa.co.jp, 2000.

Day, M., "What is PLM?," *Cadserver*, April 15, 2002, *tenlinks.com/NEWS/ARTICLES/cadserver/plm.htm* (accessed June 2003).

Degnan, C., "Best Practices in Expense Management Automation," Special Report. Boston: Aberdeen Group, January 2003, *aberdeen.com/ab_company/hottopics/emabp/default.htm* (accessed June 2003).

Ensher, E. A. et al., "Tales from the Hiring Line," *Organizational Dynamics*, October–December 2002.

europcar.com, 2001.

ford.com, 2000.

Galagan, P. A., "The Delta Force at Cisco," *Training and Development*, July 2002.

Goldman Sachs Group. Special Report, *gs.com*, February 15, 2001.

Gorton, I., *Enterprise TPS: Putting the CORBA OTS, ENGINA, and OrbixOTM to Work*. Reading, MA: Addison Wesley, 2000.

Grimes, S., "Declaration Support: The B.P.M. Drumbeat," *Intelligent Enterprise*, April 23, 2003.

Harrington, A., "Can Anyone Build a Better Monster?" *Fortune*, May 13, 2002.

Holweg, M., and F. K. Pil, "Sucessful Build-to-Order Strategies Start with the Customer," *MIS Sloan Management Review*, Fall 2001.

Howarth, B., "To Catch a Thief," *BRW*, January 15–21, 2004a.

Howarth, B., "Shopper-Cam," *BRW*, January 15–21, 2004b.

InternetWeek, July 2000.

jaguar.com (accessed October 13, 2000 and February 8, 2003).

Jandt, E. F., and Nemnich, M. B. (eds.), *Using the Internet and the Web in Your Job Search*, 2nd ed. Indianapolis, IN: Jistwork, 1999.

Jareb, E., and V. Rajkovic, "Use of an Expert System in Personnel Selection," *Information Management*, July–December 2001.

Kahn, R. H., and M. Sloan, "Twenty-First Century Training," *Sales and Marketing Management*, June 1997.

Kannan, P. K. et al., "Marketing Information on the I-Way," *Communications of the ACM*, March 1999.

Korolishin, J., "Meeting the Employee Scheduling Challenge," *Stores*, September 2003.

Korolishin, J., "Payroll Pay Cards Pay Off at Payless," *Stores*, February 2004a.

Korolishin, J., "Sheetz Keeps Tab on Training Compliance via Web Portal," *Stores*, February 2004b.

Kroll, K. M., "Video-Based Systems Seek Cleaner Focus on Store Traffic," *Stores*, April 2002.

Lawson.com, 2002.

Lee, Y. M., and E. J. Chen, "BASF Uses a Framework for Developing Web-Based Production-Planning Optimization Tools," *Interfaces*, November–December 2002.

Liao, Z., "Real Time Tax: Dispatching Using GPS," *Communications of the ACM*, May 2003.

Maxemchuk, N. F., and D. H. Shur, "An Internet Multicast System for the Stock Market," *ACM Transactions on Computer Systems*, August 2001.

McClenahen, J. S., "The Book on the One-Day Close," *Industry Week*, April 2002.

McCullough, D. C., *Oracle 9i*. New York: Hungry Minds, 2002.

McKinley, E., "Multicasting Solution Ushers in New Era of Computer-Based Training," *Stores*, April 2003.

Meredith, J. R., and S. M. Shafer, *Operations Management*. New York: Wiley, 2002.

O'Donnell, A., "Sales Force Automation iAnywhere Solutions," *Insurance & Technology*, December 2003.

Palaniswamy, R., and T. Frank, "Enhancing Manufacturing Performance with ERP Systems," *Information Management Journal*, Summer 2000.

Parks, L., "Schurman Fine Papers Rocks Up Labor Savings," *Stores*, February 2004.

Perkins-Munn, T. S., and Y. T. Chen, "Streamlining Project Management through Online Solutions," *Journal of Business Strategy*, January 2004.

pg.com (accessed February–December 2002).

Pittaras, A., "Automated Modeling," *PC AI*, January–February 1996.

qvc.com (accessed June 2003).

Rae-Dupree, J., "Case Study: 99 Cents Only Stores' Efficient IT Infrastructure," *CIO Insight*, April 1, 2004, *http:www.cio.insight.com/article2/o,1397,1456000,00.asp*.

Raskin, A., "A Faster Ride to Market," *Business* 2.0, October 2002.

Reda, S., "Evelyn Follit Fuses Technology, Business, and HR Strategies," *Stores*, March 2004.

Reda, S., "Word-of Mouth Marketing Enjoys New Life as Potent Online Advertising Strategy," *Stores*, October 2002.

Reed, C. et al., *eCFO: Sustaining Value in New Corporations*. Chichester, U.K.: Wiley, 2001.

Robb, D., "The Virtual Enterprise: How Companies Use Technology to Stay in Control of a Virtual Supply Chain," *Information Strategy*, 2003.

Sadeh, N. M., *M-Commerce: Technologies, Services, and Business Models*. New York: Wiley, 2002.

Salodof-MacNeil, J., "The Factoring Factor," *Inc. Magazine*, February 1, 2002.

Schafer, S., "Super Charged Sell," *Inc. Technology*, No. 2, 1997.

Seidman, T., "Retail Fast-Food Marketing Targets Workers on the Job," *Stores*, February 2002.

Subrahmanyam, A., "Nuts and Bolts of Transaction Processing: A Comprehensive Tutorial," *subrahmanyam.com…articles/transactions/NutsAndBoltsOfTP.html* (accessed March 2, 2002).

Strauss, J. et al., *E-Marketing*, 3rd ed. Upper Saddle River, NJ: Prentice Hall, 2003.

Sung, N. H., and J. K. Lee, "Knowledge Assisted Dynamic Pricing for Large-Scale Retailers," *Decision Support Systems*, June 2000.

Sweeney, T., "Web Kiosks Spur Spending in Stores," *Information Week.com*, March 12, 2001, *informationweek.com/828/kiosk.htm* (accessed June 2003).

Thomas, S. L., and K. Ray, "Recruiting and the Web: High-Tech Hiring," *Business Horizons*, May–June 2000.

Totty, P., "MCIF Systems Are Gaining Broader Acceptance," *Credit Union Magazine*, May 2000.

Training and Development, February 1997.

Turban, E. et al., *Electronic Commerce 2006*. Upper Saddle River, NJ: Prentice Hall, 2006.

Vijayakumar, S., "Improving Software Cost Estimation," *Project Management Today*, May 2002.

"Web Breathes Life into Medical Firm's Training Program," *Internet Week*, July 27, 1988, *internetwk.com/search/results.jhtml?queryText=Omniteche&site_id=3* (accessed October 2002).

"What EMA Systems Now Offer Accounting Departments?" *Acct. Dept. Mgt. & Administration Report,* February 2002.

Wigham, R., "98 Percent Now Use Online Recruitment," *Personnel Today,* January 27, 2004.

Wind, Y., "The Challenge of Customization in Financial Services," *Communications of the ACM,* July 2001.

Yakhou, M., and B. Rahali, "Integration of Business Functions: Roles of Cross-Functional Information Systems," *APICS,* December 1992.

Zakaria, Z., "Many Currencies, One FMIS System," *MIS Asia,* April 2002.

Zaremba, M. B., and G. Morel, "Integration and Control of Intelligence in Distributed Manufacturing," *Journal of Intelligent Manufacturing,* February 2003.

Zdnetindia.com/news, September 29, 2000.

Zipkin, P., "The Limits of Mass Customization," *MIT Sloan Management Review,* Spring 2001.

PART III
Organizational Applications

6. Transaction Processing, Functional Applications, and Integration
▶ 7. Enterprise Systems: From Supply Chains to ERP to CRM
8. Interorganizational and Global Information Systems

CHAPTER

7

Enterprise Systems: From Supply Chains to ERP to CRM

7.1 Essentials of Enterprise Systems and Supply Chains

7.2 Supply Chain Problems and Solutions

7.3 Computerized Enterprise Systems: MRP, MRP II, SCM, and Software Integration

7.4 Enterprise Resource Planning and Supply Chain Management

7.5 CRM and Its Support by IT

Minicases:
1. Northern Digital
2. QVC

LEARNING OBJECTIVES

After studying this chapter, you will be able to:

❶ Understand the essentials of enterprise systems and computerized supply chain management.

❷ Describe the various types of supply chains.

❸ Describe some major problems of managing supply chains and some innovative solutions.

❹ Describe some major types of software that support activities along the supply chain.

❺ Describe the need for integrated software and how ERP does it.

❻ Describe CRM and its support by IT.

CHEVRONTEXACO MODERNIZED ITS SUPPLY CHAIN WITH IT

➡ THE PROBLEM

ChevronTexaco, the largest U.S. oil company, is multinational in nature. Its main business is drilling, refining, transporting, and selling gasoline (oil). In this competitive business, a saving of even a quarter of a penny per gallon totals up to millions of dollars. Two problems have plagued the oil industry: running out of gasoline at individual pumps, and a delivery that is aborted because a tank at the gas station is too full (called "retain"). Run-outs and retains, known as the industry's "twin evils," have been a target for improvements for years, with little success.

The causes of the twin evils have to do with the supply chain: Gasoline flows in the supply chain start with oil hunting, drilling, and extraction. After the oil is taken from the ground, it is delivered to and then processed in refineries, and finally it goes to storage and eventually to the retail pump and to the customer. The difficulty is to match the three parts of the supply chain: oil acquisition, processing, and distribution.

ChevronTexaco owns oil fields and refineries, but it also buys both crude and refined oil to meet peak demand. Purchases are of two types: those that are made through long-term contracts, and those that are purchased "as needed," in what is called the *spot market*, at prevailing prices (usually higher than contract purchases).

In the past, ChevronTexaco acted like a mass-production manufacturing company, just trying to make lots of oil products and then sell them (a supply-driven strategy). The problem with this strategy is that each time you make too much, you are introducing extra inventory or storage costs. If you make too little, you lose sales.

➡ THE SOLUTION

The company decided to change its business model from *supply driven* to *demand driven*. Namely, instead of focusing on how much oil it would process and "push" to customers, the company started thinking about how much oil its customers wanted and then about how to get it. This change necessitated a major transformation in the business and extensive support by information technologies.

To implement the IT support, the company installed in each tank in each gas station an electronic monitor. The monitor transmits real-time information about the oil level, through a cable, to the station's IT-based management system. That system then transmits the information via a satellite to the main inventory system at the company's main office. There, an advanced DSS-based planning system processes the data to help refining, marketing, and logistics decisions. This DSS also includes information collected at trucking and airline companies, which are major customers. Using an enterprise resource planning (ERP) and business planning system (BPS), ChevronTexaco determines how much to refine, how much to buy in spot markets, and when and how much to ship to each retail station.

To combine all of these data, it is necessary to integrate the supply and demand information systems, and this is where the ERP software is useful. These data are used by planners at various points across the supply chain (e.g., refinery, terminal management, station management, transportation, and production) who process and share data constantly. This data processing and data sharing are provided by the various information systems.

Recent IT projects support the supply chain and extend it to a global reach. These projects include the NetReady initiative that enables the operations of 150 e-business projects, the Global Information Link (GIL2) that enables connectivity throughout the company, the e-Guest project that enables sharing of information with business partners, and a global human resources information system.

 THE RESULTS

The integrated system that allows data to be shared across the company has improved decision making at every point in the customer-facing and processing parts of the supply chain. It resulted in an increase in the company's profit by more than $300 million in 1999 and by more than an additional $100 million each year after.

According to Worthen (2002), studies indicate that companies in the top 20 percent of the oil industry operate their supply chains twice as efficiently as average companies. These successful companies also carry half as much inventory, can respond to a significant rise in demand (20% or higher) twice as fast, and know how to minimize the number of deliveries to the gas stations. ChevronTexaco is in this category.

Sources: Compiled from Worthen (2002); and from *chevrontexaco.com,* see "Information Technology" (accessed January 2004).

 LESSONS LEARNED FROM THIS CASE

The ChevronTexaco case illustrates the need to drastically improve the management of the supply chain. All decision makers along the supply chain need to share information and collaborate. Doing so is not a simple task, as will be seen in this chapter, but IT solutions enable even a large multinational company to manage its supply chain.

ChevronTexaco successfully implemented the concepts of *supply chain management* and *enterprise resource planning.* Figure 7.1 (page 296) shows how these two topics are interrelated. Such a system is an enterprise system. In addition, the figure shows other enterprise systems. Some are described in other chapters (Chapters 2–6, and 9–11). Enterprise systems such as supply chains, ERP, and CRM are the subjects of this chapter.

7.1 ESSENTIALS OF ENTERPRISE SYSTEMS AND SUPPLY CHAINS

Enterprise systems (also called **enterprisewide systems**) are systems or processes that involve the entire enterprise or major portions of it. This is in contrast to functional systems, which are confined to one department (functional area) each.

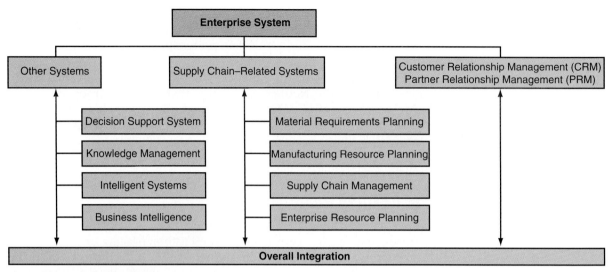

FIGURE 7.1 Overview of enterprise systems.

Several enterprise systems can be found in organizations. Typical examples are:

- Enterprise resource planning (ERP), which supports the internal supply chain.
- Extended ERP, which supports business partners as well. Most ERP systems today are extended.
- Customer relationship management (CRM), which provides customer care.
- Partner relationship management (PRM), which is designed to provide care to business partners.
- Decision support systems (DSSs), whose purpose is to support decision making throughout the enterprise, frequently with the help of a data warehouse. This category includes executive information systems.
- Knowledge management (KM) systems, whose objective is to support knowledge creation, storage, maintenance, and distribution throughout the enterprise.
- Business intelligence, which is computer-based decision analysis usually done online by managers and staff. It includes forecasting, analyzing alternatives, and evaluating risk and performance.
- Intelligent systems, which include a knowledge component, such as an expert system or neural network.

The first three systems are described in this chapter; PRM is described in Chapter 8, KM in Chapter 9, business intelligence in Chapter 10, and decision support and intelligent systems in Chapter 11.

Relevant Definitions The following definitions are helpful as you read this chapter:

SUPPLY CHAIN. *Supply chain* refers to the flow of materials, information, money, and services from raw material suppliers, through factories and warehouses, to the end customers. A supply chain also includes the *organizations* and *processes* that create and deliver products, information, and services to end customers. It includes many tasks, such as purchasing, payment flow, materials handling, production planning and control, logistics and warehousing, inventory control, and distribution and delivery.

SUPPLY CHAIN MANAGEMENT. The function of **supply chain management (SCM)** is to plan, organize, and optimize one or more of the supply chain's activities. Today the concept of SCM is usually supported by IT (see Mentzer, 2004, and Vakharia, 2002).

SCM SOFTWARE. **SCM software** refers to software intended to support specific segments of the supply chain, such as in manufacturing, inventory control, scheduling, and transportation. This software concentrates on improving decision making, optimization, and analysis.

E-SUPPLY CHAIN. When a supply chain is managed electronically, usually with Web-based software, it is referred to as an **e-supply chain.** As will be shown in this chapter, improvements in supply chains frequently involve attempts to convert a traditional supply chain to an e-supply chain, namely to automate the information flow in the chain (see Poirier and Bauer, 2000). For success factors for external adoption, see Chow (2004).

The Flows in the Supply Chain

There are typically three types of flows in the supply chain: materials, information, and financial.

1. *Materials flows.* These are all physical products, raw materials, supplies, and so forth, that flow along the chain. The concept of material flows also includes *reverse* flows—returned products, recycled products, and disposal of materials or products. A supply chain thus involves a *product life cycle* approach, from "dirt to dust."

2. *Information flows.* All data related to demand, shipments, orders, returns, and schedules, and changes in the data just cited, are information flows.

3. *Financial flows.* The financial flows are all transfers of money, payments, credit card information and authorization, payment schedules, e-payments, and credit-related data.

In some supply chains there are fewer types of flows. For example, in service industries there may be no physical flow of materials, but frequently there is flow of documents (hard and/or soft copies). In fact, the digitization of software, music, and other digital content may result in a supply chain without any physical flow. Notice, however, that in such a case, there are two types of information flows: one that replaces materials flow (e.g., digitized software) and one that is the supporting information (orders, billing, etc).

In managing the supply chain it is necessary to coordinate all the above flows among all the parties involved in the supply chain.

The Structure and Components of Supply Chains

The term *supply chain* comes from a picture of how the partnering organizations are linked together. A typical supply chain, which links a company with its suppliers and its distributors and customers, was shown in Figure 2.6 (page 64). Note that the supply chain involves three segments:

1. *Upstream,* where sourcing or procurement from external suppliers occur

2. *Internal*, where packaging, assembly, or manufacturing take place

3. *Downstream*, where distribution or dispersal takes place, frequently by external distributors

As noted earlier, a supply chain is more than just the movement of tangible inputs; it also includes the movement of information and money and the procedures that support the movement of a product or a service. Finally, the organizations and individuals involved are part of the chain as well.

Supply chains come in all shapes and sizes. They may be fairly complex, as shown in Figure 7.2. As can be seen in the figure, the supply chain for a toy manufacturer includes many suppliers, manufacturing plants (for parts) and assembly plants, wholesalers (some of which are virtual), retailers, customers, and support functions such as product design and engineering. For the sake of simplicity we do not show here the flow of payments.

Notice that in Figure 7.2 the chain is not strictly linear, as it was in Figure 2.6. Here, we see some loops in the process. In addition, sometimes the flow of information and even goods can be bidirectional. For example, the *return* of damaged or unwanted products (known as *reverse logistics*) takes place. For the toy industry that would include toys returned to the retailers in cases of defects or recalls by the manufacturer.

FIGURE 7.2 An toy industry supply chain.

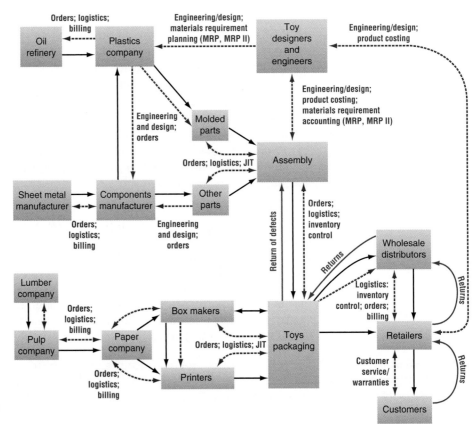

TIERS OF SUPPLIERS. An examination of Figure 2.6 (page 64) shows there are several potential tiers of suppliers. In some processes, there is only one tier of suppliers. However, in many other processes there are several tiers of suppliers. The idea of tiers of suppliers means that a supplier may have one or more subsuppliers, and the subsupplier may have its own subsupplier(s), and so on. For example, making cardboard containers involves three tiers: The cardboard container manufacturer (tier one) gets its material from the paper mill (tier two), which gets its material from the lumber company (tier three). Some supply chains can have up to a dozen tiers.

Coordinating subsuppliers can be a complex task. Use of B2B exchanges (Chapter 4), extranets, and PRM (Chapter 8) can help provide needed coordination.

Types of Supply Chains

The supply chain shown in Figure 7.2 is representative of manufacturing companies. Such companies may also have warehouses in different locations, making the chain even more complex. Types of supply chains can be classified into four categories: integrated make-to-stock, continuous replenishment, build-to-order, and channel assembly. Details are provided in Online File W7.1.

Benefits of Proper Supply Chain Management

The flow of goods, services, information, and financial resources is usually designed not only to effectively transform raw items to finished products and services, but also to do so in an *efficient manner* (e.g., by using proper planning; see Sodhi, 2003). IT makes a major contribution to both efficiency and effectiveness of information flows (see Section 7.3).

The goals of modern SCM are to reduce uncertainty and risks along the supply chain, thereby decreasing inventory levels and cycle time, and improving business processes and customer service. All of these benefits contribute to increased profitability and competitiveness, as demonstrated in the opening case. The benefits of supply chain management have long been recognized both in business and in the military. To enjoy the above benefits it is necessary to overcome the limitations and problems described in the next section of the chapter.

7.2 SUPPLY CHAIN PROBLEMS AND SOLUTIONS

Supply chain problems have been recognized in business, services, government, and the military for generations. Some even caused companies to go out of business. The problems are most evident in complex or long supply chains and in cases where many business partners are involved.

A well-known military case is the difficulties the German army encountered in World War II in the long supply chain to its troops in remote Russian territories, especially during the winter months. These difficulties resulted in a major turning point in the war and the beginning of the Germans' defeat. Note that during the 1991 war in Kuwait (and also in the war in Iraq that began in 2003), the allied armies had superb supply chains that were managed by the latest computerized technologies (including DSS and intelligent systems). These chains were a major contributor to the swift victory in Kuwait.

In the business world there are numerous examples of supply chain problems, such as companies that were unable to meet demand, had too large and expensive inventories, and so on. Some of these companies paid substantial penalties, and others even went out of business. On the other hand, some world-class companies such as Wal-Mart, Federal Express, and Dell have excellent supply chains with innovative IT-enhanced applications.

Problems along the Supply Chain

Problems along the supply chain can occur between business units within a single enterprise; they also can occur between (and among) enterprises. A major symptom of ineffective supply chains is poor customer service, which hinders people or businesses from getting products or services when and where needed or gives them poor-quality products. Other symptoms are high inventory costs, loss of revenues, extra cost of expediting shipments, and more. Let's look at an example.

Example: Problems with "Santa's Supply Chain." An example of a supply chain problem was the difficulty of fulfilling toy orders received electronically during the 1999 holiday season. During the last months of that year, online toy retailers, including eToys (now *kbtoys.com*), Amazon.com, and ToysRUs, conducted a massive advertising campaign for Internet ordering. This included $20 to $30 discount vouchers for shopping online.

Customer response was overwhelming, and the retailers that underestimated it were unable to get the necessary toys from the manufacturing plants and warehouses and deliver them to the customers' doors by Christmas Eve. ToysRUs, for example, offered each of its unhappy customers a $100 store coupon as compensation. Despite its generous gift, over 40 percent of the unhappy ToysRUs customers said they would not shop online at ToysRUs again (*Interactiveweek.com*, February 3, 2000).

REASONS FOR SUPPLY CHAIN PROBLEMS. The problems along the supply chain stem mainly from two sources: (1) from uncertainties and (2) from the need to coordinate several activities, internal units, and business partners. Here we will address several of the uncertainties that contribute to supply chain problems. Throughout the chapter we will consider how IT can help enterprises improve supply chain coordination and reduce uncertainties.

A major source of supply chain uncertainties is the *demand forecast*, as demonstrated by the 1999 toy season example. The actual demand may be influenced by several factors such as competition, prices, weather conditions, technological developments, customers' general confidence, and more. These are external, usually uncontrollable factors. ChevronTexaco, as seen earlier, overcame this uncertainty by measuring demand in real time and using a demand-driven production strategy.

Other supply chain uncertainties are delivery times, which depend on many factors, ranging from production machine failures to road conditions and traffic jams that may interfere with shipments. Quality problems in materials and parts may also create production delays, which lead to supply chain problems.

One of the major difficulties to properly setting inventory levels in various parts of the supply chain is known as the bullwhip effect.

THE BULLWHIP EFFECT. The **bullwhip effect** refers to erratic shifts in orders up and down the supply chain. This effect was initially observed by

Procter & Gamble (P&G) with its disposable diapers product (Pampers). While actual sales in retail stores were fairly stable and predictable, orders from distributors to the manufacturer, P&G, had wild swings, creating production and inventory problems. An investigation revealed that distributors' orders were fluctuating because of poor demand forecast, price fluctuation, order batching, and rationing within the supply chain. These dysfunctions resulted in unnecessary and costly inventories in various locations along the supply chain, fluctuations in P&G production levels as well as in orders to P&G's suppliers, and flow of inaccurate information. Distorted information can lead to tremendous inefficiencies, excessive inventories, poor customer service, lost revenues, ineffective shipments, and missed production schedules (Donovan, 2002/2003).

The bullwhip effect is not unique to P&G, however. Firms ranging from Hewlett-Packard in the computer industry to Bristol-Myers Squibb in pharmaceuticals have experienced a similar phenomenon. Basically, demand variables can become magnified when viewed through the eyes of managers at each link in the supply chain. If each distinct entity makes ordering and inventory decisions with an eye to its own interest above those of the chain, stockpiling may be simultaneously occurring at as many as seven or eight locations along the supply chain. Study has shown that such hoarding has led in some cases to as many as 100 days of inventory that is waiting, "just in case" (versus 10–20 days in the normal case).

A 1998 industry study projected that $30 billion in savings could materialize in grocery industry supply chains alone, by sharing information and collaborating. Thus, companies are trying to avoid the "sting of the bullwhip" as well as to solve other SCM problems.

Solutions to Supply Chain Problems

Supply chain problems can be very costly for companies, and therefore organizations are motivated to find innovative solutions. In the remaining portion of this section we will look at some of the possible solutions to supply chain problems, many of which are supported by IT.

USING INVENTORIES TO SOLVE SUPPLY CHAIN PROBLEMS. Undoubtedly, the most common solution used by companies to solve supply chain problems is *building inventories*, as "insurance" against supply chain uncertainties. The main problem with this approach is that it is very difficult to correctly determine inventory levels for each product and part. If inventory levels are set too high, the cost of keeping the inventory will be very large. (And, as we have seen, high inventories at multiple points in the supply chain can result in the bullwhip effect.) If the inventory is too low, there is no insurance against high demand or slow delivery times, and revenues (and customers) may be lost. In either event, the total cost—including cost of keeping inventories, cost of lost sales opportunities, and bad reputation—can be very high. Thus, companies make major attempts to optimize and control inventories, as discussed in the story about Littlewoods Stores, one of Britain's largest retailers of high-quality clothing, available in Online File W7.2.

INFORMATION SHARING. Another common way to solve supply chain problems, and especially to improve demand forecasts, is *sharing information* along the supply chain. Such sharing can be facilitated by EDI, extranets, and groupware technologies, as part of interorganizational information systems (IOSs, Chapter 8). Such information sharing is frequently referred to as the *collaborative supply chain* (see Simatupang and Sridharan, 2002).

One of the most notable examples of information sharing is between large manufacturers and retailers. For example, Wal-Mart provides Procter & Gamble access to daily sales information from every store for every item P&G makes for Wal-Mart. Then P&G is able to manage the *inventory replenishment* for Wal-Mart's stores. By monitoring inventory levels, P&G knows when inventories fall below the threshold for each product at any Wal-Mart store. These data trigger an immediate shipment.

Such information sharing between Wal-Mart and P&G is done automatically. It is part of a *vendor-managed inventory (VMI)* strategy. P&G has similar agreements with other major retailers. The benefit for P&G is accurate and timely demand information. Thus, P&G can plan production more accurately, minimizing the "bullwhip effect." To do so, in 2000 P&G deployed a Web-based "Ultimate-Supply System," which replaced 4,000 different EDI links to suppliers and retailers in a more cost-effective way. The VMI is an example of supply chain collaboration. Information sharing can be facilitated by RFID.

USING RFID TO IMPROVE SUPPLY CHAINS. One of the newest (and possibly revolutionary) solutions to supply chain problems is RFID. We introduced the concept of RFID in Chapter 1 by describing how Wal-Mart is mandating that its largest suppliers attach RFID tags to every pallet or box they ship to Wal-Mart. Eventually, RFIDs will be attached to every item. This can be done due to their tiny size (a grain of sand) and the low cost (less than 5 cents apiece).

How might RFIDs improve the supply chain? Look at Figure 7.3, which shows the supply chain relationships among a retailer, a manufacturer, and

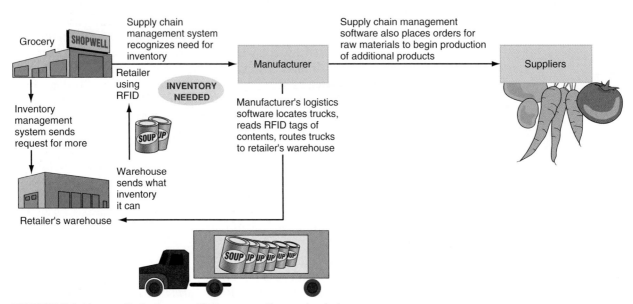

FIGURE 7.3 How radio frequency ID tags smooth supply chains.

suppliers, all of whom use RFID tags. Because the RFIDs are used by all companies in the figure, automatic alerts can be sent within each company and between companies. There is no longer a need to count inventories, and visibility of inventories is provided to all business partners. These benefits can go several tiers down the supply chain. Additional applications, such as rapid checkout in a retail store, eliminating the need to scan each item, will be available in the future.

Other applications of RFID are shown in Figure 7.4. The upper part of the figure shows how the tags are used when merchandise travels from the supplier to the retailer. Note that the RFID transmits real-time information about the location of the merchandise. The lower part of the figure shows the use of the RFID at the retailer, mainly to locate merchandise, control inventory, prevent theft, and expedite processing of relevant information.

More about RFID. The RFID tag is about the size of a pinhead or grain of sand. The tag includes an antenna and a chip that contains an electronic product code (EPC; see discussion of Auto-ID in Chapter 5). The EPC stores much more information than a regular barcode (e.g., when and where the product was made, where the components come from, and when they might perish).

Unlike barcodes, which need line-of-sight contact to be read, RFID tags also act as passive tracking devices, signaling their presence over a radio frequency when they pass within yards of a special scanner. The tags have long been used

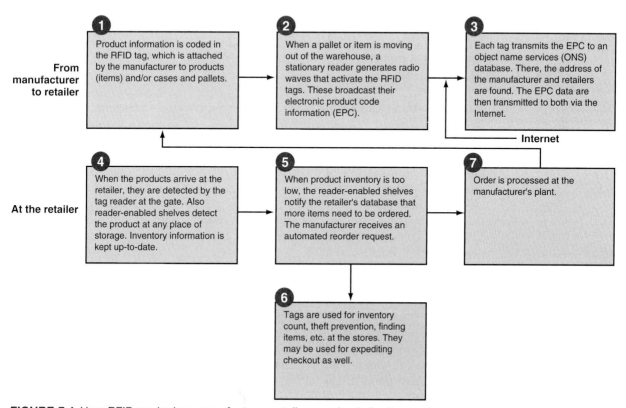

FIGURE 7.4 How RFID works in a manufacturer–retailer supply chain. (*Source:* Drawn by E. Turban.)

in high-cost applications such as automated tolling systems and security-ID badges. Recent innovations have caused the price of the tags to plummet and their performance to improve, enabling them to be used more widely.

The prospect of affordable RFID tags has retailers drooling. If every item in a shop were tagged, RFID technology could be used to locate mislaid products, to deter theft, and even to offer customers personalized sales pitches through displays mounted in dressing rooms. Ultimately, tags and readers could replace barcodes and checkout labor altogether. For more about RFID, see Kinsella (2003) and Reda (2003).

Limitations of RFID. For small companies, the cost of an RFID system may be too high (at least for some time). Also, there may be atmospheric interference (expected to be minimized in the future), as well as limited range (only 30–50 feet at this time). The fear of violating customers' privacy is another issue (see Chapter 1, Wal-Mart). Agreeing on universal standards, as well as connecting the RFIDs with existing IT systems, are technical issues to be solved. For other limitations, see Kinsella (2003).

CHANGING A LINEAR SUPPLY CHAIN TO A HUB. In linear supply chains, information is processed in a sequence, which slows down its flow. One solution is to change the linear chain into a hub, as the Chapter 1 example about Orbis Corp. (page 8) demonstrated. Recall that ProductBank.com is a digitized hub of photos, to which manufacturers, ad agencies, retailers, and printers have access. Each partner in the supply chain can directly access the images in the data bank. With the electronic hub, the transaction cost per picture (usually paid by the manufacturer) is 30 to 40 percent lower, and the cycle time is 50 to 70 percent shorter than in the traditional linear supply chain model (*productbank.com.au*). Orbis's information system is concentrated around its own supply chain; other companies provide similar services to entire industries (see *Webcor.com*, and the Asite case in Chapter 8).

SUPPLY CHAIN COLLABORATION. Proper supply chain management and inventory management require coordination of all the different activities and links of the supply chain. Successful coordination enables goods to move smoothly and on time from suppliers to manufacturers to customers, which enables a firm to keep inventories low and costs down. Collaboration of supply chain partners is needed since companies depend on each other but do not always work together toward the same goal. Both suppliers and buyers must participate together in the design or redesign of the supply chain to achieve their shared goals. As part of the collaboration effort, business partners must learn to *trust* each other.

To properly control the uncertainties associated with supply chain problems, it is necessary to identify and understand their causes, determine how uncertainties in some activities will affect other activities up and down the supply chain, and then formulate specific ways to reduce or eliminate the uncertainties. Combined with this is the need for an effective and efficient communication environment among all business partners (see Chapter 8). A rapid flow of information along a supply chain tends to improve efficiency. For example, computerized point-of-sale (POS) information can be transmitted in real time to distribution centers, suppliers, and shippers. Having real-time information enables firms to achieve optimal inventory levels.

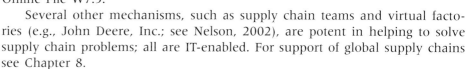

Another example of supply chain collaboration that requires system integration is product-development systems. These allow suppliers to dial into a client's intranet, pull product specifications, and view illustrations and videos of a manufacturing process. (For further discussion, see Manthou et al., 2004; Goutsos and Karacapilidis, 2004; and Hagel, 2002). For benefits to suppliers, see Subramani (2004).

An example of a well-known supply chain collaboration, the CPFR, is provided in *IT at Work 7.1* (page 306).

OTHER IT-ASSISTED SOLUTIONS TO SCM PROBLEMS. Some other generic IT-assisted solutions to solve supply chain management problems are provided in Table 7.1.

Large companies employ several methods to achieve supply chain superiority. Wal-Mart, for example, is well-known for its ability to collaborate with companies across its supply chain. It is able to combine information from its suppliers with demand and inventory data from its stores in order to minimize operating cost and reduce prices. Nestlé USA even created a vice-president-level position exclusively to manage business with Wal-Mart (Worthen, 2002). For an example of how another large company, Dell, manages its supply chain, see Online File W7.3.

Several other mechanisms, such as supply chain teams and virtual factories (e.g., John Deere, Inc.; see Nelson, 2002), are potent in helping to solve supply chain problems; all are IT-enabled. For support of global supply chains see Chapter 8.

Supply Chain Teams. The change of the linear supply chain to a hub points to the need to create **supply chain teams.** A supply chain team is a group of

TABLE 7.1 IT-Supported Solutions to Supply Chain Problems

Problem Area	Solution
Slow communication and messaging	Use wireless devices to find vehicle locations, to expedite salespeople's contact with headquarters. Use hub supply chain to enable online access to information. Use XML (Chen et al., 2004).
Difficult product configuration	Use DSS and intelligent systems for rapid and accurate analysis.
Select and coordinate suppliers	Use DSS to determine which suppliers to use; determine how to create strategic partnerships.
Supplies arrive when needed	Use just-in-time approach and collaboration with suppliers.
Handle peak demands	Use IT-enabled outsourcing. Use DSS to determine what to outsource and when to buy or when to make (see ChevronTexaco opening case). Use RFID.
Expedite lead time for buying and selling	Use e-commerce tools and business intelligence models. Use RFID and wireless.
Too many or too few suppliers	Use optimization model to decide and employ e-procurement.
Supplier relationships	Improve supplier relationships by using portals, Web-based call center, and other CRM and PRM tools.
Control inventory levels	Manufacture only after order received (build to order). Use VMI and Web Services. Use RFID.
Forecast fluctuating demand	Use collaboration (like CPFR) or intelligent systems (see ChevronTexaco opening case).
Expedite flows in the chain	Automate material, information, and money flows. Use Web Services (e.g., Dell).

IT at Work 7.1
HOW WARNER-LAMBERT APPLIES AN INTEGRATED SUPPLY CHAIN

Warner-Lambert is a major U.S. pharmaceutical company that is now owned by Pfizer (*pfizer.com*). One of its major products is Listerine antiseptic mouthwash. The materials for making Listerine come mainly from eucalyptus trees in Australia and are shipped to the Warner-Lambert (WL) manufacturing plant in New Jersey. The major problem there is to *forecast* the *overall demand* in order to determine how much Listerine to produce. Then one can figure how much raw materials are needed and when. A wrong forecast will result either in high inventories of raw materials and/or of finished products, or in shortages. Inventories are expensive to keep; shortages may result in loss of business (to competitors).

Warner-Lambert forecasts demand with the help of Manugistic Inc.'s Demand Planning Information System (an SCM product). Used with other software in Manugistics' Supply Chain Planning suite, the system analyzes manufacturing, distribution, and sales data against expected demand and business climate information. Its goal is to help WL decide how much Listerine (and other products) to make and how much of each raw ingredient is needed, and when. For example, the model can anticipate the impact of seasonal promotion or of a production line being down.

The sales and marketing group of WL also meets monthly with WL employees in finance, procurement, and other departments. The group enters the expected demand for Listerine into the Prism Capacity Planning system (now Invensys plc), which schedules the production of Listerine in the amounts needed and generates electronic purchase orders for WL's suppliers.

WL's supply chain excellence stems from the Collaborative Planning, Forecasting, and Replenishment (CPFR) program. This is a retailing industry project for which piloting was done at WL. In the pilot project, WL shared strategic plans, performance data, and market insight with Wal-Mart over private networks. The company realized that it could benefit from Wal-Mart's market knowledge, just as Wal-Mart could benefit from WL's product knowledge. In CPFR, trading partners collaborate on the demand forecast using *collaborative e-commerce* (see figure, next page). The project includes major SCM and ERP vendors such as SAP and Manugistics.

During the CPFR pilot, WL increased its products' shelf-fill rate—the extent to which a store's shelves are fully stocked—from 87 percent to 98 percent, earning the company about $8 million a year in additional sales. This was the equivalent of a new product launch, but for much less investment. WL is now using the Internet to expand the CPFR program to all its major suppliers and retail partners.

Warner-Lambert is involved in another collaborative retail industry project, the Supply Chain Operations Reference (SCOR), an initiative of the Supply Chain Council in

(continues on page 307)

tightly coordinated employees who work together to serve the customer. Each task is done by the member of the team who is best positioned, trained, and capable of doing that specific task, regardless of which company the member works for.

For example, in a supply chain team, the team member that deals with the delivery will handle a delivery problem, even if he or she works for the delivery company rather than for the retailer whose product is being delivered. This way, redundancies will be minimized. The delivery company will deal with the customer about a delivery problem, rather than passing the problem along to the retailer, who would end up having to contact the delivery company. Thus, the retailer will not have to spend valuable resources following up on the delivery. The task assignment to team members can be facilitated by IT tools such as workflow software and groupware. An example of a supply chain team in a global setting is provided in Minicase 1 in Chapter 8 (VW case).

Virtual Factories.   A **virtual factory** is a collaborative enterprise application that provides a computerized model of a factory. In the virtual factory, proposed designs can be tested, relationships with suppliers can be simulated, and manufacturing processes and how they are connected can be modeled. If potential

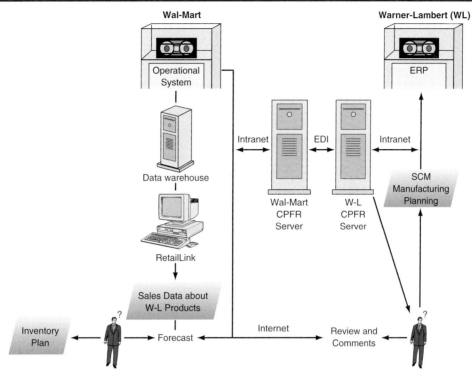

the United States. SCOR divides supply chain operations into parts, giving manufacturers, suppliers, distributors, and retailers a framework within which to evaluate the effectiveness of their processes along the same supply chains.

Sources: Compiled from Bresnahan (1998) and *Logistics Management and Distribution Report* (1998, 1999).

For Further Exploration: Why would Listerine have been a target for the pilot CPFR collaboration? For what industries, besides retailing, would such collaboration be beneficial?

problems in these areas are spotted in the digital model of the factory, simulated solutions can be worked out in the virtual model before they are implemented in the real-world factory. Usually, the virtual factory application would connect suppliers to the B2B system and clearly present the needed demand to suppliers. That "demand visibility" can help the company to focus on two important key performance indicators, lead times and transaction cost. Uniting the entire supply chain and creating visibility between suppliers and buyers can help the companies forecast and plan demand more effectively. Virtual factories also enable all companies involved to work together collaboratively using common tools, and they provide greater flexibility and responsiveness by getting information and goods flowing much more quickly.

Example: Work in a Virtual Factory. Adaptec Inc. and Taiwan Semiconductor Manufacturing Co. (TSMC) are using Extricity Alliance (from Extricity Software) to connect their internal systems through the Internet and to create a smoothly choreographed virtual factory. By means of this system-to-system communication over the Internet, the two companies accomplish several supply chain management activities, including sharing forecasts, managing orders,

IT at Work 7.2
PEACOCKS RETAILS USES WIRELESS TO SMOOTH ITS SUPPLY CHAIN

Peacocks Retails of Wales operates about 250 retail stores, selling clothes and home furniture in Wales and the south of England. The company had a problem in its internal supply chain: Its paper-based system of managing the distribution of products was prone to problems such as incorrectly completed pick-lists, wrongly picked items, transcription errors, delays in generating and receiving data, and much more. These interfered with the company's growth strategy and reduced its profit.

In 1997, Peacocks Retails consolidated its six warehouses to a single distribution center (100,000 square feet). Stores were ordering more than 4,000 SKUs (stock-keeping units) each day. These needed to be picked and shipped to stores effectively and efficiently. Using one warehouse instead of six solved some problems, but the paper-based communication system was as bad as before. With a paper-based pick system, it is easy to run out of product in a specific location. Then the picker has to either wait for more product to arrive or return to the location. There is always a built-in delay, and the company has no idea about potential stock problems until they happen.

In 1998, Peacocks Retails started to replace the paper-based system with a wireless system (from Symbol.com). Specifically, the fully automated distribution center is equipped with a hands-free and real-time putaway and picking system. It is based on a combination of 28 wearable computers and 6 truck-mounted terminals supported by wireless LAN.

The wireless system provides real-time control. Whether an item is moved by hand or by truck, Peacocks knows precisely where it is. If at any point in the process someone is at the wrong location, handling the wrong product, or trying to send it to the wrong place, the system simply sends out an alert and prevents the action. When Peacocks receives a delivery from a manufacturer, the consignment is checked, and the individual cartons from each delivery are given an identifying barcode label and scanned to report receipt. In this way, every item can be tracked through the distribution center from the minute it arrives. Immediately, the system will know if there is a requirement at a pick location. Once individual cartons are labeled, Peacocks uses an automated conveyor system to send cartons to the desired location, as directed by the wireless warehouse management system.

Each member of the picking team wears a wrist-mounted terminal that receives picking instructions via the wireless LAN from Peacocks' host system. As empty trolleys arrive in the pick area, a picker scans its barcode, and the terminal's LCD screen tells the picker which aisle to go to, which location to pick from, and which items to pick. When a picker arrives at the pick face, she first scans the barcode mounted at the end of the aisle. This verifies that she is in the correct aisle. She then scans another barcode at the product location to verify she is at the correct place. Finally, she scans each item as it is picked into the trolley. Once each pick is complete, the conveyor system takes each trolley to the dispatch area to be loaded into crates for delivery to a Peacocks store.

Because data are sent to the host in real-time, as the picking operation proceeds, the system knows when pick "face stocks" are approaching the replenishment level set by Peacocks. Once this happens, the system sends an alert to a truck-mounted terminal in the pallet store. As with the wrist-mounted terminals, an LCD screen on the truck terminal directs the driver to a precise location in the pallet racking. On arrival at the location, the driver uses a hand-held scanner to scan the location barcode. This confirms that he is at the right location and selecting the right product.

Some other benefits: The hands-free arrangement saves time; it is not necessary to keep putting down the terminals when hands are needed. Also, wearable computers are not dropped, so they are not damaged. Finally, the system is user-friendly, so training is minimal.

Source: Compiled from Peacocks Case Study (2004, accessed May 2004).

For Further Exploration: Identify all segments of the supply chain that are improved by the system and describe the improvement. Also, investigate how RFID may impact this system.

---

issuing work-in-progress reports, and transmitting shipping notices and engineering-design changes. This process results in shorter product lead times, more direct control over processes, and more accurate capacity planning.

Wireless Solutions. In the last few years we have seen an increased number of wireless solutions to supply chain problems. In addition to RFID one can use mobile devices, as illustrated in *IT at Work 7.2.*

ETHICAL ISSUES RELATING TO SUPPLY CHAIN SOLUTIONS. Conducting a supply chain management project may result in the need to lay off, retrain, or transfer employees. Should management notify the employees in advance regarding such possibilities? And what about those older employees who are difficult to retrain? Other ethical issues may involve sharing of personal information, which may be required for a collaborative organizational culture, but which some employees may resist. Finally, individuals may have to share computer programs that they designed for their personal use on the job. Such programs may be considered the intellectual property of the individuals. (Should the employees be compensated for the programs' use by others?)

To provide the solutions discussed in this section, IT utilizes a number of software packages. These are described in the next two sections.

7.3 COMPUTERIZED ENTERPRISE SYSTEMS: MRP, MRP II, SCM, AND SOFTWARE INTEGRATION

The concept of the supply chain is interrelated with the computerization of its activities, which has evolved over 50 years.

The Evolution of Computerized Aids

Historically, many of the supply chain management activities were done manually using paper, telephones, and faxes, but this can be very inefficient, slow, and error-prone. Therefore, since the time when computers first began to be used for business, people have wanted to automate the processes along the supply chain.

The first software programs, which appeared in the 1950s and early 1960s, supported short segments along the supply chain. Typical examples are inventory management systems, scheduling, and resource allocation. The supporting software was called *supply chain management (SCM) software* (see Section 7.4). The major objectives were to expedite processing, reduce errors, optimize operations, and reduce costs. Such applications were developed in the functional areas, independently of each other, and they became more and more sophisticated with the passage of time. Of special interest were inventory management systems and financial decision-making formulas (e.g., for capital budgeting).

In a short time it became clear that interdependencies exist among some of the supply chain activities. One early realization was that production scheduling is related to inventory management and purchasing plans. As early as the 1960s, the *material requirements planning (MRP)* model was devised. This planning model essentially integrates production, purchasing, and inventory management of interrelated products in an attempt to minimize costs. It became clear that computer support could greatly enhance the use of this model, which may require daily updating. This resulted in commercial MRP software packages coming on the market.

MRP packages were (and still are) useful in many cases, helping to drive inventory levels down and streamlining portions of the supply chain. However, they also failed in many cases. One of the major reasons for the failures was the realization that schedule-inventory-purchasing operations are closely related to both financial and labor resources. This realization resulted in the enhanced MRP methodology (and software) called *manufacturing resource planning (MRP II),* which adds labor requirements and financial planning to MRP (see Sheikh, 2002).

During this evolution there was more and more integration of functional information systems. This evolution continued, leading to the *enterprise resource planning (ERP)* concept, which adds functionalities to MRP II by integrating the transaction processing and other routine activities of all functional areas in the entire enterprise. We'll look at ERP in more detail in Section 7.4.

The next step in this evolution, which started in the late 1990s, is the inclusion of business intelligence and other software. At the beginning of the twenty-first century, the integration expanded to include markets and communities (e.g., see *mysap.com*).

Notice that throughout this evolution there has been increasing integration along several dimensions (e.g., more functional areas, combination of transaction processing and decision support, and inclusion of business partners). Therefore, before we describe the essentials of ERP and SCM software it may be beneficial to analyze the reasons for activities and software integration.

Why Systems Integration?

Twentieth-century computer technology was *functionally* oriented. Functional systems may not let different departments communicate with each other in the same language. Worse yet, crucial sales, inventory, and production data often have to be painstakingly entered manually into separate computer systems every time a person who is not a member of a specific department needs ad-hoc information related to the specific department. In many cases, employees using functionally oriented technology simply do not get the information they need, or they get it too late (e.g., see Minicase 1). Thus, managing the twenty-first-century enterprise cannot be done effectively with such technology.

Sandoe et al. (2001) list the following major benefits of systems integration (in order of importance):

- *Tangible benefits.* Inventory reduction, personnel reduction, productivity improvement, order management improvement, financial-close cycle improvements, IT cost reduction, procurement cost reduction, cash management improvements, revenue/profit increases, transportation logistics cost reduction, maintenance reduction, and on-time delivery improvement
- *Intangible benefits.* Information visibility, new/improved processes, customer responsiveness, standardization, flexibility, globalization, and business performance

INTERNAL VERSUS EXTERNAL INTEGRATION. There are two basic types of systems integration—internal and external. *Internal integration* refers to integration within a company between (or among) applications, and/or between applications and databases. For example, an organization may integrate inventory control with an ordering system, or a CRM suite with the database of customers. Large companies that have hundreds of applications may find it extremely difficult to integrate the newer Web-based applications with the older legacy systems.

External integration refers to integration of applications and/or databases among business partners—for example, the suppliers' catalogs with the buyers' e-procurement system. Another example of external supply chain integration is product-development systems that allow suppliers to dial into a client's intranet, pull product specifications, and view illustrations and videos of a manufacturing process. (For further discussion, see Hagel, 2002.) External integration is especially needed for B2B and for partner relationship management (PRM) systems, as will be discussed in Chapter 8. For more on integration, see Jinyoul et al. (2003) and Siau and Tian (2004).

7.4 ENTERPRISE RESOURCE PLANNING AND SUPPLY CHAIN MANAGEMENT

One of the most successful tools for managing supply chains, especially internal ones, is enterprise resource planning (ERP).

What Is ERP? With the advance of enterprisewide client/server computing comes a new challenge: how to control all major business processes in *real time* with a single software architecture. The most common *integrated software* solution of this kind is known as **enterprise resource planning (ERP)** or just **enterprise systems.** This software integrates the planning, management, and use of all resources in the entire enterprise. It is comprised of *sets of applications* that automate routine back-end operations (such as financial, inventory management, and scheduling) to help enterprises handle jobs such as order fulfillment. For example, there is a module for cost control, for accounts payable and receivable, and for fixed assets and treasury management. ERP promises benefits ranging from increased efficiency to improved quality, productivity, and profitability. (See Ragowsky and Somers, 2002, for details.)

ERP's major objective is to *integrate all departments and functional information flows across a company* onto a single computer system that can serve all of the enterprise's needs. For example, improved order entry allows immediate access to inventory, product data, customer credit history, and prior order information. Such availability of information raises productivity and increases customer satisfaction (Gattiker and Goodhue, 2004). ERP systems are in use in thousands of large and medium companies worldwide, and some ERP systems are producing dramatic results (see *erp.ittoolbox.com*). ERP initially covered all routine transactions within a company, including internal suppliers and customers. Later it was expanded, in what is known as *extended ERP software*, to incorporate external suppliers and customers.

Example: Rolls-Royce. The implementation of ERP enables Rolls-Royce not only to lower its IT costs but also to deliver to the customer on time. Timely delivery improves customer satisfaction and confidence in the company and, it is hoped, will lead to an increase of orders in the future (Yusuf et al., 2004).

Example: Comark Corp. Using ERP, Comark Corp (*comarkcorp.com*) reduced inventories and eliminated voluminous reports. It also is used to track information more accurately.

Example: Consolidation Applications via ERP. ExxonMobil consolidated 300 different information systems by implementing SAP R/3 (see below) in its U.S. petrochemical operations alone.

For businesses that want to use ERP, one option is to self-develop an integrated system, either by linking together existing functional packages or by programming a new, custom-built system. Another option, which is often quicker and/or less expensive, is to use commercially available integrated ERP software (see Minicase 1). The leading ERP software is **SAP R/3** (from SAP AG Corp.). This highly integrated software package contains more than 70 business activities modules. Oracle, Computer Associates, and PeopleSoft also make similar products. All of these products include Web modules.

Yet another way for a business to implement ERP is to lease ERP systems from *application service providers (ASPs)*. A major advantage of the leasing approach is that even a small company can enjoy ERP: A small company can lease only relevant modules, rather than buy an entire ERP package. Some companies, such as Starbucks, have chosen a *best-of-breed* approach—building their own customized ERP with ready-made components leased or purchased from several vendors.

THE SOFTWARE CONTENT OF ERP. As indicated above, an ERP system is composed of modules for managing all the routine activities performed by a business. For example, an ERP suite for a manufacturing company would include modules that cover activities such as production scheduling, inventory management, entering sales orders, coordinating shipping, and providing after-sales customer service. The modules in an ERP suite are accessed through a single interface. A list of representative ERP modules is provided in Online File W7.4.

Lately, however, there has been a trend to have the ERP functionally oriented. For example, SAP offers the following products: mySAP financial, ERP human capital management, ERP operations, and ERP service.

First-Generation ERP

The first generation of ERP concentrated on activities within the enterprise that were routine and repetitive in nature. Large companies have been successful in integrating several hundred applications using first-generation ERP software. ERP forces discipline and organization around business processes, making the alignment of IT and business goals (Chapter 12) more likely. Such change is related to business process redesign (Chapter 14). Also, by implementing ERP a company can discover and clean up the "dusty corners" of its business.

However, ERP is not a "wonder drug" for business ills. It has some drawbacks: It can be extremely complex to implement. Also, companies often need to change existing business processes to fit ERP's format. Finally, some companies require only a few of the ERP's software modules yet must purchase the entire package (unless they decide to lease individual modules from ASPs). For these reasons, ERP software may not be attractive to everyone.

As of the late 1990s, ERP systems began to be extended along the supply chain to suppliers and customers. These extended systems can incorporate functionality for customer interactions and for managing relationships with suppliers and vendors, making the system extremely fitted. (For a comprehensive treatment of ERP, see Lucas and Bishop, 2002.)

But ERP was never originally meant to fully support entire supply chains, even when suppliers and customers were added. ERP solutions are centered around *business transactions*. As such, they do not provide the computerized models needed to respond rapidly to real-time changes in supply, demand, labor, or capacity, nor to effectively integrate with e-commerce and other applications. This deficiency has been overcome by the second generation of ERP.

Second-Generation ERP

The objective of second-generation ERP is to leverage existing information systems in order to increase efficiency in handling transactions, improve decision making, and transform ways of doing business into e-business. Let's explain.

The reports generated by first-generation ERP systems gave planners statistics about business transactions, costs, and financial performance. However, the planning systems in ERP were rudimentary. Reports from first-generation ERP systems provided a snapshot of the business at a point in time. But they did not support *continuous* planning, which is central to supply chain planning. Continuous planning is more like a video than a snapshot: It continues to refine and enhance the plan as changes and events occur, up to the very last minute before the plan is executed. Attempting to come up with an optimal plan using first-generation ERP-based systems has been compared to steering a car by looking in the rear-view mirror.

This weakness of first-generation ERP created the need for planning systems oriented toward decision making. *SCM software* is specifically designed to improve decision making in segments of the supply chain. Its focus on decision making is in contrast to the focus in ERP on streamlining the flow of routine information. (For further description of the differences between SCM and ERP software, see Online File W7.5.)

COMBINING ERP WITH SCM SOFTWARE. Use of ERP and SCM software is not necessarily an either–or decision. Rather, the two can be combined and used together. To illustrate how ERP and SCM may work together, consider the task of order processing. There is a fundamental difference between SCM and ERP in order processing: The ERP approach is, "How can I best take or fulfill your order?" In contrast, the question that SCM software asks is, "Should I take your order?" The answer might be "no" if taking the order would lose money for the company or interfere with production. Thus, SCM software focuses on planning, optimization, and decision making in segments of the supply chain.

Thus, the *analytical* SCM information systems have emerged as a *complement* to ERP systems, to provide intelligent decision support or business intelligence (Chapters 10 and 11) capabilities. An SCM system is designed to overlay existing systems and to pull data from every step of the supply chain. It is therefore able to provide a clear, organizational-level picture of where the enterprise is heading.

Example: How IBM Is Using SCM. An example of a successful SCM effort is IBM's restructuring of its *global supply chain*. The goal of the restructuring was to achieve quick responsiveness to customers and to do it with minimal inventory. To support this effort, IBM developed a supply chain analysis tool, called the Asset Management Tool (AMT), for use by a number of IBM business units and their channel partners. IBM is using AMT to analyze and improve such issues as inventory budgets and turnover, customer-service targets, and new-product introductions. AMT integrates graphical process modeling, analytical performance optimization, simulation, activity-based costing, and enterprise database connectivity into a system that allows quantitative analysis of interenterprise supply chains. AMT benefits include savings of over $750 million in material costs and price-protection expenses each year (Yao et al., 2000). The system was also a prerequisite to a major e-procurement initiative at IBM.

Creating a plan from an SCM system allows companies to quickly assess the impact of their actions on the entire supply chain, including customer demand. But this can be done only if ERP software is added. Therefore, it makes sense to integrate ERP and SCM.

ALTERNATIVE WAYS TO INTEGRATE ERP AND SCM. How is integration of ERP and SCM done? One approach is to work with different software products from different vendors. For example, a business might use SAP as an ERP and add to it Manugistics' manufacturing-oriented SCM software, as shown in the Warner-Lambert case (*IT at Work 7.1*). Such an approach requires fitting together different software, which may be a complex task unless special connectors provided by middleware vendors exist. (See also Kovács and Paganelli, 2003.)

The second approach is for ERP vendors to add decision support and analysis capabilities, known as *business intelligence*, to their major product. Business intelligence (as defined in Chapter 10) refers to analysis performed by DSS, ESS, data mining, and intelligent systems. Using a combined product from a single vendor solves the integration problem. For example, Gayialis and Tatsiopoulos (2004) describe how a downstream oil company combined a supply chain management (SCM) application with a geographical information system (GIS), integrated with ERP software. The result was an innovative decision support system for routing and scheduling purposes.

However, most ERP vendors offer a combined product for another reason: It is cheaper for the customers. The added business intelligence functionalities, which create the *second-generation ERP*, include not only decision support, but also CRM, e-commerce, and data warehousing and mining. Some systems include a *knowledge management* component as well. In 2003, vendors started to add PLM (see Chapter 6) in an attempt to optimize the supply chain. An example of an ERP application that includes an SCM module is provided in *IT at Work 7.3*.

Third-Generation ERP

By 2004 ERP entered into a new generation, where projects are focused on specific business process areas. The capabilities of such ERP are:

- Combining logistics across business units with neighboring facilities
- Combining distribution centers and *less than truckloads (LTLs)* in order to fill trucks, reduce pickup/delivery lanes, and eliminate unneeded facilities
- Dynamically sourcing products from different manufacturing and distribution facilities based on inventory and capacity
- Shared services for manufacturing (like having one's own internal contract manufacturer)
- Global order management, showing a single face to global customers across business lines
- Consolidating country-based sales, marketing, and distribution operations in geographic areas, such as Europe, that have high density and falling barriers to trade
- Coordinating procurement of key commodities across business units and geographies
- Creating supplier portals that consolidate the needs of each business unit and provide a way of deepening the partnership with the supplier

These capabilities were formerly impossible. According to Swanton (2004), they are resulting in a number of benefits. For one, projects can be run in parallel, potentially generating benefits more quickly. In addition, fewer people are affected by each project, reducing retraining issues. Also, the ERP work is often to turn on or reconfigure functionality already owned, reducing the pressure to

IT at Work 7.3
COLGATE-PALMOLIVE USES ERP TO SMOOTH ITS SUPPLY CHAIN

Colgate-Palmolive is the world leader in oral-care products (toothpaste, toothbrushes, and mouthwashes) and a major supplier of personal-care products (baby care, deodorants, shampoos, and soaps). In addition, the company's Hill's Health Science Diet is a leading pet-food brand worldwide. Foreign sales account for about 70 percent of Colgate's total revenues.

To stay competitive, Colgate continuously seeks to streamline its supply chain, through which thousands of suppliers and customers interact with the company. At the same time, Colgate faces the challenges of accelerating new-product development, which has been a factor in driving faster sales growth and improved market share. Also, Colgate is devising ways to offer consumers a greater choice of better products at a lower cost to the company. To better manage the complexities of its manufacturing and the supply chains, Colgate embarked on an ERP implementation. The new system allows the company to access more timely and accurate data and to reduce costs. The structure of the ERP is pictured below.

An important factor for Colgate was whether it could use the ERP software across the entire spectrum of the business. Colgate needed the ability to coordinate globally and act locally. Colgate's U.S. division installed SAP R/3 for this purpose.

Source: Compiled from R. Kalakota and M. Robinson (2001).

For Further Exploration: What is the role of the ERP for Colgate-Palmolive? Who are the major beneficiaries of the new system? How is the SCM improved?

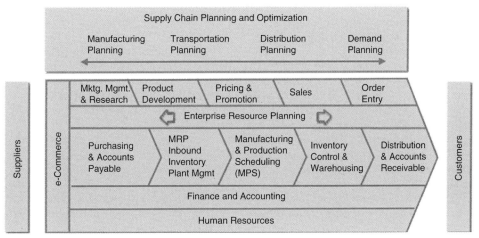

Colgate-Palmolive ERP implementation
(*Source:* R. Kalakota and M. Robinson, *E-Business 2.0,* Boston, MA, Addison Wesley, 2001.)

upgrade ERP and lowering IT costs. Note that using this new generation of ERP requires business units to give up total control and cooperate with their peers.

Integrating ERP with Other Enterprise Systems

In addition to integrating ERP with SCM systems, ERP can be integrated with other enterprise systems, most notably with e-commerce. *IT at Work 7.4* (page 316) describes the integration of ERP and EC at Cybex International.

ERP is a most common enterprisewide information system in medium and large organizations. Another enterprise system, which is adopted even by some small companies, is customer relationship management (CRM) (Section 7.5).

IT at Work 7.4
INTEGRATING EC AND ERP AT CYBEX

Cybex International (*cybexintl.com*), a global maker of fitness machines, was unable to meet the demand for its popular fitness machines, which increased dramatically in the late 1990s. To maintain its market share, the company had to work with rush orders from its nearly 1,000 suppliers. The cost of responding to rush orders was extremely high. This problem was a result of a poor demand forecast for the machine's components. The demand forecast was produced using three different legacy systems that Cybex had inherited from merger partners.

After examining existing vendors' supply chain software, Cybex decided to install an ERP system (from People-Soft Inc.) for its supply chain planning and manufacturing applications. In conjunction with the software installation, the company analyzed and redesigned some of its business processes. It also reduced the number of suppliers from 1,000 to 550.

In the new system, customers' orders are accepted at the corporate Web site. Each order is electronically forwarded to one of the company's two specialized manufacturing plants. The ERP uses its *planning module* to calculate which parts are needed for each model. Then, the ERP's *product configurator* constructs, in just a few seconds, a component list and a bill-of-materials needed for each order.

The ERP system helps with other processes as well. For example, Cybex can e-mail to a vendor a detailed purchase order with engineering changes clearly outlined. These changes are visible to everyone; if one engineer is not at work, his or her knowledge remains in the system and is easy to find. Furthermore, dealers now know that they will get deliveries in less than two weeks. They can also track the status of each order (see *www.peopletalkonline.com*,

July–September 2003), which allows Cybex to provide superb customer care.

The system also helps Cybex to better manage its 550 suppliers. For example, the planning engine looks at price variations across product lines, detecting opportunities to negotiate price reductions by showing suppliers that their competitors offer the same products at lower prices. Also, by giving suppliers projected long- and short-term production schedules, Cybex helps ensure that all parts and materials are available when needed. This also reduces the inventory level at Cybex. Furthermore, suppliers that cannot meet the required dates are replaced after quarterly reviews.

Despite intense industry price-cutting in 2002, Cybex has remained very profitable, mainly due to its improved supply chain. Some of the most impressive results were the following: Cybex cut its bill-of-material count from thousands to hundreds; reduced the number of vendors from 1,000 to 550; cut paperwork by two-thirds; and reduced build-to-order time from four to two weeks.

Implementing the system cost money, of course. In addition to the cost of the software, the technology staff increased from three to 12. Yet the company feels that the investment was worthwhile, especially because it provided for much greater harmony between Cybex and its customers and suppliers.

Sources: Compiled from Sullivan et al. (2002), and from press releases at *cybex.com*.

For Further Exploration: What are the relationships between the EC applications and ERP? What are the critical success factors for implementation?

ERP Failures and Their Prevention

Despite improvements over the years, ERP projects, especially large ones, may fail. Sarkis and Sundarraj (2003) report that CEOs believe that as many as two-thirds of all ERPs fail. The following are some examples of ERP failures. See the Nike case in Chapter 1 (page 26) for another example of an ERP failure.

Example: ERP Integration Problems at Hershey. In late 1999, Hershey Foods Corporation reported a 19 percent drop in third-quarter net earnings, due to computer problems. The major problem, according to the company, was its new order-and-distribution system, which used software from both SAP (the ERP) and Siebel Systems (the CRM). Since the integrated system went live in July 1999, Hershey had been unable to fill all orders and get products onto shelves on time. The problems continued for several months, causing Hershey to lose market share and several hundred million dollars.

Example: Rushing Resulted in Damage. In November 1999, Whirlpool Corp. reported major delays in shipment of appliances due to "bugs" in its new ERP. Orders for quantities smaller than one truckload met with snags in the areas of order processing, tracking, and invoicing. According to *cnet.com* (accessed February 16, 2001), SAP gave Whirlpool a red light twice prior to the date on which the project would go live, saying the supply chain software was not ready, but Whirlpool ignored the signals.

Example: Did ERP Bankrupt FoxMeyer? FoxMeyer, a major distributor of prescription drugs to hospitals and pharmacies, filed for bankruptcy in 1996. In August 2001, FoxMeyer sued both SAP and Accenture Consulting for $500 million each, claiming that the ERP system they constructed led to its demise. Many customers sued FoxMeyer as well. (See the complete case in Online File W7.6.)

Example: Gore's ERP Cost Too Much. W.L. Gore and Associates filed a lawsuit against PeopleSoft and Deloitte & Touche because the ERP project that the two companies developed for W.L. Gore cost twice the original estimate. The vendors claimed that the cost runup was due to unforeseeable difficulties in integration and special requirements for the ERP.

According to *thespot4sap.com,* to Sarkis and Sundarraj (2003), and to Kanakamedala (2003), in order to avoid failures and ensure success, it is necessary for the partners involved in ERP implementation (the software vendor, the management consultant, the implementing company, and the support-service vendors) to hold open and honest dialogue at the start of each project. Included in this initial dialogue should be consideration of the following factors: the company's expectations; the ERP product capabilities and limitations; the level of change the company has to go through to make the system fit; the level of commitment within the organization to see the project through to completion; the risks presented by politics within the organization, and (if applicable) the capabilities, responsibilities, and role of the implementing IT consultants. In addition, the organization and the IT consultants should nail down the critical success factors (CSFs) of the implementation. Failures can also be minimized if appropriate cost-benefit and cost justification is done in advance.

Yet another way to avoid failures, or at least to minimize their cost, is to use application service providers (ASPs). Online File W7.7 describes the use of ASPs as a way to outsource ERPs. ERP implementation may be affected by cultural and global factors, which are described in the next chapter. For more on ERP implementation, see Stevens (2003) and Duplaga and Astani (2003).

Some characteristics in a business organization often suggest the failure of ERP implemention (Ligus, 2004). Various other considerations can affect the success or failure of an ERP project. For example, failures can be minimized if appropriate cost-benefit analysis is done in advance (Oliver and Romm, 2002, and Murphy and Simon, 2002). Another way to avoid failures, or at least minimize their cost, is to use ASPs to lease rather than buy or build ERPs. ERP implementation may also be affected by cultural and global factors. Business, technical, and cultural issues should not be overlooked in ERP implementation (Yusuf et al., 2004). Top management's support is also crucial (Doane, 2004).

In whatever form it is implemented, ERP has played a critical role in getting organizations to focus on business processes, thus facilitating business process changes across the enterprise. For manufacturers, in particular, by tying together multiple plants and distribution facilities, ERP solutions have facilitated a change in thinking. This change in thinking has its ultimate expression in an enterprise that is better able to expand operations and manage its supply chain. For a successful case of implementation and the critical success factors there, see the Texas Instrument (TI) case online (Integrative Case W1).

7.5 CRM AND ITS SUPPORT BY IT

Customer relationship management (CRM) is an enterprisewide effort to acquire and retain customers. CRM recognizes that customers are the core of a business and that a company's success depends on effectively managing relationships with them (see Greenberg, 2002). CRM focuses on building long-term and sustainable customer relationships that add value both for the customer and the company. (See Fjermestad and Romano, 2003, *crm-forum.com*, and *crmassist.com*.)

What Is CRM?   Greenberg (2002), Tan et al. (2002), and Chen and Popovich (2003) provide more than 10 definitions of CRM. Why are there so many definitions? The reason is that CRM is new and still evolving. Also, it is an interdisciplinary field, so each discipline (e.g., marketing, management) defines CRM differently.

EVALUATION OF CRM.   In general, CRM is an approach that recognizes that customers are the core of the business and that the company's success depends on effectively managing relationships with them. In other words: "CRM is a business strategy to select and manage customers to optimize long-term value. CRM requires a customer-centric business philosophy and culture to support effective marketing, sales, and services processes" (Thompson, 2003). It overlaps somewhat with the concept of *relationship marketing,* but not everything that could be called relationship marketing is in fact CRM (see Peppers and Rogers, 2004). CRM is much broader in that it includes a *one-to-one* relationship between a customer and a seller. To be a genuine one-to-one marketer, a company must be willing and able to change its behavior toward a specific customer, based on what it knows about that customer. So, CRM is basically a simple idea: *Treat different customers differently,* because their needs differ and their value to the company may be different.

CRM involves much more than just sales and marketing, because a firm must be able to change how its products are configured or its service is delivered, based on the needs of individual customers. (See Minicase 2 at the end of this chapter.) Smart companies have always encouraged the active participation of customers in the development of products, services, and solutions. For the most part, however, being customer oriented has traditionally meant being oriented to the needs of the *typical* customer in the market—the average customer. In order to build enduring one-to-one relationships in a CRM initiative, a company must continuously interact with customers *individually*. One reason so many firms are beginning to focus on CRM is that this kind of service can create high customer loyalty and, additionally, help the firm's profitability (Goodhue et al., 2002). Involvement of almost all other departments and especially engineering (design), accounting, and operations, is critical in CRM. For the essentials of today's CRM, see Bergerson (2004) and Urban (2004).

Types of CRM and IT Support

We distinguish among three major types of CRM *activities* involved: operational, analytical, and collaborative. *Operational CRM* is related to typical business functions involving customer services, order management, invoice/billing, and sales/marketing automation and management. *Analytical CRM* involves activities that capture, store, extract, process, interpret, and report customer data to a corporate user, who then analyzes them as needed. *Collaborative CRM* deals with all the necessary communication, coordination, and collaboration between vendors and customers. Typical CRM activities and their IT support are listed in Online File W7.8. (For more details see Goodhue et al., 2002.)

CLASSIFICATIONS OF CRM APPLICATIONS. Another way of looking at CRM is to focus on the tools used by the CRM applications. The Patricia Seybold Group (2002) distinguishes among *customer-facing*, *customer-touching*, and *customer-centric intelligence* CRM applications. These three categories of applications are described below and are shown in Figure 7.5. The exhibit also shows how customers interact with these applications.

1. *Customer-facing applications.* These include all the areas where customers interact with the company: call centers, including help desks; sales force automation; and field service automation. Such CRM applications basically automate the information flow or they support employees in these areas.

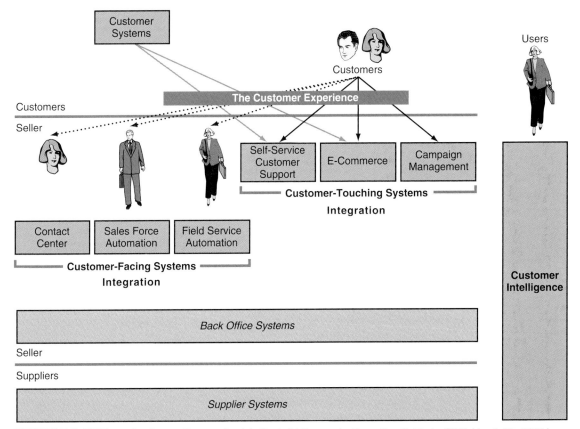

FIGURE 7.5 CRM applications. (*Source:* Patricia Seybold Group, *An Executive Guide to CRM*, March 21, 2002.)

2. **Customer-touching applications.** In this category, customers interact directly with the applications. Notable are self-service, campaign management, and general purpose e-commerce applications.

3. **Customer-centric intelligence applications.** These are applications that are intended to analyze the results of operational processing and use the results of the analysis to improve CRM applications. Data reporting and warehousing and data mining are the prime topics here.

To this classification of CRM applications we add the following fourth category:

4. **Online networking applications.** Online networking refers to methods that provide the opportunity to build personal relationships with a wide range of people in business. These include chat rooms and discussion lists.

(Further details on the first three categories can be found at *psgroup.com*, in the free download of *An Executive's Guide to CRM*.)

E-CRM

CRM has been practiced manually by corporations for generations. However, since the mid-1990s various types of information technologies have enhanced CRM. CRM technology is an evolutionary response to changes in the business environment, making use of new IT devices and tools. The term **e-CRM** (electronic CRM) was coined in the mid-1990s, when businesses started using Web browsers, the Internet, and other electronic touchpoints (e-mail, POS terminals, call centers, and direct sales) to manage customer relationships. E-CRM covers a broad range of topics, tools, and methods, ranging from the proper design of digital products and services to pricing and to loyalty programs (e.g., see *e-sj.org*, *Journal of Service Research*, and *ecrmguide.com*). The use of e-CRM technologies has made customer service, as well as service to partners, much more effective and efficient.

Through Internet technologies, data generated about customers can be easily fed into marketing, sales, and customer service applications for analysis. E-CRM also includes online applications that lead to segmentation and personalization. The success of these efforts can be measured and modified in real time, further elevating customer expectations. In the world connected by the Internet, e-CRM has become a requirement for survival, not just a competitive advantage.

THE SCOPE OF E-CRM. We can differentiate three levels of e-CRM:

1. **Foundational service.** This includes the *minimum necessary* services such as Web site responsiveness (e.g., how quickly and accurately the service is provided), site effectiveness, and order fulfillment.

2. **Customer-centered services.** These services include order tracking, product configuration and customization, and security/trust. These are the services that *matter the most* to customers.

3. **Value-added services.** These are *extra services* such as online auctions and online training and education.

CUSTOMER SERVICE ON THE WEB. A primary activity of e-CRM is customer service on the Web, which can take many forms. We describe some of these different kinds of Web-based customer service below. (For fuller details, see Greenberg, 2002.)

Search and Comparison Capabilities.   With the hundreds of thousands of online stores, it is difficult for customers to find what they want, even inside a single electronic mall. Search and comparison capabilities are provided internally in large malls (e.g., *smartmall.biz*) or by independent comparison sites (*mysimon.com*). Some of these shopping aids were described in Chapter 3.

Free Products and Services.   One approach companies use to differentiate themselves is to give away some product or service. For example, Compubank.com once offered free bill payments and ATM services. Companies can offer free samples over the Internet, as well as free entertainment, customer education, and more.

Technical and Other Information and Services.   Interactive experiences can be personalized to induce the consumer to commit to a purchase or to remain a loyal customer. For example, General Electric's Web site provides detailed technical and maintenance information and sells replacement parts for discontinued models for those who need to fix outdated home appliances. Such information and parts are quite difficult to find offline. Another example is Goodyear, which provides information about tires and their use at *goodyear.com*. The ability to download manuals and problem solutions at any time is another innovation of electronic customer service.

Customized Products and Services.   Dell Computer revolutionized the purchasing of computers by letting customers configure their own systems. This mass customization process is now used extensively by online vendors. Consumers are shown prepackaged "specials" and are given the option to "custombuild" products using online product configurators.

Other companies have found ways that are unique to their industries to offer customized products and services online. Web sites such as *gap.com* allow you to "mix and match" your entire wardrobe. Web sites such as *hitsquad.com, musicalgreeting.com*, or *surprise.com* allow consumers to handpick individual music titles from a library and customize a CD, a feature that is not offered in traditional music stores. Instant delivery of any digitized entertainment is a major advantage of EC.

Account or Order Status Tracking.   Customers can view their account balances or check merchandise shipping status at any time from their computers or cell phones. If you ordered books from Amazon, for example, you can find the anticipated arrival date. Many companies follow this model and provide similar services.

All of these examples of customer service on the Web demonstrate an important aspect of CRM: a focus on the individual customer.

OTHER TOOLS FOR CUSTOMER SERVICE.   There are many innovative Web-related tools to enhance customer service and CRM. Here are the major ones.

Personalized Web Pages.   Many companies allow customers to create their own individual Web pages. These pages can be used to record purchases and preferences, as well as problems and requests. For example, using intelligent agent techniques, American Airlines generates personalized Web pages for each of about 800,000 registered travel-planning customers.

Also, customized information (such as product and warranty information) can be efficiently delivered when the customer logs on to the vendor's Web site. Not only can the customer pull information as needed, but the vendor also can push information to the customer. Transaction information stored in the vendor's database can be used to support marketing of more products, for example.

FAQs. Frequently asked questions (FAQs) are the simplest and least expensive tool for dealing with repetitive customer questions. Customers use this tool by themselves, which makes the delivery cost minimal. However, any nonstandard question requires an e-mail.

E-Mail and Automated Response. The most popular tool of customer service is e-mail. Inexpensive and fast, e-mail is used mostly to answer inquiries from customers but also to disseminate information (e.g., confirmations), to send alerts, to send product information, and to conduct correspondence regarding any topic.

Chat Rooms. Another tool that provides customer service, attracts new customers, and increases customers' loyalty is a chat room. For example, retailer QVC offers a chat room where customers can discuss their QVC shopping experiences (see Minicase 2 at the end of this chapter).

Call Centers. One of the most important tools of customer service is the *call center*. Call centers are typically the "face" of the organization to its customers. For example, investment company Charles Schwab's call center effectively handles over 1 million calls from investment customers every day.

New technologies are extending the functionality of the conventional call center to e-mail and to Web interaction. For example, *epicor.com* combines Web channels, such as automated e-mail reply, Web knowledge bases, and portal-like self-service, with call center agents or field service personnel. Such centers are sometimes called *telewebs*.

Troubleshooting Tools. Large amounts of time can be saved by customers if they can solve problems by themselves. Many vendors provide Web-based troubleshooting software to assist customers in this task. The vendors dramatically reduce their expenses for customer support when customers are able to solve problems without further intervention of customer service specialists.

WIRELESS CRM. Many CRM tools and applications are going wireless. As shown in Chapter 5, mobile sales force automation is becoming popular. In addition, use of wireless devices by mobile service employees is enabling these employees to provide better service while they are at the customer's site. Also, using SMS and e-mail from hand-held devices is becoming popular as a means of improving CRM. Overall, we will see many CRM services going wireless fairly soon. For example, the Expedia case in Chapter 12 illustrates a wireless CRM application.

CRM Failures

As with many IT innovations, there have been initially a large number of CRM failures, which have been reported in the media. For example, according to *Zdnetindia.com/news* (2000), the founder and CEO of Customer.com estimated that 42 percent of the top 125 CRM sites experienced failures. Numerous failures have also been reported by *thinkanalytics.com*, *cio.com*, *CRM-forum.com*, and many more. However, according to *itgreycells.com*, CRM failures are declining, from a failure rate of up to 80 percent in 1998 to about 40 percent in 2003.

Some of the major issues relating to CRM failures are the following:

● Difficulty in measuring and valuing intangible benefits. There are only a few tangible benefits to CRM.

TABLE 7.2 How to Implement CRM to Avoid Its Failure

- Conduct a survey to determine how the organization responds to customers.
- Carefully consider the four components of CRM: sales, service, marketing, and channel/partner management.
- Survey how CRM accomplishments are measured; use defined metrics. Make sure quality, not just quantity, is addressed.
- Consider how CRM software can help vis-à-vis the organization's objectives.
- Decide on a strategy: refining existing CRM processes, or reengineering the CRM.
- Evaluate all levels in the organization but particularly frontline agents, field service, and salespeople.
- Prioritize the organization's requirements as one of the following: *must*, *desired*, or *not so important*.
- Select appropriate CRM software. There are more than 60 vendors. Some (like Siebel) provide comprehensive packages; others provide only certain functions. Decide whether to use the best-of-breed approach or to go with one vendor. ERP vendors (e.g., PeopleSoft and SAP) also offer CRM products.

Source: Compiled from DeFazio (2002).

- Failure to identify and focus on specific business problems.
- Lack of active senior management (non-IT) sponsorship.
- Poor user acceptance. This issue can occur for a variety of reasons such as unclear benefits (i.e., CRM is a tool for management, but it may not help a rep sell more effectively) and usability problems.
- Trying to automate a poorly defined process.

Strategies to deal with these and other problems are offered by many. (For example, see *cio.com* for CRM implementation, Kotorov, 2003, and Newell and Godin, 2003. Also see *conspectus.com* for "10 steps for CRM success.") Finally, the use of metrics to compare results is highly recommended (see Online File W7.9).

CRM failures can create substantial problems. Some companies are falling behind in their ability to handle the volume of site visitors and the volume of buyers. Managerial guidelines for implementing CRM and avoiding CRM failure are provided in Table 7.2.

→ MANAGERIAL ISSUES

1. ***Ethical issues.*** Conducting a supply chain management project may result in the need to lay off, retrain, or transfer employees. Should management notify the employees in advance regarding such possibilities? And what about those older employees who are difficult to retrain? Other ethical issues may involve sharing of personal information, which may be required for a collaborative organizational culture.

2. ***How much to integrate?*** While companies should consider extreme integration projects, including ERP, SCM, and e-commerce, they should recognize that integrating long and complex supply chain segments may result in failure. Therefore, many times companies tightly integrate the upstream, inside-company, and downstream activities, each part by itself, and loosely connect the three.

3. ***Role of IT.*** Almost all major SCM projects use IT. However, it is important to remember that in most cases the technology plays a supportive role, and the

primary role is organizational and managerial in nature. On the other hand, without IT, most SCM efforts do not succeed.

4. ***Organizational adaptability.*** To adopt ERP, organization processes must, unfortunately, conform to the software, not the other way around. When the software is changed, in a later version for example, the organizational processes must change also. Some organizations are able and willing to do so; others are not.

5. ***Going global.*** EC provides an opportunity to expand markets globally. However, it may create long and complex supply chains. Therefore, it is necessary to first check the logistics along the supply chain as well as regulations and payment issues.

6. ***The customer is king/queen.*** In implementing IT applications, management must remember the importance of the customer/end-user, whether external or internal. Some innovative applications intended to increase customers' satisfaction are difficult to justify in a traditional cost-benefit analysis. Empowering customers to enter into a corporate database can make customers happy since they can conduct self-service activities such as configuration and tracking and get quick answers to their queries. Self-services can save money for a company as well, but it may raise security and privacy concerns. Corporate culture is important here, too. Everyone in the organization must be concerned about customers. Management should consider installing a formal CRM program for this purpose.

7. ***Set CRM policies with care.*** In practicing CRM, companies may give priority to more valuable customers (e.g., frequent buyers). This may lead to perceived discrimination. For example, in one case, when a male customer found that Victoria's Secret charged him more than it did female buyers, he sued. In court it was shown that he was buying less frequently than the specific female he cited; the company was found not guilty of discrimination. Companies need to be very careful with CRM policies.

KEY TERMS

Bullwhip effect *300*

Customer relationship management (CRM) *318*

E-CRM *320*

E-supply chain *297*

Enterprise resource planning (ERP) *311*

Enterprise systems (enterprisewide systems) *295*

SAP R/3 *311*

SCM software *297*

Supply chain management (SCM) *297*

Supply chain team *305*

Virtual factory *306*

CHAPTER HIGHLIGHTS (Numbers Refer to Learning Objectives)

1 Enterprise systems are information systems that support several departments and/or the entire enterprise. The most notable are ERP, which supports supply chains, and CRM.

1 Supply chains connect suppliers to a manufacturing company, departments inside a company, and a company to its customers. The supply chain must be completely managed, from the raw material to the end customers. Typical supply chains involve three segments: upstream, internal, and downstream. Most supply chains are supported by a variety of IT application programs.

2 The major types of supply chains are integrated make-to-stock (manufacture to inventory), continuous replenishment, build-to-order, and channel assembly. Each type can be global or local.

3 It is difficult to manage the supply chain due to the uncertainties in demand and supply and the need to coordinate several (sometimes many) business partners' activities. One of the major problems is known as the bullwhip effect, in which lack of coordination and/or communication results in large, unnecessary inventories.

3 A number of solutions to supply chain problems are supported by IT, such as appropriate inventory management, vertical integration, information sharing, VMI, supply chain hubs, supply chain collaboration, RFID, supply chain teams, virtual factories, and wireless solutions.

4 During the last 50 years, software support for supply chain management (SCM) has increased both in coverage and scope. SCM supports mostly decision making in short segments, such as resource optimization and inventory management. MRP pulled together production, purchasing, and inventory management of interrelated products. MRP II software added labor requirement and financial planning to the MRP model.

4 The next step in SCM was to integrate routine transactions, including internal suppliers/customers and external suppliers/customers, in ERP and extended ERP software. The latest step in the evolution of integrated supply chain software is the addition of business intelligence and CRM applications.

5 ERP software, which is designed to improve standard business transactions from all of the functional departments, is enhanced with decision-support capabilities as well as Web interfaces, and it provides an integrated framework of all routine activities in the enterprise. ERP enables different functional applications to work seamlessly so that data can flow automatically (from production to marketing, for example). ERP also provides easy interfaces to legacy systems as well as to partners' systems.

6 CRM is an enterprisewide activity through which an organization takes care of its customers and their needs. It is based on the idea of one-to-one relationships with customers. CRM is done by providing many communication and collaboration services, most of which are IT-supported and many of which are delivered on the Web.

VIRTUAL COMPANY ASSIGNMENT

Instructions for accessing The Wireless Café on the Student Web Site:

1. Go to
   wiley.com/college/turban
2. Select Turban/Leidner/
   McLean/Wetherbe's
   *Information Technology for
   Management, Fifth Edition.*
3. Click on Student
   Resources site, in the toolbar on the left.
4. Click on the link for
   Virtual Company Web site.
5. Click on Wireless Café.

Enterprise Systems at The Wireless Café

Go to The Wireless Café's link on the Student Web Site. There you will be asked to apply some ERP principles to The Wireless Café and to propose some enterprisewide applications that could benefit the restaurant's operations.

More Resources

More resources and study tools are located on the Student Web Site. You'll find additional chapter materials and useful Web links. In addition, self-quizzes that provide individualized feedback are available for each chapter.

QUESTIONS FOR REVIEW

1. Define and list enterprise systems.
2. Define a supply chain and supply chain management (SCM).
3. List the major components of supply chains.
4. List the benefits of effective SCM.
5. Describe typical supply chain problems and the reasons for such problems.
6. What is the bullwhip effect?
7. Describe solutions to supply chain problems.
8. How does collaboration solve supply chain problems?
9. Describe how RFID improves supply chain operations.
10. Describe VMI, supply teams, and virtual factories.
11. Describe MRP and MRP II.
12. Describe the need for, and types of, systems integration.
13. Define ERP and describe its functionalities.
14. List the additions provided by second-generation ERP.
15. Describe the logic of integrating ERP and SCM software.
16. List some reasons for ERP failures.
17. Define CRM.
18. List the major types of CRM.
19. What is e-CRM?
20. List some customer-facing, customer-touching, and customer-intelligent CRM tools.

QUESTIONS FOR DISCUSSION

1. Distinguish between ERP and SCM software. In what ways do they complement each other? Relate them to system integration.
2. Discuss how cooperation between a company that you are familiar with and its suppliers can reduce inventory cost.
3. Find examples of how organizations improve their supply chains in two of the following: manufacturing, hospitals, retailing, education, construction, agribusiness, and shipping. Discuss the benefits to the organizations.
4. It is said that supply chains are essentially "a series of linked suppliers and customers; every customer is in turn a supplier to the next downstream organization, until the ultimate end-user." Explain. Use of a diagram is recommended.
5. Explain the bullwhip effect. In which type of business is it likely to occur most? How can the effect be controlled?
6. Discuss why Web-based call centers are critical for a successful CRM.
7. Discuss why RFID may completely revolutionize the management of supply chains. Can it solve the bullwhip problem? If so, how?
8. Discuss why it is difficult to justify CRM and how metrics can help. (See Online File W7.9 and Minicase 2.)

EXERCISES

1. Identify the supply chain(s) and the flow of information described in the opening case. Draw it. Also, answer the following.
   a. "The company's business is not to make the product, but to sell the product." Explain this statement.
   b. Why was it necessary to use IT to support the change?
   c. Identify all the segments of the supply chain.
   d. Identify all supporting information systems in this case.
2. Enter *aberdeen.com* and observe its "online supply chain community" (go to *supply chain access*). Most of the information there is free. Prepare an outline of the major resources available in the site.
3. Go to a bank and find out the process and steps of obtaining a mortgage for a house. Draw the supply chain. Now assume that some of the needed information, such as the value of the house and the financial status of the applicant, is found in a publicly available database (such a database exists in Hong Kong, for example). Draw the supply chain in this case. Explain how such a database can shorten the loan approval time.
4. Go to Online File W7.9 and review the CRM metrics. Select a bank or other company that provides you with services. How can the company use metrics to evaluate its CRM?

GROUP ASSIGNMENTS

1. Each group in the class will be assigned to a major ERP/SCM vendor such as SAP, PeopleSoft, Oracle, etc. Members of the groups will investigate topics such as: (a) Web connections, (b) use of business intelligence tools, (c) relationship to CRM and to EC, (d) major capabilities, and (e) availability of ASP services by the specific vendor.

   Each group will prepare a presentation for the class, trying to convince the class why the group's software is best for a local company known to the students (e.g., a supermarket chain).

2. Assign each team to one type of supply chain, such as build-to-order or continuous replenishment. The team should find two examples of the assigned type, draw the supply chains, and explain the IT and EC solutions used.

3. Create groups to investigate the major CRM software vendors, their products, and the capabilities of those products in the following categories. (Each group represents a topical area of several companies.)

- Sales force automation (Oracle, Onyx, Salesforce, Siebel, Saleslogix, Pivotal)
- Call centers (Clarify, LivePerson, NetEffect, Inference, Peoplesoft)
- Marketing automation (Annuncio, Exchange Applications, MarketFirst, Nestor)
- Customer service (Brightware, Broadvision, Primus, Silknet)
- Sales configuration (Exactium, Newtonian)

Start with *searchcrm.com* and *crmguru.com* (to ask questions about CRM solutions). Each group must present arguments to the class to convince class members to use the product(s) the group investigated.

INTERNET EXERCISES

1. Enter *ups.com*. Examine some of the IT-supported customer services and tools provided by the company. Write a report on how UPS contributes to supply chain improvements.

2. Enter *supply-chain.org, cio.com, findarticles.com,* and *google.com* and search for recent information on supply chain management integration.

3. Enter one or more of the following Web sites: *logictool.com, isourceonline.com, supplychaintoday.com,* and *tilion.com*. Find information on the bullwhip effect and on the strategies and tools used to lessen the effect.

4. Enter *mySap.com*. Identify its major components. Also review the Advanced Planning and Optimization tool. How can each benefit the management of a supply chain?

5. Enter *i2.com* and review its SCM products that go beyond ERP. Examine the OCN Network and Rhythm. Write a report.

6. Enter *siebel.com*. View the demo on e-business. Identify all e-business–related initiatives. Why is the company considered as the leader of CRM software?

7. Enter *anntaylor.com* and identify the customer service activities offered there.

8. Enter *oracle.com*. Find the ERP modules offered by Oracle and identify their connection to CRM and customer services.

9. Enter *salesforce.com* and take the tour. What enterprisewide system does the company support? How?

10. Enter *2020software.com*. Find information about the top 10 ERP applications. View the demo; write a report on your findings.

Minicase 1
ERP Helps Productivity at Northern Digital Inc.

Northern Digital Inc. (*ndigital.com*) in Ontario, Canada, is a supplier of 3D/6D measurement products. The relatively small company employs 90 people and generates over $20 million in annual revenue.

The Problem

Northern Digital Inc. (NDI) faced a challenge when rapid growth and aging technology threatened to stand in the way of company goals. Instead of enabling operational improvements, NDI's existing systems were impeding progress. Existing technology was causing missed deliveries and creating a high number of back orders. Inventory control was poor, and the planning was inaccurate. With some customers expecting shipment in as long as 9 months and others expecting shipment in as little as 9 days or even less, more sophisticated and accurate planning was critical. Customer satisfaction was at risk, and internal morale was slipping. With almost 20 years in business, NDI's well-established reputation for high-quality, high-performance products was at risk.

The Solution

NDI selected an ERP system (from Intuitive Manufacturing Systems) based on factors that directly supported corporate objectives. Intuitive's ERP provided a level of system functionality that could immediately improve inventory management and the expandability and flexibility to support NDI's growth. The software includes a complete planning system, automated inventory management, and enhanced technology infrastructure. Equally important was the system's level of ease of implementation and ease of use.

The Results

After implementing Intuitive ERP, Northern Digital experienced continued success in improving inventory management and increasing revenue. Prior to implementation, the company struggled to achieve even two inventory "turns" (turnovers) per year. Inventory turns have now more than doubled, and expectations are that the company will better that in the near future. Since implementation, Northern Digital's revenue has increased from $10 million to over $20 million with little increase in inventory value. In addition, the company has reduced order cycle time for its flagship product from 4 months to 4 weeks, an improvement of almost 80 percent. This was a result of improved planning capabilities due to the ERP.

Improvements in production control and inventory management have had a direct impact on customer delivery. The Material Requirements Planning and Forecasting capabilities of Intuitive ERP have allowed Northern Digital to better service its customers. The addition of better planning capabilities had an immediate positive impact on labor and materials. "We were able to better understand what was in stock, what we were buying, and what was needed," said Tom Kane, production manager. "Improved planning has made a huge difference in improving delivery."

Ease of use and system scalability have been important in utilizing Intuitive ERP to improve operations. When the system was first implemented, NDI needed only five user seats (user licenses). As NDI grew, that number increased to 25. Significantly increasing the number of users, and doing so without a lot of training, allowed the company to expand without worrying about putting constraints on its business infrastructure, supporting the growth strategy.

For Northern Digital, improving operations is more than just a way to reduce expenses. With the implementation of Intuitive ERP, the NDI has found a way to increase the value it provides to customers while also improving financial performance.

Sources: Compiled from *managingautomation.com* (May 10, 2004), and from *ndigital.com* (accessed June 11, 2004).

Questions for Minicase 1

1. For a small company like NDI, why is an ERP better than SCM applications?
2. Identify the supply chain segments that the ERP supports; be specific.
3. Relate this case to Porter's value chain and to its competitive model (Appendix 1A). Show the ERP's contribution.
4. Enter *intuitivemfg.com* and report on the capabilities of the company's ERP product.
5. Relate this case to business planning and strategy.

Minicase 2
QVC Provides Superb CRM

QVC (*qvc.com*) is known for its TV shopping channels, and it is selling on the Web too. It is a very competitive business, since retail selling is done in several marketing channels. In 2000, QVC served more than 6 million customers, answered 125 million phone calls, shipped about 80 million packages, and handled more than a billion page views

on its Web site. QVC's business strategy is to provide top-notch customer service in order to keep its customers loyal. QVC also appointed a senior vice president for customer service. The problem was how to provide top-notch customer care and do it economically.

To manage its huge business (about $5 billion a year), QVC must use the latest IT support. For example, QVC operates four state-of-the-art call centers, one of these for overseas operations. However, before using technology to boost loyalty and sales, QVC had to develop a strategy to put its customers at the core of corporate decision making. "Exceeding the expectations of every customer" is a sign you can see all over QVC's premises. As a matter of fact, the acronym QVC stands for Quality, Value, and Convenience—all from the customers' perspective.

In pursuit of this goal, QVC created a truly excellent service organization. Among other things, QVC provides education (demonstrating product features and functions), entertainment, and companionship. Viewers build a *social* relationship with show hosts, upon which the *commercial* relationship is built. Now QVC is also attempting to build a social relationship with its customers on the Web (see *qvc.com*).

QVC knows that building trust on the TV screen is necessary, but not sufficient to draw customers. So everyone in the company contributes to the customer service goals. QVC's president randomly checks customers' letters, including e-mail. All problems are fixed quickly. Everything is geared toward the long run. In addition, to make CRM work, QVC aligns senior executives, IT executives, and functional managers so that they work toward the same goals, collaborate, have plans that do not interfere with others' plans, and so forth. Also, the company adopts the latest IT applications and continuously offers training to its customer service reps in the new CRM applications.

QVC is using metrics to measure customer service. These include: friendliness of the call center reps; how knowledgeable the reps are about the products; clarity of the instructions about how to order and how to use the products purchased; the number of people a customer has to speak with to get a satisfactory answer; and how often a customer has to call a second time to get a problem resolved.

Data on customer service are collected in several ways, including tracking of telephone calls and Web-site movements. Cross-functional teams staff the call centers, so complete knowledge is available in one place. Corrective actions are taken quickly, to prevent repeat problems in the future.

To get the most out of the call center's employees, QVC strives to keep them very satisfied. They must enjoy the work in order to provide excellent customer service. The employees are called "customer advocates," and they are handsomely rewarded for innovative ideas.

In addition to call centers, QVC uses computer-telephony integration technology (CTI), which identifies the caller's phone number and matches it to customer information in the database. This information pops up on the rep's screen when a customer calls. The rep can greet the customer by saying, "Nice to have you at QVC again, David. I see that you have been with us twice this year, and we want you to know that you are important to us. Have you enjoyed the jacket you purchased last June?"

To know all about the customer history, QVC maintains a large data warehouse. Customers' buying history is correlated by Zip code with psychodemographic data from Experian (*experian.com*), a company that analyzes consumer information. This way, QVC can know instantly, for example, whether a new product is a hit with wealthy retirees or with young adults. The information is used for e-procurement, advertising strategy, and more. QVC also uses viral marketing (word-of-mouth of its loyal customers). In order not to bother its customers, QVC does not send any mail advertisements.

Sources: Compiled from "Nice Guys Finish First . . ." (2000), and from *qvc.com* (accessed June 2004).

Questions for Minicase 2

1. Enter *qvc.com* and identify actions that the company takes to increase trust in its e-business. Also, look at all customer-service activities. List as many as you can find.

2. List the advantages of buying online versus buying over the phone after watching QVC. What are the disadvantages? Is this a CRM service?

3. Enter the chat room of *qvc.com* and the bulletin board. What is the general mood of the participants? Are they happy with QVC? Why or why not? What is the advantage of having customers chat live online?

4. QVC is using a data warehouse to provide customer service (e.g., find what customers purchased in the past). Explain how this is done. The data warehouse now operates in real time. Why?

REFERENCES

Bresnahan, J., "The Incredible Journey," *CIO.com*, August 15, 1998, *cio.com/archive/enterprise/081598_jour.html* (accessed June 2003).

Chen, I. J., and K. Popovich, "Understanding Customer Relationship Management (CRM): People, Process, and Technology," *Business Process Management Journal*, 9(5), 2003.

Chow, W. S., "An Exploratory Study of the Success Factors for Extranet Adoption in E-supply Chains," *Journal of Global Information Management*, January–March 2004.

DeFazio, D., "The Right CRM for the Job," *Technologydecisions.com*, November 2000.

Doane, M., "Ready, Fire, Aim: A Failure of ERP Readiness Starts at the Top," *ZDNet.com*, April 19, 2004, *techupdate.zdnet.com/techupdate/stories/main/Ready_Fire_Aim.html?tag=tu.arch.link.* (accessed May 2004).

Donovan, R. M., "Supply Chain Management: Cracking the Bullwhip Effect," *Material Handling Management*, Director Issue, 2002/2003.

Duplaga, E. A., and M. Astani, "Implementing ERP in Manufacturing," *Information Systems Management*, Summer 2003.

Fjermestad, J., and N. C. Romano, "Electronic Customer Relationship Management: Revisiting the General Principles of Usability and Resistance—An Integrative Implementation Framework," *Business Process Management Journal*, 9(5), 2003.

Gattiker, T. F., and Goodhue, D. L., "Understanding the Local-Level Costs and Benefits of ERP through Organizational Information Processing Theory," *Information and Management*, 41(4), March 2004.

Gayialis, S. P., and Tatsiopoulos, I. P., "Design of an IT-Driven Decision Support System for Vehicle Routing and Scheduling," *European Journal of Operational Research*, 152(2), January 16, 2004.

Goodhue, D. L., et al., "Realizing Business Benefits through CRM: Hitting the Right Target in the Right Way," *MIS Quarterly Executive*, 1(2), June 2002.

Goutsos, S., and N. Karacapilidis, "Enhanced Supply Chain Management for e-Business Transactions," *International Journal of Production Economics*, 89(2), May 28, 2004.

Greenberg, P., *CRM at the Speed of Light: Capturing and Keeping Customers in Internet Real Time*, 2nd ed. New York: McGraw-Hill, 2002.

Hagel, J., III, *Out of the Box*. Boston: Harvard Business School Press, 2002.

Handfield, R. B., and E. L. Nichols, *Introduction to Supply Chain Management*. Upper Saddle River, NJ: Pearson Education, 1999.

Heizer, L., and B. Render, *Operations Management*, 7th ed. Upper Saddle River, NJ: Pearson Education, 2004.

Jinyoul, L., et al., "Enterprise Integration with ERP and EAI," *Communications of the ACM*, February 2003.

Kalakota, R., and M. Robinson, *E-Business 2.2: Roadmap for Success*. Boston, MA: Addison Wesley, 2001.

Kanakamedala, K., et al., "Getting Supply Chain Software Right," *McKinsey Quarterly*, No. 1, 2003.

Kinsella, B., "Wal-Mart Factor," *Industrial Engineer*, November 2003.

Kotorov, R., "Customer Relationship Management: Strategic Lessons and Future Directions," *Business Process Management Journal*, 9(5), 2003.

Kovács, G. L., and P. Paganelli, "A Planning and Management Infrastructure for Large, Complex, Distributed Products—Beyond ERP and SCM," *Computers in Industry*, 51(2), June 2003.

Ligus, R. G., "The 12 Cardinal Sins of ERP Implementation," *Supply ChainBrain.com*, February 2004, *glscs.com/archives/02.04.opinion2.htm?adcode=30* (accessed May 2004).

Logistics Management and Distribution Report, October 1998 and November 1999.

Lucas, M. E., and R. Bishop, *ERP for Dummies*. Greensboro, NC: Resource Publication, October 2002.

Manthou, V., et al., "Virtual e-Chain (VeC) Model for Supply Chain Collaboration," *International Journal of Production Economics*, 87(3), February 18, 2004.

Mentzer, J. T., *Fundamentals of Supply Chain Management: Twelve Drivers of Competitive Advantage*. Thousand Oaks, CA: Sage Publications Ltd., 2004.

Murphy, K. E., and S. J. Simon, "Intangible Benefits Valuation in ERP Projects," *Information Systems Journal*, 12, October 2002.

"Nice Guys Finish First—Customer Relationship Management," *Darwin Magazine*, October 2000.

Nelson, D., "John Deere Optimizes Operations with Supply Chain Efforts," *Journal of Organizational Excellence*, Spring 2002.

Newell, F., and S. Godin, *Why CRM Doesn't Work: How to Win by Letting Customers Manage the Relationship*, Bloomberg Press, 2003.

Oliver, D., and C. Romm, "Justifying Enterprise Resource Planning Adoption," *Journal of Information Technology*, December 2002.

Patricia Seybold Group, *An Executive's Guide to CRM*. Boston, MA: Patricia Seybold Group, 2002, *psgroup.com/freereport/imedia/resport/asp* (accessed April 15, 2003).

Peacocks Case Study, *symbol.com/uk/solutions/case_study_peacocks.html*, 2004 (accessed May 2004).

Peppers, D., and M. Rogers, *Managing Customer Relationships: A Strategic Framework*. New York: Wiley, 2004.

Poirier, C. C., and M. J. Bauer, *E-Supply Chain: Using the Internet to Revolutionize Your Business*. San-Francisco, CA: Berrett-Koehler, 2000.

Ragowsky, A., and T. M. Somers (eds.), "Enterprise Resource Planning," special issue, *Journal of Management Information Systems*, Summer 2002.

Reda, S., "The Path to RFID," *Stores*, June 2003.

Sandoe, K., et al., *Enterprise Integration*. New York: Wiley, 2001.

Sarkis, J., and R. P. Sundarraj, "Managing Large-Scale Global ERP Systems: A Case Study at Texas Instruments," *Information and Management*, 23, October–November 2003.

Sheikh, K., *Manufacturing Resource Planning (MRP II)*. Boston, MA: McGraw-Hill, 2002.

Siau, K., and Y. Tian, "Supply Chains Integration: Architecture and Enabling Technologies," *Journal of Computer Information Systems*, Spring 2004.

Simatupang, T. M., and R. Sridharan, "The Collaborative Supply Chain," *International Journal of Logistics Management*, 13(1), 2002.

Sodhi, M., "How to Do Strategic Supply-Chain Planning," *MIT Sloan Management Review*, Fall 2003.

Stevens, C. P., "Enterprise Resource Planning: A Trio of Resources," *Information Systems Management*, Summer 2003.

Subramani, M., "How Do Suppliers Benefit from IT Use in Supply Chain Relationships?" *MIS Quarterly*, March 2004.

Sullivan, M., et al., "Case Studies: Digital Do-Overs," *Forbes.com*, October 7, 2002.

Swanton, B., "Phase III ERP Benefits: The Art of the Formerly Impossible," *Tech Update, ZD Net*, April 30, 2004.

Tau, X., et al., "Internet Integrated Customer Relationship Management," *Journal of Computer Information Systems*, Spring 2002.

Thompson, B., "What Is CRM?" *CRMguru*, 2003.

Turban, E., et al., *Electronic Commerce 2006*. Upper Saddle River, NJ: Prentice Hall, in press.

Vakharia, J. (ed.), "E-business and Supply Chain Management," special issue, *Decision Sciences*, Fall 2002.

Worthen, B., "Drilling for Every Drop of Value," *CIO Management*, June 1, 2002.

Yao, D. D., et al., "Extended Enterprise Supply-Chain Management at IBM," *Interfaces*, January–February 2000.

Yusuf, Y., et al., "Enterprise Information Systems Project Implementation: A Case Study of ERP in Rolls-Royce," *International Journal of Production Economics*, 87(3), February 2004.

PART III
Organizational Application

6. Transaction Processing, Functional Applications, and Integration
7. Enterprise Systems: From Supply Chains to ERP to CRM
▶ 8. Interorganizational and Global Information Systems

CHAPTER 8

Interorganizational and Global Information Systems

8.1 Interorganizational Systems

8.2 Global Information Systems

8.3 B2B Exchanges, Hubs, and Directories

8.4 Virtual Corporations and IT Support

8.5 Electronic Data Interchange (EDI)

8.6 Extranets, XML, and Web Services

8.7 IOS Implementation Issues

Minicases:
1. Volkswagen
2. Six Flags

LEARNING OBJECTIVES

After studying this chapter, you will be able to:

❶ Define and classify interorganizational information systems.

❷ Define and classify global information systems.

❸ Present the major issues surrounding global information systems.

❹ Describe B2B exchanges, hubs, and directories.

❺ Describe virtual corporations and their IT support.

❻ Describe EDI and EDI/Internet and their benefits and limitations.

❼ Describe extranets, XML, and Web Services.

❽ Present major IOS implementation issues.

HOW DELL IS USING WEB SERVICES TO IMPROVE ITS SUPPLY CHAIN

➡ THE PROBLEM

Dell Inc. (*dell.com*) has many assembly plants. In these plants, located in various countries and locations, Dell makes PCs, servers, printers, and other computer hardware. The assembly plants rely on third-party logistics companies (3PLs), called "vendor-managed hubs," whose mission is to collect and maintain inventory of components from all of Dell's component manufacturers (suppliers). The supply chain is shown in Figure 8.1.

In the past, Dell submitted a weekly demand schedule to the 3PLs, who prepared shipments of specific components to the plants based on expected demand. Components management is critical to Dell's success for various reasons: Components become obsolete quickly, and their prices are constantly declining (by an average of 0.6 percent a week). So the fewer components a company keeps in inventory, the lower its costs. In addition, lack of components prevents Dell from delivering its build-to-order computers on time. Finally, the costs of components make up about 70 percent of a computer's cost, so managing components' cost can have a major impact on the bottom line. Because it is expensive to carry, maintain, and handle inventories, it is tempting to reduce inventory levels as low as possible. However, some inventories are necessary, both at the assembly plants and at the 3PLs' premises. Without such inventories Dell cannot meet its "five-day ship to target" goal (computer must be on a shipper's truck no later than five days after an order is received).

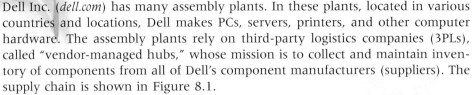

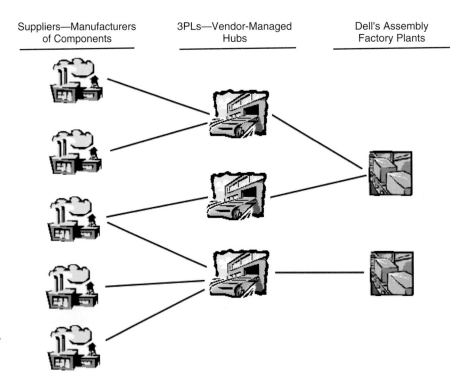

FIGURE 8.1 Dell's supply chain. (*Source:* Drawn by E. Turban.)

To minimize inventories, it is necessary to have considerable collaboration and coordination among all parties of the supply chain. For Dell, the supply chain includes hundreds of suppliers that are in many remote countries, speak different languages, and use different hardware and software platforms. Many have incompatible information systems that do not "talk" to each other.

In the past, Dell suppliers operated with 45 days of lead time. (That is, the suppliers had 45 days to ship an order after it was received.) To keep production lines running, Dell had to carry 26 to 30 hours of buffer inventory at the assembly plants, and the 3PLs had to carry 6 to 10 days of inventory. To meet its delivery target, Dell created a 52-week demand forecast that was updated every week as a guide to its suppliers.

All of these inventory items amount to large costs (due to the millions of computers produced annually). Also, the lead time was too long.

THE SOLUTION

Dell started to issue updated manufacturing schedules for each assembly plant, every two hours. These schedules reflected the actual orders received during the previous two hours. The schedules list all the required components, and they specify exactly when components need to be delivered, to which plant, and to what location of the plant (building number and exact door dock). These manufacturing schedules are published as Web Services and can be accessed by suppliers via Dell's extranet. Then, the 3PLs have 90 minutes to pick, pack, and ship the required parts to the assembly plants.

Dell introduced another Web Services system that facilitates checking the reliability of the suppliers' delivery schedules early enough in the process that corrective actions can take place. Dell can, if necessary, temporarily change production plans to accommodate delivery difficulties of components.

THE RESULTS

As a result of the new systems, inventory levels at Dell's assembly plants have been reduced from 30 hours to between 3 and 5 hours. This improvement represents a reduction of about 90 percent in the cost of keeping inventory. The ability to lower inventories also resulted in freeing up floor space that previously was used for storage. This space is now used for additional production lines, increasing factory utilization (capacity) by a third.

The inventory levels at the 3PLs have also been reduced, by 10 to 40 percent, increasing profitability for all. The more effective coordination of supply-chain processes across enterprises has also resulted in cost reduction, more satisfied Dell customers (who get computers as promised), and less obsolescence of components (due to lower inventories). As a result, Dell and its partners have achieved a more accelerated rate of innovations, which provides competitive advantage. Dell's partners are also happy that the use of Web Services has required only minimal investment in new information systems.

Sources: Compiled from Hagel (2002), and from *dell.com,* press releases (2000–2004).

LESSONS LEARNED FROM THIS CASE

Dell's success depends in large part on the information systems that connect its manufacturing plants with its suppliers and logistics providers. The construction and operation of interorganizational information systems (IOSs) that serve two or more organizations is the subject of this chapter. In today's economy, such IOSs may also be global. A new information technology, Web Services, has been successfully applied to improve the information systems that connect Dell and its vendors and the vendors and their parts' and components' manufacturers. To achieve efficient and effective communication of information, companies may select from technologies such as EDI and extranets, both of which are also described in this chapter. Finally, we describe some relevant implementation issues of interorganizational systems.

8.1 INTERORGANIZATIONAL SYSTEMS

An **interorganizational information system (IOS)** involves information flow among two or more organizations. Its major objective is efficient processing of transactions, such as transmitting orders, bills, and payments. As we will show in this chapter, an IOS can be local or global, dedicated to only one activity (e.g., transfer of funds) or intended to support several activities (e.g., to facilitate trade, communication, and collaboration).

Interorganizational systems have developed in direct response to two business pressures: the desire to reduce costs, and the need to improve the effectiveness and timeliness of business processes. More specifically, by connecting the information systems of business partners, IOSs enable both partners to: reduce the costs of routine business transactions; improve the quality of the information flow by reducing or eliminating errors; compress cycle time in the fulfillment of business transactions; eliminate paper processing and its associated inefficiencies and costs; and make the transfer and processing of information easy for users.

A major characteristic of an IOS is that the customer–supplier relationship frequently is determined in advance (as in the case of Dell), with the expectation that it will be ongoing. Advance arrangements result in agreements between organizations on the nature and format of the business documents and payments that will be exchanged. Both parties also know which communication networks will be integral to the system. Interorganizational systems may be built around privately or publicly accessible networks.

When IOSs use telecommunications companies for communication, they typically employ *value-added networks (VANs)*. These are *private*, third-party networks that can be tailored to specific business needs. However, use of *publicly accessible* networks is growing with the increased use of the Internet.

Types of Interorganizational Systems

Interorganizational information systems include a variety of business activities, from data interchange to messaging services to funds transfers. The most prominent types of interorganizational systems are the following.

- *B2B trading systems.* These systems are designed to facilitate trading between (among) business partners. The partners can be in the same or in different countries. B2B trading systems were covered in Chapter 4, where we described both company-centric (private) e-marketplaces and many-to-many public exchanges.

- *B2B support systems.* These are nontrading systems such as hubs, directories, and other services.
- *Global systems.* Global information systems connect two or more companies in two or more countries. The airline reservations system SABRE is an example of a huge global system.
- *Electronic funds transfer (EFT).* In EFT, telecommunications networks transfer money among financial institutions.
- *Groupware.* Groupware technologies (Chapter 3) facilitate communication and collaboration between and among organizations.
- *Integrated messaging.* A single transmission system can be used to deliver electronic mail and fax documents between organizations.
- *Shared databases.* Trading partners sometimes share databases in order to reduce time in communicating information between parties and to arrange cooperative activities.
- *Systems that support virtual companies.* These IOSs provide support to *virtual companies*—two or more business partners, in different locations, sharing costs and resources to provide a product or service.

IOS Support Technologies

Technology Guides are located at the book's Web site.

IOSs are also classified by the technology used. Four major IOS technologies are described in this chapter:

1. *Electronic data interchange (EDI).* The electronic movement of business documents between business partners. EDI runs on VANs (see Technology Guide 4), but it can be Internet-based, in which case it is known as EDI/Internet.
2. *Extranets.* Extended intranets that link business partners.
3. *XML.* An emerging B2B standard, promoted as a companion or even a replacement for EDI systems.
4. *Web Services.* The emerging technology for integrating B2B and intrabusiness applications (see Technology Guide 6).

The IOS systems and their supporting technologies are the subject of this chapter. Figure 8.2 provides an overview of these topics and their relationships.

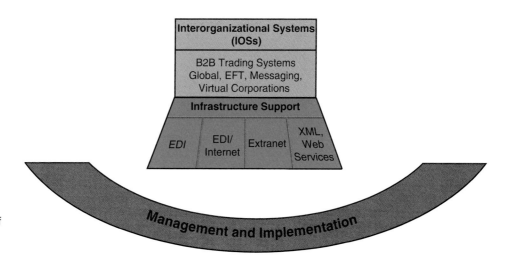

FIGURE 8.2 Overview of interorganizational information systems (IOSs).

8.2 GLOBAL INFORMATION SYSTEMS

Interorganizational systems that connect companies (or parts of one company) located in two or more countries are referred to as **global information systems.** Multinational companies, international companies, and virtual global companies typically need global information for their B2B operations. Companies that have global B2C operations usually use the Internet.

Multinational companies are those that operate in several countries. Examples are Coca-Cola, McDonald's, IBM, and SAP/AG (a German company). Multinational organizations may have sales offices and/or production facilities in several countries (e.g., see Minicase 1). They may conduct operations in locations where factory workers are plentiful and inexpensive, or where highly skilled employees are available at low salaries, or where there is a need to be close to the market. SAP/AP, for example, has a large research and development division in Silicon Valley, California, and distribution and sales offices in dozens of countries.

International companies are those that do business with other companies in different countries. For example, Boeing Corporation solicits bids from and does contract work with manufacturers in over 40 countries.

Virtual global companies are joint ventures whose business partners are located in different countries. The partners form a company for the specific purpose of producing a product or service. Such companies can be temporary, with a one-time mission (such as building an oil pipeline), or they can be permanent. (For more on virtual companies, see Section 8.4.)

All of the above companies use some global information systems. Global systems involve multiple organizations in multiple countries. Examples include airline reservation systems such as SABRE (*sabre.com*), police and immigration systems, electronic funds transfer (EFT) systems (including networks of ATMs), and many commercial and educational systems for international organizations such as the United Nations.

Benefits of Global Information Systems

Regardless of its structure, a company with global operations relies heavily on IT. The major benefits of global information systems for such organizations, made possible by IT, are:

- *Effective communication at a reasonable cost.* The partners are far from each other, yet they are able to work together, make decisions, monitor transactions, and provide controls. Business partners communicate through e-mail, EDI, Web Services (see the Dell opening case), and extranets. Communication is even more critical if the partners speak different languages. Intelligent IT systems can provide automatic translation.

- *Effective collaboration to overcome differences in distance, time, language, and culture.* Collaboration can be enhanced with groupware software (Chapter 3), group decision support systems (see Chapter 11), extranets, and teleconferencing devices (Chapter 3).

- *Access to databases of business partners and ability to work on the same projects while their members are in different locations.* Information technologies such as video teleconferencing and screen sharing (Chapter 3) are useful for this purpose.

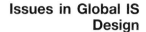

Issues in Global IS Design

The task of designing any effective interorganizational information system is complicated. It is even more complex when the IOS is a global system, because of differences in cultures, economies, and politics among parties in different countries.

Although the potential for a global economy certainly exists, some countries are erecting artificial borders through local language preference, local regulation, and access limitations. In addition, barriers of various sorts must be dealt with before global information systems can achieve their potential. Some issues to consider in designing global IOSs are cultural differences, localization, economic and political differences, and legal issues.

CULTURAL DIFFERENCES. *Culture* consists of the objects, values, and other characteristics of a particular society. It includes many different aspects ranging from tradition, to legal and ethical issues, to what information is considered offensive. When companies plan to do business in countries other than their own, they must consider the cultural environment. A well-known example is GM's car Nova. *No va* means "no go" in Spanish. GM did not pay attention to this issue, and the model's sales in Spanish-speaking countries suffered as a result.

LOCALIZATION. Many companies use different names, colors, sizes, and packaging for their overseas products and services. This practice is referred to as *localization*. In order to maximize the benefits of global information systems, the localization approach should also be used in the design and operation of such systems. For example, many Web sites offer different language and/or currency options, as well as special content. Europcar (*europcar.com*), for example, offers portals in 118 countries, each with an option for one of 10 languages (see Chapter 6, page 284).

ECONOMIC AND POLITICAL DIFFERENCES. Countries also differ considerably in their economic and political environments. One result of such variations is that the information infrastructures may differ from country to country. For example, many countries own the telephone services; others control communications very tightly. France, for example, insisted for years that French should be the sole language on French Web sites. Additional languages are now allowed, but French must also appear in every site. China controls the content of the Internet, blocking some Web sites from being viewed in China.

LEGAL ISSUES. Legal systems differ considerably among countries. Examples are copyrights, patents, computer crimes, file sharing, privacy, and data transfer. All of these issues have the potential to affect what is transmitted via global information systems, and so they must be considered. The impact of legal, economic, and political differences on the design and use of global information systems can be clearly seen in the issue of cross-border data transfer.

Transfer of Data across International Borders. Several countries, such as Canada and Brazil, impose strict laws to control **cross-border data transfer,** the flow of corporate data across nations' borders. These countries usually justify their laws as protecting the privacy of their citizens, since corporate data frequently contain personal data. Other justifications are intellectual property protection and keeping jobs within the country by requiring that data processing be done there.

The transfer of information in and out of a nation raises an interesting legal issue: Whose laws have jurisdiction when records are in a different country for reprocessing or retransmission purposes? For example, if data are transmitted by a Polish company through a U.S. satellite to a British corporation, whose laws control the data, and when? In order to solve some of these issues, governments are developing laws and standards to cope with the rapid increase of information technology, and international efforts to standardize these laws and standards are underway (e.g., see *oecd.org*). Some issues of cross-border data transfer are shown in Online File W8.1.

DESIGNING WEB SITES FOR A GLOBAL AUDIENCE.   Designing Web sites for a global audience is important. Web sites need to address cultural, legal, language, and other factors. These factors are summarized by Dubie (2003), who points out that 60 percent of all Internet users are non-English–speaking. Thus, doing business on the Internet must include *localization,* which includes translating languages, adapting content to meet cultural standards, and more. Dubie suggests how to customize Web sites and evaluates the power of machine translation (only 60% accurate).

Characteristics and Problems along Global Supply Chains

A special issue for global companies and their global information systems is how to optimize their supply chains. Supply chains that involve suppliers and/or customers in other countries are referred to as *global supply chains* (e.g., see Harrison, 2001, and Handfield and Nichols, 1999). E-commerce has made it much easier to find suppliers in other countries (e.g., by using electronic bidding) as well as to find customers in other countries (see Handfield et al., 2002, and Turban et al., 2006).

Global supply chains are usually longer than domestic ones, and they may be complex. Therefore, interruptions and uncertainties are likely. Some of the issues that may create difficulties in global supply chains are legal issues, customs fees and taxes, language and cultural differences, fast changes in currency exchange rates, and political instabilities. An example of difficulties in a global supply chain can be seen in *IT at Work 8.1.*

Information technologies have proven to be extremely useful in supporting global supply chains, but one needs to carefully design global information systems (Harrison, 2001). For example, TradeNet in Singapore connects sellers, buyers, and government agencies via electronic data interchange (EDI). (TradeNet's case is described in detail in Online File W8.2.) A similar network, TradeLink, is operating in Hong Kong, using both EDI and EDI/Internet and attempting to connect about 70,000 potential trading partners.

IT provides not only EDI and other communication infrastructure options, but also online expertise in sometimes difficult and fast-changing regulations. IT also can be instrumental in helping businesses find trading partners (via electronic directories and search engines, as in the case of *alibaba.com*). In addition, IT can help solve language problems through use of automatic Web page translation (see *A Closer Look 3.1,* page 99).

IT at Work 8.1
LEGO STRUGGLES WITH GLOBAL ISSUES

Lego Company of Denmark (*lego.com*) is a major producer of toys, including electronic ones. It is the world's best-known toy manufacturer (voted as "the toy of the 20th century") and has thousands of Web sites created by fans all over the world.

In 1999 the company decided to market its Lego Mindstorms on the Internet. This product is a unique innovation. Its users can build a Lego robot using more than 700 traditional Lego elements, program it on a PC, and transfer the program to the robot. Lego sells its products in many countries using several regional distribution centers.

When the decision to do global electronic commerce was made, the company had the following concerns. (Note that although this is a B2C example, many of the concerns are common to B2B as well.)

● It did not make sense to go to all countries, since sales are very low in some countries and some countries offer no logistical support services. In which countries should Lego sell the product?

● A supportive distribution and service system would be needed for e-commerce sales, including returns and software support.

● There was an issue of merging the offline and online operations versus creating a new centralized unit, which seemed to be a complex undertaking.

● Existing warehouses were optimized to handle distribution to commercial buyers, not to individual customers. E-commerce sales to individual customers would need to be accommodated.

● It would be necessary to handle returns around the globe.

● Lego products were selling in different countries in different currencies and at different prices. Should the product be sold on the Net at a single price? In which

currency? How would this price be related to the offline prices?

● How should the company handle the direct mail and track individual shipments?

● Invoicing must comply with the regulations of many countries.

● Should Lego create a separate Web site for Mindstorms? What languages should be used there?

● Some countries have strict regulations regarding advertising and sales to children. Also laws on consumer protection vary among countries. Lego needed to understand and deal with these differences.

● How should the company handle restrictions on electronic transfer of individuals' personal data?

● How should the company handle the tax and import duty payments in different countries?

In the rush to get its innovative product to market, Lego did not solve all of these issues before it introduced the direct Internet marketing. The resulting problems forced Lego to close the Web site for business in 1998. It took about a year to solve all global trade-related issues and eventually reopen the site. By 2001 Lego was selling online many of its products, priced in U.S. dollars, but the online service was available in only 15 countries.

As of 2003, *Lego.com* has been operating as an independent unit, allowing online design of many products (e.g., see "Train Configurator"). The site offers many Web-only deals, and it is visited by over 4 million unique visitors each day.

Sources: Compiled from *lego.com* (2003), from Damsgaard and Horluck (2000), and from Stoll (2003).

For Further Exploration: Is the Web the proper way to go global? Why does it make sense to sell the Lego products on the Internet?

In order to overcome logistics problems along the supply chain, especially global ones, companies are outsourcing logistics services to logistics vendors. Global information systems help enable tight communication and collaboration among supply chain members, as shown in *IT at Work 8.2* (page 340).

As IT technologies advance and global trade expands, more organizations will find the need to implement global information systems. We next look at three other types of IOSs (which sometimes are global)—B2B exchanges, hubs, and directories.

IT at Work 8.2

HOW BIKEWORLD USES GLOBAL INFORMATION SYSTEMS TO FULFILL ORDERS

BikeWorld (San Antonio, Texas) is a small company (16 employees) known for its high-quality bicycles and components, expert advice, and personalized service. The company opened its Web site (*bikeworld.com*) in February 1996, using it as a way to expand its reach to customers outside of Texas, including other countries.

BikeWorld encountered two of Internet retailing's biggest problems: fulfillment and after-sale customer service. Sales of its high-value bike accessories over the Internet steadily increased, including global markets. But the time BikeWorld spent processing orders manually, shipping packages, and responding to customers' order status inquiries was overwhelming for the company.

In order to focus on its core competency (making bicycles and their components), BikeWorld decided to outsource its order fulfillment. FedEx offered reasonably priced, quality express delivery, exceeding customer expectations while automating the fulfillment process. Whit Snell, BikeWorld's founder, knew that his company needed the help that FedEx's global systems could provide: "To go from a complete unknown to a reputable worldwide retailer was going to require more than a fair price. We set out to absolutely amaze our customers with unprecedented customer service. FedEx gave us the blinding speed we needed," Snell said. The shipping is free for a

normal delivery. You pay extra for expedited delivery on some items.

The nearby figure shows the five steps in the fulfillment process. (Explanations are provided in the figure.) Notice that the logistics vendor (FedEx), with its sophisticated information system, provides services to the customers (such as order tracking).

Four years after BikeWorld ventured online, its sales volume more than quadrupled. The company had sales of over $8 million in 2003 and is consistently profitable. Thanks to its outsourcing of order fulfillment, and to FedEx's world-class information systems, BikeWorld has a fully automated and scalable fulfillment system; has access to real-time order status data, which enhances customer service and leads to greater customer retention; and has the capacity to service global customers. The site offers free topographical maps (take the tour), order tracking, customer support, employment opportunities, and more.

Source: Compiled from FedEx (2000), and from *bikeworld.com* (accessed June 2004).

For Further Exploration: Identify the necessary IOSs between FedEx and the customers, and between BikeWorld and FedEx. Visit *fedex.com* and find out how FedEx can help any company in global trade.

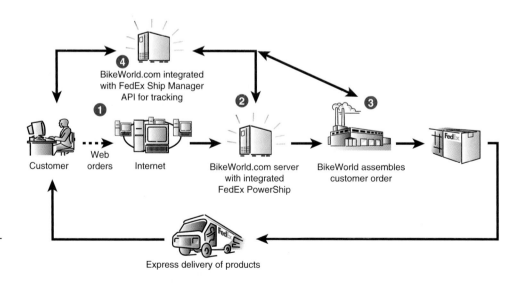

BikeWorld's order fulfillment process
(*Source:* FedEx, 2000).

BikeWorld.com integrated with FedEx Ship Manager API for tracking

Customer | Web orders | Internet

BikeWorld.com server with integrated FedEx PowerShip

BikeWorld assembles customer order

Express delivery of products

8.3 B2B Exchanges, Hubs, and Directories

IOSs are viewed by many as wireline or wireless connections between organizations. Actually they are much more than that: These systems provide for *all the interactions* among organizations including communication, collaboration, and even trading. Three IT innovations that help organizations communicate, collaborate, and trade are B2B exchanges, hubs, and directory services.

B2B Exchanges

Considerable support to B2B supply chains can be provided by electronic exchanges (see Ranganatan, 2003). *B2B exchanges*, as discussed in Chapter 4, can be either *private* (one buyer and many sellers, or one seller and many buyers) or *public* (many sellers and buyers). In either case, the communications and transactions are done on IOSs. The IOS in a private exchange is usually controlled by the sole seller or buyer; it is usually an extranet or EDI. In a public exchange, the IOS can be an extranet or the Internet, usually with a virtual private network (VPN).

A system of public exchanges is shown in Figure 8.3. Notice that in this example there are three interconnected exchanges (designated by the ovals in the center of the figure). In other cases there may be only one exchange for an entire industry.

B2B public exchanges provide an alternative to private exchanges. As described in Chapter 4, the public exchange manager provides all the necessary information systems to the participants. Thus, buyers and sellers merely have to "plug in" in order to trade. The technology used by the B2B exchange depends on its size and the nature of transactions.

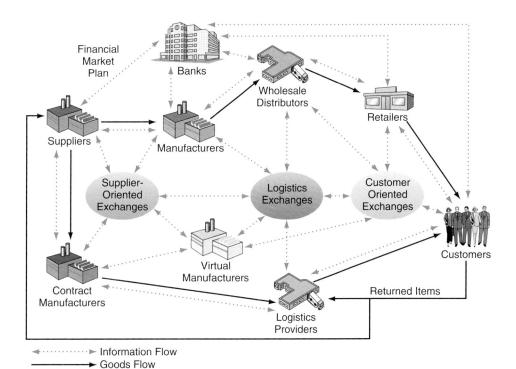

FIGURE 8.3 Web-based supply chain involving public exchanges.

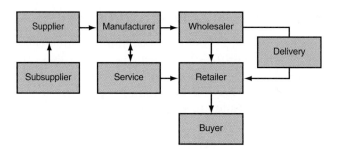

Traditional Intermediaries

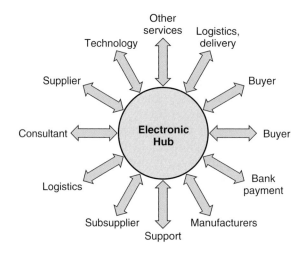

Electronic Hub

FIGURE 8.4 Electronic hub (bottom) compared to traditional intermediaries (top). (*Source:* Drawn by J. Lee and E. Turban.)

B2B public exchanges are sometimes the initial point for contacts between business partners. Once such contact is made, the partners may move to a private exchange or to the private trading rooms provided by many public exchanges to do their subsequent trading activities. Also, partners may continue to work directly with each other, avoiding the public exchange.

Electronic Hubs B2B exchanges are used mainly to facilitate trading among companies. In contrast, a *hub* is used to facilitate communication and coordination among business partners, frequently *along the supply chain*. Hubs are structured in such a way that each partner can access a Web site, usually a portal, which is used for an exchange of information. Furthermore, each partner can deposit new information, make changes, and receive or leave messages. In some hubs it is possible to conduct trade as well. A structure of an electronic hub is shown in Figure 8.4. An example of a company that provides an electronic hub as well as some public exchange capabilities is Asite, as described in *IT at Work 8.3* (next page).

A variation of a hub is *supplier networks*, which can be used for purposes such as ordering and even for training (Dyer and Hatch, 2004).

B2B hubs are popular in global trading, as illustrated in Online File W8.3 (the case of Rawmart). Hubs are related to or even combined with directories.

IT at Work 8.3
ASITE'S B2B EXCHANGE AND E-HUB FOR THE CONSTRUCTION INDUSTRY

Asite Network (*www.asite.com/community.html*) is a B2B exchange for the construction industry in the United Kingdom. The construction industry is typified by a high degree of physical separation and fragmentation, and communication among the members of the supply chain (e.g., contractors, subcontractors, architects, supply stores, and building inspectors) has long been a primary problem. Founded in February 2000 by leading players in the construction industry, Asite understands two of the major advantages of the Internet: the ability it provides to communicate more effectively, and the increase in processing power that Internet technologies make possible. Taking advantage of the functions of an online portal as information broker, Asite developed a comprehensive portal for the construction industry. The company's goal is to be the leading information and transaction hub in the European construction industry.

Asite drew on partner organizations with profound industry knowledge and expertise. It made the decision not to build its own technology, but to establish partnerships with technology vendors that have highly specialized products. It formed core partnerships with Commerce One, which provides the business solution for the portal; Microsoft, which provides the technology platform and core applications; and Attenda, which designed and manages Asite's Internet infrastructure.

Within its portal, Asite set up seven interconnected marketplaces (e.g., logistics, insurance, etc.; see the oval area in the nearby figure). These marketplaces serve the needs of the participants in the construction industry—building owners, developers, trade contractors, general contractors, engineers, architects, and materials suppliers—from design through procurement to materials delivery. Participating firms need nothing more sophisticated than a browser to connect to Asite's portal. This ease of access makes it particularly well suited to an industry such as construction, which is distinguished by a high proportion of small, and even single-person, firms.

Asite's partnerships allow it to seamlessly interact with other e-marketplaces. The open standards espoused by vendors in these e-marketplaces enable Asite's technology to be easily incorporated with participating firms' back-end technologies. Such linkages allow full visibility of the supply and demand chains.

The combination of strong backing from industry participants, experienced management from the construction industry, and the commitment to working with best-of-breed technology infrastructure providers is helping construction firms streamline their supply chains.

Sources: Compiled from Aberdeen Group (2001) and *www.asite.com* (accessed May 2004).

For Further Exploration: What type of IOS is this (per Section 8.1)? What are the advantages to the participating companies? Why is the exchange connected to the seven marketplaces?

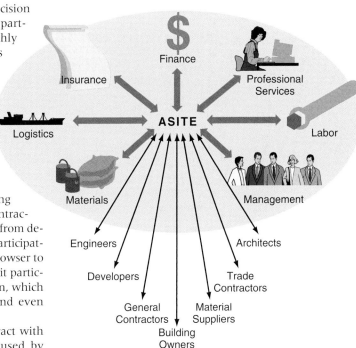

The participants in Asite's E-Marketplace (*Source:* Aberdeen Group, Inc.).

Directory Services

The B2B landscape is huge, with thousands of companies online. Directory services can help buyers and sellers manage the task of finding potential partners. Directories appear as B2B information portals, which usually include catalogues of products offered by each seller, lists of buyers and what they want, and other industry or general information. Buyers can then hyperlink to sellers' sites to complete trades. Some popular directories are listed and described in Online File W8.4. (Note that the last three entries in the table are search engines, which can be used to discover information about B2B. Some of these search engines are embedded in the directories.)

However, B2B information portals may have a difficult time generating revenue, and so they are starting to offer, for a fee, additional services that support trading. An example of a B2B portal is MyBoeingFleet.com (*myboeingfleet.com*), which is a Web portal for airplane owners, operators, and MRO (maintenance, repair, and operations) vendors (who supply indirect items such as light bulbs and cleaning materials). Developed by Boeing Commercial Aviation Services, MyBoeingFleet.com provides customers (primarily businesses) direct and personalized access to information that is essential to the operation of Boeing aircraft.

Like exchanges, information portals can be horizontal (e.g., Alibaba.com), offering a wide range of products to different industries. Or, they can be vertical, focusing on a single industry or industry segment. Vertical portals are often referred to as *vortals*.

8.4 VIRTUAL CORPORATIONS AND IT SUPPORT

Another variation of an IOS is one that supports virtual corporations.

A **virtual corporation (VC)** is an organization composed of two or more business partners, in different locations, sharing costs and resources for the purpose of producing a product or service. The VC can be temporary, with a one-time mission such as launching a satellite, or it can be permanent. Permanent virtual corporations are designed to create or assemble a broad range of productive resources rapidly, frequently, and concurrently. Each partner in a VC creates a portion of a product or service, in an area in which they have special advantage (such as expertise or low cost). The major characteristics of VCs are listed in Online File W8.5.

The concept of VCs is not new, but recent developments in IT allow new implementations. The modern VC can be viewed as a *network* of creative people, resources, and ideas connected via online services and/or the Internet, who band together to produce products or services. In a VC the resources of the business partners remain in their original locations but are integrated for the VC's use. Because the partners are in different locations, they need IOSs to support communication and collaboration. (Note: Some people use the term *virtual corporation* more narrowly, to describe a pure online company.)

How IT Supports Virtual Corporations

IT can support virtual corporations in several ways. The most obvious are those that allow communication and collaboration among the dispersed business partners. For example, e-mail, desktop videoconferencing, screen sharing, and several other groupware technologies (such as Lotus Notes) support interorganizational collaboration. Standard transactions are supported by EDI and EFT (electronic funds transfer). The Internet is the infrastructure for these and other technologies.

Also, modern database technologies and networking permit business partners to access each other's databases. In general, most VCs cannot exist without information technology.

Example: Five Companies Join IBM's Ambra. IBM's Ambra was formed to produce and market a PC clone. At Ambra's headquarters in Raleigh, North Carolina, 80 employees used global telecommunications networks to coordinate the activities of five companies that were partners in the virtual company.

Wearnes Technology of Singapore did engineering design and subsystem development services and manufacture for Ambra PC components. SCI Systems assembled the Ambra microcomputers in its assembly plants on a build-to-order basis from order data received by its computers from AI Incorporated. AI, a subsidiary of Insight Direct, a national telemarketing company based in Tempe, Arizona, received orders for Ambra computers from customers over its 800-number telephone lines or its Web site. Merisel Enterprises provided the product and delivery database used by AI and handled Ambra order fulfillment and customer delivery. Finally, another IBM subsidiary provided field service and customer support. (Note: The Ambra model has been discontinued; only service is provided by IBM.)

Example: No Need to Buy Office Furniture for Turnstone. Steelcase Inc. is a major U.S. maker of office furniture. It formed a virtual corporation subsidiary called Turnstone that sells its products through catalogs designed and printed by a third-party company (and now also available on the Web). Turnstone's customers e-mail or phone in credit card orders to a telemarketing company based in Denver, Colorado, which transmits the order data to computers at warehouses operated by Excel Logistics, Inc. in Westerville, Ohio. From there, subcontracted carriers ship the products to manufacturing plants. Excel's computer systems handle all order processing, shipment tracking, and inventory control applications. Marketing, financial management, and coordinating the virtual company's business partners are the only major functions left to Turnstone's managers. A comprehensive IOS provides seamless communication and effective collaboration among all partners.

8.5 ELECTRONIC DATA INTERCHANGE (EDI)

One of the early contributions of IT to facilitate B2B e-commerce and other IOSs is electronic data interchange (EDI).

Traditional EDI **Electronic data interchange (EDI)** is a communication standard that enables the electronic transfer of routine documents, such as purchase orders, between business partners. It formats these documents according to agreed-upon standards. EDI has been around for about 30 years in the non-Internet environment (usually VANs). EDI often serves as a catalyst and a stimulus to improve the standard of information that flows between organizations. It reduces costs, delays, and errors inherent in a manual document-delivery system.

MAJOR COMPONENTS OF EDI. The following are the major components of EDI:

- *EDI translators.* An EDI translator converts data into a standard format before it is transmitted; then the standard form is converted to the original data.
- *Business transactions messages.* These include purchase orders, invoices, credit approvals, shipping notices, confirmations, and so on.

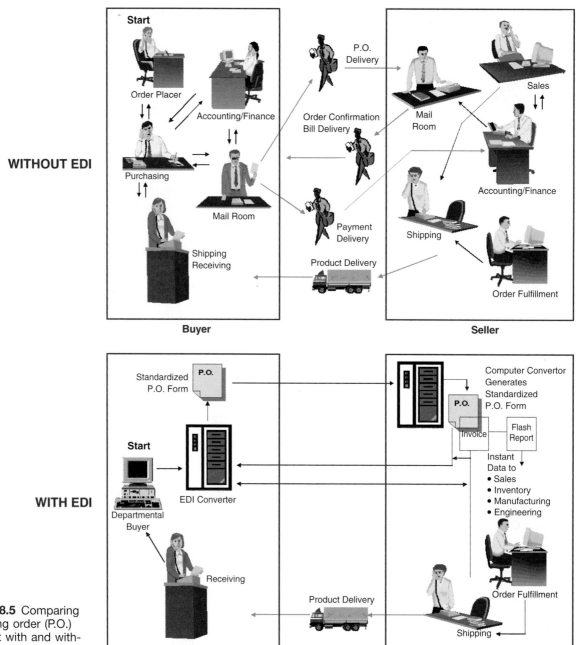

FIGURE 8.5 Comparing purchasing order (P.O.) fulfillment with and without EDI. (*Source:* Drawn by E. Turban.)

- *Data formatting standards.* Because EDI messages are repetitive, it makes sense to use formatting (coding) standards. In the United States and Canada, EDI data are formatted according to the ANSI X.12 standard. An international standard developed by the United Nations is called EDIFACT.

THE PROCESS AND BENEFITS OF EDI. The process of EDI (as compared with a non-EDI process) is shown in Figure 8.5. The figure shows that in EDI, computers talk to computers. Messages are coded using the standards before they are transmitted using a converter. Then, the message travels over a VAN or the Internet (secured). When received, the message is automatically translated into a business language.

The benefits of this process are that data entry errors are minimized (only one entry, and an automatic check by the computer), the length of the message can be shorter, the messages are secured, and EDI fosters collaborative relationships and strategic partnerships. Other benefits are: reduced cycle time, better inventory management, increased productivity, enhanced customer service, minimized paper usage and storage, and increased cash flow (per *ledisource.com*).

Applications of Traditional EDI

Traditional EDI has changed the business landscape of many industries and large corporations. It is used extensively by large corporations, sometimes in a global network such as the one operated by General Electric Information System (which has over 100,000 corporate users). Well-known retailers such as Home Depot, ToysRUs, and Wal-Mart would operate very differently without EDI, because it is an integral and essential element of their business strategies. Thousands of global manufacturers, including Procter & Gamble, Levi Strauss, Toyota, and Unilever, have been using EDI to redefine relationships with their customers through such practices as quick-response retailing and just-in-time (JIT) manufacturing. These highly visible, high-impact applications of EDI by large companies have been extremely successful.

Limitations of Traditional EDI

However, despite the tremendous impact of traditional EDI among industry leaders, the set of adopters represented only a small fraction of potential EDI users. In the United States, where several million businesses participate in commerce every day, only about 100,000 companies have adopted traditional EDI. Furthermore, most of these companies have had only a small number of their business partners on EDI, mainly due to its high cost. Therefore, in reality, few businesses have benefited from traditional EDI.

Various factors held back more universal implementation of traditional EDI. For example: Significant initial investment is needed, and ongoing operating costs are high (due to use of expensive, private VANs). Another cost is the purchase of a converter, which is required to translate business transactions to EDI code. Other major issues for some companies relate to the fact that the traditional EDI system is inflexible. For example, it is difficult to make quick changes, such as adding business partners, and a long startup period is needed. Further, business processes must sometimes be restructured to fit EDI requirements. Finally, multiple EDI standards exist, so one company may have to use several standards in order to communicate with different business partners.

These factors suggest that traditional EDI—relying on formal transaction sets, translation software, and VANs—is not suitable as a long-term solution for most corporations. Therefore, a better infrastructure was needed; *Internet-based EDI* is such an infrastructure.

Internet-Based EDI

Internet-based (or Web-based) EDI is becoming very popular (e.g., see Witte et al., 2003). Let's see why this is the case.

WHY INTERNET-BASED EDI?   When considered as a channel for EDI, the Internet appears to be a most feasible alternative to VANs for putting online B2B trading within reach of virtually any organization, large or small. There are a number of reasons for firms to create EDI ability over the Internet.

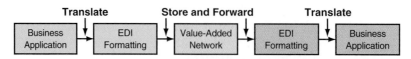

TRADITIONAL ELECTRONIC DATA INTERCHANGE (EDI)

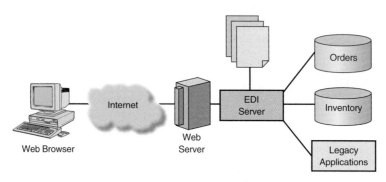

FIGURE 8.6 Traditional and Web-based EDI. (*Source:* Drawn by E. Turban.)

WEB-BASED EDI

- *Accessibility.* The Internet is a publicly accessible network with few geographical constraints. Its largest attribute, large-scale connectivity (without the need for any special company networking architecture), is a seedbed for growth of a vast range of business applications.
- *Reach.* The Internet's global network connections offer the potential to reach the widest possible number of trading partners of any viable alternative currently available.
- *Cost.* The Internet's communication cost can be 40 to 70 percent lower than that of VANs. Transmission of sensitive data can be made secure with VPN (see Technology Guide 4).
- *Use of Web technology.* Using the Internet to exchange EDI transactions is consistent with the growing interest of business in delivering an ever-increasing variety of products and services via the Web. Internet-based EDI can complement or replace many current EDI applications.
- *Ease of use.* Internet tools such as browsers and search engines are very user-friendly, and most employees today know how to use them.
- *Added functionalities.* Internet-based EDI has several functionalities not provided by traditional EDI, which include collaboration, workflow, and search engine capabilities (see Boucher-Ferguson, 2002). A comparison between EDI and EDI/Internet is provided in Figure 8.6.

TYPES OF INTERNET-BASED EDI. The Internet can support EDI in a variety of ways. For example, Internet e-mail can be used to transport EDI messages in place of a VAN. To this end, standards for encapsulating the messages within Secure Internet Mail Extension (S/MIME) exist and need to be used. Another way to use the Internet for EDI is to create an extranet that enables a company's trading partners to enter information into a Web form, the fields of which correspond to the fields in an EDI message or document.

Alternatively, companies can use a Web-based EDI hosting service, in much the same way that companies rely on third parties to host their EC sites. Harbinger Commerce (*inovis.com*) is an example of those companies that provide third-party hosting services.

The Prospects of Internet-Based EDI

Many companies that used traditional EDI in the past have had a positive experience when they moved to Internet-based EDI. With traditional EDI, companies have to pay for network transport, translation, and routing of EDI messages into their legacy processing systems. The Internet serves as a cheaper alternative transport mechanism. The combination of the Web, XML, and Java makes EDI affordable even for small, infrequent transactions. Whereas EDI is not interactive, the Web and Java were designed specifically for interactivity as well as ease of use.

The following examples demonstrate the application range and benefits of Internet-based EDI.

Example: Rapid Growth at CompuCom. CompuCom Systems, a leading IT services provider, was averaging 5,000 transactions per month with traditional EDI. In just a short time after the transition to Web-based EDI, the company was able to average 35,000 transactions. The system helped the company to grow rapidly.

Example: Recruitment at Tradelink. Tradelink of Hong Kong had a traditional EDI that communicated with government agencies regarding export/import transactions, but was successful in recruiting only several hundred of the potential 70,000 companies to the traditional system. After switching to an Internet-based system, Tradelink registered thousands of new companies to the system; hundreds were being added monthly, reaching about 18,000 by 2004.

Example: Better Collaboration at Atkins Carlyle. Atkins Carlyle Corp. a wholesaler of industrial, electrical, and automotive parts, buys from 6,000 suppliers and has 12,000 customers in Australia. The large suppliers were using three different traditional-EDI platforms. By moving to an Internet-based EDI, the company was able to collaborate with many more business partners, reducing the transaction cost by about $2 per message.

Note that many companies no longer refer to their IOSs as EDI. However, some *properties* of EDI are embedded in new e-business initiatives such as collaborative commerce, extranets, PRM, and electronic exchanges. The new generation of EDI/Internet is built around XML (see next section).

8.6 EXTRANETS, XML, AND WEB SERVICES

Companies involved in an IOS need to be connected in a secure and effective manner and their applications must be integrated with each other. This can be done by using extranets, XML, and Web services.

Extranets

In building IOSs, it is necessary to connect the internal systems of different business partners, which are usually connected to the partners' corporate intranets. A common solution is to use an extranet. Extranets are generally understood to be networks that link business partners over the Internet by providing access to certain areas of each other's corporate intranets. This arrangement is shown in Figure 8.7 (page 350). (An exception to this definition is an extranet that offers individual customers or suppliers one-way access to a company's intranet.) The term *extranet* comes from "extended intranet."

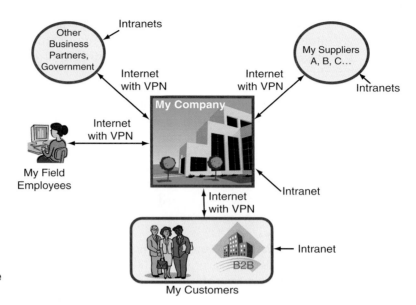

FIGURE 8.7 The structure of an extranet.

The main goal of extranets is to foster collaboration between business partners. An extranet is open to selected B2B suppliers, customers, and other business partners, who access it through the Internet. Extranets enable people who are located outside a company to work together with the company's internally located employees. An extranet enables external business partners and telecommuting employees to enter the corporate intranet, via the Internet, to access data, place orders, check status, communicate, and collaborate.

THE COMPONENTS, STRUCTURE, AND BENEFITS OF EXTRANETS. An extranet uses the same basic infrastructure components as the Internet, including servers, TCP/IP protocols, e-mail, and Web browsers. In addition, extranets use virtual private network (VPN) technology to make communication over the Internet more secure. The Internet-based extranet is far less costly than proprietary networks (VANs). It is a nonproprietary technical tool that can support the rapid evolution of electronic communication and commerce.

Why would a company allow a business partner access to its intranet? To answer this question, let's look at Dr. Pepper in the following example.

Example: Dr. Pepper Notifies Bottlers of Price Changes. Dr. Pepper/Seven Up, the $1.7 billion division of Cadbury Schweppes, uses an extranet to improve efficiency for its diverse community of 1,400 independent and franchise bottlers. The Bottler Hub/Extranet is made available to Dr. Pepper's entire group of registered bottlers and retailers. The extranet has helped automate the process of communicating price changes to retailers, in real time.

Such automation was necessary for Dr. Pepper because the company depends on contract bottlers, who set the pricing of Dr. Pepper products in stores. Customer retailers such as Wal-Mart had complained about the bottlers' practice of faxing weekly price changes. Because many bottlers were mom-and-pop organizations and did not have the resources to modernize the process, Dr. Pepper decided to put in an extranet-based centralized system that would make the pricing information available online, in real time, to retail outlets.

Dr. Pepper also uses its extranet for other purposes. In addition, the company collects sales data online, enabling merchants to report how many cases of soda

IT at Work 8.4
DEALER CONNECTION PORTAL AT FORD

Ford Motor Co. in Europe serves 7,500 dealers, speaking 15 different languages, in 18 countries. In order to connect them all, Ford created a portal, called DealerConnection. The portal provides dealers with a single point of real-time access to all the information and tools they need to manage daily tasks efficiently, such as warranty checks and parts ordering. It also frees dealers from having to access separate systems. In addition, all information on pricing, products, servicing, customer services, and marketing is now available to the dealers online. Prior to the portal, updating dealers on new information often took five days for preparation, printing, and distribution of material; thus, the portal is achieving real efficiencies for Ford in its distribution of company information.

DealerConnection provides local dealers and Ford representatives in each country with control of their own Enterprise Web application. Unlike traditional applications, Enterprise Web applications, built on Plumtree (*plumtree.com*) portal software, combine existing data and processes from enterprise systems with new shared services. These applica-

tions are managed within one administrative framework at the corporate level, allowing the company to create real, working online communities. DealerConnection also facilitates self-service among dealers, allowing Ford to implement a more streamlined and centralized back office.

Instead of creating 18 different portals for the countries in which Ford operates, the company has developed one pan-European portal with applications for each respective country and each line of business. By adopting this approach, Ford is empowering each country to create its own environment under the European umbrella of DealerConnection, even though Ford still has central control over its brand, image, and communications. The vendor believes that the portal has delivered a positive return of investment for both Ford and its network of dealers.

Source: Compiled from Plumtree Software Inc. (2003).

For Further Exploration: Why only one portal? What about the multilanguage, multicultural aspects? (Hint: See Enterprise Web at *plumtree.com.*)

---

they sell. The data are used to measure sales growth and to analyze brands and packages that are sold by a bottler within a territory to the major retail chains. The information is also used to help the national accounts department find opportunities to sell more Dr. Pepper/Seven Up brands within a particular account.

As seen in the example, the extranet enables effective and efficient real-time collaboration. It also enables partners to perform self-service activities such as checking the status of orders or inventory levels.

TYPES OF EXTRANETS. Depending on the business partners involved and the purpose, there are three major types of extranets, as described below.

A Company and Its Dealers, Customers, or Suppliers. Such an extranet is centered around one company. An example would be the FedEx extranet that allows customers to track the status of a package. To do so, customers use the Internet to access a database on the FedEx intranet. By enabling a customer to check the location of a package, FedEx saves the cost of having a human operator do that task over the phone. Ford Motor is using an extranet-based portal with its dealers in Europe, as described in *IT at Work 8.4.* Similarly, Toshiba uses an extranet with its dealers, as shown in Online File W8.6.

An Industry's Extranet. The major players in an industry may team up to create an extranet that will benefit all. The world's largest industry-based, collaborative extranet is used by General Motors, Ford, and DaimlerChrysler. That extranet, called the Automotive Network Exchange (ANX), links the carmakers with more than 10,000 suppliers. The suppliers can then use a B2B marketplace, Covisint (*covisint.com,* now a division of Compuware) located on ANX, to sell directly and efficiently to the carmakers, cutting communications costs by as much as 70 percent.

Joint Ventures and Other Business Partnerships. In this type of extranet, the partners in a joint venture use the extranet as a vehicle for communications and collaboration. An example is Bank of America's extranet for commercial loans. The partners involved in making such loans are a lender, loan broker, escrow company, title company, and others. The extranet connects lenders, loan applicants, and the loan organizer, Bank of America. A similar case is Lending Tree (*lendingtree.com*), a company that provides mortgage quotes for your home and also sells mortgages online, which uses an extranet for its business partners (e.g., the lenders).

BENEFITS OF EXTRANETS. As extended versions of intranets, extranets offer benefits similar to those of intranets, as well as other benefits. The major benefits of extranets include faster processes and information flow, improved order entry and customer service, lower costs (e.g., for communications, travel, and administrative overhead), and overall improvement in business effectiveness. Details of how these benefits are achieved are summarized in Online File W8.7.

Extranets are fairly permanent in nature, where all partners are known in advance. For on-demand relationships and one-time trades, companies can instead use B2B exchanges and hubs (Chapter 4) and directory services (see Online File W8.4).

Two emerging technologies that are extremely important for IOSs are XML and Web Services.

XML

An emerging technology that can be used effectively to integrate internal systems as well as systems of business partners is a language (and its variants) known as XML (see Raisinghani, 2002; Linthicum, 2000). **XML (eXtensible Markup Language)** is a simplified version of a general data description language known as SGML (Standard Generalized Markup Language). XML is used to improve compatibility between the disparate systems of business partners by defining the meaning of data in business documents. XML is considered "extensible" because the markup symbols are unlimited and self-defining. This new standard is promoted as a new platform for B2B and as a companion or even a replacement for EDI systems. It has been formally recommended by the World Wide Web Consortium (*W3C.org*).

XML DIFFERS FROM HTML. People sometimes wonder if XML and HTML are the same. The answer is, they are not. The purpose of HTML is to help build Web pages and display data on Web pages. The purpose of XML is to describe data and information. It does not say *how* the data will be displayed (which HTML does). XML can be used to send complex messages that include different files (and HTML cannot). See Technology Guide 2 for details.

BENEFITS OF XML. XML was created in an attempt to overcome limitations of EDI implementation. XML can overcome EDI barriers for three reasons:

1. *Flexibility.* XML is a flexible language. Its flexibility allows new requirements and changes to be incorporated into messages, thus expanding the rigid ranges of EDI.

IT at Work 8.5

FIDELITY USES XML TO STANDARDIZE CORPORATE DATA

Fidelity Investments has made all its corporate data XML-compatible. The effort helped the world's largest mutual fund company and online brokerage eliminate up to 75 percent of the hardware and software devoted to middle-tier processing and speeded the delivery of new applications.

The decision to go to XML began when Fidelity developed its Powerstreet Web trading service. At the time, Fidelity determined it would need to offer its most active traders much faster response times than its existing brokerage systems allowed. The move to XML brought other benefits as well. For example, the company was able to link customers who have 401k pension plans, brokerage accounts, and IRAs under a common log-in. In the past, they required separate passwords.

Today, two-thirds of the hundreds of thousands of hourly online transactions at *fidelity.com* use XML to link the Web to back-end systems. Before XML, comparable transactions took many seconds longer because they had to go through a different proprietary data translation scheme for each back-end system from which they retrieved data.

Fidelity's XML strategy is critical to bringing new applications and services to customers faster than rivals. By using XML as a common language into which all corporate data—from Web, database, transactional, and legacy systems—are translated, Fidelity is saving millions of dollars on infrastructure and development costs. Fidelity no longer has to develop translation methods for communications between the company's many systems. XML also has made it possible for Fidelity's different databases—including Oracle for its customer account information and IBM's DB2 for trading records—to respond to a single XML query.

Source: Compiled from "Fidelity Retrofits All Data . . ." (2001); and from *fidelity.com*.

For Further Exploration: Why did Fidelity decide to use XML? Why is it possible to develop applications faster with XML?

---

2. ***Understandability.*** XML message content can be easily read and understood by people using standard browsers. Thus, message recipients do not need EDI translators. This feature enables SMEs to receive, understand, and act on XML-based messages.

3. ***Less specialized.*** In order to implement EDI, it is necessary to have highly specialized knowledge of EDI methodology. Implementation of XML-based technologies requires less-specialized skills.

XML supports IOSs and makes B2B e-commerce a reality for many companies that were unable to use the traditional EDI. These and other benefits of XML are demonstrated in *IT at Work 8.5* and in Korolishin (2004). For more information see *xml.com*.

Despite its many potential benefits, XML has, according to McKinsey Research (Current Research Note, 2003), several serious limitations, especially when compared to EDI. These include lack of universal XML standards, lack of experience in XML implementation, and sometimes less security than EDI.

Another technology that supports IOSs and uses XML in its core is Web Services.

Web Services
As described in Chapter 2, *Web Services* are universal, prefabricated business process software modules, delivered over the Internet, that users can select and combine through almost any device, enabling disparate systems to share data and services. Web Services can support IOSs by providing easy integration for different internal and external systems. (Also see Technology Guide 6.) Such

integration enables companies to develop new applications, as the following example demonstrates.

Example: Web Services Facilitate Communication at Allstate. The Allstate Financial Group, with 41,000 employees and $29 billion in annual sales, used Microsoft.NET (a Web Services implementation) to create AccessAllstate.com (*accessallstate.com*). This Web portal allows its 350,000 sales representatives to access information about Allstate investment, retirement, and insurance products.

Before the portal was developed, independent agents had to call Allstate customer service representatives for information, and transactions were done via mail, fax, or phone. The necessary information resided on five policy-management information systems running on mainframe computers—substantial technology investments that Allstate was not willing to lose. But because Web Services enables easy communications between applications and systems, Allstate did not have to lose its mainframe investment. The agents use the Web portal to access the policy-management systems residing on the mainframe. Web Services make this connection seamless and transparent to the agents.

AccessAllstate.com has about 13,000 registered users and receives 500,000 hits per day. By unlocking the information on Allstate's proprietary mainframes, the company increases revenues and reduces costs. The Web portal eliminates the need to call the service center to perform common account service tasks. Allstate estimates that the portal will pay for itself through lower call center and mailing costs. The company is also making all printed correspondence available online via the portal. (*Sources:* Compiled from Grimes, 2003; and *allstate.com*, accessed June 2004.)

8.7 IOS IMPLEMENTATION ISSUES

Due to their complexity and the involvement of two or more organizations, IOSs and global systems face issues relating to partner relationship management, collaborative commerce, and facilitating global trade.

Partner Relationship Management

Every company that has business partners has to manage the relationships with them. Partners need to be identified, recruited, and maintained. Communication needs to flow between the organizations. Information needs to be updated and shared. **Partner relationship management (PRM)** is a business strategy that recognizes the need to develop long-term relationships with business partners, by providing each partner with the services that are most beneficial to that partner. This strategy is similar to that of CRM, and it is supported by similar IT tools.

Before the spread of Internet technology, there were few automated processes to electronically support business partnerships. Organizations were limited to manual methods of phone, fax, and mail. EDI was used by large corporations, but usually only with their largest partners. Also, there was no systematic way of conducting PRM. Internet technology changed the situation by offering a way to connect different organizations easily, quickly, and affordably.

WHAT PRM DOES. PRM solutions connect companies with their business partners (suppliers, customers, services) using Web technology to securely distribute and manage information. At its core, a PRM application facilitates partner relationships. Specific functions include: partner profiles, partner communications, management of customer leads, targeted information distribution, connecting the extended enterprise, partner planning, centralized forecasting, group planning, e-mail and Web-based alerts, messaging, price lists, and community bulletin boards. Many large companies offer suppliers or partners portals for improved communication and collaboration. (For more on PRM, see *channelwave.com*, *www.ittelecomsolutions.com*, Murtaza and Shah, 2004, and Coupey, 2001.)

Example: Supporting PRM at SkyMall. *SkyMall.com* (now a subsidiary of Gem-Star TV Guide International) is a retailer that sells from catalogs on board airplanes, over the Internet, and by mail order. It relies on its catalog partners to fill the orders. For small vendors that do not handle their own shipments and for international shipments, SkyMall contracts with distribution centers owned by fulfillment outsourcer Sykes Enterprise.

To coordinate the logistics of sending orders to thousands of customers, SkyMall uses integrated EC order-management software called Order Trust. SkyMall leases this software and pays transaction fees for its use. As orders come in, SkyMall conveys the data to Order Trust, which disseminates the information to the appropriate partners (either a vendor or a Sykes distribution center). A report about the shipment is then sent to SkyMall, and SkyMall pays Order Trust the transaction fees. This arrangement has allowed SkyMall to increase its online business by more than 3 percent annually without worrying about order fulfillment. The partners (the makers of the products) also benefit by receiving the electronically transmitted orders quickly.

A Gartner Group survey about CRM, conducted in December 2002, showed that of all sales-related applications, PRM programs had the highest return on investment (*Business Wire*, 2003). For this reason, companies are interested in finding ways to use PRM extensively, as shown in *IT at Work 8.6* (page 356).

SUPPLIER RELATIONSHIP MANAGEMENT. One of the major categories of PRM is **supplier relationship management (SRM),** where the partners are the suppliers. For many companies (e.g., retailers and manufacturers), the ability to work properly with suppliers is a major critical success factor. PeopleSoft, Inc. (*peoplesoft.com*) developed a model for managing relationships with suppliers.

PeopleSoft's SRM model. PeopleSoft's SRM model is generic and could be considered by any large company. It includes 12 steps, illustrated in Figure 8.8 (page 357). The details of the steps are shown in Online File W8.8. The core idea of this model is that an e-supply chain is based on integration and collaboration. The supply chain processes are connected, decisions are made collectively, performance metrics are based on common understanding, information flows in real time (whenever possible), and the only thing a new partner needs in order to join the SRM system is just a Web browser.

Collaborative Commerce

Collaborative commerce (c-commerce) refers to non–selling/buying electronic transactions within, between, and among organizations. An example would be a company collaborating electronically with a vendor that is designing a product or part for this company. C-commerce implies communication, information sharing, and collaboration done electronically by means of tools such as groupware and specially designed collaboration tools. That means that IOSs and c-commerce

IT at Work 8.6
CRM/PRM INITIATIVES AT NEW PIPER AIRCRAFT

Today, New Piper Aircraft is the only general-aviation manufacturer offering a complete line of business and pleasure aircraft (from trainers and high-performance aircraft for personal and business use to turbine-powered business aircraft). In 1992, the company (then Piper Aircraft) was making fewer than 50 planes per year and had $15 million in bank debt and only $1,000 in cash. However, by 2001, the company delivered 441 planes and took in $243 million in revenue. How was this possible?

The fundamental reason for the company's success was its new ownership and management that realized that its ability to provide assistance to customers and partners needed to be completely overhauled. The company purchased Siebel Systems' MidMarket, a CRM software tool, and customized it for PRM. The results were the PULSE Center. PULSE stands for Piper Unlimited Liaison via Standards of Excellence. The system tracks all contacts and communications between New Piper and its dealers and customers. It also helps meet the growing needs of its partner- and customer-care programs.

In less than one year after implementation, the Web-based call center's productivity increased 50 percent, the number of lost sales leads was reduced 25 percent, and sales representatives handled 45 percent more sales. Before the system was instituted, an 11-person call center used spiral notebooks crammed into numerous cabinets to store the data and contacts; it took 30 minutes to locate a contact. Today, the call center tracks 70,000 customers among 17 dealers, and contact information is available in less than a minute.

Development of the PULSE Center took place in stages. The first three phases had been completed by October 2002: Phase 1—loading current aircraft owners, dealers, fleet customers aircraft, and new customer service employees into the system to develop the organization infrastructure; Phase 2—enabling the Customer Service Center to process activities; and Phase 3—enabling dealers to access sales opportunities pertinent to their territory.

The company is now (June 2004) in Phases 4 and 5. Phase 4 is the opening of the Dealer Web Portal, which allows partners (aircraft dealers) access to particular areas of PULSE and provide the technology to make online service requests. Phase 5 streamlines entry of warranty claims. Phase 6, the Partner Web Portal, will allow key suppliers access to areas of the PULSE system and assist in communication with those suppliers. Phase 7 will provide for ordering parts online, and Phase 8 will be the Customer Web Portal giving customers access to open service requests, online logbooks, and product and survey information.

Piper's Vice President for Customers, Dan Snell, says, "New Piper's goal is to lead the industry with respect to quality, excellence, and customer care. It is a challenging mission, but certainly not daunting, and will be achieved through initiatives such as PULSE."

Sources: Compiled from Galante (2002); and *New Piper* news releases (2002, 2004).

For Further Exploration: Describe the major features of the CRM/PRM program. Why does the company need such an elaborate program? How would you justify it?

---

coexist. Use of c-commerce requires some IOS technology, such as an extranet, EDI, or groupware. Let's look at some areas of collaboration using IOSs.

RETAILER-SUPPLIERS. As discussed in Chapter 7, large retailers like Wal-Mart collaborate with their major suppliers to conduct production and inventory planning and forecasting of demand. Such forms of collaboration enable the suppliers to improve their production planning as well.

PRODUCT DESIGN. All the parties that are involved in a specific product design may use software tools that enable them to share data and collaborate in product design. One such tool is screen sharing (see Chapter 3), in which several people can work on the same document on a computer screen while in different locations. Changes made in one place are visible to others instantly. Documents that can be processed through a collaborative product design IOS include

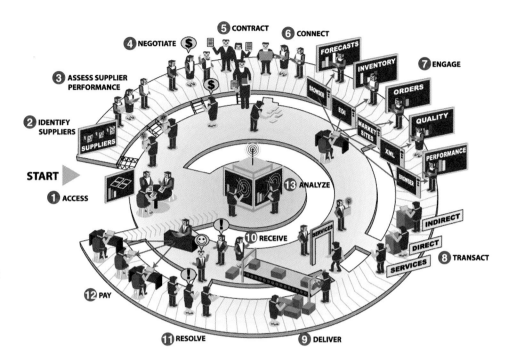

FIGURE 8.8 Supplier relationship management (SRM). (*Source:* B. Schecterle, "Managing and Extending Supplier Relationships," *People Talk*, April–June 2003.)

blueprints, bills of material, accounting and billing documents, and joint reports and statements.

COLLABORATIVE MANUFACTURING. Manufacturers can create dynamic collaborative production networks by means of IOSs. For example, original equipment manufacturers (OEMs) outsource components and subassemblies to suppliers. (For example, if you buy a Kenmore product from Sears, Sears does not make the product; it just buys and resells it. Some other manufacturer, such as Maytag, is the OEM.) In the past, these relationships often created problems in coordination, workflows, and communication. Web-based collaborative IOSs have improved the outsourcing process and are especially useful in tracking changes that may be initiated by any partner along the supply chain.

Other IOS Infrastructures

Information systems of two or more organizations can be connected in less structured ways than by EDI or extranets. As a matter of fact, most large software vendors, such as Microsoft, Oracle, SAP, and IBM, offer several solutions that can be customized to include existing systems, such as ERPs. An example can be seen in Minicase 2 at the end of the chapter, where the construction of a global system connecting 40 sites in eight countries is demonstrated. Another interesting example is the system constructed for Corning, Inc., which connects the company's 12 business units using software from PeopleSoft (see Online File W8.9). In Europe, Pierre Lang Corp. of Austria, a large jewelry company, gained control over 60 million customers throughout Western European countries by using mySAP ERP (see SAP AG, 2004). Oracle 9i is used extensively to provide infrastructure support to IOSs. Finally, one should remember that VANs, while more expensive, provide more functionalities to IOSs and are used not only for EDI but also for other types of systems (e.g., EFT).

Facilitating Global Trade

As countries' borders begin to disappear in global trading, language translation is becoming very important. This topic is very important in e-commerce, where appropriate translation of Web pages is a critical success factor. The use of intelligent systems in automatic language translation has been progressing rapidly since the mid-1990s. (For details see Chapter 3 and Online File W3.3.)

Many other systems and applications are used to facilitate international trade. An example is the use of intelligent systems to fight money laundering across international borders, or the use of a hybrid intelligent system for developing global marketing strategy. As international trade is expanding, mainly due to the Internet and trading blocks like the European Union and NAFTA, expertise will be needed in many areas, ranging from legal issues to export and import licenses. Such expertise can be provided to a global audience online. Also, expert systems can provide to users in developing countries the advice of top experts in the fields of medicine, safety, agriculture, and crime fighting. These various systems and applications work with different types of IOSs and technologies.

➡ MANAGERIAL ISSUES

1. *Selecting a system.* Companies have an option to select an IOS infrastructure from several types and vendors. Selection could follow the guidelines suggested in Chapter 14.

2. *Partners' collaboration.* An IOS has at least two participating organizations, so collaboration is critical. Many failures of EDI adoption, for example, result from lack of partners' cooperation. If you are Wal-Mart, you may be able to mandate that your partner cooperate (or be excluded from doing business with you). But most other companies need to *persuade* partners, showing them mutual benefits, or provide them with incentives.

3. *New infrastructures.* XML, Web Services, and other tools are gaining converts but are not universally accepted. Companies like Dell can lead in using such new infrastructures, but smaller companies might be better off to wait and see. However, management must assess the risk of waiting while competitors are moving.

4. *Globalization.* The issue of going global or not, or to what extent, depends on what information systems are needed for supporting the globalization. Issues such as multiple languages, different currencies, tax requirements, legal aspects, and cultural considerations need to be reflected in the supporting IT (e.g., see Minicase 2). Globalization may not be simple or inexpensive.

5. *Using exchanges, hubs, and other services.* These are viable options since the service providers provide the IOS infrastructure. Also, frequently the Internet can be used. Using third-party providers can be cheaper, but you may lose some control over the system. Again, selecting the appropriate system(s) is critical.

6. *Partner and supplier relationship management.* Modern business is increasingly using partners, as we have seen in several examples throughout the book. The trend for outsourcing, for example, means more partners. (Even

Microsoft, as seen in Minicase 2, has used a partner to implement its business solutions.) Cultivating PRM and especially SRM is not a simple task and needs to be planned for and organized properly (look again at Figure 8.8).

KEY TERMS

Cross-border data transfer *337*

Electronic data interchange (EDI) *345*

Global information systems *336*

Interorganizational information system (IOS) *334*

Partner relationship management (PRM) *354*

Supplier relationship management (SRM) *355*

Virtual corporation (VC) *344*

XML (eXtensible Markup Language) *352*

CHAPTER HIGHLIGHTS (Numbers Refer to Learning Objectives)

1 Information systems that involve two or more organizations are referred to as interorganizational information systems (IOSs). They can be local or global, dedicated to only one activity (e.g., transfer funds), or intended to support several activities (e.g., to facilitate trade, communication, or collaboration).

1 IOSs are classified into the following types: B2B trading, global systems, EFT, integrated messaging, shared databases, and systems that support virtual corporations. Technologies that support IOSs are EDI, extranets, groupware, XML, and Web Services.

2 Global information systems exist when at least two parties of an information system are in different countries.

2 Three types of companies that use global information systems exist: multinational (one company operates in two or more countries), international (at least one business partner is in a different country), and virtual global (partners in at least two countries form one company jointly).

3 Some of the major issues that affect global information systems are cultural issues, political and economic issues (including currency conversion), legal issues such as cross-border data transfer, different languages, and logistics. Global supply chains are usually longer, requiring complex supporting information systems.

4 Communication and collaboration among companies can be done via IOSs that are organized as either public or private B2B exchanges (usually designed for trading) or hubs (designed to improve the supply chain). Directories provide listings of B2B products, vendors, and services.

5 Virtual corporations are joint ventures involving several companies that create one entity for a special purpose. Since working groups of the VC are in different locations, IT is needed to facilitate coordination and collaboration.

6 EDI provides a systematic framework for information exchange between business partners. It both translates routine business documents to national or international standard formats and provides a secure transmission over VANs.

6 The major benefits of EDI and EDI/Internet include minimization of errors and cycle time, increased understanding and collaboration among business partners, reduced cost of processing information, better customer service, and improved employee productivity.

6 The major limitations of EDI and EDI/Internet are high cost and complexity, long training periods required, high investment and operating costs, and inflexibility. EDI/Internet overcomes most of the above limitations by using the Internet and its tools to reduce cost and to increase flexibility and ease of use.

7 Extranets connect the intranets of business partners by using the Internet (over secure VPNs). This connection enables partners to conveniently enter portions of their partners' intranets.

7 XML is a standard, used mainly for B2B transactions, that enables communication among business partners, regardless of the software they use.

7 Web Services support IOSs and facilitate integration of B2B applications by enabling disparate systems to share data and services.

8 Some representative IOS implementation issues are appropriate partner relationship management, c-commerce, and the use of automatic language translation and other methods to facilitate global trade.

VIRTUAL COMPANY ASSIGNMENT

Interorganizational Systems at The Wireless Café
Go to The Wireless Café's link on the Student Web Site. There you will be asked to propose some interorganizational systems that could benefit the restaurant's operations.

More Resources
More resources and study tools are located on the Student Web Site. You'll find additional chapter materials and useful Web links. In addition, self-quizzes that provide individualized feedback are available for each chapter.

QUESTIONS FOR REVIEW

1. Define an interorganizational information system (IOS).
2. List the major types of IOSs.
3. List the IT technologies that can support IOSs.
4. Define a global information system.
5. List some of the difficulties in managing global supply chains.
6. How can global information systems facilitate global trade?
7. What is a B2B exchange?
8. Why is a B2B exchange considered an IOS?
9. Define a B2B hub and contrast it with an exchange.
10. List the major benefits of a hub to the participating companies. (Hint: See *IT at Work 8.3*.)
11. Describe B2B directories.
12. Define virtual corporations (VCs).
13. Describe the support IT provides to VCs.
14. Define EDI.
15. List the major benefits of EDI.
16. List the limitations of traditional EDI.
17. Explain the benefits of Internet-based EDI.
18. Define an extranet and explain its infrastructure.
19. List and briefly define the major types of extranets.
20. Describe XML and explain how it facilitates IOSs.
21. Describe how Web Services can enhance IOSs.
22. Describe PRM and SRM.
23. Describe the major SRM activities (refer to Figure 8.8).
24. What is collaborative commerce? What are some of its areas?
25. How can global trade be facilitated by IT?

QUESTIONS FOR DISCUSSION

1. Discuss some reasons for the complexity of global trade and the potential assistance of IT.
2. In what way is a B2B exchange related to a global supply chain? To a global information system?
3. Discuss the major differences between a B2B exchange and a B2B hub.
4. Compare an EDI to an extranet and discuss the major differences.

5. When a company opens a private marketplace (for selling and/or buying), it may use EDI, an extranet, EDI/Internet, or just the Internet with regular encryption. Discuss the *criteria* a company needs to consider when making this decision.

6. Discuss the manner in which cross-border data transfer can be a limitation to a company that has manufacturing plants in other countries.

EXERCISES

1. Enter *peoplesoft.com* and find material on the different IOSs discussed in this chapter. Prepare a report.

2. General Electric Information Systems is the largest provider of EDI services. Investigate what services GEIS and other EDI vendors provide. If you were to evaluate their services for your company, how would you plan to approach the evaluation? Prepare a report.

3. Examine the Lego case and *lego.com*. Design the conceptual architecture of the relevant IOSs you think Lego needs. Concentrate on the marketing portion of the supply chain, but point out some of the suppliers of plastic, paper, electronics, and wood that Lego uses.

GROUP ASSIGNMENTS

1. Have each team locate several organizations that use IOSs, including one with a global reach. Students should contact the companies to find what IOS technology support they use (e.g., an EDI, extranet, etc.). Then find out what issues they faced in implementation. Prepare a report.

2. Team members will work on the EDI-XML connection. Start with *XML-EDI.org* and *xmlglobal.com* (see the tutorials at those sites) and find more resources. Prepare a report to convince management of a hypothetical company to use XML/EDI.

INTERNET EXERCISES

1. Enter *i2.com* and review the products presented there. Explain how some of the products facilitate collaboration.

2. Enter *collaborate.com* and read about recent issues related to collaboration. Prepare a report.

3. Enter *smarterwork.com*. Find out how collaboration is done. Summarize the benefits of this site to the participants. Then enter *vignette.com*; look at the products listed under Collaboration. Compare the two sites.

4. Enter *1edisource.com* and see the demo of WebSource. What are the benefits of this product?

5. Visit *edi-information.com* and prepare a list of educational and source material offered there.

6. Visit *xml.com* and *google.com* and find recent applications of XML. Prepare a report.

Minicase 1
How Volkswagen Runs Its Supply Chain in Brazil

The Problem

Like many other companies, Volkswagen (VW) works with several vendors in its assembly plants. However, there were problems in coordination and communication with some vendors. Vendors' materials were shipped to VW factories, where VW employees assembled trucks. But the supply chain was long, and problems with materials often developed. Each time there was a problem, VW had to wait for a partner to come to the plant to solve the problem. Also, materials arrived late, and so VW held large inventories to have extra materials on hand in the event of a delayed shipment. Finally, quality was frequently compromised. There was a need for a computer-based collaborative system.

The Solution

In its Brazilian plant truck 100 miles northwest of Rio de Janeiro, Volkswagen (VW) radically altered its supply chain in 2002. The Rio plant is relatively small: Its 1,000 workers are scheduled to produce 100 trucks per day. Only 200 of the 1,000 workers are Volkswagen employees; they are responsible for overall quality, marketing, research, and design. The other 800 workers, who are employees of suppliers such as Rockwell International and Cummins Engines, do the specific assembly work. The objective of the lean supply chain was to reduce the number of defective parts, cut labor costs, and improve efficiency.

Volkswagen's major suppliers are assigned space in the VW plant, but they supply and manage their own components, supplies, and workers. Workers from various suppliers build the truck as it moves down the assembly line. The system is illustrated in the nearby figure. At the first stop in the assembly process, workers from Iochepe-Maxion mount the gas tank, transmission lines, and steering blocks. As the chassis moves down the line, employees from Rockwell mount axles and brakes. Then workers from Remon put on wheels and adjust tire pressure. The MWM/Cummins team installs the engine and transmission. Truck cabs, produced by the Brazilian firm Delga Automotivea, are painted by Eisenmann, and then finished and upholstered by VDO, both of Germany. Volkswagen employees do an evaluation of the final truck. The various national groups still need to communicate with their headquarters, but only infrequently (mostly by e-mail).

The Results

Volkswagen's innovative supply chain has already improved quality and driven down costs, as a result of each supplier having accepted responsibility for its units and workers' compensation. Encouraged by these results, VW is trying a similar approach in plants in Buenos Aires, Argentina, and with Skoda, in the Czech Republic. Volkswagen's new level of integration in supply chain management may be the wave of the future.

Source: Compiled from Heizer and Render (2003), and from *vw.com*.

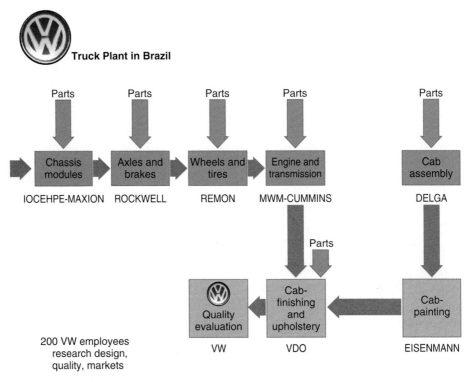

Volkswagen's truck assembly plant in Brazil.

Questions for Minicase 1

1. Draw the supply chain of VW's manufacturing plant.
2. What IOSs might be necessary to support such an arrangement? Distinguish between upstream, internal, and downstream supply chain activities. (See Chapter 7 for review of these terms.)
3. Which of the following is most appropriate for the old process: extranet, EDI, EDI/Internet, or Web Services?
4. What IT support is needed in the new arrangement?

Minicase 2
Six Flags' Global IOS

The Problem

Entertaining nearly 50 million guests annually at 39 different theme and water parks, located across eight different countries, all while growing a multinational organization, is not an easy task. Six Flags' many parks were each running different general ledger and other administrative systems. The large parks had complex ERP systems that did not "talk" with the small parks' financial packages. In addition, ticket sales on the Web had been growing rapidly, as were ticket sales by phone and in kiosks. Finally, new Six Flags parks continue to pop up around the world.

Consolidation of financial results was a challenge, and collaboration among the parks was slow, expensive, and error-prone, mainly done via faxes and express mail. This situation interfered with the explosive growth of the company and hurt its profit. In the past, Six Flags had struggled to make various systems work together, and corporate reporting included hours of data uploads and manual consolidations for distribution to managers around the globe. As a result, decisions were being delayed. For a multinational corporation, this was unacceptable.

The Solution

Six Flags elected to use Business Solutions—Great Plains (from Microsoft), which provided support to local tax codes and local currency computations, facilitating global reporting. Of all the expectations Six Flags set for a new business solution, global reporting was one of the most crucial requirements. The system was customized by Collins Computing, to address the issues of multiple languages, currencies, and localization.

Centralized on 10 Citrix servers, the system operates on Microsoft SQL Server, enabling all park management teams across the globe to work collectively, while providing scalability to support the high transaction volume generated by the various parks (especially during the summer). For example, integrated inventory planning and purchasing capabilities enable Six Flags to lower inventory overhead. The system was implemented in just two months.

The Results

The results have come on various fronts:

- *Cost savings from purchasing and inventory planning.* With one central, enterprise-level solution, purchasing and inventory planning are implemented in an integrated, shared environment. This enables Six Flags to lower inventory overhead by providing various parks around the world with the opportunity to swap high-cost parts needed to keep the complex park rides running smoothly.

- *Increased customer satisfaction at the parks.* Customer satisfaction is also on the rise with a better stream of supplies hitting the food stands on demand, rather than on a scheduled basis.

- *Ease of operation.* Microsoft Business Solutions is easy to learn, maintain, and operate, which has allowed the company to distribute valuable technical resources to other parts of the company.

- *Improved business processes.* Sharing a common system, executives around the globe can now run and create their own reports using industry-standard reporting tools. Users are able to drill down to gather greater detail, a feature that was not available in Six Flags' previous systems. Employees are spending less time on the tedious tasks of consolidating data and manually creating reports, providing for improved employee morale.

- *Annual savings.* Annual savings are estimated at $1 million, providing an extremely high ROI on the new system.

Sources: Compiled from Microsoft Case Study (2003).

Questions for Minicase 2

1. The system is used both for internal communication and for external communication (e.g., for purchasing supplies and for selling tickets). Identify what IOSs are supported by this system.

2. What are the advantages of a system from one vendor?

3. Why do you think it took only two months to build the system?

4. Explain the global-related issues handled by the system.

5. Why is rapid global reporting so critical for Six Flags?

REFERENCES

Aberdeen Group Inc., "Asite Builds E-Marketplace Using Combined Strength of Commerce One, Microsoft, and Attenda," *Aberdeen Group Profile*, 2001.

Boucher-Ferguson, R., "A New Shipping Rout (Web-EDI)," *eWeek*, September 23, 2002.

Business Wire (2003).

Coupey, P., *Marketing and the Internet*. Upper Saddle River, NJ: Prentice Hall, 2001.

Current Research Note, "The Truth about XML," *McKinsey Quarterly*, No. 3, 2003.

Damsgaard, L., and J. Horluck, "Designing *www.LEGO.com/shop*: Business Issues and Concerns," case 500-0061, *European Clearing House*, 2000.

Dell.com, press releases (2000–2003).

Dubie, D., "Going Global," *ebusinessiq.com*, News Features, March 13, 2003.

Dyer, J. H., and N. W. Hatch, "Using Supplier Networks to Learn Faster," *MIT Sloan Management Review*, Spring 2004.

"Fidelity Retrofits All Data for XML," *InternetWeek*, August 6, 2001.

Galante, D., "Case Studies: Digital Do-Overs," *Forbes*, October 7, 2002.

Grimes, B., "Microsoft.NET Case Study: Allstate Financial Group," *PC Magazine*, March 25, 2003.

Hagel, J., III, *Out of the Box*. Boston: Harvard Business School Press, 2002.

Handfield, R. B., and E. L. Nichols, Jr., *Introduction to Supply Chain Management*. Upper Saddle River, NJ: Prentice Hall, 1999.

Handfield, R. B., et al., *Supply Chain Redesign: Transforming Supply Chains into Integrated Value Systems*. Upper Saddle River, NJ: Financial Times/Prentice Hall, 2002.

Harrison, T. P., "Global Supply Chain Design," *Information Systems Frontiers*, October–December 2001.

Heizer, L., and B. Render, *Principles of Operations Management*, 5th ed. Upper Saddle River, NJ: Prentice Hall, 2003.

Korolishin, J., "Industry-Specific XML Reduces Paperwork for C-store Chain," *Stores*, February 2004.

Linthicum, D., *B2B Application Integration: E-Business-Enable Your Enterprise*. Boston, MA: Addison-Wesley, 2000.

Microsoft Case Study, "Six Flags Affords Thrill Rides in the Park, Grounded Financial Management in Operations," *microsoft.com/BusinessSolutions/casestudies/CaseStudy.aspx?CaseStudyID=1*, November 18, 2003.

Murtaza, M. B., and J. R. Shah, "Managing Information for Effective Business Partner Relationships," *Information Systems Management*, Spring 2004.

New Piper, "New Piper Rolls Out Further Customer Relations Initiatives," news release, *newpiper.com*, 2002, 2004.

Plumtree Software Inc., "Ford Connects European Dealer Network," *plumtree.com*, October 14, 2003.

Raisinghani, M. (ed.), *Cases on Worldwide E-Commerce*. Hershey, PA: The Idea Group, 2002.

Ranganatan, C., "Evaluating the Options for B2B E-Exchanges," *Information Systems Management*, Summer 2003.

SAP AG, Customer Success Story #50868084, *sap.com*, March 2004.

Schecterle, B., "Managing and Extending Supplier Relationships," *People Talk*, April–June 2003, *peoplesoft.com.au/corp/en/peopletalkonline/april_2003/sidebar2.jsp* (accessed June 2003).

Stoll, R., "How We Built LEGO.com," *Practical Internet*, March 2003.

Turban, E., et al., *Electronic Commerce 2006*. Upper Saddle River, NJ: Prentice Hall, 2006.

Witte, C. L., et al., "The Integration of EDI and the Internet," *Information Systems Management*, Fall 2003.

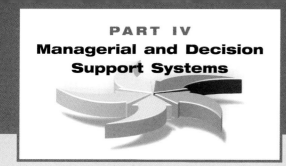

PART IV
Managerial and Decision Support Systems

▶ 9. Knowledge Management
10. Data Management: Warehousing, Analyzing, Mining, and Visualization
11. Management Decision Support and Intelligent Systems

CHAPTER

9

Knowledge Management

9.1 Introduction to Knowledge Management

9.2 Knowledge Management Initiatives

9.3 Approaches to Knowledge Management

9.4 Information Technology in Knowledge Management

9.5 Knowledge Management Systems Implementation

9.6 Roles of People in Knowledge Management

9.7 Ensuring Success of KM Efforts

Minicases:
1. DaimlerChrysler
2. Buckman Labs

LEARNING OBJECTIVES

After studying this chapter, you will be able to:

❶ Define knowledge and describe the different types of knowledge.

❷ Describe the activities involved in knowledge management.

❸ Describe different approaches to knowledge management.

❹ Describe the technologies that can be utilized in a knowledge management system.

❺ Describe the issues associated with implementing knowledge management in organizations.

❻ Describe the activities of the chief knowledge officer and others involved in knowledge management.

❼ Describe benefits as well as drawbacks to knowledge management initiatives.

KM PORTAL AT FRITO-LAY ASSISTS
DISPERSED SALES TEAMS

 THE PROBLEM

Frito-Lay, an $8.6 billion division of PepsiCo, based in Plano, Texas, had information scattered in disparate systems around the country with no simple way for geographically dispersed sales forces to access the same information. The vice president of customer development described the situation as akin to having "knowledge trapped in files everywhere." Different salespeople would be requesting the same information, but there was no means of keeping track of frequently requested information and data. For example, the corporate sales, marketing, and operations staffs were often asked for information concerning private-label trends within snack categories. These support staffs found themselves gathering the same data again and again for different salespeople. In addition, each individual salesperson often had valuable knowledge stored on his or her own laptop, which was not accessible to others. Not only that, but the ability to coordinate with other salespersons was missing. For example, "If somebody got a piece of research and wanted to get input from account executives in Baltimore and Los Angeles, the ability to collaborate [online] just wasn't there."

 THE SOLUTION

Frito-Lay decided to implement a knowledge management (KM) portal on the corporate intranet. The KM portal would enable a central point of entry for all sales-related customer and corporate information. The portal would contain information (such as sales, analysis, and news) about the team's customers and would contain profiles of individuals within Frito-Lay. The portal would help reduce the time it took to locate information on products, sales, promotions, and research. In addition, the portal would make locating an expert within the company much easier.

Following a pilot conducted with one of the highly dispersed sales teams, three goals were established for the portal: to streamline knowledge, to exploit customer-specific data, and to foster team collaboration. Navigator Systems, a consultancy based in Dallas, Texas, built a prototype in about three months using technologies such as Lotus Domino, BusinessObjects' WebIntelligence, Java, and IBM's DB2 database. A search engine called Autonomy was used. Autonomy is a natural-language search engine that allows users to search information in different repositories such as spreadsheets, Word files, and presentations.

To populate the portal, an audit was conducted that resulted in expertise profiles. The expertise profiles enable salespersons to learn who had expertise in promotion planning, activity planning, costing, or new product announcements, for example.

The portal is password-protected so that sensitive customer data is limited to the immediate sales team.

THE RESULTS

The knowledge portal has had both tangible and intangible results. For one, the portal has enabled sales teams to achieve a faster growth rate. The initial pilot team was able to double the growth rate of the customers' business in the salty snack category. A year after the pilot, the sales team was able to share documents concurrently online rather than having to fax documents to members dispersed around the country. Being able to manipulate large amounts of data online also helps reduce physical travel to the retail customers.

The tool has also contributed to a sense of camaraderie. The portal provides a personal touch for the teams, with information on team members' birthdays, best practices, and a messaging system that displays who is currently online. In addition, the portal has helped reduce turnover. Turnover has historically been quite high, attributed to the pressure on salespeople. Salespeople often became frustrated because they had no way to efficiently collaborate with their dispersed team members. Company surveys have found that salespeople enjoy the sense of connection that the portal provides. So successful is the portal, that it has now become a PepsiCo initiative.

Source: Adapted from Shein (2001).

 LESSONS LEARNED FROM THIS CASE

The case illustrates the importance of realizing value from centralizing access to organizationwide knowledge resources. By providing ready access to information that had been scattered around the organization and by providing an alternative to labor-intensive coordination mechanisms such as faxing team documents, the organization realized benefits in terms of growth rate, retention, and morale.

In this chapter we describe the characteristics and concepts of knowledge management. In addition, we will explain how firms are using information technology to implement knowledge management systems and how these systems are transforming modern organizations.

9.1 INTRODUCTION TO KNOWLEDGE MANAGEMENT

Concepts and Definitions

With roots in expert systems, organizational learning, and innovation, the idea of knowledge management is itself not new (e.g., see Cahill, 1996). Successful managers have always used intellectual assets and recognized their value. But these efforts were not systematic, nor did they ensure that knowledge gained was shared and dispersed appropriately for maximum organizational benefit. Moreover, sources such as Forrester Research, IBM, and Merrill Lynch estimate that 85 percent of a company's knowledge assets are not housed in relational databases, but are dispersed in e-mail, Word documents, spreadsheets, and presentations on individual computers (Ziff-Davis, 2002). The application of information technology tools to facilitate the creation, storage, transfer, and application of previously uncodifiable organizational knowledge is a new and major initiative in organizations.

Knowledge management (KM) is a process that helps organizations identify, select, organize, disseminate, and transfer important information and expertise that are part of the organization's memory and that typically reside within the organization in an unstructured manner. This structuring of knowledge enables effective and efficient problem solving, dynamic learning, strategic

FIGURE 9.1 Data, information, and knowledge.

planning, and decision making. Knowledge management initiatives focus on identifying knowledge, explicating it in such a way that it can be shared in a formal manner, and leveraging its value through reuse.

Through a supportive organizational climate and modern information technology, an organization can bring its entire organizational memory and knowledge to bear upon any problem anywhere in the world and at any time. For organizational success, *knowledge, as a form of capital, must be exchangeable among persons, and it must be able to grow.* Knowledge about how problems are solved can be captured, so that knowledge management can promote organizational learning, leading to further knowledge creation.

KNOWLEDGE. In the information technology context, knowledge is very distinct from data and information (see Figure 9.1 and Online File W9.1). Whereas *data* are a collection of facts, measurements, and statistics, *information* is organized or processed data that are timely (i.e., inferences from the data are drawn within the time frame of applicability) and accurate (i.e., with regard to the original data) (Holsapple, 2003). **Knowledge** is information that is *contextual, relevant,* and *actionable.*

For example, a map giving detailed driving directions from one location to another could be considered data. An up-to-the-minute traffic bulletin along the freeway that indicates a traffic slowdown due to construction could be considered information. Awareness of an alternative, back-roads route could be considered knowledge. In this case, the map is considered data because it does not contain current relevant information that affects the driving time and conditions from one location to the other. However, having the current conditions as information is useful only if the individual has knowledge that will enable him or her to avert the construction zone. The implication is that knowledge has strong experiential and reflective elements that distinguish it from information in a given context. Having knowledge implies that it can be exercised to solve a problem, whereas having information does not carry the same connotation.

An *ability to act* is an integral part of being knowledgeable. For example, two people in the same context with the same information may not have the same ability to use the information to the same degree of success. Hence there is a difference in the human capability to add value. The differences in ability may be due to differences in experiences, training, perspectives, and so on. While data, information, and knowledge may all be viewed as assets of an organization, knowledge provides a higher level of meaning about data and information. It conveys *meaning,* and hence tends to be much more valuable, yet more ephemeral.

Knowledge has the following characteristics that differentiates it from an organization's other assets (Gray, 1999; Holsapple, 2003):

- *Extraordinary leverage and increasing returns.* Knowledge is not subject to diminishing returns. When it is used, it is not consumed. Its consumers can add to it, thus increasing its value.

- *Fragmentation, leakage, and the need to refresh.* As knowledge grows, it branches and fragments. Knowledge is dynamic; it is information in action. Thus, an organization must continually refresh its knowledge base to maintain it as a source of competitive advantage.

- *Uncertain value.* It is difficult to estimate the impact of an investment in knowledge. There are too many intangible aspects.

- *Uncertain value of sharing.* Similarly, it is difficult to estimate the value of sharing the knowledge, or even who will benefit most.

- *Rooted in time.* The utility and validity of knowledge may vary with time; hence, the immediacy, age, perishability, and volatility of knowledge are important attributes.

There is a vast amount of literature about what knowledge and knowing means in epistemology (study of the nature of knowledge), the social sciences, philosophy, and psychology (Polanyi, 1958, 1966). Though there is no single definition of what knowledge and knowledge management specifically mean, the business perspective on them is fairly pragmatic. Information as a resource is not always valuable (i.e., information overload can distract from the important); knowledge is a resource when it is clear, relevant, and important to an individual processing the knowledge (Holsapple, 2003). Knowledge implies an implicit understanding and experience that can discriminate between its use and misuse. Over time, information accumulates and decays, while knowledge evolves. The word *knowledge* tends to carry positive connotations (Schultze and Leidner, 2002). However, because *knowledge is dynamic in nature,* today's knowledge may well become tomorrow's ignorance if an individual or organization fails to update knowledge as environmental conditions change. For more on the potential drawbacks of managing and reusing knowledge, see Section 9.7.

Intellectual capital (or **intellectual assets**) is another term often used for knowledge, and it implies that there is a financial value to knowledge (Edvinsson, 2003). Though intellectual capital is difficult to measure, some industries have tried. For example, the value of the intellectual capital of the property-casualty insurance industry has been estimated to be between $270 billion to $330 billion (Mooney, 2000). The Organization for Economic Co-operation and Development (OECD) has scored its 30 member nations according to their investments in intellectual capital such as R&D, education, and patents. According to OECD, those countries with the most intellectual capital activities will be the winners of future wealth (Edvinsson, 2003).

Knowledge evolves over time with experience, which puts connections among new situations and events in context. Given the breadth of the types and applications of knowledge, we adopt the simple and elegant definition that knowledge is *information in action* (O'Dell et al., 1998).

TACIT AND EXPLICIT KNOWLEDGE. Polanyi (1958) first conceptualized and distinguished between an organization's tacit and explicit knowledge. **Explicit knowledge** deals with more objective, rational, and technical knowledge (data, policies, procedures, software, documents, etc.). **Tacit knowledge** is usually in the domain of subjective, cognitive, and experiential learning; it is highly personal and difficult to formalize (Nonaka and Takeuchi, 1995). Other types of knowledge are displayed in Online File W9.2.

Explicit knowledge is the policies, procedural guides, white papers, reports, designs, products, strategies, goals, mission, and core competencies of the enterprise and the information technology infrastructure. It is the knowledge that has been codified (documented) in a form that can be distributed to others or transformed into a process or strategy without requiring interpersonal interaction. For example, a description of how to process a job application would be documented in a firm's human resources policy manual. Moreover, there is a simple relationship between the codification of knowledge and the costs of its transfer: the more that knowledge is made explicit, the more economically it can be transferred (Teece, 2003). Explicit knowledge has also been called **leaky knowledge** because of the ease with which it can leave an individual, document, or the organization, after it has been documented (Alavi, 2000).

Tacit knowledge is the cumulative store of the experiences, mental maps, insights, acumen, expertise, know-how, trade secrets, skill sets, and learning that an organization has, as well as the organizational culture that has embedded in it the past and present experiences of the organization's people, processes, and values. Tacit knowledge, also referred to as *embedded knowledge* (Madhaven and Grover, 1998), is usually either localized within the brain of an individual or embedded in the group interactions within a department or a branch office. Tacit knowledge typically involves expertise or high skill levels. It is generally slow and costly to transfer and can be plagued by ambiguity (Teece, 2003).

Sometimes tacit knowledge is easily documentable but has remained tacit simply because the individual housing the knowledge does not recognize its potential value to other individuals. Other times, tacit knowledge is unstructured, without tangible form, and therefore difficult to codify. Polanyi (1966) suggests that it is difficult to put some tacit knowledge into words. For example, an explanation of how to ride a bicycle would be difficult to document explicitly, and thus is tacit. Tacit knowledge has been called **sticky knowledge** because it may be relatively difficult to pull it away from its source.

Successful transfer or sharing of tacit knowledge usually takes place through associations, internships, apprenticeships, conversations, other means of social and interpersonal interactions, or even through simulations (e.g., see Robin, 2000). Nonaka and Takeuchi (1995) claim that intangibles like insights, intuitions, hunches, gut feelings, values, images, metaphors, and analogies are the often-overlooked assets of organizations. Harvesting this intangible asset can be critical to a firm's bottom line and its ability to meet its goals.

The Need for Knowledge Management Systems

The goal of knowledge management is for an organization to be aware of individual and collective knowledge so that it may make the most effective use of the knowledge it has (Bennet and Bennet, 2003). Historically, MIS has focused on capturing, storing, managing, and reporting explicit knowledge. Organizations now recognize the need to integrate both explicit and tacit knowledge in formal information systems. **Knowledge management systems (KMSs)** refers to the use of modern information technologies (e.g., the Internet, intranets, extranets, LotusNotes, software filters, agents, data warehouses) to systematize, enhance, and expedite intra- and interfirm knowledge management (Alavi and Leidner, 1999). KMSs are intended to help an organization cope with turnover, rapid change, and downsizing by making the expertise of the organization's human capital widely accessible. They are being built in part

IT at Work 9.1
CINGULAR CALLS ON KNOWLEDGE

How do you make sure that each of your customer service agents at 22 call centers nationwide can answer virtually any question asked by one of your 22 million clients? That was the challenge faced by Cingular Wireless (*cingular.com*), a major mobile communications provider based in Atlanta, Georgia.

To accomplish this Herculean task, Cingular Wireless turned to knowledge management. Cingular benchmarked knowledge management solutions of technology-oriented companies, such as Dell and Microsoft. Steve Mullins, vice president of customer experience for Cingular Wireless, and Monica Browning, Cingular's director of knowledge management, met with several knowledge management software vendors to learn how their tools operate. Following a review of knowledge management solutions used by other companies, Cingular chose eService Suite by ServiceWare of Edison, New Jersey.

To ensure successful implementation of the system, Cingular embarked on a campaign to obtain support of everyone involved, from senior executives to each call center agent who would use the system. A pilot program was initiated at technical support departments at three call centers. In addition, to help manage organizational changes that accompany a shift to knowledge management, Cingular enlisted the help of leading consulting firms Cap Gemini, Ernst and Young, and Innovative Management Solutions.

A major issue in developing the knowledge management system involved capturing the knowledge and storing it in the system. Cingular accomplished it by combining the efforts of its employees and an external authoring group from Innovative Management Solutions. Cingular divided the process into phases, which allowed the company to populate the knowledge base with technical support information, common topics, information on rate plans, and so on. It took about four months before the knowledge base was ready for the first group of users.

The knowledge management system uses complex algorithms to process natural language queries and provide customer service agents with lists of most likely answers to their questions. Furthermore, the software determines the relevance of possible answers by ranking them partly on exact text and phrase matching. In addition, the system can match synonyms and assign additional weight to certain things. The system attempts to provide even more focused solutions by retrieving answers from the pool of knowledge that is relevant to a particular user and his or her profile.

Understanding that knowledge must grow and evolve, Cingular encourages users to contribute their expertise to the system. The software can automatically record a sequence of steps that an agent took to find a correct solution to a certain problem and give the agent an option to provide additional feedback.

Cingular realized that ensuring validity and integrity of the knowledge stored and distributed by the knowledge management system is one of the key factors of the system's success. To that end, the company employs a knowledge management team that is responsible for monitoring, maintaining, and expanding the knowledge management system. The team consists of about 25 full-time employees based in Cingular's Atlanta headquarters. The KM team works closely with various departments of the company and subject matter experts to ensure that the knowledge base has the right answers in a user-friendly format at the right time. In addition, the team reviews contributions to the knowledge base made by the agents and makes appropriate changes or additions to the knowledge base.

Cingular's clients are often the ultimate beneficiaries of the company's knowledge. That is why Cingular plans to bring its knowledge closer to its customers by extending the knowledge management system online and to retail stores. Customers will be able to access instructions on using wireless services and features, handsets, and other devices that Cingular carries, as well as troubleshooting tips.

Source: Adapted from O'Herron (2003) and *cingular.com* (accessed May 2004).

For Further Exploration: Explain the advantages and disadvantages of a professional knowledge management team administering the content of an organization's knowledge base.

from increased pressure to maintain a well-informed, productive workforce. Moreover, they are built to help large organizations provide a consistent level of customer service, as illustrated in *IT at Work 9.1.* Many organizations have been building KM systems in order to capitalize on the knowledge and experience of employees worldwide. Online File W9.3 describes Siemens's experience with knowledge management. Online File W9.4 describes how Chevron-Texaco was able to reduce operating expenses by implementing a KMS.

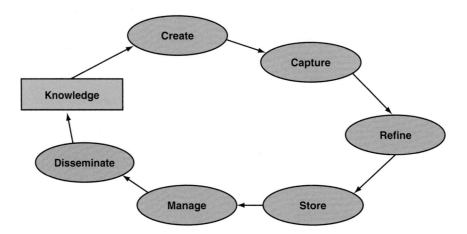

FIGURE 9.2 The knowledge management cycle.

Knowledge Management System Cycle

A functioning knowledge management system follows six steps in a cycle (see Figure 9.2). The reason the system is cyclical is that knowledge is dynamically refined over time. The knowledge in a good KM system is never finished because, over time, the environment changes, and the knowledge must be updated to reflect the changes. The cycle works as follows:

1. *Create knowledge.* Knowledge is created as people determine new ways of doing things or develop know-how. Sometimes external knowledge is brought in.
2. *Capture knowledge.* New knowledge must be identified as valuable and be represented in a reasonable way.
3. *Refine knowledge.* New knowledge must be placed in context so that it is actionable. This is where human insights (tacit qualities) must be captured along with explicit facts.
4. *Store knowledge.* Useful knowledge must then be stored in a reasonable format in a knowledge repository so that others in the organization can access it.
5. *Manage knowledge.* Like a library, the knowledge must be kept current. It must be reviewed to verify that it is relevant and accurate.
6. *Disseminate knowledge.* Knowledge must be made available in a useful format to anyone in the organization who needs it, anywhere and any time.

As knowledge is disseminated, individuals develop, create, and identify new knowledge or update old knowledge, which they replenish into the system. Knowledge is a resource that is not consumed when used, though it can age. (For example, driving a car in 1900 was different from driving one now, but many of the basic principles still apply.) Knowledge must be updated. Thus, the amount of knowledge grows over time.

9.2 KNOWLEDGE MANAGEMENT INITIATIVES

When asked why the organization was building a worldwide knowledge management system, the chief knowledge officer (CKO) of a large multinational consulting firm replied, "We have 80,000 people scattered around the world that need information to do their jobs effectively. The information they needed was too difficult to find and, even if they did find it, often inaccurate. Our intranet is meant to solve this problem" (Leidner, 2003). A survey of European firms by KPMG Peat Marwick in 1998 found that almost half of the companies reported having suffered a significant setback from losing key staff (KPMG, 1998). Similarly, a survey conducted in the same year by Cranfield University found that the majority of responding firms believed that much of the knowledge they needed existed inside the organization, but that finding and leveraging it were ongoing challenges. It is precisely these types of difficulties that have led to the systematic attempt to manage knowledge.

Most knowledge management initiatives have one of three aims: (1) to make knowledge visible mainly through maps, yellow pages, and hypertext, (2) to develop a knowledge-intensive culture, or to (3) build a knowledge infrastructure (Davenport and Prusak, 1998). These aims are not mutually exclusive, and indeed, firms may attempt all three as part of a knowledge management initiative.

There are several activities or processes that surround the management of knowledge. These include the creation of knowledge, the sharing of knowledge, and the seeking and use of knowledge. Various terms have been used to describe these processes. What is important is an understanding of how knowledge flows through an organization, rather than any particular label assigned to a knowledge activity.

Knowledge Creation

Knowledge creation is the generation of new insights, ideas, or routines. It may also be referred to as *knowledge acquisition* (Holsapple and Joshi, 2003). It is helpful to distinguish between the creation of fundamentally new knowledge versus the acquisition of existing knowledge (Ford, 2003). Nonaka (1994) describes knowledge creation as interplay between tacit and explicit knowledge and as a growing spiral as knowledge moves among the individual, group, and organizational levels.

There are four modes of knowledge creation: socialization, combination, externalization, and internalization. The *socialization* mode refers to the conversion of tacit knowledge to new tacit knowledge through social interactions and shared experience among organizational members (e.g., mentoring). The *combination* mode refers to the creation of new explicit knowledge by merging, categorizing, reclassifying, and synthesizing existing explicit knowledge (e.g., statistical analyses of market data). The other two modes involve interactions and conversion between tacit and explicit knowledge. *Externalization* refers to converting tacit knowledge to new explicit knowledge (e.g., producing a written document describing the procedures used in solving a particular client's problem). *Internalization* refers to the creation of new tacit knowledge from explicit knowledge (e.g., obtaining a novel insight through reading a document). These final two modes of knowledge creation deal less with the creation of new knowledge than with the conversion of existing knowledge to a new mode.

Holsapple and Joshi (2003) suggest that there are two important dimensions to the acquisition of knowledge: one is the identification of existing knowledge from external sources and the other, the selection of needed knowledge from an organization's existing knowledge resources. These two activities require different skills, levels of effort, and costs.

Knowledge Sharing

Knowledge sharing is the willful explication of one's ideas, insights, solutions, experiences (i.e., knowledge) to another individual either via an intermediary, such as a computer-based system, or directly. However, in many organizations, information and knowledge are not considered organizational resources to be shared, but individual competitive weapons to be kept private (Davenport et al., 1998). Organizational members may share personal knowledge with a certain trepidation—the perceived threat that they are of less value if their knowledge is part of the organizational public domain. Also, a primary constraint on an individual's knowledge sharing behaviors might simply be time. Moreover, sharing knowledge is a risky proposition since one does not know how that knowledge might be reused (Ford, 2003).

Research in organizational learning and knowledge management suggests that some facilitating conditions include trust, interest, and shared language (Hanssen-Bauer and Snow, 1996), fostering access to knowledgeable members (Brown and Duguid, 2000), and a culture marked by autonomy, redundancy, requisite variety, intention, and fluctuation (Nonaka, 1994). Several organizations have made knowledge sharing a guiding principal for the organization (Liebowitz and Chen, 2003). Johnson & Johnson has knowledge fairs designed to promote new relationships among colleagues in order to facilitate knowledge transfer. The World Bank includes such factors as openness to new ideas, continual learning, and sharing of knowledge as part of their annual performance evaluation of employees (Liebowitz and Chen, 2003).

Knowledge Seeking

Knowledge seeking, also referred to as *knowledge sourcing* (Gray and Meister, 2003), is the search for and use of internal organizational knowledge. While the lack of time or the lack of reward may hinder the sharing of knowledge, the same can be said of knowledge seeking. Individuals may sometimes feel compelled to come up with new ideas, rather than use tried-and-true knowledge, if they feel that their own performance review is based on the originality or creativity of their ideas. Such was the case for marketing employees in a global consumer goods organization described in Alavi et al. (2003).

Individuals may engage in knowledge creation, sharing, and seeking with or without the use of information technology tools. We next describe two common approaches to knowledge management.

9.3 APPROACHES TO KNOWLEDGE MANAGEMENT

There are two fundamental approaches to knowledge management: the process and the practice approaches.

The Process Approach

The **process approach** attempts to codify organizational knowledge through formalized controls, processes, and technologies (Hansen et al., 1999). Organizations adopting the process approach may implement explicit policies governing how knowledge is to be collected, stored, and disseminated throughout the organization. The process approach frequently involves the use of information technologies to enhance the quality and speed of knowledge creation and distribution in the organizations. These technologies may include intranets, data warehousing, knowledge repositories, decision support tools, and groupware (Ruggles, 1998).

There are several different levels of the process approach (van der Spek et al., 2003). At the most rudimentary, knowledge may be codified in project descriptions, stories, or other forms of documentation, but limited filtering has been done. At the next level, knowledge may be codified into structured concepts, frameworks, and theories. At the highest level, knowledge is embedded into work practices that give direction to employees (van der Spek et al., 2003).

The main criticisms of the process approach are that it fails to capture much of the tacit knowledge embedded in firms and that it forces individuals into fixed patterns of thinking (DeLong and Fahey, 2000; Brown and Duguid, 2000; Von Krogh, 2000; Hargadon, 1998). The process approach is favored by firms that sell relatively standardized products that fill common needs. Most of the valuable knowledge in these firms is fairly explicit because of the standardized nature of the products and services. For example, a kazoo manufacturer has minimal product changes or service needs over the years, and yet there is steady demand and a need to produce the item. In these cases, the knowledge is typically static in nature.

Even large firms that utilize tacit knowledge, such as Ernst & Young, have invested heavily to ensure that the process approach works efficiently. The 250 people at Ernst & Young's Center for Business Knowledge manage an electronic repository and help consultants find and use information. Specialists write reports and analyses that many teams can use. And each of Ernst & Young's more than 40 practice areas has a staff member who helps codify and store documents. The resulting area databases are linked through a network (Hansen et al., 1999). Naturally, people-to-documents is not the only way consultants in firms like Ernst & Young and Accenture share knowledge; they talk with one another as well. But they do place a high degree of emphasis on the codification strategy (Hansen et al., 1999).

The Practice Approach

In contrast, the **practice approach** to knowledge management assumes that a great deal of organizational knowledge is tacit in nature and that formal controls, processes, and technologies are not suitable for transmitting this type of understanding. Rather than building formal systems to manage knowledge, the focus of this approach is to build the social environments or communities of practice necessary to facilitate the sharing of tacit understanding (Brown and Duguid, 2000; DeLong and Fahey, 2000; Gupta and Govindarajan, 2000; Wenger and Snyder, 2000; Hansen et al., 1999). **Communities of practice (COPs)** are groups of individuals with a common professional interest who work together informally. Within such a community, individuals collaborate directly, teach each other, and share experiences (Smith and McKeen, 2003).

The practice approach is typically adopted by companies that provide highly customized solutions to unique problems. The valuable knowledge for these firms is tacit in nature, which is difficult to express, capture, and manage. In this case, the environment and the nature of the problems being encountered are extremely dynamic. For these firms, knowledge is shared mostly through person-to-person contacts. Collaborative computing methods (for example, Lotus Notes/Domino Server or e-mail) help people communicate. Because tacit knowledge is difficult to extract, store, and manage, the explicit knowledge that points to *how* to find the appropriate tacit knowledge (people contacts, consulting reports) is made available to an appropriate set of individuals who might need it.

To make their practice approach work, firms like Bain invest heavily in building networks of people and communications technology such as telephone, e-mail, and videoconferencing. Also they commonly have face-to-face meetings (Hansen et al., 1999).

TABLE 9.1 Process and Practice Approaches to Knowledge Management

	Process Approach	Practice Approach
Type of knowledge supported	Explicit knowledge—codified in rules, tools, and processes (DeLong and Fahey, 2000).	Mostly tacit knowledge—unarticulated knowledge not easily captured or codified (Leonard and Sensiper, 1998).
Means of transmission	Formal controls, procedures, and standard operating procedures with heavy emphasis on information technologies to support knowledge creation, codification, and transfer of knowledge (Ruggles, 1998).	Informal social groups that engage in story telling and improvisation (Wenger and Snyder, 2000).
Benefits	Provides structure to harness generated ideas and knowledge (Brown and Duguid, 2000). Achieves scale in knowledge reuse (Hansen et al., 1999).	Provides an environment to generate and transfer high-value tacit knowledge (Brown and Duguid, 2000; Wenger and Snyder, 2000). Provides spark for fresh ideas and responsiveness to changing environment (Brown and Duguid, 2000).
Disadvantages	Fails to tap into tacit knowledge. May limit innovation and forces participants into fixed patterns of thinking.	Can result in inefficiency. Abundance of ideas with no structure to implement them.
Role of information technology	Heavy investment in IT to connect people with reusable codified knowledge (Hansen et al., 1999).	Moderate investment in IT to facilitate conversations and transfer of tacit knowledge (Hansen et al., 1999).

Table 9.1 summarizes the process and practice approaches.

In reality, a knowledge management initiative can, and probably will, involve both process and practice approaches. The two are not mutually exclusive. Alavi et al. (2003) describe the case of an organization that began its KM effort with a large repository but evolved the knowledge management initiative into a community-of-practice approach that existed side-by-side with the repository. In fact, community members would pass information from the community forum to the organizational repository when they felt that the knowledge was valuable outside their community. *IT at Work 9.2* illustrates how Monsanto successfully manages its knowledge using a combination of the two approaches.

9.4 INFORMATION TECHNOLOGY IN KNOWLEDGE MANAGEMENT

Knowledge management is more a methodology applied to business practices than a technology or product. Nevertheless, information technology is *crucial* to the success of every knowledge management system. Information technology enables KM by providing the enterprise architecture on which it is built.

Components of Knowledge Management Systems

Knowledge management systems are developed using three sets of technologies: *communication, collaboration,* and *storage and retrieval.*

Communication technologies allow users to access needed knowledge, and to communicate with each other—especially with experts. E-mail, the Internet,

IT at Work 9.2
CULTIVATING KNOWLEDGE AT MONSANTO

Following a series of mergers and divestitures in the late 1990s and early 2000s, Monsanto transformed itself from a chemical company into a leading life sciences and biotechnology firm. Today, along with a number of other products, Monsanto develops and produces seeds with impressive genetic traits, such as herbicide tolerance and insect protection. Not surprisingly, succeeding in this knowledge-intensive field requires Monsanto to focus on knowledge management.

Monsanto's board of directors realized the need for knowledge management quite early and readily approved a substantial investment in KM. In fact, one of the company's business units was specifically created to focus on growth opportunities by creating and enabling "a learning and sharing environment where knowledge and information are effectively used across the enterprise."

The objectives of knowledge management initiatives at Monsanto included connecting people with other knowledgeable people, connecting people with information, enabling the conversion of information to knowledge, encapsulating knowledge to make it easier to transfer, and distributing knowledge around the company.

Information technology played a crucial role in achieving these objectives. Data warehousing, full-text search engines, Internet/intranet capabilities, collaborative workgroup software, and other systems contributed to creating connections among knowledgeable people, as well as between people and sources of information. Information technology also helped the company create an enterprisewide infrastructure, which enabled end-user applications to tap into the structured and unstructured knowledge available throughout the organization. In addition to technology, Monsanto used dedicated "knowledge teams" that created and maintained the guide to the company's knowledge and served as points of contact for employees seeking information.

The wealth of tacit knowledge possessed by Monsanto's highly educated scientists and researchers was colossal. However, the prevailing culture in some parts of the organization rewarded employees for their individual, specialized expertise. As a result, employees guarded their knowledge carefully. Internal KM initiatives, supported by external consultants, managed to convince employees that it is their collective knowledge that brings power, rather than the knowledge of any particular individual.

The quality of Monsanto's knowledge management programs earned the company a place on the prestigious list of Most Admired Knowledge Enterprises. More importantly, active management of knowledge contributes to the company's performance, such as increasing the speed of obtaining regulatory approvals for its innovative products.

Source: Sharp (2003), Dash (1998), Junnarkar (1997), "Most Admired Knowledge Companies Recognized," (1999), and *monsanto.com* (accessed June 2004).

For Further Exploration: Monsanto employs a variety of KM initiatives related to its people, processes, and technology. Is this multifaceted method more effective than relying on a narrower, more focused program? Review the five objectives of knowledge management at Monsanto. Discuss which of them can be accomplished best with the practice approach to KM.

corporate intranets, and other Web-based tools provide communication capabilities. Even fax machines and the telephone are used for communication, especially when the practice approach to knowledge management is adopted.

Collaboration technologies provide the means to perform group work. Groups can work together on common documents at the same time (synchronous) or at different times (asynchronous), in the same place or in different places. This is especially important for members of a community of practice working on knowledge contributions. Collaborative computing capabilities such as electronic brainstorming enhance group work, especially for knowledge contribution. Additional forms of group work involve experts working with individuals trying to apply their knowledge. This requires collaboration at a fairly high level. Other collaborative computing systems allow an organization to create a virtual space so that individuals can work online anywhere and at any time.

Storage and retrieval technologies originally meant using a database management system to store and manage knowledge. This worked reasonably well in the early days for storing and managing most explicit knowledge, and even explicit knowledge about tacit knowledge. However, capturing, storing, and managing tacit knowledge usually requires a different set of tools. Electronic document management systems and specialized storage systems that are part of collaborative computing systems fill this void.

Technologies Supporting Knowledge Management

Several technologies have contributed to significant advances in knowledge management tools. Artificial intelligence, intelligent agents, knowledge discovery in databases, and Extensible Markup Language (XML) are examples of technologies that enable advanced functionality of modern knowledge management systems and form the base for future innovations in the KM field.

ARTIFICIAL INTELLIGENCE. In the definition of knowledge management, *artificial intelligence* (Chapter 11) is rarely mentioned. However, practically speaking, AI methods and tools are embedded in a number of knowledge management systems, either by vendors or by system developers.

AI methods can assist in identifying expertise, in eliciting knowledge automatically and semiautomatically, in interfacing through natural language processing, and in intelligent search through intelligent agents. AI methods, notably expert systems, neural networks, fuzzy logic, and intelligent agents, are used in knowledge management systems to perform various functions: They assist in and enhance searching knowledge (e.g., intelligent agents in Web searches), including scanning e-mail, documents, and databases and helping establish knowledge profiles of individuals and groups. They forecast future results using existing knowledge. AI methods help determine the relative importance of knowledge, when knowledge is both contributed to and accessed from the knowledge repository, and help determine meaningful relationships in the knowledge. They identify patterns in data (usually through neural networks), induce rules for expert systems, and provide advice directly from knowledge by using neural networks or expert systems. Finally, they provide a natural language or voice command–driven user interface for a knowledge management system.

INTELLIGENT AGENTS. *Intelligent agents* are software systems that learn how users work and provide assistance in their daily tasks. For example, when these software programs are told what the user wants to retrieve, passive agents can monitor incoming information for matches with user interests, and active agents can seek out information relevant to user preferences (Gray and Tehrani, 2003). Intelligent agents of various kinds are discussed in Chapter 11.

There are a number of ways that intelligent agents can help in knowledge management systems. Typically they are used to elicit and identify knowledge. Examples are:

- IBM (*ibm.com*) offers an intelligent data mining family, including Intelligent Decision Server (IDS), for finding and analyzing massive amounts of enterprise data.
- Gentia (Planning Sciences International, *gentia.com*) uses intelligent agents to facilitate data mining with Web access and data warehouse facilities.

- Convectis (HNC Software Inc.) uses neural networks to search text data and images, to discern the meaning of documents for an intelligent agent. This tool is used by InfoSeek, an Internet search engine, to speed up the creation of hierarchical directories of Web topics.

Combining intelligent agents with enterprise knowledge portals is a powerful technique that can deliver to a user exactly what he or she needs to perform his or her tasks. The intelligent agent learns what the user prefers to see, and how he or she organizes it. Then, the intelligent agent takes over to provide it at the desktop like a good administrative assistant would (King and Jones, 1995).

KNOWLEDGE DISCOVERY IN DATABASES. **Knowledge discovery in databases (KDD)** is a process used to search for and extract useful information from volumes of documents and data. It includes tasks known as knowledge extraction, data archaeology, data exploration, data pattern processing, data dredging, and information harvesting. All of these activities are conducted automatically and allow quick discovery, even by nonprogrammers. Data are often buried deep within very large databases, data warehouses, text documents, or knowledge repositories, all of which may contain data, information, and knowledge gathered over many years. *Data mining,* the process of searching for previously unknown information or relationships in large databases, is ideal for eliciting knowledge from databases, documents, e-mail, and so on. (For more on data mining, see Chapter 11.)

AI methods are useful data mining tools that include automated knowledge elicitation from other sources. Intelligent data mining discovers information within databases and other repositories that queries and reports cannot effectively reveal. Data mining tools find patterns in data and may even (automatically) infer rules from them. Patterns and rules can be used to guide decision making and forecast the effect of these decisions. KDD can also be used to identify the meaning of data or text, using KM tools that scan documents and e-mail to build an expertise profile of a firm's employees. Data mining can speed up analysis by providing needed knowledge.

Extending the role of data mining and knowledge discovery techniques for knowledge externalization, Bolloju et al. (2002) propose a framework for integrating knowledge management into enterprise environments for next-generation decision support systems. Their framework, shown in Figure 9.3 (page 380), includes **model marts** and **model warehouses.** Both of these are repositories of knowledge created by employing knowledge-discovery techniques on past decision instances stored in data repositories. Model marts are smaller versions of model warehouses. The model marts and model warehouses capture operational and historical decision models. For example, a model mart can store decision rules corresponding to problem-solving knowledge of different decision makers in a particular domain, such as loan approvals in a banking environment. (As you will discover in Chapter 11, model marts and model warehouses are for models analogous to data marts and data warehouses for data.)

This integrated decision support–knowledge management framework accommodates different types of knowledge transformations proposed by Nonaka and Takeuchi (1995). Systems built around this framework are expected to enhance the quality of support provided to decision makers; to support knowledge management functions such as acquisition, creation, exploitation, and accumulation;

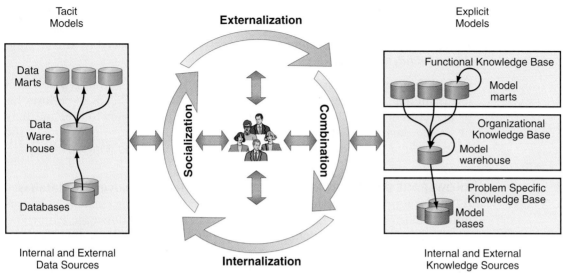

FIGURE 9.3 Framework for integrating decision support and knowledge management systems. (*Source:* Bolloju et al., 2001.)

to facilitate discovery of trends and patterns in the accumulated knowledge; and to provide means for building up organizational memory.

EXTENSIBLE MARKUP LANGUAGE (XML). *EXtensible Markup Language (XML)* enables standardized representations of data structures, so that data can be processed appropriately by heterogeneous systems without case-by-case programming. This method suits e-commerce applications and supply chain management systems that operate across enterprise boundaries. XML not only can automate processes and reduce paperwork, but also can unite business partners and supply chains for better collaboration and knowledge transfer. XML-based messages can be taken from back-end repositories and fed out through the portal interface and back again. A portal that uses XML allows the company to communicate better with its customers, linking them in a virtual demand chain, where changes in customer requirements are immediately reflected in production plans. Due to its potential to tremendously simplify systems integration, XML may become the universal language that all portal vendors embrace (see Ruber, 2001). (For more technical details on XML, see Technology Guide 2.)

Vendors are quickly moving to integrate the advantages offered by XML standards. For example, Interwoven's content management software, Teamsite, now fully supports XML, enabling organizations to provide content available in any format across the enterprise. Sequoia Software's XML Portal Server (XPS) and Hummingbird's Enterprise Portal Suite also support the XML standard for data exchange.

Technology Guides are located at the book's Web site.

9.5 KNOWLEDGE MANAGEMENT SYSTEMS IMPLEMENTATION

The KMS challenge is to identify and integrate the three essential components—communication technologies, collaboration technologies, and storage and retrieval technologies—to meet the knowledge management needs of an organization. The earliest knowledge management systems were developed with networked technology (intranets), collaborative computing tools (groupware), and databases (for the knowledge repository). They were constructed from a variety of off-the-shelf IT components (e.g., see Ruggles, 1998). Many organizations, especially large management consulting firms like Accenture and J.D. Edwards, developed their knowledge architecture with a set of tools that provided the three technology types. Collaborative computing suites such as Lotus Notes/Domino Server provide many KMS capabilities. Other systems were developed by integrating a set of tools from a single or multiple vendors. For example, J.D. Edwards used a set of loosely integrated Microsoft tools and products to implement its Knowledge Garden KMS, as did KPMG.

In the early 2000s, KMS technology has evolved to integrate the three components into a single package. These include enterprise knowledge portals and knowledge management suites.

Knowledge Management Products and Vendors

Technology tools that support knowledge management are called **knowware.** Most knowledge management software packages include one or more of the following seven tools: collaborative computing tools, knowledge servers, enterprise knowledge portals, electronic document management systems, knowledge harvesting tools, search engines, and knowledge management suites. Many packages provide several tools because several are necessary in an effective knowledge management system. For example, most electronic document management systems also include collaborative computing capabilities.

Knowledge management systems can be purchased in whole or in part from one of numerous software development companies and enterprise information systems vendors, they can be acquired through major consulting firms, or they can be outsourced to the application service providers (ASPs). All three alternatives will be discussed in the latter part of this chapter.

SOFTWARE DEVELOPMENT COMPANIES AND ENTERPRISE INFORMATION SYSTEMS VENDORS. Software development companies and enterprise information systems vendors offer numerous knowledge management packages, from individual tools to comprehensive knowledge management suites. The variety of knowware that is readily available on the market allows companies to find the tools that will meet their unique knowledge management needs. Following is a review of some software packages and their vendors in each of the seven knowware categories cited earlier.

Collaborative Computing Tools. Collaboration tools, or groupware, were the first used to enhance tacit knowledge transfer within an organization. One of the earliest collaborative computing systems, GroupSystems, provides many of the tools that support group work, including electronic brainstorming and idea categorization. Lotus Notes/Domino Server provides an enterprisewide collaborative environment. Other collaboration tools include MeetingPlace (Latitude), QuickPlace (Lotus Development Corp.), eRoom Documentum (Documentum), and PlaceWare (PlaceWare Inc.).

Knowledge Servers. A knowledge server contains the main knowledge management software, including the knowledge repository, and provides access to other knowledge, information, and data. Examples of knowledge servers include the Hummingbird Knowledge Server, the Intraspect Software Knowledge Server, the Hyperwave Information Server, the Sequoia Software XML Portal Server, and

Autonomy's Intelligent Data Operating Layer (IDOL) Server. Autonomy's IDOL Server connects people to content, content to content, and people to people through modules that enable organizations to integrate various personalization, collaboration, and retrieval features. The server provides a **knowledge repository,** a central location for searching and accessing information from many sources, such as the Internet, corporate intranets, databases, and file systems, thereby enabling the efficient distribution of time-sensitive information. The server seamlessly extends and integrates with the company's e-business suite, allowing rapid deployment applications that span the enterprise and leverage AI-assisted technology to harvest knowledge assets.

Enterprise Knowledge Portals. *Enterprise knowledge portals (EKPs)* are the doorways into many knowledge management systems. They have evolved from the concepts underlying executive information systems, group support systems, Web-browsers, and database management systems. According to an IDC report, individuals may spend as much as 30 percent of their time looking for information (Ziff-Davis, 2002). An enterprise knowledge portal presents a single access point for a vast body of explicit information, such as project plans, functional requirements, technical specifications, white papers, training materials, and customer feedback survey data (Kesner, 2003).

Enterprise knowledge portals are a means of organizing the many sources of unstructured information in an organization. Most combine data integration, reporting mechanisms, and collaboration, while document and knowledge management is handled by a server. The portal aggregates each user's total information needs: data and documents, e-mail, Web links and queries, dynamic feeds from the network, and shared calendars and task lists. The personal information portal has evolved into an enterprise knowledge portal (Silver, 2000).

One highly successful portal is Cisco's Employee Connection. The portal provides any time, anywhere access to the company's intranet; it has been credited with helping save the company $551 million, thanks primarily to improved self-service (Anderson, 2002). The intent of the system is to connect as many systems and applications as possible so that the user has a single entree into all of Cisco's information systems (Anderson, 2002).

When enterprise information portals first entered the market, they did not contain knowledge management features. Now, most do. Leading portal vendors include Autonomy, Brio, Corechange, Dataware, Intraspect, Hummingbird, InXight, IBM/Lotus, Knowmadic, OpenText, Plumtree, Verity, Viador, and Vignette. Database vendors such as Microsoft, Oracle, and Sybase are also selling knowledge portals. Portals can range in cost from less than $500,000 to $8 million (Steinberg, 2002).

The Knowledge Center (from KnowledgeTrack) offers integrated business-to-business (B2B) functions and can scale from dot-coms to large enterprises. Knowledge Center can be built into the enterprise architecture instead of simply sitting on top, the way most intranet portals do. The Knowledge Center integrates with external data sources including ERP, online analytical processing (OLAP) (see Chapter 10), and CRM systems (see Chapter 7). Knowledge Center supports communities of practice and enables them for large project management, allowing information to be shared among all of the extended enterprise value chains.

Hyperwave's Hyperwave Information Portal (HIP) aggregates information from disparate sources and features dynamic link management, which verifies the quality of the link and hides links to unauthorized content. HIP manages

IT at Work 9.3
PORTAL OPENS THE DOOR TO LEGAL KNOWLEDGE

Gowling Lafleur Henderson LLP *(gowlings.com)* is an international law firm based in Canada, which has recently expanded via mergers. As the firm became larger, formal knowledge management initiatives replaced the informal knowledge exchange that took place naturally in smaller groups. Currently, Karen Bell, knowledge management counsel at Gowlings, is responsible for the "development and implementation of a firmwide integrated program to capture, share, and leverage the firm's collective knowledge."

Although the need for active knowledge management became more pronounced after the merger, the challenge of knowledge management is not new for law firms. In fact, Smith Lyons, a Canadian law firm that merged with Gowlings in 2001, has been facing the challenge of managing the knowledge contained in its documents for a long time.

Prior to the merger, Richard Van Dyk, CIO of Smith Lyons, spent a year defining the requirements of a system to manage the firm's documents and knowledge. He wanted to take thousands of pieces of information, give people different views into that information, and have a high level of link management. Van Dyk considered document management tools to be too inflexible for the way lawyers practice law. "We needed a flexible environment that we could massage and manipulate and that would allow people to continue working as they have," says Van Dyk.

"Lawyers are basically document generators," he says. "Due to time constraints, they spend more time collecting documents than organizing them." Because the firm's 550 attorneys and support specialists each had a distinct working methodology, often reflecting the requirements of a specific area of practice, Van Dyk knew they would resent having a rigid system they could not easily personalize.

The profusion of document management, knowledge management, and portal systems makes finding the right product difficult. Each has its strengths and weaknesses. Organizations coming from a document-centric perspective, like Smith Lyons, need to organize and manage content at the back end while developing highly customized individual user interfaces at the front end.

The solution that best met Van Dyk's criteria was the Hyperwave Information Portal from Hyperwave Information Management of Westford, Massachusetts. "What I liked about Hyperwave's portal environment was that as soon as we installed it, we had a framework to begin knowledge mapping—tagging and indexing documents by subject and key words and phrases—and for building the database structures in our repositories," says Van Dyk. The firm had definite ideas on how to structure templates and specific pieces of information that are unique to a legal practice. These issues included myriad legal forms and documents generated by the proprietary software applications used for different practice areas.

Once the portal was set up, Smith Lyons' developers began to customize the views for each desktop PC by creating wizards that connect users to their own secure information areas and to intranet pages containing company activity information. "That flexibility in building our DM portal allowed Smith Lyons lawyers and specialists to be incredibly specific in their searches," says Van Dyk. Lawyers also could share their accumulated knowledge more easily with colleagues in the same practice areas, by referencing legal citations, court decisions, and winning strategies that had worked in the past.

Today, Gowlings continues to emphasize the importance of document management. Each document at Gowlings is stored with a name, an identifying number, the name of its author, the client it was prepared for, the practice area, and a description. Lawyers in any of the firm's offices can use these fields to search for documents and unlock the explicit knowledge of their colleagues.

Source: Ruber (2000), Buckler (2004), and *gowlings.com* (accessed May 2004).

For Further Exploration: How is the practice of law different from the operations of other businesses? How can enterprise knowledge portals benefit the entire legal system (courts, and so on)?

connections between information sources and makes structured and unstructured corporate information searchable via a standard browser. See *IT at Work 9.3* about how a Canadian law firm developed a successful enterprise knowledge portal. For more on such portals, see Collins (2001), Liautaud and Hammond (2000), and *InfoWorld* (2000).

Electronic Document Management. Electronic document management (EDM) systems focus on the document in electronic form as the collaborative focus of work. EDM systems allow users to access needed documents, generally via a Web-browser over a corporate intranet. EDM systems enable organizations to better manage documents and workflow for smoother operations. They also allow collaboration on document creation and revision.

Many knowledge management systems use an EDM system as the knowledge repository. There is a natural fit in terms of the purpose and benefits of the two. For example, Pfizer uses a large-scale document management system to handle the equivalent of truckloads of paper documents of drug approval applications passed between Pfizer and the FDA, its regulating agency. This EDM system dramatically cut the time required for FDA submission and review, making Pfizer more competitive in getting new and effective drugs to market (Blodgett, 2000).

Systems like DocuShare (Xerox Corporation) and Lotus Notes (Lotus Development Corporation) allow direct collaboration on a common document. Some other EDM systems include Documentum (Documentum Inc.), ViewStar (eiStream), FYI (Identitech), FileNet Content Manager (FileNet Corporation), Livelink (Open Text Corporation), PaperPort (ScanSoft Inc.), and CaseCentral.com (Document Repository Inc.).

Knowledge Harvesting Tools. Tools for capturing knowledge unobtrusively are helpful since they allow a knowledge contributor to be minimally (or not at all) involved in the knowledge-harvesting efforts. Embedding this type of tool in a KMS is an ideal approach to knowledge capture.

For example, Tacit Knowledge Systems' KnowledgeMail is an expertise-location software package that analyzes users' outgoing e-mail to parse subject expertise. It maintains a directory of expertise and offers ways to contact experts, while maintaining privacy controls for those experts. Autonomy's Active-Knowledge performs a similar analysis on e-mail and other standard document types. Intraspect Software's Intraspect platform monitors an organization's group memory, captures the context of its use (such as who used it, when, for what, how it was combined with other information, and what people said about it), and then makes the information available for sharing and reuse.

Search Engines. Search engines perform one of the essential functions of knowledge management—locating and retrieving necessary documents from vast collections accumulated in corporate repositories. Companies like Google, Verity, and Inktomi are offering a wide selection of search engines that are capable of indexing and cataloging files in various formats as well as retrieving and prioritizing relevant documents in response to user queries.

Knowledge Management Suites. Knowledge management suites are complete knowledge management solutions out-of-the-box. They integrate the communications, collaboration, and storage technologies into a single convenient package. A knowledge management suite must still access internal databases and other external knowledge sources, so some integration is required to make the software truly functional. Knowledge management suites are powerful approaches to developing a KMS because they offer one user interface, one data repository, and one vendor.

IBM/Lotus offers an extensive range of knowledge management products: the Domino platform, QuickPlace and Sametime, Discovery Server, and Learning Space, as well as the WebSphere portal. See *IT at Work 9.4* to learn how Commerce Bank implemented a knowledge management system based on the IBM/Lotus platform.

IT at Work 9.4
FINDING THE RIGHT ANSWERS WITH KNOWLEDGE MANAGEMENT

Commerce Bank (*commerceonline.com*) is a $15.4 billion financial institution that is quickly growing to become a dominant player in the financial services market of Philadelphia and southern New Jersey. During 30 years of its existence, it has developed a network of 214 branches and made ambitious plans for continuous growth. Commerce Bank names itself "America's Most Convenient Bank." It lives up to that name by maintaining a strong banking network and by empowering each branch to make business decisions in an effort to better meet the needs of its customers.

While undergoing explosive growth, Commerce Bank encouraged its associates to learn all about the customers and the right ways to service them. However, the company realized that its most important asset, knowledge, was locked away in file cabinets and in the heads of its associates. In order to support this initiative, Commerce Bank needed to tap into that knowledge and find a way to train employees consistently and conveniently across the entire branch network.

The first step for new employees is Commerce University, a "boot camp" where they are instilled with the fundamentals of customer service. But the program covers only a few of the range of issues that an associate might encounter.

The need for knowledge management at Commerce Bank was apparent. Jack Allison, VP of Systems Development, said, "We had folks in administration who could spend 70 percent of their time answering calls and clarifying answers for branches. At times, we could wait weeks or months for the right answer to certain questions. Knowing that training may not give answers for every scenario, we needed to give associates a tool that could help them find any answer to any topic at any time."

Commerce Bank envisioned a solution—a workflow-based knowledge management system that could provide instant answers to questions for the bank's employees and online customers. To make this vision a reality, Commerce chose to develop a system based on IBM's Lotus Notes, which the bank had been using since 1995. Using IBM's Domino server, the Lotus Notes client, and an application development toolkit, Commerce Bank created a full-fledged knowledge management system, called Wow Answer Guide.

Introduced in 2000, Wow Answer Guide provides a central repository of knowledge about all bank transactions, helps employees learn a process and respond to customer inquiries, and stores information electronically. In addition, the system allows employees to register for the bank's continuing education courses.

The complete Wow Answer Guide contains more than 400 applications, and Commerce plans to add even more, such as a customer relationship management system. The flexibility of the platform simplifies application development and allows adding new features and expanding functionality with minimal investments of time and effort. By drawing on the power of the Domino platform, Commerce Bank created workflow-based applications that streamline internal knowledge sharing and that route data and information to the appropriate employees within the organization. This dramatically reduces the completion time for approval-intensive transactions, improves the bank's capacity, and minimizes labor costs.

"[Wow Answer Guide] is especially good for the green associate, or the veteran who is still learning how to process a new product," says Allison. "We don't want our associates on a scavenger hunt to get the correct information."

Commerce Bank realized that knowledge management would be beneficial not only to the bank's employees, but also to the bank's clients. "We wanted to put information in our customers' hands so they could conduct [online] transactions with confidence," said Allison. In the summer of 2000, Commerce Bank deployed a new version of Wow Answer Guide that empowered the bank's online customers.

Knowledge management at Commerce Bank proved to be an effective investment. According to Allison, the application has saved the bank $20,000 per week, or approximately $1 million a year. In fact, the bank achieved a return on its investment within a month of launching Wow Answer Guide.

Source: Adapted from Amato-McCoy (2003) and *commerceonline.com* (accessed May 2004).

For Further Exploration: How do knowledge requirements of bank employees differ from those of bank customers? How would these differences influence the functionality of knowledge management systems designed to serve these two groups of users?

Several vendors also provide fairly comprehensive sets of tools for KM initiatives, which include Dataware Knowledge Management Suite, KnowledgeX by KnowledgeX, Inc., and many others. Autonomy Knowledge Management Suite offers document categorization and workflow integration. Microsoft provides central components of knowledge management solutions, and is working on developing an encompassing KM framework. Some enterprise information systems vendors, such as SAP, PeopleSoft, and Oracle, are developing knowledge-management-related technologies as a platform for business applications. Siebel Systems is repositioning itself as a business-to-employee knowledge management platform.

CONSULTING FIRMS. All of the major consulting firms (Accenture, Ernst & Young, and so on) have massive internal knowledge management initiatives. Usually these become products after they succeed internally and provide assistance in establishing knowledge management systems and measuring their effectiveness. Consulting firms also provide some direct, out-of-the-box proprietary systems for vertical markets. Most of the major consulting firms define their knowledge management offerings as a *service*. For more on consulting firm activities and products, see McDonald and Shand (2000).

KNOWLEDGE MANAGEMENT APPLICATION SERVICE PROVIDERS. Application service providers (ASPs) have evolved as a form of KMS outsourcing on the Web. There are many ASPs for e-commerce on the market.

For example, Communispace is a high-level ASP collaboration system that focuses on connecting people to people (not just people to documents) to achieve specific objectives, regardless of geographic, time, and organizational barriers. As a hosted ASP solution, it is easy to rapidly deploy within organizations. Unlike conventional KM systems that organize data and documents, or chat rooms where people simply swap information, Communispace contains a rich assortment of interactions, activities, and tools that connect people to the colleagues who can best help them make decisions, solve problems, and learn quickly. Communispace is designed to build trust online. It attempts to make a community self-conscious about taking responsibility for its actions and knowledge. Its Climate component helps participants to measure and understand how people are feeling about the community. The Virtual Café gives dispersed employees a way to meet and learn about each other through pictures and profiles.

A recent trend among application service providers is to offer a complete knowledge management solution, including a KM suite and the consulting to set it up.

Integration of KM Systems with Other Business Information Systems

Since a knowledge management system is an enterprise system, it must be integrated with other enterprise and other information systems in an organization. Obviously, when it is designed and developed, it cannot be perceived as an add-on application. It must be truly integrated into other systems. Through the structure of the organizational culture (changed if necessary), a knowledge management system and its activities can be directly integrated into a firm's business processes. For example, a group involved in customer support can capture its knowledge to provide help on customers' difficult problems. In this case, help-desk software would be one type of package to integrate into a KMS, especially into the knowledge repository.

Since a KMS can be developed on a knowledge platform consisting of communication, collaboration, and storage technologies, and most firms already have many such tools and technologies in place, it is often possible to develop a KMS in the organization's existing tools (e.g., Lotus Notes/Domino Server). Or, an enterprise knowledge portal can provide universal access and an interface into all of an individual's relevant corporate information and knowledge. In this case, the KMS effort would provide the linkage for everyone into the entire enterprise information system.

In the remainder of this section, we look at how KM systems can be integrated with other types of business information systems.

INTEGRATION WITH DECISION SUPPORT SYSTEMS. Knowledge management systems typically do not involve running models to solve problems, which is an activity typically done in decision support systems (DSSs). However, since a knowledge management system provides help in solving problems by applying knowledge, part of the solution may involve running models. A KMS could integrate into an appropriate set of models and data and activate them, when a specific problem may call for it.

INTEGRATION WITH ARTIFICIAL INTELLIGENCE. Knowledge management has a natural relationship with artificial intelligence (AI) methods and software, though knowledge management, strictly speaking, is not an artificial intelligence method. There are a number of ways in which knowledge management and artificial intelligence can integrate. For example, if the knowledge stored in a KMS is to be represented and used as a sequence of if-then-else rules, then an expert system becomes part of the KMS (see Rasmus, 2000). An expert system could also assist a user in identifying how to apply a chunk of knowledge in the KMS.

Much work is being done in the field of artificial intelligence relating to knowledge engineering, tacit-to-explicit knowledge transfer, knowledge identification, understanding, dissemination, and so on. Companies are attempting to realign these technologies and resultant products with knowledge management. The AI technologies most often integrated with knowledge management are intelligent agents, expert systems, neural networks, and fuzzy logic. Several specific methods and tools were described earlier.

INTEGRATION WITH DATABASES AND INFORMATION SYSTEMS. Since a KMS utilizes a knowledge repository, sometimes constructed out of a database system or an electronic document management system, it can automatically integrate to this part of the firm's information system. As data and information updates are made, the KMS can utilize them. Knowledge management systems also attempt to glean knowledge from documents and databases (knowledge discovery in databases) through artificial intelligence methods, as was described earlier.

INTEGRATION WITH CUSTOMER RELATIONSHIP MANAGEMENT SYSTEMS. Customer relationship management (CRM) systems help users in dealing with customers. One aspect is the help-desk notion described earlier. But CRM goes much deeper. It can develop usable profiles of customers and predict their needs, so that an organization can increase sales and better serve its clients. A KMS can certainly provide tacit knowledge to people who use CRM directly in working with customers.

INTEGRATION WITH SUPPLY CHAIN MANAGEMENT SYSTEMS. The supply chain is often considered to be the logistics end of the business. If products do not move through the organization and go out the door, the firm will fail. So it is important to optimize the supply chain and manage it properly. As discussed in Chapter 7, supply chain management (SCM) systems attempt to do so. SCM can benefit through integration with KMS because there are many issues and problems in the supply chain that require the company to combine both tacit and explicit knowledge. Accessing such knowledge will directly improve supply chain performance.

INTEGRATION WITH CORPORATE INTRANETS AND EXTRANETS. Communication and collaboration tools and technologies are necessary for KMS to function. KMS is not simply integrated with the technology of intranets and extranets, but is typically developed on them as the communications platform. Extranets are specifically designed to enhance the collaboration of a firm with its suppliers and sometimes with customers. If a firm can integrate its KMS into its intranets and extranets, knowledge will flow more freely, both from a contributor and to a user (either directly or through a knowledge repository), and the firm also can capture knowledge directly with little user involvement and can deliver it when the system "thinks" that a user needs knowledge.

9.6 ROLES OF PEOPLE IN KNOWLEDGE MANAGEMENT

Managing a knowledge management system requires great effort. Like any other information technology, getting it started, implemented, and deployed requires a champion's effort. Many issues of management, people, and culture must be considered to make a knowledge management system a success. In this section, we address those issues.

Managing the knowledge repository typically requires a full-time staff, similar to a reference-library staff. This staff examines, structures, filters, catalogues, and stores knowledge so that it is meaningful and can be accessed by the people who need it. The staff assists individuals in searching for knowledge and performs "environmental scanning": If they identify specific knowledge that an employee or client might need, they send it directly to them, thus adding value to the organization. (This is standard procedure for Accenture knowledge management personnel.) Finally, the knowledge repository staff may create communities of practice (see Minicase 1) to gather individuals with common knowledge areas to identify, filter, extract, and contribute knowledge to a knowledge repository.

Most of the issues concerning the success, implementation, and effective use of a knowledge management system are people issues. And since a knowledge management system is an enterprisewide effort, many people need to be involved in it (Robb, 2003). They include the chief knowledge officer (CKO), the CEO, the other officers and managers of the organization, members and leaders of communities of practice, KMS developers, and KMS staff. Each person or group has an important role in either the development, management, or use of a KMS. By far, the CKO has the most visible role in a KMS effort, but the system cannot succeed unless the roles of all the players are established and understood. Ensuring that a KM team is properly constituted is therefore an essential factor in the success of any KM initiative (Robb, 2003).

The Chief Knowledge Officer

Knowledge management projects that involve establishing a knowledge environment conducive to the transfer, creation, or use of knowledge attempt to build *cultural receptivity.* These attempts are centered on changing the behavior of the firm to embrace the use of knowledge management. Behavioral-centric projects require a high degree of support and participation from the senior management of the organization to facilitate their implementation. Most firms developing knowledge management systems have created a knowledge management officer, a **chief knowledge officer (CKO),** at the senior level. The objectives of the CKO's role are to maximize the firm's knowledge assets, design and implement knowledge management strategies, effectively exchange knowledge assets internally and externally, and promote system use.

A chief knowledge officer must do the following (adapted from Duffy, 1998):

● Set strategic priorities for knowledge management.
● Establish a knowledge repository of best practices.
● Gain a commitment from senior executives to support a learning environment.
● Teach information seekers how to ask better and smarter questions.
● Establish a process for managing intellectual assets.
● Obtain customer satisfaction information in near real time.
● Globalize knowledge management.

The CKO is responsible for defining the area of knowledge within the firm that will be the focal point, based on the mission and objectives of the firm (Davis, 1998). The CKO is responsible for standardizing the enterprisewide vocabulary and for controlling the knowledge directory. This is critical in areas that must share knowledge across departments, to ensure uniformity. CKOs must get a handle on the company's repositories of research, resources, and expertise, including where they are stored and who manages and accesses them. (That is, the CKO must perform a *knowledge audit.*) Then the CKO must encourage "pollination" (sharing of knowledge) among disparate workgroups with complementary resources.

The CKO is responsible for creating an infrastructure and cultural environment for knowledge sharing. He or she must assign or identify the *knowledge champions* within the business units. The CKO's job is to manage the content their group produces (e.g., the Chrysler Tech Clubs in Minicase 1), continually add to the knowledge base, and encourage their colleagues to do the same. Successful CKOs should have the full and enthusiastic support of their managers and of top management. Ultimately, the CKO is responsible for the entire knowledge management project while it is under development, and then for management of the system and the knowledge once it is deployed.

CEO, Officers, and Managers of the Organization

Vis-à-vis knowledge management, the CEO is responsible for championing the KM effort. He or she must ensure that a competent and capable CKO is found and that the CKO can obtain all the resources (including access to people with knowledge sources) needed to make the project a success. The CEO must also gain organization-wide support for the contribution to and use of the KMS. The CEO must also prepare the organization for the cultural changes that are expected to occur when the KMS is implemented. Support for the KMS and the CKO is the critical responsibility of the CEO.

The various other officers in the organization generally must make resources available to the CKO so that he or she can get the job done. The chief financial officer (CFO) must ensure that the financial resources are available. The chief operating officer (COO) must ensure that people begin to embed knowledge management practices into their daily work processes. There is a special relationship between the CKO and chief information officer (CIO). Usually the CIO is responsible for the IT vision of the organization and for the IT architecture, including databases and other potential knowledge sources. The CIO must cooperate with the CKO in making these resources available. KMSs are expensive propositions, and it is wise to use existing systems if they are available and capable.

Managers must also support the KM effort and provide access to sources of knowledge. In many KMSs, managers are an integral part of the communities of practice.

Communities of Practice

The success of many KM systems has been attributed to the active involvement of the people who contribute to and benefit from using the knowledge. Consequently, communities of practice have appeared within organizations that are serious about their knowledge management efforts. As discussed earlier, a *community of practice (COP)* is a group of people in an organization with a common professional interest. Ideally, all the KMS users should each be in at least one COP. Creating and nurturing COPs properly is one key to KMS success.

In a sense, a community of practice "owns" the knowledge that it contributes, because it manages the knowledge on its way into the system, and as owner, must approve modifications to it. The community is responsible for the accuracy and timeliness of the knowledge it contributes and for identifying its potential use.

A number of researchers have investigated how successful COPs form and function. One study, by Storck and Hill (2000), investigated one of the earliest communities of practice, at Xerox. When established at Xerox, the COP was a new organizational form. The word *community* captured the sense of responsible, independent action that characterized the group, which continued to function within the standard boundaries of the large organization. Management sponsored the community, but did not mandate it. Community members were volunteers. For more on communities of practice, see Barth (2000a), Cothrel and Williams (1999a, 1999b), Eisenhart (2000), and Smith and McKeen (2003).

KMS Developers

KMS developers are the team members who actually develop the system. They work for the CKO. Some are organizational experts who develop strategies to promote and manage the organizational culture shift. Others are involved in system software and hardware selection, programming, testing, deploying, and maintaining the system. Still others initially are involved in training users. Eventually the training function moves to the KMS staff.

KMS Staff

Enterprisewide KM systems require a full-time staff to catalogue and manage the knowledge. This staff is either located at the firm's headquarters or dispersed throughout the organization in the knowledge centers. Most large consulting firms have more than one knowledge center.

Earlier we described the function of the staff to be similar to that of reference librarians. They actually do much more. Some members are functional-area experts who are now cataloguing and approving knowledge contributions, and pushing the knowledge out to clients and employees who they believe can use the knowledge. These functional experts may also work in a liaison role with the functional areas of the communities of practice. Others work with users to train them on the system or help them with their searches. Still others work on improving the system's performance by identifying better methods with which to manage knowledge. For example, Ernst & Young has 250 people managing the knowledge repository and assisting people in finding knowledge at its Center for Business Knowledge. Some staff members disseminate knowledge, while others are liaisons with the 40 practice areas. They codify and store documents in their areas of expertise (see Hansen et al., 1999).

9.7 ENSURING SUCCESS OF KM EFFORTS

Organizations can gain several benefits from implementing a knowledge management strategy. Tactically, they can accomplish some or all of the following: reduce loss of intellectual capital due to people leaving the company; reduce costs by decreasing the number of times the company must repeatedly solve the same problem, and by achieving economies of scale in obtaining information from external providers; reduce redundancy of knowledge-based activities; increase productivity by making knowledge available more quickly and easily; and increase employee satisfaction by enabling greater personal development and empowerment. The best reason of all may be a strategic need to gain a *competitive advantage* in the marketplace (Knapp, 1998).

Knowledge Management Valuation

In general, companies take either an asset-based approach to knowledge management valuation or one that links knowledge to its applications and business benefits (Skyrme and Amidon, 1998). The former approach starts with the identification of intellectual assets and then focuses management's attention on increasing their value. The second uses variants of a *balanced scorecard*, where financial measures are balanced against customer, process, and innovation measures. Among the best-developed financial measurement methods in use are the balanced-scorecard approach, Skandia's Navigator, Stern Stewart's economic value added (EVA®), M'Pherson's inclusive valuation methodology, the return on management ratio, and Levin's knowledge capital measure. See Skyrme and Amidon (1998) for details on how these measures work in practice.

Another method of measuring the value of knowledge is to estimate its price if it were offered for sale. Most firms are reluctant to sell knowledge, unless they are expressly in the business of doing so. Generally a firm's knowledge is an asset that has competitive value, and if it leaves the organization, the firm loses its competitive advantage. However, it is possible to price the knowledge and the access to the knowledge in order to make it worth a firm's while to sell it. For example, American Airlines' Decision Technologies Corp. grew from a small internal analysis team in the 1970s. Initially the team was created to solve problems and provide decision support to American Airlines only. As it grew, it became an independent corporation within AMR Corp., and it began to provide consulting and systems to other airlines, including American's competitors. AMR evidently had decided that the revenue it could obtain by selling some knowledge overrode any competitive advantage it would lose by doing so. The major consulting firms are in the business of selling expertise. Their knowledge management efforts, which often began as internal systems, evolved into quite valuable systems that their clients use on a regular basis.

Success indicators with respect to knowledge management are similar to those for assessing the effectiveness of other business-change projects. They include growth in the resources attached to the project, growth in the volume of knowledge content and usage, the likelihood that the project will survive without the support of a particular individual or individuals, and some evidence of financial return either for the knowledge management activity itself or for the entire organization (Davenport et al., 1998).

There are in general two types of measures that can be used to assess the effectiveness of a KM initiative: results-oriented and activity-oriented (O'Dell et al., 2003). The results-oriented measures are financial in nature and might include such things as increase in goods sold. The activities-based measures consider how frequently users are accessing knowledge or contributing to knowledge (O'Dell et al., 2003).

FINANCIAL METRICS.   Even though traditional accounting measures are incomplete for measuring KM, they are often used as a quick justification for a knowledge management initiative. Returns on investment (ROIs) are reported to range from 20:1 for chemical firms to 4:1 for transportation firms, with an average of 12:1, based on the knowledge management projects assisted on by one consulting firm (Abramson, 1998). In order to measure the impact of knowledge management, experts recommend focusing KM projects on specific business problems that can be easily quantified. When the problems are solved, the value and benefits of the system become apparent and often can be measured (MacSweeney, 2002).

At Royal Dutch/Shell group, the return on investment was explicitly documented: The company had invested $6 million in a knowledge management system in 1999 and within two years obtained $235 million in reduced costs and new revenues (King, 2001). Hewlett-Packard offers another example of documented financial returns: Within six months of launching its @HP companywide portal in October 2000, Hewlett-Packard realized a $50 million return on its initial investment of $20 million. This was largely due to a reduction in volume of calls to internal call centers and to the new paperless processes (Roberts-Witt, 2002).

The financial benefit might be perceptual, rather than absolute, but it need not be documented in order for the KM system to be considered a success.

NONFINANCIAL METRICS.   Traditional ways of financial measurement may fall short when measuring the value of a KMS, because *they do not consider intellectual capital an asset.* Therefore there is a need to develop procedures for valuing the *intangible* assets of an organization, as well as to incorporate models of intellectual capital that in some way quantify innovation and the development and implementation of core competencies.

When evaluating intangibles, there are a number of new ways to view capital. In the past, only customer goodwill was valued as an asset. Now the following are also included (adapted from Allee, 1999):

- *External relationship capital:* how an organization links with its partners, suppliers, customers, regulators, and so on
- *Structural capital:* systems and work processes that leverage competitiveness, such as information systems, and so on
- *Human capital:* the individual capabilities, knowledge, skills, and so on, that people have
- *Social capital:* the quality and value of relationships with the larger society
- *Environmental capital:* the value of relationships with the environment

For example, a knowledge management initiative undertaken by Partners HealthCare System, Inc. has not resulted in quantifiable financial benefits, but has greatly increased the social capital of the company. The knowledge management system for physicians implemented by Partners reduced the number of serious medication errors by 55 percent at some of Boston's most prestigious teaching hospitals. Calculating return on investment for such a system turns out to be an extremely difficult proposition, which is why only a small fraction of hospitals use similar systems. While the company is unable to determine how the system affects its bottom line, it is willing to justify the costs based on the system's benefits to society (Melymuka, 2002).

Causes of KM Failure

No system is infallible. There are many cases of knowledge management failing. Estimates of KM failure rates range from 50 percent to 70 percent, where a failure is interpreted to mean that *all* of the major objectives were not met by the effort (Ambrosio, 2000).

Some reasons for failure include having too much information that is not easily searchable (Steinberg, 2002) and having inadequate or incomplete information in the system so that identifying the real expertise in an organization becomes foggy (Desouza, 2003). Failure may also result from an inability to capture and categorize knowledge as well as from the overmanagement of the KM process such that creativity and communities of practice are stifled (Desouza, 2003). Other issues include lack of commitment (this occurred at a large Washington, D.C., constituent lobbying organization), not providing incentive for people to use the system (as occurred at Pillsbury Co.; see Barth, 2000b, and Silver, 2000), and an overemphasis on technology at the expense of larger knowledge and people issues (Hislop, 2002). *IT at Work 9.5* (page 394) illustrates how Frito-Lay narrowly avoided failure of its KMS.

Factors Leading to KM Success

To increase the probability of success of knowledge management projects, companies must assess whether there is a strategic need for knowledge management in the first place. The next step is to determine whether the current process of dealing with organizational knowledge is adequate and whether the organization's culture is ready for procedural changes. Only when these issues are resolved should the company consider technology infrastructure and decide if a new system is needed. When the right technological solution is chosen, it becomes necessary to properly introduce the system to the entire organization and to gain participation of every employee (Kaplan, 2002).

IT at Work 9.5

ESCAPING A KNOWLEDGE MANAGEMENT FAILURE

The opening case described the successful KM portal to assist Frito-Lay's sales teams. Here we describe the near brush with failure that preceded the successful implementation of Frito-Lay's knowledge portal.

Frito-Lay selected a pilot sales team to describe the kinds of knowledge they needed. The requests ranged from simple information, such as why Frito-Lay merchandises Lays and Ruffles products in one part of a store and Doritos in another, to more complex questions on what motivates shoppers as they move through a store. To collect the required knowledge, developers searched Frito-Lay's databases in departments such as marketing, sales, and operations. They also referenced external sources such as trade publications and industry organizations, and identified in-house subject matter experts.

In October 1999, a working prototype of the system was presented to the pilot sales team. Only then did Frito-Lay discover that in the quest for speed, a classic and crippling mistake had been made: The development team had failed to obtain sufficient input from the sales team and did not involve users in the design process. The prototype had the potential to be marginally useful to any sales team, but it was not specific enough to offer fundamental benefits for the pilot team. Therefore, the pilot team was reluctant to accept the system. "Conceptually, it was a great idea," said Frito-Lay sales team leader Joe Ackerman. "But when folks are not on the front line, their view of what is valuable is different from those running 100 miles an hour in the field."

Frito-Lay learned valuable lessons from that mistake and chose to redesign the system. However, at this stage, it not only needed to add the missing features, but also had to win back the sales force and convince them that the redesigned system would indeed streamline their work by facilitating knowledge exchange. The team of developers spent the following four months working with salespeople to transform the prototype into a system they would embrace.

The redesigned portal has been a big success. Better collaboration has helped to significantly reduce turnover, while improved access to knowledge-base resources has enabled salespeople to present themselves as consultants with important knowledge to share. Today, the knowledge management portal is used for daily communication, call reporting, weekly cross-country meetings, training, document sharing, and access to data and industry news. The pilot team exceeded its sales plan for 2000 and grew its business at a rate almost twice that of Frito-Lay's other customer teams. The KMS concept is now being tailored to three other Frito-Lay sales teams and departments, and other divisions of PepsiCo have expressed interest in it as well.

Source: Adapted from Melymuka (2001).

For Further Exploration: Why did Frito-Lay find it difficult to correct the mistake identified in a late stage of the development cycle? If you were responsible for the development of a knowledge management system, what specific actions would you take to ensure that it satisfies the needs of end users?

A case study of Nortel Network's KM initiative indicated that there were three major issues that influenced the success of KM: (1) having effective managerial influence in terms of coordination, control and measurement, project management, and leadership; (2) having key resources such as financial resources and cross-functional expertise, and (3) taking advantage of technological opportunities. Together, these enabled a well-defined process, the understanding of people issues, and the successful incorporation of technology (Massey et al., 2002). Other factors that may lead to knowledge management project success are shown in Table 9.2.

Effective knowledge sharing and learning requires cultural change within the organization, new management practices, senior management commitment, and technological support. We recognize that organizational culture must shift to a culture of sharing. This should be handled through strong leadership at the top, and by providing knowledge management tools that truly make people's

---

TABLE 9.2 Major Factors that Lead to KM Project Success

- A link to a firm's economic value, to demonstrate financial viability and maintain executive sponsorship.
- A technical and organizational infrastructure on which to build.
- A standard, flexible knowledge structure to match the way the organization performs work and uses knowledge. Usually, the organizational culture must change to effectively create a knowledge-sharing environment.
- A knowledge-friendly culture leading directly to user support.
- A clear purpose and language, to encourage users to buy into the system. Sometimes simple, useful knowledge applications need to be implemented first.
- A change in motivational practices, to create a culture of sharing.
- Multiple channels for knowledge transfer—because individuals have different ways of working and expressing themselves. The multiple channels should reinforce one another. Knowledge transfer should be easily accomplished and be as unobtrusive as possible.
- A level of process orientation to make a knowledge management effort worthwhile. In other words, new, improved work methods can be developed.
- Nontrivial motivational methods, such as rewards and recognition, to encourage users to contribute and use knowledge.
- Senior management support. This is critical to initiate the project, to provide resources, to help identify important knowledge on which the success of the organization relies, and to market the project.

Source: Adapted from Davenport et al. (1998).

---

jobs better. As far as encouraging system use and knowledge sharing goes, people must be *properly* motivated to contribute knowledge. The mechanism for doing so should be part of their jobs, and their salaries should reflect this. People must also be motivated to utilize the knowledge that is in the KMS. Again, this should be part of their jobs and their reward structures.

As more companies develop their knowledge management capabilities, some of the ground rules are becoming apparent. Success depends on a clear strategic logic for knowledge sharing, the choice of appropriate infrastructure (technical or non-technical), and an implementation approach that addresses the typical barriers: motivation to share knowledge, resources to capture and synthesize organizational learning, and ability to navigate the knowledge network to find the right people and data.

Potential Drawbacks to Knowledge Management Systems

While there are many positive outcomes of managing knowledge, as discussed in examples throughout this chapter, it would be short-sighted not to consider the potential negative outcomes associated with reusing knowledge. As an example, Henfridsson and Söderholm (2000) analyzed the situation that faced Mrs. Fields cookies, as described in *A Closer Look 9.1* (page 396).

The case of Mrs. Fields illustrates that while organizations might achieve significant short-term gains through knowledge management systems, they must not neglect to allow for the creative process of new knowledge creation, lest they eventually find themselves applying yesterday's solutions to tomorrow's problems.

Closing Remarks

For millennia we have known about the effective use of knowledge and how to store and reuse it. Intelligent organizations recognize that knowledge is an intellectual asset, perhaps the only one that grows over time, and when harnessed effectively can sustain competition and innovation. Organizations can use

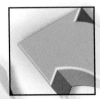

A CLOSER LOOK
9.1 ADAPTABILITY—A MISSING INGREDIENT

Mrs. Fields Cookies, a national chain of cookie stores, grew remarkably fast and successfully during the early 1980s. A key aspect of the company's strategy was to provide expertise directly from the headquarters to every store. As the number of stores increased, the only feasible way to achieve such direct control was through the use of information systems that were designed to mimic the decision making of Mrs. Fields herself. Decision-making systems were placed in each store. The system would take input (such as the temperature, the day of the week, the date, and so forth), would process the data, and would provide, as output, information to each store manager about how many cookies of each type to bake each hour. In essence, the software provided each store manager with explicit directions for planning each day's production, sales, and labor scheduling, along with inventory control and ordering. Because of the well-functioning computer systems, which in principle were systems designed to make Mrs. Fields' tacit knowledge available to all stores, the company was able to successfully function with few managerial levels.

However, as the market began to change and consumers became more health conscious, Mrs. Fields was very slow to respond. In a sense, by embedding so much knowledge into systems that were incapable of adaptation, the organization tied itself to a certain way of doing things and failed to engage in knowledge creation. That is, it failed to pick up the signals in the environment, which might have suggested a change in strategy or product focus. By the early 1990s, the company had fallen into bankruptcy.

Source: Adapted from Henfridsson and Söderholm (2000).

information technology to perform true knowledge management. Leveraging an entire organization's intellectual resources can have tremendous financial impact.

With knowledge management, the definition is clear, the concepts are clear, the methodology is clear, the challenges are clear and surmountable, the benefits are clear and can be substantial, and the tools and technology—though incomplete and somewhat expensive—are viable. Key issues are executive sponsorship and measuring success. Technological issues are minimal compared to these. Knowledge management is not just another expensive management fad. Knowledge management is a new paradigm for how organizations work.

➡ MANAGERIAL ISSUES

1. *Organizational culture change.* This issue is how we can change organizational culture so that people are willing both to contribute knowledge to and use knowledge from a KMS. There must be strong executive leadership, clearly expressed goals, user involvement in the system, and deployment of an easy-to-use system that provides real value to employees. A viable reward structure for contributing and using knowledge must also be developed.

2. *How to store tacit knowledge.* This is extremely difficult. Most KMSs (based on the network storage model) store explicit knowledge about the tacit knowledge that people possess. When the knowledgeable people leave an organization, they take their knowledge with them. Since knowledge requires active use by the recipient, it is important for the person generating knowledge to articulate it in a way that another, appropriately educated person can understand it.

3. *How to measure the tangible and intangible benefits of KMS.* Organizations need to identify ways to measure the value of intellectual assets and the value of providing them to the organization, as discussed in Section 9.7.

4. *Determining the roles of the various personnel in a KM effort.* A knowledge management staff, led by a chief knowledge officer (CKO), can provide structure to an organization's ongoing KM efforts.

5. *The lasting importance of knowledge management.* Knowledge management is extremely important. It is not another management fad. If it is correctly done, it can have massive impact by leveraging know-how throughout the organization. If it is not done, or is not correctly done, the company will not be able to effectively compete against another major player in the industry that does KM correctly.

6. *Implementation in the face of quickly changing technology.* This is an important issue to address regarding the development of many IT systems. Technology has to be carefully examined, and experiments done, to determine what makes sense. By starting now, an organization can get past the managerial and behavioral issues, which have greater impact on the eventual success (or not) of a KMS. As better and cheaper technology is developed, the KMS can be migrated over to it, just as legacy systems have migrated to the PC.

KEY TERMS

Chief knowledge officer (CKO) *389*

Communities of practice (COPs) *375*

Explicit knowledge *369*

Intellectual capital (intellectual assets) *369*

Knowledge *368*

Knowledge discovery in databases (KDD) *379*

Knowledge management (KM) *367*

Knowledge management systems (KMS) *370*

Knowledge repository *382*

Knowware *381*

Leaky knowledge *370*

Model marts *379*

Model warehouses *379*

Practice approach *374*

Process approach *374*

Sticky knowledge *370*

Tacit knowledge *369*

CHAPTER HIGHLIGHTS (Numbers Refer to Learning Objectives)

1 Knowledge is different from information and data. Knowledge is information that is contextual, relevant, and actionable. It is dynamic in nature.

1 Explicit (structured, leaky) knowledge deals with more objective, rational, and technical knowledge. Tacit (unstructured, sticky) knowledge is usually in the domain of subjective, cognitive, and experiential learning. Tacit knowledge is highly personal and hard to formalize.

2 Knowledge management is a process that helps organizations identify, select, organize, disseminate, and transfer important information and expertise that typically reside within the organization in an unstructured way.

2 Knowledge management requires a major transformation in organizational culture to create a desire to share (give and receive) knowledge, plus a commitment to KM at all levels of a firm.

2 The knowledge management model involves the following cyclical steps: create, capture, refine, store, manage, and disseminate knowledge.

2 Standard knowledge management initiatives involve the creation of knowledge bases, active process management, knowledge centers, and collaborative technologies.

2 Knowledge management is an effective way for an organization to leverage its intellectual assets.

3 The two strategies used for KM initiatives are the process approach and the practice approach.

4 A knowledge management system is generally developed using three sets of technologies: communication, collaboration, and storage.

④ A variety of technologies can make up a knowledge management system: the Internet, intranets, data warehousing, decision-support tools, groupware, and so on. Intranets are the primary means of displaying and distributing knowledge in organizations.

④ Knowledge management systems can be purchased in whole or in part from one of numerous software development companies and enterprise information systems vendors, can be acquired through major consulting firms, or can be outsourced to application service providers (ASPs).

⑤ Knowledge portals can be used to provide a central location from which various KM applications are searched.

⑥ The chief knowledge office (CKO) is primarily responsible for changing the behavior of the firm to embrace the use of knowledge management and then managing the development operation of a knowledge management system.

⑥ Knowledge management typically involves the cooperation of managers, developers, KM staff, and users.

⑥ Communities of practice (COPs) provide pressure to break down the cultural barriers that hinder knowledge management efforts.

⑦ It is difficult to measure the success of a KMS. Traditional methods of financial measurement fall short, as they do not consider intellectual capital an asset. Nonfinancial metrics are typically used to measure the success of a KM, yet some firms have been able to determine financial payoffs.

VIRTUAL COMPANY ASSIGNMENT

Instructions for accessing The Wireless Café on the Student Web Site

1. Go to **wiley.com/college/turban**
2. Select Turban/Leidner/ McLean/Wetherbe's *Information Technology for Management, Fifth Edition.*
3. Click on Student Resources site, in the toolbar on the left.
4. Click on the link for Virtual Company Web site.
5. Click on Wireless Café.

Knowledge Management at The Wireless Café
Go to The Wireless Café's link on the Student Web Site. There you will be asked to think about the problems of retaining knowledge in an organization, such as a restaurant, that experiences high turnover. You will also be asked to identify types of knowledge at the restaurant and to propose how that knowledge could be captured in information systems.

More Resources
More resources and study tools are located on the Student Web Site. You'll find additional chapter materials and useful Web links. In addition, self-quizzes that provide individualized feedback are available for each chapter.

QUESTIONS FOR REVIEW

1. Discuss what is meant by an intellectual asset.
2. Define knowledge and knowledge management.
3. Define explicit knowledge. Why is it also called leaky?
4. Define tacit knowledge. Why is it also called sticky?
5. How can tacit knowledge be transferred or shared?
6. List some ways in which organizational culture can impact a knowledge management effort.
7. What is the primary goal of knowledge management?

8. Describe the process approach to knowledge management.

9. Describe the practice approach to knowledge management.

10. Describe the roles and responsibilities of the people involved in a knowledge management system, especially the CKO.

11. What is a community of practice?

12. List the steps in the cyclical model of knowledge management. Why is it a cycle?

13. List the major knowledge management success factors.

14. Describe the role of IT in knowledge management.

QUESTIONS FOR DISCUSSION

1. Why is the term knowledge so hard to define?

2. Describe and relate the different characteristics of knowledge.

3. Explain why it is important to capture and manage knowledge.

4. Compare and contrast tacit knowledge and explicit knowledge.

5. Explain why organizational culture must sometimes change before knowledge management is introduced.

6. How does knowledge management attain its primary objective?

7. How can employees be motivated to contribute to and use knowledge management systems?

8. What is the role of a knowledge repository in knowledge management?

9. Explain the importance of communication and collaboration technologies to the processes of knowledge management.

10. Explain why firms adopt knowledge management initiatives.

11. Explain the role of the CKO in developing a knowledge management system. What major responsibilities does he or she have?

12. Discuss some knowledge management success factors.

13. Why is it hard to evaluate the impacts of knowledge management?

14. Explain how the Internet and its related technologies (Web browsers, intranets, and so on) enable knowledge management.

15. Explain the roles of a community of practice.

16. Describe an enterprise knowledge portal and explain its significance.

EXERCISES

1. Make a list of all the knowledge management methods you use during your day (work and personal). Which are the most effective? Which are the least effective? What kinds of work or activities does each knowledge management method enable?

2. Investigate the literature for information on the position of CKO. Find out what percentage of firms with KM initiatives have CKOs and what their responsibilities are.

3. Investigate the literature for new measures of success (metrics) for knowledge management and intellectual capital. Write a report on your findings.

4. Describe how each of the key elements of a knowledge management infrastructure can contribute to its success.

5. Based on your own experience or on the vendor's information, list the major capabilities of a particular knowledge management product, and explain how it can be used in practice.

6. Describe how to ride a bicycle, drive a car, or make a peanut butter and jelly sandwich. Now, have someone else try to do it based solely on your explanation. How can you best convert this knowledge from tacit to explicit (or can't you)?

7. Consider why knowledge management systems would be so important to a modern organization that firms would initiate such systems.

GROUP ASSIGNMENTS

1. Compare and contrast the capabilities and features of electronic document management with those of collaborative computing and those of knowledge management systems. Each team represents one type of system. Present the ways in which these capabilities and features can create improvements for an organization.

2. Search the Internet for knowledge management products and systems and create categories for them. Assign one vendor to each team. Describe the categories you created and justify them.

3. If you are working on a decision-making project in industry for this course (or if not, use one from another class or from work), examine some typical decisions in the related project. How would you extract the knowledge you need? Can you use that knowledge in practice? Why or why not?

4. Read the article by A. Genusa titled "Rx for Learning," available at *cio.com* (February 1, 2001), which describes Tufts University Medical School's experience with knowledge management. Determine how these concepts and such a system could be implemented and used at your college or university. Explain how each aspect would work, or if not, explain why not.

INTERNET EXERCISES

1. How does knowledge management support decision making? Identify products or systems on the Web that help organizations accomplish knowledge management. Start with *brint.com, decisionsupport.net,* and *knowledge management.ittoolbox.com.* Try one out and report your findings to the class.

2. Try the KPMG Knowledge Management Framework Assessment Exercise at *kmsurvey.londonweb.net* and assess how well your organization (company or university) is doing with knowledge management. Are the results accurate? Why or why not?

3. Search the Internet to identify sites dealing with knowledge management. Start with *google.com, kmworld.com,* and *km-forum.org.* How many did you find? Categorize the sites based on whether they are academic, consulting firms, vendors, and so on. Sample one of each and describe the main focus of the site.

4. Identify five real-world knowledge management success stories by searching vendor Web sites (use at least three different vendors). Describe them. How did knowledge management systems and methods contribute to their success? What features do they share? What different features do individual successes have?

5. Search the Internet for vendors of knowledge management suites, enterprise knowledge portals, and out-of-the-box knowledge management solutions. Identify the major features of each product (use three from each), and compare and contrast their capabilities.

6. J.D. Edwards (*jdedwards.com*) developed a knowledge management intranet initiative called the Knowledge Garden. Access both the J.D. Edwards and Microsoft Web sites and investigate its current capabilities.

Minicase 1
DaimlerChrysler EBOKs with Knowledge Management

In 1980 Chrysler Corporation came back from near bankruptcy with innovative designs and a view of a shared culture in design, development, and manufacturing. The company began new ways of looking at its business, its suppliers, and its workers. After the acquisition of American Motors Corporation (AMC) in 1987, executives developed and deployed advanced, dedicated platform design and production methods, which showed enormous potential. Jack Thompson, the technology center development director, worked closely with Chairman Lee Iacocca on the development of a new, modern engineering and design facility. Thompson designed the center around knowledge-sharing and productivity principles: open air, natural light, and escalators (people don't talk on elevators).

In 1994 the tech center opened, providing a home for a transformed engineering culture. Two years later, the corporate headquarters was moved next to the tech center so executives could be nearby. By 2000, over 11,000 people were working at the Auburn Hills, Michigan, center. In November 1998, Daimler-Benz became the majority owner of Chrysler Corporation, renaming the company Daimler-Chrysler (*daimlerchrysler.com*). Chrysler's fast, efficient, and innovative nature, as a result of the extremely successful platform approach to design and engineering, led to the buy-in—the largest merger in manufacturing history.

Platform production at DaimlerChrysler has teams of engineers focused on a single type of car platform (small car, minivan, and so on), working on new models as a system from concept to production. Cars are designed by a single team considering customer needs and preferences, as opposed to the standard practice of organizing the new designs by organizational functions (silos). Platform teams of employees work and learn together, focused on the product, with a payoff in market responsiveness, reduced cost, and increased quality. The Chrysler LH, the first model developed with the platform approach, took 39 months to produce; typically the time to market exceeds 50 months.

While the benefits were clear, Chrysler executives noticed that unexplained errors were popping up in the new platforms (like leaving a moisture barrier out of car doors). *There was an organizational memory problem:* Mentoring and peer support had become limited. Informal and formal professional collaboration had stopped. The same mistakes were being made, corrected, and repeated. People were not learning about new developments in their core areas. The typical collaboration found among groups doing similar work was sharply reduced, and so problems and solutions were not being documented or shared.

Collaboration and communication needed to be reestablished within groups that have common training, interests, and responsibilities (design, engineering, body, engine, manufacturing, and so on). The goal was to reestablish these links while becoming more competitive with even faster product-cycle times. Chrysler needed to institutionalize knowledge sharing and collaboration. In 1996 Chrysler Corporation made *knowledge management* a vital condition for design and engineering, leading to dramatic improvements in productivity.

First, engineers mapped out where the knowledge was within the organization (a knowledge audit). There were many categories, or "buckets of knowledge," ranging from product databases to CAD/CAM systems to manufacturing, procurement, and supply vehicle test data. Within each category, details were identified and codified. Sharing knowledge meant integrating these knowledge buckets, while resolving cultural issues that impeded sharing across platform boundaries. Chrysler created informal cross-platform *Tech Clubs,* functionally organized communities of practice to reunite designers and engineers with peers from other platform groups. Each community would then codify its knowledge and provide mentoring and apprenticing opportunities for learning.

The *Engineering Book of Knowledge (EBOK)* is Chrysler's intranet supporting a knowledge repository of process *best practices* and technical know-how to be shared and maintained. It was initially developed by two engineering managers but continues through encouraged employee participation in grassroots (i.e., supported at the lower levels of the organization) Tech Clubs. EBOK is written in GrapeVine (GrapeVine Technologies), running as a Lotus Notes application, and is accessed with the Netscape browser and NewsEdge.

Knowledge is explored and entered into the EBOK through an iterative team approach: the Tech Clubs. Best practices are identified, refined, confirmed, and finally entered into the EBOK in a secure interactive electronic repository. When an author proposes a best practice, users in the Tech Club responsible for that area of knowledge react by commenting on the knowledge through a discussion list. One manager, the *Book Owner,* is ultimately responsible for approving new entries and changes to the book. The Book Owner joins the conversation. The author can respond to the comments by either building a better case or going along with the discussion. Ultimately the Tech Club decides, and the Book Owner enters the new knowledge. The Book Owner is the individual who is ultimately responsible for the accuracy of the book, and therefore approves entries to, modifications to, and deletions from the book.

The EBOK is DaimlerChrysler's official design review process. The EBOK even contains best practices information about DaimlerChrysler's competitors. DaimlerChrysler has determined that EBOK is both a best practices tool (the process approach) and a collaboration tool (the practice approach). DaimlerChrysler officials recognize that because the environment changes and new methods are being continually developed, the EBOK will never be fully complete. The EBOK is a *living book.* The EBOK *leverages* technology knowledge.

The EBOK is central to DaimlerChrysler's new way of working. The plan is to have more than 5,000 users with access to 3,800 chapters, of which just over half were completed by early 1999. Through the EBOK, DaimlerChrysler reconciled its platform problems and developed a technical memory while tracking competitive information, quality information, and outside standards. Even though there is no central budget for books of knowledge and associated processes, DaimlerChrysler is deploying knowledge in other departments such as manufacturing, finance, and sales and marketing.

The EBOK is only one of several initiatives that promote and facilitate knowledge sharing at DaimlerChrysler. In early 1999, soon after the merger, the company began an information-sharing project called ProBench. The objective of ProBench was to help Chrysler and Mercedes determine how to best use each other's manufacturing expertise. Extensive collaboration enabled Chrysler to benefit from the engineering strengths of Mercedes, while Mercedes was able to learn from Chrysler's know-how in launching new vehicle models. One of the biggest accomplishments of ProBench was Chrysler's decision to use Mercedes' superior rear-wheel-drive automatic transmission on future vehicles. "We are able to save [$600 million in] investment money, get variable costs down, and gain many other advantages by not inventing the wheel twice," says Dieter Zetsche, DaimlerChrysler's Chief Executive Officer. Zetsche concludes: "[Collaboration] has been a real value to us, and it is a very positive result of the merger."

Facing global competition in a knowledge-intensive business, DaimlerChrysler needs to utilize knowledge management to support continuous improvement and innovation. Thus, KM efforts enjoy company-wide management support. DaimlerChrysler is convinced that "knowledge transfer within the Group . . . will contribute towards higher earnings in the coming years."

Sources: Adapted from Karlenzig (1999), Maynard (2001), Haas et al. (2003), *daimlerchrysler.com,* and DaimlerChrysler Annual Report (2003).

Questions for Minicase 1

1. Platform design at DaimlerChrysler led directly to a reduction in the time to market and in costs for new vehicles. Explain how it caused new problems.

2. What is meant by a community of practice? How did DaimlerChrysler leverage the knowledge within such a community?

3. Describe the Engineering Book of Knowledge (EBOK). Explain how it is updated by adding new knowledge of practice.

4. It has been said that "the proper role for all knowledge management tools is to leverage technology in service to human thinking." Explain this statement.

5. How successful was the knowledge management initiative at DaimlerChrysler?

6. Consider how a book of knowledge could impact another organization, ideally one with which you are affiliated (e.g., your university, job, part-time job, family business). Describe the potential impacts, and list the benefits. Would there be any organizational culture issues to deal with? Why or why not?

Minicase 2
Buckman Labs Improves Global Knowledge Sharing

Buckman Labs (*buckman.com*), a US$300 million chemical company with operations in 21 different countries, sells more than 1,000 different specialty chemicals. Sales in 2003 increased 10% from 2002, in spite of economic and political instability in the world. Gross profits rose by 5.7%. Buckman's 2003 annual report states, "Our ability to share knowledge within our company and use that knowledge for the benefit of our customers distinguishes Buckman Laboratories from our competitors." In the 1990s, Buckman began a global knowledge management initiative that has continued to yield positive results a decade later.

The first project was to design and implement a global forum, based on intranet technology. The resulting Tech-Forum created a taxonomy of knowledge areas based upon business functions across all of the different systems and repositories with a common interface. By the mid-90s, TechForum had become the central pivot of Buckman's global KMS. TechForum had 20 sections, each with its own message board, conference rooms to facilitate debate, and library section, where the communication threads and other pertinent knowledge were stored. Thirteen of the 20 sections were devoted to the business areas within Buckman Labs (e.g., Pulp and Paper, and Leather). These forums were expected to help improve client companies' productivity. Six of the 20 sections were primarily internal and designed to improve

the operational efficiency and effectiveness of Buckman Labs (e.g., human resources, plant operations, safety/environment, KT topics/help). The Bulab News and Breakroom sections were general discussion sections in Tech-Forum, where Buckman employees were free to discuss topics of their choice.

In terms of content design, the majority of TechForum was devoted to business-related activities designed to provide employees access to relevant knowledge needed for their tasks. Other sections, such as Breakroom, provided a social environment. Topics discussed in Breakroom ranged from support for sports teams, to requests sent to employees in foreign countries for vacation recommendations in their area, and other non-business-related activities.

Setting up the technology and forums was an important part of Buckman's KM initiative, but so too was putting in place a management structure that would ensure that the knowledge was kept valuable, current, and easy to locate. Buckman's management combined Information Services, Telecommunications, and the Technical Information Center (which included a full-fledged corporate library) to form the Knowledge Transfer Department (KTD). Forty-five KTD employees were responsible for the design, development, implementation, and maintenance of the software and hardware of the ICT-based KM system. Another five KTD employees were responsible for the monitoring and processing of the knowledge generated within the various sections of Buckman forums.

A knowledge-processing team was assembled to reduce the need for each associate to retrieve and store the accumulated knowledge that each section captured as a result of discussions within the sections. Members of the specialist knowledge-processing team included a number of forum specialists and section leaders (two or more per section from various departments). Section leaders were recruited to help manage knowledge activities. These were highly trained chemists or microbiologists with specialized industry knowledge and experience. The section leaders wrote weekly abstracts for a central database accessible to most employees. They were responsible not only for facilitating the knowledge-sharing process but also for assisting in "processing" knowledge—for example, by writing abstracts for storage and facilitating the re-use of the obtained knowledge. Members of the specialist team assumed the additional responsibility of preparing a summary of the discussion points that occurred in each section and posting the information at the end of each week.

Forums specialists facilitated the process of responding to online requests. If an online request went unattended for a few hours, two scenarios could emerge. First, one of the forum specialists would pick up the request and then identify the potential experts based on their previous industrial experience and reputation of their willingness to

share knowledge. Alternatively, a team of experts with related industrial experience who had volunteered as "section leaders" would also help answer any requests and prepare weekly summaries to be stored in the knowledge repositories for later use. When an information search was completed, responses were then formulated and presented to customers for problem solving. The request was kept on the forum for as long as there was an active discussion.

Together, Buckman's KM technology, structure, and processes enabled front-line employees to continue serving customers while a specialized knowledge-processing team devoted time to capturing company knowledge into a re-usable form.

Sources: Buckman Annual Report 2003 (*buckman.com*); Plan and Leidner (2003).

Questions for Minicase 2

1. What are the advantages to an organization of having a global knowledge management system, as opposed to having multiple systems dispersed around the world?
2. What are the key roles played by the KM staff?
3. How can management continue to show support for the volunteer section leaders?
4. How would you measure the success of Buckman Labs' KM initiative?

REFERENCES

Abramson, G., "Measuring Up," *CIO*, June 15, 1998.

Alavi, M., "Managing Organizational Knowledge," Chapter 2 in Zmud, W. R. (ed.), *Framing the Domains of IT Management: Projecting the Future*. Cincinnati, OH: Pinnaflex Educational Resources, 2000.

Alavi, M. and D. Leidner, "Knowledge Management Systems: Emerging Views and Practices from the Field," *Proceedings of 32nd Annual HICSS*, Maui, HI, January 1999, available at *computer.org/proceedings/hicss/0001/00017/00017009.pdf?SMSESSION=NO* (accessed July 2003).

Alavi, M., T. Kayworth, and D. Leidner, "An Empirical Examination of the Influence of Knowledge Management on Organizational Culture," working paper, Baylor University, 2003.

Allee, V., "Are You Getting Big Value from Knowledge?" *KMWorld*, September 1999, pp. 16–17.

Amato-McCoy, D., "Commerce Bank Manages Knowledge Profitably," *Bank Systems and Technology*, January 2003.

Ambrosio, J., "Knowledge Management Mistakes," *Computerworld*, 34(27), July 3, 2000.

Anderson, L., "Cisco Employee Connection: Saving Money, Keeping Employees," Smartbusinessmag.com, June 2002, p. 49.

Barth, S., "KM Horror Stories," *Knowledge Management*, October 2000b.

Barth, S., "Knowledge as a Function of X," *Knowledge Management*, February 2000a.

Bennet, A., and D. Bennet, "The Partnership-between Organizational Learning and Knowledge Management," in *Handbook on Knowledge Management*, Volume 1k (ed. C. W. Holsapple). New York: Springer-Verlag, 2003, pp. 439–460.

Blodgett, M., "Prescription Strength," *CIO*, February 1, 2000.

Bolloju, N., M. Khalita, and E. Turban, "Integrating Knowledge Management into Enterprise Environments for the Next Generation of Decision Support," *Decision Support Systems*, 33(2), June 2002, pp. 163–176.

Brown, S. J., and P. Duguid, "Balancing Act: How to Capture Knowledge Without Killing It," *Harvard Business Review*, May–June 2000, 73–80.

Buckler, G., "Knowledge Management Crucial Tool for Law Firms," *The Globe and Mail*, April 12, 2004.

Cahill, T., *How the Irish Saved Civilization*. New York: Anchor, 1996.

Chandler, P., "Connecting People," *CVX Magazine*, ChevronTexaco, June–July 2002.

ChevronTexaco 2004 Fact Sheet, *chevrontexaco.com*(accessed May 2004).

Cingular, *cingular.com* (accessed May 2004).

CIO.com, "The Means to an Edge: Knowledge Management—Key to Innovation," *CIO* white paper, September 15, 1999.

Collins, H., *Corporate Portals: Revolutionizing Information Access to Increase Productivity and Drive the Bottom Line*, AMACOM, 2001.

Commerce Bank, *commerceonline.com* (accessed May 2004).

Cothrel, J., and R. L. Williams, "On-line Communities: Getting the Most Out of On-line Discussion and Collaboration," *Knowledge Management Review*, No. 6, January–February 1999b.

Cothrel, J., and R. L. Williams, "On-line Communities: Helping Them Form and Grow," *Journal of Knowledge Management*, 3(1), 1999a.

Cranfield University, "The Cranfield/Information Strategy Knowledge Survey: Europe's State of the Art in Knowledge Management," *The Economist Group*, 1998.

"DaimlerChrysler 2003 Annual Report," DaimlerChrysler, 2004.

Dash, J., "Cultivating Collaboration," *Software Magazine*, March 1998.

Davenport, T. H., and L. Prusak, *Working Knowledge: How Organizations Manage What They Know*. Boston: Harvard Business School Press, 1998.

Davenport, T., D. DeLong, and M. Beers, "Successful Knowledge Management Projects," *Sloan Management Review*, 39(2), Winter 1998.

Davis, M., "Knowledge Management," *Information Strategy: The Executive's Journal*, Fall 1998.

DeLong, D. W., and L. Fahey, "Diagnosing Cultural Barriers to Knowledge Management, *Academy of Management Executive*, 14(4), November 2000, pp. 113–127.

Desouza, K.C., "Knowledge Management Barriers: Why the Technology Imperative Seldom Works," *Business Horizons*, January/February 2003, pp. 25–29.

Duffy, D., "Knowledge Champions," *CIO* (Enterprise-Section 2), November 1998.

Economist, "Business: Electronic Glue," *The Economist*, May 31, 2001, *economist.com/displaystory.cfm?story_id=638605* (accessed July 2003).

Edvinsson, L., "The Intellectual Capital of Nations" in *Handbook on Knowledge Management*, Volume 1k (ed. C. W. Holsapple). New York: Springer-Verlag, 2003, pp. 153–163.

Eisenhart, M., "Around the Virtual Water Cooler: Sustaining Communities of Practice Takes Plenty of Persistence," *Knowledge Management*, October 2000.

Ford, D. P., "Trust and Knowledge Management: The Seeds of Success," in *Handbook on Knowledge Management*, Volume 1k (ed. C. W. Holsapple). New York: Springer-Verlag, 2003, pp. 553–576.

Genusa, A., "Rx for Learning," *cio.com*, February 1, 2001, *cio.com/archive/020101/tufts.html* (accessed July 2003).

Gowlings, *gowlings.com* (accessed May 2004).

Gray, P., "Tutorial on Knowledge Management," *Proceedings of the Americas Conference of the Association for Information Systems*, Milwaukee, WI, August 1999.

Gray, P., and D. Meister, "Knowledge Sourcing Effectiveness," working paper, University of Pittsburgh, 2003.

Gray, P., and S. Tehrani, "Technologies for Disseminating Knowledge," in *Handbook on Knowledge Management*, Volume 1k (ed. C. W. Holsapple). New York: Springer-Verlag, 2003, pp. 109–128.

Gupta, A. K., and V. Govindarajan, "Knowledge Management's Social Dimension: Lessons from Nucor Steel," *Sloan Management Review*, 42(1), Fall 2000, pp. 71–80.

Haas, R., W. Aulbur, and S. Thakar, "Enabling Communities of Practice at EADS Airbus," in *Sharing Expertise: Beyond Knowledge Management* (ed. M. Ackerman, V. Pipek, and V. Wulf). Cambridge, MA: MIT Press, 2003.

Hansen, M., N. Nohria, and T. Tierney, "What's Your Strategy for Managing Knowledge?" *Harvard Business Review*, 77(2), March–April 1999.

Hanssen-Bauer, J., and C. C. Snow, "Responding to Hypercompetition: The Structure and Processes of a Regional Learning Network Organization," *Organization Science*, 7(4), 1996, pp. 413–427.

Hargadon, A. B., "Firms as Knowledge Brokers: Lessons in Pursuing Continuous Innovation," *California Management Review*, 40(3), Spring 1998, pp. 209–227.

Heier, H., *Siemens ShareNet: Change Paradigms in the Setting of Knowledge Management Systems*. Dissertation, Leiden University School of Management, 2003.

Henfridsson, O., and A. Söderholm, "Barriers to Learning: On Organizational Defenses and Vicious Circles in Technological Adoption," *Accounting, Management and Information Technologies*, 10(1), 2000, pp. 33–51.

Hislop, D., "Mission Impossible? Communicating and Sharing Knowledge via Information Technology," *Journal of Information Technology*, September 2002, pp. 165–177.

Holsapple, C. W., "Knowledge and its Attributes," in *Handbook on Knowledge Management*, Volume 1k (ed. C. W. Holsapple). New York: Springer-Verlag, 2003, pp. 165–188.

Holsapple, C. W. and K. D. Joshi, "A Knowledge Management Ontology," in *Handbook on Knowledge Management*, Volume 1k (ed. C. W. Holsapple). New York: Springer-Verlag, 2003, pp. 89–128.

InfoWorld, "Enterprise Knowledge Portals Wise Up Your Business," *InfoWorld*, 22(49), December 4, 2000, *archive .infoworld.com/gui/infographics/00/12/04/001204tcvit.gif* (accessed July 2003).

Junnarkar, B., "Creating Fertile Ground for Knowledge at Monsanto," *Perspectives on Business Innovation*. EY Center for Business Innovation, 1997.

Kaplan, S., "KM the Right Way," *CIO*, July 15, 2002.

Karlenzig, W., "Chrysler's New Know-Mobiles," *Knowledge Management*, May 1999, pp. 58–66.

Kesner, R. M., "Building a Knowledge Portal: A Case Study in Web-Enabled Collaboration," *Information Strategy: The Executive's Journal*, Winter 2003, pp. 13–23.

King, D., and K. Jones, "Competitive Intelligence, Software Robots, and the Internet: The NewsAlert Prototype," *Proceedings, 28th HICSS*, Wailea, Maui, Hawaii, January 1995.

King, J., "Shell Strikes Knowledge Gold," *Computerworld*, July–August 2001.

Knapp, E. M., "Knowledge Management," *Business and Economic Review*, 44(4), July–September 1998.

KPMG Management Consulting, *Knowledge Management: Research Report*, 1998.

KPMG Consulting (*kpmgconsulting.com/kpmgsite/service/km/publications.htm*), press release 2000.

Leidner, D. E., "Understanding Information Culture: Integrating Knowledge Management Systems into Organizations," in *Strategic Information Management* (eds. R. D. Galliers and D. E. Leidner). Oxford: Butterworth Heinemann, 2003, pp. 497–525.

Leonard, D., and S. Sensiper, "The Role of Tacit Knowledge in Group Innovations," *California Management Review*, 40(3), Spring 1998.

Liautaud, B., and M. Hammond, *E-Business Intelligence: Turning Information into Knowledge into Profit*. New York: McGraw-Hill, 2000.

Liebowitz, J., and Y. Chen, "Knowledge Sharing Proficiencies: The Key to Knowledge Management," in *Handbook on Knowledge Management*, Volume 1k (ed. C. W. Holsapple). New York: Springer-Verlag, 2003, pp. 409–438.

MacSweeney, G., "The Knowledge Management Payback," *Insurance & Technology*, June 2002.

Madhaven, R., and R. Grover, "From Embedded Knowledge to Embodied Knowledge: New Product Development as Knowledge Management," *Journal of Marketing*, 62(4), October 1998.

Massey, A. P., M. Montoya-Weiss, and T. O'Driscoll, "Knowledge Management in Pursuit of Performance: Insights from Nortel Networks," MIS *Quarterly,* 26(3), September 2002, pp. 269–289.

Maynard, M., "Amid the Turmoil, a Rare Success at Daimler-Chrysler," *Fortune,* January 2001.

McDonald, M., and D. Shand, "Request for Proposal: A Guide to KM Professional Services," *Knowledge Management*, March 2000.

Melymuka, K., "Profiting from Mistakes," *Computerworld*, April 2001.

Melymuka, K., "Knowledge Management Helps Cut Errors by Half," *Computerworld*, July 8, 2002, *computerworld.com/databasetopics/data/story/0,10801,72513,00.html* (accessed July 2003).

"Monsanto at a Glance," *monsanto.com* (accessed June 2004).

Mooney, S. F., "P-C 'Knowledge Capital' Can be Measured," *National Underwriter*, 104(51–52), December 25, 2000.

"Most Admired Knowledge Companies Recognized," *Knowledge Management Review,* January–February 1999.

Nonaka, I., "A Dynamic Theory of Organizational Knowledge Creation," *Organization Science*, 5(1), Feb. 1994, pp. 14–37.

Nonaka, I., and H. Takeuchi, *The Knowledge-Creating Company: How Japanese Companies Create the Dynamics of Innovation.* New York: Oxford University Press, 1995.

O'Dell, C., C. Grayson, and N. Essaides, *If Only We Knew What We Know: The Transfer of Internal Knowledge and Best Practice.* New York: Free Press, 1998.

O'Dell, C. S., S. Elliot, and C. Hubert, "Achieving Knowledge Management Outcomes," in *Handbook on Knowledge Management*, Volume 1k (ed. C. W. Holsapple). New York: Springer-Verlag, 2003, pp. 253–288.

O'Herron, J., "Building the Bases of Knowledge," *Call Center Magazine*, January 2003.

Plan, S. L., and D. E. Leidner, "Bridging Communities of Practice with Information Technology in Pursuit of Global Knowledge Sharing," *Journal of Strategic Information Systems*, Vol. 12, 2003, pp. 71–88.

Polanyi, M., *Personal Knowledge*. Chicago: University of Chicago Press, 1958.

Polanyi, M., *The Tacit Dimension*. London: Routledge & Kegan Paul, 1966.

Rasmus, D. W., "Knowledge Management: More than AI But Less Without It," *PC AI*, 14(2), March–April 2000.

Robb, D., "Assembling Knowledge Management Teams," *Information Strategy Executive Journal,* Winter 2003, pp. 37–48.

Roberts-Witt, S. L., "The @HP Way," *Portals Magazine*, November, 2002.

Robin, M., "Learning by Doing," *Knowledge Management*, March 2000.

Ruber, P., "Build a Dynamic Business Portal with XML," *Knowledge Management*, January 11, 2001.

Ruggles, R., "The State of the Notion: Knowledge Management in Practice," *California Management Review*, 40(3), 1998.

Schultze, U. and D. E. Leidner, "Studying Knowledge Management in Information Systems Research: Discourses and Theoretical Assumptions," *MIS Quarterly*, 26(3), September, 2002, pp. 213–242.

Sharp, D., "Knowledge Management Today: Challenges and Opportunities," *Information Systems Management,* Spring 2003.

Shein, E., "The Knowledge Crunch," CIO.com, May 1, 2001, http://www.cio.com/archive/050101/crunch.html.

Siemens, *siemens.com* (accessed May 2004).

Silver, C. A., "Where Technology and Knowledge Meet," *Journal of Business Strategy*, 21(6), November–December 2000.

Silverman, S. et al., "Reaping the Rewards," *Oil & Gas Investor*, 2000.

Skyrme, D. J., and D. Amidon, "New Measures of Success," *Journal of Business Strategy*, January–February 1998.

Smith, H. A., and J. D. McKeen, "Creating and Facilitating Communities of Practice," in *Handbook on Knowledge Management*, Vol. 1 (ed. C. W. Holsapple). New York: Springer-Verlag, 2003, pp. 393–408.

Steinberg, D., "Bringing Order to the Information Explosion," Smartbusinessmag.com, June 2002, pp. 48–53.

Storck, J., and P. A. Hill, "Knowledge Diffusion Through Strategic Communities," *Sloan Management Review*, 41(2), Winter 2000.

Teece, D. J., "Knowledge and Competence as Strategic Assets," in *Handbook on Knowledge Management*, Volume 1k (ed. C. W. Holsapple). New York: Springer-Verlag, 2003, pp. 129–152.

van der Spek, R., J. Hofer-Alfeis, and J. Kingma, "The Knowledge Strategy Process," in *Handbook on Knowledge Management*, Volume 1k (ed. C. W. Holsapple). New York: Springer-Verlag, 2003, pp. 443–466.

Vasilash, G. S., "447,000 Heads Are Better than One," *Automotive Design & Production*, June 2002.

Velker, L., "Knowledge the Chevron Way," *KMWorld*, 8(2), February 1, 1999, pp. 20–21.

Von Krogh, G. et al., eds., *Knowledge Creation: A Source of Value*. New York: St. Martin's Press, 2000.

Warner, F., "He Drills for Knowledge," *Fast Company*, September 2001.

Wenger, E. C., and W. M. Snyder, "Communities of Practice: The Organizational Frontier," *Harvard Business Review*, January–February 2000, pp. 139–145.

Williams, S., "The Intranet Content Management Strategy Conference," *Management Services*, September 2001.

Ziff Davis Smart Business, "Inside Information," *Smartbusinessmag.com,* June 2002, pp. 46–54.

PART IV
Managerial and Decision Support Systems

9. Knowledge Management
▶ 10. Data Management: Warehousing, Analyzing, Mining, and Visualization
11. Management Decision Support and Intelligent Systems

CHAPTER
10 Data Management: Warehousing, Analyzing, Mining, and Visualization

10.1 Data Management: A Critical Success Factor

10.2 Data Warehousing

10.3 Information and Knowledge Discovery with Business Intelligence

10.4 Data Mining Concepts and Applications

10.5 Data Visualization Technologies

10.6 Marketing Databases in Action

10.7 Web-Based Data Management Systems

Minicases:
1. Homeland Security
2. Sears

LEARNING OBJECTIVES

After studying this chapter, you will be able to:

① Recognize the importance of data, their managerial issues, and their life cycle.

② Describe the sources of data, their collection, and quality issues.

③ Describe document management systems.

④ Explain the operation of data warehousing and its role in decision support.

⑤ Describe information and knowledge discovery and business intelligence.

⑥ Understand the power and benefits of data mining.

⑦ Describe data presentation methods and explain geographical information systems, visual simulations, and virtual reality as decision support tools.

⑧ Discuss the role of marketing databases and provide examples.

⑨ Recognize the role of the Web in data management.

FINDING DIAMONDS BY DATA MINING AT HARRAH'S

➤ THE PROBLEM

Harrah's Entertainment (*harrahs.com*) is a very profitable casino chain. With 26 casinos in 13 states, it had $4 billion sales in 2002 and net income of $235 million. One of Harrah's casinos, located on the Las Vegas strip, typifies the marketing issues that casino owners face. The problem is very simple: how to attract visitors to come and spend money in your casino, and to do it again and again. There is no other place like the Las Vegas strip, where dozens of mega casinos and hundreds of small ones lure visitors by operating attractions ranging from fiery volcanoes to pirate ships.

Most casino operators use intuition to plan inducements for customers. Almost all have loyalty cards, provide free rooms to customers who visit frequently, give tickets for free shows, and more. The problem is that there is only little differentiation among the casinos. Casinos believe they must give those incentives to survive, but do they help casinos to excel? Harrah's is doing better than most competing casinos by using management and marketing theories facilitated by information technology, under the leadership of Gary Loveman, a former Harvard Business School professor.

➤ THE SOLUTION

Harrah's strategy is based on technology-based CRM and the use of customer database marketing to test promotions. This combination enables the company to fine-tune marketing efforts and service-delivery strategies that keep customers coming back. Noting that 82.7 percent of its revenue comes from slot machines, Harrah's started by giving each player a loyalty smart card. A smart-card reader on each slot machine in all 26 of its casinos records each customer's activities. (Readers are also available in Harrah's restaurants, gift shops, etc., to record any spending.)

Logging your activities, you earn credit, as in other loyalty programs, for which you get free hotel rooms, dinners, etc. Such programs are run by most competitors, but Harrah's goes a step further: It uses a 300-gigabyte transactional database, known as a *data warehouse,* to analyze the data recorded by the card readers. By tracking millions of individual transactions, the IT systems assemble a vast amount of data on customer habits and preferences. These data are fed into the enterprise data warehouse, which contains not only millions of transactional data points about customers (such as names, addresses, ages, genders) but also details about their gambling, spending, and preferences. This database has become a very rich repository of customer information, and it is mined for decision support.

The information found in Harrah's database indicated that a loyalty strategy based on same-store (same casino, in this case) sales growth could be very beneficial. The goal is to get a customer to visit your establishment regularly. For example, analysis discovered that the company's best customers were middle-aged and senior adults with discretionary time and income, who enjoyed playing slot machines. These customers did not typically stay in a hotel, but visited a casino on the way home from work or on a weekend night out. They responded better to an offer of $60 of casino chips than to a free room, two steak dinners, and

$30 worth of chips, because they enjoyed the anticipation and excitement of gambling itself (rather than seeing the trip as a vacation get-away).

This strategy offered a way to differentiate Harrah's brand. Understanding the lifetime value of the customers became critical to the company's marketing strategy. Instead of focusing on how much people spend in the casinos during a single visit, the company began to focus on their total spending over a long time. By gathering more and more specific information about customer preferences, running experiments and analyses on the newly collected data, and determining ways of appealing to players' interests, the company was able to increase the amount of money customers spent there by appealing to their individual preferences.

As in other casinos with loyalty programs, players are segregated into three tiers, and the biggest spenders get priorities in waiting lines and in awards. There is a visible differentiation in customer service based on the three-tier hierarchy, and every experience in Harrah's casinos was redesigned to drive customers to want to earn a higher-level card. Customers have responded by doing what they can to earn the higher-tiered cards.

However, Harrah's transactional database is doing much more than just calculating gambling spending. For example, the casino knows which specific customers were playing at particular slot machines and at what time. Using data mining techniques, Harrah's can discover what specific machines appealed to specific customers. This knowledge enabled Harrah's to configure the casino floor with a mix of slot machines that benefited both the customers and the company.

In addition, by measuring all employee performance on the matrices of speed and friendliness and analyzing these results with data mining, the company is able to provide its customers with better experiences as well as earn more money for the employees. Harrah's implemented a bonus plan to reward hourly workers with extra cash for achieving improved customer satisfaction scores. (Bonuses totaling $43 million were paid over three years.) The bonus program worked because the reward depends on everyone's performance. The general manager of a lower-scoring property might visit a colleague at a higher-scoring casino to find out what he could do to improve his casino's scores.

 THE RESULTS

Harrah's experience has shown that the better the experience a guest has and the more attentive you are to him or her, the more money will be made. For Harrah's, good customer service is not a matter of an isolated incident or two but of daily routine. So, while somewhere along the Las Vegas strip a "Vesuvian" volcano erupts loudly every 15 minutes, a fake British frigate battles a pirate ship at regular intervals, and sparkling fountains dance in a lake, Harrah's continues to enhance benefits to its Total Rewards program, improves customer loyalty through customer service supported by the *data mining,* and of course makes lots of money.

Sources: Compiled from Loveman (2003) and from Levinson (2001).

 LESSONS LEARNED FROM THIS CASE

The opening case about Harrah's illustrates the importance of data analysis to a large entertainment company. It shows that it is necessary to collect vast amounts of data, organize and store them properly in one place, and then analyze the data and use the results to make better marketing and other corporate decisions. The case shows us that new data go through a process and stages: Data are collected, processed, and stored in a data warehouse. Then, data are processed by analytical tools such as data mining and decision modeling. The findings of the data analysis direct promotional and other decisions. Finally, continuous collection and analysis of fresh data provide management with feedback regarding the success of management strategies.

In this chapter we explain how this process is executed with the help of IT. We will also deal with some additional topics that typically supplement the data management process.

10.1 DATA MANAGEMENT: A CRITICAL SUCCESS FACTOR

As illustrated throughout this textbook, IT applications cannot be done without using some kind of data. In other words, without data you cannot have most IT applications, nor can you make good decisions. Data, as we have seen in the opening case, are at the core of management and marketing operations. However, there are increasing difficulties in acquiring, keeping, and managing data.

The Difficulties of Managing Data, and Some Potential Solutions

Since data are processed in several stages and possibly places, they may be subject to some problems and difficulties.

DATA PROBLEMS AND DIFFICULTIES. Managing data in organizations is difficult for various reasons:

- The amount of data increases exponentially with time. Much past data must be kept for a long time, and new data are added rapidly. However, only small portions of an organization's data are relevant for any specific application, and that relevant data must be identified and found in order to be useful.
- Data are scattered throughout organizations and are collected by many individuals using several methods and devices. Data are frequently stored in several servers and locations, and in *different* computing systems, databases, formats, and human and computer languages. This may create problems, as demonstrated in the case of data needed for homeland security (see Minicase 1, which also discusses a solution).
- An ever-increasing amount of external data needs to be considered in making organizational decisions.
- Data security, quality, and integrity are critical, yet are easily jeopardized. In addition, legal requirements relating to data differ among countries and change frequently.
- Selecting data management tools can be a major problem because of the huge number of products available.

These difficulties, and the critical need for timely and accurate information, have prompted organizations to search for effective and efficient data management solutions.

SOLUTIONS TO MANAGING DATA. Historically, data management has been geared to supporting transaction processing by organizing the data in a *hierarchical format* in one location. This format supports secured and efficient high-volume

Technology Guides are located at the book's Web site.

processing; however, it may be inefficient for queries and other ad-hoc applications. Therefore, *relational databases*, based on organization of data in rows and columns, were added to facilitate end-user computing and decision support. (Data organization is described further in Technology Guide 3.)

With the introduction of client/server environments and Web technologies, databases became distributed throughout organizations, creating problems in finding data quickly and easily. This was the major reason that Harrah's sought the creation of a *data warehouse*. As we will see later, the intranet, extranets, and Web technologies can also be used to improve data management.

It is now well recognized that data are an asset, although they can be a burden to maintain. The purpose of appropriate data management is to ease the burden of maintaining data and to enhance the power from their use. To see how this is done, let's begin by examining how data are processed during their life cycle.

Data Life Cycle Process

Businesses do not run on raw data. They run on data that have been processed to information and knowledge, which managers apply to business problems and opportunities. As seen in the Harrah's case, *knowledge* fuels solutions. Everything from innovative product designs to brilliant competitive moves relies on knowledge (see Markus et al., 2002). However, because of the difficulties of managing data, cited earlier, deriving knowledge from accumulated data may not be simple or easy.

Transformation of data into knowledge and solutions is accomplished in several ways. In general, it resembles the process shown in Figure 10.1. It starts with new data collection from various sources. These data are stored in a database(s). Then the data are preprocessed to fit the format of a data warehouse or data marts, where they are stored. Users then access the warehouse or data mart and take a copy of the needed data for analysis. The analysis is done with data analysis and mining tools (see Chopoorian et al., 2001) which look for patterns, and with intelligent systems, which support data interpretation.

Note that not all data processing follows this process. Small and medium companies do not need data warehouses, and even many large companies do not need them. (We will see later who needs them.) In such cases data go directly from data sources or databases to an analysis (broken line in Figure 10.1). An example of direct processing is an application that uses real-time data. These can be processed as they are collected and immediately analyzed. Many Web data are of this type. In such a case, as we will see later, we use Web mining instead of data mining.

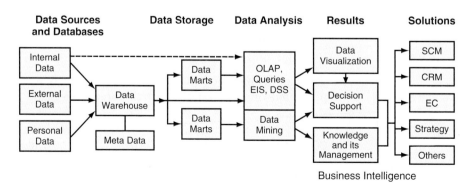

FIGURE 10.1 Data life cycle.

The result of these activities is the generating of decision support and knowledge. Both the data (at various times during the process) and the knowledge (derived at the end of the process) may need to be presented to users. The presentation can be accomplished by using different visualization tools. The created knowledge may be stored in an organizational knowledge base (as shown in Chapter 9) and used, together with decision support tools, to provide solutions to organizational problems. The elements and the process shown in Figure 10.1 are discussed in the remaining sections of this chapter and in Chapter 11.

Data Sources   The data life cycle begins with the acquisition of data from data sources. Data sources can be classified as internal, personal, and external.

INTERNAL DATA SOURCES. An organization's internal data are about people, products, services, and processes. Such data may be found in one or more places. For example, data about employees and their pay are usually stored in the corporate database. Data about equipment and machinery may be stored in the maintenance department database. Sales data can be stored in several places— aggregate sales data in the corporate database, and details at each regional database. Internal data are usually accessible via an organization's intranet.

PERSONAL DATA. IS users or other corporate employees may document their own expertise by creating personal data. These data are not necessarily just facts, but may include concepts, thoughts, and opinions. They include, for example, subjective estimates of sales, opinions about what competitors are likely to do, and certain rules and formulas developed by the users. These data can reside on the user's PC or be placed on departmental or business units' databases or on the corporate knowledge bases.

EXTERNAL DATA SOURCES. There are many sources for external data, ranging from commercial databases to sensors and satellites. Government reports constitute a major source for external data. Data are available on CD-ROMs and memory chips, on Internet servers, as films, and as sound or voices. Pictures, diagrams, atlases, and television are other sources of external data. Hundreds of thousands of organizations worldwide place publicly accessible data on their Web servers, flooding us with data. Most external data are irrelevant to any single application. Yet, much external data must be monitored and captured to ensure that important data are not overlooked. Large amounts of external data are available on the Internet.

The Internet and Commercial Database Services. Many thousands of databases all over the world are accessible through the Internet. Much of the database access is free. A user can access Web pages of vendors, clients, and even competitors. He or she can view and download information while conducting research. Some external data flow to an organization on a regular basis through EDI or through other company-to-company channels. Much external data are free; other data are available from commercial database services.

A commercial *online database publisher* sells access to specialized databases, newspapers, magazines, bibliographies, and reports. Such a service can provide external data to users in a timely manner and at a reasonable cost. Many commercial database publishers will customize the data for each user. Several thousand services are currently available, most of which are accessible via the Internet. Many consulting companies (e.g., *aberdeen.com*) sell reports online.

Methods for Collecting Raw Data

The diversity of data and the multiplicity of sources make the task of data collection fairly complex. Sometimes it is necessary to collect raw data in the field. In other cases it is necessary to elicit data from people.

Raw data can be collected manually or by instruments and sensors. Some examples of manual data collection methods are time studies, surveys, observations, and contributions from experts. Data can also be scanned or transferred electronically. Although a wide variety of hardware and software exists for data storage, communication, and presentation, much less effort has gone into developing software tools for data capture in environments where complex and unstable data exist. Insufficient methods for dealing with such situations may limit the effectiveness of IT development and use. One exception is the Web. **Clickstream data** are those that can be collected automatically, using special software, from a company's Web site or from what visitors are doing on the site (see Chapter 4, and Turban et al., 2006). In addition, the use of online polls and questionnaires is becoming very popular (see Baumer, 2003, and Ray and Tabor, 2003).

The collection of data from multiple external sources may be an even more complicated task. One way to improve it is to use a *data flow manager (DFM)*, which takes information from external sources and puts it where it is needed, when it is needed, in a usable form (e.g., see *smartdraw.com*). A DFM consists of (1) a decision support system, (2) a central data request processor, (3) a data integrity component, (4) links to external data suppliers, and (5) the processes used by the external data suppliers.

The complexity of data collection can create data-quality problems. Therefore, regardless of how they are collected, data need to be validated. A classic expression that sums up the situation is "garbage in, garbage out" (GIGO). Safeguards for data quality are designed to prevent data problems.

Data Quality and Integrity

Data quality (DQ) is an extremely important issue since quality determines the data's usefulness as well as the quality of the decisions based on the data (Creese and Veytsel, 2003). It has the following dimensions: *accuracy, accessibility, relevance, timeliness,* and *completeness* (Olson, 2003; Wang and Strong, 1996). Data are frequently found to be inaccurate, incomplete, or ambiguous, particularly in large, centralized databases. The economical and social damage from poor-quality data has actually been calculated to have cost organizations billions of dollars (see Redman, 1998, and Chapter 16). According to Brauer (2001), data quality is the cornerstone of effective business intelligence.

Interest in data quality has been known for generations. For example, according to Hasan (2002), treatment of numerical data for quality can be traced to the year 1881. An example of typical data problems, their causes, and possible solutions is provided in Table 10.1. For a discussion of data auditing and controls, see Chapter 15.

Strong et al. (1997) conducted extensive research on data quality problems. Some of the problems identified are technical ones such as capacity, while others relate to potential computer crimes. The researchers divided these problems into the following four categories and dimensions.

1. *Intrinsic DQ:* accuracy, objectivity, believability, and reputation
2. *Accessibility DQ:* accessibility and access security

TABLE 10.1 Data Problems and Possible Solutions		
Problem	**Typical Cause**	**Possible Solutions (in Some Cases)**
Data are not correct.	Raw data were entered inaccurately.	Develop a systematic way to ensure the accuracy of raw data. Automate (use scanners or sensors).
	Data derived by an individual were generated carelessly.	Carefully monitor both the data values and the manner in which the data have been generated. Check for compliance with collection rules.
	Data were changed deliberately or accidentally.	Take appropriate security measures (see Chapter 15).
Data are not timely.	The method for generating the data was not rapid enough to meet the need for the data.	Modify the system for generating the data. Move to a client/server system. Automate.
Data are not measured or indexed properly.	Raw data were gathered according to a logic or periodicity that was not consistent with the purposes of the analysis.	Develop a system for rescaling or recombining the improperly indexed data. Use intelligent search agents.
Needed data simply do not exist.	No one ever stored the data needed now.	Whether or not it is useful now, store data for future use. Use the Internet to search for similar data. Use experts.
	Required data never existed.	Make an effort to generate the data or to estimate them (use experts). Use neural computing for pattern recognition.

Source: Compiled and modified from Alter (1980).

3. **Contextual DQ:** relevancy, value added, timeliness, completeness, amount of data
4. **Representation DQ:** interpretability, ease of understanding, concise representation, consistent representation

Although business executives recognize the importance of having high-quality data, they discover that numerous organizational and technical issues make it difficult to reach this objective. For example, data ownership issues arise from the lack of policies defining responsibility and accountability in managing data. Inconsistent data-quality requirements of various standalone applications create an additional set of problems as organizations try to combine individual applications into integrated enterprise systems. Interorganizational information systems add a new level of complexity to managing data quality. Companies must resolve the issues of administrative authority to ensure that each partner complies with the data-quality standards. The tendency to delegate data-quality responsibilities to the technical teams, as opposed to business users, is another common pitfall that stands in the way of high-quality data (Loshin, 2004).

Different categories of data quality are proposed by Brauer (2001). They are: *standardization* (for consistency), *matching* (of data if stored in different places), *verification* (against the source), and *enhancement* (adding of data to increase its usefulness). Whichever system is used, once the major variables and relationships in each category are identified, an attempt can be made to find out how to better manage the data.

An area of increasing importance is the quality of data that are processed very fast in *real time*. Many decisions are being made today in such an environment.

For how to handle data in such a case, see Creese and Veytsel (2003) and Bates (2003).

Another major data quality issue is **data integrity.** Many definitions of integrity in the context of data management have been proposed in the literature. For example, Motro (1989) suggested using both validity and completeness constraints to guarantee that all false data are excluded. Moerkotte and Lockemann (1991) used the term consistency as an equivalent for integrity. In general, the concept of integrity means that data must be accurate, correct, and valid (Date, 1995). Usually, poor legacy integration or older filing systems may lack integrity. In such cases, a change made in the file in one place may not be made in a related file in another place. This results in *conflicting* data.

The relationship of data quality to information quality is described by Lee and Strong (2003–2004) and by Ballou et al. (2003–2004).

DATA QUALITY IN WEB-BASED SYSTEMS.   Data are collected from the Internet on a routine basis or for a special application. In either case, it is necessary to organize and store the data before they can be used. This may be a difficult task, especially when media-rich Web sites are involved. For a comprehensive approach on how to ensure quality of Internet-generated data, see Creese and Veytsel (2003). For an example of multimedia databases, widely used for Web applications, see Online File W10.1.

Data Privacy, Cost, and Ethics

Collecting data about employees, customers, or any other people raises the concern about privacy protection. Data need to be accessible only to authorized people. Keeping data secure costs money during collection, storage, and use. Furthermore, providing information required by the government means even more cost to organizations. An example is the situation of homeland security described in *A Closer Look 10.1.*

Document Management

There are several major problems with paper documents. For example, in maintaining paper documents, we can pose the following questions: (1) Does everyone have the current version? (2) How often does it need to be updated? (3) How secure are the documents? (4) How can the distribution of documents to the appropriate individuals be managed in a timely manner? and (5) How can a company reduce the paper usage from the viewpoints of protecting the environment and saving natural resources? The answers to these and similar questions may be difficult.

Electronic data processing overcomes some of these problems. One of the earliest IT-enabled tools of data management is called *document management.* When documents are provided in electronic form from a single repository (typically a Web server), only the current version is provided. For example, many firms maintain their telephone directories in electronic form on an intranet to eliminate the need to copy and distribute hard copies of a directory that requires constant corrections. Also, with data stored in electronic form, access to various documents can be restricted as required (see Becker, 2003).

WHAT IS DOCUMENT MANAGEMENT?   **Document management** is the automated control of electronic documents, page images, spreadsheets, voice word processing documents, and other complex documents through their entire life cycle within an organization, from initial creation to final archiving. Document management offers various benefits: It allows organizations to exert greater

A CLOSER LOOK

10.1 HOMELAND SECURITY PRIVACY AND COST CONCERNS

The U.S. government plans to apply analytical technologies on a global scale in the war on terrorism, but will these technologies prove an effective weapon? In the first year and a half after September 11, 2001, supermarket chains, home improvement stores, and other retailers voluntarily handed over massive amounts of customer records to federal law enforcement agencies, almost always in violation of their stated privacy policies. Many others responded to court orders for information, as required by law. The government has a right to gather corporate data under legislation passed after September 11, 2001.

The FBI now mines enormous amounts of data looking for activity that could indicate a terrorist plot or crime. Law-enforcement agencies expect to find results in transaction data, and American businesses are stuck in the middle. Some have to create special systems to generate the data required by law-enforcement agencies. An average-size company may spend an average of $5 million for a system. On the other hand, not complying can cost more. Western Union was fined $8 million in December 2002 for not properly complying with law-enforcement requests for corporate data.

Privacy issues abound. Since the government is acquiring personal data to detect suspicious patterns of activity, there is the prospect of improper or illegal use of the data. Many see such gathering of data as a violation of citizens' freedoms and rights. They see the need for an oversight organization to "watch the watchers," to ensure that the Department of Homeland Security (DHS) does not mindlessly acquire data. Instead, it should acquire only pertinent data and information that can be mined to identify patterns that potentially could lead to stopping terrorists' activities.

Sources: Compiled from Foley (2003), Grimes (2003), and Worthen (2003).

control over production, storage, and distribution of documents, yielding greater efficiency in the reuse of information, the control of a document through a workflow process, and the reduction of product cycle times.

Electronic delivery of documents has been around since 1999, with UPS and the U.S. Post Office playing a pioneering role in such service. They deliver documents electronically over a secured system (e-mail is not secured), and they are able to deliver complex "documents" such as large files and multimedia videos (which can be difficult to send via e-mail). The need for greater efficiency in handling business documents to gain an edge on the competition has fueled the increased availability of document management systems, also known as electronic document management. Essentially, **document management systems (DMSs)** provide information in an electronic format to decision makers. The full range of functions that a document management system may perform includes document identification, storage, and retrieval; intelligent search; tracking; version control; workflow management; and presentation. The Thomas Cook Company, for example, uses a document management system to handle travel-refund applications. The system works on the PC desktop and has automated the workflow process, helping the firm double its volume of business while adding only about 33 percent more employees (see Cole, 1996). Another example is the Massachusetts Department of Revenue, which uses imaging systems to increase productivity of tax return processing by about 80 percent (see *civic.com/pubs*, 2001). Recently, DMSs are equipped with XML capabilities (see Yao et al., 2003).

Document management deals with knowledge in addition to data and information. See Asprev and Middleton (2003) for an overview and for the relationship of document management with knowledge management.

A CLOSER LOOK
10.2 HOW COMPANIES USE DOCUMENT MANAGEMENT SYSTEMS

Here are some examples of how companies use document management systems to manage data and documents:

The Surgery Center of Baltimore stores all of its medical records electronically, providing instant patient information to doctors and nurses anywhere and any time. The system also routes charts to the billing department, whose employees can scan and e-mail any related information to insurance providers and patients. The DMS also helps maintain an audit trail, including providing records for legal purposes or action. Business processes have been expedited by more than 50 percent, the cost of such processes is significantly lower, and morale of office employees in the center is up (see *laserfiche.com/newsroom/baltimore.html*).

American Express is using a DMS to collect and process over one million customer satisfaction surveys each year. The data are collected in templates of over 600 different survey forms, in 12 languages, in 11 countries. The system (TELEform from Alchemy and Cardiff Software) is integrated with AMEX's legacy system and is capable of distributing processed results to many managers. Staff who process these forms have been reduced from 17 to 1, saving AMEX over $500,000 each year (see case studies at *imrgold.com*).

LifeStar, an ambulance service in Tulare, California, is keeping all historical paper documents on optical disks. Hundreds of boxes with documents were digitized, and so are all new documents. Furthermore, all optical disks are backed up and are kept in different locations for security purposes (see *laserfiche.com/newsroom/tulare.html*).

In Toronto, Canada, the Works and Emergency Services Department uses a Web-based record document-retrieval solution. With it, employees have immediate access to drawings and the documents related to roads, buildings, utility lines, and more. Quick access to these documents enables emergency crews to solve problems, and even save lives, much faster. Laptop computers are installed in each departmental vehicle, loaded with maps, drawings, and historical repair data (see *laserfiche.com/newsroom/torantoworks.html*).

The University of Cincinnati, a state university in Ohio, is required to provide authorized access to the personnel files of 12,000 active employees and tens of thousands of retirees. There are over 75,000 queries about the personnel records every year, and answers need to be found among 2.5 million records. Using an antiquated microfilm system to find answers took days. The solution was a DMS that digitized all paper and microfilm documents, making them available via the Internet and the intranet. An authorized employee can now use a browser and access a document in seconds (see *imrgold.com/en/case_studies/edu_Univ_of_Cin.asp*).

The European Court of Human Rights (44 countries in Europe) created a Web-based document and KM system which was originally stored on an intranet and now is stored in a separate organizational knowledge base. The DMS has had over 20 million hits in 2002 (Canada NewsWire, 2003). Millions of euros are saved each year just on printing and mailing documents.

McDonnell-Douglas (now part of the Boeing Company) distributed aircraft service bulletins to its customers around the world using the Internet. The company used to distribute a staggering volume of bulletins to over 200 airlines, using over 4 million pages of documentation every year. Now it is all on the Web, saving money and time both for the company and for its customers.

Motorola uses a DMS not only for document storage and retrieval, but also for small-group collaboration and companywide knowledge sharing. It develops virtual communities where people can discuss and publish information, all with the Web-enabled DMS.

The major tools of document management are workflow software, authoring tools, scanners, and databases (known as object-relational database management systems; see Technology Guide 3). Document management systems usually include computerized imaging systems that can result in substantial savings, as shown in Online File W10.2.

One of the major vendors of document management is Lotus Development Corporation. Its document databases and their replication property provide many advantages for group work and information sharing (see *lotus.com*). For further discussion see *imrgold.com* and *docuvantage.com*.

WEB-BASED DMS. In many organizations, documents are now viewed as multimedia objects with hyperlinks. The Web provides easy access to pages of information. DMSs excel in this area (see examples in *A Closer Look 10.2*, page 416). Web-enabled DMSs also make it easy to put information on intranets (see Yao et al., 2003), since many of them provide instantaneous conversion of documents to HTML. BellSouth, for example, saves an estimated $17.5 million each year through its intranet-enabled forms-management system. For another example of Web-enabled document management systems see Delcambre et al. (2003).

In all of the examples cited in the text and in *A Closer Look 10.2*, time and money are saved. Also, documents are not lost or mixed up. An issue related to document management systems is how to provide the privacy and security of personal data. We address that issue in Chapters 15 and 16.

10.2 DATA WAREHOUSING

Many large and even medium-size companies are using data warehousing to make it easier and faster to process, analyze, and query data.

Transactional versus Analytical Processing

Data processing in organizations can be viewed either as *transactional* or *analytical*. The data in transactions processing systems (TPSs) are organized mainly in a *hierarchical structure* (Technology Guide 2) and are centrally processed. The databases and the processing systems involved are known as *operational systems*, and the results are mainly transaction reports. This is done primarily for fast and efficient processing of routine, repetitive data.

Today, however, the most successful companies are those that can respond quickly and flexibly to market changes and opportunities, and the key to this response is the effective and efficient use of data and information, as shown in the Harrah's case. This is done not only via transaction processing, but also through a supplementary activity, called **analytical processing,** which involves analysis of accumulated data, frequently by end users. Analytical processing, also referred to as *business intelligence*, includes data mining, decision support systems (DSSs), enterprise information systems (EISs), Web applications, querying, and other end-user activities. Placing strategic information in the hands of decision makers aids productivity and empowers users to make better decisions, leading to greater competitive advantage. A good data delivery system should be able to support easy data access by the end users themselves, as well as quick, accurate, flexible and effective decision making.

There are basically two options for conducting analytical processing. One is to work directly with the operational systems (the "let's use what we have" approach), using software tools and components known as front-end tools and *middleware* (see Technology Guide 2). The other is to use a data warehouse.

The first option can be optimal for companies that do not have a large number of end users running queries and conducting analyses against the operating systems. It is also an option for departments that consist mainly of users who have the necessary technical skills for an extensive use of tools such as spreadsheets (see BIXL, 2002) and graphics. Although it is possible for those with fewer technical skills to use query and reporting tools, they may not be effective, flexible, or easy enough to use in many cases.

Since the mid-1990s, there has been a wave of *front-end tools* that allow end users to solve these problems by directly conducting queries and reporting on data stored in operational databases. The problem with this approach, however, is that the tools are only effective with end users who have a medium to high degree of knowledge about databases. This situation improved drastically with the use of Web-based tools. Yet, when data are in several sources and in several formats, it is difficult to bring them together to conduct an analysis.

The second option, a data warehouse, overcomes these limitations and provides for improved analytical processing. It involves three concepts:

1. A business representation of data for end users
2. A Web-based environment that gives the users query and reporting capabilities
3. A server-based repository (the data warehouse) that allows centralized security and control over the data

The Data Warehouse

The Harrah's case illustrates some major benefits of a **data warehouse,** which is a repository of subject-oriented historical data that are organized to be accessible in a form readily acceptable for analytical processing activities (such as data mining, decision support, querying, and other applications). Representative examples are revenue management, customer-relationship management, fraud detection, and crew payroll-management applications (Whiting, 2003). Pizza Hut, for example, builds its customer relationship management programs on a data warehouse with 40 million U.S. households, or between 40 and 50 percent of the U.S. market gleaned from point-of-sale transactions at its restaurants (Brown, 2003).

The major benefits of a data warehouse are (1) the ability to reach data quickly, since they are located in one place, and (2) the ability to reach data easily and frequently by end users with Web browsers. To aid the accessibility of data, detail-level operational data must be transformed into a relational form, which makes them more amenable to analytical processing. Thus, data warehousing is not a concept by itself, but is interrelated with data access, retrieval, analysis, and visualization. (See Eckerson, 2003, and Inmon, 2002.)

The process of building and using a data warehouse is shown in Figure 10.2. The organization's data are stored in operational systems (left side of the figure). Using special software called ETL (extraction, transformation, load), data are processed and then stored in a data warehouse. Not all data are necessarily transferred to the data warehouse. Frequently only a summary of the data is transferred. The data that are transferred are organized within the warehouse in a form that is easy for end users to access and locate. The data are also standardized. Then, the data are organized by subject, such as by functional area, vendor, or product. In contrast, operational data are organized according to a business process, such as shipping, purchasing, or inventory control and/or functional department. (Note that ERP data can be input to a data warehouse, and ERP and SCM decisions use the output from data warehouse. See Grant, 2003.)

Data warehouses provide for the storage of **metadata,** meaning data about data (see Sen, 2004). Metadata include software programs about data, rules for organizing data, and data summaries that are easier to index and search, especially with Web tools. The design and use of metadata may involve ethical issues such as organizing the metadata so that it will influence users one way or another (Brody, 2003). Finally, *middleware* tools enable access to the data warehouse (see Technology Guide 2, and Rundensteiner et al., 2000).

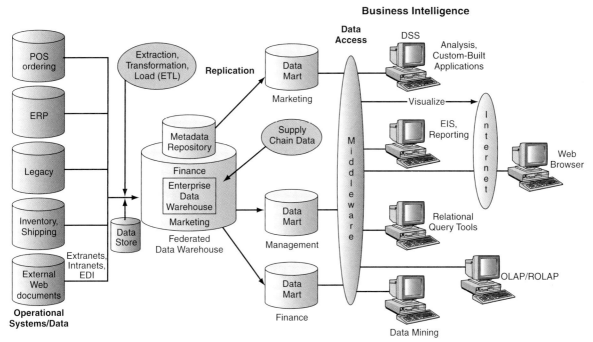

FIGURE 10.2 Data warehouse framework and views. (*Source:* Drawn by E. Turban.)

CHARACTERISTICS OF A DATA WAREHOUSE.   Nine major characteristics of data warehousing are:

1. *Organization.* Data are organized by subject (e.g., by customer, vendor, product, price level, and region), and contain information relevant for decision support only.
2. *Consistency.* Data in different operational databases may be encoded differently. For example, gender data may be encoded 0 and 1 in one operational system and "m" and "f" in another. In the warehouse they will be coded in a consistent manner.
3. *Time variant.* The data are kept for many years so they can be used for trends, forecasting, and comparisons over time.
4. *Nonvolatile.* Once entered into the warehouse, data are not updated.
5. *Relational.* Typically the data warehouse uses a relational structure.
6. *Client/server.* The data warehouse uses the client/server architecture mainly to provide the end user an easy access to its data.
7. *Web-based.* Today's data warehouses are designed to provide an efficient computing environment for Web-based applications (Rundensteiner et al., 2000).
8. *Integration.* Data from various sources are integrated. Web Services is now used to support integration (Vaughan, 2003).
9. *Real time.* Although most applications of data warehousing are not in real time, it is possible to arrange for real-time capabilities. For details, see Basu (2004) and Bonde and Kuckuk (2004).

BENEFITS.   Moving information off the mainframe presents a company with the unique opportunity to restructure its IT strategy. Companies can reinvent the way in which they shape and form their application data, empowering end users to conduct extensive analysis with these data in ways that may not have been possible before (e.g., see Minicase 2, see p. 452, about Sears). Another immediate benefit is providing a consolidated view of corporate data, which is better than providing many smaller (and differently formatted) views. For example, separate applications may track sales and coupon mailings. Combining data from these different applications may yield insights into the cost-efficiency of coupon sales promotions that would not be immediately evident from the output data of either application alone. Integrated within a data warehouse, however, such information can be easily extracted and analyzed.

Another benefit is that data warehousing allows information processing to be offloaded from expensive operational systems onto low-cost servers. Once this is done, the end-user tools can handle a significant number of end-user information requests. Furthermore, some operational system reporting requirements can be moved to decision support systems, thus freeing up production processing.

These benefits can improve business knowledge, provide competitive advantage (see Watson et al., 2002), enhance customer service and satisfaction (see Online File W10.3), facilitate decision making, and help in streamlining business processes.

COST. The cost of a data warehouse can be very high, both to build and to maintain. Furthermore, it may be difficult and expensive to incorporate data from obsolete legacy systems. Finally, there may be a lack of incentive to share data. Therefore, a careful feasibility study must be undertaken before a commitment is made to data warehousing.

ARCHITECTURE AND TOOLS. There are several basic architectures for data warehousing. Two common ones are two-tier and three-tier architectures. (See Gray and Watson, 1998.) In three-tier architecture, data from the warehouse are processed twice and deposited in an additional *multidimensional database,* organized for easy multidimensional analysis and presentation (Section 10.5) or replicated in data marts. For a Web-based architecture see Rundensteiner et al. (2000). The architecture of the data warehouse determines the tools needed for its construction (see Kimball and Ross, 2002).

PUTTING THE WAREHOUSE ON THE INTRANET. Delivery of data warehouse content to decision makers throughout the enterprise can be done via an intranet. Users can view, query, and analyze the data and produce reports using Web browsers. This is an extremely economical and effective method of delivering data (see Kimball and Ross, 2002, and Inmon, 2002).

SUITABILITY. Data warehousing is most appropriate for organizations in which some of the following apply:

- Large amounts of data need to be accessed by end users (see the Harrah's case and the Sears Minicase 2).
- The operational data are stored in different systems.
- An information-based approach to management is in use.
- There is a large, diverse customer base (such as in a utility company or a bank; for example, AT&T's 26-terabyte data warehouse is used by 3,000 employees for doing marketing analysis).

TABLE 10.2 Summary of Strategic Uses of Data Warehousing

Industry	Functional Areas of Use	Strategic Use
Airline	Operations and Marketing	Crew assignment, aircraft deployment, mix of fares, analysis of route profitability, frequent flyer program promotions
Apparel	Distribution and Marketing	Merchandising, and inventory replenishment
Banking	Product Development, Operations, and Marketing	Customer service, trend analysis, product and service promotions, reduction of IS expenses
Credit card	Product Development and Marketing	Customer service, new information service for a fee, fraud detection
Health care	Operations	Reduction of operational expenses
Investment and insurance	Product Development, Operations, and Marketing	Risk management, market movements analysis, customer tendencies analysis, portfolio management
Personal care products	Distribution and Marketing	Distribution decisions, product promotions, sales decisions, pricing policy
Public sector	Operations	Intelligence gathering
Retail chain	Distribution and Marketing	Trend analysis, buying pattern analysis, pricing policy, inventory control, sales promotions, optimal distribution channel decisions
Steel	Manufacturing	Pattern analysis (quality control)
Telecommunications	Product Development, Operations, and Marketing	New product and service promotions, reduction of IS budget, profitability analysis

Source: Park (1997), p. 19, Table 2.

- The same data are represented differently in different systems.
- Data are stored in highly technical formats that are difficult to decipher.
- Extensive end-user computing is performed (many end users performing many activities; for example, Sears has 5,000 users, as described in Minicase 2).

Some of the successful applications are summarized in Table 10.2. Hundreds of other successful applications are reported (e.g., see client success stories and case studies at Web sites of vendors such as Hyperion Inc., Business Objects, Cognos Corp., Information Builders, NCR Corp., Oracle, Computer Associates, and Software A&G). For further discussion see Gray and Watson (1998) and Inmon (2002). Also visit the Data Warehouse Institute (*dw-institute.org*).

Data Marts, Operational Data Stores, and Multidimensional Databases

Data warehouses are frequently supplemented with or substituted by the following: data marts, operational data stores, and multidimensional databases.

DATA MARTS. The high cost of data warehouses confines their use to large companies. An alternative used by many other firms is creation of a lower cost, scaled-down version of a data warehouse called a data mart. A **data mart** is a small warehouse designed for a strategic business unit (SBU) or a department.

The advantages of data marts include: low cost (prices under $100,000 versus $1 million or more for data warehouses); significantly shorter lead time for implementation, often less than 90 days; local rather than central control, conferring power on the using group. They also contain less information than the data warehouse. Hence, they have more rapid response and are more easily understood and navigated than an enterprisewide data warehouse. Finally, they allow a business unit to build its own decision support systems without relying on a centralized IS department.

There are two major types of data marts:

1. *Replicated (dependent) data marts.* Sometimes it is easier to work with a small subset of the data warehouse. In such cases one can replicate some subsets of the data warehouse in smaller data marts, each of which is dedicated to a certain area, as was shown in Figure 10.2 (page 419). In such a case the data mart is an *addition* to the data warehouse.
2. *Standalone data marts.* A company can have one or more independent data marts without having a data warehouse. Typical data marts are for marketing, finance, and engineering applications.

OPERATIONAL DATA STORES. An **operational data store** is a database for transaction processing systems that uses data warehouse concepts to provide clean data. That is, it brings the concepts and benefits of the data warehouse to the operational portions of the business, at a lower cost. It is used for short-term decisions involving mission-critical applications rather than for the medium- and long-term decisions associated with the regular data warehouse. These decisions depend on much more current information. For example, a bank needs to know about all the accounts for a given customer who is calling on the phone. The operational data store can be viewed as situated between the operational data (in legacy systems) and the data warehouse. A comparison between the two is provided by Gray and Watson (1998).

MULTIDIMENSIONAL DATABASES. **Multidimensional databases** are specialized data stores that organize facts by dimensions, such as geographical region, product line, salesperson, or time (see Online File W10.4). The data in multidimensional databases are usually preprocessed and stored in what is called a (multidimensional) *data cube*. A data cube is shown on the left side of the figure in Online File W10.4. Each cell in the cube represents some attribute of a specific mix of dimensions. (There are three dimensions in the figure.) Facts, such as quantities sold, are placed at the intersection of the dimensions. One such intersection might be the quantities of washers sold in the Central Division of the company in July 2004.

Dimensions often have a hierarchy. Sales figures, for example, might be presented by day, by month, or by year. They might also roll up an organizational dimension from store to region to company. Multidimensional databases can be incorporated in a data warehouse, sometimes as its core, or they can be used as an additional layer of storage. For further discussion of multidimensionality, see Section 10.5.

10.3 INFORMATION AND KNOWLEDGE DISCOVERY WITH BUSINESS INTELLIGENCE

Business Intelligence

Once the data are in the data warehouse and/or data marts they can be accessed by managers, analysts, and other end users. Users can then conduct several activities. These activities are frequently referred to as analytical processing or more commonly as *business intelligence*. (Note: For a glossary of these and other terms, see *Dimensional Insight*, 2003.)

Business intelligence (BI) is a broad category of applications and techniques for gathering, storing, analyzing, and providing access to data to help enterprise users make better business and strategic decisions (see Oguz, 2003, and Moss and Atre, 2003). Pizza Hut, for example, has significantly boosted its sales revenue by using BI tools (Langnau, 2003). Based on 20 years' worth of data on consumers, Pizza Hut knows what kind of pizza customers order, what kind of coupons they usually use, and how much they spend in a given time period. Marketing managers can take this information and run it through a BI system that predicts and forecasts the probability of a customer's next order. The company then uses this information to determine marketing strategies to influence the customer to buy more pizza without spending more on that marketing program than it has to. The process of BI usually, but not necessarily, involves the use, or even the construction, of a data warehouse, as seen in Figure 10.3.

HOW BUSINESS INTELLIGENCE WORKS. Operational raw data are usually kept in corporate databases. For example, a national retail chain that sells everything from grills and patio furniture to plastic utensils has data about inventory, customer information, data about past promotions, and sales numbers in various databases. Though all this information may be scattered across multiple systems—and may seem unrelated—data warehouse–building software can

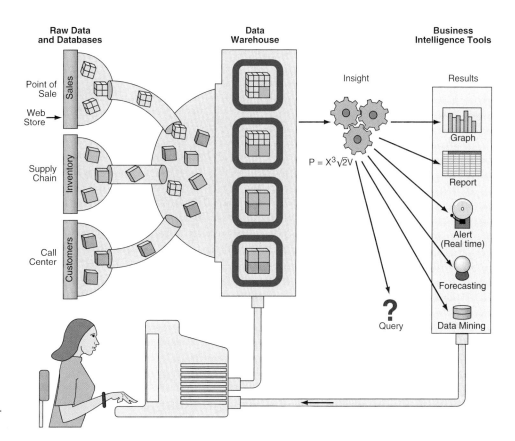

FIGURE 10.3 How business intelligence works.

IT at Work 10.1
BEN & JERRY'S KEEPS TRACK OF ITS PINTS

At the Ben & Jerry's (*benjerry.com*) factory in Waterbury, Vermont, huge pipes pump out 190,000 pints of ice cream each day. Throughout the day, refrigerated tractor trailers pull up, pick up the pints, and deliver them to depots. From there, the ice cream is shipped out to 50,000 grocery stores in the United States and 12 other countries. There, the ice cream is placed on the freezer shelves.

At the company's headquarters, the life of each pint of ice cream—from ingredients to sale—is tracked. Once the pint is stamped and sent out, Ben & Jerry's stores its tracking number in an Oracle data warehouse and later analyzes the data. Using business intelligence software, the sales team can check to see if Chocolate Chip Cookie Dough is gaining ground on Cherry Garcia for the coveted Number 1 sales position. The marketing department checks to see whether company promotions and advertis-

ing are leading to increased sales. The finance people use the tracking number in their analyses to show the profit generated from each type of ice cream. Since the company started using the software, the accounting department has sharply reduced the amount of time it takes to close the monthly books. And probably most important to a company focused on customer loyalty, the consumer affairs staff matches up each pint with the 225 calls and e-mails received each week, checking to see if there were any complaints.

Source: Compiled from Schlosser (2003).

For Further Exploration: What other analyses can Ben & Jerry's do with its business intelligence software? What is the role of Ben & Jerry's information technology department?

---

bring it together to the data warehouse. In the data warehouse (or mart), tables can be linked, and *data cubes* (another term for multidimensional databases) are formed. For instance, inventory information is linked to sales numbers and customer databases, allowing for extensive analysis of information. Some data warehouses have a dynamic link to the databases; others are static.

Using business intelligence software, the user can ask queries, request ad-hoc reports, or conduct any other analyses. For example, analysis can be carried out by performing multilayer queries. Because all the databases are linked, you can search for what products a store has too much of. You can then determine which of these products commonly sell with popular items, based on previous sales. After planning a promotion to move the excess stock along with the popular products (by bundling them together, for example), you can dig deeper to see where this promotion would be most popular (and most profitable). The results of your request can be reports, predictions, alerts, and/or graphical presentations. These can be disseminated to decision makers. For an example of an application at Ben & Jerry's, see *IT at Work 10.1*.

More advanced applications of business intelligence include outputs such as financial modeling, budgeting, resource allocation, and competitive intelligence. Advanced business intelligence systems include components such as decision models, business performance analysis, metrics, data profiling and reengineering tools, and much more. (For details see Eckerson, 2003, and *dmreview.com*.) Finally, BI can be conducted in real time (see Bonde and Kuckuk, 2004, and Microsoft's IT Business Intelligence).

THE TOOLS AND TECHNIQUES OF BUSINESS INTELLIGENCE. BI employs large numbers of tools and techniques. The major applications include the activities of

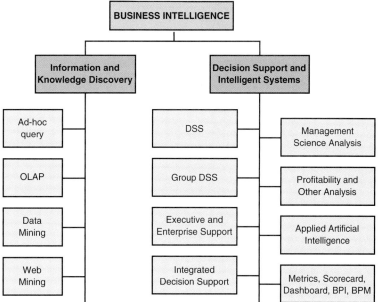

FIGURE 10.4 Categories of business intelligence.

query and reporting, online analytical processing (OLAP), DSS, data mining, forecasting, and statistical analysis. A major BI vendor is SAS (*sas.com*). Other vendors include Microstrategy (see Microstrategy, 2003a, b), Cognos, IBM, SPSS, Hyperion, and Business Objects. We have divided the BI tools into two major categories: (1) *information and knowledge discovery* and (2) *decision support and intelligent analysis*. In each category there are several tools and techniques, as shown in Figure 10.4. In this chapter we will describe the information and knowledge discovery category, while Chapter 11 is dedicated to decision support and intelligent systems. In Chapter 13 we will discuss scorecard and dashboard. For another classification of BI and its relationship to supported users, see Microstrategy (2003).

The Tools and Techniques of Information and Knowledge Discovery

Information and knowledge discovery differs from decision support in its main objective: discovery. Once discovery is done, the results can be used for decision support. Let's distinguish first between information and knowledge discovery.

THE EVOLUTION OF INFORMATION AND KNOWLEDGE DISCOVERY. *Information discovery* started in the late 1960s and early 1970s with data collection techniques. It was basically simple data collection and answered queries that involved one set of historical data. This analysis was extended to answer questions that involved several sets of data with tools such as SQL and relational database management systems (see Table 10.3, page 426, for the evolution). During the 1990s, a recognition of the need for better tools to deal with the ever-increasing amount of data was initiated. This resulted in the creation of the data warehouse and the appearance of OLAP and multidimensional databases and presentation. When the amount of data to be analyzed exploded in the mid-1990s, *knowledge discovery* emerged as an important analytical tool.

TABLE 10.3 Stages in the Evolution of Knowledge Discovery			
Evolutionary Stage	**Business Question**	**Enabling Technologies**	**Characteristics**
Data collection (1960s)	What was my total revenue in the last five years?	Computers, tapes, disks	Retrospective, static data delivery
Data access (1980s)	What were unit sales in New England last March?	Relational databases (RDBMS), structured query language (SQL)	Retrospective, dynamic data delivery at record level
Data warehousing and decision support (early 1990s)	What were the sales in region A, by product, by salesperson?	OLAP, multidimensional databases, data warehouses	Retrospective, dynamic data delivery at multiple levels
Intelligent data mining (late 1990s)	What's likely to happen to the Boston unit's sales next month? Why?	Advanced algorithms, multiprocessor computers, massive databases	Prospective, proactive information delivery
Advanced intelligent system	What is the best plan to follow?	Neural computing, advanced AI models, complex optimization, Web Services	Proactive, integrative; multiple business partners
Complete integration (2000–2004)	How did we perform compared to metrics?		

Source: Based on material from *accure.com* (Accure Software).

The process of extracting useful knowledge from volumes of data is known as *knowledge discovery in databases (KDD),* or just *knowledge discovery,* and it is the subject of extensive research (see Fayyad et al., 1996). KDD's major objective is to identify valid, novel, potentially useful, and ultimately understandable patterns in data. KDD is useful because it is supported by three technologies that are now sufficiently mature: massive data collection, powerful multiprocessor computers, and data mining and other algorithms. KDD processes have appeared under various names and have shown different characteristics. As time has passed, KDD has become able to answer more complex business questions. In this section we will describe two tools of information discovery: ad-hoc queries, and OLAP. Data mining as a KDD tool is described in Section 10.4. We discuss multidimensionality in Section 10.5, and Web-based query tools are described in Section 10.7.

AD-HOC QUERIES AND REPORTING.   Ad-hoc queries allow users to request, in real time, information from the computer that is not available in periodic reports. Such answers are needed to expedite decision making. The system must be intelligent enough to understand what the user wants. Simple ad-hoc query systems are often based on menus. More intelligent systems use structured query language (SQL) and query-by-example approaches, which are described in Technology Guide 3. The most intelligent systems are based on natural language understanding (Chapter 11), and some can communicate with users using voice recognition. Later on we will describe the use of Web tools to facilitate queries.

Querying systems are frequently combined with reporting systems that generate routine reports. For an example of such a combination in a video rental store see Amato-McCoy (2003b). For Web-based information discovery tools see Online File W10.5.

ONLINE ANALYTICAL PROCESSING. The term **online analytical processing (OLAP)** was introduced in 1993 by E. F. Codd, to describe a set of tools that can analyze data to reflect actual business needs. These tools were based on a set of 12 rules: (1) multidimensional view, (2) transparency to the user, (3) easy accessibility, (4) consistent reporting, (5) client/server architecture, (6) generic dimensionality, (7) dynamic sparse matrix handling, (8) multiuser support, (9) cross-dimensional operations, (10) intuitive data manipulation, (11) flexible reporting, and (12) unlimited levels of dimension and aggregation. (For details see Codd et al., 1993.) Let's see how these rules may work.

Assume that a business might organize its sales force by regions, say the Eastern and Western. These two regions might then be broken down into states. In an OLAP database, this organization would be used to structure the sales data so that the VP of sales could see the sales figures for each region. The VP might then want to see the Eastern region broken down by state so that the performance of individual state sales managers could be evaluated. Thus, OLAP reflects the business in the data structure.

The power of OLAP is in its ability to create these business structures (sales regions, product categories, fiscal calendar, partner channels, etc.) and combine them in such a way as to allow users to quickly answer business questions. "How many blue sweaters were sold via mail-order in New York so far this week?" is the kind of question that OLAP is very good at answering. Users can interactively slice the data and drill down to the details they are interested in.

In terms of the technology, an OLAP database can be implemented on top of an existing relational database (this is called ROLAP, for relational OLAP) or it can be implemented via a specialized multidimensional data store (this is called MOLAP, for multidimensional OLAP). In ROLAP, the data request is translated into SQL and the relational database is queried for the answer. In MOLAP, the specialized data store is preloaded with the answers to (all) possible queries so that any request for data can be returned quickly. Obviously there are performance and storage tradeoffs between these two approaches. (Another technology called HOLAP attempts to combine these two approaches.)

Unlike online transaction processing (OLTP) applications, OLAP involves examining many data items (frequently many thousands or even millions) in complex relationships. In addition to answering users' queries, OLAP may analyze these relationships and look for patterns, trends, and exceptions.

A typical OLAP query might access a multigigabyte, multiyear sales database in order to find all product sales in each region for each product type. (See Mini-case 2.) After reviewing the results, an analyst might further refine the query to find sales volume for each sales channel within region or product classifications. As a last step, the analyst might want to perform year-to-year or quarter-to-quarter comparisons, for each sales channel. This whole process must be carried out *online* with rapid response time so that the analysis process is undisturbed.

OLAP can be combined with data mining to conduct a very sophisticated multidimensional-based decision support as illustrated by Fong et al. (2002). By attaching a rule-based component to the OLAP, one can make this type of integrated system an intelligent data mining system (see Lau et al., 2001). For more information, products, and vendors, visit *olapreport.com* and *olap.com*.

Although OLAP and ad-hoc queries are very useful in many cases, they are retrospective in nature and cannot provide the automated and prospective knowledge discovery that is done by advanced data mining techniques.

10.4 DATA MINING CONCEPTS AND APPLICATIONS

Data mining is becoming a major tool for analyzing large amounts of data, usually in a data warehouse (Nemati and Barko, 2002) as well for analyzing Web data. **Data mining** derives its name from the similarities between searching for valuable business information in a large database, and mining a mountain for a vein of valuable ore. Both processes require either sifting through an immense amount of material or intelligently probing it to find exactly where the value resides. (See the Harrah's case at the start of the chapter.) For multiple definitions of data mining, see Hormozi and Giles (2004). In some cases the data are consolidated in a data warehouse and data marts. In others they are kept on the Internet and intranet servers. Usually, data may come from routine operational activities such as sales and marketing, procurement and logistics, production, and accounting. Data may also come from external, nonroutine sources such as government statistical sources, surveys, and commercial databases.

Capabilities of Data Mining

Given databases of sufficient size and quality, data mining technology can generate new business opportunities by providing these capabilities:

- *Automated prediction of trends and behaviors.* Data mining automates the process of finding predictive information in large databases. Questions that traditionally required extensive hands-on analysis can now be answered directly and quickly from the data. A typical example of a predictive problem is *targeted marketing.* Data mining can use data from past promotional mailings to identify the targets most likely to respond favorably to future mailings. Other predictive examples include forecasting bankruptcy and other forms of default, and identifying segments of a population likely to respond similarly to given events.

- *Automated discovery of previously unknown patterns.* Data mining tools identify previously hidden patterns in one step. An example of pattern discovery is the analysis of retail sales data to identify seemingly unrelated products that are often purchased together, such as baby diapers and beer. Other pattern discovery problems include detecting fraudulent credit card transactions and identifying invalid (anomalous) data that may represent data entry keying errors.

When data mining tools are implemented on high-performance parallel-processing systems, they can analyze massive databases in minutes. Larger databases, in turn, yield improved predictions (see Hirji, 2001). Often, these databases will contain data stored for several years. Faster processing means that users can experiment with more models to understand complex data.

Data mining also can be conducted by nonprogrammers. The "miner" is often an end user, empowered by "data drills" and other power query tools to ask ad-hoc questions and get answers quickly, with little or no programming skill. Data mining tools can be combined with spreadsheets and other end-user software development tools, making it relatively easy to analyze and process the mined data. Data mining appears under different names, such as knowledge extraction, data dipping, data archaeology, data exploration, data pattern processing, data dredging, and information harvesting. "Striking it rich" in data mining often involves finding unexpected, valuable results.

The Tools of Data Mining

Data mining frequently consists of two steps, building a data cube and using the cube to extract data for the mining functions that the mining tool supports. A data cube is multidimensional, as was shown in Online File W10.4. Data miners

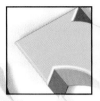

A CLOSER LOOK
10.3 DATA MINING TECHNIQUES AND INFORMATION TYPES

The most commonly used techniques for data mining are the following.

- **Case-based reasoning.** The case-based reasoning approach uses historical cases to recognize patterns (see Chapter 11). For example, customers of Cognitive Systems, Inc., utilize such an approach for helpdesk applications. One company has a 50,000-query case library. New cases are matched quickly against the 50,000 samples in the library, providing more than 90 percent accurate and automatic answers to queries.

- **Neural computing.** Neural computing is a machine learning approach by which historical data can be examined for pattern recognition. These patterns can then be used for making predictions and for decision support (details are given in Chapter 11). Users equipped with neural computing tools can go through huge databases and, for example, identify potential customers of a new product or companies whose profiles suggest that they are heading for bankruptcy. Most practical applications are in financial services, in marketing, and in manufacturing.

- **Intelligent agents.** One of the most promising approaches to retrieving information from the Internet or from intranet-based databases is the use of intelligent agents. As vast amounts of information become available through the Internet, finding the right information is more difficult. This topic is further discussed in Chapters 4 and 11.

- **Association analysis.** Association analysis is a relatively new approach that uses a specialized set of algorithms that sort through large data sets and express statistical rules among items. (See Moad, 1998, for details.)

- **Other tools.** Several other tools can be used. These include decision trees, genetic algorithms, nearest-neighbor method, and rule induction. (For details, see Inmon, 2002.)

The most common information types are:

- **Classification.** Implies the defining characteristics of a certain group (e.g., customers who have been lost to competitors).

- **Clustering.** Identifies groups of items that share a particular characteristic. Clustering differs from classification in that no predefining characteristic is given.

- **Association.** Identifies relationships between events that occur at one time (e.g., the contents of a shopping basket). (For an application in law enforcement see Brown and Hagen, 2003.)

- **Sequencing.** Similar to association, except that the relationship exists over a period of time (e.g., repeat visits to a supermarket or use of a financial planning product).

- **Forecasting.** Estimates future values based on patterns within large sets of data (e.g., demand forecasting).

There are a large number of commerical products available for conducting data mining (e.g., *dbminer.com*, *data-miner.com*, and *spss.com*). For a directory see *kdnuggets.com/software*.

---

can use several tools and techniques; see the list in *A Closer Look 10.3*. Among different data-mining software, Oracle's Darwin, SAS's Enterprise Miner, and IBM's Intelligent Miner are the dominant players, with SPSS's Clementine being used by a smaller number of Fortune 500 companies (Calderon et al., 2003).

Data Mining Applications   Large numbers of applications exist in data mining, both in business (see Apte et al., 2002) and other fields. According to a GartnerGroup report (*gartnergroup.com*), more than half of all the Fortune 1000 companies worldwide are using data mining technology. Also, a large number of commercial products is available (e.g., *data-miners.com*, *dbminer.com*).

A SAMPLER OF DATA MINING APPLICATIONS. Data mining is used extensively today for many business applications (see Hormozi and Giles, 2004, and Apte et al., 2002), as illustrated by the representative examples that follow. Note that the intent of most of these examples is to identify a business opportunity in order to create a sustainable competitive advantage.

- ***Retailing and sales.*** Predicting sales; determining correct inventory levels and distribution schedules among outlets and loss prevention. For example, retailers such as AAFES (store in military bases) use data mining to combat fraud done by employees in their 1,400 stores, using the Fraud Watch solution from a Canadian company, Triversity (see Amato-McCoy, 2003c). Eddie Bauer (see Online File W10.6) uses data mining for several applications.
- ***Banking.*** Forecasting levels of bad loans and fraudulent credit card use, credit card spending by new customers, and which kinds of customers will best respond to (and qualify for) new loan offers (see Hormozi and Giles, 2004).
- ***Manufacturing and production.*** Predicting machinery failures; finding key factors that control optimization of manufacturing capacity.
- ***Brokerage and securities trading.*** Predicting when bond prices will change; forecasting the range of stock fluctuations for particular issues and the overall market; determining when to buy or sell stocks.
- ***Insurance.*** Forecasting claim amounts and medical coverage costs; classifying the most important elements that affect medical coverage; predicting which customers will buy new insurance policies.
- ***Computer hardware and software.*** Predicting disk-drive failures; forecasting how long it will take to create new chips; predicting potential security violations.
- ***Policework.*** Tracking crime patterns, locations, and criminal behavior; identifying attributes to assist in solving criminal cases (Zdanowicz, 2004).
- ***Government and defense.*** Forecasting the cost of moving military equipment; testing strategies for potential military engagements; predicting resource consumption.
- ***Airlines.*** Capturing data on where customers are flying and the ultimate destination of passengers who change carriers in hub cities; thus, airlines can identify popular locations that they do not service and can check the feasibility of adding routes to capture lost business.
- ***Health care.*** Correlating demographics of patients with critical illnesses; developing better insights on symptoms and their causes and how to provide proper treatments.
- ***Broadcasting.*** Predicting what is best to air during prime time and how to maximize returns by interjecting advertisements.
- ***Marketing.*** Classifying customer demographics that can be used to predict which customers will respond to a mailing or buy a particular product (as illustrated in Section 10.6), as well as to predict other consumer behavior (Apte et al., 2002).

- ***Fighting terrorist activities and financing.*** Governments are fighting terrorism by using data mining to cut the financial support to terrorist groups. The same is true for money-laundering (see Zdanowicz, 2004). For a discussion of use of data mining in homeland security, see Online File W10.7.

Text Mining and Web Mining

TEXT MINING. **Text mining** is the application of data mining to nonstructured or less-structured text files (see Berry, 2002). Data mining takes advantage of the infrastructure of stored data to extract predictive information. For example, by mining a customer database, an analyst might discover that everyone who buys product A also buys products B and C, but does so six months later. Text mining, however, operates with less structured information. Documents rarely have strong internal infrastructure, and when they do, it is frequently focused on document format rather than document content. Text mining helps organizations to do the following: (1) find the "hidden" content of documents, including additional useful relationship and (2) group documents by common themes (e.g., identify all the customers of an insurance firm who have similar complaints).

WEB MINING. **Web mining** is the application of data mining techniques to discover actionable and meaningful patterns, profiles, and trends from Web resources (see Linoff and Berry, 2002). The term Web mining is used to refer to both Web-content mining and Web-usage mining. *Web-content mining* is the process of mining Web sites for information. *Web-usage mining* involves analyzing Web access logs and other information connected to user browsing and access patterns on one or more Web localities.

Web mining is used in the following areas: information filtering (e-mails, magazines, and newspapers); surveillance (of competitors, patents, technological development); mining of Web-access logs for analyzing usage (clickstream analysis); assisted browsing; and services that fight crime on the Internet.

In e-commerce, Web content mining is especially critical, due to the large number of visitors to e-commerce sites. For example, when you look for a certain book on Amazon.com, the site will use mining tools to also provide you with a list of books purchased by the customers who have bought the specific book you are looking for. By providing such mined information, the Amazon.com site minimizes the need for additional search and provides customers with a valuable service.

According to Etzioni (1996), Web mining can perform the following functions:

- *Resource discovery:* locating unfamiliar documents and services on the Web.
- *Information extraction:* automatically extracting specific information from newly discovered Web resources.
- *Generalization:* uncovering general patterns at individual Web sites and across multiple sites. Miner3D (*miner3d.com*) is a suite of visual data analysis tools including a Web-mining tool that displays hundreds and even thousands of search hits on a single screen. The actual search for Web pages is performed through any major search engine, and this add-on tool presents the resulting search in the form of a 3-D graphic instead of displaying links to the first few pages. For details on a number of Web-mining products see *Kdnuggets.com/software/web.html*. Also see *spss.com* and *bayesia.com* (free downloads).

Failures of Data Warehouses and Data Mining

Since their early inceptions, data warehouses and mining have produced many success stories. However, there have also been many failures. Carbone (1999) defined levels of data warehouse failures as follows: (1) Warehouse does not meet the expectations of those involved; (2) warehouse was completed, but went severely over budget in relation to time, money, or both; (3) warehouse failed one or more times but eventually was completed; and (4) warehouse failed with no effort to revive it.

TABLE 10.4 The Reasons Data Warehouses and Mining Fail

- Unrealistic expectations—overly optimistic time schedule or underestimation of cost.
- Inappropriate architecture.
- Vendors overselling capabilities of products.
- Lack of training and support for users.
- Omitted information.
- Lack of coordination (or requires too much coordination).
- Cultural issues were ignored.
- Use of the warehouse only for operational, not informational, purposes.
- Not enough summarization of data.
- Poor upkeep of technology.
- Improper management of multiple users with various needs.
- Failure to align data marts and data warehouses.

- Unclear business objectives; not knowing the information requirements.
- Lack of effective project sponsorship.
- Lack of data quality.
- Lack of user input.
- Use of data marts instead of data warehouses (and vice versa).
- Inexperienced/untrained/inadequate number of personnel.
- Interfering corporate politics.
- Insecure access to data manipulation (users should not have the ability to change any data).
- Inappropriate format of information—not a single, standard format.
- Poor upkeep of information (e.g., failure to keep information current).

Source: Compiled from Carbone (1999).

Carbone provided examples and identified a number of reasons for failures (which are typical for many other large information systems): These are summarized in Table 10.4. Suggestions on how to avoid data warehouse failure are provided at *datawarehouse.com,* at *bitpipe.com,* and at *teradatauniversitynetwork.com.* Suggestions on how to properly implement data mining are provided by Hirji (2001).

10.5 DATA VISUALIZATION TECHNOLOGIES

Once data have been processed, they can be presented to users as text, graphics, tables, and so on, via several data visualization technologies. A variety of methods and software packages are available to do visualization for supporting decision making (e.g., see I/S Analyzer, 2002 and Li et al., 2001).

Data Visualization Visual technologies make pictures worth a thousand numbers and make IT applications more attractive and understandable to users. **Data visualization** refers to presentation of data by technologies such as digital images, geographical information systems, graphical user interfaces, multidimensional tables and graphs, virtual reality, three-dimensional presentations, videos, and animation. Visualization is becoming more and more popular on the Web not only for entertainment, but also for decision support (see *spss.com, microstrategy.com*). *IT at Work 10.2* describes use of visualization by Danskin. Visualization software packages offer users capabilities for self-guided exploration and visual analysis of large amounts of data. By using visual analysis technologies, people may spot problems that have existed for years, undetected by standard analysis methods. Data visualization can be supported in a dynamic way (e.g., by video clips). It can also be done in real time (e.g., Bates, 2003). Visualization technologies can

IT at Work 10.2
DANSKIN'S VIRTUAL SHOWROOM

Danskin (*danskin.com*), a manufacturer of women's activewear and dancewear, needed an easier way to communicate with the company's more than 3,000 specialty store accounts. Danskin has an external sales force of 15 people for the specialty store market, but at most, the company's reps can meet or deal extensively with a total of only 150 to 250 accounts during each selling season. The remaining stores primarily receive a Danskin catalog and are asked to communicate via phone and fax with a special team of customer service reps.

Traditionally, store buyers travel to New York City four to six times a year to preview upcoming collections of apparel, accessories, and shoes. Faxes and phone calls were (and sometimes still are) the main communications channel between retailers (e.g., the specialty stores) and suppliers like Danskin. This process is very inefficient for both the retailers and suppliers. To improve the process, Danskin established a virtual online showroom where specialty store buyers can view products, read descriptions, check inventory availability, place orders, and keep abreast of changes in Danskin's product lines.

To create this visual business-to-business Web presence, Danskin formed a partnership with 7thOnline (*7thonline.com*), a company that provides visual merchandising and assortment planning technology to the global fashion industry. The 7thOnline platform streamlines the merchandising and communications process between manufacturers and retailers by offering a visual, online product catalog. 7thOnline also provides electronic data interchange integration, which enables retailers to transmit product purchase orders over the Internet.

While some "touch and feel" elements cannot be replaced by the virtual showroom, it can help decrease potential human errors and the high travel and operating costs associated with the manual buying routine. Buyers from the specialty stores now have earlier and more convenient access to product information, giving them time to plan, so that they come to market better equipped to make final purchasing decisions. Essentially, the 7thOnline system provides for much closer collaboration between Danskin and specialty stores.

And the external Danskin reps? They can now concentrate on the company's biggest, most profitable accounts as well as developing new accounts.

Source: Compiled from Buss (2003).

For Further Exploration: Why is a visual B2B solution so important for the fashion industry? Would a visual solution be as important in other industries? Provide some examples.

---

also be integrated among themselves to create a variety of presentations, as demonstrated in Online File W10.8.

Data visualization is easier to implement when the necessary data are in a data warehouse. Our discussion here will focus mainly on the data visualization techniques of multidimensionality, geographical information systems, visual interactive modeling, and virtual reality. Related topics, such as multimedia (see *informatica.com*) and hypermedia, are presented in Technology Guide 2.

Multidimensionality Visualization

Modern data and information may have several dimensions. For example, management may be interested in examining sales figures in a certain city by product, by time period, by salesperson, and by store (i.e., in five dimensions). The common tool for such situations is OLAP, and it often includes a visual presentation. The more dimensions involved, the more difficult it is to present multidimensional information in one table or in one graph. Therefore, it is important to provide the user with a technology that allows him or her to add, replace, or change dimensions quickly and easily in a table and/or graphical presentation. Such changes are known as "slicing and dicing" of data. The technology of slicing,

(a)

	Planes		Trains		Automobiles	
	This Year	Next Year	This Year	Next Year	This Year	Next Year
Canada	740	888	140	168	640	768
Japan	430	516	290	348	150	180
France	320	384	460	552	210	252
Germany	425	510	430	516	325	390

Country

(b)

		This Year	Next Year
Planes	Canada	740	888
	Japan	430	516
	France	320	384
	Germany	425	510
Trains	Canada	140	168
	Japan	290	348
	France	460	552
	Germany	430	516
Automobiles	Canada	640	768
	Japan	150	180
	France	210	252
	Germany	325	390

Travel Country

(c)

Worksheet1-View1-TUTORIAL

			This Year	Next Year
Planes	Canada		740	888
	Japan		430	516
		France	320	384
		Germany	425	510
	Europe	Total	745	894
Trains	Canada		140	168
	Japan		290	348
		France	460	552
		Germany	430	516
	Europe	Total	890	1068
Automobiles	Canada		640	768
	Japan		150	180
		France	210	252
		Germany	325	390
	Europe	Total	535	642

Travel Country

Next Year = (This Year)*1.2

- The software adds *Total* rows.
- The software calculates "Next Year" totals.

Shows how formula 1 calculates cells (in this case, the cells in the *Next Year* column.)

FIGURE 10.5 Multidimensionality views.

dicing, and similar manipulations is called *OLAP multidimensionality,* and it is available in most business intelligence packages (e.g., *hyperion.com*).

Figure 10.5 shows three views of the same data, organized in different ways, using multidimensional software, usually available with spreadsheets. Part a shows travel hours of a company's employees by means of transportation and by country. The "next year" column gives projections automatically generated by an embedded formula. In part b the data are reorganized, and in part c they are reorganized again and manipulated as well. All this is easily done by the end user with one or two clicks of the mouse.

The major advantage of multidimensionality is that data can be organized the way managers like to see them rather than the way that the system analysts do. Furthermore, different presentations of the same data can be arranged and rearranged easily and quickly.

Three factors are considered in **multidimensionality:** dimensions, measures, and time.

1. *Examples of dimensions:* products, salespeople, market segments, business units, geographical locations, distribution channels, countries, industries
2. *Examples of measures:* money, sales volume, head count, inventory profit, actual versus forecasted results
3. *Examples of time:* daily, weekly, monthly, quarterly, yearly

For example, a manager may want to know the sales of product M in a certain geographical area, by a specific salesperson, during a specified month, in terms of units. Although the answer can be provided regardless of the database structure, it can be provided much faster, and by the user himself or herself, if the data are organized in multidimensional databases (or data marts), or if the query tools are designed for multidimensionality (e.g., via OLAP). In either case, users can navigate through the many dimensions and levels of data via tables or graphs and then conduct a quick analysis to find significant deviations or important trends.

Multidimensionality is available with different degrees of sophistication and is especially popular in business intelligence software (e.g., see Campbell, 2001). There are several types of software from which multidimensional systems can be constructed, and they often work in conjunction with OLAP tools.

Geographical Information Systems

A **geographical information system (GIS)** is a computer-based system that enables capturing, modeling, storing, checking, integrating, manipulating, analyzing, and displaying of geographically referenced data using digitized maps. Its most distinguishing characteristic is that every record or digital object has an identified geographical location. By integrating maps with spatially oriented databases and other databases (called *geocoding*), users can generate information for planning, problem solving, and decision making, increasing their productivity and the quality of their decisions. Today's business geographical information systems (GISs) include applications in marketing, locational analysis, and geodemographics (Grimshaw, 1999). For example, location-based data are becoming an integral part of customer relationship management (CRM) programs.

The field of GIS can be divided into two major categories: *functions* and *applications*. There are four major functions: design and planning, decision modeling, database management, and spatial imaging. These functions support six areas of applications as shown in Figure 10.6 (page 436). Note that the functions (shown as pillars) can support all the applications. The applications they support the most are shown closest to each pillar.

GIS SOFTWARE. GIS software varies in its capabilities, from simple computerized mapping systems to enterprisewide tools for decision support data analysis (see Online Minicase W10.1). Because a high-quality graphics display and high

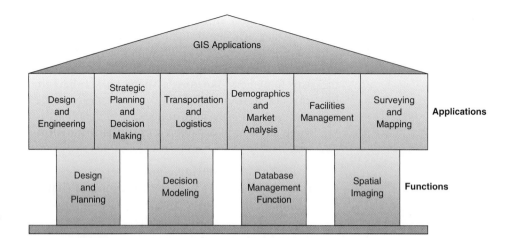

FIGURE 10.6 GIS functions and applications.

computation and search speeds are necessary, most early GIS implementations were developed for mainframes. Initially, the high cost of GISs prevented their use outside experimental facilities and government agencies. Since the 1990s, however, the cost of GIS software and its required hardware has dropped dramatically. Now relatively inexpensive, fully functional PC-based packages are readily available. Representative GIS software vendors are ESRI, Intergraph, and Mapinfo.

GIS DATA. GIS data are available from a wide variety of sources. Government sources (via the Internet and CD-ROM) provide some data, while vendors provide diversified commercial data as well. Some are free (see CD-ROMs from MapInfo, and downloadable material from *esri.com* and *gisdatadepot.com*).

GIS AND DECISION MAKING. GISs provide a large amount of extremely useful information that can be analyzed and utilized in decision making. Its graphical format makes it easy for managers to visualize the data. For example, as Janet M. Hamilton, market research administrator for Dow Elanco, a $2 billion maker of agricultural chemicals based in Indianapolis, Indiana, explains, "I can put 80-page spreadsheets with thousands of rows into a single map. It would take a couple of weeks to comprehend all of the information from the spreadsheet, but in a map, the story can be told in seconds" (Hamilton, 1996, p. 21).

There are countless applications of GISs to improve decision making in the public or private sector (see Nasirin and Birks, 2003). They include the dispatch of emergency vehicles, transit management, facility site selection, drought risk management (Goddard, 2003), and wildlife management. GISs are extremely popular in local governments, where the tools are used not only for mapping but for many decision-making applications (see O'Looney, 2000). States, cities, and counties are using a GIS application related to property assessment, mapping, and flood control (e.g., Hardester, 2002). Banks have been using GIS for over a decade to support expansion and marketing decision making (see Online File W10.9).

For many companies, the intelligent organization of data within a GIS can provide a framework to support the process of decision making and of designing alternative strategies, especially when location decisions are involved (Church, 2002).

Some examples of successful GIS applications are provided by Korte (2000) and Hamilton (1996). Other examples of successful GIS applications are summarized in Online File W10.10.

GIS AND THE INTERNET OR INTRANETS. Most major GIS software vendors are providing Web access, such as embedded browsers or a Web/Internet/intranet server that hooks directly into their software. Thus, users can access dynamic maps and data via the Internet or a corporate intranet.

A number of firms are deploying GISs on the Internet for internal use or for use by their customers. For example, Visa Plus, which operates a network of automated teller machines, has developed a GIS application that lets Internet users call up a locator map for any of the company's 300,000 ATM machines worldwide. A common application on the Internet is a store locator. Not only do you get an address near you, but you are also told how to get there in the shortest way (e.g., try *frys.com*). As GIS Web server software is deployed by vendors, more applications will be developed. Maps, GIS data, and information about GISs are available over the Web through a number of vendors and public agencies. (For design issues see Sikder and Gangopadhyay, 2002.)

EMERGING GIS APPLICATIONS. The integration of GISs and global positioning systems (GPSs) has the potential to help restructure and redesign the aviation, transportation, and shipping industries. It enables vehicles or aircraft equipped with a GPS receiver to pinpoint their location as they move (Steede-Terry, 2000). This enables autopiloting of ships and airplanes. Emerging applications of GPSs include personal automobile mapping systems, vehicle tracking (Terry and Kolb, 2003), and earth-moving equipment tracking. The price of these applications is dropping with improvements in hardware, increased demand, and the availability of more competing vendors. (A simple GPS cost less than $50 in 2003.) GPSs have also become a major source of new GIS data (see Group Assignment 1). Some researchers have developed intelligent GISs that link a GIS to an expert system or to intelligent agents (Tang et al., 2001).

L-Commerce. In Chapter 5 we introduced the concept of location-based commerce (l-commerce), a major part of mobile-commerce (m-commerce). In l-commerce, advertising is targeted to an individual whose location is known (via a GPS and GIS combination). Similarly, emergency medical systems identify the location of a car accident in seconds, and the attached GIS helps in directing ambulances to the scene. For other interesting applications, see Sadeh (2002).

CONCLUSIONS. Improvements in the GIS user interface have substantially altered the GIS "look" and "feel." Advanced visualization (three-dimensional graphics) is increasingly integrated with GIS capabilities, especially in animated and interactive maps. GISs can provide information for virtual reality engines, and they can display complex information to decision makers. Multimedia and hypermedia play a growing role in GISs, especially in help and training systems. Object linking and embedding is allowing users to import maps into any document. More GISs will be deployed to provide data and access data over the Web and organizational intranets as "Web-ready" GIS software becomes more affordable. On the relationships of GIS and Web Services, see Alameh (2003). See Korte (2000) and Ursery (2004) for an overview of GISs, their many capabilities, potential advances, and existing applications.

Visual Interactive Models and Simulation

Visual interactive modeling (VIM) uses computer graphic displays to represent the impact of different management or operational decisions on goals such as profit or market share. VIM differs from regular simulation in that the user can intervene in the decision-making process and see the results of the intervention. A visual model is much more than a communication device; it is an integral part of decision making and problem solving.

A VIM can be used both for supporting decisions and for training. It can represent a static or a dynamic system. Static models display a visual image of the result of one decision alternative at a time. (With computer windows, several results can be compared on one screen.) Dynamic models use animation or video clips to show systems that evolve over time. These are also used in real-time simulations.

VIM has been used with DSSs in several operations management decision processes (see Beroggi, 2001). The method loads the current status of a plant (or a business process) into a virtual interactive model. The model is then run rapidly on a computer, allowing management to observe how a plant is likely to operate in the future. De Lora and Alfonseca (2003) demonstrate the use of VIM in an educational Web environment.

One of the most developed areas in VIM is **visual interactive simulation (VIS),** a method in which the end user watches the progress of the simulation model in an animated form using graphics terminals. The user may interact with the simulation and try different decision strategies. (See Pritsker and O'Reilly, 1999.) VIS is an approach that has, at its core, the ability to allow decision makers to learn about their own subjective values and about their mistakes. Therefore, VIS can be used for training, as in the case of flight simulators and as shown in *IT at Work 10.3.*

Animation systems that produce realistic graphics are available from many simulation software vendors (e.g., see SAS.com and Vissim.com). The latest visual simulation technology is tied in with the concept of virtual reality, where an artificial world is created for a number of purposes—from training to entertainment to viewing data in an artificial landscape.

Virtual Reality

There is no standard definition of virtual reality. The most common definitions usually imply that **virtual reality (VR)** is interactive, computer-generated, three-dimensional graphics delivered to the user through a head-mounted display. Defined technically, virtual reality is an environment and/or technology that provides artificially generated sensory cues sufficient to engender in the user some willing suspension of disbelief. So in VR, a person "believes" that what he or she is doing is real even though it is artificially created.

More than one person and even a large group can share and interact in the same artificial environment. VR thus can be a powerful medium for communication, entertainment, and learning. Instead of looking at a flat computer screen, the VR user interacts with a three-dimensional computer-generated environment. To see and hear the environment, the user wears stereo goggles and a headset. To interact with the environment, control objects in it, or move around within it, the user wears a computerized display and hand position sensors ("gloves"). Virtual reality displays achieve the illusion of a surrounding medium by updating the display in real time. The user can grasp and move virtual objects. According to *USA Today* (2003), virtual reality (VR) literally is going to change the face of business, communication, and health care in the next 10 to 20 years.

IT at Work 10.3
COMPUTER TRAINING IN COMPLEX LOGGING MACHINES AT PARTEK FOREST

The foresting industry is extremely competitive, and countries with high labor costs must automate tasks such as moving, cutting, delimbing, and piling logs. A new machine, called the "Harvester," can replace 25 lumberjacks.

The Harvester is a highly complex machine that takes six months to learn how to operate. The trainee destroys a sizeable amount of forest in the process, and terrain suitable to practice on is decreasing. In unskilled hands, this expensive machine can also be damaged. Therefore, extensive and expensive training is needed. Sisu Logging of Finland (a subsidiary of Partek Forest) found a solution to the training problem by using a real-time simulation (*partekforest.com*).

In this simulation, the chassis, suspension, and wheels of the vehicles have to be modeled, together with the forces acting on them (inertia and friction), and the movement equations linked with them have to be solved in real time. This type of simulation is mathematically complex, and until recently it required equipment investment running into millions of dollars. However, with the help of a visual simulations program, simulation training can now be carried out for only 1 percent of the cost of the traditional method.

Inside the simulator are the Harvester's actual controls, which are used to control a virtual model of a Harvester plowing its way through a virtual forest. The machine sways back and forth on uneven terrain, and the grapple of the Harvester grips the trunk of a tree, fells it, delimbs it, and cuts it into pieces very realistically in real time.

The simulated picture is very sharp: Even the structures of the bark and annual growth rings are clearly visible where the tree has been cut. In traditional simulators, the traveling path is quite limited beforehand, but in this Harvester simulator, you are free to move in a stretch of forest covering two hectares (25,000 square yards).

In addition, the system can be used to simulate different kinds of forest in different parts of the world, together with the different tree species and climatic conditions. An additional advantage of this simulator is that the operations can be videotaped so that training sessions can be studied afterward. Moreover, it is possible to practice certain dangerous situations that cannot be done using a real machine.

Source: Condensed from *Finnish Business Report* (April 1997).

For Further Exploration: Why is the simulated training time shorter? Why is visualization beneficial?

For example, virtual videoconferencing, facemail, and "virtual humans" are three recent examples of applied VR.

VIRTUAL REALITY AND DECISION MAKING. Most VR applications to date have been used to support decision making indirectly. For example, Boeing has developed a virtual aircraft mockup to test designs. Several other VR applications for assisting in manufacturing and for converting military technology to civilian technology are being utilized at Boeing. At Volvo, VR is used to test virtual cars in virtual accidents; Volvo also uses VR in its new model-designing process. British Airways offers the pleasure of experiencing first-class flying to its Web site visitors. For a comprehensive discussion of virtual reality in manufacturing, see Banerjee and Zetu (2001).

Another VR application area is data visualization. VR helps financial decision makers make better sense of data by using visual, spatial, and aural immersion virtual systems. For example, some stock brokerages have a VR application in which users surf over a landscape of stock futures, with color, hue, and intensity indicating deviations from current share prices. Sound is used to convey other information, such as current trends or the debt/equity ratio. VR allows side-by-side comparisons with a large assortment of financial data. It is easier to make intuitive connections with three-dimensional support. Morgan Stanley & Co. uses VR to display the results of risk analyses.

VIRTUAL REALITY AND THE WEB. A platform-independent standard for VR called **virtual reality markup language (VRML)** (*vrmlsite.com*, and Kerlow, 2000) makes navigation through online supermarkets, museums, and stores as easy as interacting with textual information. VRML allows objects to be rendered as an Internet user "walks" through a virtual room. At the moment, users can utilize regular browsers, but VRML browsers will soon be in wide circulation.

Extensive use is expected in e-commerce marketing (see Dalgleish, 2000). For example, Tower Records offers a virtual music store on the Internet where customers can "meet" each other in front of the store, go inside, and preview CDs and videos. They select and purchase their choices electronically and interactively from a sales associate. Applications of virtual reality in other areas are shown in Online File W10.11.

Virtual supermarkets could spark greater interest in home grocery shopping. In the future, shoppers will enter a virtual supermarket, walk through the virtual aisles, select virtual products, and put them in their virtual carts. This could help remove some of the resistance to virtual shopping. Virtual malls, which can be delivered even on a PC (*synthonics.com*), are designed to give the user a feeling of walking into a shopping mall. In another recent virtual reality project, the National Science Foundation (NSF), a U.S. research and education organization, has revealed its plans to develop a virtual tour (Telecomworldwire, 2003). The tour will let visitors see a 3-D view of the various rooms at Thomas Jefferson's home Monticello, by "looking in" through the windows of the virtual house.

Virtual reality is just beginning to move into many business applications. An interactive, three-dimensional world on the Internet should prove popular because it is a metaphor to which everyone can relate.

10.6 MARKETING DATABASES IN ACTION

Data warehouses and data marts serve end users in all functional areas. However, the most dramatic applications of data warehousing and mining are in marketing, as seen in the Harrah's case, in what is referred to as *marketing databases* (also referred to as *database marketing*).

In this section we examine how data warehouses, their extensions, and data mining are used, and what role they play in new marketing strategies, such as the use of Web-based marketing transaction databases in interactive marketing.

The Marketing Transaction Database

Many databases are static: They simply gather and store information about customers. They appear in the following categories: operations databases, data warehouses, and marketing databases. Success in marketing today requires a new kind of database, oriented toward targeting the personalizing marketing messages in real time. Such a database provides the most effective means of capturing information on customer preferences and needs. In turn, enterprises can use this knowledge to create new and/or personalized products and services. Such a database is called a **marketing transaction database (MTD).** The MTD combines many of the characteristics of the current databases and marketing data sources into a new database that allows marketers to engage in real-time personalization and target every interaction with customers.

MTD'S CAPABILITIES. The MTD provides dynamic, or interactive, functions not available with traditional types of marketing databases. In marketing terms, a transaction occurs with the exchange of information. With interactive media, each exposure to the customer becomes an opportunity to conduct a marketing "transaction." Exchanging information (whether gathered actively through registration or user requests, or passively by monitoring customer behavior) allows marketers to refine their understanding of each customer continuously and to use that information to target him or her specifically with personalized marketing messages. This is done most frequently on the Web.

THE ROLE OF THE INTERNET. Data mining, data warehousing, and MTDs can be delivered on the Internet and intranets. The Internet does not simply represent another advertising venue or a different medium for catalog sales. Rather, it contains new attributes that smart marketers can exploit to their fullest degree. Indeed, the Internet promises to revolutionize sales and marketing. Dell Computer (see Online Minicase W10.2) offers an example of how marketing professionals can use the Internet's electronic sales and marketing channels for market research, advertising, information dissemination, product management, and product delivery. For an overview of marketing databases and the Web, see Grossnickle and Raskin (2000).

One of the leading software products in this field is DataDistilleries (*datadistilleries.com*), which helps companies that are active in the B2C market understand, build, and manage their customer relationships with the objective of optimizing their value. DataDistilleries leverages the existing marketing databases in order to analyze customer data and accurately predict individual customer behavior, needs, risks, and profitability (Siddiqui, 2003).

Implementation Examples

Fewer and fewer companies can afford traditional marketing approaches, which include big-picture strategies and expensive marketing campaigns. Marketing departments are being scaled down (and so are the traditional marketing approaches), and new approaches such as one-to-one marketing, speed marketing, interactive marketing, and relationship marketing are being employed (see Strauss et al., 2003).

The following examples illustrate how companies use data mining and warehousing to support the new marketing approaches. For other examples, see Online File W10.12.

- Through its online registry for expectant parents, Burlington Coat Factory tracks families as they grow. The company then matches direct-mail material to the different stages of a family's development over time. Burlington also identifies, on a daily basis, top-selling styles and brands. By digging into reams of demographic data, historical buying patterns, and sales trends in existing stores, Burlington determines where to open its next store and what to stock in each store.

- Au Bon Pain Company, Inc., a Boston-based chain of cafés, discovered that the company was not selling as much cream cheese as planned. When it analyzed point-of-sale data, the firm found that customers preferred small, one-serving packaging (like butter). As soon as the package size of the cream cheese was changed, sales shot up.

● Bank of America gets more than 100,000 telephone calls from customers every day. Analyzing customers' banking activities, the bank determines what may be of interest to them. So when a customer calls to check on a balance, the bank tries to sell the customer something in which he or she might be interested.

● Supermarket chains regularly analyze reams of cash register data to discover what items customers are typically buying at the same time. These shopping patterns are used for issuing coupons, designing floor layouts and products' location, and creating shelf displays.

● In its data warehouse, the *Chicago Tribune* stores information about customer behavior as customers move through the various newspaper Web sites. Data mining helps to analyze volumes of data ranging from what browsers are used to what hyperlinks are clicked on most frequently.

The data warehouses in some companies include several terabytes or more of data (e.g., at Sears; see Minicase 2). They need to use supercomputing to sift quickly through the data. Wal-Mart, the world's largest discount retailer, has a gigantic database, as described in *IT at Work 10.4.*

IT at Work 10.4
DATA MINING POWERS WAL-MART

With more than 60 terabytes of data (in 2004) on two NCR (National Cash Register) systems, Wal-Mart (*walmart.com*) manages one of the world's largest data warehouses. Besides the two NCR Corp. Teradata databases, which handle most decision-support applications, Wal-Mart has another 6 terabytes of transaction processing data on IBM and Hitachi mainframes.

Wal-Mart's formula for success—getting the right product on the appropriate shelf at the lowest price—owes much to the company's multimillion-dollar investment in data warehousing. "Wal-Mart can be more detailed than most of its competitors on what's going on by product, by store, by day—and act on it," says Richard Winter, a database consultant in Boston. "That's a tremendously powerful thing."

The systems house data on point of sale, inventory, products in transit, market statistics, customer demographics, finance, product returns, and supplier performance. The data are used for three broad areas of information discovery and decision support: analyzing trends, managing inventory, and understanding customers. What emerges are "personality traits" for each of Wal-Mart's 3,600 or so outlets, which Wal-Mart managers can use to determine product mix and inventory levels for each store.

Wal-Mart is using a data mining–based demand-forecasting application that employs neural-networking software and runs on a 4,000-processor parallel computer. The application looks at individual items for individual stores to decide the seasonal sales profile of each item. The system keeps a year's worth of data on the sales of 100,000 products and predicts which items will be needed in each store and when.

Wal-Mart is expanding its use of market-basket analysis. Data are collected on items that comprise a shopper's total purchase so that the company can analyze relationships and patterns in customer purchases. The data warehouse is available over an extranet to store managers and suppliers. In 2003, 6,000 users made over 40,000 database queries each day.

"What Wal-Mart is doing is letting an army of people use the database to make tactical decisions," says consultant Winter. "The cumulative impact is immense."

Sources: This information is courtesy of NCR Corp. (2000) and *walmart.com.*

For Further Exploration: Since small retailers cannot afford data warehouses and data mining, will they be able to compete?

10.7 WEB-BASED DATA MANAGEMENT SYSTEMS

Data management and business intelligence activities—from data acquisition (e.g., Atzeni et al., 2002), through warehousing, to mining—are often performed with Web tools, or are interrelated with Web technologies and e-business (see Liautaud, 2001). Users with browsers can log onto a system, make inquiries, and get reports in a real-time setting. This is done through intranets and, for outsiders, via extranets (see *remedy.com*).

The challenge these days for data management and business intelligence activities is information integration. The reason this is a challenging task is that today's enterprise systems extend beyond the walls of the corporate data center to include customers, suppliers, partners, and electronic marketplaces. Information integration is a technology approach that combines core elements from data management systems, content management systems, data warehouses, and other enterprise applications into a common platform (Roth et al., 2002). Web Services are a commonly used programming interface in information integration.

E-commerce software vendors are providing Web tools that connect the data warehouse with EC ordering and cataloging systems. Hitachi's EC tool suite, Tradelink (at *hitachi.com*), combines EC activities such as catalog management, payment applications, mass customization, and order management with data warehouses and marts and ERP systems. Oracle (see Winter, 2001) and SAP offer similar products.

Data warehousing and decision support vendors are connecting their products with Web technologies and EC. Examples include Web Intelligence from Business Objects, and Cognos's DataMerchant. Hyperion's Appsource "wired for OLAP" product connects OLAP with Web tools. IBM's Decision Edge makes OLAP capabilities available on the intranet from anywhere in the corporation using browsers, search engines, and other Web technologies. MicroStrategy offers DSS Agent and DSS Web for help in drilling down for detailed information, providing graphical views, and pushing information to users' desktops. Oracle's Financial Analyzer and Sales Analyzer, Hummingbird's Bi/Web and Bi/Broker, and several of the products cited above bring interactive querying, reporting, and other OLAP tasks to many users (both company employees and business partners) via the Web. Also, for a comprehensive discussion of business intelligence on the Web, see the white paper at *businessobjects.com*.

The systems described in the previous sections of this chapter can be integrated on Web-based platforms, such as the one shown in Figure 10.7 (page 444). The Web-based system is accessed via a portal, and it connects these parts: the business intelligence (BI) services, the data warehouse and marts, the corporate applications, and the data infrastructure. A security system protects the corporate proprietary data. Let's examine how all of these components work together via the corporate portal.

Enterprise BI Suites and Corporate Portals Enterprise BI suites (EBISs) integrate query, reporting, OLAP, and other tools. They are scalable, and offered by many vendors (e.g., IBM, Oracle, Microsoft, Hyperion Solution, Sagent Technology, AlphaBlox, MicroStrategy, and Crystal Decisions). EBISs are offered usually via enterprise portals.

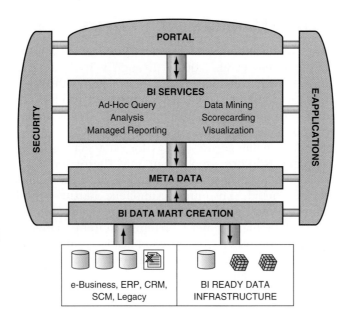

In Chapter 3 we introduced the concept of corporate portals as a Web-based gateway to data, information, and knowledge. As seen in Figure 10.8, the portal integrates data from many sources. It provides end users with a single Web-based point of personalized access to BI and other applications. Likewise, it provides IT with a single point of delivery and management of this content. Users are empowered to access, create, and share valuable information.

Intelligent Data Warehouse Web-Based Systems

The amount of data in the data warehouse can be very large. While the organization of data is done in a way that permits easy search, it still may be useful to have a search engine for specific applications. Liu (1998) describes how an intelligent agent can improve the operation of a data warehouse in the pulp and paper industry. This application supplements the monitoring and scanning of external strategic data. The intelligent agent application can serve both managers' ad-hoc query/reporting information needs and the external data needs of a strategic management support system for forest companies in Finland.

Clickstream Data Warehouse

Large and ever-increasing amounts of B2C data about consumers, products, etc. can be collected. Such data come from several sources: internal data (e.g., sales data, payroll data etc.), external data (e.g., government and industry reports), and clickstream data. *Clickstream* data (also known as *Web logs*) occur inside the Web environment, when customers visit a Web site. They provide a trail of the users' activities in the Web site, including user behavior and browsing patterns. By looking at clickstream data, an e-tailer can find out such things as which promotions are effective and which population segments are interested in specific products.

Analyzing Web logs quickly can be very useful. For example, quick analysis allows management to gauge the effectiveness of a Web-based sales promotion.

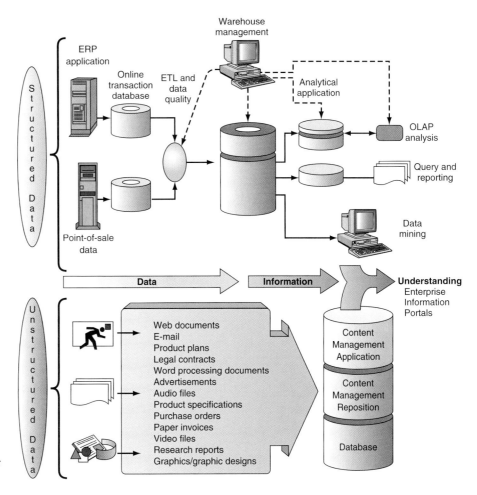

FIGURE 10.8 Sources of content for an enterprise information portal. (*Source:* Merrill Lynch, 1998.)

Popular tools are Web Trends (from NetIQ) and Mach5 Analyzer (from Mach5.com).

According to Inmon (2001), clickstream data can reveal information to answer questions such as the following: What goods has the customer looked at or purchased? What items did the customer buy in conjunction with other items? What ads and promotions were effective? Which were ineffective? Are certain products too hard to find? Are certain products too expensive? Is there a substitute product that the customer finds first?

The Web is an incredibly rich source of *business intelligence,* and many enterprises are scrambling to build data warehouses that capture the knowledge contained in the clickstream data from their Web sites. By analyzing the user behavior patterns contained in these clickstream data warehouses, savvy business can expand their markets, improve customer relationships, reduce costs, streamline operations, strengthen their Web sites, and hone their business strategies. One has two options: incorporate Web-based data into preexisting data warehouses, or build new **clickstream data warehouses** that are capable of showing both e-business activities and the non-Web aspects of the business in an integrated fashion (see Sweiger at el., 2002). For an application used by Victoria's Secret, see *IT at Work 10.5* (next page).

IT at Work 10.5
VICTORIA'S SECRET'S DATA WAREHOUSE

For direct-to-consumer merchants, the "death of an order" can occur at any time during the transaction. The "death of an order" means that customers change their minds at some point during the ordering process. By using an enterprise data warehouse to capture customer information and decision-support tools to analyze shopping patterns, however, Victoria's Secret (*victoriassecret.com*) is keeping orders alive and working to provide a better shopping experience.

Unlike a bricks-and-mortar purchase, the direct sale of products through electronic storefronts provides vast amounts of unique and diverse data elements at all stages of an order's life. To turn collected data into actionable information, the company uses a data warehouse solution from Teradata (a division of NCR Corp.). The retailer monitors all customer touches and shopping patterns.

The data warehouse holds data collected from several data streams:

- The first data source is the customer. Besides having access to all customer names, addresses, and purchase history, the company also differentiates orderers from product recipients, based on storing each different shipping address.
- The company also stores customer payment information. Victoria's Secret uses the payment data to monitor the purchasing habits of the company's shoppers.
- The third data stream comes from direct customer contacts via the firm's direct-mail operations. For example, the company has more than 50 domestic and international catalog mailings (300 million catalogs per year).
- The retailer's call center provides another data stream. Each day hundreds of fashion consultants examine

thousands of calls ranging from orders and "up-sell" opportunities (opportunities to sell customers more expensive items) to complaints and resolutions about merchandise.

- The company's online channel produces a huge amount of customer data, as it accepts thousands of orders daily for both online and catalog merchandise. Each customer's activities on the Web site are stored in the data warehouse.

Victoria's Secret puts all of these data into action in many ways. The company creates targeted e-mail messages, adding up to 150 million outbound e-mail messages each year. These messages include offers, merchandise specials, invitations, announcements, and other calls to action.

The company analyzes the status of every individual product by customer, by day, for each order. The data warehouse is enabling Victoria's Secret to improve predictions of customer behavior. The data warehouse also enables the company to stay abreast of each order's profit equation. To measure the revenue of each order, Victoria's Secret starts with the merchandise price and subtracts shipping, handling, and related taxes, as well as special service charges, such as shipping upgrades and gift wrapping. This process means that the retailer can measure the profitability of every customer, order, catalog, and product.

Source: Compiled from Amato-McCoy (2003a).

For Further Exploration: What does Victoria's Secret mean by "keeping an order alive?" Would this phrase apply to other businesses? Why or why not? Give examples. Finally, describe the various data streams that feed Victoria's Secret's data warehouse.

➡ MANAGERIAL ISSUES

1. ***Cost-benefit issues and justification.*** Some of the data management solutions discussed in this chapter are very expensive and are justifiable only in large corporations. Smaller organizations can make the solutions cost effective if they leverage existing databases rather than create new ones. A careful cost-benefit analysis must be undertaken before any commitment to the new technologies is made.

2. ***Where to store data physically.*** Should data be distributed close to their users? This could potentially speed up data entry and updating, but adds replication

and security risks. Or should data be centralized for easier control, security, and disaster recovery? This alternative offers fewer communications and single-point-of-failure risks.

3. *Legal issues.* Data mining may suggest that a company send electronic or printed catalogs or promotions to only one age group or one gender. A man sued Victoria's Secret Corp. because his female neighbor received a mail order catalog with deeply discounted items and he received only the regular catalog (the discount was actually given for volume purchasing). Settling discrimination charges can be very expensive.

4. *Internal or external?* Should a firm invest in internally collecting, storing, maintaining, and purging its own databases of information? Or should it subscribe to external databases, where providers are responsible for all data management and data access?

5. *Disaster recovery.* Can an organization's business processes, which have become dependent on databases, recover and sustain operations after a natural or other type of information systems disaster? (See Chapter 15.) How can a data warehouse be protected? At what cost?

6. *Data security and ethics.* Are the company's competitive data safe from external snooping or sabotage? Are confidential data, such as personnel details, safe from improper or illegal access and alteration? A related question is, Who owns such personal data?

7. *Ethics: Paying for use of data.* Compilers of public-domain information, such as Lexis-Nexis, face a problem of people lifting large sections of their work without first paying royalties. The Collection of Information Antipiracy Act (Bills HR 2652 and HR 354 in the U.S. Congress) may provide greater protection from online piracy. This, and other intellectual property issues, are being debated in Congress and adjudicated in the courts. (See Chapter 16.)

8. *Privacy.* Storing data in a warehouse and conducting data mining may result in the invasion of individual privacy. What will companies do to protect individuals? What can individuals do to protect their privacy? (See Chapter 16.)

9. *The legacy data problem.* One very real issue, often known as the legacy data acquisition problem, is what to do with the mass of information already stored in a variety of systems and formats. Data in older, perhaps obsolete, databases still need to be available to newer database management systems. Many of the legacy application programs used to access the older data simply cannot be converted into new computing environments without considerable expense. Basically, there are three approaches to solving this problem. One is to create a database front end that can act as a translator from the old system to the new. The second is to cause applications to be integrated with the new system, so that data can be seamlessly accessed in the original format. The third is to cause the data to migrate into the new system by reformatting it. A new promising approach is the use of Web Services (see Technology Guide 6).

10. *Data delivery.* Moving data efficiently around an enterprise is often a major problem. The inability to communicate effectively and efficiently among different groups, in different geographical locations, is a serious roadblock to

implementing distributed applications properly, especially given the many remote sites and mobility of today's workers. Mobile and wireless computing are addressing some of these difficulties.

KEY TERMS

Analytical processing *417*

Business intelligence (BI) *423*

Clickstream data *412*

Clickstream data warehouses *445*

Data integrity *414*

Data mart *421*

Data mining *428*

Data quality (DQ) *412*

Data visualization *432*

Data warehouse *418*

Document management *414*

Document management system (DMS) *415*

Geographical information system (GIS) *435*

Marketing transaction database (MTD) *440*

Metadata *418*

Multidimensional database *422*

Multidimensionality *435*

Online analytical processing (OLAP) *427*

Operational data store *422*

Text mining *430*

Virtual reality (VR) *438*

Virtual reality markup language (VRML) *440*

Visual interactive modeling (VIM) *438*

Visual interactive simulation (VIS) *438*

Web mining *431*

CHAPTER HIGHLIGHTS (Numbers Refer to Learning Objectives)

1 Data are the foundation of any information system and need to be managed throughout their useful life cycle, which converts data to useful information, knowledge, and a basis for decision support.

2 Data exist in internal and external computerized and other sources. Personal data and knowledge are often stored in people's minds.

2 The Internet is a major source of data and knowledge. Other sources are databases, paper documents, videos, maps, pictures, and more.

2 Many factors that impact the quality of data must be recognized and controlled.

3 Today data and documents are managed electronically. They are digitized, stored, and used in electronic management systems.

3 Electronic document management, the automated control of documents, is a key to greater efficiency in handling documents in order to gain an edge on the competition.

3 Multidimensional presentation enables quick and easy multiple viewing of information in accordance with people's needs.

4 Data warehouses and data marts are necessary to support effective information discovery and support of decision making. Relevant data are indexed and organized for easy access by end users.

5 Online analytical processing is a data discovery method that uses analytical approaches.

5 Business intelligence is an umbrella name for a large number of methods and tools used to conduct data analysis.

6 Data mining for knowledge discovery is an attempt to use intelligent systems to scan volumes of data to locate necessary information and knowledge and to discover relationships among data items.

7 Visualization is important for better understanding of data relationships and compression of information. Several computer-based methods exist.

7 A geographical information system captures, stores, manipulates, and displays data using digitized maps.

7 Virtual reality is 3-D, interactive, computer-generated graphics that provides users with a feeling that they are inside a certain real environment.

8 Marketing databases provide the technological support for new marketing approaches such as interactive marketing.

8 Marketing transaction databases provide dynamic interactive functions that facilitate customized advertising and services to customers.

9 Web-based systems are used extensively in supporting data access and data analysis. Also, Web-based systems are an important source of data. Finally, data visualization is frequently combined with Web systems.

VIRTUAL COMPANY ASSIGNMENT

Data Management at The Wireless Café

Go to The Wireless Café's link on the Student Web Site. There you will be asked to think about how to better manage the various types of data that the restaurant uses in its activities.

More Resources

More resources and study tools are located on the Student Web Site. You'll find additional chapter materials and useful Web links. In addition, self-quizzes that provide individualized feedback are available for each chapter.

QUESTIONS FOR REVIEW

1. List the major sources of data.
2. List some of the major data problems.
3. What is a terabyte? (Write the number.)
4. Review the steps of the data life cycle and explain them.
5. List some of the categories of data available on the Internet.
6. Define data quality.
7. Define document management.
8. Describe a data warehouse.
9. Describe a data mart.
10. Define business intelligence.
11. Define online analytical processing (OLAP).
12. Define data mining and describe its major characteristics.
13. Define data visualization.
14. Explain the properties of multidimensionality and its vizualization.
15. Describe GIS and its major capabilities.
16. Define visual interactive modeling and simulation.
17. Define a marketing transaction database.
18. Define virtual reality.

QUESTIONS FOR DISCUSSION

1. Compare data quality to data integrity. How are they related?
2. Discuss the relationship between OLAP and multidimensionality.
3. Discuss business intelligence and distinguish between decision support and information and knowledge discovery.
4. Discuss the factors that make document management so valuable. What capabilities are particularly valuable?
5. Relate document management to imaging systems.
6. Describe the process of information and knowledge discovery, and discuss the roles of the data warehouse, data mining, and OLAP in this process.
7. Discuss the major drivers and benefits of data warehousing to end users.
8. A data mart can substitute for a data warehouse or supplement it. Compare and discuss these options.
9. Why is the combination of GIS and GPS becoming so popular? Examine some applications related to data management.

10. Discuss the advantages of terabyte marketing databases to a large corporation. Does a small company need a marketing database? Under what circumstances will it make sense to have one?

11. Discuss the benefits managers can derive from visual interactive simulation in a manufacturing company.

12. What is the logic of targeted marketing, and how can data management be used in such marketing?

13. Distinguish between operational databases, data warehouses, and marketing data marts.

14. Relate the Sears minicase to the phases of the data life cycle.

15. Discuss the potential contribution of virtual reality to e-commerce.

16. Discuss the interaction between marketing and management theories and IT support in the Harrah's case.

EXERCISES

1. Review the list of data management difficulties in Section 10.1. Explain how a combination of data warehousing and data mining can solve or reduce these difficulties. Be specific.

2. Interview a knowledge worker in a company you work for or to which you have access. Find the data problems they have encountered and the measures they have taken to solve them. Relate the problems to Strong's four categories.

3. Ocean Spray Cranberries is a large cooperative of fruit growers and processors. Ocean Spray needed data to determine the effectiveness of its promotions and its advertising and to make itself able to respond strategically to its competitors' promotions. The company also wanted to identify trends in consumer preferences for new products and to pinpoint marketing factors that might be causing changes in the selling levels of certain brands and markets.

   Ocean Spray buys marketing data from InfoScan (*infores.com*), a company that collects data using barcode scanners in a sample of 2,500 stores nationwide and from A.C. Nielsen. The data for each product include sales volume, market share, distribution, price information, and information about promotions (sales, advertisements).

   The amount of data provided to Ocean Spray on a daily basis is overwhelming (about 100 to 1,000 times more data items than Ocean Spray used to collect on its own). All the data are deposited in the corporate marketing data mart. To analyze this vast amount of data, the company developed a DSS. To give end users easy access to the data, the company uses an expert system–based data-mining process called CoverStory, which summarizes information in accordance with user preferences. CoverStory interprets data processed by the DSS, identifies trends, discovers cause-and-effect relationships, presents hundreds of displays, and provides any information required by the decision makers. This system alerts managers to key problems and opportunities.

   a. Find information about Ocean Spray by entering Ocean Spray's Web site (*oceanspray.com*).

   b. Ocean Spray has said that it cannot run the business without the system. Why?

   c. What data from the data mart are used by the DSS?

   d. Enter *infores.com* or *scanmar.nl* and review the marketing decision support information. How is the company related to a data warehouse?

   e. How does Infoscan collect data? (Check the Data Wrench product.)

4. Enter *visualmining.com*. Explore the relationship of visualization and business intelligence. See how BI is related to dashboards (Chapter 13). Write a report on your findings.

GROUP ASSIGNMENTS

1. Several applications now combine GIS and GPS.

   a. Survey such applications by conducting literature and Internet searches and query GIS vendors.

   b. Prepare a list of five applications, including at least two in e-commerce (see Chapter 4).

   c. Describe the benefit of such integration.

2. Prepare a report on the topic of "data management and the intranet." Specifically, pay attention to the role of the data warehouse, the use of browsers for query, and data mining. Also explore the issue of GIS and the Internet. Finally, describe the role of extranets in support of business partner collaboration. Each group will visit one or two vendors' sites, read the white papers, and examine products (Oracle, Red Bricks, Brio, Siemens Mixdorf IS, NCR, SAS, and Information Advantage). Also, visit the Web site of the Data Warehouse Institute (*dw-institute.org*).

3. Using data mining, it is possible not only to capture information that has been buried in distant courthouses, but also to manipulate and cross-index it. This can benefit law enforcement but invade privacy. In 1996, Lexis-Nexis, the online information service, was accused of permitting access to sensitive information on individuals. The company argued that the firm was targeted unfairly, since it provided only basic residential data for lawyers and law enforcement personnel. Should Lexis-Nexis be prohibited from allowing access to such information or not? Debate the issue.

INTERNET EXERCISES

1. Conduct a survey on document management tools and applications by visiting *dataware.com, documentum.com, mobius.com,* and *aiim.org/aim/publications.*

2. Access the Web sites of one or two of the major data management vendors, such as Oracle, IBM, and Sybase, and trace the capabilities of their latest BI products.

3. Access the Web sites of one or two of the major data warehouse vendors, such as NCR or SAS; find how their products are related to the Web.

4. Access the Web site of the GartnerGroup (*gartnergroup.com*). Examine some of their research notes pertaining to marketing databases, data warehousing, and data management. Prepare a report regarding the state of the art.

5. Explore a Web site for multimedia database applications. Visit such sites as *leisureplan.com, illustra.com,* or *adb.fr.* Review some of the demonstrations, and prepare a concluding report.

6. Enter *microsoft.com/solutions/BI/customer/biwithinreach_demo.asp* and see how BI is supported by Microsoft's tools. Write a report.

7. Enter *teradatauniversitynetwork.com.* Prepare a summary on resources available there. Is it valuable to a student? To practicing managers?

8. Enter *visualmining.com* and review the support they provide to business intelligence. Prepare a report.

9. Survey some GIS resources such as *geo.ed.ac.uk/home/hiswww.html,* and *prenhall.com/stratgis/sites.html.* Identify GIS resources related to your industry, and prepare a report on some recent developments or applications. See *http://nsdi.usgs.gov/nsdi/pages/what_is_gis.html.*

10. Visit the sites of some GIS vendors (such as *mapinfo.com, esri.com, autodesk.com,* or *bently.com*). Join a newsgroup and discuss new applications in marketing, banking, and transportation. Download a demo. What are some of the most important capabilities and new applications?

11. Enter *websurvey.com, clearlearning.com,* and *tucows.com/webforms,* and prepare a report about data collection via the Web.

12. Enter *infoscan.com.* Find all the services related to dynamic warehouse and explain what it does.

13. Enter *ibm.com/software* and find their data mining products, such as DB2 Intelligent Miner. Prepare a list of products and their capabilities.

14. Enter *megapuker.com,* Read "Data Mining 101," "Text Analyst," and "WebAnalyst." Compare the two products. (Look at case studies.)

15. Enter *psgroup.com* and find the free report (by M. Kramer, 2004) on customer data mining. Prepare a summary of the applications in your area of interest.

16. Explore the issue of data quality at *dmreview.com.* See how it relates to portals, and examine the profiling and augmentation dimensions.

Minicase 1
Homeland Security Data Integration

The CIO of the U.S. Department of Homeland Security (DHS) is responsible for determining which existing applications and types of data can help the organization meet its goal, migrating the data into a secure, usable, state-of-the-art framework, and integrating the disparate networks and data standards of 22 federal agencies, with 170,000 employees, that merged to form the DHS. The real problem is that federal agencies have historically operated autonomously, and their IT systems were not designed to interoperate with one another. Essentially, the DHS needs to link large and complex silos of data together.

The challenge of moving data from legacy systems, within or across agencies, is the first challenge DHS must address. Complicating the issue is the plethora of rapidly aging applications and databases throughout government.

Data integration improvement is underway at the federal, local, and state levels. The government is utilizing tools from the corporate world.

Major problems have occurred because each agency has its own set of business rules that dictate how data are described, collected, and accessed. Some of the data are unstructured and not organized in relational databases, and they cannot be easily manipulated and analyzed. Commercial applications are used for the major integration, mostly data warehouse and data-mart technologies. Informatica, among other software vendors, has developed data integration solutions that enable organizations to combine disparate systems to make information more widely accessible throughout an organization. Such software may be suitable for such a large-scale project (see *informatica.com*).

The idea is to decide on and create an enterprise architecture for federal and state agencies involved in homeland security. The architecture will help determine the success of homeland defense. The first step in migrating data is to identify all the applications and data in use. After identifying applications and databases, the next step is to determine which to use and which to discard. Once an organization knows which data and applications it wants to keep, the difficult process of moving the data starts. First, it is necessary to identify and build on a common thread in the data. Another major challenge in the data-migration arena is data security, especially when dealing with data and applications that are decades old.

Homeland Security will also have information-analysis and infrastructure-protection components. Developing these components may be the single most difficult challenge for the DHS. Not only will Homeland Security have to make sense of a huge mountain of intelligence gathered from disparate sources, but then it will have to get that information to the people who can most effectively act on it. Many of them are outside the federal government. Data analysis, including data mining, OLAP, and more, will help in early detection of planned attacks, as well as in finding terrorists.

Even the central government recognizes that data deficiencies may plague the DHS. Moving information to where it is needed, and doing so when it is needed, is critical and exceedingly difficult. Some 650,000 state and local law enforcement officials "operate in a virtual intelligence vacuum, without proper access to terrorist watch lists provided by the State Department to immigration and consular officials," according to the October 2002 Hart-Rudman report, titled "America Still Unprepared—America Still in Danger."

Sources: Compiled from Datz (2002), Foley (2003), Nazarov (2003), Thibodeau (2003), and Peters (2003).

Questions for Minicase 1

1. List the data problems and difficulties (see Section 10.1).
2. Why is the data warehouse beneficial?
3. What kind of analysis can the government perform with the IT support? What tools do you suggest be used?
4. How can Informatica.com products help? (Visit the company's site, *informatica.com*.)
5. Would you suggest a document management system (DMS)? For what purpose?

Minicase 2
Precision Buying, Merchandising, and Marketing at Sears

The Problem

Sears, Roebuck and Company, the largest department store chain and the third-largest retailer in the United States, was caught by surprise in the 1980s as shoppers defected to specialty stores and discount mass merchandisers, causing the firm to lose market share rapidly. In an attempt to change the situation, Sears used several response strategies, ranging from introducing its own specialty stores (such as Sears Hardware) to restructuring its mall-based stores. Recently, Sears has moved to selling on the Web. It discontinued its over 100-year-old paper catalog. Accomplishing the transformation and restructuring required the retooling of its information systems.

Sears had 18 data centers, one in each of 10 geographical regions as well as one each for marketing, finance, and other departments. The first problem was created when the reorganization effort produced only seven geographical regions. Frequent mismatches between accounting and sales figures and information scattered among numerous databases forced users to query multiple systems, even when they needed an answer to a simple query. Furthermore, users found that data that were already summarized made

it difficult to conduct analysis at the desired level of detail. Finally, errors were virtually inevitable when calculations were based on data from several sources.

The Solution

To solve these problems, Sears constructed a single sales information data warehouse. This replaced the 18 old databases which were packed with redundant, conflicting, and sometimes obsolete data. The new data warehouse is a simple repository of relevant decision-making data such as authoritative data for key performance indicators, sales inventories, and profit margins. Sears, known for embracing IT on a dramatic scale, completed the data warehouse and its IT reengineering efforts in under one year—a perfect IT turnaround story.

Using an NCR enterprise server, the initial 1.7 terabyte (1.7 trillion bytes) data warehouse is part of a project dubbed the Strategic Performance Reporting System (SPRS). By 2003, the data warehouse had grown to over 70 terabytes. SPRS includes comprehensive sales data; information on inventory in stores, in transit, and at distribution centers; and cost per item. This has enabled Sears to track sales by individual items(skus) in each of its 1,950 stores (including 810 mall-based stores) in the United States and 1,600 international stores and catalog outlets. Thus, daily margin by item per store can be easily computed, for example. Furthermore, Sears now fine-tunes its buying, merchandising, and marketing strategies with previously unattainable precision.

SPRS is open to all authorized employees, who now can view each day's sales from a multidimensional perspective (by region, district, store, product line, and individual item). Users can specify any starting and ending dates for special sales reports, and all data can be accessed via a highly user-friendly graphical interface. Sears managers can now monitor the precise impact of advertising, weather, and other factors on sales of specific items. This means that Sears merchandise buyers and other specialists can examine and adjust, if needed, inventory quantities, merchandising, and order placement, along with myriad other variables, almost immediately, so they can respond quickly to environmental changes. SPRS users can also group together widely divergent kinds of products, for example, tracking sales of items marked as "gifts under $25." Advertising staffers can follow so-called "great items," drawn from vastly different departments, that are splashed on the covers of promotional circulars. SPRS enables extensive data mining, but only on sku- and location-related analysis.

In 1998 Sears created a large customer database, dubbed LCI (Leveraging Customer Information) which contained customer-related sale information (which was not available on SPRS). The LCI enables hourly records of transactions, for example, guiding hourly promotion (such as 15% discounts for early-bird shoppers).

In the holiday season of 2001, Sears decided to replace its regular 10% discount promotion by offering deep discount during early shopping hours. This new promotion, which was based on SPRS, failed, and only when LCI was used was the problem was corrected. This motivated Sears to combine LCI and SPRS in a single platform, which enables sophisticated analysis (in 2002).

By 2001, Sears also had the following Web initiatives: an e-commerce home improvement center, a B2B supply exchange for the retail industry, a toy catalog (*wishbook .com*), an e-procurement system, and much more. All of these Web-marketing initiatives feed data into the data warehouse, and their planning and control are based on accessing the data in the data warehouse.

The Results

The ability to monitor sales by item per store enables Sears to create a sharp local market focus. For example, Sears keeps different shades of paint colors in different cities to meet local demands. Therefore, sales and market share have improved. Also, Web-based data monitoring of sales at LCI helps Sears to plan marketing and Web advertising.

At its inception, the data warehouse had been used daily by over 3,000 buyers, replenishers, marketers, strategic planners, logistics and finance analysts, and store managers. By 2004, there were over 6,000 users, since users found the system very beneficial. Response time to queries has dropped from days to minutes for typical requests. Overall, the strategic impact of the SPRS-LCI data warehouse is that it offers Sears employees a tool for making better decisions, and Sears retailing profits have climbed more than 20 percent annually since SPRS was implemented.

Sources: Compiled from Amato-McCoy (2002), Beitler and Leary (1997); and press releases of Sears (2001–2004).

Questions for Minicase 2

1. What were the drivers of SPRS?
2. How did the data wareshouse solve Sears's problems?
3. Why was it beneficial to integrate the customers' database with SPRS?
4. How could RFID change Sears' operations?

REFERENCES

Alameh, N., "Chaining Geographic Information Web Services," *IEEE Internet Computing,* September–October 2003.

Alter, S. L., *Decision Support Systems.* Reading, MA: Addison Wesley, 1980.

Amato-McCoy, D. M., "Sears Combines Retail Reporting and Customer Databases on a Single Platform," *Stores,* November 2002.

Amato-McCoy, D. M., "Victoria's Secret Works to Keep Orders Alive," *Stores,* January 2003a.

Amato-McCoy, D. M., "Movie Gallery Mines Data to Monitor Associate Activities," *Stores,* May 2003b.

Amato-McCoy, D. M., "AAFES Combats Fraud with Exception Reporting Solution," *Stores,* May 2003c.

Apte, C., et al., "Business Application of Data Mining," *Communications of the ACM,* August 2002.

Asprev, L., and M. Middleton (eds.), *Integrative Document and Content Management.* Hershey, PA: The Idea Group, 2003.

Atzeni, P., et al., "Managing Web-Based Data," *IEEE Internet Computing,* July–August 2002.

Ballou, D., et al., "Assuring Information Quality," *JMIS,* Winter 2003–2004.

Banerjee, P., and D. Zetu, *Virtual Manufacturing: Virtual Reality and Computer Vision Techniques.* New York: Wiley, 2001.

Bates, J., "Business in Real Time—Realizing the Vision," *DM Review,* May 2003.

Baumer, D., "Innovative Web Use to Learn about Consumer Behavior and Online Privacy," *Communications of the ACM,* April, 2003.

Becker, S. A. (ed.), *Effective Database for Text and Document Management.* Hershey, PA: IRM Press, 2003.

Beitler, S. S., and R. Leary, "Sears' Epic Transformation: Converting from Mainframe Legacy Systems to OLAP," *Journal of Data Warehousing,* April 1997.

Beroggi, G.E., "Visual Interactive Decision Modeling in Policy Management," *Eurpoean Journal of Operational Research,* January 2001.

Berry, M., *Survey of Text Mining: Clustering, Classification and Retrieval.* Berlin: Springer–Verlag, 2002.

BIXL, *Business Intelligence for Excel,* a white paper, Business Intelligence Technologies, Inc. 2002 (*BIXL.com*).

Bonde, A., and M. Kuckuk, "Real-World Business Intelligence: The Implementation Perspective," *DM Review,* April 2004.

Brauer, J. R., "Data Quality Is the Cornerstone of Effective Business Intelligence," *DM Direct,* October 5, 2001.

Brody, R., "Information Ethics in the Design and Use of Metadata," *IEEE Technology and Society Magazine,* Summer 2003.

Brown, D. E., and S. Hagen, "Data Association Methods with Applications to Law Enforcement," *Decision Support Systems,* March 2003.

Brown, J., "Pizza Hut Delivers Hot Results Using Data Warehouse—Enterprise Computing," October 17, 2003, *articles. findarticles.com/ p/articles/mi_m0CGC/is_20_29/ai_109518376* (accessed May 2004).

Buss, D., "Donskin Launches Virtual Showroom for Retail Clients," *Stores,* March 2003.

Calderon, T. G., et. al., "How Large Corporations Use Data Mining to Create Value," *Management Accounting Quarterly,* Winter 2003, *articles.findarticles.com/p/articles/mi_m0OOL/is_2_4/ai_99824637/pg_2* (accessed May 2004).

Campbell, D., "Visualization for the Real World," *DM Review,* September 7, 2001.

Canada NewsWire, "European Court of Human Rights Saves Time and Money for a News Wire," April 29, 2003, NAICS#922110.

Carbone, P. L., "Data Warehousing: Many of the Common Failures," Presentation, *mitre.org/support/papers/tech…9_00/d-warehoulse_ presentation.htm* (May 3, 1999).

Chopoorian, J. A., et al., "Mind Your Business by Mining Your Data," *SAM Advanced Management Journal,* Spring 2001.

Church, R. L., "Geographical Information Systems and Location Science," *Computers and Operations Research,* May 2002.

Civic.com/pubs (accessed March 2001).

Codd, E. F., et al., "Beyond Decision Support," *Computerworld,* July 1993.

Cognos.com. "Platform for Enterprise Business Intelligence," Cognos Inc., 2001.

Cole, B., "Document Management on a Budget," *Network World,* Vol. 13, No. 8, September 16, 1996.

Creese, G., and A. Veytsel, *Data Quality at a Real-Time Tempo,* Special Report. Boston: Aberdeen Group, January 9, 2003.

Dalgleish, J., *Customer-Effective Web Sites.* Upper Saddle River, NJ: Pearson Technology Group, 2000.

Date, C. J., *An Introduction to Database Systems,* 6th ed. New York: Addison-Wesley, 1995.

Datz, T., "Integrating America," *CIO,* December 2002.

Delcambre, L., et al., "Harvesting Information to Sustain Forests," *Communications of the ACM,* January 2003.

De Lora, J., and M. Alfonseca, "Visual Interactive Simulation for Distance Education," *Simulation: Transactions of the Society for Modeling and Simulation International,* 79(1), January 2003.

Dimensional Insight, *Business Intelligence and OLAP Terms: An Online Glossary, dimins.com/Glossary1.html* (accessed June 15, 2003).

Eckerson, W., *The Secrets of Creating Successful Business Intelligence Solutions.* Seattle, WA: The Data Warehousing Institute, 2003.

Etzioni, O., "The WWW: Quagmire or Gold Mine," *Communications of the ACM,* November 1996.

Fayyad, U. M., et al., "The KDD Process for Extracting Useful Knowledge from Volumes of Data," *Communications of the ACM,* November 1996.

Finnish Business Report, April 1997.

Foley, J., "Data Debate," *Information Week,* May 19, 2003.

Fong, A. C. M., et al., "Data Mining for Decision Support," *IT Pro,* March–April, 2002.

GIS World, July 1993.

Goddard, S., et al., "Geospatial Decision Support for Drought Risk Management," *Communications of the ACM,* January 2003.

Grant, G. (ed.), *ERP and Datawarehousing in Organizations: Issues and Challenges.* Hershey, PA: IRM Press, 2003.

Gray, P., and H. J. Watson, *Decision Support in the Data Warehouse.* Upper Saddle River, NJ, Prentice-Hall, 1998.

Grimes, S., "Look Before You Leap," *Intelligent Enterprise,* June 2003.

Grimshaw, D. J., *Bringing Geographical Information Systems into Business,* 2nd ed. New York: Wiley, 1999.

Grossnickle, J., and O. Raskin, *The Handbook of Marketing Research.* New York: McGraw-Hill, 2000.

Hamilton, J. M., "A Mapping Feast," *CIO,* March 15, 1996.

Hardester, K. P., "Au Enterprise GIS Solution for Integrating GIS and CAMA," *Assessment Journal,* November–December 2002.

Hasan, B., "Assessing Data Authenticity with Benford's Law," *Information Systems Control Journal,* July 2002.

Hirji, K. K., "Exploring Data Mining Implementation," *Communications of the ACM,* July 2001.

Hormozi, A. M., and S. Giles, "Data Mining: A Competitive Weapon for Banking and Retail Industries," *Information Systems Management,* Spring 2004.

Inmon, W. H., "Why Clickstream Data Counts," *e-Business Advisor,* April 2001.

Inmon, W. H., *Building the Data Warehouse,* 3rd ed. New York: Wiley, 2002.

I/S Analyzer, "Visualization Software Aids in Decision Making," *I/S Analyzer,* July 2002.

Kimball, R., and M. Ross, *The Data Warehouse Tool Kit,* 2nd ed. New York: Wiley, 2002.

Kerlow, I. V., *The Art of 3D,* 2nd ed. New York: Wiley, 2000.

Korte, G. B., *The GIS Book,* 5th ed. Albany, NY: Onward Press, 2000.

Langnau, L., "Business Intelligence and Ethics: Can They Work Together? Controls & Systems Editorial—Industry Overview," November 2003, *articles.findarticles.com/p/articles/mi_m0EWQ/is_12_58/ ai_111303805* (accessed May 2004).

Lau, H. C. W., et al., "Development of an Intelligent Data-Mining System for a Dispersed Manufacturing Network," *Expert Systems,* September 2001.

Lee, W. Y., and D. M. Strong, "Knowing-Why about Data Processes and Data Quality," *JMIS,* Winter 2003–2004.

Levinson, M., "Jackpot! Harrah's Entertainment," *CIO Magazine,* February 1, 2001.

Li, T., et al., "Information Visualization for Intelligent DSS," *Knowledge Based Systems,* August 2001.

Liautaud, B., *E-Business Intelligence.* New York: McGraw-Hill, 2001.

Linoff, G. S., and J. A. Berry, *Mining the Web: Transforming Customer Data*. New York: Wiley, 2002.

Liu, S., "Data Warehousing Agent: To Make the Creation and Maintenance of Data Warehouse Easier," *Journal of Data Warehousing,* Spring 1998.

Loshin, D., "Issues and Opportunities in Data Quality Management Coordination," *DM Review*, April 2004.

Loveman, G., "Diamonds in the Data," *Harvard Business Review,* May 2003.

Markus, M. L., et al., "A Design Theory for Systems that Support Emergent Knowledge Processes," *MIS Quarterly,* September 2002.

Merrill Lynch, 1998.

MicroStrategy, *The 5 Styles of Business Intelligence,* white paper prepared by MicroStrategy, Inc., 2003a.

MicroStrategy, *Industrial-Strength Business Intelligence,* white paper prepared by MicroStrategy, Inc., 2003b.

Moad, J., "Mining a New Vein," *PC Week,* January 5, 1998.

Moerkotte, G., and P. C. Lockemann, "Reactive Consistency Control in Deductive Databases," *ACM Transactions on Database Systems,* 16(4), December 1991.

Moss, L. T., and S. Atre, *Business Intelligence Roadmap: The Complete Project Lifecycle for Decision Support Applications.* Boston: Addison Wesley, 2003.

Motro, A., "Integrity = Validity + Completeness," *ACM Transactions on Database Systems,* 14(4), December 1989.

Nasirin, S., and D. F. Birks, "DSS Implementation in the UK Retail Organizations: A GIS Perspective," *Information and Management,* March, 2003.

Nazarov, A. R., "Information Seeks Partners to Gain Traction in Fed Market," *CRN*, June 9, 2003.

NCR Corp. (2000).

Nemati, H. R., and C. D. Barko, "Enhancing Enterprise Decision through Organizational Data Mining," *Journal of Computer Information Systems,* Summer, 2002.

O'Looney, J. A., *Beyond Maps: GIS Decision Making in Local Governments.* Redlands, CA: ESRI Press, 2000.

Oguz, M. T., "Strategic Intelligence: Business Intelligence in Competitive Strategy," *DM Review,* May 31, 2003.

Olson, J. E., *Data Quality: The Accuracy Dimension*. San Francisco: Morgan Kaufman, 2003.

Park, Y. T., "Strategic Uses of Data Warehouses," *Journal of Data Warehousing,* April 1997.

Peters, K. M., "5 Homeland Security Hurdles," *Government Executive*, 35(2), February 2003.

Pritsker, A. A. B., and J. J. O'Reilly, *Simulation with Visual SLAM and Awesim,* 2nd ed. New York: Wiley, 1999.

Ray, N., and S.W. Tabor, "Cyber-Surveys Come of Age," *Marketing Research,* Spring 2003.

Redman, T. C., "The Impact of Poor Data Quality on the Typical Enterprise," *Communications of the ACM,* February 1998.

Roth, M. A., et al., "Information Integration: A New Generation of Information Technology," *IBM Systems Journal,* December 2002.

Rundensteiner, E. A., et al., "Maintaining Data Warehousing over Changing Information Sources," *Communications of the ACM,* June 2000.

Sadeh, N., *M-Commerce*. New York: Wiley, 2002.

Schlosser, J., "Looking for Intelligence in Ice Cream," *Fortune,* March 17, 2003.

Sears (2001–2003).

Sen, A., "Metadata Management: Past, Present, and Future," *Decision Support Systems,* April 2004.

Siddiqui, A., "DataDistilleries: DataDistilleries Proves that Analytics Pays in Marketing, Call Centre and Internet Environments; Customer Statistics Show DataDistilleries Users Cut Marketing Costs by a Third Whilst Increasing Conversion Rates by 60%," *M2 Presswire.* Coventry England?, June 26, 2003.

Sikder, I., and A. Gangopadhyay, "Design and Implementation of a Web-Based Collaborative Spatial Decision Support System: Organizational and Managerial Implications," *Information Resources Management Journal,* October–December 2002.

Steede-Terry, K., *Integrating GIS and GPS.* Redlands, CA: Environmental Systems Research (*eSRI.com*), 2000.

Strauss, J., et al., *E-Marketing.* Upper Saddle River, NJ: Prentice Hall, 2003.

Strong, D. M., et al., "Data Quality in Context," *Communications of the ACM,* May 1997.

Sweiger, M., et al., *Clickstream Data Warehousing.* New York: Wiley, 2002.

Tang C., et al., "An Agent-Based Geographical Information System," *Knowledge-Based Systems,* Vol. 14, 2001.

Telecomworldwire, "NSF to Introduce Virtual Reality Tour of Monticello," April 7, 2003, *articles.findarticles.com/p/articles/mi_m0ECZ/is_2003_April_7/ai_99726484* (accessed May 2004).

Terry, K., and D. Kolb, "Integrated Vehicle Routing and Tracking Using GIS-Based Technology," *Logistics,* March–April 2003.

Thibodeau, P., "DHS Sets Timeline for IT Integration," *Computer World,* June 16, 2003.

Turban, E., et al., *Decision Support Systems and Intelligent Systems.* Upper Saddle River, NJ: Prentice Hall, 2005.

Turban, E., et al., *Electronic Commerce 2006.* Upper Saddle River, NJ: Prentice-Hall, 2006.

Ursery, S., "GIS More Prevalent in Big Cities, Counties," *The American City & County*, 119(2), February 2004, *americancityandcounty. com/mag/government_gis_prevalent_big/* (accessed May 2004).

USA Today, "Virtual Reality Will Change Your Reality, Your Life," May 2003, *articles.findarticles.com/p/articles/mi_m1272/is_2696_131/ai_101497538* (accessed May 2004).

Vaughan, J., "XML Meets the Data Warehouse," January 1, 2003, *adtmag.com/article.asp?id=7116* (accessed May 2004).

Wang, R. Y., and D. M. Strong, "Beyond Accuracy: What Data Quality Means to Data Consumers," *Journal of Management Information Systems,* 12(4), Spring 1996.

Watson, H. J., et al., "The Effects of Technology-Enabled Business Strategy At First American Corporation," *Organizational Dynamics,* Winter, 2002.

Weiss, T. R., "Online Retail Sales On the Rise," *PC World,* January 2003.

Whiting, R., "The Data-Warehouse Advantage," July 28, 2003, *informationweek.com/story/showArticle.jhtml?articleID=12802974* (accessed May 2004).

Winter, R., *Large Scale Data Warehousing with Oracle 9i Database,* Special Report. Waltham MA: Winter Corp., 2001.

Worthen, B., "What to Do When Uncle Sam Wants Your Data," *CIO,* April 15, 2003.

Yao, Y. H., et al., "XML-Based IS09000 Electronic Document Management System," *Robotics and Computer-Integrated Manufacturing,* 19(4), August 2003.

Zdanowicz, J. S., "Detecting Money Laundering and Terrorist Financing via Data Mining," *Communications of the ACM,* May 2004.

PART IV
Managerial and Decision Support Systems

9. Knowledge Management
10. Data Management: Warehousing, Analyzing, Mining, and Visualization
▶ 11. Management Decision Support and Intelligent Systems

CHAPTER

11

Management Decision Support and Intelligent Systems

11.1 Managers and Decision Making

11.2 Decision Support Systems

11.3 Group Decision Support Systems

11.4 Enterprise and Executive Decision Support Systems

11.5 Intelligent Support Systems: The Basics

11.6 Expert Systems

11.7 Other Intelligent Systems

11.8 Web-Based Management Support Systems

11.9 Advanced and Special Decision Support Topics

Minicases:
1. Netherlands Railway
2. Singapore and Malaysia Airlines

Online Appendix W11.1 Intelligent Software Agents

LEARNING OBJECTIVES

After studying this chapter, you will be able to:

❶ Describe the concepts of managerial decision making and computerized support for decision making.

❷ Justify the role of modeling in decision making.

❸ Describe decision support systems (DSSs) and their benefits, and describe the DSS structure.

❹ Describe the support to group (including virtual) decision making.

❺ Describe organizational DSS and executive support systems, and analyze their role in management support.

❻ Describe artificial intelligence (AI) and list its benefits and characteristics.

❼ List the major commercial AI technologies.

❽ Define an expert system and its components, and describe its benefits and limitations.

❾ Describe natural language processing and compare it to speech understanding.

❿ Describe artificial neural networks (ANNs), their characteristics and major applications; compare them to fuzzy logic and describe their role in hybrid intelligent systems.

⓫ Describe the relationships between the Web, DSS, and intelligent systems.

⓬ Describe special decision support applications including the support of frontline employees.

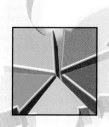

NEW BALANCE MAKES SURE
THAT SHOES FIT

 THE PROBLEM

New Balance (*newbalance.com*) is a $1.3 billion privately held athletic shoe company. As recently as 2001, New Balance executives did not have the tools to deliver accurate forecasts for the number of shoes it would sell through its various outlets.

The company's forecasting process worked like this: The person in charge of the forecasting department was supposed to collect forecasts from about half of the company's 160 sales representatives, compile them, and create overall predictions of what shoes the company's factories should turn out and when. However, she was lucky to get 20 forecasts back each month.

The problem for the sales representatives was that filling out the sheets consumed a lot of time—as much as a day for the forecasts for larger accounts. Reps had to pore through reams of printouts to plug answers into the company's spreadsheet. For salespeople paid on commission, the process took money out of their wallets, and they were unhappy.

The problems multiplied for the forecasters. The format of the company's spreadsheet was not protected. That meant, first of all, that reps would delete columns, type in the wrong style names, and move information around as they saw fit. It took at least a day for New Balance forecasters to validate the data from each sales rep's forecast, put the data into the correct form, and collate and analyze it.

In reality, New Balance forecasters produced their forecasts without much input of sales reps. This seat-of-the-pants approach caused sudden spikes in orders to factories for some products and backlogs of others. There would be deep valleys of production, when inventory that had piled up was sold off. The worst problem was that New Balance could not get orders to customers on time.

Also, the company used these forecasts to push sales quotas down from headquarters. The quota typically was the prior year's number plus some estimate of growth for the coming year. Because the quotas had little basis in reality, the sales force paid little attention to them.

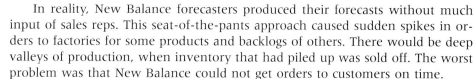 **THE SOLUTION**

New Balance turned to a decision support system (DSS) to give it the ability to manage its complex production planning by account, region, salesperson, and other criteria. The DSS helped New Balance forecasters take into account such predictors of demand as general economic indicators, current orders, and historic sales data. The DSS produces forecast numbers for each shoe style. These forecasts help the company's manufacturing managers to plan for production capacity. The forecasts are done with special mathematical and statistical models. However, the DSS includes other tools of business intelligence (Chapter 10).

Also, with the new DSS, information about customers can be gathered for each sales rep from corporate databases. The reps download that information from a secure Web site as each month ends. Using the data and consulting with business customers, each sales rep updates the forecast of each customer's orders, not just for the rest of the current year, but for the following year as well. Also, the company can assign reps to the accounts they do best.

Then, instead of using a malleable spreadsheet, sales reps enter their revisions in a locked-down template created by corporate forecasters. This template makes it easier and quicker for sales reps to fill out required information, and it is easy for forecasters to "roll up" all the sales reps' forecasts. In four hours, corporate forecasters can send out consolidated reports and breakouts by account and product.

 THE RESULTS

The DSS has produced several beneficial results for New Balance. For the first time, the company can tell which representatives can best predict orders and which representatives can best resolve problems with key business customers. In addition, the DSS has added accountability to everyone's role.

Second, New Balance now has a much more accurate picture each month of what its production should be. Because New Balance has a six-month lead time for delivery from its factories and overseas suppliers, rapid information and more accurate forecasts enable the company to react more quickly to retailers' needs. Since the implementation of the DSS, the number of shoes left in inventory when the company discontinues a style has dropped on average by 8 percent.

Third, using the DSS, the company discovered that its best-selling shoe sales had shifted from the $120-to-$160 basketball shoes to less-expensive, multipurpose shoes that cost between $60 and $90 per pair. So, the company produced styles in this price range in all widths.

Fourth, company executives now routinely call individual sales reps whose top business customers have fallen behind on purchases. The source of the executives' information is the "Top Accounts" report, an update distributed at noon every Monday that gives company executives a detailed look at sales figures for the past, present, and forecasted future. Executives have a wealth of information: a report for each style of shoe in New Balance's lineup; the to-date sales for the year and the month for each major retailer that New Balance serves; the sales of that shoe (or its predecessor) for the same period last year at that retailer; the orders for that retailer that have not been filled by New Balance's factory or warehouse; and what the sales rep had forecast for the current month. The sales force has access to the same report, meaning that everyone is on the same page and there are far fewer surprises.

The bottom line? Worldwide sales have more than doubled from $560 million in 1997 to $1.3 billion in 2002. New Balance now stands second only to Nike in the sale of running shoes. For all types of athletic shoes, New Balance ranks third, behind Nike and Reebok.

Source: Compiled from Barrett and Gallagher (2003).

 LESSONS LEARNED FROM THIS CASE

The opening case illustrates that a solution to complex production and other problems can be enhanced with the use of a decision support system (DSS). In fact, the DSS software supported several important decisions in production/ operations, marketing, and HRM. Furthermore, the case illustrates the concepts of modeling and quantitative analysis. Finally, the Web is playing an increasing role in facilitating the use of such systems.

This chapter describes computerized and Web support to *managerial decision makers.* We begin by reviewing the manager's job and the nature of today's decisions, which help explain why computerized support is needed. Then we present the concepts and methodology of the computerized decision support system for supporting individuals, groups, and whole organizations. Next, we introduce several types of intelligent systems and their role in decision support. Finally, we describe the topic of decision support in the Web environment. A discussion of intelligent software agents and their role in decision support appears in Online Appendix W11.1.

11.1 MANAGERS AND DECISION MAKING

Decisions are being made by all of us, every day. However, most major organizational decisions are made by managers. We begin with a brief description of the manager's job, of which making decisions is a major activity.

The Manager's Job
Management is a process by which organizational goals are achieved through the use of resources (people, money, energy, materials, space, time). These resources are considered to be *inputs,* and the attainment of the goals is viewed as the *output* of the process. Managers oversee this process in an attempt to optimize it.

To understand how computers support managers, it is necessary first to describe what managers do. They do many things, depending on their position in the organization, the type and size of the organization, organizational policies and culture, and the personalities of the managers themselves. Mintzberg (1973) divided the manager's roles into three categories: *interpersonal* (figurehead, leader, liaison), *informational* (monitor, disseminator, spokesperson), and *decisional* (entrepreneur, problem solver, resource allocator, and negotiator). Mintzberg and Westley (2001) also analyzed the role of decision makers in the information age. Finally, Huber (2003) describes the role of top management in today's complex, turbulent environment.

Early information systems mainly supported informational roles. In recent years, however, information systems have grown to support all three roles. In this chapter, we are mainly interested in the support that IT can provide to *decisional* roles. We divide the manager's work, as it relates to decisional roles, into two phases. Phase I is the identification of problems and/or opportunities. Phase II is the decision of what to do about them. Online File W11.1 provides a flowchart of this process and the flow of information in it.

DECISION MAKING AND PROBLEM SOLVING. A *decision* refers to a choice made between two or more alternatives. Decisions are diverse in nature and are made continuously by both individuals and groups. The purposes of decision making in organizations can be classified into two broad categories: *problem solving* and *opportunity exploiting.* In either case, managers must make decisions.

The ability to make crisp decisions was rated first in importance in a study conducted by the Harbridge House in Boston, Massachusetts. About 6,500 managers in more than 100 companies, including many large, blue-chip corporations, were asked how important it was that managers employ certain management practices. They also were asked how well, in their estimation, managers performed these practices. From a statistical distillation of these answers, Harbridge ranked "making clear-cut decisions when needed" as the *most important* of 10 management practices. Ranked second in importance was "getting to the heart of the problems rather than dealing with less important issues." Most of the remaining eight management practices were related directly or indirectly to decision making. The researchers also found that only 10 percent of the managers thought management performed "very well" on any given practice, mainly due to the difficult decision-making environment. It seems that the trial-and-error method, which might have been a practical approach to decision making in the past, is too expensive or ineffective today in many instances.

Therefore, managers must learn how to use the new tools and techniques that can help them make better decisions (see Huber, 2003). Many such techniques use a quantitative analysis (see the opening case) approach, and they are supported by computers. Several of the computerized decision aids are described in this chapter.

Computerized Decision Aids

The discussion on computerized decision aids here deals with four basic questions: (1) Why do managers need the support of information technology in making decisions? (2) Can the manager's job be fully automated? (3) What IT aids are available to support managers? (4) How are the information needs of managers determined? We answer the first three here; for answers to the fourth, see Online File W11.2. For further discussion, see Huber (2003).

WHY MANAGERS NEED THE SUPPORT OF INFORMATION TECHNOLOGY. It is very difficult to make good decisions without valid and relevant information. Information is needed for each phase and activity in the decision-making process.

Making decisions while processing information manually is growing increasingly difficult due to the following trends:

- The number of alternatives to be considered is ever *increasing*, due to innovations in technology, improved communication, the development of global markets, and the use of the Internet and e-business. A key to good decision making is to explore and compare many relevant alternatives. The more alternatives there are, the more computer-assisted search and comparisons are needed.
- Many decisions must be made under time pressure. Even in real time, frequently it is not possible to manually process the needed information fast enough to be effective.
- Due to increased fluctuations and uncertainty in the decision environment, it is frequently necessary to conduct a sophisticated analysis to make a good decision. Such analysis usually requires the use of mathematical modeling. Processing models manually can take a very long time.
- It is often necessary to rapidly access remote information, consult with experts, or have a group decision-making session, all without large expenses. Decision makers can be in different locations and so is the information. Bringing them all together quickly and inexpensively may be a difficult task.
- Decision making frequently requires an organization to conduct a forecast of prices, market share, and so on. Reliable forecasting requires analytical and statistical tools.

● Making decisions requires data. The amount of data, especially Internet clickstream data, is enormous, and growing rapidly. Data are located in multiple sources and need to be integrated from those sources.

These trends cause difficulties in making decisions, but a computerized analysis can be of enormous help. For example, a DSS can examine numerous alternatives very quickly, can support forecasting, can provide a systematic risk analysis, can be integrated with communication systems and databases, and can be used to support group work (see Kohari et al., 2003). And all this can be done with relatively low cost. *How* all this is accomplished will be shown later.

According to Bonabeau (2003), intuition plays an important role in decision making, but it can be dangerously unreliable. Therefore, one should use analytical tools such as those presented in this chapter and in Chapter 10.

Complexity of Decisions.   Decisions range from simple to very complex. Complex decisions are composed of a sequence of interrelated subdecisions. As an example, see the decision process pursued by a pharmaceutical company, Bayer Corp., regarding developing a new drug, as shown in Online File W11.3.

CAN THE MANAGER'S JOB BE FULLY AUTOMATED?   The generic decision-making process involves specific tasks (such as forecasting consequences and evaluating alternatives). This process can be fairly lengthy, which is bothersome for a busy manager. Automation of certain tasks can save time, increase consistency, and enable better decisions to be made. Thus, the more tasks we can automate in the process, the better. A logical question that follows is this: Is it possible to completely automate the manager's job?

In general, it has been found that the job of middle managers is the most likely job to be automated. Mid-level managers make fairly routine decisions, and these can be fully automated. Managers at lower levels do not spend much time on decision making. Instead, they supervise, train, and motivate non-managers. Some of their routine decisions, such as scheduling, can be automated; other decisions that involve behavioral aspects cannot. But, even if we completely automate their decisional role, we cannot automate their jobs. Note: The Web also provides an opportunity to automate certain tasks done by *front-line* employees. (This topic is discussed in Section 11.9.) The job of top managers is the least routine and therefore the most difficult to automate. For further discussion, see Huber (2003).

WHAT INFORMATION TECHNOLOGIES ARE AVAILABLE TO SUPPORT MANAGERS?
In addition to discovery, communication, and collaboration tools that provide indirect support to decision making, several other information technologies have been successfully used to support managers. The Web can facilitate them all. Collectively, they are referred to as **management support systems (MSSs)** (see Turban et al., 2005). The first of these technologies are *decision support systems*, which have been in use since the mid-1970s. They provide support primarily to analytical, quantitative types of decisions. Second, *executive (enterprise) support systems* represent a technology developed initially in the mid-1980s, mainly to support the informational roles of executives. A third technology, *group decision support systems*, supports managers and staff working in groups. A fourth technology is *intelligent systems*. These four technologies and their variants can be used independently, or they can be combined,

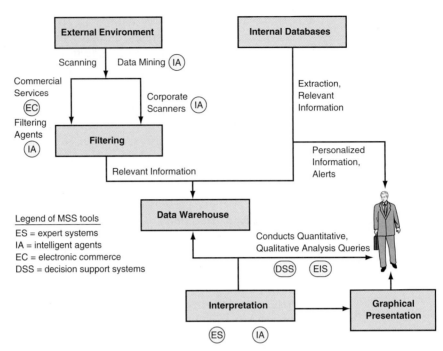

FIGURE 11.1
Computerized support for
decision making.

each providing a different capability. They are frequently related to data warehousing.

A simplified presentation of such support is shown in Figure 11.1. As Figure 11.1 shows, managers need to find, filter, and interpret information to determine potential problems or opportunities and then decide what to do about them. The figure shows the support of the various MSS tools (in yellow circles) as well as the role of a data warehouse, which was described in Chapter 10.

Several other technologies, either by themselves or when integrated with other management support technologies, can be used to support managers. One example is the **personal information manager (PIM).** A set of tools labeled PIM is intended to help managers be more organized. A PIM can play an extremely important role in supporting several managerial tasks. Lately, the use of mobile PDA tools, such as personal Palm computers, is greatly facilitating the work of managers. Several other analytical tools are being used. For example, McGuire (2001) describes the use of such tools in the retail industry, and Bonabeau (2003) describes them in complex decision situations.

The Process of Computer-Based Decision Making

When making a decision, either organizational or personal, the decision maker goes through a fairly systematic process. Simon (1977) described the process as composed of three major phases: *intelligence, design,* and *choice.* A fourth phase, *implementation,* was added later. Simon claimed that the process is general enough so that it can be supported by *decision aids* and modeling. A conceptual presentation of the four-stage modeling process is shown in Figure 11.2, which illustrates what tasks are included in each phase. Note that there is a continuous flow of information from intelligence to design to choice (bold lines), but at any phase there may be a return to a previous phase (broken lines). For details see Stonebraker (2002).

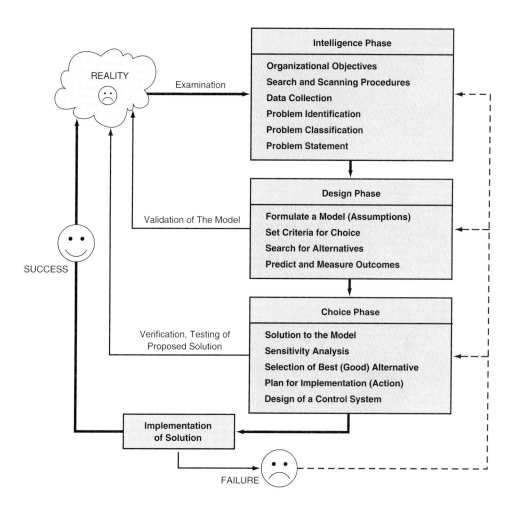

FIGURE 11.2 The process and phases in decision making/ modeling.

The decision-making process starts with the *intelligence phase,* in which managers examine a situation and identify and define the problem. In the *design phase*, decision makers construct a model that simplifies the problem. This is done by making assumptions that simplify reality and by expressing the relationships among all variables. The model is then validated, and decision makers set criteria for the evaluation of alternative potential solutions that are identified. The process is repeated for each subdecision in complex situations. The output of each subdecision is an input for the main decision. The *choice phase* involves selecting a solution, which is tested "on paper." Once this proposed solution seems to be feasible, we are ready for the last phase—*implementation*. Successful implementation results in resolving the original problem or opportunity. Failure leads to a return to the previous phases. A computer-based decision support attempts to automate several tasks in this process, in which *modeling* is the core.

MODELING AND MODELS. A **model** (in **decision making**) is a *simplified representation*, or abstraction of reality. It is usually simplified because reality is too complex to copy exactly, and because much of its complexity is actually irrelevant to a specific problem. With modeling, one can perform virtual experiments and an analysis on a model of reality, rather than on reality itself. The benefits of modeling in decision making are:

- The cost of virtual experimentation is much lower than the cost of experimentation conducted with a real system.
- Models allow for the simulated compression of time. Years of operation can be simulated in seconds of computer time.
- Manipulating the model (by changing variables) is much easier than manipulating the real system. Experimentation is therefore easier to conduct, and it does not interfere with the daily operation of the organization.
- The cost of making mistakes during a real trial-and-error experiment is much lower than when models are used in virtual experimentation.
- Today's environment holds considerable uncertainty. Modeling allows a manager to better deal with the uncertainty by introducing many "what-ifs" and calculating the risks involved in specific actions.
- Mathematical models allow the analysis and comparison of a very large, sometimes near-infinite number of possible alternative solutions. With today's advanced technology and communications, managers frequently have a large number of alternatives from which to choose.
- Models enhance and reinforce learning, and support training.

Representation by models can be done at various degrees of abstraction. Models are thus classified into four groups according to their degree of abstraction: iconic, analog, mathematical, and mental. Brief descriptions are presented in Online File W11.4.

A Framework for Computerized Decision Analysis

Gorry and Scott-Morton (1971) proposed a framework for decision support, based on the combined work of Simon (1977) and Anthony (1965). The first half of the framework is based on Simon's idea that decision-making processes fall along a continuum that ranges from highly structured (sometimes referred to as *programmed*) to highly unstructured (*nonprogrammed*) decisions. *Structured* processes refer to routine and repetitive problems for which standard solutions exist. *Unstructured* processes are "fuzzy," complex problems for which there are no cut-and-dried solutions.

In a structured problem, the intelligence, design, and choice are all structured, and the procedures for obtaining the best solution are known. Whether the solution means finding an appropriate inventory level or deciding on an optimal investment strategy, the solution's criteria are clearly defined. They are frequently cost minimization or profit maximization.

In an unstructured problem, *none* of the three phases is structured, and human intuition is frequently the basis for decision making. Typical unstructured problems include planning new services to be offered, hiring an executive, predicting markets (see Berg and Rietz, 2003), or choosing a set of research and development projects for next year.

Semistructured problems, in which only some of the phases are structured, require a combination of standard solution procedures and individual judgment. Examples of semistructured problems include trading bonds, setting marketing budgets for consumer products, and performing capital acquisition analysis. Here, a DSS is most suitable. It can improve the quality of the information on which the decision is based (and consequently the quality of the decision) by providing not only a single solution but also a range of what-if scenarios.

The second half of the decision support framework is based upon Anthony's taxonomy (1965). It defines three broad categories that encompass managerial activities: (1) *strategic planning*—the long-range goals and policies for resource allocation; (2) *management control*—the acquisition and efficient utilization of resources in the accomplishment of organizational goals; and (3) *operational control*—the efficient and effective execution of specific tasks. Anthony's and Simon's taxonomies can be combined in a nine-cell decision support framework (see Online File W11.5).

COMPUTER SUPPORT FOR STRUCTURED DECISIONS.   Structured and some semi-structured decisions, especially of the operational and managerial control type, have been supported by computers since the 1950s. Decisions of this type are made in all functional areas, especially in finance and operations management.

Problems that are encountered fairly often have a high level of structure. It is therefore possible to abstract, analyze, and classify them into standard classes. For example, a "make-or-buy" decision belongs to this category. Other examples are capital budgeting (e.g., replacement of equipment), allocation of resources, distribution of merchandise, and some inventory control decisions. For each standard class, a prescribed solution was developed through the use of mathematical formulas. This approach is called *management science* or *operations research,* and it is also executed with the aid of computers.

Management Science.   The *management science* approach takes the view that managers can follow a fairly systematic process for solving problems. Therefore, it is possible to use a scientific approach to managerial decision making. This approach, which also centers on modeling, is presented in Online File W11.6, along with a list of management science problems and tools. Management science frequently attempts to find the best possible solution, an approach known as **optimization** (see Hillier and Hillier, 2002).

11.2   DECISION SUPPORT SYSTEMS

DSS Concepts   Broadly defined, a **decision support system (DSS)** is a computer-based information system that combines models and data in an attempt to solve semistructured and some unstructured problems with extensive user involvement. But the term decision support system (DSS), like the terms MIS and MSS, means different things to different people. DSSs can be viewed as an *approach* or a *philosophy* rather than a precise methodology. However, a DSS does have certain recognized characteristics, which we will present later. First, let us look at a classical case of a successfully implemented DSS, which thought it occurred long ago is a typical scenario, as shown in *IT at Work 11.1* (page 466).

The case demonstrates some of the major characteristics of a DSS. The risk analysis performed first was based on the decision maker's initial definition of the situation, using a management science approach. Then, the executive vice president, using his experience, judgment, and intuition, felt that the model should be modified. The initial model, although mathematically correct, was incomplete. With a regular simulation system, a modification of the computer program would have taken a long time, but the DSS provided a very quick analysis. Furthermore, the DSS was flexible and responsive enough to allow managerial intuition and judgment to be incorporated into the analysis.

IT at Work 11.1
USING A DSS TO DETERMINE RISK

An oil and minerals corporation in Houston, Texas, was evaluating a proposed joint venture with a petrochemicals company to develop a chemical plant. Houston's executive vice president responsible for the decision wanted analysis of the risks involved in areas of supplies, demand, and prices. Bob Sampson, manager of planning and administration, and his staff built a DSS in a few days by means of a specialized planning language. The results strongly suggested that the project should be accepted.

Then came the real test. Although the executive vice president accepted the validity and value of the results, he was worried about the potential downside risk of the project, the chance of a catastrophic outcome. Sampson explains that the executive vice president said something like this: "I realize the amount of work you have already done,

and I am 99 percent confident of it. But I would like to see this in a different light. I know we are short of time and we have to get back to our partners with our yes or no decision."

Sampson replied that the executive could have the risk analysis he needed in less than one hour. As Sampson explained, "Within 20 minutes, there in the executive boardroom, we were reviewing the results of his what-if questions. Those results led to the eventual dismissal of the project, which we otherwise would probably have accepted."

Source: Information provided to author by Comshare Corporation (now a subsidiary of Geac Computer Corp.).

For Further Exploration: What were the benefits of the DSS? Why might it have reversed the initial decision?

Many companies are turning to DSSs to improve decision making. Reasons cited by managers for the increasing use of DSSs include the following: New and accurate information was needed; information was needed fast; and tracking the company's numerous business operations was increasingly difficult. Or, the company was operating in an unstable economy; it faced increasing foreign and domestic competition; the company's existing computer system did not properly support the objectives of increasing efficiency, profitability, and entry into profitable markets. Other reasons include: the IS department was unable to address the diversity of the company's needs or management's ad-hoc inquiries, and business analysis functions were not inherent within the existing systems. For a brief history of DSS, see Power (2002).

In many organizations that have adopted a DSS, the conventional information systems, which were built for the purpose of supporting transaction processing, were *not sufficient* to support several of the company's critical response activities, described in Chapter 1, especially those that require fast and/or complex decision making. A DSS, on the other hand, can do just that. (See Turban et al., 2005.)

Another reason for the development of DSS is the *end-user computing movement*. With the exception of large-scale DSSs, end users can build systems themselves, using DSS development tools such as Excel.

Characteristics and Capabilities of DSSs

Because there is no consensus on exactly what constitutes a DSS, there obviously is no agreement on the characteristics and capabilities of DSSs. However, most DSSs at least have some of the attributes shown in Table 11.1. DSSs also employ mathematical models and have a related, special capability, known as sensitivity analysis.

SENSITIVITY ANALYSIS: "WHAT-IF" AND GOAL SEEKING. Sensitivity analysis is the study of the impact that changes in one or more parts of a model have

TABLE 11.1 Capabilities of a DSS
A DSS provides support for decision makers at all management levels, whether individuals or groups, mainly in semistructured and unstructured situations, by bringing together human judgment and objective information.
A DSS supports several interdependent and/or sequential decisions.
A DSS supports all phases of the decision-making process—intelligence, design, choice, and implementation—as well as a variety of decision-making processes and styles.
A DSS is adaptable by the user over time to deal with changing conditions.
A DSS is easy to construct and use in many cases.
A DSS promotes learning, which leads to new demands and refinement of the current application, which leads to additional learning, and so forth.
A DSS usually utilizes quantitative models (standard and/or custom made).
Advanced DSSs are equipped with a knowledge management component that allows the efficient and effective solution of very complex problems.
A DSS can be disseminated for use via the Web.
A DSS allows the easy execution of *sensitivity analyses*.

on other parts. Usually, we check the impact that changes in input variables have on result variables.

Sensitivity analysis is extremely valuable in DSSs because it makes the system flexible and adaptable to changing conditions and to the varying requirements of different decision-making situations. It allows users to enter their own data, including the most pessimistic data (worst scenario) and to view how systems will behave under varying circumstances. It provides a better understanding of the model and the problem it purports to describe. It may increase the users' confidence in the model, especially when the model is not so sensitive to changes. A *sensitive model* means that small changes in conditions dictate a different solution. In a *nonsensitive model*, changes in conditions do not significantly change the recommended solution. This means that the chances for a solution to succeed are very high. Two popular types of sensitivity analyses are *what-if* and *goal seeking* (see Online File W11.7).

Structure and Components of DSS

Every DSS consists of at least data management, model management components, user interface, and end users. A few advanced DSSs also contain a knowledge management component. What does each component (subsystem) consist of?

DATA MANAGEMENT SUBSYSTEM. A DSS data management subsystem is similar to any other data management system. It contains all the data that flow from several sources and that usually are *extracted* prior to their entry into a DSS database or a data warehouse. In some DSSs, there is no separate database, and data are entered into the DSS model as needed (i.e., as soon as they are collected by sensors, as in the ChevronTexaco case in Chapter 7).

MODEL MANAGEMENT SUBSYSTEM. A model management subsystem contains completed models, and the building blocks necessary to develop DSSs applications. This includes standard software with financial, statistical, management science, or other quantitative models. An example is Excel, with its many mathematical and statistical functions. A model management subsystem also contains all the custom models written for the specific DSS. These models provide the system's analytical

IT at Work 11.2
WEB-BASED DECISION SUPPORT SYSTEM HELPS A BREWERY TO COMPETE

Guinness Import Co., a U.S. subsidiary of UK's Guinness Ltd. (*guinness.com*), needed a decision support system for (1) executives, (2) salespeople, and (3) analysts. The company did not want three separate systems. Using InfoAdvisor (from Platinum Technology Inc., now part of Computer Associates, *cai.com*), a client/server DSS was constructed. In the past, if manager Diane Goldman wanted to look at sales trends, it was necessary to ask an analyst to download data from the mainframe and then use a spreadsheet to compute the trend. This took up to a day and was error-prone. Now, when Diane Goldman needs such information she queries the DSS herself and gets an answer in a few minutes. Furthermore, she can quickly analyze the data in different ways. Over 100 salespeople keep track of sales and can do similar analyses, from anywhere, using a remote Internet access.

To expedite the implementation of the system, highly skilled users in each department taught others how to use the DSS. The DSS helped to increase productivity of the employees. This improved productivity enables the company to compete against large companies such as Anheuser-Busch, as well as against microbrewers. The system reduced the salespeople's paperwork load by about one day each month. For 100 salespeople, this means 1,200 extra days a year to sell. Corporate financial and marketing analysts are also using the system to make better decisions. As a result, sales increased by 20 percent every year since the system was installed.

Sources: Compiled from *Computerworld* (July 7, 1997); *platinum.com* (2000); and *dmreview.com* (2001).

For Further Exploration: What can a DSS do that other computer programs cannot do for this company?

Technology Guides are located at the book's Web site.

capabilities. Also included is a **model-based management system (MBMS)** whose role is analogous to that of a DBMS. (See Technology Guide 3.) The major functions (capabilities) of an MBMS are shown in Online File W11.8.

The model base may contain standard models (such as financial or management science) and/or customized models as illustrated in *IT at Work 11.2.*

THE USER INTERFACE. The term *user interface* covers all aspects of the communications between a user and the DSS. Some DSS experts feel that the user interface is the most important DSS component because much of the power, flexibility, and ease of use of the DSS are derived from this component. For example, the ease of use of the interface in the Guinness DSS enables, and encourages, managers and salespeople to use the system. Most interfaces today are Web-based and some are supplemented by voice.

The user interface subsystem may be managed by software called *user interface management system (UIMS),* which is functionally analogous to the DBMS.

THE USERS. The person faced with the problem or decision that the DSS is designed to support is referred to as the *user,* the *manager,* or the *decision maker.*

The user is considered to be a part of the system. Researchers assert that some of the unique contributions of DSSs are derived from the extensive interaction between the computer and the decision maker. A DSS has two broad classes of users: managers, and staff specialists (such as financial analysts, production planners, and market researchers).

DSS Intermediaries. When managers utilize a DSS, they may use it via an intermediary person who performs the analysis and reports the results. However, with Web-based systems, the use of DSSs becomes easier. Managers can use the Web-based system by themselves, especially when supported by an intelligent knowledge component.

KNOWLEDGE-BASED SUBSYSTEMS. Many unstructured and semistructured problems are so complex that they require expertise for their solutions. Such expertise can be provided by a knowledge-based system, such as an expert system. Therefore, the more advanced DSSs are equipped with a component called a *knowledge-based* (or *an intelligent*) *subsystem*. Such a component can provide the required expertise for solving some aspects of the problem, or provide knowledge that can enhance the operation of the other DSS components.

The knowledge component consists of one or more expert (or other intelligent) systems, or it draws expertise from the *organizational knowledge base* (see Chapter 9).

A DSS that includes such a component is referred to as an *intelligent DSS*, a *DSS/ES*, or a *knowledge-based DSS (KBDSS)*. An example of a KBDSS is in the area of estimation and pricing in construction. It is a complex process that requires the use of models as well as judgmental factors. The KBDSS includes a knowledge management subsystem with 200 rules incorporated with the computational models. (For details, see Kingsman and deSouza, 1997.)

How a DSS Works   The DSS components (see Figure 11.3) are all software, they run on standard hardware, and they can be facilitated by additional software (such as multimedia). Tools like Excel include some of the components and therefore can be used for DSS construction by end users.

The figure also illustrates how the DSS works. As you recall from Chapter 10, the DSS users get their data from the data warehouse, databases, and other

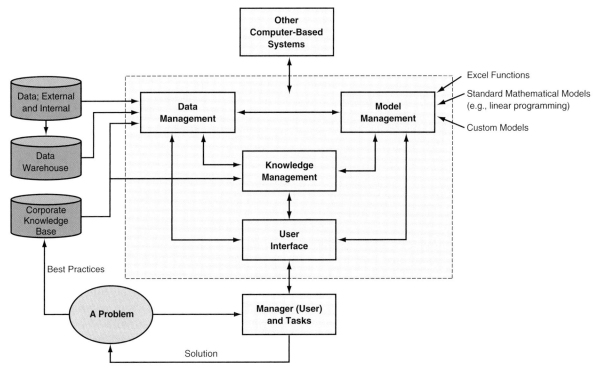

FIGURE 11.3 The DSS and its computing environment. Conceptual model of a DSS shows four main software components and their relationships with other systems.

data sources. When a user has a problem, it is evaluated by the processes described in Figures 11.1 (page 462) and 11.2 (page 463). A DSS system is then constructed. Data are entered from the sources on the left side and the models from the right side in Figure 11.3 (page 469). Knowledge can be also tapped from the corporate knowledge base. As more problems are solved, more knowledge is accumulated in the organizational knowledge base.

DSS Applications

A large number of DSS applications can be found in almost any industry, including both manufacturing and services, as shown in the following examples.

Example 1: Wells Fargo Targets Customers. Wells Fargo (*wellsfargo.com*) has become so good at predicting consumer behavior that it practically knows what customers want before they realize it themselves. The bank developed a decision support system (DSS) in-house. The DSS collects data on every transaction—whether it is over the phone, at an ATM, in a bank branch, or online—and combines that data with personal data that the customer provides. Wells Fargo then analyzes the data and models the customer's behavior to come up with prospective offerings, like a low-cost second mortgage, just at the right time for the customer. The result: Compared with the industry average of 2.2 products per customer, Wells Fargo sells four (Hovanesian, 2003).

Example 2: Schwab Targets the Rich. In 2000, Charles Schwab (*schwab.com*) changed its strategy to target high-net-worth investors. This meant turning itself from a discount brokerage into a full-service investment firm. To avoid the $20-million-per-year cost of hiring analysts, it made a onetime, $20 million investment in a decision support system. Schwab Equity Ratings, an online intelligent DSS, offers recommendations for buying and selling more than 3,000 stocks. It automatically sends e-mail alerts to Schwab customers and to Schwab analysts. Schwab says the system picks stocks as efficiently as its human counterparts. In addition, the system does away with conflicts of interest. In the wake of Wall Street scandals, the DSS makes some investors feel safer (Edwards, 2003).

Example 3: Lowering Costs in Health Care. For Owens & Minor (*owens-minor.com*), one of the largest suppliers for the health care industry, success means driving down the price of thousands of hospital supplies. The company uses its decision support system to help customers hunt for bargains. The DSS lets hospitals track purchases they make with hundreds of competing medical suppliers. The DSS pinpoints lower pricing on similar items, helping customers take advantage of discounts already negotiated. Hospitals keep better tabs on their bills and cut costs an average of 2 to 3 percent. For Owens & Minor, the DSS attracts new customers, and when existing customers find lower prices, they order more (Ante, 2003).

These examples exhibit the diversity of decisions that DSSs can support. Other examples are provided by Fagerholt (2004), Huber (2003), and McKinley (2003), and in Online File W11.9, Minicase 1 at the end of this chapter, and Online Minicase W11.1. In addition, many examples can be found at *sas.com*, where hundreds of applications (success stories) are listed by industry.

The DSS methodology just described was designed initially to support individual decision makers. However, most organizational decisions are made by groups, such as an executive committee. Next we see how IT can support such situations.

11.3 GROUP DECISION SUPPORT SYSTEMS

Decision making is frequently a shared process. For example, meetings among groups of managers from different areas are an essential element for reaching consensus. The group may be involved in making a decision or in a decision-related task, like creating a short list of acceptable alternatives or deciding on criteria for accepting an alternative. When a decision-making group is supported electronically, the support is referred to as *group decision support.* Two types of groups are considered: a same-room group whose members are in one place (e.g., a meeting room), and a virtual group (or team), whose members are in different locations.

A **group decision support system (GDSS)** is an interactive computer-based system that facilitates the solution of semistructured and unstructured problems when made by a group of decision makers. The objective of a GDSS is to support the *process* of arriving at a decision. Important characteristics of a GDSS, according to DeSanctis and Gallupe (1987), are shown in Online File W11.10. These characteristics can negate some of the dysfunctions of group processes described in Chapter 3, Table 3.2 (page 109).

The first generation of GDSSs was designed to support face-to-face meetings in what is called a *decision room.* Such a GDSS is described in Online File W11.11.

Some Applications of GDSSs

An increasing number of companies are using GDSSs, especially when virtual groups are involved. One example is the Internal Revenue Service, which used a one-room GDSS to implement its quality-improvement programs based on the participation of a number of its quality teams. The GDSS was helpful in identifying problems, generating and evaluating ideas, and developing and implementing solutions. Another example is the European automobile industry, which used a one-room GDSS to examine the competitive automotive business environment and make ten-year forecasts, needed for strategic planning. Atkins et al. (2003) report on successful application at the U.S. Air Force. A virtual GDSS application is described in *IT at Work 11.3* (page 472). For further discussion of virtual teams and IT support, see Chapter 16 and Powell et al. (2004).

11.4 ENTERPRISE AND EXECUTIVE DECISION SUPPORT SYSTEMS

Two types of enterprise decision support systems are described here: systems that support whole organizational tasks and systems that support decisions made by top-level managers and executives.

Organizational Decision Support System

The term **organizational** (or **institutional**) **decision support system (ODSS)** was first defined by Hackathorn and Keen (1981), who discussed three levels of decision support: individual, group, and organization. They maintained that computer-based systems can be developed to provide decision support for *each* of these levels. They defined an ODSS as one that focuses on an organizational task or activity involving a *sequence* of operations and decision makers, such as developing a divisional marketing plan or doing capital budgeting. Each individual's activities must mesh closely with other people's work. The computer support was primarily seen as a vehicle for improving communication and coordination, in addition to problem solving.

IT at Work 11.3
VIRTUAL MEETINGS AT THE WORLD ECONOMIC FORUM

The World Economic Forum (WEF, at *weforum.org*) is a consortium of top business, government, academic, and media leaders from virtually every country in the world. WEF's mission is to foster international understanding. Until 1998, the members conferred privately or debated global issues only at the forum's annual meeting in Davos, Switzerland, and at regional summits. Follow-up was difficult because of the members' geographic dispersion and conflicting schedules.

A WEF online strategy and operations task force developed a collaborative computing system to allow secure communication among members, making the nonprofit group more effective in its mission. Now WEF is making faster progress toward solutions for the global problems it studies. Called the World Electronic Community (WELCOM), the GDSS and its complementary videoconferencing system give members a secure channel through which to send e-mail, read reports available in a WEF library, and communicate in point-to-point or multipoint videoconferences. Forum members now hold real-time discussions and briefings on pressing issues and milestones, such as, for example, the global war against terrorism.

The WELCOM system was designed with a graphical user interface (GUI) to make it easily accessible to inexpe-

rienced computer users, because many WEF members might not be computer-literate or proficient typists. The forum also set up "concierge services," based in Boston, Singapore, and Geneva, for technical support and to arrange videoconferences and virtual meetings. To handle any time/any place meetings, members can access recorded forum events and discussions that they may have missed, as well as an extensive library, which is one of the most heavily used features of the system. The site also operates a knowledge base ("knowledge navigator") and media center.

As of 2001 the system has been completely on the Web. With *Webcasting*, all sessions of the annual meetings can be viewed in real time. The virtual meetings are done in a secured environment, and private chat rooms are also available.

Sources: Compiled from *weforum.org* (accessed June 29, 2003) and *PC Week* (August 17, 1998).

For Further Exploration: Check the Netmeeting and Netshow products of Microsoft, and see how their capabilities facilitate the WEF virtual meetings. How does an environment such as *eroom* at *documentum.com* support the process of group decision making, if at all?

Some decision support systems provide support throughout large and complex organizations (see Carter et al., 1992). A major benefit of such systems is that many DSS users become familiar with computers, analytical techniques, and decision supports, as illustrated in Online File W11.12.

The major characteristics of an ODSS are: (1) it affects several organizational units or corporate problems, (2) it cuts across organizational functions or hierarchical layers, and (3) it involves computer-based technologies and usually also communications technologies. Also, an ODSS often interacts or integrates with enterprisewide information systems such as executive support systems. Moreover, the advent of the Web has given rise to interorganizational decision support systems (Shim et al., 2002). It seems likely that mobile tools, mobile e-services, and wireless Internet protocols will mark the next major set of developments in DSS.

For further information on a very-large-scale ODSS, see El Sharif and El Sawy (1988) and Carter et al. (1992). For evidence about benefits, see Kohli and Devaraj (2004).

Executive Information (Support) Systems The majority of personal DSSs support the work of professionals and middle-level managers. Organizational DSSs provide support primarily to planners, analysts, researchers, or to some managers. For a DSS to be used by top managers it must meet the executives' needs. An executive information system (EIS), also known as an executive support system (ESS), is a technology designed in response to the specific needs of executives, as shown in Online File W11.13.

The terms *executive information system* and *executive support system* mean different things to different people, though they are sometimes used interchangeably. The following definitions, based on Rockart and DeLong (1988), distinguish between EIS and ESS:

- **Executive information system (EIS).** An EIS is a computer-based system that serves the information needs of top executives. It provides rapid access to timely and relevant information, to aid in monitoring an organization's performance by directly accessing management reports and to improve managerial growth and learning (*Business World,* 2004). An EIS is very user friendly, is supported by graphics, and provides the capabilities of *exception reporting* (reporting of only the results that deviate from a set standard) and *drill down* (investigating information in increasing detail). It is also easily connected with online information services and electronic mail.

- **Executive support system (ESS).** An ESS is a comprehensive support system that goes beyond EIS to include analysis support, communications, office automation, and intelligence support.

Capabilities and Characteristics of ESSs

Executive support systems vary in their capabilities and benefits (e.g., see Singh et al., 2002). Capabilities common to many ESSs are summarized in Table 11.2. A sample graphical presentation is provided in Figure 11.4 (page 474). One of these capabilities, the CSF, is measured by key performance indicators (KPIs), as shown in Online File W11.14.

Business Performance Management

EIS and ESS products evolved over the years to a more comprehensive technology called business (or corporate) performance management. **Business performance management (BPM)** is a methodology for measuring organizational performance, analyzing it by comparing it to some standards, and planning how to improve it. (Note that in some situations, BPM also stands for *business process management*, a topic we describe in Chapter 14. Even greater confusion occurs

---

TABLE 11.2 Capabilities of an ESS

Capability	Description
Drill down	Ability to go to details at several levels; can be done by a series of menus or by direct queries (using intelligent agents and natural language processing).
Critical success factors (CSFs)	The factors most critical for the success of business. These can be organizational, industry, departmental, etc.
Key performance indicators (KPIs)	The specific measures of CSFs. (Examples are provided in Online File W11.14.)
Status access	The latest data available on KPIs or some other metric, ideally in real time.
Trend analysis	Short-, medium-, and long-term trend of KPIs or metrics are projected using forecasting methods.
Ad-hoc analysis	Analysis made at any time, and with any desired factors and relationships.
Exception reporting	Based on the concept of management by exception, reports highlight deviations larger than certain thresholds. Reports may include only deviations.

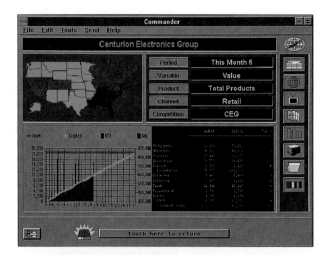

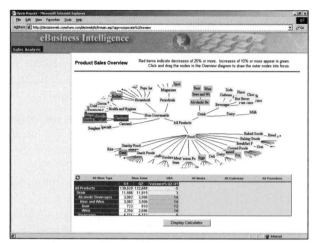

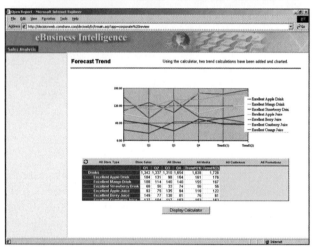

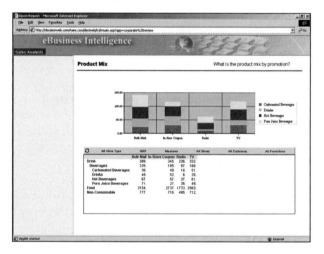

FIGURE 11.4 Sample screens from Comshare Decision (now a subsidiary of Geac Computer Corp.)—a modular system for generating a business intelligence report.

since business process management is a tool for restructuring processes, which is a business performance monitoring activity.)

The business performance management process involves the following major steps:

1. Design a BPM program, and define what you want to measure, when, and how.

2. Establish standards/metrics against which performance is to be measured (e.g., balanced scorecard; see Chapter 13).

3. Prepare a system for monitoring performance, including the finding of defects.

4. Prepare a system for analyzing performance, its trends, fluctuations, and reasons. This analysis includes comparisons against the standards and metrics.

5. Take an action, if needed. For example, adjust or restructure processes (Chapter 14), change staff, introduce incentive programs, reduce defects, optimize processes, and so forth.

The implementation of BPM can be complex due to the fact that many business processes are interrelated and to the frequent changes in the business environment. Also, the amount of impacting variables, data, and information can be very large. Therefore, the support of IT is usually a requirement (see Grimes, 2003). IT tools are available to support any of the above steps. Some are comprehensive, supporting several or all steps. Decision support systems, intelligent systems, and other tools of BI play an important role in BPM.

BPM attempts to integrate the various separate applications into a single environment. Executives use the output of BPM to create an *agile business*, a business that is able to rapidly adjust its business strategy to meet changes in circumstances (see Chapman, 2003). An example of a changing situation is the introduction of new government regulations, such as the Sarbanes–Oxley Act (see Online File W1.3). This regulation requires extensive reporting.

BUSINESS ACTIVITY MONITORING (BAM) SYSTEMS. One of the major tools of BPM is BAM. **Business activity monitoring (BAM)** systems consist of *real-time* enterprise systems that alert managers to potential opportunities, impending problems, or threats, and then empower managers to react through models and collaboration. Situations are detected in real time, quickly analyzed, and solved.

Business activity monitoring (BAM) software monitors the activities of a specific facility, such as a factory or a call center, or of a specific business process, such as logistics or sales. BAM integrates data from different processes within the company and from outside partners, using even unstructured (soft) information, and it provides collaboration capabilities for teams to make decisions. Its two major activities include detecting a developing dangerous situation as quickly as possible, and formulating a speedy response (see Keating, 2003).

As a technology layer, BAM sits on top of a BPM solution to capture and analyze business process data in real time. Events are displayed in an enterprise information portal (e.g., a dashboard). The dashboard display offers instant insight into business metrics (like CRM call center success rates or supply chain inventory levels). Real-time alerting to breakdowns in processes such as shipping schedules enables users to react to problems in real time. Like BPM, business activity monitoring evolved from the basic concepts of executive information systems. Today, mature integration and business intelligence tools, real standards (such as XML), and improved software development methods and tools make such real-time technology feasible (see Keating, 2003).

The tools of BAM are frequently combined with other BPM tools and are offered by most vendors of BI, ERP, CRM, and business integration products. Notable are Web Methods, IBM, Hyperion, Cognus, Microsoft, Business Objects, and PeopleSoft Inc. Their products use warehouses, visualization, statistical and mathematical models, sensors, intelligent systems, and dashboards.

Dashboards. Essentially, a *dashboard* is a preset OLAP display. Dashboards are set up to provide managers with the information they need in the correct format at the correct time. Ideally, each manager can use the display on the dashboard to focus on what is important in his or her job. Business intelligence systems are the foundation of dashboards, which have evolved from executive information systems into enterprise information systems that access data warehouses via OLAP systems. MQSoftware's Business Dashboard provides real-time views of data. Cognos Visualizer Series 7 is another example of a corporate dashboard that helps give managers information with which to make better decisions.

Dashboards can impact communications and company policies by measuring and displaying data that are important to the organization. For example, Southwest Airlines uses digital dashboards, called *cockpits,* that provide Southwest employees with customized views of the information they need for their work. At Honeywell Inc.'s Specialty Materials Division in Morristown, New Jersey, Cognos Inc. dashboards give everyone in sales a clear view into daily business performance. Sales representatives can see their own sales statistics, but they can also see how others are doing, as can managers. The use of dashboards has led to a move from monthly and quarterly data views to daily views. In addition, the firm now has a common definition and view of all information.

DSS Failures

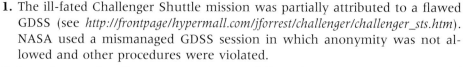

Over the years there have been many cases of failures of all types of decision support systems. There are multiple reasons for such failures, ranging from human factors to software glitches. Here are two examples:

1. The ill-fated Challenger Shuttle mission was partially attributed to a flawed GDSS (see *http://frontpage/hypermall.com/jforrest/challenger/challenger_sts.htm*). NASA used a mismanaged GDSS session in which anonymity was not allowed and other procedures were violated.

2. In an international congress on airports, failures in Denver, Hong Kong, and Malaysia airports were analyzed (*onera.fr/congress/jso2000airport*). Several DSS applications did not work as intended for reasons such as poor planning and inappropriate models.

Brezillon and Pomerol (1997) describe some failures of intelligent DSSs. Also, Briggs and Arnoff (2002) conducted a comprehensive evaluation of a DSS failure and identified areas that could create system failures. Most DSS failures can be eliminated by using appropriate planning, collaboration, and management procedures. Also, attaching an *intelligent system* makes DSSs more useful and less likely to fail.

11.5 INTELLIGENT SUPPORT SYSTEMS: THE BASICS

Intelligent systems is a term that describes the various commercial applications of artificial intelligence (AI).

Artificial Intelligence and Intelligent Behavior

Most experts (see Cawsey, 1998, and Russell and Norvig, 2002) agree that **artificial intelligence (AI)** is concerned with two basic ideas. First, it involves studying the thought processes of humans; second, it deals with representing those processes via machines (computers, robots, and so on). Following 9/11, AI has been getting lots of attention, due to its capability to assist in fighting terrorism (Kahn, 2002). Another development that helps AI to get attention is the large number of intelligent devices in the marketplace (Rivlin, 2002).

One well-publicized definition of AI is "behavior by a machine that, if performed by a human being, would be considered *intelligent.*" Let us explore the meaning of the term *intelligent behavior.* The following capabilities are considered to be signs of intelligence: learning or understanding from experience, making sense of ambiguous or contradictory messages, and responding quickly and successfully to a new situation. Using reasoning to solve problems and direct actions effectively is another indicator of intelligence. Some other indicators include dealing with complex situations, and understanding and inferring in ordinary, rational ways. Applying knowledge to manipulate the environment and recognizing the relative importance of different elements in a situation complete our list.

AI's ultimate goal is to build machines that will mimic human intelligence. So far, current intelligent systems, exemplified in commercial AI products, are far from exhibiting any significant intelligence. Nevertheless, they are getting better with the passage of time, and are currently useful in making faster, more efficient, and cheaper many cumbersome tasks that require some human intelligence.

An interesting test to determine whether a computer exhibits intelligent behavior was designed by Alan Turing, a British AI pioneer. According to the **Turing test,** a computer could be considered "smart" only when a human interviewer, conversing with both an unseen human being and an unseen computer, cannot determine which is which.

So far we have concentrated on the concept of *intelligence*. According to another definition, artificial intelligence is the branch of computer science that deals with ways of representing *knowledge*. It uses symbols rather than numbers, and *heuristics*, or rules of thumb, rather than algorithms for processing information.

KNOWLEDGE AND AI. Although a computer cannot have experiences or study and learn as a human can, it can use knowledge given to it by human experts. Such knowledge consists of facts, concepts, theories, heuristic methods, procedures, and relationships. Knowledge is also information organized and analyzed to make it *understandable* and *applicable* to problem solving or decision making. The collection of knowledge related to a specific problem (or an opportunity) to be used in an intelligent system is organized and stored in a **knowledge base.** As discussed in Chapter 9, the collection of knowledge related to the operation of an organization is called an *organizational knowledge base*.

Comparing Artificial and Natural Intelligence

The potential value of AI can be better understood by contrasting it with natural (human) intelligence. AI has several important commercial advantages over natural intelligence, but also some limitations, as shown in Table 11.3 (page 478).

Benefits of AI

Despite their limitations, AI applications can be extremely valuable. They can make computers easier to use and can make knowledge more widely available. One major potential benefit of AI is that it significantly increases the speed and consistency of some problem-solving procedures, including those problems that are difficult to solve by conventional computing and those that have incomplete or unclear data. Another benefit of AI is that it significantly increases the productivity of performing many tasks; it helps in handling information overload by summarizing or interpreting information and by assisting in searching through large amounts of data.

TABLE 11.3 Comparison of the Capabilities of Natural vs. Artificial Intelligence

Capabilities	Natural Intelligence	Artificial Intelligence
Preservation of knowledge	Perishable from an organizational point of view	Permanent
Duplication and dissemination of knowledge	Difficult, expensive, takes time	Easy, fast, and inexpensive once knowledge is in a computer
Consistency of knowledge	Can be erratic and inconsistent Incomplete at times	Consistent and thorough
Documentability of process and knowledge	Difficult	Fairly easy
Creativity	Can be very high	Low; uninspired
Use of sensory experiences	Direct and rich in possibilities	Must be interpreted first; limited
Recognizing patterns and relationships	Fast, easy to explain	Machine learning still not as good as people in most cases, but in some cases can do better than people
Reasoning	Making use of wide context of experiences	Good only in narrow, focused, and stable domains
Cost of knowledge	Expensive	Inexpensive if shared by many users

Conventional versus AI Computing

Conventional computer programs are based on algorithms. An *algorithm* is a mathematical formula or sequential procedure that leads to a solution. It is converted into a computer program that tells the computer exactly what operations to carry out. The algorithm then uses data such as numbers, letters, or words to solve problems. AI software is using knowledge and heuristics instead of, or along with, algorithms.

In addition, AI software is based on **symbolic processing** of knowledge. In AI, a symbol is a letter, word, or number that represents objects, processes, and their relationships. Objects can be people, things, ideas, concepts, events, or statements of fact. Using symbols, it is possible to create a knowledge base that contains facts, concepts, and the relationships that exist among them. Then various processes can be used to manipulate the symbols in order to generate advice or a recommendation for solving problems.

The major differences between AI computing and conventional computing are shown in Online File W11.15.

DOES A COMPUTER REALLY THINK? Knowledge bases and search techniques certainly make computers more useful, but can they really make computers more intelligent? The fact that most AI programs are implemented by search and pattern-matching techniques leads to the conclusion that *computers are not really intelligent.* You give the computer a lot of information and some guidelines about how to use this information, and the computer can then come up with a solution. But all it does is test the various alternatives and attempt to find some combination that meets the designated criteria. The computer appears to be "thinking" and often gives a satisfactory solution. But Dreyfus and Dreyfus (1988) feel that the public is being misled about AI, whose usefulness is overblown and whose goals are unrealistic. They claim, and we agree, that the human mind is just too complex to duplicate. Yet chess legend Garry Kasparov had difficulties in winning against computers and even lost to IBM's Deep Blue supercomputer in 1997 and was forced to a draw with Deep Blue and with X3D Fritz in 2003. *Computers certainly cannot think*, but they can be very useful for increasing our productivity. This is done by several commercial AI technologies.

Commercial AI Technologies

The development of machines that exhibit intelligent characteristics draws upon several sciences and technologies, ranging from linguistics to mathematics (see the roots of the tree in Online File W11.16). Artificial intelligence itself is not a commercial field; it is a collection of concepts and ideas that are appropriate for research but cannot be marketed. However, AI provides the scientific foundation for several commercial technologies.

The major intelligent systems are: expert systems, natural language processing, speech understanding, robotics and sensory systems, fuzzy logic, neural computing, computer vision and scene recognition, and intelligent computer-aided instruction. In addition, a combination of two or more of the above is considered a *hybrid* intelligent system. The major commercial intelligent systems are listed in Table 11.4 and are discussed further in Online File W11.17. A discussion of the state of the art of these systems can be found in Iserlis (2004).

SOFTWARE AND INTELLIGENT AGENTS. As described in Chapters 3 and 4, software and intelligent agents play a major role in supporting work on computers (such as search, alerts, monitor Web activities, suggestions to users) and work in general (e.g., configure complex products diagnose malfunctions in networks). Fuller coverage of the topic is provided in Online Appendix W11.1.

TABLE 11.4 Commercial AI Techniques	
Name	**Short Description**
Expert system (ES)	Computerized advisory systems usually based on rules. (See Section 11.6.)
Natural language processing (NLP)	Enables computers to recognize and even understand human languages. (See Section 11.7.)
Speech understanding	Enables computers to recognize words and understand short voice sentences. (See Section 11.7.)
Robotic and sensory systems	Programmable combination of mechanical and computer programs. Recognize their environments via sensors.
Computer vision and scene recognition	Enable computers to interpret the content of pictures captured by cameras.
Machine learning	Enables computers to interpret the content of data and information captured by sensors (see next three techniques).
Handwriting recognition	Enables computers to recognize characters (letters, digits) written by hand.
Neural computing (networks)	Using massive parallel processing, able to recognize patterns in large amount of data. (See Section 11.7.)
Fuzzy logic	Enables computers to reason with partial information. (See Section 11.7.)
Intelligent agents	Software programs that perform tasks for a human or machine master. (See Online Appendix W11.1.)
Semantic Web	An intelligent software program that "understands" content of Web pages. (See Section 11.7.)
Genetic programming	Automatic analysis and synthesis of computer programs. (See Section 11.7.)

11.6 EXPERT SYSTEMS

When an organization has a complex decision to make or a problem to solve, it often turns to experts for advice. These experts have specific knowledge and experience in the problem area. They are aware of alternative solutions, chances of success, and costs that the organization may incur if the problem is not solved. Companies engage experts for advice on such matters as equipment purchase, mergers and acquisitions, and advertising strategy. The more unstructured the situation, the more specialized and expensive is the advice. **Expert systems (ESs)** are an attempt to mimic human experts. Expert systems can either *support* decision makers or completely *replace* them (see Edwards et al., 2000). Expert systems are the most widely applied and commercially successful AI technology. A recent study by Arnold et al. (2004) suggests that intelligent decision aids may be best viewed as complements to expert decision makers during complex problem analysis and resolution.

Typically, an ES is decision-making software that can reach a level of performance comparable to a human expert in some specialized and usually narrow problem area. The basic idea behind an ES is simple: *Expertise* is transferred from an expert (or other source of expertise) to the computer. This knowledge is then organized and stored in the computer. Users can call on the computer for specific advice as needed. The computer can make inferences and arrive at a conclusion. Then, like a human expert, it advises the nonexperts and explains, if necessary, the logic behind the advice. ESs can sometimes perform better than any single expert can.

Expertise and Knowledge

Expertise is the extensive, task-specific knowledge acquired from training, reading, and experience. It enables experts to make better and faster decisions than nonexperts in solving complex problems. Expertise takes a long time (possibly years) to acquire, and it is distributed in organizations in an uneven manner. A senior expert possesses about 30 times more expertise than a junior (novice) staff member.

The transfer of expertise from an expert to a computer and then to the user involves four activities: *knowledge acquisition* (from experts or other sources), *knowledge representation* (in the computer), *knowledge inferencing*, and *knowledge transfer* to the user.

Knowledge is acquired from experts and/or from documented sources. Through the activity of knowledge representation, acquired knowledge is organized as rules or frames (object-oriented) and stored electronically in a knowledge base. Given the necessary expertise stored in the knowledge base, the computer is programmed so that it can make inferences. The inferencing is performed in a component called the **inference engine**, which is the "brain" of the ES, and results in a recommendation for novices. Thus, the expert's knowledge has been *transferred* to users.

A unique feature of an ES is its ability to explain its recommendations. The explanation and justification is done in a subsystem called the *justifier* or the *explanation subsystem* (e.g., presents the sequence of rules used by the inference engine to generate a recommendation).

The Benefits and Limitations of Expert Systems

THE BENEFITS OF EXPERT SYSTEMS. Expert systems have considerable benefits, but their use is constrained. During the past few years, the technology of expert systems has been successfully applied in thousands of organizations

TABLE 11.5 Benefits of Expert Systems

Benefit	Description/Example
Increased output and productivity	At Digital Equipment Corp. (now part of Hewlett-Packard), an ES plans configuration of components for each custom order, increasing preparation production speed fourfold.
Increased quality	ESs can provide consistent advice and reduce error rates.
Capture and dissemination of scarce expertise	Physicians in Egypt and Algeria use an eye-care ES developed at Rutgers University to diagnose ailments and to recommend treatment. Advice is provided by top physicians.
Operation in hazardous environments	ESs that interpret information collected by sensors enable human workers to avoid hot, humid, or toxic environments.
Accessibility to knowledge and help desks	ESs can increase the productivity of help-desk employees (there are over 30 million in the U.S. alone), or even automate this function.
Reliability	ESs do not become tired or bored, call in sick, or go on strike. They consistently pay attention to details and do not overlook relevant information.
Increased capabilities of other systems	Integration of an ES with other systems makes the other systems more effective.
Ability to work with incomplete or uncertain information	Even with an answer of "don't know" or "not sure," an ES can still produce an answer, though it may not be a certain one.
Provision of training	Novices who work with an ES become more experienced thanks to the explanation facility, which serves as a teaching device and knowledge base. They also can play what-if scenarios.
Enhancement of decision-making and problem-solving capabilities	ESs allow the integration of expert judgment into analysis. Successful applications are diagnosis of machine malfunction and even medical diagnosis.
Decreased decision-making time	ESs usually can make faster decisions than humans working alone. American Express authorizers can make charge authorization decisions in 3 minutes without an ES and in 30 seconds with one.
Reduced downtime	ESs can quickly diagnose machine malfunctions and prescribe repairs. An ES called Drilling Advisor detects malfunctions in oil rigs, saving most of the cost of downtime (as much as $250,000/day).

worldwide to problems ranging from AIDS research to the analysis of dust in mines. Why have ESs become so popular? It is because of the large number of capabilities and benefits they provide at a reasonable cost. The major ones are listed in Table 11.5. For examples of ES applications, see Online File W11.18.

THE LIMITATIONS OF EXPERT SYSTEMS. Despite their many benefits, available ES methodologies are not always straightforward and effective. Some factors that have slowed the commercial spread of ES are listed in Online File W11.19.

In addition, expert systems may not be able to arrive at any conclusions. For example, even some fully developed complex expert systems are unable to fulfill about 2 percent of the orders presented to it. Finally, expert systems, like human experts, sometimes produce incorrect recommendations.

Failing Expert Systems. Various organizational, personal, and economic factors can slow the spread of expert systems, or even cause them to fail, as shown in *IT at Work 11.4* (page 482).

IT at Work 11.4
EVEN AN INTELLIGENT SYSTEM CAN FAIL

Mary Kay (*marykay.com*), the multinational cosmetics company, uses teams of managers and analysts to plan its products. This process attempted to iron out potential weaknesses before production. However, the company still faced costly errors resulting from such problems as product-container incompatibility, interaction of chemical compositions, and marketing requirements with regard to packaging and distribution.

An eclectic group of Mary Kay managers, representing various functional areas, used to meet every six weeks to make product decisions. The group's decision-making process was loosely structured: The marketing team would give its requirements to the product formulator and the package engineer at the same time. Marketing's design requests often proved to be beyond the allocated budget or technical possibilities, and other problems arose as a result of not knowing the ultimate product formulation. The result was more meetings and redesign.

Mary Kay decided to implement an expert system to help. In an effort to keep costs to a minimum, it engaged the services of a research university that developed a system that consisted of a DSS computational tool plus two ES components. The decision support tool was able to select compatible packages for a given cosmetic product and to test product and package suitability. The ES component used this information to guide users through design and to determine associated production costs.

At first the system was a tremendous success. There was a clear match between the abilities of the system technology and the nature of the problem. The director of package design enthusiastically embraced the system solution. The entire decision process could have been accomplished in two weeks with no inherent redesign. By formulating what previously was largely intuitive, the ES improved understanding of the decision process itself, increasing the team's confidence. By reducing the time required for new product development, executives were freed for other tasks, and the team met only rarely to ratify the recommendations of the ES.

However, without support staff to *maintain* the ES, no one knew how to add or modify decision rules. Even the firm's IT unit was unable to help, and so the system fell into disuse. More importantly, when the director of package design left the firm, so did the enthusiasm for the ES. No one else was willing to make the effort necessary to maintain the system or sustain the project. Without managerial direction about the importance of the system to the firm's success, the whole project foundered.

Source: Condensed from Vedder et al. (2002).

For Further Exploration: What can a company do to prevent such failures? Can you speculate on why this was not done at Mary Kay?

The Components of Expert Systems

The following components exist in an expert system: knowledge base, inference engine, blackboard (workplace), user interface, and explanation subsystem (justifier). In the future, systems will include a knowledge-refining component. The relationships among components are shown in Figure 11.5 (page 483).

DESCRIPTION OF THE COMPONENTS. The major components of expert systems are described below.

The *knowledge base* contains knowledge necessary for understanding, formulating, and solving problems. It includes two basic elements: (1) *facts*, such as the problem situation and theory of the problem area, and (2) *rules* that direct the use of knowledge to solve specific problems in a particular domain.

The "brain" of the ES is the *inference engine*. This component is essentially a computer program that provides a methodology for reasoning and formulating conclusions.

The *user interface* in ESs allows for user–computer dialogue, which can be best carried out in a natural language, usually presented in a questions-and-answers format and sometimes supplemented by graphics. The dialogue triggers

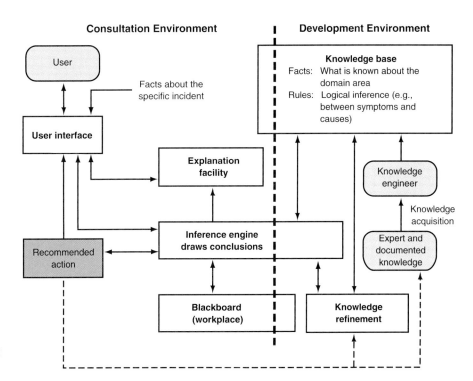

Consultation Environment | Development Environment

FIGURE 11.5 Structure and process of an expert system.

the inference engine to match the problem symptoms with the knowledge in the knowledge base and then generate advice.

The *blackboard* is an area of working memory set aside for the description of a current problem, as specified by the input data; it is also used for recording intermediate results. It is a kind of database.

The *explanation subsystem* can trace responsibility for arriving at a conclusion and explain the ES's behavior by interactively answering questions such as the following: *Why* was a certain question asked by the expert system? *How* was a certain conclusion reached? *What* is the plan to reach the solution? (See the discussion by Gregor and Benbasat, 1999.)

Human experts have a *knowledge-refining* system; that is, they can analyze their own performance, learn from it, and improve it for future consultations. Similarly, such evaluation is necessary in computerized learning so that the program will be able to improve by analyzing the reasons for its success or failure. Such a component is not available in commercial expert systems at the moment, but it is being developed in experimental systems.

The process of building and using expert systems is described in Online File W11.20, which includes an example of how an ES consultation is done.

Applications of Expert Systems

Expert systems are in use today in all types of organizations. For many examples, by industry, see *exsys.com* (in the case studies) and Jackson (1999). Expert systems are especially useful in ten generic categories, displayed in Table 11.6 (page 484). (For examples, see Minicase 2 and Online Minicase W11.2.) For other examples see Jareb and Rajkovic (2001) and Pontz and Power (2003).

EMBEDDED EXPERT SYSTEMS. One of the most useful applications of expert systems is as an embedded component in other systems, including robots. The

TABLE 11.6 Generic Categories of Expert Systems

Category	Problem Addressed
1. Interpretation	Inferring situation descriptions from observations.
2. Prediction	Inferring likely consequences of given situations.
3. Diagnosis	Inferring system malfunctions from observations.
4. Design	Configuring objects under constraints.
5. Planning	Developing plans to achieve goal(s).
6. Monitoring	Comparing observations to plans, flagging exceptions.
7. Debugging	Prescribing remedies for malfunctions.
8. Repair	Executing a plan to administer a prescribed remedy.
9. Instruction	Diagnosing, debugging, and correcting student performance.
10. Control	Interpreting, predicting, repairing, and monitoring systems behavior.

ES components are so integrated that they have turned into transparent parts of processes or systems. Actually, many software and hardware products include embedded ESs or other intelligent systems, which the users may not be aware of. IT systems are sold based on their functionalities, not on whether they include an intelligent component.

11.7 OTHER INTELLIGENT SYSTEMS

An expert system's major objective is to provide expert advice. Other intelligent systems can be used to solve problems or provide capabilities on areas in which they excel. Several such technologies are described next.

Natural Language Processing and Voice Technologies

Today, when you tell a computer what to do, you usually type commands on the keyboard. In responding to a user, the computer outputs message symbols or other short, cryptic notes of information. Many problems could be minimized or even eliminated if we could communicate with the computer in our own language. We would simply type in directions, instructions, or information. Better yet, we would converse with the computer using voice. The computer would be smart enough to interpret the input, regardless of its format. **Natural language processing (NLP)** refers to communicating with a computer in English or whatever language you may speak.

To understand a natural language inquiry, a computer must have the knowledge to analyze and then interpret the input. This may include linguistic knowledge about words, domain knowledge, common-sense knowledge, and even knowledge about the users and their goals. Once the computer understands the input, it can take the desired action. For details see Reiter and Dale (2000).

In this section we briefly discuss two types of NLP:

1. Natural language *understanding*, which investigates methods of allowing a computer to comprehend instructions given in ordinary English, via the keyboard or by voice (speech understanding), so that computers are able to understand people

2. Natural language *generation*, which strives to allow computers to produce ordinary English language, on the screen or by voice (known as voice synthesis), so people can understand computers more easily

APPLICATIONS OF NATURAL LANGUAGE PROCESSING. Natural language processing programs have been applied in several areas. The most important are human-to-computer interfaces, which include abstracting and summarizing text, analyzing grammar, understanding speech, and even composing letters by machines. These programs translate one natural language to another, or one computer language to another, and they even translate Web pages (see Chapter 3).

By far the most dominant use of NLP is "front-ends" for other software packages, especially databases that allow the user to operate the applications programs with everyday language.

SPEECH (VOICE) RECOGNITION AND UNDERSTANDING. Speech recognition is a process that allows us to communicate with a computer by speaking to it. The term **speech recognition** is sometimes applied only to the first part of the communication process, in which the computer recognizes words that have been spoken without necessarily interpreting their meanings. The other part of the process, wherein the meaning of speech is ascertained, is called **speech understanding.** It may be possible to understand the meaning of a spoken sentence without actually recognizing every word, and vice versa. When a speech recognition system is combined with a natural language processing system, the result is an overall system that not only recognizes voice input but also understands it (see Dettmer, 2003). For multiple applications in stores and warehouses, see Amato-McCoy (2003). Speech recognition is deployed today in wireless PDAs as well (see Kumagai, 2002, and Alesso and Smith, 2002).

Advantages of Speech Recognition and Understanding. The ultimate goal of speech recognition is to allow a computer to understand the natural speech of any human speaker at least as well as a human listener could understand it. Speech recognition offers several other advantages:

- *Ease of access.* Many more people can speak than can type. As long as communication with a computer depends on typing skills, many people may not be able to use computers effectively.

- *Speed.* Even the most competent typists can speak more quickly than they can type. It is estimated that the average person can speak twice as quickly as a proficient typist can type.

- *Manual freedom.* Obviously, communicating with a computer through typing occupies your hands. There are many situations in which computers might be useful to people whose hands are otherwise engaged, such as product assemblers, pilots of aircraft, and busy executives. Speech recognition also enables people with hand-related physical disabilities to use computers.

- *Remote access.* Many computers can be accessed remotely by telephones. If a remote database includes speech recognition capabilities, you could retrieve information by issuing oral commands into a telephone.

- *Accuracy.* People tend to make mistakes when typing, especially in spelling. These could be reduced with voice input.

American Express Travel Related Services (AETRS) is using interactive voice recognition (IVR) that allows its customers to check and book domestic flights by talking to a computer over the phone. The system asks customers questions such as: Where do you want to travel? When do you want to go? The system can handle 400 city and airport names, and lets callers use more than 10,000 different ways to identify a location. The reservation transaction costs were reduced about 50 percent compared to operator-handled costs. The average transaction time was reduced from 7 to 2 minutes. AETRS offers a similar service on the Web.

Limitations of Speech Recognition and Understanding. The major limitation of speech understanding is its inability to recognize long sentences, or the long time needed to accomplish it. The better the system is at speech recognition, the higher is its cost. Also, in voice recognition systems, you cannot manipulate icons and windows, so speech may need to be combined with a keyboard entry, which slows communication.

VOICE SYNTHESIS. The technology by which computers speak is known as **voice synthesis.** The synthesis of voice by computer differs from the simple playback of a prerecorded voice by either analog or digital means. As the term *synthesis* implies, sounds that make up words and phrases are electronically constructed from basic sound components and can be made to form any desired voice pattern.

The current quality of synthesized voice is very good, but the technology remains somewhat expensive. Anticipated lower cost and improved performance of synthetic voice should encourage more widespread commercial voice applications, especially those on the Web. Opportunities for its use will encompass almost all applications that can provide an automated response to a user, such as inquiries by employees pertaining to payroll and benefits. A number of banks already offer a voice service to their customers, informing them about their balances, which checks were cashed, and so on. Many credit card companies provide similar services, telling customers about current account balances, recent charges, and payments received. For a list of other voice synthesis and voice recognition applications, see Table 11.7 (page 487).

Artificial Neural Networks

Artificial neural networks (ANNs) are biologically inspired. Specifically, they borrow ideas from the manner in which the human brain works. The human brain is composed of special cells called *neurons*. Estimates of the number of neurons in a human brain cover a wide range (up to 150 billion), and there are more than a hundred different kinds of neurons, separated into groups called *networks*. Each network contains several thousand neurons that are highly interconnected. Thus, the brain can be viewed as a collection of neural networks.

Today's ANNs, whose application is referred to as **neural computing,** use a very limited set of concepts from biological neural systems. The goal is to simulate massive parallel processes that involve processing elements interconnected in a network architecture. The artificial neuron receives inputs analogous to the electrochemical impulses biological neurons receive from other neurons. The output of the artificial neuron corresponds to signals sent out from a biological neuron. These artificial signals can be changed, like the signals from the human brain. Neurons in an ANN receive information from other neurons or from external sources, transform or process the information, and pass it on to other neurons or as external outputs.

The manner in which an ANN processes information depends on its structure and on the algorithm used to process the information, as explained in Online File W11.21.

BENEFITS AND APPLICATIONS OF NEURAL NETWORKS. The value of neural network technology includes its usefulness for pattern recognition, learning, and the interpretation of incomplete and "noisy" inputs.

TABLE 11.7 Examples of Voice Technology Applications

Company	Applications
Scandinavian Airlines, other airlines	Answering inquiries about reservations, schedules, lost baggage, etc.[a]
Citibank, many other banks	Informing credit card holders about balances and credits, providing bank account balances and other information to customers[a]
Delta Dental Plan (CA)	Verifying coverage information[a]
Federal Express	Requesting pickups, ordering supplies[b]
Illinois Bell, other telephone companies	Giving information about services,[a] receiving orders[b]
Domino's Pizza	Enabling stores to order supplies, providing price information[a,b]
General Electric, Rockwell International, Austin Rover, Westpoint Pepperell, Eastman Kodak	Allowing inspectors to report results of quality assurance tests[b]
Cara Donna Provisions	Allowing receivers of shipments to report weights and inventory levels of various meats and cheeses[b]
Weidner Insurance, AT&T	Conducting market research and telemarketing[b]
U.S. Department of Energy, Idaho National Engineering Laboratory, Honeywell	Notifying people of emergencies detected by sensors[a]
New Jersey Department of Education	Notifying parents when students are absent and about cancellation of classes[a]
Kaiser-Permanente Health Foundation (HMO)	Calling patients to remind them of appointments, summarizing and reporting results[a]
Car manufacturers	Activating radios, heaters, and so on, by voice[b]
Taxoma Medical Center	Logging in and out by voice to payroll department[b]
St. Elizabeth's Hospital	Prompting doctors in the emergency room to conduct all necessary tests, reporting of results by doctors[a,b]
Hospital Corporation of America	Sending and receiving patient data by voice, searching for doctors, preparing schedules and medical records[a,b]

[a]Output device.
[b]Input device.

Neural networks have the potential to provide some of the human characteristics of problem solving that are difficult to simulate using the logical, analytical techniques of DSS or even expert systems. One of these characteristics is **pattern recognition.** Neural networks can analyze large quantities of data to establish patterns and characteristics in situations where the logic or rules are not known. An example would be loan applications. By reviewing many historical cases of applicants' questionnaires and the "yes or no" decisions made by people, the ANN can create "patterns" or "profiles" of applications that should be approved or denied. A new application can then be matched by the computer against the pattern. If it comes close enough, the computer classifies it as a "yes" or "no"; otherwise it goes to a human for a decision. Neural networks are especially useful for financial applications such as determining when to buy or sell stock (see Shadbolt, 2002, for examples), predicting bankruptcy (Gentry et al., 2002), predicting exchange rates (Davis et al., 2001), and detecting fraud (Merator, 2003).

Neural networks have several other benefits, which are described in Online File W11.22, together with typical applications. For a comprehensive coverage see Smith and Gupta (2002).

IT at Work 11.5

BANKS ARE CRACKING DOWN ON CREDIT CARD FRAUD

Only 0.2 percent of Visa International's turnover in 1995 was lost to fraud, but at $655 million it is a loss well worth addressing. Visa (*visa.com*) is now concentrating its efforts on reversing the number of fraudulent transactions by using neural network technology.

Most people stick to a well-established pattern of credit card use and only rarely splurge on expensive nonessentials. Neural networks are designed to notice when a card that is usually used to buy gasoline once a week in Hawaii is suddenly used to buy a number of tickets to the latest theater premiere on Broadway.

Visa's participating banks believe the neural network technology has been successful in combating fraud. Bank of America uses a cardholder risk identification system (CRIS) and has cut fraudulent card use by up to two-thirds. Toronto Dominion Bank found that losses were reduced, and overall customer service improved, with the introduction of neural computing. Another bank recorded savings of $5.5 million in six months. In its first year of use, Visa member banks lost 16% to counterfeiters; considering such numbers, the $2 million Visa spent to implement CRIS certainly seems worth the investment. In fact, Visa says, CRIS paid for itself in one year.

In 1995, CRIS conducted over 16 billion transactions. By 2003, VisaNet (Visa's data warehouse and e-mail operations) and CRIS were handling more than 8,000 transactions per second or about 320 billion a year. By fall 2003, CRIS was able to notify banks of fraud within a few seconds of a transaction. The only downside to CRIS is that occasionally the system prompts a call to a cardholder's spouse when an out-of-the-ordinary item is charged, such as a surprise vacation trip or a diamond ring. After all, no one wants to spoil surprises for loved ones.

Sumitomo Credit Service Co., a credit card issuer in Japan, is using a neural network-based system from *fairisaac.com*. The product works well reading Japanese characters, protecting 18 million cardholders in Japan. The system is used by many other banks worldwide.

Sources: Condensed from "Visa Stamps Out Fraud" (1995), p. viii; "Visa Cracks Down on Fraud" (1996); customer success stories at *fairisaac.com* and *visa.com* (press releases, accessed June 2004).

For Further Exploration: What is the advantage of CRIS over an automatic check against the balance in the account? What is the advantage of CRIS against a set of rules such as "Call a human authorizer when the purchase price is more than 200 percent of the average previous bill"?

Beyond its role as an alternative computing mechanism, and in data mining, neural computing can be combined with other computer-based information systems to produce powerful hybrid systems, as illustrated in *IT at Work 11.5*.

GENETIC PROGRAMMING (ALGORITHMS). Another machine learning tool related to ANN is **genetic programming,** which is an automatic domain-independent method for solving problems. It randomly creates thousands of computer programs, and then employs the Darwinian concept of natural selection (the strongest survive), applying principles such as recombination (crossover), mutation, gene selection, and duplication. It attempts to breed improved populations of programs over many generations. For details and sources see Koza et al. (2003).

Neural computing is emerging as an effective technology in pattern recognition. This capability is being translated to many applications (e.g., see Haykin, 1998; Chen, 1996; and Giesen, 2002) and is sometimes integrated with fuzzy logic.

Fuzzy Logic   **Fuzzy logic** deals with uncertainties by simulating the process of human reasoning, allowing the computer to behave less precisely and logically than conventional computers do. Fuzzy logic is a technique developed by Zadeh (1994), and its use is gaining momentum (Nguyen and Walker, 1999). The rationale behind this approach is that decision making is not always a matter of black and white, true or false. It often involves gray areas where the term *maybe* is more appropriate. In fact, creative decision-making processes are often unstructured, playful, contentious, or rambling.

According to experts, productivity of decision makers can improve many times using fuzzy logic (see Nguyen and Walker, 1999). At the present time, there are only a few examples of pure fuzzy logic applications in business, mainly in prediction-system behavior (see Peray, 1999, for investment, and Flanagan, 2000, for project evaluation). An interesting application is the use of fuzzy logic to support services for corporate travelers (see *Information Week*, May 15, 2000). More often, fuzzy logic is used together with other intelligent systems. For example, Advanced Traveler Information System (ATIS) standalone control systems use neuro-fuzzy logic to optimize overall network travel time by recommending the most suitable route based on a traveler's requirements (Dharia and Adeli, 2003; Ye, 2004).

Semantic Web
One of the major problems of the Web is the information overload, which is growing rapidly with time. Software and search agents are helpful, but they cannot (yet) understand words that have multiple meanings. Meaning depends on content, context, graphics, and even positioning on a Web page. The proposed solution is known as **semantic Web** (*w3.org/2001/sw/*). The semantic Web is an extension of the Web where information is assigned greater meaning and data can be accessed for automation, integration, and reuse.

In early 2004, the World Wide Web Consortium released two new specifications as an international standard: The Resource Description Framework (RDF) and the Web Ontology Language (OWL) (Lee, 2004). RDF is a set of rules for providing metadata, or simple descriptions of information. OWL specifies the interrelationships between objects. Using RDF and OWL, content developers can connect metadata with documents to enable better search capabilities. Other enhancements include the ability to integrate enterprise applications and to better manage Web sites (Taft, 2004). For how the process works, see Online File W11.23.

Semantic Web is expected to facilitate search, interoperability, and the composition of complex applications. It is an attempt to make the Web more homogenous, more data-like, and more amenable to computer understanding. If Web pages contained their own semantics, then software agents could conduct smarter searches. Semantic Web will enable software agents to understand Web forms and databases.

According to Cherry (2002), semantic Web, if it becomes successful, could provide "personal assistants" to people in term of software agents that will be able to conduct many useful tasks, such as completely booking your business trip.

Hybrid Intelligent Systems
Intelligent systems are frequently integrated with other intelligent systems or with conventional systems, such as DSSs. The following examples illustrate such *hybrid* systems.

DEVELOPING MARKETING STRATEGY. Developing marketing strategy is a complex process performed by several people working as a team. The process involves many tasks that must be performed sequentially, with contributions from corporate experts. Numerous marketing strategy models were developed over the

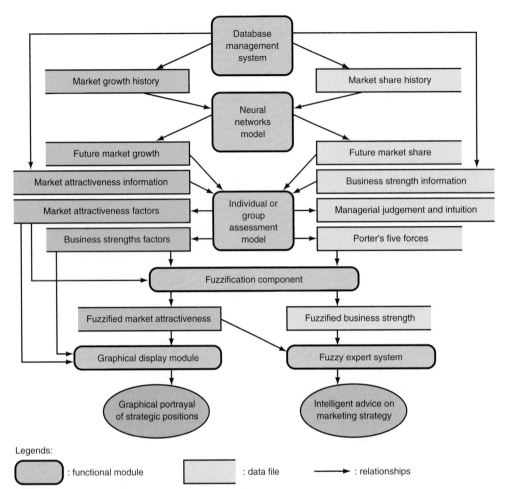

FIGURE 11.6 The architecture of a hybrid intelligent system. (*Source:* Reprinted from *Decision Support Systems*, January 2000, S. Li, "The Development of a Hybrid Intelligent System for Developing Market Strategy," p. 399. © 2000, with permission from Elsevier Science.)

years to support the process. Unfortunately, most of the models support only one IT goal (e.g., to perform forecasting). A proposal to integrate expert systems, fuzzy logic, and ANN was made by Li (2000). The process of developing marketing strategy and the support of the three technologies in that process is shown in Figure 11.6. This hybrid system is powerful enough to incorporate strategic models, such as Porter's five forces, and the directional policy matrices model. The integrated technologies and their roles are:

● *Neural networks.* These are used to predict future market share and growth.
● *Expert systems.* These provide intelligent advice on developing market strategy to individuals and to the planning team.
● *Fuzzy logic.* This helps managers to handle uncertainties and fuzziness of data and information.

The integration of the technologies helps in sharing information, coordination, and evaluation. The system is designed to support both individuals and groups. It allows for inclusion of users' judgment in implementing the model.

OPTIMIZING THE DESIGN PROCESS. Lam et al. (2000) applied an integrated fuzzy logic, ANN, and algorithmic optimization to the design of a complex design process for ceramic casting manufacturing. The ANN estimates the inputs needed by the fuzzy-rule base and also provides evaluation of the objective function of the optimization model. The system was successfully used, enabling fast and consistent production decision making.

11.8 WEB-BASED MANAGEMENT SUPPORT SYSTEMS

The Web is a perfect medium for deploying decision support capabilities on a global basis (see Power and Kaparthi, 2002 and Simic and Devedzic, 2003). Let's look at **Web-based management support systems (MSSs)** that can benefit both users and developers. These systems include decision support systems of all types, including intelligent and hybrid ones. Web-based MSSs are especially suitable for enterprise systems. An example is provided in *IT at Work 11.6.*

IT at Work 11.6
WEB-BASED MSS AT A LUXEMBOURG BANK

SEB Private Bank is the Luxembourg subsidiary of Swedish Bank SEB, an elite international bank that is quickly moving to take advantage of big growth opportunities in Europe with Internet banking. SEB discovered that customers on the Internet conducted more transactions than others, a trend that could deliver high profitability. The bank sees its greatest and most attractive opportunity in Europe, where SEB participates in a growing investment market and distinguishes itself with high-performance financial tools that empower managers to offer superior customer service. The Swedish bank has set an ambitious goal of having 5 million Internet customers by the end of 2004 with the help of a pan-European Internet partner.

To move into real-time 24/7 operations, SEB Private Bank decided to investigate an MSS software called WebFOCUS (from Information Builders). The software allows users to quickly build self-service production reporting and business analysis systems. Everything from standard to customized reports can be developed quickly and delivered immediately, internally or externally, by intranets, extranets, and over the Internet. As a result, the entire *decision-making process* is shifted onto a *real-time* transaction platform. The bank developed over 600 reports, of which more than 150 are used by the bank's managers on a day-to-day basis.

Two core elements of SEB Private Bank's information system are the IBM AS/400 hardware platform and Olympic, a Swiss-developed financial application. The combination of WebFOCUS and Information Builders' EDA (integration middleware that offers access to virtually any database) has improved information access for account managers.

Olympic software generates messages to leading stock exchanges, which in turn deliver a return message to the application, giving current financial updates. This streamlines the bank's reaction times with the outside world, giving up-to-the-minute information.

But having this intelligent information source is one thing; making full use of it is another. SEB Private Bank sees the increasing use of its intranet, with its Web-based, thin-client architecture, as a move toward fewer paper reports. For example: Through this system, the bank's managers can easily check the inventory value of a client's assets; when the DSS is asked to evaluate a dossier, it can quickly produce a result.

With reliable security and high value-added services, SEB Private Bank feels well positioned to expand its markets with new expatriate investor business.

Source: Compiled from *informationbuilders.com/applications/seb.html* (2001).

For Further Exploration: What other applications can be developed with such an MSS?

TABLE 11.8 Benefits of Web-Based MSSs

Benefit	Description
Reach rich data sources	The Web can have many resources with multimedia presentation, all accessible with a browser.
Easy data retrieval	Data can be accessed any time, from anywhere. Salespeople for example, can run proposals, using DSS models at a client's place of business.
Ease of use and learning	Use of browser, search engine, hypertext, etc., makes DSSs easy to learn and use. Even top executives are using them directly.
Reduce paperwork and processing efforts for raw data	All data are visible on the Web. If a data warehouse exists, data are organized for view.
Better decisions	With accessibility to more and current information, as well as to DSS models and technology, users of DSSs can make better decisions.
Expanding the use of ready-made DSSs	ASPs are using the Internet to lease DSS models as needed. Soon utility computing will make such distribution a common scenario. Also, more and cheaper applications are available.
Reduced development cost	Building one's own DSS can be cheaper when one uses components (Technology Guide 6) available on the Web. Also customizing vendors' products is faster and cheaper when done in the Internet environment.

The major beneficial features of Web-based MSSs are provided in Table 11.8. For examples of applications see Cohen et al. (2001). For other benefits of Web-based MSSs, see Online File W11.24.

11.9 ADVANCED AND SPECIAL DECISION SUPPORT TOPICS

Several topics are involved in implementing DSSs. The major ones are presented in this section. (For others and more details, see Turban et al., 2005.)

Simulation for Decision Making

Simulation has many meanings. In general, to *simulate* means to assume the appearance of characteristics of reality. In DSSs, **simulation** generally refers to a technique for conducting experiments (such as "what-if") with a computer on a model of a management system.

Because a DSS deals with semistructured or unstructured situations, it involves complex reality, which may not be easily analyzed by optimization or other standard models but often can be handled by simulation. Therefore, simulation is one of the most frequently used tools of DSSs. (See Law and Kelton, 1999.) For example, simulation is increasingly part of the decision support tools used in the airline industry for short-term decision making (Adelantado, 2004; Chong et al., 2003).

MAJOR CHARACTERISTICS. To begin, simulation is not a regular type of model. Models in general *represent* reality, whereas simulation usually *imitates* it closely. In practical terms, this means that fewer simplifications of reality are needed in simulation models than in other models.

Second, simulation is a technique for *conducting experiments,* especially "what-if" ones. As such, it can describe or predict the characteristics of a given system under different circumstances. Once the characteristics' values are computed, the best among several alternatives can be selected. The simulation process often consists of the repetition of an experiment many, many times to obtain an estimate of the overall effect of certain actions. It can be executed manually in some cases, but a computer is usually needed. Simulation can be used for complex decision making, as illustrated in an application of an automated underground freight transport system (Heijden, 2002) and in Online File W11.25.

Advantages of Simulation. Simulation is used for decision support because it:

- *Allows for inclusion of the real-life complexities of problems.* Only a few simplifications are necessary. For example, simulation may utilize the real-life probability distributions rather than approximate theoretical distributions.
- *Is descriptive.* This allows the manager to ask what-if type questions. Thus, managers who employ a trial-and-error approach to problem solving can do it faster and cheaper, with less risk, using a simulated problem instead of a real one.
- *Can handle an extremely wide variation in problem types,* such as inventory and staffing, *as well as higher managerial-level tasks* like long-range planning. Further, the manager can experiment with different variables to determine which are important, and with different alternatives to determine which is best.
- *Can show the effect of compressing time,* giving the manager in a matter of minutes some feel as to the long-term effects of various policies.
- *Can be conducted from anywhere* using Web tools on the corporate portal or extranet.

Of the various types of simulation, the most comprehensive is *visual interactive simulation* (see Chapter 10), which allows managers to interact with an analysis while it is in progress, making desired changes and manipulations.

Specialized Ready-Made Decisions Support

Initially, DSSs were custom-built. This resulted in two categories of DSS: The first type was small, end-user DSSs which were built by inexpensive tools such as Excel. The second type was large-scale, expensive DSSs built by IT staff and/or vendors with special tools. For many applications, however, building a custom system was not justified. As a result, vendors started to offer DSSs in specialized areas such as financial services, banking, hospitals, or profitability measurements (or combinations of these areas). The popularity of these DSSs has increased since 1999 when vendors started to offer them online as ASP services. Examples of ready-made DSS products are provided in Online File W11.26.

These tools and many more can be customized, at additional cost. However, even when customized, the total cost to users can be usually much lower than that of developing DSSs from scratch.

Decision support in ready-made expert systems is also provided on the Web. For more examples see Online File W11.27.

Frontline Decision Support Systems

Decisions at all levels in the organization contribute to the success of a business. But decisions that maximize a sales opportunity or minimize the cost of customer service requests are made on the frontlines by those interacting with customers and other business partners during the course of daily business. Whether it is an order exception, an upselling opportunity, resolving a customer complaint, or a contract that hangs on a decision, the decision maker on the frontline must be able to make effective decisions *rapidly*, while interacting with customers, sometimes in seconds, based on context and according to strategies and guidelines set forth by senior management.

FRONTLINE SYSTEMS. **Frontline decision making** is the process by which companies automate decision processes and push them down to frontline employees. It includes *empowering employees* by letting them devise strategies, evaluate metrics, analyze impacts, and make operational changes, based on information they can access in seconds. For more, see Online File W11.28.

Real-Time Decision Support

Business decisions today must be made at the right time, and frequently under time pressure. To do so, managers need to know what is going on in the business at any moment and be able to quickly select the best decision alternatives. In recent years, special decision support software has been developed for this purpose. These tools appear under different names such as *business activity monitoring (BAM)* and *extreme analytic frameworks (EAF)*. For details and examples see Bates (2003). Variants of these methods are *business performance intelligence (BPI)* (Sorensen, 2003) and *business performance management (BPM)* (Choy, 2003). Also related are *business performance measurement (BPM)* programs such as benchmarking and balanced scorecard (Chapter 13).

Creativity in Decision Support

In order to solve problems or assess opportunities it is often necessary to generate alternative solutions and/or ideas. Creativity is an extremely important topic in decision support, but it is outside the scope of this IT book. However, there is one topic that clearly belongs to IT and this is the use of computers to support the process of idea generation (some of which we discussed in Section 11.3) as well as the use of computers to generate ideas and solutions by themselves. Actually, expert systems can be considered contributors to creativity since they can generate proposed solutions that will help people generate new ideas (e.g., via association, a kind of a "brainstorming"). Interested readers are referred to Yiman-Seid and Kobsa (2003) and to Online File W11.29. Group support systems (GSSs) are another kind of groupware that is increasing the effectiveness of group decision making and fostering an environment that brings out ideas and creativity (Bose, 2003).

➡ MANAGERIAL ISSUES

1. *Cost justification; intangible benefits.* While some of the benefits of management support systems are tangible, it is difficult to put a dollar value on the intangible benefits of many such systems. While the cost of small systems is fairly low and justification is not a critical issue, the cost of medium-to-large systems can be very high, and the benefits they provide must be economically justified.

2. *Documenting personal DSS.* Many employees develop their own DSSs to increase their productivity and the quality of their work. It is advisable to have an inventory of these DSSs and make certain that appropriate documentation and security measures exist, so that if the employee is away or leaves the organization, the productivity tool remains.

3. *Security.* Decision support systems may contain extremely important information for the livelihood of organizations. Taking appropriate security measures, especially in Web-based distributed applications, is a must. End users who

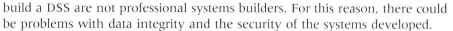

build a DSS are not professional systems builders. For this reason, there could be problems with data integrity and the security of the systems developed.

4. ***Ready-made commercial DSSs.*** With the increased use of Web-based systems and ASPs, it is possible to find more DSS applications sold off the shelf, frequently online. The benefits of a purchased or leased DSS application sometimes make it advisable to change business processes to fit a commercially available DSS. Some vendors are willing to modify their standard software to fit the customer's needs. Commercial DSSs are available both for certain industries (hospitals, banking) and for specific tasks (profitability analysis).

5. ***Intelligent DSS.*** Introducing intelligent agents into a DSS application can greatly increase its functionality. The intelligent component of a system can be less than 3 percent of the entire system (the rest is models, a database, and telecommunications), yet the contribution of the intelligent component can be incredible.

6. ***Organizational culture.*** The more people recognize the benefits of a DSS and the more support is given to it by top management, the more the DSS will be used. If the organization's culture is supportive, dozens of applications can be developed.

7. ***Embedded technologies.*** Intelligent systems are expected to be embedded in at least 20 percent of all IT applications in about 10 years. It is critical for any prudent management to closely examine the technologies and their business applicability.

8. ***Ethical issues.*** Corporations with management support systems may need to address some serious ethical issues such as privacy and accountability. For example, a company developed a DSS to help people compute the financial implications of early retirement. However, the DSS developer did not include the tax implications, which resulted in incorrect retirement decisions.

   Another important ethical issue is human judgment, which is frequently used in DSSs. Human judgment is subjective, and therefore, it may lead to unethical decision making. Companies should provide an ethical code for DSS builders. Also, the possibility of automating managers' jobs may lead to massive layoffs.

   There can be ethical issues related to the implementation of expert systems and other intelligent systems. The actions performed by an expert system can be unethical, or even illegal. For example, the expert system may advise you to do something that will hurt someone or will invade the privacy of certain individuals. An example is the behavior of robots, and the possibility that the robots will not behave the way that they were programmed to. There have been many industrial accidents, caused by robots, that resulted in injuries and even deaths. The issue is, Should an organization employ productivity-saving devices that are not 100 percent safe?

   Another ethical issue is the use of knowledge extracted from people. The issue here is, Should a company compensate an employee when knowledge that he or she contributed is used by others? This issue is related to the motivation issue. It is also related to privacy. Should people be informed as to who contributed certain knowledge?

   A final ethical issue that needs to be addressed is that of dehumanization and the feeling that a machine can be "smarter" than some people. People may have different attitudes toward smart machines, which may be reflected in the manner in which they will work together.

KEY TERMS

Artificial intelligence (AI) *476*

Artificial neural network (ANN) *486*

Business activity monitoring (BAM) *475*

Business performance management (BPM) *473*

Decision support system (DSS) *465*

Executive information system (EIS) *473*

Executive support system (ESS) *473*

Expert system (ES) *480*

Frontline decision making *494*

Fuzzy logic *488*

Genetic programming *488*

Group decision support system (GDSS) *471*

Inference engine *480*

Knowledge base *477*

Management support system (MSS) *461*

Model (in decision making) *463*

Model-based management system (MBMS) *468*

Natural language processing (NLP) *484*

Neural computing *486*

Optimization *465*

Organizational (institutional) decision support system (ODSS) *471*

Pattern recognition *487*

Personal information manager (PIM) *462*

Semantic Web *489*

Sensitivity analysis *466*

Simulation *492*

Speech recognition *485*

Speech understanding *485*

Symbolic processing *478*

Turing test *477*

Voice synthesis *486*

Web-based MSS *491*

CHAPTER HIGHLIGHTS (Numbers Refer to Learning Objectives)

1 Managerial decision making is synonymous with management.

1 In today's business environment it is difficult or impossible to conduct analysis of complex problems without computerized support.

1 Decision making is becoming more and more difficult due to the trends discussed in Chapter 1. Information technology enables managers to make better and faster decisions.

1 Decision making involves four major phases: intelligence, design, choice, and implementation; they can be modeled as such.

2 Models allow fast and inexpensive virtual experimentations with new or modified systems. Models can be iconic, analog, or mathematical.

3 A DSS is an approach that can improve the effectiveness of decision making, decrease the need for training, improve management control, facilitate communication, reduce costs, and allow for more objective decision making. DSSs deal mostly with unstructured problems. Structured decisions are solved with management science models.

3 The major components of a DSS are a database and its management, the model base and its management, and the user friendly interface. An intelligent (knowledge) component can be added.

4 Computer support to groups is designed to improve the process of making decisions in groups, which can meet face-to-face or online. The support increases the effectiveness of decisions and reduces the wasted time and other negative effects of face-to-face meetings.

5 Organizational DSSs are systems with many users throughout the enterprise. This is in contrast with systems that support one person or one functional area.

5 Executive support systems are intended to support top executives. Initially these were standalone systems, but today they are part of enterprise systems delivered on intranets.

6 The primary objective of AI is to build computers that will perform tasks that can be characterized as intelligent.

6 The major characteristics of AI are symbolic processing, use of heuristics instead of algorithms, and application of inference techniques.

6 AI has several major advantages: It is permanent; it can be easily duplicated and disseminated; it can be less expensive than human intelligence; it is consistent and thorough; and it can be documented.

7 The major application areas of AI are expert systems, natural language processing, speech understanding, intelligent robotics, computer vision, neural networks, fuzzy logic, and intelligent computer-aided instruction.

⑧ Expert system technology attempts to transfer knowledge from experts and documented sources to the computer, in order to make that knowledge available to nonexperts for the purpose of solving difficult problems.

⑧ The major components of an ES are a knowledge base, inference engine, user interface, blackboard, and explanation subsystem.

⑧ Expert systems can provide many benefits. The most important are improvement in productivity and/or quality, preservation of scarce expertise, enhancing other systems, coping with incomplete information, and providing training.

⑨ Natural language processing (NLP) provides an opportunity for a user to communicate with a computer in day-to-day spoken language.

⑨ Speech understanding enables people to communicate with computers by voice. There are many benefits to this emerging technology, such as speed of data entry and having free hands.

⑩ Neural systems are composed of processing elements called artificial neurons. They are interconnected, and they receive, process, and deliver information. A group of connected neurons forms an artificial neural network (ANN). ANNs are used to discover patterns of relationships among data, make difficult forecasts, and to fight fraud. They can process incomplete input information.

⑩ Fuzzy logic is a technology that helps analyze situations under uncertainty. The technology can also be combined with an ES and an ANN to conduct complex predictions and interpretations. ANNs, fuzzy logic, and ESs complement each other.

⑪ The Web can facilitate decision making by giving managers easy access to information and to modeling tools to process this information. Furthermore, Web tools such as browsers and search engines increase the speed of gathering and interpreting data. Finally, the Web facilitates collaboration and group decision making.

⑪ The Web helps in building decision support and intelligent systems, providing easy access to them from anywhere, reducing their per item cost, and improving information discovery and customer service.

⑫ Special applications of decision support include complex simulations, ready-made systems, and empowerment of frontline employees.

VIRTUAL COMPANY ASSIGNMENT

Instructions for accessing The Wireless Café on the Student Web Site

1. Go to
   wiley.com/college/turban
2. Select Turban/Leidner/
   McLean/Wetherbe's
   Information Technology for Management, Fifth Edition.
3. Click on Student
   Resources site, in the toolbar on the left.
4. Click on the link for
   Virtual Company Web Site
5. Click on Wireless Café.

Management Decision Support at The Wireless Café
Go to The Wireless Café's link on the Student Web Site. There you will be asked to think about how automated tools could support better decision making at the restaurant.

More Resources
More resources and study tools are located on the Student Web Site. You'll find additional chapter materials and useful Web links. In addition, self-quizzes that provide individualized feedback are available for each chapter.

QUESTIONS FOR REVIEW

1. Describe the manager's major roles.
2. Define models and list the major types used in DSSs.
3. Explain the phases of intelligence, design, and choice.
4. What are structured (programmed) and unstructured problems? Give one example of each in the following three areas: finance, marketing, and personnel administration.
5. Give two definitions of DSSs. Compare DSS to management science.
6. Explain sensitivity analysis.
7. List and briefly describe the major components of a DSS.
8. What is the major purpose of the model-based component in a DSS?
9. Define GDSS. Explain how it supports the group decision-making process.
10. What is an organizational DSS?
11. What is the difference between an EIS and an ESS?
12. What are the major benefits of an ESS?
13. Describe BPM and BAM.
14. What cause different decision support systems to fail?
15. Define artificial intelligence and list its major characteristics.
16. What is the Turing test?
17. List the major advantages and disadvantages of artificial intelligence as compared with natural intelligence.
18. List the commercial AI technologies.
19. List three major capabilities and benefits of an ES.
20. Define the major components of an ES.
21. Which component of an ES is mostly responsible for the reasoning capability?
22. List the 10 generic categories of ESs.
23. Describe some of the limitations of ESs.
24. Describe a natural language and natural language processing; list their characteristics.
25. List the major advantages of voice recognition and voice understanding.
26. What is an artificial neural network?
27. What are the major benefits and limitations of neural computing?
28. Define fuzzy logic, and describe its major features and benefits.
29. Describe simulation as a decision support tools.
30. Define semantic Web and describe its purposes.
31. How can frontline employees be supported for decision making?

QUESTIONS FOR DISCUSSION

1. What could be the biggest advantages of a mathematical model that supports a major investment decision?
2. Your company is considering opening a branch in China. List several typical activities in each phase of the decision (intelligence, design, choice, and implementation).
3. How is the term *model* used in this chapter? What are the strengths and weaknesses of modeling?
4. American Can Company announced that it was interested in acquiring a company in the health maintenance organization (HMO) field. Two decisions were involved in this act: (1) the decision to acquire an HMO, and (2) the decision of which one to acquire. How can a DSS, ES, or ESS be used in such situation?
5. Relate the concept of a knowledge subsystem to frontline decision support. What is the role of Web tools in such support?
6. Discuss how GDSSs can negate the dysfunctions of face-to-face meetings (Chapter 3).
7. Discuss the advantages of Internet-based DSSs.
8. A major difference between a conventional decision support system and an ES is that the former can explain a "how" question whereas the latter can also explain a "why" question. Discuss.
9. What is the difference between voice recognition and voice understanding?
10. Compare and contrast neural computing and conventional computing.
11. Fuzzy logic is frequently combined with expert systems and/or neural computing. Explain the logic of such integration.
12. Explain why even an intelligent system can fail.
13. Discuss the use of BPM and relate it to other enterprise systems.

EXERCISES

1. Sofmic (fictitious name) is a large software vendor. About twice a year, Sofmic acquires a small specialized software company. Recently, a decision was made to look for a software company in the area of data mining. Currently, there are about 15 companies that would gladly cooperate as candidates for such acquisitions.

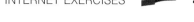

Bill Gomez, the corporate CEO, asked that a recommendation for a candidate for acquisition be submitted to him within one week. "Make sure to use some computerized support for justification, preferably from the area of AI," he said. As a manager responsible for submitting the recommendation to Gomez, you need to select a computerized tool for conducting the analysis. Respond to the following points:

a. Prepare a list of all the tools that you would consider.
b. Prepare a list of the major advantages and disadvantages of each tool, as it relates to this specific case.
c. Select a computerized tool.
d. Mr. Gomez does not assign grades to your work. You make a poor recommendation and you are out. Therefore, carefully justify your recommendation.

2. Table 11.6 provides a list of 10 categories of ES. Compile a list of 10 examples from the various functional areas in an organization (accounting, finance, production, marketing, human resources, and so on) that will show functional applications as they are related to the 10 categories.

3. Review the opening case and answer these questions:
a. Why do airlines need optimization systems for crew scheduling?
b. What role can experts' knowledge play in this case?
c. What are the similarities between the systems in Singapore and Malaysia?

4. *Debate:* Prepare a table showing all the arguments you can think of that justify the position that computers cannot think. Then, prepare arguments that show the opposite.

5. Enter *sas.com* and find the story of Quaker Chemical. View the video. Write a report about how the Strategic Performance Management tool helped the company. Relate it to the scorecard.

GROUP ASSIGNMENTS

1. Development of an organizational DSS is proposed for your university. As a group, identify the management structure of the university and the major existing information systems. Then, identify and interview several potential users of the system. In the interview, you should check the need for such a system and convince the potential users of the benefits of the system.

2. Prepare a report regarding DSSs and the Web. As a start, go to *dssresources.com*. (Take the DSS tour.) Each group represents one vendor such as *microstrategy.com*, *sas.com*, and *cai.com*. Each group should prepare a report that aims to convince a company why its DSS Web tools are the best.

3. Find recent application(s) of intelligent systems in an organization. Assign each group member to a major functional area. Then, using a literature search, material from vendors, or industry contacts, each member should find two or three recent applications (within the last six months) of intelligent systems in this area. (*Primenet. pcai.com* is a good place to search. Also try the journals *Expert Systems* and *IEEE Intelligent Systems*.)

a. The group will make a presentation in which it will try to convince the class via examples that intelligent systems are most useful in its assigned functional area.
b. The entire class will conduct an analysis of the similarities and differences among the applications across the functional areas.
c. The class will vote on which functional area is benefiting the most from intelligent systems.

4. Each group member composes a list of mundane tasks he or she would like an intelligent system to prepare. The group will then meet and compare and draw some conclusions.

5. Investigate the use of NLP and voice recognition techniques that enable consumers to get information from the Web, conduct transactions, and interact with others, all by voice, through regular and cell telephones. Investigate articles and vendors of voice portals and find the state of the art. Write a report.

INTERNET EXERCISES

1. Enter the site of *microstrategy.com* and identify its major DSS products. Find success stories of customers using these products.

2. Find DSS-related newsgroups. Post a message regarding a DSS issue that is of concern to you. Gather several replies and prepare a report.

3. Several DSS vendors provide free demos on the Internet. Identify a demo, view it, and report on its major capabilities. (Try *microstrategy.com*, *sas.com*, *hyperion.com*, and *crystaldecision.com*. You may need to register at some sites.)

4. Search the Internet for the major DSSs and business intelligence vendors. How many of them market a

Web-based system? (Try *businessobjects.com, hyperion.com, cognos.com.*)

5. Enter *asymetrix.com.* Learn about their decision support and performance management tool suite (Toolbook Assistant). Explain how the software can increase competitive advantage.

6. Find 10 case studies about DSSs. (Try *microstrategy.com, sas.com,* and *findarticles.com.*) Analyze for DSS characteristics.

7. Enter *solver.com, ncr.com, hyperion.com,* and *ptc.com.* Identify their frontline system initiatives.

8. Prepare a report on the use of ESs in help desks. Collect information from *ginesys.com, exsys.com, ilog.com,* and *pcai.com/pcai.*

9. Enter the Web site of Carnegie Mellon University (*cs.cmu.edu*) and identify current activities on the Land Vehicle. Send an e-mail to ascertain when the vehicle will be on the market.

10. At MIT (*media.mit.edu*) there is a considerable amount of interest in intelligent systems. Find the latest activities. (Look at research and projects.)

11. Visit *sas.com/pub/neural/FAZ.html/.* Identify links to real-world applications of neural computing in finance, manufacturing, health care, and transportation. Then visit *wolfram.com.* Prepare a report on current applications.

12. Visit *spss.com, informatica.com,* or *accure.com* and identify their Internet analytic solutions. Compare and comment. Relate your findings to business performance measurement.

13. Enter *del.gov/eLaws/* and *exsys.com* and identify public systems–oriented advisory systems. Summarize in a report.

14. Enter *fairisaac.com* and find how credit risk scores are calculated. Also find how fraud is treated.

Minicase 1
A DSS Reshapes the Railway in the Netherlands

More than 5,000 trains pass through 2,800 railway kilometers and 400 stations each day in the Netherlands. As of the mid-1990s, the railway infrastructure was hardly sufficient to handle the passenger flow. The problem worsened during rush hours, and trains were delayed. Passengers complained and tended to use cars, whose variable cost is lower than that of using the train. This increased the congestion on the roads, adding pollution and traffic accidents. Several other problems plagued the system. The largest railway company, Nederlandse Spoorweges (NS), was losing money in rural areas and agreed to continue services there only if the government would integrate the railways with bus and taxi systems, so that commuters would have more incentives to use the trains. Government help was needed.

Rail 21 is the name of the government's attempt to bring the system into the twenty-first century. It is a complex, multibillion-dollar project. The government wanted to reduce road traffic among the large cities, stimulate regional economies by providing a better public transportation system, stimulate rail cargo, and reduce the number of short-distance passenger flights in Europe. NS wanted to improve service and profitability. A company called Railned is managing the project, which is scheduled for completion in 2010.

Railned developed several alternative infrastructures (called "cocktails"), and put them to analysis. The analysis involved four steps: (1) use experts to list possible alternative projects, (2) estimate passenger flows in each, using an econometric model, (3) determine optimization of rail lines, and (4) test feasibility. The last two steps were complex enough that the following computerized DSSs were developed for their execution:

- **PROLOP:** This DSS was designed to do the lines optimization. It involves a database and three quantitative models. It supports several decisions regarding rails, and it can be used to simulate the scenarios of the "cocktails." It incorporates a management science model, called integer linear programming. PROLOP also compares line systems based on different criteria. Once the appropriate line system is completed, an analysis of the required infrastructure is done, using the second DSS, called DONS.

- **DONS:** This system contains a DSS database, graphical user interface, and two algorithmic modules. The first algorithm computes the arrival and departure times for each train at each station where it stops, based on "hard" constraints (must be met), and "soft" constraints (can be delayed). It represents both safety and customer-service requirements. The objective is to create a feasible timetable for the trains. If a feasible solution is not possible, planners relax some of the "soft" constraints. If this does not help, modifications in the lines system are explored.

- **STATIONS:** Routing the trains through the railway stations is an extremely difficult problem that cannot be solved simultaneously with the timetable. Thus, STATIONS, another DSS, is used. Again, feasible optimal solutions are searched for. If these do not exist, system modifications are made.

This DSS solution is fairly complex due to conflicting objectives of the government and the railway company (NS), so negotiations on the final choices are needed. To do so, Railned developed a special DSS model for conducting cost-benefit evaluations. It is based on a multiple-criteria approach with conflicting objectives. This tool can rank alternative "cocktails" based on certain requirements and assumptions. For example, one set of assumptions emphasizes NS long-term profitability, while the other one tries to meet the government requirements.

The DSSs were found to be extremely useful. They reduced the planning time and the cost of the analysis and increased the quality of the decisions. An example was an overpass that required an investment of $15 million. DONS came up with a timetable that required an investment of only $7.5 million by using an alternative safety arrangement. The DSS solution is used during the operation of the system as well for monitoring and making adjustments and improvements in the system.

Source: Compiled from Hooghiemstra et al. (1999).

Questions for Minicase 1

1. Why were management science optimizations by themselves not sufficient in this case?
2. What kinds of DSSs were used?
3. Enter *NS.nl* and find information about NS's business partners and the system. (English information is available on some pages.)
4. Given the environment described in the case, which of the DSS generic characteristics described in this chapter are likely to be useful, and how?
5. In what steps of the process can simulation be used, and for what?
6. Identify sensitivity analysis in this case.

Minicase 2
Singapore and Malaysia Airlines Expert Systems

The Problem

Airlines fly around the globe, mostly with their native crew. Singapore Airlines and Malaysia Airlines are relatively small airlines, but they serve dozens of different countries. If a crewmember is ill on route, there is a problem of quickly finding a replacement. This is just one example why crew scheduling may be complex, especially when it is subject to regulatory constraints, contract agreements, and crew preferences. Disturbances such as weather conditions, maintenance problems, etc. also make crew management difficult.

The Solution

Singapore airlines uses Web-based intelligent systems such as expert systems and neural computing to manage the company's flight crew scheduling and handle disruptions to the crew rosters. The Integrated Crew Management System (ICMS) project, implemented in Singapore since 1997, consists of three modules: one roster assignment module for cockpit crew, one for the cabin crew, and a crew tracking module. The first two modules automate the tracking and scheduling of the flight crew's timetable. The second module tracks the positions of the crew and includes an *intelligent system* that handles crew pattern disruptions.

For example, crews are rearranged if one member falls ill while in a foreign port; the system will find a backup in order to prevent understaffing on the scheduled flight. The intelligent system then determines the best way to reschedule the different crew members' rosters to accommodate the sick person. When a potentially disruptive situation occurs, the intelligent system automatically draws upon the knowledge stored in the database and advises the best course of action. This might mean repositioning the crew or calling in backup staff. The crew tracking system includes a crew disruption handling module which provides decision-support capabilities in real time.

A similar Web-based system is used by Malaysia Airlines, as of summer 2003, to optimize flight crew utilization. Also called ICMS, it leverages optimization software from *ilog.com*. Its Crew Pairing Optimization (CPO) module utilizes Ilog Cplex and Ilog Solver optimization components to ensure compliance with airline regulations, trade union agreements, and company policies, to minimize the costs associated with crew accommodations and transportation and to efficiently plan and optimize staff utilization and activities associated with long-term planning and daily operations. The Crew Duty Assignment (CDA) module provides automatic assignment of duties to all flight crews. The system considers work rules, regulatory requirements, and crew requests to produce an optimal monthly crew roster.

The Results

Despite the difficult economic times, both airlines are competing successfully in the region, and their balance sheets are better than most other airlines.

Sources: Compiled from news item at *Computerworld Singapore* (April 10, 2003), and from *ilog.com* (accessed June 9, 2003).

Questions for Minicase 2

1. Why do airlines need optimization systems for crew scheduling?
2. What role can experts' knowledge play in this case?
3. What are the similarities between the systems in Singapore and Malaysia?

REFERENCES

Adelantado, M., "Rapid Prototyping of Airport Advanced Operational Systems and Procedures Through Distributed Simulation," *Simulation: Transactions of the Society for Modeling and Simulation International*, 80(1), January 2004.

Alesso, P., and C. F. Smith, *Intelligent Wireless Web*. Boston: Addison Wesley, 2002.

Amato-McCoy, D. M., "Speech Recognition System Picks Up the Pace in Kwik Trip DC," *Stores*, May 2003.

Ante, S., "Owens & Minor", *BusinessWeek*, November 24, 2003.

Anthony, R. N., *Planning and Control Systems: A Framework for Analytics*. Cambridge, MA: Harvard University Press, 1965.

Arnold, V., et al., "Impact of Intelligent Decision Aids on Expert and Novice Decision-Makers' Judgments," *Accounting and Finance*, 44(1), March 2004.

Barrett, L., and S. Gallagher, "New Balance: Shoe Fits," *Baseline Magazine*, November 1, 2003.

Bates, J., "Business in Real Time-Realizing the Vision," *DM Review*. May 2003.

Berg, J. E., and T. A. Rietz, "Prediction Markets as Decision Support Systems," *Information Systems Frontiers*, January 2003.

Bonabeau, E., "Don't Trust Your Gut," *Harvard Business Review*, May 2003.

Bose, R., "Group Support Systems: Technology and Products Selection," *Industrial Management and Data Systems*, 103(9), November 2003.

Brezillon, P., and Pomerol, J. C., "User Acceptance of Interactive Systems: Lessons from Knowledge-Based DSS," *Failure and Lessons Learned in IT Management*, 1(1), 1997.

Briggs, D., and D. Arnoff, "DSSs Failures: An Evolutionary Perspective," *Proceedings DSI AGE 2002, Cork, Ireland*, July 2002.

Business World, "Executive Information System: The Right Move," *itmatters.com.ph/news/news_05042002f.html*, May 4, 2004 (accessed May 2004).

Carter, G. M., et al., *Building Organizational Decision Support Systems*. Cambridge, MA: Academic Press, 1992.

Cawsey, A., *The Essence of Artificial Intelligence*. Upper Saddle River, NJ: Prentice Hall PTR, 1998.

Chapman, T., "Vital Signs," *UK Microsoft Customer Magazine*, July 2003.

Chen, C. H., *Fuzzy Logic and Neural Network Handbook*. New York, McGraw-Hill, 1996.

Cherry, S. M., "Weaving a Web of Ideas," *IEEE Spectrum*. September 2002.

Chong, K. I., et al., "A Simulation-Enabled DSS for Allocating Check-In Agents," *INFOR*, 41(3), August 2003.

Choy, J., "Growing Interest in Business Performance Management," *Asia Computer Weekly, Singapore*, April 28, 2003.

Cohen, H. D., et al., "Decision Support with Web-Enabled Software," *Interfaces*, March–April 2001.

Computerworld, July 7, 1997.

Computerworld Singapore, April 10, 2003.

Davis, J. T., et al., "Predicting Direction Shifts on Canadian-US Exchange Rates with Artificial Neural Networks," *International Journal of Intelligent Systems in Accounting, Finance & Management*, Vol. 10, 2001.

DeSanctis, G., and B. Gallupe, "A Foundation for the Study of Group Decision Support Systems," *Management Science*, 33(5), 1987.

Dettmer, R., "IT's Good to Talk," *IEE Software*, June 2003.

Dharia, A., and H. Adeli, "Neural Network Model for Rapid Forecasting of Freeway Link Travel Time," *Engineering Applications of Artificial Intelligence*, October 2003.

dmreview.com, 2001.

Dreyfus, H., and S. Dreyfus, *Mind Over Machine*. New York: Free Press, 1988.

Edwards, C., "Charles Schwab," *BusinessWeek*, November 24, 2003.

Edwards, J. S., et al., "An Analysis of Expert Systems for Decision Making," *European Journal of Information Systems*, March 2000.

El Sharif, H., and O. A. El Sawy, "Issue-based DSS for the Egyptian Cabinet," *MIS Quarterly*, December 1988.

Fagerholt, K., "A Computer-Based DSS for Vessel Fleet Scheduling," *Decision Support Systems*, April 2004.

Flanagan, R., "A Fuzzy Stochastic Technique for Project Selection," *Construction Management and Economics*, January 2000.

Gentry, J. A., et al., "Using Inductive Learning to Predict Bankruptcy," *Journal of Organizational Computing and Electronic Commerce.* Vol. 12, 2002.

Giesen, L., "Artificial-Intelligence System Separates Good Check Writers from Bad," *Stores*, March 2002.

Gorry, G. A., and M. S. Scott-Morton, "A Framework for Management Information Systems," *Sloan Management Review*, 13(1), Fall 1971.

Gregor, S., and I. Benbasat, "Explanations from Intelligent Systems," *MIS Quarterly*, December 1999.

Grimes, S., "Decision Support: The BPM Drumbeat," *Intelligent Enterprise*, April 22, 2003.

Hackathorn, R. D., and P. G. Keen, "Organizational Strategies for Personal Computing in Decision Support Systems," *MIS Quarterly*, September 1981.

Harrington, A. M., "Building the Optimal Schedule at Reno-Depot," *Stores*, September 2003.

Haykin, S., *Neural Networks: A Comprehensive Foundation*. Upper Saddle River, NJ: Prentice Hall, 1998.

Heijden, M. C., et al., "Using Simulation to Design an Automated Underground System for Transporting Freight Around Schiphol Airport," *Interfaces*, July–August 2002.

Hillier, S. F., and S. M. Hillier, *Introduction to Management Science*, 2nd edition. New York: McGraw-Hill, 2002.

Hooghiemstra, J. S., et al., "Decision Support Systems Support the Search for Win–Win Solutions in Railway Network," *Interfaces*, March–April 1999.

Hovanesian, M. D., "Wells Fargo," *BusinessWeek*, November 24, 2003.

Huber, G. P., *The Necessary Nature of Future Firms: Attributes of Survivors in a Changing World*. San Francisco: Sage Publications, 2003.

ilog.com (accessed June 9, 2003).

informationbuilders.com/applications/seb.html (2001).

Information Week, May 15, 2000.

Iserlis, Y., "Intelligent Programs and Machines: A Snapshot of Where We Are," *PCAI*, March 2004.

Jackson, P., *Introduction to Expert Systems*, 3rd ed. Reading, MA: Addison Wesley, 1999.

Jareb, E., and Rajkovic, V., "Use of an Expert System in Personnel Selection," *Information Management*. Vol. 14, 2001.

Kahn. J., "It's Alive," *Wired*, March 2002.

Keating, W., "Fast Tracking," *Optimize*, March 2003.

Kingsman, B. G., and A. A. deSouza, "A KBDSS for Cost Estimation and Pricing Descision," *International Journal of Production Economics*, November 1997.

Kohli, R., and S. Devaraj, "Contribution of Institutional DSS to Organizational Performance: Evidence from a Longitudinal Study," *Decision Support Systems*, April 2004.

Koza, J. R., et al., "Genetic Programming's Human-Competitive Results," *IEEE Intelligent Systems*, May–June 2003.

Kumagai, J., "Talk to the Machine," *IEEE Spectrum*, September 2002.

Law, A. M., and D. W. Kelton, *Simulation Modeling and Analysis*. New York: McGraw-Hill, 1999.

Lam, S. S. Y., et al., "Prediction and Optimization of a Ceramic Casting Process Using a Hierarchical Hybrid System of Neural Network and Fuzzy Logic," *IIE Transactions*, January 2000.

Lee, L. Y., "W3C Releases 'Semantic Web' Specs," *Software Development Times*, March 1, 2004.

Li, S., "The Development of a Hybrid Intelligent System for Developing Marketing Strategy," *Decision Support Systems*, January 2000.

McGuire, P. A., "The Analytics Divide," *Stores*, October 2001.

McKinley, E., "Getting a Jump on the Competition," *Stores*, October 2003.

Mercator Advisory Group, "Credit Scoring and Analytic Technologies: ROI Better Than Ever," *researchandmarkets.com/reports/54412*, November 2003 (accessed May 2004).

Mintzberg, H., *The Nature of the Managerial Work*. New York: Harper & Row, 1973.

Mintzberg, H., and F. Westley, "Decision Making: It's Not What You Think," *MIT Sloan Management Review*, Spring 2001.

Nevis, C., "California DMV Streamlines Fee Processing," a case study, *Fair Isaac, Inc., blazesoft.com*, February 2003.

Nguyen, H. T., and E. A. Walker, *A First Course in Fuzzy Logic*. Boca Raton, FL: CRC Press, 1999.

O'Leary, D. E., "AI and Navigation on the Internet and Intranet," *IEEE Expert*, April 1996.

O'Leary, D. E., "Internet-based Information and Retrieval Systems," *Decision Support Systems*, December 1999.

PC Week, August 17, 1998.

Peray, K., *Investing in Mutual Funds Using Fuzzy Logic*. Boca Raton, FL: CRC Press, 1999.

platinum.com, 2000.

Pontz, C., and D. J. Power, "Building an Expert Assistance System for Examiners (EASE) at the Pennsylvania Department of Labor and Industry," *dssresources.com/cases/Penndeptlabor.html*, 2003 (accessed July 2003).

Powell, A., et al., "Virtual Teams: Review of Current Literature," *Database Journal*, Winter 2004.

Power, D. J., *Decision Support Systems: Concepts and Resources for Managers*. Westport, CT: Quorum Books, 2002.

Power, D. J., and S. Kaparthi, "Building Web-based DSSs," *Studies in Informatics and Control*, December 2002.

Reiter, E., and R. Dale, *Building Natural Language Generation Systems*. Cambridge U.K.: Cambridge University Press, 2000.

Rivlin, G., "The Things They Carry," *Fortune*, Winter 2002, *fortune.cnet.com/fortune/0,10000,0-5937473-7-7707001,00.html?tag=txt* (accessed July 2003).

Rivlin, G., "They Carry (Intelligent Devices)," *Fortune.Cnet.com*, Winter 2002.

Rockart, J. F., and D. DeLong, *Executive Support Systems*. Homewood, IL: Dow Jones–Irwin, 1988.

Russell, S. J., and P. Norvig, *Artificial Intelligence*, 2nd ed. Upper Saddle River, NJ: Prentice Hall, 2002.

Shadbolt, J., et al., *Neural Networks and the Financial Markets: Predicting, Combining, and Portfolio Optimisation (Perspectives in Neural Computing)*. New York: Springer-Verlag, 2002.

Shim, J. P., et al., "Past, Present, and Future of Decision Support Technology," *Decision Support Systems*, 33(2), June 2002.

Simic, G., and V. Devedzic, "Building an Intelligent System Using Modern Internet Technologies," *Expert System With Applications*, August 2003.

Simon, H., *The New Science of Management Decisions*, rev. ed. Englewood Cliffs, NJ: Prentice-Hall, 1977.

Singh, S. K., et al., "EIS Support of Strategic Management Process," *Decision Support Systems*, May 2002.

Smith, K., and J. Gupta (eds.), *Neural Networks in Business: Techniques and Applications*. Hershey, PA: The India Group, 2002.

Sorensen, D., "Emerging Technology Innovation and Products in the Vanguard," *CIO Magazine*, February 2003.

Stonebraker, J. S., "How Bayer Makes Decisions to Develop New Drugs," *Interfaces*, November–December 2002.

Taft, K. D., "W3C Approves Pair of Semantic Web Specs," *eWeek*, 21(7), February 16, 2004, *eweek.com/article2/0,4149,1524306,00.asp* (accessed May 2004).

Turban, E., et al., *Decision Support Systems and Intelligent Systems*, 8th ed. Upper Saddle River, NJ: Prentice Hall, 2005.

Vedder, R. G., et al., "Death of an Expert System: A Case Study of Success and Failure," *Journal of International Technology and Information Management*, 11(1), 2002.

"Visa Cracks Down on Fraud," *Information Week*, August 26, 1996.

visa.com, press releases (accessed June 19, 2003).

"Visa Stamps Out Fraud," *International Journal of Retail and Distribution Management*, 23(11), Winter 1995, p. viii.

Voth, D., "TIA Program Researches Terrorism Patterns," *IEEE Intelligent Systems*, May–June 2003.

Wang, F. Y., et al., "Toward Intelligent Transportation System for the 2008 Olympics," *IEEE Intelligent Systems*, November–December 2003.

weforum.org (accessed June 29, 2003).

w3.org/2001/sw/. 2001.

Ye, H., "A Neuro-Fuzzy Logic for ATIS Stand-Alone Control Systems: Structure, Calibration, and Analysis," *Computer-Aided Civil and Infrastructure Engineering*, 19(3), May 2004.

Yiman-Seid, D., and Kobsa, A., "Expert-Finding Systems for Organizations: Problem and Domain Analysis and the DEMOIR Approach," *Journal of Organizational Computing and Electronic Commerce*, Vol. 13, 2003.

Zadeh, L., "Fuzzy Logic, Neural Networks, and Self-Computing," *Communications of the ACM*, March 1994.

PART V

Implementing and Managing IT

12. Using IT for Strategic Advantage
13. Information Technology Economics
14. Acquiring IT Applications and Infrastructure
15. Managing Information Resources and Security
16. The Impacts of IT on Individuals, Organizations, and Society

CHAPTER
12

Using Information Technology for Strategic Advantage

12.1 Strategic Advantage and Information Technology

12.2 Porter's Value Chain Model

12.3 Strategic Resources and Capabilities

12.4 IT Planning—A Critical Issue for Organizations

12.5 Strategic IT Planning (Stage 1)

12.6 Information Requirements Analysis, Resource Allocation, and Project Planning (Stages 2–4)

12.7 Planning IT Architectures

12.8 Some Issues in IT Planning

Minicases:
1. Cisco Systems
2. National City Bank

LEARNING OBJECTIVES

After studying this chapter, you will be able to:

❶ Describe ways of interpreting the strategic impact of information systems.

❷ Describe IT-enabled strategies that companies can use to achieve competitive advantage in their industry.

❸ Describe information technology skills and resources as they relate to the achievement of sustained competitive advantage.

❹ Explain the four-stage model of information systems planning, and discuss the importance of aligning information systems plans with business plans.

❺ Describe information requirement analysis, project payoff and portfolios, resource allocation, and project planning.

❻ Discuss the meaning and importance of IT alignment.

❼ Identify the different types of IT architectures and outline the processes necessary to establish an information architecture.

❽ Discuss the major issues addressed by information systems planning.

❾ Distinguish the major Web-related IT planning issues and understand application portfolio selection.

505

DELL'S DIRECT PATH
TO SUCCESS

 ## THE PROBLEM

The value chain in place at most firms assumes a *make-to-forecast strategy*. That is, standard products are produced from long-term forecasts of customer demand. Thus, the primary activities of the value chain move from inbound logistics to operations to outbound logistics and then to marketing and sales. All of these activities are based on projections of what customers will be buying and in what quantities. A make-to-forecast strategy offers efficiencies in production, but if the forecasts are inaccurate, as they frequently are, the results are lost sales (inadequate supply) or heavy discounting to move excess product (oversupply). Then the bottom line is, literally, less profit. Another major disadvantage of the make-to-forecast strategy is the inability of the firm to track ongoing changes in customer demand.

 ## THE SOLUTION

A possible solution to the problems of the make-to-forecast strategy is the *direct business model,* which allows the company to build each product to order. It was this concept that led Michael Dell to establish Dell Computer Corporation (now Dell Inc.) in 1984. Dell is well-known for its ability to mass-produce computers that are customized to a customer's order. This production and operations process is known as *mass-customization* or, in a value-chain context, a *build-to-order (BTO) strategy*. The ability to build to order depends on how well a company can efficiently meet customer demands at each stage of the value chain.

Dell's value chain moves the marketing and sales activity forward to the front of the value chain. In its build-to-order strategy, Dell assembles the product only after the customer has placed the order, so marketing and sales come first.

At Dell the BTO process begins with receipt of the customer order from the Internet, fax, or telephone. It takes approximately one day to process the order and for production control to ensure that the necessary parts are in stock. Assembly and shipment takes another day, and delivery to the customer's home or office takes a final one to five days.

At Dell, this process depends on computer systems that link customer order information to production, assembly, and delivery operations. To support its build-to-order strategy, Dell was among the first companies to add e-commerce capabilities to its Web site in 1996. The following year, Dell became the first enterprise to record $1 million in daily online sales. Today, Dell operates one of the highest-volume Internet commerce sites in the world. The company's Web site runs entirely on Dell PowerEdge servers and uses Microsoft Windows as the software platform. The site receives more than one billion page requests each quarter at 84 country sites in 28 languages and processes transactions in 29 currencies.

Executing a build-to-order strategy is not easy, as many companies have found out. Not only must interconnected information systems be built, but also BTO frequently requires a change in organizational culture, managerial thinking, and supplier interactions and support. Inevitably, the process begins by acquiring a better understanding of customer demand; then improvements in information flow will produce the ability to increase responsiveness in all areas of the value chain.

THE RESULTS

A successful build-to-order strategy offers companies like Dell numerous bene-fits in process, product, and volume flexibility. For example, customer require-ments are linked directly to production. As a result, production decisions are based on up-to-the-minute customer demand, not long-range forecasts, which can be wildly inaccurate. This real-time linkage increases management's knowl-edge about trends in the marketplace and decreases inventory-holding costs. BTO also offers partners in Dell's value system increased visibility to the demand and flow of goods. As noted in the text, understanding this entire value system can give additional insight and opportunities for competitive advantage.

In addition, the support structures for BTO are naturally more flexible, cre-ating a higher sense of responsiveness within the firm and a more flexible and agile company. One outcome of such flexibility is that adjustable price and sales incentives can be used to manage demand levels; this gives the company more control than the strategy of having to reactively discount excess stock. Finally, be-cause the customer gets exactly what he or she wants, first-time customers are likely to become repeat customers and recommend Dell to friends and colleagues.

The primary disadvantage of the BTO strategy is system sensitivity to short-term changes in customer demand. For example, if a particular computer component suddenly becomes wildly popular or temporarily unavailable, the standard supply in inventory may diminish fast, and customer orders will not be completed on time.

Chairman Michael Dell and CEO Kevin Rollins both agree that information technology is one of the critical sources of the company's competitive advantage. For instance, Dell's information systems, aligned with appropriate business processes and controls, allow the firm to keep only three days' worth of inven-tory and achieve well over a hundred inventory turns a year. If information tech-nology were a commodity, Michael Dell argues, then every company would have a similar inventory turnover. Since this is clearly not the case, Dell derives a competitive advantage from the low inventory levels.

Effective implementation of the build-to-order strategy is largely responsible for Dell's spectacular growth. Currently, Dell Inc. enjoys annual revenues of over $40 billion and employs over 47,000 people around the globe. Dell has become the global market-share leader in certain product categories. Furthermore, in 2004, Dell topped the entire list of Fortune 500 companies in 10-year total return to investors.

Sources: Kirkpatrick (2004); Holweg and Pil (2001); *dell.com* (accessed June 2004).

LESSONS LEARNED FROM THIS CASE

The example of Dell Inc. demonstrates that a company's business strategy has crucial implications for its operations, profitability, and capacity to meet the needs of its customers. The case also illustrates that information technology can facilitate strategy implementation and can become a source of competitive ad-vantage. The most important lesson learned from this case is the importance of planning and applying information systems in a way that complements the over-all strategies and tactics of the organization.

Computer-based information systems of all kinds have been enhancing com-petitiveness and creating strategic advantage for companies over several decades (e.g., see Griffiths et al., 1998, Galliers et al., 1999, and Ward and Peppard,

2002). Through numerous examples, this chapter demonstrates how different kinds of strategic information systems work. We also present some classic models on which strategic information systems have been built and utilized from the 1970s to this very day.

12.1 STRATEGIC ADVANTAGE AND INFORMATION TECHNOLOGY

The Competitive Forces Model

Any of the information systems we have introduced thus far in the text may be used, intentionally or in some cases unintentionally, to create a strategic advantage for a firm. One way to analyze the strategic impact of information systems is to consider their influence on one or more of the five forces presented in Porter's **competitive forces model** (see Appendix 1A, page 44). Take, for example, the strategic impact of Internet initiatives. Porter (2001) and Harmon et al. (2001) suggest some ways the Internet influences competition in the five factors:

1. *The threat of new entrants.* For most firms, the Internet *increases* the threat of new competitors. First, the Internet sharply reduces traditional barriers to entry, such as the need for a sales force or a physical storefront to sell goods and services. All a competitor needs to do is set up a Web site. This threat is especially acute in industries that perform an intermediation role as well as industries in which the primary product or service is digital. Second, the geographical reach of the Internet enables distant competitors to bring competition into the local market, or even an indirect competitor to compete more directly with an existing firm.

2. *The bargaining power of suppliers.* The Internet's impact on suppliers is mixed. On the one hand, buyers can find alternative suppliers and compare prices more easily, reducing the supplier's bargaining power. On the other hand, as companies use the Internet to integrate their supply chain and join digital exchanges, participating suppliers will prosper by locking in customers and increasing switching costs.

3. *The bargaining power of customers (buyers).* The Web greatly increases a buyer's access to information about products and suppliers, Internet technologies can reduce customer switching costs, and buyers can more easily buy from downstream suppliers. These factors mean that the Internet greatly increases customers' bargaining power.

4. *The threat of substitute products or services.* Information-based industries are in the greatest danger here. Any industry in which digitalized information can replace material goods (e.g., music, books, software) must view the Internet as a threat.

5. *The rivalry among existing firms in the industry.* The visibility of Internet applications on the Web makes proprietary systems more difficult to keep secret, reducing differences among competitors. In most industries, the tendency for the Internet to lower variable costs relative to fixed costs encourages price discounting at the same time that competition migrates to price. Both are forces that encourage destructive price competition in an industry.

Porter concludes that the *overall* impact of the Internet is to increase competition, which negatively impacts profitability. According to Porter, "The great paradox of the Internet is that its very benefits—making information widely available; reducing the difficulty of purchasing, marketing, and distribution; allowing buyers and sellers to find and transact business with one another more easily—also make it more difficult for companies to capture those benefits as profits" (2001, p. 66).

In many other ways Web-based systems are changing the nature of competition and even industry structure. Consider the following.

- Bookseller Barnes & Noble, hardware sales giant The Home Depot, and other companies have created independent online divisions, which are competing against the parent companies. Such companies are termed "click-and-mortar" companies, because they combine both "brick-and-mortar" and e-commerce operations.
- Any company that sells direct to consumers is becoming a distributor (wholesaler or retailer), competing against its own traditional distributors.
- The variable cost of a digital product is close to zero. Therefore, if large quantities are sold, the product's price can be so low that it might be given away, for free. For example, some predict that commissions for online stock trading will go to zero for this reason.
- Competitors are getting together and becoming more willing to share information. Examples are the vertical exchanges owned by industry leaders. The "Big Three" auto manufacturers, for example, operate the auto exchange *covisint.com*. Similar exchanges exist in the paper, chemical, and many other industries. (See Turban et al., 2006.)

Figure 12.1 (page 510) describes some potential ways in which the use of the Internet by organizations can alter industry structure. For example, buyers may have greater bargaining power as a result of the Internet for several reasons, including: Their access to various suppliers increases, their access to price information increases, and their ability to join forces with other buyers to obtain quantity discounts increases.

In some cases it is not a specific strategic information system that changes the nature of competition, but it is the Web technology itself that renders obsolete traditional business processes, brand names, and even superior products. One example is provided in *IT at Work 12.1* (page 511).

Strategies for Competitive Advantage   Porter's model identifies the forces that influence competitive advantage in the marketplace. It can provide insight into the potential impact of information systems on an industry. Aside from analyzing the impacts of systems on the industry, of significant importance to managers is the development of a *strategy* aimed at establishing a profitable and sustainable position against these five forces. To establish such a position, a company needs to develop a strategy of performing activities differently from a competitor.

Porter (1985) proposed cost leadership, differentiation, and niche strategies. Additional strategies have been proposed by other strategic-management authors (e.g., Neumann, 1994; Wiseman, 1988; Frenzel, 1996). In Appendix 1A (in Table 1A.1 on page 45), we listed 12 general strategies for gaining competitive advantage. We discuss seven of these strategies for competitive advantage here.

1. **Cost leadership strategy:** Produce products and/or services at the lowest cost in the industry. A firm achieves cost leadership in its industry by thrifty buying practices, efficient business processes, forcing up the prices paid by competitors, and helping customers or suppliers reduce their costs. A cost leadership example is the Wal-Mart automatic inventory replenishment

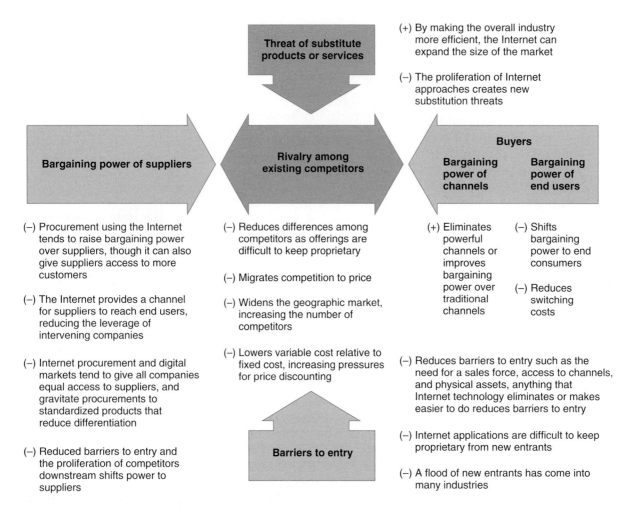

FIGURE 12.1 Porter's Competitive Forces Model: How the Internet influences industry structure. (*Source:* Reprinted by permission of *Harvard Business Review.* From "Strategy and the Internet" by Michael E. Porter, *Harvard Business Review,* March 2001. Copyright 2001 by the Harvard Business School Publishing Corporation: all rights reserved.)

system. This system enables Wal-Mart to reduce storage requirements so that Wal-Mart stores have one of the highest ratios of sales floor space in the industry. Essentially Wal-Mart is using floor space to sell products, not store them, and it does not have to tie up capital in inventory. Savings from this system and others allows Wal-Mart to provide low-priced products to its customers and still earn high profits.

2. **Differentiation strategy:** Offer different products, services, or product features. By offering different, "better" products, companies can charge higher prices, sell more products, or both. Southwest Airlines has differentiated itself as a low-cost, short-haul, express airline, and that has proven to be a winning strategy for competing in the highly competitive airline industry. Dell has differentiated itself in the personal computer market through its mass-customization strategy.

3. **Niche strategy:** Select a narrow-scope segment (niche market) and be the best in quality, speed, or cost in that market. For example, several

IT at Work 12.1
TECHNOLOGY INTRODUCES NEW COMPETITION FOR BRITANNICA

For generations *Encyclopaedia Britannica* was known for its world's-best content and brand name. However, in 1997 the company lost so much money that it was liquidated and sold for a fraction of its book value. What happened?

Microsoft started to sell a less-known encyclopedia, *Funk & Wagnalls*, on CD-ROMs for $50, under the name *Encarta*. Later on, the CD-ROMs were given away free with Microsoft PCs. In contrast, *Britannica*'s price was about $2,000. Furthermore, Encarta was media-rich. It included video clips, voices, and many pictures.

Britannica's sales declined rapidly. To compete, the company created a media-rich CD-ROM version, which was given free with the printed version. Without the print version, the CD-ROM was sold for $1,000. But very few people were willing to pay $1,000 when a competing product was available essentially for free.

Source: Venkatraman (2000).

For Further Exploration: What were the critical events that led to the demise of *Britannica*? What was the role of the Internet and Web in the demise of *Britannica*? Consult *britannica.com* to find out in what form *Britannica* has survived.

computer-chip manufacturers make customized chips for specific industries or companies. Some of the best-selling products on the Internet are niche products. For example, *dogtoys.com* and *cattoys.com* offer a large variety of pet toys that no other pet toy retailer offers.

4. **Growth strategy:** Increase market share, acquire more customers, or sell more products. Such a strategy strengthens a company and increases profitability in the long run. Web-based selling can facilitate growth by creating new marketing channels, such as electronic auctions. An example is Dell Computer (*dellauction.com*), which auctions both new and used computers mainly to individuals and small businesses.

5. **Alliance strategy:** Work with business partners in partnerships, alliances, joint ventures, or virtual companies. This strategy creates synergy, allows companies to concentrate on their core business, and provides opportunities for growth. Alliances are particularly popular in electronic commerce ventures. For example, in August 2000 Amazon.com and Toysrus.com launched a co-branded Web site to sell toys, capitalizing on each others' strengths. In spring 2001 they created a similar baby-products venture. Of special interest are alliances with suppliers, some of whom monitor inventory levels electronically and replenish inventory when it falls below a certain level (e.g., Wal-Mart, Master Builders). Alliances can also be made among competitors in a strategy known as "co-opetition" (cooperation + competition). For example, airlines in global alliances such as OneWorld and the Star Alliance compete for ticket sales on some routes, but once the ticket is sold they may cooperate by flying passengers on competitor's planes to avoid half-full planes. Additional examples of alliances are provided in Chapters 4 through 7.

6. **Innovation strategy:** Introduce new products and services, put new features in existing products and services, or develop new ways to produce them. Innovation is similar to differentiation except that the impact is much more dramatic. Differentiation "tweaks" existing products and services to offer the customer something special and different. Innovation implies

TABLE 12.1 Areas of IT Related to Technological Innovations

Innovation	Advantage
New business models	Being the first to establish a new model puts one way ahead of possible competitors. The Web enables many innovative new business models, such as Priceline's "name-your-own-price" and Auto-by-Tel's infomediary model. Creating and applying these models can provide strategic advantage.
New markets, global reach	Finding new customers in new markets. Using the Web, Amazon.com is selling books in over 200 countries, all by direct mail. Rosenbluth International, backed by its communication systems, expanded to 57 countries.
New products	Constantly innovating with new competitive products and services. Electronic Art Inc. was first to introduce CD-ROM-based video games. MP3 Inc. enabled downloading of music from its Web site.
Extended products	Leveraging old products with new competitive extensions. When a Korean company was the first to introduce "fuzzy logic" in its washing machines, sales went up 50 percent in a few months.
Differentiated products	Gaining advantage through unique products or added value. Compaq Computers at one time became the leading PC seller after providing self-diagnostic disks with its computers. Dell Computer pioneered the concept of home delivery of customized computers.
Supersystems	Erecting competitive barriers through major system developments that cannot be easily duplicated. American Airlines' reservation system, SABRE, became so comprehensive that it took years to duplicate; a supersystem always stays ahead of the competition. Caterpillar's multibillion-dollar equipment maintenance system is difficult to duplicate.
Interorganizational systems	Linking two organizational information systems together can lock out the competition. In the 1980s, American Hospital Supply installed supply-reordering systems in hospitals, to its competitive advantage.
Computer-aided sales	Offering systems that provide computer support to marketing and sales. For example, a company might equip salespeople with wireless hand-held computers that allow them to provide price quotations at the customer's location.

something so new and different that it changes the nature of the industry. A classic example is the introduction of automated teller machines (ATMs) by Citibank. The convenience and cost-cutting features of this innovation gave Citibank a huge advantage over its competitors. Like many innovative products, the ATM changed the nature of competition in the banking industry so that now an ATM network is a competitive necessity for any bank. Eight ways that IT can introduce technological innovation for competitive advantage are shown in Table 12.1.

In the late 1990s innovation became almost synonymous with electronic commerce. The Internet, especially, enabled dot-com entrepreneurs to create innovative Web-based business models, such as Priceline's name-your-own-price model, Auto-by-Tel's infomediary model, and Amazon.com's affiliate program.

A key consideration in introducing innovation is the need to continually innovate. When one company introduces a successful innovation, other companies in the industry need to respond to the threat by attempting to duplicate or better that innovation. Especially in electronic commerce, the visibility of technologies on the Web makes keeping innovations secret more difficult.

7. **Entry-barriers strategy:** Create barriers to entry. By introducing innovative products or using IT to provide exceptional service, companies can create

barriers to entry from new entrants. For example, Priceline.com has received U.S. patent 5,794,207 on its name-your-own-price business model (Lipton, 1998). Cisco's Dynamic Configuration Tool (*cisco.com/appcontent/apollo/configureHomeGuest.html*) allows prospective buyers to complete an online configuration of a Cisco product and receive intelligent feedback about compatibility and ordering. Service levels such as this make it difficult for new entrants to compete against Cisco. Firms may also create entry barriers by increasing the switching costs of customers or suppliers. A classic example is frequent-flyer and similar buyer-loyalty programs in the airline, hospitality, and retail industries. Companies that have such programs have more customers who are "locked in" by the incentives the loyalty programs offer. A business-to-business example in the car industry is e-procurement system Covisint, which locks in car manufacturers as customers and parts manufacturers as suppliers. By locking in customers, the firm is raising the barriers to entry.

These strategies may be interrelated. For example: Some innovations are achieved through alliances that reduce cost and increase growth; cost leadership improves customer satisfaction and may lead to growth; and alliances are key to locking in customers and increasing switching costs.

Almost 25 years after it was first published, Porter's competitive forces model remains the dominant framework for analyzing competitive advantage within an industry. A different way to analyze competition and the role of IT is provided in Porter's value chain model, which is the subject we turn to next.

12.2 PORTER'S VALUE CHAIN MODEL

The Model
The value chain can be diagrammed for both products and services and for any organization, private or public. (See Appendix 1A for the details of the value chain.) The initial purpose of the **value chain model** was to analyze the internal operations of a corporation, in order to increase its efficiency, effectiveness, and competitiveness. The model has since been used as a basis for explaining the support that IT can provide. It is also the basis for the *supply chain management* concept, which was presented in Chapter 8. *IT at Work 12.2* (page 514) offers a vivid example of a company that occupies a key portion of a supply chain.

The value chain model is useful in conducting a company analysis, by systematically evaluating a company's key processes and core competencies. To do so, we first determine strengths and weaknesses of performing the activities and the values added by each activity. The activities that add more value are those that might provide strategic advantage. Then we investigate whether by adding IT the company can get even greater added value and where in the chain its use is most appropriate. For example, Caterpillar uses EDI to add value to its inbound and outbound activities; it uses its intranet to boost customer service. In Chapters 4 through 11 we included many examples of how IT supports the activities of the value chain for individual firms. While initially developed with a manufacturing firm in mind, the value chain can also be applied to firms in a service industry, such as the airlines. Figure 12.2 (page 515) applies the framework to an airline.

Porter's Models in the Digital Age
The application of Porter's models is still valid today. But some adjustments may be needed to take into account the realities of business in the digital economy. Consider a company such as Amazon.com. Who are Amazon's competitors? It

IT at Work 12.2
MANAGING THE SUPPLY CHAIN AT 1-800-FLOWERS

1-800-Flowers sits in the middle of a complex and critical "customer supply chain." On one side of this supply chain are the customers who call the 1-800 number or visit the Web site (*1800flowers.com*) to order flowers or gifts. On the other side are the 1,500 floral affiliates who actually create and deliver the products. Maintaining satisfactory relationships on both sides of this supply chain is critical to 1-800-Flowers's success, and the key to those relationships is the electronic communications system the company has built.

When 1-800-Flowers opened for business in 1986 it was one of the first businesses to promote the 1-800 toll-free number system on a nationwide basis. The initial 1-800-Flowers system included a complex but effective system for directing incoming calls to agents in various call centers across the nation.

It was only natural that an intermediary that based its business on connecting customers and suppliers by a telephone network would be one of the first companies to see the potential of the Web. In 1995, 1-800-Flowers was one of the first three beta testers of the Netscape platform and launched its Web site later that year. Web-sourced orders, which amounted to approximately half of all orders in 2001, were woven into the existing telephone-based business through data-networking services. Customer purchases, customer profiles, and internal information created

an efficient, wired customer supply chain that helped 1-800-Flowers maintain a competitive advantage.

The next step was to wire-up the connection to the florists. In 1997, 1-800-Flowers initiated BloomLink, an extranet that sends orders out to affiliates and tracks progress in getting the shipments to customers. Additionally, BloomLink offers training programs and access to wholesale flower supply networks. This network helps lock in the suppliers and create switching costs. The significance of BloomLink is its ability to support both the business goal of order fulfillment and the competitive-advantage goal of supplier relationship management.

Like many companies in numerous industries, establishing and maintaining excellent relationships with customers and suppliers is critical to the success of 1-800-Flowers. By wiring up customers and suppliers on both sides of its supply chain, 1-800-Flowers has achieved its goals.

Sources: Reda (2002), Kemp (2001), and *1800flowers.com* (accessed June 2004).

For Further Exploration: Why was it necessary for the firm to develop e-commerce capabilities both upstream and downstream along its supply chain? What unique services does 1-800-Flowers offer that prevent customers from bypassing the firm and contacting the florists directly?

---

depends. In books they compete mainly against Barnes & Noble Online, in toys against Wal-Mart, Target, and Sears, and in music against CDNOW.com. Amazon.com could also be seen to compete against television, video games, and the Internet itself, because each of these compete for customers' leisure time. In that view, Amazon.com is not necessarily in the book-selling business, but in the entertainment business. Could we use one diagram such as Figure 1A.1 (p. 45) to describe Amazon.com's competitive environment? Probably not. We might need several figures, one for each of Amazon's major products. Furthermore, due to alliances (such as between Amazon.com and Toysrus.com), the competition and the value chain analysis can be fairly complex and frequently in flux.

For a presentation of strategic information systems frameworks proposed by other researchers, see Online File W12.1 at the book's Web site.

Porter's value chain provides a nice tool with which one can consider the potential impact of IT on an organization's activities. However, it is important to realize that the firm must have the appropriate resources to deploy in order to create the potential value-added applications. We next consider a framework that helps elucidate the potential of a firm's IT resources to serve as a basis for strategic advantage.

	Financial Policy	Accounting	Regulatory Compliance	Legal	Community Affairs	
Firm Infrastructure						

FIGURE 12.2 The airline industry value chain superimposed on Porter's value chain. (*Source:* Adapted by Callon, 1996, and reprinted by permission of *Harvard Business Review*. From Michael Porter, "How Competitive Forces Shape Strategy," March–April 1979. © 1979 by Harvard Business School Publishing Corporation; all rights reserved.)

12.3 STRATEGIC RESOURCES AND CAPABILITIES

IT can add value to a company in one of two general ways—either *directly* or *indirectly*. IT can add value *directly* by *reducing the costs* associated with a given activity or subset of activities. Cost reduction usually occurs when IT enables the same activity or set of activities to be performed more efficiently. Hence, the firm may reduce its workforce while not reducing its production level. Cost reduction is also possible when IT enables an activity to be redesigned such that it is performed more efficiently. In this case, personnel may also be reduced.

IT can add value *indirectly* by *increasing revenues*. The increase in revenues occurs when IT enables a firm to be more effective. This may occur when a firm is able to either produce more or service more without having to hire more employees. In other words, IT enables the firm to grow in terms of service and revenue without having to grow significantly more in terms of personnel. For example, IT can be used to enable self-service on the part of clients, which enables a firm both to decrease costs and increase revenues. The value chain is useful in visualizing those areas that may benefit from such value-added uses of IT.

However, there is another means by which IT can play a strategic role in a firm, and that is through enabling a temporary or sustained competitive advantage. Both a firm's IT and a firm's deployment of IT may provide a source of strategic advantage. The prevailing paradigm of understanding how and why firms gain and sustain competitive advantage is the **resource-based view (RBV)** of the firm (Schendel, 1994; Mahoney and Pandian, 1992). The resource-based view of the firm maintains that firms possess resources, some of which enable firms to gain competitive advantage and some of which allow firms to achieve superior long-term performance (Wade and Hulland, 2004; Barney, 1991). A firm may achieve a competitive advantage when it is implementing a strategy not currently pursued by rivals. However, the advantage will be temporary in cases where rivals may readily acquire the resources needed to implement the strategy. In cases where the resources enabling the strategy are difficult to acquire, the firm might enjoy a sustained competitive advantage.

Because of the central role played by resources in creating and sustaining strategic advantage, the resource-based view of the firm centers on understanding the nature of resources and their relationship to performance and competitiveness (Penrose, 1959; Andrews, 1971; Wernerfelt, 1984). Resources consist of assets and capabilities that are available and useful in sensing and responding to market opportunities or threats. Included as resources are physical capital (e.g., financial assets and technology), human capital (e.g., managerial skills), and various organizational resources (e.g., reputation, culture) (Barney, 1986 and 1991). Capabilities consist of a firm's capacity to *deploy* valued resources, usually in combination or in co-presence (Amit and Schoemaker, 1993; Schendel, 1994). Capabilities consist of such competencies as trustworthiness, organizational flexibility, rapid response to new customer trends, and short product life cycles. Capabilities are firm-specific and are developed over time (Barney and Hansen, 1994; Collis and Montgomery, 1995).

Three characteristics of resources give them the potential to create a strategic advantage: value, rarity, and "appropriability." Firm resources can be a source of competitive advantage only when they are *valuable*. A resource has value to the extent that it enables a firm to implement strategies that improve efficiency and effectiveness. But even if valuable, resources that are equitably distributed across organizations are commodities. Resources also must be *rare* in order to confer strategic advantages. Finally, to provide competitive advantage, a resource must be appropriable. *Appropriability* refers to the ability of the firm to create earnings through the resource. Even if a resource is rare and valuable, if the firm expends more effort to obtain the resource than it generates through the resource, then the resource will not create a strategic advantage. Wade and Hulland (2004) give the example of firms attempting to hire ERP-knowledgeable personnel during the 1999–2000 time period, only to discover that they were unable to appropriate a return on their investment because of the higher compensation demanded by these high-in-demand (and hence, rare) and valuable knowledge resources.

The three characteristics described above are used to characterize resources that can create an initial competitive advantage. In order for the competitive advantage to be sustained, however, the resources must be inimitable, imperfectly mobile, and have low substitutability. *Imitability* is the facility with which another firm can copy the resource. Factors that contribute to low imitability include firm history, causal ambiguity, and social complexity (Wade and Hulland, 2004). *Substitutability* refers to the ability of competing firms to substitute an alternative resource in lieu of the resources deployed by the first-moving firm

TABLE 12.2 Key Resource Attributes that Create Competitive Advantage

Resource Attributes	Description
Value	The degree to which a resource can help a firm improve efficiency or effectiveness.
Rarity	The degree to which a resource is nonheterogeneously distributed across firms in an industry.
Appropriability	The degree to which a firm can make use of a resource without incurring an expense that exceeds the value of the resource.
Imitability	The degree to which a resource can be readily emulated.
Mobility	The degree to which a resource is easy to transport.
Substitutability	The degree to which another resource can be used in lieu of the original resource to achieve value.

in achieving an advantage. Finally, *mobility* (or *tradability*) refers to the degree to which a firm may easily acquire the resource necessary to imitate a rival's competitive advantage. Some resources, such as hardware and software, are easy to acquire and are thus highly mobile and unlikely to generate sustained competitive advantage. Even if a resource is rare, if it is possible to either purchase the resource (or in the case of a rare expertise, hire the resource), then the resource is mobile and incapable of contributing to a sustained advantage. Table 12.2 summarizes the key attributes and their definitions.

Thus far, we have described the resource-based view of the firm; now let us consider information systems (technology, skills, management) as a resource for a firm. Through the RBV model, we can consider the ways in which information systems contribute to strategic advantages for a firm. Information systems can contribute three types of resources to a firm: technology resources, technical capabilities, and IT managerial resources.

Technology resources include the IS infrastructure, proprietary technology, hardware, and software. The IS infrastructure is "the base foundation of IT capability, delivered as reliable services shared throughout the firm and coordinated centrally, usually by the information systems group" (Weill and Broadbent, 2000, p. 333). The creation of a successful infrastructure may take several years to achieve and is somewhat different for each organization. Thus, even while competitors might readily purchase the same hardware and software, the combination of these resources to develop a flexible infrastructure is a complex task. IS infrastructure is valuable in that it enables a firm to quickly deploy new systems in a growing market (Leidner et al., 2003). It may take firms many years to catch up with the infrastructure capabilities of rivals, even as KMart has lagged consistently behind Wal-Mart in deploying IT. As such, even IS infrastructure may be viewed as having the potential for providing strategic advantage in certain industries.

Technical capabilities (skills) include IS technical knowledge (programming languages), IS development knowledge (experience with new technologies and experience with different development platforms), and IS operations (cost-effective operations and support). Technical IT skills include the expertise needed to build and use IT applications (Copeland and McKenney, 1988; Dehning and Stratopoulous, 2003). Technical skills are not considered to be valid sources of sustained competitive advantage for several reasons. Firstly, they are not heterogeneously distributed across firms, and even if they were, they are highly mobile due to the codifiable nature of technical IT skills (Dehning and

Stratopoulous, 2003). However, the ease with which technical training can be carried out in a company as well as the facility of interchanging IT personnel is highly debatable. One study found that the best programmers tended to congregate in a few highly desirable technology companies (Demarco and Lister, 1987). As a result, IT skills might not be as mobile and substitutable as appears on the surface. In this sense, IT skills may form the basis of competitive advantage to a firm in an industry where staying abreast of technology is a critical aspect of being competitive.

Managerial resources include both those related to IS and those related to IT. IS managerial resources include vendor relationships, outsourcer relationship management, market responsiveness, IS-business partnerships, and IS planning and change management. Managerial IT skills refer to management's ability to conceive, develop, and exploit IT applications (Mata et al., 1995; Dehning and Stratopoulos, 2003).

Dehning and Stratopoulous (2003) associate managerial IT skills with a sustainable competitive advantage for four reasons: First, these skills enable companies to manage the technical as well as the market risks associated with investments in IT (Bharadwaj, 2000; Mata et al., 1995). Second, they are developed over time through the accumulation of experience. Third, they are tacit and causally ambiguous; and fourth, they are the result of socially complex processes. For more details on these IS resources, see Wade and Hulland (2004).

Table 12.3 provides definitions for these IS resources and capabilities and suggests the degree to which they embody the attributes described in Table 12.2.

We have presented three models to help understand the relationship of information systems to strategic advantage. These models can be useful in providing tools for analyzing the current impact that systems are having on a firm and industry. They also may be useful in highlighting potential high-impact areas where systems are not currently used. It is the responsibility of IT management to foresee the role that new IT can play in terms of supporting business activities ahead of the competition. In order to achieve strategic advantage through IT, a firm must carefully plan its IT investments. We therefore now turn to the topic of IT planning.

TABLE 12.3 IS Resources and Capabilities

IS Resource/Capability	Description	Relationship to Resource Attributes
Technology resources	Includes infrastructure, proprietary technology, hardware, and software.	Not necessarily rare or valuable, but difficult to appropriate and imitate. Low mobility but a fair degree of substitutability.
IT skills	Includes technical knowledge, development knowledge, and operational skills.	Highly mobile, but less imitable or substitutable. Not necessarily rare but highly valuable.
Managerial IT resources	Includes vendor and outsourcer relationship skills, market responsiveness, IS-business partnerships, IS planning and management skills.	Somewhat more rare than the technology and IT skill resources. Also of higher value. High mobility given the short tenure of CIOs. Nonsubstitutable.

12.4 IT PLANNING—A CRITICAL ISSUE FOR ORGANIZATIONS

IT planning is the organized planning of IT infrastructure and applications portfolios done at various levels of the organization. The topic of IT planning is very important for both planners and end users: End-users often do IT planning for their own units, and they also frequently participate in the corporate IT planning. Therefore, end-users must understand the planning process. Corporate IT planning determines how the IT infrastructure will look. This in turn determines what applications end users can deploy. Thus the future of every unit in the organization could be impacted by the IT infrastructure.

Business Importance and Content

A survey of more than 500 IT executives, conducted in 2003 by *cio.com*, revealed that *strategic thinking and planning* was the number-one concern for CIOs (*cio.com*, 2003). It was also among the top issues in 2000 and 2001. Why does strategic planning continuously rank high as an issue of concern among IT executives? Simply put, because IT has to work closely with an organization's business side to make sure the company stays competitive. Aligning the goals of the organization and the ability of IT to contribute to those goals can deliver great gains in productivity to the organization. According to Blodgett (1998), as the demands of an increasingly competitive workplace call for closer integration of IT goals and the business mission, strategic plans for the whole enterprise become more important. In addition, with advances in Web-based supply chain collaborations and integration of e-marketplaces with buyers, sellers, and service providers, a good business strategy involves an IT strategy that keeps in mind the internal customers as well as the external customers and vendors. Aligning IT with the business is a process rather than an event, and IT strategy should be based on adding value to the organization's activities.

The Evolution of IT Planning

During the early years of information technology, in the late 1950s and 1960s, developing new applications and then revising existing systems were the focal points for the first planning and control systems. Organizations adopted methodologies for developing systems, and they installed project management systems to assist with implementing new applications. These initial mechanisms addressed *operational* planning. As organizations became more sophisticated in their use of information systems, emphasis shifted to *managerial* planning, or resource-allocation control. In the 1990s, the role of IT evolved to helping organizations to reach their business goals and to create competitive advantage. Currently the particular focus of IT strategy is on how IT creates business value.

Typically, annual planning cycles are established to identify potentially beneficial IT services, to perform cost-benefit analyses, and to subject the list of potential projects to resource-allocation analysis. Often the entire process is conducted by an IT *steering committee* (see Chapter 15). The steering committee reviews the list of potential projects, approves the ones considered to be beneficial, and assigns them relative priorities. The approved projects are then mapped onto a development schedule, usually encompassing a one- to three-year time frame. This schedule becomes the basis for determining IT resources requirements such as long-range hardware, software, personnel, facilities, and financial requirements.

Some organizations extend this planning process by developing additional plans for longer time horizons. They have a *long-range IT plan*, sometimes referred to as the *strategic IT plan* (see Ward and Peppard, 2002; and Boar, 2000). This plan typically does not refer to specific projects; instead it sets the overall directions in terms of infrastructure and resource requirements for IT activities for five to ten years in the future.

The next level down is a *medium-term IT plan*. It identifies the **applications portfolio,** a list of major, approved IS projects that are consistent with the long-range plan. Since some of these projects will take more than a year to complete, and others will not start in the current year, this plan extends over several years. For more on applications portfolios, see Online File W12.2.

The third level is a *tactical plan,* which has budgets and schedules for current-year projects and activities. In reality, because of the rapid pace of change in technology and the environment, short-term plans may include major items not anticipated in the other plans.

The planning process just described is currently practiced by many organizations. Specifics of the IT planning process, of course, vary among organizations. For example, not all organizations have a high-level IT steering committee. Project priorities may be determined by the IT director, by his or her superior, by company politics, or even on a first-come, first-served basis.

A Four-Stage Model of IT Planning

Several models have been developed to facilitate IT planning (e.g., see Ward and Peppard, 2002; Cassidy, 1998; and Papp, 2001). Of special interest is Wetherbe's (1993) **four-stage model of planning.** The model (depicted in Figure 12.3) consists of four major activities—*strategic planning, requirements analysis, resource allocation,* and *project planning*—and it is valid today. The stages involve the following activities:

- *Strategic IT planning:* establishes the relationship between the overall organizational plan and the IT plan
- *Information requirements analysis:* identifies broad, organizational information requirements to establish a strategic information architecture that can be used to direct specific application development
- *Resource allocation:* allocates both IT application development resources and operational resources
- *Project planning:* develops a plan that outlines schedules and resource requirements for specific information systems projects

Most organizations engage in all four stages, but their involvement in the specific stages tends to be sporadic and prompted by problems as they occur, instead of reflecting a systematic, stage-by-stage process. The four-stage model can be expanded to include major activities and outputs of the four stages. The model moves from a high level of abstraction to a more concrete formulation of IT planning activities. Some useful methodologies for conducting each planning stage are discussed later in this chapter.

The four-stage planning model is the foundation for the development of a portfolio of applications that is both highly aligned with the corporate goals and

FIGURE 12.3 Basic four-stage model of IS planning.

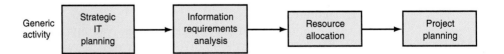

has the ability to create an advantage over competitors. There is also a relationship between the four-stage planning model and the various versions of the system development life cycle (SDLC) described in Chapter 14. The four-stage planning model identifies projects and general resource requirements necessary to achieve organizational objectives. In Sections 12.5 and 12.6, we describe the four stages in more detail.

Let's now begin at Stage 1 in the four-stage model of IT planning.

12.5 STRATEGIC IT PLANNING (STAGE 1)

The first stage of the IT planning model is **strategic information technology planning (SITP).** It includes several somewhat different types of activities. On the one hand, it refers to identifying the *applications portfolio* through which an organization will conduct its business. These applications make it possible for an organization to implement its business strategies in a competitive environment.

On the other hand, SITP can also refer to a process of searching for *strategic information systems (SIS)* applications that enable an organization to develop a competitive advantage, rather than just maintaining its position. To accomplish this goal, the organization must do some creative thinking: This involves assessing the current business environment and the organization's objectives and strategies, understanding the capabilities of existing systems, and looking ahead to how new IT systems could produce future advantages for the organization.

The output from the SITP process should include the following: a new or revised IT charter and assessment of the state of the information systems department; an accurate evaluation of the strategic goals and directions of the organization; and a statement of the objectives, strategies, and policies for the IT effort.

Ward and Peppard (2002) provided a more in-depth analysis on the strategic planning and proposed a framework for IT strategy formulation and planning. Details are found in Online File W12.3.

IT Alignment with Organizational Plans

Improving the planning process for information systems has long been one of the top concerns of information systems department management. The Society for Information Management (SIM) (*simnet.org,* 2002) found this to be the number-one issue in surveys of senior IT executives in 1997/1998. A survey of 420 organizations, conducted by NCC in 2003 (*ncc.co.uk,* 2003), found that keeping IT strategy aligned with business strategy was their number-one strategic concern.

Strategic information technology planning (SITP) must be aligned with overall organizational planning, whenever relevant, so that the IT unit and other organizational personnel are working toward the same goals, using their respective competencies (Chan, 2002; Pickering, 2000; Ward and Peppard, 2002). The primary task of IT planning is therefore to identify information systems applications that fit the objectives and priorities established by the organization. Figure 12.4 (page 522) graphically illustrates the alignment of IS strategy, business strategy, and IT strategy and deployment. *IT at Work 12.3* (page 523) demonstrates how alignment was done at Hewlett-Packard. For another example of alignment of business strategy and IT strategy, see Cale and Kanter (1998).

Aligning IT with the organization has two facets. One facet is aligning the IS function's strategy, structure, technology, and processes with those of the

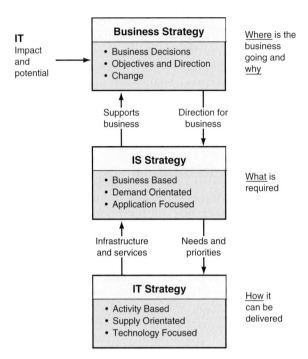

FIGURE 12.4 The relationship among business, IS, and IT strategies. (*Source:* Ward and Peppard, 2002, Figure 1.6, p. 41.)

business units so that IS and business units are working toward the same goals. This facet is referred to as *IS alignment* (Chan, 2002). Another type of alignment, referred to as *IS strategic alignment,* involves aligning IS strategy with organizational strategy. The goal of IS strategic alignment is to ensure that IS priorities, decisions, and projects are consistent with the needs of the entire business. Failure to properly align IS with the organizational strategy may result in large investments in systems that have a low payoff, or failure to invest in systems that might potentially have a high payoff.

In order to achieve IT alignment, several preconditions must be achieved. Among these is communication between the line and IS executives and interconnected planning processes, such that IS planning does not occur in a vacuum (Chan, 2002). A recent report conducted by Deloitte Consulting LLP found that 96 percent of IT executives polled indicated that significant or moderate bottom-line impact would result from aligning IT strategy with business strategy. Yet, many still felt that their alignment efforts were unsuccessful (Beal, 2004). Another precondition for successful alignment is a clear definition of IT's role in an organization. A major challenge is that the technology infrastructures built to support one strategy often outlast the strategy that they were intended to support (Beal, 2004).

CHALLENGES FOR IT ALIGNMENT. Despite the theoretical importance of IT alignment, organizations continue to demonstrate limited actual alignment. People 3 Inc. (2003) reported that about 65 percent of companies have either a negative or neutral view of the ability of IT and business managers to work together in supporting corporate goals and objectives. Alignment is a complex management activity (Hackney et al., 2000), and its complexity increases in accordance with the increasing complexity of organizations. A study conducted by

IT at Work 12.3
HEWLETT-PACKARD ALIGNS BUSINESS AND IT STRATEGIES

Hewlett-Packard (*hp.com*) developed a planning methodology in which business process strategies and technologies are defined and aligned concurrently. This methodology was designed to allow the company to make process changes regardless of the limitations of the existing technology, and it gives visibility to the impacts that new technologies and processes have on each other.

In the past, Hewlett-Packard had used a sequential process. First, it defined the business strategy and the operations and supporting strategies, including technologies. Then, all these functions were aligned and replanned, taking into consideration the technologies available. In the new methodology, the planning is performed for all areas *concurrently*. Furthermore, the entire approach is complemented by a strong focus on teamwork, specialized and objective-driven functional areas and business units, and a commitment to quality and customer satisfaction. The approach links strategy and action. The business alignment framework takes into account the necessary process changes resulting from changes in the business environment, as well as potential technological developments. But, because major changes may result in a change in value systems as well as culture and team structures of the

organization, H-P includes these factors within the planning methodology.

Target processes, technologies, and standards drive the selection of potential solutions. The participative management approach ensures effective implementation. According to the framework, business processes and information requirements are defined in parallel with technology enablers and models, which are then linked throughout the alignment process.

H-P's focus on strategic alignment is evident not only in its planning for internal technology solutions, but also in its quest for technological innovation through a centralized R&D function with an annual budget of $4 billion. The R&D function actively participates in the strategy development process, which helps the R&D department better understand what is driving customers while simultaneously offering a strong technology perspective that influences the business as a whole.

Sources: Compiled from Feurer et al. (2000), Collins (2004), and *hp.com* (June 2004).

For Further Exploration: Why is concurrent planning superior? What communication and collaboration support is needed?

Chan (2002) also found that informal organizational structure results in better IT alignment and performance. (For a listing of the fundamental assumptions upon which the SITP process is grounded, and the challenges to those assumptions, see Online File W12.4 and Hackney et al., 2000.)

Tools and Methodologies of IT Planning

Several tools and methodologies exist to facilitate IT planning. These methods are used to help organizations to align their business IT/IS strategies with the organizational strategies, to identify opportunities to utilize IT for competitive advantage, and to analyze internal processes. Most of these methodologies start with some investigation of strategy that checks the industry, competition, and competitiveness, and relates them to technology (*alignment*). Others help create and justify new uses of IT (*impact*).

Ward and Peppard (2002) further categorized these tools and methodologies with respect to their nature (see Online File W12.5). In the next section, we look briefly at some of these methodologies.

THE BUSINESS SYSTEMS PLANNING (BSP) MODEL. The **business systems planning (BSP) model** was developed by IBM, and it has influenced other planning efforts such as Andersen Consulting's (now Accenture's) *method/1* and Martin and Finkelstein's *information engineering* (Martin and Finkelstein, 1981).

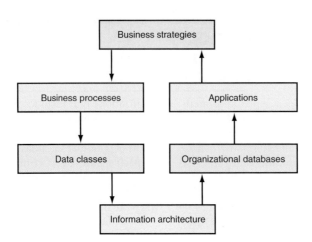

FIGURE 12.5 Business systems planning (BSP) approach. (*Source:* Derived from *Business Systems Planning—Information Systems Planning Guide,* Application Manual GE20-0527-3, 3rd ed., IBM Corporation, July 1981. Courtesy of the International Business Machines Corporation.)

BSP is a top-down approach that starts with business strategies. It deals with two main building blocks—*business processe*s and *data classes*—which become the basis of an information architecture. From this architecture, planners can define organizational databases and identify applications that support business strategies, as illustrated in Figure 12.5.

BSP relies heavily on the use of metrics in the analysis of processes and data, with the ultimate goal of developing the information architecture. (For details see Business Systems Planning, 1981.)

THE STAGES OF IT GROWTH MODEL. Nolan (1979) indicated that organizations go through six **stages of IT growth** (called "IS growth" at that time). *A Closer Look 12.1* describes these six stages. In each stage, four processes are active to varying degrees. These are the applications portfolio, users' role and awareness, IT resources, and management planning and control techniques. The *y* axis in the figure in *A Closer Look 12.1* refers to IT expenditures. Note that the growth *rate* of IT expenses is low during data administration, medium during initiation and maturity, and high during expansion (contagion) and integration. In addition to serving as a guide for expenditure, the model helps in determining the seriousness of problems. (For more on Nolan's stages of IT growth, see Online File W12.6.)

The *stages of growth model* was initially intended to explain the growth and maturity of the IT department in an organization. Another way to use the model is to consider that each major system progresses through these growth stages in such a way that an organization might be at the maturity level regarding TPS but at the integration level regarding KM. This underscores an enduring challenge for IS departments in large organizations: One unit of the organization might be predominantly at an initiation stage with its systems (such as a unit in a developing nation), whereas another unit of the same organization in a well-developed region might be mostly at the maturity level. Thus, achieving enterprisewide systems would be particularly challenging in such a situation.

CRITICAL SUCCESS FACTORS. **Critical success factors (CSFs)** are those few things that must go right in order to ensure the organization's survival and success. The *CSF approach* to IT planning was developed to help identify the

A CLOSER LOOK
12.1 NOLAN'S SIX STAGES OF IT GROWTH MODEL

The six stages of IT growth (see the figure below) are:

1. **Initiation.** When computers are initially introduced to the organization, batch processing is used to automate clerical operations in order to achieve cost reduction. There is an operational systems focus, general lack of management interest, and a centralized information systems department (ISD).

2. **Expansion (Contagion).** Centralized rapid growth takes place as users demand more applications based on high expectations of benefits. There is a move to online systems as ISD tries to satisfy all user demands and little, if any, control. IT expenses increase rapidly.

3. **Control.** In response to management concern about cost versus benefits, systems projects are expected to show a return, plans are produced, and methodologies/standards are enforced. The control stage often produces a backlog of applications and dissatisfied users. Planning and controls are introduced.

4. **Integration.** There is considerable expenditure on integrating (via telecommunications and databases)

existing systems. User accountability for systems is established, and ISD provides a service to users, not just solutions to problems. At this time there is a transition in computer use and an approach from data processing to information and knowledge processing (transition between the two curves).

5. **Data administration.** Information requirements rather than processing drive the applications portfolio, and information is shared within the organization. Database capability is exploited as users understand the value of the information and are willing to share it.

6. **Maturity.** The planning and development of IT in the organization are closely coordinated with business development. Corporate-wide systems are in place. The ISD and the users share accountability regarding the allocation of computing resources. IT has truly become a strategic partner.

Source: Compiled from R. L. Nolan, "Managing the Crises in Data Processing," *Harvard Business Review,* March–April 1979. Reprinted with permission of the *Harvard Business Review.*

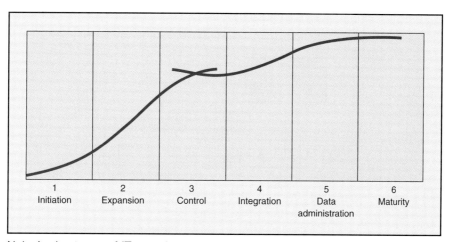

Nolan's six stages of IT growth

information needs of managers. The fundamental assumption is that in every organization there are three to six key factors that, if done well, will result in the organization's success. Therefore organizations should continuously measure performance in these areas, taking corrective action whenever necessary. CSFs also exist in business units, departments, and other organizational units.

Critical success factors vary by broad industry categories—manufacturing, service, or government—and by specific industries within these categories. For organizations in the same industry, CSFs will vary depending on whether the firms are market leaders or weaker competitors, where they are located, and what competitive strategies they follow. Environmental issues, such as the degree of regulation or amount of technology used, influence CSFs. In addition, CSFs change over time based on temporary conditions, such as high interest rates or long-term trends.

IT planners identify CSFs by interviewing managers in an initial session, and then refine these CSFs in one or two additional sessions. Sample questions asked in the CSF approach are:

- What objectives are central to your organization?
- What are the critical factors that are essential to meeting these objectives?
- What decisions or actions are key to these critical factors?
- What variables underlie these decisions, and how are they measured?
- What information systems can supply these measures?

The first step following the interviews is to determine the organizational objectives for which the manager is responsible, and then the factors that are critical to attaining these objectives. The second step is to select a small number of CSFs. Then, one needs to determine the information requirements for those CSFs and measure to see whether the CSFs are met. If they are not met it is necessary to build appropriate applications (see Figure 12.6).

The critical success factors approach encourages managers to identify what is most important to their performance and then develop good indicators of performance in these areas. Conducting interviews with all key people makes

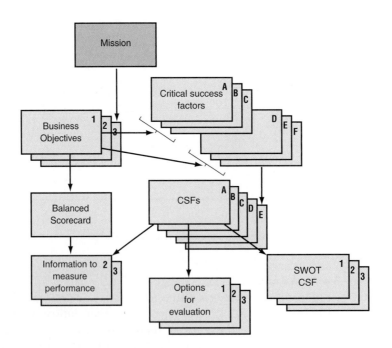

FIGURE 12.6 Critical success factors—basic processes. (*Source:* Ward and Peppard, 2002, Figure 4.7, p. 211.)

it less likely that key items will be overlooked. On the other hand, the emphasis on critical factors avoids the problem of collecting too much data, or including some data just because they are easy to collect.

SCENARIO PLANNING. **Scenario planning** is a methodology in which planners first create several scenarios, then a team compiles as many future events as possible that may influence the outcome of each scenario. This approach is used in planning situations that involve much uncertainty, like that of IT in general and e-commerce in particular. With the rapid changes of technologies and business environment, Stauffer (2002) emphasized the need for scenario planning. Five reasons to do scenario planning are: (1) to ensure that you are not focusing on catastrophe to the exclusion of opportunity, (2) to help you allocate resources more prudently, (3) to preserve your options, (4) to ensure that you are not still "fighting the last war," and (5) to give you the opportunity to rehearse testing and training of people to go through the process. Scenario planning follows a rigorous process; the essential steps are summarized in Table 12.4.

Scenario planning has been widely used by major corporations to facilitate IT planning (e.g., *ncri.com* and *gbn.com*). It also has been particularly important to e-commerce planning. For instance, creating customer scenarios helps the company better fit the products and services into the real lives of the customers, resulting in sales expansion and customer loyalty. Seybold (2001) described three cases (National Semiconductor, Tesco, Buzzsaw.com) that used customer scenarios to strengthen customer relationships, to guide business strategy, and to deliver business value.

Although EC proliferation would certainly allow any combination or variation of business scenarios, each company has to select the most appropriate model for its needs. The use of this model can help EC planners to determine the EC initiatives that best fit their organization.

TABLE 12.4 Essential Steps of Scenario Planning

- Determine the scope and time frame of the scenario you are fleshing out.
- Identify the current assumptions and mental models of individuals who influence these decisions.
- Create a manageable number of divergent, yet plausible, scenarios. Spell out the underlying assumptions of how each of these imagined futures might evolve.
- Test the impact of key variables in each scenario.
- Develop action plans based on either (a) the solutions that play most robustly across scenarios, or (b) the most desirable outcome toward which a company can direct its efforts.
- Monitor events as they unfold to test the corporate direction; be prepared to modify it as required.

The educational experience that results from this process includes:

- Stretching your mind beyond the groupthink that can slowly and imperceptibly produce a sameness of minds among top team members in any organization.
- Learning the ways in which seemingly remote potential developments may have repercussions that hit close to home.
- Learning how you and your colleagues might respond under both adverse and favorable circumstances.

Source: Compiled from Stauffer (2002).

12.6 INFORMATION REQUIREMENTS ANALYSIS, RESOURCE ALLOCATION, AND PROJECT PLANNING (STAGES 2–4)

The next three stages of the four-stage planning model are interrelated; they start with information requirements.

Information Requirements Analysis: Stage 2 of the 4-Stage Model

The second stage of the model is the **information requirements analysis,** which is an analysis of the information needs of users and how that information relates to their work. The goal of this second stage is to ensure that the various information systems, databases, and networks can be integrated to support the requirements identified in stage 1 to enable decision making.

In the first step of information requirements analysis, IT planners assess what information is needed to support current and projected decision making and operations in the organization. This is different from the detailed information requirements analysis associated with developing *individual* application systems (i.e., identifying required outputs and the inputs necessary to generate them, which we describe in Chapter 14). Rather, the stage 2 information requirements analysis is at a more comprehensive level of analysis. It encompasses infrastructures such as the data needed in a large number of applications (e.g., in a data warehouse or a data center) for the whole organization. Similarly, requirements for the intranet, extranet, and corporate part are established.

There are several alternative approaches for conducting the requirements analysis. One of them is presented as a five-step model in Table 12.5. Also, some of the methods described in Chapter 14, such as JAD, can be used here.

The results of the requirements analysis exercise are threefold: It identifies high-payoff information categories, it provides a basis for the architecture of IT, and it guides in resource allocation.

IDENTIFYING HIGH PAYOFFS. To determine which IT projects will produce the highest organizational payoff, the organization can identify categories with high

---

TABLE 12.5 The Five-Step Requirements-Analysis Model

Step 1: Define underlying organizational subsystems. The first step is to identify the underlying organizational processes, such as order fulfillment or product analysis.

Step 2: Develop a subsystem matrix. The next phase is to relate specific managers to organizational processes. This relationship can be represented by a matrix. The matrix is developed by reviewing the major decision responsibilities of each middle-to-top manager and relating them to specific processes.

Step 3: Define and evaluate information requirements for organizational subsystems. In this phase, managers with major decision-making responsibility for each process are interviewed in groups by information analysts in order to obtain the information requirements of each organizational process.

Step 4: Define major information categories and map interview results into them. The process of defining information categories is similar to the process of defining data items for individual application into entities and attributes.

Step 5: Develop an information/subsystem matrix. Mapping information categories against organizational subsystems creates an information-categories-by-organizational-process matrix. Information categories can be, for example, accounts receivable, customers' demographics, or products' warranties. In each cell of the matrix an important information category value is inserted.

importance-value scores, and should consider them first for feasibility. In order to identify high payoff, planners use a matrix that relates information categories to organizational processes. But this matrix does not indicate whether it is technically, economically, or operationally feasible to develop systems for each information category. The matrix merely indicates the relative importance of information. Feasibility studies and other project-related tasks must still be performed, as described in Chapter 14. This step requires substantial creativity (e.g., see Ruohonen and Higgins, 1998). An example of identifying high-payoff projects is provided at *IT at Work 12.4* (page 530).

PROVIDING AN ARCHITECTURE. Clearly defining the intersection of information and processes helps an organization avoid separate, redundant information systems for different organizational processes. When an organization decides to improve information for one process, other processes that need such information can be taken into consideration. By completing the conceptual work first, an organization can identify information systems projects that offer the most benefit and lead to cohesive, integrated systems. The resulting systems are far better than the fragmented, piecemeal systems that must continually be reworked or abandoned because they do not mesh with the organization's general requirements. To develop such integrated systems requires systematic planning from the top down, rather than randomly from the bottom up, and this is done in the architecture phase. In Chapter 13, we describe how this has been done in the State of Iowa (see the opening case there).

GUIDANCE IN RESOURCE ALLOCATION. Once high-payoff areas of IT have been identified, it is reasonable to give those areas high priority when the organization allocates resources. Such an allocation is described next.

Resource Allocation: Stage 3 of the 4-Stage Model

Resource allocation, the third stage of the IT planning model, consists of developing the hardware, software, data communications and networks, facilities, personnel, and financial plans needed to execute the master development plan as defined in the requirements analysis. This stage provides the framework for technology and labor procurement, and it identifies the financial resources needed to provide appropriate service levels to users. The financial aspect will be discussed briefly here (with a more in-depth discussion in Chapter 13).

Resource allocation is a contentious process in most organizations because opportunities and requests for spending far exceed the available funds. (See the opening case in Chapter 13.) This can lead to intense, highly political competition among organizational units, which makes it difficult to objectively identify the most desirable investments.

Requests for funding approval from the steering committee fall into two categories. Some projects and infrastructure are necessary in order for the organization to stay in business. For example, it may be imperative to purchase or upgrade hardware if the network, or disk drives, or the processor on the main computer are approaching capacity limits. Obtaining approval for this type of spending is largely a matter of communicating the gravity of the problems to decision makers.

On the other hand, the IT planning process identifies an information architecture that usually requires additional funding for less critical items: new projects, maintenance or upgrades of existing systems, and infrastructure to support these

IT at Work 12.4
IDENTIFYING HIGH-PAYOFF PROJECTS

Wing Fat Foods (WFF) is a wholesaler, delivering perishable and nonperishable foodstuffs, as well as hardware, kitchenware, and household goods, to restaurants, groceries, and similar businesses along the Atlantic Coast of the United States. WFF is famous for its quality and service, which is accomplished with a relatively low level of IT investment. WFF hopes that its additional IT investment will help it to sustain its edge over competitors.

In response to the need of identifying potential new IT projects, Peffers and Gengler (2003) proposed to WFF a new method, the *critical success chain (CSC) method,* for IT planning. The CSC method includes four steps:

Step 1: Pre-study preparation: Determine scope and participants and collect project idea stimuli. The analyst invited 25 IT users (6 senior managers, 11 middle managers, 5 journeyman employees, and 3 WFF customers) to participate in an in-depth interview. At the same time, she collected project ideas to serve as stimuli. For example, she asked each participant to describe the functionality of a system that would benefit WFF.

Step 2: Participant interviews: Elicit personal constructs from organization members. The analyst then conducted 25–50 minute interviews with each participant, showing the participant three system descriptions and asking them to rank the system attributes and explain their importance

to the organization. A line of questions was asked until the participants suggested a concrete feature or attribute that would become part of the project idea. This line of questions was designed to produce specific ideas for features of the system, expected performance, and related organizational values or objectives. In this study, the analyst collected about 8 chains of suggestions per participant.

Step 3: Analysis: Aggregate personal constructs into CSC models. The analyst first clustered the interview statements into constructs and mapped the constructs into a matrix. She then clustered the chains using the Ward and Peppard strategic planning framework (found in Online File W12.3). Mapping each cluster into a CSC map, she represented the constructs as nodes and the links in the chains as lines connecting the nodes. The figure on page 531 depicts an organization-specific CSC model consisting of, from left to right, descriptions of desired system attributes, resulting expected performance outcomes (CSF), and associated organizational goals.

Step 4: Idea workshops: Elicit feasible strategic IT from technical and business experts and customers. The CSC maps were used by both IT professionals from within WFF and non-IT customers as a starting point for developing a portfolio of IT proposals. Providing the technical

(continues on page 531)

systems and future needs. Approval for projects in this category may become more difficult to obtain because the ISD is already receiving funding for mandatory projects.

After setting aside funds for the first category, the organization can use the remainder of the IT budget for projects related mainly to the improved information architecture. The organization can prioritize spending among items in the architecture developed by using information requirements analysis. In addition to formally allocating resources through budgeting decisions, an organization can use chargeback mechanisms to fund corporate-level projects. In a *chargeback system,* some or all of a system's cost is charged to users. In addition, management may encourage individual units to make their own decisions about IT expenses. Chapter 13 discusses chargeback, cost-benefit analysis, and other, more sophisticated analyses that can also be used to assess investments in individual IT projects as well as infrastructure.

Another major factor in resource allocation is the *outsourcing strategy* (Chapter 13). The more that is outsourced, the less capital investment and internal resources are needed.

and business experts at WFF with the CSC maps, the workshop finally yielded 14 project ideas, including a decision support system for scheduling, routing, and loading trucks for delivery, as well as the support activities for existing systems, including training and updated equipment and maintenance support.

Sources: Compiled from Peffers and Gengler (2003).

For Further Exploration: Why is the method called the CS chain? Why is such a lengthy process, with so many participants, needed?

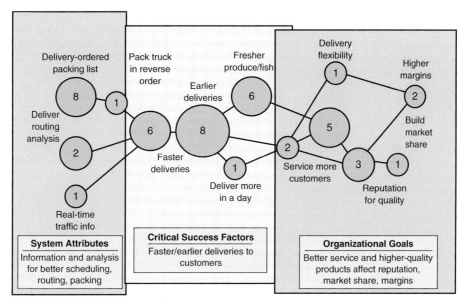

Critical success chain network map.
(*Source:* Peffers and Gengler, 2003.)

Project Planning: Stage 4 of the 4-Stage Model

The fourth and final stage of the model for IT planning is **project planning.** It provides an overall framework within which specific applications can be planned, scheduled, and controlled. Since this stage is associated with systems development, it will be covered in Chapter 14. Also, this stage depends on the outsourcing strategy. The more an organization outsources, the more vendor management and control will need to be included in project planning.

12.7 PLANNING IT ARCHITECTURES

The term *information technology architecture* refers to the overall (high-level) structure of all information systems in an organization. This structure consists of applications for various managerial levels (operational control, management planning and control, and strategic planning) and applications oriented to various functional-operational activities (such as marketing, R&D, production, and distribution). The information architecture also includes infrastructure (e.g., the databases, supporting software, and networks needed to connect

IT at Work 12.5
HOW EXPEDIA USES WEB SERVICES

Expedia.com is a leading online travel service in the United States, with localized versions in the United Kingdom, Canada, and Germany. Expedia operates in a very competitive marketplace with competition from similar services such as Travelocity and Orbitz, ticket discounters such as Priceline.com and Lastminute.com, traditional travel agencies such as Rosenbluth, and, increasingly, airlines and hotels themselves. Expedia harnesses the power of Web Services to distinguish itself in this market.

Expedia's competitive strategy is driven by nearly every traveler's need to receive up-to-the-second, diverse information at any time and any place. Expedia actively supplies travelers with dynamic and real-time personalized information, such as flight status. This information is *pushed to* travelers (sent to them from Expedia) as well as *pulled from* the company's portal (accessed by the travelers through specific inquiries). Travelers use desktop computers, cell phones, and other Web-enabled devices to receive or access the information. This multichannel provision of timely travel information is the key for attracting new customers and for keeping existing customers.

To make this happen, Expedia needs to connect to many service providers (airlines, hotels, car rental companies) as well as airports, news services, map services, and more. By using Web Services the company solves the integration problem as well as creating device-independent information delivery. This way Expedia can write information only once and then deliver it via whichever method the customer wants—eliminating the need to rewrite the information for each delivery method. Expedia also can tie information into the users' existing "buddy lists" and calendars. This way customers do not have to reconstruct their contact lists and schedules within Expedia.

The solution is based on Microsoft's .NET Passport. A single sign-in for customers provides authentication and eliminates redundant log-on procedures. Using Passport's notification service, a user can choose to receive alerts to any device, including wireless ones. Furthermore, customers can, for example, automatically send notifications of flight plans to people on their contact lists. The users can also enter their itinerary schedule to their computer calendars in a second, moving it from .NET calendar.

The architecture of the system is flexible enough to work with non-Internet devices. For example, many people with PDAs do not have wireless capabilities. So they can receive information from Expedia via a synchronized solution (the users can synchronize the information from a PC to their PDAs and vice versa). By using a system development vendor (Microsoft), Expedia did not have to build its own services such as authentication, message notification, and calendaring. This enabled the company to be a first mover in getting these services to market. Using this XML-based service, Expedia adds value for its customers, which provides Expedia with an edge over its competitors.

Source: Compiled and condensed from Microsoft (2001) (*microsoft. com/servers/evaluation/casestudies/Expedia.doc*).

For Further Exploration: How many of the competitive strategies described in this section are exemplified in this case study? What is the advantage of being the first mover in this case? How can small travel agencies that cannot build such a system (at least for several years, until technology will be affordable) respond?

Technology Guides are located at the book's Web site.

applications together). In the simplest view, an IT architecture consists of a description of the combination of hardware, software, data, personnel, and telecommunications elements within an organization, along with procedures to employ them. An information architecture for an organization should guide the long-range development as well as allow for responsiveness to diverse, short-range information systems demands. (The configuration of these architectures is discussed in Technology Guide 4.) *IT at Work 12.5* explains how Expedia utilized a flexible IT architecture to build and deploy various Web Services.

An **information architecture** is a high-level, logical plan of the information requirements and the structures or integration of information resources needed to meet those requirements. An information technology architecture specifies the technological and organizational infrastructure that physically implements an information architecture.

Three types of technology architectures are described in Technology Guide 4: *centralized, noncentralized,* and *client/server.* In this section we discuss the general considerations relating to IT infrastructure and provide some guidelines for choosing among achitecture options. We conclude the section with a look at the issue of reengineering *legacy systems* (holdover systems from earlier architectures).

IT Infrastructure Considerations

Different organizations have different IT infrastructure requirements. Broadbent et al. (1996) looked at how the characteristics and environments of organizations influenced their IT infrastructure. They identified several core *infrastructure services* provided in all of the firms, plus others provided by some of the firms. They also found the following four *infrastructure relationships* in a sample of 26 large firms:

1. *Industry.* Manufacturing firms use fewer IT infrastructure services than retail or financial firms.
2. *Market volatility.* Firms that need to change products quickly use more IT infrastructure services.
3. *Business unit synergy.* Firms that emphasize synergies (e.g., cross-selling) use more IT infrastructure services.
4. *Strategy and planning.* Firms that integrate IT and organizational planning, and track or monitor the achievement of strategic goals, use more IT infrastructure services.

Based on analysis of their data, Broadbent et al. developed a model of the relationship between firm context and IT infrastructure (shown in Online File W12.7). This model indicates that two general factors influence infrastructure levels: The first factor is *information intensity,* the extent to which products or processes incorporate information. The second factor is *strategic focus,* the level of emphasis on strategy and planning. Firms with higher levels of these two factors use more IT infrastructure services, and they have greater reach and range in their use of these services.

Choosing among Architecture Options

A poorly organized IT architecture can disrupt a business by hindering or misdirecting information flows. Each organization—even within the same industry—has its own particular needs and preferences for information. Therefore each organization requires an IT architecture specifically designed and deployed for its use.

In today's computing environment, IT architectures are becoming increasingly complex, yet they still must be responsive to changing business needs. Actually, today's IT architecture is designed around *business processes* rather than around the traditional application hierarchy of the functional departments. These requirements call for tough decisions about a number of architectural issues. The choices among *centralized computing, distributed computing,* and *blended computing* architectures are discussed below.

IN FAVOR OF CENTRALIZED COMPUTING. Centralized computing has been the foundation of corporate computing for over 30 years. **Centralized computing** puts all processing and control authority within one (mainframe) computer to which all other computing devices respond.

There are a number of benefits of centralized computing: Centralized computing can exploit the economies of scale that arise whenever there are a large number of IT applications and users in an organization. It may be more cost-effective to have one large-scale computing resource that is used by many than it is to have many small-scale computing resources. The cost of a centralized facility can be divided among many users, usually reducing duplication of effort and more efficiently managing an operation (housing the computer, providing support services, etc.). Centralized approaches can also offer easier control from an enterprise perspective. If important corporate data are stored on a centralized computing platform, a company is able to impose strict physical access controls to protect the data. When data are spread throughout an organization, securing and preserving data becomes much more difficult (see Chapter 15).

However, with increasing use of *client/server* systems, the role of the mainframe computer has shifted toward a more collaborative relationship with other computing resources within an organization. A few proponents of PCs go so far as to claim that the mainframe is dead. Many experts, though, agree that the mainframe is likely to exist for many years, particularly as a repository for data that can be centrally maintained for enterprisewide use (the data center; see Technology Guide 3). Providing access to and analyzing very large quantities of data are uses for which mainframes are still very appropriate. This is especially important in banking, insurance, airlines, and large retailing. The Internet and intranets can be extremely useful in distributing information stored on mainframe (and smaller) computers.

IN FAVOR OF DISTRIBUTED COMPUTING. **Distributed computing** gives users direct control over their own computing. This approach argues that choices for computing are best handled at the point of the computing need—that individual needs are best met with individualized computing. The rise in popularity of PCs, with their decreasing costs and increasing performance, has led many organizations to embrace distributed computing. Applications data can be entered, verified, and maintained closer to their source.

Distributed computing can also offer a high degree of flexibility and desirable system redundancy. When an organization expands, it may be much easier and less expensive to add another local, distributed processor than to replace a centralized mainframe with an even larger mainframe. Also, a computer in a decentralized environment may be noticeably faster than a centralized computer very far away from a user.

Moreover, a malfunctioning distributed computer ordinarily does not prevent other distributed computers from working, especially if data are partially or fully duplicated around the system, such as in the case of Lotus Notes/Domino or some intranets. (In contrast, a centralized approach has a single point of failure—the central computer. When it goes down, no one computes.) Consider an organization that sells online; if its order processing system goes down for a day in the holiday season, it could lose hundreds of thousands of dollars in sales.

IN FAVOR OF BLENDING CENTRALIZED AND DISTRIBUTED COMPUTING. As noted earlier, computing does not have to be entirely centralized or entirely distributed—it can be a blending of the two models. Many distributed systems are based on client/server architecture. In some circumstances, the mainframe (centralized resource) is viewed as a kind of peripheral device for other (distributed) computing resources. The mainframe can be a large file server that offers the economies of scale and data control that are desirable in most organizations, and yet still allows processing and handling of local needs via distributed computing resources. *What* to distribute *where* (and what *not* to distribute) then become key issues.

INFORMATION ARCHITECTURES AND END-USER COMPUTING. Like an automobile, a personal computer gives its user great flexibility, power, and freedom. But just as the user of an automobile needs access to an infrastructure of highways, the user of a personal computer needs access to an infrastructure of databases and communication networks, including the Internet, a corporate portal, and intranets. Creating such an architecture for end-users invariably involves PC linkage issues.

There are five basic configurations of PCs for end users:

1. Centralized computing with the PC functioning as a "dumb terminal" (or sometimes "not-so-dumb," yet not smart)—the thin PCs.
2. A single-user PC that is not connected to any other device.
3. A single-user PC that is connected to other PCs or systems, using ad hoc telecommunications (such as dial-up telephone connections).
4. Workgroup PCs connected to each other in a small *peer-to-peer network* (see Technology Guide 4).
5. Distributed computing with many PCs fully connected by LANs via wireline or Wi-Fi.

End-user computing with interconnected desktop PCs or network computers appears inevitable. Given this inevitability, it is important that organizations maximize corporate business benefits and, at the same time, minimize risks and undue constraints on user initiative, business knowledge, and organizational unity. (For more on the development of end-user computing, see Chapter 14.)

THE IMPACT OF OUTSOURCING AND UTILITY COMPUTING. As the amount of IT that is outsourced increases, and with the development of utility computing (the purchase of computing services, much as one today purchases electricity and water services; see Chapters 2 and 14), the amount of infrastructure needed by organizations will decline. Theoretically, there will be no need even for a data center. The architecture then will be comprised of LANs and PCs, intranets, corporate portals, and extranets. While outsourcing is spreading rapidly, it is mostly *selected outsourcing* (Chapter 13), namely, only some of the IT operations are outsourced. However, within about 5 to 10 years the impact of both outsourcing and utility computing are expected to be significant.

Reengineering Legacy Systems

Holdovers of earlier architectures that are still in use after an organization migrates to a new architecture are described as *legacy systems*. These systems may continue in use even after an organization switches to an architecture that is different from, and possibly incompatible with, the architectures on which they are based. They may still be capable of meeting business needs, and so might not require any immediate changes. Or they may be in need of reengineering to meet some current business needs, requiring significant changes.

Each legacy system has to be examined on its own merits, and a judgment made regarding the current and future value of the system to the organization. This type of decision—to keep, improve, or replace—can present management with agonizing alternatives. On one hand, keeping a legacy system active offers stability and return on previous investments ("If it ain't broke, don't fix it"). On the other hand, increasing processing demands and high operational costs make replacement attractive if not imperative. Newer systems, however, may be more risky and less robust.

Reverse engineering is the process of examining systems to determine their present status, and to identify what changes are necessary to allow the system to meet current and future business needs. The results of this process can then guide the redesign and redevelopment of the system. Some reverse engineering tools, when applied to legacy systems, automatically generate up-to-date documentation. Other tools in this category help programmers convert code in older programs into a more efficient form.

Legacy systems are not just mainframe systems. A legacy system might consist of PC programs that need to be reengineered and "ported" to a mainframe, a process that is called *upsizing* the system. Or a legacy system might be a mainframe application that needs to be reengineered and "rehosted" onto PCs, an example of *downsizing* a system. In each instance, a business is trying to effectively "rightsize" a legacy system to meet evolving business requirements. An important area is in the *integration* of legacy systems with enterprise systems (such as ERP, CRM, and KM) and with e-commerce systems.

Finally, organizations should reengineer legacy systems in concert with business process redesign. Changes to the computerized or automated side of a business should synchronize with changes in other business processes. While reengineering legacy systems might be justified solely on a cost or efficiency basis, significant business gains can also be made when this effort is a coordinated part of restructuring business processes to improve efficiency and effectiveness.

12.8 SOME ISSUES IN IT PLANNING

IT planning is a complex process. Major planning initiatives are likely to occur following important events such as the merger of organizations, the acquisition of a new company, unexpected poor performance, or the change in upper-level management. *IT at Work 12.6* demonstrates information technology planning that took place after a governmental institution had become private, for example. Even while major planning initiatives may not occur on a yearly basis, because of the pace of technological change, the IT portfolios resulting from an IT plan will be carefully revisited each year to ensure continued alignment with organizational goals. During periods of economic decline, firms often choose to eliminate projects from the portfolio that do not have expected returns of 6 months or less (Leidner et al., 2003).

Of the many special topics in this category, we have elected to focus on IT planning in interorganizational and international systems. Information technology planning may get more complicated when several organizations are involved, as well as when we deal with multinational corporations. In this section, we also address the problems and challenges for IT planning.

IT at Work 12.6
INSTITUTE OF TECHNOLOGY TURNS ITS FOCUS ON THE CUSTOMER

As noted in this chapter, major IT projects and planning programs are often undertaken following significant events experienced by organizations. Increasingly, an organization's ability to change and adjust to such events depends on its ability to implement new IT solutions. In 1989, the Institute of Technology (TI) in Oslo, Norway, went through a very dramatic change: It was transformed from a public, government-funded institute into a private foundation. The 260 employees of the Institute of Technology served small and medium-sized Norwegian companies by assisting them with technology development and transfer. TI's typical services included technical consulting and practical courses in such disciplines as welding, testing, and calibration, as well as ISO certification.

Following the privatization, government support was gradually reduced to 25 percent and TI was required to generate its income independently, which was a difficult task for an organization that was not accustomed to marketing and selling services.

To expand the organization's focus beyond the technical matters, TI recruited managers from the private sector, who quickly identified a potentially valuable asset: contacts with 8,000 companies and thousands of individuals. TI then developed a strategy of leveraging these contacts and relationships with the goal of transforming itself into a viable market-driven organization. In 1992, the Institute's director launched "The Customer Project." The major objectives of this initiative included better financial control of the consulting projects, more effective and efficient marketing, and development of long-term relationships with the most important customers.

Fostering relationships with the clients requires a variety of customer information and frequent communications with the customers, both of which can be facilitated by the use of information technology. Not surprisingly, TI turned to information technology for a customer relationship management (CRM) solution. The Institute implemented the Customer System which was based on SalesMaker, a system from a Norwegian company, Software Innovation. The system was extended with a specialized module developed in-house. At the time, the system was very modern: Windows-based and compatible with the financial system and with office productivity applications.

The Customer System was based on information technology tools; however, the entire project was not purely technical. The Institute dedicated considerable effort to ensure user participation and organizational alignment. In fact, the biggest challenge of the initial implementation was not technical: Since the system was not yet integrated in the day-to-day work routines, users failed to verify customer information, creating duplicate records for the same clients. This behavior resulted in serious information quality problems and undermined the users' confidence in the system.

The second CRM initiative was supported by extensive hands-on guidance for the departments and allowed the Institute to segment its market better, reduce direct marketing volume by 50 percent, and improve sales at the same time. Greater effectiveness in direct marketing led to annual savings of at least half a million NOK (Norway kroner) per year, which fully recovered TI's investment in CRM. Nevertheless, this project failed to change the culture from a focus on technical disciplines to a focus on the customer. Furthermore, the partial success that had been achieved was not self-sustaining.

In 1998, the Institute launched the third CRM initiative, in a new version of the Customer System with a new focus on supporting individual consultants with their personal contacts, document management, and calendars. Overall, the organization was able to achieve the first two of the original goals—improve financial control over projects and become more efficient in direct marketing. Unfortunately, the most important goal of establishing strong, lasting relationships with the most important customers had largely failed.

Source: Bygstad (2003).

For Further Exploration: Why did the outcome of deploying an information system (Customer System) at TI depend so heavily on the Institute's ability to change organizational culture? In addition to CRM, what other IT planning initiatives could have supported Technology Institute's strategy of becoming a profitable private organization?

Planning for Interorganizational Systems

Internal information systems of business partners must "talk" with each other effectively and do it efficiently. In Chapters 3 and 4, we introduced IT technologies such as EDI, e-mail, and extranets that facilitate communication and collaboration between companies. IT planning that involves several organizations may be complex. The problem is that some information systems may involve hundreds or even thousands of business partners. IT planners in such a case could use focus groups of customers, suppliers, and other business partners, especially during the strategic information planning as well as during the information requirements analysis.

Planning for project management of interorganization systems (IOSs) can be fairly complex. IT planners may create virtual planning teams that will work together on projects such as extranets or EDI. Such collaboration is especially important in strategic planning that involves infrastructure. Questions such as who is going to pay for what can become critical factors in cost/benefit analysis and justification of information systems applications.

A comprehensive study of global IT strategic planning was conducted by Curry and Ferguson (2000). In order to increase the success of such planning, they suggest that organizations reduce the planning horizon to two to three years (from three to five years) and that they increase the collaboration between the IT planners and end users.

Examples of joint planning for interorganizational systems can include using an extended supply chain approach and adopting the same enterprise software. If company A will use software from SAP and company B will use Oracle software, there could be additional expenses for connecting these softwares to each other. Web Services (Chapters 2 and 15) may provide the solution for such an integration.

IT Planning for Multinational Corporations

Multinational corporations face a complex legal, political, and social environment, which complicates corporate IT planning. Therefore, many multinational companies prefer to decentralize their IT planning and operations, empowering their local IT managers. However, such a policy may be self-defeating since communication, coordination, and collaboration among decentralized business units may require large expenses. ExxonMobil Corporation, for example, was forced to centralize its IT operations because of such high expenditures (see Online File W12.8).

Problems for IT Planning

IT planning can be an expensive and time-consuming process. A study of five large-scale planning projects found that such projects may involve ten or more employees, on a half-time or full-time basis, for periods lasting from ten weeks to a year. The estimated costs of these projects ranged from $450,000 to $1.9 million. In addition, a survey reported by King (2000) disclosed that more than 50 percent of the companies surveyed were conducting IS planning using obsolete methodologies.

Teo and Ang (2001) emphasized the importance of understanding IT planning problems. They argued that these problems may result in wasted resources, lost opportunities, duplicated efforts, and incompatiable systems. They studied 138 companies and identified IT planning problems at the three phases of IS planning: the launching phase, the plan development phase, and the implementation phase. In all three phases, failing to get top management support for the IS planning was the most serious problem. Other major IS planning problems included: not having free communication flow and not being able to obtain sufficiently qualified personnel in the planning phase; ignoring business goals and failing to translate goals and strategies into action plans in the plan development phase; neglecting to adjust the IS plan to reflect major environmental changes; and ignoring the IS plan once it has been developed in the implementation phase. (Details of these planning problems, as outlined in one study, are shown in Online File W12.9.)

In response to the rapid change of technology and the business environment, IT strategies have to be more flexible and more responsive in order to take advantage of opportunities quickly and in the most cost-effective way. Details in planning for Web-based system and e-commerce are described in the following section.

E-Planning

IT planning in this chapter refers mostly to corporate planning of IT infrastructure rather than to applications planning. In contrast, **e-planning** is electronically supported IT planning that touches on EC infrastructure and mostly deals with uncovering business opportunities and deciding on an applications portfolio that will exploit those opportunities (see *IT at Work 12.4,* pages 530–531).

Some of the infrastructure needed for e-commerce and Web-based systems may be already in place, as part of the organization's overall IT infrastructure. Nevertheless, e-planning may be conducted as a separate planning exercise. In such a case, ISD people will participate in the steering committee together with end users. Of course, alignment between the two processes is needed. One reason for such separation is that technology is an enabler of e-commerce, but the major objective of e-commerce is to rejuvenate organizations. If the process is controlled by IT people, the success of e-commerce may be constrained. Another reason for the separation is that e-planning is usually less formal, and it must be done quickly. Furthermore, due to rapid changes the e-planning must be more flexible.

Planning for Web-based individual applications is very similar to the planning of any IT application. However, at the macro level of planning, the emphasis is different. The areas where more attention is given in e-planning are the applications portfolio, risk analysis, and strategic planning issues such as the use of metrics. Let's elaborate.

APPLICATIONS PORTFOLIO FOR E-COMMERCE. The importance of the applications portfolio in regular IT planning may be declining. Most organizations have their mission-critical systems already in place, and IT activities are fairly distributed. In e-commerce, however, most organizations are starting from scratch. The cost of building systems is high, and so is the risk. Therefore, it is advisable to conduct centralized EC planning and to select appropriate applications and prioritize them. *IT at Work 12.7* (page 540) offers an example of planning and implementing e-commerce systems at Intel.

Another methodology for planning an applications portfolio was proposed by Tjan (2001).

Tjan's Portfolio Strategy. Tjan (2001) adopted a business project portfolio applications approach to create an Internet portfolio planning matrix. (Also see Boar, 2000.) However, instead of trading off industry growth and market position, here the strategy is based on *company fit,* which can be either low or high, and the *project's viability,* which can also be low or high. Together these create an *Internet portfolio map (matrix).*

A project's viability can be assessed by four criteria: market-value potential, time to positive cash flow, personnel requirements, and funding requirements. EC initiatives such as a B2B procurement site, a B2C store, or a portal for kids, for example, can be evaluated on a scale of 1 to 100, for each of the four metrics.

IT at Work 12.7
ACHIEVING COMPETITIVE ADVANTAGE WITH E-BUSINESS

In recent years, Intel Corp., the world's largest producer of integrated-circuit chips, has been facing intense competition from other chip makers, such as Motorola, IBM, Advanced Micro Devices (AMD), and Texas Instruments. To differentiate itself from its competitors, Intel started customizing its paper catalogs and sending the catalogs along with product availability information to potential customers. Initially, this process was performed entirely on paper. However, in 1997, Intel began to explore the feasibility of building an e-business system that would improve and enhance this paper-based process. Intel's objective was to integrate e-business technology into the firm's overall strategy in order to gain competitive advantage in both operational effectiveness and strategic positioning.

The task of designing and implementing an e-business system that would span the entire value chain of a company the size of Intel was enormous. Thus, Intel's development teams chose to focus on small projects that could be completed and deployed to the customers quickly. First, the company implemented an extranet business-to-business system to support direct customers online.

In order to improve efficiency, Intel automated its order management and information delivery system, replaced traditional phone and fax lines with PC-based communications, and enabled its value chain partners to access information online. The greatest efficiency improvement was to customers who were not already electronically connected to Intel. By providing access to real-time information, Intel allowed customers to know more about Intel's products and future direction. Online access to these resources made customers feel more connected and helped them form closer business relationships with Intel.

Furthermore, the e-business initiatives were instrumental in establishing and strengthening Intel's strategic position. By leveraging the capabilities of the e-business systems, Intel was able to build online relationships with direct customers, including original equipment manufacturers (OEMs)

and distributors. These relationships facilitated the conversion of Intel's systems and data from the conventional vendor-centric model to the new customer-centric model.

Because management, procurement, sales and marketing, and engineering functions of value chain partners and customers all have different informational needs, Intel customized its extranet for each customer account. Being able to deliver personalized information online allowed Intel to support multiple levels of the customer organization in a manner that best met the individual's needs. Customers visiting Intel's extranet find their names and specific applications available to them, based on their personal profiles. These profiles allow customers to obtain personalized confidential information and take appropriate actions.

On July 1, 1998, Intel officially began taking orders from OEMs and distribution customers using its new personalized Web sites. Having customers connected electronically brought multiple benefits for Intel. First, the company was able to move resources toward a more efficient and productive technology. For instance, the new system eliminated the need to send and receive hundreds of thousands of faxes each year, leading to significant cost reductions for Intel and its value chain partners. Second, salespeople no longer needed to hand-deliver confidential product information as they had in the past. Third, potential sales were enormous, because Intel was dealing with billions of dollars of orders per quarter. Within the first 15 days following the deployment of the e-business system, Intel was processing $1 billion in sales through the new online channel.

Sources: Phan (2003).

For Further Exploration: Why was it important for Intel to integrate e-business initiatives into the company's overall strategy? Can this system offer Intel a lasting competitive advantage?

Then, an average score (simple average) for each metric is computed. For *fit*, the following criteria are used: alignment with core capabilities, alignment with other company initiatives, fit with organizational structure, fit with company's culture and values, and ease of technical implementation. Again, each EC initiative is assessed on a scale of 1 to 100 (or on a qualitative scale of high, medium, low), and an average is computed.

The various applications initiatives are then mapped on the *Internet portfolio matrix*, based on the average scores for viability and fit. The Internet matrix is

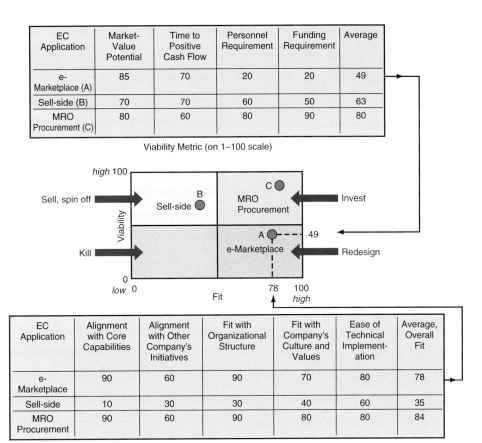

EC Application	Market-Value Potential	Time to Positive Cash Flow	Personnel Requirement	Funding Requirement	Average
e-Marketplace (A)	85	70	20	20	49
Sell-side (B)	70	70	60	50	63
MRO Procurement (C)	80	60	80	90	80

Viability Metric (on 1–100 scale)

FIGURE 12.7 Application portfolio analysis for a toy distributor. Potential applications: (A) create e-marketplace; (B) direct sale (sell-side); and (C) MRO procurement. The average results determine the location on the grid. Results (at center): invest in project C; redesign project A so it will become viable; and sell the idea (B) to someone else since it does not pay to reengineer the company. (*Source:* Drawn by E. Turban.)

EC Application	Alignment with Core Capabilities	Alignment with Other Company's Initiatives	Fit with Organizational Structure	Fit with Company's Culture and Values	Ease of Technical Implementation	Average, Overall Fit
e-Marketplace	90	60	90	70	80	78
Sell-side	10	30	30	40	60	35
MRO Procurement	90	60	90	80	80	84

Fit Metric (on 1–100 scale)

divided into four cells, as shown in Figure 12.7. If both *viability* and *fit* are low, the project is killed. If both are high, then the project is adopted. If *fit* is high, but *viability* is low, the project is sent to redesign. Finally, if the *fit* is low but the *viability* is high, the project may be sold or spun off. The figure shows how several applications were rated for an e-marketplace company for a toy company in Hong Kong.

Tjan's portfolio strategy introduces a systematic approach to EC project selection. The assessment of the points per criterion can be done by several experts to ensure quality. Cases where there is more agreement can be considered with more confidence. Organizations can add their own criteria to the methodology.

RISK ANALYSIS. The degree of risk of some Web-based systems is very high, and such risk often leads to failure. For example, Disney Inc. aborted two major EC initiatives in 2000: First, Disney closed its e-toy company (*smartkid. com*), and second, it closed its company (*go.com*) that was managing all of Disney's EC initiatives. The loss was many millions of dollars. Failures of IT applications do not usually cost so much money, especially if they are not enterprisewide in nature. Conducting an appropriate risk analysis could reduce the chance of failures. However, this was difficult to do at that time due to lack of historical data.

STRATEGIC PLANNING ISSUES. Several strategic planning issues are unique to the Web environment. Each of these may involve IT infrastructure, but the market and organizational implications may be more important. Here are some examples:

- *Who and where?* Should the EC initiatives be conducted in a completely independent division or even a separate company?
- *Use of metrics.* EC planning is difficult because the field is evolving, the history is brief, and few planners have experience. Therefore it is desirable to use industry standards, also known as *metrics,* for executing various steps of the planning process (see Plant, 2000). (Metrics are discussed in Chapters 4 and 13.)
- *Learn from failures.* During 2000/2001 there were many EC failures, both major initiatives and whole companies. Planners should study such failures, to learn what went wrong in the hope of avoiding such problems in the future. (For lessons for planners, see Useem, 2000; Agrawal et al., 2001; and Chapter 4 of this book.)
- *Use a different planning process.* The Web environment requires a different planning process, as illustrated by Turban et al. (2006).
- *Integration.* Information systems strategic planning must integrate, in many cases, e-business and knowledge management (see Galliers, 1999, for details).

Planning in a Turbulent Web Environment

The Web environment is very turbulent. Some people question the validity of formal planning in such an environment. Others insist that the turbulence makes formal planning a necessity. Samela et al. (2000) investigated the issue of planning in a turbulent environment in two organizations and concluded that a formal comprehensive approach may be more beneficial than not having a formal plan. Of course, generalizing from only two organizations may not tell the whole story. Samela and Spil (2002) recently suggested a continuous e-business planning process, with four basic planning cycles: (1) agreeing on planning objectives, (2) aligning business objectives and information objectives, (3) analyzing IS resources and IT infrastructure, and (4) authorizing actions. The four cycles are repeated each period in order to ensure continuous review and improvement of the strategies. (Details are shown in Online File W12.10.)

Whether an organization uses formal planning for the Web environment or not, the planning of Web systems frequently requires redesign of business processes, our next topic.

➡ MANAGERIAL ISSUES

1. *Sustaining competitive advantage.* As companies become larger and more sophisticated, they develop sufficient resources to quickly duplicate the successful systems of their competitors. For example, Alamo Rent-a-Car now offers a frequent-renter card similar to the one offered by National car rental.

2. *Importance.* Getting IT ready for the future—that is, planning—is one of the most challenging and difficult tasks facing all of management, including IS management. Each of the four steps of the IT strategic planning process—strategic planning, information requirements analysis, resource allocation, and project planning—presents its own unique problems. Yet, without planning, or with poor planning, the organization may be doomed.

3. ***Organizing for planning.*** Many issues are involved in planning: What should be the role of the ISD? How should IT be organized? Staffed? Funded? How should human resources issues, such as training, benefits, and career paths for IS personnel, be handled? What about the environment? The competition? The economy? Governmental regulations? Emerging technologies? What is the strategic direction of the host organization? What are its key objectives? Are they agreed upon and clearly stated? Finally, with these strategies and objectives and the larger environment, what strategies and objectives should IS pursue? What policies should it establish? What type of information architecture should the organization have: centralized or not centralized? How should investments in IT be justified? The answer to each of these questions must be tailored to the particular circumstances of the ISD and the larger organization of which it is a part.

4. ***Fitting the IT architecture to the organization.*** Management of an organization may become concerned that its IT architecture is not suited to the needs of the organization. In such a case, there has likely been a failure on the part of the IT technicians to determine properly the requirements of the organization. Perhaps there has also been a failure on the part of management to understand the type and manner of IT architecture that they have allowed to develop or that they need.

5. ***IT architecture planning.*** IT specialists versed in the technology of IT must meet with business users and jointly determine the present and future needs for the IT architecture. In some cases, IT should lead (e.g., when business users do not understand the technical implications of a new technology). In other cases, users should lead (e.g., when technology is to be applied to a new business opportunity). Plans should be written and published as part of the organizational strategic plan and as part of the IT strategic plan. Plans should also deal with training, career implications, and other secondary infrastructure issues.

6. ***IT policy.*** IT architectures should be based on corporate guidelines or principles laid out in policies. These policies should include the roles and responsibilities of IT personnel and users, security issues, cost-benefit analyses for evaluating IT, and IT architectural goals. Policies should be communicated to all personnel who are managing or directly affected by IT.

7. ***Ethical and legal issues.*** Conducting interviews for finding managers' needs and requirements must be done with full cooperation. Measures to protect privacy must be taken.

    In designing systems one should consider the people in the system. Reengineering IT means that some employees will have to completely reengineer themselves. Some may feel too old to do so. Conducting a supply chain or business process reorganization may result in the need to lay off, retrain, or transfer employees. Should management notify the employees in advance regarding such possibilities? And what about those older employees who may be difficult to retrain?

    Other ethical issues may involve sharing of computing resources (in a client/server environment, for example) or of personal information, which may be part of the new organizational culture. Finally, individuals may have to share computer programs that they designed for their departmental use, and may resist doing so because they consider such programs their intellectual property. Appropriate planning must take these and other issues into consideration.

Implementing organizational transformation by the use of IT may tempt some to take unethical or even illegal actions. Companies may need to use IT to monitor the activities of their employees and customers, and in so doing may invade the privacy of individuals. When using business intelligence to find out what competitors are doing, companies may be engaged in unethical tactics such as pressuring competitors' employees to reveal information, or using software that is the intellectual property of other companies (frequently without the knowledge of these other companies).

8. ***IT strategy.*** In planning IT it is necessary to examine three basic strategies: (1) *Be a leader in technology.* Companies such as FedEx, Dell, and Wal-Mart are known for their leading strategy. The advantages of being a leader are the ability to attract customers, to provide unique services and products, and to be a cost leader. However, there is a high development cost of new technologies and high probability of failures. (2) *Be a follower.* This is a risky strategy because you may be left behind. However, you do not risk failures, and so you usually are able to implement new technologies at a fraction of the cost. (3) *Be an experimenter, on a small scale.* This way you minimize your research and development investment and the cost of failure. When new technologies prove to be successful you can move fairly quickly for full implementation.

KEY TERMS

Alliance strategy *511*	E-planning *539*	Project planning *531*
Applications portfolio *520*	Entry-barriers strategy *512*	Resource allocation *529*
Business systems planning (BSP) model *523*	Four-stage model of planning *520*	Resource-based view (RBV) *516*
	Growth strategy *511*	Reverse engineering *536*
Centralized computing *533*	Information architecture *532*	Scenario planning *527*
Competitive forces model *508*	Information requirements analysis *528*	Stages of IT growth *524*
Cost leadership strategy *509*		Strategic information technology planning (SITP) *521*
Critical success factors (CSFs) *524*	Innovation strategy *511*	
Differentiation strategy *510*	IT planning *519*	Value chain model *513*
Distributed computing *534*	Niche strategy *510*	

CHAPTER HIGHLIGHTS (Numbers Refer to Learning Objectives)

❶ Information systems support or shape competitive strategies.

❶ Porter's value chain model can be used to identify areas in which IT can provide strategic advantage.

❷ Cost leadership, differentiation, and niche were Porter's first strategies for gaining a competitive advantage, but today many other strategies exist. All of the competitive strategies can be supported by IT.

❷ The Internet has changed the nature of competition, altering the traditional relationships between customers, suppliers, and firms within an industry.

❸ The resource-based view of the firm can help identify those IT-based resources and capabilities that are critical to creating, and sustaining, a competitive advantage.

3 Acquiring competitive advantage is hard, and sustaining it can be just as difficult because of the innovative nature of technology advances.

4 IT planning methods have evolved over time. Today they are centered around e-planning.

4 The four-stage IT planning model includes strategic planning, requirements analysis, resource allocation, and project planning.

5 IS planning requires analysis of the information needed by the organization. Several methods exist for doing it. Also, implementing the planning requires planning—including resource allocation, cost-benefit analysis, and project management (using software).

6 Aligning IT plans with business plans makes it possible to prioritize IS projects on the basis of contribution to organizational goals and strategies.

7 Information technology architecture can be centralized or distributed. When it is distributed, it often follows the client/server architecture model.

7 Organizations can use enterprise architecture principles to develop an information technology architecture.

8 Strategic information systems planning involves methodologies such as business systems planning (BSP), stages of IT growth, and critical success factors (CSFs).

8 The major information systems planning issues are strategic alignment, architecture, resource allocation, and time and budget considerations.

9 To prioritize an e-commerce applications portfolio, IT planners can use the validity of the application and its fit with the organization, plotting it on a grid that indicates company fit and project viability and suggests one of four strategies.

VIRTUAL COMPANY ASSIGNMENT

Strategic Advantage at The Wireless Café
Go to The Wireless Café's link on the Student Web Site. There you will be asked to think about how the competitive forces model and IT planning could contribute to strategic advantage for the restaurant.

More Resources
More resources and study tools are located on the Student Web Site. You'll find additional chapter materials and useful Web links. In addition, self-quizzes that provide individualized feedback are available for each chapter.

QUESTIONS FOR REVIEW

1. What has been the impact of the digital economy on competition?
2. What has been the impact of the Internet on Porter's competitive forces model?
3. List five strategies for competitive advantage.
4. List two reasons why it is difficult for businesses to sustain a competitive advantage.

5. What are the characteristics of resources that enable a competitive advantage? Contrast those with the characteristics of resources that enable a sustainable competitive advantage.

6. List the types of IS resources that a firm might possess.

7. What are some of the problems associated with IT planning?

8. Define and discuss the four-stage model of IT planning.

9. Identify the methods used for strategic planning and review their characteristics.

10. What is information technology architecture and why is it important? List the major types.

11. What are the advantages and disadvantages of centralized computing architectures?

12. What is a legacy system? Why do companies have legacy systems?

13. Define scenario planning.

QUESTIONS FOR DISCUSSION

1. Discuss the relationship between the critical organizational responses of Chapter 1 and a *differentiation* strategy.

2. Give two examples that show how IT can help a defending company *reduce* the impact of the five forces in Porter's model.

3. Give two examples of how attacking companies can use IT to *increase* the impact of the five forces in Porter's model.

4. Discuss the idea that an information system by itself can rarely provide a sustainable competitive advantage.

5. Discuss how strategic planning, as described in this chapter, could help an electric utility plan its future.

6. How might an organization with a good strategic idea be limited in its ability to implement that idea if it has an inferior or inappropriate information architecture? Provide an example.

7. What type of problems might an organization encounter if it focuses only on resource allocation planning and project planning?

8. Why is it so important to align the IT plan with organizational strategies? What could happen if the plan is not aligned with these strategies?

9. Discuss the advantages of using Tjan's approach to an applications portfolio.

10. Some organizations feel that IT planning is a waste of time, because the competitive environment and technologies are changing so rapidly. They argue that their plans will be obsolete before they are completed. Discuss.

11. Should there be a correlation between a firm's architecture structure (and chart) and its IT architecture (e.g., centralized IT for a centralized structure)?

EXERCISES

1. One area of intensive competition is selling cars online (see Slater, 1999). Examine the strategy of the players cited in the paper (available at *cio.com*). Identify the related new business models and relate them to the strategies promoted in this chapter.

2. Study the Web sites of Amazon.com and Barnes & Noble online (*bn.com*). Also, find some information about the competition between the two. Analyze Barnes & Noble 's defense strategy using Porter's model. Prepare a report.

3. Identify the major competitors of Rosenbluth International. Visit three other travel agent Web sites, and compare their strategies and offerings to those of Rosenbluth.

4. Using the CSF method of strategic planning, identify new strategic initiatives that a university might take using information technology.

5. What kind of IT planning is done in your university or place of work to ensure that the Internet demand in the future will be met? Does the university have a CIO? Why or why not?

6. Examine *IT at Work 12.7* and Tjan's applications portfolio method. Compare the two, showing the advantages and limitations of each.

GROUP ASSIGNMENTS

1. Assign group members to each of the major car rental companies. Find out their latest strategies regarding customer service. Visit their Web sites and compare the findings. Have each group prepare a presentation on why its company should get the title of "best customer service provider." Also, each group should use Porter's forces model to convince the class that its company is the best competitor in the car rental industry.

2. The competition in online retailing is growing rapidly, as evidenced in goods such as books, toys, and CDs. Assign groups to study online competition in the above industries and more. Identify successes and failures. Compare the various industries. What generalizations can you make?

3. Assign each group member to a company to which he or she has access, and have each member prepare a value-chain chart. The objective is to discover how specific IT applications are used to facilitate the various activities. Compare these charts across companies in different industries.

4. Divide the class into groups of six people or less. Each group will be entrepreneurs attempting to start some kind of nationwide company. Each group should describe the IT architecture it would build, as well as the expected benefits from, and potential problems with, the IT architecture it has chosen.

5. Assign groups to the following industries: banking, airlines, health care, insurance, and large retailing. Each group will investigate the use of the mainframe in one industry and prepare a report on the future of the mainframe. Also, include information on how client/server architecture is used in the industry.

INTERNET EXERCISES

1. McKesson Drugs is the largest wholesale drug distributor in the world. Visit the company Web site (*mckesson.com*). What can you learn about its strategy toward retailers? What is its strategy toward its customers? What e-commerce initiatives are evidenced?

2. Enter some EDGAR-related Web sites (*edgar-online.com, hottools.com, edgar.stern.nyu.edu*). Prepare a list of the documents that are available, and discuss the benefits one can derive in using this database for conducting a competitive intelligence (see Kambil and Ginsburg, 1998).

3. Go to *dwinc.com/strat.htm* and read the content. Compare and contrast the approach on this page to other approaches to strategic information systems planning.

4. Enter *cio.com*. Review the latest IT planning surveys and reviews reported. Start with the October 1997 survey conducted by CIO Communications Inc.

5. Enter *truserv.com* and find "news" in the media relations section. Identify all IT-related plans announced by the company in the last six months. Comment on your findings.

Minicase 1
Net Readiness at Cisco Systems

Cisco Systems (*cisco.com*) richly deserves its self-designated title of "the worldwide leader in networking for the Internet." Virtually all of the data packets that swirl through the Internet pass through a Cisco-manufactured router on their way to their destination. However, Cisco does not see itself as a computer hardware company. Instead, Cisco considers its main product to be networking solutions. Through initiatives such as its Internet Business Solutions Group, Cisco provides businesses with the software, support, service, training, and, yes, hardware, they need to create an information infrastructure to become e-businesses. In 2004, Cisco sold its products in over 100 countries and employed over 34,000 employees. In fiscal year 2003, Cisco Systems had almost $19 billion in revenues and ranked 95 on the Fortune 500.

To fulfill its vision of being a complete network solutions provider, Cisco Systems relies on a broad strategy of establishing a dominant networking standard in the Internet era. Cisco has used the Internet, electronic commerce, and infor-

mation systems to support this strategy in several ways: (1) to create a business environment that reinforces Cisco's control over key networking standards; (2) to create a virtual organization, outsourcing various manufacturing and customer service functions, while focusing its own resources on core product innovation; (3) to showcase its own use of networking technologies and the Internet as a marketing tool. Three of Cisco's information systems described below are properly aligned with the company's strategy and fully support the process of strategy implementation.

Cisco Connection Online (CCO) is its customer-facing information system. The Cisco Web site (*cisco.com*) is the gateway for customers to price and configure orders, place orders, and check order status. CCO also offers customers the opportunity to help themselves to the information they need to do business with Cisco. And they do access it: CCO is accessed over 1.5 million times each month by its 150,000 active registered users. Customers use CCO to get answers to questions, diagnose network problems, and collaborate with other customers and Cisco staff. Currently Cisco is working with its major customers to integrate their enterprise applications directly into Cisco's back-end systems. The goals of this project are to provide better and speedier customer service, lock in customers, and generate operating expense savings of $350 million per year.

Manufacturing Connection Online (MCO) is an extranet application that links Cisco's partners up and down its supply chain. Its purpose is to provide real-time manufacturing information to Cisco's suppliers and employees in support of the manufacturing, supply, and logistics functions. MCO delivers forecast data, real-time inventory data, purchase orders, and related information through a secure connection and a graphical user interface. One of the most successful aspects of MCO is direct fulfillment. The old process had all products coming to Cisco for storage and then shipment to the customer. MCO's connections to Cisco's suppliers allows Cisco to forward a customer's order to a third-party supplier, who ships it directly to the customer. By pushing information down the supply chain instead of product up the supply chain, Cisco is able to reduce shipping time, save money, and make customers happy.

Cisco Employee Connection (CEC) is Cisco's inward-looking SIS, an intranet that addresses the unique needs of every Cisco employee. CEC offers ubiquitous communications (e.g., distribution of marketing materials, major corporate announcements), streamlined business processes (e.g., travel expense reimbursement), and integrated business systems (e.g., scheduling meetings, a problem-reporting system).

One application that illustrates CEC's benefits to both Cisco and its employees is Metro, a travel-expense reporting system. Assume an employee uses a corporate credit card to charge an expense. Metro displays all expenses on a current credit card statement, and the employee can then move all relevant charges to an expense report. In pre-Metro days, a travel reimbursement took four to five weeks; Metro reimburses the employee in two to three days.

Cisco has benefited richly from these strategic information systems. For example:

- Eighty percent of technical support requests are filled electronically, reducing help desk labor costs and almost always with a customer satisfaction rate that exceeds that of human intervention.
- Providing technical support to customers over the Internet has enabled Cisco to save more than $200 million annually, more money than what some of its competitors spend on research and development.

- CCO metrics show 98 percent accurate, on-time repair shipments, and customer satisfaction increased by 25 percent between 1995 and 2000.
- By outsourcing 70 percent of its production means, Cisco has quadrupled output without the time and investment required to build new plants.
- MCO has allowed Cisco to lower business costs in processing orders (from $125 per order to less than $5), improved employee productivity, and reduced order cycle times.
- Metro not only reimburses employees faster, it increases employee productivity and saves Cisco auditing costs. Today Cisco employs only two auditors to audit expenses for 15,000 Metro users per month.
- Cisco estimates total annual savings from CEC at $58 million, including $25 million in employee training savings and $16 million in employee communication.
- Overall, in fiscal 2003, Cisco saved US $2.1 billion by relying on the Internet and information systems to provide customer support, offer employee services, sell products, provide training, and manage finances and manufacturing processes.

A recent Cisco advertising campaign featured children and adults from all over the world asking the viewer, "Are you ready?" for the Internet. Cisco not only promotes Net readiness through its advertising, but also lives Net readiness by applying network connectivity throughout the company. This close integration of the company's strategy and its use of the Internet and information systems allows Cisco to maintain its competitiveness in network technology.

Sources: Hartman and Sifonis (2000); Kraemer and Dedrick (2002); *newsroom.cisco.com* (accessed June 2004).

Questions for Minicase 1

1. How does each of Porter's five forces apply to Cisco?
2. The case emphasizes benefits to Cisco. How do suppliers benefit? How do customers benefit?
3. Are the initiatives in place at Cisco available only to such a high-tech company? Specifically, what difficulties would a more traditional company face in becoming Net-ready?
4. How can Cisco use the knowledge it has acquired from internal implementation of these systems to fulfill its goal to be a network solution provider to its customers?

Minicase 2
Scenario Planning at National City Bank Aligns IT with Business Planning

The banking industry is very competitive. National City Corp. (*national-city.com*), one of the largest U.S. bank holding companies, based in Cleveland, Ohio, was confronting three challenges: (1) It needed new ways to generate earnings; (2) it faced increasing competition for market share; and (3) the bank was losing customers who wanted to do banking using the Internet.

National City saw the customer information system it was developing with IBM as a solution to these problems. The bank hoped to use this system to develop new, high-revenue products, tailor programs for customers, and cross-sell products to appropriate customers. But to design it, the bank had to know what kind of information the system would be aggregating. Would it track information about the products the bank offered or the people who bought them? If it was product-focused, it would have to include detailed descriptions of each financial service, whether credit cards or mortgages. If the system was customer-focused, it would track whether they used ATMs, branch offices, or call centers, and would indicate demographics in order to build customer profiles. Furthermore, the bank would need to set up business rules to determine customer profitability.

Management quickly realized that they simply could not answer these questions because the answers were linked to a larger issue: Management didn't have a clear sense of the bank's strategic direction. The required investment in technology was $40 million, so planning to invest it properly was critical.

To clarify the business direction, the bank hired a consulting company, *ncri.com*, to employ scenario planning. The planning process involved six phases used by an implementation team:

Phase I: Alternative Visions (Scenarios)

In this phase, a few possible visions of the future are selected. In the case of National City, the scenarios were:

- *Utilize a CRM-based strategy.* This was a major industry trend in which everything would be geared to individual customer need. This business model is complex and expensive to pursue.
- *Specialize solely in certain financial services.* This is a low-cost option, but may not bring new customers and may even result in losing existing customers.
- *Create a separate online bank.*

Phase II: Events Generation

Next, a list of 150 internal and external events that might influence any of the outcomes was generated by the team. Events included new regulations and technological developments (e.g., wireless). These events were simulated as newspaper headlines (e.g., "Demand for real-time banking information via cell phones is skyrocketing"). These events were used later to create scenarios.

Phase III: The Workshop

A three-day workshop with the 24 top executives was conducted. The participants were divided into three groups. The first task was to rank all 150 events by the *chance that they will occur*. Once done, all participants met to discuss the rankings and, after appropriate discussion, reach a consensus. This process can be lengthy, but it is essential.

Then, each team was assigned one of the bank's three scenarios and was asked to analyze the impact of the most-likely-to-occur events on that scenario, within a five-year planning horizon.

Phase IV: Presentation

Each group made an oral presentation, in which their goal was to convince the other groups that their vision was the most feasible. This was a difficult task since some team members, who had to play the role of supporters, actually did not like the scenario they were supposed to "sell."

Phase V: Deliberation and Attempt to Reach a Consensus

The entire group of participants needed to agree on which alternative was the best for the bank. After long deliberation, the group decided to support alternative #1, the CRM-based strategy.

Phase VI: IT Support

To facilitate the IT planning, an IS plan was devised in which a data warehouse was planned, so that customers' profiles could be built. Data mining was planned for identifying the bank's most profitable customers, and a Web-based call center was designed to provide personalized services.

All in all, the scenario planning process was an exercise in contingency thinking that resulted in prosperity when the system was eventually deployed.

Sources: Condensed from Levinson (2000), *ncri.com*, and *national-city.com*.

Questions for Minicase 2

1. One critique of this approach is that some members who are asked to "sell" a specific scenario may not be enthusiastic to do so. Find information in the scenario planning literature on this issue, or e-mail a scenario consultant (*ncri.com* or *gbn.com*). Write a report on your findings.

2. Can group decision support systems (Chapter 9) be used in this case? Why and what for, or why not?

3. How can the end users learn about technology in scenario planning?

4. What can IT tools be used to facilitate this scenario planning process, which was done manually?

5. How did the scenario planning help the IT people to better understand the business?

6. Why is scenario planning considered a risk-management tool?

REFERENCES

1800flowers.com (accessed June 2004).

Agrawal, V., L. D. Arjona, and R. Lemmens, "E-Performance: The Path to Rational Exuberance," *McKinsey Quarterly,* First Quarter, 2001.

Amit, R., and P. J. H. Schoemaker, "Strategic Assets and Organizational Rent," *Strategic Management Journal,* Vol. 14, 1993.

Andrews, K., *The Concept of Corporate Strategy.* Homewood, IL: Dow Jones–Irwin, 1971.

Barney, J. B., "Organizational Culture: Can It Be a Source of Sustained Competitive Advantage?" *Academy of Management Review,* Vol. 11, 1986.

Barney, J. B., "Firm Resources and Sustained Competitive Advantage," *Journal of Management,* Vol. 17, 1991.

Barney, J. B., and M. H. Hansen, "Trustworthiness as a Source of Competitive Advantage," *Strategic Management Journal,* Vol. 15, 1994.

Beal, B., "IT-business Alignment Elusive for Some," *searchCIO.com,* March 24, 2004.

Bharadwaj, A. S., "A Resource-Based Perspective on Information Technology Capability and Firm Performance: An Empirical Investigation," *MIS Quarterly,* Vol. 24, 2000.

Blodgett, M., "Game Plans (Strategic Plans)," *CIO Magazine,* January 1998.

Boar, B. H., *The Art of Strategic Planning for Information Technology,* 2nd ed. New York: Wiley, 2000.

Broadbent, M., P. Weill, and D. St. Clair, "Firm Context and Patterns of IT Infrastructure Capability," *Proceedings of the 17th International Conference on Information Systems,* Cleveland, December 16–18, 1996.

Business Systems Planning—Information Systems Planning Guide, Application Manual GE20-0527-3, 3rd ed., IBM Corporation, July 1981.

Bygstad, B., "The Implementation Puzzle of CRM Systems in Knowledge-Based Organizations," *Information Resources Management Journal* 16(4), October–December 2003.

Cale, E. G., and J. Kanter, "Aligning Information Systems and Business Strategy: A Case Study," *Journal of Information Technology Management,* 9(1), 1998.

Callon, J. D., *Competitive Advantage through Information Technology.* New York: McGraw-Hill, 1996.

Carry, J., and J. Ferguson, "Increasing the Success of the IT Strategic Planning Process," *Proceedings, 33rd Hawaiian International Conference on Systems Sciences (HICSS),* Hawaii, January 2000.

Cassidy, A., *A Practical Guide to IT Strategic Planning.* Boca Raton, FL: CRC Press, 1998.

Chan, Y. E., "Why Haven't We Mastered Alignment? The Importance of the IT Informal Organization Structure," *MIS Quarterly Executive,* June 2002.

CIO.com, *cio.com/archive(040103)strategy.html* (accessed July 2003).

Cisco.com.

Collins, L., "Efficient and Effective," *IEE Review,* 50(1), January 2004.

Collis, D., and C. Montgomery, "Competing on Resources: Strategy in the 1990s," *Harvard Business Review,* 73(4), 1995.

Copeland, D. G., and J. L. McKenney, "Airline Reservation Systems: Lessons from History," *MIS Quarterly,* 12(3), September 1988.

Dehning, B., and T. Stratopoulos, "Determinants of a Sustainable Competitive Advantage Due to an IT-enabled Strategy," *Journal of Strategic Information Systems,* Vol. 12, 2003.

Dell.com.

Demarco, T., and T. Lister, *Peopleware: Productive Projects and Teams.* New York: Dorset House Publishing, 1987.

Feurer, R., K. Chaharbaghi, M. Weber, and J. Wargin, "Aligning Strategies, Processes, and IT: A Case Study," *Information Systems Management,* Winter 2000.

Frenzel, C. W., *Management of Information Technology,* 2nd ed. Cambridge, MA: Course Technology, 1996.

Galliers, B., "Towards the Integration of E-Business, KM, and Policy Considerations Within an Information Systems Strategy Framework," *Strategic Information Systems,* Vol. 8, 1999.

Galliers, R., and D. Leidner, *Strategic Information Systems: Challenges and Strategies in Managing Information Systems,* 3rd ed. Woburn, MA: Butterworth-Heinemann, 2003.

Griffiths, P. M., et al. (eds.), *Information Management in Competitive Success.* New York: Pergamon Press, 1998.

Hackney, R. A., J. Buru, and G. Dhillon, "Challenging Assumptions for Strategic Information Systems Planning," *Communications of AIS,* 3(9), 2000.

Hackney, R. A., G. Griffiths, and J. Buru, "Strategic Information Systems Planning: A Resource and Capabilities-Based View for Sustainability of Competitiveness," *Proceedings of British Academy of Management (BAM99)*, Manchester Metropolitan University (UK), September 1999.

Harmon, P., et al., *Developing E-Business Systems and Architectures: A Manager's Guide.* San Francisco: Morgan Kaufmann, 2001.

Hartman, A., and J. Sifonis, *Net Ready: Strategies for Success in the E-conomy.* New York: McGraw-Hill, 2000.

Holweg, M., and F. K. Pil, "Successful Build-to-Order Strategies: Start with the Customer," *Sloan Management Review*, Fall 2001, pp. 74–83.

HP.com.

Kambil, A., and M. Glasburg, "Public Access Web Information Systems: Lessons from the Internet EDGAR Project," *Communications of the ACM*, July 1998.

Kemp, T., "Online Retailers Smell the Roses," *InternetWeek.com*, September 17, 2001, *internetweek.com/customers/customers091701.htm* (accessed May 20, 2003).

King, W. R., "Assessing the Efficiency of IS Strategic Planning," *Information Systems Management*, Winter 2000.

Kirkpatrick, D., "Dell and Rollins: The $41 Billion Buddy Act," *Fortune*, 149(8), April 19, 2004.

Kraemer, K., and J. Dedrick, "Strategic Use of the Internet and E-Commerce: Cisco Systems," *Journal of Strategic Information Systems*, 11(1), 2003.

Leidner, D., R. Beatty, and J. Mackay, "How CIOs Manage IT during Economic Decline: Surviving and Thriving amid Uncertainty," *MIS Quarterly Executive*, March 2003.

Levinson, M., "Don't Stop Thinking about Tomorrow," *CIO Magazine*, January 1, 2000.

Mahoney, J. T., and J. R. Pandian, "The Resource-Based View within the Conversation of Strategic Management," *Strategic Management Journal*, Vol. 13, 1992.

Martin, J., and C. Finkelstein, "Information Engineering," Technical Report, two volumes, November 1981. Lancs, UK: Savant Institute, Carnforth.

Mata, F. J., W. Fuerst, and J. Baruey, "Information Technology and Sustained Competitive Advantage: A Resource-Based Analysis," *MIS Quarterly*, December 1995.

Microsoft, "XML Web Services Provide Travelers with Unprecedented Advantages," May 1, 2001, *microsoft.com/servers/evaluation/casestudies/Expedia.doc* (accessed May 20, 2003).

Neumann, S., *Strategic Information Systems—Competition through Information Technologies.* New York: Macmillan, 1994.

Nolan, R. L., "Managing the Crises in Data Processing," *Harvard Business Review*, March–April 1979.

Papp, R. (ed.), *Strategic Information Technology: Opportunities for Competitive Advantage.* Hershey, PA: Idea Group, 2001.

Peffers, K., and C. E. Gengler, "How to Identify New High-Payoff Information Systems for the Organization," *Communications of the ACM*, 46(1), January 2003.

People 3 Inc., "Achieving IT and Business Alignment: A Human Capital Management View," 2003.

Phan, D. D., "E-Business Development for Competitive Advantages: A Case Study," *Information and Management*, Vol. 40, 2003.

Penrose, E. T., *The Theory of Growth of the Firm.* Oxford, England: Blackwell Publishers, 1959.

Pickering, C., *E-Business Success Strategies: Achieving Business and IT Alignment.* Charleston, S.C.: Computer Technology Research, 2000.

Plant, T., *E-Commerce: Formulation of Strategy.* Upper Saddle River, NJ: Prentice Hall, 2000.

Porter, M. E., *Competitive Advantage: Creating and Sustaining Superior Performance.* New York: Free Press, 1985.

Porter, M. E., "What Is a Strategy?" *Harvard Business Review*, November–December 1996.

Porter, M. E., "Strategy and the Internet," *Harvard Business Review*, March 2001.

Reda, S., "1-800-Flowers.com and AT&T Cultivate Relationship Rooted in Common Business Objectives," *Stores*, October 2002, pp. 54–58.

Ruohonen, M., and L. F. Higgins, "Application of Creativity Principles to IS Planning," *Proceedings HICSS*, Hawaii, January 1998.

Samela, H., A. L. Lederer, and T. Reponen, "Information Systems Planning in a Turbulent Environment," *European Journal of Information Systems*, 9(1), 2000.

Samela, H., and T. A. M. Spil, "Dynamic and Emergent Information Systems Strategy Formulation and Implementation," *International Journal of Information Management*, December 2002.

Schendel, D., "Introduction to Competitive Organizational Behavior: Toward an Organizationally-Based Theory of Competitive Advantage," *Strategic Management Journal*, Vol. 15 (1994).

Seybold, P. B., "Get Inside the Lives of Your Customers," *Harvard Business Review*, May 2001.

Slater, D., "Car Wars," *CIO Magazine*, September 15, 1999.

Stauffer, D., "Five Reasons Why You Still Need Scenario Planning," *Harvard Business Review*, June 2002.

Teo, T. S. H., and J. S. K. Ang, "An Examination of Major IS Planning Problems," *International Journal of Information Management*, December 2001.

Tjan, A. K., "Finally, A Way to Put Your Internet Portfolio in Order," *Harvard Business Review*, February 2001.

Turban, E., D. King, and J. K. Lee, *Electronic Commerce 2006.* Upper Saddle River, NJ: Prentice Hall, 2006.

Useem, J., "Dot-coms: What Have We Learned?" *Fortune*, October 30, 2000.

Venkatraman, N., "Five Steps to a Dot-Com Strategy: How to Find Your Footing on the Web," *Sloan Management Review*, Spring 2000.

Wade, M., and J. Hulland, "The Resource-based View and Information Systems Research: Review, Extension, and Suggestions for Future Research," *MIS Quarterly*, March 2004.

Ward, J., and J. Peppard, *Strategic Planning for Information Systems*, 3rd ed. New York: Wiley, 2002.

Weill, P., and M. Broadbent, "Managing IT Infrastructure: A Strategic Choice." In R. W. Zmud (ed.), *Framing the Domains of IT Management*, pp. 329–353. Cincinnati, OH: Pinnaflex Educational Resources, 2000.

Wernerfelt, B., "A Resource-Based View of the Firm," *Strategic Management Journal*, Vol. 5 (1984).

Wetherbe, J. C., "Four-Stage Model of MIS Planning Concepts, Techniques, and Implementation." In R. Banker, R. Kaufman, and M. Mahmood (eds.), *Strategic Information Technology Management: Perspectives on Organizational Growth and Competitive Advantage.* Harrisburg, PA: Idea Group, 1993.

Wiseman, C., *Strategic Information Systems.* Burr Ridge, IL: Richard D. Irwin, 1988.

PART V
Implementing and Managing IT

12. Using IT for Strategic Advantage
▶ 13. Information Technology Economics
14. Acquiring IT Applications and Infrastructure
15. Managing Information Resources and Security
16. The Impacts of IT on Individuals, Organizations, and Society

CHAPTER 13

Information Technology Economics

13.1 Financial and Economic Trends and the Productivity Paradox

13.2 Evaluating IT Investment: Benefits, Costs, and Issues

13.3 Methods for Evaluating and Justifying IT Investment

13.4 IT Economics Strategies: Chargeback and Outsourcing

13.5 Economics of Web-Based Systems and E-Commerce

13.6 Other Economic Aspects of Information Technology

Minicases:
1. The "Invest First, Analyze Later" Approach
2. Kone Inc.

LEARNING OBJECTIVES

After studying this chapter, you will be able to:

❶ Identify the major aspects of the economics of information technology.

❷ Explain and evaluate the productivity paradox.

❸ Describe approaches for evaluating IT investment and explain why is it difficult to do it.

❹ Explain the nature of intangible benefits and the approaches to deal with such benefits.

❺ List and briefly describe the traditional and modern methods of justifying IT investment.

❻ Identify the advantages and disadvantages of approaches to charging end users for IT services (chargeback).

❼ Identify the advantages and disadvantages of outsourcing.

❽ Describe the economic impact of EC.

❾ Describe economic issues related to Web-based technologies including e-commerce.

❿ Describe causes of systems development failures, the theory of increasing returns, and market transformation through new technologies.

JUSTIFYING IT INVESTMENT
IN THE STATE OF IOWA

➡️ **THE PROBLEM**

For years there was little planning or justification for IT projects developed by agencies of the state of Iowa. State agencies requested many projects, knowing that they would get only a few. Bargaining, political favors, and pressures brought to bear by individuals, groups, and state employees determined who would get what. As a result some important projects were not funded, some unimportant ones were funded, and there was very little incentive to save money.

This situation existed in Iowa until 1999, and it exists even today in many other states, countries, counties, cities, and other public institutions. Any agency that needed money in Iowa for an IT project slipped it into its budget request. A good sales pitch would have resulted in approval. But, this situation, which cost taxpayers lots of money, changed in 1999 when a request for $22.5 million to fix the Y2K problem was made. This request triggered work that led Iowans to realize that the state government needed a better approach to planning and justifying IT investments.

➡️ **THE SOLUTION**

The solution that Iowa chose is an *IT value model.* The basic idea was to promote *performance-based government,* an approach that measures the results of government programs. Using the principles deployed to justify the investment in the Y2K fix, a methodology was developed to measure the value an IT project would create. The system is based on the return on investment (ROI) financial model, and is known as R.O. Iowa (a play on words). Its principles are described below.

First, new IT investments are paid for primarily from a pot of money called the Pooled Technology Account, which is appropriated by the legislature and is controlled by the state's IT department. Pooling the funds makes budget oversight easier and helps avoid duplication of systems. Second, the IT department reimburses agencies for expenses from this fund only after verifying that they are necessary. If an agency's expenditures are not in line with the project schedule, it's a red flag for auditors that the project could be in trouble.

To support spending decisions, agency managers have to document the expected costs and benefits according to a standard set of factors. The score for each factor ranges from 5 to 15 points, for a maximum total score of 100 points. In addition they must specify metrics related to those factors to justify requests and later to determine the project's success. The scores are based on ten criteria that are used to determine values. Besides asking for standard financial data, the ROI program also requires agencies to detail their technology requirements and functional needs. This level of detail enforces standards, but it also helps officials identify duplicative expenditures. For example, in 2001 several agencies were proposing to build pieces of an ERP system, such as electronic procurement and human resources management. The IS department suggested that, for less money, the state could deploy a single ERP system that agencies could share. The project, which had an estimated cost of $9.6 million, could easily have cost many times that amount, if agencies were allowed to go it alone.

As noted earlier, once a project is funded, the state scrutinizes agencies' expenses. Agencies have to submit their purchase orders and invoices to the Enterprise Quality Assurance Office for approval before they can be reimbursed.

 THE RESULTS

The R.O. Iowa system became, by 2002, a national model for documenting value and prioritizing IT investments in the U.S. public sector. In 2002 the program was named the "Best State IT Management Initiative" by the National Association of State CIOs. It saved Iowa taxpayers more than $5 million in less than 4 years (about 16 percent of the spending on new IT projects).

The process has changed users' behavior as well. For example, during the fiscal-year 2003 budget approval process, agencies asked for 17 IT projects, and were granted only six. For the year 2004 they asked for only four projects, all of which were granted. Also, there is considerable collaboration among agencies and use of cross-functional teams to write applications, so the need to "play games" to get project funding is largely gone. Another improvement is elimination of duplicated systems. Finally, the methodology minimizes politics and political pressures.

The success of R.O. Iowa led to the Iowa Accounting Government Act, which requires establishing similar methodology in all state investments, not just for IT projects.

Source: Compiled form Varon (2003).

 LESSONS LEARNED FROM THIS CASE

Justifying the cost of IT is a major financial decision that organizations must make today. The unique aspects of IT make its justification and economics different in many respects from the economics of other aspects of business. This chapter explores the issues related to IT economics.

In order to understand the factors that determine the IT investment justification, we need to understand the technological trends of increasing investment in technology and the changes that IT makes to productivity. These are the first topics we address in the chapter.

A major problem in making IT-related economic decisions is the measurement and comparison of performance under alternative methods. This is done with approaches such as scoring (used in R.O. Iowa), benchmarking, and metrics. Other important issues are assessing intangible variables and dealing with costs, including chargeback and outsourcing, which are viable strategies that are explored in this chapter. We also deal with e-commerce, whose economic foundations are also explained here. Finally, we discuss some failure issues which, as pointed out throughout the book, are common in IT and can cost dearly.

13.1 FINANCIAL AND ECONOMIC TRENDS AND THE PRODUCTIVITY PARADOX

Technological and Financial Trends

Information technology capabilities are advancing at a rapid rate, and this trend is likely to continue for the foreseeable future. Expanding power and declining costs enable new and more extensive applications of information technology, which makes it possible for organizations to improve their efficiency and effectiveness.

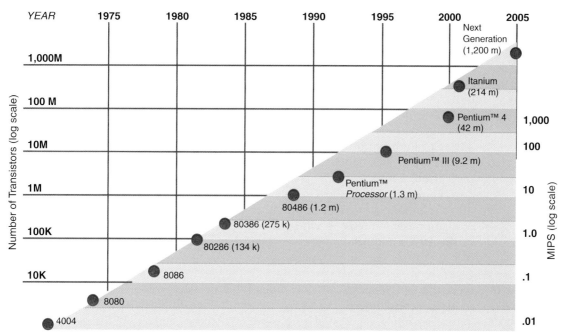

FIGURE 13.1 Moore's Law as it relates to Intel microprocessors. (*Source:* Modified from Intel Corporation, *intel.com.research/silicon/mooreslaw.htm*. Reprinted by permission of Intel Corporation, ©Intel Corporation.)

On the hardware side, capabilities are growing at an exponential rate. As discussed in Chapter 1, *Moore's Law,* named for one of the founders of Intel Corp., postulated that the number of transistors, and thus the power, of an integrated circuit (now, computer chip) would double every year, while the cost remained the same. Moore later revised this estimate to a slightly less rapid pace: doubling every 18 months. Figure 13.1 illustrates Moore's Law as it relates to the power of Intel microprocessors, measured in MIPS, or millions of (computer) instructions per second (on the right) and transistors count (on the left). Moore has also applied the law to the Web, electronic commerce, and supply chain management (see Moore, 1997). Others applied it, with slight modifications, to storage capability.

Assuming the current rate of growth in computing power (see Hamilton, 2003), organizations will have the opportunity to buy, for the same price, twice the processing power in $1\frac{1}{2}$ years, four times the power in 3 years, eight times the power in $4\frac{1}{2}$ years, and so forth. Another way of saying this is that the **price-to-performance ratio** will continue to decline exponentially. Limitations associated with current technologies could end this trend for silicon-based chips in 10 or 20 years (or possibly earlier; see Pountain, 1998), but new technologies will probably allow this phenomenal growth to continue. Advances in network technologies and storage, as compared to those in chip technology, are even more profound, as shown in Chapter 2.

What does this growth in computing power mean in economic terms? First, most organizations will perform existing functions at decreasing costs over time and thus become more efficient. Second, creative organizations will find new uses for information technology—based on the improving price-to-performance ratio—and thus become more effective. They will also apply technology to activities that are technically feasible at current power levels but will not be economically feasible until costs are reduced. Information technology will become an even more significant factor in the production and distribution of almost every product and service. This will increase the attractiveness of automating more manual jobs. Will it also result in more unemployment?

These new and enhanced products and services will provide competitive advantage to organizations that have the creativity to exploit the increasing power of information technology. They will also provide major benefits to consumers, who will benefit from the greater functionality and lower costs (e.g., see Farrell, 2003).

The remainder of this chapter focuses on evaluating the costs, benefits, and other economic aspects of information technology. Productivity is a major focus of economists, and those who studied the payoff from massive IT investments in the 1970s and 1980s observed what has been called the *productivity paradox.* It is that topic we address next.

What Is the Productivity Paradox?

Over the last 50 years, organizations have invested trillions of dollars in information technology. By the start of the twenty-first century, total worldwide *annual* spending on IT had surpassed two trillion dollars (ITAA, 2000). As this textbook has demonstrated, these expenditures have unquestionably transformed organizations: The technologies have become an integral aspect of almost every business process. The business and technology presses publish many "success stories" about major benefits from information technology projects at individual organizations or even industries (e.g., electronic ticketing). It seems self-evident that these investments must have increased productivity, not just in individual organizations, but throughout the economy.

On the other hand, it is very hard to demonstrate, at the level of a national economy, that the IT investments really have increased outputs or wages. Most of the investment went into the service sector of the economy which, during the 1970s and 1980s, was showing much lower productivity gains than manufacturing. Fisher (2001) reports on a study that showed that only 8 percent of total IT spending actually delivers value. Nobel prize winner in economics Robert Solow quipped, "We see computers everywhere except in the productivity statistics." The discrepancy between measures of investment in information technology and measures of output at the national level has been called the **productivity paradox.**

To understand this paradox, we first need to understand the concept of productivity. Economists define *productivity* as outputs divided by inputs. Outputs are calculated by multiplying units produced (for example, number of automobiles) by their average value. The resulting figure needs to be adjusted for price inflation and also for any changes in quality (such as increased safety or better gas mileage). If inputs are measured simply as hours of work, the resulting ratio of outputs to inputs is *labor productivity.* If other inputs—investments and materials—are included, the ratio is known as *multifactor productivity. A Closer Look 13.1* shows an example of a simple productivity calculation.

Explaining the Productivity Paradox

Economists have studied the productivity issue extensively in recent years and have developed a variety of possible explanations of the apparent paradox (e.g., see Olazabal, 2002). These explanations can be grouped into several categories:

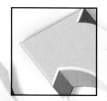

A CLOSER LOOK
13.1 CALCULATING LABOR PRODUCTIVITY AT THE DRISCOLL COMPANY

Assume that The Driscoll Company uses 10 employees who manually process 1,000 customer service inquiries per day. Unit sales are increasing at 5 percent per year, and the number of customer inquiries is increasing at about the same rate. Turnover among customer service representatives is 20 percent: On the average, two of these employees leave the company every year.

The company purchased an automated call-answering and customer-service system, which should make it possible to increase output per employee by 50 percent. That increase will make it possible to answer the calls using fewer customer-service reps. However, rather than having a layoff to achieve the 50 percent productivity gain right away, the company will rely on attrition; it will wait until employees leave on their own and then just not replace them. The following calculations compare productivity with the previous system and new systems.

PRODUCTIVITY WITH THE MANUAL SYSTEM:

1,000 inquiries/10 employees = 100 inquiries handled per employee per day

PRODUCTIVITY WITH THE AUTOMATED SYSTEM (ONE YEAR LATER):

1,050 inquiries/8 employees = 131 inquiries handled per employee per day

The productivity increase is 31 percent (131 − 100 = 31 ÷ 100 calls = 31%). Productivity will increase further as additional employees leave, up to the 50 percent increase determined by the technology.

(1) Problems with data or analyses hide productivity gains from IT, (2) gains from IT are offset by losses in other areas, and (3) IT productivity gains are offset by IT costs or losses. We discuss these explanations in more detail next.

DATA AND ANALYSIS PROBLEMS HIDE PRODUCTIVITY GAINS. Productivity numbers are only as good as the data used in their calculations. Therefore, one possible explanation for the productivity paradox is that the data, or the analysis of the data, is actually hiding productivity gains.

For manufacturing, it is fairly easy to measure outputs and inputs. General Motors, Ford, and DaimlerChrysler, for example, produce motor vehicles, relatively well-defined products whose quality changes gradually over time. It is not difficult to identify, with reasonable accuracy, the inputs used to produce these vehicles. However, the trend in the United States and other developed countries is away from manufacturing and toward services.

In service industries, such as finance or health care delivery, it is more difficult to define what the products are, how they change in quality, and how to allocate to them the corresponding costs. For example, banks now use IT to handle a large proportion of deposit and withdrawal transactions through automated teller machines (ATMs). The ability to withdraw cash from ATMs 24 hours per day, 7 days per week is a substantial quality increase in comparison to the traditional 9 A.M. to 4 P.M. hours for live tellers. But what is the value of this quality increase in comparison with the associated costs? If the incremental value exceeds the incremental costs, then it represents a productivity gain; otherwise the productivity impact is negative.

Similarly, the productivity gains may not be apparent in all processes supported by information systems. Mukhopadhyay et al. (1997), in an assessment of productivity impacts of IT on a toll-collection system, found that IT had a significant impact on the processing of complex transactions, but not on simple transactions. Based on an investigation of IT performance in 60 construction-industry firms in Hong Kong, Li et al. (2000) found productivity improvements in architecture and quantity-surveying firms (which perform a wide range of functions involved in the estimation and control of construction project costs) and no evidence of productivity improvement in engineering firms.

Another important consideration is the amount of time it takes to achieve the full benefits of new technologies. Economists point out that it took many decades to start achieving the full productivity impacts of the Industrial Revolution. Productivity actually may decrease during the initial learning period of new software and then increase over a period of a year or longer.

Hitt and Brynjolfsson (1996) point out that answers to questions about the value of IT investments depend on how the issue is defined. They emphasize that productivity is not the same thing as profitability. Their research indicates that IT increases productivity and value to consumers but does not increase organizational profitability. Brynjolfsson and Hitt (1998) suggest using alternate measures, other than traditional productivity measures, to measure productivity.

IT PRODUCTIVITY GAINS ARE OFFSET BY LOSSES IN OTHER AREAS.   Another possible explanation of the productivity paradox is that IT produces gains in certain areas of the economy, but that these gains are offset by losses in other areas. One company's IT usage could increase its share of market at the expense of the market share of other companies. Total output in the industry, and thus productivity, remains constant even though the competitive situation may change.

Offsetting losses can also occur within organizations. Consider the situation where an organization installs a new computer system that makes it possible to increase output per employee. If the organization reduces its production staff but increases employment in unproductive overhead functions, the productivity gains from information technology will be dispersed.

IT PRODUCTIVITY GAINS ARE OFFSET BY IT COSTS OR LOSSES.   The third possibility is that IT in itself really does not increase productivity. This idea seems contrary to common sense: Why would organizations invest tremendous amounts of money in something that really does not improve performance? On the other hand, there are considerations that support this possibility. Strassmann (1997) compared relative IT spending at a sample of corporations and found little or no relationship between IT spending and corporate profitability. (See Online File W13.1.)

To determine whether IT increases productivity, it is not enough simply to measure changes in outputs for a new system. If outputs increase 40 percent but inputs increase 50 percent, the result is a decline in productivity rather than a gain. Or consider a situation where a new system is developed and implemented but then, because of some major problems, is replaced by another system. Even though the second system has acceptable performance, an analysis that includes the costs of the unsuccessful system could indicate that IT did not increase productivity, at least in the short run.

Therefore, productivity evaluations must include changes in inputs, especially labor, over the total life cycle, including projects that are not implemented. These inputs need to include not just the direct labor required to develop and operate the system, but also indirect labor and other costs required to maintain the system. Examples of factors that, under this broader perspective, reduce productivity are provided in Online File W13.2.

Other possible explanations of the productivity paradox have been noted. A number of researchers have pointed out, for example, that time lags may throw off the productivity measurements (Reichheld and Scheffer, 2000; Qing and Plant, 2001). Many IT investments, especially those in CRM, for example, take five or six years to show results, but many studies do not wait that long to measure productivity changes. Another possible explanation was suggested by Devaraj and Kohli (2003), who tried to relate the actual use of a system, rather than the potential use, to the paradox. For a list of other explanations of the paradox proposed by Devaraj and Kohli (2002), see Online File W13.3.

Conclusion: Does the Productivity Paradox Matter?

The productivity-offsetting factors described earlier largely reflect problems with the administration of IT, rather than with the technologies themselves. In many cases these problems in administration are controllable through better planning or more effective management techniques. For organizations, the critical issue is not whether and how IT increases productivity *in the economy as a whole*, but how it improves their own productivity. Lin and Shao (2000) find a robust and consistent relationship between IT investment and efficiency, and they support evaluating IT investments in terms of organizational efficiency rather than productivity. For the results of a comprehensive study on the economic value of IT in Europe see Legrenzi (2003).

Some of the difficulties in finding the relationship between IT investment and organizational performance can be seen in Figure 13.2. The relationships are basically indirect, via IT assets and IT impacts. The figure shows that the relationships between IT investment and performance are not direct; other factors exist in between. This could be the reason why the productivity paradox exists, since these intermediary factors (in the middle of the figure) can moderate and influence the relationship.

The inconclusiveness of studies about the value of IT investment and inaccuracies in measurements have prompted many companies to skip formal evaluations (see Seddon et al., 2002, and Sawhney, 2002). However, as became apparent during the dot-com bubble, when many dot-coms were started and almost as many quickly failed, this can be a very risky approach. Therefore, before

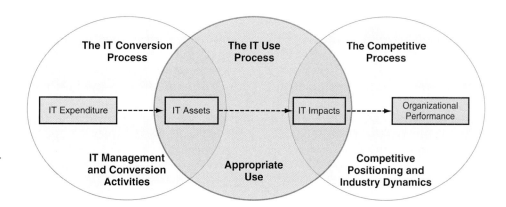

FIGURE 13.2 Process approach to IT organizational investment and impact. (*Source:* Soh and Markus, 1995.)

deciding to skip evaluation, an organization should examine some of the new methods that may result in more accurate evaluation (see Section 13.3).

Many believe that the productivity paradox as it relates to IT is no longer valid, since we are able to explain what caused it. Others believe that the issue is still very relevant, especially on the level of the economy as a whole. They claim that the paradox still matters because IT has failed to lift productivity growth throughout the economy, although it may have improved productivity at the level of firms or of industries. We may not at this point be able to provide a final answer to the question about whether the paradox still matters. The important conclusion that we can draw is that we need to be careful in measuring the economic contributions of information technology on all three levels—firms, industries, and economies. Because almost 50 percent of all capital investment in the United States is in IT and it is growing with time, it is even more important to properly assess its benefits and costs, and that is what this chapter is attempting to do.

The next two sections cover ways organizations can evaluate IT benefits and costs and target their IT development and acquisition toward systems that will best contribute to the achievement of organizational goals.

13.2 EVALUATING IT INVESTMENT: BENEFITS, COSTS, AND ISSUES

Evaluating IT investment covers many topics. Let's begin by categorizing types of IT investment.

IT Investment Categories

One basic way to segregate IT investment is to distinguish between investment in infrastructure and investment in specific applications.

IT infrastructure provides the foundations for IT applications in the enterprise. Examples are a data center, networks, data warehouse, and knowledge base. Infrastructure investments are made for a long time, and the infrastructure is shared by many applications throughout the enterprise (see Broadbent and Weill, 1997). *IT applications* are specific systems and programs for achieving certain objectives—for example, providing a payroll or taking a customer order. The number of IT applications is large and they can be in one functional department, or they can be shared by several departments, which makes evaluation of their costs and benefits more complex.

Another way to look at IT investment categories is proposed by Ross and Beath (2002). As shown in Online File W13.4, their categories are based on the purpose of the investment (called "drivers" in the table). They also suggest a cost justification (funding approach) as well as the probable owner. Still other investment categories are offered by Devaraj and Kohli (2002), who divide IT investments into operational, managerial, and strategic types, and by Lucas (1999), whose types of investment are shown in Online File W13.5. The variety of IT investment categories demonstrates the complex nature of IT investment.

The Value of Information in Decision Making

People in organizations use information to help them make decisions that are better than they would have been if they did not have the information. Senior executives make decisions that influence the profitability of an organization for years to come; operational employees make decisions that affect production on a day-to-day basis. In either case, the value of information is the difference between the *net benefits* (benefits adjusted for costs) of decisions made using information and the net benefits of decisions made without information. The value of the net benefits with information obviously needs to reflect the additional costs of obtaining the information. Thus, the value of information can be expressed as follows:

> Value of information = Net benefits with information
>   − Net benefits without information

It is generally assumed that systems that provide relevant information to support decision making will result in better decisions, and therefore they will contribute toward the return on investment. But, this is not always the case. For example, Dekker and de Hoog (2000) found that the return on most knowledge assets created for loan evaluation decisions in a large bank was negative. However, as technology gets cheaper and applications get more sophisticated, it becomes more attractive to use technology not only to improve service but also to increase profit.

A popular alternative to measure the value of information is to have the decision maker subjectively estimate it. This person is most familiar with the situation and has the most to lose from a bad decision. However, to make sure the estimates are not inflated in order to get an approval for more IT, the organization needs to hold the decision maker *accountable* for the cost and benefits of the information. Before we deal with such accountability we will examine the methodologies of evaluating automation of business processes with IT.

Evaluating IT Investment by Traditional Cost-Benefit Analysis

Automation of business processes is a major area where it is necessary to define and measure IT benefits and costs. For example, automation was implemented in the organization's business offices when word processing replaced typing and spreadsheet programs replaced column-ruled accounting pads and 10-key calculators. In the factory, robots weld and paint automobiles on assembly lines. In the warehouse, incoming items are recorded by RFID readers. The decision of whether to automate is an example of a *capital investment* decision. Another example is replacement of an old information system by a new or improved one. Traditional tools used to evaluate capital investment decisions are net present value and return on investment.

USING NPV IN COST-BENEFIT ANALYSIS.   Capital investment decisions can be analyzed by **cost-benefit analyses,** which compare the total value of the benefits with the associated costs. Organizations often use net present value (NPV) calculations for cost-benefit analyses. In an NPV analysis, analysts convert future values of benefits to their present-value equivalent by discounting them at the organization's cost of funds. They then can compare the present value of the future benefits to the cost required to achieve those benefits, in order to determine whether the benefits exceed the costs. (For more specific guidelines and decision criteria on how NPV analysis works, consult financial management textbooks.)

The NPV analysis works well in situations where the costs and benefits are well defined or "tangible," so that it is not difficult to convert them into monetary values. For example, if human welders are replaced by robots that produce work of comparable quality, the benefits are the labor cost savings over the usable life of the robots. Costs include the capital investment to purchase and install the robots, plus the operating and maintenance costs.

RETURN ON INVESTMENT. Another traditional tool for evaluating capital investments is *return on investment (ROI)*, which measures the effectiveness of management in generating profits with its available assets. The ROI measure is a percentage (and the higher this percentage return, the better). It is calculated essentially by dividing net annual income attributable to a project by the cost of the assets invested in the project. For an overview, see Paton and Troppito (2004). An example of a detailed study of the ROI of a portal, commissioned by Plumtree Software and executed by META group, can be found at *plumtree.com* (also white papers at *metagroup.com*). Davamanirajan et al. (2002) found an average 10 percent annual rate of return on investment in IT projects in the financial services sector. For a comprehensive study see Kudyba and Vitaliano (2003).

**Costing
IT Investment**

Placing a dollar value on the cost of IT investments may not be as simple as it may sound. One of the major issues is to allocate fixed costs among different IT projects. *Fixed costs* are those costs that remain the same in total regardless of change in the activity level. For IT, fixed costs include infrastructure cost, cost of IT services (Gerlach et al., 2002), and IT management cost. For example, the salary of the IT director is fixed, and adding one more application will not change it.

Another area of concern is the fact that the cost of a system does not end when the system is installed. Costs for keeping it running, dealing with bugs, and for improving and changing the system may continue for some time. Such costs can accumulate over many years, and sometimes they are not even anticipated when the investment is made. An example is the cost of the Y2K reprogramming projects that cost billions of dollars to organizations worldwide. (For a discussion see Read et al., 2001.)

The fact that organizations use IT for different purposes further complicates the costing process (see DiNunno, 2002, for discussion). There are multiple kinds of values (e.g., improved efficiency, improved customer or partner relations); the return on a capital investment measured in numeric terms (e.g., dollar or percentage) is only one of these values. In addition, the probability of obtaining a return from an IT investment also depends on the probability of implementation success. These probabilities reflect the fact that many systems are not implemented on time, within budget, and/or with all the features orginally envisioned for them. Finally, the expected value of the return on IT investment in most cases will be less than that originally anticipated. For this reason, Gray and Watson (1998) point out that managers often make substantial investments in projects like data warehousing by relying on intuition when evaluating investment proposals rather than on concrete evaluation.

After the dot-com problems of 2000–2002 it become almost mandatory to justify IT projects with a solid business case, including ROI. However, according to Sawhney (2002), and others, this may have little value due to the difficulties in dealing with intangible benefits. These are real and important, but it is not easy to accurately estimate their value. (For further guidelines on cost-benefit analysis, see Clermont, 2002.)

**The Problem of
Intangible Benefits**

As indicated above, in many cases IT projects generate **intangible benefits** such as faster time to market, employee and customer satisfaction, easier distribution, greater organizational agility, and improved control. These are very desirable benefits, but it is difficult to place an accurate monetary value on them. For example, many people would agree that e-mail improves communications, but it is not at all clear how to measure the value of this improvement. Managers are very conscious of the bottom line, but no manager can prove that e-mail is responsible for so many cents per share of the organization's total profits.

Intangible benefits can be very complex yet substantial. For example, according to Arno Penzias, a Nobel Laureate in physics, the New York Metropolitan Transit Authority (MTA) had not found the need to open another airport for almost two decades, even when traffic had tripled. This, according to his study, was due to productivity gains derived from improved IT systems (quoted by Devaraj and Kohli, 2002). IT systems added by the MTA played critical roles in ticket reservations, passenger and luggage check-in, crew assignment and scheduling, runway maintenance and management, and gate assignments. These improvements enabled MTA to cope with increased traffic without adding new facilities, saving hundreds of millions of dollars. Many similar examples of increased capacity exist. Intangible benefits are especially common in service and government applications (see Steyaert, 2004).

One class of intangible benefits, according to Ryan and Gates (2004), is *social subsystem issues*, such as comfort to employees, impact on the environment, changes to the power distribution in an organization, and invasion of the privacy of employees and customers.

An analyst could ignore intangible benefits, but doing so implies that their value is zero and may lead the organization to reject IT investments that could substantially increase revenues and profitability. Therefore, financial analyses need to consider not just tangible benefits but also intangible benefits in such a way that the decision reflects their potential impact. The question is how to do it.

HANDLING INTANGIBLE BENEFITS. The most straightforward solution to the problem of evaluating intangible benefits in cost-benefit analysis is to make *rough estimates* of monetary values for all intangible benefits, and then conduct a NVP or similar financial analysis. The simplicity of this approach is attractive, but in many cases the assumptions used in these estimates are debatable. If the technology is acquired because decision makers assigned too high a value to intangible benefits, the organization could find that it has wasted some valuable resources. On the other hand, if the valuation of intangible benefits is too low, the organization might reject the investment and then find that it is losing market share to competitors who did implement the technology. (See Plumtree Corp., 2001, for a study on translating intangible benefits to dollar amounts.)

There are many approaches to handling intangibles (e.g., see Read et al., 2001). Sawhney (2002) suggests the following solutions:

- ***Think broadly and softly.*** Supplement hard financial metrics with soft ones that may be more strategic in nature and may be important leading indicators of financial outcomes. Measures such as customer and partner satisfaction, customer loyalty, response time to competitive actions, and improved responsiveness are examples of soft measures. Subjective measures can be objective if used consistently over time. For instance, customer satisfaction measured consistently on a five-point scale can be an objective basis for measuring the performance of customer-facing initiatives.

- ***Pay your freight first.*** Think carefully about short-term benefits that can "pay the freight" for the initial investment in the project. For example, a telecom company found that it could justify its investment in data warehousing based on the cost savings from data mart consolidation, even though the real payoffs from the project would come later from increased cross-selling opportunities.

● *Follow the unanticipated.* Keep an open mind about where the payoff from IT and e-business projects may come from, and follow opportunities that present themselves. Eli Lilly & Co. created a Web site called InnoCentive (*innocentive.com*) to attract scientists to solve problems in return for financial rewards ("bounties"). In the process, Lilly established contact with 8,000 exceptional scientists, and Lilly's HR department has used this list of contacts for recruiting.

The Business Case Approach

One method used to justify investments in projects, or even in entire new companies, is referred to as the *business case approach*. The concept of a business case received lots of attention in the mid-1990s when it was used to justify funding for investment in dot-coms. In 2002–2003, it has become clear that one of the reasons for the collapse of the dot-com bubble was improper business cases submitted to investors. Nevertheless, if done correctly, business cases can be a useful tool.

A **business case** is a written document that is used by managers to garner funding for one or more specific applications or projects. Its major emphasis is the justification for a specific required investment, but it also provides the bridge between the initial plan and its execution. Its purpose is not only to get approval and funding, but also to provide the foundation for tactical decision making and technology risk management. A business case is usually conducted in existing organizations that want to embark on new IT projects (for example, an e-procurement project). The business case helps to clarify how the organization will use its resources in the best way to accomplish the IT strategy. It helps the organization concentrate on justifying the investment, on risk management, and on fit of an IT project with the organization's mission. Software for preparing a business case for IT (and for EC in particular) is commercially available (e.g., from *paloalto.com* and from *bplans.com*).

A business case for IT investment can be very complex. Gunasekaran et al. (2001) divided such justification into five parts as shown in Figure 13.3.

Sometimes an IT project is necessary in order for the organization to stay in business, and in those instances, the business case is very simple: "We must do it, we have no choice." For example, the U.S. Internal Revenue Service is requiring businesses to switch to electronic systems for filing their tax returns. Both Wal-Mart and the U.S. federal government mandate that large suppliers must use RFIDs if they want to do business. Sometimes an organization must invest because its competitors have done so and if it does not follow, it will lose customers. Examples are e-banking and some CRM services. These types of investments do not require firms to do a lot of analysis.

For a description of business cases in e-commerce, see Turban et al. (2006). For a tool for building a business case, see Wang and Shiang (2002) and *sap.com/solutions/case builder*. For a discussion of how to conduct a business case for global expansion, see DePalma (2001). An example of a business case for wireless networks, prepared by Intel Corp. (2002), is presented in Online File W13.6.

Evaluating IT Investment: Conclusions

This section has shown that several traditional methods can be used to assess the value of IT information and IT investment. Table 13.1 lists some of the traditional financial evaluation methods with their advantages and disadvantages.

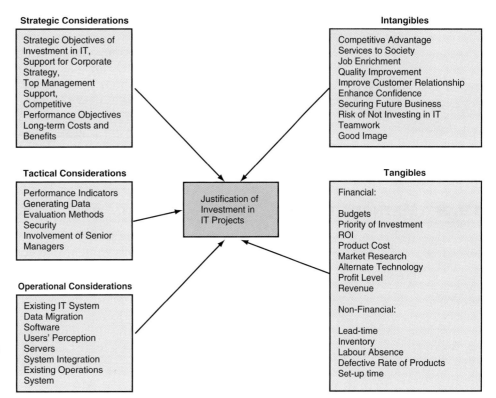

FIGURE 13.3 A model for investment justification in IT projects. (*Source:* Gunasekaran et al., 2001, p. 354.)

TABLE 13.1 Traditional Methods of Evaluating Investments

Method	Advantages	Disadvantages
Internal rate of return (IRR)	Brings all projects to common footing. Conceptually familiar.	Assumes reinvestment at same rate. Can have multiple roots. No assumed discount rate.
Net present value or net worth (NPV or NW)	Very common. Maximizes value for unconstrained project selection.	Difficult to compare projects of unequal lives or sizes.
Equivalent annuity (EA)	Brings all project NPVs to common footing. Convenient annual figure.	Assumes projects repeat to least common multiple of lives, or imputes salvage value.
Payback period	May be discounted or non-discounted. Measure of exposure.	Ignores flows after payback is reached. Assumes standard project cash flow profile.
Benefit-to-cost ratio	Conceptually familiar. Brings all projects to common footing.	May be difficult to classify outlays between expense and investment.

Source: Compiled from *Capital Budgeting and Long-Term Financing Decisions*, 2nd ed., by N. E. Seitz © 1995. Reprinted with permission of South-Western College Publishing, a division of Thomson Learning.

Different organizations use different methods, which often are chosen by management and may change over time as an organization's finance personnel come and go. For example, many companies have automated programs that use company-specific inputs and hurdles for making ROI calculations.

However, traditional methods may not be useful for assessing some of the newest technologies (e.g., see Violino, 1997). (An example of such a case—acquiring expert systems—is shown in Online File W13.7.) Because traditional methods may not be useful for evaluating new technologies, there are special methodologies (some of them incorporated in computerized models) for dealing with investment in IT. We will address some of these methods next.

13.3 METHODS FOR EVALUATING AND JUSTIFYING IT INVESTMENT

As indicated earlier, evaluating and justifying IT investment can pose problems different from traditional capital investment decisions such as whether to buy a new delivery truck. However, even though the relationship between intangible IT benefits and performance is not clear, some investments should be better than others. How can organizations increase the probability that their IT investments will improve their performance?

A comprehensive list of over 60 different appraisal methods for IT investments can be found in Renkema (2000). For details of some methods, see McKay and Marshall (2004). The appraisal methods are categorized into the following four types.

1. *Financial approach.* These appraisal methods consider only impacts that can be monetary-valued. They focus on incoming and outgoing cash flows as a result of the investment made. Net present value and return on investment are examples of financial-approach methods.

2. *Multicriteria approach.* These appraisal methods consider both financial impacts and nonfinancial impacts that cannot be (or cannot easily be) expressed in monetary terms. These methods employ quantitative and qualitative decision-making techniques. Information economics and value analysis are examples.

3. *Ratio approach.* These methods use several ratios (e.g., IT expenditures vs. total turnover) to assist in IT investment evaluation.

4. *Portfolio approach.* These methods apply portfolios (or grids) to plot several investment proposals against decision-making criteria. The portfolio methods are more informative compared to multicriteria methods and generally use fewer evaluation criteria.

The following specific evaluation methods that are particularly useful in evaluating IT investment are discussed in this section: total cost of ownership, value analysis, information economics, use of benchmarks, management by maxim, and real-option valuation. Other methods are cited briefly at the end of the section.

Total Cost of Ownership   As mentioned earlier, the costs of an IT system can sometimes accumulate over many years. An interesting approach for IT cost evaluation is the **total cost of ownership (TCO).** TCO is a formula for calculating the cost of owning, operating, and controlling an IT system, even one as simple as a PC. The cost includes *acquisition cost* (hardware and software), *operations cost* (maintenance, training, operations, evaluation, technical support, installation, downtime, auditing, virus damage, and power consumption), and *control cost* (standardization, security, central services). The TCO can be a hundred percent higher than just the cost of the hardware, especially for PCs (David et al., 2002). By identifying these various costs, organizations can make more accurate cost-benefit analyses. A methodology for calculating TCO is offered by David et al. (2002). They also provide a detailed example of the items to be included in the TCO calculations (see Online File W13.8). For further discussion, see Vijayan (2001) and Blum (2001), and for a comprehensive study, see Ferrin and Plank (2002).

A concept similar to TCO is **total benefits of ownership (TBO).** These benefits cover both tangible and the intangible benefits. By calculating and comparing both TCO and TBO, one can compute the payoff of an IT investment [Payoff = TBO − TCO]. For details on the calculations, see Devaraj and Kohli (2002) and also Online File W13.8.

Value Analysis

The **value analysis** method evaluates intangible benefits on a low-cost, trial basis before deciding whether to commit to a larger investment in a complete system. Keen (1981) developed the value analysis method to assist organizations considering investments in decision support systems (DSSs). The major problem with justifying a DSS is that most of the benefits are intangible and not readily convertible into monetary values. Some—such as better decisions, better understanding of business situations, and improved communication—are difficult to measure even in nonmonetary terms. These problems in evaluating DSSs are similar to the problems in evaluating intangible benefits for other types of systems. Therefore, value analysis could be applicable to other types of IT investments in which a large proportion of the added value derives from intangible benefits.

The value analysis approach includes eight steps, grouped into two phases. As illustrated in Figure 13.4, the first phase (first four steps) works with a low-cost prototype. Depending on the initial results, this prototype is followed by a full-scale system in the second phase.

In the first phase the decision maker identifies the desired capabilities and the (generally intangible) potential benefits. The developers estimate the cost of providing the capabilities; if the decision maker feels the benefits are worth this cost, a small-scale prototype of the DSS (or other IT application) is constructed. The prototype then is evaluated.

The results of the first phase provide information that helps with the decision about the second phase. After using the prototype, the user has a better understanding of the value of the benefits, and of the additional features the full-scale system needs to include. In addition, the developers can make a better estimate of the cost of the final product. The question at this point is: What

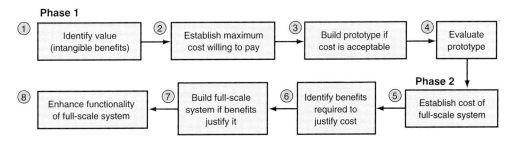

FIGURE 13.4 Steps in the value analysis approach.

benefits are necessary to justify this cost? If the decision maker feels that the system can provide these benefits, development proceeds on the full-scale system.

Though it was designed for DSSs, the value analysis approach is applicable to any information technology that can be tested on a low-cost basis before deciding whether to make a full investment. The current trend of buying rather than developing software, along with the increasingly common practice of offering software on a free-trial basis for 30 to 90 days, provide ample opportunities for the use of this approach. Organizations may also have opportunities to pilot the use of new systems in specific operating units, and then to implement them on a full-scale basis if the initial results are favorable. For further discussion see Fine et al. (2002).

Information Economics

The **information economics** approach is similar to the concept of critical success factors in that it focuses on key organizational objectives, including intangible financial benefits, impacts on the business domain, and impact on IT itself. Each area has several components (see Figure 13.5). In addition, more areas can be added (see McKay and Marshall, 2004). Information economics incorporates the familiar technique of *scoring* methodologies, which are used in many evaluation situations.

A **scoring methodology** evaluates alternatives by assigning weights and scores to various aspects and then calculating the weighted totals. The analyst first identifies all the key performance issues and assigns a weight to each one. Each alternative in the evaluation receives a score on each factor, usually between zero and 100 points, or between zero and 10. These scores are multiplied by the weighting factors and then totaled. The alternative with the highest score is judged the best (or projects can be ranked, as in the R.O. Iowa case at the beginning of the chapter). Then one can perform sensitivity analysis, to see the impact of changing weights. Online File W13.9 shows an example of using a scoring methodology to evaluate two different alternatives.

The information economics approach uses *organizational objectives* to determine which factors to include, and what weights to assign, in the scoring methodology. The approach is flexible enough to include factors in the analysis such as impacts on customers and suppliers (the value chain). Executives in an organization determine the relevant objectives and weights at a given point in time, subject to revision if there are changes in the environment. These factors

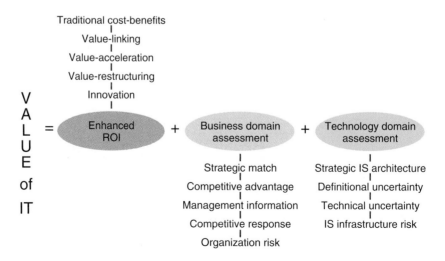

FIGURE 13.5 Information economics. (*Source:* Willcocks, 1994, p. 376.)

and weights are then used to evaluate IT alternatives; the highest scores go to the items that have the greatest potential to improve organizational performance.

Note that this approach can incorporate both tangible and intangible benefits. If there is a strong connection between a benefit of IT investment (such as quicker decision making) and an organizational objective (such as faster product development), the benefit will influence the final score even if it does not have a monetary value. Thus the information economics model helps solve the problem of assessing intangible benefits by linking the evaluation of these benefits to the factors that are most important to organizational performance.

Approaches like this are very flexible. The analyst can vary the weights over time; for example, tangible benefits might receive heavier weights at times when earnings are weak. The approach can also take risk into account, by using negative weights for factors that reduce the probability of obtaining the benefits. Information economics studies appear in various shapes depending on the circumstances. An example in banking is provided by Peffers and Sarrinen (2002). Note that in this study, as in many others, special attention is paid to the issue of *risk assessment.* (See also Gaulke, 2002.) Online File W13.10 shows an analysis of a decision of whether to develop a system in-house or buy it. Information economics can be implemented by software packages such as Expert Choice (*expertchoice.com*).

Assessing Investments in IT Infrastructure

Information systems projects are usually not standalone applications. In most cases they depend for support on enabling infrastructures already installed in the organization. These infrastructure technologies include mainframe computers, operating systems, networks, database management systems, utility programs, development tools, and more. Since many of the infrastructure benefits are intangible and are spread over many different present and future applications, it is hard to estimate their value or to evaluate the desirability of enhancements or upgrades. In other words, it is much more difficult to evaluate infrastructure investment decisions than investments in specific information systems application projects (see Lewis and Byrd, 2003). Two methods are recommended: use of benchmarks and management by maxim.

USING BENCHMARKS TO ASSESS INFRASTRUCTURE INVESTMENTS. One approach to evaluating infrastructure is to focus on *objective* measures of performance known as **benchmarks.** These measures are often available from trade associations within an industry or from consulting firms. A comparison of measures of performance or of an organization's expenditures with averages for the industry or with values of the more efficient performers in the industry indicates how well the organization is using its infrastructure. If performance is below standard, corrective action is indicated. The benchmark approach implicitly assumes that IT infrastructure investments are justified if they are managed efficiently.

Benchmarks come in two very different forms: *Metrics* and *best-practice benchmarks.* **Metric benchmarks** provide numeric measures of performance; for example: (1) IT expenses as percent of total revenues, (2) percent of downtime (time when the computer is unavailable), (3) central processing unit (CPU) usage as a percentage of total capacity, and (4) percentage of IS projects completed on time and within budget. These types of measures are very useful to managers, even though sometimes they lead to the wrong conclusions. For example, a ratio of IT expenses to revenues that is lower than the industry average might indicate that a firm is operating more efficiently than its competitors. Or it might indicate that the company is investing less in IT than it should and will become less competitive as a result. An illustration of typical support expected from benchmarking tools in complex IT environments is described in Online File W13.11.

Metric benchmarks can help diagnose problems, but they do not necessarily show how to solve them. Therefore, many organizations also use **best-practice benchmarks.** Here the emphasis is on how information system activities are actually performed rather than on numeric measures of performance. For example, an organization might feel that its IT infrastructure management is very important to its performance. It then could obtain information about best practices about how to operate and manage IT infrastructure. These best practices might be from other organizations in the same industry, from a more efficient division of its own organization, or from another industry entirely. The organization would then implement these best practices for all of its own IT infrastructure, to bring performance up to the level of the leaders.

MANAGEMENT BY MAXIM FOR IT INFRASTRUCTURE. Organizations that are composed of multiple business units, including large, multidivisional ones, frequently need to make decisions about the appropriate level and types of infrastructure that will support and be shared among their individual operating units. These decisions are important because infrastructure can amount to over 50 percent of the total IT budget, and because it can increase effectiveness through synergies across the organization. However, because of substantial differences among organizations in their culture, structure, and environment, what is appropriate for one will not necessarily be suitable for others. The fact that many of the benefits of infrastructure are intangible further complicates this issue.

Broadbent and Weill (1997) suggest a method called **management by maxim** to deal with this problem. This method brings together corporate executives, business-unit managers, and IT executives in planning sessions to determine appropriate infrastructure investments through five steps that are diagrammed in Figure 13.6. In the process, managers articulate *business maxims*—short, well-defined statements of organizational strategies or goals—and develop corresponding *IT maxims* that explain how IT could be used to support the business maxims. The five steps are further discussed in Online File W13.12.

Notice that Figure 13.6 also shows a line at the bottom flowing through an item labeled "Deals." This represents a theoretical alternative approach in the absence of appropriate maxims, where the IT manager negotiates with individual business units to obtain adequate funding for *shared infrastructure*. This approach can work where there is no shared infrastructure, or where the infrastructure category is a utility. However, Broadbent and Weill (1997) have not found any cases of firms that developed an enabling infrastructure via deals.

Real-Option Valuation of IT Investment

A promising new approach for evaluating IT investments is to recognize that they can increase an organization's performance in the future. This is especially important for emerging technologies that need time to mature. The concept of real options comes from the field of finance, where financial managers have applied it to capital budgeting decisions. Instead of using only traditional measures like NPV to make capital decisions, financial managers are looking for opportunities that may be *embedded in* capital projects. These opportunities, if taken, will enable the organization to alter future cash flows in a way that will increase profitability. These opportunities are called **real options** (to distinguish them from *financial options* that give investors the right to buy or sell a financial asset at a stated

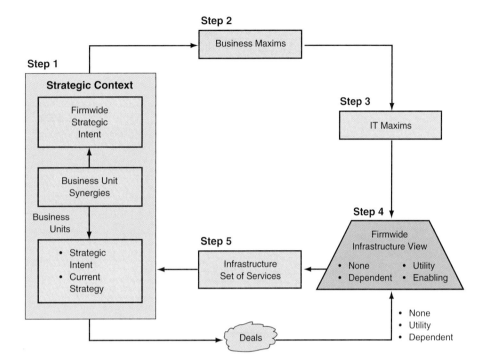

FIGURE 13.6
Management by maxim: Linking strategy and infrastructure. (*Source:* M. Broadbent and P. Weill, "Management by Maxim," *Sloan Management Review,* Spring 1997, p. 79, by permission of publisher. ©2001 by Massachusetts Institute of Technology. All rights reserved.)

price on or before a set date). Common types of real options include the option to expand a project (so as to capture additional cash flows from such growth), the option to terminate a project that is doing poorly (in order to minimize loss on the project), and the option to accelerate or delay a project (e.g., the delay of airport expansion cited earlier). Current IT investments, especially for infrastructure, can be viewed as another type of real option. Such capital budgeting investments make it possible to respond quickly to unexpected and unforeseeable challenges and opportunities in later years. If the organization waits in its investment decisions until the benefits have been established, it may be very difficult to catch up with competitors that have already invested in the infrastructure and have become familiar with the technology.

Applying just the NPV concept (or other purely financial) measure to an investment in IT infrastructure, an organization may decide that the costs of a proposed investment exceed the tangible benefits. However, if the project creates opportunities for additional projects in the future—that is, if it creates opportunities for real options—the investment also has an options value that should be added to its other benefits (see Benaroch, 2002, and Devaraj and Kohli, 2002).

The mathematics of real-option valuation are well established but unfortunately are too complex for many managers. (See Dixit and Pindyck, 1995, for details.) For a discussion on using real-option pricing analysis to evaluate a real-world IT project investment in four different settings, see Benaroch and Kauffman (1999). Li and Johnson (2002) use a similar approach. For an example of DSS evaluation using real-option theory, see Kumar (1999). Rayport and Jaworski (2001) applied the method for evaluating EC initiatives (see Online File W13.13).

The Balanced Scorecard and Similar Methods

The **balanced scorecard method** evaluates the overall health of organizations and projects. Initiated by Kaplan and Norton (1996), the method advocates that managers focus not only on short-term financial results, but also on four other

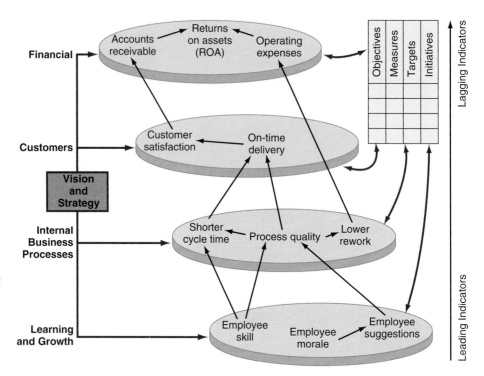

FIGURE 13.7 The logic of the balanced scorecard. (*Source:* Compiled from Dutta and Manzoni, 1999, p. 215; and from The Balanced Scorecard Institute, 2004.)

areas for which metrics are available. These areas are: (1) finance, including both short- and long-term measures; (2) customers (how customers view the organization); (3) internal business processes (finding areas in which to excel); and (4) learning and growth (the ability to change and expand). The key idea is that an organization should consider all four strategic areas when considering IT investments.

The balanced scorecard, similar to *information economics*, assumes that in addition to financial results (which are *lagging indicators*, see Figure 13.7), IT investments in people, skills and capabilities, creating databases, knowledge, and so forth, are measures of the success of organizations (*leading indicators*). The scorecard method (Kaplan and Norton, 2000) offers a series of interlinked measures (shown in the figure) that are derived from both short-term operational requirements and long-term vision and strategy. The financial measures show current success (and/or problems), while the other measures point to the future. In his framework, van Grembergen (2003) relates the balanced scorecard to the results of IT investment.

Swamy (2002) attempted to use the balanced scorecard to measure the performance of EC systems, including intangible benefits. He examined the EC systems from two perspectives: that of the e-business and that of the user. Rayport and Jawarski (2001) developed a variant of the balanced scorecard called *performance dashboard,* which they advocate for evaluation of EC strategy. Several other attempts to fit the balanced scorecard approach to IT project assessment have been made (e.g., see van Grembergen et al., 2003, and *balancedscorecard.org*). The methodology actually is embedded in several vendors' products (e.g., *sas.com/solutions/bsc/*). For demos see *corvu.com*. For more on the balanced scorecard, see Lawson et al. (2004).

Other Methods and Tools

Several other methods exist for evaluating IT investment. For example, most large vendors provide proprietary *calculators for ROI*. However, according to King (2002), those may be biased (and may lead to a sometimes-unjustified decision to adopt a project). To make the decision less biased, some companies use a third-party evaluator, such as IDC (*idc.com*) or META Group (*metagroup.com*) to conduct ROI studies. An example of such a calculator is SAP Business Case Builder. (For details see *sap.com/solutions/casebuilder*.) Several independent vendors offer ROI calculators (e.g., CIO View Corporation). CIO.com (2004) offers many tools via Nucleuse Research Inc. for calculating ROI of different IT systems.

According to Rubin (2003), every IT project *must* be tied to a specific business objective, with its priority indicated, so as to measure the project's success in terms of a specific primary business value. Rubin developed a special "whiteboard" that includes metrics and their stakeholders. For details and examples, see Rubin (2003).

In addition, there are other popular methods (e.g., see Irani and Love, 2000–2001), a few of which we describe briefly next.

IT Metrics

A **metric** is a specific, measurable standard against which actual performance is compared. Metrics can produce very positive results in organizations by driving behavior in a number of ways. According to Rayport and Jaworski (2001), metrics can:

- Define the value proposition of business models.
- Communicate the strategy to the workforce through performance targets.
- Increase accountability when metrics are linked to performance-appraisal programs.
- Align the objectives of individuals, departments, and divisions to the enterprise's strategic objectives.

An example of IT metrics implementation can be found in a white paper that analyzed the impact of a new online service on the profitability of Axon Computertime, a small computer services business in New Zealand (Green, 2002). Axon found the following results were obtained from the implementation of this service as part of their EC strategy:

- *Revenue growth.* Product revenue increased over 40 percent in the first 12 months of operation.
- *Cost reduction.* Selling costs were reduced by 40 percent for each dollar of margin generated.
- *Cost reduction.* Expenditures on brochure design and production were reduced by 45 percent.
- *Cost avoidance.* Obsolete stock write-offs as percentage of revenue were reduced by 93 percent.
- *Customer fulfillment.* Average days to delivery were reduced by 20 percent over 2 years.
- *Customer service.* Customer satisfaction with the delivery process is consistently in excess of 80 percent.
- *Customer communications.* Customer response to e-mail communications is five times the response rate to postal mail.

The last few metrics in this list highlight the importance of including nonfinancial measures in the measurement of organizational performance.

THE EXPLORATION, INVOLVEMENT, ANALYSIS, AND COMMUNICATIONS (EIAC) MODEL. Devaraj and Kohli (2002) propose a methology for implementing IT payoff initiatives. The method is composed of nine phases, divided into four categories: exploration (E), involvement (I), analysis (A), and communication (C). These are shown in Online File W13.14 at the book's Web site. For details see Devaraj and Kohli (2002).

ACTIVITY-BASED COSTING. A fairly recent approach for assessing IT investment is proposed by Gerlach et al. (2002) and Roberts (2003), who suggest use of the *activity-based costing (ABC)* approach to assist in IT investment analysis. (For details on how ABC works, see a management or managerial accounting textbook.) Using a case study, Gerlach et al. showed that the company that utilized ABC derived significant benefits from a better understanding of IT delivery costs and a rationale for explaining IT costs to department managers. Mutual understanding of IT costs is a necessary condition for shared responsibility of IT, which in turn leads to effective economic decision making that optimizes resource utilization and the alignment of IT with business strategy. In addition, the use of ABC helps in reducing operational costs.

EXPECTED VALUE ANALYSIS. It is relatively easy to estimate **expected value (EV)** of possible future benefits by multiplying the size of each benefit by the probability of its occurrence. For example, an organization might consider investing in a corporate portal only if there is a 50 percent probability that this would result in new business worth $10 million in additional profits and the cost will be less than $5 million. The value of this specific benefit would be 50 percent times $10 million, or $5 million. This method is simple but like any EV approach, it can be used only for *repetitive investments*.

Unfortunately, none of the above methods is perfect, and it is not simple for organizations to decide which method to use in which case.

13.4 IT ECONOMICS STRATEGIES: CHARGEBACK AND OUTSOURCING

In addition to identifying and evaluating the benefits of IT, organizations also need to account for its costs. Ideally, the organization's accounting systems will effectively deal with two issues: First, they should provide an accurate measure of total IT costs for management control purposes. Second, they should charge users for shared (usually infrastructure) IT investments and services in a manner that contributes to the achievement of organization goals. These are two very challenging goals for any accounting system, and the complexities and rapid pace of change make them even more difficult to achieve in the context of IT.

In the early days of computing it was much easier to identify costs than it is today. Computers and other hardware were very expensive and were managed by centralized organizational units with their own personnel. Most application software was developed internally rather than purchased. IT was used only for a few well-defined applications, such as payroll, inventory management, and accounts payable/receivable. In contrast, nowadays computers are cheap, and software is increasingly purchased or leased. The overwhelming majority of the total processing power is located on the collective desktops of the organization rather than in centralized computer centers, and it is managed by individual organizational units rather than a centralized IS department. A large proportion of the costs are in "hidden," indirect costs that are often overlooked (e.g., see Barthelemy, 2001).

These trends make it very difficult just to identify, let alone effectively control, the total costs of IT. As a practical matter, many organizations track costs associated with centralized IS and leave management accounting for desktop IT to the user organizations. However, the trend toward attaching personal computers to networks, and the availability of network management software, make it easier to track and manage costs related to desktop IT. Some organizations indicate "six-digits" savings by using network management software to identify which computers use what software, and then reducing the site licenses to correspond to the actual usage (see Coopee, 2000, for details).

In this section we look at two strategies for costing of IT services: chargeback and outsourcing.

Chargeback

In some organizations, the ISD functions as an unallocated cost center: All expenses go into an overhead account. The problem with this approach is that IT is then a "free good" that has no explicit cost, so there are no incentives to control usage or avoid waste.

A second alternative is called **chargeback** (also known as chargeout or cost recovery). In this approach, all costs of IT are allocated to users as accurately as possible, based on actual costs and usage levels. Accurate allocation sounds desirable in principle, but it can create problems in practice (see Wheatley, 2003). The most accurate measures of use may reflect technological factors that are totally incomprehensible to the user. If fixed costs are allocated on the basis of total usage throughout the organization, which varies from month to month, charges will fluctuate for an individual unit even though its own usage does not change. These considerations can reduce the credibility of the chargeback system.

Nevertheless, organizations can use chargeback systems to influence organizational IT usage in desirable directions. So the way users are charged for these services will influence how much they use them.

BEHAVIOR-ORIENTED CHARGEBACK. A third approach is to employ a **behavior-oriented chargeback** system. Such a system sets IT service costs in a way that meets organizational objectives, even though the charges may not correspond to actual costs. The primary objective of this type of system is influencing users' behavior. For example, it is possible to encourage (or discourage) usage of certain IT resources by assigning lower (or higher) costs. For example, the organization may wish to encourage use of central processing in off-peak hours, and so it might decide to charge business units less for processing from 1 to 4 A.M. than from 9 A.M. to noon. Or, the organization may encourage use of wireline over wireless technologies, or encourage the use of a central printer rather than a departmental one.

Although more difficult to develop, a behavior-oriented chargeback system recognizes the importance of IT—and its effective management—to the success of the organization. It not only avoids the unallocated cost center's problem of overuse of "free" resources; it can also reduce the use of scarce resources where demand exceeds supply, even with fully allocated costs. For more on behavior-oriented chargeback see Online File W13.15.

There are other methods of chargeback. The reason for the variety of methods is that it is very difficult to approximate costs, especially in companies where multiple independent operating units are sharing a centralized system. Therefore, organizations have developed chargeback methods that make sense to their managers and their particular needs. For a review of methods, see McAdam (1996).

The difficulties in applying chargeback systems may be one of the drivers of IT outsourcing.

Outsourcing as an Economic Strategy

Information technology is now a vital part of almost every organization and plays an important supporting role in most functions. However, IT is not the primary business of many organizations. Their core competencies—the things they do best and that represent their competitive strengths—are in manufacturing, or retailing, or services, or some other function. IT is an *enabler* only, and it is complex, expensive, and constantly changing. IT is difficult to manage, even for organizations with above-average management skills. For such organizations, the most effective strategy for obtaining the economic benefits of IT and controlling its costs may be **outsourcing,** which is obtaining IT services from outside vendors rather than from internal IS units within the organization (see Harmozi, 2003). According to a survey reported by Corbett (2001), the major reasons cited by large U.S. companies for use of outsourcing are: focus on core competency (36%), cost reduction (36%), improved quality (13%), increased speed to market (10%), and faster innovation (4%).

Companies typically outsource many of their non-IT activities, from contract manufacturing to physical security. But most of all they outsource IT activities (see Minicases 1 and 2 at the end of the chapter, and Online Minicase W13.1). Outsourcing is more than just purchasing hardware and software. It is a long-term result-oriented relationship for whole business activities, over which the provider has a large amount of control and managerial direction. For an overview of the past, present, and future of outsourcing, see Lee et al. (2003).

Outsourcing IT functions, such as payroll services, has been around since the early days of data processing. Contract programmers and computer timesharing services are longstanding examples. What is new is that, since the late 1980s, many organizations are outsourcing the majority of their IT functions rather than just incidental parts. The trend became very visible in 1989 when Eastman Kodak announced it was transferring its data centers to IBM under a 10-year, $500 million contract. This example, at a prominent multibillion-dollar company, gave a clear signal that outsourcing was a legitimate approach to managing IT. Since then, many mega outsourcing deals were announced, some for several billion dollars. (For a list of some recent outsourcing deals and the story of a 10-year, $3 billion contract between Procter & Gamble and Hewlett-Packard, see Cushing, 2003. For the case of outsourcing at Pilkington, see Online File W13.16.)

In a typical situation, the outsourcing firm hires the IS employees of the customer and buys the computer hardware. The cash from this sale is an important incentive for outsourcing by firms with financial problems. The outsourcer then provides IT services under a 5- to 10-year contract that specifies a baseline level of services, with additional charges for higher volumes or services not identified in the baseline. Many smaller firms provide limited-scale outsourcing of individual services, but only the largest outsourcing firms can take over large proportions of the IT functions of major organizations. In the mid-1990s, IBM, EDS, and Computer Sciences Corp. were winning approximately two-thirds of the largest outsourcing contracts. Today other vendors (e.g., HP and Oracle) also provide such services.

Offshore outsourcing of software development has become a common practice in recent years. About one-third of Fortune 500 companies have started to outsource software development to software companies in India (Carmel and Agrawal, 2002). This trend of offshore outsourcing is largely due to the emphasis of Indian companies on process quality by adhering to models such as Software Engineering Institute's Software Capability Maturity Model (SW-CMM) and through ISO 9001 certification. India has 15 of the 23 organizations worldwide that have achieved Level 5, the highest in SW-CMM ratings. Davidson (2004) highlighted that offshore outsourcing can reduce IT expenditures by 15 to 25 percent within the first year, and in the long term, outsourcing can help reduce cost and improve the quality of IT services delivered. However, organizations must balance the risks and uncertainties involved in offshore outsourcing, including: (1) cost-reduction expectations, (2) data/security and protection, (3) process discipline, (4) loss of business knowledge, (5) vendor failure to deliver, (6) scope creep, (7) government oversight/regulation, (8) differences in culture, (9) turnover of key personnel, and (10) knowledge transfer. For further details on offshore outsourcing, see Gillin (2003) and Carmel and Agrawal (2002).

In addition to the traditionally outsourced services, Brown and Young (2000) identify two more scenarios for future outsourcing: creation of shared environments (e.g., exchanges, portals, e-commerce backbones), and providing access to shared environments (e.g., application service providers, Internet data centers). For example, Flooz.com, an online gift-currency store, outsourced its storage requirements to StorageNetworks, a storage service provider (Wilkinson, 2000). See *outsourcing-center.com* for details on practices in outsourcing of various types of services. Finally, outsourcing of call centers, especially of high-tech companies, mainly to India, has accelerated since 2003.

A popular approach is *strategic outsourcing,* whereby you can generate new business, retain skilled employees, and effectively manage emerging technologies. Strategic outsourcing facilitates the leveraging of knowledge capabilities and investments of others by exploiting intellectual outsourcing in addition to outsourcing of traditional functions and services (Quinn, 1999).

ASPs AND UTILITY COMPUTING. The concept behind an *application service provider (ASP)* is simple: From a central, off-site data center, a vendor manages and distributes software-based services and solutions, via the Internet. Your data seem to be run locally, whereas they are actually coming from the off-site data center. The user company pays subscription and/or usage fees, getting IT services on demand (utility computing). In other words, ASPs are a form of outsourcing.

ASP services are becoming very popular, but they do have potential pitfalls. Focacci et al. (2003) provided some contingency guidelines for organizations to use to make their specific decision to adopt ASP services. According to Lee et al. (2003), the ASP approach is the future of outsourcing. The authors provide a list of ASPs in different areas and suggest a collaborative strategy with the users. For further discussion see Chapter 14 and Walsh (2003).

MANAGEMENT SERVICE PROVIDERS. A **management service provider (MSP)** is a vendor that remotely manages and monitors enterprise applications—ERP, CRM, firewalls, proprietary e-business applications, network infrastructure, etc. Like ASPs, MSPs charge subscription fees. But they claim to be an improvement over the ASP model because they permit companies to outsource the *maintenance* of their applications. MSPs make sure that applications are up and running, thus providing a relatively cheap, easy, and unobtrusive way for an organization to prevent outages and malfunctions. Meanwhile, because MSPs provide 24/7 monitoring, companies do not have to worry about staffing up to handle that nonrevenue-producing task. And if the MSP suddenly shuts its doors, as has happened all too often in the ASP world (and recently in the MSP world too), the organization can continue with minimal disruption because it still controls its applications.

OUTSOURCING AND E-COMMERCE.   Consider the following story, described by Palvia (2002): In the spring of 1996 the competitors of Canadian Imperial Bank of Commerce (CIBC) were ahead in implementing Internet banking, and CIBC was starting to lose market share. The bank needed to move quickly to implement its own Internet capabilities. But, being a bank and not an IT expert, this was a challenge. So the bank decided to outsource the job to IBM's Global Services. Together, CIBC and IBM were able to implement home banking in six months. By 1998 the bank regained market share, having 200,000 online clients.

CIBC's dilemma is becoming a familiar story in just about every industry. Time constraints brought on by competitive challenges, security issues, and a shortage of skilled system developers in the Internet/intranet field contribute to a boom in the outsourcing business. Some organizations may decide to outsource because they need to sell off IT assets to generate funds. In addition, implementing EC applications forces companies to outsource mission-critical applications on a scale never before seen. According to the Gartner Group, this need for EC applications will result in the tripling of IT outsourcing in three years. Forrester Research found that 90 percent of the companies they polled use or plan to use Internet-related outsourcing (Palvia, 2002).

A special EC outsourcing consideration is the implementation of extranets. Implementing an extranet is very difficult due to security issues and the need to have the system be rapidly expandable.

OUTSOURCING ADVANTAGES AND DISADVANTAGES.   The use of IT outsourcing is still very controversial (e.g., see Hirschheim and Lacity, 2000). Outsourcing advocates describe IT as a commodity, a generic item like electricity or janitorial services. They note the potential benefits of outsourcing, in general, as listed in Table 13.2.

In contrast, others see many limitations of outsourcing (e.g., see Cramm, 2001). One reason for the contradicting opinions is that many of the benefits of outsourcing are intangible or have long-term payoffs. Clemons (2000) identifies the following risks associated with outsourcing:

- *Shirking* occurs when a vendor deliberately underperforms while claiming full payment (e.g., billing for more hours than were worked, providing excellent staff at first and later replacing them with less qualified ones).

- *Poaching* occurs when a vendor develops a strategic application for a client and then uses it for other clients (e.g., vendor redevelops similar systems for other clients at much lower cost, or vendor enters into client's business, competing against it).

- *Opportunistic repricing ("holdup")* occurs when a client enters into a long-term contract with a vendor and the vendor changes financial terms at some point or overcharges for unanticipated enhancements and contract extensions.

TABLE 13.2 Potential Outsourcing Benefits

FINANCIAL
  ● Avoidance of heavy capital investment, thereby releasing funds for other uses.
  ● Improved cash flow and cost accountability.
  ● Cost benefits from economies of scale and from sharing computer housing, hardware, software, and personnel.
  ● Less need for expensive office space.

TECHNICAL
  ● Access to new information technologies.
  ● Greater freedom to choose software due to a wider range of hardware.
  ● Ability to achieve technological improvements more easily.
  ● Greater access to technical skills.
  ● Faster application development.

MANAGEMENT
  ● Concentration on developing and running core business activity.
  ● Delegation of IT development (design, production, and acquisition) and operational responsibility to supplier.
  ● Elimination of need to recruit and retain competent IT staff.

HUMAN RESOURCES
  ● Opportunity to draw on specialist skills, available from a pool of expertise, when needed.
  ● Enriched career development and opportunities for staff.

QUALITY
  ● Clearly defined *service levels* (see Chapter 15).
  ● Improved performance accountability.
  ● Quality accreditation.

FLEXIBILITY
  ● Quick response to business demands.
  ● Ability to handle IT peaks and valleys more effectively.

Other risks are: irreversibility of the outsourcing decision, possible breach of contract by the vendor or its inability to deliver, loss of control over IT decisions, loss of critical IT skills, vendor lock-in, loss of control over data, loss of employee morale and productivity, and uncontrollable contract growth.

Another possible risk of outsourcing is failure to consider all the costs. Some costs are hidden. Barthelemy (2001) discusses the following hidden costs: (1) vendor search and contracting, (2) transitioning from in-house IT to a vendor, (3) cost of managing the effort, and (4) transition back to in-house IT after outsourcing. These costs can be controlled to some extent, however.

Despite the risks and limitations, the extent of IT outsourcing is increasing rapidly together with the use of ASPs. We will return to these topics in Chapter 14.

STRATEGIES FOR OUTSOURCING. There are five major risk areas that executives should consider when making the decision to outsource. They are: (1) higher developmental or operational costs than anticipated, (2) inability to provide the expected service levels at implementation, (3) exceeding the time anticipated for development or transition, (4) allowing technical failure to continue, and (5) neglecting to navigate the internal politics of the company (Rubin, 2003). Therefore, organizations should consider the following strategies in managing the risks associated with outsourcing contracts.

1. *Understand the project.* Clients must have a high degree of understanding of the project, including its requirements, the method of its implementation, and the source of expected economic benefits. A common characteristic of successful outsourcing contracts is that the client was generally capable of developing the application but chose to outsource simply because of constraints on time or staff availability (Clemons, 2000).

2. *Divide and conquer.* Dividing a large project into smaller and more manageable pieces will greatly reduce outsourcing risk and provides clients with an exit strategy if any part of the project fails (Clemons, 2000).

3. *Align incentives.* Designing contractual incentives based on activities that can be measured accurately can result in achieving desired performance (Clemons, 2000).

4. *Write short-period contracts.* Outsourcing contracts are often written for 5- to 10-year terms. Because IT and the competitive environment change so rapidly, it is very possible that some of the terms will not be in the customer's best interests after 5 years. If a long-term contract is used, it needs to include adequate mechanisms for negotiating revisions where necessary (Marcolin and McLellan, 1998).

5. *Control subcontracting.* Vendors may subcontract some of the services to other vendors. The contract should give the customer some control over the circumstances, including choice of vendors, and any subcontract arrangements (Marcolin and McLellan, 1998).

6. *Do selective outsourcing.* This is a strategy used by many corporations who prefer not to outsource the majority of their IT, but rather to outsource certain areas (such as system integration or network security). Cramm (2001) suggests that an organization *insource* important work, such as strategic applications, investments, and HRM.

At this point of time, the phenomenon of large-scale IT outsourcing is approximately 20 years old. The number of organizations that have used it for at least several years is growing. Business and IT-oriented periodicals have published numerous stories about their experiences. Outsourcing is also popular on a global basis, as is demonstrated in Minicase 2 and as described by Zviran et al. (2001). The general consensus of the various sources of anecdotal information is that the cost savings of outsourcing are not large (perhaps around 10 percent) and that not all organizations experience savings. This still leaves the question of whether outsourcing IT can improve organizational performance by making it possible to focus more intensely on core competencies. Further research is necessary to answer this question.

13.5 ECONOMICS OF WEB-BASED SYSTEMS AND E-COMMERCE

As indicated throughout this text, Web-based systems can considerably increase productivity and profitability. In order to understand the economic logic of this, let us first examine the cost curves of digital products versus nondigital products, as shown in Figure 13.8. As the figure shows, for regular physical products (a), the average per-unit cost declines up to a certain quantity, but then, due to increased overhead (e.g., adding a manager) and marketing costs, the cost will start to increase. For digital products (b), the cost will continue to decline

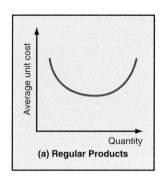
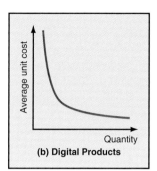

FIGURE 13.8 Cost curves of regular and digital products.

with increased quantity. The variable cost in the case of digital products is very little, so once the fixed cost is covered, an increase in quantity produces a continuous decrease in average cost.

However, even for nondigital products, e-commerce can shift economic curves, as shown in Figure 13.9. The production function will decline (from L1 to L2 in part a) since you can get the same quantity with less labor and IT cost. The *transaction cost* for the same quantity (size) will be lower due to computerization (part b). And finally, the administrative cost for the same quantity will also be lower (part c).

The justification of EC applications can be difficult. Usually one needs to prepare a business case, as described earlier in the chapter. A proper business case develops the baseline of desired results against which actual performance can and should be measured. The business case should cover both the financial and non-financial performance metrics against which to measure the e-business implementation. For further details on use of metrics to justify e-commerce, see Straub et al. (2002a and 2002b), Sterne (2002), Tjan (2001), and Turban et al. (2006).

The benefits and costs of EC depend on its definitions. If we use the broad definition, there are substantial benefits to buyers, sellers, and society (see Chapter 4). The complexity of the EC payoff can be seen in Online File W13.17. (For a discussion, see Devaraj and Kohli, 2002.) But even when the applications are well defined, we still have measurement complexities. It is difficult even to conduct risk analysis, not to mention cost-benefit analysis. (See insights from Thomas Mesenbourg, of the Economic Programs of the U.S. Bureau of the Census, at *census.gov/epdc/www/ebusins.htm*.)

Web-based systems are being implemented by many organizations. However, hardly any efforts are being made to perform cost-benefit analysis or measure

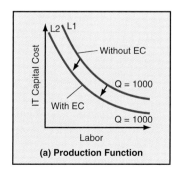
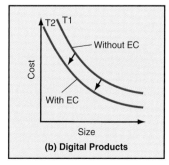
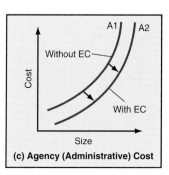

FIGURE 13.9 Economic effects of e-commerce.

return on investment (ROI) on Web-based systems. Instead, most decisions to invest in Web-based systems are based on the assumption that the investments are needed for strategic reasons and that the expected returns cannot be measured in monetary values. Raskin (1999) advocates determining a return on investment (ROI) for extranet projects, though it is a difficult task, and suggests strategies for calculating ROI. Online File W13.18 illustrates that some organizations calculate ROIs for their intranets and extranets and others do not.

As indicated earlier, many vendors provide ROI examples, proprietary methodologies, and calculators for IT projects, including EC, such as for portals (e.g., *plumtree.com*). Although use of third-party evaluators, such as IDC, is common, the reported high ROIs should be considered with care. As noted earlier, bias is possible. For a comprehensive discussion of the economics of e-commerce, see Vulkan (2003) and Kohli et al. (2003).

13.6 OTHER ECONOMIC ASPECTS OF INFORMATION TECHNOLOGY

In this final section of the chapter, we look at some other associated economic aspects of information technology. The first of these is IT failures and runaway projects, many of which occur for economic reasons.

IT Failures and "Runaway" Projects

Information technology is difficult to manage and can be costly when things do not go as planned. Indeed, a high proportion of IS development projects either fail completely or fail to meet some of the original targets for features, development time, or cost. Many of these are related to economic issues, such as an incorrect cost-benefit analysis.

Many failures occur in smaller systems that handle internal processes within an organization, and they usually remain corporate secrets. The total investment is not large, the failure does not have a major economic impact, and the effects are generally not visible to outsiders so we do not know about them. On the other hand, some IS failures result in losses in excess of 10 million dollars and may severely damage the organization, as well as generate a lot of negative publicity, as in the Nike case in Chapter 1 or the ERP cases cited in Chapter 7. Failures in large public organizations such as the IRS and Social Security Administration have also been well advertised. A large-scale failure at a university is described in *IT at Work 13.1*. A failure in a new airport is described in Online File W13.19.

Because of the complexity and associated risks of developing computer systems, some IT managers refuse to develop systems in-house beyond a certain size. The "one, one, ten rule" says not to develop a system if it will take longer than one year, has a budget over one million dollars, and will require more than ten people. Following this strategy, an organization will need to buy rather than develop large systems, or do without them.

The economics of software production suggest that, for relatively standardized systems, purchasing or leasing can result in both cost savings and increased functionality. Purchasing or leasing can also be the safest strategy for very large and complex systems, especially those that involve multiple units within an organization. For example, the SAP AG software firm offers a family of integrated, enterprise-level, large-scale information systems. These systems are available in versions tailored for specific industries, including aerospace, banking, utilities, retail, and so forth, as well as for SMEs. Many organizations feel that buying from a good vendor reduces their risk of failure,

IT at Work 13.1
A UNIVERSITY ACCOUNTING SYSTEM FAILED

A large British university (requested to be unnamed) developed a new computer-based accounting system that did not work at all for its first six weeks of operation. Several months later it was evaluated as "failing to do what it was supposed to do" and as "unreliable." This failure led to a major investigation, which concluded that basic project management procedures had not been followed and that it would take at least two years to put things right. A series of smaller oversights and failures led to the catastrophic failure of the system as a whole, because of the interdependent nature of the tasks and responsibilities in the project.

Here are two of the findings of the investigation related to IT justification:

1. *Overspending.* The purchase of new hardware, software, and networks for the accounting system appears to have been planned without any serious attempt to calculate the cost or to identify where the money to pay for it was to come from. This was one reason for the significant overrun of costs for the whole project.

    Lesson learned: There was a failure to budget for the cost of these particular project deliverables. An initial costing should have been part of a business case, which was not done. By presenting a full business case before the project is started, a commitment to resources is obtained from stakeholders and senior management. The construction of a business case also ensures that time is allowed to fully assess costs and benefits of any proposed new system before the project gets underway.

2. *Tendering and contracts.* Consultants seem to have been employed without proper tendering practices being done. It appeared that a contract committing the university to an expenditure of millions of pounds was signed with the database software suppliers without the university having taken legal advice about its contents. Also, no attempt was made to justify the purchases.

    Lesson learned: A university is expected to demonstrate best value for money in the same way as a commercial organization, and this can be demonstrated only if the organization's procurement procedures are adhered to. The procurement process is itself a project to which basic project management principles should be applied.

Sources: Compiled from Laurie (2003).

For Further Exploration: Which of the methods of this chapter could be used for the IT justification? Why are the problems related to project management?

---

even if they have to change their business processes to be compatible with the new system.

The Economics of the Web

In the preceding sections, our focus has been on the economics of *the use of IT* in organizations as an enabler. In this section, we turn to the economics of IT *as a product in itself,* rather than in a supporting role.

In 1916, David Sarnoff attempted to persuade his manager that the American Marconi Company should produce inexpensive radio receivers to sell to the consumer market. Others in the company (which subsequently became RCA) opposed the idea because it depended on the development of a radio broadcasting industry. They did not expect such an industry to develop because they could not see how broadcasters could generate revenues by providing a service without any charges to the listeners. The subsequent commercial development of radio, and the even greater success of television, proved that Sarnoff was right. If it is possible to provide a popular service to a large audience at a low cost per person, there will be ways of generating revenues. The only question is, How?

The World Wide Web on the Internet resembles commercial broadcasting in its early days. Fixed costs—initial investments and production costs—can be high in themselves, but they are low in terms of average cost per potential customer.

The incremental or variable costs of delivering content to individual customers or of processing transactions are very low (see Choi and Whinston, 2000).

The market for the Web is large. About 60 percent of the U.S. population, plus many foreign countries, now have access to the Internet. Many people who do not have computers at home can access the Internet through computers at work, schools, libraries, or via mobile devices. The arrival of Web TV adapters for TV sets made it possible for homes without computers to get on the Internet for as little as $300. By 2003, the cost of the Simputer and other thin computers has come down to about $200. These trends could lead to a situation of "universal connectivity," in which almost every citizen in the industrialized countries has access to the Net. Using Internet-enabled cellphones, nearly universal connectivity can be achieved in developing countries as well.

Increasing Returns   Stanford University economist Brian Arthur (1996) is the leading proponent of the economic theory of *increasing returns,* which applies to the Web and to other forms of information technology. He starts with the familiar concept that the economy is divided into different sectors, one that produces physical products and another that focuses on information. Producers of physical products (e.g., foodstuffs, petroleum, automobiles) are subject to what are called diminishing returns: Although they may have initial increasing economies of scale, they eventually reach a point where costs go up and additional production becomes less profitable.

Arthur notes that in the information economy the situation is very different. For example, initial costs to develop new software are very high, but the cost of producing additional copies is very low. The result is **increasing returns,** where profitability rises more rapidly than production increases. Figure 13.10 illustrates the difference between increasing and decreasing returns. A firm with a high market share can use these higher profits to improve the product or to enhance the marketing in order to strengthen its leading position.

In addition to higher profitability, two other factors favor firms with higher market share. The first is **network effects.** The leading products in an industry attract a base of users, and this base leads to development of complementary products, further strengthening the position of the dominant product.

The second factor is the **lock-in effect.** Most new software is hard to learn, so users typically will not switch to a different product unless it is much more powerful or they are forced into making the change. The end result of these factors is that when a firm establishes a clear lead over its competitors, it tends to become stronger and stronger in its market.

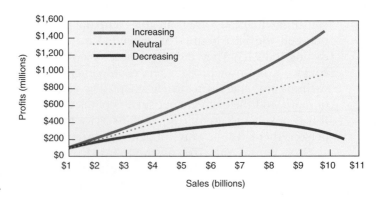

FIGURE 13.10 Increasing versus decreasing returns.

The potential for increasing returns requires management strategies that are very different from those in other industries. Arthur (1996) suggests strategies for producing increasing returns which are shown in Online File W13.20.

Market Transformation through New Technologies

In some cases, IT has the potential to completely transform the economics of an industry. For example, until recently the hard-copy encyclopedia business consisted of low-volume sales, primarily to schools and libraries. The physically very bulky product (20–30 volumes) resulted in relatively high manufacturing and shipping costs, which made the price even higher. The high price, the need for periodic updating, and the space required to store the books, reduced potential sales to the home market.

Two things happened to change this situation. First, CD-ROM technology was adapted from storing music to storing other digital data, including text and images. Second, since the mid-1990s use of CD-ROMs has been a standard component of a majority of computers sold for the home market. Encyclopedia producers began selling their products on CD-ROMs, in some cases at reduced prices that reflected the lower production costs. These CD-ROM versions include new features made possible by the technology, most notably sound, easy search, and hyperlink cross-references to related material in other sections. Lower prices and additional features have the potential to substantially increase the size of the total market, especially when the encyclopedia is placed online, as an electronic book, which is easy to update and requires no shipping cost. The hypothetical example in Online File W13.21 shows how the economics of this business could change.

MANAGERIAL ISSUES

Information technology has certain characteristics that differentiate it, and its economics, from other aspects of the organizational world. Therefore IT requires management practices that are more effective than, and in some cases different from, those that are adequate for non-IT activities. For example, organizational resistance on many fronts can turn the most promising system into a failure (Watson and Haley, 1998). Managers need to be aware of and responsive to the following issues.

1. *Constant growth and change.* The power of the microprocessor chip doubles every two years, while the cost remains constant. This ever-increasing power creates both major opportunities and large threats as its impacts ripple across almost every aspect of the organization and its environment. Managers need to continuously monitor developments in this area to identify new technologies relevant to their organizations and to keep themselves up-to-date on their potential impacts.

2. *Shift from tangible to intangible benefits.* Few opportunities remain for automation projects that simply replace manual labor with IT on a one-for-one basis. The economic justification of IT applications will increasingly depend on intangible benefits, such as increased quality or better customer service. In contrast to calculating cost savings, it is much more difficult to accurately estimate the value of intangible benefits prior to the actual implementation. Managers need to understand and use tools that bring intangible benefits into the decision-making processes for IT investments.

3. *Not a sure thing.* Although IT offers opportunities for significant improvements in organizational performance, these benefits are not automatic. Managers need to very actively plan and control implementations to increase the return on their IT investments.

4. *Chargeback.* Users have little incentive to control IT costs if they do not have to pay for them at all. On the other hand, an accounting system may allocate costs fairly accurately to users but discourage exploration of promising new technologies. The solution is to have a chargeback system that has the primary objective of encouraging user behaviors that correspond to organizational objectives.

5. *Risk.* Investments in IT are inherently more risky than investments in other areas. Managers need to evaluate the level of risk before committing to IT projects. The general level of management involvement as well as specific management techniques and tools need to be appropriate for the risk of individual projects.

6. *Outsourcing.* The complexities of managing IT, and the inherent risks, may require more management skills than some organizations possess. If this is the case, the organization may want to outsource some or all of its IT functions. However, if it does outsource, the organization needs to make sure that the terms of the outsourcing contract are in its best interests both immediately and throughout the duration of the agreement.

7. *Increasing returns.* Industries whose primary focus is IT (digital products), or that include large amounts of IT in their products, often operate under a paradigm of increasing returns. In contrast, industries that primarily produce physical outputs are subject to diminishing returns. Managers need to understand which paradigm applies to the products for which they are responsible and apply management strategies that are most appropriate.

KEY TERMS

Balanced-scorecard method *571*

Behavior-oriented chargeback *575*

Benchmarks *569*

Best-practice benchmarks *570*

Business case *564*

Chargeback *575*

Cost-benefit analysis *561*

Expected value (EV) *574*

Increasing returns *584*

Information economics *568*

Intangible benefits *562*

Lock-in effect *584*

Management by maxim *570*

Management service provider (MSP) *577*

Metric *573*

Metric benchmarks *569*

Network effects *584*

Offshore outsourcing *577*

Outsourcing *576*

Price-to-performance ratio *555*

Productivity paradox *556*

Real options *570*

Scoring methodology *568*

Total benefits of ownership (TBO) *567*

Total cost of ownership (TCO) *566*

Value analysis *567*

CHAPTER HIGHLIGHTS (Numbers Refer to Learning Objectives)

❶ The power of computer hardware should continue increasing at an exponential rate for at least 10 years, doubling every 18 months, while costs remain at the same levels as before. Also the performance/cost ratio of storage and networks behaves in a similar way.

❷ Although organizations have spent tremendous amounts of money on IT, it is difficult to prove that this spending has increased national or industry productivity. The discrepancy between measures of IT investment and measures of output is described as the productivity paradox, and it can be explained.

③ Evaluating IT investment requires finding the total costs of ownership and the total benefits of ownership and subtracting the costs from the benefits. The value of information to an organization should be part of that calculation.

③ The major difficulty in evaluating IT investment is assessing the intangible benefits. Also, some costs are difficult to relate to specific projects.

③ Traditional financial approaches can be used to evaluate IT investment, but in many cases methods such as value analysis, benchmarking, or real option analysis fit better, especially for investment in infrastructures.

④ Intangible benefits cover many areas ranging from customer satisfaction to deferring IT investments. To include intangible benefits in IT justification, one may attempt to quantify them, to list them as arguments for justification, or to ignore them. Specific methodologies may be useful.

⑤ The NPV and ROI methods work well with tangible benefits. When intangible benefits are involved, one may try one of the following: value analysis, information economics, benchmarks, management by maxim, real option valuation, balanced scorecard, and activity-based costing.

⑥ Chargeback systems may be used to regulate the use of shared information systems. Behavior-oriented chargeback systems, if properly designed, encourage efficient and effective usage of IT resources.

⑦ Outsourcing may reduce IT costs and can make it possible for organizations to concentrate their management efforts on issues related to their core competencies. However, outsourcing may reduce the company's flexibility to find the best IT fit for the business, and it may also pose a security risk.

⑧ EC enables electronic delivery of digital products at very low cost. Also, many nondigital products can be produced and delivered with lower overhead and with less administrative cost.

⑨ Web-based technologies may be approached differently for conducting cost-benefit analysis due to their different economic curves, lack of baseline data, frequent changes, etc. Modifying existing concepts, such as is done in portfolio selection, is advisable.

⑩ Several topics are related to the economics of IT. IT failures are frequently the result of poor cost-benefit analysis, and IT projects sometimes linger because of poor planning of economic resources.

VIRTUAL COMPANY ASSIGNMENT

IT Economics at The Wireless Café

Go to The Wireless Café's link on the Student Web Site. There you will be asked to analyze some IT economics issues as you think about how the many useful and innovative technologies that could be implemented at the restaurant will fit into its budget.

More Resources

More resources and study tools are located on the Student Web Site. You'll find additional chapter materials and useful Web links. In addition, self-quizzes that provide individualized feedback are available for each chapter.

Instructions for accessing The Wireless Café on the Student Web Site

1. Go to
   wiley.com/college/turban
2. Select Turban/Leidner/ McLean/Wetherbe's *Information Technology for Management, Fifth Edition.*
3. Click on Student Resources site, in the toolbar on the left.
4. Click on the link for Virtual Company Web site.
5. Click on Wireless Café.

QUESTIONS FOR REVIEW

1. Describe Moore's Law.
2. Define productivity.
3. Describe the productivity paradox. Why is it important?
4. List three major explanations of the productivity paradox.
5. Define information infrastructure and list some of its costs.
6. Define cost-benefit analysis.
7. What is TCO? What is TBO?
8. List some tangible and intangible benefits of IT.
9. Describe the value analysis method.
10. Define information economics.
11. Define IT benchmarks and metrics.
12. Describe best-practice benchmarks.
13. What is management by maxim?
14. What is real-option valuation in IT?
15. Describe the balanced scorecard method.
16. Describe IT chargeback.
17. Define behavior-oriented chargeback.
18. Define IT outsourcing.
19. List five benefits of outsourcing.
20. List five drawbacks or limitations of outsourcing.
21. Describe increasing returns in IT.

QUESTIONS FOR DISCUSSION

1. What are the general implications for managers, organizations, and consumers of constantly increasing computer capabilities and declining costs?
2. What are the impacts of exponentially increasing computer hardware power and declining price-to-performance ratios on business production activities and new-product development?
3. Discuss what is necessary in order to achieve productivity gains from IT investments.
4. Why is it more difficult to measure productivity in service industries?
5. Compare and contrast metrics and best practices. Give an example of each in an IT in a university.
6. Discuss what may happen when an organization does not charge users for IT services.
7. Identify circumstances that could lead a firm to outsource its IT functions rather than continue with an internal IS unit.
8. Identify arguments for including estimated values for intangible benefits in net present value (NPV) analyses of IT investments, and contrast them with the arguments for excluding such estimates.
9. What is IT infrastructure, and why is it difficult to justify its cost?
10. Discuss the economic advantages of digital products compared to nondigital ones.
11. Explain how a behavior-oriented chargeback system can be superior to an accounting system that charges users fairly accurate estimates of the costs of services they use.
12. Discuss the pros and cons of outsourcing IT, including alternatives to outsourcing.
13. Compare information economics with the balanced scorecard method.
14. Discuss the value of offshore outsourcing. Summarize the benefits and the risks.

EXERCISES

1. Conduct research on how many more years exponential growth in computer hardware capabilities (Moore's Law) will continue.
2. Create a scoring methodology that reflects your personal requirements, and use it to evaluate two competing software products in the same category (for example, two Web browsers or two corporate portal development environments).
3. If you have access to a large organization, conduct research on the methods it uses to charge users for IT services and how the users feel about these charges.
4. Enter *ibm.com* and find information about how IBM measures the ROI on WebSphere. Then examine ROI from CIOView Corporation (*CIOview.com*). Identify the variables included in the analysis (at both *ibm.com* and *CIOview.com*). Prepare a report about the fairness of such a tool.
5. A small business invests $50,000 in robotic equipment. This amount is shown as a negative value in Year 0. Projected cash flows of $20,000 per year in Year 1 through Year 5 result from labor savings, reduced material costs, and tax benefits. The business plans to replace the robots with more modern ones after 5 years and does not expect

them to have any scrap value. The equipment generates a total of $100,000 in savings over 5 years, or $50,000 more than the original investment. However, a dollar saved in the future is worth less than a dollar invested in the present. If the business estimates its return on investment as 15 percent, then $1.00 should be worth $1.15 in one year, $1.32 after 2 years with compound interest, and so on. Cash flows are divided by these "discount factors" to estimate what they are worth at present. Calculate the total cash flow after this discounting, and discuss whether the investment can be justified.

GROUP ASSIGNMENTS

1. Considerable discussions and disagreements occur among IS professionals regarding outsourcing. Divide the group into two parts: One will defend the strategy of large-scale outsourcing. One will oppose it. Start by collecting recent material at *google.com* and *cio.com*.

2. Each group is assigned to an ROI calculator (e.g., from PeopleSoft, Oracle, IBM, etc.). Each group should prepare a list of the functionalities included and the variables. Make a report that shows the features and limitations of each tool.

INTERNET EXERCISES

1. Enter *google.com* and *itgovernance.com,* and search for material on the use of the balanced scorecard method for evaluating IT investments. Prepare a report on your findings.

2. Enter the Web sites of the Gartner Group (*gartnergroup.com*), The Yankee Group (*yankeegroup.com*), and *CIO* (*cio.com*). Search for recent material about outsourcing, and prepare a report on your findings.

3. Enter the Web site of IDC (*idc.com*) and find how they evaluate ROI on intranets, supply chain, and other IT projects.

4. Visit the Web site of Resource Management Systems (*rms.net*) and take the IT investment Management Approach Assessment Self-Test (*rms.net/self_test.htm*) to compare your organization's IT decision-making process with those of best-practices organizations.

5. Enter *plumtree.com* and see how they conduct ROI on portals. List major elements of the analysis. Is it biased?

6. Enter *sap.com* and use the casebuilder calculator for a hypothetical (or real) IT project. Write a report on your experience.

7. Enter *searchcio.techtarget.com* and find free ROI analysis tools. Download a tool of your choice and identify its major components. Write a report.

Minicase 1
Intranets: Invest First, Analyze Later?

The traditional approach to information systems projects is to analyze potential costs and benefits before deciding whether to develop the system. However, for moderate investments in promising new technologies that could offer major benefits, organizations may decide to do the financial analyses after the project is over. A number of companies took this latter approach in regard to intranet projects initiated prior to 1997.

Judd's

Located in Strasburg, Virginia, Judd's is a conservative, family-owned printing company that prints *Time* magazine, among other publications. Richard Warren, VP for IS, pointed out that Judd's "usually waits for technology to prove itself . . . but with the Internet the benefits seemed so great that our decision proved to be a no-brainer." Judd's first

implemented Internet technology for communications to meet needs expressed by customers. After this it started building intranet applications to facilitate internal business activities. One indication of the significance of these applications to the company is the bandwidth that supports them. Judd's increased the bandwidth by a magnitude of about 900 percent in the 1990s without formal cost-benefit analysis.

Eli Lilly & Company

A very large pharmaceutical company with headquarters in Indianapolis, Eli Lilly has a proactive attitude toward new technologies. It began exploring the potential of the Internet in 1993. Managers soon realized that, by using intranets, they could reduce many of the problems associated with developing applications on a wide variety of hardware platforms and network configurations. Because the benefits were so obvious, the regular financial justification process was waived for intranet application development projects. The IS group that helps user departments develop and maintain intranet applications increased its staff from three to ten employees in 15 months.

Needham Interactive

Needham, a Dallas advertising agency, has offices in various parts of the country. Needham discovered that, in developing presentations for bids on new accounts, employees found it helpful to use materials from other employees' presentations on similar projects. Unfortunately, it was very difficult to locate and then transfer relevant material in different locations and different formats. After doing research on alternatives, the company identified intranet technology as the best potential solution.

Needham hired EDS to help develop the system. It started with one office in 1996 as a pilot site. Now part of DDB Needham, the company has a sophisticated corporate-wide intranet and extranet in place. Although the investment was "substantial," Needham did not do a detailed financial analysis before starting the project. David King, a managing partner, explained, "The system will start paying for itself the first time an employee wins a new account because he had easy access to a co-worker's information."

Cadence Design Systems

Cadence is a consulting firm located in San Jose, California. It wanted to increase the productivity of its sales personnel by improving internal communications and sales training. It considered Lotus Notes but decided against it because of the costs. With the help of a consultant, it developed an intranet system. Because the company reengineered its sales training process to work with the new system, the project took somewhat longer than usual.

International Data Corp., an IT research firm, helped Cadence do an after-the-fact financial analysis. Initially the analysis calculated benefits based on employees meeting their full sales quotas. However, IDC later found that a more appropriate indicator was having new sales representatives meet half their quota. Startup costs were $280,000, average annual expenses were estimated at less than $400,000, and annual savings were projected at over $2.5 million. Barry Demak, director of sales, remarked, "We knew the economic justification . . . would be strong, but we were surprised the actual numbers were as high as they were."

Sources: Compiled from Korzenioski (1997) and the cited companies' Web sites.

Questions for Minicase 1

1. Where and under what circumstances is the "invest first, analyze later" approach appropriate? Where and when is it inappropriate? Give specific examples of technologies and other circumstances.

2. How long do you think the "invest first, analyze later" approach will be appropriate for intranet projects? When (and why) will the emphasis shift to traditional project justification approaches? (Or has the shift already occurred?)

3. What are the risks of going into projects that have not received a thorough financial analysis? How can organizations reduce these risks?

4. Based on the numbers provided for Cadence Design System's intranet project, use a spreadsheet to calculate the net present value of the project. Assume a 5-year life for the system.

5. Do you see any relationship between the "invest first, analyze later" approach to financial analysis and the use of behavior-oriented chargeback systems?

6. Relate the Needham case to the concept of a repository knowledge base.

Minicase 2
Outsourcing Its IT, Kone Is Focusing on Its Core Competencies

The Problem

Kone Inc. is a multinational corporation, based in Finland. Kone makes over 20,000 new escalators and elevators each year, installing and servicing them in more than 40 countries, with about 30 percent of Kone's business in the

United States. The company embarked on a globalization strategy several years ago, and soon discovered that the internal IT processes were insufficient to support the expansion. The same was true with the IT for the company's value-added private communication networks. IT costs were growing rapidly, yet their contribution to reducing the administrative cost of global sales was minimal. Kone was managing different IT platforms around the world with a variety of home-grown and nonstandard applications. None of the regional IT infrastructures was integrated, nor were they connected or compatible. Kone's global strategy was in danger.

The Solution

Kone Inc. realized that it must implement and manage a global-standard IT environment. But the company also realized that its business is about escalators and elevators, not IT, so it decided to pursue IT outsourcing. Kone had had an experience with IT outsourcing before, when it outsourced its mainframe operations to Computer Science Corp. But this time the scope of outsourcing was much larger, so the company solicited proposals and finally decided to partner with two global IT providers, SAP AG from Germany and Hewlett-Packard (HP) from the United States.

As described in Chapter 7, SAP is the world's largest ERP provider, and almost all of the 72 modules of SAP R/3 software (including a data warehouse) were deployed at Kone. The SAP environment is deployed in 16 countries, with 4,300 users, in all functional areas.

HP was hired to provide and manage the hardware on which SAP is run. The decision to use two vendors was not easy. IBM and Oracle each could have provided both the software and hardware, but using two separate vendors promised the best-of-breed approach.

HP manages 20 Kone Unix Servers in three data centers (one in Atlanta for North America, one in Singapore for Asia, and one in Brussels for Europe). HP uses its latest technology. HP's OpenView network and system manage-

ment and security software are also deployed with the system to ensure high availability environment. The system is linked with EMC storage and backup. The annual cost of this global outsourcing is $5 million.

The entire global IT infrastructure is connected and integrated, and it supports identical business processes and practices in all countries. The system provides management with real-time data on product sales, profitability, and backlogs—on a country, regional, or global basis.

Kone maintains some IT competencies to allow it to actively manage its outsourcing partners. The internal team meets online regularly, and SAP and HP collaborate and work closely together.

The Results

The outsourcing arrangement allows Kone to concentrate on its core competencies. The cost is only 0.02 percent of sales. Large fixed costs in infrastructure and people have been eliminated. The company has better cost control, as well as flexible opportunity for business process redesign, thus speeding up restructuring. The outsourcing vendors guarantee to have the system available 99.5 percent of the time. Actual uptime has been very close to 100 percent.

Sources: Compiled from "The Elevation of IT Outsourcing Partnership" (2002), and *rsleads.com/208cn-254* (accessed February 13, 2003).

Questions for Minicase 2

1. What were the major drivers of the outsourcing at Kone?
2. Why did Kone elect to work with several vendors?
3. What are some of the risks of this outsourcing?
4. How can Kone control its vendors?

REFERENCES

Arthur, W. B., "Increasing Returns and the New World of Business," *Harvard Business Review,* July–August 1996.

Barthelemy, J., "The Hidden Costs of IT Outsourcing," *MIT Sloan Management Review,* Spring 2001.

Benaroch, M., "Management Information Technology Investment Risk: A Real Options Perspective," *Journal of Management Information Systems,* Fall 2002.

Benaroch, M., and R. J. Kauffman, "A Case for Using Real Options Pricing Analysis to Evaluate Information Technology Project Investments," *Information Systems Research,* 10(1), March 1999.

Blum, R., *Network and System Management TCO.* Murray Hill, NJ: Lucent Technologies, 2001.

Broadbent, M., and P. Weill, "Management by Maxim: How Business and IT Managers Can Create IT Infrastrucures," *Sloan Management Review,* Spring 1997.

Brown, R. H., and A. Young, "Scenarios for the Future of Outsourcing," GartnerGroup, December 12, 2000.

Brynjolfsson, E., and L. M. Hitt, "Beyond the Productivity Paradox," *Communications of the ACM,* August 1998.

Carmel, E., and R. Agrawal, "The Maturation of Offshore Sourcing of Information Technology Work," *MIS Quarterly Executive,* June 2002.

Choi, S. Y., and A. B. Whinston, *The Internet Economy: Technology and Practice.* Austin, TX: SmartEcon, 2000.

CIO.com, "ROI Analysis Tools," Nucleuse Research Inc., *nucleuseresearch.com* (accessed July 2004).

Clemons, E. K., "The Build/Buy Battle," *CIO Magazine,* Dec. 1, 2000.

Clermont, P., Cost-Benefit Analysis: IT's Back in Fashion, Now Let's Make It Work. *Information Strategy: The Executive's Journal,* Winter 2002.

Coopee, T., "Building a Strong Foundation," *Network World,* January 31, 2000.

Corbett, M. F., "Taking the Pulse of Outsourcing," *Firmbuilder.com* (Data and Analysis from the 2001 Outsourcing World Summit), December 6, 2001.

Cramm, S. H., "The Dark Side of Outsourcing," *CIO Magazine*, November 15, 2001.

Cushing, K., "Procter & Gamble's 3bn HP Deal Shows Mega IT Outsourcing Is Still Tempting Some," *Computer Weekly*, April 22, 2003.

Davamanirajan, P., et al., "Assessing the Business Value of Information Technology in Global Wholesale Banking: Case of Trade Service," *Journal of Organizational Computing and Electronic Commerce*, January–March 2002.

David, J. S. et al., "Managing Your IT Total Cost of Ownership," *Communications of the ACM*, January 2002.

Davidson, D., "Top 10 Risks of Offshore Outsourcing," MetaGroupInc., 2004, *http://www2.cio.com/analyst/report2224.html*.

Dekker, R., and R. de Hoog, "The Monetary Value of Knowledge Assets: A Micro Approach," *Expert Systems with Applications*, Vol. 18, 2000.

DePalma, D., "Make the Business Case for Global Expansion," *e-Business Advisor*, April 1, 2001.

Devaraj, S., and R. Kohli, *The IT Payoff*. New York: Financial Times/Prentice Hall, 2002.

Devaraj, S., and R. Kohli, "Information Technology Payoff Paradox and System Use: Is Actual Usage the Missing Link?" *Management Science*, 49(3), 2003.

DiNunno, D., "Measuring Return of IT Projects," *CIO Magazine*, September 25, 2002.

Dixit, A. K., and Pindyck, R. S., "The Options Approach to Capital Investment," *Harvard Business Review*, May–June 1995.

Dutta, S., and J. F. Manzoni, *Process Re-engineering, Organizational Change, and Performance Improvement* (Insead Global Management Series). Boston: McGraw-Hill, Irwin, 1999.

Farrell, D., "IT Investments that Pay Off," *Special Report of Harvard Business School to Search CIO.com*, November 26, 2003.

Ferrin, B. G., and R. E. Plank, "Total Cost of Ownership Models: An Exploratory Study," *Journal of Supply Chain Management*, Summer 2002.

Fine, C. H., et al., "Rapid-Response Capability in Value-Chain Design," *MIT Sloan Management Review*, Winter 2002.

Fisher, A., "A Waste of Money?" *Financial Times*, October 25, 2001.

Focacci, L., et al., "Using Application Service Providers: Yes or No?" *Strategic Change*, 2003.

Gaulke, M., "Risk Management in TI Projects, *Information Systems Control Journal*, November–December 2002.

Gerlach, J., et al., "Determining the Cost of IT Services," *Communications of the ACM*, September 2002.

Gillin, P., "Offshore Outsourcing Becoming 'In' Thing for CIOs," *CIO News & Analysis*, June 24, 2003.

Gray, P., and H. Watson, "Present and Future Directions in Data Warehousing," *Database*, Summer 1998.

Green, S., *Profit on the Web*. Auckland, New Zealand: Computertime, 2002.

Gunasekaran, et al., "A Model for Investment Justification in Information Technology Projects," *International Journal of Information Management*, March 2001.

Hamilton, S., "Intel Research Expands Moore's Law," *Computer*, January 2003.

Harmozi, A., et al., "Outsourcing Information Technology: Assessing Your Options," *SAM Advanced Management Journal*, Autumn 2003.

Hirschheim, R., and M. Lacity, "Information Technology Insourcing: Myths and Realities," *Communications of the ACM*, February 2000.

Hitt, L. M., and E. Brynjolfsson, "Productivity, Business Profitability, and Consumer Surplus: Three Different Measures of Information Technology Value," *MIS Quarterly*, June 1996.

Intel Corp., "Building the Foundation for Anytime, Anywhere Computing," white paper #251290–002, *Intel Information Technology Publication*, June 13, 2002.

Irani, Z., and P. E. D. Love, "The Propagation of Technology Management Taxonomies for Evaluating Investments in Information Systems," *Journal of Management Information Systems*, Winter 2000–2001.

ITAA (Information Technology Association of America), "Skills Study 2000—Bridging the Gap: Information Technology Skills for a New Millennium," *uen.org/techday/html/technology.html*, April 2000.

Kaplan, R. S., and D. Norton, *The Balanced Scorecard*, rev. ed. Boston, MA: Harvard Business School Press, 2000; e-book.

Kaplan, R. S., and D. Norton, *The Balanced Scorecard*. Boston. MA: Harvard Business School Press, 1996.

Keen, P. G. W., "Value Analysis: Justifying DSS," *Management Information Systems Quarterly*, March 1981.

King, J., "User Beware," *Computerworld*, March 18, 2002.

Kohli, R., et al., "IT Investment Payoff in E-Business Environments: Research Issues," *Information Systems Frontiers*, September 2003.

Korzenioski, P., "Intranet Bets Pay Off," *InfoWorld*, January 13, 1997.

Kudyba, S., and D. Vitaliano, "Information Technology and Corporate Profitability: A Focus on Operating Efficiency." *Information Resources Management Journal*, January–March 2003.

Kumar, R. L., "Understanding DSS Value: An Options Perspective," *Omega*, June 1999.

Laurie, J., "Why Projects Fail," *JISC InfoNet (jiscinfonet.ac.uk)*, Northumbria University, Newcastle Upon Tyne, UK.

Lawson, R., et al., "Automating the Balanced Scorecard," *CMA Management*, February 2004.

Lee, J. N., et al., "IT Outsourcing Evaluation—Past, Present and Future," *Communications of the ACM*, May 2003.

Legrenzi, C., "The 2nd Edition of the European Survey on the Economic Value of IT," *Information Systems Control Journal*, May–June 2003.

Lewis, B. C., and T. A. Byrd, "Development of a Measure for IT Infrastructure Construct," *European Journal of Information Systems*, June 2003.

Li, H., et al., "The IT Performance Evaluation in the Construction Industry," *Proceedings, 33rd Hawaiian International Conference on Systems Sciences (HICSS)*, Maui, HI, January 2000.

Li, X., and J. D. Johnson, "Evaluate IT Investment Opportunities Using Real Options Theory." *Information Resources Management Journal*, July–September 2002, pp. 32–47.

Lin, W. T., and B. M. Shao, "Relative Sizes of Information Technology Investments and Productivity Efficiency: Their Linkage and Empirical Evidence," *Journal of AIS*, September 2000.

Lucas, H. C., *Information Technology and the Productivity Paradox: Assessing the Value of Investing in IT*. New York: Oxford University Press, 1999.

Marcolin, B. L., and K. L. McLellan, "Effective IT Outsourcing Arrangements," *Proceedings, 31st HICSS*, January 1998.

McAdam, J. P., "Slicing the Pie: Information Technology Cost Recovery Models," *CPA Journal*, February 1996.

McKay, J., and P. Marshall, *Strategic Management of e-Business.* Milton, Australia: Wiley, 2004.

Moore, G. E., "Moore's Law," *CIO,* January 1, 1997.

Mukhopadhyay, T., et al., "Assessing the Impact of Information Technology on Labor," *Decision Support Systems,* Vol. 19, 1997.

Olazabal, N. G., "Banking: the IT Paradox," *The McKinsey Quarterly,* January–March 2002.

Palvia, S., "Is E-Commerce Driving Outsourcing to Its Limits?" *Journal of IT Cases & Applications,* January 2002.

Paton, D., and D. Troppito, "Eye on ROI: ROI Review," *DM Review,* March 2004.

Peffers, K., and T. Saarinen, "Measuring the Business Value of IT Investments: Inferences from a Study of a Senior Bank Executive." *Journal of Organizational Computing and Electronic Commerce* January–March 2002.

Plumtree Corp., "MyAPlus.com: A Return-on-Investment Study of Portals," *A Meta Group White Paper,* November 12, 2001.

Pountain, D., "Amending Moore's Law," *Byte,* March 1998.

Qing, H. U., and R. Plant, "An Empirical Study of the Casual Relationship Between IT Investment and Firm Performance," *Information Resources Management Journal,* July–September 2001.

Quinn, J. B., "Strategic Outsourcing: Leveraging Knowledge Capabilities," *Sloan Management Review,* Summer 1999.

Raskin, A., "The ROIght Stuff," *CIO Web Business Magazine,* February 1, 1999.

Rayport, J., and B. J. Jaworski, *E-Commerce.* New York: McGraw-Hill, 2001.

Read, C., et al., *eCFO: Sustaining Value in the New Corporation.* Chichester, U.K.: Wiley, 2001.

Reichheld, F., and P. Schefter, "E-loyalty—Your Secret Weapon on the Web," *Harvard Business Review,* July–August 2000.

Renkema, T. J. W., *The IT Value Quest: How to Capture the Business Value of IT-Based Infrastructure.* Chichester, England: Wiley, 2000.

Roberts, A., "Project Aquarius: Measuring the Impact of Technology," *Management Services,* 2003.

Ross, J. W., and C. M. Beath, "Beyond the Business Case: New Approaches to IT Investment," *MIT Sloan Management Review,* Winter 2002.

Rothfeder, J., "Supply and Demand: Software Pricing," *eWeek,* February 26, 2004.

Rubin, H. A., "How to Measure IT Value," *CIO Insight,* May 1, 2003.

Rubin, R., "Outsourcing Imperative: Do or Die," *Optimize,* 2003.

Ryan S. D., and M. S. Gates, "Inclusion of Social Subsystem Issues in IT Investment Decisions: An Empirical Assessment," *Information Resources Management Journal,* January–March 2004.

sap.com (accessed June 27, 2003).

Sawhney, M., "Damn the ROI, Full Speed Ahead," *CIO Magazine,* July 15, 2002.

Seddon, P., et al., "Measuring Organizational IS Effectiveness: An Overview and Update of Senior Management Perspectives," *The Data BASE for Advances in Information Systems,* Spring 2002.

Seitz, N. E., *Capital Budgeting and Long-Term Financing Decisions,* 2nd ed. Cincinnati: South-Western Publishing, 1995.

Soh, C., and L. M. Markus, "How IT Creates Business Value: A Process Theory Synthesis," *Proceedings of the 16th International Conference on Information Systems,* December 1995.

Standish Group, "Chaos," Standish Research Paper, *standish-group.com/visitor/chaos.htm,* 1995.

Sterne, J, *Web Metrics.* New York: Wiley, 2002.

Steyaert, J. C., "Measuring the Performance of Electronic Government Services," *Information and Management,* January–February 2004.

Strassmann, P. A., *The Squandered Computer.* New Canaan, CT: Information Economics Press, 1997.

Straub, D. W., et al., "Measuring e-Commerce in Net-Enabled Organizations, *Information Systems Research,* June 2002a.

Straub, D. W., et al., "Toward New Metrics for Net-Enhanced Organizations," *Information Systems Research,* September 2002b.

Swamy, R., "Strategic Performance Measurement in the New Millennium," *CMA Management,* May 2002.

The Balanced Scorecard Institute, "What Is the Balanced Scorecard?" *balancedscorecard.org/basics/bsc1.html* (accessed July 2004).

"The Elevation of IT Outsourcing Partnership: With HP/SAP Trained Staff, Kone's Global Strategy In Top Level," *Communication News,* August 2002.

Tjan, A. K., "Put Your Internet Portfolio in Order," *Harvard Business Review,* February 2001.

Turban, E., et al., *E-Commerce 2006.* Upper Saddle River, NJ: Prentice Hall, 2006.

Van Grembergen, W. V., et al., "Linking the IT Balanced Scorecard to the Business Objectives at a Major Canadian Financial Group," *Journal of Information Technology Cases and Applications,* 2003.

Varon, E., "R. O. Iowa," *CIO Magazine,* June 1, 2003.

Vijavan, J., "The New TCO Metric," *Computerworld,* June 18, 2001.

Violino, B., "Return on Investment Profiles: The Intangible Benefits of Technology Are Emerging as the Most Important of All," *Information Week,* June 30, 1997.

Vulkan, N., *The Economics of e-Commerce.* Princeton, NJ: Princeton University Press, 2003.

Walsh, K. R., "Analyzing the Application ASP Concept: Technologies, Economics, and Strategies," *Communications of the ACM,* August 2003.

Wang, A. L., and D. Shiang, "SAP Business Case Builder," *An IDC Case Study* (sponsored by SAP), *IDC.com,* May 2002.

Watson, H. J., and B. J. Haley, "Managerial Considerations," *Communications of ACM,* September 1998.

Wheatley, M., "Chargeback for Good or Evil; Charging Users for IT Costs Can Rein in Budgets and Bring Rigor to Planning, but It Can Also Turn You into an Unpopular Bean Counter," *CIO,* March 1, 2003.

Wilkinson, S., "Phone Bill, Electricity Bill . . . Storage Bill? Storage Utilities Attract New Economy Companies with Pay-as-you-Go Service," *Earthweb.com,* October 24, 2000.

Willcocks, J., "Managing Information Technology Evaluation—Techniques and Processes," in R. G. Galliers and B. S. H. Baker (eds.), *Strategic Information Management: Challenges and Strategies in Managing Information Systems.* Oxford: Butterworth Heinemann, 1994.

Zviran, M., et al., "Building Outsourcing Relationships Across the Global Community: The UPS-Motorola Experience," *Journal of Strategic Information Systems,* December 2001.

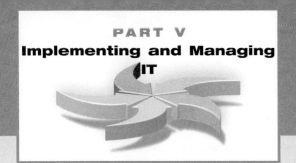

PART V
Implementing and Managing IT

12. Using IT for Strategic Advantage
13. Information Technology Economics
▶ 14. Acquiring IT Applications and Infrastructure
15. Managing Information Resources and Security
16. The Impacts of IT on Individuals, Organizations, and Society

CHAPTER

14 Acquiring IT Applications and Infrastructure

14.1 The Landscape and Framework of IT Application Acquisition

14.2 Identifying, Justifying, and Planning Information System Applications

14.3 Acquiring IT Applications: Available Options

14.4 Outsourcing and Application Service Providers

14.5 Vendor and Software Selection and Other Implementation Issues

14.6 Connecting to Databases and Business Partners: Integration

14.7 Business Process Redesign

14.8 The Role of IT in Business Process Redesign

14.9 Restructuring Processes and Organizations

Minicases:
1. Pioneer Inc.
2. McDonald's

LEARNING OBJECTIVES

After studying this chapter, you will be able to:

❶ Describe the process of IT acquisition or development.

❷ Describe IT project identification, justification, and planning.

❸ List the major IT acquisition options and the criteria for option selection.

❹ Describe the use of criteria for selecting an acquisition approach.

❺ Describe the role of ASPs.

❻ Describe the process of vendor and software selection.

❼ Understand some major implementation issues.

❽ Understand the issue of connecting IT applications to databases, other applications, networks, and business partners.

❾ Describe the need for business process redesign and the methodologies for doing it.

❿ Explain the IT support for process redesign and BPR, and describe redesign efforts, successes, and failures.

HOW STERNGOLD ACQUIRED AN E-COMMERCE SYSTEM

Sterngold (*sterngold.com*), a century-old manufacturer of dental materials, is a subsidiary of London-based Cookson Group PLC. Sterngold is based in Attleboro, Massachusetts; it has only 90 employees but has offices in Europe and South America.

 THE PROBLEM

The company sells more than 4,000 products either directly to 350,000–400,000 dental professionals or through distributors to another 5 million dental professionals. Orders come in small quantities, very frequently from repeat customers, with a frequent demand for same-day shipment. Sterngold realized that moving its sales online might create easy ordering for its customers, reduce its own transaction costs, and enable customers to get its products faster—all of which could provide a competitive advantage. The company had a Web site, but without selling capabilities. Sterngold decided that it had two choices to solve this problem: (1) to develop an e-commerce application in-house, or (2) to find an outsourcer to provide the application.

 THE SOLUTION

The company wanted a technology solution that allowed it fast time to market, access to best-of-breed technology and people, high security, superb reliability, and the ability to focus on core competency. Having only one IT person, the company knew that the in-house solution required hiring additional personnel, creating a temporary large IT department. Therefore, Sterngold decided to use an application outsourcing.

The question then became how to select a trusted business partner who understood the need to move quickly, but carefully. After long deliberation and interviews with potential outsourcers, the company selected Surebridge Inc. to develop and then host the e-commerce application. The selection was "blessed" by the parent company, Cookson Group.

THE PROCESS

Surebridge followed its own proprietary eMethodology approach. First, a vendor's implementation team was created. The team started by evaluating Sterngold's business needs, using interviews to gather the information. Then goals and a timetable were created. A major consideration was to finish the project before the industry's annual trade show, so that Sterngold would be able to demonstrate to its customers how easy it is to order products in the online store.

The next step was to create an architecture. This step included a front-end ordering system (phase I) and its integration with the back-office systems (phase II). This was not an easy task, given that there were over 4,000 products whose information attributes resided in disparate areas of the company. The relevant information was channeled into a large database. A major task was the creation of a search engine that would be useful to diverse groups of customers (e.g., dentists, dental labs). Each group of customers had different knowledge, requirements, and buying habits. Working hand-in-hand, Sterngold and Surebridge completed phase I in less than three months.

To execute phase II there were many challenges to meet. First, expertise was needed on how financial, inventory, and order fulfillment could best be integrated with the ordering system. This required the services of a consultant and resulted in redesign of some business processes. Also, several internal policies were modified to support the Web initiative. For example, a complex pricing policy was simplified by creating clear rules about discounting.

THE RESULTS

The new system offers a number of major capabilities: Because the ordering system was integrated with the back office, the system reduces errors due to manual data entry. Real-time inventory status is given to customers before they place an order, and a tracking feature provides real-time status of orders. Discounts are related to specific customers, so they know what they will pay as soon as they log in. Real-time authorization of customers' credit cards is provided when orders are placed. In addition, the company now can offer promotions to its customers without the need to send letters. The site also offers the ability to track customer clickstream movements, allowing the company to personalize products and to offer cross-sell and up-sell products and services. Also, the site includes capabilities for conducting e-mail marketing campaigns using permission marketing.

By 2004, two years after implementation, Sterngold has recorded the following results:

- By offering free shipping, Sterngold has encouraged more and more customers to order online, thus increasing the customer base (at the expense of the competitors).
- More product promotion (which has been easy to do online) has resulted in more customers and sales.
- Both the company and the customers have experienced increasing efficiencies and savings on administrative costs.
- Much fax and snail mail have been eliminated.
- The online presence has resulted in greater exposure to business partners.
- A strong relationship with the technology partners has been created. (Since Sterngold owns the IT infrastructure and Surebridge just operates it, finger pointing in case of problems is minimized.)

Use of an outside vendor enabled Phase I to be finished in less than three months, rather than two to three years if it had been done in-house. This enabled Sterngold to be the *first mover* in its industry. The Web site is now being translated into several languages for the global market.

Sources: Compiled from Craig (2003) and from *sterngold.com* (accessed July 2004).

LESSONS LEARNED FROM THIS CASE

First the case demonstrates how an IT application starts. Then it describes how a company selects an alternative for building an IT application. In this case, an outsourcer was selected to build a custom-made application. Then, a team is created to implement the application. The implementation requires a study of existing processes and redesign of some. Critical to the project is the need to integrate the ordering system with the back office (order fulfillment, inventory, accounting, payment). Finally, we learn that being first mover can be advantageous. All of these issues and a few related ones are the subject of this chapter.

14.1 THE LANDSCAPE AND FRAMEWORK OF IT APPLICATION ACQUISITION

Our attention in this chapter is focused on information systems *acquisition*. We include in "acquisition" all approaches to obtaining systems: *buying, leasing,* or *building*. The acquisition issue is complex for various reasons: There is a large variety of IT applications, they keep changing over time, and they may involve several business partners. In addition, there is no single way to acquire IT applications: They can be developed in-house, outsourced (obtained or leased from an external organization), or a combination of the two. Another strategy that is becoming very popular is to build applications from components. When components are used, the appropriate ones must be found, and even a single application may have many components from several different vendors.

The diversity of IT applications requires a variety of development approaches. For example, small EC storefronts can be developed with HTML, Java, or other programming languages. Or they can be quickly implemented with commercial packages, leased from application service providers (ASPs) for a small monthly fee, or purchased "on demand" as water or electricity are purchased. Larger applications can be outsourced or developed in-house. Building medium-to-large applications requires extensive integration with existing information systems such as corporate databases, intranets, enterprise resource planning (ERP), and other application programs. Therefore, developing IT projects can be rather complex (Xia and Lee, 2004).

The Acquisition Process

The acquisition process of a typical IT application has five major steps, which are shown in Figure 14.1 (page 598). The steps in the acquisition process are outlined and discussed below.

STEP 1: IDENTIFYING, JUSTIFYING, AND PLANNING INFORMATION SYSTEMS. Information systems are usually built as *enablers* of some business process(es). Therefore, their planning must be aligned with that of the organization's overall business plan and the specific processes involved. Such processes may need to be restructured to fully reap the benefits of the supporting IT (see Section 14.8). Furthermore, each application must be carefully analyzed, using the methods described in Chapter 13, to ensure that it will have the needed functionality to meet the requirements of the business processes and the users, and that its benefits justify its cost. Both of these activities may be complex, but they are necessary, especially for systems that require high investment to acquire, operate, and maintain. The output of this step is a decision to go with the specific application, with a timetable, budget, and assigned responsibility. This step is described in Technology Guide 6 and in Section 14.2. For further details, see Kendall and Kendall (2005). This step is usually done in-house (with consultants if needed). All other steps can be done in-house or outsourced.

Technology Guides are located at the book's Web site.

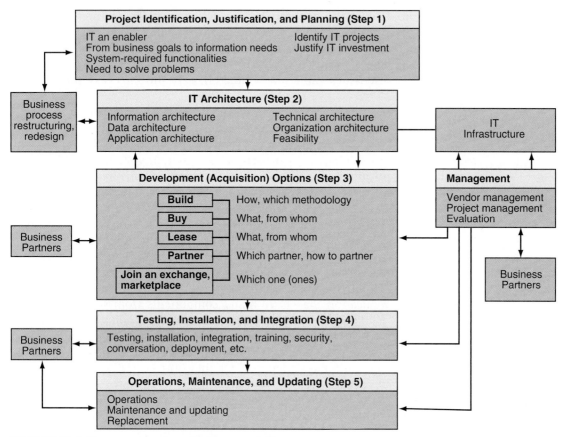

FIGURE 14.1 The process of application acquisition.

STEP 2: IT ARCHITECTURE CREATION—A SYSTEMS ANALYSIS APPROACH. The major objective of this step is to create the IT architecture. *IT architecture,* as described in Chapters 2 and 12, is the conceptualization of how the organization's information objectives are met by the capabilities of the specific applications. A detailed description of this step is provided in Technology Guide 6 (see Section TG6.1).

The results obtained from Step 2 are routed to the strategic planning level (e.g., to a steering committee). As a result, the application portfolio may be changed. For example, the steering committee may defer or scale down the specific project because it is too risky. Once the architecture is compiled and the project gets a final approval, a decision about *how* to develop the specific application has to be made.

STEP 3: SELECT A DEVELOPMENT OPTION AND ACQUIRE THE APPLICATION. IT applications can be developed through several alternative approaches that will be introduced in this chapter and in Technology Guide 6. The major options are:

- Build the system in-house. (This can be done in several ways.)
- Have a vendor build a custom-made system for you.

- Buy an application and install it (with or without modifications) by yourself or by a vendor.
- Lease software from an application service provider (ASP) or lease via utility computing.
- Enter into a partnership or alliance that will enable the company to use someone else's application.
- Join a third-party e-marketplace, such as an auction site, a bidding (reverse auction) site, or an exchange, that provides needed capabilities to participants.
- Use a combination of these listed approaches.

For further details, see Sections 14.3 and 14.4.

The consideration criteria for selecting among the various options are presented in Section 14.5. Once an option is decided on, the system is acquired. At the end of this step, an application is ready to be installed and deployed. See Technology Guide 6 for procedures.

No matter what option you choose, you most likely will have to select some vendor(s) and/or software, and then you will need to work with and manage the vendors (Section 14.5).

STEP 4: INSTALLING, CONNECTING, AND MORE. IT applications need to be connected to the corporate intranet and/or extranets, to databases, and to other applications. Connection to business partners or public exchanges may also be required. Details of the connection process are provided in Section 14.6 under the topic of integration.

During this step the applications are also tested, and user reactions are examined. Once the applications pass all of the tests, they can be deployed. In the deployment process one may deal with issues such as conversion strategies, training, and resistance to change (see Whitten et al., 2003).

STEP 5: OPERATION AND MAINTENANCE. Operation and maintenance can be done in-house and/or outsourced (Kendall and Kendall, 2005). Software maintenance can be a big problem due to rapid changes in the IT technology field. Because of the scope of this topic, it is not discussed in this textbook. For full discussion, see Kendall and Kendall (2005).

MANAGING THE DEVELOPMENT PROCESS. The development process can be fairly complex, and it must be managed properly. For medium-to-large applications a project team is usually created to manage the process and the vendors. Collaboration with business partners is also critical. As shown in various chapters, some IT failures are the result of lack of cooperation by business partners. For example, you can install a superb e-procurement system, but if your vendors will not use it properly, the system will collapse. Projects can be managed with project management software (e.g., *office.microsoft.com/project,* and *primavera.com*).

Appropriate management also includes periodic evaluations of system performance. Standard project management techniques and tools are useful for this task. Finally, implementing an IT project may require restructuring of one or more business processes. This topic is addressed in Sections 14.7 and 14.9. For further discussion see Kanter and Walsh (2004).

Let's now look at some of the steps (1, 3, and 4) in more detail.

14.2 IDENTIFYING, JUSTIFYING, AND PLANNING INFORMATION SYSTEM APPLICATIONS (STEP 1)

In Chapter 12 we described the process of IT planning from a *macro* point of view—that is, looking at the entire IT resources in the organization. When we look at a specific application or a specific infrastructure, we need to go through an application-by-application planning process as well. Note that the need to acquire an application can be the result of the macro planning, usually due to its inclusion in the proposed new applications in the *application portfolio* (Chapter 12). However, applications can be initiated for other reasons, such as to solve a recurrent problem, as illustrated in the Swedish bank case described in *IT at Work 14.1*.

IT at Work 14.1
WEB SERVICES GET SWEDISH BANKING APPLICATIONS TALKING TO EACH OTHER

Centrala Studie Stodsnamnden (CSN) is the Swedish government's banking authority responsible for providing student loans and grants to Swedes who are pursuing higher education. Each year, CSN loans out SEK$2.5 billion to a half-million people and delivers a host of financial services to thousands more. In January 2002, at the start of the new school semester, when online traffic to the organization is typically four to five times greater than in other months, CSN's Web site went down. Students were forced to phone CSN representatives directly to receive help with new loan and grant applications and payback information. The voice-response system, that was designed to meet a much lower demand, had proved inadequate.

A group of technicians led by the production team worked hard to stabilize the Web site and ease the burden caused by overuse of the voice-response system. "We found the load problem and tried to tame it by adding servers, but the solution was like patchwork—and in the following weeks we could see the same pattern with instability occur," says Orjan Carlsson, Chief Architect of CSN's information technology department. Consistently poor Web site performance coupled with long waits on the telephone was enough to cause a public outcry.

Given CSN's heterogeneous enterprise environment—which comprised everything from IBM mainframes to UNIX-based applications, to systems running Microsoft Windows NT—a solution that could support cross-platform communication was a necessity. Only a flexible, scalable, open-standards–based integration architecture could supply the level of interoperability the organization desired, especially for the high volume during the start of a semester.

A locally based IBM team worked closely with CSN to investigate solution possibilities. Together, the technical teams decided that the best way for the organization to realize cross-platform, program-to-program communication was through Web Services built on IBM WebSphere. This architecture allows CSN's disparate applications to exchange information with each other without human intervention. The team implemented a system that also eliminated the organization's reliance on an outsourced application service provider for its voice-response system. The system leverages Web Services to enable the Windows NT–based voice-response system to execute transactions that are easily recognized by CSN's back-end (back-office) operations.

The new Web Services–enabled system allows CSN to deliver student account status and transaction information to phones (voice response) and to CSN's portal at a significantly reduced cost. "Web Services are essential for us today and in the future," says Carlsson. According to Carlsson, Web Services enable a loosely coupled architecture, resulting in a highly integrated solution.

Reuse of code also gives CSN an advantage. One interface can serve several business systems using different channels, making it easy to modify existing channels or add new ones, a feature that significantly reduces total cost of ownership. CSN dramatically saves on developer costs as well as gets new functionality to market faster and with more frequency. The result is a flexible and scalable Web services–enabled architecture that is essentially transparent to end users, giving CSN the cross-platform communication system it needs to operate efficiently, serve its customers, and lower costs.

Source: Compiled from *http://www-3.ibm.com/software/success/cssdb.nsf/ CS/LEOD-5KKTRX?OpenDocument&Site=admain* (accessed November 25, 2003).

For Further Exploration: How did this application arise? What does the solution provide? What role does the business partner play?

Other sources of IT project applications can be any of the following: requests from user departments (see the R.O.I. Iowa case in Chapter 13); vendors' recommendations; need to comply with new government regulations; auditors' recommendations; recommendation of the steering committee; recommendation of the IS department; top management requests (orders); or search for high-payoff projects. For more discussion see Carroll (2004).

Identifying High-Payoff Projects

It is natural that organizations will prefer to search for high-payoff applications, especially if they are not difficult to implement. Some organizations use a systematic approach for such a search, as described in Online File W14.1.

Project Justification

Once potential projects are identified, they usually need to be justified. To do so, one can use some of the methods described in Chapter 13. Since organizations have limited resources, they cannot embark on all projects at once. Therefore, all proposed projects must be scrutinized. This may not be an easy task due to the complexity of IT projects (see Xia and Lee, 2004).

Information system applications may be expensive. Therefore, an organization must analyze the need for applications and justify it in terms of cost and benefits. Because most organizations operate with tight budgets, this analysis must be carefully done. The investigation is usually divided into two parts. First, it is necessary to explore the need for each system (i.e., find the information needs of the users and how the application will meet those needs). Second, it is necessary to justify it from a cost-benefit point of view. The need for information systems is usually related to organizational planning and to the analysis of its performance vis-à-vis its competitors (see Chapter 12). The cost-benefit justification must look at the wisdom of the specific IT investment vis-à-vis investing in alternative IT or other projects.

Both of these topics are complex, involving many issues. For example, organizational and IT planning may involve business processes redesign (e.g., see Sections 14.7 and 14.9, and El Sawy, 2001). Both issues are also related to marketing and corporate strategy. For example, Ward and Peppard (2002) developed a framework for deciding on what specific IT applications to choose, based on their strategic versus high potential values. Such investigation is the subject of special IS courses and will not be dealt with here. However, what is important to stress is that such an investigation determines the relative importance of each IT application.

Once justification is done, a plan for the application acquisition can be made.

Planning for the Specific Application

Before a project is implemented, or even before a company decides how to acquire the software, it is necessary to understand the organization's current way of doing business (the business process) in the area the application is going to be used. For example, if you plan to install an e-procurement application, it makes sense to study the ins and outs of procurement in your business. This can be done in a systematic way as part of *system analysis,* as described in Technology Guide 6.

The planning process includes documenting system requirements, studying data and information flows, and studying the users' community and their specific objectives. Also included is the risk of failure and how to manage that risk. This then leads to the creation of a timetable (schedule) and milestones (which are needed in order to determine how to acquire the application). For example, if you need the system very quickly, you will favor buying or leasing one. The planning process covers resources other than time—specifically, money (budget), labor, and equipment (if needed). Project planning also examines the issue of connectivity to databases and to partners' systems, relevant government regulations, what to do if some employees lose their jobs as a result of the implementation of the application, and so on. Online File W14.2 describes more about milestones and about project properties and priorities.

Issues such as connecting to business partners and databases are the foundations for step 2, the creation of the IT architecture. This step is discussed in detail in Technology Guide 6.

14.3 ACQUIRING IT APPLICATIONS: AVAILABLE OPTIONS (STEP 3)

There are several options for acquiring IT applications. The major options are: buy, lease, and develop in-house. Each of these is described in this section, with some other minor options.

Buy the Applications (Off-the-Shelf Approach)

Standard features required by IT applications can be found in many commercial packages. Buying an existing package can be a cost-effective and time-saving strategy compared with in-house application development. The "buy" option should be carefully considered and planned for to ensure that all critical features for current and future needs are included in the selected package. Otherwise such packages may quickly become obsolete.

However, organizational needs are rarely fully satisfied by one software package. It is therefore sometimes necessary to acquire multiple packages to support even one business process. These packages then need to be integrated with each other as well as with existing software (see Section 14.6).

The buy option is especially attractive if the software vendor allows for modifications. However, even this option may not be attractive in cases of high obsolescence rates or high software cost. The advantages and limitations of the buy option are summarized in Table 14.1.

TABLE 14.1 Advantages and Limitations of the "Buy" Option

Advantages of the "Buy" Option	Disadvantages of the "Buy" Option
• Many different types of off-the-shelf software are available.	• Software may not exactly meet the company's needs.
• Much time can be saved by buying rather than building.	• Software may be difficult or impossible to modify, or it may require huge business process changes to implement.
• The company can know what it is getting before it invests in the software.	• The company will not have control over software improvements and new versions. (Usually it may only recommend.)
• The company is not the first and only user.	
• Purchased software may avoid the need to hire personnel specifically dedicated to a project.	• Purchased software can be difficult to integrate with existing systems.
• The vendor updates the software frequently.	• Vendors may drop a product or go out of business.
• The price is usually much lower for a buy option.	

Lease the Applications

Compared with the buy option and the option to develop applications in-house (to be discussed soon), the "lease" option can result in substantial cost and time savings. Leased packages may not always exactly fit the application requirements (the same is true with the buy option). But many common features that are needed by most organizations are usually included in leased packages. (It usually is more comprehensive than a "buy" package.)

In those cases where extensive software maintenance is required or where the cost of buying is very high, leasing is more advantageous than buying. Leasing can be especially attractive to SMEs that cannot afford major investments in IT software. Large companies may also prefer to lease packages in order to test potential IT solutions before committing to heavy investments. Also, because there is a shortage of IT personnel with appropriate skills for developing novel IT applications (such as EC or wireless), many companies choose to lease instead of develop software in-house. Even those companies that have in-house expertise may not be able to afford the long wait for strategic applications to be developed in-house. Therefore, they lease (or buy) applications from external resources to establish a quicker presence in the market.

TYPES OF LEASING VENDORS. Leasing can be done in one of two ways. The first way is to lease the application from an outsourcer and install it on the company's premises. The vendor can help with the installation and frequently will offer to also contract for the operation and maintenance of the system. Many conventional applications are leased this way. The second way, using an application system provider (ASP), is becoming more popular. ASPs are explored in Section 14.4.

UTILITY COMPUTING. Tapping into computing resources with a simplicity equal to plugging an electrical lamp into an outlet has been a goal of many companies for years. The approach is known as *utility computing* (or *on-demand computing*). See Chapter 2 and *A Closer Look 14.1* (page 604). The idea is to provide unlimited computing power and storage capacity that can be used and reallocated for any application—and billed on a pay-per-use basis.

Utility computing consists of a pool of "self-managing" IT resources that can be continually reallocated to meet the organization's changing business and service needs. These resources can be located anywhere and managed by an organization's IT staff or a third-party service provider. Equally important, usage of these resources can be tracked and billed down to the level of an individual user or group.

As shown in Figure 14.2 (page 604), utility computing consists of three layers of tools and two types of value-added services. Each tool must be seamlessly integrated to create a comprehensive solution, but will usually be implemented separately. These three tools are:

1. *Policy-based service-level-management tools.* These coordinate, monitor, and report on the ways in which multiple infrastructure components come together to deliver a business service.
2. *Policy-based resource-management tools.* These automate and standardize all types of IT management best practices, from initial configuration to ongoing fault management and asset tracking.
3. *Virtualization tools.* These allow server, storage, and network resources to be deployed and managed as giant pools, and seamlessly changed as needs change.

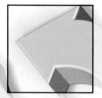

A CLOSER LOOK
14.1 UTILITY COMPUTING: "THE NEXT BIG THING"

Imagine this scene. It's noon on Friday and you just found out that your relatives are coming to spend the weekend. It's time to contact the electric company to let them know that you will need extra electricity for the weekend. You're told you have to fill out a purchase order and it will be five to seven days before you can get extra electricity. Of course, life is not like this, because basic utilities have extra capacity built into their delivery systems. But this *would* be a likely scenario if you were to find out at noon on Friday that you were expecting a major spike in usage on your servers. You'd have to call your provider, do a bunch of paperwork, and maybe in a few days you could get the extra capacity you need. That's the kind of problem that utility computing aims to solve.

THE TECHNOLOGY. Utility computing vendors are looking toward a future in which computing capacity is as easy to acquire as electricity. Rather than having a fixed amount of computing resources, you would have access to computing resources on an as-needed basis—just like with electricity. Many IT market leaders are now starting to catch on to the concept of utility computing as a bullet-proof utility service that we can virtually take for granted. IBM announced it is spending $10 billion on its on-demand computing initiatives. HP also announced its Utility Data Center architecture, and Sun has its own N1 data virtualization center plans. Sun, HP, and IBM are

"duking it out" over how best to meet utility computing requirements and command a leadership position.

IMPLEMENTATION. Already present in a variety of capacity-based pricing models, utility computing is poised to expand throughout the enterprise as various key technologies—such as Web Services, grid computing, and provisioning—intersect. Growth of utility computing in the enterprise will deliver to the industry not only equal access to supercomputing resources, but also new revenue streams for commercial data centers, new application pricing models based on metered use, and an open computing infrastructure for companies with little or no standing IT maintenance budget. Utility computing is on track to be the "next big thing" for IT vendors and services companies that sell to large enterprises.

CONCLUSION. Utility computing (also called "on-demand computing") has become one of the hot topics in the IT community and, increasingly, in larger enterprises that are looking for ways to reduce the fixed costs and complexity of IT. Utility computing tools provide total flexibility in information systems development, from in-house and self-managed to fully outsourced, with everything in between—including a hybrid deployment model in which in-house capacity can be supplemented by third-party resources to handle peak needs.

Sources: Compiled from Zimmerman (2003) and from Neel (2002).

These tools share multisourcing delivery and framework services (left side of figure) and provide for customer access and management services (right side of figure).

Utility computing still faces daunting obstacles. One obstacle is the immaturity of the tools. Another is the fact that each vendor prefers to tout its own unique

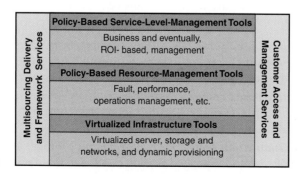

FIGURE 14.2 Utility computing. (*Source:* Here, 2003.)

variation on the utility-computing vision, with different (often confusing) names and terminology. However, utility computing will accelerate acceptance of ASPs, which may distribute it. For more, see *utilitycomputing.itworld.com.*

Develop the Applications In-House (Insourcing)

A third development strategy is to develop ("build") applications in-house. Although this approach is usually more time-consuming and may be more costly than buying or leasing, it often leads to a better fit with the specific organizational requirements. Companies that have the resources and time to develop their own IT applications in-house may follow this approach as a strategy to differentiate themselves from the competition, which may be using standard applications that are bought or leased. In-house development, however, is a challenging task, as many applications are novel, have users from outside the organization, and involve multiple organizations. Before selecting a development approach, a company needs to complete IT design (see Briggs, 2004).

IN-HOUSE DEVELOPMENT APPROACHES. There are two major approaches to in-house development: building from scratch or building from components.

1. *Build from scratch.* This option should be considered only for specialized applications for which components are not available. It is an expensive and slow process, but it will provide the best fit.

2. *Build from components.* Companies with experienced IT staff can use standard components (e.g., a secure Web server), some software languages (e.g., Java, Visual Basic, or Perl), and third-party subroutines to create and maintain applications on their own. (Or, companies can outsource the entire development process to an integrator that assembles the components.) From a software standpoint, using components offers the greatest flexibility and can be the least expensive option in the long run. However, it can also result in a number of false starts and wasted experimentations. For this reason, even those companies with experienced staff are frequently better off modifying and customizing one of the packaged solutions as part of the "buy" option. For details about using components see Technology Guide 6 and Ravichandran (2003).

In building in-house, one can use various methodologies, described below.
    Systems Development Life Cycle (SDLC). Large IT projects, especially ones that involve infrastructure, are developed according to a systematic set of procedures known as the *systems development life cycle (SDLC)* using several tools, notably CASE tools. Details about this approach are provided in Technology Guide 6.2.
    Prototyping Methodology. With a *prototyping* methodology, an initial list of basic system requirements is defined and used to build a prototype, which is then improved in several iterations based on users' feedback. This approach can be very rapid.
    Many companies have used this approach to develop their IT, and especially their EC, applications mainly for three reasons: (1) Clear-cut information requirements, which are necessary for SDLC, are not available. For example, requirements are clear in building a payroll system, but they are not so clear in building a complex scheduling decision support system. (2) Time is important, and they want to be the first to market. (3) It is usually beneficial to involve the users (employees, suppliers, and customers) in the design of the applications. By quickly building a prototype instead of a full-fledged application, a company

can, for example, establish an online presence more quickly than its competitors. The initial prototype is then tested and improved, tested again and developed further, based on the users' feedback.

The prototyping approach, however, is not without drawbacks. There is a risk of getting into an endless loop of prototype revisions, as users may never be fully satisfied. Such a risk should be planned for because of the rapid changes in IT technology and business models. Another drawback is the risk of idiosyncratic design; the prototype may be revised based on the feedback of only a small group of users who are not necessarily representative of the entire user population. Such a risk can be alleviated by embedding a systematic feedback mechanism in the application itself, such as click trails and online feedback forms to elicit input from as many users as possible.

In-house development can be done by IS department personnel, by outsourcers, or by end users (usually small systems).

End-User Development

In the early days of computing, an organization housed its computer in a climate-controlled room (computer center), with locked doors and restricted access. The only people who interacted with the computer (most organizations had only one computer) were specialists: programmers, computer operators, and data entry personnel. Over the years, computers became cheaper, smaller, and more widely dispersed throughout the organization. Now almost everybody who works at a desk or in the field has a computer in addition to, or instead of, the computer center.

Along with this proliferation of hardware, many computer-related activities shifted out into the work area. Users now handle most of their own data entry. They create many of their own reports and print them locally, instead of waiting for them to arrive in the interoffice mail after a computer operator has run them at a remote computer data center. They provide unofficial training and support to other workers in their area. Users also design and develop an increasing proportion of their own applications, sometimes even relatively large and complex systems. End-user computing is ever-increasing (see Online File W14.3).

Beneficial as this trend is to both workers and the organization as a whole, end-user computing has some limitations. End users may not be skilled enough in computers, so quality and cost may be jeopardized unless proper controls are installed. Also, many end users do not take time to document their work and may neglect proper security measures. For complete coverage, see Regan and O'Connor (2002) and Sutcliffe and Mehandjiev (2004). For the different types of end-user computing, see Online File W14.4.

END-USER COMPUTING AND WEB-BASED SYSTEMS DEVELOPMENT. The development of client/server applications in the 1980s and 1990s was characterized by user-driven systems development. Either directly or indirectly, end users made decisions for systems designers and developers on how the programs should operate. Web-based systems development in the twenty-first century, however, is *application driven* rather than *user driven*. The end user can still determine what the *requirements* will be and has some input into the design of the applications. But because of the nature of the technologies used in Web-based application design, the required functions, not the user, determines what the application will look like and how it will perform.

An innovative way of managing end-user computing is described in *IT at Work 14.2*. In this case, an outside vendor helped to *manage* the end-user computing.

IT at Work 14.2
ANSETT AUSTRALIA AND IBM COLLABORATE IN END-USER COMPUTING

Ansett Australia, one of Australia's leading airlines, had chosen IBM Global Services Australia to manage its end-user computing support functions. Ansett (*ansett.com.au*), based in Melbourne, operates an extensive range of domestic airline services and also flies to Japan, Hong Kong, Taiwan, Bali, and Fiji.

Ansett Australia's General Manager for IT Infrastructure and Operations, Hal Pringle, said that IBM Global Services Australia's appointment significantly improved desktop services to the airline's end users while at the same time delivering substantial cost savings. Such service was previously delivered by a mixture of external contractors and in-house staff.

Mr. Pringle said the decision to hire an external provider of end-user computing (EUC) support arose from a benchmarking study conducted earlier by Ansett. The study showed that a move to a single external provider of the caliber of IBM would do the following: achieve a more consistent end-to-end delivery of applications; assist the implementation of best-practice EUC support at the best cost; deliver substantial cost savings; allow Ansett to better manage EUC supply and demand; and deliver a more consistent and better quality support service to end users.

"The study highlighted the fact that Ansett had in effect 'outgrown' the level of end-user service provided at that time, and that a quantum leap in service was required to ensure a full return on our end-user computing investment," Pringle said.

"Improving delivery of services to end users and enhancing end-user productivity are becoming key focus areas for many Australian corporations. I am very pleased that we have been chosen to deliver these additional services to Ansett," said Mr. Bligh, General Manager of IBM Global Services Australia, Travel and Transportation Services.

Sources: Compiled from Sachdeva (2000) and *ansett.com.au* (accessed December 2003).

For Further Exploration: What strategic advantages can Ansett Australia gain by ensuring consistent and reliable support to its end-user computing? Why does a large company like Ansett use a vendor to manage EUC?

Other Acquisition Options

A number of other acquisition options are available to IT developers, and in particular for e-commerce applications.

JOIN AN E-MARKETPLACE OR AN E-EXCHANGE. With this option, the company "plugs" itself into an e-marketplace. For example, a company can place its catalogs in Yahoo's marketplace. Visitors to Yahoo's store will find the company's products and will be able to buy them. The company pays Yahoo a monthly fee for the catalog space. (Yahoo is "hosting" the company's selling portal.)

JOIN A THIRD-PARTY AUCTION OR REVERSE AUCTION. Similar to the previous option, a company can plug into a third-party auction or reverse auction site fairly quickly. Many companies use this option for certain e-procurement activities or to liquidate products. Alternatively, a company can join a B2B exchange that offers auctions, as described in Chapter 4.

ENGAGE IN JOINT VENTURES. There are several different partnership or joint venture arrangements that may facilitate EC application development. For example, four banks in Hong Kong have developed a joint e-banking system. In some cases, companies can team up with a company that already has the needed application in place.

JOIN A PUBLIC EXCHANGE OR A CONSORTIUM. Finally, a company can join a public exchange (Chapter 4), for selling and/or buying, by simply plugging into the public exchange. Another option is for a company to join a consortium (a vertical exchange owned by a group of big players in an industry), which may have applications developed to fit the needs of companies in the industry.

HYBRID APPROACH. A hybrid approach combines the best of what the company does internally with an outsourced strategy. Hybrid models work best when the outsourced partner offers higher security levels, faster time-to-market, and superb service level agreements.

Criteria for selecting a development strategy are provided in Section 14.5. However, before proceeding to that topic, let's look further at the recent trend of outsourcing and ASPs.

14.4 OUTSOURCING AND APPLICATION SERVICE PROVIDERS

Outsourcing

Small or medium-sized companies with few IT staff and smaller budgets are best served by outside contractors. Outside contractors have also proven to be a good selection for large companies in certain circumstances. Use of outside contractors or external organizations to acquire IT services is called *outsourcing* (Chapter 13). Large companies may choose outsourcing when they want to experiment with new IT technologies without a great deal of up-front investment, to protect their own internal networks, or to rely on experts. Outsourcers can perform any or all tasks in IT development. For example, they can plan, program, build applications, integrate, operate, and maintain. The benefits and problems of outsourcing are presented in Online File W14.5. It is useful to develop good relationships with the outsourcers (see Kishore et al., 2003).

Several types of vendors offer services for creating and operating IT systems including e-commerce applications:

- *Software houses.* Many software companies, from IBM to Oracle, among others, offer a range of outsourcing services for developing, operating, and maintaining IT applications.
- *Outsourcers and others.* IT outsourcers, such as EDS, offer a variety of services. Also, the large CPA companies and management consultants (e.g., Accenture) offer some outsourcing services.
- *Telecommunications companies.* Increasingly, the large telecommunications companies are expanding their hosting services to include the full range of IT and EC solutions. MCI, for example, offers Web Commerce services for a monthly fee.

While the trend to outsource is rising, so is the trend to do it *offshore,* mainly in India and China. Offshore outsourcing is certainly less expensive, but it includes risks as well (see *cio.com,* "The 10 most important issues in 2003," and Overby, 2003).

One of the most common types of IT outsourcing is the use of application service providers.

Application Service Providers

An **application service provider (ASP)** is a vendor who assembles the software needed by enterprises and packages it, usually with outsourced development, operations, maintenance, and other services (see Kern and Kreijger, 2001). The essential difference between an ASP and an outsourcer is that an

ASP will manage application servers in a centrally controlled location, rather than on a customer's site. Applications are then accessed via the Internet or VANs through a standard Web browser interface. Such an arrangement provides a full range of services for the company using the ASP: Applications can be scaled, upgrades and maintenance can be centralized, physical security over the applications and servers can be guaranteed, and the necessary critical mass of human resources can be efficiently utilized.

Monthly fees are paid by the end-user businesses to the ASP. In general, the fees include payment for the application software, hardware, service and support, maintenance, and upgrades. The fee can be fixed or be based on utilization. According to Scott McNealy, Sun Microsystems' CEO, by 2005, "if you're a CIO with a head for business, you won't buy software or computers anymore. You'll rent all your resources from a service provider" (staff interview, *CIO* magazine, November 2000).

ASPs are especially active in enterprise computing and EC applications, which may be too complex to build and too cumbersome to modify and maintain. Therefore, the major providers of ERP software, such as SAP and Oracle, are offering ASP options. IBM, Microsoft, and Computer Associates also offer ASP services.

BENEFITS OF LEASING FROM ASPS. Leasing from an ASP is a particularly desirable option for SME businesses, for which in-house development and operation of IT applications can be time-consuming and expensive. Leasing from ASPs saves various expenses (such as labor costs) in the initial development stage. It also helps reduce the software maintenance and upgrading and user training costs in the long run. A company can select other software products from the same ASP to meet its changing needs and does not have to invest further in upgrading the existing one. Thus, overall business competitiveness can be strengthened through reducing the time-to-market and enhancing the ability to adapt to changing market conditions. ASPs are particularly effective for IT applications for which timing and flexibility and agility are crucial. For a list of benefits and potential risks, see Online File W14.6.

Leasing from ASPs does have its disadvantages. Many companies are concerned with the adequacy of protection offered by the ASP against hackers, theft of confidential information, and virus attacks. Also, leased software often does not provide the perfect fit for the desired application. It is also important to ensure that the speed of the Internet connection is compatible with that of the application, to avoid distortions in its performance. For example, it is not advisable to run heavy-duty applications on a modem link below a T1 line or a high-speed DSL.

From the ASP vendor's point of view, the benefits presented by the ASP model are many. For one, revenues are squeezed due to heavy competition in the long-distance carrier and Internet service providers (ISP) markets. These companies are looking to generate revenues from sources other than connectivity and transport, and ASP services offer a new outlet. An interesting institution is the *ASP Industry Consortium,* whose founding members include AT&T, Cisco, Citrix Systems, Ernst & Young, Verizon, IBM, Marimba, Sharp Electronics, Sun Microsystems, UUNET, and Verio.

Criteria for Selecting an Acquisition Approach

A major issue faced by any company is which method(s) of acquisition to select. To do so the company must consider many criteria, such as those provided in Table 14.2 (page 610). Some criteria may conflict with others, so the company

TABLE 14.2 Criteria for Determining Which Application Development Approach to Use

- The functionalities of packages
- Information requirements
- User friendliness of the application
- Hardware and software resources
- Installation difficulties; integration
- Maintenance services requirements
- Vendor quality and track record
- Estimated total costs of ownership
- Ability to measure tangible benefits
- Personnel needed for development
- Forecasting and planning for technological evolution (what will come next)
- Scaling (ease, cost, limits)
- Sizing requirements
- Performance requirements
- Reliability requirements
- Security requirements

TABLE 14.3 Advantages and Disadvantages of Various Systems Acquisition Methods

Advantages	Disadvantages
External Acquisition (Buy or Lease)	
• Software can be tried out.	• Controlled by another company with its own priorities and business considerations.
• Software has been used for similar problems in other organizations.	• Package's limitations may prevent desired business processes.
• Reduces time spent for analysis, design, and programming.	• May be difficult to get needed enhancements.
• Has good documentation that will be maintained.	• Lack of intimate knowledge in the purchasing company about how the software works and why it works that way.
End-User Development	
• Bypasses the IS department and avoids delays.	• May eventually require maintenance assistance from IT department.
• User controls the application and can change it as needed.	• Documentation may be inadequate.
• Directly meets user requirements.	• Poor quality control.
• Increased user acceptance of new system.	• System may not have adequate interfaces to existing systems.
• Frees up IT resources.	
• May create lower-quality systems.	
Traditional Systems Development (SDLC)	
• Forces staff to systematically go through every step in a structured process.	• May produce excessive documentation.
• Enforces quality by maintaining standards.	• Users may be unwilling or unable to study the specifications they approve.
• Has lower probability of missing important issues in collecting user requirements.	• Takes too long to go from the original ideas to a working system.
	• Users have trouble describing requirements for a proposed system.
Prototyping	
• Helps clarify user requirements.	• May encourage inadequate problem analysis.
• Helps verify the feasibility of the design.	• Not practical with large number of users.
• Promotes genuine user participation.	• User may not give up the prototype when the system is completed.
• Promotes close working relationship between systems developers and users.	• May generate confusion about whether the system is complete and maintainable.
• Works well for ill-defined problems.	• System may be built quickly, which may result in lower quality.
• May produce part of the final system.	

must decide which criteria are most important to its needs. For a discussion of the criteria in the table, see Online File W14.7.

Using all the previous criteria, an organization can select one or more methods for acquiring systems. Comparison of the various methods is given in Table 14.3. (For description of additional systems development methods, see Technology Guide 6.)

14.5 VENDOR AND SOFTWARE SELECTION AND OTHER IMPLEMENTATION ISSUES

Vendor and Software Selection

Few organizations, especially SMEs, have the time, financial resources, or technical expertise required to develop today's complex IT or e-business systems. This means that many applications are built with hardware, software, hosting services, and development expertise provided by outside vendors. Thus, a major aspect of developing an IT application revolves around the selection and management of these vendors and their software offerings.

Martin et al. (2000) identified six steps in selecting a software vendor and an application package.

STEP 1: IDENTIFY POTENTIAL VENDORS. Potential software application vendors can be identified from software catalogs, lists provided by hardware vendors, technical and trade journals, consultants experienced in the application area, peers in other companies, and Web searches.

These sources often yield so many vendors and packages that one must use some preliminary evaluation criteria to eliminate all but a few of the most promising ones from further consideration. For example, one can eliminate vendors that are too small or that have no track record or have a questionable reputation. Also, packages may be eliminated if they do not have the required features or will not work with available hardware, operating system, communications network, or database management software.

STEP 2: DETERMINE THE EVALUATION CRITERIA. The most difficult and crucial task in evaluating a vendor and a software package is to determine a set of detailed criteria for choosing the best vendor and package. Some areas in which detailed criteria should be developed are: characteristics of the vendor, functional requirements of the system, technical requirements the software must satisfy, amount and quality of documentation provided, and vendor support of the package.

These criteria should be set out in a **request for proposal (RFP)**, a document that is sent to potential vendors inviting them to submit a proposal describing their software package and how it would meet the company's needs. The RFP provides the vendors with information about the objectives and requirements of the system: It describes the environment in which the system will be used, the general criteria that will be used to evaluate the proposals, and the conditions for submitting proposals. The RFP may also request a list of current users of the package who may be contacted, describe in detail the form of response that is desired, and require that the package be demonstrated at the company's facilities using specified inputs and data files.

STEP 3: EVALUATE VENDORS AND PACKAGES. The multivendor responses to an RFP generate massive volumes of information that must be evaluated. The goal of this evaluation is to determine the gaps between the company's needs (as specified by the requirements) and the capabilities of the vendors and their application packages. Often, the vendors and packages are given an overall score by assigning an importance weight to each of the criteria, ranking the vendors on each of the weighted criteria (say 1 to 10), and then multiplying the ranks by the associated weights. A short list of potential suppliers can be chosen from those vendors and packages with the highest overall scores.

STEP 4: CHOOSE THE VENDOR AND PACKAGE. Once a short list has been prepared, negotiations can begin with vendors to determine how their packages might be modified to remove any discrepancies with the company's IT needs. Thus, one of the most important factors in the decision is the additional development effort that may be required to tailor the system to the company's needs or to integrate it into the company's computing environment. Additionally, the opinions of the users who will work with the system and the IT personnel who will have to support the system have to be considered.

Selecting software depends on the nature of the application. Thus, several selection methods exist. For a list of general criteria, see Table 14.4. Details of some of the criteria are provided in Online File W14.8. For an example of selecting enterprise systems, see Sarkis and Sundarraj (2003).

Several third-party organizations evaluate software and make their findings public. For example, see eWeekLabs at *eweek.com.* Many other IT trade journals provide periodic software evaluation. Also, professional associations and interest groups provide evaluations and rankings, as do organizations such as Software Testing Institute (*sti.com*), *metagroup.com, technologyevaluation.com,* and *knowledgestorm.com.*

TABLE 14.4 Criteria for Selecting a Software Application Package
● Usability and reusability
● Cost and financial terms (cost/benefit ratio)
● Upgrade policy and cost
● Vendor's reputation and availability for help
● Vendor's success stories (visit vendor's Web site, contact clients)
● System flexibility and scalability
● Manageability, such as ease of Internet interface, and user acceptance
● Availability and quality of documentation
● Necessary hardware and networking resources
● Required training (check if provided by vendor)
● Security
● Required maintenance cost
● Learning (speed of) for developers and users
● Performance
● Interoperability and data handling
● Ease of integration
● Minimal negative cross-impact (on other applications)

STEP 5: NEGOTIATE A CONTRACT. The contract with the software vendor is very important. It specifies both the price of the software and the type and amount of support to be provided by the vendor. The contract will be the only recourse if the system or the vendor does not perform as expected. Furthermore, if the vendor is modifying the software to tailor it to the company's needs, the contract must include detailed specifications (essentially the requirements) of the modifications. Also, the contract should describe in detail the acceptance tests the software package must pass.

Contracts are legal documents, and they can be quite tricky. Experienced contract negotiators and legal assistance may be needed. Many organizations have software-purchasing specialists who assist in negotiations and write or approve the contract. They should be involved in the selection process from the start. If an RFP is used, these purchasing specialists may be very helpful in determining its form and in providing boilerplate sections of the RFP.

STEP 6: ESTABLISH A SERVICE LEVEL AGREEMENT. **Service level agreements (SLAs)** are formal agreements regarding the division of work between a company and its vendors. Such division is based on a set of agreed-upon milestones, quality checks, and "what-if" situations; they describe how checks will be made and what is to be done in case of disputes. If the vendor is to meet its objectives of installing IT applications, it must develop and deliver support services to meet these objectives. An effective approach to managing vendors must achieve both facilitation and coordination. SLAs do this by (1) defining the partners' responsibilities, (2) providing a framework for designing support services, and (3) allowing the company to retain as much control as possible over their own systems. Such SLAs are similar to what companies use internally, between the ISD and end users (see Chapter 15).

Other Implementation Issues

The following implementation issues are related to IT resource acquisition.

- *In-house or outsource Web site?* Many large enterprises are capable of running their own publicly accessible Web sites for advertising purposes. However, Web sites for online selling may involve complex integration, security, and performance issues. For those companies venturing into such Web-based selling, a key issue is whether the site should be built in-house, thus providing more direct control, or outsourced to a more experienced provider. Outsourcing services, which allow companies to start small and evolve to full-featured functions, are available through many ISPs, telecommunications companies, Internet malls, and software vendors.

- *Consider an ASP.* The use of ASPs is recommended for SMEs and should be considered by many large companies as well. However, care must be used in selecting a vendor due to the newness of the concept.

- *Do a detailed IT architecture study.* Some companies rush this process, and this can be a big mistake. If the high-level conceptual planning is wrong, the entire project is at great risk.

- *Security and ethics.* During the application development process, pay close attention to security. It is likely that vendors and business partners will be involved. Protecting customers' privacy is a must, and the issue of how to use clickstream and other data is essential.

● *Evaluate the alternatives to in-house systems development.* In-house systems development requires highly skilled employees to undertake a complex process. Organizations may sometimes find it preferable to acquire IT resources rather than build in-house. Methods for acquiring IT resources outside the information systems department include purchase, lease, outsourcing, use of ASPs, and end-user development.

14.6 CONNECTING TO DATABASES AND BUSINESS PARTNERS: INTEGRATION (STEP 4)

EC applications must be connected to internal information systems, infrastructure (including databases), ERP, and so on (see Coffee, 2004). They also must be connected to such items as partners' systems or to public exchanges. Such connections are referred to as *integration* and are the subject of this section. (See also Chapters 6 and 7, and Rogers, 2003 and Brobst, 2002 for related discussion.)

Connecting to Databases

Many IT applications need to be connected to a database. For example, when you receive a customer's order, you want to immediately find out if the item is in stock. To do so, you need to connect your ordering system to your inventory system. Several possibilities exist regarding such a connection. The connection technology enables customers with a Web browser to access catalogs in the seller's database, request specific data, and receive an instant response. Here the application server manages the client's requests. The application server also acts as the front end to complex databases.

Connecting to Business Partners

Connecting to business partners is critical to the success of IT, especially for B2B e-commerce. As described in Chapter 8, such connection is done via EDI, EDI/Internet, XML, and extranets.

Connection to business partners is done usually along the supply chain. It typically involves connecting a company's front- and back-office e-commerce applications, as shown in Figure 14.3.

In addition to the networking problem, one must deal with issues of connectivity, compatibility, security, scalability, and more.

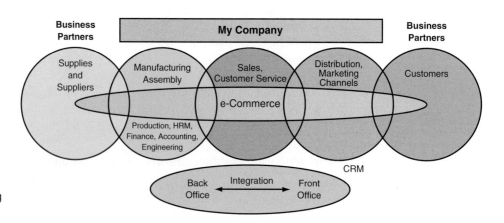

FIGURE 14.3 Connecting to databases.

IT at Work 14.3
LINCOLN FINANCIAL EXCELS BY USING WEB SERVICES

incoln Financial is a $5 billion provider of life insurance, retirement products, and wealth management services. It distributes its offering through financial advisors, banks, and independent brokers. In most of the insurance industry, if consumers want to access their accounts or download a form from a broker site, they click on a link that takes them to the insurance provider's site, where they input a separate password or user ID. To become a "partner of choice" on such sites, Lincoln Financial wanted tighter integration with brokers' Web sites. But Lincoln also wanted to go a step further, providing content and account access within its partners' Web sites, as well as single sign-on for consumers.

This was not simple. Outlining the Lincoln content in an HTML frame would not provide the partner's look and feel. A pure Web Services approach was also out, since most of Lincoln's clients could not support that kind of system, since the partner then had to process the XML/SOAP messages. For a short time, Lincoln maintained subsites for its partners that wanted them, and those sites linked to requested content. However, maintenance of the subsites was burdensome.

The ultimate answer was Service Broker. It took three developers four months to build the pilot of Service Broker, which is a Web Services–based application with a front end that the company calls a *servlet*. When the servlet is installed on a partner's server, it provides a wrapper that can accept Lincoln's content and applications and still maintain the partner's look and feel.

The servlet manages in a Web Services application many of the functions the partner would have to manage, such as authentication, digital signature, passwords, and page rendering. When the partner wants to include Lincoln content or an application, it needs to add just one line of code.

In Spring 2004, Lincoln was the only insurer that did not require customers to leave a partner's Web site to access information. This capability provided Lincoln with competitive advantage.

Source: Compiled from Brandel (2004).

For Further Exploration: What systems were connected between the business partners? Why was it important to maintain the partner's look and feel?

Companies are connected to business partners for many reasons. A common reason is to better work with vendors' designers, as in the case of Boeing described in Online File W14.9. Another example is content visualization from a partner's Web site; see *IT at Work 14.3.* Both internal and external connectivity can be improved by using Web Services. For details, see Technology Guide 6 and Casati (2003).

14.7 BUSINESS PROCESS REDESIGN

Of the organizational responses to environmental pressures (Chapter 1), business process redesign and its variants have received lots of management attention (e.g., see Evangelista and Burke, 2003, and Rajaram and Corbett, 2002). (One variant, and predecessor, of business process redesign is *business process reengineering.*) In this section we will explore the topic of business process redesign. Let's begin by looking at some of its drivers.

The Drivers of Process Redesign

A **business process** is a collection of activities that take one or more kinds of inputs and create an output. Here are some representative drivers behind the need for business process redesign:

● *Fitting commercial software.* To reap the best benefit of buying or leasing software, it is frequently best to use the software as it is rather than to modify it.

(Remember the Nike disaster discussed in Chapter 1.) But what if the software does not fit your business processes, and it is not possible or advisable to change the software? The best solution sometimes is to redesign the affected business processes. Typical software in this category are the functional information systems, ERP, business intelligence, and business performance management software.

- ***Streamlining the supply chain.*** As seen in Chapter 7, it is frequently necessary to change segments in the supply chain to streamline its operations and to better collaborate with business partners. Redesign is frequently done on small segments of the chain, but sometimes the entire chain is redesigned (e.g., the Orbis case of Chapter 1, where a linear chain was changed to a hub).

- ***Participating in private or public e-marketplaces.*** With the increased trend to use e-marketplaces comes the need to get connected to them, as well as to the organization's back-end processes. To enable such integration it is frequently necessary to redesign internal as well as external processes. The same is true with participation in auction sites. Not changing the processes results in manual operations (e.g., data entry) which may be expensive, slow, and error-prone.

- ***Improving customer service.*** To properly introduce CRM, it is often necessary to change business processes. As will be seen later in this chapter, centralizing 800 numbers and empowering frontline employees involve process restructuring.

- ***Conducting e-procurement.*** Introduction of e-procurement methods frequently requires complete redesign of the purchasing process (requisition, approval, control, and payment for purchases).

- ***Enabling direct online marketing.*** Many manufacturers as well as retailers are using direct marketing to consumers, mostly via the Internet. Moving to such a business model requires design or redesign of order taking and order fulfillment.

- ***Reducing cost and improving productivity.*** For generations, companies have sought to reduce costs and increase productivity. An example is industrial engineering methods. Many of these are part of continuous small improvements, while others require radical changes in business processes (e.g., see Barua et al., 2001, and Salladurai, 2002). This is part of the BPM process (Chapter 11).

- ***Restructuring old processes prior to automation.*** Many organizations believe that the solution to their problem is to automate business processes. While in some cases it make sense to do it, in many others it does not. Automating ineffective processes can result in only small savings, whereas restructuring can result in a much larger savings.

- ***Transformation to e-business.*** When organizations transform themselves to e-business, usually by automating processes or collaborating electronically, they frequently need to change their business processes.

Several other drivers may contribute to the need for redesign. In the following sections we will describe some of them: reducing cycle time, need for customization, and empowering employees. Another of these drivers, the *problem of the stovepipe*, is described in Online File W14.10.

Methodologies for Restructuring

As indicated earlier, business process redesign was preceded by **business process reengineering (BPR),** a methodology in which an organization *fundamentally* and *radically* changes its business processes to achieve *dramatic improvement.* Initially, attention in BPR was given to *complete restructuring* of organizations (Hammer and Champy, 2001). Later on, the concept was changed to include only one of a few processes (rather than an entire organization) due to numerous failures of BPR projects (e.g., Sarker and Lee, 1999) and the emergence of Web-based applications that solved many of the problems that BPR was supposed to solve.

Today, the concept of BPR has been modified to *business process redesign,* which can focus on anything from the redesign of an individual process, to redesign of a group of processes (e.g., all the processes involved in e-procurement), to redesign of the entire enterprise (see El Sawy, 2001). The redesign of several processes became a necessity for many companies aspiring to transform themselves to e-businesses. For El Sawy's principles of redesign, see Online File W14.11. We will return to BPR in Section 14.9.

BUSINESS PROCESS MANAGEMENT. **Business process management** is a new method for restructuring that combines workflow systems (Chapter 3) and redesign methods. This emerging methodology covers three process categories—people-to-people, systems-to-systems, and systems-to-people interactions—all from a process-centered perspective. In other words, BPM is a blending of workflow, process management, and applications integration. Le Blond (2003) describes the use of BPM in McDonald's Singapore operations. One area of redesign there was the scheduling of crews at McDonald's restaurants; several other successful applications related to performance improvements. (Staffware Inc., a BPM software vendor and consultant, provides a free online demo as well as case studies at *staffware.com.*) For comprehensive coverage see also Smith and Fingar (2003) and Perry (2004).

The conduct of a comprehensive business process redesign, or even of the redesign of only one process, is almost always enabled by IT, which we address in the next section.

14.8 THE ROLE OF IT IN BUSINESS PROCESS REDESIGN

IT has been used for several decades to improve productivity and quality by automating existing processes. However, when it comes to restructuring or redesign, the traditional process of looking at problems first and then seeking technology solutions for them may need to be reversed. A new approach is first to recognize powerful solutions that make redesign and BPR possible, and then to seek the processes that can be helped by such solutions. This approach requires *inductive* rather than *deductive* thinking. It also requires innovation, since a company may be looking for problems it does not even know exist.

Process redesign can break old rules that limit the manner in which work is performed. Some typical rules are given in Table 14.5 (page 618). IT-supported redesign and BPR examples can be found in any industry, private or public (e.g., MacIntosh, 2003 and Khan, 2000). The role of IT in redesigning business processes can be very critical and is increasing due to the Internet and intranets (Salladurai, 2002).

TABLE 14.5 Changes in Business Processes Brought by IT

Old Rule	Intervening Technology	New Rule
Information appears in only one place at one time.	Shared databases, client/server architecture, Internet, intranets	Information appears simultaneously wherever needed.
Only an expert can perform complex work.	Expert systems, neural computing	Novices can perform complex work.
Business must be either centralized or distributed.	Telecommunications and networks: client/server, intranet	Business can be both centralized and distributed.
Only managers make decisions.	Decision support systems, enterprise support systems, expert systems	Decision making is part of everyone's job.
Field personnel need offices to receive, send, store, and process information.	Wireless communication and portable computers, the Web, electronic mail	Field personnel can manage information from any location.
The best contact with potential buyers is a personal contact.	Interactive videodisk, desktop teleconferencing, electronic mail	The best contact is the one that is most cost-effective.
You have to locate items manually.	Tracking technology, groupware, workflow software, search engines	Items are located automatically.
Plans get revised periodically.	High-performance computing systems, intelligent agents	Plans get revised instantaneously whenever needed.
People must come to one place to work together.	Groupware and group support systems, telecommunications, electronic mail, client/server	People can work together while at different locations.
Customized products and services are expensive and take a long time to develop.	CAD/CAM, CASE tools, online systems for JIT decision making, expert systems	Customized products can be made quickly and inexpensively (mass customization).
A long period of time is spanned between the inception of an idea and its implementation (time-to-market).	CAD/CAM, electronic data interchange, groupware, imaging (document) processing	Time-to-market can be reduced by 90 percent.
Organizations and processes are information-based.	Artificial intelligence, expert systems	Organizations and processes are knowledge-based.
Move labor to countries where labor is inexpensive (off-shore production).	Robots, imaging technologies, object-oriented programming, expert systems, geographical information systems (GIS)	Work can be done in countries with high wages and salaries.

Source: Compiled from M. Hammer and J. Champy, *Re-engineering the Corporation* (New York: Harper Business, 2001).

Need for Information Integration

One objective of redesign is to overcome problems (such as that of the stovepipe) by *integrating* the fragmented information systems. Besides creating inefficient redundancies, information systems developed along departmental or functional boundaries cause difficulties in generating the information that is required for effective decision making. For instance, consider a case where the management of a bank wants to offer more mortgage loans to better utilize large savings deposits. Management decides to send letters encouraging specific customers to consider buying homes, using convenient financing available through the bank. Management also decides that the best customers to whom to send such letters are: customers who do not currently have mortgage loans or who have loans for a very small percentage of the value of their homes; customers who have good checking account records (e.g., few or no overdrafts); customers with sufficient funds in their savings accounts to make

IT at Work 14.4
VW OF MEXICO SHIFTED TO E-PROCUREMENT

Facing strong competition and the North American Free Trade Agreement (NAFTA) environment, Volkswagen of Mexico (*vw.com.mx*) turned to IT. In 1996, VW implemented an ERP system, using SAP R/3 software. By 1998, the company integrated its enterprise system, which was used to cut inventory and production costs, with an extranet, which streamlined spare-parts ordering by its dealers in Mexico. The major reason for the project was the increased demand that resulted from NAFTA and from VW's decision to market the Beetle (called the "New Beetle") in the United States and Canada. These cars are manufactured in Mexico, where labor and services are cheaper.

The integrated system allows people at every level of the company, from manufacturing to car servicing at the dealership, to take advantage of the SAP system. The SAP system integrates the manufacturing, finance, marketing, and other departments among themselves and, thanks to the extranet, now also links these departments with the dealers and business partners. In order to implement SAP, VW had to redesign many of its production, accounting, and sales processes. This was done using some of the methods we describe later in this chapter.

The R/3 system orchestrates all the different areas of the manufacturing and parts-ordering tasks, such as supplier orders, receiving, warehousing, client orders, packing, and billing. By tapping into R/3 modules, the dealers can cut the turnaround time for ordering spare parts from 10 days to fewer than 5—a very important competitive advantage. The dealers can check the status of their orders on the computer.

One problem with the integrated system is that some of the dealers in Mexico were not ready to buy, install, and use computers. However, the fact that the new system means a low inventory level, which can save the dealers considerable money, motivated them to join in. The company estimated that the application resulted in $50 million in cost savings for the dealers over the first three years.

Sources: Compiled from *PC Week* (1998), and from press releases of *vw.com.mx* (1999–2002).

For Further Exploration: Can VW's suppliers be added to the system? What competitive advantage could be realized with such an addition?

---

a down payment on a home; and customers with good payment records on installment loans with the bank.

Because the data necessary to identify such customers may be available in different files of different information systems, there may be no convenient or economical way to integrate them. Using innovations such as *data warehouses* and special integrated software can be helpful, but expensive. Therefore, extensive programming and clerical work are required to satisfy such an information request. The scenario of the bank can be translated into other organizational settings.

Integration should cross not only departmental boundaries but also organizational ones, reaching suppliers and customers. Namely, it should work along the *extended supply chain*. This is especially important in company-centric B2B e-marketplaces and in B2B exchanges. An example of an internal integration followed by integration with dealers is provided in *IT at Work 14.4*.

The integration of an organization's information systems enables redesign innovations such as the introduction of a single point of contact for customers, called a *case manager* or a *deal structurer*. We can see how this single point of contact works by looking at a credit-approval process at IBM. The old process took seven days and eight steps. It involved creation of a paper folder that was routed, sequentially, through four departments (sales, credit check, business practices, finance, and back to sales). In the redesigned process, one person, the deal structurer, conducts all the necessary tasks. This one generalist replaces four specialists. To enable one person to execute the above steps, an expert system provides the deal structurer with the guidance needed. The program guides the generalist in finding information in the databases, plugging numbers into an evaluation model, and pulling standardized clauses—"boilerplates"—from a file. For difficult situations, the generalist can get help from a specialist. As a result, the turnaround time has been slashed from seven days to four hours.

IT Software for Business Process Redesign

CHANGING EXISTING INFORMATION SYSTEMS. Redesign of business processes often means a need to change some or all of the organizational information systems. The reason for this is that information systems designed along hierarchical lines may be ineffective in supporting the redesigned organization. Therefore, it is often necessary to redesign the information systems. This process is referred to as *retooling*. See Online File W14.12.

IT TOOLS FOR BUSINESS PROCESS REDESIGN AND BPR. A large variety of IT tools can be used to support redesign and BPR. Some of these tools are generic and can be used for other purposes, while others are specifically designed for redesign and BPR. Let's elaborate.

Special BPR and Process Redesign Software. According to El Sawy (2001), special BPR software enables the capture of the key elements of a business process in a visual representation made up of interconnected objects on a time line. The elements of this visual representation usually include activities, sequencing, resources, times, and rules. BPR software is much more than drawing or flowcharting software in that the objects on the screen are intelligent and have process and organizational data and rules associated with them. The software is also interactive, in real time. BPR software may incorporate some aspects of project management in terms of allocating resources and costs to work activities and their time sequencing. BPR software also has "what-if" capabilities in that it enables process simulation and performance comparison of alternative process designs. The better BPR software packages are quite intuitive and relatively easy to learn. The 10 major reasons why special BPR software is of value for business process redesign are summarized in Online File W14.13.

The most comprehensive special BPR suite, which includes many functionalities, was BPR Workflow from Holosofx (now a part of IBM's WebSphere). For a detailed description of this package and usable software, see El Sawy (2001). In addition to BPR Workflow one can find integrated BPR tool kits in some ERP software (e.g., see Oracle 9i and SAP R/3).

Some people believe that BPR can be done with CASE tools (Technology Guide 6). This is not the case, since CASE tools can be used to execute only a few BPR activities, and they are difficult to use. Other believe that workflow tools can be used. Again, this is true only for some redesign activities. Furthermore, the workflow capabilities in custom-designed BPR software are usually superior to those of generic tools. However, for many projects there is no need for a comprehensive suite; in those situations, generic tools or special tools designed to be used for only one or two BPR activities are both efficient and effective. For a listing of some generic and single-activity tools that may be of use in business process redesign, see Online File W14.14.

14.9 RESTRUCTURING PROCESSES AND ORGANIZATIONS

Redesign, restructuring, and reengineering efforts involve many activities, three of which are described in this section: redesign of one or a few processes, cycle time reduction, and restructuring the entire organization. In this section we also look at some BPR failures.

Redesign of One or a Few Processes

Redesign efforts frequently involve only one or a few processes. One of the most publicized examples of process redesign is the accounts payable process at Ford Motor Company, described in Online File W14.15. The Ford example demonstrates changes in a simple process. Khan (2000) describes the restructure of an air cargo process that was much more complicated and involved several IT tools.

Cycle Time Reduction

Cycle time refers to the time it takes to complete a process from beginning to end. As discussed earlier, competition today focuses not only on cost and quality, but also on speed. Time is recognized as a major element that provides competitive advantage, and therefore **cycle time reduction** is a major business objective. For a discussion of how this is done with IT, see Online File W14.16.

Restructuring the Whole Organization

One recurrent problem in many organizations is communication breakdowns in vertical structures. How should a contemporary organization be organized? There are several alternatives. Let's look at how it can be done with business process redesign.

The fundamental problem with the hierarchical organizational structure is that any time a decision needs to be made, it must climb up and down the hierarchy. If one person says "no" to a pending decision, everything comes to a screeching halt. Also, if information is required from several "functional sources," getting all the right information coordinated can be a time-consuming and frustrating process for employees and customers alike.

So, how is organizational redesign done? It varies, depending on the organization and the circumstances. For example, providing each customer with a single point of contact can solve the stovepipe problem (Online File W14.10). In the traditional bank, for example, each department views the same customer as a separate customer. Figure 14.4 (page 622) depicts a redesigned bank in which the customer deals with a single point of contact, the account manager. The account manager is responsible for all bank services and provides all services to the customer, who receives a single statement for all of his or her accounts and can access all accounts on the same Web page ("My Accounts"). Notice that the role of IT is to back up the account manager by providing her with expert advice on specialized topics, such as loans. Also, by having easy access to the different databases, the account manager can answer queries, plan, and organize the work with customers.

An alternative to the single-point contact is a networked structure. In this structure, regardless of where and when a client contacts the company, the networked agents would have access to all customer data, so that *any* employee can provide excellent customer service. Companies such as USAA, Otis Elevator, and others have all agents located in one city and give customers around the country the same toll-free number and a centralized Web address. In this model, the company also can install a computer-based call-center technology,

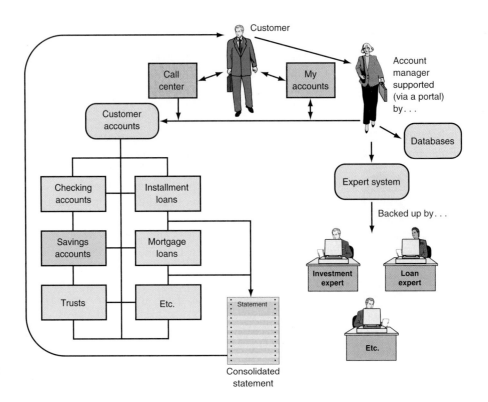

FIGURE 14.4
Reengineered bank with integrated system.

which brings up complete customer information (or information about a customer's elevator in the case of Otis) on the computer screen, whenever a customer calls. This means that anyone who answers the call would know all the information necessary to make a quick, frontline decision (see Chapter 11). There is no need to ask questions of the customer, and any agent can give personalized and customized service. This is especially important in services such as reservation systems for hotels or airlines, as well as for utility companies, financial services, universities, and health care services.

Reengineering and restructuring is not limited to a specific type of organization. Studies indicate that 70 percent of all large U.S. corporations are restructuring or considering some major redesign projects. In addition, the public sector, including the U.S. federal government, is continuously implementing restructuring projects. See Online File W14.17, which describes one such project by the U.S. federal government.

BPR Failures and Successes

During the 1990s, there were many success stories of BPR (Grant, 2002, El Sawy, 2001) and just as many cases of failures.

FAILURES. The PROSCI organization conducted a survey of several hundred companies to learn the best BPR practices and the reasons for BPR failures, which can be found at the organization's Web site (*prosci.com*). Another summary of research into business process redesign failure is available at *managingchange. com/bpr/bprcult/4bprcult.htm.* The summary indicates a failure rate of 50 to 80 percent. According to Grant (2002), at least 70 percent of all BPR projects fail. Some of the reasons cited for failure are high risk, inappropriate change management, failure to plan, internal politics, high cost of IT retooling, lack of participation and leadership, insufficient stakeholder involvement, poor analyses of business processes, inflexible software, lack of motivation, and lack of top management support. Highly detailed case studies on BPR failures are provided by Sarker and Lee (1999) and by Hengst and Vreede (2004). For more on BPR failures and suggestions on how to avoid them, see El Sawy (2001).

BPR SUCCESSES. Despite the high failure rate of business process redesign, there are many cases of success, especially when less than the entire organization is restructured. While BPR failures tend to get more widespread publicity, success stories are published mostly by vendors and in academic and trade journals. For example, there is evidence of the success of BPR in the public sector (MacIntosh, 2003). Khong and Richardson (2003) report on extensive BPR activities and successes in banking and finance companies in Malaysia; Mohanty and Deshmukh (2001) found successful BPR initiatives in a large cement manufacturing plant in India. (For details, see Online File W14.18.)

Organizations should consider restructuring their business processes or sometimes the entire business. When successful, redesign has great potential to improve an organization's competitive position.

MANAGERIAL ISSUES

1. *Importance.* Some general and functional managers believe that system development is a technical topic that should be of interest only to technical people. This is certainly not the case. Appropriate construction of systems is necessary for their success. Functional managers must participate in the development process and should understand all the phases. They must also participate in the make-or-buy decisions and software selection decisions. Inappropriate development methodologies can result in the system's failure.

2. *Ethical and legal issues.* Developing systems across organizations and countries could result in problems in any phase of system development. For example, in developing the Nagano Olympics system in 1998, IBM found at the last minute that pro-North-Korea groups in Japan took offense at a reference to the Korean War written on the Web site. Although the material was taken from the *World Book Encyclopedia,* it offended some people. IBM had to delete the reference and provide an apology. IBM commented, "Next time we're going to do a ton of research first versus just do it and find out the hard way." A special difficulty exists with Internet-related projects, where legislation is still evolving.

3. *User involvement.* The direct and indirect users of a system are likely to be the most knowledgeable individuals concerning requirements and which alternatives will be the most effective. Users are also the most affected by a new information system. IS analysts and designers, on the other hand, are likely to be the most knowledgeable individuals concerning technical and data-management issues as well as the most experienced in arriving at viable systems solutions. The right mixture of user involvement and information systems expertise is crucial.

4. *Tool use by developers.* Development tools and techniques can ensure that developers consider all necessary factors and standardize development, documentation, and testing. Forcing their use, on the other hand, may unnecessarily constrain innovation, development efficiency, and personnel productivity.

5. *Quality assurance vs. schedules.* Quality counts in the short term and the long term, but it can lengthen development and increase developmental costs. Trying to meet tight development schedules can induce poor quality with even worse schedule, cost, and morale problems. Control is done with ISO 9000 standards (see Online File W14.19).

6. *Behavior problems.* People use information systems and often become quite used to how existing systems work. They may react to new systems in unexpected ways, making even the best technically designed systems useless. Changes brought about by information systems need to be managed effectively. Of special interest is the issue of motivating programmers to increase their productivity by learning new tools and reusing preprogrammed modules.

7. *Perpetual development.* Information systems are designed to meet organizational needs. When they don't accurately meet these needs, or these needs change, information systems need to be redeveloped. Developing a system can be a major expense, but perpetually developing a system to maintain its usefulness is usually much more expensive.

8. *Risk level.* Building information systems involves risk. Systems may not be completed, completed too late, or require more resources than planned. The risk is large in enterprise systems. For how to manage such risk, see Scott and Vessey (2002) and Levine (2004).

9. *Business process redesign.* Business process redesign can be driven by the need to prepare for IT or by many other reasons. It can be done by methodologies ranging from BPR to BPM.

10. *Structural changes.* IT helps not only to automate existing processes but also to introduce innovations that change structure (e.g., create case managers and interdisciplinary teams), reduce the number of processes, combine tasks, enable economic customization, and reduce cycle time.

11. *Ethical and legal issues.* Conducting interviews for finding managers' needs and requirements must be done with full cooperation. Measures to protect privacy must be taken.

In designing systems one should consider the people in the system. Reengineering IT means that some employees will have to completely reengineer themselves. Some may feel too old to do so. Conducting a supply chain or business process reorganization may result in the need to lay off, retrain, or transfer employees. Should management notify the employees in advance regarding such possibilities? And what about those older employees who may be difficult to retrain?

Other ethical issues may involve sharing of computing resources or of personal information, which may be part of the new organizational culture. Finally, individuals may have to share computer programs that they designed for their departmental use, and may resist doing so because they consider such programs their intellectual property. Appropriate planning must take these and other issues into consideration.

12. *Integration: The role of IT in redesign and BPR.* Almost all major supply chain management (SCM) and/or BPR projects use IT. However, it is important to remember that in most cases the technology plays a *supportive* role. The primary role is organizational and managerial in nature. On the other hand, without IT, most SCM and BPR efforts do not succeed.

KEY TERMS

Application service provider
(ASP) *608*

Business process *615*

Business process management
(BPM) *617*

Business process reengineering
(BPR) *617*

Cycle time reduction *621*

Request for proposal (RFP) *611*

Service level agreements (SLAs) *613*

CHAPTER HIGHLIGHTS (Numbers Refer to Learning Objectives)

1 Information systems acquisition includes all approaches to obtaining systems: buying, leasing, or building. The objective of IT application acquisition is to create (or buy) applications and implement them.

1 The process of acquiring IT applications can be divided into five steps: planning and justification; IT architecture creation; selecting development options; testing, installing, and integrating new applications; and conducting operations and maintenance. This process needs to be managed.

2 There are several sources of identifying new projects (applications) such as the need to solve a business problem. The justification process is basically a comparison of the expected costs versus the benefits of each application. While measuring cost may not be complex, measuring benefits is, due to the many intangible benefits involved. The planning of projects involves schedules, milestones, and resource allocation.

3 The major options for acquiring applications are buy, lease, and build (develop in-house). Other options are joint ventures and use of e-marketplaces or exchanges (private or public).

3 Building in-house can be done by using the SDLC, by using prototyping or other methodologies, and it can be done by outsourcers, the IS department employees, or end users (individually or together).

4 In deciding how to acquire applications, companies must consider several, sometimes many, criteria. These criteria may conflict among themselves (e.g., quality and price). Companies need to make sure that all criteria are considered and to evaluate the importance of each criterion for the company.

5 ASPs lease software applications, usually via the Internet. Fees for the leased applications can be the same each month or can be based on actual usage (like electricity). (This is the basic idea of utility computing which will be provided by ASPs or by software vendors.)

6 The process of vendor and software selection is composed of six steps: identify potential vendors, determine evaluation criteria, evaluate vendors and packages, choose the vendor and package, negotiate a contract, and establish service level agreements.

7 Most of the implementation issues are related to decisions regarding selection of development options and vendor and software selection. Also, security and ethics need to be considered.

8 New applications need to be connected to existing applications, databases, and so on inside the organization. They may also be connected to partners' information systems.

8 Issues of connectivity, compatibility, and security make connections difficult. Several tools and methods exist to alleviate the problem.

9 Introducing new technology may require restructure or redesign of processes. Also, processes may need to be redesigned to fit standard software.

9 Several methodologies exist for redesigning processes, notably BPR, BPM, and work flow.

10 IT can help in analyzing, combining, improving, and simplifying business processes.

10 Redesign may be a large and complex effort resulting in failure if not planned and managed properly.

10 One or a few business processes are easier to redesign than redesigning processes on a larger scale. Limiting the scale of redesign projects helps ensure successful implementation of IT applications.

VIRTUAL COMPANY ASSIGNMENT

Acquiring Information Systems for The Wireless Café
Go to The Wireless Café's link on the Student Web Site. There you will be asked to plan and recommend how to proceed in upgrading and adding information systems for the restaurant.

More Resources
More resources and study tools are located on the Student Web Site. You'll find additional chapter materials and useful Web links. In addition, self-quizzes that provide individualized feedback are available for each chapter.

Instructions for accessing The Wireless Café on the Student Web Site

1. Go to
   wiley.com/college/turban
2. Select Turban/Leidner/ McLean/Wetherbe's *Information Technology for Management,* Fifth Edition.
3. Click on Student Resources site, in the toolbar on the left.
4. Click on the link for Virtual Company Web site
5. Click on Wireless Café.

QUESTIONS FOR REVIEW

1. List and briefly discuss the five steps of the information systems acquisition process.
2. List the options of system acquisition.
3. Describe some implementation and management issues.
4. What is involved in identifying IT projects? How is such identification done?
5. What is the basic idea of justifying an application?
6. Describe IT project planning.
7. List the major acquisition and development strategies.
8. Compare the buy option against the lease option.
9. List the in-house development approaches.
10. Describe end-user development and cite its advantages and limitations.
11. List other acquisition options.
12. What type of companies provide outsourcing service?
13. Define ASPs and list their advantages to companies using them.
14. List some disadvantages of ASPs.
15. List five criteria for assessing a buy option.

16. List five criteria for selecting a development option.
17. List the major steps of selection of a vendor and a software package.
18. Describe a request for proposal (RFP).
19. Describe SLAs.
20. List three major implementation issues.
21. List some internal systems that usually need to be connected to new applications.
22. Why is it especially important to connect to databases?
23. What is mainly connected between business partners?
24. Define business process and BPR.
25. List the drivers of process redesign.
26. Describe the stovepipe problem. (See the related on-line file.)
27. Define BPM.
28. Describe the enabling role of IT in BPR.
29. Define cycle time and discuss its reduction.
30. Why do so many BPR projects fail?

QUESTIONS FOR DISCUSSION

1. Discuss the advantages of a lease option over a buy option.

2. Why is it important for all business managers to understand the issues of IT resource acquisition?

3. List some of the new options for acquiring IT resources. (See Table 14.1, page 602.)

4. Discuss the role of ASPs. Why is their attractiveness increasing? (Hint: Consider utility computing.)

5. Review the opening case. What approach was used to develop an information systems plan?

6. Explain why IT is an important enabler of business process redesign.

7. Some people say that BPR is a special case of a strategic information system, whereas others say that the opposite is true. Comment.

8. What are some of the reasons for maintaining a functional structure in an organization?

9. Discuss the relationship between IT planning (Chapter 12) and project (application) planning.

10. Discuss the relationship between system acquisition and business process restructuring.

11. Discuss why BPM is useful for restructuring.

12. Discuss why IT is an enabler of redesign and restructuring while it also requires retooling for its implementation.

EXERCISES

1. Enter *ecommerce.internet.com*. Find the product review area. Read reviews of three software payment solutions. Assess them as possible components.

2. Prepare a comparison of the following utility computing initiatives: IBM's On-Demand, H-P's Adaptive Enterprise, and Fujitsu's Triole Utility. What is the focus of each? What are their strategies?

3. Examine some business processes in your university or company. Identify two processes that need to be redesigned. Employ some of El Sawy's 10 principles (see Online File W14.11) to plan the redesign. Be innovative.

GROUP ASSIGNMENTS

1. Assessment of the functionality of an application is a part of the planning process (Step 1). Select three to five Web sites catering to the same type of buyer (for instance, several sites that offer CDs or computer hardware), and divide the sites among the teams. Each team will assess the functionality of its assigned Web site by preparing an analysis of the different sorts of functions provided by the site. In addition, the team should assess the strong and weak points of its site from the buyer's perspective.

2. Divide into groups, with each group visiting a local company (include your university). At each firm, study the systems acquisition process. Find out the methodology or methodologies used by each organization and the types of application to which each methodology applies. Prepare a report and present it to the class.

3. As a group, design an information system for a startup business of your choice. Describe your chosen IT resource acquisition strategy, and justify your choices of hardware, software, telecommunications support, and other aspects of a proposed system.

4. Have teams from the class visit IT project-development efforts at local companies. Team members should interview members of the project team to ascertain the following information.

   a. How does the project contribute to the goals and objectives of the company?

   b. Is there an information architecture in place? If so, how does this project fit into that architecture?

   c. How was the project justified?

   d. What project planning approach, if any, was used?

   e. How is the project being managed?

INTERNET EXERCISES

1. Enter *ibm.com/software*. Find the WebSphere product. Read recent customers' success stories. What makes this software so popular?

2. Enter the Web sites of the Gartner Group (*gartnergroup.com*), the Yankee Group (*yankeegroup.com*), and CIO (*cio.com*). Search for recent material about ASPs and outsourcing, and prepare a report on your findings.

3. Enter the Web site of IDC (*idc.com*) and find out how the company evaluates ROI on portals, supply chain, and other IT projects.

4. Visit the Web site of Resource Management Systems (*rms.net*) and take the IT investment Management Approach Assessment Self-Test (*rms.net/self_test.htm*). Compare your organization's IT decision-making process with those of best-practices organizations.

5. StoreFront (*storefront.net*) is the leading vendor of e-business software. At its site, the company provides demonstrations illustrating the types of storefronts that it can create for shoppers. The site also provides demonstrations of how the company's software is used to create a store.

   a. Run either the StoreFront 5.0 or StoreFront 6.0 demonstration to see how this is done.

   b. What sorts of features does StoreFront 5.0 provide?

   c. Does StoreFront 5.0 support larger or smaller stores?

   d. What other products does StoreFront offer for creating online stores? What types of stores do these products support?

6. Surf the Internet to find some recent material on the role IT plays in support BPR. Search for products and vendors and download an available demo.

7. Identify some newsgroups that are interested in BPM. Initiate a discussion on the role of IT in BPM.

8. Enter *gensym.com* and find their modeling products. Explain how they support BPR and redesign.

9. Enter *xelus.com/index.asp* and find how Xelus Corporation software can facilitate planning (e.g., see the Cisco case).

Minicase 1
Enterprise Web at Pioneer Inc.

Pioneer is a large, global oil and gas company that needed IT tools to streamline business processes, automate workflows, and improve communication internally and with business partners. The company also needed IT infrastructure that would be the foundation for building enterprise Web applications. The employees needed a system that would enable them to collaborate and that would give them an up-to-date view of the company's finance and production activities. The company selected a comprehensive software suite, Enterprise Web (from Plumtree.com). The suite includes a corporate portal, a content server, and a collaboration server. The suite fulfilled the above requirements, and it also helped to better manage the oil exploration and extraction processes. All of these capabilites resulted in higher productivity and profit.

The portal is bringing fundamental changes to the way Pioneer works, from empowering employees in remote locations to collaborate on data analysis, to giving executives and key employees the ability to monitor oil and gas field production volumes in near real time. The new system simplifies access to information, freeing Pioneer employees from the complexity of underlying systems.

Using Open Architecture

To integrate information and functionality from systems running on different application servers and coded in different languages, Pioneer needed the openness provided by Plumtree's Web Services Architecture. In addition, the Enterprise Web technologies offer an integrated solution of portal and collaboration technologies, giving users a unified, interactive environment and project sponsors a low total cost of ownership.

Enterprise Web applications are hosted on different application servers but managed within one framework. They differ from traditional applications in three ways: First, Enterprise Web applications combine existing data and processes from diverse enterprise systems with new shared services, providing greater return on assets. Second, Enterprise Web applications are assembled dynamically, incorporating new capabilities on-the-fly, allowing for greater agility in solving business problems. Finally, Enterprise Web applications are designed to be integrated into an enterprisewide environment, providing greater economies of scale; users can easily navigate between or search across applications, and Web Services developed for one enterprise Web application can be reused as-is in other applications. Special functionalities of Enterprise Web applications are the ability to unlock data hidden in complex systems, provide real-time production monitoring via dashboards, capture knowledge in collaborative communities, and provide balanced-scorecard applications.

Pioneer selected Plumtree for the functionalities listed above, as well as because of its published success with other companies in the oil and gas industry. Pioneer leases the software from Plumtree, paying a monthly fee based on the number of users.

Source: Compiled from a press release from Plumtree Software Inc. (*plumtree.com*), October 14, 2003.

Questions for Minicase 1

1. What acquisition option was selected? Why?
2. Why was Plumtree selected?
3. Relate the case to the issue of integration.
4. Why did the company need the collaboration server?
5. What is the role of Web Services?
6. Which problems were solved by the use of the software?

Minicase 2
McDonald's Global Network Comes Up Short

The Problem

McDonald's (*mcdonalds.com*), a $15.4 billion company, has more than 30,000 restaurants in 121 countries serving more than 46 million customers a day. However, the company had a number of operational problems.

First and foremost, McDonald's scores from the American Customer Satisfaction Index (ASCI) were lower than those of Wendy's, Burger King, Pizza Hut, and Kentucky Fried Chicken, its major competitors. Customer complaints centered on slow service and an "old, tired" menu. McDonald's wanted to speed up service and develop a menu offering more "healthy" options. Second, data that were batch-processed on the McDonald's proprietary mainframe system at headquarters every night did not offer the details that executives needed, and it took as long as a week for data to be analyzed and distributed to managers. Although McDonald's collects daily sales data, the company's decade-old financial reporting systems were not built with *real-time business* intelligence in mind. Third, unskilled workers and employee turnover mandate training new employees quickly and making the assembly-line method of food preparation extremely easy to understand.

The Proposed IT Solution

McDonald's planned to spend $1 billion over five years to tie all its operations into an Internet-based, global, real-time digital network called Innovate. This system would be the most expensive and extensive information technology project in the company's history. Headquarters wanted to create a means of controlling the key quality that makes a fast-food chain successful: consistency. In addition, executives needed to know, as soon as possible, what was going on in its stores.

"Innovate" was designed to be a Web-based network of computers and monitors connected to every key piece of information in every store. Information delivered instantly would give executives the ability to monitor, and possibly to affect in real time, the company's ability to get a consistent product to customers as fast as possible. McDonald's hoped that the new system would let company executives see at any time of day how sales of any product at any store were proceeding, see where backup supplies sat anywhere between its stores and its suppliers' plants, and manage its stores accordingly.

The hub of Innovate was to be an Oracle ERP system, which would replace the company's homegrown IBM mainframe general ledger accounting system and the company's finance, supply chain management, and human resources systems. The network would link all of the company's restaurants and all of its more than 300 major vendors, 24 hours a day, seven days a week, to the back-office system at its headquarters. Also, the system would simplify the scheduling of crew members because it would tell managers, for example, exactly how many customers order Big Macs or Quarter Pounders between noon and 2:00 P.M. every day of the week. It would also streamline the delivery of employee training and benefits data over the Web.

McDonald's also hoped to use Innovate to make life easier for its franchisees. For example, the system would automatically generate historical temperature logs for food-safety reports required by the Food and Drug Administration. It could also alert owner-operators in the event of an unusually large voided transaction at the drive-through window point-of-sale system (suggesting that a crew member might be pocketing money instead of putting it in the register).

The Results

After just two years, though, McDonald's wrote off its $170 million investment in the system when the company discontinued Innovate even before its development had been completed. Because it had never been on the cutting edge of technology, the company had a lack of experience in this area. Though the company had shown little or no expertise in large-scale information systems implementations when Innovate was initiated, its executives thought they could easily and completely revamp their entire core technology infrastructure. Further, its executives did not understand technology and made it a low priority for the company. McDonald's had fallen victim to some of the classic pitfalls that face corporations trying to justify and implement information systems projects of this size for the first time.

Source: Compiled from Barrett and Gallagher (2003).

Questions for Minicase 2

1. What are the major IOS and global information systems that the company needed?
2. What information requirements were needed by the company?
3. What were the major problems that led to the failure of Innovate?
4. Relate the case to Figure 14.1 (page 598). In which of the steps did the company fail?
5. If McDonald's were choosing from among today's technologies, it probably would have selected Oracle Information Architecture (Chapter 2) instead of Oracle ERP. Examine the new architecture. Speculate on what contribution it could have provided to McDonald's.

REFERENCES

Barrett, L., and S. Gallagher, "McBusted," *Baseline* (July 2, 2003).

Barua, A., et al., "Driving E-Business Excellence," *MIT Sloan Management Review*, 43(1), 2001.

Benaroch, M., "Managing Information Technology Investment Risk: A Real Options Perspective," *Journal of MIS*, 19(2), Fall 2002.

Brandel, M., "Lincoln Financial Syndicates Content with Web Services," *Computerworld*, March 15, 2004.

Briggs, R. O., "Information Systems Design—Theory and Methodology," Special issue, *JMIS*, Spring 2004.

Broadbent, M., and P. Weill, "Management by Maxim: How Business and IT Managers Can Create IT Infrastructures," *Sloan Management Review*, Spring 1997.

Brobst, S., "Enterprise Application Integration and Active Data," *TDWI Flashpoint* (Newsletter), *dw-institute.com*, September 11, 2002.

Carroll, C. T., "Structured Project Requests for Control, Analysis and Training," *Information Strategy—The Executive Journal*, Summer 2004.

Casati, F., et al., "Business-Oriented Management of Web Services," *Communications of the ACM*, October 2003.

CIO.com, *cio.com/archive(040103)strategy.html* (accessed July 2003).

CIO Magazine, November 2000.

Coffee, P., "Data Integration Is IT's Frontier," *eWeek*, February 23, 2004.

Craig, G., "Old Dental Manufacturer Adopts New IT Tricks," *Outsourcing Magazine*, November–December 2003.

Database, "5-Minute Briefing: Data Integration," *Database: Trends and Application, dbta.com/5_minute_briefing/3–10–03.html* (accessed December 2003).

Devaraj, S., and R. Kohli, *The IT Payoff: Measuring Business Value of Information Technology Investments*. Upper Saddle River, NJ: Financial Times Prentice Hall, 2002.

El Sawy, O., *The BPR Workbook*. New York: McGraw-Hill, 1999.

El Sawy, O., *Redesigning Enterprise Processes for E-Business*. New York: McGraw-Hill, 2001.

Evangelista, A. S., and L. A. Burke, "Work Redesign and Performance Management in Times of Downsizing," *Business Horizons*, 46(2), 2003.

Gerlach, R., et al., "Determining the Cost of IT Services," *Communications of the ACM*, 45(9), September 2002.

Grant, D., "A Wilder View of Business Process Reengineering," *Association for Computing Machinery*, 45(2) 2002.

Gunasekaran, A., et al., "A Model for Investment Justification in Information Technology Products," *International Journal of Information Management*, March 2001.

Hammer, M., and J. Champy, *Re-engineering the Corporation*. New York: Harper Business, 2001.

Hengst, M. D., and G. D. Vreede, "Collaborative Business Engineering: A Decade of Lessons from the Field," *Journal of Management Information Systems*, 2004.

Here, T., "Utility Computing," *Analyst Views*, February 2003. *-analystviews.com/data/web/av/JSP/AnalystContent?SummitStrategies_20030207.jsp*.

Kanter, J., and J. J. Walsh, "Toward More Successful Project Management," *Information Strategy—The Executive Journal*, Summer 2004.

Kaplan, R. S., and D. P. Norton, *The Balanced Scorecard: Translating Strategy into Action*. Boston: Harvard Business School Press, 1996. Enhanced edition (e-book), 2001.

Kendall, K. E., and J. E. Kendall, *Systems Analysis and Design*, 6th ed. Upper Saddle River, NJ: Prentice Hall, 2005.

Kern, T., and T. Kreijger, "An Exploration of Application Service Provision Outsourcing Option," *Proceedings of 34th HICSS*, Maui, January 2001.

Khan, M. R. R., "BPR of an Air Cargo Handling Process," *International Journal of Production Economics*, January 2000.

Khong, K. W., and S. Richardson, "BPR in Malaysian Banks and Finance Companies," *Managing Service Quality*, January 2003.

Kishore, R., et al., "A Relationship Perspective on IT Outsourcing," *Communications of the ACM*, December 2003.

LeBlond, R., "BPM: Look Under the Hood," CIO Asia, March 2003, *cio-asia.com*.

Levine, R., "Risk Management Systems: Understanding the Needs," *Information Strategy—The Executive Journal*, Summer 2004.

MacIntosh, R., "BPR: Alive and Well in the Public Sector," *International Journal of Operations and Production Management*, 23(3/4), 2003.

Martin, E. W., et al., *Managing Information Technology.* Upper Saddle River, NJ: Prentice Hall, 2000.

Mohanty, R. P., and S. G. Deshmukh, "Reengineering of Materials Management System: A Case Study," *International Journal of Production Economics*, 70(3), 2001.

Overby, S., "Bringing I.T. Back Home," *CIO Magazine*, March 1, 2003, *cio.com/archive/030103/home.html* (accessed January 2004).

PC Week, 1998.

Perry, R., "The Future of BPM," *ebizQ* (*ebizQ.net*), April 19, 2004.

Plumtree Software Inc., *plumtree.com*, October 14, 2003.

Rajaram, K., and C. J. Corbett, "Achieving Environmental and Productivity Improvements Through Model-based Process Redesign," *Operations Research*, 50(5), 2002.

Ravichandran, T., "Component-Based Software Development," Special issue. *Data Base, Fblazesoft.com*, February 2003.

Regan, E. A., and B. N. O'Connor, *End User-Information Systems*, 2nd ed. Upper Saddle River, NJ: Prentice Hall, 2002.

Rogers, S., *InterSystems Ensemble: Integration for Today's Rapidly Changing Enterprise*, special report. Framingham, MA: IDC, 2003.

Sachdeva S., "Outsourcing Strategy Helps Ansett Australia Streamline Its Business," *IBM Success Story*, 2000, *ibm.com/services/successes/ansett.html* (accessed January 2004).

Salladurai, R., "An Organizational Profitability, Productivity, Performance (PPP) Model: Going Beyond TQM and BPR," *Total Quality Management*, 13(5), 2002.

Sarker, S., and A. S. Lee, "It-Enabled Organizational Transformation: A Case Study of BPR Failure at TELECO," *Journal of Strategic Information Systems*, Vol. 8, 1999.

Sarkis, J., and R. P. Sundarraj, "Evaluating Componentized Enterprise Information Technologies: A Multiattribute Modeling Approach," *Information Systems Frontiers*, 5(3), 2003.

Smith, H., and P. Fingar, *Business Process Management (BPM): The Third Wave*. Tampa, FL: Meghan-Kiffar, 2003.

Sterlicchi, J., and E. Wales, "Custom Chaos: How Nike Just Did It Wrong," *Business Online* (*BolWeb.com*), June 2001.

Sutcliffe, A., and N. Mehandjiev (eds.), "End User Computer," Special Issue, *Communications of the ACM*, September 2004.

Ward, J., and J. Peppard, *Strategic Planning for Information Systems, 3/e*, New York: Wiley, 2002.

Whitten, J., et al., *Systems Analysis and Design Methods*, 6th ed. New York: Irwin/McGraw-Hill, 2003.

Xia, W., and G. Lee, "Grasping the Complexity of IS Development Projects," *Communications of the ACM*, May 2004.

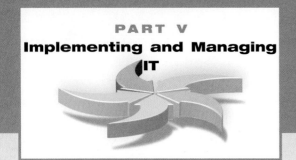

PART V
Implementing and Managing IT

12. Using IT for Strategic Advantage
13. Information Technology Economics
14. Acquiring IT Applications and Infrastructure
▶ 15. Managing Information Resources and Security
16. The Impacts of IT on Individuals, Organizations, and Society

CHAPTER

15

Managing Information Resources and Security

15.1 The IS Department and End Users

15.2 The CIO in Managing the IS Department

15.3 IS Vulnerability and Computer Crimes

15.4 Protecting Information Resources: From National to Organizational Efforts

15.5 Securing the Web, Intranets, and Wireless Networks

15.6 Business Continuity and Disaster Recovery Planning

15.7 Implementing Security: Auditing and Risk Management

15.8 Information Technology in Counterterrorism

Minicases:
1. Home Depot
2. Zions Bancorporation

LEARNING OBJECTIVES

After studying this chapter, you will be able to:

❶ Recognize the difficulties in managing information resources.

❷ Understand the role of the IS department and its relationships with end users.

❸ Discuss the role of the chief information officer.

❹ Recognize information systems' vulnerability, attack methods, and the possible damage from malfunctions.

❺ Describe the major methods of defending information systems.

❻ Describe the security issues of the Web and electronic commerce.

❼ Describe business continuity and disaster recovery planning.

❽ Understand the economics of security and risk management.

❾ Describe the role of IT in supporting counterterrorism.

CYBERCRIME IN THE NEW MILLENNIUM

On January 1, 2000, the world was relieved to know that the damage to information systems due to the YK2 problem was minimal. However, only about six weeks into the new millennium, computer systems around the world were attacked by criminals.

On February 6, 2000, the biggest e-commerce sites were falling like dominos. First was Yahoo, which was forced to close down for three hours. Next were eBay, Amazon.com, E*Trade, and several other major EC and Internet sites that had gone dark.

The attacker(s) used a method called *denial of service (DoS)*. By hammering a Web site's equipment with too many requests for information, an attacker can effectively clog a system, slowing performance or even crashing a site. All one needs to do is to get the DoS software (available for free in many hacking sites), break into unrelated unprotected computers and plant some software there, select a target site, and instruct the unprotected computers to repeatedly send requests for information to the target site. It is like constantly dialing a telephone number so that no one else can get through. It takes time for the attacked site to identify the sending computers and to block e-mails from them. Thus, the attacked site may be out of service for a few hours.

The magnitude of the damage was so large (several billion dollars per Yankee Group; see Panko, 2004), that on February 9, the U.S. Attorney General pledged to track down the criminals and ensure that the Internet remains secure. This assurance did not last too long, as can be seen from the following story told by Professor Turban:

> When I opened my e-mail on May 4, 2000, I noticed immediately that the number of messages was larger than usual. A closer observation revealed that about 20 messages were titled I LOVE YOU, and most of them came from faculty, secretaries, and administrators at City University of Hong Kong. It was not my birthday and there was no reason to believe that so many people would send me love messages the same day. My initial thought was to open one message to find out what's going on. But, on second thought I remembered the "Melissa" virus and the instructions not to open any attachment of a strange e-mail. I picked up the telephone and called one of the senders, who told me not to open the attachment since it contained a deadly virus.

Although Professor Turban's system escaped the virus, thousands of users worldwide opened the "love" attachment and released the bug. It is interesting to note that the alleged attacker, from the Philippines, was not prosecuted because he did not break any law in the Philippines. The damage, according to Zetter and Miastkowski (2000), was estimated at $8.7 billion worldwide.

Sources: Compiled from news items during May 3–11, 2000, and from Zetter and Miastkowski (2000).

→ LESSONS LEARNED FROM THIS CASE

Every year there have been more than a dozen major virus attacks, and hundreds of small ones, causing damage to organizations and individuals (see Richardson, 2003). The frequency and magnitude of these and other cybercrimes are increasing rapidly, threatening the welfare of the Internet and e-business.

Clearly, information resources, including computers, networks, programs, and data, are vulnerable to unforeseen attacks. Attackers can zero in on a single company, or can attack many companies and individuals without discrimination, using various attack methods. Although variations of the attack methods are known, the defense against them is difficult and/or expensive. As the story of the "love" virus demonstrated, many countries do not have sufficient laws to deal with computer criminals. For all of these reasons, protection of networked systems can be a complex issue.

The actions of people or of nature can cause an information system to function in a way different from what was planned. It is important, therefore, to know how to ensure the continued operation of an IS and to know what to do if the system breaks down. These and similar issues are of concern to the management of information resources, the subject of this chapter.

In this chapter we also look at how the IS department and end users work together; the role of the chief information officer; and the issue of information security and control in general and of Web systems in particular. Finally, we deal with plans of business continuity after a disaster, and the costs of preventing computer hazards.

15.1 THE IS DEPARTMENT AND END USERS

Throughout this book, we have seen that information systems are used to increase productivity and help achieve quality, timeliness, and satisfaction for both employees and customers. Most large, many medium, and even some small organizations around the world are strongly dependent on IT. Their information systems have considerable strategic importance.

The IS Department in the Organization

IT resources are very diversified; they include personnel assets, technology assets, and IT relationship assets. The management of information resources is divided between the information services department (ISD) and the end users. **Information resources management (IRM)** encompasses all activities related to the planning, organizing, acquiring, maintaining, securing, and controlling of IT resources (see Luftman, 2004). The division of responsibility depends on many factors, beginning with the amount of IT assets and nature of duties involved in IRM, and ending with outsourcing policies. Decisions about the roles of each party are made during the IS planning (Chapter 12). (For some insights, see also Sambamurthy et al., 2001.)

A major decision that must be made by senior management is where the ISD is to report in the organizational hierarchy. Partly for historical reasons, a common place to find the ISD is in the accounting or finance department. In such situations, the ISD normally reports to the controller or the chief financial officer. The ISD might also report to one of the following: (1) a vice president or chief officer of technology, (2) an executive vice president (e.g., for administration), or (3) the CEO.

THE IS DIRECTOR AS A "CHIEF." To show the importance of the IS area, some organizations call the director of IS a *chief information officer (CIO),* a title similar to chief financial officer (CFO) and chief operating officer (COO). Typically, only important or senior vice presidents receive this title. Other common titles are *vice president for IS, vice president for information technology,* or *director of information systems.* Unfortunately, as Becker (2003) reports, some companies provide the title CIO, but do not accord the position the importance other "chiefs" are getting. The *title* of CIO and the position to whom this person reports reflect, in many cases, the degree of support being shown by top management to the ISD. The *reporting relationship* of the ISD is important in that it reflects the focus of the department. If the ISD reports to the accounting or finance area, there is often a tendency to emphasize accounting or finance applications at the expense of those in the marketing, production, and logistics areas. In some organizations the IS functions are distributed, depending on their nature (see Minicase 1). To be most effective, the ISD needs to take as broad a view as possible. (See Kern, 2003, for the ideal ISD.)

THE NAME AND POSITION OF THE IS DEPARTMENT.   The *name* of the ISD is also important. Originally it was called the Data Processing (DP) Department. Then the name was changed to the Management Information Systems (MIS) Department and then to the Information Systems Department (ISD). In addition, one can find names such as Information Technology Department, Corporate Technology Center, and so on. In very large organizations the ISD can be a division, or even an independent corporation (such as at Bank of America and at Boeing Corp.).

Some companies separate their e-commerce activities, creating a special online division. This is the approach taken by Qantas Airways, for example. In others, e-commerce may be combined with ISD in a technology department or division. Becker (2003) reports on a study that shows that companies get the largest return from IT when they treat the ISD like any other important part of their business.

The status of the ISD also depends on its mission and internal structure. Agarwal and Sambamurthy (2002) found in a survey that companies usually organize their IT functions in one of the following ways: making IT an active partner in business innovation, providing IT resources for innovation and global reach, or seeking flexibility via a considerable amount of outsourcing.

The increased role and importance of IT and its management, both by a centralized unit and by end users, require careful understanding of the manner in which ISD is organized as well as of the relationship between the ISD and end users. (See the case of Texaco at Hirschheim et al., 2003.) These topics are discussed next. Also, for more on the connection between the ISD and the organization, see the IRM feedback model in Online File W15.1 at the book's Web site.

The IS Department and End Users

It is extremely important to have a good relationship between the ISD and end users. Unfortunately, though, this relationship is not always optimal. The development of end-user computing and outsourcing was motivated in part by the poor service that end users felt they received from the ISD. (For the issue of how to measure the quality of IS services, see Murrays, 2004, and Jiang et al., 2002). Conflicts occur for several reasons, ranging from the fact that priorities of the ISD may differ from those of the end users, to lack of communication. Also, there are some fundamental differences between the personalities, cognitive styles, educational backgrounds, and gender proportion of the end users versus the ISD staff (generally more males in the ISD) that could contribute to conflicts. An example of such conflict is illustrated in *IT at Work 15.1* (page 636).

IT at Work 15.1
MINNESOTA'S DEPARTMENT OF TRANSPORTATION VIOLATES PROCEDURES

The Department of Transportation in Minnesota (*dot. state.mn.us*) had come across a hybrid PC system that would allow road surveys to be accomplished with less time and effort, and greater accuracy. The system would require two people to conduct a survey instead of the usual three, and because of the precision of the computer-based system, the survey could be done in half the time.

The department ran into a problem because the ISD for the State of Minnesota had instituted standards for all PCs that could be purchased by any state agency. Specifically, a particular brand of IBM PC was the only PC purchase allowed, without going through a special procedure. The red tape, as well as the unwillingness of the ISD to allow any deviation from the standard, caused a great deal of frustration.

As a last resort, the Department of Transportation procured the hybrid PC and camouflaged the transaction as engineering equipment for conducting surveys. From that point on, its staff decided they would do what they needed to do to get their jobs done, and the less the ISD knew about what they were doing, the better. When asked why they behaved this way, the administrator of the Department of Transportation simply said, "We have to do it this way because the ISD will either try to stop or hold up for a long period of time any decision we want to make, because they just are not familiar enough with the issues that we are facing in our department."

For Further Exploration: What are the organizational risks when the Transportation Department takes this attitude? How can the conflict be resolved?

The situation described in *IT at Work 15.1* used to be common. One of this book's authors, when acting as a consultant to an aerospace company in Los Angeles, found that end users frequently bought nonstandard equipment by making several smaller purchases instead of one large purchase, because the smaller purchases did not require authorization by the ISD. When asked if the ISD and top management knew about this circumventing of the rules, a violating manager answered, "Of course they know, but what can they do—fire me?" Fortunately, the situation is now improving (see Ragsdale, 2004).

Generally, the ISD can take one of the following four approaches toward end-user departments:

1. ***Let them sink or swim.*** Don't do anything; let the end user beware.
2. ***Use the stick.*** Establish policies and procedures to control end-user computing so that corporate risks are minimized, and try to enforce them.
3. ***Use the carrot.*** Create incentives to encourage certain end-user practices that reduce organizational risks.
4. ***Offer support.*** Develop services to aid end users in their computing activities.

Each of these responses presents the IS executive with different opportunities for facilitation and coordination, and each has its advantages and disadvantages.

Fostering the ISD/End-User Relationships

The ISD is a *service organization* that manages the IT infrastructure needed to carry on enterprise and end-user IT applications. Therefore, a partnership between the ISD and the end users is a must. This is not an easy task since the ISD is basically a technical organization that may not understand the business and the users. The users, on the other hand, may not understand information technologies. Also, there could be differences between the ISD (the provider) and the end users in terms of agreement on how to measure the IT services provided (quality, quantity) (see Murrays, 2004, and Jiang et al., 2002). Another major reason for tense relationships in many organizations is the difficulties discussed in Chapter 13 regarding the evaluation of IT investment (Seddon et al., 2002).

To improve collaboration, the ISD and end users may employ three common arrangements: the steering committee, service-level agreements, and the information center. (For other strategies, see Online File W15.2.)

THE STEERING COMMITTEE. The corporate **steering committee** is a group of managers and staff representing various organizational units that is set up to establish IT priorities and to ensure that the ISD is meeting the needs of the enterprise (see Minicase 1). The committee's major tasks are:

- *Direction setting.* In linking the corporate strategy with the IT strategy, planning is the key activity (see Chapter 12 and Willcocks and Sykes, 2000).
- *Rationing.* The committee approves the allocation of resources for and within the information systems organization. This includes outsourcing policy.
- *Structuring.* The committee deals with how the ISD is positioned in the organization. The issue of centralization–decentralization of IT resources is resolved by the committee.
- *Staffing.* Key IT personnel decisions involve a consultation-and-approval process made by the committee. Notable is the selection of the CIO and major IT outsourcing decisions.
- *Communication.* Information regarding IT activities should flow freely.
- *Evaluating.* The committee should establish performance measures for the ISD and see that they are met. This includes the initiation of *service-level agreements.*

The success of steering committees largely depends on the establishment of **IT goverance,** a formally established set of statements that should direct the policies regarding IT alignment with organizational goals, risk determination, and allocation of resources (Cilli, 2003). For more on IT governance see *A Closer Look 15.1* (page 638).

SERVICE-LEVEL AGREEMENTS. *Service-level agreements (SLAs)* are formal agreements regarding the division of computing responsibility between end users and the ISD, and the expected services to be rendered by the ISD. A service-level agreement can be viewed as a *contract* between each end-user unit and the ISD. If a chargeback system exists, it is usually spelled out in the SLA. The process of establishing and implementing SLAs may be applied to each of the *major* computing resources: hardware, software, people, data, networks, and procedures.

The divisions of responsibility in SLAs are based on critical computing decisions that are made by *end-user managers,* who agree to accept certain computing responsibilities and to turn over others to the ISD. Since end-user managers make these decisions, they are free to choose the amount and kind of support they feel they need. This freedom to choose provides a check on the ISD and encourages it to develop and deliver support services to meet end-user needs.

An approach based on SLAs offers several advantages. First, it reduces "finger pointing" by clearly specifying responsibilities. When a PC malfunctions, everyone knows who is responsible for fixing it. Second, it provides a structure for the design and delivery of end-user services by the ISD. Third, it creates incentives for end users to improve their computing practices, thereby reducing

A CLOSER LOOK
15.1 IT GOVERNANCE

Managing information resources is becoming more important and more complex. Organizations must understand and manage the risks associated with new technologies. The following are five critical issues:

1. Aligning IT strategy with the business strategy (see Chapter 12)
2. Cascading strategy and goals down into the enterprise (Chapter 12)
3. Measuring IT's performance (Chapter 13)
4. Providing organizational structures that facilitate the implementation of strategy and goals (Chapters 15 and 16)
5. Insisting that an IT control framework be adopted and implemented (Chapter 15)

Addressing these issues is at the core of *IT governance.* According to Luftman et al. (2004):

IT governance is the operating model for how the organization will make decisions about the use of information technology. IT governance addresses decisions about the allocation of resources, the evaluation of business initiatives and risk, prioritization of projects, performance measurements and tracking mechanisms, determinations of cost and their assignment (i.e., how IT costs are allocated), and the assessment

of the value of an IT investment. Also, just as business governance is concerned with make–buy decisions in business strategy, IT governance is also concerned with external relationships for obtaining IT resources. These relationships may embrace mechanisms such as strategic alliances, partnerships, outsourcing, spin-offs, joint ventures (for developing new IT capabilities), and licensing activities. (Luftman et al., 2004, p. 295)

According to the IT Governance Institute (*itgi.org*), IT governance is an integral part of the enterprise governance, and it is the responsibility of the board of directors and executive management. Since IT governance involves many activities, there are several interpretations of what it includes. The IT Governance Institute provides a tutorial about the role of IT governance and the tools (including software) available for its implementation (see "Board Briefing on IT Governance" at *itgi.org*).

Luftman et al. (2004) provide a list of dozens of IT governance tasks ranging from budget and training to alliance management. The steering committee is part of IT governance as are activities such as security risk assessment (to be described later). Assessing the risk of new technology and risk mitigation is clearly a major task of IT governance.

---

computing risks to the firm. SLAs are useful to both the ISD and the user community (see White, 2004, and Luftman et al., 2004).

Establishing SLAs requires the following steps: (1) Define service levels. (2) Divide computing responsibility at each level. (3) Design the details of the service levels, including measurement of quality (see Jiang et al., 2002). (4) Implement service levels. Kesner (2002) adds to these: (5) Assign SLA owner (the person or department that gets the SLA), (6) monitor SLA compliance, (7) analyze performance, (8) refine SLAs as needed, and (9) improve service to the department or company.

Due to the introduction of Web-based tools for simplifying the task of monitoring enterprise networks, more attention has recently been given to service-level agreement (Adams, 2000). (For an overview of SLAs, see Pantry and Griffiths, 2002; for suggestions of how to control SLAs, see Diao et al., 2002.)

THE INFORMATION CENTER. The concept of **information center (IC)** (also known as the user's service center, technical support center, or IS help center) was conceived by IBM Canada in the 1970s as a response to the increased number of end-user requests for new computer applications. This demand created a huge backlog in the IS department, and users had to wait several *years* to get their systems built. Today, ICs concentrate on end-user support with PCs, client/server applications, and the Internet/intranet, helping with installation, training, problem resolution, and other technical support.

The IC is set up to help users get certain systems built quickly and to provide tools that can be employed by users to build their own systems. The concept of the IC, furthermore, suggests that the people in the center should be especially oriented toward the users in their outlook. This attitude should be shown in the training provided by the staff at the center and in the way the staff helps users with any problems they might have. There can be one or several ICs in an organization, and they report to the ISD and/or the end-user departments.

The New IT Organization

To carry out its mission in the digital economy, the ISD needs to adapt. Rockart et al. (1996) proposed eight imperatives for ISDs, which are still valid today. These imperatives are summarized in Online File W15.3.

Information technology, as shown throughout this book, is playing a critical role in the livelihood of many organizations, small and large, private and public, throughout the world. Furthermore, the trend is for even more IT involvement. Effective ISDs will help their firms apply IT to transform themselves to e-businesses, redesign processes, and access needed information on a tight budget. For more on managing IT in the digital era, see Sambamurthy et al. (2001).

15.2 THE CIO IN MANAGING THE IS DEPARTMENT

Managing the ISD is similar to managing any other organizational unit. The unique aspect of the ISD is that it operates as a service department in a rapidly changing environment, thus making the department's projections and planning difficult. The IT resources are scattered all over the enterprise, adding to the complexity of ISD management. Here we will discuss only one issue: the CIO and his or her relationship with other managers and executives.

The Role of the Chief Information Officer

The changing role of the ISD highlights the fact that the CIO is becoming an important member of the organization's top management team (Ross and Feeny, 2000). Also, the experience of 9/11 changed the role of the CIO, placing him or her in a more important organizational position (see Ball, 2002) because of the organization's realization of the need for IT-related disaster planning and the importance of IT to the organization's activities (see Luftman et al., 2004).

The prime role of the CIO is to align IT with the business strategy. Secondary roles are to implement state-of-the-art solutions and to provide and improve information access. These roles are supplemented today by several strategic roles because IT has become a strategic resource for many organizations. Coordinating this resource requires strong IT leadership and ISD/end-user collaboration within the organization. In addition, CIO–CEO relationships are crucial for effective, successful utilization of IT, especially in organizations that greatly depend on IT, where the CIO joins the top management "chiefs" group (e.g., see Roberts, 2004, and Potter, 2003). For an example of the importance of the CIO role, see Online Minicase W15.1.

The CIO in some cases is a member of the corporate *executive committee,* the most important committee in any organization, which has responsibility for strategic business planning. Its members include the chief executive officer and the senior vice presidents. The executive committee provides the top-level oversight for the organization's information resources. It guides the IS steering committee that is usually chaired by the CIO. Related to the CIO is the emergence of the chief

The CIO in the Web-Based Era

knowledge officer (CKO, see Chapter 9). A CIO may report to the CKO, or the same person may assume both roles, especially in smaller companies.

Major responsibilities that are part of the CIO's evolving role are listed in Online File W15.4.

According to Ross and Feeny (2000), Luftman et al. (2004), and Earl (1999–2000), the CIO's role in the Web-based era is influenced by the following three factors:

- *Technology and its management are changing.* Companies are using new Web-based business models. Conventional applications are being transformed to Web-based. There is increasing use of B2B e-commerce, supply chain management, CRM, ERP (see Willcocks and Sykes, 2000), and knowledge management applications.
- *Executives' attitudes are changing.* Greater attention is given to opportunities and risks. At the very least, CIOs are the individuals to whom the more computer literate executives look for guidance, especially as it relates to e-business. Also, executives are more willing to invest in IT, since the cost-benefit ratio of IT is improving with time.
- *Interactions with vendors are increasing.* Suppliers of IT, especially the major ones (HP, Cisco, IBM, Microsoft, Sun, Intel, and Oracle), are influencing the strategic thinking of their corporate customers.

The above factors shape the roles and responsibilities of the CIO in the following eight ways: (1) The CIO is taking increasing responsibility for defining the strategic future. (2) The CIO needs to understand (with others in the organization) that the Web-based era is more about fundamental business change than about technology. (3) The CIO is responsible for protecting the ever-increasing IT assets, including the Web infrastructure, against ever-increasing hazards, including terrorists' attacks. (4) The CIO is becoming a *business visionary* who drives business strategy, develops new business models on the Web, and introduces management processes that leverage the Internet, intranets, and extranets. (5) The CIO needs to argue for a greater measure of central control. For example, placing inappropriate content on the Internet or intranets can be harmful and needs to be monitored and coordinated. (6) The IT asset-acquisition process must be improved. The CIO and end users must work more closely than ever before. (7) The increased networked environment may lead to disillusionment with IT—an undesirable situation that the CIO should help to avoid. (8) The CIO must lead the exploration of new computing environments, such as mobile enterprises and utility computing. These eight challenges place lots of pressure on CIOs, especially in times of economic decline (see Leidner et al., 2003).

As a result of the considerable pressures they face, CIOs may earn very high salaries (up to $1,000,000/year in large corporations), but there is high turnover at this position (see Earl, 1999/2000). As technology becomes increasingly central to business, the CIO becomes a key mover in the ranks of upper management. For example, in a large financial institution's executive committee meeting, attended by one of the authors, modest requests for additional budgets by the senior vice presidents for finance and for marketing were turned down after long debate. But, at the same meeting the CIO's request for a tenfold addition was approved in only a few minutes.

With the growth of utility computing and outsourcing, some question the future of the ISD as an in-house organization. Horner-Reich and Nelson (2003)

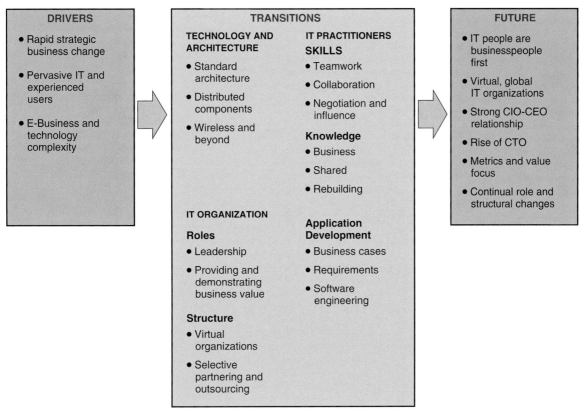

FIGURE 15.1 The transition environment (*Source:* Horner-Reich and Nelson, 2003.)

visualize a major change in the makeup and working of the ISD, and we are in the midst of a transition, as shown in Figure 15.1.

It is interesting to note that CEOs are acquiring IT skills. According to Duffy (1999), a company's best investment is a CEO who knows technology. If both the CIO and the CEO have the necessary skills for the information age, their company has the potential to flourish. For this reason some companies promote their CIOs to CEOs.

According to *eMarketer Daily* (May 12, 2003), CEOs see *security* as the second most important area for IT over the next two to three years. We will now turn our attention to that area, where the CIO is expected to lead—the security of data and information systems in the enterprise.

15.3 IS VULNERABILITY AND COMPUTER CRIMES

Information resources are scattered throughout the organization. Furthermore, employees travel with and take home corporate computers and data. Information is transmitted to and from the organization and among the organization's components. IS physical resources, data, software, procedures, and any other information resources may therefore be vulnerable, in many places at any time. (See Online Minicase W15.2.)

TABLE 15.1 IT Security Terms	
Term	**Definition**
Backup	An extra copy of the data and/or programs, kept in a secured location(s).
Decryption	Transformation of scrambled code into readable data after transmission.
Encryption	Transformation of data into scrambled code prior to its transmission.
Exposure	The harm, loss, or damage that can result if something has gone wrong in an information system.
Fault tolerance	The ability of an information system to continue to operate (usually for a limited time and/or at a reduced level) when a failure occurs.
Information system controls	The procedures, devices, or software that attempt to ensure that the system performs as planned.
Integrity (of data)	A guarantee of the accuracy, completeness, and reliability of data. System integrity is provided by the integrity of its components and their integration.
Risk	The likelihood that a threat will materialize.
Threats (or hazards)	The various dangers to which a system may be exposed.
Vulnerability	Given that a threat exists, the susceptibility of the system to harm caused by the threat.
Malware	General term for software that enables malicious acts against a computing system.

Before we describe the specific problems with information security and some proposed solutions, it is necessary to know the key terminology in the field. Table 15.1 provides an overview of that terminology.

Information Systems Breakdowns

Most people are aware of some of the dangers faced by businesses that are dependent on computers. Information systems, however, can be damaged for many other reasons. The following incidents illustrate representative cases of breakdowns in information systems.

INCIDENT 1. On September 12, 2002, Spitfire Novelties Corp. fell victim to what is called a "brute force" credit card attack. On a normal day, the Los Angeles–based company generates between 5 and 30 transactions. That Thursday, Spitfire's credit card transaction processor, Online Data Corporation, processed 140,000 fake credit card charges, worth $5.07 each. Of these, 62,000 were approved. The total value of the approved charges was around $300,000. Spitfire found out about the transactions only when they were called by one of the credit card owners who had been checking his statement online and had noticed the $5.07 charge.

Brute force credit card attacks require minimal skill. Hackers simply run thousands of small charges through merchant accounts, picking numbers at random. (For details on a larger credit card scam see *money.cnn.com/2003/02/18/technology/creditcards/index.htm.*)

INCIDENT 2. In January 2003 a hacker stole from the database of Moscow's MTS (mobile phone company) the personal details (passport number, age, home address, tax ID number, and more) of 6 million customers, including Russia's president V. V. Putin, and sold them on CD-ROMs for about $15 each. The database can be searched by name, phone number, or address. The information can be used for crimes such as **identity theft,** where someone uses the personal information of others to create a false identify and then uses it for some fraud (e.g., to get a fake credit card). However, in Russia, neither the theft of such information nor its sale was illegal (see Walsh, 2003).

INCIDENT 3. Destructive software (viruses, worms, and their variants, which are defined and discussed more fully later in the chapter) is flooding the Internet. Here are some examples of the 2003 vintage: SQL Slammer is a worm that carries a self-regenerating mechanism that enables it to multiply quickly across the Internet. It is so good at replicating that it quickly generates a massive amount of data, which slowed Internet traffic mainly in South Korea, Japan, Hong Kong, and some European countries in January 2003. It is a variation of Code Red, which slowed traffic on the Internet in July 2001. On May 18, 2003, a new virus that masqueraded as an e-mail from Microsoft technical support attacked computers in 89 countries. In June 2003, a high-risk virus w32/ Bugbear started to steal VISA account information (see "Bugbear worm steals...," 2003).

INCIDENT 4. On March 15, 2003, a student hacked into the University of Houston computer system and stole Social Security numbers of 55,000 students, faculty, and staff. The student was charged with unauthorized access to protected computers using someone else's ID, with intent to commit a federal crime. The case is still in the courts, and prison time is a possibility.

INCIDENT 5. On February 29, 2000, hundreds of automated teller machines (ATMs) in Japan were shut down, a computer system at a nuclear plant seized up, weather-monitoring devices malfunctioned, display screens for interest rates at the post offices failed, seismographs provided wrong information, and there were many other problems related to programming for "leap year." The problem was that years that end in "00" do not get the extra day, added every four years, unless they are divisible by 400 (2000 is such a leap year, but not 1900, or 2100). This rule was not programmed properly in some old programs in Japan, thus creating the problems.

INCIDENT 6. For almost two weeks, a seemingly legitimate ATM operating in a shopping mall near Hartford, Connecticut, gave customers apologetic notes that said, "Sorry, no transactions are possible." Meanwhile, the machine recorded the card numbers and the personal identification numbers that hundreds of customers entered in their vain attempts to make the machine dispense cash. On May 8, 1993, while the dysfunctional machine was still running in the shopping mall, thieves started tapping into the 24-hour automated teller network in New York City. Using counterfeit bank cards encoded with the numbers stolen from the Hartford customers, the thieves removed about $100,000 from the accounts of innocent customers. The criminals were successful in making an ATM machine do what it was supposedly designed not to do: breach its own security by recording bank card numbers together with personal security codes.

INCIDENT 7. Princeton University's director of admissions admitted hacking into Yale University's admissions program in 2002. Posing as students, and using data of students who applied to Princeton, he logged in several times, reviewing confidential data at Yale's site. All he needed to enter the system was a student name, birth date, and Social Security number.

INCIDENT 8. In 1994 a Russian hacker (who did not know much English) broke into a Citibank electronic funds transfer system and stole more than $10 million by wiring it to accounts around the world. Since then, Citibank, a giant bank that moves about a trillion dollars a day, increased its security measures, requiring customers to use electronic devices that create new passwords very frequently.

INCIDENT 9. On April 30, 2000, the London Stock Exchange was paralyzed by its worst computer system failure, before finally opening nearly eight hours late. A spokesman for the exchange said the problem, which crippled the supply of prices and firm information, was caused by corrupt data. He gave no further details. Dealers were outraged by the fault, which came on the last day of the tax year and just hours after violent price swings in the U.S. stock markets. The British Financial Services Authority said it viewed the failure seriously, adding it would insist any necessary changes to systems be made immediately and that lessons be "learned rapidly" to ensure the breakdown would not be repeated.

INCIDENT 10. On July 21, 2004, a man named Scott Levine was indicted on 144 charges of conspiracy, unauthorized access to a protected computer, and access-device fraud. Levine is accused of hacking into the systems of Acxion Corp., a company that manages personal, financial, and corporate data of clients. He took a megabyte of data (including many mailing list addresses), which he then sold to marketing firms, causing a $7 million loss to Acxion.

INCIDENT 11. On August 1, 2004, a computer glitch grounded thousands of American Airlines and U.S. Airways flights for about three hours. EDS Corporation, to whom the system involved was outsourced, was checking the cause of the problem (Associated Press, August 1, 2004).

These incidents and the two in the opening case (for more see *cybercrime.gov*) illustrate the vulnerability of information systems, the diversity of causes of computer security problems, and the substantial damage that can be done to organizations anywhere in the world as a result. The fact is that computing is far from secure (e.g., see Austin and Darby, 2003, Online Minicase W15.2, and the 2003 and 2004 FBI reports; Richardson, 2003, and Gordon et al., 2004).

System Vulnerability
Information systems are made up of many components that may be housed in several locations. Thus, each information system is vulnerable to many potential *hazards* or *threats*. Figure 15.2 presents a summary of the major threats to the security of an information system. Attacks on information systems can be either on internal systems (suffered by about 30% of the responding organizations in the CSI/FBI survey, as reported in Richardson, 2003), or via remote dial-ins (18%), or on Internet-based systems (78%). (See also *sons.org/*, for the most critical (top 20) Internet security vulnerabilites.)

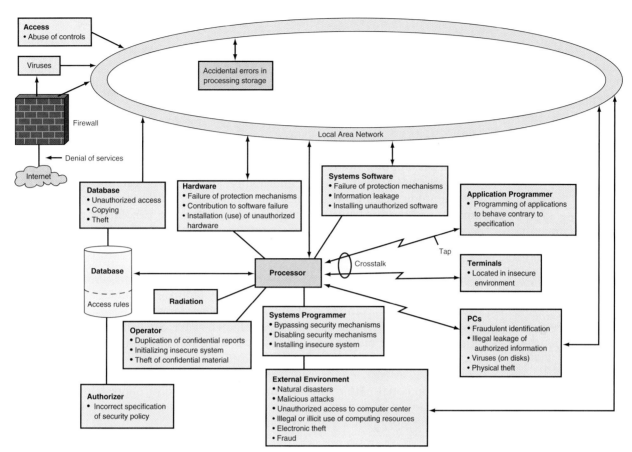

FIGURE 15.2 Areas of security threats.

According to CVE (Common Vulnerabilities and Exposure, an organization based at Mitre Corp. that provides information, education, and advice regarding IT vulnerabilities and exposure)(*cve.mitre.org/about/terminology.html*), there is a distinction between vulnerability and exposure:

A universal **vulnerability** is a state in a computing system (or set of systems) which either: allows an attacker to execute commands as another user; allows an attacker to access data that is contrary to the specified access restrictions for that data; allows an attacker to pose as another entity; or allows an attacker to conduct a denial of service.

An **exposure** is a state in a computing system (or set of systems) which is not a universal vulnerability, but either: allows an attacker to conduct information gathering activities; allows an attacker to hide activities; includes a capability that behaves as expected, but can be easily compromised; is a primary point of entry that an attacker may attempt to use to gain access to the system or data; and is considered a problem according to some reasonable security policy.

We will use the term vulnerability here to *include* exposure as well (including unintentional threats). Incidentally, by 2002, CVE identified more than 5,000 different security issues and problems (see Mitre, 2002). Whitman (2003) classified all the threats into 12 categories. These are shown in Online File W15.5.

The vulnerability of information systems is increasing as we move to a world of networked and especially wireless computing. Theoretically, there are hundreds of points in a corporate information system that can be subject to some threats. And actually, there are thousands of different ways that information systems can be attacked or damaged. These threats can be classified as *unintentional* or *intentional.*

UNINTENTIONAL THREATS. Unintentional threats can be divided into three major categories: human errors, environmental hazards, and computer system failures.

Many computer problems result from *human errors.* Errors can occur in the design of the hardware and/or information system. They can also occur in the programming, testing, data collection, data entry, authorization, and instructions. Human errors contribute to the *majority* (about 55 percent) of control- and security-related problems in many organizations.

Environmental hazards include earthquakes, severe storms (e.g., hurricanes, snow, sand, lightning, and tornadoes), floods, power failures or strong fluctuations, fires (the most common hazard), defective air conditioning, explosions, radioactive fallout, and water-cooling-system failures. In addition to damage from combustion, computer resources can incur damage from other elements that accompany fire, such as smoke, heat, and water. Such hazards may disrupt normal computer operations and result in long waiting periods and exorbitant costs while computer programs and data files are recreated.

Computer systems failures can occur as the result of poor manufacturing or defective materials. Unintentional malfunctions can also happen for other reasons, ranging from lack of experience to inappropriate testing. See *A Closer Look 15.2* for the story about some systems failures at airports.

INTENTIONAL THREATS. As headlines about computer crime indicate, computer systems can be damaged as a result of intentional actions as well. These account for about 30 percent of all computer problems, according to the Computer Security Institute (*gocsi.com*), but the monetary damage from such actions can be

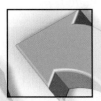

A CLOSER LOOK
15.2 COMPUTER GLITCHES DELAY AIRPORT OPENINGS

When the multibillion-dollar airport was opened in Hong Kong on July 6, 1998, a combination of computer glitches and unprepared personnel turned the airport into chaos. Both travelers and cargo were affected. For example, one software bug erased all inventory records, leaving no clue as to who owned what. Another software bug erased flight information from monitors, preventing passengers from finding flights. Computer problems in the baggage system resulted in 10,000 lost bags. Fresh food and seafood being shipped to restaurants

and hotels got spoiled, and considerable business was lost. In the United States, Denver's airport, which opened in 1995, had been plagued by computer glitches as well. Similarly, in Malaysia, when a new facility opened on July 1, 1999, a computerized total airport management system collapsed on the first day.

In all these airport cases, the problem was not external hackers' attacks or internal intentional acts. The bugs resulted from poor IS planning, lack of coordination, and insufficient testing.

extremely large. Examples of intentional threats include: theft of data; inappropriate use of data (e.g., manipulating inputs); theft of mainframe computer time; theft of equipment and/or programs; deliberate manipulation in handling, entering, processing, transferring, or programming data; labor strikes, riots, or sabotage; malicious damage to computer resources; destruction from viruses and similar attacks; and miscellaneous computer abuses and Internet fraud. In addition, while terrorists' attacks do not usually directly target computers, the computers and information systems can be destroyed in such cases, as happened in the 9/11 disaster in New York and Washington, D.C. Intentional threats can even be against whole countries. Many fear the possibility of *cyberattacks* by some countries against others.

Computer Crimes

According to the Computer Security Institute (*gocsi.com*), 64 percent of all corporations experienced computer crimes in 1997. The figures in the years 1998 through 2003 were even higher—about 96 percent in 2003 (per Richardson, 2003). The number, magnitude, and diversity of computer crimes are increasing. Lately, increased fraud related to the Internet and e-commerce is in evidence. For an overview of computer crime, see Loundy (2003); for FBI statistics for 2002–2004, see Richardson (2003) and Gordon et al. (2004).

TYPES OF COMPUTER CRIMES AND CRIMINALS. In many ways, computer crimes resemble conventional crimes. They can occur in various ways. First, the computer can be the *target* of the crime. For example, a computer may be stolen or destroyed, or a virus may destroy data. The computer can be the *medium* or *tool* of the attack, by creating an environment in which a crime or fraud can occur. For example, false data are entered into a computer system to mislead individuals examining the financial condition of a company. Finally, the computer can be used to *intimidate* or *deceive*. For instance, a stockbroker stole $50 million by convincing his clients that he had a computer program with which he could increase their return on investment by 60 percent per month. Crimes done on the Internet, called cybercrimes (discussed later), can fall into any of these categories.

Crimes can be performed by *outsiders* who penetrate a computer system (frequently via communication lines) or by *insiders* who are authorized to use the computer system but are misusing their authorization. **Hacker** is the term often used to describe an outside person who penetrates a computer system. For an overview of hacking and the protection against it, see Fadia (2002). Not all hackers are criminals. *White-hat hackers* perform ethical hacking, doing penetrating tests on their clients' systems to find the weak points, so that they can be fixed. *Black-hat hackers*, also referred to as crackers, are the criminals. A **cracker** is a *malicious hacker*, who may represent a serious problem for a corporation.

Hackers and crackers may involve in their crimes unsuspecting insiders. In a strategy called **social engineering,** computer criminals or corporate spies build an inappropriate trust relationship with insiders for the purpose of gaining sensitive information or unauthorized access privileges. For description of social engineering and some tips for prevention, see Damle (2002) and Online File W15.6.

Computer criminals, whether insiders or outsiders, tend to have a distinct profile and are driven by several motives (see Online File W15.7). Ironically, many employees fit this profile, but only a few of them are criminals. Therefore, it is difficult to predict who is or will be a computer criminal.

A large proportion of computer crimes are performed by insiders. According to Richardson (2003), the likely sources of attacks on U.S. companies are:

independent hackers (82%), disgruntled employees (78%), U.S. competitors (40%), foreign governments (28%), and foreign corporations (25%).

In addition to computer crimes against organizations, there is an alarming increase of fraud committed against individuals, on the Internet. These are a part of cybercrimes.

CYBERCRIMES. The Internet environment provides an extremly easy landscape for conducting illegal activities. These are known as **cybercrimes,** meaning crimes executed on the Internet. Hundreds of different methods and "tricks" are used by innovative criminals to get money from innocent people, to buy without paying, to sell without delivering, to abuse people or hurt them, and much more.

According to Sullivan (2003), between January 1 and April 30, 2003, agencies of the U.S. government uncovered 89,000 victims from whom Internet criminals bilked over $176 million. As a result, on May 16, 2003, the U.S. Attorney General announced that 135 people were arrested nationwide and charged with cybercrime. The most common crimes were investment swindles and identity theft. The Internet with its global reach has also resulted in a growing amount of cross-border fraud (see Online File W15.8).

Identity Theft. A growing cybercrime problem is *identity theft,* in which a criminal (the *identity thief*) poses as someone else. The thief steals Social Security numbers and credit card numbers, usually obtained from the Internet, to commit fraud (e.g., to buy products or consume services) that the victim may be required to pay for. The biggest damage to the person whose identity was stolen is to restore the damaged credit rating. For details and commercial solutions see *idthief.com* and Buell and Sandhu (2003).

CYBERWAR. There is an increasing interest in the threat of **cyberwar,** also known as *warefare*, in which a country's information systems could be paralyzed by a massive attack of destructive software. The target systems can range from the ISs of business, industry, government services, and the media, to military command systems (e.g., see Elbirt, 2003/2004).

One aspect of cyberwar is **cyberterrorism,** which refers to Internet terrorist attacks. These attacks, like cyberwar, can risk the national information infrastructure. The U.S. presidential Critical Infrastructure Protection Board (CIPB) is preparing protection plans, policies, and strategies to deal with cyberterrorism. The CIPB is recommending investment in cybersecurity programs. Some of the areas of the CIPB report are: a general policy on information security; asset protection requirements, including controls to ensure the return or destruction of information; technology insurance requirements; intellectual property rights; the right to monitor, and revoke, user activity; specification of physical and technical security standards; and communication procedures in time of emergency. (For more details and debates, see *cdt.org/security/critinfra*. For more details on cyberterrorism, see Verton and Brownlow, 2003.) The topic of countering cyberterrorism is presented in Section 15.8.

Methods of Attack on Computing Facilities

There are many methods of attack, and new ones appear regularly. Of the many methods of attack on computing facilities, the CSI/FBI reports (per Richardson, 2003) the following as most frequent (percentage of responding companies): virus (82%), insider abuse of Internet access (80%), unauthorized access by insiders (45%), theft of laptop (59%), denial of service (DoS) attack

(42%), system penetration (36%), sabotage (21%), and theft of proprietary information (21%). In this section we look at some of these methods. Two basic approaches are used in deliberate attacks on computer systems: data tampering and programming attack.

Data tampering, the most common means of attack, refers to entering false, fabricated, or fraudulent data into the computer or changing or deleting existing data. This is the method often used by insiders. For example, to pay for his wife's drug purchases, a savings and loan programmer transferred $5,000 into his personal account and tried to cover up the transfer with phony debit and credit transactions.

Programming attack is popular with computer criminals who use *programming techniques* to modify a computer program, either directly or indirectly. For this crime, programming skills and knowledge of the targeted systems are essential. *Programming attacks* appear under many names, as shown in Table 15.2. Several of the methods were designed for Web-based systems. Viruses merit special discussion here, due to their frequency, as do denial of service attacks, due to the effects they have had on computer networks.

VIRUSES. The most publicized and most common attack method is the **virus.** It receives its name from the program's ability to attach itself to ("infect") other computer programs, without the owner of the program being aware of the

TABLE 15.2 Methods of Programming Attack on Computer Systems

Method	Definition
Virus	Secret instructions inserted into programs (or data) that are innocently run during ordinary tasks. The secret instructions may destroy or alter data, as well as spread within or between computer systems.
Worm	A program that replicates itself and penetrates a valid computer system. It may spread within a network, penetrating all connected computers.
Trojan horse	An illegal program, contained within another program, that "sleeps" until some specific event occurs, then triggers the illegal program to be activated and cause damage.
Salami slicing	A program designed to siphon off small amounts of money from a number of larger transactions, so the quantity taken is not readily apparent.
Superzapping	A method of using a utility "zap" program that can bypass controls to modify programs or data.
Trap door	A technique that allows for breaking into a program code, making it possible to insert additional instructions.
Logic bomb	An instruction that triggers a delayed malicious act.
Denial of service	Too many requests for service, which crashes a Web site.
Sniffer	A program that searches for passwords or content in a packet of data as they pass through the Internet.
Spoofing	Faking an e-mail address or Web page to trick users to provide information or send money.
Password cracker	A password that tries to guess passwords (can be very successful).
War dialing	Programs that automatically dial thousands of telephone numbers in an attempt to identify one authorized to make a connection with a modem; then someone can use that connection to break into databases and systems.
Back doors	Invaders to a system create several entry points; even if you discover and close one, they can still get in through others.
Malicious applets	Small Java programs that misuse your computer resources, modify your file, send fake e-mail, etc.

Just as a biological virus disrupts living cells to cause disease, a computer virus—introduced maliciously—invades the inner workings of computers and disrupts normal operations of the machines.

2 The virus attaches itself and travels anywhere that the host program or piece of data travels, whether on floppy disk, local area networks, or bulletin boards.

1 A virus starts when a programmer writes a program that embeds itself in a host program.

3 The virus is set off by either a time limit or some set of circumstances, possibly a simple sequence of computer operations by the user (e.g., open an attachment). Then it does whatever the virus programmer intended, whether it is to print "Have a nice day" or erase data.

FIGURE 15.3 How a computer virus can spread.

infection (see Figure 15.3). When the software is used, the virus spreads, causing damage to that program and possibly to others.

According to Bruno (2002), 93 percent of all companies experienced virus attacks in 2001, with an average loss of $243,845 per company. A virus can spread throughout a computer system very quickly. Due to the availability of public-domain software, widely used telecommunications networks, and the Internet, viruses can also spread to many organizations around the world, as shown in the incidents listed earlier. Some of the most notorious viruses are "international," such as Michelangelo, Pakistani Brain, Chernobyl, and Jerusalem. (For the history of viruses and how to fight them, see Zetter and Miastkowski, 2000.)

When a virus is attached to a legitimate software program, the legitimate software is acting as a **Trojan horse,** a program that contains a hidden function that presents a security risk. The name is derived from the Trojan horse in Greek legend. The Trojan horse programs that present the greatest danger are those that make it possible for someone else to access and control a person's computer over the Internet.

Trojan horses, like viruses, are getting more sophisticated over time. For example, on July 14, 2004, *computerweekly.com* reported a "mass Trojan on the loose." The program, called Backdoor CGT, placed malicious code on thousands of computers.

Another virus, called "Bin Laden's suicide," also spread rapidly. It purported to show images of Osama Bin Laden's suicide, designed to entice recipients to open a file that would unleash a malicious software code. According to ABC Online News (July 24, 2004), the virus was posted on over 30,000 newsgroups. The fake file, when opened, launches a Trojan horse program that allows attackers to take over infected personal computers running Microsoft operating systems.

We'll look at viruses and how to fight them later in the chapter, when we describe security on networks.

DENIAL OF SERVICE. The opening case of this chapter described a denial of service incident. In a **denial-of-service (DoS)** attack, an attacker uses specialized software to send a flood of data packets to the target computer, with the aim of overloading its resources. Many attackers rely on software that has been created by other hackers and made available free over the Internet.

With a **distributed denial of service (DDoS)** attack, the attacker gains illegal administrative access to unsuspecting computers on the Internet. With access to a large number of such computers, the attacker loads the specialized DDoS software onto these computers. The software lies in wait for a command to begin the attack. When the command is given, the distributed network of computers begins sending out requests to one or more target computers. The requests can be legitimate queries for information or can be very specialized computer commands designed to overwhelm specific computer resources.

The machines on which DDoS software is loaded are known as **zombies** (Karagiannis, 2003). Zombies are often located at university and government sites. Increasingly, with the rise of cable modems and DSL modems, home computers that are connected to the Internet and left on all the time have become good zombie candidates.

DoS attacks are not new. In 1996, a New York Internet service provider had service disrupted for over a week by a DoS attack, denying service to over 6,000 users and 1,000 companies. A recent example of a DoS attack is the one on RIAA (Recording Industry Association of America) whose site (*riaa.org*) was rendered largely unavailable for a week starting January 24, 2003. The attack was done mainly by those who did not like the RIAA's attempts to fight pirated music done by file sharing. Due to the widespread availability of free intrusion tools and scripts and the overall interconnectivity on the Internet, the intruder population now consists of virtually anyone with minimal computer experience (often a teenager with time on his hands). A sophisticated large-scale DDoS attack on Akamai was reported by SearchSecurity.com, on June 16, 2004. It bogged down several of its client's Web sites (e.g., FedEx, Microsoft, and Google). Unfortunately, a successful DoS attack can literally threaten the survival of an EC site, especially for SMEs. Panko (2004) reports that one company went out of business because of DoS attacks. A report by the FBI (Gordon et al., 2004) found that companies lost more money due to DoS than from any other type of attack.

ATTACKS VIA MODEMS. In many companies employees who are on the road use modems for dial-in access to the company intranet. Two types of modems exist: authorized and not authorized (known as *rogue modems*). The latter are installed by employees when there are no authorized modems, when it is inconvenient to use the authorized modems, or when the authorized modems provide only limited access.

Modems are very risky. It is quite easy for attackers to penetrate them, and it is easy for employees to leak secret corporate information to external networks via rogue modems. In addition, software problems may develop, such as downloading programs with viruses or with a "back door" to the system. Back doors are created by hackers to repenetrate a system, once a successful penetration is made. For ways to protect systems that use modems, see White (1999).

15.4 PROTECTING INFORMATION RESOURCES: FROM NATIONAL TO ORGANIZATIONAL EFFORTS

Organizations and individuals can protect their systems in many ways. Indeed, reported attacks on computer systems have been steadily decreasing over time (Gordon et al., 2004). Let's look first at what protections the national efforts can provide. Then we will look at what organizations can do to protect information resources. (For an overview, see Panko, 2004.)

Representative Federal Laws Dealing with Computer Crime and Security

A "crime" means breaching the law. In addition to breaking regular law related to physically stealing computers or conducting fraud, computer criminals may break the specially legislated computer crime laws. According to the FBI, an average robbery involves about $3,000; an average white-collar crime involves $23,000; but an average computer crime involves about $600,000. Table 15.3 lists some key U.S. federal statutes dealing with computer crime. (For more on these laws, see *epic.org/security* and Volonino and Robinson, 2004.)

Legislation can be helpful but not sufficient. Therefore, the FBI has formed the *National Infrastructure Protection Center (NIPC)*. This joint partnership

TABLE 15.3 Key U.S. Federal Statutes Dealing with Computer Crime

Federal Statute	Key Provisions
Privacy Act of 1974	Prohibits the government from collecting information secretly. Information must be used only for a specific purpose.
Counterfeit Access Device and Computer Crime Control Act (passed in October 1984)	Prohibits fraud in online transactions.
Computer Fraud and Abuse Act (1986), 18 USC, section 1030	Prohibits unauthorized access to computer systems.
Electronic Communications Privacy Act of 1986	Prohibits interception of private e-mail without a court order.
Computer Security Act of 1987	Requires security of information of individuals.
Video Privacy Protection Act of 1988	Protects privacy in transmission of pictures.
Computer Abuse Amendment Act of 1994	Prohibits knowing transmission of computer viruses.
National Information Infrastructure Protection Act of 1996	Protects proprietary economic information.
Gramm-Leach-Bliley Act of 1999	Specifies when a financial institution must give notice to a customer that their personal information has been accessed.
Computer Security Enhancement Act of 2000	Policy on digital signatures.
Patriot Act (sections 202, 209)	Gives authority to monitor communication, stored data.
E-Mail Threats and Harassment Act (18 USC, 47 USC)	Prohibits transmission of damaging threat and harassment via e-mail.
Wire Fraud Act (18 USC #1343)	Prohibits use of wire communications to defraud; amended to include wireless.

between government and private industry is designed to protect the nation's infrastructure—its telecommunications, energy, transportation, banking and finance, emergency, and governmental operations. The FBI has also established *Regional Computer Intrusion Squads,* which are charged with the task of investigating violations of the Computer Fraud and Abuse Act. The squads' activities are focused on intrusions to public switched networks, major computer network intrusions, privacy violations, industrial espionage, pirated computer software, and other cybercrimes.

Another national organization is the *Computer Emergency Response Team (CERT)* at Carnegie Mellon University (*cert.org*). The CERT Coordination Center (CC) consists of three teams: the Incident Handling Team, the Vulnerability Handling Team, and the Artifact Analysis Team. The Incident Handling Team receives incident reports of cyberattacks from Internet sites and provides information and guidance to the Internet community on combating reported incidents. The Vulnerability Handling Team receives reports on suspected computer and network vulnerabilities, verifies and analyzes the reports, and works with the Internet community to understand and develop countermeasures to those vulnerabilities. The Artifacts Analysis Team focuses on the code used to carry out cyberattacks (e.g., computer viruses), analyzing the code and finding ways to combat it.

Organizing for Information Security

Information security problems are increasing rapidly, causing damages to many organizations. According to the Computer Security Institute (*gocsi.com*), the average reported annual loss in 2004 was 200 percent to 400 percent higher, depending on the category, than in 1999. Protection may be expensive and complex. Therefore, companies must not only use controls to prevent or detect security problems, they must do so in an organized way, starting with assigning responsibilities and authority throughout the organization (e.g., see Talleur, 2001 and Atlas and Young, 2002). Any program that is adopted must be supported by three organizational components: people, technology, and process (see Doughty, 2003).

One way to approach the problem of organizing for security is similar to the familiar total quality management approach—namely, recognizing the importance of a corporatewide security program, which will deal with all kinds of security issues, including protecting the information assets. Doll et al. (2003) present this approach as having six major characteristics:

- *Aligned.* The program must be aligned with the organizational goals.
- *Enterprisewide.* Everyone in the organization must be included in the security program.
- *Continuous.* The program must be operational all the time.
- *Proactive.* Do not wait for trouble; be aware and ready; use innovative, preventive, and protective measures.
- *Validated.* The program must be tested and validated to ensure it works.
- *Formal.* It must be a formal program with authority, responsibility, and accountability.

A corporate security model proposed by Doll et al. (2003) is illustrated in Figure 15.4 (page 654). Obviously, only very large organizations can afford such a comprehensive security structure. We will present several of the components and concepts in the figure in the remaining portions of this chapter. A case study

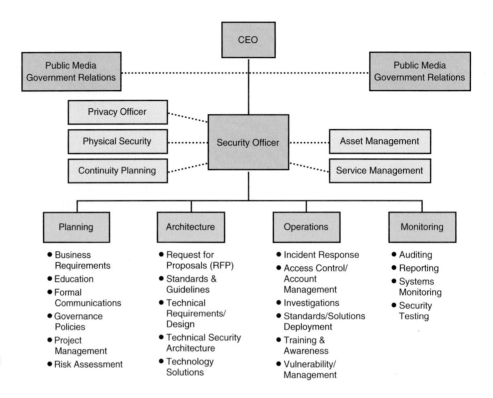

FIGURE 15.4 Corporate security plan. (*Source:* Doll et al., 2003.)

for implementing enterprise security is provided by Doughty (2003). A major issue is the role the person responsible for security (the chief security officer) is going to assume (see Robinson, 2003).

Controls and Awareness

Knowing about major potential threats to information systems is necessary, but understanding ways to defend against these threats is equally critical (see *cert.org* and *sans.com*). Defending information resources is not a simple or inexpensive task. The major difficulties of protecting information are listed in Table 15.4. Because of its importance to the entire enterprise, organizing an appropriate defense system is one of the major activities of any prudent CIO and of the functional managers who control information resources. As a matter of fact, IT security is the business of *everyone* in an organization (see Pooley, 2002).

Protection of information resources is accomplished mostly by inserting *controls* (defense mechanisms) intended to prevent accidental hazards, deter intentional acts, detect problems as early as possible, enhance damage recovery, and correct problems. Controls can be integrated into hardware and software during the system development phase (an efficient approach). They can also be added on once the system is in operation, or during its maintenance. The important point is that defense should stress *prevention*; defense does no good *after the crime has occurred*.

In addition to controls, a good defense system must include security *awareness*. All organizational members must be aware of security threats and watch constantly for potential problems and crimes. Suggestions of how to develop such programs are offered by security consultants (e.g., see Wiederkehr, 2003). Awareness training is recommended by Talleur (2001).

TABLE 15.4 The Difficulties in Protecting Information Resources
● Hundreds of potential threats exist, and they keep changing.
● Computing resources may be situated in many locations.
● Many individuals own or control information assets.
● Computer networks can be outside the organization and difficult to protect.
● Rapid technological changes make some controls obsolete as soon as they are installed. New threats (e.g., viruses) appear constantly.
● Many computer crimes are undetected for a long period of time, so it is difficult to learn from experience.
● People tend to violate security procedures because the procedures are inconvenient.
● Many computer criminals who are caught go unpunished, so there is no deterrent effect.
● The amount of computer knowledge necessary to commit computer crimes is usually minimal. As a matter of fact, one can learn hacking, for free, on the Internet.
● The cost of preventing some hazards can be very high. Therefore, most organizations simply cannot afford to protect against all possible hazards.
● It is difficult to conduct a cost-benefit justification for controls before an attack occurs since it is difficult to assess the value of a hypothetical attack.

Since there are many security threats, there are also many defense mechanisms. Controls are designed to protect all the components of an information system, specifically data, software, hardware, and networks. In the next section, we describe the major defense strategies.

Defense Strategy: How Do We Protect?

The selection of a specific defense strategy and controls depends on the objective of the defense and on the perceived cost-benefit. The following are the major objectives of *defense strategies:*

1. *Prevention and deterrence.* Properly designed controls may prevent errors from occurring, deter criminals from attacking the system, and better yet, deny access to unauthorized people. Prevention and deterrence are especially important where the potential damage is very high (see Scalet, 2003). They are the most desirable controls.

2. *Detection.* It may not be economically feasible to prevent all hazards, and deterrence measures may not work. Therefore, unprotected systems are vulnerable to attack. Like a fire, the earlier an attack is detected, the easier it is to combat, and the less damage is done. Detection can be performed in many cases by using special diagnostic software, at a minimal cost.

3. *Limitation of damage.* This strategy is to minimize (limit) losses once a malfunction has occurred (damage control). This can be accomplished, for example, by including a *fault-tolerant system* that permits operation in a degraded mode until full recovery is made. If a fault-tolerant system does not exist, a quick (and possibly expensive) recovery must take place. Users want their systems back in operation as fast as possible (e.g., see Kelly, 2004).

4. *Recovery.* A recovery plan explains how to fix a damaged information system as quickly as possible. Replacing rather than repairing components is one route to fast recovery. For a recovery manager, see Kelly (2004).

5. *Correction.* Correcting the causes of damaged systems can prevent the problem from occurring again.

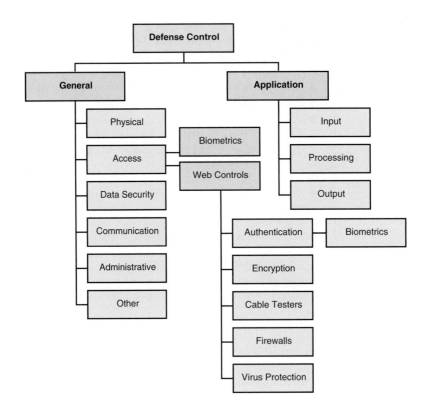

FIGURE 15.5 Major defense controls.

6. *Awareness and compliance.* All organization members must be educated about the hazards and must comply with the security rules and regulations.

Any defense strategy that aims to attain one or more of these objectives may involve the use of several controls. The defense controls are divided in our discussion into two major categories: *general controls* and *application controls*. Each has several subcategories, as shown in Figure 15.5. **General controls** are established to protect the system regardless of the specific application. For example, protecting hardware and controlling access to the data center are independent of the specific application. **Application controls** are safeguards that are intended to protect specific applications. In the next two sections, we discuss the major types of these two groups of information systems controls.

General Controls

The major categories of general controls are physical controls, access controls, data security controls, communications (networks) controls, and administrative controls.

PHYSICAL CONTROLS. Physical security refers to the protection of computer facilities and resources. This includes protecting physical property such as computers, data centers, software, manuals, and networks. Physical security is the first line of defense and usually the easiest to construct. It provides protection against most natural hazards as well as against some human hazards. Appropriate physical security may include several controls such as the following:

● Appropriate design of the data center. For example, the site should be noncombustible and waterproof.
● Shielding against electromagnetic fields.

● Good fire prevention, detection, and extinguishing systems, including sprinkler system, water pumps, and adequate drainage facilities. A better solution is fire-enveloping Halon gas systems.

● Emergency power shutoff and backup batteries, which must be maintained in operational condition.

● Properly designed, maintained, and operated air-conditioning systems.

● Motion detector alarms that detect physical intrusion.

Another example of physical controls is the need to protect against theft of mobile computers. Such protection is important not only because of the loss of the computer but also because of loss of data. Several interesting protection devices are offered by *targus.com.* For more details, see Panko (2004).

ACCESS CONTROL. Access control is the restriction of unauthorized user access to a portion of a computer system or to the entire system. It is the major defense line against unauthorized insiders as well as outsiders. To gain access, a user must first be *authorized.* Then, when the user attempts to gain access, he or she must be *authenticated.*

Access to a computer system basically consists of three steps: (1) physical access to a terminal, (2) access to the system, and (3) access to specific commands, transactions, privileges, programs, and data within the system. Access control software is commercially available for large mainframes, personal computers, local area networks, mobile devices, and dial-in communications networks. Access control to *networks* is executed through firewalls and will be discussed later.

Access procedures match every valid user with a *unique user-identifier (UID).* They also provide an authentication method to verify that users requesting access to the computer system are really who they claim to be. User identification can be accomplished when the following identifies each user:

● Something only the user *knows,* such as a password.

● Something only the user *has,* for example, a smart card or a token.

● Something only the user *is,* such as a signature, voice, fingerprint, or retinal (eye) scan. It is implemented via *biometric controls,* which can be physiological or behavioral (see Alga, 2002) and whose cost is relativly very small.

Biometric Controls. A **biometric control** is an automated method of verifying the identity of a person, based on physiological or behavioral characteristics. Most biometric systems match some personal characteristic of a person against a pre-stored profile (in a template). A comparison of the characteristics against the pre-stored template produces a "matching score," which indicates how closely the actual and pre-stored data match. The process is shown in Figure 15.6 (page 658). The most common biometrics are the following:

● ***Photo of face.*** The computer takes a picture of your face and matches it with a prestored picture. In 2002, this method was successful in correctly identifying users except in cases of identical twins.

● ***Fingerprints.*** Each time a user wants access, a fingerprint (finger scan) is matched against a template containing the authorized person's fingerprint to identify him or her. Note that in 2001 Microsoft introduced a software program, now a part of Windows, that allows users to use Sony's fingerprint recognition device. Computer manufacturers started shipping laptops secured

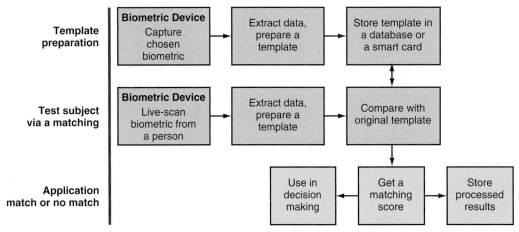

FIGURE 15.6 How a biometric system works. (*Source:* Drawn by E. Turban.)

by fingerprint-scanning touchpads in 2004. These devices reject unauthorized access (see *synaptics.com*).

- **Hand geometry.** This biometric is similar to fingerprints except that the verifier uses a television-like camera to take a picture of the user's hand. Certain characteristics of the hand (e.g., finger length and thickness) are electronically compared against the information stored in the computer.
- **Iris scan.** This technology uses the colored portion of the eye to identify individuals (see *iriscan.com*). It is a noninvasive system that takes a photo of the eye and analyzes it and is a very accurate method.
- **Retinal scan.** A match is attempted between the pattern of the blood vessels in the back-of-the-eye retina that is being scanned and a prestored picture of the retina.
- **Voice scan.** A match is attempted between the user's voice and the voice pattern stored on templates.
- **Signature.** Signatures are matched against the prestored authentic signature. This method can supplement a photo-card ID system.
- **Keystroke dynamics.** A match of the person's keyboard pressure and speed is made against prestored information.

Several other methods, such as *facial thermography,* exist.

Biometric controls are now integrated into many e-business hardware and software products. For an overview and comparison of technologies, see Jain et al. (1999 and 2000) and Alga (2002). Biometric controls do have some limitations: they are not accurate in certain cases, and some people see them as an invasion of privacy (see Caulfield, 2002).

DATA SECURITY CONTROLS.   Data security is concerned with protecting data from accidental or intentional disclosure to unauthorized persons, or from unauthorized modification or destruction. Data security functions are implemented through operating systems, security access control programs, database/data communications products, recommended backup/recovery procedures, application programs, and external control procedures. Data security must address the following issues: confidentiality of data, access control, critical nature of data, and integrity of data.

Two basic principles should be reflected in data security.

- *Minimal privilege.* Only the information a user needs to carry out an assigned task should be made available to him or her. This principle is also referred to as "need to know."
- *Minimal exposure.* Once a user gains access to sensitive information, he or she has the responsibility of protecting it by making sure only people whose duties require it obtain knowledge of this information while it is processed, stored, or in transit.

Data integrity is the condition that exists as long as accidental or intentional destruction, alteration, or loss of data *does not* occur. It is the preservation of data for their intended use.

COMMUNICATIONS AND NETWORK CONTROLS. Network protection is becoming extremely important as the use of the Internet, intranets, and electronic commerce increases. We will discuss this topic in more detail in Section 15.5.

ADMINISTRATIVE CONTROLS. While the previously discussed general controls were technical in nature, administrative controls deal with issuing guidelines and monitoring compliance with the guidelines. Representative examples of such controls are shown in Table 15.5.

OTHER GENERAL CONTROLS. Several other types of controls are considered general. Representative examples include the following:

Programming Controls. Errors in programming may result in costly problems. Causes include the use of incorrect algorithms or programming instructions, carelessness, inadequate testing and configuration management, or lax security. Controls include training, establishing standards for testing and configuration management, and enforcing documentation standards.

Documentation Controls. Manuals are often a source of problems because they are difficult to interpret or may be out of date. Accurate writing, standardization updating, and testing are examples of appropriate documentation controls. Intelligent agents can be used to prevent documentation problems.

System Development Controls. System development controls ensure that a system is developed according to established policies and procedures. Conformity

---

TABLE 15.5 Representative Administrative Controls

- Appropriately selecting, training, and supervising employees, especially in accounting and information systems
- Fostering company loyalty
- Immediately revoking access privileges of dismissed, resigned, or transferred employees
- Requiring periodic modification of access controls (such as passwords)
- Developing programming and documentation standards (to make auditing easier and to use the standards as guides for employees)
- Insisting on security bonds or malfeasance insurance for key employees
- Instituting separation of duties, namely dividing sensitive computer duties among as many employees as economically feasible in order to decrease the chance of intentional or unintentional damage
- Holding periodic random audits of the system

with budget, timing, security measures, and quality and documentation require-ments must be maintained.

Application Controls

General controls are intended to protect the computing facilities and provide security for hardware, software, data, and networks regardless of the specific application. However, general controls do not protect the *content* of each specific application. Therefore, controls are frequently built into the applications (that is, they are part of the software) and are usually written as validation rules. They can be classified into three major categories: *input controls, processing controls,* and *output controls.* Multiple types of application controls can be used, and management should decide on the appropriate mix of controls.

INPUT CONTROLS. Input controls are designed to prevent data alteration or loss. Data are checked for accuracy, completeness, and consistency. Input controls are very important; they prevent the GIGO (garbage-in, garbage-out) situation.

Four examples of input controls are:

1. *Completeness.* Items should be of a specific length (e.g., nine digits for a Social Security number). Addresses should include a street, city, state, and Zip code.
2. *Format.* Formats should be in standard form. For example, sequences must be preserved (e.g., Zip code comes after an address).
3. *Range.* Only data within a specified range are acceptable. For example, Zip code ranges between 00000 to 99999; the age of a person cannot be larger than, say, 120; and hourly wages at the firm do not exceed $50.
4. *Consistency.* Data collected from two or more sources need to be matched. For example, in medical history data, males cannot be pregnant.

PROCESSING CONTROLS. Processing controls ensure that data are complete, valid, and accurate when being processed and that programs have been prop-erly executed. These programs allow only authorized users to access certain pro-grams or facilities and monitor the computer's use by individuals.

OUTPUT CONTROLS. Output controls ensure that the results of computer pro-cessing are accurate, valid, complete, and consistent. By studying the nature of common output errors and the causes of such errors, security and audit staff can evaluate possible controls to deal with problems. Also, output controls ensure that outputs are sent only to authorized personnel.

15.5 SECURING THE WEB, INTRANETS, AND WIRELESS NETWORKS

Some of the incidents described in Section 15.3 point to the vulnerability of the Internet and Web sites (see Sivasailam et al., 2002). As a matter of fact, the more networked the world becomes, the more security problems we may have. Security is a race between "lock makers" and "lock pickers." Unless the lock makers have the upper hand, the future of the Internet's credibility and of e-business is in danger.

Over the Internet, messages are sent from one computer to another (rather than from one network to the other). This makes the network difficult to pro-tect, since at many points people can tap into the network and the users may never know that a breach had occurred. An example of the magnitude of the problem is the announcement in July 2004 that hackers can find your account number and password if you use the Explorer Internet browser. For details, see *ecommercetimes.com* (news item, June 28, 2004) and *cert.org*. For a list of techniques attackers can use to compromise Web applications, in addition to what was described in Section 15.3, see Online File W15.9. The table covers the major security measures of the Internet. Security issues regarding e-business are discussed in Chapters 4 and 5.

McConnell (2002) divides Internet security measures into three layers: *border security* (access), *authentication,* and *authorization.* Details of these layers are shown in Figure 15.7. Several of these are discussed in some detail in the remainder of this chapter. For more details and other measures, see Panko (2004). Some commercial products include security measures for all three levels—all in one product (e.g., WebShield from McAfee, and Firewall/VPN Appliance from Symantec; see Slewe and Hoogenboom, 2004).

Many security methods and products are available to protect the Web. We briefly describe the major ones in the following sections.

Border Security

The major objective of border security is access control, as seen in Figure 15.7. Several tools are available. First we consider firewalls.

FIREWALLS. Hacking is a growing phenomenon. Even the Pentagon's system, considered a very secure system, experiences more than 250,000 hacker infiltrations per year, many of which are undetected (*Los Angeles Times,* 1998). It is believed that hacking costs U.S. industry several billion dollars each year. Hacking is such a popular activity that over 80,000 Web sites are dedicated to it. Firewalls provide the most cost-effective solution against hacking (see Fadia, 2002).

A **firewall** is a system, or group of systems, that enforces an access-control policy between two networks. It is commonly used as a barrier between a secure corporate intranet or other internal networks and the Internet, which is assumed to be unsecured.

Firewalls are used to implement access-control policies by 98 percent of U.S. corporations (Gordon et al., 2004). The firewall follows strict guidelines that either permit or block traffic; therefore, a successful firewall is designed with clear and specific rules about what can pass through. Several firewalls may exist in one information system.

Firewalls are also used as a place to store public information. While visitors may be blocked from entering the company networks, they can obtain information about products and services, download files and bug-fixes, and so forth.

1st layer	**2nd layer**	**3rd layer**
Border security	Authentication	Authorization
Network layer security	**Proof of identity**	**Permissions based on identity**
• Virus scanning	• User name/password	• User/group permissions
• Firewalls	• Password synchronization	• Enterprise directories
• Intrusion	• Public key	• Enterprise user administration
• Virtual private networking	• Tokens	• Rules-based access control
• Denial-of-service protection	• Biometrics	
	• Single sign-on	

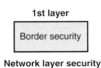

FIGURE 15.7 Three layers of Internet security measures. (*Source:* McConnell, 2002.)

TABLE 15.6 Protecting Against Viruses	
Possible Mode of Entrance	**Countermeasure**
● Viruses pass through firewalls undetected (from the Internet).	● User must screen all downloaded programs and documents before use.
● Virus may be resident on networked server; all users are at risk.	● Run virus scan daily; do comprehensive backup to restore data; maintain audit trail.
● Infected floppy; local server system at risk; files shared or put on server can spread virus.	● Use virus checker to screen floppies locally.
● Mobile or remote users exchange or update large amounts of data; risk of infection is greater.	● Scan files before upload or after download; make frequent backups.
● Virus already detected.	● Use a clean starter disk or recovery disk.

Source: Compiled from Nance (1996, updated 2003), p. 171.

Useful as they are, firewalls do not stop viruses that may be lurking in networks. Viruses can pass through the firewalls, usually hidden in an e-mail attachment. For more on firewalls, see Panko (2004).

VIRUS CONTROLS. Many viruses exist (over 120,000 known in 2004), and the number is growing by 30 percent a year according to the International Computer Security Association (reported by *statonline*, 2003). So the question is, What can organizations do to protect themselves against viruses? Some solutions against virus penetrations are provided in Zenkin (2001) and in Table 15.6. The most common solution used by over 99 percent of all U.S. companies (Gordon et al., 2004) is to use antivirus software (e.g., from *symantec.com*). However, antivirus software provides protection against viruses only after they have attacked someone and their properties are known. New viruses are difficult to detect in their first attack.

The best protection against viruses is to have a comprehensive plan such as shown in *A Closer Look 15.3.*

INTRUSION DETECTING. Because protection against denial of service (see the opening vignette) is difficult, the sooner one can detect an usual activity, the better. Therefore, it is worthwhile to place an *intrusion detecting* device near the entrance point of the Internet to the intranet (close to a firewall). The objective is early detection, and this can be done by several devices (e.g., Caddx from Caddx Controls, and IDS from Cisco). Intrusion detecting is done by different tools, such as statistical analysis or neural networks. Biermann et al. (2001) provide a comparison of 10 different methods and discuss which methods are better at detecting different types of intrusions. For details see *dshield.org, sans.org,* and *acm.org.*

PROTECTING AGAINST DENIAL OF SERVICE ATTACKS. After the February 6, 2000, DoS attack, the industry started to find solutions. A special task force of experts was formed at the Internet Engineering Task Force (IETF); it included vendors and companies that were attacked. The IETF group developed procedures on what to do in the event of such attack. One approach suggested was tracking the attacker in real time (e.g., by tracking the flow of data packets through the Net).

Automated Attack Traceback. Investigation to find attackers can be done manually or can be automated. **Attack traceback** refers to a system that would identify the person responsible for a virus, DoS, or other attacks. For

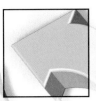

A CLOSER LOOK
15.3 HOW TO MINIMIZE THE DAMAGE FROM VIRUSES

To minimize the damage from viruses, take the following preventive actions:

1. Install a good antivirus program. These are also known as *gateway virus scanners* (e.g., Norton AntiVirus, McAfee VirusScan).
2. Scan the hard drive for viruses at least weekly.
3. Write-protect your floppy disks and scan them before using them.
4. Write-protect your program disks.
5. Back up data fully and frequently.
6. Don't trust outside PCs.
7. Virus scan before "laplinking" or synchronizing files.
8. Develop an antivirus policy.
9. Identify the areas of risk in case of virus attack. These are:
   a. Direct losses (e.g., time spent to restore systems)
   b. Losses your customers and suppliers suffer when your system is down
   c. Losses to a third party to which your company had passed on a virus, possibly due to your employees' negligence
10. Minimize losses by the following measures:
    a. Install strict employee guidelines dealing with e-mail viruses. Use an e-mail service that scans the incoming e-mails (e.g., *yahoomail*).
    b. Use an Internet service provider to handle virus detection and control. This way you get the latest technology, make it more difficult for insiders to perform crimes, and may transfer the risk to the service provider.
    c. Have contracts that will protect you from a legal action by your customers/suppliers who suffer damage when your systems are damaged (called a "force majeure" clause).
    d. Instruct your employees on how to scan all outgoing e-mails to your business partners.
11. The SANS Institute (*sans.org*) is an IT cooperative research and education organization for system administrators and security professionals; it has more than 100,000 members. SANS recommends the following guidelines for action during virus attacks:
    a. *Preparation.* Establish policy, design a form to be filed when a virus is suspected (or known), and develop outside relationships.
    b. *Identification.* Collect evidence of attack, analyze it, notify officals (e.g., at *cert.org*).
    c. *Containment.* Back up the system to capture evidence, change passwords, determine the risk of continuing operations.
    d. *Eradication.* Determine and remove the cause, and improve the defense.
    e. *Recovery.* Restore and validate the system.
    f. *Follow up.* Write a follow-up report detailing lessons learned.
12. Get information and sometimes free software at the following sites:

antivirus.com	*cert.org*	*pgp.com*
symantec.com	*ncsa.com*	*rsa.com*
mcafee.com	*iss.net*	*tis.com*

example, it would identify the computer host that is the source of the attack. Attackers usually try to hide their identity. The automatic traceback attempts to circumvent the methods used by attackers (such as zombies, discussed earlier, and using a false IP address; see Panko, 2004). According to Lee and Shields (2002), however, the use of automatic attack traceback programs may raise legal issues (e.g., what data you can legally track).

VIRTUAL PRIVATE NETWORKING (VPN). The last major method of border security described here is a virtual private network (VPN). A VPN uses the Internet to carry information within a company that has multiple sites and among known business partners, but it increases the security of the Internet by using a combination of encryption, authentication, and access control. It replaces the traditional private leased line and/or remote access server (RAS) that provide

Technology Guides are located at the book's Web site.

direct communication to a company's LAN (see Technology Guide 4). According to Prometheum Technologies (2003), costs can be reduced by up to 50 percent by using the VPN, which can also be used by remote workers (here the savings can reach 60–80 percent). Confidentiality and integrity are assured by the use of protocol tunneling for the encryption (McKinley 2003). For further details on VPNs, see Garfinkel (2002), Fadia (2002), and McKinley (2003).

Authentication

As applied to the Internet, an *authentication* system guards against unauthorized dial-in attempts. Many companies use an access protection strategy that requires authorized users to dial in with a preassigned personal identification number (PIN). This strategy is usually enhanced by a unique and frequently changing password. A communications access control system authenticates the user's PIN and password. Some security systems proceed one step further, accepting calls only from designated telephone numbers. Access controls also include biometrics.

HOW AUTHENTICATION WORKS. The major objective of authentication is the proof of identity (see Figure 15.7, page 661). The attempt here is to identify the legitimate user and determine the action he or she is allowed to perform, and also to find those posing as others. Such programs also can be combined with authorization, to limit the actions of people to what they are authorized to do with the computer once their identification has been authenticated.

Authentication systems have five key elements (Smith, 2002): (1) a person (or a group) to be authenticated; (2) a distinguishing characteristic that differentiates the person (group) from others; (3) a proprietor responsible for the system being used; (4) an authentication mechanism; and (5) an access control mechanism for limiting the actions that can be performed by the authenticated person (group).

A stronger system is *two-factor-authentication,* which combines something one knows (password, answer to a query) with something one has (tokens, biometrics). An access card is an example of a passive token, carried to enter into certain rooms or to gain access to a network. *Active tokens* are electronic devices that can generate a one-time password after being activated with a PIN. Note that public key systems (PKI, see Panko, 2004) include an authentication feature.

Authorization

Authorization refers to permission issued to individuals or groups to do certain activities with a computer, usually based on verified identity. The security system, once it authenticates the user, must make sure that the user operates within his or her authorized activities. This is usually done by monitoring user activities and comparing them to the list of authorized ones.

Other Methods of Protection

Other methods of protecting the Web and intranets include the following.

ENCRYPTION. **Encryption** encodes regular digitized text into unreadable scrambled text or numbers, which are decoded upon receipt. Encryption accomplishes three purposes: (1) identification (helps identify legitimate senders and receivers), (2) control (prevents changing a transaction or message), and (3) privacy (impedes eavesdropping). Encryption is used extensively in e-commerce for protecting payments and for privacy.

A widely accepted encryption algorithm is the Data Encryption Standard (DES), produced by the U.S. National Bureau of Standards. Many software products also are available for encryption. *Traffic padding* can further enhance encryption. Here a computer generates random data that are intermingled with real data, making it virtually impossible for an intruder to identify the true data.

To ensure secure transactions on the Internet, VeriSign and VISA developed encrypted digital certification systems for credit cards. These systems allow customers to make purchases on the Internet without giving their credit card number. Cardholders create a digital version of their credit card, called *virtual credit card* (see Chapter 4), VeriSign confirms validity of the buyer's credit card, and then it issues a certificate to that effect. Even the merchants do not see the credit card number. For further discussion of encryption, see *sra.co* and *verisign.com*, Young (2003), and Panko (2004).

TROUBLESHOOTING.   A popular defense of local area networks (LANs) is troubleshooting. For example, a *cable tester* can find almost any fault that can occur with LAN cabling. Another protection can be provided by *protocol analyzers,* which allow the user to inspect the contents of information packets as they travel through the network. Recent analyzers use *expert systems,* which interpret the volume of data collected by the analyzers. Some companies offer integrated LAN troubleshooting (a tester and an intelligent analyzer).

PAYLOAD SECURITY.   *Payload security* involves encryption or other manipulation of data being sent over networks. *Payload* refers to the contents of messages and communication services among dispersed users. An example of payload security is Pretty Good Privacy (PGP), which permits users to inexpensively create and encrypt a message. (See *pgp.com* for free software.)

HONEYNETS.   Companies can trap hackers by watching what the hackers are doing. These traps are referred to as **honeypots;** they are traps designed to work like real systems but to attract hackers. A network of honeypots is called a **honeynet.**

FIGHTING HACKERS.   Secure Networks (*snc-net.com*) developed a product that is essentially a honeynet, a decoy network within network. The idea is to lure the hackers into the decoy to find what tools they use and detect them as early as possible. For details, see Piazza (2001) and *honeynet.org.*

Securing Your PC   Your PC at home is connected to the Internet and needs to be protected (Luhn and Spanbauer, 2002). Therefore, solutions such as antivirus software (e.g., Norton Antivirus 2002) and a personal firewall are essential. (You can get a free Internet connection firewall with Microsoft Windows or pay $30–$50 for products such as McAfee Firewall.) For an overview see Sullivan (2003).

If you use a gateway or router at home, you need to protect it as well, if it does not have built-in protection. You need protection against stealthware as well. **Stealthware** refers to hidden programs that come with free software you download. These programs track your surfing activities, reporting them to a marketing server. Programs such as Pest Control (*pestcontrol.com*) and Spy Blocker (*spyblocker-software.com*) can help. Finally you need an antispam tool (e.g., SpamKiller, *spamkiller.com*).

All of the tools just mentioned can be combined in suites (e.g., Internet Security from McAFee or Symantec).

Securing Wireless Networks

Wireless networks are more difficult to protect than wireline ones. While many of the risks of desktop Internet-based commerce will pervade m-commerce, m-commerce itself presents new risks. This topic was discussed in Chapter 5. In addition, lately there is recognition that malicious code may penetrate wireless networks. Such a code has the ability to undermine controls such as authentication and encryption (Ghosh and Swaminatha, 2001 and Biery and Hager, 2001). The first viruses in cell phones were discovered in summer 2004. For a comprehensive commercial suite to protect wireless networks, see MebiusGuard at *symbal.com.*

Summary

It should be clear from this chapter how important it is for organizations to secure networks. What protective measures are actually employed? What security technologies are used the most? According to the CSI/FBI report (Richardson, 2003), 99 percent of all companies use antivirus software, 92 percent use access

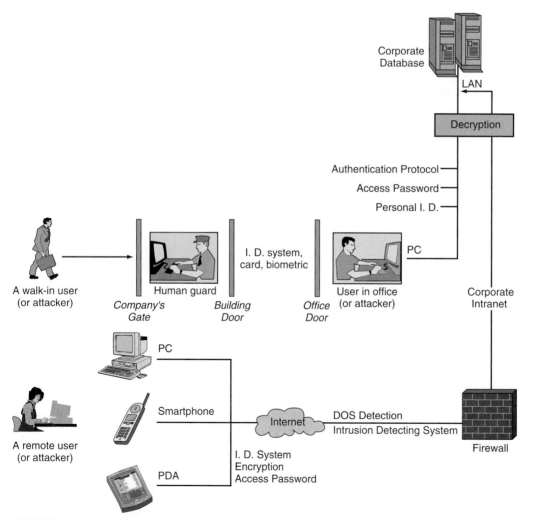

FIGURE 15.8 Defense mechanisms: where they are located. (*Source:* Drawn by E. Turban.)

control, 98 percent use firewalls, 91 percent use physical security, 73 percent use intrusion detection, 69 percent use encrypted files, 58 percent use encrypted login, 47 percent use reusable passwords, and only 11 percent use biometrics. While some measures are commonly used, others, especially new ones such as biometrics, are not yet in regular use. (However, the use of biometrics is now rapidly increasing.) A schematic view of all major defense mechanisms, which protect against attackers of all types, is shown in Figure 15.8 (page 666).

15.6 BUSINESS CONTINUITY AND DISASTER RECOVERY PLANNING

Disasters may occur without warning. According to Strassman (1997), the best defense is to be prepared. Therefore, an important element in any security system is the **business continuity plan,** also known as the **disaster recovery plan.** Such a plan outlines the process by which businesses should recover from a major disaster. Destruction of all (or most) of the computing facilities can cause significant damage. Therefore, it is difficult for many organizations to obtain insurance for their computers and information systems without showing a satisfactory disaster prevention and recovery plan. It is a simple concept that advance crisis planning can help minimize losses (Gerber and Feldman, 2002). The comprehensiveness of a business recovery plan is shown in Figure 15.9.

Business Continuity Planning

Disaster recovery is the chain of events linking the business continuity plan to protection and to recovery. The following are some key thoughts about the process:

● The purpose of a business continuity plan is to keep the business running after a disaster occurs. Both the ISD and line management should be involved in preparation of the plan. Each function in the business should have a valid recovery capability plan.

● Recovery planning is part of *asset protection.* Every organization should assign responsibility to management to identify and protect assets within their spheres of functional control.

● Planning should focus first on recovery from a total loss of all capabilities.

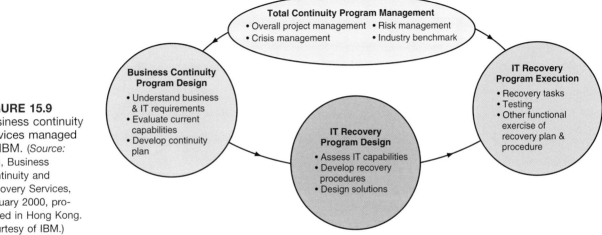

FIGURE 15.9
Business continuity services managed by IBM. (*Source:* IBM, Business Continuity and Recovery Services, January 2000, produced in Hong Kong. Courtesy of IBM.)

- Proof of capability usually involves some kind of what-if analysis that shows that the recovery plan is current (see Lam, 2002).
- All critical applications must be identified and their recovery procedures addressed in the plan.
- The plan should be written so that it will be effective in case of disaster, not just in order to satisfy the auditors.
- The plan should be kept in a safe place; copies should be given to all key managers, or it should be available on the intranet. The plan should be audited periodically.

For a methodology of how to conduct business continuity planning, see *A Closer Look 15.4.* Other methodologies can be found in Volonino and Robinson (2004), Rothstein (2002), and Luftman et al. (2004).

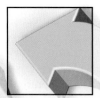

A CLOSER LOOK
15.4 HOW TO CONDUCT BUSINESS CONTINUITY PLANNING

There are many suggestions of how to conduct business continuity planning (BCP). Lam (2002) suggests an 8-step cyclical process shown in the figure below.

In conducting BCP one should devise a policy which is central to all steps in the process. One also must test the plan on a worst-case scenario, for each potential disaster (e.g., system failure, information hacking, terrorist attack). Disruptions are analyzed for their impact on technology, information, and people.

Finally, it is important to recognize the potential pitfalls of BCP. These include:

- An incomplete BCP (may not cover all aspects).
- An inadequate or ineffective BCP (unable to provide remedy).
- An impractical BCP (e.g., does not have enough time and money).

- Overkill BCP (usually time consuming and costly).
- Uncommunicated BCP (people do not know where to find it or do not know its details).
- Lacking defined process (not clearly defined, chain of needed events not clear).
- Untested (may look good on paper, but no one knows, since it was never tested).
- Uncoordinated (it is not a team's work, or the team is not coordinated).
- Out of date (it was good long ago, but what about today?).
- Lacking in recovery thinking (no one thinks from A to Z about how to do it).

For details see Lam (2002).

Business continuity plan.
(*Source:* Lam (2002), Fig. 1.)

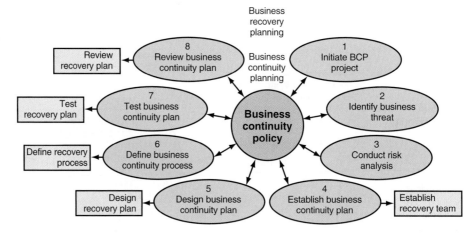

Disaster recovery planning can be very complex, and it may take several months to complete. Using special software, the planning job can be expedited.

Backup Arrangements

One of the most logical ways to deal with loss of data is to *back them up*. A business continuity plan includes backup arrangements. Organizations should make copies of all important files and keep them separately. In addition to backing up data, organizations should be interested in quick recovery. Also, as part of business continuity one can back up an entire computer or data center. Let's look at these two arrangements.

BACKING UP DATA FILES.   While everyone knows how important it is to back up data files, many neglect to do so because the process is cumbersome and time consuming. Several programs make this process easier, and some restore data as well (e.g., Ontrack.com provides EasyRecovery and File repair, 10mega.com provides QuickSync, and Officerecovery.com provides for office recovery). For tips how to avoid data loss by backing up data files, see Spector (2002). Backup arrangements may also include the use of network attached storage (NAS) and storage area networks (SANs) (see Technology Guide 4 and Hunton, 2002).

BACKING UP COMPUTER CENTERS.   As preparation for a major disaster, such as in the 9/11 case, it is often necessary for an organization to have a *backup location.* External *hot-site* vendors provide access to a fully configured backup data center.

To appreciate the usefulness of a hot-site arrangement, consider the following example: On the evening of October 17, 1989, when a major earthquake hit San Francisco, Charles Schwab and Company was ready. Within a few minutes, the company's disaster plan was activated. Programmers, engineers, and backup computer tapes of October 17 transactions were flown on a chartered jet to Carlstadt, New Jersey. There, Comdisco Disaster Recovery Service provided a hot site. The next morning, the company resumed normal operations. Montgomery Securities, on the other hand, had no backup recovery arrangement. On October 18, the day after the quake, the traders had to use telephones rather than computers to execute trades. Montgomery lost revenues of about $500,000 in one day.

A less costly alternative arrangement is external *cold-site* vendors that provide empty office space with special flooring, ventilation, and wiring. In an emergency, the stricken company moves its own (or leased) computers to the site.

One company that did its disaster planning right is Empire Blue Cross and Blue Shield, as explained in *IT at Work 15.2* (pages 670–671).

Physical computer security is an integral part of a total security system. Cray Research, a leading manufacturer of supercomputers (now a subsidiary of Silicone Graphics, Inc.), has installed a corporate security plan, under which the corporate computers are automatically monitored and centrally controlled. *Graphic displays* show both normal status and disturbances. All the controlled devices are represented as icons on floor-plan graphics. These icons can change colors (e.g., green means normal, red signifies a problem). The icons can flash as well. Corrective-action messages are displayed whenever appropriate. The alarm system includes over 1,000 alarms. Operators can be alerted, even at remote locations, in less than one second.

Of special interest is disaster planning for Web-based systems, as shown in an example in Online File W15.10. For some interesting methods of recovery, see the special issue of *Computers and Security* (2000). Finally, according to Brassil (2003), mobile computing and other innovations are changing the business

IT at Work 15.2
9/11 DISASTER RECOVERY AT EMPIRE BLUE CROSS/BLUE SHIELD

Empire Blue Cross and Blue Shield (*empireblue.com*) provides health insurance coverage for 4.7 million people in the northeastern United States. It is a regional arm of the Blue Cross/Blue Shield Association (*bcbs.com*). On September 11, 2001, the company occupied an entire floor of the World Trade Center (WTC). Information assets there included the e-business development center as well as the enterprise network of 250 servers and a major Web-enabled call center. Tragically, nine employees and two consultants lost their lives in the terrorist attack. But the company's operations were not interrupted. Let's see why.

The company had built redundancy into all its applications and had moved much of its business to Internet technology for connecting workforce, clients, and partners. Forty applications are available on its corporate intranet; Web-enabled call centers handle 50,000 calls each day; and Web-based applications connect the huge system of hospitals and health-care providers.

Immediately after the terrorist attack, a senior server specialist in Albany, NY, made a quick decision to switch the employee profiles to the Albany location. This action saved the company days of downtime and the need to rebuild the profiles by hand. As employees moved to temporary offices, they were able to log on as if they were sitting at their desks in the WTC.

The disaster recovery protocol, which is shown in the figure on the next page, worked without a glitch. Calls to the customer support center in the WTC were rerouted to centers in Albany and on Long Island; customers' access to the Web site experienced no interruptions; and 150 servers, 500 laptops, and 500 workstations were ordered within an hour of the attack, to replace the equipment lost at the WTC. In off-facility sites, the main data center was not affected, and the backup tapes allowed full restoration of data. The network restructured automatically when the private enterprise network was destroyed, and all necessary information needed at the main off-site data center was rerouted, bypassing the WTC.

Besides building the redundancy into the system, the company had also tested different disaster scenarios frequently, making sure everything worked. As a result, the company and the technoloy were prepared to deal with the disaster. Everything was backed up, so once the servers were rebuilt, all information was available, and all applications were functioning within days thanks to a 300-member IT team working around the clock. Three days after the attack, a new VPN was running, enabling employees to work at home.

Since that experience, Empire has made even more use of Internet technology to connect the staff that is dispersed

(continues on page 671)

continuity industry by quickly reaching a large number of people, wherever they are, and by the ability of mobile devices to help in quick restoration of service.

DISASTER AVOIDANCE.   **Disaster avoidance** is an approach oriented toward *prevention.* The idea is to minimize the chance of avoidable disasters (such as fire or other human-caused threats). For example, many companies use a device called *uninterrupted power supply (UPS),* which provides power in case of a power outage.

15.7   IMPLEMENTING SECURITY: AUDITING AND RISK MANAGEMENT

Implementing controls in an organization can be a very complicated task, particularly in large, decentralized companies where administrative controls may be difficult to enforce. Of the many issues involved in implementing controls, three are described here: auditing information systems, risk analysis, and IT security trends, including use of advanced intelligent systems.

Controls are established to ensure that information systems work properly. Controls can be installed in the original system, or they can be added once a

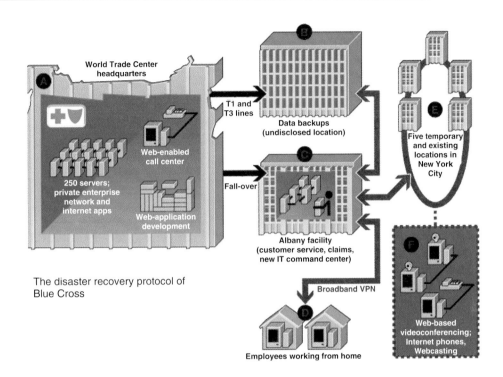

World Trade Center headquarters

T1 and T3 lines

Web-enabled call center

250 servers; private enterprise network and internet apps

Web-application development

Data backups (undisclosed location)

Fall-over

Five temporary and existing locations in New York City

Albany facility (customer service, claims, new IT command center)

The disaster recovery protocol of Blue Cross

Broadband VPN

Employees working from home

Web-based videoconferencing; Internet phones, Webcasting

among five temporary offices in Manhattan, and it does more business by Internet-based videoconferencing, Webcasting, and IP-based phones.

Source: Compiled from Levin (2002).

For Further Exploration: Explore the usefulness of Internet technology for disaster planning. What is its advantage over older technology? Why are people the most important part when a disaster strikes?

system is in operation. Installing controls is necessary but not sufficient. It is also necessary to answer questions such as the following: Are controls installed as intended? Are they effective? Are they working reliably? Did any breach of security occur? If so, what actions are required to prevent reoccurrence? These questions need to be answered by independent and unbiased observers. Such observers perform the information system *auditing* task (e.g., see Stone and Marotta, 2003).

Auditing Information Systems

An **audit** is an important part of any control system. In an organizational setting, it is usually referred to as a periodical *examination and check* of financial and accounting records and procedures. Specially trained professionals execute an audit. In the information system environment, auditing can be viewed as an additional layer of controls or safeguards. Auditing is considered as a deterrent to criminal actions (Wells, 2002), especially for insiders. According to Gordon et al. (2004), 82 percent of U.S. corporations conduct security audits.

TYPES OF AUDITORS AND AUDITS. There are two types of auditors (and audits): internal and external. An *internal auditor* is usually a corporate employee who is not a member of the ISD.

An *external auditor* is a corporate outsider. This type of auditor reviews the findings of the internal audit and the inputs, processing, and outputs of information systems. The external audit of information systems used to be a part of the overall external auditing performed by a certified public accounting (CPA) firm, but now it is frequently performed by *certified information systems auditors* (CISAs) (see *isaca.org*).

IT auditing can be very broad, so only its essentials are presented here. Auditing looks at all potential hazards and controls in information systems. It focuses attention on topics such as new systems development, operations and maintenance, data integrity, software application, security and privacy, disaster planning and recovery, purchasing, budgets and expenditures, chargebacks, vendor management, documentation, insurance and bonding, training, cost control, and productivity. Several guidelines are available to assist auditors in their jobs. *SAS No. 55* is a comprehensive guide provided by the American Institute of Certified Public Accountants and by *isaca.org*. Also, guidelines are available from the Institute of Internal Auditors, Orlando, Florida. (See Frownfelter-Lohrke and Hunton, 2002, for a discussion of new directions in IT auditing.)

Auditors attempt to answer questions such as these:

Are there sufficient controls in the system? Which areas are not covered by controls?

Which controls are not necessary?

Are the controls implemented properly?

Are the controls effective? That is, do they check the output of the system?

Is there a clear separation of duties of employees?

Are there procedures to ensure compliance with the controls?

Are there procedures to ensure reporting and corrective actions in case of violations of controls?

Other items that IT auditors may check include: the data security policies and plans, the business continuity plan (Von-Roessing, 2002), the availability of a strategic information plan, what the company is doing to ensure compliance with security rules, the responsibilities of IT security, the measurement of success of the organization's IT security scheme, the existence of a security awareness program, and the security incidents reporting system.

Two types of audits are used to answer these questions. The *operational audit* determines whether the ISD is working properly. The *compliance audit* determines whether controls have been implemented properly and are adequate. In addition, auditing is geared specifically to general controls and to application controls (see Sayana, 2002). For details on how auditing is executed, see Online File W15.11.

AUDITING WEB SYSTEMS AND E-COMMERCE. According to Morgan and Wong (1999), auditing a Web site is a good preventive measure to manage the legal risk. Legal risk is important in any IT system, but in Web systems it is even more important due to the content of the site, which may offend people or be in violation of copyright laws or other regulations (e.g., privacy protection). Auditing EC is also more complex since in addition to the Web site one needs to audit order taking, order fulfillment, and all support systems (see Blanco, 2002). For more about IT auditing see Woda (2002).

Security Assessment. Security assessment is part of risk management; a check of security typically is done as part of a financial audit. One way to assess your company's security is to compare its status to standards. A most common standard is BS7799 and its modification ISO17799 (used for certification). ISO17799 recognized the differences in security needs of organizations due to their size, dependency on networks, and so forth.

Tse (2004) proposed an improvement of the above standards by assimilating all tasks from BS7799, as key process areas, into five levels, like the *capability maturing model* (CMM). This model can help organizations assess their own security practices as well as those of their trading partners.

An example of risk assessment is the case of Allstate, a major U.S. insurance company (see "COBIT and IT Governance Case Study: Allstate," at *itgi.org*, 2004). The case connects IT auditing, controls, investment decisions, and collaboration. The detailed process of security and risk assessment is described by Volonino and Robinson (2004).

Risk Management and Cost-Benefit Analysis

It is usually not economical to prepare protection against every possible threat. Therefore, an IT security program must provide a process for assessing threats and deciding which ones to prepare for and which ones to ignore or provide reduced protection against. The CSI/FBI 2004 survey (Gordon et al., 2004) revealed that most organizations conduct some form of economic evaluation of their security expenditure (mostly ROI). Installation of control measures is based on a balance between the cost of controls and the need to reduce or eliminate threats. Such analysis is basically a **risk-management** approach, which helps identify threats and selects cost-effective security measures (see Hiles, 2002, Volonino and Robinson (2004), and Minicase 2).

Major activities in the risk-management process can be applied to existing systems as well as to systems under development. These are summarized in Figure 15.10 (page 674). A more detailed structure for a strategic risk management plan suggested by Doughty (2002) is provided in Online File W15.12.

RISK-MANAGEMENT ANALYSIS. Risk-management analysis can be enhanced by the use of DSS software packages. A simplified computation is shown here:

$$\text{Expected loss} = P_1 \times P_2 \times L$$

where:

P_1 = probability of attack (estimate, based on judgment)
P_2 = probability of attack being successful (estimate, based on judgment)
L = loss occurring if attack is successful

Example:

$$P_1 = .02, \ P_2 = .10, \ L = \$1,000,000$$

Then, expected loss from this particular attack is:

$$P_1 \times P_2 \times L = 0.02 \times 0.1 \times \$1,000,000 = \$2,000$$

The amount of loss may depend on the duration of a system being out of operation. Therefore, some add duration to the analysis (e.g., see Volonino and Robinson, 2004).

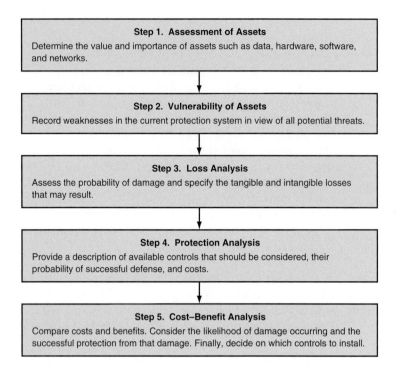

FIGURE 15.10 The risk management process.

The expected loss can then be compared with the cost of preventing it. The value of software programs lies not only in their ability to execute complex computations, but also in their ability to provide a structured, systematic framework for ranking both threats and controls.

HOW MUCH TO SECURE? The National Computer Security Center (NCSC) of the U.S. Department of Defense published guidelines for security levels. The government uses these guidelines in its requests for bids on jobs where vendors must meet specified levels. The seven levels are shown in Online File W15.13 at the book's Web site. Vendors are required to maintain a certain security level depending on the security needs of the job. The decision of how much to secure can be treated as an insurance issue (see Kolodzinski, 2002, and Gordon et al., 2004). For further discussion see Volonino and Robinson (2004).

IT Security in the Twenty-first Century

Computer control and security have recently received increased attention. For example, the story of the "I Love You" bug captured the headlines of most newspapers, TV, and computer portals in May 2000, and other wide-scale viruses since then have received similar media play. Almost 98 percent of the world's major corporations battled computer viruses in 2004. Several important IT-security trends are discussed in this section.

INCREASING THE RELIABILITY OF SYSTEMS. The objective relating to reliability is to use **fault tolerance** to keep the information systems working, even if some parts fail. Several PC manufacturers provide a feature that stores data on more than one disk drive at the same time; if one disk fails or is attacked, the data are still available. Several brands of PCs include a built-in battery that is automatically activated in case of power failure.

Some information systems today have 10,000 to 20,000 components, each of which can go a million hours without a failure, but a combined system may go only 100 hours until it fails. With future systems of 100,000 components, the mathematical odds are that systems will fail every few minutes—clearly, an unacceptable situation. Therefore, it is necessary to improve system reliability.

SELF-HEALING COMPUTERS. As computing systems become more complex, they require higher amounts of human intervention to keep operating. Since the level of complexity is accelerating (e.g., see grid computing in Chapter 2), there is an increasing need for **self-healing computers.** Ideally, recovery can be done instantly if computers can find their problems and correct them themselves, before a system crashes.

According to Van (2003), IBM is engaged in a project known as *automatic computing,* which aims at making computers more self-sufficient and less fragile. The basic idea is borrowed from the human body and its immune system. IBM's first known self-healing computer is called eLiza; it is attached to a huge supercomputer, called Blue Sky, at the National Center for Atmospheric Research in the United States. For further discussion see Pescovitz (2002). However, do not expect your PC to "self-heal" problems. It is still too expensive a capability and is used only with very large systems.

INTELLIGENT SYSTEMS FOR EARLY INTRUSION DETECTION. Detecting intrusion at its beginning is extremely important, especially for classified information and financial data. Expert systems and neural networks are used for this purpose. For example, *intrusion-detecting systems* are especially suitable for local area networks and client/server architectures. This approach compares users' activities on a workstation network against historical profiles and analyzes the significance of any discrepancies. The purpose is to detect security violations. If you use a good Internet security system, it will detect intrusions.

The intrusion-detecting approach is used by several government agencies (e.g., Department of Energy and the U.S. Navy) and large corporations (e.g., Citicorp, Rockwell International, and Tracor). It detects other things as well, for example, compliance with security procedures. People tend to ignore security measures (20,000–40,000 violations were reported each month in a large aerospace company in California). The system detects such violations so that improvements can be made.

INTELLIGENT SYSTEMS IN AUDITING AND FRAUD DETECTION. Intelligent systems are used to enhance the task of IS auditing. For example, expert systems evaluate controls and analyze basic computer systems, while neural networks and data mining are used to detect fraud (e.g., see Sheridan, 2002).

ARTIFICIAL INTELLIGENCE IN BIOMETRICS. Expert systems, neural computing, voice recognition, and fuzzy logic can be used to enhance the capabilities of several biometric systems. For example, Fujitsu of Japan developed a computer mouse that can identify users by the veins of their palms, detecting unauthorized users.

EXPERT SYSTEMS FOR DIAGNOSIS, PROGNOSIS, AND DISASTER PLANNING.
Expert systems can be used to diagnose troubles in computer systems and to suggest solutions. The user provides the expert systems with answers to questions about symptoms. The expert system uses its knowledge base to diagnose the source(s) of the trouble. Once a proper diagnosis is made, the computer provides a restoration suggestion. For example, Exec Express (*e-exec.co.uk*) sells intranet-based business recovery planning expert systems that are part of a bigger program called Self-Assessment. The program is used to evaluate a corporation's environment for security, procedures, and other risk factors.

SMART CARDS. Smart card technology can be used to protect PCs on LANs. For examples, see *cryptocard.com* and *hidcorp.com*.

ETHICAL ISSUES. Implementing security programs raises many ethical issues (see Azari, 2003). First, some people are against any monitoring of individual activities. Imposing certain controls is seen by some as a violation of freedom of speech or other civil rights. Reda (2002) cited a Gartner Group study that showed that even after the terrorist attacks of 9/11/2001, only 26 percent of Americans approved a national ID database. Using biometrics is considered by many a violation of privacy. Finally, using automated traceback programs, described earlier, may be unethical in some cases or even illegal (Lee and Shields, 2002).

15.8 INFORMATION TECHNOLOGY IN COUNTERTERRORISM

In Chapters 10 and 11 we discussed the role of data mining and intelligent systems in counterterrorism. In Section 15.3 we called attention to cyberterrorism and cyberwar. Several of the technologies cited in Sections 15.4 through 15.6 can be used to combat terrorism as well. Terrorists use many methods; many are non-IT related (e.g., planting a bomb in a building). Some are attacks against information resources, or they use IT to plan and conduct terrorist acts. Fortunately, IT provides multiple counterterrorism tools, mostly to absorb, process, and analyze massive amounts of data and information (Chapter 10) and then to support recommendations for action.

The major IT areas considered crucial for counterterrorism (by Popp et al., 2004) are: collaboration, analysis, and decision support tools; foreign language translation and analysis; pattern-analysis tools (such as data mining); and predictive models tools. Most of these topics were discussed in Chapters 10 and 11. In Online File W15.14 we present a schematic view of these IT tools. Some other tools, including those discussed in this chapter, are summarized in Table 15.7 (pages 677–678). For additional information see Lawrence (2004), Yen (2004), Volonino and Robinson (2004), and Newell (2004).

MANAGERIAL ISSUES

1. *To whom should the IS department report?* This issue is related to the degree of IS decentralization and to the role of the CIO. Having the IS department reporting to a functional area may introduce biases in providing IT priorities to that functional area, which may not be justifiable. Having the IS report to the CEO is very desirable.

TABLE 15.7 Other Information Technologies Considered Important for Counterterrorism

Information Technology	Description
Biometrics	Identify and or verify human terrorist (or watchlist) subjects using 2D and 3D modeling approaches over a variety of biometric signatures: face, gait, iris, fingerprint, voice. Also exploit multiple sensor modalities, EQ, IR, radar, hyper-spectral.
Categorization, clustering	Employ numerous technical approaches (natural language processing, AI, machine learning, pattern recognition, statistical analysis, probabilistic techniqes) to automatically extract meaning and key concepts from (un)structured data and categorize via an information model (taxonomy, ontology). Cluster documents with similar contents.
Database processing	Ensure platform, syntactic and semantic consistency, and interoperability of multiple types of data stored on multiple storage media (disk, optical, tape) and across multiple database management systems. Desirable aspects include flexible middleware for: data location transparency and uncertainty management, linguistically relevant querying tuned for knowledge discovery and monitoring scalability and mediation, scheme evolution and metadata management, and structuring unstructured data.
Event detection and notification	Monitor simple and complex events and notify users (or applications) in real time of their detection. Monitoring can be scheduled a priori, or placed on an ad hoc basis driven by user demands. When an event is detected, automatic notifications can range from simple actions (sending an alert, page, or email) to more complex ones (feeding information into an analytics system).
Geospatial information exploitation	Fuse, overlay, register, search, analyze, annotate, and visualize high-resolution satellite and aerial imagery, elevation data, GPS coordinates, maps, demographics, land masses, and political boundaries to deliver a streaming 3D map of the entire globe.
Information management and filtering	Collect, ingest, index, store, retrieve, extract, integrate, analyze, aggregate, display, and distribute semantically enhanced information from a wide variety of sources. Allow for simultaneous search of any number of information sources, sorting and categorizing various items of information according to query relevance. Provide an overall view of the different topics related to the request, along with the ability to visualize the semantic links relating the various items of information to each other.
Infrastructure	Provide comprehensive infrastructure for capturing, managing, and transferring knowledge and business processes that link enterprise software packages, legacy systems, databases, workflows, and Web Services, both within and across enterprises. Important technologies include Web Services, service-oriented grid-computing concepts, extensible component-based modules, P2P techniques, and platforms ranging from enterprise servers to wireless PDAs, Java, Microsoft, and NET implementations.
Knowledge management, context development	Use Semantic Web, associative memory, and related technologies to model and make explicit (expose via Web Services) an analyst's personal preferences, intellectual capital, multidimensional knowledge, and tacit understanding of a problem domain.
Predictive modeling	Predict future terrorist group behaviors, events, and attacks, based on past examples and by exploiting a variety of promising approaches, including neural networks, AI, and behavioral sciences techniques, subject matter expertise, and red teams.
Publishing	Generate concise accurate summaries of recent newsworthy items, ensuring users see topics only once, regardless of how many times the item appears in data or in the press.
Searching	Alow users to perform more complete and meaningful searches (free text, semantic, similarity, partial or exact match) across a multitude of geographically dispersed, multilingual and diverse (un)structured information repositories within and across enterprises (any document type located on file servers, groupware systems, databases, document management systems, Web servers).
Semantic consistency, resolving terms	Exploit ontologies, taxonomies, and definitions for words, phrases, and acronyms using a variety of schemes so users have a common and consistent understanding of the meaning of words in a specific context. Resolve semantic heterogeneity by capitalizing on Semantic Web technologies.

Continues

Information Technology	Description
	TABLE 15.7 Other Information Technologies Considered Important for Counterterrorism Continues
Video processing	Analyze, detect, extract, and digitally enhance (reduce noise, improve image color and contrast, and increase resolution in selected areas) user-specified behaviors or activities in video (suspicious terrorist-related activities).
Visualization	Provide graphical displays, information landscapes, time-based charts, and built-in drill-down tools to help analysts and investigators discover, discern, and visualize networks of interrelated information (associations between words, concepts, people, places, or events) or visually expose nonobvious patterns, relationships, and anomalies from large data sets.
Workflow management	Create optimized workflows and activities-based business process maps using techniques, such as intelligent AI engines by watching, learning, and recording/logging the activities of multiple users using multiple applications in multiple sessions.

Source: Popp et al. (2004).

2. *Who needs a CIO?* This is a critical question that is related to the role of the CIO as a senior executive (chief executive) in the organization. Giving a title without authority can damage the ISD and its operation. Asking the IS director to assume a CIO's responsibility, but not giving the authority and title, can be just as damaging. Any organization that is heavily dependent on IT should have a CIO.

3. *End users are friends, not enemies, of the IS department.* The relationship between end users and the ISD can be very delicate. In the past, many ISDs were known to be insensitive to end-user needs. This created a strong desire for end-user independence, which can be both expensive and ineffective. Successful companies develop a climate of cooperation and friendship between the two parties.

 4. *Ethical issues.* The reporting relationship of the ISD can result in some unethical behavior. For example, if the ISD reports to the finance department, the finance department will have access to information about individuals or other departments that could be misused.

5. *Responsibilities for security should be assigned in all areas.* The more an organization uses the Internet, extranets, and intranets, the greater are the security issues. It is important to make sure that employees know who is responsible and accountable for what information and that they understand the need for security control. In many organizations, the vast majority of information resources is in the hands of end users. Therefore, functional managers must understand and practice IT security management and other proper asset management tasks.

6. *Security awareness programs are important for any organization, especially if it is heavily dependent on IT.* Such programs should be corporatewide and supported by senior executives. In addition, monitoring security measures and ensuring compliance with administrative controls are essential to the success of any security plan. For many people, following administrative controls means additional work, which they prefer not to do.

7. *Auditing information systems should be institutionalized into the organizational culture.* Organizations should audit IS not because the insurance company may ask for it, but because it can save considerable amounts of money. On the other hand, overauditing is not cost-effective.

8. *Multinational corporations.* Organizing the ISD in a multinational corporation is a complex issue. Some organizations prefer a complete decentralization, having an ISD in each country or even several ISDs in one country. Others keep a minimum of centralized staff. Some companies prefer a highly centralized structure. Legal issues, government constraints, and the size of the IS staff are some factors that determine the degree of ISD decentralization.

9. *Sarbanes–Oxley.* The Sarbanes–Oxley Act, according to the CSI/FBI survey (Gordon et al., 2004), is having a major impact on IT, especially in the financial, utility, and telecommunications sectors (see Minicase 2).

KEY TERMS

Application controls *656*

Attack traceback *662*

Audit *671*

Biometric control *657*

Business continuity plan *667*

Cracker *647*

Cybercrime *648*

Cyberterrorism *648*

Cyberwar *648*

Data tampering *649*

Denial of service (DoS) *651*

Disaster avoidance *670*

Disaster recovery plan *667*

Distributed denial of service (DDoS) *651*

Encryption *664*

Exposure *645*

Fault tolerance *674*

Firewall *661*

General controls *656*

Hacker *647*

Honeynets *665*

Honeypots *665*

Identity theft *643*

Information center (IC) *638*

Information resources management (IRM) *634*

IT governance *637*

Programming attack *649*

Risk management *673*

Self-healing computers *675*

Social engineering *647*

Stealthware *665*

Steering committee *637*

Trojan horse *650*

Virus *649*

Vulnerability *645*

Zombies *651*

CHAPTER HIGHLIGHTS (Numbers Refer to Learning Objectives)

❶ Information resources scattered throughout the organization are vulnerable to attacks and difficult to coordinate and control, and therefore they are difficult to manage.

❷ The responsibility for IRM is divided between the ISD and end users. They must work together.

❷ Steering committees, information centers, and service-level agreements can reduce conflicts between the ISD and end users.

❷ ISD reporting locations can vary, but a preferred location is to report directly to administrative senior management or even to the CEO.

❸ The chief information officer (CIO) is a corporate-level position demonstrating the importance and changing role of IT in organizations.

❹ Data, software, hardware, and networks can be threatened by many internal and external hazards.

❹ The attack to an information system can be caused either accidentally or intentionally.

❹ There are many potential computer crimes; some resemble conventional crimes (embezzlement, vandalism, fraud, theft, trespassing, and joyriding).

❹ Computer criminals are driven by economic, ideological, egocentric, or psychological factors. Most of the criminals are insiders, but outsiders (such as hackers, crackers, and spies) can cause major damage as well.

❹ A virus is a computer program hidden within a regular program that instructs the regular program to change or destroy data and/or programs. Viruses spread very quickly along networks worldwide.

⑤ Information systems are protected with controls such as security procedures, physical guards, or detecting software. These are used for *prevention, deterrence, detection, recovery,* and *correction* of information systems.

⑤ General controls include physical security, access controls, data security controls, communications (network) controls, and administrative controls.

⑤ Biometric controls are used to identify users by checking physical characteristics of the user (e.g., fingerprints and voice pattern).

⑤ Application controls are usually built into the software. They protect the data during input, processing, or output.

⑥ Encrypting information is a useful method for protecting transmitted data.

⑥ The Internet is not protected; therefore anything that comes from the Internet can be hazardous.

⑥ Firewalls protect intranets and internal systems from hackers, but not from viruses.

⑥ Access control, authentication, and authorization are the backbone of network security.

⑦ Disaster recovery planning is an integral part of effective control and security management.

⑦ Business continuity planning includes backup of data and computers and a plan for what to do when disaster strikes.

⑧ It is extremely difficult and expensive to protect against all possible threats to IT systems. Therefore, it is necessary to use cost-benefit analysis to decide how many and which controls to adopt.

⑧ A detailed internal and external IT audit may involve hundreds of issues and can be supported by both software and checklists.

⑨ A large variety of IT tools, ranging from data mining to intelligent systems, assist governments and organizations to combat terrorism and cyberterrorism.

VIRTUAL COMPANY ASSIGNMENT

Managing Information Resources and Security at The Wireless Café

Go to The Wireless Café's link on the Student Web Site. There you will be asked to analyze security vulnerabilities of the restaurant's information resources.

More Resources

More resources and study tools are located on the Student Web Site. You'll find additional chapter materials and useful Web links. In addition, self-quizzes that provide individualized feedback are available for each chapter.

Instructions for accessing The Wireless Café Web Site on the Student Web Site

1. Go to **wiley.com/college/turban**
2. Select Turban/Leidner/ McLean/Wetherbe's *Information Technology for Management,* Fifth Edition.
3. Click on Student Resources site, in the toolbar on the left.
4. Click on the link for Virtual Company Web Site.
5. Click on Wireless Café.

QUESTIONS FOR REVIEW

1. What are possible reporting locations for the ISD?
2. Why has the ISD historically reported to finance or accounting departments?
3. List the mechanisms for ISD–end users cooperation.
4. Summarize the new role of the CIO.
5. List Rockart's eight imperatives (see Online File W15.3).

6. What is a steering committee?

7. Define SLAs and discuss the roles they play.

8. What are the services to end users that are usually provided by an information (help) center?

9. Define controls, threats, vulnerability, and backup.

10. What is a computer crime?

11. List the four major categories of computer crimes.

12. What is a cybercrime?

13. What is the difference between hackers and crackers?

14. Explain a virus and a Trojan horse.

15. Explain a corporatewide security system.

16. Define controls.

17. Describe prevention, deterrence, detection, recovery, and correction.

18. Define biometrics; list five of them.

19. Distinguish between general controls and application controls.

20. What is the difference between authorized and authenticated users?

21. Explain DoS and how to defend against it.

22. How do you protect against viruses?

23. Define firewall. What is it used for?

24. Explain encryption.

25. Define a business continuity plan.

26. Define and describe a disaster recovery plan.

27. What are "hot" and "cold" recovery sites?

28. Describe auditing of information systems.

29. List and briefly describe the steps involved in risk analysis of controls.

30. Define cyberterrorism. List five IT tools that can help to fight terrorism.

QUESTIONS FOR DISCUSSION

1. What is a desirable location for the ISD to report to, and why?

2. What information resources are usually controlled by the ISD, and why?

3. Discuss the new role of the CIO and the implications of this role to management.

4. Why should information control and security be of prime concern to management?

5. Compare the computer security situation with that of insuring a house.

6. Explain what firewalls protect and what they do not protect. Why?

7. What is the purpose of biometrics? Why are they popular?

8. Describe how IS auditing works and how it is related to traditional accounting and financial auditing.

9. Why are authentication and authorization important in e-commerce?

10. Some insurance companies will not insure a business unless the firm has a computer disaster recovery plan. Explain why.

11. Explain why risk management should involve the following elements: threats, exposure associated with each threat, risk of each threat occurring, cost of controls, and assessment of their effectiveness.

12. Some people have recently suggested using viruses and similar programs in wars between countries. What is the logic of such a proposal? How could it be implemented?

13. How important is it for a CIO to have an extensive knowledge of the business?

14. Why is it necessary to use SLAs with vendors? What are some of the potential problems in such situations?

15. Compare a corporatewide security plan to another enterprisewide IT-based plan (such as KM or CRM). What is similar? What is different?

16. Why do intelligent systems play an increasing role in securing IT?

17. Why is cross-border cybercrime expanding rapidly? Discuss some possible solutions.

18. Discuss why the Sarbanes–Oxley Act is having an impact on information security.

EXERCISES

1. Examine Online File W15.4. Read some new material on the CIO and add any new roles you find in your reading. Which of the roles in the list seem to have gained importance and which seem to have lost importance?

2. Assume that the daily probability of a major earthquake in Los Angeles is .07%. The chance of your computer center being damaged during such a quake is 5%. If the center is damaged, the average estimated damage will be $1.6 million.

   a. Calculate the expected loss (in dollars).

   b. An insurance agent is willing to insure your facility for an annual fee of $15,000. Analyze the offer, and discuss whether to accept it.

3. The theft of laptop computers at conventions, hotels, and airports is becoming a major problem. These categories of protection exist: physical devices (e.g., *targus.com*), encryption (e.g., *networkassociates.com*), and security policies (e.g., at *ebay.com*). Find more information on the problem and on the solutions. Summarize the advantages and limitations of each method.

4. Expert systems can be used to analyze the profiles of computer users. Such analysis may enable better intrusion detection. Should an employer notify employees that their usage of computers is being monitored by an expert system? Why or why not?

5. Ms. M. Hsieh worked as a customer support representative for the Wollongong Group, a small software company (Palo Alto, California). She was fired in late 1987. In early 1988, Wollongong discovered that someone was logging onto its computers at night via a modem and had altered and copied files. During investigation, the police traced the calls to Ms. Hsieh's home and found copies there of proprietary information valued at several million dollars. It is interesting to note that Ms. Hsieh's access code was canceled the day she was terminated. However, the company suspects that Ms. Hsieh obtained the access code of another employee. (*Source*: Based on *BusinessWeek*, August 1, 1988, p. 67.)

   a. How was the crime committed? Why were the controls ineffective? (State any relevant assumptions.)

   b. What can Wollongong, or any company, do in order to prevent similar incidents in the future?

6. Guarding against a distributed denial of service attack is not simple. Examine the major tools and approaches available. Start by downloading software from *nipc.gov*. Also visit *cert.org, sans.org,* and *ciac.llnl.gov*. Write a report summarizing your findings.

7. Twenty-five thousand messages arrive at an organization each year. Currently there are no firewalls. On the average there are 1.2 successful hackings each year. Each successful hacking results in loss to the company of about $130,000.

   A major firewall is proposed at a cost of $66,000 and a maintenance cost of $5,000. The estimated useful life is 3 years. The chance that an intruder will break through the firewall is 0.0002. In such a case, the damage will be $100,000 (30%) or $200,000 (50%), or no damage. There is annual maintenance cost of $20,000 for the firewall.

   a. Should management buy the firewall?

   b. An improved firewall that is 99.9988 percent effective costs $84,000, with a life of 3 years and annual maintenance cost of $16,000, is available. Should this one be purchased instead of the first one?

8. In spring 2000 the U.S. government developed an internal intrusion detection network (*fidnet.gov*) to protect itself from hackers. The Center for Democracy and Technology (*cdt.org*) objected, claiming invasion of privacy. Research the status of the project (FIDNet) and discuss the claims of the center.

9. Review the incidents in Section 5.3. Which controls could have prevented each (especially incident 7)?

GROUP ASSIGNMENTS

1. With the class divided into groups, have each group visit an IS department. Then present the following in class: an organizational chart of the department; a discussion on the department's CIO (director) and her or his reporting status; information on a steering committee (composition, duties); information on any SLAs the department has; and a report on the extent of IT decentralization in the company.

2. Each group is to be divided into two parts. The first part will interview students and businesspeople and record the experiences they have had with computer security problems. The second part of each group will visit a computer store (and/or read the literature or use the Internet) to find out what software is available to fight different computer security problems. Then, each group will prepare a presentation in which they describe the problems and identify which of the problems could have been prevented with the use of commercially available software.

3. Create groups to investigate the latest development in IT and e-commerce security. Check journals such as *CIO.com* (available free online), vendors, and search engines such as *techdata.com.* and *google.com*.

4. Research the Melissa attack in 1999. Explain how the virus works and what damage it causes. Examine Microsoft's attempts to prevent similar future attacks. Investigate similarities between the 2003 viruses (Slammer, Bugbear, etc.) and earlier ones (e.g., "I Love You" and Melissa). What preventive methods are offered by security vendors?

INTERNET EXERCISES

1. Explore some job-searching Web sites (such as *brassring.com,* and *headhunter.com*), and identify job openings for CIOs. Examine the job requirements and the salary range. Also visit *google.com* and *cio.com*, and find some information regarding CIOs, their roles, salaries, and so forth. Report your findings.

2. Enter *scambusters.org.* Find out what the organization does. Learn about e-mail scams and Web site scams. Report your findings.

3. Access the site of *comdisco.com.* Locate and describe the latest disaster recovery services.

4. Enter *epic.org/privacy/tools.html,* and examine the following groups of tools: Web encryption, disk encryption, and PC firewalls. Explain how these tools can be used to facilitate the security of your PC.

5. Access the Web sites of the major antivirus vendors (*symantec.com, mcafee.com,* and *antivirus.com*). Find out what the vendors' research centers are doing. Also download VirusScan from McAfee and scan your hard drive with it.

6. Many newsgroups are related to computer security (*groups.google.com; alt.comp.virus; comp.virus; maous.comp. virus*). Access any of these sites to find information on the most recently discovered viruses.

7. Check the status of biometric controls. See the demo at *sensar.com.* Check what Microsoft is doing with biometric controls.

8. Enter *v:l.nai.com/vil/default.asp.* Find information about viruses. What tips does McAfee (*mcafee b2b.com*) give for avoiding or minimizing the impact of viruses?

9. You have installed a DSL line in your home and want to find out if you need a firewall. Enter *securitydogs.com, macafee.com,* or *symantec.com.* Find three possible products. Which one do you like best? Why?

10. Access a good search engine (e.g., *google.com* or *findart icles.com*). Find recent articles on disaster planning. Prepare a short report on recent developments in disaster recovery planning.

11. The use of smart cards for electronic storage of user identification, user authentication, changing passwords, and so forth is on the rise. Surf the Internet and report on recent developments. (For example, try the Web sites *microsoft.com/windows/smartcards, litronic.com, gemplus.com,* or *scia.org.*)

12. Access the Web site *2600.com* and read the *2600 Magazine.* Also try *waregone.com* and *skynamic.com.* Prepare a report that shows how easy it is to hack successfully.

13. Enter *ncsa.com* and find information about "why hackers do the things they do." Write a report.

14. Enter *biopay.com* and other vendors of biometrics and find the devices they make that can be used to access control into information systems. Prepare a list of major capabilities.

15. Enter *cybercrime.gov* and find five recent incidents in which the criminals were convicted. Write a summary of your findings.

16. Enter *cert.org* and prepare a report on the organization's mission and mode of operations.

Minicase 1
Putting IT to Work at Home Depot

Home Depot is the world's largest home-improvement retailer, a global company that is expanding rapidly (about 200 new stores every year). With over 1,500 stores (mostly in the United States and Canada, and now expanding to other countries) and about 50,000 kinds of products in each store, the company is heavily dependent on IT, especially since it started to sell online.

To align its business and IT operations, Home Depot created a business and information service model, known as the Special Projects Support Team (SPST). This team collaborates both with the ISD and business colleagues on new projects, addressing a wide range of strategic and tactical needs. These projects typically occur at the intersection of business processes. The team is composed of highly skilled employees. Actually, there are several teams, each with a director and a mix of employees, depending on the project. For example, system developers, system administrators, security experts, and project managers can be on a team. The teams exist until the completion of a project;

then they are dissolved and the members are assigned to new teams. All teams report to the SPST director, who reports to a VP of Technology.

To ensure collaboration among end users, the ISD and the SPST created structured (formal) relationships. The basic idea is to combine organizational structure and process flow, which is designed to do the following:

● Achieve consensus across departmental boundaries with regard to strategic initiatives.
● Prioritize strategic initiatives.
● Bridge the gap between business concept and detailed specifications.
● Result in the lowest possible operational costs.
● Achieve consistently high acceptance levels by the end-user community.
● Comply with evolving legal guidelines.
● Define key financial elements (cost-benefit analysis, ROI, etc.).

- Identify and render key feedback points for project metrics.
- Support very high rates of change.
- Support the creation of multiple, simultaneous threads of work across disparate time lines.
- Promote known, predictable, and manageable work-flow events, event sequences, and change management processes.
- Accommodate the highest possible levels of operational stability.
- Leverage the extensive code base, and leverage function and component reuse.
- Leverage Home Depot's extensive infrastructure and IS resource base.

There is a special EC steering committee which is connected to the CIO (who is a senior VP), to the VP for marketing and advertising, and to the VP for merchandising (merchandising deals with procurement). The SPST is closely tied to the ISD, to marketing, and to merchandising. The data center is shared with non-EC activities.

The SPST migrated to an e-commerce team in August 2000 in order to construct a Web site supporting a national catalog of products, which was completed in April 2001. (This catalog contains over 400,000 products from 11,000 vendors.) This project required the collaboration of virtu-

ally every department in Home Depot (e.g., see finance/accounting, legal, loss prevention, etc., in the figure). Also contracted services were involved.

Since 2001, SPST has been continually busy with EC initiatives, including improving the growing Home Depot online store. The cross-departmental nature of the SPST explains why it is an ideal structure to support the dynamic, ever-changing work of the EC-related projects. The structure also considers the skills, strengths, and weaknesses of the IT employees. The company offers both online and offline training aimed at improving those skills. Home Depot is consistently ranked among the best places to work for IT employees.

Sources: Compiled from Alberts (2001) and from *homedepot.com* (2003).

Questions for Minicase 1

1. Relate this case to the ISD–users relationship discussed in this chapter.
2. The new organizational structure means that the SPST reports to both marketing and technology. This is known as a matrix structure. What are the potential advantages and problems of reporting to two bosses?
3. How is collaboration facilitated by IT in this case?
4. Why is the process flow important in this case?

Minicase 2
Risk Management at Zions Bancorporation

Operating over 400 branches in eight western states and protecting the privacy of its customers and the security of its information, while complying with the requirements of the Sarbanes–Oxley Act, is not an easy task for Zions, a financial services company headquartered in Salt Lake City, Utah. The company realized that it needed a corporatewide, comprehensive risk management and assessment program.

Zions outlined three goals for its operational risk framework:

1. Enable the company to better manage risk and reduce loss.
2. Strengthen customer service and shareholder value.
3. Meet a variety of regulatory requirements, including internal control assessment and attestation required by Sarbanes–Oxley, Section 404, and operational risk

guidelines under Basel II. (Basel II is a set of international banking standards for security, capital measurement, and intercountry banking transactions; see *bis.org/publ/bcbsca.htm*.)

After thorough analysis, the company decided to deploy a Web-based risk assessment system. The first step was to determine the system requirements. Extensive consultations were made with all user departments as well as with U.S. government agencies and internal auditing professional societies and experts. The company's internal audit department played a major role and worked closely with the risk management team. For example, the auditors provided feedback on the system's functionality, screen design, risk scoring and rating methodology, work flow, reporting mechanisms, user guidelines, and alert capabilities. In addition, the auditors helped define the system's internal audit interface and evaluate vendor software.

A major idea was that the program should encourage business departments to take responsibility for identifying, assessing, and managing their security risks. In addition, the tool represented a way of establishing an audit trail for risks, controls, and actions, thus expediting tracking and problem resolution.

Zions established the following system requirements:

- Develop an automated enterprise risk management system covering operation risk and other risk categories.
- Integrate a variety of risk tools such as risk assessment, key risk indicators (KRI), and loss data capture and analysis to strengthen data integrity.
- Deliver intuitive screen designs to reduce training and enhance ease of use.
- Provide flexible, robust reporting so that anyone from the board of directors to line management could use the system for their respective needs.
- Create automatic alerts to enhance communication, escalate critical issues, and provide accountability.
- Ensure the system is Web-based and scalable, enabling use across multiple states and lines of business.
- Enable data feeds from multiple systems.

These requirements created the foundation on which the company built its risk management tool. Once the parameters were established, Zions hired an outside vendor, Providus Software Solutions Inc., to develop the system.

The program is based on the Committee of Sponsoring Organizations of the Treadway Commission's (COSO) *International Control-Integrated Framework* model (see *coso.org*), which provides an effective and straightforward approach to assessing risk and controls. The model is consistent with Zions' philosophy that business lines are responsible for assessing and managing their risks. For these reasons, the system's structure was modeled after COSO's method of operational risk evaluation.

Based on this framework, Zions developed four main stages for its risk management process: (1) Identify business objectives and related risks; (2) list and assess the strength of controls; (3) determine actions needed to close control gaps; and (4) ensure accountability and sustainability. Members of the company's business units provided input at each of these stages to help assess key risks and ensure those risks are managed effectively. (The details of these stages are provided by Stone and Marotta, 2003.)

With more than 350 users, including executives, business-line management, and internal audit, compliance, and business-continuity teams, the system has proved to be a significant enhancement over Zions' previous risk management process. Integrating electronic alerts and action-tracking capabilities within the system, for example, has made it an effective tool that business lines and internal auditors use to address existing and emerging risk issues. In addition, because the system acts as a common forum for discussing risks among departments, it provides greater disclosure to auditors earlier in the process, uncovering issues more quickly while minimizing surprises. The system also became increasingly useful as a means of gathering an enterprise view of key exposures that enhance the organization's ability to manage risk proactively for the long term.

As Zions' risk management process has evolved, the firm has combined various risk tools that were once separate and disjointed into a single, Web-based system that enables the company to better manage risk and strengthen customer service.

Sources: Compiled from Stone and Marotta (2003).

Questions for Minicase 2

1. Compare the project initiation to what you learned about the topic in Chapter 14, and discuss your findings
2. Comment on the idea of "pushing" the responsibility of risk assessment to the users. Relate it to the discussion in Section 15.1.
3. There was no attempt to do a cost-benefit analysis to justify the program. Can you speculate why?
4. How can such a program assist the internal auditors?
5. Relate the case to Section 15.7. Can you recommend improvements in Zions' program?

REFERENCES

ABC Online News (July 24, 2004).

Adams, S., "Effective SLAs Define Partnership Roles," *Communications News*, June 2000, *comnews.com* (accessed August 2003).

Agarwal R., and V. Sambamurthy, "Principles and Models for Organizing the IT function," *MIS Querterly Executive*, March 2002.

Alberts, B., "Home Depot's Special Projects Support Team Powers Information Management for Business Needs," *Journal of Organization Excellence*, Winter 2001.

Alga, N., "Increasing Security Levels," *Information Systems Control Journal*, March–April 2002.

Associated Press, news item (August 1, 2004).

Atlas, R. I., and S. A. Young, "Planting and Shaping Security Success," *Security Management*, August 2002.

Austin R.D., and C. A. R. Darby, "The Myth of Secure Computing," *Harvard Business Review*, June 2003.

Ball, L. D., "CIO on Center Stage: 9/11 Changes Everything," *Information Systems Management*, Spring 2002.

Becker, D., "Equal Rights for CIOs," *CNET News.Com*, June 16, 2003.

Biermann E., et al., "A Comparison of Intrusion Detection Systems," *Computers and Security*, Vol. 20, 2001.

Biery K., and D. Hager, "The Risks of Mobile Communication," *Security Management*, December 2001.

Blanco L., "Audit Trail in an E-Commerce Environment," *Information Systems Control Journal*, September–October 2002.

Brassil, R. A., "The Changing Realities of Recovery: How Onsite and Mobile Options Have Revolutionized the Business Continuity Industry," *Information Systems Control Journal*, March–April 2003.

Bruno L., "Out, Out Damned Hacker!" *Red Herring*, January 2002.

"Bugbear Worm Steals Credit Card and Password Details," *Information Management and Computer Security*, June 2003.

Buell, D. A., and R. Sandhu, "Identity Management," *IEEE Internet Computing*, November–December 2003.

Caulfield, B., "The Trouble with Biometrics," *Business 2.0*, September 2002.

Cilli, C., "IT Governance: Why a Guideline?" *Information Systems Control Journal*, May–June 2003.

Computers and Security, special issue, 19(1), 2000.

Computerweekly.com, article 131966 (July 14, 2004).

Damle, P., "Social Engineering: A Tip of the Iceberg," *Information Systems Control Journal*, March–April 2002.

Diao Y., et al., "Using Fuzzy Control to Maximize Profits in Service Level Agreement, *IBM Systems Journal*, XYZ, 2002.

Doll, M. W., et al., *Defending the Digital Frontier*. New York: Wiley, 2003.

Doughty, K., "Business Continuity: A Business Survival Strategy, *Information Systems Control Journal*, January–February 2002.

Doughty, K., "Implementing Enterprise Security," *Information Systems Control Journal*, May–June 2003.

Duffy, D., "Chief Executives Who Get IT," *CIO*, July 15, 1999.

Earl, M. J., "Blue Survivors (the CIO's)," *CIO*, December 15, 1999–January 1, 2000.

ecommercetimes.com, news item (June 28, 2004).

Elbirt, A. J., "Information Warfare: Are You at Risk?" *IEEE Technology and Society Magazine*, Winter 2003/2004.

Fadia, A., *Network Security: A Hacker's Perspective*. Boston, MA: Premier Press, 2002.

Frownfelter–Lohrke, C., and J. E. Hunton, "New Opportunities for Information Systems Auditors," *Information Systems Control Journal*, May–June 2002.

Garfinkel, S., *Web Security, Privacy and Commerce*. Sebastopal, CA: O'Reilly and Associates, 2002.

Gerber, J. A., and E. R. Feldman, "Is Your Business Prepared for the Worst?" *Journal of Accountancy*, April 2002.

Ghosh, A. K., and T. M. Swaminatha, "Software Security and Privacy Risks in Mobile E-Commerce," *Communications of the ACM*, February 2001.

Gordon, L. A., et al., *2004 CSI/FBI Computer Crime and Security Survey*. San Francisco: Computer Security Institute, 2004.

Hiles, A., *Enterprise Risk Assessment and Business Impact Analysis*. Rothstein Assoc., 2002.

Hirschheim, R., et al., "The Evolution of the Corporate IT Function and the Role of the CIO at Texaco," *Data Base*, Fall 2003.

Horner-Reich, B., and K. M. Nelson, "In Their Own Words: CIO Visions About the Future of In-house IT Organizations," *Data Base*, Fall 2003.

Hunton, J. E., "Back Up Your Data to Survive a Disaster," *Journal of Accountancy*, April 2002.

Jain, A., et al., "Biometric Identification," *Communications of the ACM*, February 2000.

Jain, A., et al. (eds.), *Biometrics: Personal Identification in Networked Security*. New York: Kluwer, 1999.

Jiang, J. J., et al., "Measuring Information Systems Service Quality," *MIS Quarterly*, June 2002.

Karagiannis, K., "DDoS: Are You Next?" *PC Magazine*, January 1, 2003, *pcmag.com/article2/0,4149,768385,00.asp* (accessed August 2003).

Kelly, D. A., "Always Available," *Oracle Magazine*, March–April 2004.

Kern, H., "10 Commandments for Building the Ideal IT Organization," *Search CIO.com*, September 30, 2003.

Kesner, R. M., "Running Information Services as a Business: Managing IS Commitments within the Enterprise," *Information Strategy: The Executive Journal*, Summer 2002.

Kolodzinski, O., "Aligning Information Security Imperatives with Business Needs," *The CPA Journal*, July 2002, *luca.com/cpajournal/2002/0702/nv/nv10.htm* (accessed August 2003).

Lam, W., "Ensuring Business Continuity," *IT Pro*, June 2002.

Lawrence, S., "Detecting Bioterrorism," *eWeek*, June 7, 2004.

Lee, S. C., and C. Shields, "Technical Legal and Societal Challenges to Automated Attack Traceback," *IT Pro*, May–June 2002.

Leidner, D. E., et al., "How CIOs Manage IT During Economic Decline: Surviving and Thriving Amid Uncertainty," *MIS Quarterly Executive*, March 2003.

Levin, C., "The Insurance Plan that Came to the Rescue," *PC Magazine*, January 29, 2002.

Los Angeles Times, April 24, 1998.

Loundy, D. L., *Computer Crime, Information Warfare and Economic Espionage*. Durham, N.C: Carolina Academic Press, 2003.

Luftman, J. N., et al., *Managing the Information Technology Resources*. Upper Saddle River, NJ: Pearson Education, 2004.

Luhn, R., and S. Spanbauer, "Protect Your PC," *PC World*, July 2002.

McConnell, M., "Information Assurance in the Twenty-first Century," *Supplement to Computer*, February 2002.

McKinley, E., "VPN Provides Rent-A-Center with a Multitude of Positive Changes," *Stores*, May 2003.

Mitre, "CVE List Exceeds 5,000 Security Issues," September 9, 2002, *cve.mitre.org/news/*(accessed July 20, 2003).

Morgan, J. P., and N. A. Wong, "Conduct a Legal Web Audit," *e-Business Advisor*, September 1999.

Murrays, J. P., "Judging IT Department Performance," *Information Strategy*, Summer 2004.

Nance, B., "Keep Networks Safe from Viruses," *Byte*, November 1996, p. 171. Updated June 2003.

Newell, A., "Cybersecurity Warning Service Launches," *PCWorld*, January 28, 2004.

Panko, R. R., *Corporate Computer and Network Security*. Upper Saddle River, NJ: Prentice Hall, 2004.

Pantry, S., and P. Griffiths, *A Complete Guide for Preparing and Implementing Service Level Agreements*, 2nd Ed. London: Library Association Publishing, 2002.

Pescovitz, D., "Helping Computers Help Themselves," *IEEE Spectrum*, September 2002.

Piazza, P., "Honeynet Attracts Hacker Attack," *Security Management*, November 2001.

Pooley, J., "Blocking Information Passes," *Security Management*, July 2002.

Popp, R., et al., "Countering Terrorism through Information Technology," *Communications of the ACM*, March 2004.

Potter, R. E., "How CIOs Manage Their Superior Expectations," *Communications of the ACM*, August 2003.

Prometheum Technologies, "How Does a Virtual Private Network (VPN) Work?" April 2003, *prometheum.com/m_vpn.htm* (accessed August 2003).

Ragsdale, J., "IT Relationship Management: Position Defined, But Where Are the Tools?" Research Paper #0,7211,34352,00, Forrester Research, May 4, 2004.

Reda, S., "Brave New World of Biometrics," *Stores*, May 2002.

Richardson, R., *2003 CSI/FBI Computer Crime and Security Survey*. San Francisco: Computer Security Institute (*gocsi.com*), 2003.

Roberts, B., "Side by Side," *HR Magazine*, March 2004.

Robinson, C., "The Role of a Chief Security Officer," *CIO Asia*, April 2003 (*cio-asia.com*).

Rockart, J. F., et al., "Eight Imperatives for the New IS Organization," *Sloan Management Review*, Fall 1996.

Ross, J. W., et al., "Develop Long-Term Competitiveness Through IT Assets," *Sloan Management Review*, Fall 1996.

Ross, J. W., and D. F. Feeny, "The Evolving Role of the CIO," in R. Zmud (ed.), *Framing the Domain of IT Management*. Cincinnati, OH: Pinnaflex Educational Resources, 2000.

Rothstein, P. J., *Develop a Disaster Recovery/Business Continuity Plan*, Brookfield, CT: Rothstein Assoc., 2002.

Sambamurthy, V., et al., "Managing in the Digital Era," in G. Dickson and G. DeSanctis, *Information Technology and the Future Enterprise*. Upper Saddle River, NJ: Prentice Hall, 2001.

sans.org, "The Twenty Most Critical Internet Security Vulnerabilities," SANS Institute, *sans.org/top20* (accessed April 2003).

Sayana, S. A., "Auditing General and Application Controls," *Information Systems Control Journal*, September–October 2002.

Scalet, S. D., "Immune Systems," *CIO*, June 1, 2003.

Seddon, P. B., et al., "Measuring Organizational IS Effectiveness," *Data Base*, Spring 2002.

Sheridan, R. M., "Working the Data Mines," *Security Management*, April 2002.

Sivasailam, N., et al., "What Companies Are(n't) Doing about Web Site Assurance," *IT Pro*, May–June 2002.

Slewe, T., and M. Hoogenboom, "Who Will Rob You on the Digital Highway?" *Communications of the ACM*, May 2004.

Smith, R., *Authentication: From Password to Public Keys*. Boston: Addison Wesley, 2002.

South China Morning Post, news item, Hong Kong, May 21, 1999.

Spector, L., "How to Avoid Data Disaster," *PC World*, June 2002.

Statonline, "Technology Facts and Links," *statonline.com/technologies/facts.asp* (accessed August 2003).

Stone, D. L., and D. L. Marotta, "Leveraging Risk Technology," *Internal Auditing*, December 2003.

Strassman, P., "What Is the Best Defense? Being Prepared," *ComputerWorld*, March 31, 1997.

Sullivan A., "U.S. Arrests 135 in Nationwide Cybercrime Sweep," *Yahoo!News*, provided by Reuters, May 16, 2003.

Sullivan, B., "How to Protect Your Home Network," *Technology and Science*, *msnbc.com/news/875670* (accessed September 29, 2003).

Talleur, T., "Can Your Organization Survive a Cybercrime?" *e-Business Advisor*, September 2001.

Tse, D., "Security Assessment Model for Information Security Practices," *Proceedings, 8th PACIS Conference*, Shanghai, China, July 7–11, 2004.

Van, J., "Self Healing Computers Seen as Better Fix," *Chicago Tribune*, January 2, 2003.

Verton, E., and J. Brownlow, *Black Ice: The Invisible Threat of Cyberterrorism*. New York: McGraw-Hill, 2003.

Volonino, L., and S. R. Robinson, *Principles and Practice of Information Security*. Upper Saddle River, NJ: Prentice Hall, 2004.

Von-Roessing, R., *Auditing Business Continuity: Global Best Practices*, Brookfield, CT: Rothstein Assoc., 2002.

Walsh, N. P., "Stolen Details of 6 Million Phone Users Hawked on Moscow Streets," *The Guardian*, January 27, 2003.

Wells, J. T., "Occupational Fraud: The Audit as a Deterrent," *Journal of Accountancy*, April 2002.

White, G. B., "Protecting the Real Corporate Networks," *Computer Security Journal*, 1(4), 1999.

White, D., "SLA Strategies from the Buyer's Perspective," *Outsourcing Magazine*, January– February 2004.

Wiederkehr, B., "IT Security Awareness Programme," *Information Systems Control Journal*, May–June 2003.

Willcocks, L. P., and R. Sykes "The Role of the CIO and IT Function in ERP," *Communications of the ACM*, April 2000.

Woda, A., "The Role of the Auditor in IT Governance," *Information Systems Control Journal*, Vol. 2, 2002.

Yen, J., "Emerging Technologies for Homeland Security," Special Issue, *Communications of the ACM*, March 2004.

Young, A., "The Future of Cryptography," *IT Pro*, July–August 2003.

Zenkin, D., "Guidelines for Protecting the Corporation Against Viruses," *Computers and Security*, August 2001.

Zetter, K., and S. Miastkowski, "Viruses: The Next Generation," *PC World*, December 2000.

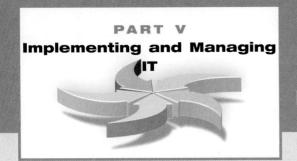

PART V
Implementing and Managing IT

12. Using IT for Strategic Advantage
13. Information Technology Economics
14. Acquiring IT Applications and Infrastructure
15. Managing Information Resources and Security
▶ 16. The Impacts of IT on Individuals, Organizations, and Society

CHAPTER
16
The Impacts of Information Technology on Individuals, Organizations, and Society

16.1 Introduction

16.2 IT Is Eliminating the Barriers of Space and Distance

16.3 Information Is Changing from a Scarce Resource to an Abundant Resource

16.4 Machines Are Performing Functions Previously Performed by Humans

16.5 Information Technology Urges People to Reexamine Their Value Systems

16.6 Conclusion

Minicases:
1. ChoicePoint
2. Australian Fishing Community

LEARNING OBJECTIVES

After studying this chapter, you will be able to:

❶ Describe some of the major impacts of information technology on individuals, organizations, and society.

❷ Understand the changes that take place in the workplace and the lives of individuals when information technology eliminates geographical and spatial barriers.

❸ Discuss the positive and negative effects associated with the abundance of information made available by IT.

❹ Identify the issues that arise due to uneven diffusion of information technology across countries and socioeconomic classes.

❺ Understand the complexity of effects of technological progress on labor markets and individual employees.

❻ Discuss the impacts of information technology on the quality of life and interpersonal relationships.

❼ Recognize the legal, ethical, and moral issues that become particularly critical due to proliferation of information technology.

MOVIE PIRACY

 THE PROBLEM

Generations of moviegoers grew up with the idea that a movie theater is the right place to enjoy the latest films. They also accepted the idea of paying for their movies. However, movie piracy, which has been greatly accelerated by information technology, is challenging this notion. Now, movie pirates are bringing the latest motion picture releases to an Internet-connected computer near you.

For years, movie studios suffered minor losses due to high-tech **piracy** (theft of digital content) that was carried out by people duplicating videotapes and DVDs. The need to produce and distribute physical media presented a number of technical and logistical difficulties for movie pirates, which limited the scope of their operations. Thus, picture studios largely ignored these activities. When Napster.com and other sites began to use the Web and peer-to-peer technologies to share pirated music, movie producers felt reasonably immune to this trend. After all, it would take more than a week to download a 5-gigabyte DVD-quality movie using a 56-kilobits-per-second modem.

However, as information technology continued to evolve, video compression algorithms made it possible to shrink the size of the movies to 650 megabytes, while the explosion of high-speed Internet connections made it much easier to download and share large files. Today, a user with a broadband connection can download a movie in 2 to 8 hours. The Motion Picture Association of America (MPAA) reports that in 2003 more than 50 major films were illegally copied and released even before they came out in movie theaters (Ripley, 2004).

Some individuals argue that piracy does not hurt film studios but, rather, makes movies available to those people who would not be able to enjoy them otherwise. Nevertheless, the MPAA estimates that the losses from movie piracy exceeded $3.5 billion in 2003 and are expected to reach $5.4 billion in 2005 (Ripley, 2004). Information technology that enables movie piracy raises a number of significant issues, such as intellectual property rights, fair use, and the role of government in regulating these issues. Furthermore, information technology makes it easier than ever to cross national borders, adding international implications to the issue of movie piracy.

 THE SOLUTION

To deal with movie piracy, picture studio executives attacked several aspects of the problem simultaneously. First, media companies tried to shape public opinion in a way that would discourage movie piracy. For instance, to raise public awareness of the issue, filmmakers launched an advertising campaign with the slogan "Movies. They're worth it." Moreover, by supporting several state laws prohibiting such practices as videotaping films in movie theaters, the MPAA emphasized that movie piracy is not only wrong but also illegal (McBride, 2004).

Second, the movie industry performed a number of activities that made it more difficult to copy and distribute pirated movies without being noticed. For instance, enhanced physical security at movie theaters, which may include the use of metal detectors and physical searches for recording devices, helps the film

689

industry deter piracy at "sneak previews" and movie premieres (Ripley, 2004). Technology plays an important part in this process. For example, movie theaters started installing hidden surveillance cameras integrated with image recognition software that can pinpoint camcorder lenses in the audience (McBride, 2004).

In addition, copy protection software makes it difficult to duplicate DVDs and other digital media using personal computers and standard video players. However, pirates develop software and hardware capable of disabling or ignoring anticopying codes (Delaney, 2004). Consequently, illegal copying does take place. To address this problem, movie studios use watermarks embedded in images or audio streams in order to identify the sources of unauthorized copies (Ripley, 2004). In addition, picture studios try to impede distribution of pirated movies online by posting thousands of dummy files to file sharing networks. These actions divert the attention of prospective pirates away from the actual movies (Ripley, 2004).

Finally, the movie industry is willing to prosecute pirates who managed to defeat the protective mechanisms set up by studios and theaters. In 2003, 10 lawsuits related to movie piracy were filed under federal law. In addition, 1,461 defendants were charged with film piracy under state laws (McBride and Orwall, 2004).

 THE RESULTS

Technology used by film studios made movie piracy a more difficult and more dangerous activity. Nevertheless, pirates are responding with countermeasures aimed at defeating the barriers raised by the movie industry. Software used to break copy protection codes provides an excellent example of this trend. The effectiveness of legal measures has been quite limited as well. For instance, the Digital Millennium Copyright Act requires VCRs to support technology to prevent unauthorized copying; however, the Act does not specifically address recording video to a hard drive. This allowed a French company, Archos SA, to design and sell video recording devices that comply with the letter of the law yet bypass many piracy safeguards (Delaney, 2004). Furthermore, the threat of litigation has not fully discouraged interested individuals from downloading and sharing digital movies. As of March 2004, movie download activity on peer-to-peer networks such as Kazaa, BitTorrent, and Gnutella continued to pick up the pace ("Online movie piracy . . .," 2004).

Sources: McBride and Orwall (2004), Ripley (2004), Delaney (2004), McBride (2004), and "Online movie piracy . . ." (2004).

 LESSONS LEARNED FROM THIS CASE

Obviously, information technology is not the *cause* of movie piracy, just as it is not the cause of music piracy. (See Online File W16.1 for a discussion of music piracy.) However, it is the tool that tremendously heightens the importance of legal, ethical, and regulatory issues related to this phenomenon.

Copyright, trademark, and patent infringement, freedom of thought and speech, theft of property, and fraud are not new issues in modern societies. However, as this opening case illustrates, information technology adds to the scope and scale of these issues. It also raises a number of questions about what constitutes *illegal* behavior versus unethical, intrusive, or undesirable behavior. This chapter examines these and numerous other impacts of information technology on individuals, organizations, and society.

16.1   INTRODUCTION

Concern about the impact of technology on people, organizations, and society is not new. As early as the 1830s, English intellectuals expressed philosophical arguments about the effects of technologies that had given rise to the Industrial Revolution some 60 to 70 years earlier. Samuel Butler, in his 1872 book *Erehwon* (an anagram for *nowhere*), summarized the anxiety about the disruptive influences of technology on the lives of people. The book described a society that made a conscious decision to reject machines and new technology; in it, people have "frozen" technology at a predetermined level and outlawed all further technological development.

While there are many philosophical, technological, social, and cultural differences between society at the start of the Industrial Revolution and the society of the middle of the *Information Age* in which we now live, there are, nevertheless, people who continue to believe that humankind is threatened by the evolution of technology. Overall, however, our society has not rejected technology but, rather, has embraced it. Most of us recognize that technology and information systems are essential to maintaining, supporting, and enriching many aspects of the lives of individuals, operations of organizations, and functioning of societies. Humans are involved in a symbiotic relationship with technology. All the same, we must be aware of its effect on us as individuals and as members of organizations and society.

Throughout this book, we have noted how information systems are being rationalized, developed, used, and maintained to help organizations meet their needs and reach their goals. In all these discussions, we have assumed that development and implementation of information technology produce only positive results and leave no major negative consequences. However, is this really true? Abundant evidence unmistakably points to potential negative effects of technology in general, and information technology in particular. Information technology has raised a multitude of negative issues, ranging from illegal copying of software programs to surveillance of employees' e-mail. The impact of IT on employment levels is of major concern, as are the effects on sociability and the quality of life.

A more critical issue, however, involves questions such as: Will proliferation of technology cause irreversible changes to the society as we know it? Will humans benefit from the new capabilities of information technology, or will they be harmed by machines playing more and more prominent roles in the society? Who will investigate the costs and risks of technologies? Will society have any control over the decisions to deploy technology?

This chapter will discuss several major themes that can be identified among the countless effects of information technology. We will discuss how information technology removes spatial and geographic barriers, transforms information into an abundant resource, enables machines to perform "human" tasks, and forces people to reconsider their value systems. Each of these trends is comprised of the effects of multiple technologies and has far-reaching implications for various groups of people.

16.2 IT IS ELIMINATING THE BARRIERS OF TIME, SPACE, AND DISTANCE

One of the most noticeable developments precipitated by information technology is the elimination of numerous barriers that traditionally separated individuals, organizations, and societies at different geographic locations. In essence, information technology is redefining the entire concept of time, space, and distance. Proliferation of high-speed data communication networks that span the globe enables companies to integrate geographically distant manufacturing and research facilities, link international financial markets, and even provide customer service from halfway around the world.

Globalization

Offshore outsourcing is one of the manifestations of the trend toward **globalization**—blurring of geographic barriers—that is accelerated by information technology. Well-educated English-speaking employees residing in countries like India and the Philippines can perform services demanded by firms based in the United States, the Great Britain, or any other country. In fact, outsourcing of white-collar services has already become mainstream, with software development and call-center operations being among the most prevalent. Furthermore, the outsourcing trends are naturally expanding into such activities as processing of insurance claims, transcription of medical records, engineering and design work, financial analysis, market research, and many others ("The Remote Future," 2004).

In the future, advances in information technology will make it possible to perform numerous seemingly improbable activities remotely, such as medical diagnosis, treatment, and surgery. For instance, in 2001, doctors in New York performed the first successful cross-Atlantic telesurgery on a patient in Strasbourg, France. The removal of the patient's gallbladder was conducted via a robotic arm that was remotely controlled by the surgeons. A fiber-optic cable operated by France Telecom enabled the high-speed link so that the images from the operating table in France were on display in front of the doctors in New York, with an average time delay of only 150 milliseconds (Johnson, 2002).

From a macroeconomic perspective, the effects of offshore outsourcing are quite positive: It facilitates a more efficient allocation of human resources by removing the imperfections introduced by geographical boundaries. On a microeconomic level, numerous companies will benefit from lower costs of outsourced activities. For example, by outsourcing back-office work to Costa Rica, the Philippines, and Great Britain, Procter & Gamble was able to realize $1 billion in cost reductions (La Londe, 2004).

Nevertheless, outsourcing, as any other impact of information technology, raises an array of complex interrelated issues that are not always positive. For instance, outsourcing may be advantageous to some groups of people, but detrimental to others. Nasscom, the Indian IT industry lobby, forecasts that employment in the "IT-enabled services" industry in India will grow from 770,000 in 2004 to 2 million in 2008 ("The Remote Future," 2004). Yet, employees and trade unions in Western nations are expressing concerns about job losses resulting from offshore outsourcing. The U.S. federal government and the majority of individual states are already considering laws that would prevent government agencies from contracting their services out to foreign firms (Schroeder, 2004).

As the volume of sensitive data processed offshore increases, outsourcing will raise the questions of privacy and confidentiality. *Privacy standards* in a country where data originate may vary dramatically from the privacy laws and privacy

IT at Work 16.1
GLOBAL FIRM RESPONDS TO GLOBAL THREATS

Trend Micro Incorporated, a leading network antivirus and Internet content security firm, offers an excellent example of how information technology can force a company to become global, and yet help it succeed once the firm transcends geographic boundaries. Founded in California in 1988, Trend Micro has grown into a transnational corporation with financial headquarters in Tokyo, product development headquarters in Taiwan, and sales headquarters in Silicon Valley. The company's main virus response center is located in the Philippines, while additional response and engineering labs are scattered across the United States, Japan, Taiwan, Germany, and China. Trend Micro distributed its top executives, engineering teams, and support staff around the globe in order to enhance its ability to respond to new virus threats. "With the Internet, viruses became global. To fight them, we had to become a global company," states Steve Chang, founder, chairman, and CEO.

Even though Trend Micro's 1,800 employees speak different languages and live in different time zones, they communicate in real time using the Internet, e-mail, instant messaging, and videoconferencing. Obviously, the transnational nature of the company presents its own challenges. "We like to joke that we communicate here in a mix of C++ and broken English," says Eva Chen, Trend

Micro's chief technology officer. "For example, we recently had our German and Japanese engineering teams working on a product for the Korean market. They communicated together in English about a product that would be presented in Korean."

Nevertheless, being transnational equips Trend Micro with several impressive capabilities. Having access to engineering talent from around the world helps the company win patents and industry awards. Six response centers operating around the clock make it possible for Trend Micro to be among the first responders to new virus threats, often delivering pattern files and fixes 30 minutes before market leader Symantec Corp. By placing sales headquarters in the massive U.S. market, Trend Micro was able to add about 70 percent of the Fortune 500 companies to the ranks of its customers and grow its revenues from $241 million in 2001 to $454 million in 2003.

Sources: Compiled from Hamm (2003), Rombel (2003), Carroll (2000), and *trendmicro.com* (2004).

For Further Exploration: How does the organizational structure of Trend Micro differ from structures of most other multinational companies? What types of companies stand to benefit from fragmenting their corporate functions and spreading them across the globe?

---

safeguards in the country where the data are processed. An incident in which a disgruntled worker in Pakistan threatened to post medical records of U.S. patients on the Internet highlights the seriousness of this issue (Mintz, 2004).

The remarkable communications capabilities delivered by IT promote globalization not only through offshore outsourcing but also through enabling firms to distribute core corporate functions around the globe. A number of companies have been able to leverage the capabilities of information technologies to become successful transnational corporations, as illustrated in *IT at Work 16.1.*

Telecommuting
Broadband Internet access, secure virtual private networks, and mobile computing technologies are making it possible for many professionals to **telecommute,** or work from outside the office. According to some estimates, by the year 2010 more than half of workers in the United States will spend 2 or more days a week working away from the office. However, experts estimate that even in 10 years it would be uncommon to find workers who telecommute 5 days a week, suggesting that telecommuting would not fully eliminate the need for central office locations (Cole et al., 2003).

The benefits of teleworking are clear: It lowers employers' real estate expenditures, offers greater flexibility to the worker, and reduces the amount of time spent commuting to work. Another benefit is that telecommuting results for many in greater productivity. For example, an employee spending 40 minutes a day traveling to and from work would save over 160 hours a year by working from home, which is equivalent to over 4 weeks of full-time work. In addition, the opportunity to work from home helps parents with young children or other homebound people assume more responsible positions in organizations.

Along with the noticeable benefits, telecommuting places unique demands on the employee who works a room or two away from her bed. Teleworking requires the discipline, initiative, and energy to get the work done in an informal home environment (Garrett, 2003). Furthermore, telecommuting reduces the opportunities for daily face-to-face human interaction that workplaces typically provide. Thus, telecommuting may contribute to social isolation, leading to such serious personal consequences as loneliness and depression (Nie, 2001 and Garrett, 2003). Telecommuting also may contribute to lack of workplace visibility, lower pay (in some cases), and the potential of slower promotions. Telecommuting also forces both employees and managers to focus on results, not just time put in at a desk.

Growth in telecommuting raises the questions of whether the benefits of working from home outweigh the costs, and whether telecommuting is appropriate for everyone or only for workers with certain individual qualities and personality types. Moreover, few of us want to work around the clock, 24 hours a day, seven days a week, 365 days a year, but the pressure to do so could be considerable if the facility exists. Indeed, another pressure may be to work anti-social hours—night shifts, for example, or weekends—which can adversely impact the quality of social interactions and interpersonal relationships. (For more on teleworking, see Online File W16.2.)

Globalization and telecommuting are only two examples of how information technology removes the barriers of time, space, and distance. Far-reaching results of this trend are changing the way we live, work, play, and do business, bringing both improvements that we can enjoy and the challenges that we need to overcome. In the context of organizations, these changes have important implications for structure, authority, power, job content, and personnel issues.

Structure, Authority, Power, Job Content, and Personnel Issues

The IT revolution may result in many changes in structure, authority, power, and job content, as well as personnel management and human resources management. Details of these changes are shown in Table 16.1.

In addition, other changes are expected in organizations. For example, as the corporate culture in the Internet age is changing (see Kleiner, 2000), IT managers are assuming a greater leadership role in making business decisions (see Dalton, 1999). For a comprehensive analysis of business leadership in the information age, see Nevins and Stumpf (1999). Moreover, the impact goes beyond one company or one supply chain, to influence entire industries. For example, the use of profitability models and optimization is reshaping retailing, real estate, banking, transportation, airlines, and car renting, to mention just a few. For more on organizational issues see Mora (2002) and Huang (2001).

These and other changes are impacting personnel issues, as shown in Table 16.2. Many additional personnel-related questions could surface as a result of using IT. For example: What will be the impact of IT on job qualifications and on training requirements? How can jobs that use IT be designed so that they present an acceptable level of challenge to users? How might IT be used to personalize or enrich jobs? What can be done to make sure that the introduction

TABLE 16.1 Impacts of IT on Structure, Authority, Power, and Job Content

Impact	Effect of IT
Flatter organizational hierarchies	IT increases *span of control* (more employees per supervisor), increases productivity, and reduces the need for technical experts (due to expert systems). Fewer managerial levels will result, with fewer staff and line managers. Reduction in the total number of employees, reengineering of business processes, and the ability of lower-level employees to perform higher-level jobs may result in flatter organizational hierarchies.
Change in blue-to-white-collar staff ratio	The ratio of white- to blue-collar workers increases as computers replace clerical jobs, and as the need for information systems specialists increases. However, the number of professionals and specialists could *decline* in relation to the total number of employees in some organizations as intelligent and knowledge-based systems grow.
Growth in number of special units	IT makes possible technology centers, e-commerce centers, decision support systems departments, and/or intelligent systems departments. Such units may have a major impact on organizational structure, especially when they are supported by or report directly to top management.
Centralization of authority	Centralization may become more popular because of the trend toward smaller and flatter organizations and the use of expert systems. On the other hand, the Web permits greater empowerment, allowing for more decentralization. Whether use of IT results in more centralization or in decentralization may depend on top management's philosophy.
Changes in power and status	Knowledge is power, and those who control information and knowledge are likely to gain power. The struggle over who controls the information resources has become a conflict in many organizations. In some countries, the fight may be between corporations that seek to use information for competitive advantage and the government (e.g., Microsoft vs. the Justice Dept.). Elsewhere, governments may seek to hold onto the reins of power by not letting private citizens access some information (e.g., China's restriction of Internet usage).
Changes in job content and skill sets	*Job content* is interrelated with employee satisfaction, compensation, status, and productivity. Resistance to changes in job skills is common, and can lead to unpleasant confrontations between employees and management (see Routt, 1999).

of IT does not demean jobs or have other negative impacts from the workers' point of view? What principles should be used to allocate functions to people and machines, especially those functions that can be performed equally well by either one? Should cost or efficiency be the sole or major criterion for such allocation? All these and more issues could be encountered in any IT implementation.

TABLE 16.2 Impacts of IT on Personnel Issues

Impact	Effect of IT
Shorter career ladders	In the past, many professionals developed their abilities through years of experience and a series of positions that exposed them to progressively more complex situations. The use of IT, and especially Web-based computer-aided instruction, may short-cut this learning curve.
Changes in supervision	IT introduces the possibility for greater electronic supervision. In general, the supervisory process may become more formalized, with greater reliance on procedures and measurable (i.e., quantitative) outputs and less on interpersonal processes. This is especially true for knowledge workers and telecommuters.
Job mobility	The Web has the potential to increase job mobility. Sites such as *techjourney.com* can tell you how jobs pay in any place in the U.S. Sites like *monster.com* offer places to post job offerings and résumés. Using videoconferencing for interviews and intelligent agents to find jobs is likely to increase employee turnover.

16.3 INFORMATION IS CHANGING FROM A SCARCE RESOURCE TO AN ABUNDANT RESOURCE

Information technology has brought about major improvements in the ability of humans to collect, store, process, and disseminate information. The trend toward increased reliance on information started decades ago. In fact, the United States entered the Information Age in 1957 when the number of U.S. employees whose primary job responsibilities involved handling of information exceeded the number of industrial workers (Porat, 1977).

However, this impact of information technology became particularly pronounced with the rapid development of the Internet and the World Wide Web. Development of the telecommunications infrastructure, coupled with the explosive growth of personal computers and ubiquitous mobile computing devices, is bringing vast amounts of information to people any time, anywhere. The number of Web servers mushroomed from 23,500 in mid-1995 to 38.1 million by early 2002 (Kessler, 2003). The number of publicly accessible Web pages approached 4.3 billion in 2004 (Google, 2004), while billions of other documents were available through company intranets and proprietary databases.

Furthermore, the number of people linked by this global network is expected to climb from 597 million in 2002 to 963 million in 2006 (Kessler, 2003). Thanks to information technology, millions of people have instantaneous access to information ranging from up-to-the-minute news from every part of the world, to stock quotes, to office documents, to personal e-mail. Unquestionably, information is becoming an abundant resource that is playing a critical part in the functioning of individuals, businesses, and societies.

Information Overload

Few people disagree with the notion that information is a valuable resource and that increased availability of information can be beneficial for individuals and organizations alike. However, information technology's capability to introduce ever-growing amounts of data and information into our lives can exceed our capacity to keep up with them, leading to **information overload.** Business users are not suffering from the scarcity of data; instead, they are discovering that the process of finding the information they need in massive collections of documents can be complicated, time consuming, and expensive. Some researchers report that this process takes up to a third of an employee's workday (Turocy et al., 2002).

Attempts to absorb the wealth of readily available information force people to *multitask*. A study conducted at a financial institution suggests that, on average, employees switched tasks every three minutes, either from interruptions or by their own choice. Moreover, people frequently attend meetings or talk on the phone while being distracted by surfing the Web, reading e-mails, or exchanging instant messages (Berman, 2003). These and other forms of "absent presence" may have adverse effects on job performance and the quality of interpersonal communications.

The impact of information overload is felt not only in business circles but also in many other parts of the society, including the military intelligence community. At the onset of the Information Age, intelligence professionals acquired never-before-seen data collection tools, including high-resolution satellite imagery and versatile sensors capable of penetrating natural and manmade barriers. Furthermore, information technology enabled the intelligence community to establish high-speed communication links to transfer the data, build vast databases to store the data, and use powerful supercomputers with intelligent software to process the data. Clearly, information technology has greatly increased both the amount of information available to the intelligence community and the speed at which it can analyze this information.

However, existing computer systems and human analysts are unable to deal with the increasing volumes of data, creating the information-overload problem. For instance, according to MacDonald and Oettinger (2002), "information that might have prevented some of the September 11 attacks apparently existed somewhere within the vast quantity of data collected by the intelligence community, but the systems for using such information have lagged far behind the ability to collect the data."

Ironically, experts believe that the problem of information overload created by information technology may also be solved by information technology (Turocy et al., 2002). Enterprise content management tools, knowledge management systems (KMSs), and decision support systems (DSSs) hold the promise of organizing the data into concise, actionable pieces of information that the users need. In fact, as we discussed in Chapters 10 through 12, numerous organizations are already benefiting from the improvements in the ability to manage data, information, and knowledge that these systems and related technologies can offer.

However, most existing systems that employ summarization and ranking as the primary methods of reducing the volume of information suffer from serious limitations. These systems may provide a view of the "big picture" but omit critical details or relevant pieces of information, thereby distorting the overall picture. To be effective at solving the problem of information overload, information systems must differentiate between the data that can be safely summarized and the data that should be viewed in its original form (DeSouza et al., 2004).

While the high-tech solutions to information overload are still under development, some organizations are trying to minimize the negative impacts of this phenomenon by promoting "e-mail-free Wednesdays" or encouraging employees to limit their Web surfing and e-mail use to reasonable amounts (Berman, 2003).

Information Quality

As organizations and societies continue to generate, process, and rely on the rapidly increasing amounts of information, they begin to realize the importance of information quality. **Information quality** is a somewhat subjective measure of the utility, objectivity, and integrity of gathered information. Quality issues affect both the simple collections of facts (data) and the more complex pieces of processed data (information). To be truly valuable, both data and information must possess a number of essential characteristics, such as being complete, accurate, up-to-date, and "fit for the purpose" for which they are used (Ojala, 2003). (See also the discussion of data quality in Chapter 10.) The value and usability of data and information that do not satisfy these requirements are severely limited.

Issues relating to information quality have become sufficiently significant that they now occupy a notable place on the government's legislative agenda. The Data Quality Act of 2001 and the Sarbanes–Oxley Act of 2002 impose stringent information quality requirements on government agencies and publicly traded corporations (Loshin, 2004). For example, one of the provisions of the Sarbanes–Oxley Act makes chief executive and financial officers personally responsible and liable for the quality of financial information that firms release to stockholders or file with the Securities and Exchange Commission. This rule emphasizes the importance of controlling and measuring data quality and information quality in business intelligence, corporate performance management, and record management systems (Logan and Buytendijk, 2003).

Information quality problems are not limited to corporate data. Millions of individuals face information quality issues on a daily basis as they try to find information online, whether on publicly available Web pages or in specialized research databases. According to Wurman (2000), between 60 and 80 percent of the people searching for specific information on the Web cannot find what they need from the various types of information available.

Among the most common problems that plague online information sources is omission of materials. A number of online "full-text" periodicals databases may omit certain items that appeared in the printed versions of those publications. In addition, online sources of information leave out older documents, which are not available in digital form. Thus, one cannot be assured of having access to a complete set of relevant materials. Even materials that are available from seemingly reputable sources present information quality concerns. Information may have been reported wrong, whether intentionally or unintentionally, or the information may have become out of date (Ojala, 2003). These and other information quality issues are contributing to the frustration and anxiety that for some have become the unfortunate side effect of the Information Age.

Spam   Speed and low cost of modern information technologies that are enhancing our access to valuable information are also responsible for introducing growing amounts of "information noise" to our lives. *Spamming*, the practice of indiscriminately broadcasting unsolicited messages via e-mail and over the Internet, is one of the most widespread forms of digital noise. Spam is typically directed at a person and presents a considerable annoyance, with 70 percent of users indicating that "spam makes being online unpleasant" (Davies, 2004).

In February 2004, unsolicited commercial e-mail comprised two-thirds of all messages, as compared to only 7 percent two years earlier ("Spam . . .," 2004). This volume of messages significantly impairs the bandwidth of Internet service providers and places excessive capacity demands on mail servers. In electronic commerce, spam can delay transactions and can cause problems in supply chains where business data are exchanged through specially configured e-mail accounts (Davies, 2004). Spam hurts businesses even more by lowering the productivity of employees who have to deal with unwanted messages.

The potential adverse effect of unsolicited commercial e-mail was recognized quite early. One major piece of U.S. legislation addressing online marketing practices is the Electronic Mailbox Protection Act, passed in 1997. The primary thrust of this law is that commercial speech is subject to government regulation, and that spamming, which can cause significant harm, expense, and annoyance, should be controlled. The Electronic Mailbox Protection Act requires those sending spam to identify it as advertising, to indicate the name of the sender prominently, and to include valid routing information. Recipients of spam have the right to request termination of future spam from the same sender and to bring civil action if necessary.

However, the effectiveness of the Electronic Mailbox Protection Act has been quite limited because spammers operate globally. A recent anti-spam act passed in Australia explicitly acknowledges the global nature of spam, by considering it a violation to send any unsolicited commercial electronic communication that can be accessed in Australia, regardless of its origin or intended destination (Fiedler, 2004). Enforcement of this law may remain problematic, though. Viable regulation will require cooperation of governments worldwide (Davies, 2004). See Online File W16.3 for discussion of the U.S. Can-Spam Act.

Internet service providers and software companies have embarked on a technological campaign to eradicate spam. Mail-filtering software and other technologies have made it more difficult for spammers to distribute their messages. However, spammers have responded with creative new schemes to defeat the anti-spam solutions. The battle of innovations and counterinnovations between spammers and anti-spam companies continues.

The Digital Divide

The arrival of the Information Age made information a considerably more abundant resource; however, technologies enabling access to information are not distributed evenly among various groups of people. For some people, information continues to be a scarce resource, which puts them at a comparative economic and social disadvantage. The gap in computer technology in general, and now in Web technology in particular, between those who have such technology and those who do not is referred to as the **digital divide.**

According to UN and ITU reports, more than 90 percent of all Internet hosts are in developed countries, where only 15 percent of the world's population resides. In 2001, the city of New York, for example, had more Internet hosts than the whole continent of Africa. Venkat (2002) asserted that the digital divide has consistently followed the income divide all over the world. More than 96 percent of those with Internet access are in the wealthiest nations, representing 15 percent of the world's population.

The digital divide exists not only between countries, but also within them. Internet access is highly correlated with education, wealth, and other socioeconomic status characteristics. In the United States, only 31 percent of those without a high school diploma and only 53 percent of high school graduates use the Internet, as compared to 86 percent of college graduates. A similar relationship exists between Internet access and household income. Only 40 percent of individuals with household incomes of $15,000 or less access the Internet, whereas 88 percent of individuals earning more than $100,000 are Internet users (Nie, 2001).

The U.S. federal and state governments are attempting to close this gap within the country by encouraging training and by supporting education and infrastructure improvements. For example, the U.S. Department of Education reports that the percentage of public schools with Internet access rose from 50 percent in 1995 to 99 percent in 2001, with little difference among schools regardless of their location, size, or socioeconomic makeup (Kessler, 2003).

Many other government and international organizations are also trying to close the digital divide around the world. Furthermore, a number of for-profit technology companies have realized that supporting the adoption of information technology in developing countries not only benefits local residents but also presents new profitable opportunities. Hewlett-Packard is one of the leaders in developing low-cost computing and communications devices targeted at the

4 billion people in developing countries. The company's "e-inclusion" initiatives create social value, while improving the firm's brand image, sales, and profitability ("Beyond the digital divide," 2004). Efforts to bridge the global digital divide are beginning to show encouraging results. International Data Corporation projects that the Asia-Pacific hardware market (excluding Japan) will grow at a compounded annual rate of 17.2 percent for the 2001–2006 period, as compared to the rate of 7.0 percent in the United States (Graham-Hackett, 2003).

Impacts on Individuals

Together, the increasing amounts of information and information technology use have potential impacts on job satisfaction, dehumanization, and information anxiety as well as impacts on health and safety. Although many jobs may become substantially more "enriched" with IT, other jobs may become more routine and less satisfying. For example, as early as 1970, researchers predicted that computer-based information systems would reduce managerial discretion in decision making and thus create dissatisfied managers. This dissatisfaction may be the result of perceived dehumanization.

DEHUMANIZATION AND OTHER PSYCHOLOGICAL IMPACTS. A frequent criticism of traditional data processing systems was their impersonal nature and their potential to *dehumanize* and depersonalize the activities that have been computerized. Many people felt, and still feel, a loss of identity, a **dehumanization,** because of computerization; they feel like "just another number" because computers reduce or eliminate the human element that was present in the noncomputerized systems. Some people also feel this way about the Web.

On the other hand, while the major objective of newer technologies, such as e-commerce, is to increase productivity, they can also create *personalized,* flexible systems that allow individuals to include their opinions and knowledge in the system. These technologies attempt to be people-oriented and user-friendly.

The Internet threatens to have an even more isolating influence than has been created by television. If people are encouraged to work and shop from their living rooms, then some unfortunate psychological effects, such as depression and loneliness, could develop. Some people have become so addicted to the Web that they have dropped out of their regular social activities, at school or work or home, creating new societal and organizational problems.

Another possible psychological impact relates to distance learning. In some countries, it is legal to school children at home through IT. Some argue, however, that the lack of social contacts could be damaging to the social, moral, and cognitive development of school-age children who spend long periods of time working alone on the computer.

INFORMATION ANXIETY. One of the negative impacts of the Information Age is **information anxiety.** This disquiet can take several forms, such as frustration with our *inability to keep up with the amount of data* present in our lives. Information anxiety can take other forms as well. One is frustration with the quality of the information available on the Web, which frequently is not up-to-date or is incomplete. Another is frustration or guilt associated with not being better informed, or being informed too late ("How come others knew this before I did?"). A third form of information anxiety stems from information overload (too many online sources). For some Internet users, anxiety resulting from information overload may even result in inadequate or poor sleep. (For some possible solutions, see *sleepfoundation.org*.)

According to Wurman (2000), between 60 and 80 percent of the people searching for specific information on the Web cannot find what they want among the various types of information available. This adds to anxiety, as does the data glut that obscures the distinction between data and information, and between facts and knowledge. Wurman (2001) prescribes solutions to ease the problem of information anxiety, ranging from better access to data to better design of Web sites.

IMPACTS ON HEALTH AND SAFETY. Computers and information systems are a part of the environment that may adversely affect individuals' health and safety. To illustrate, we will discuss the effects of three issues: *job stress, video display terminals*, and *long-term use of the keyboard*. (For further discussion see the *Wall Street Journal*, April 9, 1996, p. 1.)

Job Stress. An increase in workload and/or responsibilities can trigger job stress. Although computerization has benefited organizations by increasing productivity, it has also created an ever-increasing workload for some employees. Some workers, especially those who are not proficient with computers but who must work with them, feel overwhelmed and start feeling anxious about their jobs and their job performance. These feelings of anxiety can adversely affect workers' productivity. Management's responsibility is to help alleviate these feelings by providing training, redistributing the workload among workers, or by hiring more individuals.

Video Display Terminals. Exposure to video display terminals (VDTs) raises the issue of the risk of radiation exposure, which has been linked to cancer and other health-related problems. Exposure to VDTs for long periods of time is thought to affect an individual's eyesight, for example. Also, lengthy exposure to VDTs has been blamed for miscarriages in pregnant women. However, results of the research done to investigate these charges have been inconclusive.

Repetitive Strain (Stress) Injuries. Other potential health and safety hazards are repetitive strain injuries such as backaches and muscle tension in the wrists and fingers. *Carpal tunnel syndrome* is a painful form of repetitive strain injury that affects the wrists and hands. It has been associated with the long-term use of keyboards. According to Kome (2001), 6 million Americans suffered repetitive strain injuries on the job between 1991 and 2001.

Lessening the Negative Impact on Health and Safety. Designers are aware of the potential problems associated with prolonged use of computers. Consequently, they have attempted to design a better computing environment. Research in the area of **ergonomics** (the science of adapting machines and work environments to people) provides guidance for these designers. For instance, ergonomic techniques focus on creating an environment for the worker that is safe, well lit, and comfortable. Devices such as antiglare screens have helped alleviate problems of fatigued or damaged eyesight, and chairs that contour the human body have helped decrease backaches (see *A Closer Look 16.1*, page 702).

OTHER IMPACTS. Interactions between individuals and computers are so numerous that entire volumes can be written on the subject. An overview of such interactions is provided by Kanter (1992). As he describes, and as this book

A CLOSER LOOK
16.1 ERGONOMIC AND PROTECTIVE PRODUCTS

Many products are available to improve working conditions for people who spend much of their time at a computer. The following photos illustrate some ergonomic solutions.

Wrist support

Back support

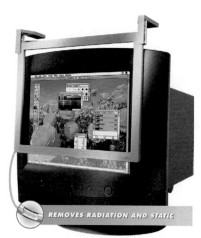

Eye-protection filter (optically coated glass).

Adjustable foot rest

has shown, computers have affected nearly every aspect of our lives—shopping and commerce, business and financial systems, education, medicine, delivery of public and private services, leisure activities, and even the homes in which we live. For a review of individual acceptance of information technologies, see Agarwal (2000).

16.4 MACHINES ARE PERFORMING FUNCTIONS PREVIOUSLY PERFORMED BY HUMANS

One of the distinguishing traits of humankind is the continuous quest to find tools and techniques to replace human work and manual labor. Information technology greatly accelerates this process and allows machines to perform a variety of complex functions, which, in the past, could be performed only by humans. Robotics offers a clear example of information technology eliminating the need for human labor. Computerized transaction processing systems, automated teller machines, intelligent scheduling software, and voice recognition systems illustrate information technology's capability to replace administrative and clerical work. Moreover, artificial intelligence and expert systems are now able to perform the work of white-collar professionals. As functionality of machines and computer systems continues to evolve, it will transform societies by influencing such critical factors as the quality of life, the dynamics of labor markets, and the nature of human interactions.

Quality of Life
Quality of life refers to measures of how well we achieve a desirable standard of living. For example, the use of robots in uncomfortable or dangerous environments is one of the primary ways of improving the quality of life with information technology. For decades, robots have been used to replace physically demanding or tedious activities in manufacturing plants. In recent years, robots and other quasi-autonomous devices have become increasingly common on farm fields, in hospitals, and even in private homes, improving the quality of life of numerous people. A type of robot works at the University of California Hospital at San Francisco. The five-foot-tall machine, which can drive down the hallways and call an elevator to travel to other floors, carries medicine and blood samples around the building (Stone, 2003). Specialized robots that can relieve people of the need to perform certain household tasks are becoming commercially available. For instance, robotic vacuum cleaners capable of finding their way around furniture and other obstacles in any room are already sweeping the floors in thousands of homes around the world.

Military applications of robotics hold the potential not only to improve the quality of life but also to save the lives of soldiers. The Pentagon is researching self-driving vehicles and bee-like swarms of small surveillance robots, each of which would contribute a different view or angle of a combat zone. In March 2004, DARPA, the research arm of the U.S. Department of Defense, held a race of fully autonomous land vehicles across a challenging 150-mile stretch of the Mojave Desert. Thirteen entrants designed vehicles that could navigate and drive themselves without humans at the remote controls. This race ended without any winners. The machine that traveled the farthest—12 km—was built by Carnegie Mellon University ("Robots, start your engines," 2004). These initial results suggest that significant advances in IT will need to be made before robots can handle complex, unfamiliar situations and operate entirely autonomously. Nevertheless, the Department of Defense plans another race for 2006 and expects that by 2015 one-third of U.S. combat ground vehicles will be autonomous ("Science and Technology . . .," 2004).

Somewhat less obvious, but very noticeable improvements in the quality of life arise from the ability of computers to "make decisions"—an activity that used to be in the exclusive domain of human beings. Although such decisions are typically limited in scope and are based on rules established by people, they are successfully employed in a variety of practical applications. For example, automobile navigation systems may be incapable of guiding a vehicle across the unpredictable desert terrain, but they are quite adept at finding the optimal route to the desired destination using a network of existing roadways. Onboard global positioning systems (GPSs) integrated with geographic information systems (GISs) available in many modern vehicles allow the driver to hand over navigational decisions to the computer, thereby offering an additional level of safety and convenience (Kageyama, 2000).

Expert systems used in the healthcare industry offer another example of quality of life improvements that follow from machines' abilities to perform "human" work. For instance, some systems can improve the diagnosis process by analyzing the set of symptoms experienced by the patient. Other systems can supplement a physician's judgment by analyzing prescriptions for dosage and potential drug interactions, thus reducing the frequency and severity of medication errors, which translates into a higher quality of life for the patients. Partners HealthCare System, Inc., for example, reported a 55 percent reduction in the number of serious medication errors following the implementation of such a system (Melymuka, 2002).

Whether robots will be of the quality of R2D2 (the *Star Wars* robot) is another issue. It probably will be a long time before we see robots making decisions by themselves, handling unfamiliar situations, and interacting with people. Nevertheless, robots are around that can do practical tasks. Carnegie Mellon University, for example, has developed self-directing tractors that harvest hundreds of acres of crops around the clock in California, using global positioning systems combined with video image processing that identifies rows of uncut crops. Robots are especially helpful in hazardous environments, as illustrated in *IT at Work 16.2.*

The fact that machines can now answer the phone, receive and forward voice mail messages, automatically filter e-mail, process standard transactions, and perform numerous other repetitive and inflexible tasks implies that humans are less likely to have these responsibilities. As information technology improves organizational efficiency, it also alters the nature of the workplace by expanding it from the traditional 9-to-5 jobs at a central location to 24 hours a day at any location. This expansion provides an exceptional level of flexibility that can significantly improve the quality of leisure time, even if the total amount of leisure time is not increased.

Impact on Labor Markets

Rapid diffusion of information technology and its increasing potential to replicate the roles previously performed by human workers draw attention to IT's impact on labor markets. One of the most prominent concerns is the fear that due to technological advances, machines will replace millions of workers, leading to mass unemployment. Robots and office automation systems are effectively competing with humans for blue-collar and clerical jobs. It is important to note that white-collar occupations are not immune to the impact of information technology either. In fact, machines are beginning to challenge scientists, interpreters, computer programmers, lawyers, aircraft pilots, and other professionals in their jobs.

Researchers in Great Britain, for instance, have built a robot-scientist capable of performing simple genetic experiments. The computer-controlled robot

IT at Work 16.2
THE WORKING LIVES OF ROBOTS

LAYING FIBER OPTIC CABLES. Cities around the world are transforming themselves to the digital era by replacing copper wires with fiber-optic cables or by installing fiber optics where there were no wires before. Because fiber-optic cables are a choice method to deliver high-speed voice and data communication (see Technology Guide 4), demand for them is expanding. Cities know that in order to attract and hold on to high-tech business they must provide fiber-optic access to all commercial buildings. You may have seen this activity many times without realizing it: Workers cut up the street, creating noise, dust, and traffic problems. But the worst part of it is that the disruption to people may take weeks, or even months, just to complete one city block. Now, robots are changing it all.

One company that invented a technology to improve the situation is City Net Telecommunications (*citynettelecom .com*). The idea is to use the existing sewer system to lay the cables. This way no trenches need to be dug in the streets. Pioneering work has been done in Albuquerque, New Mexico, Omaha, Nebraska, and Indianapolis, Indiana (in spring 2001). How do the robots help? Robots are waterproof and do not have noses, and so they are not bothered by working in the sewer. They do not complain, nor do they get sick. As a matter of fact, they work faster than humans when it comes to laying the fiber-optic cables inside the sewer system.

What does it cost? The company claims that laying the fiber-optic cable with robots costs about the same as the old method. The major advantage is that it can be done 60 percent faster and without disruption to people's lives.

CLEANING TRAIN STATIONS IN JAPAN. With growing amounts of rubbish to deal with at Japanese train stations and fewer people willing to work as cleaners, officials have started turning the dirty work over to robots. Since May 1993, the Central Japan Railway Company and Sizuko Company, a Japanese machinery maker, have been using robots programmed to vacuum rubbish. A railway official said the robots, which are capable of doing the work of 10 people each, have been operating at the Sizuko station in Central Japan. The robots measure about 1.5 meters wide and 1.2 meters long. The railway and Sizuko spent 70 million yen to develop the machines and are planning to program them for other tasks, such as sweeping and scrubbing.

Sources: Compiled from the *New York Times* (March 6, 2001); from the *Wall Street Journal* (November 21, 2000); and from "Robots Used to Clean Train Station in . . .," (1993). See also "The Robot Revolution Is on the Way" (2000).

For Further Exploration: If robots are so effective, what will be the impact on unemployment when more tasks are robotized? What will people do if robots take over?

---

independently formulated hypotheses about the functions of unknown genes, designed experiments to test them, manipulated laboratory equipment to conduct the experiments, analyzed the results, and accepted or rejected hypotheses based on the evidence it obtained. The robot's performance was comparable to the performance of graduate students working on similar tasks (Begley, 2004).

Translators and interpreters also face competition from information technology in the form of speech- and text-based machine translation systems. While existing machine translation software cannot rival the accuracy, clarity, eloquence, and vividness of human translations, it is typically able to convey the gist of the message and comply with the major rules of grammar and syntax (Schwartz, 2004). (Visit *online-translator.com, google.com/language_tools,* and *world.altavista.com* to review several online translation services.)

Similarly, information technology is expanding into other job areas as well. New software applications might be written by other software programs with minimal input from humans, thus vying for the jobs of certain computer programmers (Challenger, 2000). Legal professionals may also discover some unusual contenders, eager to take over their jobs. Some software packages used by law firms rely on artificial intelligence to analyze facts, determine applicable regulations, and prepare drafts of appropriate documents—all of which are activities traditionally performed by entry-level lawyers and paralegals (Challenger, 2000). And, although information technology is not expected to displace airline pilots in the near future, this may be a plausible scenario over a longer time horizon. In fact, computer-controlled airplanes have already left the realm of science fiction. In March 2003, Boeing X-45, a stealth unmanned military aircraft, performed a successful test flight. The plane took off, completed its mission, and landed without human intervention (Stone, 2003).

These and other examples illustrate a valid threat that information technology presents to workers in numerous occupations. In addition, they prompt the question of whether you should be concerned about the prospects of computers acquiring the capabilities of doing your job more effectively and efficiently. Following the introduction of new technologies that mimic the functions of human workers, it is common to observe some job losses as old jobs are replaced by computerized equipment. However, this negative impact on employment levels offers a very simplistic and incomplete picture of the chain of events associated with technological advances.

One of the more straightforward positive side-effects of technological advances is the creation of new jobs, which takes place in other sectors of the economy that produce and operate the new equipment and computer systems. Furthermore, introduction of new information technologies results in more efficient allocation of scarce resources, such as labor, capital, and raw materials. As the production processes become more efficient, they apply downward pressure on price levels, which leads to higher demand, as consumers respond to lower prices. To satisfy the growing demand, producers tend to increase the output of goods and services, which is frequently accomplished by hiring more workers. Other entities in the affected supply chains react to increased demand and instigate further employment growth. Thus, from the macroeconomic perspective, technological progress generally increases the aggregate level of employment (Soete, 2001).

Empirical data support this theory: Total employment in the United States has been steadily increasing, from less than 60 million in 1948 to more than 135 million in 2000. The rate of employment growth has not weakened, even in the 1980s and 1990s, when the use of information technology rose dramatically in virtually every sector of the economy. Moreover, fluctuations in unemployment rates are generally associated with business cycles and do not indicate that information technology is likely to displace a large number of workers (Handel, 2003). *IT at Work 16.3* demonstrates one of the impacts of information technology on employment in the retailing industry.

Although the net effect of information technology proliferation is generally positive for the economy as a whole, on a personal level, IT-induced *job displacement* may be a disruptive experience. Individual workers may need to develop new areas of expertise, acquire new skill sets, and seek employment in unfamiliar industries and occupations. For some, this presents a threat to their current lifestyles; for others, this may be an opportunity to improve their well-being and quality of life. One thing is clear—information technology has already changed the nature of countless jobs and is likely to eliminate certain jobs altogether, leaving a lasting impact on individuals and societies.

IT at Work 16.3
DO-IT-YOURSELF RETAILING

The concept of allowing shoppers to scan and bag their own items at retail stores has been around for quite a while. In the 1980s, technology necessary to implement self-checkout systems was already available. However, at that time, the costs of such systems were prohibitively high, and consumer acceptance was extremely low. As this technology continued to evolve and mature, self-checkout registers turned into attractive propositions for supermarkets, grocery stores, and other retailers. In winter of 1997, Wal-Mart was among the first merchants to test the self-checkout systems in Fayetteville, Arkansas, and other selected markets.

The self-checkout machines were developed by Optimal Robotics based in Montreal, Canada. Each register included a holding area with a conveyer belt, a barcode reader, a touch-screen display, and a voice synthesizer to provide the customer with vocal and visual instructions, as well as a bagging area, which rested on scales that checked whether the weight of the scanned item corresponded with the weight of the item placed in the bag. The checkout stations also included currency readers and equipment to accept credit and debit cards, which allowed the customer to pay for the goods.

The results of the initial tests were quite encouraging; thus, in 2002 the company began a large-scale rollout of self-checkout units. Wal-Mart is installing self-checkout machines in most new Supercenters and Neighborhood Market Stores. A significant number of existing stores were also retrofitted with the new technology. Typically, the company installs from four to eight self-checkout stations in a store, depending on its size and sales volume.

The main reasons that persuade retailers to adopt the new systems include the desire to provide a better customer experience and the need to control costs. Self-checkout stations occupy 25 percent less space than traditional registers, which allows retailers to place more stations within the same floor space. Furthermore, with only one employee overseeing four machines, the store is able to keep a sufficient number of registers open while driving down labor costs. A set of four registers, which costs $80,000 to $100,000, has a payback period of only 6 to 12 months, if implemented correctly.

Consumers enjoy shorter lines, faster service, and greater control over the checkout process. In a 2003 survey by ACNielsen, 61 percent of respondents reported using self-checkout machines. Of these, 32 percent characterized them as "great" and 52 percent labeled them as "okay." However, 30 percent of consumers who had tried self-checkout indicated that they were not planning to use the systems again. Yet, even those consumers who do not wish to use the self-checkout machines benefit from having them in their stores, because they open up regular lanes for the "old-fashioned" customers.

IHL Consulting Group estimates that by the end of 2002, approximately 25 percent of U.S. grocery chains were equipped with self-checkout stations. By 2005, the market for self-checkout systems will exceed $1.3 billion, and by 2006, nearly all supermarket chains are expected to offer some degree of self-checkout service.

As self-checkout machines gain the capabilities to perform the functions of human cashiers (with some help from shoppers), they gradually displace store employees from their jobs. Most consumers acknowledge the time savings and convenience of self-checkout systems, and most business managers recognize the cost savings associated with their use. Nevertheless, the effectiveness and efficiency of self-checkout will mean little to a cashier who lost her job right after the systems were introduced at her previous place of work.

Sources: Compiled from King (2004), McCartney (1999), "Self-checkout gets mixed bag of results" (2003), "Self-checkout's 'explosive' growth . . ." (2004).

For Further Exploration: What types of stores are likely to derive the greatest benefit from self-checkout systems? What other technologies may replace a substantial number of workers in the retailing industry? How will the self-checkout process change when retailers place radio frequency identification (RFID) tags on each individual store item?

Human–Computer Interactions   With continuously expanding capabilities of computers and IT-enabled devices, people are spending a greater proportion of their time interacting with machines, as opposed to interacting with other people face-to-face. The range of common *human–computer interactions* is quite extensive. In education, for example, computer-based training and Web-based course delivery systems are commonly supplementing or even entirely replacing the conventional interactions with professors, instructors, and other students that typically occur in the classroom. In fact, certain educational institutions offer degree programs (including associate's, bachelor's, master's, and even doctoral), in which the entire curriculum is offered via the Internet.

Online shopping and e-commerce provides another illustration of information technology taking over person-to-person contacts and replacing them with human–computer interactions. International Data Corporation estimates that in 2003, individuals and organizations made more than $1.4 trillion worth of online purchases (Rudy, 2003b). Books, shoes, groceries, cars, medicines, airplane tickets, and, of course, ever-more-powerful computers are commonly purchased through Web-based retailers, which minimizes the contact with human workers. Proliferation of automated teller machines as well as online banking and brokerage services reflects a similar trend in the financial services industry and other sectors of the economy.

Furthermore, a growing number of firms are relying on machines to provide basic customer service to their clients. Computers with voice recognition software, natural language processing technologies, and text-to-speech capabilities commonly replace customer service representatives at call centers of various organizations. Alternatively, companies frequently direct consumers to their Web sites for service and customer care in order to reduce the costs of support personnel.

Many working professionals have discovered that voice mail systems, software organizers, automatic scheduling applications, and personal digital assistants (PDAs) are replacing administrative assistants and eliminating another aspect of interpersonal interactions that formerly existed in the workplace.

With the advent of high-definition television, home theater systems, digital video recorders, and on-demand programming, consumers can enjoy high-quality music and motion pictures in the privacy of their own homes, which tends to substitute for going to the movies and participating in other social activities. Rising popularity of video games demonstrates another significant shift toward interactions with computers that takes place at the expense of interpersonal activities. For a long time, parents, educators, and psychologists have been expressing concerns about the possible negative consequences of video game obsession on the physical, psychological, and social development of children and young adults.

The movement toward increased interaction with machines is likely to expand into many other spheres of the society. One of the most interesting issues related to this trend is the role of humans in the operation of stock markets. The New York Stock Exchange (NYSE) is one of the few exchanges that have preserved a traditional floor-based manual trading model in which multiple specialists participate in every transaction. Most other exchanges, such as NASDAQ, have adopted fully electronic trading systems in which buyers and sellers communicate with each other using computers and secure communication networks. Proponents of the computerized trading model argue that removing the unnecessary layer of human interaction leads to a more efficient, more consistent, and more transparent system for trading financial instruments. Defenders of the manual system, on the other hand, insist that it is human judgment and discretion that helped the NYSE maintain its prominent position among global financial markets. One of the feasible solutions to this controversy is to develop a computerized trading system with its inherent efficiency, while using the human judgment to establish and enforce trading rules (Greifeld, 2003).

As demonstrated by electronic stock exchanges, even interactions between two or more humans increasingly involve machines as intermediaries. E-mail, voice mail, online bulletin boards, Web logs, instant messaging, and video conferencing are among the most widely accepted information technologies that people use to communicate with each other.

An innovative combination of these communication tools can be used to create a *virtual community.* A community is a group of people with some common interests who interact with one another. **Virtual communities** parallel typical physical communities, such as neighborhoods, clubs, or associations, except that people do not meet face-to-face. Instead, community members meet online using digital tools to communicate and collaborate. Similar to the click-and-mortar e-commerce model, many physical communities also have an online presence for Internet-related activities.

Pure-play Internet communities (those that exist solely online) may have thousands or even millions of members. For instance, GeoCities—an advertising-supported community that allows members to set up free personal homepages—grew to 10 million members in less than 2 years and had over 45 million members in 2002 (*geocities.yahoo.com*). This is one major difference from purely physical communities, which are usually smaller. Another difference is that offline communities are frequently confined to one geographical location, whereas online communities can go beyond geographical constraints.

Virtual communities can be classified in several ways. The most common classification is the one proposed by Armstrong and Hagel (1996). They recognized four types of Internet communities: communities of transactions, communities of interest, communities of practice (or relations), and communities of fantasy. (For other classifications see Hummel and Lechner, 2002.) Examples of these communities are provided in Table 16.3. In addition, *IT at Work 16.4* (page 710) describes the operation of a virtual gaming community.

TABLE 16.3 Types of Virtual Communities

Community Type	Description
Transactions	Facilitates buying and selling (e.g., *ausfish.com.au*). Combines information portal with infrastructure for trading. Members are buyers, sellers, intermediaries, etc. Focused on a specific commercial area (e.g., fishing).
Purpose or interest	No trading, just exchange of information on a topic of mutual interest. *Examples:* Investors consult The Motley Fool (*fool.com*) for investment advice; *Geocities.yahoo.com* is a collection of several areas of interest in one place.
Relations or practice	Members are organized around certain life experiences. For example *ivillage.com* caters to women. Professional communities also belong to this category. *Example: isworld.org* for information systems faculty, students, and professionals.
Fantasy	Members share imaginary environments. *Examples:* sport fantasy teams at *espn.com;* over 80,000 members of Utopia (*games.swirve.com/utopia/*) can pretend to be kings of medieval provinces in an online multiplayer game.

Sources: Compiled from Armstrong and Hagel (1996) and Hagel and Armstrong (1997).

IT at Work 16.4
NET FUN: VIRTUAL GAME PLAYER COMMUNITY

Net Fun (*netfun.com*) is an online entertainment Web site founded in 1994. In 1996, the firm launched its flagship product, CyberCity. Installing CyberCity on the user's PC enables the user to access a variety of online games available from the Web site. CyberCity also provides other functions such as chat rooms, scoreboards, and searching for online game-playing partners. The site provides a three-dimensional (3-D) virtual reality interface between the user and the games and other facilities available on the Web site.

Membership shot up quickly, reaching 180,000 within two years. At that time, the total Internet user population was only around one million. However, the firm was incurring substantial losses. By 1997, losses had mounted up to over US$2.56 million, and the firm changed ownership. In 1998, the new owner of the firm, Peggy Chan, changed its revenue model from advertising-based to subscription-based. Membership dropped rapidly by almost 95 percent to a low of 10,000 but then gradually picked up again, growing to about 45,000 in July 2003. As of April 2002, Net Fun became a profitable firm with a digital product delivered online. Today, Net Fun is an associated company of Cheung Kong Ltd., a Hong-Kong based blue-chip conglomerate.

Net Fun operates in the Chinese multiplayers online games (MPOG) industry. Although there are numerous players operating in the MPOG industry and many of them offer free online games, surprisingly almost none focuses exclusively on classical Chinese games (e.g., mah-jongg). The global Chinese online game player community is the target of Net Fun, as the user market is huge.

In addition, the interactive multiplayer nature of most online games would be conducive to the building up of an interactive online community. Indeed, Net Fun not only provides games, but it is also a virtual community in which game players can interact with each other through game competitions, chat rooms, private messaging, and even online voice messaging. The high level of customer "stickiness" to the online gaming Web site helped the firm successfully switch a failing advertising-based revenue model to a successful subscription-based model.

Sources: Lee (2002) and *netfun.com* (2003).

For Further Exploration: Why are advertising revenue models generally ineffective? (See Chapter 4 for a review of the revenue models.) Are the community aspects helpful? Why or why not? How could such a site be even more profitable?

The fact that frequency and variety of human–computer interactions as well as computer-assisted interactions between humans have increased over the past few decades is well established. What may not be entirely clear is the effect that information technology has on sociability and the quality of interpersonal relations. Does information technology isolate people from society by capturing the time that humans used to spend with one another? Or does it improve sociability by offering humans better connectivity and more free time?

In the past few years, a number of researchers conducted empirical studies to find the answers to these questions. Most of these studies focused somewhat more narrowly on the impact of Internet use on sociability. Surprisingly, these studies arrived at diametrically opposite conclusions on this issue. Some studies found that Internet use reduces sociability, since time spent on the Internet is, in part, replacing time previously spent interacting with family and friends, as well as socializing outside the home. Other studies argue that Internet users become more socially engaged and improve their relationships with families and friends thanks to the substantial enhancements to interpersonal connectivity that e-mail and the Internet have to offer.

An attempt to reconcile these studies was made by Norman Nie of Stanford University, who claims that younger, more affluent, and better educated individuals are more likely to exhibit a greater degree of sociability. At the same time, they are more likely to adopt and use the Internet and other new technologies (an example of the digital divide). Thus, the use of the Internet does not make people more sociable, but rather reflects the higher level of social activity that Internet users already display (Nie, 2001).

16.5 INFORMATION TECHNOLOGY URGES PEOPLE TO REEXAMINE THEIR VALUE SYSTEMS

As we discussed earlier, people can use information technology to achieve the outcomes that they value highly. For example, information technology can be utilized to increase security and to enhance society's ability to fight crime and terrorism. At the same time, however, members of the society may be forced to sacrifice other important values, such as privacy. The first step in integrating information technology into one's value system involves identifying the outcomes that are legal, ethical, desirable, and socially acceptable. However, when information technology helps to promote one worthy value at the expense of another, it creates a serious dilemma: Which one of the conflicting values should take precedence over the other? Do the social benefits of upholding a particular principle justify the loss of benefits resulting from suppressing another principle?

Undeniably, information technology is only one of numerous factors that constantly challenge and redefine human value systems. Nonetheless, IT has a particularly significant impact on some values that are important in modern society, including security and privacy, freedom of speech and protection against inappropriate content, as well as respect for intellectual property and fair use.

Security versus Privacy

The issue of security versus privacy is at the forefront of the debate about clashing values that are heavily influenced by information technology. The terrorist attacks against the United States on September 11, 2001, which resulted in the loss of thousands of lives, demonstrate the tragic consequences of terrorist activities and the critical threats they present to the safety of entire countries and their citizens. Violent crime and organized criminal rings inflict enormous pain and suffering on thousands of victims every year, illustrating another threat to physical safety and security. White-collar crimes, ranging from accounting irregularities to embezzlement, jeopardize the financial security of investors and employees of various companies. The collapse of the energy giant, Enron, the bankruptcy of MCI-WorldCom, and the dissolution of Arthur Andersen exemplify the magnitude of potential losses resulting from such illegal activities.

An extensive array of computer crimes has been recently added to the list of factors that infringe on the security of organizations and individuals. Intrusions into corporate computer systems by hackers, theft and destruction of data by both insiders and outsiders, denial of service attacks against Web sites, release of malicious worms and viruses, and numerous other computer crimes endanger the operations of corporations and government agencies. For instance, the

Internet Fraud Prevention Advisory Council reports that losses from online fraud incidents may be as much as 40 times higher than in conventional face-to-face transactions (Rombel, 2004). The damage from a single virus, Code Red, is estimated to have amounted to $1.2 billion (Rudy, 2003a). Furthermore, a growing number of computer crimes are perpetrated against individuals, with identity theft and investment fraud being the most prevalent. According to a 2003 survey conducted for the Federal Trade Commission, nearly 10 million Americans had become victims of identity theft in the preceding year (Coleman, 2004).

Information technology produces a number of impressive **electronic surveillance** weapons that could be used to combat crime and other security threats. At the corporate level, network intrusion detection systems, keystroke logging, biometric identification devices, and surveillance cameras represent some of the feasible control mechanisms that may reduce the incidence of white-collar and computer crimes (Cole et al., 2003). Law-enforcement agencies could improve their response time to criminal acts by using integrated databases containing records on suspects and convicts from multiple states and multiple agencies. One such system, known as Matrix, currently connects certain law-enforcement data from several states.

One application of technology to reduce crime was used during the January 2001 Super Bowl game in Tampa, Florida. Video cameras took pictures of each of 100,000 fans as they entered the stadium. Within seconds, thousands of photos were compared with digital portraits of known criminals and suspected terrorists; several matches were found. The technology was not new, but never before had such a large number of people been photographed and the photos analyzed in such a short time. However, the fact that permission to take the photos was not obtained struck critics as an example of Big Brother watching. Others were not troubled, feeling that scanning crowds for criminals was for the greater public good.

An even more impressive application of information technology was proposed by the U.S. Department of Defense in the antiterrorism program dubbed "Total Information Awareness" (TIA). Advocates of the program claimed that it would be able to recognize the electronic footprints of would-be terrorists by analyzing police records, travel records, financial transactions, medical records, telephone conversations, e-mail and instant messages, and other types of data stored in governmental and commercial databases (MacDonald, 2004). Clearly, these tools and systems promise to enhance the safety and security of individuals, organizations, and nations.

Nevertheless, opponents of IT-enabled security systems caution about the loss of privacy that these systems may cause. Ubiquitous surveillance systems may violate the expectations of the right to be left alone and to be free from unreasonable personal intrusions. These concerns are valid in the workplace, where nearly 80 percent of major U.S. corporations monitor their employees electronically (Farmer and Mann, 2003). In Great Britain, over four million video cameras installed by municipal governments watch people outside of their homes and offices. In fact, an average visitor to London is captured on camera 300 times in a single day (Shenk, 2003). The U.S. Department of Defense was ready to explore the possibility of creating a nationwide biometric "Human ID at a Distance" program that would use face recognition and other technologies to take electronic surveillance to a completely new level ("With any luck . . .," 2002).

Another aspect of privacy—the right to determine when, and to what extent, information about oneself can be distributed to others—becomes particularly relevant with the advent of technologies that make it possible to link previously disjointed databases into a single network of (ominously?) detailed information. The major concerns surrounding large surveillance databases include the lack of accountability in their use and the possibility that information collected for a worthwhile cause will be used for other, potentially damaging purposes (Farmer and Mann, 2003). A surveillance system implemented in London, England, illustrates how quickly the scope of a system can expand to new, unanticipated purposes. The system comprised digital video cameras and optical character recognition software and was originally designed to read license plate numbers and impose a "congestion fee" on vehicles that enter certain areas of the city. Then, video feeds from the system were made available to the police and the military, who used facial recognition software to search for criminals and terrorists (Farmer and Mann, 2003).

The American Civil Liberties Union and other privacy advocates are alarmed that electronic surveillance systems will completely destroy privacy and will evolve into the instruments of totalitarian control. Privacy activists in the United States have succeeded at canceling the Total Information Awareness program and limiting the scope of the Matrix program for law-enforcement agencies. Now, they direct their efforts to Capps II (Computer-Assisted Passenger Pre-screening System II), which analyzes the profiles of all domestic and international air travelers in an attempt to boost security (MacDonald, 2004). The society will need to reconsider its values to decide whether the benefits of enhanced security justify the corresponding sacrifices of privacy.

POLITICAL CONTRIBUTIONS. Thanks to the Web site *fundrace.org*, individuals can investigate the campaign-giving activities of neighbors, friends, or strangers. The site is based on publicly available information—the names, addresses, occupations, and contribution amounts—of individual contributors. This information is supplied by the Federal Election Commission. Using geocoding, the site enables various searches. For example, by entering your own address, the site will display other addresses in the area that have made campaign contributions. While the site is based on public data, most individuals would not easily access this data were it not provided in such a readily searchable format. Some individuals might have a fear of being harassed if strangers in their neighborhood with opposite political viewpoints discover their campaign contributions. Others might worry that their bosses can discover the amount, and recipient, of their political contributions. Such a site forces us to consider the meaning of public information. (Three other Web sites provide additional information on individual campaign contributions: *opensecrets.org*, *politicalmoneyline.com*, and *fec.gov*. For more on political campaign contribution Web sites, see McNichol, 2004.)

Freedom of Expression versus Censorship

Freedom of expression, or the right to say what one thinks, is generally regarded as one of the most valuable rights in a democratic society. Since the passage of the First Amendment to the U.S. Constitution in 1789, Congress has been prohibited from introducing any laws "abridging the freedom of speech." The arrival of the Information Age has contributed to this First Amendment right. Individual citizens now have access to the Internet and various communication technologies that allow them to voice their opinions and to be heard by millions of people around the globe. The volume and variety of content accessible through the Internet can be viewed as a triumph for the freedom of speech. However, this very factor provokes an important question regarding the suitability of the information found on the Internet for those who can access it.

Governments of certain countries consider it their responsibility to shield their citizens from "inappropriate content." The Chinese government, for example, fears that free speech and free flow of information will undermine the political legitimacy of the Chinese Communist Party, resulting in undesirable consequences for the Chinese society. The number of Internet users in China is expected to reach 300 million by 2006, which represents a substantial proportion of the country's population of 1.3 billion. The government of China acknowledges the crucial role of the Internet for the nation's technological and economic development. Nevertheless, it believes that careful control must be exercised over Internet content and online activities in order to maintain political stability (Qiang, 2003).

To that end, the Chinese government has established an advanced technical infrastructure, known as the "Great Firewall," which prevents access to over 500,000 "harmful" Web sites. It also monitors users' online activities, including private e-mail messages and chat room conversations. Furthermore, the government of China has enacted more than 60 laws that regulate Internet activities in the country. The Surveillance Center for National Information Security and over 30,000 state employees are constantly scrutinizing what citizens read and write online. As a result of this scrutiny, nearly half of the country's Internet cafés were closed in 2002 and dozens of people have been arrested for visiting "subversive" Web sites or distributing "inappropriate" information online (Qiang, 2003). Although the government's attempts to censor the Internet have been largely successful, the decentralized nature of the Internet helped to expose Chinese citizens to more diverse sources of information and new opportunities to express their views. Thus, information technology has helped to expand freedom of speech, despite efforts to suppress it (Qiang, 2003).

POLITICS AND PRIVACY. Most people from democratic societies would consider the censorship of the Internet with the motive of maintaining an authoritarian political regime to be unjustified. Nevertheless, attempts to protect certain individuals from other types of inappropriate content may have valid reasons, making the issue of Internet censorship considerably more controversial.

The Children's Internet Protection Act of 2001 is intended to guard children from sexually explicit and obscene materials available online. The Act requires public libraries to install filtering software in order to be eligible for federal funds. The idea of shielding minors from offensive content is generally perceived as commendable. In fact, public libraries are already screening their collections of books, periodicals, and movies to exclude questionable materials.

However, the American Library Association (ALA), library patrons, and civil liberty groups expressed concerns that Internet filtering violates the First Amendment right to free speech and blocks access to vast amounts of legitimate information due to the imperfections in filtering technology (Swartz, 2003). The ALA challenged the constitutionality of this law in a high-profile court case. In June 2003, the U.S. Supreme Court upheld the Act as constitutional, but gave libraries the ability to disable filters at the request of adult patrons (Kenney, 2003). It is estimated that 10 percent of the American online population accesses the Internet through local libraries (Swartz, 2003). Therefore, the Act will directly affect millions of Internet users.

Intellectual Property, Piracy, and Fair Use

One of the fundamental changes that took place at the dawn of the Information Age is the shift in the nature of outputs produced by individuals and organizations. Instead of tangible goods and physical objects, a substantial proportion of companies and individual workers are producing intangible **intellectual property.** Computer software, books, news articles, music, movies, paintings, and myriad other forms of intellectual property are becoming the dominant product of modern economic systems. Furthermore, information technology is introducing entirely new ways in which intellectual property can be used, transmitted, and manipulated. Ironically, the same technology greatly enhances the possibilities to abuse the information and infringe on the rights of authors and owners of the intellectual property (Strickland, 2003).

Current issues surrounding intellectual property emphasize that the laws and practices established for tangible assets are entirely out of place in a world transformed by information technology (Strickland, 2003). Seemingly simple concepts of ownership, piracy, and fair use need to be redefined to make them applicable to intellectual property. Equally important are the issues of responsibility of content creators, distributors, service providers, users, government agencies, and other entities in maintaining a favorable environment for a society revolving around intellectual property.

In contrast to purchasing tangible goods, the purchase of a computer disk or other media containing some type of intellectual property, such as a software program, does not constitute the transfer of ownership. The program has simply been *licensed for use* in accordance with existing laws and any additional agreements specified by the copyright owner.

Certain laws passed prior to the explosion of information technology can be directly applied to intellectual property in the digital age. For instance, unauthorized duplication of audio cassettes would be considered a violation of the Copyright Act of 1976 (Hinduja, 2003). The same Act would directly apply to the electronic copying and distribution of MP3 recordings. However, other laws, such as the Audio Home Recording Act would not apply, because a computer hard drive is not recognized as a recording device by the Act. In order to address such issues, legislators have passed a number of laws, including the No Electronic Theft Act of 1997 and the Digital Millennium Copyright Act of 1998 (Strickland, 2003).

Despite the new regulations, infringements on the intellectual property owners' rights are quite commonplace. Sharing of music, movies, and software through the Internet and peer-to-peer networks are among the most frequent offenses. Although individuals engaging in piracy justify their actions by claiming that copyright owners do not suffer any financial losses (Hinduja, 2003), the issue of piracy is of critical importance to companies and individuals whose main occupations involve producing creative works. The Recording Industry Association of America (RIAA) and the Motion Picture Association of America (MPAA) have been at the forefront of the fight against piracy (Strickland, 2003).

Resolving the issue of piracy raises two additional questions: Who should be responsible for preventing piracy? Who should be liable for the damages incurred by the copyright owners when piracy does occur? In recent lawsuits against file-sharing networks such as Napster and Aimster, the courts made it clear that businesses that intentionally facilitate piracy should be accountable for copyright infringements. However, a similar case won by StreamCast Networks (distributor of Morpheus) suggests that peer-to-peer networks that have valid noninfringing functions and that do not exercise close control over individual users are not considered to be contributors to piracy (Strickland, 2003). Another possible set of defendants in piracy cases includes various service providers, such as operators of telecommunications networks, educational institutions or employers that own computers, and even public libraries. In addition, hundreds of lawsuits filed against individuals who download copyrighted work without proper authorization indicate that these people should be directly responsible for their own actions (Strickland, 2003).

A different approach to controlling piracy is to delegate the responsibility for preventing unauthorized copying to the *creators* of intellectual property. Various copy protection mechanisms and **digital rights management (DRM) systems** demonstrate a feasible approach to limiting piracy. Unfortunately, this method is not perfect. As discussed in the opening case for this chapter, pirates may devise techniques to disable or bypass the copy protection systems. Even more important are the potential constraints that DRM solutions will place on the concept of *fair use*. Traditional copyright laws allowed users to duplicate a copyrighted work for educational or research purposes, so long as the work is not used for profit and its value is not diminished (Hinduja, 2003). Restrictive digital rights management systems may be unable to differentiate between unlawful piracy and legal fair use. Thus, the systems may deny educators and researchers the opportunity to use copyrighted materials, thereby limiting their ability to advance academic, scientific, and cultural progress that follows from teaching and scholarship (Russell, 2003).

16.6 CONCLUSION

The discussion of the effects of information technology presented in this chapter is far from comprehensive. Information technology influences people, organizations, and societies in innumerable other ways. Perhaps you can identify some unique effects that IT has on the way you live, learn, work, and play. Nevertheless, the examples presented in this chapter are sufficient to recognize that the changes caused by information technology introduce a variety of new issues for individuals and societies and radically alter the importance of certain preexisting issues. Each technology is likely to affect multiple groups of people, whether directly or indirectly. Moreover, the effects of any given technology are rarely only beneficial or only detrimental; they typically create a complex web of consequences that may be both positive and negative.

This chapter and the entire textbook reveal that evolution of information technology is not happening in a vacuum. Information technology has developed into an integral part of modern society, becoming interrelated with numerous aspects of the socioeconomic environment. Further advances in information technology will inevitably reverberate in the lives of individuals, operations of commercial enterprises, and functioning of societies. In the same manner, changes in the society will create new demands that will encourage the development of new technologies.

➡ MANAGERIAL ISSUES

1. ***The effects of offshore outsourcing.*** Offshore outsourcing may be either an opportunity or a threat to an organization. To improve organizational efficiency, companies should explore the opportunities to outsource certain noncore activities to firms in other parts of the world. However, managers should be aware of various legal and ethical considerations surrounding this issue as well as the impact of outsourcing on the size and morale of their workforce.

2. ***Managing and evaluating remote workers.*** Telecommuting increases the number of employees working away from the office. To manage these employees, it is vital to place a greater emphasis on regular formal communications. Effective performance evaluation is also different and requires a closer examination of the actual outputs produced by each employee.

3. ***Dealing with information overload.*** In many workplaces, the capacity of information systems to collect and generate information has outpaced the ability of human employees to absorb it. The resulting information overload negatively impacts employees and their productivity. A greater investment in knowledge management systems, decision support systems, and related tools may help to solve this problem.

4. ***Providing high-quality information.*** As companies continue to rely on increasingly larger volumes of information, the issue of information quality becomes critically important to the success of the organizations. Furthermore, recent laws, such as the Sarbanes–Oxley Act, make CEOs and CFOs personally liable for the quality and accuracy of financial information disclosed to the public.

5. ***Displacement of employees with information technology.*** In any occupation—blue-collar, clerical, or white-collar—machines are acquiring the capabilities to perform "human" tasks more effectively and efficiently. Although this trend is unlikely to result in massive worldwide unemployment, it can have dramatic results on individual organizations and on individual employees. Thus, managers should be aware of the potentially disruptive technologies that may displace them or their colleagues and subordinates.

6. ***Use of electronic surveillance.*** Proliferation of computer and white-collar crime impels employers to use information technology to monitor their employees. While electronic surveillance may reduce the incidence of unlawful activities, it may also result in employee resentment and other unintended consequences.

KEY TERMS

Dehumanization *700*

Digital divide *699*

Digital rights management (DRM) systems *716*

Electronic surveillance *712*

Ergonomics *701*

Globalization *692*

Information anxiety *700*

Information overload *696*

Information quality *697*

Intellectual property *715*

Piracy *689*

Quality of life *703*

Telecommuting *693*

Virtual community *709*

CHAPTER HIGHLIGHTS (Numbers Refer to Learning Objectives)

1 Information technology significantly impacts individuals, organizations, and societies. Any given technology is likely to affect multiple entities in ways that may be both positive and negative.

2 Globalization and telecommuting are transforming the ways in which people work and organizations operate. Now, work can be performed at any time, in any part of the globe, which tends to make organizations more efficient. Organizational structure, job content, and the nature of management and supervision are altered significantly by this trend.

3 Vast amounts of data and information made available in the Information Age are exceeding the capacity of people to absorb and process them. Spam and other forms of electronic noise only exacerbate the problem. As the quantity of information rises, the issue of information quality takes center stage.

4 Uneven diffusion of information technology results in a digital divide. The digital divide generally follows the income distribution, educational levels, and several other characteristics of people both within and across countries. People and countries with limited access to information technology are unable to benefit from this valuable resource.

5 Machines and information systems can displace humans from their jobs, both blue- and white-collar. Such changes can be extremely disruptive for an individual employee or an organization. However, on the macroeconomic level, increased efficiency of IT-enabled machines promotes lower prices and greater consumption, and ultimately results in a higher aggregate level of employment for the economy as a whole.

6 Robotics, decision support systems, and other manifestations of information technology are improving the quality of human lives by relieving people from tedious and hazardous tasks. At the same time, increased interaction with computers replaces the conventional forms of face-to-face interaction among people. This trend may adversely impact interpersonal relationships and other aspects of the quality of life.

7 Information technology challenges traditional value systems by emphasizing the significance of issues, such as security and privacy, freedom of speech and protection against inappropriate content, as well as respect for intellectual property and fair use.

VIRTUAL COMPANY ASSIGNMENT

Instructions for accessing The Wireless Café on the Student Web Site

1. Go to
   wiley.com/college/turban
2. Select Turban/Leidner/ McLean/Wetherbe's *Information Technology for Management,* Fifth Edition.
3. Click on Student Resources site, in the toolbar on the left.
4. Click on the link for Virtual Company Web site
5. Click on Wireless Café.

Impacts of IT at The Wireless Café
Go to The Wireless Café's link on the Student Web Site. There you will be asked to look back over your recommendations for the restaurant and think about some of the social consequences of these changes.

More Resources
More resources and study tools are located on the Student Web Site. You'll find additional chapter materials and useful Web links. In addition, self-quizzes that provide individualized feedback are available for each chapter.

QUESTIONS FOR REVIEW

1. Identify several major themes that describe the impact of information technology on individuals, organizations, and societies.
2. List two positive and two negative effects of globalization.
3. What causes the problem of information overload, and what can be done to solve this problem?
4. What essential characteristics describe high-quality data and information?
5. Why are country-specific laws generally ineffective in fighting spam?
6. Define *digital divide*.
7. Provide three examples of quality of life improvements brought about by robotics.

8. Describe the chain of events in the labor markets that follows the introduction of a new technology that replaces human work.
9. In what types of occupations are people facing competition from machines and information systems?
10. Why did some studies conclude that information technology led to a greater level of sociability and interpersonal interaction?
11. Describe the tradeoffs involved in using information technology to increase security versus maintaining a high level of privacy.
12. Discuss the concerns of the American Library Association related to the Children's Internet Protection Act.
13. Describe the capabilities and limitations of digital rights management (DRM) systems.

QUESTIONS FOR DISCUSSION

1. Information technology makes it possible to copy and distribute copyrighted material. What impact would large-scale copyright infringement have on authors and producers of creative works?
2. In the aftermath of the September 11 attacks, government agencies and individuals alike have turned to information technology for solutions to improve security. Do you think security measures currently in place provide adequate security as well as privacy, or is one of these issues being emphasized at the expense of the other?
3. Consider a typical day in your life and list all the instances when you interact with computers or computer-controlled machines. Discuss whether these interactions enhance your ability to interact with other people or whether they isolate you from other individuals.
4. If you were an employee in a company that offered telecommuting options, would you prefer to work from home or from the office? Why?

5. Clerks at 7-Eleven stores enter data regarding customers' gender, approximate age, and so on into a computer system. However, names are not keyed in. These data are then aggregated and analyzed to improve corporate decision making. Customers are not informed about this, nor are they asked for permission. Do you see any problems with this practice?
6. Discuss what aspects of your current job (or a hypothetical future job) are most likely to be replaced by machines.
7. Certain groups of people claim that globalization has predominantly positive effects, while others assert the opposite. Which of these two arguments do you find more compelling? Why?
8. Discuss whether information overload is a problem in your work or education. Based on your experience, what solutions can you recommend to this problem?
9. Explain why it may be difficult for an organization to reach the goal of having high-quality information.

EXERCISES

1. You would like to set up a personal Web site. Using legal reference sites such as *elexica.com*, prepare a report summarizing the types of materials you can and cannot use (e.g., logos, photographs, animations, sound clips) without breaking the copyright laws.
2. One low-tech way of alleviating the information overload problem is to limit the usage of information technology. Try spending one day without using the Internet, reading your e-mail, or exchanging text messages via your cell phone. Write a report about your experience.

3. Make a list of all the opportunities to work remotely that are available at your workplace or educational institution. If you take advantage of these opportunities to telecommute, describe what impact they have on your life. If you choose not to work remotely, explain why not.
4. Review the policies of your university or your company concerning electronic surveillance. Do these policies invade your privacy? Explain how these policies influence your behavior.

5. Create a log of all your activities on a typical weekday. Calculate the amount of time you spent interacting with computers and other machines. Compute the amount of time you spent interacting with others using telecommunications technologies (e.g., reading or writing e-mail, sending instant messages, and so on). Compare these numbers with the amount of time you spent in face-to-face interactions with other humans. Discuss how information technology impacts your social life.

GROUP ASSIGNMENTS

1. In small groups, arbitrarily select any information system or information technology (e.g., e-mail, the Internet, robotics, artificial intelligence, etc.). Working individually, each group member should consider all possible implications of this technology on people, organizations, and society. Taking the previous considerations into account, each group member should decide whether the net effect of the technology is positive or negative. Then, discuss the issue as a group and see if the group can come to a consensus about the impact of the technology.

2. The opening case for this chapter discussed some of the techniques used by movie studios to prevent movie piracy. In groups, discuss these methods and decide which of them are likely to be the most effective at limiting movie piracy.

3. The State of California maintains a database of people who allegedly abuse children. (The database also includes names of the alleged victims.) The list is made available to dozens of public agencies, and it is considered in cases of child adoption and employment decisions. Because so many people have access to the list, its content is easily disclosed to outsiders. An alleged abuser and her child, whose case was dropped but whose names had remained on the list, sued the State of California for invasion of privacy. With the class divided into groups, debate the issues involved. Specifically:

   a. Is there a need to include names of people on the list in cases that were dismissed or declared unfounded?
   b. Who should make the decision about what names should be included, and what should the criteria be?
   c. What is the potential damage to the abusers (if any)?
   d. Should the State of California abolish the list? Why or why not?

INTERNET EXERCISES

1. Visit the Web site of the American Civil Liberties Union (*aclu.org*). Browse through the site and identify five issues that are significantly influenced by the development and proliferation of information technology.

2. Visit the Web site of the Defense Advanced Research Projects Agency (DARPA) at *darpa.mil*. Browse through the list of DARPA programs and find a program intended to replace human soldiers with robots or other automated systems.

3. Browse the Web sites of Wipro Technologies (*wipro.com*) and Infosys Technologies (*infosys.com*). Determine what types of offshore outsourcing services the two companies offer. Learn how these firms affect the operations of their clients.

4. Visit the following virtual communities: *geocities.yahoo.com, fool.com, ivillage.com, startrek.com*, and *espn.com*. Join one of the communities and participate in the community activities. Report on your experience.

Minicase 1
ChoicePoint: Building a Safer Society or Destroying Your Privacy?

Headquartered outside of Atlanta, Georgia, ChoicePoint is a leading provider of decision-making information that helps businesses as well as federal, state, and local government agencies reduce fraud and control risk. The company's main line of business is gathering, analyzing, and selling of information about people.

The firm collects huge amounts of data from an extremely broad range of sources. Birth records, marriage licenses, job applications, tax return filings, vehicle registrations, educational records, home ownership data, applications for insurance policies and credit cards, criminal records, and numerous other pieces of information are collected by the company directly, bought from other firms, or obtained from public sources. Currently, ChoicePoint holds 19 billion records—an average of 65 for every American. At the request of its customers, the company is ready to apply its sophisticated data-mining technologies to assemble a profile of practically any person in the United States. Enormous electronic databases assembled and maintained by ChoicePoint contain considerably more information than is kept by any government agency. Moreover, it would be unlawful for government bodies to gather some of the data that the company collects about ordinary citizens.

Derek Smith, ChoicePoint's CEO, believes that one of the goals of the company is "to create a safer, more secure society." Undeniably, the company's pool of information and data-mining capabilities help it achieve that objective. Businesses refer to ChoicePoint to mitigate the risks they face. Insurance companies use ChoicePoint's data in underwriting insurance policies; property managers rely on ChoicePoint to screen potential tenants; and a growing number of companies turn to ChoicePoint to perform background checks on prospective employees.

In addition, the company works closely with government agencies that depend on ChoicePoint for tasks ranging from tracking down criminals to finding tax evaders. The Federal Bureau of Investigation, the Department of Defense, the Homeland Security Department, the Internal Revenue Service, the Social Security Administration, and dozens of other government offices are among ChoicePoint's clients. In the wake of the September 11 attacks, ChoicePoint joined forces with the Transportation Security Administration and U.S. intelligence agencies to prescreen tens of thousands of suspicious airline passengers and other individuals.

One of the troubling issues about the operations of companies such as ChoicePoint is that of privacy. The Fourth Amendment to the U.S. Constitution grants citizens a valuable right to be secure "against unreasonable searches and seizures." Strict safeguards were traditionally applied to government agencies in order to preserve this right. However, ChoicePoint blurs the line of what constitutes a legal search. Does a ChoicePoint report represent a "search," or is it just a product purchased from a vendor? Does ChoicePoint have a responsibility in verifying the legitimacy of information requests? These and other questions need to be addressed in order to maintain an acceptable level of privacy.

Another critical issue relates to the quality of information collected and sold by ChoicePoint. In 1998, 8,000 Florida residents were in danger of becoming ineligible to vote because ChoicePoint incorrectly identified them as convicted felons. The negative consequences that an individual may experience if she is erroneously labeled as "dangerous" are quite severe, since a growing number of businesses and government agencies are relying on data from ChoicePoint and similar providers. In addition, if the system labels a person who presents a real threat as "trusted," the society at large may suffer significant losses. Who should be responsible for the accuracy of the data—ChoicePoint, the third party that supplied the data, or the end user who bought the data?

Currently, ChoicePoint is actively acquiring other firms to extend its databases, improve its analytical tools, and boost its market power, which earned the company a place on the 2003 list of the 100 fastest-growing technology companies in America. As the company continues to expand, privacy, information quality, and numerous other issues will grow in importance.

Sources: Harris (2004), and *choicepoint.com* (accessed May 2004).

Questions for Minicase 1

1. What information systems and information technologies are essential for the operation of ChoicePoint?
2. How does the business of ChoicePoint differ from the Total Information Awareness program proposed by the U.S. Department of Defense?
3. What implications does identity theft have for the usability of data provided by ChoicePoint?
4. Is there a conflict of interests between the profit motive of this corporation and the obligation to use information responsibly?

Minicase 2
The Australian Fishing Community

Recreational fishing in Australia is popular both for residents and for international visitors. Over 700,000 Australians regularly fish. The Australian Fishing Shop (AFS) (*http://ausfish.com.au*) is a small e-tailer, founded in 1994 as a hobby site carrying information about recreational fishing. During the last few years, the site has evolved into a fishing portal, and it has formed a devoted community around itself.

A visit to the site immediately shows that the site is not a regular storefront, but rather an information portal with substantial information resources for the recreational fishing community. In addition to the sale of products (rods, reels, clothing, boats, and fishing-related books, software, and CD-ROMs) and services (fishing charters and holiday packages), the site provides the following information:

- Hints and tips for fishing
- A photo gallery of people's catches
- Chat boards—general and specialized
- Directions for boat building, tackle manufacturing, etc.
- Recipes for cooking fish
- Information about relevant newsgroups and a mailing list
- Free giveaways and competitions
- Links to fishing-related government bodies, other fishing organizations (around the globe and in Australia), and daily weather maps and tides reports
- General information site and frequently asked questions
- List of fishing sites around the globe
- Free e-mail
- Web page hosting

Moreover, the site offers an auction mechanism for fishing equipment and provides answers to inquiries.

The company is fairly small, with total revenues of about AU$500,000 a year. How can such a small company survive? The answer can be found in its strategy of providing value-added services to the recreational fishing community. These services attract over 8.3 million visitors each month, from all over the world, of which about 1 percent make a purchase. In addition, several advertisers sponsor the site. This is sufficient to survive. Another interesting strategy employed by the site is that of targeting the global markets. Most of the profit is derived from customers in the United States and Canada who buy fishing trips and holiday packages.

In terms of products, the company acts as a referral service to vendors, so it does not have to carry an inventory. When AFS receives an order, it orders the products from the suppliers. Then, it aggregates the orders from the suppliers, repacks them, and sends them via a delivery service to customers. To streamline operations, some orders are shipped directly from vendors to the customers.

Source: ausfish.com.au (accessed July 2003 and May 2004).

Questions for Minicase 2

1. Why is the Australian Fishing Shop considered an Internet community?
2. How does the community aspect facilitate revenue generation?
3. What is the critical success factor of this company?
4. What is the advantage of being a referral service? What is the disadvantage?
5. Compare the services offered at the AFS Web site with services offered by companies in other countries such as: *daytickets.co.uk*, *fishing-boating.com*, and *http://www.fishinginnewzealand.com/*.

REFERENCES

Agarwal, R., "Individual Acceptance of Information Technology," in R. Zmud, ed., *Framing the Domain of IT Management.* Cincinnati, OH: Pinnaflex Educational Resources, 2000.

Armstrong, A. G., and J. Hagel, "The Real Value of Online Communities," *Harvard Business Review,* May–June 1996.

Australian Fishing Shop, *http://ausfish.com.au* (accessed July 2003 and May 2004).

Begley, S., "This Robot Can Design, Perform, and Interpret a Genetic Experiment," *Wall Street Journal,* January 16, 2004, p. A7.

Berman, D., "Portals: Technology Has Us So Plugged Into Data We Have Turned Off," *Wall Street Journal,* November 10, 2003, p. B1.

"Beyond the Digital Divide," *The Economist,* 370(8366), March 13, 2004.

Carroll, M., "Color Me Global, Says Trend Micro CTO," *Electronic Engineering Times,* Issue 1107, April 3, 2000, p. 163.

Challenger, J. A., "24 Trends Reshaping the Workplace," *The Futurist,* 34(5), September–October 2000, p. 35.

Cole, C. L., S. F. Gale, S. Greengard, P. J. Kiger, C. Lachnif, T. Raphael, D. P. Shuit, and J. Wiscombe, "Fast Forward: 25 Trends that Will Change the Way You Do Business," *Workforce,* 82(6), June 2003, p. 43.

Coleman, T., "Identity Theft Investigation and Penalties," *FDCH Congressional Testimony, House Judiciary Committee,* March 23, 2004.

"Corporate Data Sheet," Trend Micro Incorporated, *trendmicro.com* (accessed 2004).

Dalton, G., "E-Business Revolution," *InformationWeek,* June 7, 1999.

Davies, C., "Spam—the Death of E-Commerce," *Supply Chain Europe,* February 2004, pp. 46–47.

Delaney, K. J., "Hand-Held Device for DVD Movies Raises Legal Issues," *Wall Street Journal,* January 7, 2004, p. B1.

DeSouza, K., T. Hensgen, and Y. Awazu, "Lost in the Big Picture," *Across the Board,* 41(1), January–February 2004.

Farmer, D., and C. C. Mann, "Surveillance Nation," *Technology Review,* 106(4), May 2003.

Fiedler, D., "Australian Spam Act Goes Into Effect," *InternetWeek,* April 9, 2004.

Garrett, D., "In or Out: The Pros and Cons of Home Offices," *Certification Magazine,* October 2003, pp. 52–55.

Geocities, *http://geocities.yahoo.com* (accessed 2002).

Google, *google.com* (accessed April 2004).

Graham-Hackett, M., "Standard & Poor's Industry Surveys: Computers: Hardware Industry Trends," *Standard & Poor's*, June 2003.

Greifeld, R., "Man, Machines, Markets," *Wall Street Journal*, December 23, 2003, p. A14.

Hagel, J., III, and A. G. Armstrong, *Net Gain: Expanding Markets through Virtual Communities*. Boston: Harvard Business School Press, 1997.

Hamm, S., "Borders Are So 20th Century," *Business Week*, issue 3850, September 22, 2003.

Handel, M., "Complex Picture of Information Technology and Employment Emerges," *SRI International*, July 2003.

Harris, S., "Private Eye," *Government Executive*, 36(4), March 2004, p. 30.

Hinds, P. J., and D. E. Bailey, "Out of Sight, Out of Sync: Understanding Conflict in Distributed Teams," *Organization Science*, 14(6), 2003, pp. 615–632.

Hinduja, S., "Trends and Patterns Among Online Software Pirates," *Ethics and Information Technology*, 5(1), 2003, p. 49.

Huang, J., "A New Blueprint for Business Architecture," *Harvard Business Review*, April 2001.

Hummel, J., and U. Lechner, "Social Profiles of Virtual Communities," *Proceedings of the 35th Hawaii International Conference on System Sciences*, 2002.

Johnson, D., "The Telesurgery Revolution," *The Futurist*, 36(1), January–February 2002, p. 6.

Kageyama, Y., "CyberCars Hit Streets," *Associated Press* release, July 26, 2000.

Kanter, J., *Managing with Information*, 4th ed. Englewood Cliffs, NJ: Prentice Hall, 1992.

Kenney, B., "ALA Leaders/Staff Meet on CIPA: A Time to Regroup," *Library Journal*, 128(15), September 15, 2003, p. 16.

Kessler, S. H., "Standard & Poor's Industry Surveys: Computers: Consumer Services and the Internet: Industry Trends," *Standard & Poor's*, September 2003.

King, R., "Stores Stocking Up on Self-Help: Modern Checkout Means Shorter Lines," *Times-Picayune*, May 2, 2004.

Kleiner, A., "Corporate Culture in Internet Time," *Strategy-Business* (Booz-Allen & Hamilton Quarterly), *strategy-business.com*, First Quarter, 2000.

Kome, P., "New Repetitive Strain Rules May Be Challenged," *Women's eNews*, January 29, 2001, *womensenews.org/article/cfm?aid=421* (accessed September 2003).

La Londe, B., "From Outsourcing to "Offshoring"—Part 1," *Supply Chain Management Review*, 8(2), March 2004, p. 6.

Lee, M. K. O., "Internet Retailing in Hong Kong, China," *Electronic Commerce B2C Strategies and Models*. Singapore: Wiley, 2002.

Logan, D., and F. Buytendijk, "The Sarbanes–Oxley Act Will Impact Your Enterprise," *Gartner Inc.*, March 20, 2003.

Loshin, D., "Issues and Opportunities in Data Quality Management Coordination," *DM Review*, April 2004, pp. 14–16.

MacDonald, H., "The 'Privacy' Jihad," *Wall Street Journal*, April 1, 2004, p. A14.

MacDonald, M., and A. Oettinger, "Information Overload: Managing Intelligence Technologies," *Harvard International Review*, Fall 2002, pp. 44–48.

McBride, S., "The Hunt for Movie Pirates. Hollywood Tests New Tricks, Including Spying on Audience to Find Camcorders in Crowd," *Wall Street Journal*, April 12, 2004, p. B1.

McBride, S., and B. Orwall, "Movie Industry Steps Up Drive Against Pirates," *Wall Street Journal*, January 27, 2004, p. B1.

McCartney, J., "Self-Scanning Tests at Wal-Mart, Supermarkets Register Approval," *Shopping Center Today*, November 1, 1999.

McNichol, T., "Street Maps in Political Hues," *New York Times*, May 20, 2004, p. 1.

Melymuka, K., "Knowledge Management Helps Cut Errors by Half," *Computerworld*, July 8, 2002, *computerworld.com/databasetopics/data/story/0,10801,72513,00.html* (accessed July 2003).

Mintz, S., "The Ethical Dilemmas of Outsourcing," *CPA Journal*, 74(3), March 2004, p. 6.

Mora, M., "Management and Organizational Issues for Decision Making Support Systems," *Information Resources Management Journal*, special issue, October–December 2002.

Net Fun, *netfun.com* (accessed 2003).

Nevins, M. D., and S. A. Stumpf, "21st Century Leadership: Redefining Management Education," Strategy-Business (Booz-Allen & Hamilton Quarterly), *strategy-business.com*, Third Quarter, 1999.

New York Times (March 6, 2001).

Nie, N. H., "Sociability, Interpersonal Relations, and the Internet: Reconciling Conflicting Findings," *American Behavioral Scientist*, 45(3), November 2001, p. 420.

Ojala, M., "Information Quality Matters," *Online*, 27(6), November–December 2003, p. 43.

"Online Movie Piracy on the Up Despite Legal Action Threats," *New Media Age*, April 15, 2004, p. P4.

Porat, M. U., "The Information Economy," Office of Telecommunication Policy, U.S. Department of Commerce, Washington, D.C., 1977.

Qiang, X., "Cyber Speech: Catalyzing Free Expression and Civil Society," *Harvard International Review*, Summer 2003, pp. 70–75.

Ripley, A., "Hollywood Robbery," *Time*, 163(4), January 26, 2004, p. 56.

"Robots, Start Your Engines," *The Economist*, 370(8366), March 13, 2004, p. 4.

"Robots Used to Clean Train Station in Japan," *Sunday Times* (Singapore), June 6, 1993.

Rombel, A., "Japan: Trend Micro Adapts to Meet Evolving Security Threats," *Global Finance*, 17(2), February 2003, p. 12.

Rombel, A., "Security and Fraud Become Top Tech Issues," *Global Finance*, April 2004, pp. 40–42.

Routt, C., "The Jobs They Are A-Changing," *The Banker*, December 1999.

Rudy, J., "Standard & Poor's Industry Surveys: Computers: Software: Current Environment." Standard & Poor's, April 2003a.

Rudy, J., "Standard & Poor's Industry Surveys: Computers: Software: Industry Trends." Standard & Poor's, April 2003b.

Russell, C., "Fair Use Under Fire," *Library Journal*, 128(13), August 2003, p. 32.

Sabre, Inc., *sabre-holdings.com* (accessed May 2004).

Schroeder, M., "States' Efforts to Curb Outsourcing Stymied," *Wall Street Journal*, April 16, 2004, p. A4.

Schwartz, K. D., "Fighting a War of Words," *Government Executive*, 36(4), March 2004, p. 62.

"Science and Technology: None Shall Have Prizes; Wacky Races," *The Economist*, 370(8367), March 20, 2004, p. 109.

"Self-Checkout Gets Mixed Bag of Results," *DSN Retailing Today*, 42(22), November 24, 2003, p. 10.

"Self-Checkout's 'Explosive' Growth: An Interview with Norman Tsang, IBM Worldwide Self-Checkout Executive," *Chain Store Age*, February 2004, p. 27.

Shenk, D., "Watching You," *National Geographic,* 204(5), November 2003, p. 2.

Soete, L., "ICTs, Knowledge Work and Employment: The Challenges to Europe," *International Labour Review,* 140(2), 2001, p. 143.

"Spam Makes Up Two-Thirds of All Email Worldwide," *New Media Age,* March 11, 2004, p. 12.

Stone, B., "Real-World Robots," *Newsweek,* 141(12), March 24, 2003, p. 42.

Strickland, L. S., "Copyright's Digital Dilemma Today: Fair Use or Unfair Constraints? Part I: The Battle Over File Sharing," *Bulletin of the American Society for Information Science and Technology,* 30(1), October–November 2003, p. 7.

Swartz, N., "Should Libraries Censor Patrons' Surfing?" *Information Management Journal,* 37(3), May–June 2003, p. 6.

"The Remote Future," *The Economist,* 370(8363), February 21, 2004, p. 14.

"The Robot Revolution Is on the Way," *International Herald Tribune,* September 18, 2000.

Turocy, P., J. Phillips, and B. Anders, "No More Information Overload," *Information Week,* December 16, 2002, pp. 50–51.

Venkat, K., "Delving into the Digital Divide," *IEEE Spectrum,* February 2002.

Wall Street Journal (November 21, 2000).

"With Any Luck, It Won't Work," *Fortune,* 146(13), December 30, 2002, p. 204.

Wurman, R. S., *Information Anxiety 2.* Indianapolis: Macmillan, 2001.

Wurman, R. S., "Redesign the Data Dump," *Business 2.0* (*business2.com*), November 28, 2000.

Glossary

Affinity portals Gateways to the Internet that support an entire community of affiliated interests.

Alliance strategy The competitive strategy of working with business partners in partnerships, alliances, joint ventures, or virtual companies.

Analytical processing Analysis of accumulated data, frequently by end users, through data mining, decision support systems (DSSs), enterprise information systems (EISs), and Web applications; also referred to as *business intelligence.*

Application controls Security controls designed to protect specific applications.

Application program A set of computer instructions written in a programming language, the purpose of which is to support a specific task or business process or another application program.

Application service provider (ASP) Company that provides business applications (standard or customized) over the Internet for a per-use or fixed monthly fee.

Applications portfolio The collection of major, approved IS projects that are consistent with an organization's long-range plan.

Artificial intelligence (AI) A subfield of computer science concerned with symbolic reasoning and problem solving.

Artificial neural network (ANN) A computer technology attempting to build computers that will operate like a human brain; ANN programs can work with ambiguous information.

Asynchronous communication The sending and receiving of messages in which there is a time delay between the sending and receiving; as opposed to *synchronous communication.*

Attack traceback A system that can trace and identify the person or computer responsible for a virus, DOS, or other attack.

Auction A competitive process in which either a seller solicits consecutive bids from buyers or a buyer solicits bids from sellers, and prices are determined dynamically by competitive bidding.

Audit (of ISs) A regular examination or check of systems, their inputs, outputs, and processing.

Auto Identification Center (Auto-ID) Joint partnership among global companies and research universities to create an Internet of things.

Automatic crash notification (ACN) Still-experimental device that would automatically notify police of the location of an ACN-equipped car involved in an accident.

Balanced-scorecard method Method that evaluates the overall health of organizations and projects by looking at metrics in finance, customers' view of the organization, internal business processes, and ability to change and expand.

Banners Electronic billboards, which typically contain a short text or graphical message to promote a product or a vendor.

Batch processing Processing system that processes inputs at fixed intervals as a file and operates on it all at once; contrasts with *online* (or *interactive*) processing.

Behavior-oriented chargeback Accounting system that sets IT service costs in a way that encourages usage consistent with organizational objectives, even though the charges may not correspond to actual costs.

Benchmarks Objective measures of performance, often available from industry trade associations.

Best-practice benchmarks Activities and methods that the most effective organizations use to operate and manage various IT functions.

Biometric controls Security controls that verify the identity of a person based on physiological or behavioral characteristics, such as fingerprints or voice.

Blog A personal Web site, open to the public, in which the owner expresses his or her feelings or opinions.

Blogging (Weblogging) A technology that offers an opportunity for individuals to do personal publishing on the Internet.

Bluetooth Chip technology that enables voice and data communications between many wireless devices through low-power, short-range, digital two-way radio frequency.

Brick-and-mortar organizations Organizations in which the product, the process, and the delivery agent are all physical.

Bullwhip effect Erratic shifts in orders up and down the supply chain.

Business activity monitoring (BAM) system A BPM tool that alerts managers in real time to opportunities, threats, or problems and provides collaboration tools to address these issues.

Business architecture Organizational plans, visions, objectives, and problems, and the information required to support them.

Business case A written document that is used by managers to justify funding for a specific investment and also to provide the bridge between the initial plan and its execution.

Business continuity plan A comprehensive plan for how a business and IT systems will operate in case a disaster strikes.

Business intelligence Category of applications for gathering, storing, analyzing, and providing access to data to help enterprise users make better decisions.

Business model A method by which a company generates revenue to sustain itself.

Business performance management (BPM) A methodology for measuring organizational performance, analyzing it through comparison to standards, and planning how to improve it.

Business pressures Forces in the organization's environment, such as global competition, that create pressures on the organization's operations; also called *drivers.*

Business process A collection of activities that take one or more kinds of inputs and create an output.

Business process management (BPM) Method for business restructuring that combines workflow systems and redesign methods; covers three process categories—people-to-people, systems-to-systems, and systems-to-people interactions.

Business process reengineering (BPR) A methodology for introducing a fundamental and radical change in specific business processes, usually supported by an information system.

Business systems planning (BSP) model An IBM top-down planning model that starts with business strategies and uses business processes and data classes to define organizational databases and identify applications that support business strategies.

Business-to-business EC (B2B) E-commerce in which both the sellers and the buyers are business organizations.

Business-to-business-to-consumers (B2B2C) EC E-commerce in which a business sells to a business but delivers the product or service to an individual consumer.

Business-to-consumers (B2C) EC E-commerce in which the sellers are organizations and the buyers are individuals; also known as *e-tailing.*

Business-to-employees (B2E) EC A special type of intra-business e-commerce in which an organization delivers products or services to its employees.

Buy-side marketplace B2B model in which organizations buy needed products or services from other organizations electronically, often through a reverse auction.

Centralized computing IS architecture that puts all processing and control authority within one (mainframe) computer to which all other computing devices respond.

Channel conflict The alienation of existing distributors when a company decides to sell to customers directly online.

Channel systems (in marketing) A network of the materials and product distribution systems involved in the process of getting a product or service to customers.

Chargeback System that treats the IT function as a service bureau or utility, charging organizational subunits for IT services with the objective of recovering IT expenditures.

Chat room A Web page where people can interact ("chat") in real time; a virtual meeting place.

Chief information officer (CIO) The director of the IS department in a large organization, analogous to a CEO, COO, or CFO; also known as *chief technology officer.*

Chief knowledge officer (CKO) The director assigned to manage an organization's knowledge management (KM) program.

Click-and-mortar organizations Organizations that do business in both the physical and digital dimensions.

Clickstream data The data collected on users' activities on a Web site, captured automatically by various methods, including *cookies,* and mined by advertisers.

Clickstream data warehouses Data warehouses capable of showing both e-business activities and the non-Web aspects of a business in an integrated fashion.

Client A computer such as a PC attached to a network, which is used to access shared network resources.

Client/server architecture A type of distributed architecture where end-user PCs (clients) request services or data from designated processors or peripherals (servers).

Code Division Multiple Access (CDMA) Wireless communication protocol, used with most 2.5G and 3G systems, that separates different users by assigning different codes to the segments of each user's communications.

Collaboration The mutual efforts by two or more individuals who perform activities in order to accomplish certain tasks.

Collaborative commerce (c-commerce) E-commerce in which business partners collaborate electronically.

Commercial (public) portals Gateways to the Internet that offer content for broad and diverse audiences; these are the most popular portals on the Internet, such as *yahoo.com* and *msn.com.*

Communities of practice (COPs) Groups of people in an organization with a common professional interest.

Competitive advantage An advantage over a competitor, such as lower cost or quicker deliveries.

Competitive forces model A business framework devised by Michael Porter, depicting five forces in a market (e.g., bargaining power of customers), used for analyzing competitiveness.

Computer-based information system (CBIS) Information system that includes a computer for some or all of its operation.

Computer-integrated manufacturing (CIM) Integrates several computerized systems, such as CAD, CAM, MRP, and JIT into a whole, in a factory.

Consumer-to-business (C2B) EC E-commerce in which consumers make known a particular need for a product or service, and suppliers compete to provide the product or service to consumers; an example is Priceline.com.

Consumer-to-consumer (C2C) EC E-commerce in which an individual sells products or services to other individuals (not businesses).

Context awareness Capturing a broad range of contextual attributes to better understand what the consumer needs, and what products or services he or she might possibly be interested in.

Contextual computing Enhancement of the computational environment for each user, at each point of computing.

Cookie A text string stored on the user's hard drive file to record the history of the user's computer visits to particular Web sites.

Cooperative processing Teams two or more geographically dispersed computers to execute a specific task.

Corporate portal The gateway for entering a corporate Web site. It is usually a home page, which allows for communication, collaboration, and access to diversified information. Companies may have separate portals for outsiders and for employees.

Cost-benefit analysis   Study that helps in decisions on IT investments by determining if the benefits (possibly including intangible ones) exceed the costs.

Cost leadership strategy   The competitive strategy of producing products and/or services at the lowest cost in its industry group.

Cracker   A malicious hacker.

Critical response activities   The major activities used by organizations to counter *business pressures.*

Critical success factors (CSFs)   Those few things that must go right in order to ensure the organization's survival and success.

Cross-border data transfer   The flow of corporate data across nations' borders.

Customer relationship management (CRM)   The entire process of maximizing the value proposition to the customer through all interactions, both online and traditional. Effective CRM advocates one-to-one relationships and participation of customers in related business decisions.

Cyberbanking   Various banking activities conducted electronically from home, a business, or on the road instead of at a physical bank location.

Cybercrime   Illegal activities executed on the Internet.

Cybersquatting   Registering domain names in the hope of selling them later at a higher price.

Cyberterrorism   Terrorist attack conducted via the Internet.

Cyberwar   War in which a country's information systems would be paralyzed by a massive attack of destructive software.

Cycle time reduction   The reduction of the time required to execute a task or produce a product; usually accomplished by use of IT.

Data   Raw facts that can be processed into accurate and relevant information.

Data conferencing   Teleconferencing that enables data to be sent along with voice and/or video; makes it possible to work on documents together during videoconferences.

Data integrity   The accuracy, correctness, and validity of data.

Data item   An elementary description of things, events, activities, and transactions that are recorded, classified, and stored, but not organized to convey any specific meaning; can be numeric, alphanumeric, figures, sounds, or images.

Data mart   A subset of the data warehouse, usually originated for a specific purpose or major data subject.

Data mining   The process of searching for unknown information or relationships in large databases using tools such as neural computing or case-based reasoning.

Data quality (DQ)   A measure of the accuracy, accessibility, relevance, timeliness, completeness, and other characteristics that describe useful data.

Data tampering   Deliberately entering false data, or changing and deleting true data.

Data visualization   Visual presentation of data and information by graphics, animation, or any other multimedia.

Data warehouse   A repository of historical data, subject-oriented and organized so as to be easily accessed and manipulated for decision support.

Data workers   Clerical workers who use, manipulate, or disseminate information, typically using document management, workflow, e-mail, and coordination software to do so.

Database   A collection of stored data items organized for retrieval.

Decision room   A face-to-face arrangement for a group DSS in which terminals are available to the participants.

Decision support system (DSS)   A computer-based information system that combines models and data in an attempt to solve semistructured problems with extensive user involvement.

Dehumanization   A condition that makes people feel a loss of identity when working with computers and information systems.

Denial of service (DoS)   Cyber attack in which an attacker sends a flood of data packets to the target computer, with the aim of overloading its resources.

Desktop purchasing   E-procurement method in which suppliers' catalogs are aggregated into an internal master catalog on the buyer's server for use by the company's purchasing agents.

Differentiation strategy   The competitive strategy of offering different products, services, or product features than those offered by competitors.

Digital cities   Regional communities in which people can interact and share knowledge, experiences, and mutual interests via computing technologies.

Digital divide   The gap in computer technology in general and in Web technology in particular between those who have information technology and those who do not.

Digital economy   Another name for today's Web-based, or Internet, economy.

Digital rights management (DRM) systems   Computer systems that prevent the unauthorized copying of intellectual property.

Directory   An Internet search facility that is a hierarchically organized collection of links to Web pages.

Disaster avoidance   An approach oriented toward preventing or minimizing a controllable catastrophe.

Disaster recovery plan   See *Business continuity plan.*

Disintermediation   The elimination of intermediaries in EC; removing the layers of intermediaries between sellers and buyers.

Distance learning   A learning situation in which teachers and students are in different locations.

Distributed computing   IS architecture that gives users direct control over their own computing; puts computing choices at the point of the computing need.

Distributed processing   Computing architecture that divides processing work between two or more computers that may not be (and usually are not) functionally equal.

Distributed denial of service (DDoS)   A DoS attack in which the attacker gains illegal access to unsuspecting computers and uses these computers to send a flood of data packets to the target computers.

Document management The automated control of digitized documents throughout their life cycle.

Document management system (DMS) A system that provides information in an electronic format to decision makers.

Domain name An Internet address, whose top level identifies the name of the company or organization, followed by *.com, .org,* etc.

E-business A company that performs most of its business functions electronically; the broadest definition of e-commerce, including intrabusiness, interorganizational business, and e-commerce; many use the term interchangeably with e-commerce.

eCRM (electronic CRM) The use of Web browsers, the Internet, and other electronic touchpoints to manage customer relationships.

802.11b Standard, developed by the IEEE, on which most of today's wireless LANs run.

E-government The use of e-commerce to deliver information and public services to citizens, business partners, and suppliers of government entities, and those working in the public sector.

E-learning Learning supported by the Web, in a variety of settings (either in physical classrooms or in virtual classrooms from home).

Electronic banking See *Cyberbanking.*

Electronic bartering The electronically supported exchange of goods or services without a monetary transaction.

Electronic benefits transfers (EBT) Transfer of direct payments made by the government or other organization to recipients' bank accounts or smart cards.

Electronic cash (e-cash) A computerized stored value that can be used as cash, such as in stored-value money cards.

Electronic certificates Verification, provided by a trusted third party, that a specific public encryption key belongs to a specific individual.

Electronic checks (e-checks) Payment mechanism made with electronic rather than paper checks.

Electronic commerce (e-commerce, EC) The process of buying, selling, transferring, or exchanging products, services, or information via computer networks, including the Internet; business conducted online.

Electronic credit cards Payment mechanism that enables online payments with the characteristics of regular credit cards (e.g., pay within 30 days).

EDI (electronic data interchange) A communication standard that enables the electronic transfer of routine documents between business partners.

Electronic funds transfer (EFT) The transmission of funds, debits and credits, and charges and payments electronically among banks and between banks and their customers.

Electronic mall A collection of individual shops under one Internet address.

Electronic market A network of interactions and relationships over which products, services, information, and payments are exchanged.

Electronic retailing (e-tailing) The direct sale of products and services through electronic storefronts or electronic malls, usually designed around an electronic catalog format and/or auctions.

Electronic storefront The Web site of a single company, with its own Internet address, at which orders can be placed.

Electronic surveillance The tracking of people's activities, online or offline; often done with the aid of computers (e.g., monitoring e-mail).

E-mail agent Agent that manages users' e-mail by routing, deleting, prioritizing, or blocking e-mail.

Employee relationship management (ERM) The use of Web-based applications to streamline the human resources process and to better manage employees.

Encryption Scrambling of data so that they cannot be recognized by unauthorized readers.

End-user computing The use or development of information systems by the principal users of the systems' outputs or by their staffs.

Enhanced Messaging Service (EMS) An extension of SMS capable of simple animation, tiny pictures, and short tunes.

Enterprisewide computing A client/server architecture that connects data that are used throughout the enterprise.

Enterprise resource planning (ERP) Software that integrates the planning, management, and use of all resources in the entire enterprise; also called *enterprise systems.*

Enterprise software An integrated software that supports enterprise computing and ERP. The most notable example is SAP R/3.

Enterprise system Information system that encompasses the entire enterprise, implemented on a companywide network. Also called *enterprisewide system.*

Enterprise Web The sum of a company's systems, information, and services that are available on the Web, working together as one entity.

Enterprisewide system (EIS) See *Enterprise system.*

Entry-barriers strategy The competitive strategy of creating barriers to entry of new market entrants.

E-planning Electronically supported IT planning that touches on EC infrastructure and mostly deals with uncovering business opportunities and deciding on an applications portfolio that will exploit those opportunities.

E-procurement Purchasing by using electronic support.

Ergonomics The science of adapting machines and work environments to people.

E-supply chain A supply chain that is managed electronically, usually with Web-based software.

E-tailers Electronic retailers; business-to-consumer (B2C) sellers in online stores. Engaging in such activity is termed *e-tailing.*

Ethics A branch of philosophy that deals with what is considered to be right and wrong.

E-wallets (digital wallets) A software component in which a user stores secured personal and credit card information for one-click reuse.

Exception reporting Management reporting system that calls attention only to results that deviate from a standard by a certain percentage or exceed a threshold.

Electronic exchanges Web-based public e-marketplaces, where many business buyers and many sellers interact dynamically.

Executive information system (EIS) System specifically designed to support information needs of executives.

Executive support system (ESS) A comprehensive executive support system that includes some analytical and communication capabilities.

Expected value (EV) A weighted average, computed by multiplying the size of a possible future benefit by the probability of its occurrence.

Expense management automation (EMA) Systems that automate data entry and processing of travel and entertainment expenses.

Expert system (ES) A computer system that applies reasoning methodologies or knowledge in a specific domain to render advice or recommendations—much like a human expert.

Explicit knowledge The knowledge that deals with objective, rational, and technical knowledge (data, policies, procedures, software, documents, etc.).

Exposure The state in a computing system which is not a universal vulnerability, but is considered a problem according to some reasonable security policy.

Extranet A secured network that allows business partners to access portions of each other's intranets. It is usually Internet-based.

Fault tolerance The ability to continue operating satisfactorily in the presence of faults or partial system failure.

Financial value chain management (FVCM) The combination of financial analysis with operations analysis, which analyzes all financial functions in order to provide better financial control.

Firewalls Security systems that protect organizations' internal networks from unauthorized access coming from the Internet.

Flaming Sending anonymous insulting or angry messages on the Internet.

Forward auction An auction that sellers use as a selling channel to many potential buyers; the highest bidder wins the items.

4G The expected next generation of wireless technology.

Four-stage model of planning A generic IS planning model based on four major, generic activities: strategic planning, information requirements analysis, resource allocation, and project planning.

Frequency Division Multiple Access (FDMA) Wireless communication protocol, used by 1G systems, that gives each user a different frequency on which to communicate.

Frontline decision making The process by which companies automate decision processes and push them down to frontline employees.

Functional management information system (functional MIS) An information system for a functional area, such as a marketing information system.

Fuzzy logic A way of reasoning that can cope with uncertain or partial information; a characteristic of human thinking and some expert systems.

General controls Security controls aimed at defending a computer system in general rather than protecting specific applications.

Genetic programming Automatic problem-solving method that randomly creates thousands of computer programs and then applies natural selection to choose the strongest.

Geographical information system (GIS) Computer-based system that integrates GSP data onto digitized map displays.

Global information systems Interorganizational systems that connect companies located in two or more countries.

Global positioning system (GPS) A wireless system that uses satellites to enable users to determine their position anywhere on the earth.

Globalization The elimination of geographic barriers that separated individuals, organizations, and societies.

Government-to-business (G2B) EC E-commerce in which a government does business with other governments as well as with businesses.

Government-to-citizens (G2C) EC E-commerce in which a government provides services to its citizens via EC technologies.

Government-to-government (G2G) EC E-commerce in which government units do business with other government units.

Grid computing The use of networks to harness the unused processing cycles of all computers in a given network to create powerful computing capabilities.

Group decision support system (GDSS) An interactive, computer-based system that facilitates finding solutions to semistructured problems by using a set of decision makers working together as a group.

Group purchasing The aggregation of purchasing orders from many buyers so that a volume discount can be obtained.

Group support systems (GSSs) Information systems that support the working processes of groups (e.g., communication and decision making).

Groupware Software products that support people working in groups and enable groups to share resources and opinions.

Growth strategy The competitive strategy of increasing market share, acquiring more customers, or selling more products.

Hackers People who illegally or unethically penetrate a computer system.

Honeynets A network of *honeypots*.

Honeypots Traps designed to work like real systems but to attract hackers.

Hotspot A wireless access point that provides service to a number of users within a small geographical perimeter (up to a couple hundred feet).

Increasing returns A concept in economics that expects profitability to rise more rapidly than production increases.

Inference engine The component of an expert system that performs a reasoning function.

Information Data that have been organized so they have meaning and value to the recipient.

Information anxiety The disquiet resulting from inability to cope with the quantity or quality of information and data in our lives.

Information architecture A high-level, logical plan of the information requirements and the structures or integration of information resources needed to meet those requirements.

Information center Facility that trains and supports business users with end-user tools, testing, technical support information, and standards certification.

Information economics An approach to cost-benefit analysis that incorporates organizational objectives in a scoring methodology.

Information infrastructure The physical arrangement of hardware, software, databases, networks, and information management personnel.

Information overload The introduction of more data and information than a person can handle.

Information portal Generic term for a single point of access through a Web browser to critical business information located inside and outside of an organization; content can vary from narrow to broad, and audience can also vary.

Information quality For data and information, the characteristics of completeness, accuracy, currency, and fitness for use.

Information requirements analysis An analysis of the information needs of users and how that information relates to their work; stage 2 of the four-stage planning model.

Information resources management (IRM) All activities related to the planning, organizing, acquiring, maintaining, securing, and controlling of IT resources.

Information superhighway A national information infrastructure to interconnect computer users; now usually simply called the Internet.

Information system (IS) A physical process that supports an organization by collecting, processing, storing, and analyzing data, and disseminating information to achieve organizational goals.

Information technology (IT) The technology component of an information system (a narrow definition); or the collection of the computing systems in an organization (the broad definition used in this book).

Information technology architecture High-level map or plan of the information assets in an organization; on the Web, it includes the content and architecture of the site.

Innovation strategy The competitive strategy of introducing new products and services, putting new features in existing products and services, or developing new ways to produce them.

Intangible benefits Benefits that are hard to place a monetary value on (e.g., greater design flexibility).

Intellectual capital (intellectual assets) The valuable knowledge of employees.

Intellectual property Intangible outputs such as software, books, music, movies, articles, and paintings.

Intelligent agents Software agents that exhibit intelligent behavior and learning.

Intelligent systems Information systems that include a commercial application of artificial intelligence; examples are expert systems and neural networks.

Internet A self-regulated global network of computer networks connecting millions of businesses, individuals, government agencies, schools, and other organizations all over the world.

Internet economy See *Digital economy.*

Internet telephony (voice-over IP) Technology that makes it possible to talk long distance on the Internet without paying normal long-distance telephone charges.

Internet of things A network that connects computers to objects in order to be able to track individual items through the supply chain.

Internet relay chat (IRC) An e-mail–based type of chat program that allows users to see everything that other users say.

Internet2 A U.S. government initiative supporting the creation of a high-speed computer network connecting various research facilities across the country.

Interorganizational information systems (IOSs) Information systems that support information flow between two or more organizations.

Intrabusiness E-commerce done *within* an organization (between an organization and its employees or among business units).

Intrabusiness (intraorganizational) commerce E-commerce in which an organization uses EC internally to improve its operations.

Intranet A corporate network that functions with Internet technologies, such as browsers and search engines, using Internet protocols.

IT governance A formally established set of statements intended to direct policies regarding IT alignment with organizational goals, risk determination, and resource allocation.

IT planning The organized planning of IT infrastructure and applications portfolios done at various levels of the organization.

Just-in-time (JIT) An inventory scheduling system in which material and parts arrive at a work place when needed, minimizing inventory, waste, and interruptions.

Key-word banner Banner advertising that appears when a predetermined word is queried from a search engine.

Knowledge Data and/or information that have been organized and processed to convey understanding, experience, accumulated learning, and expertise.

Knowledge audit The process of identifying the knowledge an organization has, who has it, and how it flows (or does not flow) through the enterprise.

Knowledge base A collection of facts, rules, and procedures, related to a specific problem, organized in one place.

Knowledge discovery See *Knowledge discovery in databases*.

Knowledge discovery in databases (KDD) The process of extracting knowledge from volumes of data in databases (e.g., in data warehouses); includes data mining.

Knowledge management The process that helps organizations identify, select, organize, disseminate, and transfer important information and expertise that are part of the organization's memory and that may reside in unstructured form within the organization.

Knowledge management suites Software packages that consist of a comprehensive set of KM tools that can be used out-of-the-box.

Knowledge management system (KMS) A system that organizes, enhances, and expedites intra- and interfirm knowledge management; centered around a corporate knowledge base or depository.

Knowledge repository The software system that is a collection of both internal and external knowledge in a KMS.

Knowledge workers People who create and use knowledge as a significant part of their work responsibilities.

Knowware A name for knowledge management (KM) software.

L-commerce See *Location-based commerce*.

Leaky knowledge Another name for explicit knowledge, due to the ease with which it can leave its source after it has been documented.

Legacy systems Older systems that have become central to business operations and may be still capable of meeting these business needs; they may not require any immediate changes, or they may be in need of reengineering to meet new business needs.

Location-based commerce (1-commerce) M-commerce transactions targeted to individuals in specific locations, at specific times.

Lock-in effect The difficulty of switching to a competing product due to the need to learn how to use a different product or to other factors that discourage change.

Lotus Notes Domino An integrated groupware software suite that provides various tools for groupwork, such as document management, online collaboration, e-mail, and application sharing.

Management by maxim Method that guides investment in IT infrastructure by identifying infrastructure requirements that correspond to organizational strategies and objectives.

Management information systems (MISs) Systems designed to provide past, present, and future routine information appropriate for planning, organizing, and controlling the operations of functional areas in an organization.

Management service provider (MSP) A vendor that, for a subscription fee, remotely manages and monitors enterprise applications (e.g., ERP, CRM, firewalls, proprietary e-business applications).

Management support systems (MSSs) Major IT technologies designed to support managers: decision support systems, executive support systems, group decision support systems, and intelligent systems.

Manufacturing resource planning (MRPII) A planning model that adds labor requirements and financial planning to MRP.

Marketing transaction database (MTD) An interactive database oriented toward targeting marketing messages in real time.

Mass customization The production of a very large quantity of customized products (e.g., Dell computers).

Material requirements planning (MRP) A planning model (usually computerized) that integrates production, purchasing, and inventory management of interrelated products.

M-commerce See *Mobile commerce*.

M-wallet See *Mobile wallet*.

Metadata Data about data, such as indices or summaries.

Metasearch engines Special indexing agents that integrate the findings of various search engines to answer queries posted by users.

Metcalfe's Law Maxim that states that the value of a network grows roughly in line with the square of the number of its users.

Metric A specific, measurable standard against which actual performance is compared.

Metric benchmarks Numeric measures of IT performance relative to other numeric factors (e.g., organizational revenues, CPU capacity, etc).

Mobile commerce (m-commerce, m-business) Any e-commerce done in a wireless environment, especially via the Internet.

Mobile computing Information system applications in a wireless environment.

Mobile handset A mobile system consisting of two parts—equipment that hosts the applications (e.g., a PDA) and a mobile terminal (e.g., a cell phone) that connects to the mobile network.

Mobile portal A gateway to the Internet accessible from mobile devices; aggregates content and services for mobile users.

Mobile wallet (m-wallet) Technology that enables cardholders to make purchases with a single click from their mobile devices; also known as *wireless wallet*.

Model (in decision making) A simplified representation or abstraction of reality; can be used to perform virtual experiments and analysis.

Model-based management system (MBMS) A software program to establish, update, and use a model base.

Model marts Small, generally departmental or topical repositories of knowledge created by employing knowledge-discovery techniques on past decision instances. Analogous to *data marts*.

Model warehouses Large, generally enterprisewide repositories of knowledge created by employing knowledge-discovery techniques on past decision instances. Analogous to *data warehouses.*

Moore's Law The expectation that the power of a microprocessor will double every 18 months, while the cost stays at the same level.

Multidimensional database Specialized data stores that organize facts by dimensions such as geographical region, time, product line, or salesperson.

Multidimensionality Analysis of data by looking at multiple factors: dimensions (e.g., place, products, customers, channels), measures (e.g., sales volume, head count), and time.

Multimedia messaging service (MMS) The next generation of wireless messaging, which will be able to deliver rich media.

Natural language processor (NLP) A knowledge-based user interface that allows the user to carry on a conversation with a computer-based system in much the same way as he or she would converse with another human.

Network effects The support that leading products in an industry receive from their large user base and the complementary products marketed to these users.

Network storage devices Storage devices that are attached to the corporate network (usually intranets) and that can be accessed from network applications throughout the enterprise for data sharing.

Networked computing A corporate information infrastructure that provides the necessary networks for distributed computing. Users can easily contact each other or databases and communicate with external entities.

Neural computing The technology that attempts to achieve knowledge representations and processing based on massive parallel processing, fast retrieval of large amounts of information, and the ability to recognize patterns based on experiences.

Niche strategy The competitive strategy of selecting a narrow-scope segment (niche market) and being the best in quality, speed, or cost in that market.

Object technology Technology that enables development of self-contained units of software that can be shared, purchased, and/or reused; includes object-oriented programming, object-oriented databases, and other object-oriented-based components and activities.

Offshore outsourcing Use of vendors in other countries, usually where labor is inexpensive, to do programming or other system development tasks.

1G The first generation of wireless technology, which was analog-based.

Online analytical processing (OLAP) The processing and analyzing of data to reflect business needs as transactions occur.

Online processing Processing system that operates on a transaction as soon as it occurs, possibly even in real time.

Online transaction processing (OLTP) A transaction processing system, created on a client/server architecture, that allows suppliers to enter the TPS and look at the firm's inventory level or production schedule.

Operational data store A database that provides clean data to the operational, mission-critical, short-term-oriented applications.

Optimization An approach used by management science to find the best possible solution.

Organizational (institutional) decision support system (ODSS) A network system that provides decision support for organizational, group, and individual tasks or activities.

Organizational knowledge base The collection of knowledge related to the operation of an organization.

Outsourcing Acquiring IS services from an external (outside) organization rather than through internal IS units.

Partner-relationship management (PRM) Business strategy that recognizes the need to develop long-term relationships with business partners, by providing each partner with the services that are most beneficial.

Pattern recognition The ability of a computer to classify an item to a predetermined category by matching the item's characteristics with that of a stored category.

Peer-to-peer (P2P) architecture A type of network in which each client computer shares files or computer resources *directly* with others *but not through a central server.*

Permission marketing Method of marketing that asks consumers to give their permission to voluntarily accept online advertising and e-mail.

Personal digital assistant (PDA) A small, handheld wireless computer.

Personal information manager (PIM) A software package for a manager's personal use.

Personal portals Gateways to the Internet that target specific filtered information for individuals.

Person-to-person payment A form of e-cash that enables the transfer of funds between two individuals, or between an individual and a business, without the use of a credit card.

Pervasive computing Invisible, everywhere computing that is embedded in the objects around us.

Piracy Theft of digital content.

Pop-under ad An advertisement that is automatically launched by some trigger and appears underneath the active window.

Pop-up ad An advertisement that is automatically launched by some trigger and appears in front of the active window.

Portals Web-based personalized gateways to information and knowledge in network computing.

Practice approach Knowledge management approach that assumes that much organizational knowledge is tacit in nature and so builds communities of practice necessary to facilitate the sharing of tacit understanding.

Price-to-performance ratio The relative cost, usually on a per-mips (millions of instructions per second) basis, of the processing power of a computer.

Primary activities In Porter's value chain model, those activities in which materials are purchased and processed to products, which are then delivered to customers. Secondary activities, such as accounting, support the primary ones.

Process approach Knowledge management approach that attempts to codify organizational knowledge through formalized controls, processes, and technologies.

Process-centric integration Integration solutions designed, developed, and managed from a business-process perspective, instead of from a technical or middleware perspective.

Product lifecycle management (PLM) A business strategy that enables manufacturers and logistics providers to collaborate on product development efforts, typically using Web-based technologies.

Productivity paradox The seeming discrepancy between extremely large IT investments in the economy and relatively low measures of productivity output.

Programming attack Criminal use of programming techniques to modify a computer program, either directly or indirectly; examples are computer worms, viruses, and denial of service attacks.

Project planning Planning framework within which specific applications can be planned, scheduled, and controlled; stage 4 of the four-stage planning model.

Public exchange E-marketplace in which there are many sellers and many buyers, and entry is open to all; frequently owned and operated by a third party.

Publishing portals Gateways to the Internet that are intended for communities with specific interests; involve little content customization but provide extensive online search in a specific area.

Quality of life The measure of how well we achieve a desirable standard of living.

Radio frequency identification (RFID) Generic term for technologies that use radio waves to automatically identify individual items.

Random banner Banner advertising that appears randomly, not as a result of the viewer's action.

Real options Business opportunities embedded in capital projects; if taken, these opportunities will alter future cash flows to increase profitability.

Reintermediation Occurs where intermediaries such as brokers provide value-added services and expertise that cannot be eliminated when EC is used.

Request for proposal (RFP) Document sent to potential vendors inviting them to submit a proposal describing their products or services.

Resource-based view (RBV) Competitive-advantage paradigm that maintains that firms possess resources, some of which enable firms to gain competitive advantage and some of which allow firms to achieve superior long-term performance.

Resource allocation Developing the hardware, software, data communications, facilities, personnel, and financial plans needed to execute the master development plan; stage 3 of the four-stage planning model.

Reverse auction An auction in which one buyer, usually an organization, seeks to buy a product or a service, and suppliers submit bids; the lowest bidder wins.

Reverse engineering The process of examining legacy systems to identify what changes are needed to enable the system to meet current and future business needs.

RFID See *Radio frequency identification.*

Risk management Approach that determines the potential risk associated with a project or a problem and considers this risk in cost-benefit analysis.

Sales automation software Productivity software used to automate the work of salespeople.

Sales-force automation The hardware and software used by salespeople, usually in the field and often wireless, to automate some of their tasks.

SAP R/3 The leading EPR software (from SAP AG Corp.); a highly integrated package containing more than 70 business activities modules.

Scenario planning A planning methodology for dealing with an uncertain environment by examining different scenarios; a what-if analysis.

SCM software Applications programs specifically designed to improve decision making in segments of the supply chain.

Scoring methodology Methodology that evaluates alternatives by assigning weights and scores to various aspects and then calculating the weighted totals for comparison.

Screen sharing Technology that enables two or more participants to see the same screen and make changes on it that can be seen by all.

Screenphone A telephone equipped with a color screen, possibly a keyboard, e-mail, and Internet capabilities.

Search engines Software agents whose task is to find information by searching through an index of hundreds of Web pages to match a set of user-specified keywords.

Self-healing computers Computers that can find their problems and correct them themselves, before a system crashes.

Sell-side marketplace B2B model in which organizations sell to other organizations from their own private e-marketplace and/or from a third-party site.

Semantic Web An extension of the Web where information is assigned greater meaning, and data can be accessed for automation, integration, and reuse.

Sensitivity analysis Study of the effect of a change in one or more input variables on a proposed solution.

Server Machine, attached to a network, that provides some services to client machines on the network.

Service-level agreements (SLAs) Formal agreements (contracts) regarding the division of work between a company and its vendors.

Short messaging service (SMS) Technology that allows for sending of short text messages on some cell phones.

Simulation A technique for conducting experiments that imitate reality using a model of a management system.

Smart appliances Appliances that can be controlled by computing devices via a home network or the Internet.

Smart card A card that contains a microprocessor (chip) that enables the card to store a considerable amount of information (including stored funds) and to conduct processing.

Smart terminal A terminal that contains a keyboard, screen, and disk drive that enables it to perform limited processing tasks, yet whose core processing power is the central mainframe computer to which it is networked.

Smartphone Internet-enabled cell phones that can support mobile applications.

Social engineering Getting around security systems by tricking computer users into providing information or carrying out actions that seem innocuous but are not.

Social software Software that supports actual human interactions; includes groupware, knowledge management, and other communication tools.

Softbots Software robots that create and update indexes used by search engines.

Software agents Computer programs that carry out a set of routine tasks for the benefit of their users. Also known as *intelligent agents*.

Spamming Indiscriminate distribution of electronic messages without permission of the receiver.

Speech recognition The ability of a computer to recognize spoken words.

Speech understanding The ability of a computer to understand the meaning of sentences, in contrast with merely *recognizing* individual words.

Spyware Advertising-supported software (adware).

Stages of IT growth Six commonly accepted stages, suggested by Nolan, that all organizations seem to experience in implementing and managing an information system from conception to maturity over time.

Stealthware Hidden programs that come with free software that users download, and that then track their surfing activities, reporting them to a marketing server.

Steering committee Group of key managers and staff, representing organizational units, set up to establish IT priorities and to ensure that the IS department is meeting the enterprise's needs.

Sticky knowledge Another name for tacit knowledge because it may be relatively difficult to pull away from its source.

Stored-value money card A form of e-cash on which a fixed amount of prepaid money is stored; the amount is reduced each time the card is used.

Strategic information technology planning (SITP) The identification of an IT-based strategic applications portfolio and the search for SIS applications that develop competitive advantage.

Subscription (service) computing A type of *utility computing* that puts the pieces of a computing platform together as services, rather than as a collection of separately purchased components.

Supplier relationship management (SRM) A PRM in which the partners are the company's suppliers.

Supply chain Flow of materials, information, money, and services from raw material suppliers, through factories and warehouses, to the end customers; includes the organizations and processes involved.

Supply chain management (SCM) The management of all the activities along the supply chain, from suppliers, to internal logistics within a company, to distribution, to customers. This includes ordering, monitoring, and billing.

Supply chain team A group of tightly coordinated employees who work together to serve the customer; each task is done by the member of the team who is best capable of doing the task.

Support activities Business activities that do not add value directly to a firm's product or service under consideration but support the primary activities that do add value.

Symbolic processing The use of symbols, rather than numbers, combined with rules of thumb (or heuristics) to process information and solve problems.

Synchronous (real-time) communication The nearly simultaneous sending and receiving of messages.

Tacit knowledge The knowledge that is usually in the domain of subjective, cognitive, and experiential learning; it is highly personal and hard to formalize.

Telecommuting (teleworking) Working from outside the office.

Teleconferencing The use of electronic communication to enable people in different locations to confer simultaneously.

Telematics The integration of computers and wireless communications to improve information flow using the principles of telemetry.

Text mining The application of data mining analysis to nonstructured or less-structured text files and documents.

3G The third generation of digital wireless technology; supports rich media such as video clips.

Time Division Multiple Access (TDMA) Wireless communication protocol, used with some 2G systems, that assigns different users different time slots on a given communications channel.

Total benefits of ownership (TBO) An approach for calculating the payoff of an IT investment by calculating both the tangible and intangible benefits and subtracting the costs of ownership: TBO − TCO = Payoff.

Total cost of ownership (TCO) A formula for calculating the cost of owning and operating an IT system; includes acquisition cost, operations cost, and control cost.

Transaction processing systems (TPSs) An information system that processes an organization's basic business transactions such as purchasing, billing, and payroll.

Trojan horse Software program that contains a hidden function that presents a security risk.

Turing test Named after the English mathematician Alan Turing, a test designed to measure if a computer is intelligent or not. A computer is considered intelligent only when a human interviewer, conversing with both an unseen human being and an unseen computer, cannot determine which is which.

2G The second generation of digital wireless technology; accommodates mainly text.

2.5G Interim wireless technology that can accommodate limited graphics.

Utility computing Unlimited computing power and storage capacity that, like electricity, water, and telephone services, can be obtained on demand, used and reallocated for any application, and billed on a pay-per-use basis.

Value analysis Method that evaluates intangible benefits on a low-cost, trial basis prior to committing to development of a complete system.

Value chain model Model developed by Michael Porter that shows the primary activities that sequentially add value to the profit margin; also shows the support activities.

Value system In Porter's value chain model, the stream of activities that includes the producers, suppliers, distributors, and buyers (all with their own value chains).

Vendor-managed inventory (VMI) Strategy used by retailers of allowing suppliers to monitor the inventory levels and replenish inventory when needed, eliminating the need for purchasing orders.

Video teleconferencing (videoconferencing) Teleconferencing with the added capability of the participants to see each other.

Viral marketing Online "word-of-mouth" marketing.

Virtual close The ability of a company to close its books (accounting records) any time, on short notice.

Virtual collaboration The use of digital technologies to collaboratively plan, design, develop, manage, and research products, services, and innovative IT and EC applications.

Virtual community A group of people with some common interests who interact with one another using digital tools to communicate and collaborate.

Virtual corporation (VC) An organization composed of two or more business partners, in different locations, sharing costs and resources for the purpose of producing a product or service; can be temporary or permanent.

Virtual credit card A payment mechanism that allows a buyer to shop with an ID number and a password instead of with a credit card number, yet the charges are made to the credit card.

Virtual factory Collaborative enterprise application that provides a computerized model of a factory.

Virtual group (team) A group whose members are in different locations and who "meet" electronically.

Virtual meetings Electronically supported meetings whose members are in different locations, frequently in different countries.

Virtual organizations Organizations in which the product, the process, and the delivery agent are all digital; also called *pure-play organizations*.

Virtual reality A pseudo-3-D interactive technology that provides a user with a feeling that he or she is physically present in a computer-generated world.

Virtual Reality Markup Language (VRML) A platform-independent standard for virtual reality.

Virtual universities Online universities from which students take classes from home or an off-site location via the Internet.

Virus Software that attaches itself to other programs and can damage or destroy data or software.

Visual interactive modeling (VIM) Use of computer graphic displays to represent the impact of different decisions on organizational goals.

Visual interactive simulation (VIS) A VIM where simulation is used as the problem-solving tool.

Voice portal (vortal) A Web site with audio interface, accessed by a standard or cell phone call.

Voice synthesis The technology that transforms computer output to voice or audio output.

Voice-over IP See *Internet telephony*.

Vulnerability (in security) A system's exposure to potential hazards, either intentional or accidental.

Wearable devices Mobile wireless computing devices for employees who work on buildings and other difficult-to-climb places.

Web conferencing Videoteleconferencing that is conducted solely on the Internet (not on telephone lines) for as few as two and as many as thousands of people.

Web economy See *Digital economy*.

Web mining The application of data mining techniques to discover meaningful and actionable patterns from Web resources.

Web Services Modular business and consumer applications, delivered over the Internet, that users can select and combine through almost any device, enabling disparate systems to share data and services.

Web-based DSS A DSS that is supported by the Web, either for developing applications and/or disseminating and using them. Both the Internet and intranets can be used.

Web-based management support systems (MSSs) Systems designed to support managers' decision making and delivered via the Web.

Web-based system An application delivered on the Internet or intranet using Web tools, such as a search engine.

Weblogging See *Blogging*.

Whiteboard (electronic) An area on a computer display screen on which multiple users can write or draw; multiple users can use a single document "pasted" onto the screen.

Wireless access point Transmitter with an antenna connecting a mobile device (laptop or PDA) to a wired local area network.

Wireless Application Protocol (WAP) A set of communications protocols designed to enable different kinds of wireless devices to talk to a server installed on a mobile network, so users can access the Internet.

Wireless mobile computing   Use of mobile computing devices in a wireless environment.

Wireless Encryption Protocol (WEP)   Built-in security system in wireless devices, which encrypts communications between the device and a wireless access point.

Wireless fidelity (Wi-Fi)   The standard on which most of today's WLANs run, developed by the IEEE (Institute of Electrical and Electronic Engineers). Also known as *802.11b*.

Wireless LAN (WLAN)   LAN without the cables; used to transmit and receive data over the airwaves, but only from short distances.

Wireless 911 (e-911)   Calls from cellular phones to providers of emergency services.

Wireless wide area networks (WWANs)   Wide area networks for mobile computing.

Workflow   The movement of information as it flows through the steps that make up an organization's work procedures.

Workflow systems   Business process automation tools that automate information processing tasks and place system controls in the hands of user departments.

World Wide Web (WWW, the Web)   The most widely used application that uses the transport functions of the Internet.

Workflow management   Automation of workflows, so that documents, information, or tasks are passed from one participant to another in a way that is governed by the organization's rules or procedures.

XML (eXtensible Markup Language)   A simplified version of the general data description language, SGML; used to improve compatibility between the disparate systems of business partners by defining the meaning of data in business documents.

Zombies   The machines on which distributed denial of service software is loaded.

 **Photo Credits**

Chapter 1
Page 33: Courtesy of Symbol Technologies.

Chapter 2
Page W33: ©AP/Wide World Photos. Page 51: PhotoDisc, Inc./Getty Images.

Chapter 4
Page 167: Courtesy of Chicago Transit Authority (CTA).

Chapter 5
Page 209: Brian Willer Photography.

Chapter 6
Page 265: Sonda Dawes/The Image Works.

Chapter 16
Page 702 (all photos): Courtesy WorkSmart. Page 718: Michael Freeman/Digital Vision.

Name Index

A

Abramson, G., 392
Adams, S., 638
Adelantado, M., 492
Adeli, H., 489
Afuah, A., 11
Agarwal, R., 635, 702
Agrawal, M. T. V., 87
Agrawal, R., 577
Agrawal, V. L., 542
Agre, P. E., 71
Ahmad, L., 67
Alameh, N., 437
Alavi, M., 370, 374, 376
Albalooshi, F., 121
Alberts, B., 684
Alesso, P., 485
Alexander, S., 109
Alfonseca, M., 438
Alga, N., 657, 658
Allee, V., 393
Allison, Jack, 385
Alter, S. L., 413
Amato-McCoy, D., 67, 256, 262, 289, 385, 430, 446, 453, 485
Ambrosio, J., 393
Amidon, D., 391
Amiri, A., 154
Amit, R., 516
Anderson, C., 197
Anderson, D., 18
Anderson, L., 382
Andrews, K., 516
Aneja, A., 101, 103
Ang, J. S. K., 538
Ante, S., 470
Anthony, R. N., 464, 465
Apte, C., 429, 430
Arens, Y., 12
Armstrong, A. G., 709
Arnoff, D., 476
Arnold, V., 480
Arthur, Brian, 584
Arthur, W. B., 585
Asprev, L., 415
Astani, M., 317
Athitakis, M., 176
Atkins, M., 471
Atlas, R. I., 653
Atre, S., 423
Atzeni, P., 443
Austin, R. D., 644
Avriel, M., 273
Azari, R., 676

B

Baard, M., 216
Bailey, D. E., 110
Baker, W., 266
Ball, L. D., 78, 639
Ballou, D., 414
Banerjee, P., 439
Banks, E., 270
Bantz, D. F., 75
Barko, C. D., 428
Barney, J. B., 516
Barrett, L., 458, 630
Barth, S., 390, 393
Barthelemy, J., 575, 579
Bartram, L., 114
Barva, A., 25, 616
Basu, A., 7, 17, 116, 419
Bates, J., 414, 432, 494
Bauer, M. J., 297
Baumer, D., 412
Bayers, C., 149
Bayles, D. L., 169, 170
Beal, B., 522
Beath, C. M., 560
Becker, D., 215, 635
Becker, S. A., 414
Beckett, H., 123
Bednarz, A., 75
Beitler, S. S., 453
Belanger, F., 123
Benaroch, M., 571
Benbasat, I., 483
Benbya, H., 101
Benford, S., 75
Benjaafar, S., 2002
Bennet, A., 370
Bennet, D., 370
Berg, J. E., 464
Bergerson, 318
Berman, D., 696, 697
Berners-Lee, T. J., 97
Bernstein, P. A., 250
Beroggi, G. E., 438
Berry, M., 430, 431
Bezos, Jeff, 149
Bharadwaj, A. S., 518
Bielski, L., 258
Biermann, E., 662
Biery, K., 666
Bills, S., 69
Birks, D. F., 436
Bishop, R., 312
Blackstock, M., 114
Blanco, L., 672
Blodgett, M., 384, 519
Blum, R., 567
Boar, B. H., 520, 539
Bochenek, G. M., 115
Boisvert, L., 281
Bolloju, N., 379
Bonabeau, E., 461, 462
Bonde, A., 419, 424
Boothroyd, D., 100
Borck, J. R., 278
Bose, R., 494
Boucher-Ferguson, R., 273, 348
Boyett, J. H., 12
Boyett, J. T., 12
Bradley, P., 115
Brandberry, A. A., 146
Brandel, M., 615
Brandt, A., 197
Brassil, R. A., 669
Brauer, J. R., 412, 413
Bresnahan, J., 307
Bretz, E., 228
Brewin, B., 266
Brezillon, P., 476
Briggs, D., 476
Briggs, R. O., 605
Broadbent, M., 66, 517, 533, 560, 570
Brobst, S., 614
Brody, R., 418
Brookman, F., 103, 104
Brown, D. E., 418, 429
Brown, M., 116
Brown, R. H., 577
Brown, S. J., 374, 375, 376
Brownlow, J., 648
Brue, G., 18
Bruno, L., 650
Brynjolfsson, E., 4, 11, 558
Buckler, G., 383
Buckley, N., 268
Buckman, 402
Buell, D. A., 648
Buffett, Warren, 10
Bughin, J., 207
Burke, L. A., 615
Buss, D., 282, 433
Bussler, L., 276, 279, 281
Buytendijk, F., 698
Bygstad, B., 537
Byrd, T. A., 569

C

Calderon, T. G., 429
Cale, E. G., 521
Callaghan, D., 117
Callon, J. D., 17, 515
Campbell, D., 435
Carbone, P. L., 431, 432
Carmel, E., 116, 577
Carr, N. G., 4, 7, 15
Carroll, C. T., 601
Carroll, M., 693
Carroll, S., 98
Carter, G. M., 472
Cassidy, A., 520
Caton, M., 214
Caulfield, B., 658
Cawsey, A., 476
Champy, J., 18, 617, 618
Chan, J. K. Y., 121

Chan, Peggy, 710
Chan, Y. E., 521, 522, 523
Chapman, T., 475
Chatterjee, A., 221
Chaudhury, A., 263
Chen, A., 230
Chen, C. H., 488
Chen, E. J., 259
Chen, I. J., 318
Chen, Y., 374
Chen, Y. T., 258
Cherry, S. M., 489
Choi, S. Y., 5, 91, 139, 165, 584
Chong, K. I., 492
Chopoorian, J. A., 410
Chow, W. S., 94, 297
Choy, J., 494
Church, R. L., 436
Cilli, C., 637
Clemons, E. K., 578, 580
Clermont., P., 562
Codd, E. F., 427
Coffee, P., 614
Cohen, A., 188, 194
Cohen, H. D., 492
Cole, B., 415
Cole, C. L., 693, 712
Coleman, T., 712
Collins, H., 383
Collins, L., 523
Collis, D., 516
Cone, E., 75
Cone, J. W., 123
Conley, William L., 50
Conrad, D., 216
Cooper, T., 575
Copeland, D. G., 517
Corbett, C. J., 615
Corbett, M. F., 576
Costa, D., 169
Cothrel, J., 390
Coupey, P., 355
Coursaris, C., 192, 214
Craig, G., 596
Creese, G., 412, 414
Croxton, K. L., 169
Cuban, Mark, 22–23
Curry, J., 538

D

Daisey, M., 149
Dale, R., 484
Dalgleish, J., 440
Dalton, G., 694
Damle, P., 647
Damsgaard, L., 339
Darby, C. A. R., 644
Dash, J., 377
Date, C. J., 414
Datz, T., 452
Davamanirajan, P., 562
Davenport, T. H., 373, 374, 392, 395
David, J. S., 567

Davidson, D., 577
Davies, C., 698
Davies, N., 232, 233
Davis, 276, 279, 281
Davis, B., 14
Davis, J. T., 487
Davis, M., 389
Davison, R., 114, 116
Day, M., 259
De Hoog, R., 561
De Vreede, G., 114, 116
Deans, P. C., 187
Dedrick, J., 548
Degnan, C., 273
Dehning, B., 517, 518
Deitel, H. M., 147
Dekker, R., 561
Delahoussaye, M., 123, 133
Delaney, K. J., 690
Delcambre, L., 417
Dell, Michael, 506, 507
DeLong, D., 375, 376, 473
DeLora, J., 438
Demarco, T., 518
DePalma, D., 564
DeSanctis, G., 4, 105, 471
Deshmukh, S. G., 623
DeSouza, A. A., 469
DeSouza, K., 697
Desouza, K. C., 393
Dettmer, R., 485
Devaraj, S., 472, 559, 560, 563, 567, 571, 574, 581
Devedzic, V., 491
DeYoung, J., 101
Dharia, A., 489
Diao, Y., 638
Dick, Philip K., 222
Dickson, G. W., 4
DiNunno, D., 562
D'Inverno, M., 96
Divitini, M., 114
Dixit, A. K., 571
Doane, M., 317
Dogac, A., 191
Doll, M. W., 653
Donofrio, N., 27
Donovan, R. M., 301
Doughty, K., 653, 654, 673
Dreyfus, H., 478
Dreyfus, S., 478
Drucker, Peter, 4, 12, 14, 15, 19, 176
Duan, M., 223
Dubie, D., 75, 338
Duffy, D., 389, 641
Duguid, P., 374, 375, 376
Dunne, D., 196
Duplaga, E. A., 317
Dyer, J. H., 342

E

Earl, M., 19, 640
Eckerson, W., 418, 424

Edgington, C., 224
Edvinsson, L., 369
Edwards, C., 470
Edwards, J. S., 480
Eisenhart, M., 390
Eklund, 207, 211
El Sawy, O., 18, 472, 601, 617, 620, 622, 623
El Sharif, H., 472
Elbirt, A. J., 648
Ellison, C., 213
Elrad, T., 29
Ensher, E. A., 276, 277
Erlikh, L., 70, 71
Estrada, M., 188, 208
Estrin, D., 224, 226
Etzioni, D., 431
Evangelista, A.S., 615
Evans P. B., 4, 15

F

Fadia, A., 647, 661, 664
Fagerholt, K., 470
Fahey, L., 375, 376
Farhoomand, Ali F., 50
Farmer, D., 712, 713
Farrell, D., 556
Fayad, M., 232
Fayyad, U. M., 426
Feeny, D. F., 639, 640
Feldman, E. R., 667
Ferelli, M., 32
Ferguson, J., 538
Ferguson, M., 102
Ferrin, B. G., 567
Feurer, R., 523
Fiedler, D., 699
Fine, C. H., 568
Fingar, P., 617
Finkelstein, C., 523
Fjermestad, J., 318
Fleck, M., 232
Focacci, L., 577
Foley, J., 415, 452
Fong, A. C. M., 427
Ford, D. P., 373, 374
Frank, M., 114
Frank., T., 283
Frenzel, C. W., 44, 509
Frownfelter-Lohrke, C., 672
Fusco, P., 193

G

Galagan, P. A., 133
Galante, D., 356
Gale, S. F., 122
Gallagher, S., 458, 630
Gallaugher, J. M., 145
Galliers, B., 542
Galliers, R., 507
Gallupe, B., 105, 471

Gangopadhyay, A., 437
Garfinkel, S., 664
Garrett, D., 694
Gartner G2, 12
Gates, B., 74
Gates, H. B., 14
Gates, M. S., 563
Gattiker, T. F., 311
Gaulke, M., 569
Gayialis, S. P., 314
Gellersen, H. W., 233
Gengler, C. E., 530, 531
Gentry, J. A., 487
Gerber, J. A., 667
Gerlach, J., 562, 574
Ghosh, A. K., 666
Gibson-Paul, L., 115
Giesen, L., 488
Gilbert, J., 173
Gilden, J., 172
Giles, S., 428, 429, 430
Gillin, P., 577
Gilmore, J., 87
Girishankar, S., 69
Goddard, S., 436
Godin, S., 323
Goodhue, D. L., 311, 318, 319
Gordon, L. A., 644, 647, 652, 661, 662, 671, 674
Gorry, G. A., 464
Goutsos, S., 305
Govindarajan, V., 375
Graham-Hackett, M., 700
Grant, D., 622
Grant, G., 418
Gray, P., 368, 374, 378, 420, 421, 422, 562
Green, S., 573
Greenberg, P., 15, 318, 320
Greenmeier, L., 75
Gregor, S., 483
Greifeld, R., 708
Griffiths, P., 638
Griffiths, P. M., 507
Grimes, B., 354
Grimes, S., 246, 415, 475
Grimshaw, D. J., 435
Grossnickle, J., 441
Grover, R., 370
Gunasekaran, A., 564, 565
Gupta, A. K., 375
Gupta, J., 487

H

Haas, R., 402
Hackathorn, R. D., 471
Hackney, R. A., 522, 523
Hagel, J., 305, 310, 333, 709
Hagen, S., 429
Hager, D., 666
Haley, B. J., 585
Hamblen, M., 85, 222, 234
Hamilton, J. M., 436, 437
Hamm, S., 693

Hammer, M., 18, 617, 618
Hammond, M., 383
Handel, M., 706
Handfield, R. B., 338
Hansen, M., 374, 375, 376, 391
Hansen, M. H., 516
Hanssen-Bauer, J., 374
Hardester, K. P., 436
Hargadon, A. B., 375
Harmon, P., 44, 508
Harmozi, A., 576
Harrington, A., 279
Harris, S., 721
Harrison, T. P., 338
Harsh, A., 201
Hartley, D. E., 123
Hartman, A., 548
Hasan, B., 412
Hashimi, A., 15
Hassanein, H., 192, 214
Hatch, N. W., 342
Haugseth, C., 94
Haykin, S., 488
Hedlund, T., 99
Heijden, M. C., 493
Heizer, L., 362
Helmstetter, G., 11
Henfridsson, O., 395, 396
Hengst, M. D., 623
Henning, T., 213
Higgins, L. F., 529
Hiles, A., 673
Hill, K., 211
Hill, P. A., 390
Hillier, S. F., 465
Hillier, S. M., 465
Hinds, P. J., 110
Hinduja, S., 715, 716
Hirji, K. K., 428, 432
Hirschheim, R., 578, 635
Hislop, D., 393
Hitt, L. M., 558
Hoffman, D. L., 11
Hofmann, D. W., 122
Holsapple, C. W., 368, 369, 373
Holweg, M., 87, 262, 507
Hoogenboom, M., 661
Hoogewelgen, 177
Hooghiemstra, J. S., 501
Horluck, J., 339
Hormozi, A. M., 428, 429, 430
Hornberger, M., 202
Horner-Reich, B., 640, 641
Houck, J., 216
Hovanesian, M. D., 470
Howarth, B., 267
Hricko, M. F., 121
Huang, H., 121
Huang, J., 694
Huber, G., 4, 13, 14, 18, 459, 460, 461, 470
Huff, S. L., 176
Hulland, 516, 518
Hummel, J., 709
Hunter, R., 233
Hunton, J. E., 669, 672

I

Iacocca, Lee, 400
Imhoff, C., 102
Inmon, W. H., 418, 420, 421, 429, 445
Irani, Z., 573
Iserlis, Y., 479
Ishida, T., 230
Islam, N., 232

J

Jackson, P., 483
Jafair, A., 101
Jain, A., 658
Jandt, E. F., 278
Jareb, E., 279, 483
Jarvenpaa, S., 110
Jaworski, B. J., 571, 572, 573
Jefferson, Thomas, 440
Jiang, J. J., 635, 636, 638
Jiang, X., 233
Jimyoul, L., 311
Johnson, D., 692
Johnson, J. D., 571
Jones, J., 211
Jones, K., 379
Jones, W. D., 228
Joshi, K. D., 373
Judge, P., 200
Junnarkar, B., 377

K

Kageyama, Y., 704
Kahn, J., 476
Kalakota, R., 189, 315
Kambil, A., 145
Kanakamedala, K., 317
Kannan, P. K., 268
Kanter, J., 521, 599, 701
Kaparthi, S., 491
Kaplan, P. J., 25
Kaplan, R. S., 571, 572
Kaplan, S., 153, 159, 393
Kapp, K., 123
Karacapilidis, N., 305
Karagiannis, K., 651
Karlenzig, W., 402
Kasparov, Gary, 478–479
Kauffman, R. J., 571
Kawahara, Y., 71
Kayworth, T., 110
Keart, K., 121
Keating, W., 475
Keen., P. G., 471
Kehlenbeck, C., 202
Kellner, M., 200
Kelly, D. A., 655
Kelly, K., 29

Kelton, D. W., 492
Kemp, T., 514
Kendall, J. E., 597, 599
Kendall, K. E., 597, 599
Kenney, B., 715
Kerlow, I. V., 439
Kern, H., 635
Kern, T., 608
Kesner, R. M., 102, 382, 638
Kessler, S. H., 696, 699
Khan, B., 19
Khan, M. R. R., 617, 621
Kharif, O., 230
Khong, K. W., 623
Kimball, R., 420
King, D., 379
King, J., 392, 573
King, R., 707
King, W. R., 538
Kingsman, B. G., 469
Kini, R. B., 71
Kinsella, B., 304
Kirkman, B., 111
Kirkpatrick, D., 507
Kishore, R., 608
Kleiner, A., 694
Knapp, E. M., 391
Kobsa, A., 494
Kogen, Don, 6, 10
Kohari, 461
Kohli, R., 472, 559, 560, 563, 567, 571,
    574, 581, 582
Kolb, D., 437
Kolodzinski, O., 674
Kome, P., 701
Kontzer, T., 211
Koontz, C., 66
Koppius, O. R., 54
Korolishin, J., 259, 280, 282, 353
Korte, G. B., 437
Korzenioski, P., 590
Kotorov, R., 323
Kounadis, T., 101, 103
Kovács, G. L., 314
Koza, J. R., 488
Kraemer, K., 18, 548
Kreijger, T., 608
Kridel, T., 194
Kroll, K. M., 265
Kuckuk, M., 419, 424
Kudyba, S., 562
Kumagai, J., 201, 202, 485
Kumar, A., 96, 116
Kumar, R., 75
Kumar, R. L., 571

L

La Londe, B., 692
Lacity, M., 578
Lam, S. S. Y., 491
Lam, W., 668
Landay, J. A., 233
Landoline, K., 42

Langnau, L., 423
Lau, H. C. W., 427
Laurie, J., 583
Law, A. M., 492
Lawrence, S., 676
Lawson, R., 572
Le Gal, C., 230
Leary, R., 453
LeBlond, R., 617
Lechner, U., 709
Lederer, A. D., 17
Lederer, A. L., 7
Lee, A. S., 617, 623
Lee, G., 597, 601
Lee, J. K., 266
Lee, J. N., 576, 577
Lee, M. K. O., 710
Lee, S. C., 146, 663, 676
Lee, W. Y., 414
Lee, Y., 171
Lee, Y. M., 259
Legrenzi, C., 559
Leidner, D., 110, 369, 370, 373, 402,
    517, 536, 640
Leonard, D., 376
Levin, C., 671
Levine, R., 624
Levine, Scott, 644
Levinson, M., 408, 550
Lewin, J., 108
Lewis, B. C., 569
Li, H., 558
Li, S., 490
Li, T., 432
Li, X., 571
Li, Y. N., 7, 17
Liao, Z., 254
Liautaud, B., 383, 443
Liaw, S., 121
Lieberman, H., 96
Liebowitz, J., 374
Liebowitz, S., 4
Liegle, J. O., 123
Ligus, R. G., 317
Lin, W. T., 559
Linoff, G. S., 431
Linthicum, D., 352
Lipset, V., 202, 204
Lipton, B., 513
Lister, T., 518
Liu, S., 444
Lockemann, P. C., 414
Logan, D., 698
Lohr, S., 75
Loshin, D., 413, 698
Loundy, D. L., 647
Love, P. E. D., 573
Loveman, Gary, 407, 408
Lucas, H. C., 560
Lucas, M. E., 312
Luck, M., 96
Ludorf, C., 210
Luftman, J. N., 634, 638, 639, 640,
    668
Luhn, R., 665
Luo, W., 153

M

Maamar, Z., 97
MacDonald, H., 713
MacDonald, M., 697
MacDonald, N., 108
MacIntosh, R., 617, 623
MacSweeney, G., 392
Madhaven, R., 370
Mahoney, J. T., 516
Mankins, M., 232
Mann, C. C., 712, 713
Manninen, M., 115
Manthou, V., 305
Marcolin, B. L., 580
Margulius, D., 75
Markus, L. M., 559
Markus, M. L., 410
Marotta, D. L., 671, 685
Marshall, P., 566, 568
Martin, C. F., 70
Martin, E. W., 611
Martin, J., 523
Martin, J. A., 240
Massey, A. P., 394
Mata, P. J., 518
Mathieson, R., 222
Maxemchuk, N. F., 272
Maynard, M., 402
Mayor, M., 216
McAdam, J. P., 576
McBride, S., 689, 690
McCartney, J., 707
McCleanahen, J., 14
McClenahen, J. S., 273
McConnell, M., 661
McCoy, Jack, 240
McCullough, D. C., 283
McDonald, M., 386
McGarvey, J., 27
McGuire, P. A., 462
McKay, J., 566, 568
McKeen, J. D., 375, 390
McKenney, J. L., 517
McKinley, E., 280, 470, 664
McLaughlin, L., 98
McLellan, L., 580
McNealy, Scott, 609
McNichol, T., 713
Mehandijev, N., 606
Meister, D., 374
Melymuka, K., 393, 394, 704
Mennecke, B. E., 187, 189, 196
Menon, S., 154
Mentzer, J. T., 297
Merator, 487
Meredith, J. R., 255
Mesenbourg, T., 581
Meso, P. N., 123
Metcalfe, Robert, 29
Metivier, P., 11
Mevedoth, R., 6
Miastkowski, S., 633, 650
Middleton, M., 415
Mintz, S., 693
Mintzberg, H., 459

Moad, J., 429
Moerkotte, G., 414
Mohanty, R. P., 623
Mol, M. J., 54
Moneymaker, Chris, 10
Montgomery, C., 516
Mooney, S. F., 369
Moore, Gordon, 27, 555
Moore, J. F., 228
Mora, M., 694
Morel, G., 259
Morgan, J. P., 672
Moss, L. T., 423
Moss-Kantor, R., 17
Motiwalla, L., 15
Motro, A., 414
Mukhopadhyay, T., 557
Murphy, J. V., 115
Murphy, K. E., 317
Murrays, J. P., 635, 636
Murtaza, M. B., 355
Muylle, S., 7, 17

N

Najdawi, M., 153
Nance, B., 662
Nasirin, S., 436
Nazarov, A. R., 452
Neel, D., 604
Nelson, D., 305
Nelson, K. M., 640, 641
Nelson, M., 213
Nemati, H. R., 428
Nemnich, M. B., 278
Neumann, S., 44, 509
Nevins, M. D., 694
Newcomer, E., 250
Newell, A., 676
Newell, F., 323
Ng, Pauline S. P., 50
Nguyen, H. T., 489
Nichols, E. L., Jr., 338
Nie, N. H., 694, 699, 710, 711
Nolan, R. L., 524, 525
Nonaka, I., 370, 373, 374, 379
Norton, 571, 572
Norvig, P., 476
Novak, T. P., 11
Null, C., 197

O

O'Connor, B. N., 606
O'Dell, C., 369, 392
O'Donnell, A., 266
O'Donovan, B., 52
Oettinger, A., 697
Oguz, M. T., 423
O'Herron, J., 371
Ojala, M., 103, 697, 698
Olazabal, N. G., 556
O'Leary, Dennis, 69

Oliver, D., 317
O'Looney, J. A., 436
Olson, J. E., 412
O'Reilly, J. J., 438
Orwall, B., 690
Ovans, A., 159
Overby, S., 608

P

Paganelli, P., 314
Palaniswamy, R., 283
Palvia, S., 578
Pandian, J. R., 516
Panko, R. R., 633, 651, 652, 657, 661, 662, 663, 664, 665
Pantry, S., 638
Papp, R., 520
Park, Y. T., 421
Parks, L., 259
Paton, D., 562
Peffers, K., 530, 531, 569
Penrose, E. T., 516
Penzias, Arno, 563
Peppard, J., 507, 520, 521, 522, 523, 526, 601
Peppers, D., 318
Peray, K., 489
Perkins-Munn, T. S., 258
Perry, R., 198, 617
Pescovitz, D., 675
Peters, K. M., 452
Phan, D. D., 540
Piazza, P., 665
Piccoli, G., 121
Pickering, C., 521
Pil, F. K., 87, 262, 507
Pindyck, R.S., 571
Pine, B. J., 87
Pinto, J., 227
Piskurich, G. M., 123
Pitkow, J., 224
Pitt, L. F., 14
Pittaras, A., 274
Plan, S. L., 402
Plank. R. E., 567
Plant, R., 559
Plant, T., 542
Poirier, C. C., 110, 113, 114, 297
Polanyi, M., 369, 370
Pollock, J., 35
Pomerol, J. C., 476
Pontz, C., 483
Pooley, J., 654
Popovich, K., 318
Popp, R., 78, 676, 678
Porat, M. U., 696
Poropudas, T., 204
Porter, Michael E., 44–46, 508, 509, 510, 513, 514, 515
Potter, R. E., 639
Powell, A., 112, 471
Power, D. J., 466, 483, 491
Prince, M., 24

Princi, M., 113
Pringle, Hal, 607
Pritsker, A. A. B., 438
Procaccino, J. D., 167
Prusak, L., 373

Q

Qiang, X., 714
Qing, H. U., 559
Quinn, J. B., 577

R

Rae-Dupree, J., 290
Ragowsky, A., 311
Ragsdale, J., 636
Ragusa, J. M., 115
Rahali, B., 283
Raina, K., 201
Raisinghani, M., 352
Rajaram, K., 615
Rajkovic, V., 279, 483
Raskin, A., 220, 232, 260, 582
Raskin, O., 441
Rasmus, D. W., 387
Ravichandran, T., 605
Ray, K., 276, 278
Ray, N., 412
Rayport, J., 571, 572, 573
Read, C., 562, 563
Reda, S., 138, 139, 165, 263, 281, 304, 514, 676
Redman, T. C., 412
Reed, C., 269, 276
Reeder, J., 123
Regan, E. A., 606
Reichheld, F., 559
Reiter, E., 484
Render, B., 362
Renkema, T. J., 566
Rhey, E., 74
Richardson, R., 633, 644, 647, 648, 666
Richardson, S., 623
Rietz, T. A., 464
Ripley, A., 690
Rivlin, G., 476
Robb, D., 256, 388, 389
Roberts, B., 639
Roberts-Witt, S. L., 392
Robin, M., 370
Robinson, C., 654
Robinson, D. G., 123
Robinson, M., 189, 315
Robinson, S. R., 652, 668, 673, 674, 676
Rockart, J. F., 473
Rockart, J. P., 639
Rogers, M., 318
Rogers, S., 614
Rollins, Kevin, 507

Romano, N. C., 318
Rombel, A., 693
Romm, C., 317
Roode, D., 52
Rosenbaum, D., 169
Rosenbloom, P. S., 12
Rosencrance, L., 232
Ross, J. W., 560, 639, 640
Ross, M., 420
Roth, M. A., 443
Rothstein, P. J., 668
Ruber, P., 380, 383
Rubin, H. A., 573
Rubin, R., 579
Rudy, J., 708, 712
Ruggles, R., 374, 376, 381
Rundensteiner, E. A., 418, 419, 420
Ruohonen, M., 529
Rupp, W. T., 18, 204
Russell, C., 716
Russell, S. J., 476
Ryan, S. D., 563
Ryan, T., 230

S

Saarinen, T., 569
Sachdeva, S., 607
Sadeh, N., 30, 187, 189, 192, 196, 202, 203, 204, 207, 214, 225, 262
Salladurai, R., 616, 617
Salodof-MacNeil, J., 272
Sambamurthy, V., 634, 635, 639
Samela, H., 542
Sampson, Bob, 466
Sandhu, R., 648
Sandoe, K., 310
Sappenfield, D., 116
Sarkar, D., 221
Sarker, S., 617, 623
Sarkis, J., 316, 317, 612
Sarnoff, D., 583
Sarshar, A., 189
Saunders, Michael, 23–24
Sawhney, M., 141, 159, 559, 562, 563
Sayana, S. A., 672
Scalet, S. D., 655
Scanlon, J., 199, 211
Schecterle, B., 357
Schefter, P., 559
Schendel, D., 516
Schlosser, J., 424
Schoemaker, P. J. H., 516
Schroeder, M., 692
Schultze, U., 369
Schwartz, J., 69
Schwartz, K. D., 705
Schwartz, Peter, 222
Scott, J. E., 624
Scott-Morton, M. S., 464
Seddon, P., 559, 637
Seidman, T., 264
Seitz, N. E., 565
Sen, A., 418

Sensiper, S., 376
Seybold, P. B., 527
Shadbolt, J., 487
Shafer, S. M., 255
Shah, J. R., 355
Shand, D., 386
Shao, B. M., 559
Sharke, P., 228
Sharp, D., 106, 377
Sheikh, K., 309
Shein, E., 367
Shelter, K. M., 167
Shenk, D., 712
Sheridan, R. M., 675
Shi, N., 189
Shiang, D., 564
Shields, C., 663, 676
Shim, J. P., 472
Shin, N., 121
Shipley, Peter, 200
Shur, D. H., 272
Siau, K., 311
Siddiqui, A., 441
Siekmann, S., 122
Sifonis, J., 548
Sikder, I., 437
Silver, C. A., 382, 393
Simic, G., 491
Simon, H., 462, 464
Simon, S. J., 317
Simpson, R. L., 12
Singh, S. K., 473
Sipior, J. C., 15
Skyrme, D. J., 391
Slewe, T., 661
Smailagic, A., 208
Smith, A. D., 18, 204
Smith, C. F., 485
Smith, Fred, 49
Smith, H., 617
Smith, H. A., 375, 390
Smith, K., 24, 487
Smith, R., 664
Snow, C. C., 374
Snyder, W. M., 375, 376
Sõderholm, A., 395, 396
Sodhi, M., 299
Soete, L., 706
Soh, C., 559
Solow, R., 556
Somers, T. M., 311
Sorensen, D., 494
Spanbauer, S., 665
Spector, L., 669
Spielberg, Steven, 222
Spil, T. A. M., 542
Spivey-Overby, 230
Stackpole, B., 102
Stafford, A., 197
Stanford, V., 33, 206, 230, 232
Stauffer, D., 527
Stauffer, T., 108
Stead, B. A., 173
Steede-Terry, K., 219, 437
Steinberg, D., 382, 393
Sterlicchi, J., 26

Sterne, J., 581
Stevens, C. P., 317
Steyaert, J. C., 563
Stoll, R., 339
Stone, B., 108, 703, 706
Stone, D. L., 671, 685
Stonebraker, J. S., 462
Storck, J., 390
Strader, T. J., 187, 189, 196
Strassman, P., 667
Strassmann, P. A., 558
Stratopoulos, T., 517, 518
Straub, D. W., 581
Strauss, J., 154, 262, 441
Strickland, L. S., 715, 716
Strong, D. M., 412, 414
Stumpf, S. A., 694
Subrahmanyam, A., 250, 251
Sullivan, A., 648
Sullivan, B., 665
Sullivan, D., 98, 99, 101, 132
Sullivan, M., 316
Sundarraj, R. P., 316, 317, 612
Sung, N. H., 266
Sutcliffe, A., 606
Swaminatha, T. M., 666
Swamy, R., 572
Swanton, B., 314
Swartz, N., 714, 715
Sweeney, T., 265
Sweiger, M., 445
Sykes, R., 637, 640
Szekely, B., 114

T

Tabor, S. W., 412
Taft, K. D., 489
Takeuchi, H., 370, 379
Talleur, T., 653, 654
Tan, P. N., 96
Tan, X., 318
Tang, C., 437
Tapscott, D., 4, 12
Tatsiopoulos, I. P., 314
Tedeschi, B., 100
Teece, D. J., 370
Tehrani, S., 378
Teo, T. S. H., 538
Terry, K., 437
Thibodeau, P., 452
Thomas, S. L., 276, 278
Thompson, B., 318
Thompson, Jack, 400
Tian, Y., 311
Tjan, A. K., 539, 540, 581
Totty, P., 266
Troppito, D., 562
Tucci, C. L., 11
Turban, E., 11, 19, 65, 110, 139, 153, 164, 165, 169, 338, 412, 461, 466, 492, 542, 564, 581, 633
Turing, Alan, 477
Turner, A., 191

Turocy, P., 696, 697
Tynan, D., 120

U

Udell, J., 120
Urban, 318
Urdan, T., 121
Ursery, S., 437
Useem, J., 175, 542

V

Vakharia, J., 297
Vallés, J., 114
Van, J., 29, 675
Van Den Heuvel, W. J., 97
Van der Aalst, W. M. P., 116
Van der Spek, R., 374, 375
Van Dyk, Richard, 383
Van Grembergen, W. V., 572
Van Heck, E., 145
Varney, S. E., 266
Varon, E., 554
Varshney, U., 189
Vaughan, J., 419
Vedder, R. G., 482
Venkatraman, N., 510
Verton, E., 648
Vessey, I., 624
Vetter, R., 189
Veytsel, A., 412, 414
Vijayakumar, S., 258, 276
Vijayan, J., 567
Vinas, T., 117
Violino, B., 566
Vitale, M. R., 11, 66
Vitaliano, D., 562
Volonino, L., 652, 668, 673, 674, 676
Von Krogh, G., 375
Von Pierer, Heinrich, 3
Von-Roessing, R., 672
Vreede, G. D., 623
Vulkan, N., 582

W

Wade, M., 516, 518
Wagenaar, 177
Wainewright, P., 75
Wales, E., 26
Walker, E. A., 489
Walsh, J. J., 599
Walsh, K. R., 577
Walsh, N. P., 643
Walton, B., 113
Wang, A. L., 564
Wang, R. Y., 412
Ward, J., 507, 520, 521, 522, 523, 526, 601
Warren, Richard, 589
Watson, H., 562, 585
Watson, H. J., 420, 421, 422
Weaver, P., 121
Weggen, C., 121
Weidlich, T., 108
Weill, P., 11, 66, 517, 560, 570
Weise, E., 232
Weiser, M., 222, 230, 232
Wells, J. T., 671
Wenger, E. C., 375, 376
Wernerfelt, B., 516
Westley, F., 459
Wetherbe, J. C., 520
Wheatley, M., 575
Whinston, A. B., 5, 91, 584
Whipple, L. C., 66
White, D., 638
White, G. B., 651
Whiting, R., 418
Whitman, 645
Whitten, J., 599
Wiederkehr, B., 654
Wilkinson, S., 577
Willcocks, L. P., 637, 640
Williams, R. L., 390
Willis, D., 124
Wind, Y., 262, 263
Winter, R., 443
Wiseman, C., 44, 509
Witte, C. L., 347
Woda, A., 672

Wong, N. A., 672
Wong, W. Y., 163
Wooldridge, M., 96
Worthen, B., 295, 305
Worthen, R., 415
Wreden, N., 4
Wurman, R. S., 698, 701
Wurster, T. S., 4, 15

X

Xia, W., 597, 601

Y

Yakhou, M., 283
Yao, Y. H., 415
Ye, H., 489
Yen, J., 676
Yiman-Seid, D., 494
Young, A., 577
Young, S. A., 653, 665
Yusuf, Y., 311, 317

Z

Zadeh, L., 488
Zakaria, Z., 272
Zaremba, M. B., 259
Zdanawicz, J. S., 430
Zemke, R., 123, 133
Zenkin, D., 662
Zetter, K., 633, 650
Zetu, D., 439
Zhao, Y., 221
Zhu, K., 18
Zimmerman, J., 604
Zipkin, P., 87, 262
Zviran, M., 580

Subject Index

A

Accenture Consulting, 317, 375, 381, 386
Access controls, 657–658
Accounting/finance functions, 269–276, 583
ACCPAC International, 273
Acquiring IT applications:
  available options, 602–608
  developing in-house, 605–606
  identifying projects, 601
  implementation issues, 611–614
  insourcing, 605–606
  integration issues, 614–615
  justifying projects, 601
  leases, 603–605, 609
  off-the-shelf purchases, 602
  outsourcing, 608–611
  overview, 597
  planning projects, 601–602
  process summary, 597–599
  redesigning processes, 615–623
  vendor selection, 611–613
Activity-based costing, 574
Acxion Corp., 644
Adaptec, 307
Ad-hoc queries, 426
Administrative controls, 659
Advertising, online:
  classified ads, 163–164
  location-based, 220
  overview, 153, 262–263
  and permission marketing, 155–156
  targeting mobile users, 205–207
  via banners, 154
  via electronic catalogs and brochures, 154–155
  via e-mail, 154
  via pop-up and pop-under ads, 154
  Web site events and promotions, 156–157
Affiliate marketing business model, 141
Affiliate marketing programs, 11
Affinity portals, 100, G–1
Agents. See Intelligent agents
Aggregators, 11
AI. See Artificial intelligence (AI)
Aimster, 716
AirIQ, 209
Airports:
  delayed openings, 646
  Denver International Airport, 646
  Hong Kong airport, 646
  Minneapolis-St. Paul International Airport, 199
  Wi-Fi access, 199
Alaska Airlines, 216
Alien Technology, 229
Allbusiness.com, 11
Alliances, business, 19, 511
Alliance strategy, 511, G–1
Alloy.com, 148, 176

Allstate, 354
Altavista, 96
Amazon.com, 11, 140, 145, 148, 149, 151, 300, 511, 512, 513–514
American Airlines, 54, 391–392, 644
American Express, 416, 485
American Library Association, 714
American Marconi Company, 583
America Online (AOL), 100, 101, 153, 163, 167, 169, 207
Ameritrade, 150
Analytical processing, 417, G–1
Ansett Australia, 607
Anticybersquatting Consumer Protection Act, 173
AOL (America Online), 100, 101, 153, 163, 167, 169, 207
Applets, Java, 649
Application controls, 656, 660, G–1
Application programs:
  buying off-the-shelf, 602
  defined, 51
  development options, 605–611
  glossary definition, G–1
  insourcing development, 605–606
  leasing, 603–605, 609
  outsourcing development, 608
  overview, 51
  suites, 119–120
Application service providers (ASPs):
  defined, 608
  as form of outsourcing, 577, 608–609
  glossary definition, G–1
  IBM as, 75
  and knowledge management, 386
  overview, 608–609
  and utility computing, 577
Applications portfolios, 520, 539–541, G–1
Architecture. See Client/server architecture; Information architecture
Arthur Andersen, 711
Artificial intelligence (AI):
  benefits, 477
  commercial technologies, 479
  vs. conventional computing, 478–479
  glossary definition, G–1
  integrating with knowledge management, 387
  and intelligent behavior, 476–477
  vs. natural intelligence, 477, 478
  overview, 476–477
  role in knowledge management, 477
Artificial neural networks (ANNs):
  applications, 486–488
  benefits, 486–488
  defined, 486
  glossary definition, G–1
  overview, 378, 486
Asda, 114
Asite Network, 343

Ask Jeeves, 97
ASPs. See Application service providers (ASPs)
Asynchronous communication, 105, G–1
@Home project, SETI, 76
Atkins Carlyle Corporation, 349
ATMs (automated teller machines), 168
Attachable keyboards, 193
Attack tracebacks, 662–663, G–1
Au Bon Pain Company, 441
Auctions:
  defined, 145
  eBay example, 147
  forward, 145–146
  fraud problem, 172
  glossary definition, G–1
  overview, 145
  reverse, 11, 146
Audio Home Recording Act, 715
Audits, 275, 671–673, 675, G–1
Australia:
  Ansett Australia, 607
  CAMS online, 162
  fishing community, 721–722
  Qantas Airlines, 19, 635
Authentication, 664
Authorization, 664
Auto-by-Tel, 512
Autodesk, 90
Auto Identification Centers (Auto-IDs), 229, G–1
Automated teller machines (ATMs), 168
Automatic crash notification (ACN), 221, G–1
Automatic translators, 99
Automobiles, smart, 227–228
Automotive Network Exchange (ANX), 351
Autonomy KM software, 384
AvantGo, 206

B

Babel Fish Translation, 99
Back doors, 649
Back-office operations, integrating with front-office operations, 283–284
Backups, 642, 669–670
Balanced scorecard method, 571–572, G–1
BAM. See Business activity monitoring (BAM) systems
Banamex, 202
Banking. See also Cyberbanking
  Banamex, 202
  Bank of America, 442
  Bank One, 167
  Canadian Imperial Bank of Commerce, 578
  Centrala Studie Stodsnamnden, 600–602
  Chase Manhattan Bank, 69

Banking (*cont.*)
    Citibank, 202
    Commerce Bank, 385
    Handelsbanken of Sweden, 24–25
    HDFC Bank of India, 204
    international, 149–150
    Merita Bank, 202
    mobile, 202–203
    multiple-currency, 149–150, 272
    National City Corporation, 549–550
    Royal Bank of Scotland, 202
    SEB Private Bank, 491
    virtual, 149–150
    Wells Fargo Bank, 470
    Zions Bancorporation, 684–685
Bank of America, 442
Bank One, 167
Banners, G–1
Barcodes, 228–229
Barnes & Noble, 509, 514
Bartering, online, 141, 146
Bartering online, 141, 146
BASF, 160
Batch processing, 250, G–1
Behavior-oriented chargeback, 575–576, G–1
Bell Canada, 209
BellSouth, 416
Benchmarks:
    assessing infrastructure investments, 569–570
    best-practice, 570
    defined, 569
    glossary definition, G–1
    metric, 569–570
Benefits, 281–282. *See also* Cost-benefit analysis; Intangible benefits
Ben & Jerry's, 424
Best Buy, 227
Best-practice benchmarks, 570, G–1
Best Software, 271, 272, 284
Bidding, online. *See* Auctions
"Big Brother" concerns, 170, 712
BikeWorld, 340
Bills, paying online, 168, 273
Biometric controls, 657–658, 675, 677, G–1
Bizworks, 259
Blackberry hand-helds, 194
Blackboard, Inc., 122
Black & Decker, 171
Blogging (Weblogging), 107–108, G–1
Blogs, 107, G–1
Blue Cross and Blue Shield, 670
Bluetooth, 190, 195, G–1
Boeing Company, 115, 416, 615
Borders Books & Music, 199
Bosch, 2
BPM. *See* Business performance management (BPM); Business process management (BPM)
BPR. *See* Business process reengineering (BPR)
Brick-and-mortar organizations, 140, G–1. *See also* Click-and-mortar organizations

Bristol-Myers Squibb, 301
Britannica, 511
British Airways, 439
British Petroleum, 160
BSP. *See* Business systems planning (BSP) model
Buckman Labs, 402–403
Budgeting, 270–271, 275
Build-to-order, 18, 87
Bullwhip effect, 300–301, G–1
Burger King, 87
Burlington Coat Factory, 441
Business activity monitoring (BAM) systems, 475–476, G–1
Business alliances, 19, 511
Business architecture, 66, G–1
Business cases, 564, G–1
Business continuity plans, 667–669, G–1
Business drivers. *See* Business pressures
Business intelligence, 55, 56, 422–425, G–1
Business models:
    defined, 10
    for e-commerce, 141
    glossary definition, G–1
    new economy examples, 11
Business performance management (BPM), 276, 473–475, G–1
Business pressures:
    defined, 12
    glossary definition, G–2
    organizational responses, 17–20
    types, 13–17
Business processes:
    changes brought by IT, 617, 618
    defined, 615
    glossary definition, G–2
    need for information integration, 618–620
    restructuring, 621–623
Business process management (BPM), 617, G–2
Business process reengineering (BPR):
    defined, 18, 617
    factors driving, 615–616
    failures, 622–623
    glossary definition, G–2
    legacy systems, 535–536
    methodologies, 617
    need for information integration, 618–620
    overview, 621–623
    redesigning processes, 615–623
    role of IT in, 617–620
    successes, 623
Business reengineering. *See* Business process reengineering (BPR)
Business systems planning (BSP) model, 523–524, G–2
Business-to-business e-commerce (B2B):
    buy-side model, 158
    defined, 140
    directory services, 344
    exchange model, 11, 151–161, 341–342, 343
    glossary definition, G–2
    mobile applications, 214

    as model, 140
    role of hubs, 342, 343
    sell-side model, 157–158
Business-to-business-to-consumers e-commerce (B2B2C), 140
Business-to-consumers e-commerce (B2C):
    defined, 140
    electronic retailing, 146–148
    glossary definition, G–2
    as model, 140
Business-to-its-employees e-commerce (B2E), 140, 161, G–2
Buyerzone.com, 11
Buy-side marketplace, 158, G–2
Buzzsaw, 90–91

C

Cabir virus, 201
CAD (computer-aided design), 55
Cadence Design Systems, 590
California Department of Motor Vehicles, 252
California Private Transportation Company, 217
Call centers, 106, 322
CAM (computer-aided manufacturing), 55
Campusfood.com, 23–24
Canadian Imperial Bank of Commerce, 578
Canadian Tire, 152
Can-Spam Act, 699
Capital budgeting, 270–271
Cardiff Software, 416
Carnegie Mellon University, 225, 653
Carnival Line, 252
Cars, smart, 227–228
Cash, electronic, 166
Catalogs, electronic, 143, 145, 154–155
Caterpillar Inc., 115
CBIS. *See* Computer-based information systems (CBIS)
C-commerce. *See* Collaborative commerce (c-commerce)
CDMA. *See* Code Division Multiple Access (CDMA)
CDNow.com, 11, 148, 514
Cellbucks, 203
Cell phones:
    convergence with PDAs, 194–195
    overview, 193
    paying bills from, 204
    security issues, 200–201
Cellular phones. *See* Cell phones
Censorship, 713–715
Centra EMeeting, 118
Centrala Studie Stodsnamnden (CSN), 600–602
Centralized computing, 533–534, G–2
Centrino chip, 188
Champion Chip, 223
Channel conflicts, 152, G–2
Channel systems, 260–261, G–2
Chargeback, 575–576, G–2
Chargeout. *See* Chargeback

Charles Schwab, 150, 322, 470, 669
Chase Manhattan Bank, 69
Chat rooms:
  as customer service tool, 106
  defined, 106
  glossary definition, G–2
  overview, 106–107
  software, 106
Checks. *See* Electronic checks (e-checks)
ChemConnect.com, 11, 159, 160
Chemical Bank, 69
ChevronTexaco, 160, 294–295, 300, 371
Chicago Tribune, 442
Chief information officers (CIOs), 519,
    634–635, 639–641, G–2
Chief knowledge officers (CKOs), 389, G–2
Children's Internet Protection Act, 714
ChoicePoint, 720–721
Christian Dior, 173
Chrysler. *See* DaimlerChrysler
Cignos, Inc., 476
CIM. *See* Computer-integrated
    manufacturing (CIM)
Cingular, 207, 371
CIOs. *See* Chief information officers
    (CIOs)
Cisco Systems, 132–133, 227, 273, 382,
    547–548
Citibank, 202, 512, 644
Citicorp, 175
Cities, digital, 230–232
Classified ads, 163–164
Click-and-mortar organizations:
  defined, 140
  glossary definition, G–2
  resolving conflicts, 152
Clickstream data, 412, G–2
Clickstream data warehouses, 444–445,
    G–2
Clients, 68, G–2
Client/server architecture:
  defined, 68
  Europcar example, 284
  glossary definition, G–2
  overview, 68
Cmmunispace, 386
Coca-Cola, 336
Code Division Multiple Access (CDMA),
    197, G–2
Cognos, 421, 425, 443
Colgate-Palmolive, 268, 315
Collaboration:
  benefits, 109, 110
  defined, 108
  dysfunctions and barriers, 109, 115–116
  glossary definition, G–2
  implementation issues, 120
  as Internet application category, 93
  and knowledge management, 377
  in manufacturing, 357
  nature of group work, 108–110
  overview, 108
  real-time tools, 118–119
  Sabre, Inc. example, 111
  Safeway example, 90–91
  and supply chain, 304–305

tools and methodologies, 116–120
  traditional *vs.* networked, 112–114
  virtual, 110–116
Collaborative commerce (c-commerce),
    110–116, 140, 355–357, G–2
Comark Corp., 311
Commerce Bank, 385
Commercial (public) portals, 100, G–2
Communication. *See also* Wireless
    communications
  and information technology, 104–106
  as Internet application category, 93
  and knowledge management, 376–377
  media characteristics, 104
  modes, 104
  overview, 104
  synchronous *vs.* asynchronous
    transmission, 105
  time/place framework, 105–106
Communications controls, 659
Communities, electronic. *See* Virtual
    communities
Communities of practice (COPs), 375,
    390, G–2
Competitive advantage:
  glossary definition, G–2
  old *vs.* new model, 263
  strategies for, 509
Competitive forces model:
  defined, 44, 508
  examples of use, 509–513
  glossary definition, G–2
  Internet influences, 508–509, 510
  overview, 44, 508
  response strategies, 509–513
CompuCom Systems, 349
Computer Abuse Amendment Act, 652
Computer Associates, 312, 421
Computer-based information systems
    (CBIS), 20–21, G–2. *See also*
    Information systems (IS)
Computer crimes:
  IS vulnerability, 641–651
  new millenium example, 633–634
  overview, 647–648
Computer Emergency Response Team
    (CERT), 653
Computer Fraud and Abuse Act, 652, 653
Computer-integrated manufacturing
    (CIM), 259, G–2
Computers. *See* Information technology
    (IT)
Computer Sciences Corp., 576
Computer Security Act, 652
Computer Security Enhancement Act, 652
Computer Security Institute, 653
Computer viruses. *See* Viruses
Comshare Corporation, 466
Consumers. *See also* Customers
  in e-commerce models, 140, 163–164
  mobile applications, 214–217
  tracking Internet activity, 170–171
Consumer-to-business (C2B)
    e-commerce, 140, G–2
Consumer-to-consumer (C2C)
    e-commerce, 140, 163–164, G–2

Context awareness, 223, 225–226, G–2
Contextual computing, 223–224, G–2
Continuous improvement, 18
Contracts, 613
Controls, information system, 656–660
Convectis, 379
Cookies, 171, G–2
Cookson Group, 595
Cooperative processing, 67, G–2
Copernic Agent Basic, 99
COPs. *See* Communities of practice
    (COPs)
Copyright, 124–125, 173, 715–716
Corporate portals:
  applications, 101–102, 103
  for customers, 102
  defined, 32, 72, 101
  for employees, 102
  Ford example, 351
  glossary definition, G–2
  illustrated, 103
  industrywide, 103–104
  integrating, 103
  Kaiser Permanente example, 98
  overview, 72, 101
  for supervisors, 102
  for suppliers, 102
  types, 102
Cost-benefit analysis, 561, 673–674, G–3
Costco, 265
Cost leadership strategy, 509–510, G–3
Cost recovery. *See* Chargeback
Counterfeit Access Device and Computer
    Crime Control Act, 652
Counterterrorism, 676, 677–678
Coupons, online, 157
Crackers, 647, G–3
Cray Research, 669
Credit cards. *See also* Smart cards
  electronic, 165–166
  virtual, 169
Crime, computer:
  IS vulnerability, 641–651
  new millenium example, 633–634
Critical response activities, 12, G–3
Critical success factors (CSFs), 524–527,
    G–3
CRM. *See* Customer relationship
    management (CRM)
Cross-border data transfer, 337, G–3
CSFs. *See* Critical success factors (CSFs)
Culture, 337
Currency. *See* Multiple-currency
    banking
Customer relationship management
    (CRM):
  defined, 318
  failures, 322–323
  glossary definition, G–3
  integrating knowledge management
    systems, 387
  overview, 318
  Piper Aircraft example, 356
  role of information technology, 319–322
  role of mobile computing, 211–212
  types of applications, 319–320

Customers. *See also* Consumers
 behavior on Internet, 262
 powerful, 14–15
 preference analysis, 261–262
 profiling, 261–262
 tracking Internet activity, 170–171
 viewed as royalty, 261–263
Customer service. *See also* Customer
  relationship management (CRM)
 e-commerce examples, 151–152
 Web-based, 320–321
Customer service life cycle, 151–152
Customization. *See* Mass customization
Customized catalogs, 145, 154–155
CVS Corp., 199, 217
Cyberbanking, 149–150, G–3
Cybercrimes, 648. *See also* Computer
  crimes
Cybermalls, 148
Cybersquatters, 173, G–3
Cyberterrorism, 648, G–3
Cyberwar, 648, G–3
Cybex International, 316
Cycle time reduction, G–3

D

DaimlerChrysler, 351, 400–402, 557
Dairy Queen, 280
Daiwa Securities, 274
Dallas Mavericks, 22–23
Danskin, 433
Dartmouth College, 40–41
Dartmouth-Hitchcock Medical Center
  (DHMC), 245–246
Dashboards, 475–476
Data. *See also* Data items
 collection methods, 412
 glossary definition, G–3
 vs. information, 52
 managing, 409–417
 problems and difficulties, 409, 413
 solutions to problems, 409–410, 413
 transborder flow, 337
Databases:
 connecting to, 614
 defined, 21
 glossary definition, G–3
 integrating knowledge management
   systems, 379–380, 387
 as knowledge repositories, 381–382, 387
 marketing example, 262
 multidimensional, 422
Data centers. *See* Information centers
Data conferencing, 117–118, G–3
DataDistilleries, 441
Data encryption. *See* Encryption
Data integrity, 414, G–3
Data items, 52, G–3
Data life cycle, 410–411
Data management, 409–417
Data marts, 421–422, G–3. *See also* Data
  warehouses
Data mining:
 applications, 429–430

defined, 97, 428
failure, 431–432
glossary definition, G–3
in knowledge discovery in databases,
  379–380
overview, 428
tools and techniques, 428–429
Wal-Mart example, 442
Web-based, 431
Data quality (DQ), 412–414, G–3
Data security controls, 658–659
Data sources, 411–412
Data tampering, 649, G–3
Data visualization, 432–433, G–3
Dataware, 386
Data Warehouse Institute, 421
Data warehouses:
 architecture, 420
 benefits, 419–420
 characteristics, 419
 cost, 420
 vs. data marts, 421–422
 defined, 55, 56, 418
 framework and views, 419
 glossary definition, G–3
 on intranets, 420
 as knowledge repositories, 381–382, 387
 overview, 418
 role of intelligent Web-based agents,
   444
 Sears example, 452–453
 Victoria's Secret example, 446
 when to use, 420–421
Data workers, 63, G–3
Decentralized computing. *See* Distributed
  computing
Decision making. *See also* Decision
  support systems (DSS)
 computerizing, 460–462
 and managers, 459–460
 models for, 463–464
 process of, 462–464
 and simulation, 492–493
 structured, 465
 value of information, 560–561
 and virtual reality, 439
Decision rooms, G–3
Decision support systems (DSS):
 applications, 470
 capabilities, 466–467
 characteristics, 466–467
 Charles Schwab example, 470
 Comshare example, 466
 data management subsystem, 467
 defined, 55, 465
 examples, 470
 vs. executive information systems,
   472–473
 vs. expert systems, 480
 failures, 476
 framework, 464–465
 frontline, 493–494
 glossary definition, G–3
 group aspect, 55, 471
 Guinness Import example, 468
 how they work, 469–470

integrating knowledge management
  systems, 387
knowledge management subsystem,
  469
model management subsystem, 467–468
Nederlandse Spoorweges example,
  500–501
New Balance example, 457–459
organizational, 471–472
overview, 465–470
Owens & Minor example, 470
ready-made, 493
real-time, 494
SEB Private Bank example, 491
user interface, 468
users, 468
Wells Fargo example, 470
Decryption, 642
Deep discounters business model, 141
Dehumanization, 700, G–3
Dell Computer, 14, 87, 148, 151, 157,
  158, 253, 257, 258, 305, 321,
  332–333, 441, 506–508, 511
Deloitte & Touche, 163, 317
Denial of service (DoS), 633, 649, 651,
  662–663, G–3
Denver International Airport, 646
Desktop publishing, 55
Desktop purchasing, 158, 166, G–3
Deutsche Bank, 173
DHS. *See* U.S. Department of Homeland
  Security (DHS)
Differentiation strategy, 510, G–3
Digital cities, 230–232, G–3
Digital divide, 699–700, G–3
Digital economy. *See also* Electronic
  commerce (e-commerce)
 defined, 4
 glossary definition, G–3
 vs. old economy, 7–10
 overview, 4–6
Digital Millenium Copyright Act, 715
Digital rights management (DRM)
  systems, 716, G–3
Digital wallets. *See* E-wallets (digital
  wallets)
Directories, 96, G–3
Disaster avoidance, G–3
Disaster recovery plans, 667, G–3
Discovery, as Internet application
  category, 92, 95–104
Disintermediation, 171–172, G–3
Disney Company, 25, 175, 541
Distance learning:
 defined, 121
 vs. e-learning, 121
 glossary definition, G–3
 online corporate training, 123
 overview, 121
Distributed computing, 67–68, 70, 534,
  G–3. *See also* Networked
  computing
Distributed denial of service (DDoS),
  651, G–3
Distributed processing, 67–68, 70, G–4.
  See also Networked computing

Distributed work, 123–124
Distribution channels, 263–265
Division of labor, 87
DoCoMo, 100, 200, 207
Documentation controls, 659
Document management, 414–417, G–4
Document management systems (DMS), 55, 415, 416, 417, G–4
Dollar General, 289
Domain names, 172–173, G–4
Donatos Pizzeria, 205
Dot-com models, 153. *See also* Electronic commerce (e-commerce)
Dow Chemical, 160
DPS-Promatic, 203
Dr. Pepper/Seven Up, 350–351
Driscoll Company, 557
Drivers. *See* Business pressures
DSS. *See* Decision support systems (DSS)

E

E-911, 221, G–12
Eastman Kodak. *See* Kodak Corporation
EBay, 147, 167, 205
E-biz. *See* E-business
EBizSearch, 98
E-bonds, 272
E-business. *See also* Electronic commerce (e-commerce)
    vs. e-commerce, 139
    FedEx example, 49–51
    glossary definition, G–4
    Maybelline example, 83–84
    and strategic systems, 62
EC. *See* Electronic commerce (e-commerce)
E-cash, 166
E-checks, 165
E-collaboration. *See* Virtual collaboration
E-commerce. *See* Electronic commerce (e-commerce)
E-CRM (electronic CRM), 320–322, G–4
EDI. *See* Electronic data interchange (EDI)
EDS, 576
E-government, 141, 161–163, G–4
EIAC (exploration, involvement, analysis, and communications) model, 574
802.11b standard, 197, G–4
EKPs (enterprise knowledge portals), 382
Elder care, 230, 231
E-learning:
    benefits, 121
    Cisco Systems example, 132–133
    Dartmouth College example, 40–41
    defined, 120
    vs. distance learning, 121
    drawbacks, 121
    glossary definition, G–4
    online corporate training, 123
    virtual universities, 122
Electronic aggregators, 11
Electronic auctions. *See* Auctions
Electronic banking. *See* Cyberbanking
Electronic bartering, 146, G–4

Electronic benefits transfers (EBT), G–4
Electronic bill presentment and payments (EBPP), 168, 272–273
Electronic cash, 166, G–4
Electronic certificates, G–4
Electronic chat rooms. *See* Chat rooms
Electronic checks (e-checks), 165, G–4
Electronic commerce (e-commerce). *See also* Digital economy; Information technology (IT)
    advertising, 153–157
    applications portfolio, 539–541
    auditing systems, 672–673
    benefits, 143, 144, 581
    business-to-business model, 140
    business-to-consumers model, 140, 146–148
    ChemConnect example, 11, 159, 160
    consumer-to-business model, 140
    consumer-to-consumer model, 140, 163–164
    and cybercrime, 633–634
    defined, 139
    vs. e-business, 139
    economics, 580–582
    ethical issues, 170–174
    failures, 174–175
    financial transactions, 272–273
    FreeMarkets.com example, 158, 181–182
    glossary definition, G–4
    Godiva.com example, 138–139
    government model, 141, 161–163
    Hi-Life example, 182–183
    history, 142
    intraorganizational model, 140
    Lego example, 339
    limitations, 143, 144
    and mass customization, 87–88
    mechanisms, 143–146
    mobile commerce model, 141, 205
    models, 140–141
    and outsourcing, 578
    overview, 19–20, 139–143
    payment systems, 164–169
    protecting buyers and sellers, 173–174
    pure *vs.* partial, 139–140
    scope, 142–143
    Sterngold example, 595–597
    success stories, 176
    support services, 164–170
    vs. traditional retailing, 146
    types of transactions, 140–141
Electronic Communications Privacy Act, 652
Electronic communities. *See* Virtual communities
Electronic credit cards, 165–166, G–4
Electronic data interchange (EDI):
    benefits, 346–347, 349
    defined, 56, 345
    examples, 349
    glossary definition, G–4
    how it works, 348
    Internet-based, 347–349

    limitations, 347
    traditional, 345–347
Electronic exchanges. *See* Exchanges
Electronic funds transfer (EFT), G–4
Electronic Mailbox Protection Act, 698–699
Electronic mail (e-mail). *See also* Instant messaging
    advertising via, 154
    ethical issues, 124
    glossary definition, G–4
    privacy issues, 124
Electronic malls, 148
Electronic marketplaces and exchanges, as EC business model, 141
Electronic markets, 11, 73, G–4
Electronic meeting systems, 117. *See also* Virtual meetings
Electronic (online) catalogs, 143, 145, 154–155
Electronic payment cards. *See* Smart cards
Electronic payments, 164–169, 272, 273. *See also* Wireless bill payments
Electronic retailing (e-tailing):
    customer service aspect, 151–152
    defined, 146
    glossary definition, G–4
    issues, 152–153
    malls, 148
    overview, 146–147
    storefronts, 147–148
Electronic storefronts, 147–148, G–4
Electronic surveillance, 712, G–4
Electronic teleconferencing, 117–118
Electronic tendering system business model, 141
Electronic wallets. *See* E-wallets (digital wallets)
Eli Lilly, 589–590
Elite Care, 230, 231
EMA. *See* Expense management automation (EMA)
E-mail. *See* Electronic mail (e-mail)
E-mail agents, G–4
E-Mail Threats and Harassment Act, 652
E-marketplace (electronic markets). *See* Electronic markets
EMKE Groups, 94
Empire Blue Cross and Blue Shield, 670
Employee relationship management (ERM), 282, G–4
Employees. *See also* Business-to-its-employees e-commerce (B2E)
    e-commerce among, 161
    health and safety issues, 701
    impacts of information technology on, 694–695
    job content, 694–695
    mobile workers, 208–211
    monitoring Internet use, 125–126
    personnel issues, 694–695
    recruiting, 276–280
    training online, 123
Employment opportunities:
    impact of information technology, 704–706
    online job market, 150

EMS. *See* Enhanced Messaging Service (EMS)
Encarta, 511
Encryption, 642, 664–665, G–4
Encyclopedia Britannica, 511
End-user computing:
  Ansett Austrailia example, 607
  application development, 606
  defined, 56
  glossary definition, G–4
  and information architecture, 535
  vs. information systems departments, 635–639
Enhanced Messaging Service (EMS), 190, G–4
Enron, 711
Enterprise knowledge portals (EKPs), 382
Enterprise portals. *See* Corporate portals
Enterprise resource planning (ERP):
  combining with SCM software, 313–314
  defined, 65–66
  examples, 311
  failures, 316–318
  first-generation, 312
  glossary definition, G–4
  history, 310
  overview, 311–312
  SAP R/3 software, 311–312
  second-generation, 312–314
  third-generation, 314–315
Enterprise software, G–4. *See also* SAP R/3
Enterprise systems:
  defined, 54, 295
  examples, 296
  vs. functional systems, 295
  glossary definition, G–4
  overview, 295–297
Enterprise Web, 73–74, G–4
Enterprisewide computing, 70, G–4
Enterprisewide systems. *See* Enterprise systems
Entry-barriers strategy, 512–513, G–4
E-planning, 539–542, G–4
E-procurement, 158, 159, G–4
Ergonomics, 701, 702, G–4
Ernst & Young, 375, 386, 391
ERP. *See* Enterprise resource planning (ERP)
ES. *See* Expert systems (ES)
ESS. *See* Executive support systems (ESS)
E-supply chain, 297, G–4
E-tailers, G–4. *See also* Electronic retailing (e-tailing)
Ethics:
  and data privacy, 170
  defined, 16
  and electronic commerce, 170–174
  as e-mail issue, 124
  glossary definition, G–4
  and mobile computing, 232–233
  and networked computing, 124–126
  and SCM, 309
  and security issues, 675
  as societal pressure, 16–17
Etiquette. *See* Netiquette
E*Trade, 150

Europcar, 284
European Court of Human Rights, 416
European Union, 358
EV. *See* Expected value (EV)
E-wallets (digital wallets), 169, G–5
Exception reporting, G–5
Exchanges:
  as B2B model, 11, 151–161, 341–342, 343
  defined, 73
  glossary definition, G–5
Executive information systems (EIS), 472–473, G–5
Executive support systems (ESS), 55, 56, 473, G–5. *See also* Executive information systems (EIS)
Expected value (EV), 574, G–5
Expedia.com, 151, 532
Expense management automation (EMA), 273, G–5
Expertise, 480
Expert systems (ES):
  applications, 483–484
  benefits, 480–481
  blackboard, 482
  components, 482–483
  vs. decision support systems, 480
  defined, 55, 56, 480
  elements, 482–483
  embedded, 483–484
  examples of use, 483–484
  failure, 481, 482
  glossary definition, G–5
  in hybrid systems, 490
  inference engine, 480, 482
  knowledge base, 482
  limitations, 481
  Malaysia Airlines example, 501–502
  Mary Kay example, 482
  overview, 480
  security applications, 676
  Singapore Airlines example, 501–502
  user interface, 482
Explicit knowledge, G–5
Exploration, involvement, analysis, and communications (EIAC) model, 574
Exposure, 642, 645, G–5
EXtensible Markup Language. *See* XML (eXtensible Markup Language)
External data sources, 411
Extranets:
  benefits, 352
  components, 350–351
  defined, 30, 72
  Dr. Pepper/Seven Up example, 350–351
  Ford example, 351
  glossary definition, G–5
  integrating knowledge management systems, 387
  overview, 94, 349–350
  structure, 350–351
  types, 351–352
Extricity Software, 307
ExxonMobil, 265, 311, 538

F

Factoring, 272
Failures:
  business process reengineering, 622–623
  customer relationship management, 322–323
  data mining, 431–432
  decision support systems, 476
  Denver International Airport example, 646
  e-commerce, 174–175
  enterprise resource planning, 316–318
  expert systems, 481, 482
  Go.com example, 25
  knowledge management systems, 393, 394
  mobile computing, 233–234
  Nike example, 26
  overview, 582–583
  university accounting system example, 583
FAQ agents, 96–97
Fault tolerance, 642, 674–675, G–5
FDMA. *See* Frequency Division Multiple Access (FDMA)
Federal Express. *See* FedEx
Federal laws, 652–653
Federal Trade Commission (FTC), 172
FedEx, 17–18, 49–51, 340, 351
Fidelity Investments, 151–152, 353
FileNet, 384
Finance. *See* Accounting/finance functions
Financial analysis, 274–275
Financial planning, 269–270
Financial ratios, 275–276
Financial value chain management (FVCM), 275, G–5
Findarticles.com, 99
Find-the-best-price business model, 141
Fingerprints, 169
Firewalls, 661–662, G–5
Fishing, Australia, 721–722
Fitsense Technology, 223
Flaming, 125, G–5
Flattened organizations, 695
Food.com, 205
Ford Motor Company, 171, 351, 557
Foreign languages, 99
Forward auctions, 145–146, G–5
4G, 196, G–5
Four-stage model of planning:
  defined, 520
  glossary definition, G–5
  information requirements analysis stage, 520, 528–529
  overview, 520–521
  project planning stage, 520, 531
  resource allocation stage, 520, 529–530
  strategic planning stage, 520, 521–527
FoxMeyer, 317
Framatome, 2
Fraud:
  buyer protection, 173–174

Internet, 172
seller protection, 173–174
FreeMarkets.com, 158, 181–182
Free speech, 124, 713–715
Freeware, 125
Frequency Division Multiple Access (FDMA), 196, G–5
Frito-Lay, 366–367, 394
Frontline decision making, G–5
Front-office operations, integrating with back-office operations, 283–284
Fry Multimedia, 138
Fujitsu, 2
Functional areas:
accounting and finance, 269–276
characteristics of information systems, 53–54, 247–249
human resources, 276–282
integrating information systems, 282–284
marketing and sales, 260–268
overview, 247–249
production/operations and logistics, 255–260
and supply chain, 248
transaction processing, 249–255
and value chain model, 248
Functional MIS, 59–60, G–5. *See also* Management information systems (MIS)
Funk & Wagnalls, 511
Fuzzy logic:
defined, 488
glossary definition, G–5
in hybrid systems, 490
MATLAB example, 274
overview, 488–489

G

Gambling, online, 215
Gameboy, 215
Games, mobile, 215
Games, online, 710
GDSS. *See* Group decision support systems (GDSS)
Geac Computer Corp., 466
Gemstar TV Guide International, 355
General controls, 656–660, G–5
General Electric, 11, 321, 347
General Motors, 131–132, 221, 228, 351, 557
General Packet Radio Service (GPRS), 191
Generations, wireless technology, 196
Genesys Meeting Center, 118
Genetic programming, 488, G–5
Gentia, 378
Geographical information systems (GIS):
data sources, 436
and decision making, 436–437
defined, 219, 435
glossary definition, G–5
and Internet, 437
and intranets, 437

overview, 219–220, 435
software, 435–436
Gibson Musical Instruments, 171
Gillette, 229
GIS. *See* Geographical information systems (GIS)
Global competition, 13–14
Global information systems, 336–340, G–5
Globalization, 692–693, G–5
Global Mobile Suppliers Association, 207
Global positioning systems (GPS), 189, 205, 218–219, 254, G–5
Global stock exchanges, 272
GO2Online, 206
Goal-seeking analysis, 466–467
Go.com, 25
Godiva.com, 138–139, 148, 176
Google, 10, 96, 98, 153, 384
Google Toolbar, 99
Government regulation and deregulation, 16
Government-to-business (G2B), 141, 161–163, G–5
Government-to-citizen (G2C), 141, 161–163, G–5
Government-to-government (G2G), 141, 161–163
Gowling Lafleur Henderson LLP, 383
GPRS (General Packet Radio Service), 191
GPS. *See* Global positioning systems (GPS)
Gramm-Leach-Bliley Act, 652
Great Plains software, 272
Grid computing, 75–76, 85, G–5
Grokker, 99
Group decision support systems (GDSS):
applications, 471
defined, 55, 471
glossary definition, G–5
overview, 471
Group purchasing, 11, 158, G–5
Group purchasing business model, 141
Group support systems (GSS), G–5
Groupware. *See also* Group decision support systems (GDSS); Work groups
defined, 116
glossary definition, G–5
overview, 116–117
product examples, 117–120
Group work, 108–110. *See also* Collaboration
Growth strategy, 511, G–5
GTE Corporation. *See* Verizon
Guinness Import Company, 468

H

Hackers, 647, 665, G–5
Handelsbanken of Sweden, 24–25
Hand-held computers, 193–194
Hands-free computers, 209, 308
Handwriting recognition, 479
Harbridge House, 459–460
Hardware, 21. *See also* Information technology (IT)

Harrah's, 407–409
HDFC Bank of India, 204
Hershey Foods, 316
Hertz Corporation, 239–240
Hewlett-Packard, 280, 301, 392, 523, 576
High Beam, 98
High-payoff projects, 528–529, 530, 601
Highway 91 project, California, 217
Hi-Life Corporation, 182–183
Hitachi, 443
HNC Software, 379
Home Depot, 148, 171, 176, 265, 347, 509, 683–684
Homeland security, 16. *See also* U.S. Department of Homeland Security (DHS)
Honeynets, 665, G–5
Honeypots, 665, G–5
Hong Kong airport, 646
Hong Kong and Shanghai Bank, 150
Hotels.com, 151
Hotel services, wireless, 215–216
Hotspots, 197, G–6
Howstuffworks.com, 99
HTML (Hypertext Markup Language) *vs.* XML, 352
Hubs, electronic, 342, 343
Human-computer interaction, 707–711
Human resource systems. *See also* Employees
benefits administration, 281–282
job portals, 279
labor-management negotiation, 281
overview, 276
performance evaluation, 280
planning, 281–282
recruitment, 276–280
traditional *vs.* electronic, 277
training employees, 123, 280–281
Hummingbird, 381, 382, 443
Hyatt Hotels, 160
Hybrid intelligent systems, 489–491
Hyperion, 421, 425, 443
Hypertext Markup Language (HTML) *vs.* XML, 352
Hyperwave, 382
Hyundai, 160

I

I2 Technology, 2, 26
IBM, 29, 75, 103, 158, 227, 253, 260, 267, 281, 313, 336, 345, 378, 425, 443, 479, 523–524, 576, 619–620. *See also* Lotus Notes/Domino
Identity theft, 643, 648
Immigration, 7–8
Increasing returns, 584–585, G–6
Indexing agents, 97
Industrywide portals, 103–104
Inference engines, 480, 482, G–6
In-flight medical emergencies, 216
Information:
vs. data, 52
defined, 52

Information (*cont.*)
  glossary definition, G–6
  vs. knowledge, 52
  scarcity *vs.* abundance, 696–702
Information anxiety, 700–701, G–6
Information architecture. *See also*
    Client/server architecture;
    Information technology
    architecture
  centralized *vs.* noncentralized, 533–534
  Chase Manhattan Bank example, 69
  defined, 532
  glossary definition, G–6
  legacy systems, 535–536
  overview, 531–533
  types, 533–535
Information brokers business model, 141
Information centers, 638–639, G–6
Information discovery, 425
Information economics, 568–569, G–6
Information infrastructure. *See also*
    Information architecture
  assessing investments, 569–570
  defined, 66
  glossary definition, G–6
  vs. information architecture, 66
  management by maxim, 570, 571
  overview, 66
Information management. *See*
    Information systems (IS)
Information overload, 15, 696–697, G–6
Information portals, 100–101, 344, G–6
Information quality, 697–698, G–6
Information requirements analysis,
    528–529, G–6
Information resources management
    (IRM), 77–78, 634, 638, G–6
Information superhighway, 29, G–6.
    See also Internet
Information system controls, 642
Information systems (IS). *See also*
    Information technology (IT)
  acquiting, 597–623
  architecture overview, 66, 531–533
  Campusfood.com example, 23–24
  centralized *vs.* decentralized, 533–534
  classification, 53–54
  and computer crime, 633–634, 641–667
  vs. computers, 21
  configurations, 52–53
  defined, 20, 51
  departmental issues (*See* Information
    systems department (ISD))
  examples, 22–25
  failures, 25, 582–583
  formal *vs.* informal, 20
  functional, 53–54, 247–249
  glossary definition, G–6
  history, 54, 56–57
  vs. information technology (IT), 21–22
  integrated, 310–311
  integrating knowledge management
    systems, 386–388
  interorganizational (*See*
    Interorganizational information
    systems (IOS))

organizational activities supported, 60–63
  and organizational structure, 53
  overview, 20, 51–53
  resources and capabilities, 516–518
  role of controls, 656–660
  security breakdown examples, 642–644
  stages of growth, 524, 525
  types of support provided, 54, 55
  vulnerability of, 641–651
Information systems department (ISD):
  chief information officer, 78, 634–635
  and end users, 77–78, 634, 635–639
  future of, 78
  managing information resources,
    77–78, 634, 638
  overview, 77–78, 634
  role of, 78, 634–635
Information technology architecture:
  choosing among options, 533–535
  considerations, 533
  defined, 66, 531
  distributed approach, 534
  and end-user computing, 535
  glossary definition, G–6
  and legacy systems, 535–536
  overview, 531–533
Information technology (IT). *See also* IT
    planning
  acquiring applications, 597–623
  and business process reengineering,
    617–620
  capabilities, 5
  defined, 4, 21
  direct *vs.* indirect value, 515
  economic strategies, 574–580
  economic trends, 554–556
  evaluating investments, 560–566
  financial trends, 554–556
  general technological trends, 27–29
  glossary definition, G–6
  impacts on people and organizations,
    691–716
  vs. information systems (IS), 21–22
  learning about, 34–35
  managing resources, 77–78, 634, 638
  McDonald's example, 629–630
  networked and distributed computing
    trends, 29–34
  productivity paradox, 556–560
  project failures, 25, 582–583
  runaway projects, 582–583
  as source of strategic advantage,
    515–518
  state of Iowa example, 553–554
  studying, 34–35
  value in decision making, 460–461
Information warehousing. *See* Data
    warehouses
Infrastructure. *See* Information
    infrastructure
Inktomi, 384
Innovation strategy, 511–512, G–6
Input controls, 660
Insourcing, 605–606
Instant messaging, 107. *See also* Short
    messaging service (SMS)

Instant video, 119
Institutional decision support systems. *See*
    Organizational decision support
    systems (ODSS)
Intangible benefits:
  defined, 562
  glossary definition, G–6
  handling, 563–564
  and management by maxim, 570, 571
  overview, 562–563
Integrated software suites, 119–120
Integration, information systems:
  and business processs redesign, 618–620
  Europcar example, 284
  internal *vs.* external, 310–311
  overview, 310
Integrity, data, 642
Intel Corporation, 175, 188, 281, 540, 564
Intellectual assets. *See* Intellectual capital
Intellectual capital, 369, G–6
Intellectual property, 715–716, G–6
Intelligence, natural *vs.* artificial. *See*
    Artificial intelligence (AI);
    Intelligent agents
Intelligent agents:
  and data mining, 444
  defined, 96
  examples, 378–379
  glossary definition, G–6
  overview, 378–379
  Web-based, 444
Intelligent support systems (ISSs), 56
Intelligent systems. *See also* Expert
    systems (ES)
  defined, 476
  glossary definition, G–6
  hybrid, 479, 489–491
  for intrusion detection, 675
  overview, 476–477
  security applications, 675
  types, 479
Interactive marketing (intermarketing), 156
Interactive pagers, 194
Interfaces. *See* User interfaces
Internal data sources, 411
International banking, 149–150
International business:
  banking, 149–150
  global information systems, 336–340
  transborder data flow, 337
International Information Products
    Company Ltd. (IIPC), 24
Internet. *See also* Electronic commerce
    (e-commerce); Web-based systems;
    World Wide Web
  commercial applications, 92–93
  defined, 72, 91
  glossary definition, G–6
  as job market tool, 150
  manners, 125
  monitoring employee use, 125–126
  monitoring student use, 126
  next-generation, 91
  overview, 91
  tracking individual activities, 170–171
  using for advertising, 153–157

Internet2, 91, G–6
Internet economy. *See* Digital economy
Internet fraud, 172
Internet of things, 229, G–6
Internet Relay Chat (IRC), 106–107,
    G–6
Internet telephony (voice-over IP),
    107, G–6
Interorganizational information systems
    (IOS):
  defined, 54, 334
  global, 336–340, 363
  glossary definition, G–6
  implementation issues, 354–358
  overview, 54, 334
  planning, 537–538
  support technologies, 335
  types, 334–335
Intrabusiness, 161, G–6
Intrabusiness (intraorganizational)
    e-commerce, 140, G–6
Intranets:
  defined, 30, 72
  glossary definition, G–6
  integrating knowledge management
    systems, 387
  investing before analyzing, 589–590
  overview, 93
Intraspect Software, 384
Intrusion detection, 662, 675
Inventory management. *See also* Position
    inventory
  medical center example, 245–246
  overview, 256–257
  solving supply chain problems, 301
  vendor-managed, 257
Investments:
  Daiwa Securities example, 274
  evaluating and justifying IT, 560–574
  financial analysis, 274–275
  managing, 273–275
  obtaining information, 274
  trading online, 150
"Invisible" computing. *See* Pervasive
    computing
IOS. *See* Interorganizational information
    systems (IOS)
Iowa (state), 553–554
IPaq, 33
IRC (Internet Relay Chat), 106–107
ISD. *See* Information systems department
    (ISD)
Isteelasia.com, 159
IT governance, 637, 638, G–6
IT planning:
  defined, 519
  design of architecture, 531–536
  vs. e-planning, 539–542
  evolution, 519–520
  four-stage model, 520–531
  glossary definition, G–6
  for interorganizational systems, 537–538
  issues, 536–542
  for multinational corporations, 538
  overview, 519
  problems, 538–539

J

Jaguar, 264
J.D. Edwards, 381
JIT. *See* Just-in-time (JIT)
Job content, 694–695
Job dispatch, 208–210
Job market, online, 150
Jobs. *See* Employment opportunities
Job stress, 701
John Deere Corporation, 305
Johnson & Johnson, 374
J.P. Morgan Chase, 69, 85
Judd's, 589
Junk mail, 125
Just-in-time (JIT), 258, G–6

K

Kaiser Permanente, 98
KartOO, 97, 99
Kemper Insurance Company, 213
Keyboards, attachable, 193
Keyword banners, G–6
Kinko's, 252
Knowledge:
  characteristics, 368–369
  creating, 373
  vs. data, 52
  defined, 52
  glossary definition, G–6
  vs. information, 52, 368
  leaky *vs.* sticky, 370
  overview, 52, 368–369
  seeking, 374
  sharing, 373–374
  tacit *vs.* explicit, 369–370
Knowledge audits, G–7
Knowledge bases, 477, G–7
Knowledge databases. *See* Knowledge bases
Knowledge discovery, 425–426, G–7
Knowledge discovery in databases
    (KDD), 379–380, G–7
Knowledge management (KM). *See also*
    Expert systems (ES)
  approaches, 374–376
  and artificial intelligence, 387
  DaimlerChrysler example, 400–402
  defined, 367
  Frito-Lay example, 366–367
  glossary definition, G–7
  implementing strategy, 380–388
  initiatives, 372–374
  law firm example, 383
  overview, 367–370
  role of information technology, 376–380
Knowledge management suites, 384,
    386, G–7
Knowledge management systems (KMS):
  and application service providers, 386
  Buckman Labs example, 402–403
  Cingular example, 371
  Commerce Bank example, 385
  components, 376–378
  defined, 370

failure, 393, 394
  Frito-Lay example, 394
  glossary definition, G–7
  Gowling Lafleur Henderson example,
    383
  implementing, 380–388
  integrating, 386–388
  overview, 370–371
  potential drawbacks, 395
  role of chief knowledge officers, 389
  role of developers, 390
  steps in cycle, 372
  success factors, 393–395
Knowledge repositories, 381–382, 387,
    G–7
KnowledgeTrack, 382
Knowledge workers, 63, G–7
Knowledge work systems, 55, 56
KnowledgeX, Inc., 386
Knowware, 381, G–7
Kodak Corporation, 61
Kone, Inc., 590–591

L

Labor markets, 704–706
Labor productivity, 557–559
Languages, foreign, 99
LANs (local area networks), 67, 94, 190,
    197
Laundry, old *vs.* new economy
    experience, 9–10
Law firms, and knowledge management,
    383
L-commerce. *See* Location-based
    commerce (l-commerce)
Leaky knowledge, 370, G–7. *See also*
    Explicit knowledge
Leasing applications, 603–605, 609
Legacy systems:
  defined, 70
  glossary definition, G–7
  reengineering, 535–536
Legal issues:
  in global information systems, 337–338
  in mobile computing, 232–233
Lego Company, 339
Le Saunda Holding Company, 22
Levi Strauss, 175, 347
Liberty Alliance, 169
Licensing software, 125, 715
Life cycle. *See* Data life cycle; Systems
    development life cycle (SDLC)
LifeStar, 416
Littlewoods Stores, 301
Local area networks (LANs), 67, 94, 190,
    197
Localization, 337
Location-based advertising, 220
Location-based commerce (l-commerce),
    191, 218–222, G–7
Lock-in effect, 584, G–7
Log files, 170–171
Logging machines, 439
Logic bombs, 649

London Stock Exchange, 644
Longs Drug Stores, 58
Lotus Development Corporation, 416
Lotus Notes/Domino, 119–120, 375, 381,
    382, 384, 387, G–7
Lufthansa, 199
Lutron Electronics, 227
Lycos.com, 100

M

Machine learning, 479. *See also* Fuzzy
    logic; Neural computing
Mainframe computers, 67
Make-to-order, 18
Malaysia Airlines, 501–502
Malicious applets, 649
Malls. *See* Electronic malls
Malware, 642
Management by maxim, 570, 571, G–7
Management decision systems. *See*
    Decision support systems (DSS)
Management information systems (MIS),
    54, 55, G–7. *See also* Information
    systems (IS)
Management science, 465
Management service providers (MSPs),
    577–578, G–7
Management support systems (MSS),
    461, 491, G–7
Managerial systems, 60–61
Managers:
    and decision-making, 459–460
    impacts of information technology,
        460–461
    IT support, 461–462
Manners, Internet, 125
Manufacturing resource planning
    (MRP II), 258, 309, G–7. *See also*
    Material requirements planning
    (MRP)
Marketing databases, 262
Marketing management, 266–268
Marketing transaction database (MTD),
    440, G–7
Market pressures, 13–15
Marriott International, 114, 160, 215
Mary Kay Cosmetics, 482
Mass customization:
    defined, 18
    Dell Computer example, 87
    and electronic commerce, 87–88
    glossary definition, G–7
    vs. mass production, 87, 88
    overview, 87–88, 262
Mass production, 87
MasterCard Wallet, 169
Material requirements planning (MRP),
    257, 309, G–7. *See also*
    Manufacturing resource planning
    (MRP II)
MATLAB, 274
Maybelline, 83–84
McDonald's, 199, 336, 629–630

McDonnell Douglas, 416
MCI-WorldCom, 711
M-commerce. *See* Mobile commerce
    (m-commerce)
Medicine. *See* Dartmouth-Hitchcock
    Medical Center (DHMC);
    Telemedicine, wireless
Megabeam, 215
Membership business model, 141
Merita Bank, 202
Merrill Lynch, 175, 258
Messaging. *See* Instant messaging; Short
    messaging service (SMS)
MetaCrawler, 96, 97
Metadata, 418, G–7
Metasearch engines, 97, G–7
Metcalfe's Law:
    defined, 29
    glossary definition, G–7
    Kelly's Extension, 29
Metric benchmarks, 559–570, G–7
Metrics:
    defined, 573
    glossary definition, G–7
    IT implementation, 573–574
    for knowledge management, 392–393
Micropayments, 203
Microsoft Corporation, 173, 382. *See also*
    MSN
Microsoft Encarta, 511
Microsoft.NET, 77, 354
Microsoft Passport, 169, 204
MicroStrategy, Inc., 443
Microstrategy, Inc., 267, 425
Milestones, 601–602
Millstone Coffee, 188
Minneapolis-St. Paul International
    Airport, 199
Minnesota Department of Transportation,
    636
Minority Report (movie), 222
Mitre Corporation, 645
MMS. *See* Multimedia Messaging Service
    (MMS)
MobileAria, 221
Mobile commerce (m-commerce):
    advertising applications, 205–207
    defined, 30, 73
    as e-commerce model, 141
    factors driving, 191–192
    fee-based content, 207
    financial services applications, 202–204
    glossary definition, G–7
    overview, 30, 189
    representative applications, 189
    retail shopping applications, 205
    security issues, 200–201
    specific attributes, 190–191
    value chain and revenue models,
        192–193
    voice systems, 201–202
Mobile computing. *See also* Wireless
    communications
    B2B applications, 214
    and CRM, 211–212
    defined, 55, 56, 73

enterprise applications, 208–212
ethical issues, 232–233
examples of applications, 31
factors driving, 191–192
failures, 233–234
fee-based content, 207
financial services applications, 202–204
fire department example, 240–241
glossary definition, G–7
hardware, 193–195
Hertz example, 239–240
hotel services, 215–216
infrastructure, 193–202
inhibitors and barriers, 232–234
intrabusiness applications, 212–213
job dispatch, 208–210
legal issues, 232–233
location-based, 218–222
medical center example, 245–246
NextBus example, 186–187
overview, 187–189
security issues, 200–201
software, 195
specific attributes, 190–191
supply chain applications, 214
telemedicine applications, 216–217
usability issues, 232
Mobile games, 215
Mobile handsets, 195, G–7
Mobile portals, 100, 207, G–7
Mobile Positioning Center (MPC), 218
Mobile wallets (m-wallets), 203–204, G–7
Mobil Oil. *See* Exxon Mobil
Mobil Travel Guides, 75
Model-based management system
    (MBMS), G–7
Model marts, 379, G–7
Models, in decision making, G–7
Model warehouses, 379, G–8
Modems, as security issue, 651
Monster.com, 150
Moore's Law:
    defined, 27
    extension to optical communication
        networks, 27
    extension to storage, 28
    glossary definition, G–8
    illustrated, 555
Mooter tool, 97
Morgan Stanley & Co., 439
Morrison Supermarkets, 90
Motion Picture Association of America,
    689, 715
Motorola, 205, 213, 281, 416
Movie piracy, 689–690, 715–716
MPC (Mobile Positioning Center), 218
MQSoftware, 475
MRP. *See* Manufacturing resource
    planning (MRP II); Material
    requirements planning (MRP)
Mrs. Fields Cookies, 396
MSN, 100, 153, 163, 207
MSPs. *See* Management service providers
    (MSPs)
Multidimensional databases, 422, G–8
Multidimensionality, 435, G–8

Multimedia Messaging Service (MMS), 190, G–8
Multinational corporations, 336
Multiple-currency banking, 149–150, 272
M-wallets. *See* Mobile wallets (m-wallets)

N

NAFTA (North American Free Trade Agreement), 13, 358, 619
Name-your-own-price business model, 11, 141
Nanotechnology, 29
Napster, 716
National Association of Chain Drug Stores, 103–104
National City Corporation, 549–550
National Computer Security Center (NCSC), 674
National Information Infrastructure Protection Act, 652
National Institute for Standards and Technology, 176
National Science Foundation (NSF), 440
NATO, 229
Natural language processing (NLP), 484–485, G–8
NCR Corp., 421, 442, 446
Nederlandse Spoorweges, 500–501
Needham Interactive, 590
NetCaptor, 96
Net Fun, 710
Netgain, 266
NetIQ, 445
Netiquette, 125
Net present value (NPV), 561
Network computers, 32
Network controls, 659
Networked computing:
    Cisco Systems example, 547–548
    defined, 4, 32
    ethical issues, 124–126
    glossary definition, G–8
    integration issues, 126
    overview, 91–95
Network effects, 584, G–8
Networks, 21. *See also* Client/server architecture; Distributed computing
Network storage devices, 32, G–8
Neural computing, 486, G–8
Neural networks, 55, 486–488, 490
New Balance shoes, 457–459
New economy. *See also* Digital economy
    business models, 10–11
    vs. old economy, 7–10
    opportunities, 5–6
    overview, 4–5
New Line Cinema, 181–182
New Piper Aircraft, 356
New York City transit, 9
New York Stock Exchange, 21, 273
NextBus, 186–187
Next-generation Internet, 91
Niche strategy, 510–511, G–8
Nike, 14, 26, 173

99 Cents Only stores, 290
Nintendo, 215
No Electronic Theft Act, 715
Nokia, 10, 200, 215, 221
Noncentralized computing. *See* Distributed computing
Nortel Network, 394
North American Free Trade Agreement (NAFTA), 13, 358, 619
Northeast Utilities, 234
Northern Digital, 327–328
Northwest Airlines, 267
NPV (net present value), 561
Nygaard of Canada, 114

O

Object-oriented environment, 28
Object technology, 28, G–8
ODSS. *See* Organizational decision support systems (ODSS)
Office automation systems (OAS), 54, 55
Officedepot.com, 148
Offshore outsourcing, 577, G–8
Off-the-shelf application purchases, 602
OLAP. *See* Online analytical processing (OLAP)
OLTP. *See* Online transaction processing (OLTP)
1G, 196, G–8
One-to-one marketing, 318
Online advertising. *See* Advertising, online
Online analytical processing (OLAP), 427, 475, G–8
Online auction business model, 141
Online banking. *See* Cyberbanking
Online bill-paying, 168, 273
Online communities. *See* Virtual communities
Online corporate training, 123
Online coupons, 157
Online direct marketing business model, 141
Online (electronic) catalogs, 143, 145, 154–155
Online gambling, 215
Online games, 710
Online job market, 150
Online processing, 251, G–8
Online service industries, 148–151
Online shopping. *See* Electronic commerce (e-commerce)
Online stock trading, 150
Online transaction processing (OLTP), 251–252, G–8
OnStar, 228
Operational data stores, 422, G–8
Operational systems, 60
Optical networks, 32
Optimal Robotics, 707
Optimization, 465, G–8
Opti-Money, 273
Oracle Corporation, 283–284, 312, 357, 382, 421, 443, 576
Orbis, Inc., 8–9

Orbitz.com, 151
Order fulfillment, 169–170
Organizational decision support systems (ODSS), 471–472, G–8
Organizational knowledge base, G–8
Otis Elevator Company, 253, 621, 622
Output controls, 660
Outsourcing:
    advantages and disadvantages, 578–579
    and ASPs, 577, 608–609
    Canadian Imperial Bank of Commerce example, 578
    defined, 576
    and e-commerce, 578
    as economic strategy, 576–580
    glossary definition, G–8
    impact on IT architecture, 535
    Kone example, 590–591
    and MSPs, 577–578
    offshore, 577
    overview, 576
    potential benefits, 579
    risk areas, 579
    Sterngold example, 595–597
    strategies for, 579–580
Overload, information. *See* Information overload
Owens & Minor, 470

P

Pagers, interactive, 194
Panera Bread Company, 199, 200
Papersite.com, 159
Partek Forest, 439
Partnering. *See* Business alliances
Partner-relationship management (PRM), 354–355, G–8
Partners HealthCare System, 393
Password crackers, 649
Patriot Act, 652
Pattern recognition, 487, G–8
Payless Shoes, 282
Payload security, 665
PayPal, 167–168
Payroll, 281
PCs, in information systems, 67, 665. *See also* Information technology (IT)
PDAs. *See* Personal digital assistants (PDAs)
PDE (position determining equipment), 218
Peacocks Retails, 308
Peapod, 157
Peer-to-peer (P2P) architecture, 70–71, G–8
PeopleSoft, 24, 312, 317, 355, 357
Pepsi Bottling Group, 74
Performance evaluation, 280
Permission marketing, 155–156, G–8
Personal computers, in information systems, 67, 665. *See also* Information technology (IT)
Personal data, 411
Personal digital assistants (PDAs), 190, 194, G–8

Personal information managers (PIMs), 462, G–8
Personalization, 262
Personal portals, 100, G–8
Personal services, 164, 214–217
Personnel. *See* Employees; Human resource systems
Person-to-person payments, 167–168, G–8
Pervasive computing, 30, 33, 76, 222–232, G–8
Pfizer, 384
Photography, old *vs.* new economy experience, 8–9
Physical controls, 656
PictureTel Corporation, 119
Pierre Lang Corp., 357
Pioneer, Inc., 628–629
Piper Aircraft, 356
Piracy, 689–690, 715–716, G–8
Pizza Hut, 423
PlaceWare, 118
Planning Sciences International, 378
Plasticsnet.com, 159
Playstation, 215
PLM. *See* Product lifecycle management (PLM)
Plumtree Software, 562, 628–629
Political contributions, 713
Pop-under ads, G–8
Pop-up ads, G–8
Portable computers. *See* Mobile computing
Portals, 100, G–8. *See also* Corporate portals; Information portals
PortalsCommunity.com, 100
Porter's competitive forces model. *See* Competitive forces model
Porter's value chain model. *See* Value chain model
Position determining equipment (PDE), 218
Position inventory, 278–279
Practice approach, 375, 376, G–8
Prada, 222
Pressures. *See* Business pressures
Priceline.com, 11, 151, 512, 513
Price-to-performance ratio, 555, G–8
PriceWaterhouseCoopers, 176
Pricing, 266, 276
Primary activities, 44, 46, G–9
Princeton University, 644
Privacy:
    "Big Brother" concerns, 170, 712
    as e-mail issue, 124
    as ethical issue, 170
    and patient information, 125
    and politics, 714–715
    vs. security, 711–713
Privacy Act, 652
PRM. *See* Partner-relationship management (PRM)
Procedures, defined, 21
Process approach, 374, 376, G–9
Process-centric integration, 283–284, G–9
Processing controls, 660
Procter & Gamble, 114, 267, 268, 302, 347, 576

Product customization business model, 141
Production and operations management (POM):
    computer-integrated manufacturing, 259
    inventory management, 256–257
    logistics management, 256
    materials management, 256–257
    overview, 255–256
    planning, 257–259
    product lifecycle management, 259–260
Productivity:
    Driscoll Company example, 557
    gains *vs.* losses, 557–559
    labor example, 557
Productivity paradox, 556–560, G–9
Product lifecycle management (PLM), 259–260, G–9
Product pricing, 266, 276
Profitability analysis, 276
Programming attacks, 649, G–9
Programming controls, 659
Programs. *See* Software
Project planning, 258, 531, G–9. *See also* IT planning
Project teams. *See* Collaboration
Proximity cards, 217
PTC Corp., 259, 260
Public exchanges, 159–161, 341–342, 343, G–9
Public portals. *See* Commercial (public) portals
Public transportation, 9
Publishing portals, 100, G–9
Pull-based supply system, 87, 88
Purchasing cards, 166
Push-based supply system, 87, 88

Q

Qantas Airlines, 19, 635
Quality control, 257. *See also* Data quality (DQ)
Quality of life, 703–704, G–9
Quantas Airlines. *See* Qantas Airlines
Quantum computing, 29
QVC, 6, 328–329

R

Radio frequency identfication (RFID), 30, 32, 41–42, 223, 229–230, 302–304, G–9
Radio Shack, 281
Random banners, G–9
RBV. *See* Resource-based view (RBV)
Reader's Digest, 119
Real estate, online, 151
Real options, 570–571, G–9
Real-time collaboration (RTC) tools, 118–119
Recording Industry Association of America, 715
Recruitment, 276–280
Reengineering. *See* Business process reengineering (BPR)

Reintermediation, 171–172, G–9
Relationship marketing, 318
RE/MAX, 114
Repetitive strain injuries, 701
Requests for proposal (RFPs), 611, G–9
Requests for quotation (RFQs), 11
Requirements analysis. *See* Information requirements analysis
Resource allocation, 529–530, G–9
Resource-based view (RBV), 516–518, G–9
Response management. *See* Critical response activities
Restaurant.com, 148
Restructuring business processes, 18, 621–623
Restructuring organizations. *See* Business process reengineering (BPR)
Resumix, 278
Retailing, electronic, 146–148. *See also* Electronic commerce (e-commerce)
Retailing, traditional *vs.* electronic, 146, 707
Retail stores, improving shopping and checkout, 264–265
Return on investment (ROI), 562
Reverse auctions:
    glossary definition, G–9
    overview, 146
    tendering via, 11
Reverse engineering, 536, G–9
RFID (radio frequency identification), 30, 32, 41–42, 223, 229–230, 302–304, G–9
RFQs (requests for quotation), 11
Risk, 275, 541, 642
Risk management, 673–674, G–9
Robots, 705
ROI (return on investment), 562
Rolls-Royce, 311
Royal Bank of Scotland, 202
Royal Mile Pub, 33
RTC (real-time collaboration) tools, 118–119
Runaway IT projects, 582–583

S

Sabre, Inc., 111
Safeway (UK), 90–91
Salami slicing, defined, 649
Salary surveys, 279
Sales automation software, 267, G–9
Sales-force automation:
    defined, 266
    glossary definition, G–9
    role of mobile computing, 211–212
Samsung Electronics, 281
SAP, 260, 317, 336, 582
SAP R/3, 2, 284, 311–312, G–9
Sarbanes-Oxley Act, 16, 475, 684, 698
SAS, 425
Scenario planning, 527, G–9
Schlumberger, 159
SCM. *See* Supply chain management (SCM)

SCM software, 297, 313–314, G–9
Scoring methodology, 568, G–9
Screenphones, 194, G–9
Screen sharing, 119, 356, G–9
SDLC (systems development life cycle), 605–606
Search engines:
   attracting visitors to Web sites, 156–157
   defined, 96
   glossary definition, G–9
Search for Extraterrestrial Intelligence (SETI), 76
Sears, 452–453
SEB Private Bank, 491
Securities. *See* Online stock trading; Security issues
Security issues:
   auditing, 671–673
   computer crime, 633–634, 641–667
   disaster planning, 667–670
   firewalls, 661–662
   implementing controls, 656–660
   IS breakdown examples, 642–644
   vs. privacy, 711–713
   systems vulnerability, 641–651
   viruses, 649–650, 662, 663
   Web-based systems, 660–667
Sega, 215
Self-checkout machines, 265, 707
Self-healing computers, 29, 675, G–9
Sell-side marketplace, 157–158, G–9
Semantic Web, 489, G–10
Sensitivity analysis, 466–467, G–10
September 11 attacks, 16, 117
Sequoia Software, 380
Servers, 68, G–9. *See also* Client/server architecture
Service computing. *See* Subscription (service) computing
Service industries, online, 148–151
Service-level agreements (SLA), 613, 637–638, G–9
Service-oriented architecture, 76
SETI (Search for Extraterrestrial Intelligence), 76
Shareware, 125
Sharper Image, 148
Sheetz convenience stores, 280
Shoney's, 280
Shopping. *See* Electronic commerce (e-commerce); Retail stores, improving shopping and checkout
Short messaging service (SMS), 190, 205, 211, G–9
Siebel Systems, 267
Siemens AG, 2–3, 371
Silicon Graphics, 669
Simulation, 492–493, G–9. *See also* Visual interactive simulation (VIS)
Singapore:
   satellite taxi dispatch, 254
   Singapore Airlines, 501–502
   TradeNet, 338
SingTel, 207

SITP. *See* Strategic information technology planning (SITP)
Six Flags, 363
Six Sigma, 18
Six-stages of IS growth, 524, 525
Skandia, 391
SkyMall, 355
Smart appliances, 227, G–10
Smart cards:
   defined, 167
   glossary definition, G–10
   Highway 91 example, 217
   overview, 167
   security applications, 675
Smart cars, 227–228
Smart homes, 224, 227
Smartphones, 190, 193, G–10
Smart terminals, 67, G–10
SMS. *See* Short Messaging Service (SMS)
Sniffers, 649
Social context, 21
Social engineering, 647, G–10
Social responsibility, 15
Social software, 120, G–10
Societal pressures, 15–17
Society for Information Management (SIM), 521
Softbots, 96, G–10
Software, 21. *See also* Application programs
Software A&G, 421
Software agents, 96–97, G–10. *See also* Intelligent agents
Software suites, 119–120
Southwest Airlines, 176, 476, 510
Spalding, 115
Spamming, 125, 155, 698–699, G–10
Speech recognition, 485–486, G–10. *See also* Voice synthesis
Speech understanding, 485–486, G–10
Spiders, 156
Spitfire Novelties Corp., 642
Spoofing, 649
Sprint, 207, 252
SPSS, 425
Spyware, 155, 171, G–10
Stages of IT growth, 524, 525, G–10
Staples, 176
Starbucks, 199, 312
Starwood Hotels & Resorts, 216
Stealthware, 665, G–10
Steelcase, 345
Steering committees, 637, G–10
Sterngold, 595–597
Stern Stewart, 391
Sticky knowledge, 370, G–10. *See also* Tacit knowledge
Storage networks, 32, 34
Stored-value money cards, 166–167, G–10
Storefronts, electronic, 147–148
Stovepipe problem, 616, 618, 621
Strategic alliances, 511
Strategic business units (SBUs), 161
Strategic information technology planning (SITP), 521, G–10
Strategic management, 17–18
Strategic planning. *See* IT planning

Strategic systems, 17–18
Streamcast Networks, 716
Subscription (service) computing, 75, G–10
Suites. *See* Software suites
Sumitomo, 160
Sunbeam, 227
Sun Microsystems, 77
Superzapping, 649
Supply chain:
   1-800-FLOWERS example, 514
   collaboration, 304–305
   components, 64–65, 297–299
   defined, 63, 296–297
   Dell example, 332–334
   downstream portion, 65, 298
   flows in, 297
   and functional areas, 248
   glossary definition, G–10
   internal, 65, 298
   IT support, 65–66
   linear *vs.* hub, 304
   managing, 65–66
   medical center example, 245–246
   mobile applications, 214
   old *vs.* new economy, 8–9
   overview, 63–65
   problems with, 299–301
   push model *vs.* pull model, 87, 88
   solutions to problems, 301–309
   structure, 297–299
   tiers of suppliers, 299
   types, 299
   upstream portion, 64–65, 297–298
   vs. value chain, 65
   and value chain model, 514
   Volkswagen example, 361–363
Supply-chain improvers business model, 141
Supply chain management (SCM):
   benefits, 299
   defined, 66, 297
   ethical issues, 309
   glossary definition, G–10
   history, 309–310
   integrating knowledge management systems, 387
   Warner-Lambert example, 306–307
Supply chain teams, 305, G–10
Support activities, 46, G–10. *See also* Decision support systems (DSS)
Surebridge, Inc., 595–596
Suretrade, 150
Surgery Center of Baltimore, 416
Swiss Federal Institute of Technology, 216
Sybase, 382
Sykes Enterprises, 355
Symbolic processing, 478, G–10
Symbol Technologies, 33
Synchronous (real-time) communication, 105, G–10
Synco Software, 284
System development controls, 659
Systems. *See* Information systems (IS)
Systems development life cycle (SDLC), 605–606

T

Tacit knowledge, G–10
Tacit Knowledge Systems, 384
Taco Bell, 211
Tactical systems. *See* Managerial systems
Taiwan Semiconductor Manufacturing
        Co., 307
Taj Hotels, 215
Tampering. *See* Data tampering
Targeted advertising, 205–207
Taxes, Internet, 173
Taxicabs, satellite dispatch, 254
TBO. *See* Total benefits of ownership (TBO)
TCO. *See* Total cost of ownership (TCO)
TDMA. *See* Time Division Multiple Access
        (TDMA)
Teams. *See* Collaboration
Technological innovation, 15
Technology pressures, 15
Techweb.com, 100
Telecom Italia Mobile, 212
Telecommuting:
    defined, 123
    glossary definition, G–10
    overview, 123–124
    pros and cons, 693–694
Teleconferencing:
    defined, 117
    glossary definition, G–10
    overview, 117–118
    via Web, 118
    video, 117–118
Telematics, 221, G–10
Telemedicine, wireless, 216–217
TeleVend, Inc., 203
Teleworking. *See* Telecommuting
Tellme.com, 202
Tendering systems, 11
Terrorism, 16
Texas Instruments, 318
Text mining, 430–431, G–10
Thaigem.com, 6, 10
Thomas Cook Co., 415
Threats, 642, 646–647
3G, 196, G–10
Tiffany's, 6
Time Division Multiple Access (TDMA),
        196, G–10
T-Mobile, 199, 207
Toolbars, 99
Total benefits of ownership (TBO), 567,
        G–10
Total cost of ownership (TCO), 566–567,
        G–10
Total quality management (TQM), 18
Tower Records, 440
Toyota, 258, 347
Toysrus.com, 300, 347, 511, 514
TPS. *See* Transaction processing systems
        (TPS)
TQM (total quality management), 18
Tracking Web activity, 170–171
TradeCard, 150
TradeLink, 338, 349
TradeNet, 338

Training, employee, 123, 280–281
Transaction processing systems (TPS):
    activities and methods, 250–251
    vs. analytical processing, 417–418
    defined, 55, 58, 249
    examples, 59, 252, 253, 254, 255
    flow of information, 251
    vs. functional information systems, 59
    glossary definition, G–10
    objectives, 250
    object-oriented
    online, 251–253
    overview, 58–59, 249–250
    software, 253
    typical tasks, 253
    Web-based, 252–253
Transit systems:
    New York City, 9
    NextBus, 186–187
Translating Web pages, 99
Trap doors, 649
Travelocity.com, 151
Travel services, online, 151
Trend Micro Inc., 693
Trojan horses, 155, 649, 650, G–10
Troubleshooting, 665
Turing test, 477, G–10
2G, 196, G–11
2.5G, 196, G–11

U

Unilever, 115, 347
United Sourcing Alliance, 158
Universal Product Code (UPC), 228–229
Universal Studios, 199
University accounting system failure, 583
University of California at Los Angeles, 230
University of Cincinnati, 416
Unsolicited advertising. *See* Spamming
UPS Stores, 252
U.S. Airways, 644
U.S. Department of Defense (DOD), 229,
        230
U.S. Department of Homeland Security
        (DHS), 415, 451–452
U.S. Department of Transportation
        (DOT), 228
U.S. Federal Bureau of Investigation
        (FBI), 415
U.S. Federal Communications
        Commission (FCC), 221
U.S. Federal Trade Commission (FTC),
        172
U.S. Fleet Services, 210
U.S. National Science Foundation (NSF),
        440
U.S. Postal Service, 223
User-developed systems. *See* End-user
        computing
User interfaces, 707–711
USX (U.S. Steel), 281
Utility computing, 74–75, 535, 603–605,
        G–11
Uvine.com, 148

V

Value-added networks (VANs), 93
Value analysis, 567–568, G–11
Value-chain integrators, as EC business
        model, 141
Value chain model:
    airline industry example, 515
    defined, 44
    and digital economy, 513–514
    examples of use, 513–514, 515
    and functional areas, 248
    glossary definition, G–11
    overview, 44, 46, 513
    and supply chain, 514
Value-chain service providers, as EC
        business model, 141
Value systems, 46, G–11
VANs. *See* Value-added networks (VANs)
Vendor-managed inventory (VMI), 257,
        G–11
Verity, 384
Verizon, 207
Victoria Secret, 446
Video display terminals (VDTs), 701
Video Privacy Protection Act, 652
Video teleconferencing, 117–118, G–11
VIM. *See* Visual interactive modeling
        (VIM)
Vindigo, 206
Viral marketing, 141, 156, G–11
Virtual banks. *See* Cyberbanking
Virtual close, 273, G–11
Virtual collaboration, 110–116, G–11
Virtual communities, 709, G–11
Virtual corporations:
    defined, 344
    glossary definition, G–11
    IT support, 344–345
    overview, 344
Virtual credit cards, 169, G–11
Virtual (distributed) work, 123–124
Virtual factories, 306–308, G–11
Virtual groups (teams), 108, 109–110,
        111, G–11
Virtual meetings, 108, 117, 472, G–11
Virtual organizations, 140, G–11. *See
        also* Electronic commerce
        (e-commerce)
Virtual private networks (VPNs),
        663–664
Virtual reality, 438, 439, 440, G–11
Virtual Reality Markup Language
        (VRML), 440, G–11
Virtual society. *See* Virtual communities
Virtual teams. *See* Virtual groups (teams)
Virtual universities, 123, G–11
Viruses, 649–650, 662, 663, G–11
Visa International, 488
Visual interactive modeling (VIM), 438,
        G–11
Visual interactive simulation (VIS), 438,
        439, G–11
Vivisimo, 97
Vodafone, 207
Voice communication, 107

Voice-over IP. *See* Internet telephony (voice-over IP)
Voice portals, 100, 202, G–11
Voice recognition. *See* Speech recognition
Voice synthesis, 201–202, 486, 487, G–11
Voice understanding. *See* Speech understanding
Voice XML, 195
Volkswagen, 361–363
Vortals, 100
VPNs (virtual private networks), 663–664
VRML. *See* Virtual Reality Markup Language (VRML)
Vulnerability (in security), 642, 644–647, G–11

W

Wallets, electronic. *See* E-wallets (digital wallets); Mobile wallets (m-wallets)
Wal-Mart:
    check-writers in stores, 265
    data mining example, 442
    and e-commerce, 140, 148, 171
    and EDI, 347
    and Procter & Gamble, 114, 302
    RFID application, 41–42, 229, 230
    and Thaigem.com, 6
    vendor-managed inventory, 257, 356, 510–511
WANs (wide area networks). *See* Wireless wide area networks (WWANs)
WAP. *See* Wireless application protocol (WAP)
War chalking, 200
War dialing, 649
War driving, 200
Warehouses. *See* Data warehouses
Warner-Lambert, 306–307
Washington Township (Ohio) Fire Department, 240–241
Wearable devices, 208, 209, G–11
Wearnes Technology, 345
Web-based DSS, G–11
Web-based management support systems (MSSs), 491–492, G–12
Web-based systems. *See also* Electronic commerce (e-commerce); Extranets; Internet; Intranets
    application-based *vs.* end-user-based, 606
    auditing, 672–673
    for corporate training, 123
    for customer service, 320–322
    data quality issue, 414
    decision support systems, 468
    defined, 57, 71
    for document management, 417
    e-commerce (*See* Electronic commerce (e-commerce))
    economics, 580–582
    electronic exchanges, 73

electronic markets, 73
electronic storefronts, 147–148
for financial transactions, 272–273
global issues, 338–339
glossary definition, G–11
overview, 71–72
product economics, 583–584
for recruitment, 278
risk issue, 541
security issues, 660–667
strategic planning, 542
for transaction processing, 252–253
and virtual reality, 440
WebBrain, 97
Web-browsing-assisting agents, 96
WebCertificate, 167
Web conferencing, 118, G–11
WebCT, 122
WebDAV, 120
Web economy. *See* Digital economy
WebEx Meeting Center, 118
Weblogging. *See* Blogging (Weblogging)
Web mining, 431, G–11
Webopedia, 98
Web pages, automatic translation, 99
Web Services, 34, 76, 353–354, 532, 600–602, G–11
Web tracking, 170–171
Wells Fargo Bank, 470
What-if analysis, 466–467
What Is tool, 98
Whirlpool Corporation, 227, 317
Whiteboards, 118, G–11
Wide area networks (WANs). *See* Wireless wide area networks (WWANs)
Wi-Fi (wireless fidelity), 190, 197–200, G–12. *See also* Mobile computing
Wing Fat Foods, 530
Wire Fraud Act, 652
Wireless 911 (e-911), 221, G–12
Wireless access points, 197, G–11
Wireless advertising, 205–207
Wireless application protocol (WAP), 190, 195, G–11
Wireless bill payments, 203, 204
Wireless communications. *See also* Mobile commerce (m-commerce)
    cellular technology (*See* Cell phones)
    Dartmouth College example, 40–41
    examples of applications, 31
    securing networks, 666
    wearable computer example, 208, 209
Wireless Encryption Protocol (WEP), 200
Wireless fidelity (Wi-Fi), 190, 197–200, G–12
Wireless LANs, 94, 190, 197, G–12
Wireless Markup Language (WML), 195
Wireless (mobile) computing, 188, G–12. *See also* Mobile computing
Wireless personal area networks (WPANs), 197–198

Wireless telemedicine, 216–217
Wireless wallets. *See* Mobile wallets (m-wallets)
Wireless wide area networks (WWANs). *See also* Mobile computing
    communication generations, 196
    communication protocols, 196–197
    defined, 195
    glossary definition, G–12
    overview, 195, 196
    Pepsi example, 74
    and Wi-Fi, 197–200
WiseNet, 97
W.L. Gore and Associates, 317
WLANs. *See* Wireless LANs
WML (Wireless Markup Language), 195
Word processing systems, 55
Work. *See* Collaboration; Groupware
Workers. *See* Employees
Workflow, 116, G–12
Workflow management, 116, G–12
Workflow systems:
    before and after wireless examples, 213
    defined, 116
    glossary definition, G–12
Workforce, changing nature of, 14
Workgroups, 108. *See also* Collaboration; Virtual groups (teams)
World Bank, 272, 374
World Economic Forum, 472
WorldPoint Passport, 99
World Wide Web, 91–92, G–12. *See also* Electronic commerce (e-commerce); Internet; Web-based systems
Worms, defined, 649
WPANs (wireless personal area networks), 197–198
WWANs. *See* Wireless wide area networks (WWANs)

X

Xerox Corporation, 222, 384, 390
XML (eXtensible Markup Language), 352–353, 380, G–12
Xybernaut, 209

Y

Yahoo, 11, 100, 148, 153, 163, 167, 207
Yahoo Companion, 99
Yankee Group, 207

Z

Zdnet.com, 100
Zions Bancorporation, 684–685
Zombies, 651, G–12